COLORADO REAL ESTATE MANUAL

DEPARTMENT OF REGULATORY AGENCIES
Barbara Kelley, Executive Director

THE COLORADO DIVISION OF REAL ESTATE
Marcia Waters, Director

REAL ESTATE COMMISSION
Douglas Ring, Pueblo – Chair

Kristin Bronson, Denver
Christopher McElroy, Fort Collins
Gina Piccoli, Durango
Jill Ozarski, Denver

BOARD OF REAL ESTATE APPRAISERS
Robin Anderson, Denver – Chair

Frank Beltran, Pueblo
Debbie Delaney, Fort Collins
Wayne L. Hunsperger, Englewood
Anthony Navarro, Denver
Susan E. Secrest, Denver
Bruce Willard, Greeley

BOARD OF MORTGAGE LOAN ORIGINATORS
Bart Bartholomew, Arvada – Chair

Cheryl Dingwell-Keckritz, Colorado Springs
Rosemary Marshall, Denver
Leslie Mitchell, Denver
Julie Piepho, Fort Collins

CONSERVATION EASEMENT OVERSIGHT COMMISSION
Martha Cochran, Glenwood Springs – Chair

Lise Aangeenbrug,
Great Outdoors Colorado
CindyLair,
Colorado Department of Agriculture
Doug Robotham,
Colorado Department of Resources
William Boortz, Denver
Kent Holsinger, Denver
Chris West, Denver
Janis Whisman, Longmont
Jay Winner, Pueblo

PREFACE

The Colorado Division of Real Estate and Bradford Publishing have prepared this manual with assistance from members of the Real Estate Commission, the Board of Real Estate Appraisers, the Board of Mortgage Loan Originators, and the Conservation Easement Oversight Commission. We gratefully acknowledge the help of the many who have contributed their time and experience, especially Marcia Waters and the dedicated staff at the Division of Real Estate for their commitment to making this publication available to the industry.

We hope this manual will be helpful to new applicants for licensure and also a benefit to practicing real estate brokers, appraisers and mortgage professionals as a ready reference.

The information contained in this manual is fundamental to a sound introduction to the real estate industry. It is not intended as an all-inclusive real estate text; nor should it be relied upon as a source of legal advice.

For those who desire to increase their educational and professional competency, there are many classes and courses of instruction available throughout the State of Colorado and a number of colleges and universities that offer four-year programs leading to a degree in real estate and related fields. Suggestions, corrections and criticisms for and of this publication are solicited and will receive careful consideration.

Bradford Publishing Co.
1743 Wazee Street
Denver, CO 80202
www.bradfordpublishing.com
Printers and Distributors

ISBN: 978-1-932779-74-5

TABLE OF CONTENTS

Chapter 1:
Real Estate Broker License Law

An * in the left margin indicates a change in the statute, rule, or text since the last publication of the manual.

I. Reason for Its Enactment

The Colorado Real Estate Broker License Law was passed to protect the people of the State of Colorado. Through licensing, the law seeks competency and integrity on the part of those engaged in the real estate business. The law has had the effect of raising the general standing of the real estate business and has helped to safeguard the interests of both the public and those engaged in the business.

II. What the Law Does Not Cover

The law does not dictate the ethical standards that should be observed in the real estate industry, or generally of any trade, business, or profession. The law imposes responsibility for one's moral misconduct only indirectly, through the law of crimes (public wrongs) and of torts (private wrongs). As an example, one entrusted with another's money may be held responsible for its misuse in two ways:

1. Through the crime of theft by deception, for which a person may be fined and imprisoned; and
2. Through the tort of conversion, for which a person may be required to return the money and provide compensation for any harm caused by the wrongful use of the rightful owner's money.

Codes of ethics have been voluntarily adopted by various real estate organizations as guiding standards of high moral and ethical practice. Adherence to such codes is recommended to all who are licensed to engage in real estate business.

III. The Commission Office

The Division of Real Estate has a five-member Commission that meets bi-monthly to conduct rulemaking hearings, make policy decisions, consider licensing matters, review complaints, and take disciplinary action against real estate brokers. Rules are promulgated after notice and public hearings at which all interested parties may participate. The five Commission members consist of three real estate brokers and two members of the public. Commission members serve a three-year term.

The Division of Real Estate is part of the Department of Regulatory Agencies and is responsible for budgeting, purchasing, and related management functions. The director of the Division is an administrative officer who executes the directives of the Commission and is given statutory authority in all matters delegated by the Commission.

The Division of Real Estate is the licensing, regulation, and enforcement agency for real estate brokers, appraisers, mortgage loan originators, subdivision developers, and conservation easement holders. To become licensed, individuals must comply with education and/or experience requirements, qualify for reciprocity, and/or pass a general and/or state portion of the licensing exam.

The Division's objectives are to:

- Provide protection to consumers and other stakeholders
- Educate consumers on their rights and promote consumer awareness throughout the State of Colorado
- Enforce state and federal laws, rules, regulations, and standards and impose disciplinary action when recommended
- License real estate brokers
- License real estate appraisers
- License mortgage loan originators
- Register timeshares, raw land subdivisions developers and homeowners' associations
- Certify the holders of conservation easements
- Investigate complaints
- Enforce compliance with state and federal laws
- Impose recommended disciplinary actions against licensees

The Commission exercises its duties and authorities independently through the following programs or activities.

A. The Master File

The Division staff records the historical and day-to-day information concerning the licensing status of employers, employees, corporations, limited liability companies and partnership entities, trade names, office locations, and disciplinary actions. The computerized master file supplies public information and is used as evidence in lawsuits concerning real estate transactions.

B. Licensing

The Licensing section's major responsibility is the data entry and upkeep of nearly 50,000 real estate broker, appraiser, and mortgage loan originator licensing records, as well as registration of subdivision/timeshare developers, homeowners' associations and conservation easement holders. The Licensing staff reviews and processes all incoming applications, which are screened for required qualifications, including education, experience, examinations, errors & omission (E&O), and criminal history background checks. The Licensing section also issues license histories to licensees who need to prove their credentials to other jurisdictions.

Colorado recognizes real estate licenses issued by all other U.S. and Canadian jurisdictions if the licensee in the other jurisdiction has held that license for 2 years or more. Licensing currently administers this program and offers a limited recognition program to these licensees. The Division also reciprocates with most other appraisal jurisdictions.

Applicants with a past civil judgment or criminal conviction may request a "preliminary advisory opinion" regarding the likelihood of receiving a license before completing the requirements to apply for a license (Commission Rule A-12). The Commission/board may issue either a favorable or unfavorable opinion.

Both "preliminary advisory" applicants and license applicants are subject to pre-licensing investigations and fingerprinting to safeguard the statutory mandate for truthfulness, honesty, and good moral character. (See §§ 12-61-102, -103(3), -709(1), and -905(1) C.R.S) All applications that disclose civil or criminal violations or any form of previous license discipline in any jurisdiction are reviewed and investigated thoroughly.

Licenses issued by the section include:

- Real estate broker
- Corporate/LLC real estate brokerage
- Partnership real estate brokerage
- Temporary real estate broker
- Registered appraiser
- Licensed appraiser
- Certified residential appraiser
- Certified general appraiser
- Temporary appraiser
- Mortgage loan originator

The Division also reviews and registers:

- Raw ground subdivision developers
- Timeshare and vacation club developers
- Condominium conversion developers
- Homeowners' associations
- Conservation easement holders

Information on licensing is located on the Division of Real Estate website at:
http://www.dora.state.co.us/real-estate

C. Enforcement Section

The Real Estate Commission has the power upon its own motion to investigate any licensee's real estate activities. If a written complaint is filed, the office is compelled to investigate.

If the complaint against the licensee is of such a serious nature that it may result in disciplinary action against a licensee, a hearing will be held before an administrative law judge. The judge is appointed by the Department of Personnel and Administration. The administrative law judge will make an initial decision of revocation, suspension, censure, or dismissal. Education courses, probation, and fines can also be mandated. If written objections are not filed with the Commission within 30 days, the initial decision becomes final. If written objections are filed, the Commission may adopt the findings and initial decision of the administrative law judge, modify the disciplinary action, or refer the matter back for rehearing. The Commission can also issue letters of admonishment in instances where conduct does not warrant formal disciplinary proceedings.

This program also includes:

- Investigation of applicants
- Evaluation of complaints
- Investigation of complaints
- Routine and investigative audits
- Recommendations for dismissal or disciplinary action
- Preparation and execution of subpoenas, and other legal documents
- Preparation of cases for formal hearing, restraining orders, injunctions, or complaints for filing with district attorneys and local law enforcement agencies
- Working with federal agencies, *e.g.*, the Securities and Exchange Commission or Housing and Urban Development, the Federal Bureau of Investigation, or the Internal Revenue Service.

The Real Estate Commission should *not* be confused with the Colorado Association of REALTORS®, which is a private trade organization affiliated with the National Association of REALTORS® whose members are the only licensees authorized to use the registered trademark "REALTOR"®.

IV. License Law

A. Part 1 – Brokers

§ 12-61-101, C.R.S. Definitions.

As used in this part 1, unless the context otherwise requires:

(1) "Employing real estate broker" or "employing broker" means a broker who is shown in real estate commission records as employing or engaging another broker.

(1.2) "HOA" or "homeowners' association" means an association or unit owners' association formed before, on, or after July 1, 1992, as part of a common interest community as defined in section 38-33.3-103, C.R.S.

(1.3) "Limited liability company" shall have the same meaning as it is given in section 7-80-102(7), C.R.S.

(1.5) "Option dealer" means any person, firm, partnership, limited liability company, association, or corporation who, directly or indirectly, takes, obtains, or uses an option to purchase, exchange, rent, or lease real property or any interest therein with the intent or for the purpose of buying, selling, exchanging, renting, or leasing said real property or interest therein to another or others whether or not said option is in that person's or its name and whether or not title to said property passes through the name of said person, firm, partnership, limited liability company, association, or corporation in connection with the purchase, sale, exchange, rental, or lease of said real property or interest therein.

(1.7) "Partnership" includes, but is not limited to, a registered limited liability partnership.

(2) (a) "Real estate broker" or "broker" means any person, firm, partnership, limited liability company, association, or corporation who, in consideration of compensation by fee, commission, salary, or anything of value or with the intention of receiving or collecting such compensation, engages in or offers or attempts to engage in, either directly or indirectly, by a continuing course of conduct or by any single act or transaction, any of the following acts:

(I) Selling, exchanging, buying, renting, or leasing real estate, or interest therein, or improvements affixed thereon;

(II) Offering to sell, exchange, buy, rent, or lease real estate, or interest therein, or improvements affixed thereon;

(III) Selling or offering to sell or exchange an existing lease of real estate, or interest therein, or improvements affixed thereon;

(IV) Negotiating the purchase, sale, or exchange of real estate, or interest therein, or improvements affixed thereon;

(V) Listing, offering, attempting, or agreeing to list real estate, or interest therein, or improvements affixed thereon for sale, exchange, rent, or lease;

(VI) Auctioning or offering, attempting, or agreeing to auction real estate, or interest therein, or improvements affixed thereon;

(VII) Buying, selling, offering to buy or sell, or otherwise dealing in options on real estate, or interest therein, or improvements affixed thereon or acting as an "option dealer";

(VIII) Performing any of the foregoing acts as an employee of, or in behalf of, the owner of real estate, or interest therein, or improvements affixed thereon at a salary or for a fee, commission, or other consideration;

(IX) Negotiating or attempting or offering to negotiate the listing, sale, purchase, exchange, or lease of a business or business opportunity or the goodwill thereof or any interest therein when such act or transaction involves, directly or indirectly, any change in the ownership or interest in real estate, or in a leasehold interest or estate, or in a business or business opportunity which owns an interest in real estate or in a leasehold unless such act is performed by any broker-dealer licensed under the provisions of article 51 of title 11, C.R.S., who is actually engaged generally in the business of offering, selling, purchasing, or trading in securities or any officer, partner, salesperson, employee, or other authorized representative or agent thereof;

(X) Soliciting a fee or valuable consideration from a prospective tenant for furnishing information concerning the availability of real property, including apartment housing which may be leased or rented as a private dwelling, abode, or place of residence. Any person, firm, partnership, limited liability company, association, or corporation or any employee or authorized agent thereof engaged in the act of soliciting a fee or valuable consideration from any person other than a prospective tenant for furnishing information concerning the availability of real property, including apartment housing which may be leased or rented as a private dwelling, abode, or place of residence, is exempt from this definition of "real estate broker" or "broker". This exemption applies only in respect to the furnishing of information concerning the availability of real property.

(b) "Real estate broker" does not apply to any of the following:

(I) Any **attorney-in-fact** acting without compensation under a power of attorney, duly executed by an owner of real estate, authorizing the consummation of a real estate transaction;

(II) Any **public official** in the conduct of his or her official duties;

(III) Any **receiver**, **trustee**, **administrator**, **conservator**, **executor**, or **guardian** acting under proper authorization;

(IV) Any **person**, **firm**, **partnership**, **limited liability company**, or **association** acting personally or a corporation acting through its officers or regular salaried employees, on behalf of that person or on its own behalf as principal in acquiring or in negotiating to acquire any interest in real estate;

(V) An **attorney-at-law** in connection with his or her representation of clients in the practice of law;

(VI) Any **person**, **firm**, **partnership**, **limited liability company**, **association**, or **corporation**, or any **employee** or **authorized agent** thereof, engaged in the act of negotiating, acquiring, purchasing, assigning, exchanging, selling, leasing, or dealing in **oil and gas or other mineral leases** or interests therein or other severed mineral or royalty interests in real property, including easements, rights-of-way, permits, licenses, and any other interests in real property for or on behalf of a third party, for the purpose of, or facilities related to, intrastate and interstate pipelines for oil, gas, and other petroleum products, flow lines, gas gathering systems, and natural gas storage and distribution;

(VII) A **natural person** acting personally with respect to property owned or leased by that person or a natural person who is a **general partner of a partnership**, a **manager of a limited liability company**, or **an owner of twenty percent or more** of such partnership or limited liability company, and authorized to sell or lease property owned by such partnership or limited liability company, except as provided in subsection (1.5) of this section;

(VIII) A **corporation with respect to property owned or leased by it**, acting through its officers or regular salaried employees, when such acts are incidental and necessary in the ordinary course of the corporation's business activities of a non-real estate nature (but only if the corporation is not engaged in the business of land transactions), except as provided in subsection (1.5) of this section. For the purposes of this subparagraph (VIII), the term "officers or regular salaried employees" means persons regularly employed who derive not less than seventy-five percent of their compensation from the corporation in the form of salaries.

(IX) A **principal officer of any corporation** with respect to property owned by it when such property is located within the state of Colorado and when such principal officer is the owner of twenty percent or more of the outstanding stock of such corporation, except as provided in subsection (1.5) of this section, but this exemption does not include any corporation selling previously occupied one-family and two-family dwellings;

(X) A **sole proprietor**, **corporation**, **partnership**, or **limited liability company**, acting through its officers or partners, or through regular salaried employees, with respect to property owned or leased by such sole proprietor, corporation, partnership, or limited liability company on which has been or will be erected a commercial, industrial, or **residential building which has not been previously occupied and where the consideration paid for such property includes the cost of such building, payable, less deposit or down payment, at the time of conveyance of such property and building**;

(XI) (A) A **corporation**, **partnership**, or **limited liability company** acting through its officers, partners, managers, or regularly salaried employees receiving no additional compensation therefor, or its wholly owned subsidiary or officers, partners, managers, or regular salaried employees thereof receiving no additional compensation, with respect to property located in Colorado which is owned or leased by such corporation, partnership, or limited liability company and on which has been or will be erected a **shopping center**, **office building**, or **industrial park** when such shopping center, office building, or industrial park is sold, leased, or otherwise offered for sale or lease in the ordinary course of the business of such corporation, partnership, limited liability company, or wholly owned subsidiary.

(B) For the purposes of this subparagraph (XI), "shopping center" means land on which buildings are or will be constructed which are used for commercial and office purposes around or adjacent to which off-street parking is provided; "office building" means a building used primarily for office purposes; and "industrial park" means land on which buildings are or will be constructed for warehouse, research, manufacturing, processing, or fabrication purposes.

(XII) A **regularly salaried employee** of an owner of an apartment building or complex who acts as an **on-site manager of such an apartment building** or complex. This exemption applies only in respect to the customary duties of an on-site manager performed for his or her employer.

(XIII) A **regularly salaried employee of an owner of condominium units who acts as an on-site manager** of such units. For purposes of this subparagraph (XIII) only, the term "owner" includes a **homeowners' association** formed and acting pursuant to its recorded condominium declaration and bylaws. This exemption applies only in respect to the customary duties of an on-site manager performed for his or her employer.

(XIV) A **real estate broker licensed in another state** who receives a share of a commission or finder's fee on a cooperative transaction from a licensed Colorado real estate broker;

(XV) A **sole proprietor**, **corporation**, **partnership**, or **limited liability company**, acting through its officers, partners, or regularly salaried employees, with respect to property located in Colorado, where the **purchaser** of such property **is in the business of developing land** for residential, commercial, or industrial purposes;

(XVI) Any **person**, **firm**, **partnership**, **limited liability company**, **association**, or **corporation**, or any **employee** or **authorized agent** thereof, engaged in the act of negotiating, purchasing, assigning, exchanging, selling, leasing, or acquiring rights-of-way, permits, licenses, and any other interests in real property for or on behalf of a third party for the purpose of, or facilities related to:

(A) Telecommunication lines;

(B) Wireless communication facilities;

(C) CATV;

(D) Electric generation, transmission, and distribution lines;

(E) Water diversion, collection, distribution, treatment, and storage or use; and

(F) Transportation, so long as such person, firm, partnership, limited liability company, association, or corporation, including any employee or authorized agent thereof, does not represent any displaced person or entity as an agent thereof in the purchase, sale, or exchange of real estate, or an interest therein, resulting from residential or commercial relocations required under any transportation project, regardless of the source of public funding

§ 12-61-102, C.R.S. License required.

It is unlawful for any person, firm, partnership, limited liability company, association, or corporation to engage in the business or capacity of real estate broker in this state without first having obtained a license from the real estate commission. No person shall be granted a license until such person establishes compliance with the provisions of this part 1 concerning education, experience, and testing; truthfulness and honesty and otherwise good moral character; and, in addition to any other requirements of this section, competency to transact the business of a real estate broker in such manner as to safeguard the interest of the public and only after satisfactory proof of such qualifications, together with the application for such license, is filed in the office of the commission. In determining such person's character, the real estate commission shall be governed by section 24-5-101, C.R.S.

§ 12-61-103, C.R.S. Application for license.

(1) (a) All persons desiring to become real estate brokers shall apply to the real estate commission for a license under the provisions of this part 1. Application for a license, as a real estate broker shall be made to the commission upon forms or in a manner prescribed by it.

(b) (I) Prior to submitting an application for a license pursuant to paragraph (a) of this subsection (1), each applicant shall submit a set of fingerprints to the Colorado bureau of investigation for the purpose of conducting a state and national fingerprint-based criminal history record check utilizing records of the Colorado bureau of investigation and the federal bureau of investigation. The applicant shall pay the fee established by the Colorado bureau of investigation for conducting the fingerprint-based criminal history record check to the bureau. Upon completion of the criminal history record check, the bureau shall forward the results to the real estate commission. The real estate commission may acquire a name-based criminal history record check for an applicant who has twice submitted to a fingerprint-based criminal history record check and whose fingerprints are unclassifiable. *(Ed. Note: See Rule A-16)*

(II) For purposes of this paragraph (b), "applicant" means an individual, or any person designated to act as broker for any partnership, limited liability company, or corporation pursuant to subsection (7) of this section.

(2) Every real estate broker licensed under this part 1 shall maintain a place of business within this state, except as provided in section 12-61-107. In case a real estate broker maintains more than one place of business within the state, the broker shall be responsible for supervising all licensed activities originating in such offices.

(3) The commission is authorized by this section to require and procure any such proof as is necessary in reference to the truthfulness, honesty, and good moral character of any applicant for a real estate broker's license or, if the applicant is a partnership, limited liability company or corporation, of any partner, manager, director, officer, member, or stockholder if such person has, either directly or indirectly, a substantial interest in such applicant prior to the issuance of such license.

(4) (a) An applicant for a broker's license shall be at least eighteen years of age. The applicant must furnish proof satisfactory to the commission that the applicant has either received a degree from an accredited degree-granting college or university with a major course of study in real estate or has successfully completed courses of study, approved by the commission, at any accredited degree granting college or university or any private occupational school that has a certificate of approval from the private occupational school division in accordance with the provisions of article 59 of this section or that has been approved by the commission or licensed by an official state agency of any other state as follows:

(I) Forty-eight hours of classroom instruction or equivalent correspondent hours in real estate law and real estate practice; and

(II) Forty-eight hours of classroom instruction or equivalent correspondent hours in understanding and preparation of Colorado real estate contracts; and

(III) A total of seventy-two hours of instruction or equivalent correspondence hours from the following areas of study: (*Ed. Note: See also Rule A-17*)

(A) Trust accounts and record-keeping;
(B) Real estate closings;
(C) Current legal issues; and
(D) Practical applications.

(b) An applicant for a broker's license who has been licensed as a real estate broker in another jurisdiction shall be required to complete only the course of study comprising the subject matter areas described in subparagraphs (II) and (III) (B) of paragraph (a) of this subsection (4).

(c) An applicant for a broker's license who has been licensed as a real estate salesperson in another jurisdiction shall be required to complete only the course of study required in subparagraphs (II) and (III) of paragraph (a) of this subsection.

(d) Repealed (effective 1-1-97)

(5) Repealed (effective 1-1-97)

(6) (a) The applicant for a broker's license shall submit to and pass an examination designated to determine the competency of the applicant and prepared by or under the supervision of the real estate commission or its designated contractor. The commission may contract with an independent testing service to develop, administer, or grade examinations, or to administer licensee records. The contract may allow the testing service to recover the costs of the examination and the costs of administering exam and license records from the applicant. The commission may contract separately for these functions and allow recovered costs to be collected and retained by a single contractor for distribution to other contractors. The commission shall have the authority to set the minimum passing score that an applicant must receive on the examination, and said score shall reflect the minimum level of competency required to be a broker. Said examination shall be given at such times and places as the commission prescribes. The examination shall include, but not be limited to, ethics, reading, spelling, basic mathematics, principles of land economics, appraisal, financing, a knowledge of the statutes and law of this state relating to deeds, trust deeds, mortgages, listing contracts, contracts of sale, bills of sale, leases, agency, brokerage, trust accounts, closings, securities, the provisions of this part 1, and the rules of the commission. The examination for a broker's license shall also include the preparation of a real estate closing statement.

(b) An applicant for a broker's license who has held a real estate license in another jurisdiction that administers a real estate broker's examination and the applicant has been licensed for two years prior to applying for a Colorado license may be issued a broker's license if the applicant establishes that he or she possesses credentials and qualifications that are substantively equivalent to the requirements in Colorado for licensure by examination.

(c) In addition to all other applicable requirements, the following provisions apply to brokers that did not hold a current and valid broker's license on December 31, 1996.

(I) No such broker shall engage in an independent brokerage practice without first having served actively as a real estate broker for at least two years. The commission shall adopt rules requiring an employing broker to ensure that a high level of supervision is exercised over such a broker during such two-year period. (*Ed. Note: See Rule E-32*)

(II) No such broker shall employ another broker without first having completed twenty-four clock hours of instruction, or the equivalent in correspondence hours, as approved by the commission, in brokerage administration.

(7) (a) Real estate brokers' licenses may be granted to individuals, partnership, limited liability companies, or corporations. A partnership, limited liability company or corporation, in its

application for a license, shall designate a qualified, active broker to be responsible for management and supervision of the licensed actions of the partnership, limited liability company or corporation and all licensees shown in commission records as being in the employ of such entity. The application of the partnership, limited liability company or corporation and the application of the broker designated by it shall be filed with the real estate commission.

(b) No license shall be issued to any partnership, limited liability company or corporation unless and until the broker so designated by the partnership, limited liability company or corporation submits to and passes the examination required by this part 1 on behalf of the partnership, limited liability company or corporation. Upon such broker's successfully passing the examination and upon compliance with all other requirements of law by the partnership, limited liability company or corporation, as well as by the designated broker, the commission shall issue a broker's license to the partnership, limited liability company or corporation, which shall bear the name of such designated broker, and thereupon the broker so designated shall conduct business as a real estate broker only through the said partnership, limited liability company or corporation and not for the broker's account.

(c) If the person so designated is refused a license by the real estate commission or ceases to be the designated broker of such partnership, limited liability company or corporation, such entity may designate another person to make application for a license. If such person ceases to be the designated broker of such partnership, limited liability company or corporation, the director may issue a temporary license to prevent hardship for a period not to exceed ninety days to the licensed person so designated. The director may extend a temporary license for one additional period not to exceed ninety days upon proper application and a showing of good cause; if the director refuses, no further extension of a temporary license shall be granted except by the commission. If any broker or employee of any such partnership, limited liability company or corporation, other than the one designated as provided in this section, desires to act as a real estate broker, such broker or employee shall first obtain a license as a real estate broker as provided in this section and shall pay the regular fee therefor. (*Ed. Note: See Rule A-26*)

(8) The broker designated to act as broker for any partnership, limited liability company or corporation is personally responsible for the handling of any and all earnest money deposits or escrow or trust funds received or disbursed by said partnership, limited liability company or corporation. In the event of any breach of duty by the said partnership, limited liability company or corporation as a fiduciary, any person aggrieved or damaged by the said breach of fiduciary duty shall have a claim for relief against such partnership, limited liability company or corporation, as well as against the designated broker, and may pursue said claim against the partnership, limited liability company or corporation and the designated broker personally. The said broker may be held responsible and liable for damages based upon such breach of fiduciary duty as may be recoverable against the said partnership, limited liability company or corporation, and any judgment so obtained may be enforced jointly or severally against said broker personally and the said partnership, limited liability company or corporation.

(9) No license for a broker registered as being in the employ of another broker shall be issued to a partnership, limited liability company or a corporation or under a fictitious name or trade name; except that a woman may elect to use her birth name.

(10) No person shall be licensed as a real estate broker under more than one name, and no person shall conduct or promote a real estate brokerage business except under the name under which such person is licensed. (*Ed. Note: See also Rule C-19*)

(11) Repealed (effective 7-1-79)

(12) A licensed attorney shall take and pass the examination referred to in this section after having completed twelve hours of classroom instruction or equivalent correspondent hours in trust

accounts, record-keeping, and real estate closings. (*Ed. Note: Attorney may be licensed at any bar*)

§ 12-61-103.6, C.R.S. Errors and omissions insurance – duties of the commission – certificate of coverage, when required – group plan made available – effect – repeal.

(1) Every licensee under this part 1, except an inactive broker or an attorney licensee who maintains a policy of professional malpractice insurance that provides coverage for errors and omissions for their activities as a licensee under this part 1, shall maintain errors and omissions insurance to cover all activities contemplated under parts 1 to 8 of this article. The commission shall make the errors and omissions insurance available to all licensees by contracting with an insurer for a group policy after a competitive bid process in accordance with article 103 of title 24, C.R.S. Any group policy obtained by the commission shall be available to all licensees with no right on the part of the insurer to cancel any licensee. Any licensee may obtain errors and omissions insurance independently if the coverage complies with the minimum requirements established by the commission.

(2) (a) If the commission is unable to obtain errors and omissions insurance coverage to insure all licensees who choose to participate in the group program at a reasonable annual premium, as determined by the commission, a licensee shall independently obtain the errors and omissions insurance required by this section.

(b) The commission shall solicit and consider information and comments from interested persons when determining the reasonableness of annual premiums.

(3) The commission shall determine the terms and conditions of coverage required under this section, including the minimum limits of coverage, the permissible deductible, and permissible exemptions. Each licensee shall be notified of the required terms and conditions at least thirty days prior to the annual premium renewal date as determined by the commission. Each licensee shall file a certificate of coverage showing compliance with the required terms and conditions with the commission by the annual premium renewal date, as determined by the commission.

(4) In addition to all other powers and duties conferred upon the commission by this article, the commission shall adopt such rules as it deems necessary or proper to carry out the provisions of this section. (*Ed. Note: See Rule D-14*)

§ 12-61-104, C.R.S. Licenses – issuance – contents – display.

(1) The commission shall make available for each licensee a license in such form and size as said commission shall prescribe and adopt. The real estate license shall show the name of the licensee and shall have imprinted thereon the seal, or a facsimile, of the department of regulatory agencies and, in addition to the foregoing, shall contain such other matter as said commission shall prescribe.

(2) Repealed (effective 3-9-01)

(3) Repealed (effective 3-9-01)

§ 12-61-105, C.R.S. Commission – compensation – immunity – subject to termination.

(1) There shall be a commission of five members, appointed by the governor, which shall administer parts 1, 3, and 4 of this article. This commission shall be known as the real estate commission, also referred to in this part 1 as the "commission", and shall consist of three real estate brokers who have had not less than five years' experience in the real estate business in Colorado and two representatives of the public at large. Members of the commission shall hold office for a period of three years. Upon the death, resignation, removal, or otherwise of any

member of the commission, the governor shall appoint a member to fill out the unexpired term. The governor may remove any member for misconduct, neglect of duty, or incompetence.

(2) Each member of the commission shall receive the same compensation and reimbursement of expenses as those provided for members of boards and commissions in the division of registrations pursuant to section 24-34-102(13), C.R.S. Payment for all such per diem compensation and expenses shall be made out of annual appropriations from the division of real estate cash fund provided for in section 12-61-111.5.

(2.5) Members of the commission, consultants, expert witnesses, and complainants shall be immune from suit in any civil action based upon any disciplinary proceedings or other official acts they performed in good faith.

(3) No real estate broker's license shall be denied, suspended, or revoked except as determined by a majority vote of the members of the commission.

(4) The provisions of section 24-34-104, C.R.S., concerning the termination schedule for regulatory bodies of the state unless extended as provided in that section, are applicable to the real estate commission created by this section.

§ 12-61-106, C.R.S. Director, clerks, and assistants.

(1) The executive director of the department of regulatory agencies is authorized by this section to employ, subject to the provisions of the state personnel system laws of the state, a director for the commission, who in turn shall employ such attorneys, deputies, investigators, clerks, and assistants as are necessary to discharge the duties imposed by parts 1, 3, and 4 of this article. The division of real estate, which shall be a division in the department of regulatory agencies, and the director of the division shall exercise their powers and perform their duties and functions under the department of regulatory agencies as if they were transferred to the department by a **type 2** transfer.

(2) It is the duty of the director, personally, or his designee to aid in the administration and enforcement of parts 1, 3, and 4 of this article and in the prosecution of all persons charged with violating any of their provisions, to conduct audits of business accounts of licensees, to perform such duties of the commission as the commission prescribes, and to act in behalf of the commission on such occasions and in such circumstances as the commission directs.

§ 12-61-107, C.R.S. Resident licensee – nonresident licensee – consent to service.

(1) A nonresident of the state may become a real estate broker in this state by conforming to all the conditions of this part 1; except that the nonresident broker shall not be required to maintain a place of business within this state if that broker maintains a definite place of business in another state.

(2) If a broker has no registered agent registered in this state, such registered agent is not located under its registered agent name at its registered agent address, or the registered agent cannot with reasonable diligence be served, the broker may be served by registered mail or by certified mail, return receipt requested, addressed to the entity at its principal address. Service is perfected under this subsection (2) at the earliest of:

- (a) The date the broker receives the process, notice, or demand;
- (b) The date shown on the return receipt, if signed by or on behalf of the broker; or
- (c) Five days after mailing.

(3) All such applications shall contain a certification that the broker is authorized to act for the corporation.

§ 12-61-108, C.R.S. List of licensees – publications.

The commission shall maintain a record of the names and addresses of all licensees licensed under the provisions of parts 1 and 4 of this article, together with such other information relative to the enforcement of said provisions as deemed by the commission to be necessary. Publication of the record and of any other information circulated in quantity outside the executive branch shall be in accordance with the provisions of section 24-1-136, C.R.S.

§ 12-61-108.5, C.R.S. Compilation and publication of passing rates per educational institution for real estate licensure examinations – rules.

(1) The commission shall have the authority to obtain information from each educational institution authorized to offer courses in real estate for the purpose of compiling the number of applicants who pass the real estate licensure examination from each educational institution. The information shall include the name of each student who attended the institution and a statement of whether the student completed the necessary real estate courses required for licensure. The commission shall have access to such other information as necessary to accomplish the purpose of this section. For the purposes of the section, an "applicant" is a student who completed the required education requirements and who applied for and sat for the licensure examination.

(2) The commission shall compile the information obtained in subsection (1) of this section with applicant information retained by the commission. Specifically, the commission shall compile whether the student applied for the licensure examination and whether the applicant passed the licensure examination. The commission shall create statistical data setting forth:

(a) The name of the educational institution;

(b) The number of students who completed the necessary real estate course required for licensure;

(c) Whether the student registered and sat for the licensure examination; and

(d) The number of those applicants who passed the licensure examination.

(3) The commission shall publish this statistical data and make it available to the public quarterly.

(4) The commission shall retain the statistical data for three years.

(5) Specific examination scores for an applicant will be kept confidential by the commission unless the applicant authorizes release of such information.

(6) The Commission may promulgate rules for the administration of this section.

§ 12-61-109, C.R.S. Change of license status – inactive – cancellation.

(1) Immediate notice shall be given in a manner acceptable to the commission by each licensee of any change of business location or employment. A change of business address or employment without notification to the commission shall automatically inactivate the licensee's license.

(2) A broker who transfers to the address of another broker or a broker applicant who desires to be employed by another broker shall inform the commission if said broker is to be in the employ of the other broker. The employing broker shall have the control and custody of the employed broker's license. The employed broker may not act on behalf of said broker or as broker for a partnership, limited liability company or corporation during the term of such employment; but this shall not affect the employed broker's right to transfer to another employing broker or to a location where the employed broker may conduct business as an independent broker or as a broker acting for a partnership, limited liability company or corporation.

(3) In the event that any licensee is discharged by or terminates employment with a broker, it shall be the **joint duty of both** such parties to immediately notify the commission. Either party may furnish such notice in a manner acceptable to the commission. The party giving notice shall notify the other party in person or in writing of the termination of employment.

(4) It is unlawful for any such licensee to perform any of the acts authorized under the license in pursuance of this part 1, either directly or indirectly, on or after the date that employment has been terminated. When any real estate broker whose employment has been terminated is employed by another real estate broker, the commission shall, upon proper notification, enter such change of employment in the records of the commission. Not more than one employer or place of employment shall be shown for any real estate broker for the same period of time.

§ 12-61-110, C.R.S. License fees – partnership, limited liability company and corporation licenses – rules.

(1) Fees established pursuant to section 12-61-111.5 shall be charged by and paid to the commission or the agent for the commission for the following:

(a) Each broker's examination;

(b) Each broker's original application and license;

(c) Each three-year renewal of a broker's license;

(d) Any change of name, address or employing broker requiring a change in commission records;

(e) A new application which shall be submitted when a licensed real estate broker wishes to become the broker acting for a partnership, limited liability company or a corporation.

(2) The proper fee shall accompany each application for licensure. The fee shall not be refundable. Failure by the person taking an examination to file the appropriate broker's application within one year of the date such person passed the examination will automatically cancel the examination, and all rights to a passing score will be terminated.

(3) Each real estate broker's license granted to an individual shall entitle such individual to perform all the acts contemplated by this part 1, without any further application on his part and without the payment of any fee other than the fees specified in this section.

(4) (a) The commission shall require that any person licensed under this part 1, whether on an active or inactive basis, renew said license on an anniversary date every three years. Renewal shall be conditioned upon fulfillment of the continuing education requirements set forth in section 12-61-110.5 and submission of fingerprints as required in section 12-61-110.8; except that any person licensed under this part 1 who maintains an inactive license and wants to renew to an active status shall only submit fingerprints as required in section 12-61-110.8 upon application to an active status and, except that, the real estate commission may acquire a name-based criminal history record check for an applicant who has twice submitted to a fingerprint-based criminal history record check and whose fingerprints are unclassifiable. For persons renewing or reinstating an active license, written certification verifying completion for the previous three-year licensing period of the continuing education requirements set forth in said section shall accompany and be submitted to the commission with the application for renewal or reinstatement. For persons who did not submit certification verifying compliance with section 12-61-110.5 at the time a license was renewed or reinstated on an inactive status, written certification verifying completion for the previous three-year licensing period of the continuing education requirements set forth in said section shall accompany and be submitted with any future application to reactivate the license. The commission may by rule establish procedures to facilitate such a renewal. Until such procedures are established, every license issued under the provisions of this part 1 shall expire at 12 midnight on December 31 of the year in which issued; except that each renewal of such license shall be for three years and shall expire at 12 midnight on December 31 of the third year. In the absence of any reason or condition that might warrant the refusal of the granting of a license or the revocation thereof, the commission shall issue a new license upon receipt by the commission of the written request of the applicant and the fees therefor, as required by

this section. Applications for renewal will be accepted thirty days prior to January 1. A person who fails to renew a license before January 1 of the year succeeding the year of the expiration of such license may reinstate the license as follows: (*Ed. Note: See Rules D-11 and D-13*)

(I) If proper application is made within thirty-one days after the date of expiration, by payment of the regular three-year renewal fee;

(II) If proper application is made more than thirty-one days but within one year after the date of expiration, by payment of the regular three-year renewal fee and payment of a reinstatement fee equal to one-half the regular three-year renewal fee;

(III) If proper application is made more than one year but within three years after the date of expiration, by payment of the regular three-year renewal fee and payment of a reinstatement fee equal to the regular three-year renewal fee.

(a.5) Repealed by Laws 1990, H.B.90-1131, § 4, eff. April 24, 1990.

(b) Any reinstated license shall be effective only as of the date of reinstatement. Any person who fails to apply for reinstatement within three years after the expiration of a license shall, without exception, be treated as a new applicant for licensure.

(c) All reinstatement fees shall be transmitted to the state treasurer, who shall credit same to the division of real estate cash fund, as established by section 12-61-111.5.

(5) The suspension, expiration, or revocation of a real estate broker's license shall automatically inactivate every real estate broker's license where the holder of such license is shown in the commission records to be in the employ of the broker whose license has expired or has been suspended or revoked pending notification to the commission by the employed licensee of a change of employment.

(6) Deleted by Laws 1991, H.B.91-1107, § 8, eff. July 1, 1991.

§ 12-61-110.5, C.R.S. Renewal of license – continuing education requirement.

(1) Commencing January 1, 1992, except as otherwise provided in subsection (4) of this section, a broker applying for renewal of a license pursuant to section 12-61-110 (4) shall include with such application a certified statement verifying successful completion of real estate courses in accordance with the following schedule:

(a) Repealed 4/1/04

(b) Repealed 4/1/04

(c) For licensees applying for renewal in 1994 and thereafter, passage within the previous three years of the Colorado portion of the real estate exam or completion of a minimum of twenty-four hours of credit, twelve of which shall be the credits developed by the real estate commission pursuant to subsection (2) of this section.

(2) The real estate commission shall develop twelve hours of credit designed to assure reasonable currency of real estate knowledge by licensees, which credits shall include an update of the current statutes and the rules promulgated by the commission that affect the practice of real estate. If a licensee takes a course pursuant to rule 260 of the Colorado rules of civil procedure and such course concerns real property law, such licensee shall receive credit for such course toward the fulfillment of such licensee's continuing education requirements pursuant to this section. Such credits shall be taken from an accredited Colorado college or university; a Colorado community college; a Colorado private occupational school holding a certificate of approval from the state board for community colleges and occupational education; or an educational institution or an educational service described in section 12-59-104. Successful completion of such credits shall require satisfactory passage of a written examination or written examinations of the materials covered. Such examinations shall be audited by the commission

to verify their accuracy and the validity of the grades given. The commission shall set the standards required for satisfactory passage of the examinations. (*Ed. Note: See Rule B-3(c)*)

(3) All credits, other than the credits specified in subsection (2) of this section, shall be acquired from educational programs approved by the commission that contribute directly to the professional competence of a licensee. Such credits may be acquired through successful completion of instruction in one or more of the following subjects:

(a) Real estate law;

(b) Property exchanges;

(c) Real estate contracts;

(d) Real estate finance;

(e) Real estate appraisal;

(f) Real estate closing;

(g) Real estate ethics;

(h) Condominiums and cooperatives;

(i) Real estate time-sharing;

(j) Real estate marketing principles;

(k) Real estate construction;

(*l*) Land development;

(m) Real estate energy concerns;

(n) Real estate geology;

(o) Water and waste management;

(p) Commercial real estate;

(q) Real estate securities and syndications;

(r) Property management;

(s) Real estate computer principles;

(t) Brokerage administration and management;

(u) Agency; and

(v) Any other subject matter as approved by the real estate commission.

(4) A licensee applying for renewal of a license which expires on December 31 of the year in which it was issued is not subject to the education requirements set forth in subsection (1) of this section.

(5) The real estate commission shall promulgate rules and regulations to implement this section.

§ 12-61-110.6, C.R.S. Repealed 7-1-01.

§ 12-61-110.8, C.R.S. Renewal of license – fingerprint based criminal history record check – repeal. (Repealed)

§ 12-61-111, C.R.S. Disposition of fees.

All fees collected by the real estate commission under parts 1 and 4 of this article, not including administrative fees that are in the nature of an administrative fine and fees retained by contractors pursuant to contracts entered into in accordance with section 12-61-103 or 24-34-101, C.R.S., shall be transmitted to the state treasurer, who shall credit the same to the division of real estate cash fund. Pursuant to section 12-61-111.5, the general assembly shall make annual appropriations from said fund for expenditures of the commission incurred in the performance of its duties under parts 1 and 4 of this article. The commission may request an appropriation specifically designated for educational and enforcement purposes. The expenditures incurred by the commission under parts 1 and 4 of this article shall be made out of such appropriations upon vouchers and warrants drawn pursuant to law.

§ 12-61-111.5, C.R.S. Fee adjustments.

(1) This section shall apply to all activities of the division under parts 1, 3, 4 and 7 of this article.

(2) (a) (I) The division shall propose, as part of its annual budget request, an adjustment in the amount of each fee that it is authorized by law to collect under parts 1, 3, 4 and 7 of this article. The budget request and the adjusted fees for the division shall reflect direct and indirect costs.

(II) The costs of the HOA information and resource center, created in section 12-61-406.5, shall be paid from the HOA information and resource center cash fund created in section 12-61-406.5. The division of real estate shall estimate the direct and indirect costs of operating the HOA information and resource center and shall establish the amount of the annual registration fee to be collected under section 38-33.3-401, C.R.S. The amount of the registration fee shall be sufficient to recover such costs, subject to a maximum limit of fifty dollars and subject to adjustment to reflect the actual direct and indirect costs of operating the HOA information and resource center pursuant to the general directive to adjust fees to avoid exceeding the statutory limit on uncommitted reserves in administrative agency cash funds as set forth in section 24-75-401 (3), C.R.S.

(b) Based upon the appropriation made and subject to the approval of the executive director of the department of regulatory agencies, the division of real estate shall adjust its fees so that the revenue generated from said fees approximates its direct and indirect costs. Such fees shall remain in effect for the fiscal year for which the budget request applies. All fees collected by the division not including fees retained by contractors pursuant to contracts entered into in accordance with section 12-61-103 or 24-34-101, C.R.S., shall be transmitted to the state treasurer, who shall credit the same to the division of real estate cash fund, which fund is hereby created. All moneys credited to the division of real estate cash fund shall be used as provided in this section and shall not be deposited in or transferred to the general fund of this state or any other fund.

(c) Beginning July 1, 1979, and each July 1 thereafter, whenever moneys appropriated to the division for its activities for the prior fiscal year are unexpended, said moneys shall be made a part of the appropriation to the division for the next fiscal year, and such amount shall not be raised from fees collected by the division. If a supplemental appropriation is made to the division for its activities, its fees, when adjusted for the fiscal year next following that in which the supplemental appropriation was made, shall be adjusted by an additional amount which is sufficient to compensate for such supplemental appropriation. Funds appropriated to the division in the annual long appropriations bill shall be designated as a cash fund and shall not exceed the amount anticipated to be raised from fees collected by the division.

§ 12-61-112, C.R.S. Records – evidence – inspection.

(1) The executive director of the department of regulatory agencies shall adopt a seal by which all proceedings authorized under parts 1, 3, and 4, of this article shall be authenticated. Copies of records and papers in the office of the commission or department of regulatory agencies relating to the administration of parts 1, 3, and 4 of this article, when duly certified and authenticated by the seal, shall be received as evidence in all courts equally and with like effect as the originals. All records kept in the office of the commission or department of regulatory agencies, under authority of parts 1, 3, and 4 of this article, shall be open to public inspection at

such time and in such manner as may be prescribed by rules and regulations formulated by the said commission.

(2) Repealed (1996)

(3) The commission shall not be required to maintain or preserve licensing history records of any person licensed under the provisions of this part 1 for any period of time longer than seven years.

§ 12-61-113, C.R.S. Investigation – revocation – actions against licensee – repeal.

(1) The commission, upon its own motion, may, and, upon the complaint in writing of any person, shall, investigate the activities of any licensee or any person who assumes to act in such capacity within the state, and the commission, after the holding of a hearing pursuant to section 12-61-114, has the power to impose an administrative fine not to exceed two thousand five hundred dollars for each separate offense and to censure a licensee, to place the licensee on probation and to set the terms of probation, or to temporarily suspend or permanently revoke a license when the licensee has performed, is performing, or is attempting to perform any of the following acts and is guilty of:

(a) Knowingly making any misrepresentation or knowingly making use of any false or misleading advertising;

(b) Making any promise of a character which influences, persuades, or induces another person when he could not or did not intend to keep such promise;

(c) Knowingly misrepresenting or making false promises through agents, advertising, or otherwise;

(c.5) Violating any provisions of the "Colorado Consumer Protection Act", article 1 of title 6, C.R.S.;

(d) Acting for more than one party in a transaction without the knowledge of all parties thereto;

(e) Representing or attempting to represent a real estate broker other than the licensee's employer without the express knowledge and consent of that licensee's employer;

(f) In the case of a broker registered as in the employ of another broker, failing to place, as soon after receipt as is practicably possible, in the custody of that licensed broker-employer any deposit money or other money or fund entrusted to the employee by any person dealing with the employee as the representative of that licensed broker-employer;

(g) Failing to account for or to remit, within a reasonable time, any moneys coming into the licensee's possession that belong to others, whether acting as real estate brokers or otherwise, and failing to keep records relative to said moneys, which records shall contain such information as may be prescribed by the rules of the commission relative thereto and shall be subject to audit by the commission;

(g.5) Converting funds of others, diverting funds of others without proper authorization, commingling funds of others with the broker's own funds, or failing to keep such funds of others in an escrow or a trustee account with some bank or recognized depository in this state, which account may be any type of checking, demand, passbook, or statement account insured by an agency of the United States government, and to so keep records relative to the deposit which contain such information as may be prescribed by the rules and regulations of the commission relative thereto, which records shall be subject to audit by the commission; (*Ed. Note: See Rule E-1(f)*)

(h) Failing to provide the purchaser and seller of real estate with a closing statement of the transaction, containing such information as may be prescribed by the rules and regulations of the commission or failing to provide a signed duplicate copy of the listing contract and the contract of sale or the preliminary agreement to sell to the parties thereto;

(i) Failing to maintain possession, for future use or inspection by an authorized representative of the commission, for a period of four years, of the documents or records prescribed by the rules and regulations of the commission or to produce such documents or records upon reasonable request by the commission or by an authorized representative of the commission;

(j) Paying a commission or valuable consideration for performing any of the functions of a real estate broker, as described in this part 1, to any person not licensed under this part 1; except that a licensed broker may pay a finder's fee or a share of any commission on a cooperative sale when such payment is made to a real estate broker licensed in another state or country. If a country does not license real estate brokers, then the payee must be a citizen or resident of said country and represent that the payee is in the business of selling real estate in said country;

(k) Disregarding or violating any provision of this part 1 or part 8 of this article, violating any reasonable rule or regulation promulgated by the commission in the interests of the public and in conformance with the provisions of this part 1 or part 8 of this article; violating any lawful commission orders; or aiding and abetting a violation of any rule, regulation, commission order, or provision of this part 1 or part 8 of this article;

(l) Repealed, effective July 1, 1989;

(m) Conviction of, entering a plea of guilty to, or entering a plea of nolo contendere to any crime in article 3 of title 18, C.R.S.; parts 1, 2, 3, and 4 of article 4 of title 18, C.R.S.; part 1, 2, 3, 4, 5, 7, 8, or 9 of article 5 of title 18, C.R.S.; article 5.5 of title 18, C.R.S.; parts 1, 3, 4, 6, 7, and 8 of article 6 of title 18, C.R.S.; parts 1, 3, 4, 5, 6, 7, and 8 of article 7 of title 18, C.R.S.; part 3 of article 8 of title 18, C.R.S.; article 15 of title 18, C.R.S.; article 17 of title 18, C.R.S.; section 18-18-404, 18-18-405, 18-18-406, 18-18-411, 18-18-412.5, 18-18-412.7, 18-18-412.8, 18-18-415, 18-18-416, 18-18-422, or 18-18-423, C.R.S., or any other like crime under Colorado law, federal law, or the laws of other states. A certified copy of the judgment of a court of competent jurisdiction of such conviction or other official record indicating that such plea was entered shall be conclusive evidence of such conviction or plea in any hearing under this part 1.

(Editor's note: The numbered articles in Title 18 of Colorado Revised Statute shown in this Part "m" refer to the following types of crimes:

<u>Article 3</u> is titled Offenses Against the Person and consists of four parts: homicide, assault, kidnapping and unlawful sexual behavior.

*<u>Article 4</u> deals with **offenses against property**, under which part 1 is arson, part 2 is burglary, part 3 robbery, and part 4 is theft.*

*<u>Article 5</u> consists of **offenses involving fraud**, including part 1 – forgery, obtaining a signature by deception, offering a false instrument for recording, et al, part 2 – fraud obtaining property or services (dual contracts), part 3 – fraudulent sales and business practices (unlawful activity concerning the sale of land), part 4 – bribery, part 5 – offenses relating to the uniform commercial code, part 7 – financial transaction device crime act (ATM's, et al), and part 8 – equity skimming*

*<u>Article 5.5</u> consists of **computer crime offenses**.*

*<u>Article 6</u> consists of **offenses involving family relations**.*

*<u>Article 7</u> consists of **offenses relating to morals**.*

*<u>Article 8</u> – part 3 refers to **government operations**, specifically bribery and corrupt influence.*

*<u>Article 15</u> deals with making, financing and collecting of **loans**.*

*<u>Article 17</u> is the Colorado **organized crime** control act.*

*<u>Article 18</u> is the Uniform Controlled Substances Act, part 4 deals with **offenses** and **penalties**.)*

(m.5) Violating or aiding and abetting in the violation of the Colorado or federal fair housing laws;

(m.6) Failing to immediately notify the commission in writing of a conviction, plea, or violation pursuant to paragraph (m) or (m.5) of this subsection (1);

(n) Having demonstrated unworthiness or incompetency to act as a real estate broker by conducting business in such a manner as to endanger the interest of the public;

(o) In the case of a broker licensee, failing to exercise reasonable supervision over the activities of licensed employees; (*Ed. Note: See also Rule E-31*)

(p) Procuring, or attempting to procure, a real estate broker's license or renewing, reinstating, or reactivating, or attempting to renew, reinstate, or reactivate, a real estate broker's license by fraud, misrepresentation, or deceit or by making a material misstatement of fact in an application for such license;

(q) Claiming, arranging for, or taking any secret or undisclosed amount of compensation, commission, or profit or failing to reveal to the licensee's principal or employer the full amount of such licensee's compensation, commission, or profit in connection with any acts for which a license is required under this part 1;

(r) Using any provision allowing the licensee an option to purchase in any agreement authorizing or employing such licensee to sell, buy, or exchange real estate for compensation or commission, except when such licensee, prior to or coincident with election to exercise such option to purchase, reveals in writing to the licensee's principal or employer the full amount of the licensee's profit and obtains the written consent of such principal or employer approving the amount of such profit;

(s) (I) Fraud, misrepresentation, deceit, or conversion of trust funds that results in the payment of any claim pursuant to part 3 of this article. This subparagraph (I) is repealed, effective when the last final judgment from any of the civil actions allowed pursuant to section 12-61-302(2) becomes effective and any resulting claim has been paid according to law. The director of the division of real estate shall notify the revisor of statutes, in writing, when the condition specified in this paragraph (s) has been satisfied.

(II) Effective on and after the repeal of part 3 of this article, fraud, misrepresentation, deceit, or conversion of trust funds that results in the entry of a civil judgment for damages.

(t) Any other conduct, whether of the same or a different character than specified in this subsection (1), which constitutes dishonest dealing;

(u) Repealed, effective May 30, 1986

(v) Having had a real estate broker's or a subdivision developer's license suspended or revoked in any jurisdiction, or having had any disciplinary action taken against the broker or subdivision developer in any other jurisdiction if the broker's or subdivision developer's action would constitute a violation of this subsection (1). A certified copy of the order of disciplinary action shall be prima facie evidence of such disciplinary action.

(w) Failing to keep records documenting proof of completion of the continuing education requirements in accordance with section 12-61-110.5 for a period of **four years** from the date of compliance with said section.

(x) (I) Violating any provision of section 12-61-113.2.

(II) In addition to any other remedies available to the commission pursuant to this title, after notice and a hearing pursuant to section 24-4-105, C.R.S., the commission may assess a penalty for a violation of section 12-61-113.2 or of any rule promulgated pursuant to section 12-61-113.2. The penalty shall be the amount of remuneration improperly paid and shall be transmitted to the state treasurer and credited to the general fund.

(y) Within the last five years, having a license, registration, or certification issued by Colorado or another state revoked or suspended for fraud, deceit, material misrepresentation, theft, or the breach of a fiduciary duty, and such discipline denied the person authorization to practice as:

(I) A mortgage broker or mortgage loan originator;

(II) A real estate broker or salesperson;

(III) A real estate appraiser, as defined by section 12-61-702(5);

(IV) An insurance producer, as defined by section 10-2-103(6), C.R.S.;

(V) An attorney;

(VI) A securities broker-dealer, as defined by section 11-51-201(2), C.R.S.;

(VII) A securities sales representative, as defined by section 11-51-201(14), C.R.S.;

(VIII) An investment advisor, as defined by section 11-51-201(9.5), C.R.S.; or

(IX) An investment advisor representative, as defined by section 11-51-201(9.6), C.R.S.

(1.5) Every person licensed pursuant to section 12-61-101(2) (a) (X) shall give a prospective tenant a contract or receipt; and such contract or receipt shall include the address and telephone number of the real estate commission in prominent letters and shall state that the regulation of rental location agents is under the purview of the real estate commission.

(2) In the event a firm, partnership, limited liability company, association, or corporation operating under the license of a broker designated and licensed as representative of said firm, partnership, limited liability company, association, or corporation is guilty of any of the foregoing acts, the commission may suspend or revoke the right of the said firm, partnership, limited liability company, association, or corporation to conduct its business under the license of said broker, whether or not the designated broker had personal knowledge thereof and whether or not the commission suspends or revokes the individual license of said broker.

(3) Upon request of the commission, when any real estate broker is a party to any suit or proceeding, either civil or criminal, arising out of any transaction involving the sale or exchange of any interest in real property or out of any transaction involving a leasehold interest in the real property and when such broker is involved in such transaction in such capacity as a licensed broker, it shall be the duty of said broker to supply to the commission a copy of the complaint, indictment, information, or other initiating pleading and the answer filed, if any, and to advise the commission of the disposition of the case and of the nature and amount of any judgment, verdict, finding, or sentence that may be made, entered, or imposed therein.

(4) This part 1 shall not be construed to relieve any person from civil liability or criminal prosecution under the laws of this state.

(5) Complaints of record in the office of the commission and the results of staff investigations may, in the discretion of the commission, be closed to public inspection, except as provided by court order, during the investigatory period and until dismissed or until notice of hearing and charges are served on a licensee.

(6) When a complaint or an investigation discloses an instance of misconduct which, in the opinion of the commission, does not warrant formal action by the commission but which should not be dismissed as being without merit, the commission may send a letter of admonition by certified mail, return receipt requested, to the licensee against whom a complaint was made and a copy

thereof to the person making the complaint, but the letter shall advise the licensee that the licensee has the right to request in writing, within twenty days after proven receipt, that formal disciplinary proceedings be initiated to adjudicate the propriety of the conduct upon which the letter of admonition is based. If such request is timely made, the letter of admonition shall be deemed vacated, and the matter shall be processed by means of formal disciplinary proceedings.

(7) All administrative fines collected pursuant to this section shall be transmitted to the state treasurer, who shall credit the same to the division of real estate cash fund.

(8) Any application for licensure from a person whose license has been revoked shall not be considered until the passage of one year from the date of revocation.

(9) When the division of real estate becomes aware of facts or circumstances that fall within the jurisdiction of a criminal justice or other law enforcement authority upon investigation of the activities of a licensee, the division shall, in addition to the exercise of its authority under this part 1, refer and transmit such information, which may include originals or copies of documents and materials, to one or more criminal justice or other law enforcement authorities for investigation and prosecution as authorized by law. (Editor Note: This provision is effective January 1, 2007.)

§ 12-61-113.2, C.R.S. Affiliated business arrangements – definitions – disclosures – enforcement and penalties – reporting – rules – investigation information shared with the division of insurance.

(1) As used in this section, unless the context otherwise requires:

(a) "Affiliated business arrangement" means an arrangement in which:

(I) a provider of settlement services or an associate of a provider of settlement services has either an affiliate relationship with or a direct beneficial ownership interest of more than one percent in another provider of settlement services; and

(II) a provider of settlement services or the associate of a provider directly or indirectly refers settlement service business to another provider of settlement services or affirmatively influences the selection of another provider of settlement services.

(b) "Associate" means a person who has one or more of the following relationships with a person in a position to refer settlement service business:

(I) a spouse, parent, or child of such person;

(II) a corporation or business entity that controls, is controlled by, or is under common control with such person;

(III) an employer, officer, director, partner, franchiser, or franchisee of such person, including a broker acting as an independent contractor; or

(IV) anyone who has an agreement, arrangement, or understanding with such person, the purpose or substantial effect of which is to enable the person in a position to refer settlement service business to benefit financially from referrals of such business.

(c) "Settlement service" means any service provided in connection with a real estate settlement including, but not limited to, the following:

(I) title searches;

(II) title examinations;

(III) the provision of title certificates;

(IV) title insurance;

(V) services rendered by an attorney;

(VI) the preparation of title documents;

(VII) property surveys;

(VIII) the rendering of credit reports or appraisals;

(IX) real estate appraisal services;

(X) home inspection services;

(XI) services rendered by a real estate broker;

(XII) pest and fungus inspections;

(XIII) the origination of a loan;

(XIV) the taking of a loan application;

(XV) the processing of a loan;

(XVI) underwriting and funding of a loan;

(XVII) escrow handling services;

(XVIII) the handling of the processing; and

(XIX) closing of settlement.

(2) (a) An affiliated business arrangement is permitted where the person referring business to the affiliated business arrangement receives payment only in the form of a return on an investment and where it does not violate the provisions of section 12-61-113.

(b) If a licensee or the employing broker of a licensee is part of an affiliated business arrangement when an offer to purchase real property is fully executed, the licensee shall disclose to all parties to the real estate transaction the existence of the arrangement. The disclosure shall be written, shall be signed by all parties to the real estate transaction, and shall comply with the federal "Real Estate Settlement Procedures Act of 1974", as amended, 12 U.S.C. sec. 2601 *et seq*.

(c) A licensee shall not require the use of an affiliated business arrangement or a particular provider of settlement services as a condition of obtaining services from that licensee for any settlement service. For the purposes of this paragraph (c), "Require the use" shall have the same meaning as "required use" in 24 CFR 3500.2 (b).

(d) No licensee shall give or accept any fee, kickback, or other thing of value pursuant to any agreement or understanding, oral or otherwise, that business incident to or part of a settlement service involving an affiliated business arrangement shall be referred to any provider of settlement services.

(e) Nothing in this section shall be construed to prohibit payment of a fee to:

(I) an attorney for services actually rendered;

(II) a title insurance company to its duly appointed agent for services actually performed in the issuance of a policy of title insurance;

(III) a lender to its duly appointed agent for services actually performed in the making of a loan.

(f) Nothing in this section shall be construed to prohibit payment to any person of:

(I) a bona fide salary or compensation or other payment for goods or facilities actually furnished or for services actually performed;

(II) a fee pursuant to cooperative brokerage and referral arrangements or agreements between real estate brokers.

(g) It shall not be a violation of this section for an affiliated business arrangement:

(I) to require a buyer, borrower, or seller to pay for the services of any attorney, credit reporting agency, or real estate appraiser chosen by the lender to represent the lender's interest in a real estate transaction; or

(II) if an attorney or law firm represents a client in a real estate transaction and issues or arranges for the issuance of a policy of title insurance in the transaction directly as agent or through a separate corporate title insurance agency that may be established by that attorney or law firm and operated as an adjunct to his or her law practice.

(h) No person shall be liable for a violation of this section if such person proves by a preponderance of the evidence that such violation was not intentional and resulted from a bona fide error notwithstanding maintenance of procedures that are reasonably adopted to avoid such error,

(3) On and after July 1, 2006, a licensee shall disclose at the time the licensee enters into or changes an affiliated business arrangement, in a form and manner acceptable to the commission, the names of all affiliated business arrangements to which the licensee is a party. The disclosure shall include the physical location of the affiliated businesses.

(4) On and after July 1, 2006, an employing broker, in a form and manner acceptable to the commission, shall at least annually disclose the names of all affiliated business arrangements to which the employing broker is a party. The disclosure shall include the physical location of the affiliated businesses.

(5) The commission may promulgate rules concerning the creation and conduct of an affiliated business arrangement, including, but not limited to, rules defining what constitutes a sham affiliated business arrangement. The commission shall adopt the rules, policies, or guidelines issued by the United States Department of Housing and Urban Development concerning the federal "Real Estate Settlement Procedures Act of 1974", as amended, 12 U.S.C. sec. 2601 *et seq*. Rules adopted by the commission shall be at least as stringent as the federal rules and shall ensure that consumers are adequately informed about affiliated business arrangements. The commission shall consult with the insurance commissioner pursuant to section 10-11-124 (2), C.R.S., concerning rules, policies, or guidelines the insurance commissioner adopts concerning affiliated business arrangements. Neither the rules promulgated by the commissioner nor the real estate commission may create a conflicting regulatory burden on an affiliated business arrangement.

(6) The division may share information gathered during an investigation of an affiliated business arrangement with the division of insurance.

§ 12-61-113.5, C.R.S. Mobile home transaction – requirements. Repealed (effective 4-19-94)

§ 12-61-114, C.R.S. Hearing – administrative law judge – review – rule-making authority.

(1) Except as otherwise provided in this section, all proceedings before the commission with respect to disciplinary actions and denial of licensure under this part 1 and part 8 of this article and certifications issued under part 4 of this article shall be conducted by an administrative law judge pursuant to the provisions of sections 24-4-104 and 24-4-105, C.R.S.

(2) Such proceedings shall be held in the county where the commission has its office or in such other place as the commission may designate. If the licensee is an employed broker, the commission shall also notify the broker employing the licensee by mailing, by first-class mail, a copy of the written notice required under section 24-4-104(3), C.R.S., to the employing broker's last-known business address.

(3) An administrative law judge shall conduct all hearings for denying, suspending, or revoking a license or certificate on behalf of the commission, subject to appropriations made to the department of personnel. Each administrative law judge shall be appointed pursuant to part 10 of article 30 of title 24, C.R.S. The administrative law judge shall conduct the hearing pursuant

to the provisions of sections 24-4-104 and 24-4-105, C.R.S. No license shall be denied, suspended, or revoked until the commission has made its decision by a majority vote.

(4) The decision of the commission in any disciplinary action or denial of licensure under this section is subject to review by the court of appeals by appropriate proceedings under section 24-4-106(11), C.R.S. In order to effectuate the purposes of parts 1, 3, 4, and 8 of this article, the commission has the power to promulgate rules and regulations pursuant to article 4 of title 24, C.R.S. The commission may appear in court by its own attorney.

(5) Pursuant to said proceeding, the court has the right, in its discretion, to stay the execution or effect of any final order of the commission; but a hearing shall be held affording the parties an opportunity to be heard for the purpose of determining whether the public health, safety, and welfare would be endangered by staying the commission's order. If the court determines that the order should be stayed, it shall also determine at said hearing the amount of the bond and adequacy of the surety, which bond shall be conditioned upon the faithful performance by such petitioner of all obligations as a real estate broker and upon the prompt payment of all damages arising from or caused by the delay in the taking effect of or enforcement of the order complained of and for all costs that may be assessed or required to be paid in connection with such proceedings.

(6) In any hearing conducted by the commission in which there is a possibility of the denial, suspension, or revocation of a license because of the conviction of a felony or of a crime involving moral turpitude, the commission shall be governed by the provisions of section 24-5-101, C.R.S.

§ 12-61-114.5, C.R.S. Rules and regulations.

All rules adopted or amended by the commission on or after July 1, 1979, shall be subject to sections 24-4-103(8)(c) and (8)(d) and 24-34-104(9)(b)(II), C.R.S.

§ 12-61-115, C.R.S. Subpoena compelling attendance of witnesses, records and documents (Repealed 5-24-2002)

§ 12-61-116, C.R.S. Failure to obey subpoena (Repealed 5-24-2002)

§ 12-61-117, C.R.S. Broker remuneration.

It is unlawful for a real estate broker registered in the commission office as in the employ of another broker to accept a commission or valuable consideration for the performance of any of the acts specified in this part 1 from any person except the broker's employer, who shall be a licensed real estate broker.

§ 12-61-118, C.R.S. Acts of third parties – broker's liability.

Any unlawful act or violation of any of the provisions of this part 1 upon the part of an employee, officer, or member of a licensed real estate broker shall not be cause for disciplinary action against a real estate broker, unless it appears to the satisfaction of the commission that the real estate broker had actual knowledge of the unlawful act or violation or had been negligent in the supervision of employees.

§ 12-61-119, C.R.S. Violations.

Any natural person, firm, partnership, limited liability company, association or corporation violating the provisions of this part 1 by acting as real estate broker in this state without having obtained a license or by acting as real estate broker after the broker's license has been revoked or during any period for which said license may have been suspended is guilty of a misdemeanor and, upon conviction thereof, if a natural person, shall be punished by a fine of not more than five hundred dollars, or by imprisonment in the county jail for not more than six months, or by both such fine and imprisonment and, if an entity, shall be punished by a fine of not more than five thousand dollars. A second violation, if by a natural person, shall be punishable by a fine of not more than one thousand dollars, or by imprisonment in the county jail for not more than six months, or by both such fine and imprisonment.

§ 12-61-120, C.R.S. Subpoena compelling attendance of witnesses and production of records and documents.

The commission, the director for the commission, or the administrative law judge appointed for hearings may issue a subpoena compelling the attendance and testimony of witnesses and the production of books, papers, or records pursuant to an investigation or hearing of such commission. Such subpoenas shall be served in the same manner as subpoenas issued by district courts and shall be issued without discrimination between public or private parties requiring the attendance of witnesses and the production of documents at hearings. If a person fails or refuses to obey a subpoena issued by the commission, the director, or the appointed administrative law judge, the commission may petition the district court having jurisdiction for issuance of a subpoena in the premises, and the court shall, in a proper case, issue its subpoena. Any person who refuses to obey such subpoena shall be punished as provided in section 12-61-121.

§ 12-61-121, C.R.S. Failure to obey subpoena – penalty.

Any person who willfully fails or neglects to appear and testify or to produce books, papers, or records required by subpoena, duly served upon him in any matter conducted under parts 1, 3, and 4 of this article, is guilty of a misdemeanor and, upon conviction thereof, shall be punished by a fine of twenty-five dollars, or imprisonment in the county jail for not more than thirty days for each such offense, or by both such fine and imprisonment. Each day such person so refuses or neglects shall constitute a separate offense.

§ 12-61-122, C.R.S. Powers of commission – injunctions.

The commission may apply to a court of competent jurisdiction for an order enjoining any act or practice which constitutes a violation of parts 1, 3, and 4 of this article, and, upon a showing that a person is engaging or intends to engage in any such act or practice, an injunction, restraining order, or other appropriate order shall be granted by such court regardless of the existence of another remedy there for. Any notice, hearing, or duration of any injunction or restraining order shall be made in accordance with the provisions of the Colorado rules of civil procedure.

§ 12-61-123, C.R.S. – Repeal of part.

This part 1 is repealed effective July 1, 2017. Prior to such repeal, the real estate division, including the real estate commission shall be reviewed as provided for in section 24-34-104, C.R.S.

B. Part 2 – Brokers Commissions

§ 12-61-201, C.R.S. When entitled to commission.

No real estate agent or broker is entitled to a commission for finding a purchaser who is ready, willing, and able to complete the purchase of real estate as proposed by the owner until the same is consummated or is defeated by the refusal or neglect of the owner to consummate the same as agreed upon.

§ 12-61-202, C.R.S. Objections on account of title.

No real estate agent or broker is entitled to a commission when a proposed purchaser fails or refuses to complete his contract of purchase because of defects in the title of the owner, unless such owner, within a reasonable time, has said defects corrected by legal proceedings or otherwise.

§ 12-61-203, C.R.S. When owner must perfect title.

The owner shall not be required to begin legal or other proceedings for the correction of such title, until such agent or broker secures from the proposed purchaser an enforceable contract in writing, binding him to complete the purchase whenever the defects in the title are corrected.

§ 12-61-203.5, C.R.S. Referral fees – interference with brokerage relationship

(1) No licensee under parts 1 to 4 of this article shall pay a referral fee unless reasonable cause for payment of the referral fee exists. A reasonable cause for payment means:

(a) An actual introduction of business has been made;

(b) A contractual referral fee relationship exists; or

(c) A contractual cooperative brokerage relationship exists.

(2) (a) No person shall interfere with the brokerage relationship of a licensee,

(b) As used in this subsection (2):

(I) "Brokerage relationship" means a relationship entered into between a broker and a buyer, seller, landlord, or tenant under which the broker engages in any of the acts set forth in section 12-61-101(2). A brokerage relationship is not established until a written brokerage agreement is entered into between the parties or is otherwise established by law.

(II) "Interference with the brokerage relationship" means demanding a referral fee from a licensee without reasonable cause.

(III) "Referral fee" means any fee paid by a licensee to any person or entity, other than a cooperative commission offered by a listing broker to a selling broker or vice versa.

(3) Any person aggrieved by a violation of any provision of this section may bring a civil action in a court of competent jurisdiction. The prevailing party in any such action shall be entitled to actual damages and, in addition, the court may award an amount up to three times the amount of actual damages sustained as a result of any such violation plus reasonable attorney fees.

§ 12-61-204, C.R.S. Repeal of part.

This part 2 is repealed, effective July 1, 2017. Prior to such repeal, the provisions in this part 2 shall be reviewed as provided for in section 24-34-104, C.R.S.

C. Part 3 – Recovery Fund

§ 12-61-301, C.R.S. Real estate recovery fund – fees – repeal.

§ 12-61-302, C.R.S. Limitation on payments out of the real estate cash fund – repeal.

(1) No payment shall be made from the general fund pursuant to this part 3 unless:

(a) The applicant has notified the commission, in writing, of the commencement of a civil action for a judgment that may result in an application for recovery from the fund. Such written notice shall be given no later than ninety days after commencement of the civil action.

(b) The revenues, if any, transferred to the division of real estate cash fund pursuant to subsection (11) of this section have first been exhausted. As used in this part 3, "fund" shall mean in the first instance such revenues transferred pursuant to subsection (11) of this section and then, if such revenues have been exhausted, the general fund.

(2) No payment shall be made from the fund unless the underlying civil action, on the basis of which payment from the fund is sought, was commenced within the time period prescribed in section 13-80-103, C.R.S., and by thirty days after May 27, 2005.

(3) (a) No payment shall be made from the fund unless the order of judgment in the underlying civil action contains specific findings of fact and conclusions of law that the licensed real estate broker or salesperson committed negligence, fraud, willful misrepresentation, or conversion of trust funds.

(b) Notwithstanding the provisions of paragraph (a) of this subsection (3), no payment for negligence shall be made from the fund if said licensed real estate broker or salesperson had in effect a complying policy of errors and omissions insurance coverage pursuant to section 12-61-103.6 at the time of the negligent act or omission.

(4) The fund shall be liable to pay only for reimbursement of actual and direct out-of-pocket losses, court costs and reasonable attorney fees that remain unpaid on the judgment, and postjudgment interest as provided by law. The fund shall not be liable for the payment of prejudgment interest of any kind.

(5) The fund shall not be liable for losses attributable to pain and suffering or mental anguish.

(6) Attorney fees recoverable pursuant to this section shall not exceed twenty-five percent of the amount of actual and direct out-of-pocket losses paid from the fund.

(7) The fund shall be liable only for claims based on judgments against natural persons.

(8) The fund shall not be subject to a claim by a licensee involving a transaction in which the applicant performed acts for which a broker's or salesperson's license is required.

(9) Notwithstanding any provision of this part 3 to the contrary, the liability of the fund shall not exceed:

(a) For applications filed after July 1, 1987, and before July 1, 1991, fifteen thousand dollars per claimant;

(b) For applications filed on or after July 1, 1991 and before July 1, 1995, fifteen thousand dollars per transaction, regardless of the number of persons aggrieved or the number of real estate licensees or parcels of real estate involved in such transactions;

(c) For applications filed on or after July 1, 1995, and before July 1, 1999 twenty thousand dollars per transaction, regardless of the number of persons aggrieved, the number of parcels, or the number of real estate licensees involved in such transaction;

(c.5) For applications filed on or after July 1, 1999, fifty thousand dollars per transaction, regardless of the persons aggrieved, the number of parcels, or the number of real estate licensees involved in such transactions;

(d) One hundred fifty thousand dollars for any one licensee, regardless of the number of judgments entered against the licensee, parcels of real estate involved, number of licensees involved, or number of persons aggrieved in such transactions.

(10) (a) If the validly filed applications exceed the limitation on liability set forth in paragraphs (a) to (d) of subsection (9) of this section, then payment from the fund shall be distributed among such applicants in the ratio that their respective claims bear to the aggregate of such valid claims or in such other manner as a court of record may deem equitable. Distribution of such moneys shall be among the persons entitled to share therein without regard to the order of priority in which their respective judgments may have been obtained or their applications may have been filed.

(b) If the commission issues an administrative order which directs payment from the fund in accordance with section 12-61-303 and this subsection (10), any prospective applicant affected by such order may file a petition with the appropriate court pursuant to section 12-61-304. In that proceeding, the commission may then move the court for an order consolidating or joining all applicants and prospective applicants whose judgments have been entered against a common licensee judgment debtor into one action so that the respective rights of all such applicants may be equitably adjudicated and settled.

(11) (a) The unexpended and unencumbered balance of the real estate recovery fund, as such balance existed prior to its repeal, shall be transferred to the division of real estate cash fund.

(b) This part 3 is repealed, effective when the last final judgment from any of the civil actions allowed pursuant to subsection (2) of this section becomes effective and any resulting claim has been paid according to law. The director of the division of real estate shall notify the revisor of statutes when the condition specified in this paragraph (b) has been satisfied.

§ 12-61-303, C.R.S. Simplified procedure – application for administrative order for payment from the fund – rules.

(1) A person who obtains a final judgment in any court of competent jurisdiction against a real estate broker or salesperson may file a verified application with the Colorado real estate commission for an administrative order for payment from the fund of any amount remaining unpaid on the judgment. The burden shall be upon such applicant to show the validity of the application under this part 3 and to provide the commission with such information as the commission may deem necessary to determine the validity of the application.

(2) The application shall be made on a form provided by the commission, which form shall be sufficient to provide the applicant with a reasonable opportunity to show compliance with this part 3 and shall require that the applicant submit the following information:

(a) The name, address, and telephone number of the applicant;

(b) If the applicant is represented by an attorney, the name, business address, telephone number, and Colorado supreme court registration number of the attorney;

(c) Identification of the underlying judgment forming the basis of the application, including the named parties, case number, and court entering judgment;

(d) The amount of the claim and an explanation of the applicant's computation of the claim; and

(e) Any other information the commission reasonably deems necessary to determine the validity of the application.

(3) The form provided to the applicant by the commission shall contain, in a prominent place, the following notice to the licensee judgment debtor:

"Notice: based on a judgment entered against you in the above-captioned matter, an application for an administrative order directing payment has been filed with the real estate commission.

If the real estate commission issues an administrative order for payment, your real estate license will automatically be revoked when the order is issued and payment is made to the applicant. Any subsequent application for a license shall not be granted until the amount paid has been reimbursed, plus interest at the statutory rate, and the passage of one year from the date of revocation.

If you wish to object to the application, you must file a written objection, setting forth the specific grounds for such objection, with the commission within thirty

days after having been served with a copy of the application. If you do not file a written objection, you waive your right to defend against the claim."

(4) The applicant shall also be required to show that:

(a) There is no collusion between the applicant and the judgment debtor or any other person liable to the applicant in the transaction for which the applicant seeks payment from the fund;

(b) The judgment debtor was licensed as a real estate broker or salesperson at the time of the transaction;

(c) The judgment debtor was acting in a real estate transaction as a real estate broker or salesperson, performing acts for which a real estate broker's or salesperson's license is required under this article, or that the transaction involved acts for which a real estate license was required and the judgment debtor was acting as a principal, not an agent, in that transaction;

(d) The judgment debtor committed fraud, willful misrepresentation, or conversion of trust funds;

(d.5) The judgment debtor committed negligence and did not, at the time of the negligent act or omission, have in effect a complying policy of errors and omissions insurance coverage pursuant to section 12-61-103.6;

(e) The application was not filed more than one year after finality of the judgment against the judgment debtor, including appeals;

(f) The applicant has reasonably sought to obtain a judgment against all persons and entities that are liable to the applicant for losses suffered in the transaction upon which the fund claim is based;

(g) The applicant has made reasonable searches and inquiries to ascertain whether there exists real or personal property or other assets available to satisfy the judgment in the underlying civil action and has undertaken reasonable legal means to reach such assets or other property in satisfaction of the judgment;

(h) The judgment debtor has been served with a copy of the application as required by subsection (5) of this section.

(5) When any person files an application with the commission requesting the issuance of an administrative order for payment from the fund, a copy of the verified application including the notice required by subsection (3) of this section and any other documents filed with the application shall be served upon the licensee judgment debtor by the applicant within twenty days after the date upon which the application is filed. A certificate or affidavit of such service shall be filed with the commission. Service upon a licensee judgment debtor shall be made according to the Colorado rules of civil procedure and subsection (6) of this section.

(6) (a) Service upon any real estate broker who is licensed or who renews a license under part 1 of this article on or after January 1, 2008, and upon whom personal service cannot be made with reasonable diligence shall be upon the registered agent of such real estate broker. If the real estate broker has no registered agent, the registered agent is not located under its registered agent name at its registered agent address, or the registered agent cannot with reasonable diligence be served, the real estate broker may be served by registered mail or by certified mail, return receipt requested, addressed to the entity at its principal address. Service is perfected under this subsection (6) at the earliest of:

(I) The date the real estate broker receives the process, notice, or demand;

(II) The date shown on the return receipt, if signed by or on behalf of the real estate broker; or

(III) Five days after mailing.

(b) Deleted by Laws 2008, Ch. 151, § 6, eff. April 17, 2008.

(7) The judgment debtor shall have thirty days after being served with the application within which to file a written objection to payment from the fund by the commission. Such objection shall be served upon the commission in accordance with the Colorado rules of civil procedure and shall clearly set forth the grounds upon which the objection is made. Failure to file such an objection shall constitute waiver of any right to proceed under section 12-61-304.

(8) (a) If the commission determines that an application is complete and valid, the commission may, by administrative order:

(I) Pay the requested amount or such lesser amount as the commission may deem appropriate;

(II) Settle the claim with the applicant for an appropriate agreed amount; or

(III) Deny the application on the grounds that the application does not demonstrate compliance with this part 3.

(b) Such administrative determination shall be promptly made by the commission or its designee in writing in the form of an administrative order and, if the application is denied, setting forth the general grounds therefor.

(c) Such administrative order shall be sent by regular mail to the applicant and the judgment debtor at their last known addresses according to records of the commission.

(9) The commission may adopt rules implementing this part 3 in accordance with article 4 of title 24, C.R.S.

§ 12-61-304, C.R.S. Procedure upon objection to payment or denial of application.

(1) If the commission issues an administrative order that denies an application for payment from the fund in whole or in part, the applicant may file a verified petition for payment from the fund in the court that entered the judgment on which the application is based. When an applicant files such a petition, the applicant shall serve a copy of the verified petition, including the notice required by subsection (2) of this section upon the real estate commission and upon the licensee judgment debtor in accordance with the Colorado rules of civil procedure and section 12-61-303 (6). A certificate or affidavit of such service shall be filed with the court.

(2) When a petition is filed with the court pursuant to subsection (1) of this section, the petition shall be accompanied by a notice that shall state as follows:

> **"Notice: based on a judgment entered against you in the above captioned matter, a petition for an order directing payment has been filed with the court.**
>
> **If the real estate commission makes a payment pursuant to a court order based upon this petition, your real estate license will automatically be revoked when the court order becomes final and payment is made. Any subsequent application for a license shall not be granted until the amount paid has been reimbursed, plus interest at the statutory rate, and the passage of one year from the date of revocation.**
>
> **If you wish to defend against this claim, you must file a written response with the court and mail a copy to the party filing the petition and to the real estate commission within thirty days after having been served with this notice. If you do not file a written response, you waive your right to defend against the claim."**

(3) If the judgment debtor files an objection to the issuance of an administrative order for payment from the fund in accordance with section 12-61-303 (7) and the commission issues an administrative order directing payment from the fund, the judgment debtor may file a verified petition objecting to payment from the fund in the court that entered the judgment on which the application was based. When a judgment debtor files such a petition, the judgment debtor shall

serve a copy of the petition upon the real estate commission and the applicant in accordance with the Colorado rules of civil procedure. A certificate or affidavit of such service shall be filed with the court.

(4) A petition filed with a court pursuant to subsection (1) or (2) of this section shall be in the form of a pleading and shall comply with the rules of procedure applicable to the court in which it is filed. Such petition shall be filed in the appropriate court no later than thirty days from the date upon which the administrative order is mailed by the commission pursuant to section 12-61-303 (8). The petition shall be accompanied by a verified copy of the application form and any attached documents that were filed with the commission.

(5) The real estate commission and any person served with a petition pursuant to this section shall have thirty days after service of the petition within which to file a written answer. The court shall thereafter set the matter for hearing.

(6) At a hearing under subsection (5) of this section the party filing the petition shall be required to show compliance, or lack thereof, with sections 12-61-302 to 12-61-304. Such hearing shall be on the merits of the application and shall not be in the nature of judicial review of the administrative order issued by the commission or of the procedure employed in issuing such order.

§ 12-61-305, C.R.S. Commission may defend against petition – burden of proof – presumption – compromise of claims.

The real estate commission may, on behalf of the fund, defend against a petition filed pursuant to section 12-61-304 and shall have recourse to all appropriate means of defense and appeal, including examination of witnesses and the right to relitigate any issues that were material and relevant to the proceeding against the fund and that were finally adjudicated in the underlying action on which the judgment in favor of the applicant was based. If such judgment was by default, stipulation, or consent, or whenever the action against the licensee judgment debtor was defended by a trustee in bankruptcy, the applicant shall have the burden of producing evidence of, and the burden of proving, the negligence, fraud, willful misrepresentation, or conversion of trust funds by the licensee judgment debtor; otherwise, the judgment shall create a rebuttable presumption of the negligence, fraud, willful misrepresentation, or conversion of trust funds by the licensee, and such presumption shall affect the burden of producing evidence. The real estate commission may, subject to court approval, settle a claim based upon the petition of an applicant and shall not be bound by any prior compromise of the judgment debtor.

§ 12-61-306, C.R.S. Defense against petition – conclusive adjudication of issues.

The judgment debtor may defend an action against the fund and shall have recourse to all appropriate means of defense and appeal, including examination of witnesses; except that matters finally adjudicated in the underlying action, including, but not limited to, the issues of negligence, fraud, willful misrepresentation, or conversion of trust funds, are conclusive against both the licensee judgment debtor and the applicant and may not be relitigated.

§ 12-61-307, C.R.S. Automatic revocation of license – reinstatement.

(1) Should the real estate commission pay from the fund any amount in settlement of a claim or toward satisfaction of a judgment against a licensed broker or salesperson, either by administrative order or by order of the court, the license of the broker or salesperson shall be automatically revoked upon the final date of such order.

(2) No such broker or salesperson shall be eligible to be licensed again until such broker or salesperson has repaid in full, plus interest at the statutory rate, the amount paid from the fund on the broker or salesperson's account and one year has passed from the date of revocation.

§ 12-61-308, C.R.S. Distribution from fund – fund insufficient to pay claims – delayed distribution authorized.

(1) Upon the issuance by the commission of an administrative order directing that payment be made out of the fund, or upon the entry of such an order by a court of competent jurisdiction, the controller is authorized to draw a warrant for the payment of the same upon a voucher approved by the real estate commission, and the state treasurer is authorized to pay the same out of the fund.

(2) If at any time the balance remaining in the fund is insufficient to satisfy any duly authorized claim or portion thereof, the real estate commission, when sufficient money has been deposited in the fund, shall satisfy such unpaid claims or portions thereof, in the order that such claims or portions thereof were originally filed, plus accumulated interest at the rate of four percent per year.

(3) After an administrative order for payment from the fund has been issued by the commission, the commission may delay payment in order to allow the filing periods in section 12-61-304 to expire. In the event that a petition is filed pursuant to section 12-61-304, payment pursuant to the administrative order shall be withheld pending the outcome of the court proceeding on the petition.

§ 12-61-309, C.R.S. Subrogation of rights.

(1) When, upon administrative order of the real estate commission or of any court, the real estate commission has made payment from the fund to an applicant, the real estate commission shall be subrogated to the rights of the applicant with respect to the amount so paid.

(2) Up to an amount equal to five percent of the payment to an applicant may be drawn from the fund and expended by the real estate commission for the purpose of enforcing the rights of a particular applicant to which the commission is subrogated pursuant to this section.

D. Part 8 – Brokerage Relationships

§ 12-61-801, C.R.S. Legislative declaration.

(1) The general assembly finds, determines, and declares that the public will best be served through a better understanding of the public's legal and working relationships with real estate brokers and by being able to engage any such real estate broker on terms and under conditions that the public and the real estate broker find acceptable. This includes engaging a broker as a single agent or transaction-broker. Individual members of the public should not be exposed to liability for acts or omissions of real estate brokers than have not been approved, directed, or ratified by such individuals. Further, the public should be advised of the general duties, obligations, and responsibilities of the real estate broker they engage.

(2) This part 8 is enacted to govern the relationships between real estate brokers and sellers, landlords, buyers, and tenants in real estate transactions.

§ 12-61-802, C.R.S. Definitions as used in this part 8, unless the context otherwise requires:

(1) "Broker" shall have the same meaning as set forth in section 12-61-101(2), except as otherwise specified in this part 8.

(1.3) "Customer" means a party to a real estate transaction with whom the broker has no brokerage relationship because such party has not engaged or employed a broker.

(1.5) "Designated Broker" means an employing broker or employed broker who is designated in writing by an employing broker to serve as a single agent or transaction-broker for a seller, landlord, buyer, or tenant in a real estate transaction. "Designated broker" does not include a real estate brokerage firm that consists of only one licensed natural person.

(2) "Dual agent" means a broker who, with the written informed consent of all parties to a contemplated real estate transaction, is engaged as a limited agent for both the seller and buyer or both the landlord and tenant.

(3) "Limited agent" means an agent whose duties and obligations to a principal are only those set forth in section 12-61-804, 12-61-805, with any additional duties and obligations agreed to pursuant to section 12-61-803 (5).

(4) "Single agent" means a broker who is engaged by and represents only one party in a real estate transaction. A single agent includes the following:

- (a) "Buyer's agent", which means a broker who is engaged by and represents the buyer in a real estate transaction;
- (b) "Landlord's agent", which means a broker who is engaged by and represents the landlord in a leasing transaction;
- (c) "Seller's agent", which means a broker who is engaged by and represents the seller in a real estate transaction; and
- (d) "Tenant's agent", which means a broker who is engaged by and represents the tenant in a leasing transaction.

(5) "Subagent" means a broker engaged to act for another broker in performing brokerage tasks for a principal. The subagent owes the same obligations and responsibilities to the principal as does the principal's broker.

(6) "Transaction-broker" means a broker who assists one or more parties throughout a contemplated real estate transaction with communication, interposition, advisement, negotiation, contract terms, and the closing of such real estate transaction without being an agent or advocate for the interests of any party to such transaction. Upon agreement in writing pursuant to section 12-61-803 (2) or a written disclosure pursuant to section 12-61-808 (2) (d), a transaction-broker may become a single agent.

§ 12-61-803, C.R.S. Relationships between brokers and the public.

(1) When engaged in any of the activities enumerated in section 12-61-101 (2), a broker may act in any transaction as a single agent or transaction-broker. The broker's general duties and obligations arising from that relationship shall be disclosed to the seller and the buyer or to the landlord and the tenant pursuant to section 12-61-808.

(2) A broker shall be considered a transaction-broker unless a single agency relationship is established through a written agreement between the broker and the party or parties to be represented by such broker.

(3) A broker may work with a single party in separate transactions pursuant to different relationships including, but not limited to, selling one property as a seller's agent and working with that seller in buying another property as a transaction-broker or buyer's agent, but only if the broker complies with this part 8 in establishing the relationships for each transaction.

(4) A broker licensed pursuant to part 1 of this article, whether acting as a single agent or transaction-broker, may complete standard forms including those promulgated by the Colorado real estate commission and may advise the parties as to effects thereof if the broker is performing the activities enumerated or referred to in section 12-61-101 (2) in the transaction in which the forms are to be used. In any such transaction, the broker shall advise the parties that the forms have important legal consequences and that the parties should consult legal counsel before signing such forms.

(5) Nothing contained in this section shall prohibit the public from entering into written contracts with any broker which contain duties, obligations, or responsibilities which are in addition to those specified in this part 8.

(6) (a) If a real estate brokerage firm has more than one licensed natural person, the employing broker or an individual broker employed or engaged by that employing broker shall be designated to work with the seller, landlord, buyer or tenant as a designated broker. The employing broker may designate more than one of its individual brokers to work with a seller, landlord, buyer or tenant.

(b) The brokerage relationship established between the seller, landlord, buyer or tenant and a designated broker, including the duties, obligations, and responsibilities of that relationship, shall not extend to the employing broker nor to any other broker employed or engaged by that employing broker who has not been so designated and shall not extend to the firm, partnership, limited liability company, association, corporation or other entity that employs such broker.

(c) A real estate broker may have designated brokers working as single agents for a seller or landlord and a buyer or tenant in the same real estate transaction without creating dual agency for the employing real estate broker, or any broker employed or engaged by that employing real estate broker.

(d) An individual broker may be designated to work for both a seller or landlord and a buyer or tenant in the same transaction as a transaction-broker for both, as a single agent for the seller or landlord treating the buyer or tenant as a customer, or as a single agent for a buyer or tenant treating the seller or landlord as a customer, but not as a single agent for both. The applicable designated brokerage relationship shall be disclosed in writing to the seller or landlord and buyer or tenant in a timely manner pursuant to rules promulgated by the real estate commission.

(e) A designated broker may work with a seller or landlord in one transaction and work with a buyer or tenant in another transaction.

(f) When a designated broker serves as a single agent pursuant to section 12-61-804 or 12-61-805, there shall be no imputation of knowledge to the employing or employed broker who has not been so designated.

(g) The extent and limitations of the brokerage relationship with the designated broker shall be disclosed to the seller, landlord, buyer or tenant working with that designated broker pursuant to section 12-61-808.

(7) No seller, landlord, buyer or tenant shall be vicariously liable for a broker's acts or omissions that have not been approved, directed or ratified by such seller, buyer, landlord or tenant.

(8) Nothing in this section shall be construed to limit the employing broker's or firm's responsibility to supervise licensees employed by such broker or firm nor to shield such broker or firm from vicarious liability

§ 12-61-804, C.R.S. Single agent engaged by seller or landlord.

(1) A broker engaged by a seller or landlord to act as a seller's agent or a landlord's agent is a limited agent with the following duties and obligations:

(a) To perform the terms of the written agreement made with the seller or landlord;

(b) To exercise reasonable skill and care for the seller or landlord;

(c) To promote the interests of the seller or landlord with the utmost good faith, loyalty, and fidelity, including, but not limited to:

(I) Seeking a price and terms which are acceptable to the seller or landlord; except that the broker shall not be obligated to seek additional offers to purchase the property while the property is subject to a contract for sale or to seek additional offers to lease the property while the property is subject to a lease or letter of intent to lease;

(II) Presenting all offers to and from the seller or landlord in a timely manner regardless of whether the property is subject to a contract for sale or a lease or letter of intent to lease;

(III) Disclosing to the seller or landlord adverse material facts actually known by the broker;

(IV) Counseling the seller or landlord as to any material benefits or risks of a transaction which are actually known by the broker;

(V) Advising the seller or landlord to obtain expert advice as to material matters about which the broker knows but the specifics of which are beyond the expertise of such broker;

(VI) Accounting in a timely manner for all money and property received; and

(VII) Informing the seller or landlord that such seller or landlord shall not be vicariously liable for the acts of such seller's or landlord's agent that are not approved, directed or ratified by such seller or landlord.

(d) To comply with all requirements of this article and any rules promulgated pursuant to this article; and

(e) To comply with any applicable federal, state, or local laws, rules, regulations, or ordinances including fair housing and civil rights statutes or regulations.

(2) The following information shall not be disclosed by a broker acting as a seller's or landlord's agent without the informed consent of the seller or landlord:

(a) That a seller or landlord is willing to accept less than the asking price or lease rate for the property;

(b) What the motivating factors are for the party selling or leasing the property;

(c) That the seller or landlord will agree to financing terms other than those offered;

(d) Any material information about the seller or landlord unless disclosure is required by law or failure to disclose such information would constitute fraud or dishonest dealing; or

(e) Any facts or suspicions regarding circumstances which may psychologically impact or stigmatize any real property pursuant to section 38-35.5-101, C.R.S.

(3) (a) A broker acting as a seller's or landlord's agent owes no duty or obligation to the buyer or tenant; except that a broker shall, subject to the limitations of section 38-35.5-101, C.R.S., concerning psychologically impacted property, disclose to any prospective buyer or tenant all adverse material facts actually known by such broker. Such adverse material facts may include but shall not be limited to adverse material facts pertaining to the title and the physical condition of the property, any material defects in the property, and any environmental hazards affecting the property which are required by law to be disclosed.

(b) A seller's or landlord's agent owes no duty to conduct an independent inspection of the property for the benefit of the buyer or tenant and owes no duty to independently verify the accuracy or completeness of any statement made by such seller or landlord or any independent inspector.

(4) A seller's or landlord's agent may show alternative properties not owned by such seller or landlord to prospective buyers or tenants and may list competing properties for sale or lease and not be deemed to have breached any duty or obligation to such seller or landlord.

(5) A designated broker acting as a seller's or landlord's agent may cooperate with other brokers but may not engage or create any subagents.

§ 12-61-805, C.R.S. Single agent engaged by buyer or tenant.

(1) A broker engaged by a buyer or tenant to act as a buyer's or tenant's agent shall be a limited agent with the following duties and obligations:

(a) To perform the terms of the written agreement made with the buyer or tenant;

(b) To exercise reasonable skill and care for the buyer or tenant;

(c) To promote the interests of the buyer or tenant with the utmost good faith, loyalty, and fidelity, including, but not limited to:

(I) Seeking a price and terms which are acceptable to the buyer or tenant; except that the broker shall not be obligated to seek other properties while the buyer is a party to a contract to purchase property or while the tenant is a party to a lease or letter of intent to lease;

(II) Presenting all offers to and from the buyer or tenant in a timely manner regardless of whether the buyer is already a party to a contract to purchase property or the tenant is already a party to a contract or a letter of intent to lease;

(III) Disclosing to the buyer or tenant adverse material facts actually known by the broker;

(IV) Counseling the buyer or tenant as to any material benefits or risks of a transaction which are actually known by the broker;

(V) Advising the buyer or tenant to obtain expert advice as to material matters about which the broker knows but the specifics of which are beyond the expertise of such broker;

(VI) Accounting in a timely manner for all money and property received; and

(VII) Informing the buyer or tenant that such buyer or tenant shall not be vicariously liable for the acts of such buyer's or tenant's agent that are not approved, directed, or ratified by such buyer or tenant;

(d) To comply with all requirements of this article and any rules promulgated pursuant to this article; and

(e) To comply with any applicable federal, state, or local laws, rules, regulations, or ordinances including fair housing and civil rights statutes or regulations.

(2) The following information shall not be disclosed by a broker acting as a buyer's or tenant's agent without the informed consent of the buyer or tenant:

(a) That a buyer or tenant is willing to pay more than the purchase price or lease rate for the property;

(b) What the motivating factors are for the party buying or leasing the property;

(c) That the buyer or tenant will agree to financing terms other than those offered;

(d) Any material information about the buyer or tenant unless disclosure is required by law or failure to disclose such information would constitute fraud or dishonest dealing; or

(e) Any facts or suspicions regarding circumstances which would psychologically impact or stigmatize any real property pursuant to section 38-35.5-101, C.R.S.

(3) (a) A broker acting as a buyer's or tenant's agent owes no duty or obligation to the seller or landlord; except that such broker shall disclose to any prospective seller or landlord all adverse material facts actually known by the broker including but not limited to adverse material facts concerning the buyer's or tenant's financial ability to perform the terms of the transaction and whether the buyer intends to occupy the property to be purchased as a principal residence.

(b) A buyer's or tenant's agent owes no duty to conduct an independent investigation of the buyer's or tenant's financial condition for the benefit of the seller or landlord and owes no duty to independently verify the accuracy or completeness of statements made by such buyer or tenant or any independent inspector.

(4) A buyer's or tenant's agent may show properties in which the buyer or tenant is interested to other prospective buyers or tenants without breaching any duty or obligation to such buyer or tenant. Nothing in this section shall be construed to prohibit a buyer's or tenant's agent from showing competing buyers or tenants the same property and from assisting competing buyers or tenants in attempting to purchase or lease a particular property.

(5) A broker acting as a buyer's or tenant's agent owes no duty to conduct an independent inspection of the property for the benefit of the buyer or tenant and owes no duty to independently verify the accuracy or completeness of statements made by the seller, landlord, or independent inspectors; except that nothing in this subsection (5) shall be construed to limit the broker's duties and obligations imposed pursuant to subsection (1) of this section,

(6) A broker acting as a buyer's or tenant's agent may cooperate with other brokers but may not engage or create any subagents.

§ 12-61-806, C.R.S. Dual agent.

(1) A broker shall not establish dual agency with any seller, landlord, buyer or tenant.

§ 12-61-807, C.R.S. Transaction-broker.

(1) A broker engaged as a transaction-broker is not an agent for either party.

(2) A transaction-broker shall have the following obligations and responsibilities:

(a) To perform the terms of any written or oral agreement made with any party to the transaction;

(b) To exercise reasonable skill and care as a transaction-broker, including, but not limited to:

(I) Presenting all offers and counteroffers in a timely manner regardless of whether the property is subject to a contract for sale or lease or letter of intent;

(II) Advising the parties regarding the transaction and suggesting that such parties obtain expert advice as to material matters about which the transaction-broker knows but the specifics of which are beyond the expertise of such broker;

(III) Accounting in a timely manner for all money and property received;

(IV) Keeping the parties fully informed regarding the transaction;

(V) Assisting the parties in complying with the terms and conditions of any contract including closing the transaction;

(VI) Disclosing to all prospective buyers or tenants any adverse material facts actually known by the broker including but not limited to adverse material facts pertaining to the title, the physical condition of the property, any defects in the property, and any environmental hazards affecting the property required by law to be disclosed;

(VII) Disclosing to any prospective seller or landlord all adverse material facts actually known by the broker including but not limited to adverse material facts pertaining to the buyer's or tenant's financial ability to perform the terms of the transaction and the buyer's intent to occupy the property as a principal residence; and

(VIII) Informing the parties that as seller and buyer or as landlord and tenant they shall not be vicariously liable for any acts of the transaction-broker;

(c) To comply with all requirements of this article and any rules promulgated pursuant to this article; and

(d) To comply with any applicable federal, state, or local laws, rules, regulations, or ordinances including fair housing and civil rights statutes or regulations.

(3) The following information shall not be disclosed by a transaction-broker without the informed consent of all parties:

(a) That a buyer or tenant is willing to pay more than the purchase price or lease rate offered for the property;

(b) That a seller or landlord is willing to accept less than the asking price or lease rate for the property;

(c) What the motivating factors are for any party buying, selling, or leasing the property;

(d) That a seller, buyer, landlord, or tenant will agree to financing terms other than those offered;

(e) Any facts or suspicions regarding circumstances which may psychologically impact or stigmatize any real property pursuant to section 38-35.5-101, C.R.S.; or

(f) Any material information about the other party unless disclosure is required by law or failure to disclose such information would constitute fraud or dishonest dealing.

(4) A transaction-broker has no duty to conduct an independent inspection of the property for the benefit of the buyer or tenant and has no duty to independently verify the accuracy or completeness of statements made by the seller, landlord, or independent inspectors.

(5) A transaction-broker has no duty to conduct an independent investigation of the buyer's or tenant's financial condition or to verify the accuracy or completeness of any statement made by the buyer or tenant.

(6) A transaction-broker may do the following without breaching any obligation or responsibility:

(a) Show alternative properties not owned by the seller or landlord to a prospective buyer or tenant;

(b) List competing properties for sale or lease;

(c) Show properties in which the buyer or tenant is interested to other prospective buyers or tenants; and

(d) Serve as a single agent or transaction-broker for the same or for different parties in other real estate transactions.

(7) There shall be no imputation of knowledge or information between any party and the transaction-broker or among persons within an entity engaged as a transaction-broker.

(8) A transaction-broker may cooperate with other brokers but shall not engage or create any subagents.

§ 12-61-808, C.R.S. Broker disclosures.

(1) (a) Any person, firm, partnership, limited liability company, association, or corporation acting as a broker shall adopt a written office policy that identifies and describes the relationships offered to the public by such broker.

(b) A broker shall not be required to offer or engage in any one or in all of the brokerage relationships enumerated in sections 12-61-804, 12-61-805, or 12- 61-807.

(c) Written disclosures and written agreements required by subsection (2) of this section shall contain a statement to the seller, landlord, buyer, or tenant that different brokerage relationships are available that include buyer agency, seller agency, or status as a transaction-broker. Should the seller, landlord, buyer, or tenant request information or ask questions concerning a brokerage relationship not offered by the broker pursuant to the broker's written office policy enumerated in subsection (1) (a) of this section, the broker shall provide to the party a written definition of that brokerage relationship that has been promulgated by the Colorado real estate commission.

(d) Disclosures made in accordance with this part 8 shall be sufficient to disclose brokerage relationships to the public.

(2) (a) (I) Prior to engaging in any of the activities enumerated in section 12-61-101 (2), a transaction-broker shall disclose in writing to the party to be assisted that such broker is not acting as agent for such party and that such broker is acting as a transaction-broker.

(II) As part of each relationship entered into by a broker pursuant to subparagraph (I) of this paragraph (a), written disclosure shall be made which shall contain a signature block for the buyer, seller, landlord, or tenant to acknowledge receipt of such disclosure. Such disclosure and acknowledgment, by itself, shall not constitute a contract with the broker. If such buyer, seller, landlord, or tenant chooses not to sign the acknowledgment, the broker shall note that fact on a copy of the disclosurc and shall retain such copy.

(III) If the transaction-broker undertakes any obligations or responsibilities in addition to or different from those set forth in section 12-61-807, such obligations or responsibilities shall be disclosed in a writing which shall be signed by the involved parties.

(b) Prior to engaging in any of the activities enumerated in section 12-61-101 (2), a broker intending to establish a single agency relationship with a seller, landlord, buyer, or tenant shall enter into a written agency agreement with the party to be represented. Such agreement shall disclose the duties and responsibilities specified in section 12-61-804 or 12-61-805, as applicable. Notice of the single agency relationship shall be furnished to any prospective party to the proposed transaction in a timely manner.

(c) Deleted.

(d) (I) Prior to engaging in any of the activities enumerated in section 12-61-101 (2), a broker intending to work with a buyer or tenant as an agent of the seller or landlord shall provide a written disclosure to such buyer or tenant that shall contain the following:

(A) A statement that the broker is an agent for the seller or landlord and is not an agent for the buyer or tenant;

(B) A list of the tasks that the agent intends to perform with the buyer or tenant; and

(C) A statement that the buyer or tenant shall not be vicariously liable for the acts of the agent unless the buyer or tenant approves, directs, or ratifies such acts.

(II) The written disclosure required pursuant to subparagraph (I) of this paragraph (d), shall contain a signature block for the buyer or tenant to acknowledge receipt of such disclosure. Such disclosure and acknowledgment, by itself, shall not constitute a contract with the broker. If the buyer or tenant does not sign such disclosure, the broker shall note that fact on a copy of such disclosure and retain such copy.

(e) Deleted.

(f) A broker who has already established a relationship with one party to a proposed transaction shall advise at the earliest reasonable opportunity any other potential parties or their agents of such established relationship.

(g) (I) Prior to engaging in any of the activities enumerated in section 12-61-101 (2), the seller, buyer, landlord or tenant shall be advised in any written agreement with a broker that the brokerage relationship exists only with the designated broker, does not extend to the employing broker or to any other brokers employed or engaged by the employing broker who are not so designated, and does not extend to the brokerage company.

(II) Nothing in this paragraph (g) shall be construed to limit the employing broker's or firm's responsibility to supervise licensees employed by such broker or firm nor to shield such broker or firm from vicarious liability.

§ 12-61-809, C.R.S. Duration of relationship.

(1) (a) The relationships set forth in this part 8 shall commence at the time that the broker is engaged by a party and shall continue until performance or completion of the agreement by which the broker was engaged.

(b) If the agreement by which the broker was engaged is not performed or completed for any reason, the relationship shall end at the earlier of the following:

(I) Any date of expiration agreed upon by the parties;

(II) Any termination or relinquishment of the relationship by the parties; or

(III) One year after the date of the engagement.

(2) (a) Except as otherwise agreed to in writing and pursuant to paragraph (b) of this subsection (2), a broker engaged as a seller's agent or buyer's agent owes no further duty or obligation after termination or expiration of the contract or completion of performance.

(b) Notwithstanding paragraph (a) of this section (2), a broker shall be responsible after termination or expiration of the contract or completion of performance for the following:

(I) Accounting for all moneys and property related to and received during the engagement; and

(II) Keeping confidential all information received during the course of the engagement which was made confidential by request or instructions from the engaging party unless:

(A) The engaging party grants written consent to disclose such information;

(B) Disclosure of such information is required by law; or

(C) The information is made public or becomes public by the words or conduct of the engaging party or from a source other than the broker.

(3) Except as otherwise agreed to in writing, a transaction-broker owes no further obligation or responsibility to the engaging party after termination or expiration of the contract for performance or completion of performance; except that such broker shall account for all moneys and property related to and received during the engagement.

§ 12-61-810, C.R.S. Compensation.

(1) In any real estate transaction, the broker's compensation may be paid by the seller, the buyer, the landlord, the tenant, a third party, or by the sharing or splitting of a commission or compensation between brokers.

(2) Payment of compensation shall not be construed to establish an agency relationship between the broker and the party who paid such compensation.

(3) A seller or landlord may agree that a transaction-broker or single agent may share the commission or other compensation paid by such seller or landlord with another broker.

(4) A buyer or tenant may agree that a single agent or transaction-broker may share the commission or other compensation paid by such buyer or tenant with another broker.

(5) A buyer's or tenant's agent shall obtain the written approval of such buyer or tenant before such agent may propose to the seller's or landlord's agent that such buyer's or tenant's agent be compensated by sharing compensation paid by such seller or landlord.

(6) Prior to entering into a brokerage or listing agreement or a contract to buy, sell, or lease, the identity of those parties, persons, or entities paying compensation or commissions to any broker shall be disclosed to the parties to the transaction.

(7) A broker may be compensated by more than one party for services in a transaction, if those parties have consented in writing to such multiple payments prior to entering into a contract to buy, sell, or lease.

§ 12-61-811, C.R.S. Violations.

The violation of any provision of this part 8 by a broker constitutes an act pursuant to section 12-61-113 (1) (k) for which the real estate commission may investigate and take administrative action against any such broker pursuant to sections 12-61-113 and 12-61-114.

Chapter 2:
Commission Rules and Regulations

An * in the left margin indicates a change in the statute, rule, or text since the last publication of the manual.

DEPARTMENT OF REGULATORY AGENCIES
DIVISION OF REAL ESTATE
COLORADO REAL ESTATE COMMISSION

4 CCR 725-1

RULES OF THE COLORADO REAL ESTATE COMMISSION

Rule A. License Qualifications, Applications and Examinations

A-1. Repealed (1-6-00)

* ***A-2. Requirements must precede exam and application***

Educational requirements for an initial license imposed by 12-61-103(4) and (6)(c)(II), C.R.S., must be completed and proof of completion filed in a method or manner as prescribed by the Commission prior to taking the examination and applying for a license.

A-3. Exams given only to those qualified

Examinations will be given only to duly qualified applicants for a real estate broker license, licensees upgrading a license, or licensees meeting the continuing education requirement; however, one instructor from each real estate school offering real estate courses required of applicants under section 12-61-103(4) C.R.S. may write the examination one time during any 12-month period.

A-4. Repealed

* ***A-5. Exam has two parts / Passing score on either part good for one year***

The real estate license examination is made up of two parts, a general portion and a state portion. If an applicant fails one or both parts of the exam, the applicant may retake the failed portion(s) at a subsequent time. passing score for either part of the exam is valid for one year only. An application received by the Division must be accompanied by the statutory fee, proof of completion of the required education and experience requirements, and proof of successful completion of the appropriate portion(s) of the exam within the year prior to the application being received by the Division. No exam score for either portion of the exam will be considered valid after one year.

A-6. Repealed

A-7. Exam results certified only if licensed (Repealed 5-5-04, Re-Adopted 10-5-04)

The Real Estate Commission will not certify to any person, state or agency any information concerning the results of any examination as it pertains to any person who has written the examination unless such person is or has been licensed as a Colorado real estate broker pursuant to such examination; except, that the Commission may authorize a special examination for existing licensees for certification purposes.

* ***A-8. Repealed***

A-9. License processing time frames

Provided the applicant has submitted a complete and satisfactory application in compliance with 12-61-102 C.R.S., the Commission will issue a license within 10 business days after receipt by the Commission of satisfactory results from the fingerprint-based criminal history record check. If the application or record check is not complete or satisfactory, the applicant will be mailed a notice of deferred status. The license of a broker whose application has been approved by the Commission subject to the receipt of certain compliance items shall be issued on an inactive status if such compliance items are not submitted within 20 days after written notification by the Commission.

A-10. Application denied or deferred; exam score extension

The Commission may deny or defer an original license application pursuant to 12-61-103(3) C.R.S. Under no circumstances will an examination be recognized by the Commission as complying with 12-61-103(6) C.R.S. after 18 months from the date an applicant took the examination which resulted in a passing score.

* ***A-11. Certificate of license history required***

An applicant for a Colorado real estate license, who has been licensed as a real estate broker or salesperson in any other state must file with the application for a Colorado license a "certification of licensing history" issued by each state where the applicant is currently or was previously licensed as a real estate broker or salesperson. If currently licensed, such certificate must bear a date of not more than 90 days prior to the submission date of the application. If no longer licensed, such certificate must bear a date subsequent to the expiration date.

A-12. Applicant with prior legal involvement

(a) Pursuant to 12-61-103 C.R.S., an applicant who has been convicted or pleaded nolo contendere to a misdemeanor or a felony, or any like municipal code violation, or has such charges pending or has agreed to a deferred prosecution, a deferred judgment, or a deferred sentence (violations) (excluding misdemeanor traffic violations) within the last ten years must file prior to or with his or her application for licensing the following information and documentation:

(1) A written and signed personal explanation and detailed account of the facts and circumstances surrounding each violation, which shall include the statement: "I have been charged with no other criminal violations either past or pending, other than those I have stated on the application."

(2) The completed Commission form number REC-BAA, including results of court hearing(s), in the form of copies of charges, disposition, pre-sentencing report and most recent probation or parole report.

(3) If the applicant is to be employed by another licensee, the employing broker must submit a letter stating that he/she is aware of the specific charge(s) or convictions(s).

(b) (1) At any time prior to submission of a formal application for licensure a person may request that the Commission issue a preliminary advisory opinion regarding the potential effect that previous conduct, criminal conviction(s) or violation(s) of the real estate license law may have on a future formal application for licensure. Such opinion may be issued by the Commission, in its discretion, in order to provide preliminary advisory guidance. Any such opinion shall not be binding on the Commission or limit the Commission's authority to investigate a future formal application for licensure. However, if the Commission issues a favorable advisory opinion, the Commission may elect to adopt such advisory opinion as the final decision of the Commission without further investigation or hearing.

(2) An individual seeking a preliminary advisory opinion under this rule is not an applicant for licensure and the issuance of an unfavorable opinion shall not prevent such individual from making application for licensure pursuant to the real estate licensing law and the rules and regulations of the Commission.

A-13. Repealed Effective October 2, 2005

A-14. Repealed Effective October 30, 2008

A-15. Criminal history check required prior to renewal

Any broker who has not submitted fingerprints to the Colorado Bureau of Investigation to be used to complete a one-time only criminal history record check, must do so prior to renewal of an active license. Renewed licenses will remain on inactive status until the Commission has received the results of a criminal record check. Fingerprints may be submitted for processing prior to renewal either electronically or on Card No. FD-258 in a manner acceptable to the Colorado Bureau of Investigation. The Commission may acquire a name-based criminal history record check for a renewing licensee who has twice submitted to a fingerprint-based criminal history record check and whose fingerprints are unclassifiable.

* ***A-16. Criminal history check required prior to application***

Applicants for an initial license must submit a set of fingerprints to the Colorado Bureau of Investigation and Federal Bureau of Investigation for the purpose of conducting a state and national criminal history record check prior to submitting an application for a license. Fingerprints must be submitted to the Colorado Bureau of Investigation for processing either electronically or on Card No. FD-258 in a manner acceptable to the Colorado Bureau of Investigation. Fingerprints must be readable and all personal identification data completed in a manner satisfactory to the Colorado Bureau of Investigation.

A-17. Pre-license education requirements

The seventy two hours of instruction or equivalent distance learning hours required in 12-61-103(4)(a)(III) C.R.S. must be satisfied by successful completion of courses of study approved by the Commission as follows:

(a) A minimum of 24 hours in Real Estate Closings; and

(b) A minimum of 8 hours in Trust Accounts and Record Keeping; and

(c) A minimum of 8 hours in Current Legal Issues; and

(d) A minimum of 32 hours in Practical Applications.

A-18. Repealed (effective 1-1-96)

A-19. Repealed (effective 3-4-99)

A-20. Denied license notice required

If the applicant for licensure is denied by the Commission for any reason, the applicant will be informed of the denial and the reason therefore.

A-21. Repealed (effective 1-1-97)

A-22. Repealed.

A-23. Pre-license and brokerage administration courses must be acceptable to commission

Completion of the courses of study approved by the Commission as required in 12-61-103(4)(a)(I), (II), (III), & 6(c) (II) C.R.S., whether through classroom or distance learning, must be based upon educational principles acceptable to the Real Estate Commission.

A-23.5. Repealed (effective 5-3-05)

A-24. Commission has course audit authority

The Commission may audit courses and may request from each school offering a Commission approved course of study under 12-61-103(4)(a) and (b), C.R.S., all instructional material related thereto and student attendance records as may be necessary for an investigation in the enforcement of Section 103 of the License Law and Commission Rules and Regulations. The purpose of the audit shall be to ensure that schools adhere to the approved course of study, offer course material and instruction consistent with acceptable education standards and instruct in such a manner that the desired learning objectives are met. Failure to comply with the provisions of this rule may result in the withdrawal of Commission course approval.

A-25. NSF check voids application

If the fees accompanying any application or registration made to the Commission (including fees for the recovery fund, renewals, transfers, etc.) are paid for by check and the check is not immediately paid upon presentment to the bank upon which the check was drawn, the application shall be canceled; the application may be reinstated only at the discretion of the Commission and upon full payment of any fees together with payment of the fee required by state fiscal rules for the clerical services necessary for reinstatement.

A-26. Temporary broker license

Pursuant to 12-61-103(7)(c) C.R.S., a temporary broker's license maybe issued to a corporation, partnership or limited liability company to prevent hardship. No application for a temporary broker's license will be approved unless the designated individual is a Colorado real estate broker with two years of active license experience as indicated by the records of the Real Estate Commission. No more than two temporary licenses may be issued to any corporation, partnership or limited liability company, whether consecutive or not, during any 18 month period, except by the Commission.

Rule B. Continuing Education

* ***B-1. When continuing education is required***

The Commission has determined that the license renewal process can be made more efficient by apportioning license renewals throughout the entire calendar year. Brokers must satisfy the continuing education requirements prior to applying to renew an active license, to activate an inactive license or to reinstate an expired license to active status. All license renewals shall be for a full three-year period called the "anniversary date renewal period". This period shall commence on the broker's initial date of issuance, i.e. the anniversary date, and expire three years later on the broker's anniversary date.

B-2. Methods of completing continuing education

Licensed brokers must satisfy the continuing education requirement before applying to renew an active license, to activate an inactive license or to reinstate an expired license to active status. Licensed brokers may satisfy the entire continuing education requirement through one of the following options:

(a) Completing the 12 hours required by C.R.S. 12-61-110.5(1)(c) and (2) required by this rule in annual four (4) hour increments developed by the Commission and called the "Annual Commission Update" course. Licensees choosing this option must complete an additional 12 hours of elective credit hours to meet the 24 hour total continuing education requirement during the license period in subject areas listed in C.R.S. 12-61-110.5(3).

* (b) A licensee may not take the same version of the Annual Update Course more than once. If a licensed broker takes more than 12 hours of the Annual Commission Update course during a license period, the licensee will receive elective credit hours for any additional hours.

(c) Completing the Commission-approved 24-hour "Broker Transition" course. (This option is permitted once to each licensee in lieu of the requirements of rule B-2 (a)).

(d) Completing the Commission-approved 24-hour "Brokerage Administration" course. (This option is permitted once to each licensee in lieu of the requirements of rule B-2 (a)).

(e) Passing the Colorado state portion of the licensing exam.

(f) Completing 72 total hours in the Colorado Contracts & Regulations course (48 hours) AND Real Estate Closings (24 hours) during the license period.

* ***B-3. Annual Commission Update course standards***

(a) Pursuant to 12-61-110.5(2), C.R.S. and Rule B-2(a), the 4-hour "Annual Commission Update" course shall be developed and presented by the Division of Real Estate and furnished to approved providers. Said course shall be presented without additional development by the provider or instructor.

(b) Any provider specified in commission rule B-6(a) or B-7(a) may request and offer the "Annual Commission Update" course. All other providers must apply annually for approval to offer the course using the commission-approved form and procedures in commission rule B-12, except that the course outline (B-12(a)) and course exam (B-12(b)) will be furnished by the Commission.

(c) Each active licensed broker must complete the "Annual Commission Update" course by achieving a passing score of 70% on a written or on-line course examination developed by the Commission. The Commission shall provide multiple course examinations for successive use by licensed brokers failing the end-of-course examination.

B-4. Distance learning permitted, defined

All continuing education courses may be offered and completed by distance learning. (*i.e.*, courses outside the traditional classroom setting in which the instructor and learner are separated by distance and/or time).

B-5. Courses excluded from continuing education credit

The following types of courses will not qualify for continuing education credit:

(a) Sales or marketing meetings conducted in the general course of a real estate brokerage practice.

(b) Orientation, personal growth, self-improvement, self-promotion or marketing sessions.

(c) Motivational meetings or seminars.

(d) Examination preparation or exam technique courses.

B-6. Courses automatically accepted for continuing education credit

The following courses, subject to all other provisions of Rule B, if within the topic areas listed in 12-61-110.5 (3) C.R.S., will be accepted for elective continuing education credit without Commission pre-approval.

(a) Courses offered by accredited colleges, universities, community or junior colleges, public or parochial schools or government agencies.

(b) Courses developed and offered by quasi-governmental agencies.

(c) Courses approved by and taken in satisfaction of another occupational licensing authority's education requirements.

(d) Courses in real property law by a provider approved by the Colorado Board of Continuing Legal and Judicial Education.

(e) Repealed

(f) Repealed

B-7. The following continuing education courses must receive Commission approval prior to offering: (Effective 05/01/2008)

(a) Courses offered proprietary real estate schools approved by the Colorado Division of Private Occupational Schools.

(b) Currently approved courses that are affected by any substantive changes.

(c) Courses offered by any provider proposing to offer course(s) on subjects not listed in C.R.S. 12-61-110.5(3)

(d) Courses offered by proprietary real estate schools approved as out of state providers by the Colorado Department of Private Occupational Schools, and are not approved pursuant to Rule B-6.

(e) Courses offered by employing brokers to their employed brokers.

(f) Courses offered by providers exempt under the provisions of 12-59-104, C.R.S.

(g) Courses offered by local, state or national REALTOR® Associations.

B-8. Administrative rules for continuing education courses

The following course format and administrative requirements apply to all Colorado continuing real estate education for licensed brokers:

(a) Courses must be at least 1 hour in length, containing at least 50 instructional minutes.

(b) A maximum of 8 hours of credit may be earned per day.

(c) No course may be repeated for credit in the same calendar year.

(d) Instructors may receive credit for classroom teaching hours once per course taught per year.

(e) Hours in excess of 24 may not be carried forward to satisfy a subsequent renewal requirement.

(f) No school/provider may waive, excuse completion of, or award partial credit for the full number of course hours.

(g) No challenge exam or equivalency may substitute for the full course outline.

(h) No credit may be earned for remedial education stipulated to between a licensed broker and the Commission as part of a disciplinary action, or alternative to disciplinary action.

(i) No course offering by a provider will be accepted unless the provider has either been granted a certificate of approval by the Colorado Department of Higher Education,

Division of Private Occupational Schools, or is exempt from such requirement pursuant to C.R.S.12-59-104.

* (j) Courses approved for continuing education must maintain and improve a broker's skill, knowledge, and competency in real estate practice.

B-9. Term of course approval

Course approval certification shall be for a period of three years, except that an annual or one-time seminar or conference offering may be approved for a specific date or dates.

B-10. Proof of course completion

Each Colorado licensed broker is responsible for securing from the provider evidence of course completion in the form of an affidavit, certificate or official transcript of the course. Said documentation must be in sufficient detail to show the name of the licensee, course subject, content, duration, date(s) and contain the authentication of the provider. Licensees must retain proof of continuing education completion for 4 years, and provide said proof to the Commission upon request.

* ***B-11. Provider must retain records***

Each approved provider must retain copies of course outlines or syllabi and complete records of attendance for a period of four (4) years, and provide the records to the Commission upon request.

B-12. Course approval application process

Continuing education providers required to have Commission course approval must, in accordance with all of the provisions of this Rule B, submit an application form prescribed by the Commission, along with the following information at least 30 days prior to the proposed class dates:

(a) Detailed course outline or syllabus, including the intended learning outcomes, the course objectives and the approximate time allocated for each topic.

(b) A copy of the course exam(s) and instructor answer sheet if applicable. In the absence of an exam, the criteria used in evaluating a person's successful completion of the course objectives.

(c) Copy of instructor teaching credential; if none, a résumé showing education and experience which evidence mastery of the material to be presented.

(d) A copy of advertising or promotional material used to announce the offering.

(e) Upon Commission request, a copy of textbook, manual, audio or videotapes, or other instructional material.

(f) Effective January 1, 2001, providers of continuing education offered through distance learning must submit evidence in a form prescribed by the real estate commission that the method of delivery and course structure is consistent with acceptable education standards assuring that the desired learning objectives are met. The Commission will approve methods of delivery certified by the Association of Real Estate License Law Officials (ARELLO), or by a substantially equivalent authority and method.

B-13. Providers subject to statute, rule and course audit

By offering real estate continuing education in Colorado, each provider agrees to comply with relevant statutes and Commission rules and to permit Commission audit of said courses at any time and at no cost.

B-14. Licensee attests to compliance by submitting application

The act of submitting an application for renewal, activation or reinstatement of a real estate license shall mean that the licensee attests to compliance with the continuing education requirements of C.R.S. 12-61-110.5.

Rule C. Licensing – Office

C-1. Individual proprietor must be sole owner

A broker licensed as an individual or as an individual doing business under a trade name shall be the sole owner of the brokerage business or such brokerage business will be considered as a partnership and the partnership shall apply for a broker's license under 12-61-103(7) C.R.S.

C-2. Resident broker required to have office; exceptions

Every resident Colorado real estate broker shall maintain and supervise a brokerage practice available to the public, except those brokers registered in the Commission office as in the employ of another broker or those brokers registered as inactive.

* ***C-3. Responsible broker availability***

Any broker licensed as an individual proprietorship or the acting broker for a corporation, partnership or limited liability company must be reasonably available to manage and supervise such brokerage practice.

C-4. Repealed effective 1-1-97

C-5. Repealed effective 1-1-97

C-6. Repealed effective 1-1-97

C-7. Repealed effective 1-1-97

C-8. Repealed effective 1-1-97

C-9. Repealed

C-10. Repealed

C-11. Repealed

C-12. Repealed

C-13. Repealed

* ***C-14. Repealed***

C-15. Repealed

C-16. License non-transferable

No agreement shall be entered into by any licensee whereby an individual licensee lends their name or license for the benefit of another person, partnership, limited liability company or corporation, whereby the provisions of the Colorado Real Estate Broker License Law and Commission Rules relating to licensing are circumvented.

C-17. Corporate license name may not duplicate suspended/revoked license

The Commission may refuse to issue a license to a partnership, limited liability company or corporation if the name of said corporation, partnership or limited liability company is the same as that of any person or entity whose license has been suspended or revoked or is so similar as to be easily confused with that of the suspended or revoked person or entity by members of the general public.

* ***C-18. Brokerage activity only in trade name or full licensed name***

An independent or employing broker may adopt a trade name according to Colorado law and such trade name will appear on the face of the independent or employing broker's license, however, pursuant to 12-61-103(10), C.R.S. such independent or employing broker must conduct brokerage business only under such trade name or conduct brokerage business under the entire name appearing on the face of the license. Employed brokers, who are licensed under an employing broker that is doing business under a trade name, shall be licensed under the entire name appearing on the face of the license, and not under the brokerage's or individual's trade name.

C-19. Name rules

(a) The purpose of this rule is to provide interpretation for Section 12-61-103(10), C.R.S., as amended.

(b) For the purposes of this rule, the following definitions shall apply:

(i) The term "broker" shall mean any sole proprietor, partnership, limited liability company, or corporation licensed by the Real Estate Commission.

(ii) The term "trade name" shall include trademark, service mark, trade identification, or, any portion thereof which is recognizable as a trade name, trademark, service mark, or trade identification.

(c) Pursuant to 12-61-103(10) C.R.S., no person shall be licensed under more than one name, and no person shall conduct or promote a real estate brokerage business except under the name under which such person or brokerage business is licensed; however, the use of a trade name with the permission of the owner of such trade name may be used concurrently with the licensed name of the broker in the promotion or conduct of the licensed broker's business.

(d) Repealed

(e) No broker shall advertise or promote its business in such a manner as to mislead the public as to the identity of the licensed broker, nor shall a portion of the licensed name of any broker be advertised or promoted in a manner which would mislead the public as to the identity of the licensed broker.

(f) Any broker using a trade name, the use of which requires obtaining permission from another who has an existing and continuing right in that trade name by virtue of any state of federal law, in advertising other than of specific properties for sale and in advertising of specific properties for sale jointly with other brokers under a trade name shall cause the following legend to appear in a conspicuous and reasonable manner calculated to attract the attention of the public:

"Each (Actual Trade Name) brokerage business is independently owned and operated."

(This legend may be re-phrased if the consent of the Commission is secured.)

(g) Any broker using a trade name owned by another on "for sale" or "for lease" signs on specific property or in advertising specific property for sale or rent in any media shall clearly and unmistakably include said broker's name, as registered with the Commission, in a conspicuous and reasonable manner calculated to attract the attention of the public. The broker's name shall appear where specific property is advertised for sale so that the public may unmistakably identify the broker responsible for the handling of the listing of the specific property.

(h) Any broker using a trade name owned by another on business cards, letterheads, contracts, or other documents relating to real estate transactions, shall clearly and unmistakably include said broker's name as registered with the Commission in a conspicuous and reasonable manner calculated to attract the attention of the public and shall also include the following legend:

> "Each (Actual Trade Name) brokerage business is independently owned and operated."

(This legend may be re-phrased if the consent of the Commission is secured.)

(i) Any broker using a trade name owned by another on signs displayed at a place of business shall clearly and unmistakably include said broker's name as registered with the Commission on such signs in a conspicuous and reasonable manner calculated to attract the attention of the public and shall also include the following legend:

> "Each (Actual Trade Name) brokerage business is independently owned and operated."

(This legend may be re-phrased if the consent of the Commission is secured.)

C-20. No license name identical to one previously issued

No broker's license will be issued to a broker under a trade name, corporate name, partnership name or limited liability company name which is identical to another licensed broker's trade name, corporate, partnership or limited liability company name.

C-21. Individual proprietor may not appear to be corporate

A broker licensed as an individual proprietorship shall not adopt a trade name which includes the following words: Corporation, Partnership, Limited Liability Company, Limited, Incorporated, or the abbreviations thereof.

C-22. Employing broker qualifications for business entities

When a broker applicant submits an application to qualify:

(a) A corporation as a real estate brokerage company, the broker applicant must certify that:

1. The corporation has been properly incorporated with the Colorado Secretary of State and is in good standing, proof of which shall be included with the application;
2. If an assumed or trade name is to be used, it has been properly filed with and accepted by the Colorado Secretary of State, proof of which shall be included with the application;
3. The broker applicant has been appointed by the board of directors to act as broker for the corporation.

(b) A partnership as a real estate brokerage company, the broker applicant must certify that:

1. The partnership has been properly registered with the Colorado Department of Revenue or properly filed with the Colorado Secretary of State and is in good standing, proof of which shall be included with the application;
2. If an assumed or trade name is to be used, it has been properly filed with Colorado Department of Revenue or filed and accepted by the Colorado Secretary of State, proof of which shall be included with the application;

3. The broker applicant has been appointed the real estate broker for the partnership by all general partners or managers/officers;

(c) A limited liability company as a real estate brokerage company, the broker applicant must certify that:

1. The limited liability company has been properly registered with the Colorado Secretary of State and is in good standing, proof of which shall be included with the application;
2. If an assumed or trade name is to be used, it has been properly filed with the Colorado Secretary of State, proof of which shall be included with the application;
3. The broker applicant has been appointed the real estate broker for the limited liability company by all managers, or if management has been reserved to the members in the articles of organization, by all members;

* ***C-23. Unlicensed on-site manager***

Pursuant to 12-61-101(2), C.R.S., offering to rent or lease real estate or renting or leasing real estate requires a Colorado real estate broker's license. If a brokerage firm employs an unlicensed on-site manager, the employing broker must:

(a) Actively and diligently supervise all activities of the on-site manager or delegate the supervisory responsibility in writing to a qualified employed broker;

(b) Require the on-site manager to report directly to either the employing broker or the delegated employed broker;

(c) Require the on-site manager account for and remit all monies, including rents and security deposits, collected on behalf of the broker or owner to the employing broker or the delegated employed broker;

(d) Ensure that property maintenance scheduled by the on-site manager is performed in accordance with the executed property management agreement;

(e) Engage the on-site manager, either as a regularly salaried employee or as an independent contractor, and pay the on-site manager through the real estate brokerage firm. The salary may include rent value or other non-commission income.

(f) Instruct the on-site manager to not negotiate any of the material terms of a lease or rental agreement with a tenant or prospective tenant.

The unlicensed on-site manager may show prospective tenants available units, quote rental prices established by the owner or broker, arrange for maintenance, and collect monies, including security deposits and rents.

* ***C-24. Repealed***

C-25. Notice of termination; employing broker

The employing broker of a licensed corporation, partnership or limited liability company must immediately notify the Commission in a manner acceptable to the Commission, of the employing broker's termination of employment with such licensed corporation, partnership or limited liability company, or upon the employing broker's failure to continue to comply with 12-61-103, C.R.S. and applicable rules. Upon such notification, the employing broker and all employed licensees shall be placed on inactive status.

C-26. Inactive license

A broker license may be issued on an inactive status.

Rule D. Renewal, Transfer, Inactive License, Errors and Omissions Insurance

D-1. Repealed

D-2. Inactive license request

A real estate licensee may request that the Commission records show their license inactive until proper request for reactivation has been made.

D-3. Inactive license must be renewed

A real estate licensee whose license is on inactive status must apply for renewal of such inactive license and pay the regular renewal fees.

D-4. Renew using method approved by commission

Renewal of all licenses can be effected by use of the renewal application form provided by the Commission or by other methods acceptable to the Real Estate Commission.

* ***D-5. Repealed***

* ***D-6. License renewal notification***

Notification that a license will expire, unless renewed, will be sent to the electronic mail address on file with the Commission.

D-7. Direct compensation from previous broker

When a real estate license is on inactive status or has been transferred to a subsequent employing broker, a licensee may be compensated directly by a previous employing broker for commissions earned during that term of employment.

D-8. Repealed

D-9. Form and fees required to change license

No changes in the license status will be made except in a manner acceptable to the Commission to effect such change and upon payment of the statutory fees for such changes in addition to the license renewal fees.

D-10. Repealed

* ***D-11. Initial license renewal***

An initial license will be issued for a three-year period commencing on the issuance date and expiring three years from the date of issuance.

D-12. Renewal fees non-refundable

All fees paid for the renewal of a license shall be non-refundable.

D-13. Anniversary Date Renewals and Reinstatements

* License renewal periods shall begin on the ANNIVERSARY date of issuance and continue for three full years. An expired license may be reinstated as follows:

(a) If proper application is made within thirty-one days after the date of expiration, by payment of the regular renewal fee;

(b) If proper application is made more than thirty-one days but within one year after the date of expiration, by payment of the regular renewal fee and payment of a reinstatement fee equal to one-half the regular renewal fee;

(c) If proper application is made more than one year but within three years after the date of expiration, by payment of the regular renewal fee and payment of a reinstatement fee equal to the regular renewal fee.

D-14. Errors and omissions (E&O) insurance (See 12-61-103.6 C.R.S.)

Every active real estate licensee, including licensed real estate companies, shall have in effect a policy of errors and omissions insurance to cover all acts requiring a license.

(a) The Commission shall enter into a contract with a qualified insurance carrier to make available to all licensees and license applicants a group policy of insurance under the following terms and conditions:

(1) The insurance carrier is licensed and authorized by the Colorado Division of Insurance to write policies of errors and omissions insurance in this state.

(2) The insurance carrier maintains an A.M. Best rating of "B" or better.

(3) The insurance carrier will collect premiums, maintain records and report names of those insured and a record of claims to the Commission on a timely basis and at no expense to the state.

(4) The insurance carrier has been selected through a competitive bidding process.

(5) The contract and policy are in conformance with this rule and all relevant Colorado statutory requirements.

(b) The group policy shall provide, at a minimum, the following terms of coverage:

(1) Coverage for all acts for which a real estate license is required, except those illegal, fraudulent or other acts which are normally excluded from such coverage.

(2) Deleted 10/1/03.

(3) That the coverage cannot be canceled by the insurance carrier except for non-payment of the premium or in the event a licensee becomes inactive or is revoked or an applicant is denied a license.

(4) Pro-ration of premiums for coverage which is purchased during the course of a calendar year but with no provision for refunds of unused premiums.

(5) Not less than $100,000 coverage for each licensed individual and entity per covered claim regardless of the number of licensees or entities to which a settlement or claim may apply.

(6) An annual aggregate limit of not less than $300,000 per licensed individual or entity.

(7) A deductible amount for each occurrence of not more than $1,000 for claims and no deductible for legal expenses and defense.

(8) The obligation of the insurance carrier to defend all covered claims and the ability of the insured licensee to select counsel of choice subject to the written permission of the carrier, which shall not be unreasonably withheld.

(9) Coverage of a licensee's use of lock boxes, which coverage shall not be less than $25,000 per occurrence.

(10) The ability of a licensee, upon payment of an additional premium, to obtain higher or excess coverage or to purchase additional coverage from the group carrier as may be determined by the carrier.

(11) That coverage is individual and license specific and will cover the licensee regardless of changes in employing broker.

(12) The ability of a licensee, upon payment of an additional premium to obtain an extended reporting period of not less than 365 days.

(13) A conformity endorsement allowing a Colorado resident licensee to meet the errors and omissions insurance requirement for an active license in another group mandated state without the need to purchase separate coverage in that state.

(c) Licensees or applicants may obtain errors and omissions coverage independent of the group plan from any insurance carrier subject to the following terms and conditions:

(1) The insurance carrier is licensed and authorized by the Colorado division of insurance to write policies of errors and omissions insurance in this state and is in conformance with all Colorado statutes.

(2) The insurance provider maintains an A.M. Best rating of "B" or better.

(3) The policy, at a minimum, complies with all relevant conditions set forth in this rule and the insurance carrier so certifies in an affidavit issued to the insured licensee or applicant in a form specified by the Commission and agrees to immediately notify the Commission of any cancellation or lapse in coverage. Independent coverage must provide, at a minimum, the following:

(i) The contract and policy are in conformance with all relevant Colorado statutory requirements.

(ii) Coverage includes all acts for which a real estate license is required, except those illegal, fraudulent or other acts which are normally excluded from such coverage.

(iii) Coverage cannot be canceled by the insurance provider, except pursuant to and in conformance with 10-4-109.7 CRS

(iv) Coverage is for not less than $100,000 for each licensed individual and entity per covered claim, regardless of the number of licensees or entities to which a settlement or claim may apply, with an annual aggregate limit of not less than $300,000 per licensed individual and entity.

(v) Payment of claims by the provider shall be on a first dollar basis and the provider shall look to the insured for payment of any deductible.

(vi) The ability of a licensee, upon payment of an additional premium to obtain an extended reporting period of not less than 365 days.

(vii) That the provider of the independent policy has executed an affidavit in a form or manner specified by the commission attesting that the independent policy is in force and, at a minimum, complies with all relevant conditions set forth herein and that the provider will immediately notify the commission in writing of any cancellation or lapse in coverage of any independent policy.

(viii) Coverage of a licensee's use of lock boxes, which coverage shall not be less than $25,000 per occurrence.

(d) Applicants for licensure, activation, renewal and reinstatement shall certify compliance with this rule and 12-61-103.6 C.R.S. on forms or in a manner prescribed by the Commission. Any active licensee who so certifies and fails to obtain errors and omissions coverage or to provide proof of continuous coverage, either through the group carrier or directly to the Commission, shall be placed on inactive status:

(1) immediately, if certification of current insurance coverage is not provided to the Commission; or,

(2) immediately upon the expiration of any current insurance when certification of continued coverage is not provided.

Rule E. Separate Accounts – Records – Accountings – Investigations

E-1. Trust accounts; requirements and purposes

All "money belonging to others" accepted by a resident or non-resident broker doing business in this state shall be deposited in one or more accounts separate from other money belonging to the broker or brokerage entity. The broker shall identify the fiduciary nature of each separate account in the deposit agreement with the recognized bank or institution by the use of the word "trust" or "escrow" and a label identifying the purpose/type of such account, *i.e.*, "sales escrow", "rental escrow", "security deposit escrow", "owners association escrow", or other abbreviated form defined in the deposit agreement. Unless otherwise permitted by other subsections of this rule, all money belonging to others shall be deposited according to the purpose of the transaction in separate types of escrow accounts. The broker shall retain a copy of each account deposit agreement executed for inspection by an authorized representative of the Commission.

(a) Accounts in name of broker and business entity

Such separate trust accounts must be maintained in the name of the licensed broker or if the licensed broker is a partnership, corporation or limited liability company, such account shall be maintained in the name of the broker acting for such partnership, corporation or limited liability company and in the name of the licensed partnership, limited liability company or corporation. The licensed broker must be able to withdraw money from such separate account, but may authorize other licensed or unlicensed co-signers. However, such authorization shall not relieve the broker of any responsibility under the licensing act.

(b) Credit Unions not for escrowed money

Credit union escrow or trust accounts do not meet the escrow requirements of 12-61-113 (1) (g.5) C.R.S., and are therefore not suitable depositories for money belonging to others.

(c) Accounts in name of employing broker only

When a broker is registered in the office of the Real Estate Commission as in the employ of another broker the responsibility for the maintenance of a separate account shall be the responsibility of the employing broker.

(d) Escrow funds must be available immediately without penalty

Money belonging to others shall not be invested in any type of account or security or certificate of deposit which has a fixed term for maturity or imposes any fee or penalty for withdrawal prior to maturity unless the written consent of all parties to the transaction has been secured.

(e) Repealed (effective 1 -1 -96)

(f) Commingling prohibited

A broker's personal funds shall not be commingled with money belonging to others except that an arrangement may be made with a depository to deposit a sufficient amount of the broker's funds to maintain such account. One or more separate escrow or trust bank accounts may be maintained by a broker pursuant to the following duties and limitations:

(1) Money held in an escrow or trust account which is due and payable to the broker shall be withdrawn promptly.

(2) An escrow or trust account shall not be used as a depository for money belonging to licensees employed by a broker except pursuant to an executory sales contract,

nor shall it be used for money the broker owes their licensees, or for bonuses or investment plans for the benefit of their licensees.

(3) Collections for insurance premiums and/or IRS employee's withholding funds shall not be deposited in a separate trust account established pursuant to 12-61-113 (g) and (g.5) C.R.S.

(4) Money advanced by a broker for the benefit of another may be placed in the trust account and identified as an advance but may be withdrawn by the broker only on behalf of such person. Any amount advanced to an escrow or trust account must be identified and recorded in the escrow journal, the beneficiary ledger and disclosed in periodic accounting to the beneficiary.

(5) Funds of others received by a broker relating to real estate partnerships, joint ventures and syndications in which the broker has an ownership interest and also receives compensation for selling or leasing the property shall be maintained in a trust account separate from any other trust account maintained by such broker.

(6) In the absence of a specific written agreement to the contrary, commissions, fees and other charges collected by a broker for performing any service on behalf of another are considered "earned" and available for use by the broker only after all contracted services have been performed and there is no remaining right of recall by others for such money. The broker shall identify and record all commissions, fees, or other charges withdrawn from a trust or escrow account on the account journal and individual ledgers of those against whom the fees or commissions are charged. If a single disbursement of fees or commissions includes more than one transaction, rental period or occupancy or includes withdrawals from the account of more than one trust or escrow account beneficiary, the broker, upon request, shall produce for inspection by an authorized representative of the Real Estate Commission a schedule which details (1) the individual components of all amounts included in the sum of such disbursement and (2) specifically identifies the affected beneficiary or property ledgers. Ledger entries must detail such disbursements in accordance with Rule E-l(p)(2), including the date or time period for each individual transaction, rental or occupancy.

(g) Money belonging to others defined

Money belonging to others which is received by the broker includes but is not limited to money received in connection with: property management contracts; partnerships; limited liability companies; syndications; rent or lease contracts; advance fee contracts; guest deposits for short term rentals; escrow contracts; collection contracts; earnest money contracts; or, money belonging to others received by the broker for future investment or other purpose.

(h) Earnest money on new construction

If a broker who is also acting as a builder receives deposit money under an executory sales contract which provides for the construction of a house, the deposit money must be placed in the trust account and not used for construction purposes unless the written consent of the purchaser is secured.

(i) Separate escrow accounts required for managing 7 or more residences

A broker who manages less than seven (7) single-family residential units may deposit rental receipts and security deposits and disburse money collected for such purposes in the "sales escrow" account.

(j) Repealed (effective 1-1-96)

(k) Installment land contract

If a conveyance is made by an installment contract for a deed and if such contract contains a provision whereby the broker signs the installment contract as the receipting broker, the broker must escrow the receipted money pursuant to Rule E-l until the owner signs acceptance of the contract and a copy of the fully executed contract is delivered to the purchaser.

(l) Encumbrance before delivery of deed

When a sales contract or an installment contract for the sale of an interest in real estate is signed by the parties to the transaction and the purchaser also executes a promissory note and/or a mortgage or trust deed encumbering such property before the seller delivers the deed, then all payments received by the broker pursuant to such contract shall be deposited in a trust account in a recognized depository until delivery of such deed to the purchaser unless the broker receives specific written consent from all parties concerning disposition of such funds. This rule shall apply whether or not the broker and seller are one and the same.

(m) Earnest money

Checks received as earnest money under an earnest money contract must be identified as a check in the contract and may be withheld from presentment for payment only if so disclosed in the contract or pursuant to the written instructions of the seller. If a note is received as earnest money under an earnest money contract, the seller must be informed by identifying the note in the contract and by informing the seller of the date such note becomes due by stating the due date in the contract or attaching a copy of the note to the contract. The broker must present the note or check for payment in a timely manner and if payment is not made, the broker shall promptly notify the seller.

(n) Time limits for deposit of money belonging to others

Except as provided in Rule E-l (o), all money belonging to others which is received by a broker as a property manager shall be deposited in such broker's escrow or trust account not later than five business days following receipt. All other money belonging to others which is received by a broker shall be deposited in such broker's escrow or trust account not later than the third business day following receipt.

(o) Listing broker holds escrow funds; delivery to third party

Except as otherwise agreed to in writing, in any real estate transaction in which one broker holds a listing contract on a property and where the selling broker receipts for earnest money under a contract, the selling broker shall deliver the contract and the earnest money to the listing broker who shall deposit the earnest money in the broker's escrow or trustee account in a recognized depository not later than the third business day following the day on which the broker receives notice of acceptance of such contract. If such selling broker receipts for a promissory note, or thing of value, such note or thing of value shall be delivered with the contract to the listing broker to be held by the listing broker. Any check or note shall be payable to, or assigned to, the listing broker.

(1) The broker receipting for the earnest money deposit, if instructed in writing by the parties to the contract, shall deliver the earnest money to a third party or entity so identified in writing. If the broker is instructed in writing by the parties to the contract to deliver an earnest money deposit to such third party or entity, the broker shall retain in the office transaction file a copy of the earnest money check, note or other thing of value, including any endorsement, and obtain a dated and signed receipt from the person or entity to whom the broker has been instructed to deliver the deposit.

(p) Recordkeeping requirements

A broker shall supervise and maintain, at the broker's licensed place of business, a record keeping system, subject to subsection (7) of this rule, consisting of at least the following elements for each required escrow or trust account:

(1) A record called an "escrow or trust account journal" or an equivalent accounting system which records in chronological sequence all money belonging to others which is received or disbursed by the broker. For funds received, the records maintained in the system must include the date of receipt and deposit, the name of the person who is giving the money, the name of the person and property for which the money was received, the purpose of the receipt, the amount, and. a resulting cash balance for the account. For funds disbursed, the records maintained in the system must include the date of payment, the check number, the name of the payee, a reference to vendor documentation or other physical records verifying purpose for payment, the amount paid, and a resulting cash balance for the account.

(2) A record collectively called a "ledger" or an equivalent component of an accounting system which records in chronological sequence all money which is received or disbursed by the broker on behalf of each particular beneficiary of a trust account. This record must show the monetary transactions affecting each individual beneficiary and must segregate such transactions from those pertaining to other beneficiaries of the trust account. The ledger record for each beneficiary must contain the same transactional information as is prescribed in subsection (1). No ledger may ever be allowed to have a negative cash balance and the sum of all ledger balances must at all times agree with the corresponding cash balance in the journal after each transaction has been posted.

(3) A written monthly record called the "bank reconciliation worksheet" which proves agreement, on the date of reconciliation, between (1) the cash balance shown in the account journal; (2) the sum of the cash balances for all ledgers; and (3) the corresponding bank account balance. This worksheet must be maintained in hard copy form for later inspection and list each beneficiary's ledger balance on the date of reconciliation. The broker is not required to reconcile any trust account when no money belonging to others has been received or no banking activity has occurred.

(4) When managing property, if summary totals are reported to others, the broker must maintain supporting records which accurately detail all cash received and disbursed under the terms of the management and rental agreements. Such summary totals must be reconcilable to detailed supporting records. Any accounting report furnished to others must be prepared and delivered according to the terms of the management agreement or, in the absence of a provision in the written management agreement to the contrary, within thirty (30) days after the end of the month in which funds were either received or disbursed.

(5) If a broker has on deposit personal funds sufficient to maintain the trust account pursuant to Rule E-l(f), an entry showing such money shall be made in the journal and on a "broker's ledger record" per subsections (1) and (2). Such money shall be included in the bank reconciliation worksheet.

(6) All deposits of funds into an escrow or trust account must be documented (*i.e.*, bank deposits) including confirmation of electronic and telephonic transfers or on detailed schedules attached to the deposit slips or confirmations. The documentation must identify each person tendering funds to the broker for deposit, the amount of funds tendered, types of funds received from each person,

and the property address, affected. All disbursements of funds from an escrow or trust account must be supported by source documents such as bids, invoices, contracts, etc. that identify the payees, property addresses affected and amount of funds transferred for each property. Real estate licensees shall produce for inspection by an authorized representative of the real estate commission any cancelled checks (or front and back copies) or hardcopy confirmations of electronic or telephonic transfers as may be reasonably necessary to complete audits or investigations.

(7) In the absence of a written agreement to the contrary, the "cash basis" of accounting shall be used for maintaining all required escrow or trust accounts and records. If the "accrual basis" of accounting is requested by the beneficiary of funds entrusted to a broker, such request must be in writing and the broker shall maintain separate accrual basis accounts and sets of records for each person or entity affected; such accounts and records shall be separate from other accounts and records maintained on the cash basis.

(8) Pursuant to C.R.S. 12-61-113(l)(c.5),(q) and 6-1-105, the broker must obtain prior written consent to assess and receive mark-ups and/or other compensation for services performed by any third party or affiliated business entity. The broker must retain accurate on-going office records which verify disclosure and consent, and which fully account for the amounts or percentage of compensation assessed or received.

(q) Diversion/Conversion prohibited

Money belonging to one beneficiary of a separate trust or escrow account shall not be used for the benefit of another beneficiary of a trust, or escrow account.

(r) Items in lieu of cash

Any instrument or equity or thing of value taken in lieu of cash shall be held by the broker except as otherwise agreed.

(s) Branch office trust accounts require branch office recordkeeping

In the event a branch office maintains a trust account, separate from the trust account(s) maintained by the main office, a separate record keeping system must be maintained in the branch office.

(t) Repealed (effective 1-1-96)

(u) Number of separate accounts may vary from zero to unlimited

A broker is not limited as to the number of separate accounts which may be maintained for money belonging to others and if the broker is not in possession of money belonging to others, there is no obligation to maintain a separate account.

E-2. Payment earned after performance; Account within 30 days; non-refundable retainers

When money is collected by a broker for the performance of specific services or for the expenses of performing such services, or for any other expense including but not limited to advertising expenses in regard to the sale or management of real property or a business opportunity and such money is collected before the advertising or other services have been performed, the broker shall deposit such money in an escrow or trust account pursuant to 12-61-113(l)(g.5) C.R.S. No money may be withdrawn from such person's funds, except for actual authorized expenses paid to perform the service, or on behalf of that person, until the broker has fully performed the services agreed upon. A full and itemized accounting must be furnished the person within 30 days of any withdrawal of funds from the escrow or trust account. Nothing in this section shall prohibit a licensee from taking a non-refundable retainer which need not be deposited into an escrow or trust account provided this is specifically agreed to in writing between the licensee and the person paying the retainer.

E-3. Licensee must produce records; HOA records belong to HOA

A real estate licensee shall produce for inspection by an authorized representative of the Real Estate Commission any document or record as may be reasonably necessary for investigation or audit in the enforcement of Title 12 Article 61 and in enforcement of the rules and regulations of the Real Estate Commission. Failure to submit such documents or records within the time set by the Commission in its notification shall be grounds for disciplinary action unless the Commission has granted an extension of time for such production. However, a broker who is also acting as a manager for an owners association shall turn all association management records and supporting documentation over to the association at the end of the broker's term of management. Such records are the property of the owners association and if the broker wishes to maintain copies for the broker's own files these must be made at the broker's expense.

E-4. Document preparation and duplicates

Contracting instruments for all real estate or business opportunity transactions in which a real estate broker participates, including agency and sales contracts, shall accurately reflect the financial terms of the transaction by itemizing things of value paid or received and identifying the party or parties conveying, receiving and/or ultimately benefitting from such things of value. All such terms made subsequent to the original contracting document shall be disclosed in an amending instrument. For the purpose of this rule, the term "things of value" shall include monetary considerations as well as the exchange of tangible, non-monetary assets. [*Eff. 04/30/2009*]

A real estate broker shall immediately deliver a duplicate of the original of any instrument (except deeds, notes and trust deeds or mortgages, prepared by and for the benefit of third party lenders) to all parties executing the same when such instrument has been prepared by the broker or the broker's employed licensee or closing entity and relates to the employment or engagement of the broker or pertains to the consummation of the leasing, purchase, sale or exchange of real property in which the broker may participate as a broker. For purposes of this rule, duplicate shall mean legible photocopy, carbon copy, facsimile, or electronic copies which contain a digital or electronic signature as defined in 24-71-101(1) C.R.S. Such broker shall retain a copy of the duplicate instruments for future use or inspection by an authorized representative of the Real Estate Commission. If a broker or the broker's agent prepares a mortgage or trust deed for the benefit of a buyer or seller, an unsigned duplicate of such security instrument, together with a copy of the note, unsigned or prominently marked "copy," shall be furnished to the purchaser; copies shall also be retained in such broker's office for further use or inspection by an authorized representative of the Real Estate Commission. Cooperating brokers, including brokers acting as agents for buyers in a specific real estate transaction, shall have the same requirements for retention of copies as stated above, except that a cooperating broker who is not a party to the listing contract need not retain a copy of the listing contract or the seller's settlement statement. Pursuant to Rule E-3, a broker is not required to obtain and retain copies of existing public records, title commitments, loan applications, lender required disclosures or related affirmations from independent third party closing entities after the settlement date. [*Eff. 04/30/2009*]

E-5. Closing responsibility; closing statement distribution

Pursuant to 12-61-113 (l)(h), at time of closing, the individual licensee who has established a brokerage relationship with the buyer or seller or who works with the buyer or seller as a customer, either personally or on behalf of an employing broker, shall be responsible for the proper closing of the transaction and shall provide, sign and be responsible for an accurate, complete and detailed closing statement as it applies to the party with whom the brokerage relationship has been established. If signed by an employed licensee, closing statements shall be delivered to the employing broker immediately following closing. Nothing in this rule shall relieve an employing broker of the responsibility for fulfilling supervisory responsibilities pursuant to 12-61-103(6)(c), 12-61-113(1)(o), 12-61-118 C.R.S, and Rules E-31 and E-32.

(a) Subject to Rule E-4, an employing or independent broker with whom a brokerage relationship has been established, either personally or through an employed licensee, shall retain a copy of all closing statements approved by the respective buyers or sellers for future use or for inspection by an authorized representative of the Real Estate Commission.

(b) The closing statement or statements of all real estate or business opportunity transactions in which a real estate broker participates shall show the date of closing, the total purchase price of the property, itemization of all adjustments, money, or things of value received or paid showing to whom each item is credited and/or to whom each item is debited, the dates of the adjustments shall be shown if not the same as the date of the closing, also shown shall be the balances due from the respective parties to the transaction, and the names of the payees, makers and assignees of all notes paid or made or assumed; the statements furnished to each party to the transaction shall contain an itemization of such credits and such debits as pertain to each respective party. THE CREDITS AND DEBITS CONCERNING THE SALE OF A PREOWNED HOME WARRANTY SERVICE CONTRACT SHALL BE DISCLOSED ON THE CLOSING STATEMENTS.

(c) Closing statements shall be delivered to the respective parties at the time of the delivery and acceptance of the title whether such delivery and acceptance be effected by bill of sale, deed or by an installment contract to give a deed at a future date.

(d) If closing documents and statements are prepared by, and the closing is conducted by, an employing broker's company such broker is primarily responsible for the accuracy and completeness of the settlement statements and documents.

(e) If a licensee with whom a brokerage relationship has been established is unable to attend a closing or review closing documents, another licensee may agree or be designated by an employing broker to review and sign a closing statement and will assume joint responsibility with the absent licensee for its accuracy, completeness and delivery.

(f) A broker may transfer funds pertinent to a real estate transaction from a trust or escrow account to a lawyer or a closing entity acting on behalf of the broker at or before closing or final settlement. The broker will not be relieved of responsibilities in regard thereto. The broker delivering an earnest money deposit to a lawyer or a closing entity providing settlement services shall obtain a dated and signed receipt from the person or entity providing settlement services and retain a copy of the receipt in the office transaction file. The settlement statements prepared by the lawyer or closing entity shall bear the names of the licensee who signs the statement and the employing broker if applicable.

(g) If the real estate transaction involves a new loan made by the purchaser from a lending institution which deducts costs before disbursing the loan proceeds prior to final settlement, the loan proceeds must be reconciled with money due to or paid by the buyer and money due the seller after final settlement. A copy of this reconciliation must be kept in the broker's files and available for audit by a representative of the Commission.

E-6. Electronic Records

Records as required under Title 12, Article 61, Parts 1-8 C.R.S. and rules promulgated by the Commission, may be maintained in electronic format. An electronic record as defined in 24-71.7-103 C.R.S. means a record generated, communicated, received or stored by electronic means. Such electronic records shall be produced upon request by the Commission and must be in a format that has the continued capability to be retrieved and legibly printed. Upon request of the Commission, or by any principal party to a transaction, printed records shall be produced.

***E-7. Repealed* (Effective February 1, 2001)**

E-8. Advertising

A real estate licensee who performs any act requiring a license, including advertising services or advertising property belonging to another, shall do so in the name of the employing broker; except that a licensed employee may advertise property owned by such employee without complying with this rule if the property is not listed for sale with the employing broker. General advertising which recaps sales activity over a period of time in a given subdivision or geographical area shall cite the source of the data and include a disclaimer that all reported sales were not necessarily listed or sold by the licensee and are intended only to show trends in the area or shall separately identify the licensee's own sales activity.

E-9. Repealed effective 1-1-97

E-10. License non-transferable. Associates not independent or employing

A broker license is non-transferable. No licensee shall, and no broker shall permit, employed licensees to present or to hold themselves out to the public as an employing or independent real estate broker.

E-11. Listing must have termination date

When a licensee secures a written agreement to perform activities requiring a license, a definite date for termination shall be included therein.

E-12. Holdover agreement

When a written agreement contains a provision entitling the broker to a commission on a sale or purchase made after the expiration of the agreement, such provision must refer only to those persons or properties with whom or on which the broker negotiated during the term of the agreement, and whose names or addresses, were submitted in writing to the seller or buyer during the term of the agreement, including any extension thereof.

E-13. Sign-crossing rule

A real estate licensee shall not negotiate a sale, exchange, lease or listing contract of real property directly with an owner for compensation from such owner if such licensee knows that such owner has a written unexpired contract in connection with such property which grants to another licensee an exclusive right to sell or lease or which grants an exclusive agency right to sell or lease. However, when a licensee is contacted by an owner regarding the sale, exchange, lease or listing of property that is exclusively listed with another broker, and the licensee has not initiated the discussion, the licensee may negotiate the terms upon which to take a future listing or, alternatively, may take a listing to become effective upon expiration of any existing exclusive listing. Additionally, a real estate licensee shall not negotiate a purchase, exchange, lease or exclusive right to buy contract with a buyer if such licensee knows that such buyer has a written, unexpired contract which grants to another licensee an exclusive right to buy. However, when a licensee is contacted by a buyer regarding the purchase, exchange or lease of property, and the licensee has not initiated the discussion, the licensee may enter into or negotiate the terms upon which to enter into a future exclusive right to buy contract to become effective upon expiration of any existing exclusive right to buy contract.

E-14. Licensee must recommend title exam & legal counsel

A real estate licensee shall recommend, before the closing of a real estate transaction, the examination of title and shall advise the use of legal counsel.

E-15. No broker right to earnest money return

When for any reason the owner fails, refuses, neglects or is unable to consummate the transaction as provided for in the contract, and through no fault or neglect of the purchaser the real estate transaction cannot be completed, the broker has no right to any portion of the deposit money which was deposited by the purchaser, even though the commission is earned, and such deposit should be returned to the purchaser at once and the broker should look to the owner for compensation.

E-16. Owner-held security deposits

A broker receipting for security deposits shall not deliver such deposits to an owner without the tenant's written authorization in a lease or unless written notice has been given to the tenant by first class mail. Such notice must be given in a manner so that the tenant will know who is holding the security deposit and the specific requirements for the procedure in which the tenant may request return of the deposit. If a security deposit is delivered to an owner, the management agreement must place financial responsibility on the owner for its return, and in the event of a dispute over ownership of the deposit, must authorize disclosure by the broker to the tenant of the owner's true name and current mailing address. The broker shall not contract with the tenant to use the security deposit for the broker's own benefit.

E-17. Repealed effective 6/30/04

E-18. Fees from mortgage lenders require prior written approval

A licensee shall not accept, directly or indirectly, a placement fee, commission or other valuable consideration for placing a loan with a mortgage lender or its representative in any real estate transaction in which the licensee, directly or indirectly, received, or is entitled to receive a commission as a result of the sale of property in such transaction unless the licensee fully informs any party with whom they have established a brokerage relationship, or worked with as a customer, and obtains prior written consent of such party.

All licensees should comply with the RESPA statute and regulations regarding receipt of referral fees. To the extent Rule E-18 on referral fees differs from that of RESPA and HUD, licensees should comply with RESPA and HUD to avoid jeopardizing their standing with respect to federally related loan programs and are advised to contact HUD for further clarification.

E-19. Fees from title insurance companies prohibited

A licensee shall not accept a commission, fee, or other valuable consideration from an abstract or title insurance company or its representative in any real estate transaction in which the licensee, directly or indirectly, receives, or is entitled to receive, a real estate commission as a result of the sale of property in such transaction.

E-20. Property list price must be set by owner

The licensee shall not submit or advertise property without authority, and, in any offering, the price quoted should not be other than that agreed upon with the owners as the offering price.

E-21. Licensee must respond to complaint or audit notice in writing

When a licensee has received written notification from the Commission that a complaint has been filed against the licensee, the licensee has been selected for an audit, or that an audit has identified record keeping or trust account deficiencies, such licensee shall submit a written answer to the Commission. Failure to submit a written answer within the time set by the Commission in its notification shall be grounds for disciplinary action unless the Commission has granted an extension of time for the answer in writing and regardless of the question of whether the underlying complaint warrants further investigation or subsequent action by the Commission. The licensee's written answer shall contain the following:

(a) A complete and specific answer to the factual recitations, allegations or averments made in the complaint filed against the licensee, whether made by a member of the public, on the Commission's own motion or by an authorized representative of the Commission.

(b) A complete and specific response to any additional questions, allegations or averments presented in the notification letter.

(c) Any documents or records requested in the notification letter.

(d) Any further information relative to the complaint that the licensee believes to be relevant or material to the matters addressed in the notification letter.

E-22. Inducements from settlement producers prohibited

A. In addition to the provisions of section 12-61-113.2, C.R.S., and the federal Real Estate Settlement Procedures Act, 12 U.S.C. sec. 2601 *et seq.*, no licensed real estate broker, whether or not engaged in a prohibited affiliated business arrangement, shall pay, furnish, impose, or agree to pay or furnish or impose, or accept, agree to accept or arrange to accept, either directly or indirectly, any incentive, disincentive, remuneration, commission, fee or other thing of value to or from another person or entity in any form in connection with any past, present, or future title insurance business, any closing and settlement services or any other title insurance business except for "services actually rendered" as defined in section 12-61-113.2 (2) (e), C.R.S., to or on behalf of any of the following:

1. Any "settlement producer" as defined in section 10-11-102(6.5), C.R.S., or a person that provides settlement services as defined in section 12-61-113.2 (1) (c), C.R.S.
2. Any owner or prospective owner, lessee or prospective lessee of real property or any interest in the real property;
3. Any obligee or prospective obligee of any obligation secured or to be secured either in whole or in part by real property or any interest in the real property; or,
4. Any person who is acting as or who is in the business of acting as agent, representative, attorney or employee of any of the persons described in 1, 2 or 3 above, or any other party to the instant transaction.

B. The factors the Commission will consider when determining whether incentive, disincentive, remuneration, commission, fee or other thing of value for the referral of title insurance business exists or will exist include, but are not limited to:

1. Whether the costs of any settlement producer are being or will be defrayed by the licensee's actions;
2. Whether the remuneration is being or will be given to a discrete settlement producer as opposed to a bona fide association of settlement producers;

3. Whether a pattern or practice of referrals to the real estate broker exists or will exist; and
4. Consideration of the advertising value of the incentive, disincentive, remuneration, commission, fee or other thing of value.

C. Bona fide advertising, marketing, or other acts in furtherance of maintenance and development of client relationships are not prohibited unless such conduct otherwise constitutes violation of the statutes or rules applicable to licensed real estate brokers.

D. Section 12-61-113.2 (2)(a), C.R.S., permits an affiliated business arrangement where the person referring the business to the affiliated business arrangement receives payment only in the form of a return on an investment and where it does not violate section 12-61-113, C.R.S.

E. Prohibited acts, practices, incentives, disincentives, remuneration, commissions, fees or other things of value include, but are not limited to, the following:

1. Affiliated business arrangements prohibited by section 12-61-113.2, C.R.S., that mandate the referral of title insurance business. Prohibited arrangements include, but are not limited to the following:
    a. Arrangements in which the amount of the return on the ownership interest is in some fashion conditioned on the number of or premium volume of referrals made, such as where owners or stockholders receive dividends or bonuses based on the number of referrals generated or achievement of certain referral plans or goals;
    b. Arrangements in which the ownership interests themselves are conditioned on the referrals, such as where the stock certificates are distributed based on the number of or premium volume of the referrals made in the past or to be made in the future;
    c. Arrangements in which owners or stockholders receive anything of value that is directly tied to the referral of business; and
    d. Arrangements in which the cost of the ownership opportunity is not equivalent for all investors.
2. "Sham" affiliated business arrangements as defined in Commission Rule E-46.
3. Receiving, attempting to receive, or arranging for, from a settlement producer, discounts primarily based on the volume of business the broker refers to the provider of settlement services.
4. Violation of Commission Rule E-36 regarding "good funds".
5. Except as otherwise permitted in Section 38-35-125 (2), C.R.S., arranging for the disbursement of closing and settlement services funds before all necessary conditions of the transaction have been met.
6. Arranging for or accepting a title commitment without charge or at a reduced charge, unless, within a reasonable time after the date of issuance, appropriate title insurance coverage is issued for which the scheduled rates and fees are paid. Any title commitment charge must have a reasonable relation to the cost of production of the commitment and cannot be less than the minimum rate or fee for the type of policy applied for, as set forth in the insurer's current schedule of rates and fees. This provision does not apply where a title commitment is furnished in good faith in furtherance of a bona fide sale, purchase or loan transaction that for good reason is not consummated.

7. Accepting or arranging for any portion of the following:
   a. Advertising or promotional material or activity, including, but not limited to, any obligation, product, service, seminar, convention or publication for the benefit of any settlement producer, or ostensibly for the benefit of the real estate broker, the end result of which is the substantial subsidization of an obligation, product, service, seminar, convention or publication of any settlement producer. This prohibition applies to ads placed in subdivision or tract brochures, multiple listing services or books, exchange bulletins, newsletters, information sheets, programs, announcements and periodicals or similar matter associated with meetings, seminars or conventions of such settlement producers as well as registers and directories of such persons;
   b. The cancellation fee for a title report or other fee before or after inducing such settlement producer to cancel an order with another title entity;
   c. Furniture, equipment, office supplies, telephones, or automobiles, including any portion of the cost of renting, leasing, operating or maintaining the above-mentioned items, unless such provider of settlement services pays no more than its allocable share of the actual costs for such goods and services commensurate with the actual usage of such goods services, and facilities actually furnished;
   d. Rent to or from any settlement producer for premises wherever situated, regardless of the purpose, at a rent that is materially in excess of or materially below market value when compared with the amount paid per square foot for comparable space in the geographic area;
   e. Incentives, gifts, prizes, retreats, transportation and vacations, including, but not limited to other similar things of value;
   f. Salary, compensation or services, except for services actually rendered, including, but not limited to:
      i. All or any part of the time or productive effort of any employee or affiliate of the real estate broker (*e.g.*, office manager, secretary, clerk, messenger) to any settlement producer at less than the fair market value of the services;
      ii. Compensation of a settlement producer or associate of a settlement producer;
      iii. The salary or any part of the salary of a relative of any settlement producer which payment is in excess of the reasonable value of the work actually performed by such relative on behalf of the real estate broker; and
      iv. Services by any settlement producer which services are required to be performed by such settlement producer in his or her professional capacity, and for which the settlement producer would not normally charge the real estate broker.
8. Paying a settlement producer or other person described in Section A of this rule to make an inspection and appraisal of property, except for services actually rendered.
9. Any transaction in which any person receives, or is to receive, securities of the settlement producer or its affiliates at prices below the normal market price, or bonds or debentures that guarantee a higher than normal interest rate, whether or not the consummation of such transaction is directly or indirectly related to the number of closing and settlement services or title orders coming to the title entity through the efforts of such person.
10. Accepting or arranging for less than the scheduled rate or fee for a specified real estate or closing and settlement service, or for a policy of title insurance.

11. Accepting or arranging for waiver of all or any part of the title entity's established rate or fee for services that are not the subject of rates or fees filed with the Colorado Commissioner of Insurance required to be maintained on the entity's schedules of rates and fees.
12. Except as otherwise permitted by 12-61-113(1), C.R.S., and the rules and regulations of the Commission, accepting or arranging for information, including, but not limited to, farm packages, appraisals, estimates of income production potential, information kits or similar packages containing information about one or more parcels of real property without a charge that is commensurate with the actual cost of the work performed and the material furnished, and making a good faith effort to collect payment in the amount of such charge.
13. Accepting or arranging for accumulation, credit or deferral of the charge for a title policy or closing and settlement services in order to "qualify" the charge for said policy and a later transaction for a lower rate, except to the extent that a properly filed and justified rate or fee is in place for a deferred rate.
14. Accepting or arranging for a guarantee, either directly or indirectly, of any loan to any settlement producer, regardless of the terms of the note or guarantee.
15. Accepting or arranging for a guarantee of the performance of closing and settlement services, or the performance of any other undertaking that are to be performed by any settlement producer.
16. Accepting or arranging for, either directly or indirectly, a "compensating balance" or deposit in a lending institution either for the express or implied purpose of influencing the extension of credit by such lending institution to any settlement producer, or for the express or implied purpose of influencing the placement or channeling of title insurance business by such lending institution.
17. Accepting or arranging for the payment of the fees or charges of an outside professional (*e.g.*, an attorney, engineer, appraiser, or surveyor) whose services are required by any settlement producer to structure or complete a particular transaction.
18. Accepting or arranging for real estate broker services (*e.g.*, computerized bookkeeping, forms management, computer programming, or any similar benefit) to or from any settlement producer at less than the fair market value of the services.
19. Accepting, or arranging for payment for, any business form provided to any settlement producer other than a form regularly used in the conduct of the real estate broker that form is furnished solely for the convenience of the real estate broker and does not constitute a direct monetary benefit to any settlement producer.
20. Accepting or arranging for the payment into escrow of any of the title entity funds or "closing short", except as provided in Section 38-35-125 (2), C.R.S.
21. Accepting or arranging for charges that are less than the actual cost of the closing and settlement service of the real estate broker.

F. To the extent the activities and information are provided on a nondiscriminatory basis, that such acts and practices have not been provided in a manner to circumvent the intent of this rule, and are in no way conditioned, directly or indirectly, upon prohibited referrals, prohibited acts, practices, incentives, disincentives, remuneration, commissions, fees or other things of value do not include, but may not be limited to, the following:

1. Accepting or arranging for, either orally or in writing, an ownership and encumbrance report ("O&E") or a copy of an instrument of public record, including but not limited to, a deed, deed of trust, mortgage, contract, map, plat, or

declaration of covenants, conditions and restrictions. Any such report or instrument may be accepted without charge provided and to the extent that:

a. All persons requesting such information are treated equally; and

b. The information is provided as presented by the public records and nothing of material value is added to the information; and

c. The information furnished contains no advertising or promotional material on behalf of the settlement producer to whom the information is provided.

d. Commission rules do not prohibit a real estate broker from imposing a reasonable charge for any and all of the above information, or for additional information, provided the charge is the same for all persons, and is assessed on a nondiscriminatory basis.

2. Accepting or arranging for an insured closing letter or closing protection letter that substantially conforms to an American Land Title Association ("ALTA") promulgated form.

3. Accepting or arranging for published or printing real estate industry related educational information or accepting or arranging for educational seminars for the benefit of settlement producers, as long as consistent with all other provisions of this rule.

4. Accepting or arranging for advertising or marketing in furtherance of the development of client relationships, when performed in the bona fide and legitimate promotion of the real estate broker's business, as long as consistent with all other provisions of this rule including, but not limited to:

   a. Things of reasonable value given to a bona fide trade or industry association.

   b. Advertising novelties and promotional gift items that bear the name of the real estate broker (but not the name of the recipient) to settlement producers, provided and to the extent that:

      i. The items constitute advertising directed impersonally at the general consumer public, and are provided to settlement producers on a non-discriminatory basis; and

      ii. The items are valued at no more than $10; and,

      iii. Distribution, if by mail, is made on a nonselective basis to all persons known or reasonably believed to be members of the business or professional group in the natural geographic area or political subdivision toward which the advertising effort is directed.

   c. Customer entertainment provided that:

      i. It is interactive, personal contact between a real estate broker representative who is physically present and a settlement producer; and

      ii. It is conducted to promote real estate products and services of the real estate broker; and

      iii. Any benefit conferred to a settlement producer is incidental to the promotion of the real estate broker's products and services; and

      iv. The expenditure bears a reasonable relationship to the benefit derived by the real estate broker from the activity.

5. Accepting or arranging for the use of office space or other accommodations within a settlement producer's office or business space, provided that rent is paid in accordance with this rule and the arrangement is consistent with the intent of this rule. In determining whether an office or accommodations sharing arrangement is

permitted under this rule, the Commission shall consider the following factors, including, but not limited to:

a. Whether written notice has been provided to the consumer disclosing that an office or accommodations sharing arrangement exists and that the consumer has the right to use another real estate broker;

b. Whether the real estate broker's space is clearly and conspicuously identified separately from the settlement producer's space;

c. Whether the real estate broker's space can be readily locked and secured independently from the settlement producer's space;

d. Whether the real estate broker's space is directly and easily accessible to the public without entering the settlement producer's primary workspace, such as where the real estate broker's entrance leads to or from a common area or the exterior of the premises; and

e. Whether the real estate broker, directly or indirectly pays for or subsidizes the settlement producer's expenses as proscribed by § 12-1-113.2, C.R.S.

G. Nothing herein shall be construed in a manner that conflicts with the provisions of §§ 10-11-108(2)(b) or 12-61-113.2, C.R.S. or the rules and regulations of the Colorado Real Estate Commission or the Colorado Division of Insurance.

H. For the purposes of this rule, "title entity" means a "title insurance company" as defined in section 10-11-102 (10), C.R.S., and a "title insurance agent" as defined in section 10-11-102 (9), C.R.S.

I. Noncompliance with this rule, whether defined or reasonably implied under this rule E-22, may result, after proper notice and hearing, in the imposition of any of the sanctions available in the Colorado statutes pertaining to the business of real estate brokers or other laws which include the imposition of fines and/or discipline of a license.

J. The following are hereby incorporated by reference as written on or before the effective date of this rule. This rule does not include later amendments to or editions of the incorporated material. A copy of these references may be examined at any state publications depository library. For additional information regarding how to obtain a copy please contact Rulemaking Coordinator, Colorado Division of Real Estate, 1560 Broadway Ste. 925, Denver, CO 80202.

1. The federal Real Estate Settlement Procedures Act, 12 U.S.C. sec. 2601 *et seq.*
2. The American Land Title Association (ALTA) Closing Protection Letter (rev. 3/27/97); the ALTA Closing Protection Letter – Regulatory (rev. 10-17-98); the ALTA Closing Protection Letter – Non-Residential Limitations (rev. 10-17-98); and the ALTA Closing Protection Letter – Single Transaction Limited Liability (rev. 10-17-98).

E-23. Payment to out-of-state brokers

A licensed Colorado broker who cooperates with a broker who is licensed in another state or country but is not licensed in Colorado may pay such out-of-state broker a finder's fee or share of the commission under these circumstances:

(a) The broker licensed in the other state or country must reside and maintain an office in the other state or country.

(b) All advertising, negotiations, contracting and conveyancing done in Colorado must be performed in the name of the licensed Colorado broker.

(c) All money collected from the parties to the transaction prior to closing shall be deposited in the name of the licensed Colorado broker according to Commission rules.

This rule shall also apply to payment made to citizens or residents of a country which does not license real estate brokers if the payee represents that they are in the business of selling real estate in said country.

E-24. Fraudulent application subject to discipline

A real estate licensee who procures or attempts to procure a real estate license by fraud, misrepresentation, deceit or by making a material misstatement of fact in an application for such license, will be subject to disciplinary action pursuant to 12-61-113(p), C.R.S., as amended.

E-25. Continuing duty to disclose conflict of interest and license status

When acting in a licensed capacity or when a licensee sells, buys or leases real property on the licensce's own account, such licensee shall have a continuing duty to disclose any known conflict of interest that may arise in the course of the transaction. In addition, when a licensee sells, buys or leases real property on the licensee's own account, such licensee shall disclose in the contracting instrument, or in a separate concurrent writing, that they are a real estate licensee.

E-26. Repealed

E-27. No representation of future status of property

No licensee shall make misrepresentations regarding future availability or costs of services, utilities, character and/or use of real property for sale or lease which is in the surrounding area.

E-28. Fees from home warranty companies

A licensee shall not accept, directly or indirectly, a fee, commission or other valuable consideration from a pre-owned home warranty service company or its affiliate for services rendered in connection with the sale of a pre-owned home warranty service contract.

E-29. Employing broker exercises authority, direction and control

The terms "employment", "in the employ of", "employed", "employing", "placed under contract", or "engaged", as used in the licensing statutes (12-61-101 C.R.S. *et seq.*) and Commission Rules, shall refer to any contractual relationship by or between a real estate broker and another licensee, which may be with or without limitation as to the time, place, or manner of performance of the licensee's activities, but which shall not relieve the real estate broker from the statutory requirement that the real estate broker shall exercise authority, direction and control over licensee's conformance to the licensing statutes and Commission Rules in the performance of such licensee's activities pursuant to 12-61-103(6)(c)(I) C.R.S, 12-61-113(1)(o) C.R.S, 12-61-118 C.R.S., and Commission rules. Whenever a complaint is filed with the Real Estate Commission against an employed licensee, the Commission shall cause an investigation to be made to ascertain whether there may have been a violation of 12-61-113(l)(o) C.R.S. by the employing real estate broker in failing to exercise a reasonable or high level of supervision over such licensee's 'activities with reference to the licensing statutes and Commission Rules. Such supervision, pursuant to 12-61-118 C.R.S. shall include all broker employees, including but not limited to secretaries, bookkeepers and personal assistants of licensed employees.

E-30. Employing broker responsibilities

To ensure compliance with Commission statutes and rules regarding supervision, employing brokers shall have the following responsibilities:

(a) Maintain all trust accounts and trust account records;

(b) Maintain all transaction records;

(c) Develop an office policy manual and periodically review office policies with all employees; (*Ed. Note: See CP-21 in Chapter 3)*

(d) Provide for a high level of supervision of newly licensed persons pursuant to Rule E-32;

(e) Provide for a reasonable level of supervision for experienced licensees pursuant to Rule E-31;

(f) Take reasonable steps to ensure that violations of statutes, rules and office policies do not occur or reoccur;

(g) Provide for adequate supervision of all offices operated by the broker, whether managed by licensed or unlicensed persons.

E-31. Reasonable supervision

Pursuant to section 12-61-113(l)(o), C.R.S., and in addition to the requirements of Commission Rule E-30, "reasonable supervision" of licensees with two or more years of experience shall include, but not be limited to, compliance with the following:

(a) Maintaining a written office policy describing the duties and responsibilities of licensees employed by the broker. A copy of the written policy shall:

 (1) be given to, read and signed by each licensee;

 (2) be available for inspection, upon request, by any authorized representative of the Commission.

(b) Reviewing all executed contracts in order to maintain assurance of competent preparation.

(c) Reviewing transaction files to ensure that required documents exist.

(d) Nothing in this rule shall prohibit an employing broker from delegating supervisory authority to other experienced licensees.

 (1) Employed licensees who accept supervisory authority from an employing broker shall bear responsibility with the employing broker for ensuring compliance with the Commission statutes and rules by all supervised licensees.

 (2) Any such delegation of authority shall be in writing and signed by the employed licensee to whom such authority is delegated. A copy of such delegation shall be maintained by the employing broker for inspection, upon request, by any authorized Commission representative.

 (3) An employing broker shall not contract with any employed licensee so as to circumvent the requirement that the broker supervise employed licensees.

E-32. High-level of supervision

In addition to the requirements of Rule E-31 and pursuant to section 12-61-103(6)(c)(I) C.R.S., an employing broker shall provide a "high level of supervision" for licensed persons with less than two years experience as follows:

(a) Provide specific training in office policies and procedures;

(b) Be reasonably available for consultation;

(c) Provide assistance in preparing contracts;

(d) Monitor transactions from contracting to closing;

(e) Review documents in preparation for closing;

(f) Ensure that the employing broker or an experienced licensee attends closings or is available for assistance.

(g) Nothing in this rule shall prohibit an employing broker from delegating supervisory authority to other experienced licensees.

(1) Employed licensees who accept supervisory authority from an employing broker shall bear responsibility with the employing broker for ensuring compliance with the Commission statutes and rules by all supervised licensees.

(2) Any such delegation of authority shall be in writing and signed by the employed licensee to whom such authority is delegated. A copy of such delegation shall be maintained by the employing broker for inspection upon request by an authorized Commission representative

E-33. Ministerial tasks

Following proper disclosure pursuant to 12-61-808 C.R.S., a broker engaged as a single agent for one party to a transaction may assist the other party by performing such ministerial tasks as showing a property, preparing and conveying written offers and counteroffers, making known the availability of financing alternatives and providing information related to professional, governmental and community services which will contribute to completion of the transaction and successful fulfillment of the agency. Performing such ministerial tasks shall not of themselves violate the terms of an agency relationship between a broker and a buyer, seller, tenant or landlord and shall not create an agency or transaction-broker relationship with the person being assisted.

E-34. Purchase offers must go to listing broker

A licensee must present all offers to purchase or lease to the owner's listing broker only if such owner has a written unexpired contract in connection with the sale or lease of real property which grants to the owner's listing broker an exclusive right to sell or lease.

E-35. Brokerage relationship disclosure in writing

Written disclosures pursuant to C.R.S. 12-61-808 shall be made to a buyer or tenant prior to engaging in activities enumerated in C.R.S. 12-61-101 (2) and (3).

(a) For purposes of this rule, such activities occur when a licensee elicits or accepts confidential information from a buyer or tenant concerning the buyer's or tenant's real estate needs, motivation, or financial qualifications.

(b) Such activities do not include a bona fide "open house" showing, preliminary conversations or "small talk" concerning price range, location and property styles, or responding to general factual questions from a potential buyer or tenant concerning properties which have been advertised for sale or lease.

E-36. Good funds at closing

Pursuant to 38-35-125, a real estate licensee who provides closing services shall not disburse funds or instruct an agent to disburse funds until those funds have been received and are either:

(1) available for immediate withdrawal as a matter of right from the financial institution in which the funds have been deposited or

(2) available for immediate withdrawal as a consequence of an agreement of a financial institution in which the funds are to be deposited or a financial institution upon which the funds are to be drawn. Such agreement with a financial institution must be for the benefit of the licensee providing the closing service. If the agreement contains contingencies or reservations no disbursements can be made until these are satisfied.

E-37. No fees to licensee/agent for legal document preparation

There is no obligation for a licensee to prepare any legal documents as part of a real estate transaction. However, if a licensee or the licensee's agent prepares any legal document, the licensee or the licensee's agent may not charge a separate fee for preparation of such documents. A licensee shall not be responsible for fees charged for the preparation of legal documents where they are prepared by an attorney representing the purchaser or seller. Costs of closing not related to preparation of legal documents may be paid by the licensee or by any other person. A broker who closes transactions and charges separately for costs of closing not related to the preparation of legal documents must specify the costs and obtain the written consent of the parties to be charged.

E-38. Office Policy may contain designation of brokerage relationship

For purposes of this rule, seller shall include landlord, and buyer shall include tenant. Pursuant to C.R.S. 12-61-803(6)(a), an employing broker or employed broker must be designated in writing by the employing broker to serve as a single agent or transaction-broker for a seller or buyer. Employing brokers comply with the statute if they make such written designation, as appropriate to the broker's business, in an office policy that states:

(1) Listing contracts by single individuals: that the individual broker entering into the listing contract is the seller's designated agent or designated transaction broker.

(2) Right to buy or tenant contracts by individual: that the individual broker entering into the right to buy or tenant contract is the buyer's designated agent or transaction broker, whichever is appropriate.

(3) Listing contracts by teams: that the individual team member(s) entering into the listing contract is the seller's designated agent or transaction-broker, whichever is appropriate, in which case that designation and brokerage relationship shall apply to all members of the team.

(4) Right to buy or tenant contracts by teams: that the individual team member(s) entering into the right to buy or tenant contract is the buyer's designated agent or transaction-broker, whichever is appropriate, in which case that designation and brokerage relationship shall apply to all members of the team

(5) Individuals or teams working with both buyer and seller:

  (a) that the individual(s) or team is a transaction-broker for both buyer and seller, or;

  (b) that the individual(s) or team is a single agent for the seller or buyer, and that the other party is a customer.

(6) Substitute or additional brokers: that the employing broker reserves the right to substitute or add other designated brokers, as appropriate, which shall be disclosed to the buyer or seller.

(7) Transaction-broker – written disclosure: that a broker working with a buyer or seller as a Transaction-Broker as the result of a written disclosure is the designated broker for that buyer or seller.

E-39. Office brokerage relationship policy must be written

Pursuant to 12-61-803 and 12-61-808 C.R.S., a broker shall adopt a written office policy which identifies and describes the relationships in which such broker and any employed licensee may engage with any seller, landlord, buyer or tenant as part of any real estate brokerage activities. A broker may adopt any policy suitable to the broker's business, subject to the following:

(a) An office policy shall apply to all licensees in the office;

(b) An office policy shall be given and explained to each licensee and shall be read, agreed to, and signed by each licensee;

(c) An office policy shall, in a manner compliant with Commission Rule E-38, identify the procedures for the designation of brokers who are to work with a seller, landlord, buyer or tenant pursuant to 12-61-803(6) C.R.S., except office policies of real estate brokerage firms that consist of only one licensed natural person.

(d) An office policy shall identify and provide adequate means and procedures for the maintenance and protection of confidential information that:

(1) The seller or landlord is willing to accept less;

(2) The buyer or tenant is willing to pay more;

(3) Information regarding motivating factors for the parties;

(4) Information that a party will agree to other financing terms;

(5) Material information about a party not required by law to be disclosed;

(6) Facts or suspicions which may psychologically impact or stigmatize a property;

(7) All information required to be kept confidential pursuant to sections 12-61-804(2), 12-61 805(2) and 12-61-807(3), C.R.S.

(e) An office policy may permit an employing broker to supervise a transaction and to participate in the same transaction as a designated broker.

E-40. Double-ended brokerage relationships

A broker shall not enter into a brokerage relationship with one party as an agent and the other party as a transaction broker. A broker who works with both the buyer and seller in the same real estate transaction may do so as (1) a transaction-broker for both buyer and seller (2) a single agent for the seller, treating the buyer as a customer or (3) a single agent for the buyer, treating the seller as a customer. These options shall be disclosed and made a part of the agreement between the parties to the listing contract, right to buy contract or tenant contract, whichever is appropriate. (*Ed. Note: See 12-61-803(6)(d)*)

E-41. Change of status disclosure in writing

A broker working with both the buyer and seller in the same real estate transaction who changes from working as a party's agent to assisting the parties as a Transaction-Broker shall either: check the box for "Transaction- Broker" and the box "This is a Change of Status" in the Commission-approved form, Contract to Buy and Sell Real Estate, if applicable, or provide the written "Change of Status (Transaction-Brokerage Disclosure)" to the party that has the changed relationship (seller and buyer) with the broker, at the time the broker begins to assist as a Transaction-Broker, but not later than at the time the party signs the contract. For purposes of this rule, seller shall include landlord, and buyer shall include tenant.

E-42. Notice required on CMA's for other than marketing

When a real estate licensee prepares a competitive market analysis (CMA) for any reason other than the anticipated sale or purchase of the property, the licensee must include a notice stating: "The preparer of this evaluation is not registered, licensed or certified as a real estate appraiser by the state of Colorado".

E-43. Square footage disclosure *(Effective 4/30/2009)*

This rule applies to transactions involving the sale and purchase of residences, new or existing. It requires the listing licensee to disclose the square footage of the floor space of the living area of the residence to the buyer and seller when a licensee disseminates such information, including submission to a multiple listing service. If the licensee personally measures or provides information from another source of measurement of the residence's square footage the licensee shall use the Commission approved form for such disclosure. The licensee listing the property is responsible for accurately representing any source of square footage. *[Eff. 04/30/2009]*

(a) Licensee measurement. A licensee is not required to measure the square footage of a property. If the licensee takes an actual measurement it does not have to be exact, however, the licensee's objective must be to measure accurately and calculate competently in a manner that is not misleading, and: *[Eff. 04/30/2009]*

   i. The standard, methodology or manner in which the measurement was taken must be accurately disclosed to the buyer and seller; *[Eff. 04/30/2009]*

   ii. The buyer and seller must be advised that the measurement is for purposes of marketing and is not a measurement for loan, valuation or any other purpose; and *[Eff. 04/30/2009]*

   iii. The buyer and seller must be advised that if exact square footage is a concern, the property should be independently measured. *[Eff. 04/30/2009]*

(b) Other sources of square footage. If a buyer or seller is provided information from another source for square footage, that source (whether an actual measurement, building plans, prior appraisals, assessors office, etc.) shall include the date of issuance if any and must be disclosed to the buyer and seller in writing by the licensee, in a timely manner. Such disclosure must be on the Commission approved form and must advise the recipient to verify the information. A licensee may not provide information to a person from a source known to be unreliable and is responsible for indicating obvious mismeasurement by others. *[Eff. 04/30/2009]*

(c) A licensee working with a buyer must advise that if exact square footage is a concern, the property should be independently measured. This requirement is fulfilled by the licensee supplying such buyer a copy of the Commission approved form for disclosing square footage. *[Eff. 04/30/2009]*

E-44. Actions when license is revoked, expired or inactive *(Renumbered from E-42-10/1/02)*

Upon suspension, revocation, expiration or transfer to inactive status of a real estate license, the licensee is responsible for immediate compliance with the following:

(1) Cease any activities requiring a license.

(2) Return the license and pocket card to the commission. If an employing broker, return the licenses of all employed licensees and inform such licensees of the action taken.

(3) Cease all advertising, including but not limited to, use of office signs, yard signs, billboards, newspapers, magazines, the Internet, direct mailings, and multiple listing services:

(4) Inform all owners, buyers and tenants of the action taken. If an employing broker, release all principals from any listings, management agreements, or other contractual obligations which require a license.

(5) If an employing broker, ensure that all entrusted funds have been properly accounted for and that all closings are properly completed.

(6) Commissions or fees may be received by licensees only for transactions where the commission or fee was earned prior to the suspension, revocation, expiration or transfer to inactive status.

E-45. Supervising Broker – Confidential Information

A designated broker shall be permitted to reveal to a supervising broker, and a supervising broker shall be permitted to receive, confidential information as authorized by the informed consent of the party the designated broker is assisting or working with, without changing or extending the designated brokerage relationship beyond the designated broker. A supervising broker, for the purposes of this rule, is a broker performing the responsibilities set forth in Rules E-30, 31, and 32. Confidential information includes the information referenced in Sections 12-61-804 (2), 805 (2) and 807 (3), C.R.S.

E-46. Affiliated Business Arrangements

A. This rule concerns creation and conduct of an "affiliated business arrangement" as defined in Section 12-61-113.2(1)(a). This rule governs real estate licensees and is not intended to extend the regulatory authority of the Commission or the Division to any person other than real estate licensees.

B. A "provider of settlement services" for purposes of Section 12-61-113.2, *et seq.*, includes but is not limited to brokers acting as agents or transaction brokers, real estate brokerage firms, and employing brokers.

C. A licensee or employing broker of a licensee shall disclose the existence of an affiliated business arrangement pursuant to Section 12-61-113.2(2)(b) by disclosing the affiliation to the party they are referring, either seller, buyer or both, by using and having that party sign the Affiliated Business Arrangement Disclosure Statement promulgated by HUD pursuant to the Real Estate Settlement Procedures Act. The disclosure shall be made prior to, but no later than, the referral of settlement services business.

D. A copy of the signed disclosure shall be retained in the file and a copy given to the referred party.

E. Sham affiliated business arrangements are prohibited.

1. In considering whether a real estate broker is a legitimate affiliated business arrangement or a "sham" affiliated business arrangement, the factors the Commission will consider include the following:

   a. Whether the real estate broker operates in a manner that evidences a good faith effort to conform to applicable real estate laws;

   b. Whether the title entity maintains a separate and distinct, verifiable physical location. In the event the real estate broker shares office space with another settlement service provider, the Commission may consider the factors set forth in paragraph F5 of Rule E22, inclusive, in determining compliance with this provision.

   c. Whether the employees of the real estate broker are shared with other settlement service providers within the affiliated business arrangement. In determining whether an individual is an employee of the real estate broker, the Commission may consider the following factors:

      i. Whether the real estate broker issues or causes to be issued an annual Internal Revenue Service Form W-2 to the employee;

      ii. Whether the employee is subject to the real estate broker's supervision and control;

      iii. Whether the employee devotes fixed periods of time exclusively to the business of the real estate broker or whether the employee is compensated on a fluctuating per hour basis or per transaction basis;

      iv. Whether the employee is physically located in the office of the real estate broker.

   d. Whether the real estate broker performs core title services, by and through its employees. In accordance with the HUD Statement of Policy 1996-4 the real estate broker shall not collect premiums for services not actually performed.

e. What, if any, the settlement services the real estate broker has contracted to other sources.

2. In addition to the above factors, the Commission will consider the guidelines set forth in the HUD statement of Policy 1996-2, Sham Controlled Business Arrangements (commonly referred to as the "HUD 10-Step Sham Test") and that statement is incorporated by reference. A copy of this document is available for public inspection at the office of the Division of Real Estate, 1560 Broadway, Ste. 925, Denver, CO, 80202, weekdays between 8 a.m. and 5 p.m.; excluding state observed holidays. The Commission may also consider any other relevant facts and circumstances relating to the above factors and to those elements set forth in the 10-Step Sham Test.

3. The disclosures to the Commission required by Section 12-61-113.2 (3) and (4) shall be made in a form or manner required by the Commission and shall be:

   a. At the time of a new application for active licensure or at the time of activation of an inactive license, the licensee shall disclose to the Commission the names of all affiliated business arrangements to which the licensee is a party. The written disclosure shall include the physical location of the affiliated business.

   b. Upon the transfer of an active license to another brokerage firm, the active licensee shall disclose to the Commission the names of all affiliated business arrangements to which the licensee is a party. The written disclosure shall include the physical location of the affiliated business.

   c. On an annual basis, each employing broker shall disclose to the Commission the names of all affiliated business arrangements to which the employing broker is a party. The written disclosure shall include the physical location of the affiliated business.

F. Noncompliance with this rule, whether defined or reasonably implied under this rule E-46, may result, after proper notice and hearing, in the imposition of any of the sanctions available in the Colorado statutes pertaining to the business of real estate brokers or other laws which include the imposition of fines and/or discipline of a license.

G. The following are hereby incorporated by reference as written on or before the effective date of this rule. This rule does not include later amendments to or editions of the incorporated material. A copy of these references may be examined at any state publications depository library. For additional information regarding how to obtain a copy please contact Rulemaking Coordinator, Colorado Division of Real Estate, 1560 Broadway Ste. 925, Denver, CO 80202.

1. The HUD policy statement 1996-2, which is the Policy Statement on Sham Controlled Business Arrangements.

2. The HUD policy statement 1996-4, which is the Statement of Enforcement Standards: Title Insurance Practices in Florida; Final Rule.

E-48. No licensee shall file a lien, a lis pendens or record a listing contract to secure the payment of a commission or other fee associated with real estate brokerage duties in a residential transaction. A licensee involved in a residential transaction shall not cause the title to a property to become clouded or otherwise interfere with the transfer of title when the licensee is not a principal in the transaction. A licensee involved in a commercial transaction, pursuant to §38-22.5-101, may file such a lien or lis pendens.

E-49. A licensee shall make written notification to the Commission within 30 calendar days of any of the following:

(a) A plea of guilt, a plea of nolo contendere or a conviction of any crime identified by 12-61-113(1)(m), C.R.S.

(b) A violation or aiding and abetting in the violation of the Colorado or federal fair housing laws.

(c) Any disciplinary action taken against a licensee in any other jurisdiction, if the licensee's

(d) A suspension or revocation of a license, registration, or certification by Colorado or another state, within the last five years, for fraud, deceit, material misrepresentation, theft, or the breach of a fiduciary duty that denied the licensee the authorization to practice as a mortgage broker, a real estate broker or salesperson, a real estate appraiser, an insurance producer, an attorney, a securities broker-dealer, a securities sales representative, an investment advisor, or an investment advisor representative. (Effective October 30, 2008)

Commission Approved Forms

Through the adoption and promulgation of Commission Rule F, it became compulsory for all real estate brokers licensed by the State of Colorado to use Commission approved forms in most of their contracting. 12-61-803(4) C.R.S. grants the Colorado Real Estate Commission statutory authority to promulgate standard forms for use by licensees.

One of the major purposes of the rule is to help to insure broker compliance with the Colorado Supreme Court Conway-Bogue decision. (See case summary in Chapter 5) A second purpose is to help promote uniformity in contracting to the end that the public is better protected. The privileges granted should not be abused by the real estate broker.

Rule F. Use of Commission Approved Forms

* ***F-1. Permitted and Prohibited Form Modifications***

(a) No modifications shall be made to a Commission-approved form by a broker except as provided in rules promulgated by the Commission and as set forth in this Rule F-1 through F-7. For purposes of Rule F-1 through F-7, the term "Commission-approved form" means any form promulgated by the Commission; the term "broker" shall also include brokerage firm.

(b) A broker may add its firm name, address, telephone, e-mail, trademark or other identifying information on a Commission-approved form.

(c) A broker may add initial lines at the bottom of a page of any Commission-approved form.

(d) Any deletion to the printed body of a Commission-approved form, or any "Additional Provision" or "Addenda" which by its terms serves to amend or delete portions of the approved language, must result from negotiations or the instruction(s) of a party to the transaction and must be made directly on the printed body of the form by striking through the amended or deleted portion in a legible manner that does not obscure the deletion that has been made.

(e) Blank spaces on a Commission-approved form may be lengthened or shortened to accommodate the applicable data or information.

(f) Provisions that are inserted into blank spaces must be printed in a style of type that clearly differentiates such insertions from the style of type used for the Commission-approved form language.

(g) A broker may omit part or all of the following provisions of a Commission-approved "Contract to Buy and Sell Real Estate"(even if the provision is identified by a different

Section number), or corresponding provisions in other Commission-approved forms, if such provisions do not apply to the transaction. In the event any provision is omitted, the provision's caption or heading must remain unaltered on the form followed by the word "OMITTED".

* 1. Section 2.5 Inclusions in its entirety or any of its subsections
* 2. Section 2.6 Exclusions

3. Section 4.4 Seller Concessions
4. Section 4.5 New Loan in its entirety or any of its subsections
5. Section 4.6 Assumption
6. Section 4.7 Seller or Private Financing
7. Section 5 Financing Conditions and Obligations in its entirety or any of its sections
8. Section 6 Appraisal Provisions in its entirety or any of its subsections

* 9. Section 7.3 Homeowners' Association Documents in its entirety or any of its subsections

10. Section 8.4 Special Taxing Districts

* 11. Section 8.5 Right of First Refusal or Contract Approval
* 12. Section 10.6 Due Diligence Documents
* 13. Section 10.7 Due Diligence Documents Conditions in its entirety or any of its subsections
* 14. Section 10.8 Due Diligence—Environmental, ADA (CBS2, CBS3, CBS4)
* 15 Section 10.7.3 Source of Potable Water (CBS4)
* 16. Section 10.9 Existing Leases; Modification of Existing Leases; New Leases (CBS3, CBS4)
* 17. [Deleted]
* 18. [Deleted]
* 19. [Deleted]
* 20. Section 10.15 Existing Leases; Modification of Existing Leases; New Leases (CBS2)
* 21. Section 11 Tenant Estoppel Statements in its entirety or any of its subsections (CBS2, CBS3, CBS4)

22. Section 15.3 Status and Transfer Letter Fees
23. Section 15.4 Local Transfer Tax

* 24. Section 15.6 Sales and Use Tax

25. Section 16.2 Rents
26. Section 16.3 Association Assessments

(h) A broker may add an additional page to the "Contract to Buy and Sell Real Estate", "Counterproposal" and the "Agreement to Amend/Extend Contract", following such document, that contains the dates and deadlines information set forth in §3, arranged in chronological date sequence.

(i) A broker may omit part or all of the following provisions of the "Counterproposal" and the "Agreement to Amend/Extend Contract" if such provisions do not apply to the transaction. In the event any provision is omitted, the provision's caption or heading must remain unaltered on the form followed by the words "OMITTED".

1. Section 3 Dates and Deadlines table
2. Section 4 Purchase Price and Terms [in the Counterproposal only]

(j) A broker may substitute the term "Landlord" for the term "Seller" and the term "Tenant" for the term "Buyer" in the Brokerage Disclosure to Buyer form, in the Brokerage Disclosure to Seller and Definitions of Working Relationships form when making disclosures in a lease transaction (or use the separate Brokerage Disclosure to Tenant form).

(k) A broker may add signature lines and identifying labels for the parties signature on a Commission-approved form.

(l) A broker may modify, strike or delete such language on a Commission-approved form as the Commission may from time to time authorize to be modified, stricken or deleted.

F-2. Additional Provisions

(a) The "Additional Provisions" section of a Commission-approved form must contain only those transaction-specific terms or acknowledgments that result from negotiations or the instruction(s) of the party(ies) to the transaction.

(b) A broker who is not a principal party to the contract may not insert personal provisions, personal disclaimers or exculpatory language in favor of the broker in the "Additional Provisions" section of a Commission-approved form.

F-3. Addenda

(a) If a broker originates or initiates the use of a preprinted or prepared addendum that modifies or adds to the terms of a Commission-approved contract form which does not result from the negotiations of the parties, such addendum must be prepared by:

(1) an attorney representing the broker or brokerage firm; or

(2) a principal party to the transaction; or

(3) an attorney representing a principal party.

(b) An addendum permitted by this Rule F- 3 (a), shall not be included within the body of, or in the "Additional Provisions" section of, a Commission-approved form.

(c) A broker who is not a principal party to the contract may not insert personal provisions, personal disclaimers or exculpatory language in favor of the broker in an addendum.

(d) If an addendum is prepared by a broker's attorney, the following disclosure must appear on the first page of the addendum in the same sized type as the size of type used in the addendum: "This addendum has not been approved by the Colorado Real Estate Commission. It was prepared by (insert licensed name of broker or brokerage firm's) legal counsel."

(e) If an addendum to a listing, tenant or right to buy contract, is prepared by a broker or brokerage firm, the following disclosure must appear on the first page of the addendum in the same sized type as the size of type used in the addendum:

> "This addendum has not been approved by the Colorado Real Estate Commission. It was prepared by (insert licensed name of broker or brokerage firm)."

F-4. Prohibited Provisions

No contract provision, including modifications permitted by Rules F-1 through F-3, shall relieve a broker from compliance with the real estate license law, section 12-61-101, et. seq., or the Rules of the Commission.

Pursuant to Rule E-12, when a written agreement contains a provision entitling the broker to a commission on a sale or purchase made after the expiration of the agreement, such provision must refer only to those persons or properties with whom or on which the broker negotiated during the term of the agreement, and whose names or addresses, were submitted in writing to the seller or buyer during the term of the agreement, including any extension thereof.

F-5. Explanation of Permitted Modifications

The broker shall explain all permitted modifications, deletions, omissions, insertions, additional provisions and addenda to the principal party and must recommend that the parties obtain expert advice as to the material matters that are beyond the expertise of the broker.

F-6. Commission-Approved Form Reproduction

(a) Commission-approved forms used by a broker, including permitted modification made by a broker, shall be legible.

(b) Brokers generating Commission-approved forms through the use of a computer shall ensure that a security software program is utilized that prevents inadvertent change or prohibited modification of Commission-approved forms by the broker or other computer user.

* ***F-7. Commission Approved Forms***

> Ed. Note: The most current version of approved forms can be found on the Division of Real Estate website at: **www.dora.state.co.us/real-estate/contracts/contracts2012.htm.**

Real estate brokers are required to use Commission-approved forms as appropriate to a transaction or circumstance to which a relevant form is applicable. Commission-approved forms are posted on the Division of Real Estate's website. Effective June 2009, the Commission will no longer post forms in the Code of Colorado Regulations. The Commission hereby withdraws all forms from the Code of Colorado Regulations. In instances when the Commission has not developed an approved form within the purview of this rule, and other forms are used, they are not governed by Rule F. Other forms used by a broker shall not be prepared by a broker, unless otherwise permitted by law.

* To obtain the forms promulgated by the real estate commission that are within the purview of Rule F, visit the Division of Real Estate website at: http://www.dora.state.co.us/real-estate/broker licensing.htm or the Division of Real Estate's offices at 1560 Broadway, Suite 925, Denver, Colorado 80202.

Rule G. Brokers Acting Under 12-61-101(2)(j) C.R.S. (Rental Referrals)

G-1. Repealed (1-6-00)

G-2. Receipt for advance fees

Pursuant to 12-61-113(1.5) C.R.S., every person licensed acting under 12-61-101(2)(j) C.R.S. shall give a prospective tenant a contract or receipt. At the time of acceptance of an advance fee from a prospective tenant, a broker shall provide the prospective tenant with a written contract or receipt which shall include at least the following:

(a) Name, business address and telephone number of the brokerage company.

(b) Acknowledgment of receipt of advance fee.

(c) A description of the services to be performed by the broker, including significant conditions, restrictions and limitations where applicable, and hours of operation.

(d) The prospective tenant's specifications for the rental property, including but not limited to:

(1) Type of structure, *e.g.*, detached single family, apartment, duplex, condominium, mobile home, et cetera.

(2) Location by commonly accepted residential area name, by designation of boundary streets and municipality or in any other manner affording a reasonable means of identifying acceptable locations.

(3) Furnished or unfurnished.

(4) Number of bedrooms.

(5) Earliest occupancy date desired.

(6) Maximum acceptable monthly rental.

(7) Pets.

(8) Garage, carport or off-street parking.

(e) Contract expiration date.

(f) Date of execution.

(g) Signatures of the prospective tenant, the broker, and if negotiated by a licensee in the employ of a broker, then the employed licensee shall sign on behalf of the employing broker.

(h) The address and the phone number of the Real Estate Commission in prominent letters.

(i) A statement that the regulation of rental location services is under the jurisdiction of the Real Estate Commission.

(j) Recital in bold face and capitals that:

IF THE INFORMATION CONCERNING RENTAL FURNISHED BY THE BROKER IS SHOWN TO BE NOT CURRENT OR ACCURATE IN REGARD TO THE TYPE OF RENTAL DESIRED, THE FULL FEE SHALL BE REPAID OR REFUNDED TO THE PROSPECTIVE TENANT UPON WRITTEN DEMAND. CURRENT RENTALS HAVE BEEN VERIFIED AS TO AVAILABILITY WITHIN THE PAST FOUR BUSINESS DAYS.

G-3. Broker must retain copy of referral lists given in person

Whenever the prospective tenant visits the broker's office, a list of all addresses given to the prospective tenant shall be prepared in duplicate. A copy shall be given to the prospective tenant and the original shall be retained by the broker for a period of 90 days and either affixed to the client's contract or receipt or be placed in the client's file if a separate file is kept. The list shall clearly indicate the following:

(a) The date the addresses were furnished to the prospective tenant.

(b) The type of unit, *e.g.*, detached single-family residence, apartment, duplex, condominium, mobile home, etc.

(c) Whether the unit is furnished or unfurnished.

(d) The date when the unit will be available for occupancy.

(e) The date when the unit was most recently entered on the agency's listing records.

(f) The date when the housing accommodation was last verified by the agency to be available for rent.

(g) The address and municipality of the housing accommodation.

(h) The name and address of the property owner or their authorized agent and the telephone number, if available.

(i) The monthly rent required by the landlord.

(j) The number of bedrooms and total number of rooms.

(k) Whether a written lease is required and, if so, the minimum lease term required by the landlord.

(l) Any lawful restrictions as to pets, children, furnishings, occupants or activities imposed by the landlord.

G-4. Repealed effective 1-1-97

G-5. Broker must retain copy of referral lists given by phone

Where addresses are furnished to the prospective tenant by telephone or any other manner not requiring the prospective tenant's presence at the broker's office, the addresses shall be noted on the broker's copy of the list. The list shall indicate by which broker or employee of the broker the addresses were furnished and the broker's copy shall be retained for a period of one year.

G-6. Advertising

Each broker engaged in locating or assisting in locating rental properties for an advance fee shall abide by the following regulations regarding advertising practices:

(a) Licensee shall make written registries, posted in a conspicuous place or otherwise disclosed to fee payers, of all advertisements or other publications published or caused to be published by the broker, together with address of each property advertised, the name of the party who offered the property for rent and his or her telephone, if any.

(b) No property shall be advertised which has not been verified for availability four business days or less before said advertisement shall be printed.

(c) Each property advertised for rent or lease through the use of any media form shall be assigned a code (and one code only) in accordance with a uniform coding system adopted by the broker, which code shall also appear in any media advertising placed by said broker. Coding of municipalities shall be included within the uniform system so as to be accurately reflected in media advertising.

(d) A copy of all advertising submitted to any media group for publication (including television, radio, newspaper and mimeographed sheets), together with the name of the person submitting the same, shall be maintained by a broker for a period of one year after publication.

(e) No licensee acting under 12-61-101(2)(j) C.R.S. shall advertise or furnish a prospective tenant with the address of a prospective rental unless such licensee has received specific authorization to list said property from the owner or owner's authorized agent. Specific authorization may be by writing, signed by the owner or owner's agent, or orally, if the broker notes the name of the owner or owner's agent, the date of authorization, and the telephone number of the person so authorizing.

G-7. Grounds for finding unworthiness or incompetence

Pursuant to 12-61-113(l)(n) C.R.S., a licensee acting under 12-16-101(2)(j) C.R.S. shall be considered unworthy or incompetent in the conduct of their business where:

(a) The licensee violates Rule G-6.

(b) With particular respect to media advertising:

  (1) The property is not actually located in the area represented.

  (2) The rental price shown is less than that asked by the owner of the available property.

(3) The property is non-existent or cannot be verified as currently for rent by the licensee.

(4) The specifics of the property advertised differ materially from the property as it exists.

(5) A property is advertised in such a way or under such a heading as to indicate the property is of a different type than it actually is. The word "type" refers to such designations as: single family detached residence, duplex, apartment, condominium, townhouse, or mobile home.

(c) The licensee fails or refuses to abide by the terms of the contract or receipt between himself and a prospective purchaser.

(d) The broker fails or refuses to refund money pursuant to the terms of the contract or receipt.

(e) The broker has failed to keep accurate records as specified in these rules or has failed to retain said records for the prescribed time periods.

Rule H. Repealed

Rule I. Declaratory Orders

I-1. Any person may petition for an order

Any person may petition the Commission for a declaratory order to terminate controversies or to remove uncertainties as to the applicability to the petitioner of any statutory provision or of any rule or order of the Commission.

I-2. Commission determines whether to rule

The Commission will determine, in its discretion and without prior notice to the petitioner, whether to rule upon any such petition. If the Commission determines it will not rule upon such a petition, the Commission shall issue its written order disposing of the same, stating therein its reasons for such action. A copy of such order shall forthwith be transmitted to the petitioner.

I-3. Commission considerations

In determining whether to rule upon a petition filed pursuant to this rule, the Commission will consider the following matters, among others:

(a) whether a ruling on the petition will terminate a controversy or remove uncertainties as to the applicability to petitioner of any statutory provision or rule or order of the Commission;

(b) whether the petition involves any subject, question or issue which is the subject of formal or informal matter or investigation currently pending before the Commission or a court involving one or more of the petitioners which will terminate the controversy or remove the uncertainties as to the applicability to the petitioner of any statutory provision or of any rule or order of the Commission, which matter or investigation shall be specified by the Commission;

(c) whether the petition involves any subject, question or issue which is the subject of a formal matter or investigation currently pending before the Commission or a court but not involving any petitioner which will terminate the controversy or remove the uncertainties as to the applicability to the petitioner of any statutory provision of any rule or order of the Commission, which matter or investigation shall be specified by the Commission and in which petitioner may intervene;

(d) whether the petition seeks a ruling on a moot or hypothetical question and will result in merely an advisory ruling or opinion;

(e) whether the petitioner has some other adequate legal remedy, other than an action for declaratory relief pursuant to Rule 57, Colo. R. Civ. P., which will terminate the controversy or remove any uncertainty as to the applicability to the petitioner of the statute, rule or order in question.

I-4. Petition contents

Any petition filed pursuant to this rule shall set forth the following:

(a) the name and address of the petitioner and whether the petitioner is licensed pursuant to 12-61-101 C.R.S., *et seq*.

(b) the statute, rule or order to which the petition relates;

(c) a concise statement of all the facts necessary to show the nature of the controversy or uncertainty and the manner in which the statute, rule or order in question applies or potentially applies to the petitioner.

I-5. Procedures if the Commission will rule

If the Commission determines that it will rule on the petition the following procedures shall apply:

(a) The Commission may rule upon the petition based solely upon the facts presented in the petition. In such a case:

(1) any ruling of the Commission will apply only to the extent of the facts presented in the petition and any amendment to the petition;

(2) the Commission may order the petitioner to file a written brief, memorandum or statement of opposition;

(3) the Commission may set the petition, upon due notice to petitioner, for a non-evidentiary hearing;

(4) the Commission may dispose of the petition on the sole basis of the matters set forth in the petition;

(5) the Commission may request the petitioner to submit additional facts in writing. In such event, such additional facts will be considered as an amendment to the petition;

(6) the Commission may take administrative notice of facts pursuant to the Administrative Procedure Act 24-4-105(8) C.R.S. and utilize its experience, technical competence and specialized knowledge in the disposition of the petition;

(7) if the Commission rules upon the petition without a hearing, it shall issue its written order, stating herein its basis for the order. A copy of such order shall forthwith be transmitted to the petitioner.

(b) The Commission may, in its discretion, set the petition for hearing, upon due notice to the petitioner, for the purpose of obtaining additional facts or information or to determine the truth of any fact set forth in the petition or to hear oral argument on the petition. Notice to the petitioner setting such hearing shall set forth, to the extent known, the factual or other matters into which the Commission intends to inquire. For the purpose of such a hearing, to the extent necessary, the petitioner shall have the burden of providing all of the facts stated in the petition, all of the facts necessary to show the nature of the controversy or uncertainty and the manner in which the statute, rule or order in question applies or potentially applies to petitioner and any other facts the petitioner desires the Commission to consider.

I-6. ***Parties to proceedings***

The parties to any proceeding pursuant to this rule shall be the Commission and the petitioner. Any other person may seek leave of the Commission to intervene in such a proceeding, and leave to intervene will be granted at the sole discretion of the Commission. A petition to intervene shall set forth the same matters as required by section 4 of this rule. Any reference to a "petitioner" in this rule also refers to any person who has been granted leave to intervene by the Commission.

I-7. ***Orders subject to judicial review***

Any declaratory order or other order disposing of a petition pursuant to this rule shall constitute agency action subject to judicial review pursuant to 24-4-106 C.R.S.

Rule J. Repealed

Rule K. Exceptions and Commission Review of Initial Decisions

K-1. ***Written Form, Service and Filing Requirements***

1. All Designations of Record, Requests, Exceptions and Responsive Pleadings ("Pleadings") must be in written form, mailed with a certificate of mailing to the Commission.
2. All Pleadings must be filed with the Commission by 5:00 p.m. on the date the filing is due. These rules do not provide for any additional time for service by mail. Filing is in receipt of a pleading by the Commission.
3. Any Pleadings must be served on the opposing party by mail or by hand delivery on the date which the Pleading is filed with the Commission.
4. All Pleadings must be filed with the Commission and not with the Office of Administrative Courts. Any Designations of Record, Requests, Exceptions or Responsive Pleadings filed in error with the Office of Administrative Courts will not be considered. The Commission's address is:

   Colorado Real Estate Commission
   1560 Broadway, Suite 925
   Denver, CO 80202

K-2. ***Authority to review***

1. The Commission hereby preserves the Commission's option to initiate a review of an initial decision on its own motion pursuant to § 24-4-105(14)(a)(II) and (b)(III), C.R.S. outside of the thirty day period after service of the initial decision upon the parties without requiring a vote for each case.
2. This option to review shall apply regardless of whether a party files exceptions to the initial decision.

K-3. ***Designation of record and transcripts***

1. Any party seeking to reverse or modify the initial decision of the administrative law judge shall file with the Commission a designation of the relevant parts of the record for review ("Designation of Record"). Designations of Record must be filed with the Commission within twenty days of the date on which the Commission mails the initial decision to the parties' address of record with the Commission.
2. Even if no party files a Designation of Record, the record shall include the following:
   a. All pleadings;

b. All applications presented or considered during the hearing;
c. All documentary or other exhibits admitted into evidence;
d. All documentary or other exhibits presented or considered during the hearing;
e. All matters officially noticed;
f. Any findings of fact and conclusions of law proposed by any party; and
g. Any written brief filed.

3. Transcripts: Transcripts will not be deemed part of a Designation of Record unless specifically identified and ordered. Should a party wish to designate a transcript or portion thereof, the following procedures will apply:
   a. The Designation of Record must identify with specificity the transcript or portion thereof to be transcribed. For example, a party may designate the entire transcript, or may identify witness(es) whose testimony is to be transcribed, the legal ruling or argument to be transcribed, or other information necessary to identify a portion of the transcript.
   b. Any party who includes a transcript or a portion thereof as part of the Designation of Record must order the transcript or relevant portions by the date on which the Designation of Record must be filed (within twenty days of the date on which the Commission mails the initial decision to the parties).
   c. When ordering the transcript, the party shall request a court reporter or transcribing service to prepare the transcript within thirty days. The party shall timely pay the necessary fees to obtain and file with the Commission an original transcription and one copy within thirty days.
   d. The party ordering the transcript shall direct the court report or transcribing service to complete and file with the Commission the transcript and one copy of the transcript within thirty days.
   e. If a party designates a portion of the transcript, the opposing party may also file a Supplemental Designation of Record, in which the opposing party may designate additional portions of the transcript. This Supplemental Designation of Record must be filed with the Commission and served on the other party within ten days after the date on which the original Designation of Record was due.
   f. An opposing party filing a Supplemental Designation of Record must order and pay for such transcripts or portions thereof within the deadlines set forth above. An opposing party must also cause the court reporter to complete and file with the Commission the transcript and one copy of the transcript within thirty days.
   g. Transcripts that are ordered and not filed with the Commission in a timely manner by the reporter or the transcription service due to non-payment, insufficient payment or failure to direct as set forth above will not be considered by the Commission.

K-4. Filing of Exceptions and Responsive Pleadings

1. Any party wishing to file exceptions shall adhere to the following timelines:
   a. If no transcripts are ordered, exceptions are due within thirty days from the date on which the Commission mails the initial decision to the parties. Both parties' exceptions are due on the same date.
   b. If transcripts are ordered by either party, the following procedure shall apply. Upon receipt of transcripts identified in all Designations of Record, the Commission shall mail notification to the parties stating that the transcripts have been received by the Commission. Exceptions are due within thirty days from the

date on which such notification is mailed. Both parties' exceptions are due on the same date.

2. Either party may file a responsive pleading to the other party's exceptions. All responsive pleadings shall be filed within ten days of the date on which the exceptions were filed with the Commission. No other pleadings will be considered except for good cause shown.

3. The Commission may in its sole discretion grant an extension of time to file exceptions or responsive pleadings, or may delegate the discretion to grant such an extension of time to the Commission's designee.

K-5. Request for Oral Argument

1. All requests for oral argument must be in writing and filed by the deadline for responsive pleadings.

2. It is within the sole discretion of the Commission to grant or deny a request for oral argument. If oral argument is granted, both parties shall have the opportunity to participate.

3. Each side shall be permitted ten minutes of oral argument unless such time is extended by the Commission or its designee.

Chapter 3: Commission Position Statements

An * in the left margin indicates a change in the statute, rule or text since the last publication of the manual.

CP-1 Commission Policy on Homebuilder's Exemption from Licensing

Corporations that build structures on land they own may sell the land and building together without licensing, provided that the sales are made by corporate officers or regularly salaried employees. The land and building must be sold as a unit and the building must not have been previously occupied. This exemption is usually referred to as the homebuilder's exemption. Since employees who sell must be regularly salaried employees, the question often arises as to what a regular salary is. This is the position of the Commission: 12-61-101(2)(b)(X) C.R.S., among other requirements, requires that a corporation use "regular salaried employees" to sell or negotiate the sale of real property.

It is the position of the Commission that the phrase, "regular salaried employees" means that:

1. The salary must be an actual and stated amount and must not be a draw or advance against future commissions.
2. The salary must be regularly paid (*i.e.*, weekly, monthly, etc.).
3. Although the amount of salary may vary, an employee must be paid at least the prevailing federal minimum wage.
4. The corporation should deduct amounts for state and federal withholding taxes, FICA taxes, and other commonly deductible expenses, which the corporation would employ with respect to other employees.

Payment of a commission, in addition to a regular salary, will not invalidate the exemption if the above guidelines are met.

CP-2 Commission Position on Referral Fees and Advertising Services

(Revised Position 11/08)

Section 12-61-113(1)(j) of the license law forbids a broker from paying a commission or valuable consideration, for performing brokerage functions, to any person who is not licensed as a real estate broker.

Pursuant to Colorado case law "negotiating" means "the act of bringing two parties together for the purpose of consummating a real estate transaction" *Brakhage vs. Georgetown Associates, Inc.*, 523 P 2d 145 (1974). Therefore, any unlicensed person who directly or indirectly brings a buyer and seller together, is negotiating and would need a broker's license in order to be compensated. This includes, but is not limited to, such activities as referring potential time-share purchasers to a developer or referring potential purchasers to a homebuilder.

Payment for general promotion of a real estate business is not prohibited. Contracting with newspapers, catalog companies of general circulation or with institutional advertisers such as radio, television or any other media, is not prohibited provided the activity does not otherwise constitute offering, negotiating, listing, selling, or leasing real estate as defined in 12-61-101(2). Payment based on the successful sale or lease of real estate does not in itself constitute brokering as so defined. However, in the past, the Commission has determined that many so-called advertising services actually involved brokering activities. The method of payment is often an important factor in determining whether the activity requires a license.

Payment for providing a name to a licensed broker is not specifically addressed in the license law. However, it would be illegal to pay such a fee to anyone performing acts that require a license (*i.e.*, negotiating, listing, and contracting). Care should be taken. At best, the unlicensed referrer can have no active involvement in the transaction beyond merely giving to a licensee the name of a prospective buyer, seller or tenant.

If the payment is simply for the referral of a name to a licensee, with no further activity on the part of the referrer, and the referrer is not a provider of a settlement service, the Commission will not consider it to be a violation of the license law. Complaints and inquiries are dealt with on a case-by-case basis.

Section 8 of RESPA prohibits kickbacks and unearned fees. No person shall give and no person shall accept any fee, kickback, or thing of value pursuant to any agreement or understanding, oral or otherwise, that business incident to or a part of a real estate settlement service involving a federally related mortgage loan shall be referred to any person.

The Commission has received a number of inquiries from licensees regarding its position on referral fees as related to the RESPA position prohibiting certain types of payments. All licensees must comply with RESPA statute and regulations regarding payment of referral fees. A payment pursuant to a cooperative brokerage and referral arrangements or agreements between real estate brokers is acceptable when all parties are acting in a real estate brokerage capacity. The referral fee is therefore earned compensation for the performance of brokerage duties.

CP-3 Position Statement Concerning Commission Rule E-13

Commission Rule E-13, commonly referred to as the "sign-crossing" rule, states as follows:

"A real estate licensee shall not negotiate a sale, exchange, lease or listing contract of real property directly with an owner for compensation from such owner if such licensee knows that such owner has a written unexpired contract in connection with such property which grants to another licensee an exclusive right to sell or lease or which grants an exclusive agency right to sell or lease. However, when a licensee is contacted by an owner regarding the sale, exchange, lease or listing of property that is exclusively listed with another broker, and the licensee has not initiated the discussion, the licensee may negotiate the terms upon which the licensee might take a future listing or, alternatively, may take a listing to become effective upon expiration of any existing exclusive listing."

The Commission's intent in promulgating Rule E-13 was (1) to prevent brokers from interfering with existing listing contracts to the detriment of the owner and (2) to protect the owner from possible claims that two commissions are owed.

Many owners are extremely dependent on the expertise of the licensee. They may sincerely believe an existing listing contract is not in effect when, in fact, it is. The burden of inquiry is on the licensee.

Earlier versions of E-13 had been criticized for being too restrictive. The current rule still provides that licensees shall not negotiate directly with an owner if they know that the owner has a written unexpired Exclusive Right to Sell or Lease. However, the licensee is now allowed to negotiate the terms for a future listing or take a listing effective upon expiration of a current listing so long as the licensee is first contacted by the owner.

This recognizes the fact that an owner with property currently listed may initiate the negotiations concerning a future listing. In addition, the current rule recognizes that in some instances owners become dissatisfied with the services of the broker with whom they have a listing and wish to cancel the listing. If a knowledgeable and informed seller wishes to cancel a listing and list with another company, this cannot be prevented. Of course, the seller runs the risk that improper cancellation of a listing contract can result in legal consequences. Brokers should never independently advise a seller in this area. Instead, an inquiring seller should be advised to seek legal counsel to explain the consequences of canceling an unexpired listing.

If the rule is followed closely it will provide greater opportunities for licensees to negotiate listings where a seller does not wish to re-list with the same broker while maintaining the integrity of the principal/agent brokerage relationship.

CP-4 Commission Position on Interest Bearing Trust Accounts

(Revised Position 8-04)

Section 12-61-113 (l)(g.5) C.R.S. permits brokers to place entrusted money in an interest bearing account.

The Commission has taken the position that in the absence of a contract signed by the proper parties to the contrary, any interest accumulating on a trust account does not belong to the broker who is acting as escrow agent. (This position is based upon 12-61-113(l)(q) and upon the well-established tenet of agency that the agent may not profit personally from the agency relationship except for agreed upon compensation.)

Contracts calling for large earnest money deposits or other payments should contain a provision specifying which party is entitled to interest earned and under what conditions. In the absence of such a provision, accrued interest normally belongs to the seller if the contract is consummated or if the seller is successful in declaring a forfeiture. The entrusted money normally belongs to the purchaser if the contract fails.

In a property management trust account, the accrued interest on that portion of rental money received that belongs to the lessor beneficiary (landlord), would belong to the lessor beneficiary. The accrued interest on security deposits would belong to the respective tenants unless the lessor can establish a right to the security deposit (in the absence of a contract to the contrary).

However, in the case of the property management of mobile homes, by Colorado statute, the interest earned on security deposits may be retained by the landlord of a mobile home park as compensation for administering the trust account. (38-12-209(2)(b) C.R.S.)

Nothing in this position statement precludes a real estate broker from voluntarily transferring interest earned on a trust account to a fund established for the purpose of providing affordable housing to Colorado residents if such a fund is established.

CP-5 Commission Position on Advance Rentals and Security Deposits

Pursuant to C.R.S. 12-61-113 (l)(g.5) and Commission Rule E-l and E-16, all money belonging to others which is received by a broker must be placed in an escrow or trust account. This applies to tenant security deposits and advance rental deposits, including credit card receipts, held by a broker.

A broker may not deliver a security deposit to an owner unless notice is given to the tenant in the lease, rental agreement, or in a separate written notice that the security deposit will be held by the owner. Such notice must be given in a manner so that the tenant will know who is holding the security deposit, and shall include either the true' name and current mailing address of the owner or the true name and current mailing address of a person authorized to receive legal notices on behalf of such owner, along with specific requirements for how the tenant is to request return of the deposit.

If, after receipt by the broker, the security deposit is to be transferred to the owner or used for the owner's benefit, the broker, in addition to properly notifying the tenant, must secure the consent of the owner to assume full financial responsibility for the return of any deposit which may be refundable to the tenant. The broker shall not withhold the identity of the owner from the tenant if demand for the return of the deposit is properly made according to the lease, rental agreement, or separate notice, and the owner has refused to return the security deposit. The lease, rental agreement, or separate notice may also give notice that the security deposit will be transferred upon the happening of certain events, *e.g.*, sale of the property or the naming of a new property manager.

Delivery of the security deposit to the owner or to anyone (including a succeeding broker/manager of the property) without proper notice to the tenant, in addition to subjecting the broker to possible civil liability, will constitute a violation of the license law escrow statute cited above. The licensee must retain copies of such notices for inspection by the Commission.

Under a property management contract, the broker must transfer all escrowed money belonging to the owner of the property at reasonable and agreed upon intervals and with proper accounting pursuant to statutory requirements and Commission Rules E-l and E-2. If advance rental money is held by a broker but is subject to recall by the tenant or occupant, it must be escrowed until such time as it is earned and rightfully transferred or credited to the owner. A broker has no claim on or right to use advance deposits which are subject to recall by a tenant or prospective occupant. Deposits which are not subject to recall are the property of the owner and may not be transferred to the broker's account or used for the broker's benefit unless specifically authorized and agreed to by the owner in the management agreement.

If litigation concerning escrow money commences, the money may be placed with the court. The jurisdiction of the court will, of course, supersede the statutory requirement for escrowing money belonging to others.

CP-6 Commission Position on Release of Earnest Money Deposits

(Revised Position 8-6-2008)

Rule E-15 states in part that: "When for any reason the owner fails, refuses, neglects or is unable to consummate the transaction as provided for in the contract, and through no fault or neglect of the purchaser the real estate transaction cannot be completed, . . . the deposit should be returned to the purchaser at once . . ."

The Commission will not pursue disciplinary action against a broker for refusal to disburse disputed funds when the broker is acting in accordance with the language of the appropriate Commission-approved contract to buy and sell. It is clear in the contract to buy and sell real estate that the broker holds the earnest money on behalf of both buyer and seller. If there is no dispute, the broker should disburse to the appropriate party immediately.

Some brokers unnecessarily require a signed release by both parties even when there is no disagreement. Audits have disclosed many instances where brokers have held deposits for extended periods just because one or both parties will not sign a release. While good judgment is always urged, releases are not a requirement of the Real Estate Commission. In addition, where one party has given written authorization for the release of a deposit to another, a written release by the other party is not required.

Exculpatory provisions holding the broker harmless do not belong in an agreement for the release of earnest money and should not be used to relieve the broker from liability unrelated to earnest money.

In the case of a dispute between the parties, the broker is authorized by the contract to buy and sell to obtain mutual written instructions (such as a release) before turning a deposit over to a party. The Commission has approved an optional use "Earnest Money Release" form when such a written release might help facilitate expeditious disbursement.

Unless otherwise indicated in the Commission-approved contract to buy and sell, a broker is not required to take any action regarding the release of the earnest money deposit when there is a controversy. If the following provisions are included in the contract, the broker may exercise three options in the event of an earnest money dispute, if the broker is the holder of the earnest money deposit. One option is that the broker may await any proceeding between the parties. Another option for the broker is to interplead all parties and deposit the earnest money into a court of competent jurisdiction. If included in the contract to buy and sell, the broker is entitled to recover court costs and reasonable attorney and legal fees. However, if this provision is struck from the contract to buy and sell, the broker may not be entitled to recover those costs. A third option available to the broker is to provide notice to the buyer and seller that unless the broker receives a copy of the Summons and Complaint or Claim (between the buyer and seller) containing a case number of the lawsuit within one hundred twenty (120) days of the broker's notice to the parties, the broker will be authorized to return the earnest money to the buyer.

If the broker is unable to locate the party due the refund, the broker may be required to transfer the deposit to the Colorado State Treasurer under the provisions of the Colorado "Unclaimed Property Act" C.R.S. 38-13-101. Notice of funds held is published in local newspapers under the "Great Colorado Payback Program" each year. Further information and reporting forms may be obtained from that office.

CP-7 Commission Position on Closing Costs

In the past, the Commission's position had been that real estate licensees were responsible for all costs of closing. This position has been modified after a re-examination of the Colorado Supreme Court case of Conway-Bogue vs. The Denver Bar Association and after the adoption of Rule E-37.

Commission Rule E-37 states:

> "There is no obligation for a licensee to prepare any legal documents as part of a real estate transaction. However, if a licensee or the licensee's agent prepares any legal document, the licensee or the licensee's agent may not charge a separate fee for preparation of such documents. A licensee shall not be responsible for fees charged for the preparation of legal documents where they are prepared by an attorney representing the purchaser or seller. Costs of closing not related to preparation of legal documents may be paid by the licensee or by any other person. A broker

who closes transactions and charges separately for costs of closing not related to the preparation of legal documents must specify the costs and obtain the written consent of the parties to be charged."

Based on the new rule the position is as follows:

1. Licensees are still responsible for paying the costs of legal document preparation when they are preparing such documents for their clients. If the broker delegates this function to an agent (title company or closing service) the broker is still responsible for bearing the cost.
2. Other costs associated with closings can be paid for by the licensee or any other party. The Commission will no longer require that licensees bear these costs. Licensees are urged to use the Closing Instructions and Earnest Money Receipt form developed by the Commission.
3. It is now permissible for brokers to close their own transactions and make additional charges for providing closing services so long as the charges are not tied to legal document preparation. If a licensee does this it must be with the consent of the parties and all charges must be specified. This consent may be obtained through the Listing Contract, the Contract to Buy and Sell, the Closing Instructions and Earnest Money Receipt form, or otherwise.
4. Licensees are not responsible for bearing the cost of legal document preparation where the documents are prepared by an attorney representing the parties to the transaction. However, the broker should not designate the broker's own attorney to prepare legal documents for the parties and then charge as if the attorney had prepared the documents on behalf of a client.
5. The broker must still provide accurate closing statements.

Particular note should be paid to the first sentence of the rule. While there is no legal obligation for a broker to prepare the legal documents in a transaction the Commission strongly advises that licensees make this clear in the Listing Contract. Many persons, purchasers and sellers alike, normally look to the broker for the preparation of these documents. If the broker has not made it clear that the broker's company will not undertake the preparation of legal documents, the parties might well assume that the broker will do so at the broker's cost.

CP-8 Commission Position on Assignment of Contracts and Escrowed Funds

Assignments of contracts and escrowed funds usually occur when one real estate company is purchased or taken over by another real estate company.

The following reflects the general position of the Commission concerning the assignment of contracts and escrowed funds as it concerns the brokers.

1. All parties to a contract must be informed of assignments and all beneficiaries of escrowed funds must be informed of any transfer of escrowed funds.
2. Listing contracts may not be assigned by the listing broker to another broker (without the consent of the owner), because the listing contract is a personal contract of a type which would not be entered into except when the owner relies on the personal skills and expertise of the broker.
3. The broker concerned with an executory contract is not a party principal to the contract itself and, therefore, has no voice in its assignment. The broker signs the sales contract only as the receipting agent.
4. The right of entitlement of a broker to a commission, pursuant to a contract between the broker and a seller, is assignable. In the Commission approved form of executory contract, the agreement of the seller in regard to a commission is placed outside the body of the contract between the purchaser and seller.
5. The contract between the seller and the broker concerning commissions does not affect the contract between the principal parties in the sale.

6. Earnest money taken pursuant to an executory contract is money belonging to others and falls within the purview of 12-61-113(l)(g) and (g.5), C.R.S. Earnest money being held by the broker is not transferable to any party except to a closing agent as immediately prior to closing as is practicable.
7. The maintenance of earnest money held in escrow must be pursuant to the rules of the Commission. The broker may, for convenience, authorize other persons to withdraw money from this escrow account (see Commission Rule E-l(a)), but the withdrawal must be pursuant to law and Commission rules.
8. Unless contracted to the contrary, the mechanical act of closing the transaction may be performed by any qualified person or persons with the agreement of the principal parties to the contract.
9. The absence of the closing broker or the Broker's agent will not relieve such broker from the broker's responsibilities of approving the Statement of Settlement. (See Commission Rule E-5). However, the absence of the broker cannot impede the closing of the transaction pursuant to the executory contract.
10. If a licensed broker receipts for earnest money pursuant to an executory contract and then transfers such earnest money to an unauthorized person, who is also a licensed broker, the licensed transferee, (as well as the transferor), is also subject to the law and rules of the Commission in regard to money belonging to others. Such licensed transferee is obligated to retain such money in a trust account until the transaction is consummated, defeated, or settlement has occurred, or unless directed otherwise by a court of law. If litigation concerning escrowed money commences, the money may be placed with the court. The jurisdiction of the court will supersede the statutory requirements and the Commission Rules.
11. If the seller and the buyer, who are the sole beneficiaries of the escrowed money, both agree that such escrowed money be transferred, then settlement has occurred and the broker must transfer the money according to the wishes of the beneficiaries. This does not defeat the broker's right to a commission whether by original contract with the seller or by assignment of such contract right.

CP-9 Commission Position on Record Keeping by Brokers

The Commission is often asked what documents must be kept in the broker's files which concern a particular transaction.

A duplicate means photocopy, carbon copy, or facsimile, or electronic copies which contain a digital or electronic signature as defined in 24-71-101(1) C.R.S. Pursuant to Rule E-4 and E-5, a broker shall maintain a duplicate of the original of any document (except deeds, notes and trust deeds or mortgages prepared for the benefit of third party lenders) which was prepared by or on behalf of the licensee and pertains to the consummation of the leasing, purchase, sale or exchange of real property in which the broker participates as a broker. The payoff statement and new loan statement monetarily affect the settlement statements and should be retained by the respective broker concerned. Cooperating brokers, including brokers acting as agents for buyers in a specific real estate transaction, shall have the same requirements for retention of duplicate records as is stated above, except that a cooperating broker who is not a party to the listing contract need not retain a copy of the listing contract or the seller's settlement statement. A broker is not required to obtain and retain copies of existing public records, title commitments, loan applications, lender required disclosures or related affirmations from independent third party closing entities after the settlement date. The broker shall retain documents bearing a duplicate signature for the disclosures required by Commission Rule F-7. The broker engaged by a party shall insure that the final sales agreement, settlement statement, or amendment of the settlement, delivered at closing for that party's tax reporting or future use, shall bear duplicate signatures as authorized by the parties concerned.

A complete listing of the documents normally required by the Commission for sales transactions and management activities can be found in the current edition of the Colorado Real Estate Manual, Chapter 19, and at the website address: http://www.dora.state.co.us/real-estate.

CP-10 Commission Position on Compensation Agreements Between Employing and Employed Brokers

In regard to an employed broker's claim for compensation from an employing broker, the Real Estate Commission has no legal authority to render a monetary judgment in a money dispute nor will it arbitrate such a matter. A broker's failure to pay an employee does not warrant disciplinary action.

The Commission's position is:

1. An employed broker is an employee of the employing broker.
2. That an employed broker may not accept a commission or valuable consideration for the sale of real property except from his or her employing broker. (12-61-117 C.R.S.)
3. That a commission or compensation paid to the employing or independent broker for real estate services is money belonging to such broker and is not money belonging to others as defined in 12-61-113(l)(g) and (g.5) C.R.S.
4. That a claim by an employed licensee for money allegedly owed by an employing broker must be decided by the civil courts on the basis of contract or "quantum merit."
5. That an employing broker pays their licensed or unlicensed employees pursuant to an oral or written employment contract.

Therefore, the contractual relationship between employing and employed brokers, as well as the office policy manual, should adequately cover the compensation of employed brokers.

CP-11 Commission Position on Assignments of Broker's Rights to a Commission

The Real Estate Commission recognizes and will enforce the statutory obligation of employed licensees as described in (12-61-113(1), C.R.S.), and more particularly:

> "12-61-113(l)(f) C.R.S. In the case of a broker registered as in the employ of another broker, failing to place, as soon after receipt as is practicably possible, in the custody of that licensed broker-employer any deposit money or other money or fund entrusted to the employee by any person dealing with the employee as the representative of that licensed broker-employer."

The Commission recognizes and will enforce the prohibition described in 12-61-117 C.R.S.:

> "12-61-117 C.R.S. It is unlawful for a real estate broker registered in the commission office as in the employ of another broker to accept a commission or valuable consideration for the performance of any of the acts specified in this part 1 from any person except the broker's employer, who shall be a licensed real estate broker."

However: If a broker is entitled to a commission pursuant to 12-61, Part 2, C.R.S., or, a broker is entitled to a commission in a transaction and title has passed from a seller to a buyer, the broker may assign any or all legal rights to such commission to any person including employed licensees and no disciplinary action will be invoked against such broker for having made such an assignment.

CP-12 Commission Position on the Broker's Payment or Rebating a Portion of an Earned Commission

The License Law forbids a broker from paying a commission or valuable consideration for performing brokerage functions to any person who is not licensed as a real estate broker. Thus, "referral fees" or "finder's fees" paid as the result of performing brokerage activities are prohibited.

The question of whether or not a broker may make payments from their earned commission to a buyer or a seller in a particular transaction will arise because usually neither the buyer nor the seller is licensed.

However, the License Law also permits any person to sell or acquire real property on such person's own account.

In a listing contract, the broker is principal party to the contract and the consideration offered is the brokerage services. The broker may add to this consideration the payment of money to the property owner in order to secure the listing. This is not a violation of the License Law.

Also, in a particular real estate transaction, the broker may pay a portion of commission to the unlicensed seller. This is merely a reduction in the amount of the earned commission and does not violate the License Law.

Payment to the unlicensed purchaser is often referred to as "rebating" and the intention to pay money to the purchaser is sometimes advertised and promoted as a sales inducement. The payment to the purchaser in itself is not a violation of the License Law because the broker is licensed to negotiate and the purchaser may negotiate on their own account. However, a broker representing the seller in a transaction should take care to insure that such payments do not conflict with fiduciary duties. For example, the "rebate" of a portion of a commission to a purchaser to be used by the purchaser as a down payment could distort the purchaser's financial qualifications and ultimately harm the seller. Additionally, a purchaser who does not receive a promised rebate of a partial commission may try to hold the seller liable for the wrongdoing of the broker on the theory of respondent superior. The Commission recommends that brokers disclose such payments to the seller and obtain the seller's consent prior to acceptance of any offer to purchase.

Gratuitous gifts to a purchaser subsequent to closing and not promised or offered as an inducement to buy would also be allowed (*i.e.*, a door knocker or dinner). Such gifts would not require disclosure and consent inasmuch as fiduciary duties would not be involved.

CP-13 Commission Policy on Single-Party Listings

Brokers often secure single-party listings because they have what they believe to be a good prospect for purchase. These listings are usually only for a few days, but occasionally the broker wishes to be protected for a longer period while the broker is negotiating with a particular prospective purchaser.

A single-party listing, when placed on a Commission approved form for an Exclusive Right to Sell or Exclusive Agency, results in greater protection to the broker than the broker needs to have and the owner is placed in a position which is unfair. The owner may not realize that if the owner signs a listing contract with another broker, the owner may become liable for the payment of two commissions even though the owner has excepted a sale to the person mentioned in a single-party listing contract.

In any and all contracting, the intent of the parties is paramount in its importance, in a listing contract, a broker is dealing with those less informed than the broker, and the broker has a duty to disclose the true meaning of the listing contract.

The Commission does not wish to limit any owner of the freedom to contract. However, the broker should fully disclose to the owner the effect of the exclusive right to sell listing contract or the exclusive agency contract.

Usually, when an owner signs an exclusive right to sell or exclusive agency agreement concerning a single party, the owner wishes to limit the rights of the broker under the listing contract. Therefore, in the space provided for additional provisions, one, two, or all of the following limitations should be inserted in this space:

1. The provisions of this listing contract shall apply only in the event a sale is made to ______________________.
2. The termination date shall not be extended by the "Holdover Period" of this listing contract.
3. In the event a sale is made by the owner or their broker to any other party than the above names, this listing contract is void.

If an owner is misled to their disadvantage, the broker may be found guilty of endangering the public.

CP-14 Commission Position on Sale of Modular Homes by Licensees

The Commission is aware that many services rendered by licensees may or may not, in themselves, require licensing. Such services as collection of rents on real property, subdivision development services other than sales, or the general management of real property not involving renting or leasing may all be performed independently by an unlicensed person. When performed by a licensee, these services are all so integrated with real estate brokerage that all money received in connection therewith must be held or disbursed according to the law and rules of the Real Estate Commission.

Therefore, it is the position of the Commission that a licensee who sells land and a modular home to be affixed to the land, to the purchaser in concurrent or an arranged or pre-arranged or packaged transaction, is subject to the laws and rules of the Commission. Consequently, all money received concerning the integrated transaction, including the modular home, should be processed through the broker or the employing broker pursuant to 12-61-117, C.R.S. and 12-61-113(l)(f), C.R.S. and Commission Rules E-l and E-5.

It is also the position of the Commission that if a licensee sells to an owner of land, a modular home to be affixed to the land, and there has been no brokerage relationship between the owners of the land and the licensee, such licensee in such a sale will not be required to comply with the requirements of 12-61-117, C.R.S. or 12-61-113(l)(f), C.R.S. or Commission Rules E-l and E-5.

CP-15 Commission Position on Sale of Items Other Than Real Estate

Inquiries have been made to the Commission as to the proper handling of sales, made by licensees, of items or services other than real estate. The following is the position of the Commission:

If the item, appliance, repair, remodeling or installation is performed in conjunction with a management contract or lease for a particular party or pursuant to an oral or written contingency in a specific executed contract of sale of the property, the employed licensee must process any fees or commissions received from the vendor or contractor through the employing broker. Also, disclosure must be made by the licensee to both the buyer and the seller of the property that the licensee is compensated by the vendor or contractor.

It is also the position of the Commission that if the sale of the item, appliance, repair, remodeling or installation is performed pursuant to a separate contract, and without reference to a specific contract of sale of the property, then the employed licensee may receive compensation directly from the vendor, or contractor and payment need not be made through the employing broker. However, if the sale of items or services is made to a buyer of real property during the term of the brokerage agreement with the seller of such property, then disclosure must be made by the licensee to both the buyer and the seller of the property that the licensee is compensated by the vendor or contractor.

The Commission takes no position when the licensee engages in selling items or services unconnected with real estate sales.

In any of the above situations the employed licensee may be subject to any requirements or prohibitions imposed by the employment agreement with the employing broker.

CP-16 Commission Position on Access to Properties Offered for Sale

(Revised November 1, 2005)

The Commission approved listing agreements (LC series) include a section titled OTHER BROKERAGE FIRMS ASSISTANCE – MULTIPLE LISTING SERVICE – MARKETING.

Provisions of this section allow the seller and listing broker to agree on whether or not to submit the property to a multiple listing service, information exchange, and whether there are limitations on the methods of marketing the property.

The provisions of the section also allow for discussion and the establishment of "Other Instructions" regarding access to the property by other brokerage firms such as through a lock box, for example.

It is the position of the Commission that the access information, and adherence to the Other Instructions, whether through lock box code or other means, is the responsibility of the listing broker. Listing brokers should take every effort to safeguard the access information on behalf of the seller. The listing agreements also include a section titled MAINTENANCE OF THE PROPERTY, which addresses the broker's liability for damage of any kind occurring to the property caused by the broker's negligence. Brokers are advised that failure to safeguard the access information and adhere to the instructions of the Seller related to access by other brokerage firms could result in a claim of negligence brought against the listing broker.

Selling brokers who obtain access information should safeguard that information at all times. At no time should a selling broker share the access information with a third party (inspector, appraiser, buyer, etc.) without the listing broker's authorization. Selling brokers are reminded that pursuant to the Contract to Buy and Sell, the Buyers indemnify the Seller against damage to the property in connection with the property inspection provision.

CP-18 Commission Position on Payments to a Wholly Owned Employee's Corporation

The Commission has received several inquiries concerning the payment of commissions or fees by an employing broker to a corporation that is wholly owned by an employed licensee.

12-61-103(9) which prohibits the licensing of an employed broker as a corporation, partnership or limited liability company and the limitations on the payment or receipt of real estate fees, as described in 12-61-113(l)(j) and 12-61-117, are recognized by the Commission; however, it is the position of the Commission that:

An employing broker's payment of earned real estate fees to a corporation which is solely owned by an employed licensee of such employing broker shall not be considered by the Commission as a violation of 12-61-113(l)(j) or 12-61-117; however, a contract between the employing broker and such corporation or employed licensee shall not relieve the broker of any obligation to supervise such employed licensee or any other requirement of the licensing statute and Commission rules. It is not the intent of this position statement that the employed licensee be relieved from personal civil responsibility for any licensed activities by interposing the corporate form.

It must be stressed that the above position statement does not allow such corporations to be licensed under a broker and specifically refers only to corporations which are owned solely by the employed licensee.

CP-19 Commission Position on Short Term Occupancy Agreements

The Commission has been asked for its position concerning the need for a real estate broker to escrow funds coming into their possession involving short-term occupancies.

A short-term occupancy can be distinguished from a lease in that it is in the nature of a hotel reservation and a license to use. Short-term occupancy agreements, if properly treated, are not considered lease agreements. Activities relating to these agreements are exempt from the definition of real estate brokerage. Concerns arise when a licensed real estate broker wants to engage in short term occupancy activities either exclusively or as part of their separate brokerage practice. In some instances brokers have objected to holding money belonging to others in their trust accounts or accounting for these funds if the activity itself is exempt.

C.R.S. 12-61-113(l)(g) subjects a licensee to disciplinary action for "Failing to account for or to remit, within a reasonable time, any moneys coming into the licensee's possession that belong to others, whether acting as real estate brokers or otherwise, and failing to keep records relative to said moneys...." In addition, the case of Seibel vs. Colorado Real Estate Commission, 533 P.2nd 1290, gives the Commission jurisdiction over the acts of a licensed broker even where those acts would otherwise exempt the person from original licensure.

Based on the above, it is the position of the Commission that a licensed real estate broker engaging in short term occupancy agreements must escrow and account for funds coming into their possession which belong to others. To hold otherwise, would be to invite further confusion and mistrust on the part of the public in an already confusing real estate related practice. It has been the Commission's experience that most brokerage companies engaging in short term occupancy activities combine those activities with those requiring a license (*i.e.*, long term rental and lease agreements, sales). In addition, brokers continually hold themselves out to the public as being both licensed and professional. The public does not distinguish between an activity technically exempt from licensure and the overall business practices of a licensed real estate broker.

CP-20 Commission Position Statement on Personal Assistants

(Revised October 13, 2009)

The use of personal assistants has grown considerably in recent years. Personal assistants are generally thought of as unlicensed persons performing various functions as employees (including clerical support) or independent contractors of a real estate broker within the framework of a real estate transaction. The Commission recognizes the growth in the utilization of such assistants. Inquiries generally fit into two categories: (1) whether the activity performed is one which requires a license, and (2) what are the supervisory responsibilities of the licensed broker who employs the assistant.

The license law prohibits unlicensed persons from negotiating, listing or selling real property. Therefore, foremost to the use of personal assistants is careful restriction of their activities so as to avoid illegal brokerage practice. Personal assistants may complete forms prepared for and as directed by licensees but should never independently draft legal documents such as listing and sales contracts, nor should they offer opinions, advice or interpretations. In addition, they should not distribute information on listed properties other than that prepared by a broker.

On the other hand, they may:

1. perform clerical duties for a broker which may include the gathering of information for a listing;
2. provide access to a property and hand out preprinted, objective information, so long as no negotiating, offering, selling or contracting is involved:
3. distribute preprinted, objective information at an open house, so long as no negotiating, offering, selling or contracting is involved;
4. distribute information on listed properties when such information is prepared by a broker;
5. deliver paperwork to other brokers;
6. deliver paperwork to sellers or purchasers, if such paperwork has already been reviewed by a broker;
7. deliver paperwork requiring signatures in regard to financing documents that are prepared by lending institutions; and
8. prepare market analyses for sellers or buyers on behalf of a broker, but disclosure of the name of the preparer must be given, and it must be submitted by the broker.

With respect to the above duties, when a personal assistant interacts with individuals outside the brokerage, it should be promptly disclosed that the personal assistant is not a real estate broker, and the employing broker should be identified. The employing broker should ensure that such disclosures are made not just to clients, or potential clients, but also to other real estate brokers and industry professionals such as lenders, appraisers and mortgage brokers.

As an example, if the brokerage showing desk assigns a personal assistant to provide property access, it should be disclosed up front that such individual is not a real estate broker. The same policy should be utilized when real property is advertised with the personal assistant as an initial contact.

Licensed brokers who employ personal assistants need to be especially aware of their supervisory duties under the license law. Supervisory duties apply whether the assistant is an employee or independent contractor.

An employing broker should have a written office policy explaining the duties, responsibilities and limitations on the use of personal assistants. This policy should be reviewed by and explained to all employees.

Licensees should not share commissions with unlicensed assistants. Although this may not technically be a violation of the licensing act if the activity is not one which requires a license, the temptation to "cross over" into the area of negotiating and other prohibited practices is greatly increased where compensation is based on the success of the transaction.

If brokers develop adequate policies for the use of assistants and routine procedures for monitoring their activities, the assistant can serve as a valuable tool in the success of the transaction. As with any other activity involving the delegation of an act to another, the freedom and convenience afforded the broker in allowing the use of assistants carries with it certain responsibilities for that person's actions.

CP-21 Commission Position on Office Policy Manuals

(Revised and Adopted 4-1-2003)

12-61-Part 8 C.R.S. and Commission Rules E-29, E-30, E-31 E-32, E38 and E29 set out a broker's supervising responsibilities. (See Rules E-29, E-30, E-31 and Rule E-32 in chapter 2 of this manual.) In order to help brokers comply with the rules it is suggested that a policy manual contain procedures for at least the following:

1) typical real estate transactions
   a) review of contracts
   b) handling of earnest money deposits, including the release thereof
   c) back-up contracts
   d) closings
2) non-qualifying assumptions and owner financing
3) guaranteed buyouts
4) investor purchases
5) identifying brokerage relationships offered to public (required by 12-61-808 C.R.S.)
6) procedures for designation of brokers who are to work with a seller, landlord, buyer or tenant, individually or in teams (required by Rule E-38) (Does not apply to brokerage firms that consist of only one licensed natural person.)
7) identify and provide adequate means and procedures for the maintenance and protection of confidential information (required by Rule E-39)
8) licensee's purchase and sale of property
9) monitoring of license renewals and transfers
10) delegation of authority
11) property management
12) property listing procedures, including release of listings
13) training
   a) dissemination of information
   b) staff meetings
14) use of personal assistants
15) fair housing/affirmative action marketing

Brokers are encouraged to add other policies as appropriate to their practice.

In the event that one or several of these suggested topics (*e.g.*, guaranteed buyouts) are not applicable in a particular office, they should be addressed by stating that the office does not participate in that activity.

The Commission does not become involved in matters relating to independent contractor agreements, and disputes over earned commissions. Office policies in these areas do not fall within the purview of Commission rules.

(See additional discussion of office policy manuals in Chapter 19)

CP-22 Commission Position Statement on Handling of Confidential Information in Real Estate Brokerage

(Adopted October 1, 2003)

Prior to designated brokerage, it was common for brokers to share the motivations of a buyer or seller during office sales meetings, for example. Under designated brokerage, the law specifically prohibits sharing of such information. Confidential information, and the broker responsibility thereto, are defined in C.R.S. 12-61-804 (2), 12-61-805 (2), 12-61-807 (3), and Rules E-32 and E-39. Confidential information can include, but is not limited to, motivation of the parties.

Brokers are required to have a written office policy that identifies and provides adequate means and procedures for the maintenance and protection of confidential information. Situations where inadvertent disclosure of confidential information may occur, include, but are not limited to:

- sales meetings or marketing sessions,
- shared fax or copy machines,
- shared computer networks, printers and file directories,
- in-office mail boxes,
- hand written telephone messages,
- phone conversations or meetings with clients,
- relocation, divorce, pending foreclosure and other sensitive documents,
- conversations with affiliated business providers,
- production boards,
- social functions

Brokers must develop office policies and procedures to address the handling of confidential information. For example, some offices may have "locked" transaction files that include confidential information and other offices may elect not to include confidential information in transaction files.

A designated broker is permitted to share confidential information with a supervising broker without changing or extending the brokerage relationship beyond the designated broker. Brokers may want to consult legal counsel regarding the necessity of securing the authorization of the party to whom the information is confidential before the designated broker shares that confidential information with the supervising broker. Such advice could include modifications to the listing agreement or buyer agreement that create such authorization.

CP-23 Commission Position on Use of "Licensee Buyout Addendum"

(Revised January 17, 2006)

Rule F-7 requires real estate licensees to use the Commission approved "Licensee Buyout Addendum to Contract to Buy and Sell Real Estate", when purchasing certain listed properties.

It is the Commission's position that Rule F-7 requires use of the Buyout Addendum under the following circumstances:

1. When a licensee enters into a contract to purchase a property concurrent with the listing of such property.
2. When a licensee enters into a contract to purchase a property as an inducement or to facilitate the property owner's purchase of another property, the purchase or sale of which will generate a commission or fee to the licensee.
3. When a licensee enters into a contract to purchase a property from an owner but continues to market that property on behalf of the owner under an existing listing contract.

Unless one of the above situations exists, licensees are not required to use the Buyout Addendum.

The term "licensee", as used above, refers to the individual licensee who has personally taken a listing or to the listing broker or brokerage entity if the buyout is to be accomplished by that broker or brokerage entity. If the listing licensee or broker desires to acquire a listed property solely for personal use or future resale and not as an inducement to the owner, the licensee or broker is advised to (1) clearly sever their agency or listing relationship in writing; (2) renounce the right to any commission, fee or compensation in conjunction with acquisition of the listed property; and, (3) advise the owner to seek other assistance, representation or legal advice.

Future resale of a purchased property, as referred to above, means resale to a third party purchaser with whom the licensee has not negotiated during the listing period. Resale to a person with whom a licensee has conducted previous negotiations concerning the subject property during the listing period (often referred to as a "pocket buyer"), would constitute a violation of 12-61-113(l)(n) in the absence of full written disclosure and acknowledgment by the owner.

CP-24 Commission Position on Preparation of Market Analyses and Real Estate Evaluations Used for Loan Purposes

The Colorado Real Estate Appraiser Licensing Act contains special provisions which allow licensed real estate brokers to perform certain real estate valuation related activities without being registered, licensed or certified as real estate appraisers. These provisions are found in Sections 12-61-702 and 12-61-718, C.R.S.

The first of these allows a broker to prepare an "estimate of value" which is not represented as an appraisal and is not used to obtain financing. The position of the Commission is that this provision allows a broker to prepare a market analysis for use in the real estate brokerage process and to offer their estimate as to the value or market price of real estate for court testimony or tax purposes.

The second provision allows a broker to prepare what are termed "evaluations" in federal banking regulations. These evaluations may be used for lending purposes. This provision is very narrow in scope--a broker may prepare such an evaluation only for a federally regulated bank, savings and loan or credit union with whom they have a contract. The loan amount must be below the threshold which invokes the requirement for a true appraisal.

As the authority to prepare such estimates of value and evaluations is tied to the holding of a Colorado real estate broker license, the Colorado Real Estate Commission has jurisdiction over the activities of brokers engaged in such activities. The Commission will consider the conduct of licensees who prepare estimates of value and evaluations in light of Sections 12-61-113(l)(n) and (t), which speak to unworthiness, incompetency and dishonest dealing.

It is the position of the Commission that the mere holding of a broker license does not in itself assure the competency necessary to prepare more complex estimates of value or evaluations. Licensees preparing estimates of value and evaluations have a responsibility to possess training and experience commensurate with the complexity of the assignment undertaken.

Investigations undertaken by the Commission relating to unworthiness, incompetency and dishonest dealing will take into account the following:

- Brokers preparing estimates of value and evaluations must act independently at all times. The estimate or evaluation must be unbiased.
- The broker preparing an estimate or evaluation must not represent themselves as an appraiser, nor represent the work product as being an appraisal.
- The broker preparing an estimate or evaluation must at all times comply with the statutory requirement in Sections 12-61-702 and 12-61-718, Colorado Revised Statutes, for a written notice that they are not an appraiser. The wording and use of the written notice are specified in Chapter 15 of the Rules of the Board of Real Estate Appraisers. The required wording is:

  "NOTICE: The preparer of this appraisal is not registered, licensed or certified as a real estate appraiser by the State of Colorado".

- The broker must not prepare an estimate of value or evaluation of real property which requires a level of competency beyond the level of training and experience possessed by the licensee.

CP-25 Commission Position on Recording Contracts

Over the years the Commission has received many inquiries and complaints concerning the recording of listing contracts to protect claims for commissions. In addition, some licensees have attempted more "creative" ways of holding up a closing, such as filing mechanics liens or notices of lis pendens, as well as recording demand letters or purchase contracts. The end result is usually a cloud on the title and sometimes a slander of title action.

Some states have passed statutes authorizing the filing of such liens. Colorado has not. Filings and recordings such as these are inappropriate and will result in Commission action.

Here is a typical scenario: Broker lists a property at $125,000 for 120 days and actively markets it. No offers come in during the first 30 days. Broker advises her seller to lower the price by $5,000 to encourage some activity. The seller is adamant that the property is worth the list price and refuses. After another 15 days with no offers, the seller reluctantly lowers the price. He also tells the broker that he doesn't feel she is trying hard enough to sell the property and he's going to take it off the market if nothing happens.

A week later an offer for $100,000 comes in from another company, which is presented and rejected. The seller is quite upset at the low offer and demands to be released from the listing. There is no further communication between the parties, but the listing is never formally terminated. Three weeks later the broker learns that the seller has entered into a contract with the same buyer for $110,000 and closing is set. The broker is very upset and wants to protect her commission. What can she do?

1. File a mechanics lien?

   ANS: No. Real estate licensees are not a protected class of lien claimant under the statute except as provided in C.R.S. 38-22.5 (Commerical Real Estate Brokers Commission Security Act).

2. File a lis pendens (notice of pending lawsuit)?

   ANS: No. A lis pendens relates to a title or ownership dispute involving the land itself. The broker has no legal interest in the real estate.

3. Record the listing contract?

   ANS: No. This will usually have the effect of clouding title to the property, which in turn affects the closing between buyer and seller. The broker should not interfere in the process of transferring title to property.

4. Escrow the disputed commission?

   ANS: Maybe. This is a touchy area. If the broker makes demand on the seller for the commission prior to closing and states her possible rights (mediation; arbitration; civil action) the parties may agree to an escrow pending settlement of the dispute. However, there is no legal requirement that the closing entity escrow funds absent an agreement.

5. Commence mediation, arbitration or civil action (as appropriate).

   ANS: Yes. Nothing prevents a licensee from asserting any legal claim against a principal.

A commission dispute is an emotional issue. Sometimes a licensee has put in considerable time on a listing only to be faced with a seller who refuses to pay, attempts to renegotiate or is outright deceitful. On the other side, the Commission has witnessed instances in which the licensee had no legitimate right to a commission and was using superior knowledge and scare tactics to force payment. Clearly this is a time to consult a good real estate attorney and avoid the risk of a complaint based on a hasty decision.

CP-26 Commission Position on Auctioning

(Adopted 5-1-97)

Real estate experts predict that the next decade will see a significant increase in the sale of real estate through auctions. For many years auctioning was associated with rural or distressed properties. However, forecasts are for a proliferation of sales activity in both residential and commercial real estate. Sales by auction are already occurring in the residential market in Colorado and other parts of the country.

The brokers act requires that real estate auctions be conducted by a licensed broker and defines the activity as ". . .offering, attempting or agreeing to auction real estate, or interest therein, or improvements affixed thereon. . ." (CRS 12-61-101(2)(VI)).

A long-standing Attorney General's opinion allows an unlicensed auctioneer to "cry" the bid at a real estate auction in the presence of a broker or seller. However, the control of the sale, including listing, advertising, showing the property and writing contracts must remain with the broker or the auctioneer will be violating the law.

Based on the statute and Attorney General's opinion, the following guidelines are established for unlicensed persons involved in the auction process:

1. Auctioneers should never hold themselves out as providing real estate brokerage services to the public (*e.g.*, listing, advertising, negotiating, contracting, legal document preparation);
2. Inquiries from sellers should be referred to a licensed broker or attorney;
3. Inquiries from buyers should be referred to the seller, listing broker or sellers attorney;
4. Only auctioning services should be advertised to buyers and sellers;
5. A potential buyer may be chauffeured to a property, so long as the property is shown by the seller or a licensed broker;
6. Information on listed properties may be distributed when such information has been prepared by a broker;
7. Auctioneers may "cry" the sale, but may not engage in subsequent negotiations, document drafting and the handling of earnest money;
8. Payment should be based on auctioning services performed regardless of the success of a sale.

CP-27 Commission Position on the Performance of Residential Property Management Functions

(Adopted August 1998)

Pursuant to C.R.S. 12-61-101(2)(a)&(b), the leasing and subsequent management of real estate for a fee or compensation, is included among the activities for which a license is required. Employing brokers involved in these activities should include provisions for the efficient, orderly conduct of this phase of business in their office policy manual. These activities must be done in the name of the employing broker only. All monies received from these activities shall be turned into the employing broker to be accounted for pursuant to Commission Rule E-l.

The **management contract** should be in writing and outline the duties and responsibilities of both parties. The contract should, at the very minimum, address the:

- Duration of the contract;
- Identities of the parties;
- Address of the property to be managed;
- Fees for the manager's services, including disclosure of any mark-ups (Commission Rule E-1 (p)(8));
- Disclosure of broker's ownership interest in any company which will be providing maintenance or related services;

- Identity of the entity responsible for the holding of the security deposit, and if interest is earned on security deposit escrow accounts, who benefits from such interest;
- Process to be followed in any subsequent transfer of owner's monies, security deposits, keys and documents (Commission Rule E-l6); and,
- Requirement that the owner receive regular monthly accounting of all funds received and disbursed.

Employing brokers supervising property managers should have an awareness of and comply with the proper procedures involved in C.R.S. 38-12-101, Security Deposits-Wrongful Withholding. (See also the Commission Position on Advance Rentals and Security Deposits (CP-5) within this chapter)

When ownership of a property changes or if ownership remains the same but transfer of management services occurs, it is recommended that the:

- Outgoing broker should maintain written verification of such change or transfer;
- Outgoing broker shall transfer pertinent documents to incoming broker as soon as practically possible, but in any case, not to exceed ten (10) days as it relates to items "a through e" below and not to exceed sixty (60) days as it relates to item "f" below.
- Pertinent documents shall include, but are not limited to:

(a) Copy of existing lease
(b) Copy of check-in condition report
(c) Keys
(d) Outstanding tenant balances
(e) Tenant(s) security deposit(s)
(f) Owner's funds (subject to outstanding obligations)

In those situations wherein there may be the potential for conflict of interest (*e.g.*, managing property for a family member), the broker should disclose that information to all parties, pursuant to Commission Rule E-25.

Employing brokers as well as property managers should be familiar with Chapters 19, 20, and 24 of the Colorado Real Estate Manual.

CP-28 Commission Position on Showing Properties

(Adopted March 4th 1999)

The Real Estate Commission reminds licensees that the Brokerage Relationships Act imposes duties on agents to promote the interests of their buyers or sellers with the utmost good faith as well as to counsel their principals on material benefits or risks of a transaction. A transaction-broker must exercise reasonable skill and care, advise the parties and keep the parties fully informed regarding the transaction. Whether working as an agent or a transaction-broker, these duties include disclosing the accessibility of and actual access to a property or properties.

Working With a Seller: Pursuant to the section in the various listing contracts entitled, "OTHER BROKERS, ASSISTANCE", the licensee should advise the seller of the advantages and disadvantages of using multiple listing services and other methods of making the property accessible by other brokers (*e.g.*, using lock boxes, by appointment only showings, etc.). If applicable, it should be explained that some methods may limit the ability of a selling broker to access and show a particular property. The chosen methods of cooperating with other brokers should be included in the listing agreement.

Working With a Buyer: A licensee working with a buyer has an obligation to explain the possible methods used by a listing broker and seller to show a particular property. These methods may include limitations on the buyer and selling broker being able to access a property due to the type of lock box placed on the property, the seller's choice to have the property shown by appointment only, etc. The selling broker should include such showing limitations in the Exclusive Right to Buy Contract (agency or transaction-broker).

There should be no instances of a listing broker refusing to allow a property to be shown, unless the seller has given prior explicit, written authorization to do so.

CP-29 Commission Position on "Megan's Law"

(Adopted July 1, 1999)

The Commission has been asked for its position as to the disclosure requirements for real estate licensees with regard to "Megan's Law." In 1994, and primarily as a response to the murders of two young girls, a federal law was passed creating a registration and notification procedure to alert the public as to the presence of certain types of convicted sex offenders living in a neighborhood. This is commonly referred to as "Megan's Law." Identified sex offenders are required to register with local law enforcement officials. The federal law also required states to establish registries of convicted sex offenders. It contains no disclosure requirements for real estate licensees when working with the public.

In compliance with federal law, Colorado enacted legislation that sets procedures and timeframes for local registration. The office of chief of police is the designated place of registration for those offenders residing within any city, town or city and county. The office of the county sheriff is the designated place of registration for those living outside any city, town or city and county, in addition, the law enforcement agency is required to release information regarding registered persons. However, the duty to release information may differ depending on whether the inquiring party does or does not live within that jurisdiction.

While legislation in a few states has specifically imposed disclosure requirements on real estate licensees working with buyers and sellers, Colorado's legislation imposes no such requirements. Colorado's legislation clearly places the duty to release information on the local law enforcement agency, after considering a request.

It is the position of the Real Estate Commission that all real estate licensees should inform a potential buyer to contact local law enforcement officials for further information if the presence of a registered sex offender is a matter of concern to the buyer.

Editor's Note:

C.R.S. 18-3-412.5 requires the Colorado Bureau of Investigation to post on the Internet identifying information, including a picture, of each sex offender:

- *Sentenced as a sexually violent predator; or*
- *Convicted of a sexual offense involving children*

CP-30 State of Colorado Real Estate Commission and Board of Real Estate Appraisers Joint Position Statement

(Revised January 8, 2009)

The Colorado Real Estate Commission and the Colorado Board of Real Estate Appraisers have issued this Joint Position Statement to address mutual concerns pertaining to practices of real estate brokers and real estate appraisers with regard to residential sales transactions involving seller assisted down payments, seller concessions, personal property transferred with real property and other items of value included in the sale of residential real property.

A residential real estate transaction has a life well beyond closing and possession of the property. Accurate sales data is crucial for appraisals and comparative market analysis (CMA) work products. Both appraisers and real estate brokers can effectively work together to maintain the safeguards that accurate sold data affords.

A **real estate broker** can facilitate these safeguards by adherence to the following:

- Note the amount of any seller paid costs (including a seller assisted down payment or fee paid to a charitable organization on behalf of the buyer) or other seller concession in the proper transaction documents, including the Buy/Sell Contract, Closing Statements, and Real Property Transfer Declaration.
- Utilize all available fields in the multiple listing service to report sold information including all transaction terms and seller concessions. Sold information should be entered promptly following

closing and be specific and detailed particularly when the sold price includes a seller assisted down payment or concessions.

- Advise buyers and sellers to consult legal and tax counsel for advice on tax consequences of seller contributions and inducements to purchase.
- Cooperate with appraisers as they perform their due diligence in asking questions about sales.

An **appraiser** can facilitate these safeguards by adherence to the following:

- Research and confirm subject property and comparable sales, including obtaining details of the contract and financing terms.
- Research and confirm all relevant information about a transaction, including determination of seller paid costs.
- Utilize all available data search tools, including the listing history and seller contributions features of multiple listing services.
- Make appropriate adjustments to comparables with seller contributions and inducements to purchase when developing work products.
- Comply with the applicable provisions of the Ethics Rule and Standards 1 & 2 of the Uniform Standards of Professional Appraisal Practice.
- Comply with any scope of work requirements required by agencies such as the Federal Housing Administration.

CP-31 Commission Position on Acting as a Transaction Broker or Agent in Particular Types of Transactions

(Adopted 9-8-04)

The public may enter into either a Transaction-Broker relationship or an Agency relationship with a Broker. Fundamental among the differences between Agency and Transaction-Brokerage is that an Agent is an advocate with fiduciary duties, while a Transaction-Broker should remain neutral, not advocate. However, in some situations the relationship of the Broker with a particular party or property may make a particular relationship inappropriate or problematic.

Before acting as a Transaction-Broker in transactions where neutrality is difficult, the Broker should consider whether the Transaction-Brokerage arrangement is suitable, consult with the Broker's supervising Broker and then make the necessary disclosures. Some examples of these situations include:

1. Selling or purchasing for one's own account (whether the property is solely or partially owned or to be acquired by the Broker), (See Rule E-25 regarding proper disclosures);
2. Selling or purchasing for the account of a spouse or family member of the Broker;
3. Selling or purchasing for the account of a close personal friend, business associate, or other person where it would be difficult for the Broker to remain neutral; or
4. Selling or purchasing for the account of a repeat or regular client/party where it would be difficult for the Broker to remain neutral (*i.e.*, undertaking as a Transaction-Broker the listing of multiple units, lots or properties such as listing a real estate development or condominium complex for a single developer, listing multiple residential or commercial properties for the same seller that will be sold to different buyers, or listing for lease a multiple unit residential or commercial property that will be leased to different tenants).

An agency relationship between a Broker and a seller or landlord, buyer or tenant, requires a written agency agreement. The duties of an agent go beyond facilitation of the transaction as a neutral party and require representing the interests of the Broker's principal over the interests of the other party. In certain circumstances, fulfilling the duties of an Agent including acting as an advocate may be difficult. A Broker who enters into an agency relationship must fulfill the duties of advocacy, fidelity, loyalty and other fiduciary duties associated with a single agency relationship. In circumstances where the Broker may not be able to fulfill the duties imposed on an agent the Broker should consider whether the agency arrangement is appropriate, consult with the Broker's supervising Broker and act accordingly.

This Position Statement applies to relationships where Brokers are working with landlords or tenants, as well as sellers and buyers. It applies equally to residential and commercial transactions.

CP-32 Commission Position on Brokerage Disclosures

(Adopted 9-8-04)

The Commission believes that a broker who intends to act as a buyer's or tenant's agent in a transaction should attempt to secure a written agency agreement as early in the brokerage relationship as possible. However, the Commission also recognizes that in some instances, the buyer or tenant will not immediately execute such a written agency agreement.

In these situations, the broker should initially function as a transaction-broker by either entering into:

BC 60: Exclusive Right-to-Buy Contract (All Types of Properties); or
LC 57: Exclusive Right-to-Lease Listing Contract (All Types of Properties; or
ETC 59: Exclusive Tenant Contract (All Types of Properties)

With any of the three forms the broker should check the box "Transaction-Brokerage" whereby only the brokerage services and duties contained in Section 4 of the agreement would apply; or present a buyer or tenant with BD24 Brokerage Disclosure to Buyer.

The broker may then engage as a transaction-broker and may perform any of the activities enumerated in section 12-61-101 (2), C.R.S., which are the acts of real estate brokerage.

However, **before** the broker begins to work as the buyer's or tenant's **agent** and advocate to secure the best possible price or lease rate and terms for the buyer or tenant, the parties must execute one of the above listed agreements with the "Agency" box checked. In an agency relationship the broker has the duties and responsibilities contained in Section 4 of the agreement, and the additional duties of an agent contained in Section 5 of the agreement.

CP-33 Joint Position Statement from the Division of Real Estate and Division of Insurance Concerning Application of the Good Funds Laws

Issued: July 10, 2002

I. Background and Purpose

The purpose for this bulletin is to clarify the Division of Insurance and the Division of Real Estate's position with respect to application of Colorado's good funds laws to real estate transactions involving regulated entities. In particular, there is confusion in the industry regarding reconciliation of § 38-35-125, C.R.S., Colorado's good funds laws, with Division of Insurance regulation 3-5-1(6)(F) and the current practice of disbursing cashier's checks drawn on a title entity's account, pursuant to instructions of the parties and in connection with closing a real estate transaction.

Bulletins are the agencies' interpretations of existing laws or general statements of policy. Bulletins themselves establish neither binding norms nor finally determine issues or rights.

II. Applicability and Scope

This bulletin concerns all title insurance entities and real estate licensees involved in real estate closings.

III. Position Statement

The good funds statute provides, in relevant part:

*No person or entity that provides closing and settlement services for a real estate transaction shall disburse funds as a part of such services until those funds have been **received** and are either: **available for immediate withdrawal as a matter of right** from the financial institution in*

> *which the funds have been deposited; or available for immediate withdrawal as a consequence of an agreement of a financial institution in which the funds are to be deposited or a financial institution upon which the funds are to be drawn.*

§ 38-35-125(2), C.R.S. The same statute defines funds "available for immediate withdrawal as a matter of right" to include any wire transfer or any certified check, cashier's check or teller's check. Thus, a cashier's check or wired funds (most typically used) that have been received by the entity providing closing and settlement services are considered "good funds".

Division of Insurance regulation 3-5-1(6)(F) parallels § 38-35-125, C.R.S. and provides that "All title insurance entities shall comply with the 'good funds law'." In addition, Division of Insurance regulation 3-5-1(5)(A)(3) specifies that failure to comply with the good funds laws constitutes an unlawful inducement for the referral of title insurance business proscribed by § 10-11-108, C.R.S.

The federal courts interpreted Colorado's good funds laws in *Guardian Title v. Matrix*, 141 F.Supp.2d 1277 (D.Colo. 2001). The court held that good funds laws govern title entities that engage in closing and settlement services. *See id.* at 1279. Failure to comply with the good funds statute is a deceptive trade practice and violates insurance regulation 3-5-1. *See id.* at 1280-81. The court stated: "The Good Funds law was developed as a solution to 'the need to insure that the title company or other party responsible for real estate closings has 'good funds' **in hand** before closing the transactions'". *Id.* at 1281.

Based on the above, it is the position of the Division of Real Estate and Division of Insurance that Colorado's good funds law and insurance regulation 3-5-1(6)(F) require that a title entity must have good funds **"in hand"** (*e.g.*, wired funds, certified check, cashier's check, tellers check) **before it disburses funds** as part of its settlement services.

Further, it is the position of the Division of Real Estate and Division of Insurance that a title company which withdraws funds from its account in the form of a cashier's check, but (1) maintains complete control and possession of the check; and (2) does not disburse (pay out) until **delivery** and receipt of "good funds" relating to the specific transaction, complies with the good funds laws.

By way of example, it is common in a real estate transaction for funds to come to the closing from at least two sources, the buyer and the lender. It is also common for a seller to ask for closing proceeds in the form of a cashier's check, drawn on the title entity's account. Applying the 'good funds' law and insurance regulation 3-5-1, the title company could cause a cashier's check to be issued from its account and have the check available for the seller at closing. The title entity could not disburse to the seller until "good funds" were received or "in hand" from the buyer and lender. "In hand" means that a cashier's check has been received by the title entity or, in the case of a wire transfer, has been wired into the title entity's account.

Once the transaction closes and the cashier's check is paid to the seller, the title entity is responsible for immediately depositing the buyer's "good funds" into its account. If the transaction does not close, the title entity is responsible for immediately redepositing its cashier's check into its account. In that manner, no other customer of the title entity is harmed.

IV. For more information:

Division of Insurance
1560 Broadway, Suite 850
Denver CO 80202
Phone: 303-894-7499
Internet:
www.dora.state.co.us/insurance

Division of Real Estate
1560 Broadway, Suite 925
Denver CO 80202
Phone: 303-894-2166
Internet:
http://www.dora.state.co.us/real-estate

CP-34 Joint Position Statement from the Division of Real Estate and Division of Insurance Concerning Closing Instructions

Issued: December 2, 2008

I. Background and Purpose.

The purpose for this bulletin (Position Statement) is to clarify the Division of Insurance and the Division of Real Estate's position with respect to the current practice involving the preparation and execution of Closing Instructions. In particular, there are two areas of confusion in the real estate industry with regard to Closing Instructions: The two areas are:

1) Who is responsible for preparing the Closing Instructions?
2) When is it necessary to prepare and execute the Closing Instructions?

The purpose for this bulletin is also to (1) promote the public welfare by proscribing practices which, if not proscribed, could result in public harm, which may prove detrimental to consumers; and (2) level the playing field in the real estate industry to ensure a fair and competitive market place.

Furthermore, this bulletin offers the following protection against: (1) potential risk of unexpected loss and/or forfeiture of good funds while increasing the consumer's understanding and awareness of the terms and conditions of the Closing Instructions; and (2) increase the understanding and awareness of the settlement service provider's obligations and how and when funds are disbursed.

Bulletins are the agencies' interpretations of existing laws and general statements of policy. Bulletins themselves establish neither binding norms nor finally determine issues or rights.

II. Applicability and Scope

This bulletin concerns all title insurance entities and real estate licensees involved with the receipt or disbursement of earnest money in a real estate closing.

III. Position Statement

The Division of Insurance's Regulation 3-5-1(H) states:

> "No title entity shall provide closing and settlement services without receiving written instructions from all necessary parties. In the event all parties to the real estate transaction execute written closing instructions, including those closing instructions approved by the Colorado Real Estate Commission, and such closing instructions have been delivered to the title entity in advance of the closing and settlement, the title entity shall also execute such closing instructions and furnish copies to all parties to the closing instructions, to the extent allowed by laws. Nothing in this provision shall prohibit amendments to existing Closing Instructions."

Regulation 3-5-1(H) parallels with the Division of Real Estate's Rule F-7 concerning Commission Approved Forms that states, in relevant part:

> "Real Estate Brokers are required to use Commission-approved forms as appropriate to a transaction or circumstance to which a relevant form is applicable."

The Closing Instructions form is a form that is promulgated by the real estate commission and is within the purview of Commission Rule F-7. The Closing Instructions, under section 11, includes language that addresses earnest money disputes when the earnest money is held by a closing company.

Based on the above statements, it is the position of the Division of Real Estate and the Division of Insurance that title insurance entities must maintain compliance with Regulation 3-5-1(H), by receiving written instructions prior to providing closing and settlement services, including the acceptance/receipt of earnest money.

Further, it is the position of the Division of Real Estate and the Division Insurance that real estate licensees must provide reasonable skill and care and maintain compliance with Commission Rule F-7 by preparing and executing Closing Instructions prior to delivery of the earnest money, for which a closing company is the earnest money holder pursuant to section 4(a) of the Contract to Buy and Sell Real Estate.

Moreover, it is the position of the Division of Real Estate and the Division of Insurance that real estate licensees ensure that the buyer, seller and closing company understand the terms and conditions regarding the acceptance and release of earnest money deposits.

For more information:

Division of Insurance
1560 Broadway, Suite 850
Denver, CO 80202
(303) 894-7499
www.dora.state.co.us/insurance

Division of Real Estate
1560 Broadway, Suite 925
Denver, CO 80202
(303)894-2166
www.dora.state.co.us/real-estate

CP-35 Commission Position on Brokers as Principals

The Commission regularly receives public complaints regarding real estate transactions involving a licensed real estate broker acting as a principal. Predominantly these complaints allege that the broker, who is a principal to the transaction, and may or may not also be serving as a broker in the transaction, has failed to disclose an adverse material fact; has failed to disclose brokerage relationships (when acting as more than a principal); has failed to ensure that the contract documents and/or settlement statements accurately reflect the terms of the transaction; has filed a document that unlawfully clouds the title to the property; has failed to disclose the broker's licensed status; has mismanaged funds belonging to others; and/or has falsified information used for the purpose of obtaining financing.

The Commission reminds licensees that the Commission may investigate and discipline a license if a licensee is acting in the capacity of a principal in a real estate transaction and violations of the license law occur. The Commission's authority to investigate and impose discipline in these transactions was determined by the Colorado Court of Appeals. See *Seibel v. Colorado Real Estate Commission*, 34 Colo.App. 415, 530 P.2d 1290 (1974). The court's decision affirmed that licensed real estate brokers are subject to the real estate brokers licensing act and rules adopted by the Commission when they participate in real estate matters as principals. In such cases, licensees need to be mindful of Rule E-25 (regarding conflict of interest and license status disclosures) and position statement CP-31 (regarding acting as a transaction broker).

* CP-36 Commission Position on Minimum Service Requirements

The Commission has received numerous inquiries regarding the minimum services that brokers must provide to buyers or sellers of real property. §12-61-803, C.R.S. requires that any broker performing the activities requiring a real estate broker's license as set forth in §12-61-101(2), C.R.S., act in the capacity of either a transaction broker or a single agent in the transaction. The minimum duties required to be performed by a real estate broker acting in the capacity of a single agent are set forth in §§12-61-804 and 12¬61-805, C.R.S. §12-61-804, C.R.S. Single agent engaged by seller or landlord states, in part:

(1) A broker engaged by a seller or landlord to act as a seller's agent or a landlord's agent is a limited agent with the following duties and obligations:

- *(a) To perform the terms of the written agreement made with the seller or landlord;*
- *(b) To exercise reasonable skill and care for the seller or landlord;*
- *(c) To promote the interests of the seller or landlord with the utmost good faith, loyalty, and fidelity, including, but not limited to:*
  - *(I) Seeking a price and terms which are acceptable to the seller or landlord; except that the broker shall not be obligated to seek additional offers to purchase the property while the property is subject to a contract for sale or to seek additional offers to lease the property while the property is subject to a lease or letter of intent to lease;*
  - *(II) Presenting all offers to and from the seller or landlord in a timely manner regardless of whether the property is subject to a contract for sale or a lease or letter of intent to lease;*

(III) *Disclosing to the seller or landlord adverse material facts actually known by the broker;*

(IV) *Counseling the seller or landlord as to any material benefits or risks of a transaction which are actually known by the broker;*

(V) *Advising the seller or landlord to obtain expert advice as to material matters about which the broker knows but the specifics of which are beyond the expertise of such broker;*

(VI) *Accounting in a timely manner for all money and property received; and*

(VII) *Informing the seller or landlord that such seller or landlord shall not be vicariously liable for the acts of such seller's or landlord's agent that are not approved, directed or ratified by such seller or landlord.*

(d) *To comply with all requirements of this article and any rules promulgated pursuant to this article; and*

(e) *To comply with any applicable federal, state, or local laws, rules, regulations, or ordinances including fair housing and civil rights statutes or regulations.*

§12-61-805, C.R.S. Single agent engaged by buyer or tenant states, in part:

(1) *A broker engaged by a buyer or tenant to act as a buyer's or tenant's agent shall be a limited agent with the following duties and obligations:*

(a) *To perform the terms of the written agreement made with the buyer or tenant;*

(b) *To exercise reasonable skill and care for the buyer or tenant;*

(c) *To promote the interests of the buyer or tenant with the utmost good faith, loyalty, and fidelity, including, but not limited to:*

(I) *Seeking a price and terms which are acceptable to the buyer or tenant; except that the broker shall not be obligated to seek other properties while the buyer is a party to a contract to purchase property or while the tenant is a party to a lease or letter of intent to lease;*

(II) *Presenting all offers to and from the buyer or tenant in a timely manner regardless of whether the buyer is already a party to a contract to purchase property or the tenant is already a party to a contract or a letter of intent to lease;*

(III) *Disclosing to the buyer or tenant adverse material facts actually known by the broker;*

(IV) *Counseling the buyer or tenant as to any material benefits or risks of a transaction which are actually known by the broker;*

(V) *Advising the buyer or tenant to obtain expert advice as to material matters about which the broker knows but the specifics of which are beyond the expertise of such broker;*

(VI) *Accounting in a timely manner for all money and property received; and*

(VII) *Informing the buyer or tenant that such buyer or tenant shall not be vicariously liable for the acts of such buyer's or tenant's agent that are not approved, directed, or ratified by such buyer or tenant;*

(d) *To comply with all requirements of this article and any rules promulgated pursuant to this article; and*

(e) *To comply with any applicable federal, state, or local laws, rules, regulations, or ordinances including fair housing and civil rights statutes or regulations.*

The minimum duties required to be performed by a real estate broker acting in the capacity of a transaction broker are set forth in §12-61-807, C.R.S. which states, in part:

(1) *A broker engaged as a transaction-broker is not an agent for either party.*

(2) *A transaction-broker shall have the following obligations and responsibilities:*

(a) *To perform the terms of any written or oral agreement made with any party to the transaction;*

(b) *To exercise reasonable skill and care as a transaction-broker, including, but not limited to:*

(I) *Presenting all offers and counteroffers in a timely manner regardless of whether the property is subject to a contract for sale or lease or letter of intent;*

(II) *Advising the parties regarding the transaction and suggesting that such parties obtain expert advice as to material matters about which the transaction-broker knows but the specifics of which are beyond the expertise of such broker;*

(III) *Accounting in a timely manner for all money and property received;*

(IV) *Keeping the parties fully informed regarding the transaction;*

(V) *Assisting the parties in complying with the terms and conditions of any contract including closing the transaction;*

(VI) *Disclosing to all prospective buyers or tenants any adverse material facts actually known by the broker including but not limited to adverse material facts pertaining to the title, the physical condition of the property, any defects in the property, and any environmental hazards affecting the property required by law to be disclosed;*

(VII) *Disclosing to any prospective seller or landlord all adverse material facts actually known by the broker including but not limited to adverse material facts pertaining to the buyer's or tenant's financial ability to perform the terms of the transaction and the buyer's intent to occupy the property as a principal residence; and*

(VIII) *Informing the parties that as seller and buyer or as landlord and tenant they shall not be vicariously liable for any acts of the transaction-broker;*

(c) *To comply with all requirements of this article and any rules promulgated pursuant to this article; and*

(d) *To comply with any applicable federal, state, or local laws, rules, regulations, or ordinances including fair housing and civil rights statutes or regulations.*

§12-61-803, C.R.S. allows real estate brokers to perform duties in addition to those established in §§12-61-804, 12-61-805 and 12-61-807, C.R.S. The additional duties may include, but are not limited to, holding open houses, property showings, providing a lockbox, use of multiple listing services or other information exchanges, etc. Additional services that brokers agree to provide their clients must be documented in writing. A broker is not allowed to solely perform "additional" services which require a real estate broker's license, i.e. offering the real property of another for sale through advertisements, without providing the minimum duties required by single agency or transaction brokerage. The Commission does not regulate the fees or commissions charged by brokers for minimum or additional services provided. Fees and commissions are negotiable between the broker and the principal.

* CP-37 Commission Position on Survey and Lease Objections to the Contract to Buy and Sell Real Estate

The intention of the Commission in adopting the Contract to Buy and Sell Real Estate (CBS1-8-10 and the other versions of the Contract) is set forth below.

1. As background, under Section 8.1, Buyer has the right to object to title matters up to the **Title Objection Deadline**. Under Section 8.5, Seller has the obligation and right to use reasonable efforts to correct such objections and bear nominal expense prior to Closing. If any unsatisfactory title condition is not corrected prior to Closing, Buyer may either terminate the Contract or waive objection to any unsatisfactory title condition prior to Closing.
2. Under Section 8.2, if Buyer objects to any off-record matter on or before the **Off-Record Matters Objection Deadline**, the Contract will terminate. Seller has no right to cure such off-record matters. Seller does not have a right to cure any objection to existing surveys or leases under Section 8.2. Section 8.5 does not apply to objections under Section 8.2.
3. Under Section 7.3, Buyer may obtain a new, updated or recertified Survey (Current Survey) on or before the **Survey Deadline**. Current Surveys are different than existing surveys, surveys which are

not current and which may be delivered to Buyer under Section 8.2 as an off-record matter; objections to existing surveys must be made on or before the **Off-Record Matters Objection Deadline**. Buyer may object to the Current Survey on or before the **Survey Objection Deadline**. If Buyer timely objects to the Current Survey, the Contract will terminate. Buyer's objection to the Current Survey is governed by Section 8.3.2, and Seller has no right to cure any objection to the Survey. Section 8.5 does not apply to objections under Section 8.3.2.

4. Under Sections 10.8.2 (Survey) and 10.8.3 (Leases) Buyer has a right to "terminate" the Contract. Seller has no right to cure any such objection. Section 8.5 does not apply to objections under Sections 10.8.2 and 10.8.3.

Conclusion: Buyer has a right terminate the Contract due to objections with any Survey (Existing or Current) or to any Lease. Seller has no right to cure any objection to the Survey or Lease (whether such objection is based on Section 7, 8 or 10 as Section 8.5 does not apply to Survey or Lease objections).

* **CP-38 Commission Position on Disclosure of Affiliated Business Arrangements and Conflicts of Interest (4-5-2011)**

This statement supplements Rule E-46 Affiliated Business Arrangements. §12-61-113.2, C.R.S. *Affiliated Business Arrangements* was enacted in Colorado to provide transparency, accountability, and consumer protection through disclosure and consistency concerning affiliated business arrangements. Affiliated business arrangements have also been regulated for many years by the Real Estate Settlement Procedures Act (RESPA). RESPA was precipitated by significant reforms identified by Congress as necessary to ensure that consumers did not pay disproportionately high settlement costs as the result of certain deleterious business practices by settlement service providers. RESPA is applicable to any residential mortgage transaction involving a federally related mortgage loan. However, Colorado law requires disclosure of affiliated business arrangements to consumers even if the transaction does not involve a federally related residential mortgage loan.

Colorado law C.R.S. 12-61-113.2(1)(a) defines an "affiliated business arrangement" as an arrangement in which:

> *"A provider of settlement services or an associate of a provider of settlement services has either an affiliate relationship with or a direct beneficial ownership interest of more than one percent in another provider of settlement services;"*

and the provider directly or indirectly refers business to the other provider or affirmatively influences the selection of another provider of settlement services.

It is the Commission's position that real estate brokers must disclose affiliated business arrangements to consumers in all transactions intended to result in the transfer of title from one party to another. RESPA requires that affiliated business arrangements be disclosed before or at the time a referral is made to a provider of settlement services. Colorado law requires a licensee to disclose any affiliated business arrangement when an offer to purchase real property is fully executed. In Colorado, the disclosure is required to be in writing, must be given to both agents and transaction brokers, must comply with RESPA and Colorado law, and must be made using the Federal RESPA disclosure form. Colorado law requires real estate brokers to disclose their affiliated business arrangements to all parties to the real estate transaction and all parties are expected to sign the disclosure form. The Commission recommends that real estate brokers disclose their affiliated business arrangements to the party with whom they are working early in their relationship, i.e. at the time brokerage relationships are disclosed or when the listing contract or buyer broker agreement is negotiated. In those transactions where the broker does not deal with another party until the time of contracting written disclosure should be made to all parties at the time the purchase contract is fully executed.

Additionally, real estate brokers are required to make certain disclosures to the Division of Real Estate regarding their affiliated business arrangements. Colorado law requires every licensee to disclose to the Commission when they enter into or change an affiliated business arrangement. All affiliated business arrangements to which the licensee is a party must be disclosed. Disclosure is required at the time of a new application for licensure or at the time of activation of an inactive license. The disclosure must include the physical location of the affiliated business. Employing brokers are required to disclose the names of all affiliated business arrangements to which the employing broker is a party on an annual basis, at the least. The disclosure must include the physical location of the affiliated businesses. The Commission has determined that these disclosures shall be made electronically through the Division of Real Estate's website at www.dora.state.co.us/pls/real/AFB_Web.Logon?p_div=REC.

It is the Commission's position that Rule E-25 *Continuing duty to disclose conflict of interest and license status*, applies to all licensees including real estate brokers who perform licensed property management services and are affiliated with businesses or vendors that provide services applicable to lease transactions. For example, a real estate broker acting on behalf of a landlord is required to disclose to the landlord that the real estate broker has partial ownership of the maintenance company that the real estate broker utilizes for the landlord's property repairs. The Commission strongly recommends that this type of information be disclosed to the principal early in the business relationship, i.e. at the time brokerage relationships are disclosed or when the listing contract is negotiated. Additionally, this disclosure should be made in writing.

* CP-39 Commission Position on Lease Options, Lease Purchase Agreements and Installment Land Contracts (4-5-2011)

The Commission recognizes that in order to maintain the resilience of the real estate market during times when conventional lending requirements are rigorous, alternative funding practices are utilized to sustain the market conditions of supply and demand. The Commission has received and investigated numerous complaints pertaining to lease options, lease purchase agreements and installment land contracts. Although the Commission does not have the authority to prohibit the types of real estate transactions that real estate brokers participate in, the Commission strongly cautions real estate brokers to utilize the services of an attorney licensed to practice law within the State of Colorado. It has been the Commission's observation, based on complaints received, that lease option and lease purchase transactions are complex and generally contain provisions with significant financial risk posed to the prospective buyer and seller. Installment land contracts and the other transactions mentioned in this position statement afford buyers the opportunity to take possession of the real property and make installment payments to the seller. There is a significant potential for harm to the seller, buyer or assignee if the installment land contract is not properly drafted. In all of the above transactions, the seller retains legal title to the property while the buyer may acquire equitable title. The Commission does not have an approved contract form necessary to memorialize the terms and nuances related to these complex transactions, or any jurisdictional regulations that may be germane. Pursuant to Rule F, the appropriate provisions of the license law and the brokerage relationship act (§§12-61-113, 12-61-804, 805 and 807, C.R.S.), real estate brokers are prohibited from drafting a contract document that would reflect the terms of such a transaction as it would exceed their level of competency and is a matter requiring the expertise and advice of an attorney. Additionally, such behavior may be construed as the unauthorized practice of law by the real estate broker and subject to civil penalties. The contracts for these transactions should not be prepared by a real estate broker; rather, the documents should be drafted by a licensed Colorado attorney-at-law engaged for each particular transaction.

* CP-40 Commission Position on Teams (4-5-2011)

The Commission recognizes that there are benefits to both real estate brokers and consumers in the usage of real estate broker teams. Teams may be formed within a licensed brokerage firm with the approval of the employing broker. Real estate brokers operating as teams need to ensure that they are compliant with Commission rules regarding advertising, name usage and supervision.

Advertising and name usage:

While there is no prohibition of teams, real estate brokers need to ensure that they do not advertise in a manner that misleads the public as to the identity of the brokers' licensed brokerage. Real estate brokers that function as teams should not advertise teams using the terms "realty", "real estate", "company", "corporation", "corp.", "inc.", "LLC" or other similar language that would indicate a company other than the employing brokerage firm. Advertising includes, but is not limited to, websites, signage, property flyers, mailings, business cards, letterhead and contracts. The advertising of team names should never give the impression that the team is an entity separate from the licensed real estate brokerage. If the identity of the employing broker or the brokerage firm is difficult for the public or the Commission to ascertain, the team may be in violation of Rule E-8 Advertising.

Supervision:

In addition to the supervision requirements set forth in Rules E-31 and E-32, Rule E-30 Employing broker responsibilities requires that the broker designated to act as the broker for any partnership, limited liability company or corporation, i.e. the employing broker, fulfill the following duties:

1) Maintain all trust accounts and trust account records;
2) Maintain all transaction records;
3) Develop an office policy manual and periodically review office policies with all employees;
4) Provide for a high level of supervision for newly licensed persons pursuant to Rule-32;
5) Provide for a reasonable level of supervision for experienced licensees pursuant to Rule E-31;
6) Take reasonable steps to ensure that violations of statutes, rules and office policies do not occur or reoccur;
7) Provide for adequate supervision of all offices operated by the broker, whether managed by licensed or unlicensed persons.

Pursuant to §12-61-118, C.R.S. and Rule E-29, employing brokers are also responsible for providing supervision over such activities with reference to the licensing statutes and Commission rules for all brokerage employees, including but not limited to administrative assistants, bookkeepers and personal assistants of licensed employees. Thus, employing brokers are responsible for the actions of unlicensed persons who perform functions within the real estate broker team. Employing brokers need to ensure that any unlicensed person acting within the team is not engaged in practices that require a real estate broker's license. Employing brokers also need to establish that the compensation paid to an unlicensed person for services provided is not in the form of a commission. Compensation paid to an unlicensed person is not required to to be paid solely by the employing broker. However, §12-61-117, C.R.S. requires that all licensee compensation or valuable consideration for the performance of any acts requiring a broker's license is paid solely by the employing broker.

* CP-41 Commission Position on Competency (December 6, 2011)

Pursuant to sections 12-61-804, 12-61-805 and 12-61-807, C.R.S. , which are the laws that govern the duties of a real estate broker acting in the capacity of a single agent or transaction broker, real estate brokers are required to perform the terms of written or oral agreements they make with certain parties to a real estate transaction. Pursuant to sections 12-61-804 and 12-61-805, C.R.S., real estate brokers acting in the capacity of a single agent have a duty to promote the interests of their clients with the utmost good faith, loyalty, and fidelity. Pursuant to section 12-61-113(1)(n), C.R.S., it is a violation of the license law if a licensee demonstrates unworthiness or incompetency to act as a real estate broker by conducting business in such a manner as to endanger the interest of the public.

Prior to performing any acts that require a real estate broker's license, a broker should determine whether he or she possesses the knowledge, experience, and/or training necessary to perform the terms of the transaction and maintain compliance with the applicable federal, state or local laws, rules, regulations, or ordinances. If the broker does not have the requisite knowledge, experience and/or training necessary to consummate the terms of the agreement, the broker should either decline to provide brokerage services or seek the assistance of another real estate broker who does have the necessary experience, training, and/or knowledge. The Commission will have grounds to discipline a broker's license if a broker fails to take the measures necessary to gain competence and violations of the license law are substantiated.

Chapter 4:
Subdivision Laws

An * in the left margin indicates a change in the statute, rule, or text since the last publication of the manual.

I. Subdivision Statute

§ 12-61-401, C.R.S. Definitions.

As used in this part 4, unless the context otherwise requires:

(1) "Commission" means the real estate commission established under section 12-61-105.

(2) "Developer" means any person, as defined in section 2-4-401 (8), C.R.S. which participates as owner, promoter, or sales agent in the promotion, sale, or lease of a subdivision or any part thereof.

(2.5) "HOA" or "homeowners' association" means an association or unit owners' association formed before, on, or after July 1, 1992, as part of a common interest community as defined in section 38-33.3-103, C.R.S.

(3) (a) "Subdivision" means any real property divided into twenty or more interests intended solely for residential use and offered for sale, lease, or transfer.

(b) (I) The term "subdivision" also includes:

(A) The conversion of an existing structure into a common interest community of twenty or more residential units, as defined in Article 33.3 of Title 38, C.R.S.;

(B) A group of twenty or more time shares intended for residential use; and

(C) A group of twenty or more proprietary leases in a cooperative housing corporation, as defined in article 33.5 of title 38, C.R.S.

(II) The term "subdivision" does not include:

(A) The selling of memberships in campgrounds;

(B) Bulk sales and transfers between developers;

(C) Property upon which there has been or upon which there will be erected residential buildings that have not been previously occupied and where the consideration paid for such property includes the cost of such buildings;

(D) Lots which, at the time of closing of a sale or occupancy under a lease, are situated on a street or road and street or road system improved to standards at least equal to streets and roads maintained by the county, city, or town in which the lots are located; have a feasible plan to provide potable water and sewage disposal; and have telephone and electricity facilities and systems adequate to serve the lots, which facilities and systems are installed and in place on the lots or in a street, road, or easement adjacent to the lots and which facilities and systems comply with applicable state, county, municipal, or other local laws, rules, and regulations; or any subdivision that has been or is required to be approved after September 1, 1972 by a regional, county, or municipal planning authority pursuant to Article 28 of Title 30 or Article 23 of Title 31,C.R.S.;

(E) Sales by public officials in the official conduct of their duties.

(4) "Time Share" means a time share estate, as defined in section 38-33-110(5) C.R.S., or a time share use, but the term does not include group reservations made for convention purposes as a single transaction with a hotel, motel, or condominium owner or association. For the purpose of this subsection (4), "time share use" means a contractual or membership right of occupancy (which cannot be terminated at the will of the owner) for life or for a term of years, to the recurrent, exclusive use or occupancy of a lot, parcel, unit, or specific or nonspecific segment of real property, annually or on some other periodic basis, for a period of time that has been or will be allotted from the use or occupancy periods into which the property has been divided.

§ 12-61-402, C.R.S. Registration required.

(1) Unless exempt under the provisions of section 12-61-401 (3), a developer, before selling, leasing, or transferring or agreeing or negotiating to sell, lease, or transfer, directly or indirectly, any subdivision or any part thereof, shall register pursuant to this part 4.

(2) Upon approval by the commission, a developer who has applied for registration pursuant to section 12-61-403 may offer reservations in a subdivision during the pendency of such application and until such application is granted or denied if the fees for such reservations are held in trust by an independent third party and are fully refundable.

§ 12-61-403, C.R.S. Application for registration.

(1) Every person who is required to register as a developer under this part 4 shall submit to the commission an application which contains the information described in subsections (2) and (3) of this section. If such information is not submitted, the commission may deny the application for registration. If a developer is currently regulated in another state that has registration requirements substantially equivalent to the requirements of this part 4 or that provide substantially comparable protection to a purchaser, the commission may accept proof of such registration along with the developer's disclosure or equivalent statement from the other state in full or partial satisfaction of the information required by this section. In addition, the applicant shall be under a continuing obligation to notify the commission within ten days of any change in the information so submitted, and a failure to do so shall be a cause for disciplinary action.

(2) (a) Registration information concerning the developer shall include:

(I) The principal office of the applicant wherever situate;

(II) The location of the principal office and the branch offices of the applicant in this state;

(III) Repealed, effective July 1, 1989

(IV) The names and residence and business addresses of all natural persons who have a twenty-four percent or greater financial or ultimate beneficial interest in the business of the developer either directly or indirectly, as principal, manager, member, partner, officer, director, or stockholder, specifying each such person's capacity, title, and percentage of ownership. If no natural person has a twenty-four percent or greater financial or beneficial interest in the business of the developer, the information required in this subparagraph (IV) shall be submitted regarding the natural person having the largest single financial or beneficial interest.

(V) The length of time and the locations where the applicant has been engaged in the business of real estate sales or development;

(VI) Any felony of which the applicant has been convicted within the preceding ten years, In determining whether a certificate of registration shall be issued to an applicant who has been convicted of a felony within such period of time, the commission shall be governed by the provisions of section 24-5-101, C.R.S.

(VII) The states in which the applicant has had a license or registration similar to the developer's registration in this state granted, refused, suspended, or revoked or is currently the subject of an investigation or charges that could result in refusal, suspension or revocation.

(VIII) Whether the developer or any other person financially interested in the business of the developer as principal, partner, officer, director, or stockholder has engaged in any activity that would constitute a violation of this part 4.

(b) If the applicant is a corporate developer, a copy of the certificate of authority to do business in this state or a certificate of incorporation issued by the secretary of state shall accompany the application.

(3) Registration information concerning the subdivision shall include:

(a) The location of each subdivision from which sales are intended to be made;

(b) The name of each subdivision and the trade, corporate, or partnership name used by the developer;

(c) Evidence or certification that each subdivision offered for sale or lease is registered or will be registered in accordance with state or local requirements of the state in which each subdivision is located;

(d) Copies of documents evidencing the title or other interest in the subdivision;

(e) If there is a blanket encumbrance upon the title of the subdivision, or any other ownership, leasehold, or contractual interest that could defeat all possessory or ownership rights of a purchaser, a copy of the instruments creating such liens, encumbrances, or interests, with dates as to the recording, along with documentary evidence that any beneficiary, mortgagee or trustee of a deed of trust or any other holder of such ownership, leasehold, or contractual interest will release any lot or time share from the blanket encumbrance or, has subordinated its interest in the subdivision to the interest of any purchaser or has established any other arrangement acceptable to the real estate commission that protects the rights of the purchaser;

(f) A statement that standard commission-approved forms will be used for contracts of sale, notes, deeds, and other legal documents used to effectuate the sale or lease of the subdivision or any part thereof, unless the forms to be used were prepared by an attorney representing the developer;

(g) A true statement by the developer that, in any conveyance by means of an installment contract, the purchaser shall be advised to record the contract with the proper authorities in the jurisdiction in which the subdivision is located. In no event shall any developer specifically prohibit the recording of the installment contract;

(h) A true statement by the developer of the provisions for and availability of legal access, sewage disposal, and public utilities, including water, electricity, gas, and telephone facilities, in the subdivision offered for sale or lease, including whether such are to be a developer or purchaser expense;

(i) A true statement as to whether or not a survey of each lot, site, or tract offered for sale or lease from such subdivision has been made and whether survey monuments are in place;

(i.5) A true statement by the developer as to whether or not a common interest community is to be or has been created within the subdivision, and whether or not such common interest community is or will be a small cooperative or small and limited and limited expense planned community created pursuant to section 38-33.3-116 C.R.S.

(j) A true statement by the developer concerning the existence of any common interest community association, including whether the developer controls funds in such association.

(3.5) The commission may disapprove the form of the documents submitted pursuant to paragraph (3)(f) of this section and may deny an application for registration until such time as the applicant submits such documents in a form that is satisfactory to the commission.

(4) Repealed, effective July 1, 1989.

(5) Each registration shall be accompanied by fees established pursuant to section 12-61-111.5.

§ 12-61-404, C.R.S. Registration of developers.

(1) The commission shall register all applicants who meet the requirements of this part 4 and provide each applicant so registered with a certificate indicating that the developer named therein is registered in the state of Colorado as a subdivision developer. The developer which will sign as seller or lessor in any contract of sale, lease, or deed purporting to convey any site, tract, lot, or divided or undivided interest from a subdivision shall secure a certificate before offering, negotiating, or agreeing to sell, lease, or transfer before such sale, lease, or transfer is made. If such person or entity is acting only as a trustee, the beneficial owner of the subdivision shall secure a certificate. A certificate issued to a developer shall entitle all sales agents and employees of such developer to act in the capacity of a developer as agent for such developer. The developer shall be responsible for all actions of such sales agents and employees.

(2) All certificates issued under this section shall expire on December 31 following the date of issuance. In the absence of any reason or condition under this part 4 that might warrant the denial or revocation of a registration, a certificate shall be renewed by payment of a renewal fee established pursuant to section 12-61-111.5. A registration that has expired may be reinstated within two years after such expiration upon payment of the appropriate renewal fee if the applicant meets all other requirements of this part 4.

(3) All fees collected under this part 4 shall be deposited in accordance with section 12-61-111.

(4) With regard to any subdivision for which the information required by section 12-61-403(3) has not been previously submitted to the commission, each registered developer shall register such subdivision by providing the commission with such information before sale, lease, or transfer, or negotiating or agreeing to sell, lease, or transfer, any such subdivision or any part thereof.

§ 12-61-405, C.R.S. Refusal, revocation, or suspension of registration – letter of admonition – probation.

(1) The commission may impose an administrative fine not to exceed two thousand five hundred dollars for each separate offense; may issue a letter of admonition; may place a registrant on probation under its close supervision on such terms and for such time as it deems appropriate; and may refuse, revoke, or suspend the registration of any developer or registrant if, after an investigation and after notice and a hearing pursuant to the provisions of section 24-4-104, C.R.S., the commission determines that the developer or any director, officer, or stockholder with controlling interest in the corporation:

- (a) Has used false or misleading advertising or has made a false or misleading statement or a concealment in his application for registration;
- (b) Has misrepresented or concealed any material fact from a purchaser of any interest in a subdivision;
- (c) Has employed any device, scheme, or artifice with intent to defraud a purchaser of any interest in a subdivision;
- (d) Has been convicted of or pled guilty or nolo contendere to a crime involving fraud, deception, false pretense, theft, misrepresentation, false advertising, or dishonest dealing in any court;

(e) Has disposed of, concealed, diverted, converted, or otherwise failed to account for any funds or assets of any purchaser of any interest in a subdivision or any homeowners' association under the control of such developer or director, officer, or stockholder;

(f) Has failed to comply with any stipulation or agreement made with the commission;

(g) Has failed to comply with or has violated any provision of this article, including any failure to comply with the registration requirements of section 12-61-403, or any lawful rule or regulation promulgated by the commission under this article;

(h) Deleted by amendment, effective July 1, 1989

(i) Has refused to honor a buyer's request to cancel a contract for the purchase of a time share or subdivision or part thereof if such request was made within five calendar days after execution of the contract and as made either by telegram, mail, or hand delivery. A request is considered made if by mail when postmarked, if by telegram when filed for telegraphic transmission, or if by hand delivery when delivered to the seller's place of business. No developer shall employ a contract that contains any provision waiving a buyer's right to such a cancellation period.

(j) Has committed any act that constitutes a violation of the "Colorado Consumer Protection Act", article 1 of title 6, C.R.S.;

(k) Has employed any sales agent or employee who violates the provision of this part 4;

(l) Has used documents for sales or lease transactions other than those described in section 12-61-403(3)(f);

(m) Has failed to disclose encumbrances to prospective purchasers or has failed to transfer clear title at the time of sale, if the parties agreed that such transfer would be made at that time.

(1.5) A disciplinary action relating to the business of subdivision development taken by any other state or local jurisdiction or the federal government shall be deemed to be prima facie evidence of grounds for disciplinary action, including denial of registration, under this part 4. This subsection (1.5) shall apply only to such disciplinary actions as are substantially similar to those set out as grounds for disciplinary action or denial of registration under this part 4.

(2) Any hearing held under this section shall be in accordance with the procedures established in sections 24-4-105 and 24-4-106, C.R.S.

(2.5) When a complaint or investigation discloses an instance of misconduct that, in the opinion of the commission, does not initially warrant formal action by the commission but which should not be dismissed as being without merit, the commission may send a letter of admonition by certified mail, return receipt requested, to the registrant who is the subject of the complaint or investigation and a copy thereof to any person making such complaint. Such letter shall advise the registrant that he has the right to request in writing, within twenty days after proven receipt, that formal disciplinary proceedings be initiated against him to adjudicate the propriety of the conduct upon which the letter of admonition is based. If such request is timely made, the letter of admonition shall be deemed vacated, and the matter shall be processed by means of formal disciplinary proceedings.

(3) All administrative fines collected pursuant to this section shall be transmitted to the state treasurer, who shall credit the same to the division of real estate cash fund.

§ 12-61-406, C.R.S. Powers of commission – injunction – rules.

(1) The commission may apply to a court of competent jurisdiction for an order enjoining any act or practice which constitutes a violation of this part 4, and, upon a showing that a person is engaging or intends to engage in any such act or practice, an injunction, restraining order, or other appropriate order shall be granted by such court, regardless of the existence of another

remedy therefore. Any notice, hearing, or duration of any injunction or restraining order shall be made in accordance with the provisions of the Colorado rules of civil procedure.

(1.2) The commission may apply to a court of competent jurisdiction for the appointment of receiver if it determines that such appointment is necessary to protect the property or interests of purchasers of a subdivision or part thereof.

(1.5) The commission shall issue or deny a certificate or additional registration within sixty days from the date of receipt of the application by the commission. The commission may make necessary investigations and inspections to determine whether any developer has violated this part 4 or any lawful rule or regulation promulgated by the commission. If, after an application by a developer has been submitted pursuant to section 12-61-403 or information has been submitted pursuant to section 12-61-404, the commission determines that an inspection of a subdivision is necessary, it shall complete the inspection within sixty days from the date of filing of the application or information, or the right of inspection is waived and the lack thereof shall not be grounds for denial of a registration.

(1.6) The commission, the director for the commission, or the administrative law judge appointed for a hearing may issue a subpoena compelling the attendance and testimony of witnesses and the production of books, papers, or records pursuant to an investigation or hearing of such commission. Any such subpoena shall be served in the same manner as for subpoenas issued by district courts.

(2) The commission has the power to make any rules necessary for the enforcement or administration of this part 4.

(2.5) The commission shall adopt, promulgate, amend, or repeal such rules and regulations as are necessary to:

(a) Require written disclosures to any purchasers as provided in subsection (3) of this section and to prescribe and require that standardized forms be used by subdivision developers in connection with the sale or lease of a subdivision or any part thereof, except as otherwise provided in section 12-61-403(3) (f); and

(b) Require that developers maintain certain business records for a period of at least seven years.

(3) The commission may require any developer to make written disclosures to purchasers in their contracts of sale or by separate written documents if the commission finds that such disclosures are necessary for the protection of such purchasers.

(4) The commission or its designated representative may audit the accounts of any homeowner association the funds of which are controlled by a developer.

§ 12-61-407, C.R.S. Violation – penalty.

Any person who fails to register as a developer in violation of this part 4 commits a class 6 felony and shall be punished as provided in section 18-1-105, C.R.S. Any agreement or contract for the sale or lease of a subdivision or part thereof shall be voidable by the purchaser and unenforceable by the developer unless such developer was duly registered under the provisions of this part 4 when such agreement or contract was made. (*Ed Note: Effective July 1,1993, a class 6 felony is punishable by a minimum one year and maximum eighteen months imprisonment. (18-1.3-401 (1) (a) (V) (A), C.R.S.) The minimum fine is $1,000.00; the maximum $100,000.00. (18-1.3-401 (1) (a)(III)(A), C.R.S.)*)

§ 12-61-408, C.R.S. Repeal of part.

This part 4 is repealed, effective July 1, 2017. Prior to such repeal, the provisions in this part 4 shall be reviewed as provided for in section 24-34-104, C.R.S.

II. Rules and Regulations for Subdivision Developers

Adopted, and Published by the

COLORADO REAL ESTATE COMMISSION

Approved by the Attorney General and the Executive Director of the Department of Regulatory Agencies.

In pursuance of and in compliance with Title 12, Article 61, C.R.S. 1973, as amended, and in pursuance of and in compliance with Title 24, Article 4, C.R.S. 1973, as amended.

S-1. The Registration and Certification of Subdivision Developers under Title 12, Article 61, Part 4, C.R.S. does not exempt the subdivision developer from the requirements for the licensing of real estate brokers under Title 12, Article 61, Part 1, C.R.S. Exemptions from the licensing of real estate brokers are made only under 12-61-101(4) C.R.S.

S-2. The person, firm, partnership, joint venture, limited liability company, association, corporation or other legal entity, or combination thereof, who will sign as seller or lessor in any contract of sale, lease or on any deed purporting to convey any site, tract, lot or divided or undivided interest from a subdivision, as defined in 12- 61- 401(3) C.R.S., must secure a Subdivision Developer's Certificate before negotiating or agreeing to sell, lease or transfer and before any sale, lease or transfer is made. If such person is acting only as a trustee, the beneficial owner of the Subdivision must secure a Subdivision Developer's Certificate.

S-3. If an applicant is a corporation, the individual applying on behalf of the corporation shall be an officer or director authorized to apply on behalf of said corporation.

S-4. If the applicant is a partnership, one of the general partners of the partnership shall apply on behalf of the partnership.

S-5. If the applicant is a joint owner of the subdivision, such applicant may apply on behalf of all joint owners of such subdivision.

S-6. If the applicant is a limited liability company, one of the managers or member-managers shall apply on behalf of the company.

S-7. The Real Estate Commission shall issue a certificate, refuse certification or demand further information within sixty (60) days from the date or receipt of the application by the Commission.

S-8. If additional information is required by the Real Estate Commission, the Commission shall give written notice in detail of the information so required and shall allow an additional sixty (60) days to present such material before cancellation of the application, which period may be extended only upon showing of good cause.

S-9. Repealed.

S-10. Repealed.

S-11. Notification must be made to the Real Estate Commission within 10 days of any change in the principal office address of the developer or the natural person.

S-12. Pursuant to 12-61-405 C.R.S., any subdivision developer who has received written notification from the Commission that a complaint has been filed against the developer, shall submit a written answer to the Commission within a reasonable time set by the Commission.

S-13. Repealed.

S-14. Failure to submit any written response required by S-12 shall be grounds for disciplinary action unless the Commission has granted an extension of time or, unless such answer would subject such person to a criminal penalty.

S-15. Records as required under Title 12, Article 61, Parts 1-8 C.R.S. and rules promulgated by the Commission, may be maintained in electronic format. An electronic record as defined in 24-71.7-103 C.R.S. means a record generated, communicated, received, or stored by electronic means. Such electronic records must be in a format that has the continued capability to be retrieved and legibly printed. Upon request of the Commission, or by any principal party to a transaction, printed records shall be produced.

S-16. Repealed.

S-17. In compliance with 12-61-403 the applicant for a subdivision developer's certificate shall provide the Commission with the following information concerning the subdivision(s) to be registered:

(a) The address or actual physical location of each subdivision from which sales are intended to be made.

(b) Copies of a recorded deed or other documents evidencing the title or other interest in the subdivision and a title commitment, policy or report, abstract and opinion, or other evidence acceptable to the Commission documenting the condition of such title or interest.

(c) Sample copies of contracts of sale, notes, deeds and other legal documents prepared by the developer or an attorney representing the developer which are to be used to effectuate the sale or lease. The Commission may disapprove the form of the documents submitted and may deny an application for registration until such time as the applicant submits such documents in a form that is satisfactory to the Commission.

(d) In compliance with 12-61-403(3)(e) C.R.S., a subdivision developer of time share use projects shall submit to the Commission a "Nondisturbance Agreement" by which the holder of a blanket encumbrance against the project agrees that its rights in the time share use project shall be subordinate to the rights of the purchasers. From and after the recording of a nondisturbance agreement, the person executing the same, such person's successors and assigns, and any person who acquires the property through foreclosure or by deed in lieu of foreclosure of the blanket encumbrance, shall take the time share use project subject to the rights of purchasers. Every nondisturbance agreement shall contain the covenant of the holder of the blanket encumbrance that such person or any other person acquiring through such blanket encumbrance shall not use or cause the time share use project to be used in a manner which would prevent the purchasers from using and occupying the time share use project in a manner contemplated by the time share use plan. Any other "trust" or "escrow" arrangement which fully protects the purchasers' interest in the project as contemplated by 12-61-403(3)(e) C.R.S. will be approved by the Real Estate Commission.

(e) If the developer of a subdivision is other than a natural person, proof of registration in accordance with state and local requirements shall accompany the application.

(f) Copies of the recorded declaration, covenants, filed articles of incorporation and bylaws of any owners association.

S-18. Repealed (1-1-95)

S-19. Repealed (1-1-95)

S-20. Pursuant to 12-61-403(3)(e) C.R.S. where a subdivision developer receives cash or receivables from a purchaser for an uncompleted project, the Commission will register such developer only after:

(a) The developer establishes an escrow account, with an independent escrow agent, of all funds and receivables received from purchasers: or,

(b) The developer obtains a letter of credit or bond payable to an independent escrow agent or any other financial arrangement, the purpose of which is to ensure completion of accommodations and facilities and to protect the purchaser's interest in the accommodations and facilities.

S-21. A subdivision developer shall furnish to the Commission such additional information as the Commission shall from time to time deem necessary for the enforcement of Title 12, Article 61, Part 4, C.R.S.

S-22. Renewal of the registration and certification as a subdivision developer can be executed only on the renewal application provided by the Commission accompanied by the proper fees by December 31st of each year.

S-23. Pursuant to 12-61-406(2.5)(a) C.R.S. and 12-61-406(3) C.R.S., subdivision developers shall supply the following information to the Commission in addition to the requirements of 12-61-403 C.R.S. and 404(4) C.R.S. and prior to contracting with the public shall disclose to prospective purchasers in the sales contract or in a separate written disclosure document, the following:

(a) The name and address of the developer and of the subdivision lots or units;

(b) An explanation of the type of ownership or occupancy rights being offered;

(c) A general description of all amenities and accommodations. The description must include the specific amenities promised, ownership of such amenities, the projected completion date of any amenities to be constructed, and a statement setting forth the type of financial arrangements established in compliance with Rule S-20;

(d) In compliance with 12-61-405 (1)(i), a statement in bold print immediately prior to the purchaser's signature line on the sales contract disclosing the rescission right available to purchasers and that the rescission right cannot be waived; the minimum allowable rescission period in Colorado is five days;

(e) A general description of all judgments and administrative orders issued against the seller, developer, homeowners association or managing entity which are material to the subdivision plan;

(f) Any taxes or assessments, existing or proposed, to which the purchaser may be subject or which are unpaid at the time of contracting, including obligations to special taxing authorities or districts.

(g) A statement that sales will be made by brokers licensed by the State of Colorado unless specifically exempted pursuant to C.R.S. 12-61-101(4) and the sales contract shall disclose the name of the real estate brokerage firm and the name of the broker establishing a brokerage relationship with the developer;

(h) When a separate document is used to make any of the disclosures required in this Rule S-23, this statement must appear in bold print on the first page of the document and preceding the disclosure: **"The State of Colorado has not prepared or issued this document nor has it passed on the merits of the subdivision described herein"**;

(i) A statement that all funds paid by the purchaser prior to delivery of deed will be held in trust by the licensed real estate broker named in the contract or a clear statement specifically setting forth who such funds shall be delivered to, when such delivery will occur, the use of said funds and whether or not there is any restriction on the use of such funds (This must be disclosed in contract);

(j) A statement that immediately following the date of closing, the purchaser's deed will be delivered to the Clerk and Recorder's office for recording or a clear statement specifically setting forth when such delivery will occur; for the purposes of this Rule, the date of closing is defined as the date the purchaser has either paid the full cash purchase price or has made partial cash payment and executed a promissory note or other evidence of indebtedness for the balance (See Rule S-30) (This must be disclosed in the contract);

(k) A statement that a title insurance policy, at no expense to the purchaser, will be delivered within sixty days following recording of deed unless specifically agreed to the contrary in the contracting instrument (See Rule S-31) (This must be disclosed in contract);

(l) Where an installment contract is used:

(i) Whether or not the purchaser's deed is escrowed with an independent escrow agent and if so the name and address of the escrow agent (This must be disclosed in contract);

(ii) The amount of any existing encumbrance(s), the name and address of the encumbrancer, and the conditions, if any, under which a purchaser may cure a default caused by non-payment;

(iii) A clear statement that a default on any underlying encumbrance(s) could result in the loss of the purchaser's entire interest in the property; and

(iv) A clear statement advising the purchaser to record the installment contract.

(v) Pursuant to 12-61-403(3)(e) C.R.S., an agreement by which the holder of any blanket encumbrance against the project agrees that its rights and the rights of its successors or assigns in the project shall be subordinate to the rights of purchasers, or any other "trust", "escrow" or release arrangement which fully protects the purchasers' interest in the project.

(m) The provisions for and availability of legal access, roads, sewage disposal, public utilities, including water, electricity, gas, telephone and other promised facilities in the subdivision, and whether these are to be an expense of the developer, the purchaser or a third party;

(n) If the subdivision has a homeowners or similar association:

(i) Whether membership in such association is mandatory;

(ii) An estimate of association dues and fees which are the responsibility respectively of the purchaser and the developer;

(iii) A description of the services provided by the association;

(iv) Whether the developer has voting control of the association and the manner in which such control can or will be transferred; and

(v) Whether the developer has any financial interest in or will potentially derive any income or profit from such association, including the developer's right to borrow or authorize borrowing from the association.

(o) In addition to the disclosures in (a) through (n) above, if sales are to be made from a time share project as defined in 12-61-401 (4):

(i) A description of the time share units including the number of time share units, the length and number of time share interests in each unit, and the time share periods constituting the time share plan;

(ii) The name and business address of the managing entity under the time share plan, a description of the services that the managing entity will provide, and a statement as to whether the developer has any financial interest in or will potentially derive any income or profit from such managing entity, and the manner, if any, by which the purchaser or developer may change the managing entity or transfer the control of the managing entity;

(iii) An estimate of the dues, maintenance fees, real property taxes and similar periodic expenses which are the responsibility respectively of the purchaser and the developer and a general statement of the conditions under which future changes or additions may be imposed. Such estimate will include a statement as to whether a maintenance reserve fund has been or will be established; the manner in which such reserve fund is financed if not cash funded; an accounting of any outstanding obligations either in favor of or against the fund; the developer's right to borrow or authorize borrowing from the fund; and the method of periodic accounting which will be provided to the purchaser;

(iv) A description of any insurance coverage provided for the benefit of purchasers; and

(v) That mechanic's liens law may authorize enforcement of the lien by selling the entire time share unit.

(p) In addition to the disclosures in (a) through (o) above, if sales are to be made from a time share use project as defined in 12-61-401(4):

(i) The specific term of the contract to use and what will happen to a purchaser's interest upon termination of said contract;

(ii) A statement as to the effect a voluntary sale, by the developer to a third party, will have on the contractual rights of time share owners;

(iii) A statement that an involuntary transfer by bankruptcy of the developer may have a negative effect on the rights of the time share owners; and

(iv) A statement that a Federal tax lien could be enforced against the developer by compelling the sale of the entire time share project.

(q) If time shares, as defined in 12-61-401(4), are to be sold from a subdivision which:

(1) contains two or more component sites situated at different geographic locations or governed by separate sets of declarations, by-laws or equivalent documents; and

(2) does not include, subject to agreed upon rules and conditions, a guaranteed, recurring right of use or occupancy at a single component site:

(i) For each component site, the information and disclosures required by Rule S-23(a) through (p);

(ii) A general description of the subdivision;

(iii) For each term of usage or interest offered for sale, the total annual number of available daily use periods within the entire subdivision and within each component site for that term, regardless of whether such use periods are offered to a purchaser by days, weeks, points or otherwise, and a calculation represented on a chart or grid showing each component site's annual daily use periods as a percentage of the entire subdivision's annual daily use periods;

(iv) A clear description in the sales contract of the interest and term of usage being purchased and a definite date of termination of the purchaser's interest in the subdivision, which date will be not later than the termination date of the subdivision's interest in a specifically identified component site;

(v) A clear disclosure and description of any component site which is not legally guaranteed to be available for the purchaser's use, subject to the by-laws and rules of the subdivision, for the full term of the purchaser's usage interest;

(vi) The system and method in place to assure maintenance of no more than a one-to-one ratio of purchasers' use rights to the number of total use rights in the subdivision for each term of usage being offered for sale, including provisions for compensation to purchasers resulting from destruction of a component site or loss of use rights to any component site;

(vii) Whether the developer maintains any type of casualty insurance for the component sites in addition to that maintained by the site owners association or other interested parties, including the manner of disposition of any proceeds of such insurance resulting from the destruction or loss of use rights to any component site;

(viii) A description of the system or program by which a purchaser obtains a recurring right to use and occupy accommodations and facilities in any component site through use of a reservation system or otherwise, including any restrictions on such rights or any method by which a purchaser is denied an equal right with all other users to obtain the use of any accommodation in the subdivision;

(ix) A description of the management and ownership of such reservation system or program, whether through the developer, an owners' association, a club or otherwise, including the purchaser's direct or indirect ownership interest or rights of control in such reservation system;

(x) Whether the developer, club or association which controls the reservation system or any other person has or is granted any interest in unsold, non-reserved orunused use rights and whether the developer, club, association or other person may employ such rights to compete with purchasers for use of accommodations in the subdivision or any component site and, if so, the nature and specifics of those rights, including the circumstances under which they may be employed;

(xi) The method and frequency of accounting for any income derived from unsold, non-reserved or unused use rights in which the purchaser, either directly or indirectly, has an interest;

(xii) The system and method in place, including business interruption insurance or bonding, to provide secure back-up or replacement of the reservation system in the event of interruption, discontinuance or failure;

(xiii) The amount and details of any component site, reservation system or other periodic expense required to be paid by a purchaser, the name of the person or entity to which such payments shall be made, and the method by which the purchaser shall receive a regular periodic accounting for such payments;

(xiv) If component site expenses are included in those periodic payments made by a purchaser, a statement for each component site from the owners association or other responsible agency acknowledging that payment of such expenses as taxes, insurance, dues and assessments are current and are being made in the name of the subdivision;

(xv) Evidence that an escrow system with an independent escrow agent is in place for receipt and disbursement of all moneys collected from purchasers that are necessary to pay such expenses as taxes, insurance and common expenses and assessments owing to component site owners associations or others or a clear description of the method by which such funds will be paid, collected, held, disbursed and accounted for;

(xvi) A clear statement in the sales contract as to whether a purchaser's rights, interests or terms of usage for any component site within the subdivision can subsequently be modified from those terms originally represented and a description of the method by which such modification may occur;

(xvii) If the subdivision documents allow additions or substitutions of accommodations or component sites, a clear description of the purchaser's rights and obligations concerning such additions or substitutions and the method by which such additions or substitutions will comply with the provisions of this rule;

(xviii) A clear description of any existing incidental benefits or amenities which are available to the purchaser at the time of sale but to which the purchaser has no guaranteed right of recurring use or enjoyment during the purchaser's full term of interest in the subdivision.

S-24. A time share developer shall disclose to the public whether or not a time share plan involves an exchange program and, if so, shall disclose and deliver to prospective purchasers, a separate written document, which may be provided by an exchange company if the document discloses the following information:

(a) The name and the business address of the exchange company;

(b) Whether the purchaser's contract with the exchange program is separate and distinct from the purchaser's contract with the time share developer;

(c) Whether the purchaser's participation in the exchange program is dependent upon the time share developer's continued affiliation with the exchange program;

(d) Whether or not the purchaser's participation in the exchange program is voluntary;

(e) The specific terms and conditions of the purchaser's contractual relationship with the exchange program and the procedure by which changes, if any, may be made in the terms and conditions of such contractual relationship;

(f) The procedure of applying for and effecting changes;

(g) A complete description of all limitations, restrictions, accrual rights, or priorities employed in the operation of the exchange program, including but not limited to limitations on exchanges based on seasonability, unit size, or levels of occupancy; and if the limitations, restrictions or priorities are not applied uniformly by the exchange program, a complete description of the manner of their application;

(h) Whether exchanges are arranged on a space-available basis or whether guarantees of fulfillment of specific requests for exchanges are made by the exchanging company;

(i) Whether and under what conditions, a purchaser may, in dealing with the exchange program, lose the use and occupancy of the time share period in any properly applied for exchange without being offered substitute accommodations by the exchange program;

(j) The fees for participation in the exchange program, whether the fees may be altered and the method of any altering;

(k) The name and location of each accommodation or facility, including the time sharing plans participating in the exchange program.

S-25. All approvals for the use of reservation agreements issued pursuant to 12-61-402(2) C.R.S. shall expire on December 31 following the date of issuance. Approval shall be renewed, except as provided in section 12-61-405 C.R.S., by payment of a renewal fee established pursuant to section 12-61-111.5 and completion of a renewal application.

S-26. Upon request of the Commission pursuant to an investigation, a subdivision developer shall file with the Real Estate Commission an audited financial statement in conformity with accepted accounting principles, and sworn to by the developer as an accurate reflection of the financial condition of the developer and/or the owners association controlled by the developer.

S-27. Any adverse order, judgment, or decree entered in connection with the subdivided lands by any regulatory authority or by any court of appropriate jurisdiction shall be filed with the Real Estate Commission by the developer within thirty (30) days of such order, judgment or decree being final.

S-28. (a) A subdivision developer is not required to file amendments to its registration filed with the Real Estate Commission when revisions are made to documents previously submitted to the Commission so long as the revised documents continue to (i) comply with Title 12, Article 61, Part 4 C.R.S. and the rules and regulations promulgated thereunder; and (ii) to reflect accurately the subdivision offering.

(b) Notwithstanding the above, and in addition to the notice requirements under Rule S-11 and Rule S-27, subdivision developers shall provide the Commission with noticc of the following events within ten (10) days after such event, unless otherwise provided below:

(1) A change in the information provided in the registration pursuant to Sections 12-61-403 (2)(a)(IV), (VI), (VII) or (VIII) C.R.S.;

(2) A change in the terms of any non-disturbance agreements or partial release provisions in connection with any documents previously submitted to the Commission pursuant to Section 12-61-403 (3)(e) C.R.S. and Rule S-17 (d);

(3) Any new lien encumbering the subdivision or any part thereof other than encumbrances created or permitted by purchasers;

(4) The termination or transfer of any escrow account, letter of credit, bond, or other financial assurance approved by the Commission pursuant to Rule S-20, notice of which shall be filed with the Commission prior to the effective date of such termination or transfer;

(5) Cancellation, revocation, suspension, or termination of the subdivision developer's authority to do business in this state; and

(6) Any lis pendens, lawsuit or other proceeding filed against the subdivision or subdivision developer affecting the subdivision developer's ability (i) to convey marketable title to the registered subdivision or any interest therein or (ii) to perform the subdivision developer's obligations in connection with the registered subdivision.

(c) Notification under this Rule S-28 shall be made on a form approved by the Commission. The subdivision developer shall have a period of ten (10) days after receipt of notice to take such action as may be required by the Commission in connection with any filings made under this Rule S-28.

(d) Within ten (10) days after receipt of a written request from the Commission, a subdivision developer shall have the duty to provide to the Commission copies of all documents then in use at the subdivision.

S-29. No subdivision developer shall make misrepresentations regarding future availability or costs of services, utilities, character and/or use of real property for sale or lease of the surrounding area.

S-30. (a) Unless sale is by means of an installment contract the delivery of deed shall be made within sixty days after closing. For the purposes of this Rule, the date of closing is defined as the date the purchaser has either paid the full cash purchase price or has made partial cash payment and executed a promissory note or other evidence of indebtedness for the balance (This must be disclosed in the contract).

(b) If sale is by means of an installment contract, the delivery of deed shall be made within sixty days after completion of payments. A contract which requires the execution of a promissory note or other evidence of indebtedness that accrues interest and/or requires payments prior to the recording of a deed shall be deemed to be an installment contract pursuant to 12-61-403(3)(g) C.R.S. and Commission Rule S-23.

S-31. An abstract of title or title insurance policy shall be delivered within a reasonable time after completion of payments by a purchaser. Any period of time exceeding sixty days shall be deemed unreasonable for purposes of this rule. The parties may contract to eliminate this requirement, but such waiver must be in writing and in a conspicuous manner and/or print. The presence of waiver on the back of a contract shall not be deemed conspicuous for purposes of this rule.

S-32. All developers shall provide a title insurance commitment or other evidence of title approved by the Commission within a reasonable time after execution of any contract to purchase. Any period of time in excess of ninety (90) days shall be deemed unreasonable for purposes of this rule. This requirement may be waived by the parties in writing if the waiver is made in a conspicuous manner and/or print. The presence of the waiver on the back of a contract shall not be deemed conspicuous for purposes of this rule.

S-33. Declaratory Orders

1. Any person [1] may petition the Commission for a declaratory order to terminate controversies or to remove uncertainties as to the applicability to the petitioner of any statutory provision or of any rule or order of the Commission.

[1] refers to existing definition of "person" in APA, rule or statute, if any.

2. The Commission will determine, in its discretion and without prior notice to the petitioner, whether to rule upon any such petition. If the Commission determines it will not rule upon such a petition, the Commission shall issue its written order disposing of the same, stating therein its reasons for such action. A copy of such order shall forthwith be transmitted to the petitioner.

3. In determining whether to rule upon a petition filed pursuant to this rule, the Commission will consider the following matters, among others:

   (a) Whether a ruling on the petition will terminate a controversy or remove uncertainties as to the applicability to petitioner of any statutory provision or rule or order of the Commission;

   (b) Whether the petition involves any subject, question or issue which is the subject of a formal or informal matter or investigation currently pending before the Commission or a court involving one or more of the petitioners which will terminate the controversy or remove the uncertainties as to the applicability to the petitioner of any statutory provision or of any rule or order of the Commission, which matter or investigation shall be specified by the Commission;

   (c) Whether the petition involves any subject, question or issue which is the subject of a formal matter or investigation currently pending before the Commission or a court but not involving any petitioner which will terminate the controversy or remove the uncertainties as to the applicability to the petitioner of any statutory provision or of any rule or order of the Commission, which matter or investigation shall be specified by the Commission and in which petitioner may intervene;

   (d) Whether the petition seeks a ruling on a moot or hypothetical question and will result in merely an advisory ruling or opinion;

   (e) Whether the petitioner has some other adequate legal remedy, other than an action for declaratory relief pursuant to rule 57, Colo. R. Civ. P., which will terminate the controversy or remove any uncertainty as to the applicability to the petitioner of the statute, rule or order in question.

4. Any petition filed pursuant to this rule shall set forth the following:
    (a) The name and address of the petitioner and whether the petitioner is licensed pursuant to 12-61-401, C.R.S. *et seq.*;
    (b) The statute, rule or order to which the petition relates;
    (c) A concise statement of all the facts necessary to show the nature of the controversy or uncertainty and the manner in which the statute, rule or order in question applies or potentially applies to the petitioner.
5. If the Commission determines that it will rule on the petition, the following procedures shall apply:
    (a) The Commission may rule upon the petition based solely upon the facts presented in the petition. In such a case:
        1. Any ruling of the Commission will apply only to the extent of the facts presented in the petition and any amendment to the petition;
        2. The Commission may order the petitioner to file a written brief, memorandum or statement of position;
        3. The Commission may set the petition, upon due notice to petitioner, for a non-evidentiary hearing;
        4. The Commission may dispose of the petition on the sole basis of the matters set forth in the petition;
        5. The Commission may request the petitioner to submit additional facts in writing. In such event, such additional facts will be considered as an amendment to the petition;
        6. The Commission may take administrative notice of facts pursuant to the Administrative Procedure Act (24-4-105(8) C.R.S.) and utilize its experience, technical competence and specialized knowledge in the disposition of the petition;
        7. If the Commission rules upon the petition without a hearing, it shall issue its written order, stating therein its basis for the order. A copy of such order shall forthwith be transmitted to the petitioner.
    (b) The Commission may, in its discretion, set the petition for hearing, upon due notice to the petitioner, for the purpose of obtaining additional facts or information or to determine the truth of any fact set forth in the petition or to hear oral argument on the petition. Notice to the petitioner setting such hearing shall set forth, to the extent known, the factual or other matters into which the Commission intends to inquire. For the purpose of such a hearing, to the extent necessary, the petitioner shall have the burden of proving all of the facts stated in the petition, all of the facts necessary to show the nature of the controversy or uncertainty and the manner in which the statute, rule or order in question applies or potentially applies to petitioner and any other facts the petitioner desires the Commission to consider.
6. The parties to any proceeding pursuant to this rule shall be the Commission and the petitioner. Any other person may seek leave of the Commission to intervene in such a proceeding, and leave to intervene will be granted at the sole discretion of the Commission. A petition to intervene shall set forth the same matters as required by section 4 of this rule. Any reference to a "petitioner" in this rule also refers to any person who has been granted leave to intervene by the Commission.
7. Any declaratory order or other order disposing of a petition pursuant to this rule shall constitute agency action subject to judicial review pursuant to 24-4-106, C.R.S.

S-34. Repealed.

S-35. Failure to disclose to subdivision purchasers the availability of legal access, sewage disposal, public utilities, including water, electricity, gas and telephone facilities in the subdivision and at whose expense, when proven, is a violation of C.R.S. 12-61-405(1)(b). (Statement of Basis and Purpose as adopted by the Real Estate Commission on October 5, 1988.)

S-36. Pursuant to 12-61-405(1)(e) C.R.S., 12-61-406(2.5) (b) C.R.S. and 12-61-406(4) C.R.S., a developer shall maintain in a Colorado place of business, and produce for inspection upon reasonable request by an authorized representative of the Commission, copies of the following documents and business records:

(1) The sales contract, transfer or lease agreement, installment sale agreement, financing agreement, buyer and seller settlement statement, title policy or commitment, trust deed, escrow agreement, and other documents executed by the parties or on behalf of the developer in the sale, lease or transfer of any interest in a subdivision.

(2) Records showing the receipt and disbursement of any money or assets received or paid on behalf of any homeowner or similar association managed or controlled by a developer.

III. Jurisdiction of Commission

A. Introduction

The Subdivision Developer's Act affects the types of subdivisions that must be registered with the Commission. The following types of subdivisions within the State of Colorado, and subdivisions located outside the state if being offered for sale in Colorado, must be registered before offering, negotiating, or agreeing to sell, lease, or transfer any portion of the subdivision:

1. Any division of real property into 20 or more interests for residential use;
2. Subdivisions consisting of 20 or more time-share interests (a time share interest includes a fee simple interest, a leasehold, a contract to use, a membership agreement, or an interest in common);
3. Subdivisions consisting of 20 or more residential units created by converting an existing structure (*e.g.*, condominium conversions); and
4. Subdivisions created by cooperative housing corporations with 20 or more shareholders with proprietary leases, whether the project is completed or not.

B. Exempt from Registration under the Subdivision Developer's Act

1. The selling of memberships in campgrounds;
2. Bulk sales and transfers between developers;
3. Property upon which there has been or upon which there will be erected residential buildings that have not been previously occupied and where the consideration paid by the purchaser for such property includes the cost of such buildings (this does not apply to conversions, time share, or cooperative housing projects);
4. Lots that, at the time of closing of a sale or occupancy under a lease, are situated on a street or road and the street or road system is improved to standards at least equal to streets and roads maintained by the county, city, or town in which the lots are located; have a feasible plan to provide potable water and sewage disposal; and have

telephone and electricity facilities and systems adequate to serve the lots, which facilities and systems are installed and in place on the lots or in a street, road, or easement adjacent to the lots and which facilities and systems comply with applicable state, county, municipal, or other local laws, rules, and regulations; or any subdivision that has been or is required to be approved after September 1, 1972 by a regional, county, or municipal planning authority pursuant to Article 28 of Title 30 or Article 23 of Title 31, C.R.S.; and

5. Sales by public officials in the official conduct of their duties.

C. Additional Provisions of the Subdivision Act

1. A registration expires December 31 unless renewed. A registration that has expired may be reinstated within two years after such expiration upon payment of the appropriate renewal fee if the applicant meets all other requirements of the Act. A subdivision developer is not authorized to transact business during the period between expiration of the registration and reinstatement.
2. The Act requires a *five-day cancellation period* after the execution of a contract, which right cannot be waived, and applies to any subdivision regulated pursuant to the Subdivision Act. This cancellation period runs until midnight on the fifth day following execution of the contract.
3. Any agreement or contract for the sale or lease of a subdivision or part thereof shall be voidable by the purchaser and unenforceable by the developer unless such developer was duly registered under the provisions of the Subdivision Act when such agreement or contract was made.

IV. HOA Registration and the HOA Information and Resource Center

Beginning January 1, 2011, every homeowners' association organized under § 38-33.3-301, C.R.S., must register with the Division of Real Estate on an annual basis. Some associations may be exempt from paying the prescribed fee, but still must register with the Division of Real Estate. An association is not allowed to enforce a lien for assessment under § 38-33.3-316, C.R.S., until it is properly registered.

In addition, the HOA Information and Resource Center is created within the Division of Real Estate, which acts as a clearinghouse for information concerning the basic rights and duties of unit owners, declarants, and associations.

§ 12-61-406.5, C.R.S. HOA information and resource center – creation – duties – rules – cash fund – repeal.

(1) There is hereby created, within the division of real estate, the HOA information and resource center, the head of which shall be the HOA information officer. The HOA information officer shall be appointed by the executive director of the department of regulatory agencies pursuant to section 13 of article XII of the state constitution.

(2) The HOA information officer shall be familiar with the "Colorado Common Interest Ownership Act", article 33.3 of title 38, C.R.S., also referred to in this section as the "act". No person who is or, within the immediately preceding ten years, has been licensed by or registered with the division of real estate or who owns stocks, bonds, or any pecuniary interest in a corporation

subject in whole or in part to regulation by the division of real estate shall be appointed as HOA information officer. In addition, in conducting the search for an appointee, the executive director of the division of real estate shall place a high premium on candidates who are balanced, independent, unbiased, and without any current financial ties to an HOA board or board member or to any person or entity that provides HOA management services. After being appointed, the HOA information officer shall refrain from engaging in any conduct or relationship that would create a conflict of interest or the appearance of a conflict of interest.

(3) (a) The HOA information officer shall act as a clearing house for information concerning the basic rights and duties of unit owners, declarants, and unit owners' associations under the act.

(b) The HOA information officer:

(I) May employ one or more assistants, up to a maximum of 1.0 FTE, as may be necessary to carry out his or her duties; and

(II) Shall track inquiries and complaints and report annually to the director of the division of real estate regarding the number and types of inquiries and complaints received.

(4) The operating expenses of the HOA information and resource center shall be paid from the HOA information and resource center cash fund, which fund is hereby created in the state treasury. The fund shall consist of annual registration fees paid by unit owners' associations and collected by the division of real estate pursuant to section 38-33.3-401, C.R.S. Interest earned on moneys in the fund shall remain in the fund, and any unexpended and unencumbered moneys in the fund at the end of any fiscal year shall not revert to the general fund or any other fund. Payments from the fund shall be subject to annual appropriation.

(5) The director of the division of real estate may adopt rules as necessary to implement this section and section 38-33.3-401, C.R.S. This subsection (5) shall not be construed to confer additional rule-making authority upon the director for any other purpose.

(6) This section is repealed, effective September 1, 2020. Prior to such repeal, the HOA information and resource center and the HOA information officer's powers and duties under this section shall be reviewed in accordance with section 24-34-104, C.R.S.

§ 38-33.3-401, C.R.S. Registration – annual fees.

(1) Every unit owners' association organized under section 38-33.3-301 shall register annually with the director of the division of real estate, in the form and manner specified by the director.

(2) (a) Except as otherwise provided in paragraph (b) of this subsection (2), the annual registration shall be accompanied by a fee in the amount set by the director in accordance with section 12-61-111.5, C.R.S., and shall include the information required to be disclosed under section 38-33.3-209.4 (1). The information shall be updated within ninety days of any change, in accordance with section 38-33.3-209.4 (1).

(b) A unit owners' association shall be exempt from the fee, but not the registration requirement, if the association:

(I) Has annual revenues of five thousand dollars or less; or

(II) Is not authorized to make assessments and does not have any revenue.

(3) A registration shall be valid for one year. An association that fails to register, or whose annual registration has expired, is ineligible to impose or enforce a lien for assessments under section 38-33.3-316 or to pursue any action or employ any enforcement mechanism otherwise available to it under section 38-33.3-123 until it is again validly registered pursuant to this section. A lien for assessments previously filed during a period in which the association was validly registered or before registration was required pursuant to this section shall not be extinguished by a lapse in the association's registration, but any pending enforcement proceedings related to such lien

shall be suspended, and any applicable time limits tolled, until the association is again validly registered pursuant to this section.

(4) Administratively final determinations by the director of the division of real estate concerning the validity or timeliness of registrations under this section are subject to judicial review pursuant to section 24-4-106 (11), C.R.S.

Editor's note: This section is effective January 1, 2011.

Position Statement – HOA 1.1 – Registration Requirements for CCIOA-Exempt Homeowners' Associations

§ 38-33.3-401, C.R.S. requires "every unit owners' association organized under § 38-33.3-301" to register with the Division of Real Estate. § 38-33.3-103(3), C.R.S. defines a unit owners' association as an association organized under § 38-33.3-301. C.R.S., which became effective on July 1, 1992. This particular statute provides that entities that were not formed prior to that date are exempt from the jurisdiction of the Colorado Common Interest Ownership Act (the "CCIOA-Exempt") with the exception of those enumerated provisions in § 38-33.3-117, C.R.S. Therefore, it is the position of the Director of the Division of Real Estate that homeowners' associations formed prior to July 1, 1992, that have not elected treatment under CCIOA, are not required to comply with the registration requirement set forth in §38-33.3-401(1), C.R.S. (*Issued March 1, 2011*)

V. Licensee's Responsibilities

A real estate licensee cannot be expected to be completely familiar with all county and municipal planning laws, regulations, ordinances, and zoning requirements. However, the licensee in negotiations should be very much aware of the existence of these laws, ordinances, zoning requirements, etc. It is very easy to misrepresent property through ignorance. If uninformed, the licensee should seek the information from the proper source before making a representation, or refer prospective clients to the proper source of the information.

Some facts should be known to the licensee through reading or logic, such as:

1. The sale of a portion of a seller's land divides the land into two parcels and a subdivision is created that must be approved by the proper authorities.
2. If a structure is suitable for conversion into a duplex and/or a four-plex, it does not in itself mean that such a conversion does not violate the law.
3. If an area is zoned for keeping horses, it does not necessarily follow that the acreage of the property is great enough for this purpose.
4. Even if an area is zoned for a home business, there may be a prohibition against having employees. Other complexities may also arise through various branches of local government involving utilities existent and future utilities. Representations concerning future services, zoning variances, etc. may endanger both the public and the licensee.

The following may also be subdivisions under county planning laws: the conversion of an existing building into a common interest community complex or the division of a single condominium unit into "time shares" or "interval estates." These are subdivisions as defined in § 12-61-401(3), C.R.S., and are subject to the registration requirements of §§ 12-61-401, *et seq.*, C.R.S.

A stock cooperative or cooperative housing corporation is defined in this chapter, and in Colorado is considered a subdivision of real estate. The sale of these "apartments" is accomplished by transfer of a stock certificate, together with a proprietary lease. In most states, the sale of the stock, together with the lease, would be considered the sale of a security and would fall under the jurisdiction of the division of securities. In Colorado, such sales are exempt from the Securities Act and are declared real estate (see §§ 38-33.5-101, *et seq.*, C.R.S., printed in this chapter). Therefore, such cooperatives must be registered as subdivisions, and the sale of the stock and proprietary leases must be performed by licensed real estate brokers. The act also provides that commercial banks and savings and loan associations may make a first mortgage loan on the stock and proprietary lease of each "apartment" owner.

VI. Condominium Ownership Act

Title 38, Article 33, C.R.S. – Condominium Ownership Act

Also see Colorado Common Interest Ownership Act in Part X of this chapter

Note: The portions printed below are only those portions of the old condominium act that pertain to timeshare and conversion projects and that are still in place. This Condominium Act was *superseded* by the Colorado Common Interest Ownership Act July 1, 1992.

§ 38-33-110, C.R.S. Time-sharing – definitions.

As used in this section and section 38-33-111, unless the context otherwise requires:

(1) (a) "Interval estate" means a combination of:

(I) An estate for years terminating on a date certain, during which years title to a time share unit circulates among the interval owners in accordance with a fixed schedule, vesting in each such interval owner in turn for a period of time established by the said schedule, with the series thus established recurring annually until the arrival of the date certain; and

(II) A vested future interest in the same unit, consisting of an undivided interest in the remainder in fee simple, the magnitude of the future interest having been established by the time of the creation of the interval estate either by the project instruments or by the deed conveying the interval estate. The estate for years shall not be deemed to merge with the future interest, but neither the estate for years nor the future interest shall be conveyed or encumbered separately from the other.

(b) "Interval estate" also means an estate for years as described in subparagraph (1) of paragraph (a) of this subsection (1), where the remainder estate, as defined either by the project instruments or by the deed conveying the interval estate, is retained by the developer or his successors in interest.

(2) "Interval owner" means a person vested with legal title to an interval estate.

(3) "Interval unit" means a unit the title to which is or is to be divided into interval estates.

(4) "Project instruments" means the declaration, the bylaws, and any other set of restrictions or restrictive covenants, by whatever name denominated, which limit or restrict the use or occupancy of condominium units. "Project instruments" includes any lawful amendments to such instruments. "Project instruments" does not include any ordinance or other public regulation governing subdivisions, zoning, or other land use matters.

(5) "Time share estate" means either an interval estate or a time-span estate.

(6) "Time share owner" means a person vested with legal title to a time share estate.

(7) "Time share unit" means a unit the title to which is or is to be divided either into interval estates or time-span estates.

(8) "Time-span estate" means a combination of:

(a) An undivided interest in a present estate in fee simple in a unit, the magnitude of the interest having been established by the time of the creation of the time-span estate either by the project instruments or by the deed conveying the time-span estate; and

(b) An exclusive right to possession and occupancy of the unit during an annually recurring period of time defined and established by a recorded schedule set forth or referred to in the deed conveying the time-span estate.

(9) "Time-span owner" means a person vested with legal title to a time-span estate.

(10) "Time-span unit" means a unit the title to which is or is to be divided into time-span estates.

(11) "Unit owner" means a person vested with legal title to a unit, and in the case of a time share unit, "unit owner" means all of the time share owners of that unit. When an estate is subject to a deed of trust or a trust deed "unit owner" means the person entitled to beneficial enjoyment of the estate and not to any trustee or trustees holding title merely as security for an obligation.

§ 38-33-111, C.R.S. Special provisions applicable to time share ownership.

(1) No time share estates shall be created with respect to any condominium unit except pursuant to provisions in the project instruments expressly permitting the creation of such estates. Each time share estate shall constitute for all purposes an estate or interest in real property, separate and distinct from all other time share estates in the same unit or any other unit, and such estates maybe separately conveyed and encumbered.

(2) Repealed.

(3) With respect to each time share unit, each owner of a time share estate therein shall be individually liable to the unit owners' association or corporation for all assessments, property taxes both real and personal, and charges levied pursuant to the project instruments against or with respect to that unit, and such association or corporation shall be liable for the payment thereof, except to the extent that such instruments provide to the contrary. However, with respect to each other, each time share owner shall be responsible only for a fraction of such assessments, property taxes both real and personal, and charges proportionate to the magnitude of his undivided interest in the fee to the unit.

(4) No person shall have standing to bring suit for partition of any time share unit except in accordance with such procedures, conditions, restrictions, and limitations as the project instruments and the deeds to the time share estates may specify. Upon the entry of a final order in such a suit, it shall be conclusively presumed that all such procedures, conditions, restrictions, and limitations were adhered to.

(5) In the event that any condemnation award, any insurance proceeds, the proceeds of any sale, or any other sums shall become payable to all of the time share owners of a unit, the portion payable to each time share owner shall be proportionate to the magnitude of his undivided interest in the fee to the unit.

§ 38-33-112, C.R.S. Notification to residential tenants.

(1) A developer who converts an existing multiple-unit dwelling into condominium units, upon recording of the declaration as required by section 38-33-105, shall notify each residential tenant of the dwelling of such conversion.

(2) Such notice shall be in writing and shall be sent by certified or registered mail, postage prepaid, and return receipt provided. Notice is complete upon mailing to the tenant at the tenant's last known address. Notice may also be made by delivery in person to the tenant of a copy of such written notice, in which event notice is complete upon such delivery.

(3) Said notice constitutes the notice to terminate the tenancy as provided by section 13-40-107, C.R.S.; except that no residential tenancy shall be terminated prior to the expiration date of the existing lease agreement, if any, unless consented to by both the tenant and the developer. If the term of the lease has less than ninety days remaining when notification is mailed or delivered, as the case may be, or if there is no written lease agreement, residential tenancy may not be terminated by the developer less than ninety days after the date the notice is mailed or delivered, as the case may be, to the tenant, unless consented to by both the tenant and the developer. The return receipt shall be prima facie evidence of receipt of notice. If the term of the lease has less than ninety days remaining when notification is mailed or delivered, as the case may be, the tenant may hold over for the remainder of said ninety-day period under me same terms and conditions of the lease agreement if the tenant makes timely rental payments and performs other conditions of the lease agreement.

(4) The tenancy may be terminated within the ninety days prescribed in subsection (3) of this section upon agreement by the tenant in consideration of the payment of all moving expenses by the developer or for such other consideration as mutually agreed upon. Such tenancy may also be terminated within the ninety days prescribed in subsection (3) of this section upon failure by the tenant to make timely rental or lease payments.

(5) Any person who applies for a residential tenancy after the recording of the 'declaration shall be informed of this recording at the time of application, and any leases executed after such recording may provide for termination within less than ninety days provided that the terms of the lease conspicuously disclose the intention to convert the property containing the leased premises to condominium ownership.

(6) The general assembly hereby finds and declares that the notification procedure set forth in this section is a matter of statewide concern. No county, municipality, or other political subdivision whether or not vested with home rule powers under article XX of the Colorado constitution, shall adopt or enforce any ordinance, rule, regulation, or policy which conflicts with the provisions of this section.

§ 38-33-113, C.R.S. License to sell condominiums and time-shares.

The general assembly hereby finds and declares that the licensing of persons to sell condominiums and time-shares is a matter of statewide concern.

VII. Municipal Planning and Zoning Laws

Sections 31-23-101 through -313, C.R.S., address municipal planning and zoning in incorporated areas of the state. A "subdivision" also is defined as a division of a parcel of land into two or more parcels. The definition includes condominiums, apartments, and multiple-dwelling units.

Sections 31-23-201, *et seq.*, C.R.S., authorize the creation of a municipal planning commission, which must make or adopt a master plan that, among other things, includes a zoning plan. This planning commission has all the powers of a zoning commission.

The zoning commission must approve subdivisions. Developers who sell land from an unapproved subdivision are subject to a financial penalty, and the zoning commission may also enjoin any such sale. Note that even though the Subdivision Act, in § 12-61-402(2), C.R.S., allows for the use of a reservation agreement prior to final approval by the Real Estate Commission, the developer should check with the municipality regarding the use of reservation agreements. The governing body of a municipality provides for the appointment of a board of adjustment that hears appeals made from any ordinance or order of any administrative official. This board may grant variances from an ordinance or reverse an order.

VIII. County Planning Laws

In addition to the provisions of the Subdivision Act, jurisdiction concerning the use of land within Colorado also falls within the powers of the county commissioners of each county. The county commissioners have the authority to enact zoning law for un-incorporated areas, and many counties have done so. Prior to surveying and offering subdivided property, a developer or real estate licensee should contact the county planning and zoning department regarding compliance with the county's requirements.

In regard to a county commissioner's jurisdiction, §§ 30-28-101 through -209, C.R.S., define a subdivision as any parcel of land that is divided into two or more parcels, separate interests, or interests in common. "Interests" means interests in surface land or in the air above the surface of the land, but excludes sub-surface interests. Divisions of land that create parcels of 35 acres or more and of which none is intended for use by multiple owners are exempt.

Condominiums, apartments, and multiple dwellings are included in the definition, unless they had been previously included in a filing with substantially the same density.

Subdivisions must submit the following information to the county authorities before sales within the subdivision are made:

1. Survey and ownership;
2. Site characteristics, such as topography;
3. A plat showing the plan of development and plan of the completed development;
4. Estimates of the water and sewage requirements, streets, utilities, and related facilities and estimated construction cost;
5. Evidence to ensure an adequate supply of potable water; and
6. Dedication of areas for public facilities.

Upon request of a complete preliminary plan, copies will be distributed to 10 interested public agencies for recommendations. An approved plat must be recorded before any lots are sold.

No plat will be approved until the subdivision has submitted a subdivision improvement contract agreeing to construct the required improvements, accompanied by collateral sufficient to ensure completion of the improvements.

The county commissioners must approve a final plat of the subdivision before it can be filed and recorded. Violations by a subdivider or agent of a subdivider are punishable by a fine of up to $1,000 for each parcel sold or offered for sale by a subdivider or agent of a subdivider. A sale made before a final plat is approved is considered prima facie evidence of a fraudulent sale and is grounds for the purchaser voiding the sale. The county commissioners also have the power to bring an action to enjoin any subdivider from offering to sell undivided land before a final plat has been approved.

IX. Special Types of Subdivisions

A. Condominiums as Subdivisions

"Estates above the surface" may be created in areas above the surface of the ground, and title to such "air rights" may be conveyed separate from title to the surface of the ground.

It follows that a division of air rights is a subdivision under county planning laws. A declaration must be recorded with the county and must be approved by county authorities. The declaration must provide for the recording of a map properly locating the condominium units. It is similar to the filing of a plat of surface land insofar as it describes each unit. The division however, is a division of the air space.

The conversion of an existing building into a condominium complex or the division of a single condominium unit into "time shares" or "interval estates" also may be a subdivision under county planning laws, and are considered a subdivision as defined in § 12-61-401(3), C.R.S., and subject to the registration requirements of §§ 12-61-401, *et seq.*, C.R.S.

X. Colorado Common Interest Ownership Act

§ 38-33.3-101, C.R.S. Short title.

This article shall be known and may be cited as the "Colorado Common Interest Ownership Act".

§ 38-33.3-102, C.R.S. Legislative declaration.

(1) The general assembly hereby finds, determines, and declares, as follows:

- (a) That it is in the best interests of the state and its citizens to establish a clear, comprehensive, and uniform framework for the creation and operation of common interest communities;
- (b) That the continuation of the economic prosperity of Colorado is dependent upon the strengthening of homeowner associations in common interest communities financially through the setting of budget guidelines, the creation of statutory assessment liens, the granting of six months' lien priority, the facilitation of borrowing, and more certain powers in the association to sue on behalf of the owners and through enhancing the financial stability of associations by increasing the association's powers to collect delinquent assessments, late charges, fines, and enforcement costs;
- (c) That it is the policy of this state to give developers flexible development rights with specific obligations within a uniform structure of development of a common interest community that extends through the transition to owner control;
- (d) That it is the policy of this state to promote effective and efficient property management through defined operational requirements that preserve flexibility for such homeowner associations;
- (e) That it is the policy of this state to promote the availability of funds for financing the development of such homeowner associations by enabling lenders to extend the financial services to a greater market on a safer, more predictable basis because of standardized practices and prudent insurance and risk management obligations.

§ 38-33.3-103, C.R.S. Definitions.

As used in the declaration and bylaws of an association, unless specifically provided otherwise or unless the context otherwise requires, and in this article:

(1) "Affiliate of a declarant" means any person who controls, is controlled by, or is under common control with a declarant. A person controls a declarant if the person: is a general partner, officer, director, or employee of the declarant; directly or indirectly, or acting in concert with one or more other persons or through one or more subsidiaries, owns, controls, holds with power to vote, or holds proxies representing more than twenty percent of the voting interests of the declarant; controls in any manner the election of a majority of the directors of the declarant, or has contributed more than twenty percent of the capital of the declarant. A person is controlled by a declarant if the declarant: is a general partner, officer, director, or employee of the person; directly or indirectly, or acting in concert with one or more other persons or through one or more subsidiaries, owns, controls, holds with power to vote, or holds proxies representing more than twenty percent of the voting interests of the person; controls in any manner the election of a majority of the directors of the person; or has contributed more than twenty percent of the capital of the person. Control does not exist if the powers described in this subsection (1) are held solely as security for an obligation and are not exercised.

(2) "Allocated interests" means the following interests allocated to each unit:

(a) In a condominium, the undivided interest in the common elements, the common expense liability, and votes in the association;

(b) In a cooperative, the common expense liability and the ownership interest and votes in the association; and

(c) In a planned community, the common expense liability and votes in the association.

(2.5) "Approved for Development" means that all or some portion of a particular parcel of real property is zoned or otherwise approved for construction of residential and other improvements and authorized for specified densities by the local land use authority having jurisdiction over such real property and includes any conceptual or final planned unit development approval.

(3) "Association" or "unit owners' association" means a unit owners' association organized under section 38-33.3-301.

(4) "Bylaws" means any instruments, however denominated, which are adopted by the association for the regulation and management of the association, including any amendments to those instruments.

(5) "Common elements" means:

(a) In a condominium or cooperative, all portions of the condominium or cooperative other than the units; and

(b) In a planned community, any real estate within a planned community owned or leased by the association, other than a unit.

(6) "Common expense liability" means the liability for common expenses allocated to each unit pursuant to section 38-33.3-207.

(7) "Common expenses" means expenditures made or liabilities incurred by or on behalf of the association, together with any allocations to reserves.

(8) "Common interest community" means real estate described in a declaration with respect to which a person, by virtue of such person's ownership of a unit, is obligated to pay for real estate taxes, insurance premiums, maintenance or improvement of other real estate described in a declaration. Ownership of a unit does not include holding a leasehold interest in a unit of less than forty years, including renewal options. The period of the leasehold interest, including renewal options, is measured from the date the initial term commences.

(9) "Condominium" means a common interest community in which portions of the real estate are designated for separate ownership and the remainder of which is designated for common ownership solely by the owners of the separate ownership portions. A common interest community is not a condominium unless the undivided interests in the common elements are vested in the unit owners.

(10) "Cooperative" means a common interest community in which the real property is owned by an association, each member of which is entitled by virtue of such member's ownership interest in the association to exclusive possession of a unit.

(11) "Dealer" means a person in the business of selling units for such person's own account.

(12) "Declarant" means any person or group of persons acting in concert who:

(a) As part of a common promotional plan, offers to dispose of to a purchaser such declarant's interest in a unit not previously disposed of to a purchaser; or

(b) Reserves or succeeds to any special declarant right.

(13) "Declaration" means any recorded instruments however denominated, that create a common interest community, including any amendments to those instruments and also including, but not limited to, plats and maps.

(14) "Development rights" means any right or combination of rights reserved by a declarant in the declaration to:

(a) Add real estate to a common interest community;

(b) Create units, common elements, or limited common elements within a common interest community;

(c) Subdivide units or convert units into common elements; or

(d) Withdraw real estate from a common interest community.

(15) "Dispose" or "disposition" means a voluntary transfer of any legal or equitable interest in a unit, but the term does not include the transfer or release of a security interest.

(16) "Executive board" means the body, regardless of name, designated in the declaration to act on behalf of the association.

(16.5) "Horizontal boundary" means a plane of elevation relative to a described benchmark that defines either a lower or an upper dimension of a unit such that the real estate respectively below or above the defined plane is not a part of the unit.

(17) "Identifying number" means a symbol or address that identifies only one unit in a common interest community.

(17.5) "Large planned community" means a planned community that meets the criteria set forth in section 38-33.3-116.3(1).

(18) "Leasehold common interest community" means a common interest community in which all or a portion of the real estate is subject to a lease, the expiration or termination of which will terminate the common interest community or reduce its size.

(19) "Limited common element" means a portion of the common elements allocated by the declaration or by operation of section 38-33.3-202 .(1) (b) or (1) (d) for the exclusive use of one or more units but fewer than all of the units.

(19.5) "Map" means that part of a declaration that depicts all or any portion of a common interest community in three dimensions, is executed by a person that is authorized by this title to execute a declaration relating to the common interest community, and is recorded in the real estate records in every county in which any portion of the common interest community is located. A map is required for a common interest community with units having a horizontal boundary. A map and a plat may be combined in one instrument.

(20) "Master association" means an organization that is authorized to exercise some or all of the powers of one or more associations on behalf of one or more common interest communities or for the benefit of the unit owners of one or more common interest communities.

(21) "Person" means a natural person a corporation, a partnership, an association, a trust or any other entity or any combination thereof.

(21.5) "Phased Community" means a common interest community in which the declarant retains development rights.

(22) "Planned community" means a common interest community that is not a condominium or cooperative. A condominium or cooperative may be part of a planned community.

(22.5) "Plat" means that part of a declaration that is a land survey plat as set forth in section 38-51-106 depicts all or any portion of a common interest community in two dimensions is executed by a person that is authorized by this title to execute a declaration relating to the common interest community, and is recorded in the real estate records in every county in which any portion of the common interest community is located. A plat and a map may be combined in one instrument.

(23) "Proprietary lease" means an agreement with the association pursuant to which a member is entitled to exclusive possession of a unit in a cooperative.

(24) "Purchaser" means a person, other than a declarant or a dealers who by means of a transfer acquires a legal or equitable interest in a unit, other than:

(a) A leasehold interest in a unit of less than forty years, including renewal options, with the period of the leasehold interests including renewal options, being measured from the date the initial term commences; or

(b) A security interest.

(25) "Real estate" means any leasehold or other estate or interest in, over, or under land including structures, fixtures, and other improvements and interests that, by customs usage, or laws pass with a conveyance of land though not described in the contract of sale or instrument of conveyance. "Real estate" includes parcels with or without horizontal boundaries and spaces that may be filled with air or water.

(26) "Residential use" means use for dwelling or recreational purposes but does not include spaces or units primarily used for commercial income from, or service to, the public.

(27) "Rules and regulations" means any instruments, however denominated, which are adopted by the association for the regulation and management of the common interest community, including any amendment to those instruments.

(28) "Security interest" means an interest in real estate or personal property created by contract or conveyance which secures payment or performance of an obligation. The term includes a lien created by a mortgage, deed of trust, trust deed, security deed, contract for deed, land sales contract, lease intended as security, assignment of lease or rents intended as security, pledge of an ownership interest in an association, and any other consensual lien or title retention contract intended as security for an obligation.

(29) "Special declarant rights" means rights reserved for the benefit of a declarant to perform the following acts as specified in parts 2 and 3 of this article: To complete improvements indicated on plats and maps filed with the declaration; to exercise any development right; to maintain sales offices, management offices, signs advertising the common interest community, and models; to use easements through the common elements for the purpose of making improvements within the common interest community or within real estate which may be added to the common interest community; to make the common interest community subject to a master association; to merge or consolidate a common interest community of the same form of ownership; or to appoint or remove any officer of the association or any executive board member during any period of declarant control.

(30) "Unit" means a physical portion of the common interest community which is designated for separate ownership or occupancy and the boundaries of which are described in or determined from the declaration. If a unit in a cooperative is owned by a unit owner or is sold, conveyed, voluntarily or involuntarily encumbered, or otherwise transferred by a unit owner, the interest in that unit which is owned, sold, conveyed, encumbered, or otherwise transferred is the right to

possession of that unit under a proprietary lease, coupled with the allocated interests of that unit, and the association's interest in that unit is not thereby affected.

(31) "Unit owner" means the declarant or other person who owns a unit, or a lessee of a unit in a leasehold common interest community whose lease expires simultaneously with any lease, the expiration or termination of which will remove the unit from the common interest community but does not include a person having an interest in a unit solely as security for an obligation. In a condominium or planned community, the declarant is the owner of any unit created by the declaration until that unit is conveyed to another person, in a cooperative, the declarant is treated as the owner of any unit to which allocated interests have been allocated pursuant to section 38-33.3-207 until that unit has been conveyed to another person, who may or may not be a declarant under this article.

(32) "Vertical boundary" means the defined limit of a unit that is not a horizontal boundary of that unit.

§ 38-33.3-104, C.R.S. Variation by agreement.

Except as expressly provided in this article, provisions of this article may not be varied by agreement, and rights conferred by this article may not be waived. A declarant may not act under a power of attorney or use any other device to evade the limitations or prohibitions of this article or the declaration.

§ 38-33.3-105, C.R.S. Separate titles and taxation.

(1) In a cooperative, unless the declaration provides that a unit owner's interest in a unit and its allocated interests is personal property, that interest is real estate for all purposes.

(2) In a condominium or planned community with common elements, each unit that has been created, together with its interest m the common elements, constitutes for all purposes a separate parcel of real estate and must be separately assessed and taxed. The valuation of the common elements shall be assessed proportionately to each unit, in the case of a condominium in accordance with such unit's allocated interests in the common elements, and in the case of a planned community in accordance with such unit's allocated common expense liability, set forth in the declaration, and the common elements shall not be separately taxed or assessed. Upon the filing for recording of a declaration for a condominium or planned community with common elements, the declarant shall deliver a copy of such filing to the assessor of each county in which such declaration was filed.

(3) In a planned community without common elements, the real estate comprising such planned community may be taxed and assessed in any manner provided by law.

§ 38-33.3-106, C.R.S. Applicability of local ordinances, regulations, and building codes.

(1) A building code may not impose any requirement upon any structure in a common interest community which it would not impose upon a physically identical development under a different form of ownership; except that a minimum one hour fire wall may be required between units,

(2) In condominiums and cooperatives, no zoning, subdivision, or other real estate use law, ordinance, or regulation may prohibit the condominium or cooperative form of ownership or impose any requirement upon a condominium or cooperative which it would not impose upon a physically identical development under a different form of ownership.

§ 38-33.3-106.5, C.R.S. Prohibitions contrary to public policy – patriotic and political expression – emergency vehicles – fire prevention – renewable energy generation devices – affordable housing – definitions.

(1) Notwithstanding any provision in the declaration, bylaws, or rules and regulations of the association to the contrary, an association shall not prohibit any of the following:

(a) The display of the American flag on a unit owner's property, in a window of the unit, or on a balcony adjoining the unit if the American flag is displayed in a manner consistent with the federal flag code, P.L. 94-344; 90 stat. 810; 4 U.S.C. secs. 4 to 10. The association may adopt reasonable rules regarding the placement and manner of display of the American flag. The association rules may regulate the location and size of flags and flagpoles, but shall not prohibit the installation of a flag or flagpole.

(b) The display of a service flag bearing a star denoting the service of the owner or occupant of the unit, or of a member of the owner's or occupant's immediate family, in the active or reserve military service of the United States during a time of war or armed conflict, on the inside of a window or door of the unit. The association may adopt reasonable rules regarding the size and manner of display of service flags; except that the maximum dimensions allowed shall be not less than nine inches by sixteen inches.

(c) (I) The display of a political sign by the owner or occupant of a unit on property within the boundaries of the unit or in a window of the unit; except that:

(A) An association may prohibit the display of political signs earlier than forty-five days before the day of an election and later than seven days after an election day; and

(B) An association may regulate the size and number of political signs in accordance with subparagraph (II) of this paragraph (c).

(II) The association shall permit at least one political sign per political office or ballot issue that is contested in a pending election. The maximum dimensions of each sign may be limited to the lesser of the following:

(A) The maximum size allowed by any applicable city, town, or county ordinance that regulates the size of political signs on residential property; or

(B) Thirty-six inches by forty-eight inches.

(III) As used in this paragraph (c), "political sign" means a sign that carries a message intended to influence the outcome of an election, including supporting or opposing the election of a candidate, the recall of a public official, or the passage of a ballot issue.

(d) The parking of a motor vehicle by the occupant of a unit on a street, driveway, or guest parking area in the common interest community if the vehicle is required to be available at designated periods at such occupant's residence as a condition of the occupant's employment and all of the following criteria are met:

(I) The vehicle has a gross vehicle weight rating of ten thousand pounds or less;

(II) The occupant is a bona fide member of a volunteer fire department or is employed by a primary provider of emergency fire fighting, law enforcement, ambulance, or emergency medical services;

(III) The vehicle bears an official emblem or other visible designation of the emergency service provider; and

(IV) Parking of the vehicle can be accomplished without obstructing emergency access or interfering with the reasonable needs of other unit owners or occupants to use streets, driveways, and guest parking spaces within the common interest community.

(e) The removal by a unit owner of trees, shrubs, or other vegetation to create defensible space around a dwelling for fire mitigation purposes, so long as such removal complies with a written defensible space plan created for the property by the Colorado state forest service, an individual or company certified by a local governmental entity to create such a plan, or the fire chief, fire marshal, or fire protection district within whose jurisdiction the unit is located, and is no more extensive than necessary to comply with such plan. The plan shall be registered with the association before the commencement of work. The association may require changes to the plan if the association obtains the consent of the person, official, or agency that originally created the plan. The work shall comply with applicable association standards regarding slash removal, stump height, revegetation, and contractor regulations.

(f) (Deleted by amendment, L. 2006, p. 1215, § 2, effective May 26, 2006.)

(g) Reasonable modifications to a unit or to common elements as necessary to afford a person with disabilities full use and enjoyment of the unit in accordance with the federal "Fair Housing Act of 1968", 42 U.S.C. sec. 3604 (f) (3) (A).

(h) (I) The right of a unit owner, public or private, to restrict or specify by deed, covenant, or other document:

(A) The permissible sale price, rental rate, or lease rate of the unit; or

(B) Occupancy or other requirements designed to promote affordable or workforce housing as such terms may be defined by the local housing authority.

(II) (A) Notwithstanding any other provision of law, the provisions of this paragraph (h) shall only apply to a county the population of which is less than one-hundred thousand persons and that contains a ski lift licensed by the passenger tramway safety board created in section 25-5-703 (1), C.R.S.

(B) The provisions of this paragraph (h) shall not apply to a declarant-controlled community.

(III) Nothing in subparagraph (I) of this paragraph (h) shall be construed to prohibit the future owner of a unit against which a restriction or specification described in such subparagraph has been placed from lifting such restriction or specification on such unit as long as any unit so released is replaced by another unit in the same common interest community on which the restriction or specification applies and the unit subject to the restriction or specification is reasonably equivalent to the unit being released in the determination of the beneficiary of the restriction or specification.

(IV) Except as otherwise provided in the declaration of the common interest community, any unit subject to the provisions of this paragraph (h) shall only be occupied by the owner of the unit.

(1.5) Notwithstanding any provision in the declaration, bylaws, or rules and regulations of the association to the contrary, an association shall not effectively prohibit renewable energy generation devices, as defined in section 38-30-168.

(2) Notwithstanding any provision in the declaration, bylaws, or rules and regulations of the association to the contrary, an association shall not require the use of cedar shakes or other flammable roofing materials.

§ 38-33.3-106.7, C.R.S. Unreasonable restrictions on energy efficiency measures – definitions.

(1) (a) Notwithstanding any provision in the declaration, bylaws, or rules and regulations of the association to the contrary, an association shall not effectively prohibit the installation or use of an energy efficiency measure.

(b) As used in this section, "energy efficiency measure" means a device or structure that reduces the amount of energy derived from fossil fuels that is consumed by a residence or business located on the real property. "Energy efficiency measure" is further limited to include only the following types of devices or structures:

(I) An awning, shutter, trellis, ramada, or other shade structure that is marketed for the purpose of reducing energy consumption;

(II) A garage or attic fan and any associated vents or louvers;

(III) An evaporative cooler;

(IV) An energy-efficient outdoor lighting device, including without limitation a light fixture containing a coiled or straight fluorescent light bulb, and any solar recharging panel, motion detector, or other equipment connected to the lighting device; and

(V) A retractable clothesline.

(2) Subsection (1) of this section shall not apply to:

(a) Reasonable aesthetic provisions that govern the dimensions, placement, or external appearance of an energy efficiency measure. In creating reasonable aesthetic provisions, common interest communities shall consider:

(I) The impact on the purchase price and operating costs of the energy efficiency measure;

(II) The impact on the performance of the energy efficiency measure; and

(III) The criteria contained in the governing documents of the common interest community.

(b) Bona fide safety requirements, consistent with an applicable building code or recognized safety standard, for the protection of persons and property.

(3) This section shall not be construed to confer upon any property owner the right to place an energy efficiency measure on property that is:

(a) Owned by another person;

(b) Leased, except with permission of the lessor;

(c) Collateral for a commercial loan, except with permission of the secured party; or

(d) A limited common element or general common element of a common interest community.

§ 38-33.3-107, C.R.S. Eminent domain.

(1) If a unit is acquired by eminent domain or part of a unit is acquired by eminent domain leaving the unit owner with a remnant which may not practically or lawfully be used for any purpose permitted by the declaration, the award must include compensation to the unit owner for that unit and its allocated interests whether or not any common elements are acquired. Upon acquisition, unless the decree otherwise provides, that unit's allocated interests are automatically reallocated to the remaining units in proportion to the respective allocated interests of those units before the taking. Any remnant of a unit remaining after part of a unit is taken under this subsection (1) is thereafter a common element.

(2) Except as provided in subsection (1) of this section, if part of a unit is acquired by eminent domain, the award must .compensate the unit owner for the reduction in value of the unit and its interest in the common elements whether or not any common elements are acquired. Upon acquisition, unless the decree otherwise provides:

(a) That unit's allocated interests are reduced in proportion to the reduction in the size of the unit or on any other basis specified in the declaration; and

(a) The portion of allocated interests divested from the partially acquired unit is automatically reallocated to that unit and to the remaining units in proportion to the respective interests of those units before the taking, with the partially acquired unit participating in the reallocation on the basis of its reduced allocated interests.

(3) If part of the common elements is acquired by eminent domain, that portion of any award attributable to the common elements taken must be paid to the association. Unless the declaration provides otherwise, any portion of the award attributable to the acquisition of a limited common element must be equally divided among the owners of the units to which that limited common element was allocated at the time of acquisition. For the purposes of acquisition of a part of the common elements other than the limited common elements under this subsection (3), service of process on the association shall constitute sufficient notice to all unit owners, and service of process on each individual unit owner shall not be necessary.

(4) The court decree shall be recorded in every county in which any portion of the common interest community is located.

(5) The reallocations of allocated interests pursuant to this section shall be confirmed by an amendment to the declaration prepared, executed, and recorded by the association.

§ 38-33.3-108, C.R.S. Supplemental general principles of law applicable.

The principles of law and equity, including, but not limited to, the law of corporations and unincorporated associations, the law of real property, and the law relative to capacity to contract, principal and agent, eminent domain, estoppel, fraud, misrepresentation, duress, coercion, mistake, receivership, substantial performance, or other validating or invalidating cause supplement the provisions of this article, except to the extent inconsistent with this article.

§ 38-33.3-109, C.R.S. Construction against implicit repeal.

This article is intended to be a unified coverage of its subject matter, and no part of this article shall be construed to be impliedly repealed by subsequent legislation if that construction can reasonably be avoided.

§ 38-33.3-110, C.R.S. Uniformity of application and construction.

This article shall be applied and construed so as to effectuate its general purpose to make uniform the law with respect to the subject of this article among states enacting it.

§ 38-33.3-111, C.R.S. Severability.

If any provision of this article or the application thereof to any person or circumstances is held invalid, the invalidity shall not affect other provisions or applications of this article which can be given effect without the invalid provisions or application, and, to this end, the provisions of this article are severable.

§ 38-33.3-112, C.R.S. Unconscionable agreement or term of contract.

(1) The court, upon finding as a matter of law that a contract or contract clause relating to a common interest community was unconscionable at the time the contract was made, may refuse to enforce the contract, enforce the remainder of the contract without the unconscionable clause, or limit the application of any unconscionable clause in order to avoid an unconscionable result.

(2) Whenever it is claimed, or appears to the court, that a contract or any contract clause relating to a common interest community is or may be unconscionable, the parties, in order to aid the court in making the determination, shall be afforded a reasonable opportunity to present evidence as to:

(a) The commercial setting of the negotiations;

(b) Whether the first party has knowingly taken advantage of the inability of the second party reasonably to protect such second party's interests by reason of physical or mental infirmity, illiteracy, or inability to understand the language of the agreement or similar factors;

(c) The effect and purpose of the contract or clause; and

(d) If a sale, any gross disparity at the time of contracting between the amount charged for the property and the value of that property measured by the price at which similar property was readily obtainable in similar transactions. A disparity between the contract price and the value of the property measured by the price at which similar property was readily obtainable in similar transactions does not, of itself, render the contract unconscionable.

§ 38-33.3-113, C.R.S. Obligation of good faith.

Every contract or duty governed by this article imposes an obligation of good faith in its performance or enforcement.

§ 38-33.3-114, C.R.S. Remedies to be liberally administered.

(1) The remedies provided by this article shall be liberally administered to the end that the aggrieved party is put in as good a position as if the other party had fully performed. However, consequential, special, or punitive damages may not be awarded except as specifically provided in this article or by other rule of law.

(2) Any right or obligation declared by this article is enforceable by judicial proceeding.

§ 38-33.3-115, C.R.S. Applicability to new common interest communities.

Except as provided in section 38-33.3-116, this article applies to all common interest communities created within this state on or after July 1, 1992. The provisions of sections 38-33-101 to 38-33-109 do not apply to common interest communities created on or after July 1, 1992. The provisions of sections 38-33-110 to 38-33-113 shall remain in effect for all common interest communities.

§ 38-33.3-116, C.R.S. Exception for new small cooperatives and small and limited expense planned communities.

(1) If a cooperative created in this state on or after July 1, 1992, but prior to July 1, 1998, contains only units restricted to nonresidential use, or contains no more than ten units and is not subject to any development rights, it is subject only to sections 38-33.3-105 to 38-33.3-107, unless the declaration provides that this entire article is applicable.If a planned community created in this state on or after July 1, 1992, but prior to July 1, 1998, contains no more than ten units and is not subject to any development rights or if a planned community provides, in its declaration, that the annual average common expense liability of each unit restricted to residential purposes, exclusive of optional user fees and any insurance premiums paid by the association, may not exceed three hundred dollars, it is subject only to sections 38-33.3-105 to 38-33.3-107, unless the declaration provides that this entire article is applicable.

(2) If a cooperative or planned community created in this state on or after July 1, 1998, contains only units restricted to nonresidential use, or contains no more than twenty units and is not subject to any development rights, it is subject only to sections 38-33.3-105 to 38-33.3-107, unless the declaration provides that this entire article is applicable. If a planned community created in this state after July 1, 1998, provides, in its declaration, that the annual average common expense liability of each unit restricted to residential purposes, exclusive of optional user fees and any insurance premiums paid by the association, may not exceed four hundred

dollars, as adjusted pursuant to subsection (3) of this section, it is subject only to sections 38-33.3-105 to 38-33.3-107, unless the declaration provides that this entire article is applicable.

(3) The four-hundred-dollar limitation set forth in subsection (2) of this section shall be increased annually on July 1, 1999, and on July 1 of each succeeding year in accordance with any increase in the United States department of labor, bureau of labor statistics final consumer price index for the Denver-Boulder consolidated metropolitan statistical area for the preceding calendar year. The limitation shall not be increased if the final consumer price index for the preceding calendar year did not increase and shall not be decreased if the final consumer price index for the preceding calendar year decreased.

§ 38-33.3-116.3, C.R.S. Large planned communities – exemption from certain requirements.

(1) A planned community shall be exempt from the provisions of this article as specified in subsection (3) of this section or as specifically exempted in any other provision of this article, if, at the time of recording the affidavit required pursuant to subsection (2) of this section, the real estate upon which the planned community is created meets both of the following requirements:

- (a) It consists of at least two hundred acres;
- (b) It is approved for development of at least five hundred residential units, excluding any interval estates, time-share estates, or time-span estates but including any interval units created pursuant to sections 38-33-110 and 38-33-111, and at least twenty thousand square feet of commercial use.
- (c) deleted by amendment effective 7-1-95
- (d) It is zoned for development of at least two hundred residences and at least twenty thousand square feet of commercial use at the time of recording the affidavit required pursuant to subsection (2) of this section; and
- (e) It meets the definition of a planned community pursuant to section 38-33.3-103 (22).

(2) For an exemption authorized in subsection (1) of this section to apply, the property must be zoned within each county in which any part of such parcel is located, and the owner of the parcel shall record with the county clerk and recorder of each county in which any part of such parcel is located an affidavit setting forth the following:

- (a) The legal description of such parcel of land;
- (b) A statement that the party signing the affidavit is the owner of the parcel in its entirety in fee simple, excluding mineral interests;
- (c) The acreage of the parcel;
- (d) The zoning classification of the parcel, with a certified copy of applicable zoning regulations attached; and
- (e) A statement that neither the owner nor any officer, director, shareholder, partner, or other entity having more than a ten-percent equity interest in the owner has been convicted of a felony within the last ten years.

(3) A large planned community for which an affidavit has been filed pursuant to subsection (2) of this section shall be exempt from the following provisions of this article:

- (a) Section 38-33.3-205 (1) (e) to (1) (m);
- (b) Section 38-33.3-207 (3);
- (c) Section 38-33.3-208;
- (d) Section 38-33.3-209 (2)(b), (2)(c), (2)(d), (2)(f) (2)(g), (4), and (6);
- (e) Section 38-33.3-210;

(f) Section 38-33.3-212;

(g) Section 38-33.3-213;

(h) Section 38-33.3-215;

(i) Section 38-33.3-217(1);

(j) Section 38-33.3-304.

(4) Section 38-33.3-217 (4) shall be applicable as follows: Except to the extent expressly permitted or required by other provisions of this article, no amendment may create or the uses to which any unit is restricted, in the absence of unanimous consent of the unit owners.

(5) (a) The exemption authorized by this section shall continue for the large planned community so long as the owner signing the affidavit is the owner of the real estate described in subsection (2) of this section; except that:

(I) Upon the sale, conveyance, or other transfer of any portion of the real estate within the large planned community, the portion sold, conveyed, or transferred shall become subject to all the provisions of this article;

(II) Any common interest community created on some but not all of the real estate within the large planned community shall be created pursuant to this article; and

(III) When a planned community no longer qualifies as a large planned community, as described in subsection (1) of this section, the exemptions authorized by this section shall no longer be applicable.

(b) Notwithstanding the provisions of subparagraph (HI) of paragraph (a) of this subsection (5), all real estate described in a recorded declaration creating a large planned community shall remain subject to such recorded declaration.

(6) The association established for a large planned community shall operate with respect to large planned community-wide matters and shall not otherwise operate as the exclusive unit owners' association with respect to any unit.

(7) The association established for a large planned community shall keep in its principal office and make reasonably available to all unit owners, unit owners' authorized agents, and prospective purchasers of units a complete legal description of all common elements within the large planned community.

§ 38-33.3-117, C.R.S. Applicability to preexisting common interest communities.

(1) Except as provided in section 38-33.3-119, the following sections shall apply to all common interest communities created within this state before July 1, 1992; with respect to events and circumstances occurring on or after July 1, 1992:

(a) 38-33.3-101 and 38-33.3-102;

(b) 38-33.3-103, to the extent necessary in construing any of the other sections of this article;

(c) 38-33.3-104 to 38-33.3-111;

(d) 38-33.3-114;

(e) 38-33.3-118;

(f) 38-33.3-120;

(g) 38-33.3-122 and 38-33.3-123;

(h) 38-33.3-203; and 38-33.3-217 (7);

(i) 38-33.3-302 (1) (a) to (1) (f), (1) (j) to (1) (m), and (1) (o) to (1) (q);

(i.5) 38-33.3-221.5;

(i.7) 38-33.3-303 (1) (b) and (3) (b);

(j) 38-33.3-311;

(k) 38-33.3-316;

(l) 38-33.-317 as it existed prior to January 1, 2006, 38-33.3-318, and 38-33.3-319.

(1.5) Except as provided in section 38-33.3-119, the following sections shall apply to all common interest communities created within this state before July 1, 1992, with respect to events and circumstances occurring on or after January 1, 2006:

(a) Deleted (May 26, 2006)

(b) 38-33.3-124;

(c) 38-33.3-209.4 TO 38-33.3-209.7;

(d) 38-33.3-217 (1);

(e) Deleted (May 26, 2006);

(f) 38-33.3-301;

(g) 38-33.3-302 (3) and (4);

(h) 38-33.3-303 (1) (b), (3) (b), and (4) (b);

(i) 38-33.3-308 (1), (2) (b), (2.5), and (4.5);

(j) 38-33.3-310 (1) and (2);

(k) 38-33.3-310.5;

(l) 38-33.3-315 (7); and

(m) 38-33.3-317.

(1.7) Except as provided in section 38-33.3-119, section 38-33.3-209.5 (1) (b) (IX) shall apply to all common interest communities created within this state before July 1, 1992, with respect to events and circumstances occurring on or after July 1, 2010.

(2) The sections specified in paragraphs (a) to (j) and (1) of subsection (1) of this section shall be applied and construed to establish a clear, comprehensive, and uniform framework for the operation and management of common interest communities within this state and to supplement the provisions of any declaration, bylaws, plat or map in existence on June 30, 1992. In the event of specific conflicts between the provisions of the sections specified in paragraphs (a) to (j) and (1) of subsection (1) of this section and express requirements or restrictions in a declaration, bylaws, a plat, or a map in existence on June 30, 1992, such requirements or restrictions in the declaration, bylaws, plat, or map shall control, but only to the extent necessary to avoid invalidation of the specific requirement or restriction in the declaration, bylaws, plat, or map. Sections 38-33.3-316 shall be applied and construed as stated in such sections.

(3) Except as expressly provided for in this section, this article shall not apply to common interest communities created within this state before July 1,1992.

(4) Section 38-33.3-308 (2) to (7) shall apply to all common interest communities created within this state before July 1, 1995, and shall apply to all meetings of the executive board of such a community or any committee thereof occurring on or after said date. In addition, said section 38-33.3-308 (2) to (7) shall apply to all common interest communities created on or after July 1, 1995, and shall apply to all meetings of the executive board of such a community or any committee thereof occurring on or after said date.

§ 38-33.3-118, C.R.S. Procedure to elect treatment under the "Colorado common interest ownership act".

(1) Any organization created prior to July 1, 1992, may elect to have the common interest community be treated as if it were created after June 30, 1992, and thereby subject the common interest community to all of the provisions contained in this article, in the following manner:

(a) If there are members or stockholders entitled to vote thereon, the board of directors may adopt a resolution recommending that such association accept this article and directing that the question of acceptance be submitted to a vote at a meeting of the members or stockholders entitled to vote thereon, which may be either an annual or special meeting. The question shall also be submitted whenever one-twentieth, or, in the case of an association with over one thousand members, one-fortieth, of the members or stockholders entitled to vote thereon so request. Written notice stating that the purpose, or one of the purposes, of the meeting is to consider electing to be treated as a common interest community organized after June 30,1992, and thereby accepting the provisions of this article, together with a copy of this article, shall be given to each person entitled to vote at the meeting within the time and in the manner provided in the articles of incorporation, declaration, bylaws, or other governing documents for such association for the giving of notice of meetings to members. Such election to accept the provisions of this article shall require for adoption at least sixty-seven percent of the votes that the persons present at such meeting in person or by proxy are entitled to cast.

(b) If there are no persons entitled to vote thereon, the election to be treated as a common interest community under this article may be made at a meeting of the board of directors pursuant to a majority vote of the directors in office.

(2) A statement of election to accept the provisions of this article shall be executed and acknowledged by the president or vice-president and by the secretary or an assistant secretary of such association and shall set forth:

(a) The name of the common interest community and association;

(b) That the association has elected to accept the provisions of this article;

(c) That there were persons entitled to vote thereon, the date of the meeting of such persons at which the election was made to be treated as a common interest community under this article, that a quorum was present at the meeting, and that such acceptance was authorized by at least sixty-seven percent of the votes that the members or stockholders present at such meeting in person or by proxy were entitled to cast;

(d) That there were no members or stockholders entitled to vote thereon, the date of the meeting of the board of directors at which election to accept this article was made, that a quorum was present at the meeting, and that such acceptance was authorized by a majority vote of the directors present at such meeting;

(e) (deleted by amendment effective 4-30-93)

(f) The names and respective addresses of its officers and directors; and

(g) If there were no persons entitled to vote thereon but a common interest community has been created by virtue of compliance with section 38-33.3-103 (8), that the declarant desires for the common interest community to be subject to all the terms and provisions of this article.

(3) The original statement of election to be treated as a common interest community subject to the terms and conditions of this article shall be duly recorded in the office of the clerk and recorder for the county in which the common interest community is located.

(4) Upon the recording of the original statement of election to be treated as a common interest community subject to the provisions of this article, said common interest community shall be subject to all provisions of this article. Upon recording of the statement of election, such common interest community shall have the same powers and privileges and be subject to the same duties, restrictions, penalties, and liabilities as though it had been created after June 30, 1992.

(5) Notwithstanding any other provision of this section, and with respect to a common interest community making the election permitted by this section, this article shall apply only with

respect to events and circumstances occurring on or after July 1, 1992, and does not invalidate provisions of any declaration, bylaws, or plats or maps in existence on June 30,1991.

§ 38-33.3-119, C.R.S. Exception for small preexisting cooperatives and planned communities.

If a cooperative or planned community created within this state before July 1, 1992, contains no more than ten units and is not subject to any development rights, it is subject only to sections 38-33.3-105 to 38-33.3-107 unless the declaration is amended in conformity with applicable law and with the procedures and requirements of the declaration to take advantage of the provisions of section 38-33.3-120, in which case all the sections enumerated in section 38-33.3-117 apply to that planned community.

§ 38-33.3-120, C.R.S. Amendments to preexisting governing instruments.

(1) In the case of amendments to the declaration, bylaws, or plats and maps of any common interest community created within this state before July 1, 1992, which has not elected treatment under this article pursuant to section 38-33.3-118:

  (a) If the substantive result accomplished by the amendment was permitted by law in effect prior to July 1, 1992, the amendment may be made either in accordance with that law, in which case that law applies to that amendment, or it may be made under this article; and

  (b) If the substantive result accomplished by the amendment is permitted by this article, and was not permitted by law in effect prior to July 1, 1992, the amendment may be made under this article.

(2) An amendment to the declaration, bylaws, or plats and maps authorized by this section to be made under this article must be adopted in conformity with the procedures and requirements of the law that applied to the common interest community at the time it was created and with the procedures and requirements specified by those instruments. If an amendment grants to any person any rights, powers, or privileges permitted by this article, all correlative obligations, liabilities, and restrictions in this article also apply to that person.

(3) An Amendment to the declaration may also be made pursuant to the procedures set forth in section 38-33.3-217 (7).

§ 38-33.3-120.5, C.R.S. Extension of declaration term.

(1) If a common interest community has a declaration in effect with a limited term of years that was recorded prior to July 1,1992, and if, before the term of the declaration expires, the unit owners in the common interest community have not amended the declaration pursuant to section 38-33.3-120 and in accordance with any conditions or fixed limitations described in the declaration, the declaration may be extended as provided in this section.

(2) The term of the declaration may be extended:

  (a) If the executive board adopts a resolution recommending that the declaration be extended for a specific term not to exceed twenty years and directs that the question of extending the term of the declaration be submitted to the unit owners, as members of the association; and

  (b) If an extension of the term of the declaration is approved by vote or agreement of unit owners of units to which at least sixty-seven percent of the votes in the association are allocated or any larger percentage the declaration specifies.

(3) Except for the extension of the term of a declaration as authorized by this section, no other provision of a declaration may be amended pursuant to the provisions of this section.

(4) For any meeting of unit owners at which a vote is to be taken on a proposed extension of the term of a declaration as provided in this section, the secretary or other officer specified in the

bylaws shall provide written notice to each unit owner entitled to vote at the meeting stating that the purpose, or one of the purposes, of the meeting is to consider extending the term of the declaration. The notice shall be given in the time and manner specified in section 38-33.3-308 or in the articles of incorporation, declaration, bylaws, or other governing documents of the association.

(5) The extension of the declaration, if approved, shall be included in an amendment to the declaration and shall be executed, acknowledged, and recorded by the association in the records of the clerk and recorder of each county in which any portion of the common interest community is located. The amendment shall include:

(a) A statement of the name of the common interest community and the association;

(b) A statement that the association has elected to extend the term of the declaration pursuant to this section and the term of the approved extension;

(c) A statement that indicates that the executive board has adopted a resolution recommending that the declaration be extended for a specific term not to exceed twenty years, that sets forth the date of the meeting at which the unit owners elected to extend the term of the declaration, and that declares that the extension was authorized by a vote or agreement of unit owners of units to which at least sixty- seven percent of the votes in the association are allocated or any larger percentage the declaration specifies;

(d) A statement of the names and respective addresses of the officers and executive board members of the association.

(6) Upon the recording of the amendment required by subsection (5) of this section, and subject to the provisions of this section, a common interest community is subject to all provisions of the declaration, as amended.

§ 38-33.3-121, C.R.S. Applicability to nonresidential planned communities.

This article does not apply to a planned community in which all units are restricted exclusively to nonresidential use unless the declaration provides that the article does apply to that planned community. This article applies to a planned community containing both units that are restricted exclusively to nonresidential use and other units that are not so restricted, only if the declaration so provides or the real estate comprising the units that may be used for residential purposes would be a planned community in the absence of the units that may not be used for residential purposes.

§ 38-33.3-122, C.R.S. Applicability to out-of-state common interest communities.

This article does not apply to common interest communities or units located outside this state

§ 38-33.3-123, C.R.S. Enforcement.

(1) (a) If any unit owner fails to timely pay assessments or any money or sums due to the association, the association may require reimbursement for collection costs and reasonable attorney fees and costs incurred as a result of such failure without the necessity of commencing a legal proceeding.

(b) For any failure to comply with the provisions of this article or any provision of the declaration, bylaws, articles, or rules and regulations, other than the payment of assessments or any money or sums due to the association, the association, any unit owner, or any class of unit owners adversely affected by the failure to comply may seek reimbursement for collection costs and reasonable attorney fees and costs incurred as a result of such failure to comply, without the necessity of commencing a legal proceeding.

(c) In any civil action to enforce or defend the provisions of this article or of the declaration, bylaws, articles, or rules and regulations, the court shall award reasonable attorney fees, costs, and costs of collection to the prevailing party.

(d) Notwithstanding paragraph (c) of this subsection (1), in connection with any claim in which a unit owner is alleged to have violated a provision of this article or of the declaration, bylaws, articles, or rules and regulations of the association and in which the court finds that the unit owner prevailed because the unit owner did not commit the alleged violation:

(I) The court shall award the unit owner reasonable attorney fees and costs incurred in asserting or defending the claim; and

(II) The court shall not award costs or attorney fees to the association. In addition, the association shall be precluded from allocating to the unit owner's account with the association any of the association's costs or attorney fees incurred in asserting or defending the claim.

(e) A unit owner shall not be deemed to have confessed judgment to attorney fees or collection costs.

(2) Notwithstanding any law to the contrary, no action shall be commenced or maintained to enforce the terms of any building restriction contained in the provisions of the declaration, bylaws, articles, or rules and regulations or to compel the removal of any building or improvement because of the violation of the terms of any such building restriction unless the action is commenced within one year from the date from which the person commencing the action knew or in the exercise of reasonable diligence should have known of the violation for which the action is sought to be brought or maintained.

§ 38-33.3-124, C.R.S. Legislative declaration – alternative dispute resolution encouraged.

(1) (a) (I) The general assembly finds and declares that the cost, complexity, and delay inherent in court proceedings make litigation a particularly inefficient means of resolving neighborhood disputes. Therefore, common interest communities are encouraged to adopt protocols that make use of mediation or arbitration as alternatives to, or preconditions upon, the filing of a complaint between a unit owner and association in situations that do not involve an imminent threat to the peace, health, or safety of the community.

(II) The general assembly hereby specifically endorses and encourages associations, unit owners, managers, declarants, and all other parties to disputes arising under this article to agree to make use of all available public or private resources for alternative dispute resolution, including, without limitation, the resources offered by the office of dispute resolution within the Colorado judicial branch through its web site.

(b) On or before January 1, 2007, each association shall adopt a written policy setting forth its procedure for addressing disputes arising between the association and unit owners. The association shall make a copy of this policy available to unit owners upon request.

(2) (a) Any controversy between an association and a unit owner arising out of the provisions of this article may be submitted to mediation by agreement of the parties prior to the commencement of any legal proceeding.

(b) The mediation agreement, if one is reached, may be presented to the court as a stipulation. Either party to the mediation may terminate the mediation process without prejudice.

(c) If either party subsequently violates the stipulation, the other party may apply immediately to the court for relief.

(3) The declaration, bylaws, or rules of the association may specify situations in which disputes shall be resolved by binding arbitration under the "Uniform Arbitration Act", part 2 of article

22 of title 13, C.R.S., or by another means of alternative dispute resolution under the "Dispute Resolution Act", part 3 of article 22 of title 13, C.R.S.

A. Creation, Alteration, and Termination

§ 38-33.3-201, C.R.S. Creation of common interest communities.

(1) A common interest community may be created pursuant to this article only by recording a declaration executed in the same manner as a deed and, in a cooperative, by conveying the real estate subject to that declaration to the association. The declaration must be recorded in every county in which any portion of the common interest community is located and must be indexed in the grantee's index in the name of the common interest community and in the name of the association and in the grantor's index in the name of each person executing the declaration. No common interest community is created until the plat or map for the common interest community is recorded.

(2) In a common interest community with horizontal unit boundaries, a declaration, or an amendment to a declaration, creating or adding units shall include a certificate of completion executed by an independent licensed or registered engineer, surveyor, or architect stating that all structural components of all buildings containing or comprising any units thereby created are substantially completed.

§ 38-33.3-202, C.R.S. Unit boundaries.

(1) Except as provided by the declaration:

(a) If walls, floors, or ceilings are designated as boundaries of a unit, all lath, furring, wallboard, plasterboard, plaster, paneling, tiles, wallpaper, paint, and finished flooring and any other materials constituting any part of the finished surfaces thereof are a part of the unit, and all other portions of the walls, floors, or ceilings are a part of the common elements.

(b) If any chute, flue, duct, wire, conduit, bearing wall, bearing column, or other fixture lies partially within and partially outside the designated boundaries of a unit, any portion thereof serving only that unit is a limited common element allocated solely to that unit, and any portion thereof serving more than one unit or any portion of the common elements is a part of the common elements.

(c) Subject to the provisions of paragraph (b) of this subsection (1), all spaces, interior partitions, and other fixtures and improvements within the boundaries of a unit are apart of the unit.

(d) Any shutters, awnings, window boxes, doorsteps, stoops, porches, balconies, and patios and all exterior doors and windows or other fixtures designed to serve a single unit, but located outside the unit's boundaries, are limited common elements allocated exclusively to that unit.

§ 38-33.3-203, C.R.S. Construction and validity of declaration and bylaws.

(1) All provisions of the declaration and bylaws are severable.

(2) The rule against perpetuities does not apply to defeat any provision of the declaration, bylaws, or rules and regulations.

(3) In the event of a conflict between the provisions of the declaration and the bylaws, the declaration prevails, except to the extent the declaration is inconsistent with this article.

(4) Title to a unit and common elements is not rendered un-marketable or otherwise affected by reason of an insubstantial failure of the declaration to comply with this article. Whether a substantial failure impairs marketability is not affected by this article.

§ 38-33.3-204, C.R.S. Description of units.

A description of a unit may set forth the name of the common interest community, the recording data for the declaration, the county in which the common interest community is located, and the identifying number of the unit. Such description is a legally sufficient description of that unit and all rights, obligations, and interests appurtenant to that unit which were created by the declaration or bylaws. It shall not be necessary to use the term "unit" as a part of a legally sufficient description of a unit.

§ 38-33.3-205, C.R.S. Contents of declaration.

(1) The declaration must contain:

(a) The names of the common interest community and the association and a statement that the common interest community is a condominium, cooperative, or planned community;

(b) The name of every county in which any part of the common interest community is situated;

(c) A legally sufficient description of the real estate included in the common interest community;

(d) A statement of the maximum number of units that the declarant reserves the right to create;

(e) In a condominium or planned community, a description, which may be by plat or map, of the boundaries of each unit created by the declaration, including the unit's identifying number; or, in a cooperative, a description, which may be by plat or map, of each unit created by the declaration, including the unit's identifying number, its size or number of rooms, and its location within a building if it is within a building containing more than one unit;

(f) A description of any limited common elements, other than those specified in section 38-33.3-202 (1) (b) and (1) (d) or shown on the map as provided in section 38-33.3-209 (2) (j) and in a planned community, any real estate that is or must become common elements;

(g) A description of any real estate, except real estate subject to development rights, that may be allocated subsequently as limited common elements, other than limited common elements specified in section 38-33.3-202 (1) (b) and (1) (d), together with a statement that they may be so allocated;

(h) A description of any development rights and other special declarant rights reserved by the declarant, together with a description sufficient to identify the real estate to which each of those rights applies and the time limit within which each of those rights must be exercised,

(i) If any development right may be exercised with respect to different parcels of real estate at different times, a statement to that effect together with:

(I) either a statement fixing the boundaries of those portions and regulating the order in which those portions may be subjected to the exercise of each development right or a statement that no assurances are made in those regards; and

(II) a statement as to whether, if any development right is exercised in any portion of the real estate subject to that development right, that development right must be exercised in all or in any other portion of the remainder of that real estate;

(j) Any other conditions or limitations under which the rights described in paragraph (h) of this subsection (1) may be exercised or will lapse;

(k) An allocation to each unit of the allocated interests in the manner described in section 38-33.3-207;

(l) Any restrictions on the use, occupancy, and alienation of the units and on the amount for which a unit may be sold or on the amount that may be received by a unit owner on sale, condemnation, or casualty loss to the unit or to the common interest community or on termination of the common interest community;

(m) The recording data for recorded easements and licenses appurtenant to, or included in, the common interest community or to which any portion of the common interest community is or may become subject by virtue of a reservation in the declaration;

(n) All matters required by sections 38-33.3-201, 38-33.3-206 to 38-33.3-209, 38-33.3-215, 38-33.3-216, and 38-33.3-303 (4);

(o) Reasonable provisions concerning the manner in which notice of matters affecting the common interest community may be given to unit owners by the association or other unit owners.

(p) A statement, if applicable, that the planned community is a large planned community and is exercising certain exemptions from the "Colorado Common Interest Ownership Act" as such a large planned community.

(q) In a large planned community:

(I) A general description of every common element that the declarant is legally obligated to construct within the large planned community together with the approximate date by which each such common element is to be completed. The declarant shall be required to complete each such common element within a reasonable time after the date specified in the declaration, unless the declarant, due to an act of God, is unable to do so. The declarant shall not be legally obligated with respect to any common element not identified in the declaration.

(II) A general description of the type of any common element that the declarant anticipates may be constructed by, maintained by, or operated by the association. The association shall not assess members for the construction, maintenance, or operation of any common element that is not described pursuant to this subparagraph (If) unless such assessment is approved by the vote of a majority of the votes entitled to be cast in person or by proxy, other than by declarant, at a meeting duly convened as required by law.

(2) The declaration may contain any other matters the declarant considers appropriate.

(3) The plats and maps described in section 38-33.3-209 may contain certain information required to be included in the declaration by this section.

(4) A declarant may amend the declaration, a plat, or a map to correct clerical, typographical, or technical errors.

(5) A declarant may amend the declaration to comply with the requirements, standards, or guidelines of recognized secondary mortgage markets, the department of housing and urban development, the federal housing administration, the veterans administration, the federal home loan mortgage corporation, the government national mortgage association, or the federal national mortgage association.

§ 38-33.3-206, C.R.S. Leasehold common interest communities.

(1) Any lease, the expiration or termination of which may terminate the common interest community or reduce its size, must be recorded. In a leasehold condominium or leasehold planned community, the declaration must contain the signature of each lessor of any such lease in order for the provisions of this section to be effective. The declaration must state:

(a) The recording data for the lease;

(b) The date on which the lease is scheduled to expire;

(c) A legally sufficient description of the real estate subject to the lease;

(d) Any rights of the unit owners to redeem the reversion and the manner whereby those rights may be exercised or state that they do not have those rights;

(e) Any rights of the unit owners to remove any improvements within a reasonable time after the expiration or termination of the lease or state that they do not have those rights; and

(f) Any rights of the unit owners to renew the lease and the conditions of any renewal or state that they do not have those rights.

(2) After the declaration for a leasehold condominium or leasehold planned community is recorded, neither the lessor nor the lessor's successor in interest may terminate the leasehold interest of a unit owner who makes timely payment of a unit owner's share of the rent and otherwise complies with all covenants which, if violated, would entitle the lessor to terminate the lease. A unit owner's leasehold interest in a condominium or planned community is not affected by failure of any other person to pay rent or fulfill any other covenant.

(3) Acquisition of the leasehold interest of any unit owner by the owner of the reversion or remainder does not merge the leasehold and fee simple interests unless the leasehold interests of all unit owners subject to that reversion or remainder are acquired.

(4) If the expiration or termination of a lease decreases the number of units in a common interest community, the allocated interests shall be reallocated in accordance with section 38-33.3-107 (1), as though those units had been taken by eminent domain. Reallocations shall be confirmed by an amendment to the declaration prepared, executed, and recorded by the association.

§ 38-33.3-207, C.R.S. Allocation of allocated interests.

(1) The declaration must allocate to each unit:

(a) In a condominium, a fraction or percentage of undivided interests in the common elements and in the common expenses of the association and, to the extent not allocated in the bylaw's of the association, a portion of the votes in the association;

(b) In a cooperative, an ownership interest in the association, a fraction or percentage of the common expenses of the association and, to the extent not allocated in the bylaws of the association, a portion of the votes in the association;

(c) In a planned community, a fraction or percentage of the common expenses of the association and, to the extent not allocated in the bylaws of the association, a portion of the votes in the association; except that, in a large planned community, the common expenses of the association may be paid from assessments and allocated as set forth in the declaration and the votes in the association may be allocated as set forth in the declaration.

(2) The declaration must state the formulas used to establish allocations of interests. Those allocations may not discriminate in favor of units owned by the declarant or an affiliate of the declarant.

(3) If units may be added to or withdrawn from the common interest community, the declaration must state the formulas to be used to reallocate the allocated interests among all units included in the common interest community after the addition or withdrawal.

(4) (a) The declaration may provide:

(I) That different allocations of votes shall be made to the units on particular matters specified in the declaration;

(II) For cumulative voting only for the purpose of electing members of the executive board;

(III) For class voting on specified issues affecting the class including the election of the executive board; and

(IV) For assessments including, but not limited to, assessments on retail sales and services not to exceed six percent of the amount charged for the retail sale or service, and real estate transfers not to exceed three percent of the real estate sales price or its equivalent.

(b) A declarant may not utilize cumulative or class voting for the purpose of evading any limitation imposed on declarants by this article, nor may units constitute a class because they are owned by a declarant.

(c) Assessments allowed under subparagraph (IV) of paragraph (a) of this subsection (4) shall be entitled to the lien provided for under section 38-33.3-316 (1) but shall not be entitled to the priority established by section 38-33.3-316 (2) (b).

(d) Communities with classes for voting specified in the declaration as allowed pursuant to subparagraph (III) of paragraph (a) of this subsection (4) may designate classes of members on a reasonable basis which do not allow the declarant to control the association beyond the period provided for in section 38-33.3-303, including, without limitation, residence owners, commercial space owners, and owners of lodging space and to elect members to the association executive board from such classes.

(5) Except for minor variations due to the rounding of fractions or percentages, the sum of the common expense liabilities and, in a condominium, the sum of the undivided interests in the common elements allocated at any time to all the units shall each equal one if stated as fractions or one hundred percent if stated as percentages. In the event of discrepancy between an allocated interest and the result derived from application of the pertinent formula, the allocated interest prevails.

(6) In a condominium, the common elements are not subject to partition, except as allowed in section 38-33.3-312, and any purported conveyance, encumbrance, judicial sale, or other voluntary or involuntary transfer of an undivided interest in the common elements not allowed for in section 38-33.3-312, that is made without the unit to which that interest is allocated is void.

(7) In a cooperative, any purported conveyance, encumbrance, judicial sale, or other voluntary or involuntary transfer of an ownership interest in the association made without the possessory interest in the unit to which that interest is related is void.

§ 38-33.3-208, C.R.S. Limited common elements.

(1) Except for the limited common elements described in section 38-33.3-202 (1) (b) and (1) (d), the declaration shall specify to which unit or units each limited common element is allocated. That allocation may not be altered without the consent of the unit owners whose units are affected.

(2) Subject to any provisions of the declaration, a limited common element may be reallocated between or among units after compliance with the procedure set forth in this subsection (2). In order to reallocate limited common elements between or among units, the unit owners of those units, as the applicants, must submit an application for approval of the proposed reallocation to the executive board, which application shall be executed by those unit owners and shall include:

(a) The proposed form for an amendment to the declaration as may be necessary to show the reallocation of limited common elements between or among units;

(b) A deposit against attorney fees and costs which the association will incur in reviewing and effectuating the application, in an amount reasonably estimated by the executive board; and

(c) Such other information as may be reasonably requested by the executive board. No reallocation shall be effective without the approval of the executive board. The reallocation shall be effectuated by an amendment signed by the association and by those unit owners between or among whose units the reallocation is made, which amendment shall be recorded as provided in section 38-33.3-217 (3). All costs and attorney fees incurred by the association as a result of the application shall be the sole obligation of the applicants.

(3) A common element not previously allocated as a limited common element may be so allocated only pursuant to provisions in the declaration made in accordance with section 38-33.3-205 (1) (g). The allocations must be made by amendments to the declaration prepared, executed, and recorded by the declarant.

§ 38-33.3-209, C.R.S. Plats and maps.

(1) A plat or map is a part of the declaration and is required for all common interest communities except cooperatives. A map is required only for a common interest community with units having a horizontal boundary. The requirements of this section shall be deemed satisfied so long as all of the information required by this section is contained in the declaration, a map or a plat, or some combination of any two or all of the three. Each plat or map must be clear and legible. When a map is required under any provision of this article, the map, a plat, or the declaration shall contain a certification that all information required by this section is contained in the declaration, the map or a plat, or some combination of any two or all of the three.

(2) In addition to meeting the requirements of a land survey plat as set forth in section 38-51-106, each map shall show the following, except to the extent such information is contained in the declaration or on a plat:

(a) The name and a general schematic plan of the entire common interest community;

(b) The location and dimensions of all real estate not subject to development rights, or subject only to the development right to withdraw, and the location and dimensions of all existing improvements within that real estate;

(c) A legally sufficient description, which may be of the whole common interest community or any portion thereof, of any real estate subject to development rights and a description of the rights applicable to such real estate;

(d) The extent of any existing encroachments across any common interest community boundary;

(e) To the extent feasible, a legally sufficient description of all easements serving or burdening any portion of the common interest community;

(f) The location and dimensions of the vertical boundaries of each unit and that unit's identifying number;

(g) The location, with reference to established data, of the horizontal boundaries of each unit and that unit's identifying number;

(g.5) Any units in which the declarant has reserved the right to create additional units or common elements, identified appropriately;

(h) A legally sufficient description of any real estate in which the unit owners will own only an estate for years;

(i) The distance between non-contiguous parcels of real estate comprising the common interest community; and

(j) The approximate location and dimensions of limited common elements, including porches, balconies, and patios, other than the limited common elements described in section 38-33.3-202 (1) (b) and (1) (d).

(3) (deleted by amendment effective 4-30-93)

(4) (deleted by amendment effective 7-1-07)

(5) Unless the declaration provides otherwise, the horizontal boundaries of any part of a unit located outside of a building have the same elevation as the horizontal boundaries of the inside part and need not be depicted on the plats and maps.

(6) Upon exercising any development right, the declarant shall record an amendment to the declaration with respect to mat real estate reflecting change as a result of such exercise necessary to conform to the requirements of subsections (1), (2), and (4) of this section or new certifications of maps previously recorded if those maps otherwise conform to the requirements of subsections (1), (2), and (4) of this section.

(7) Any certification of a map required by this article must be made by a registered land surveyor.

(8) The requirements of a plat or map under this article shall not be deemed to satisfy any subdivision platting requirement enacted by a county or municipality pursuant to section 30-28-133, C.R.S., part 1 of article 23 of title 31, C.R.S., or a similar provision of a home rule city, nor shall the plat or map requirements under this article be deemed to be incorporated into any subdivision platting requirements enacted by a county or municipality.

(9) Any plat or map that was recorded on or after July 1, 1998, but prior to July 1, 2007, and that satisfies the requirements of this section in effect on July 1, 2007, is deemed to have satisfied the requirements of this section at the time it was recorded.

§ 38-33.3-209.4, C.R.S. Public disclosures required – identity of association – agent – manager – contact information.

(1) Within ninety days after assuming control from the declarant pursuant to section 38-33.3-303 (5), the association shall make the following information available to unit owners upon reasonable notice in accordance with subsection (3) of this section. In addition, if the association's address, designated agent, or management company changes, the association shall make updated information available within ninety days after the change:

(a) The name of the association;

(b) The name of the association's designated agent or management company, if any;

(c) A valid physical address and telephone number for both the association and the designated agent or management company, if any;

(d The name of the common interest community;

(e) The initial date of recording of the declaration; and

(f) The reception number or book and page for the main document that constitutes the declaration.

(2) Within ninety days after assuming control from the declarant pursuant to Section 38-33.3-303 (5), and within ninety days after the end of each fiscal year thereafter, the association shall make the following information available to unit owners upon reasonable notice in accordance with subsection (3) of this section:

(a) The date on which its fiscal year commences;

(b) Its operating budget for the current fiscal year;

(c) A list, by unit type, of the association's current assessments, including both regular and special assessments;

(d) Its annual financial statements, including any amounts held in reserve for the fiscal year immediately preceding the current annual disclosure;

(e) The results of its most recent available financial audit or review;

(f) A list of all association insurance policies, including, but not limited to, property, general liability, association director and officer professional liability, and fidelity policies. Such list shall include the company names, policy limits, policy deductibles, additional named insureds, and expiration dates of the policies listed.

(g) All the association's bylaws, articles, and rules and regulations;

(h) The minutes of the executive board and member meetings for the fiscal year immediately preceding the current annual disclosure; and

(i) The association's responsible governance policies adopted under Section 38-33.3-209.5.

(3) It is the intent of this section to allow the association the widest possible latitude in methods and means of disclosure, while requiring that the information be readily available at no cost to unit owners at their convenience. Disclosure shall be accomplished by one of the following means: posting on an internet web page with accompanying notice of the web address via first-class mail or e-mail; the maintenance of a literature table or binder at the association's principal place of business; or mail or personal delivery. The cost of such distribution shall be accounted for as a common expense liability.

(4) Notwithstanding Section 38-33.3-117 (1) (h.5), this section shall not apply to a unit, or the owner thereof, if the unit is a time-share unit, as defined in section 38-33-110 (7).

§ 38-33.3-209.5, C.R.S. Responsible governance policies

(1) To promote responsible governance, associations shall:

(a) Maintain accurate and complete accounting records; and

(b) Adopt policies, procedures, and rules and regulations concerning:

(I) Collection of unpaid assessments;

* (II) Handling of conflicts of interest involving board members, which policies, procedures, and rules and regulations must include, at a minimum, the criteria described in subsection (4) of this section;

(III) Conduct of meetings, which may refer to applicable provisions of the nonprofit code or other recognized rules and principles;

(IV) Enforcement of covenants and rules, including notice and hearing procedures and the schedule of fines;

(V) Inspection and copying of association records by unit owners;

(VI) Investment of reserve funds;

(VII) Procedures for the adoption and amendment of policies, procedures, and rules; and

(VIII) Procedures for addressing disputes arising between the association and unit owners.

(IX) When the association has a reserve study prepared for the portions of the community maintained, repaired, replaced, and improved by the association; whether there is a funding plan for any work recommended by the reserve study and, if so, the projected sources of funding for the work; and whether the reserve study is based on a physical analysis and financial analysis. For the purposes of this subparagraph (IX), an internally conducted reserve study shall be sufficient.

(2) Notwithstanding any provision of the declaration, bylaws, articles, or rules and regulations to the contrary, the association may not fine any unit owner for an alleged violation unless:

(a) The association has adopted, and follows, a written policy governing the imposition of fines; and

(b) (I) The policy includes a fair and impartial factfinding process concerning whether the alleged violation actually occurred and whether the unit owner is the one who should be held responsible for the violation. This process may be informal but shall, at a minimum, guarantee the unit owner notice and an opportunity to be heard before an impartial decision maker.

(II) As used in this paragraph (b), "impartial decision maker" means a person or group of persons who have the authority to make a decision regarding the enforcement of the association's covenants, conditions, and restrictions, including its architectural requirements, and the other rules and regulations of the association and do not have any direct personal or financial interest in the outcome. A decision maker shall not be deemed to have a direct personal or financial interest in the outcome if the decision maker will not, as a result of the outcome, receive any greater benefit or detriment than will the general membership of the association.

(3) If, as a result of the factfinding process described in subsection (2) of this section, it is determined that the unit owner should not be held responsible for the alleged violation, the association shall not allocate to the unit owner's account with the association any of the association's costs or attorney fees incurred in asserting or hearing the claim. Notwithstanding any provision in the declaration, bylaws, or rules and regulations of the association to the contrary, a unit owner shall not be deemed to have consented to pay such costs or fees.

* (4) (a) The policies, procedures, and rules and regulations adopted by an association under subparagraph (II) of paragraph (b) of subsection (1) of this section must, at a minimum:

(I) Define or describe the circumstances under which a conflict of interest exists;

(II) Set forth procedures to follow when a conflict of interest exists, including how, and to whom, the conflict of interest must be disclosed and whether a board member must recuse himself or herself from discussing or voting on the issue; and

(III) Provide for the periodic review of the association's conflict of interest policies, procedures, and rules and regulations.

(b) The policies, procedures, or rules and regulations adopted under this subsection (4) must be in accordance with section 38-33.3-310.5.

§ 38-33.3-209.6, C.R.S. Executive board member education

The board may authorize, and account for as a common expense, reimbursement of board members for their actual and necessary expenses incurred in attending educational meetings and seminars on responsible governance of unit owners' associations. The course content of such educational meetings and seminars shall be specific to Colorado, and shall make reference to applicable sections of this article.

§ 38-33.3-209.7, C.R.S. Owner education

(1) The association shall provide, or cause to be provided, education to owners at no cost on at least an annual basis as to the general operations of the association and the rights and responsibilities of owners, the association, and its executive board under Colorado law. The criteria for compliance with this section shall be determined by the executive board.

(2) Notwithstanding section 38-33.3-117 (1.5) (c), this section shall not apply to an association that includes time-share units, as defined in section 38-33-110 (7).

§ 38-33.3-210, C.R.S. Exercise of development rights.

(1) To exercise any development right reserved under section 38-33.3-205 (1) (h), the declarant shall prepare, execute, and record an amendment to the declaration and, in a condominium or planned community, comply with the provisions of section 38-33.3-209. The declarant is the unit owner of any units thereby created. The amendment to the declaration must assign an identifying number to each new unit created and, except in the case of subdivision or conversion of units described in subsection (3) of this section, reallocate the allocated interests

among all units. The amendment must describe any common elements and any limited common elements thereby created and, in the case of limited common elements, designate the unit to which each is allocated to the extent required by section 38-33.3-208.

(2) Additional development rights not previously reserved may be reserved within any real estate added to the common interest community if the amendment adding that real estate includes all matters required by section 38-33.3-205 or 38-33.3-206, as the case may be, and, in a condominium or planned community, the plats and maps include all matters required by section 38-33.3-209. This provision does not extend the time limit on the exercise of development rights imposed by the declaration pursuant to section 38-33.3-205 (1) (h).

(3) Whenever a declarant exercises a development right to subdivide or convert a unit previously created into additional units, common elements, or both:

(a) If the declarant converts the unit entirely to common elements, the amendment to the declaration must reallocate all the allocated interests of that unit among the other units as if that unit had been taken by eminent domain; and

(b) If the declarant subdivides the unit into two or more units, whether or not any part of the unit is converted into common elements, the amendment to the declaration must reallocate all the allocated interests of the unit among the units created by the subdivision in any reasonable manner prescribed by the declarant.

(4) If the declaration provides, pursuant to section 38-33.3-205, that all or a portion of the real estate is subject to a right of withdrawal:

(a) If all the real estate is subject to withdrawal, and the declaration does not describe separate portions of real estate subject to that right, none of the real estate may be withdrawn after a unit has been conveyed to a purchaser; and

(b) If any portion' of the real estate is subject to withdrawal, it may not be withdrawn after a unit in that portion has been conveyed to a purchaser.

(5) If a declarant fails to exercise any development right within the time limit and in accordance with any conditions or fixed limitations described in the declaration pursuant to section 38-33.3-205 (1) (h), or records an instrument surrendering a development right, that development right shall lapse unless the association, upon the request of the declarant or the owner of the real estate subject to development right, agrees to an extension of the time period for exercise of the development right or a reinstatement of the development right subject to whatever terms, conditions, and limitations the association may impose on the subsequent exercise of the development right. The extension or renewal of the development right and any terms, conditions, and limitations shall be included in an amendment executed by the declarant or the owner of the real estate subject to development right and the association.

§ 38-33.3-211, C.R.S. Alterations of units.

(1) Subject to the provisions of the declaration and other provisions of law, a unit owner:

(a) May make any improvements or alterations to his unit that do not impair the structural integrity, electrical systems, or mechanical systems or lessen the support of any portion of the common interest community;

(b) May not change the appearance of the common elements without permission of the association; or

(c) After acquiring an adjoining unit or an adjoining part of an adjoining unit, may remove or alter any intervening partition or create apertures therein, even if the partition in whole or in part is a common element, if those acts do not impair the structural integrity, electrical systems, or mechanical systems or lessen the support of any portion of the common interest community removal of partitions or creation of apertures under this paragraph (c) is not an alteration of boundaries.

§ 38-33.3-212, C.R.S. Relocation of boundaries between adjoining units.

(1) Subject to the provisions of the declaration and other provisions of law, and pursuant to the procedures described in section 38-33.3-217, the boundaries between adjoining units may be relocated by an amendment to the declaration upon application to the association by the owners of those units.

(2) In order to relocate the boundaries between adjoining units, the owners of those units, as the applicant, must submit an application to the executive board, which application shall be executed by those owners and shall include:

(a) Evidence sufficient to the executive board that the applicant has complied with all local rules and ordinances and that the proposed relocation of boundaries does not violate the terms of any document evidencing a security interest;

(b) The proposed reallocation of interests, if any;

(c) The proposed form for amendments to the declaration, including the plats or maps, as may be necessary to show the altered boundaries between adjoining units, and their dimensions and identifying numbers;

(d) A deposit against attorney fees and costs which the association will incur in reviewing and effectuating the application, in an amount reasonably estimated by the executive board; and

(e) Such other information as may be reasonably requested by the executive board.

(3) No relocation of boundaries between adjoining units shall be effected without the necessary amendments to the declaration, plats, or maps, executed and recorded pursuant to section 38-33.3-217 (3) and (5).

(4) All costs and attorney fees incurred by the association as a result of an application shall be the sole obligation of the applicant.

§ 38-33.3-213, C.R.S. Subdivision of units.

(1) If the declaration expressly so permits, a unit may be subdivided into two or more units. Subject to the provisions of the declaration and other provisions of law, and pursuant to the procedures described in this section, a unit owner may apply to the association to subdivide a unit.

(2) In order to subdivide a unit, the unit owner of such unit, as the applicant, must submit an application to the executive board, which application shall be executed by such owner and shall include:

(a) Evidence that the applicant of the proposed subdivision shall have complied with all building codes, fire codes, zoning codes, planned unit development requirements, master plans, and other applicable ordinances or resolutions adopted and enforced by the local governing body and that the proposed subdivision does not violate the terms of any document evidencing a security interest encumbering the unit;

(b) The proposed reallocation of interests, if any;

(c) The proposed form for amendments to the declaration, including the plats or maps, as may be necessary to show the units which are created by the subdivision and their dimensions, and identifying numbers;

(d) A deposit against attorney fees and costs which the association will incur in reviewing and effectuating the application, in an amount reasonably estimated by the executive board; and

(e) Such other information as may be reasonably requested by the executive board.

(3) No subdivision of units shall be effected without the necessary amendments to the declaration, plats, or maps, executed and recorded pursuant to section 38-33.3-217 (3) and (5).

(4) All costs and attorney fees incurred by the association as a result of an application shall be the sole obligation of the applicant.

§ 38-33.3-214, C.R.S. Easement for encroachments.

To the extent that any unit or common element encroaches on any other unit or common element, a valid easement for the encroachment exists. The easement does not relieve a unit owner of liability in case of willful misconduct or relieve a declarant or any other person of liability for failure to adhere to the plats and maps.

§ 38-33.3-215, C.R.S. Use for sales purposes.

A declarant may maintain sales offices, management offices, and models in the common interest community only if the declaration so provides. Except as provided in a declaration, any real estate in a common interest community used as a sales office, management office, or model that is not designated a unit by the declaration is a common element. If a declarant ceases to be a unit owner, such declarant ceases to have any rights with regard to any real estate used as a sales office, management offices or model, unless it is removed promptly from the common interest community in accordance with a right to remove reserved in the declaration. Subject to any limitations in the declaration, a declarant may maintain signs on the common elements advertising the common interest community. This section is subject to the provisions of other state laws and to local ordinances.

§ 38-33.3-216, C.R.S. Easement rights.

(1) Subject to the provisions of the declaration, a declarant has an easement through the common elements as may be reasonably necessary for the purpose of discharging a declarant's obligations or exercising special declarant rights, whether arising under this article or reserved in the declaration.

(2) In a planned community, subject to the provisions of the declaration and the ability of the association to regulate and convey or encumber the common elements as set forth in sections 38-33.3-302 (1) (f) and 38-33.3-312, the unit owners have an easement:

(a) In the common elements for the purpose of access to their units; and

(b) To use the common elements and all other real estate that must become common elements for all other purposes.

§ 38-33.3-217, C.R.S. Amendment of declaration.

(1) (a) (I) Except as otherwise provided in subparagraphs (II) and (III) of this paragraph (a), the declaration, including the plats and maps, may be amended only by the affirmative vote or agreement of unit owners of units to which more than fifty percent of the votes in the association are allocated or any larger percentage, not to exceed sixty-seven percent, that the declaration specifies. Any provision in the declaration that purports to specify a percentage larger than sixty-seven percent is hereby declared void as contrary to public policy, and until amended, such provision shall be deemed to specify a percentage of sixty-seven percent. The declaration may specify a smaller percentage than a simple majority only if all of the units are restricted exclusively to nonresidential use. Nothing in this paragraph (a) shall be construed to prohibit the association from seeking a court order, in accordance with subsection (7) of this section, to reduce the required percentage to less than sixty-seven percent.

(II) If the declaration provides for an initial period of applicability to be followed by automatic extension periods, the declaration may be amended at any time in accordance with subparagraph (I) of this paragraph (a).

(III) This paragraph (a) shall not apply:

(A) To the extent that its application is limited by subsection (4) of this section;

(B) To amendments executed by a declarant under section 38-33.3-205 (4) and (5), 38-33.3-208 (3), 38-33.3-209 (6), 38-33.3-210, or 38-33.3-222;

(C) To amendments executed by an association under section 38-33.3-107, 38-33.3-206 (4), 38-33.3 208 (2), 38-33.3-212, 38-33.3-213, or 38-33.3-218 (11) and (12);

(D) To amendments executed by the district court for any county that includes all or any portion of a common interest community under subsection (7) of this section; or

(E) To amendments that affect phased communities or declarant-controlled communities.

(b) (I) If the declaration requires first mortgagees to approve or consent to amendments, but does not set forth a procedure for registration or notification of first mortgagees, the association may:

(A) Send a dated, written notice and a copy of any proposed amendment by certified mail to each first mortgagee at its most recent address as shown on the recorded deed of trust or recorded assignment thereof; and

(B) Cause the dated notice, together with information on how to obtain a copy of the proposed amendment, to be printed in full at least twice, on separate occasions at least one week apart, in a newspaper of general circulation in the county in which the common interest community is located.

(II) A first mortgagee that does not deliver to the association a negative response within sixty days after the date of the notice specified in subparagraph (I) of this paragraph (b) shall be deemed to have approved the proposed amendment.

(III) The notification procedure set forth in this paragraph (b) is not mandatory. If the consent of first mortgagees is obtained without resort to this paragraph (b), and otherwise in accordance with the declaration, the notice to first mortgagees shall be considered sufficient.

(2) No action to challenge the validity of an amendment adopted by the association pursuant to this section may be brought more than one year after the amendment is recorded.

(3) Every amendment to the declaration must be recorded in every county in which any portion of the common interest community is locate and is effective only upon recordation. An amendment must be indexed in the grantee's index in the name of the common interest community and the association and in the grantor's index in the name of each person executing the amendment.

(4) (a) Except to the extent expressly permitted or required by other provisions of this article, no amendment may create or increase special declarant rights, increase the number of units, or change the boundaries of any unit or the allocated interests of a unit in the absence of a vote or agreement of unit owners of units to which at least sixty-seven percent of the votes in the association, including sixty-seven percent of the votes allocated to units not owned by a declarant, are allocated or any larger percentage the declaration specifies. The declaration may specify a smaller percentage only if all of the units are restricted exclusively to nonresidential use.

(b) The sixty-seven-percent maximum percentage stated in paragraph (a) of subsection (1) of this section shall not apply to any common interest community in which one unit owner, by virtue of the declaration, bylaws, or other governing documents of the association, is allocated sixty-seven percent or more of the votes in the association.

(4.5) Except to the extent expressly permitted or required by other provisions of this article, no amendment may change the uses to which any unit is restricted in the absence of a vote or agreement of unit owners of units to which at least sixty-seven percent of the votes in the association are allocated or any larger percentage the declaration specifies. The declaration may specify a smaller percentage only if all of the units are restricted exclusively to nonresidential use.

(5) Amendments to the declaration required by this article to be recorded by the association shall be prepared, executed, recorded, and certified on behalf of the association by any officer of the association designated for that purpose or, in the absence of designation, by the president of the association.

(6) All expenses associated with preparing and recording an amendment to the declaration shall be the sole responsibility of:

(a) In the case of an amendment pursuant to sections 38-33.3-208 (2), 38-33.3-212, and 38-33.3-213, the unit owners desiring the amendment; and

(b) In the case of an amendment pursuant to section 38-33.3-208 (3), 38-33.3-209 (6), or 38-33.3-210, the declarant; and

(c) In all other cases, the association.

(7) (a) The association, acting through its executive board pursuant to section 38-33.3-303 (1), may petition the district court for any county that includes all or any portion of the common interest community for an order amending the declaration of the common interest community if:

(I) The association has twice sent notice of the proposed amendment to all unit owners that are entitled by the declaration to vote on the proposed amendment or are required for approval of the proposed amendment by any means allowed pursuant to the provisions regarding notice to members in sections 7-121-402 and 7-127-104, C.R.S., of the "Colorado Revised Nonprofit Corporation Act", articles 121tol37oftitle7,C.R.S.;

(II) The association has discussed the proposed amendment during at least one meeting of the association; and

(III) Unit owners of units to which are allocated more than fifty percent of the number of consents, approvals, or votes of the association that would be required to adopt the proposed amendment pursuant to the declaration have voted in favor of the proposed amendment.

(b) A petition filed pursuant to paragraph (a) of this subsection (7) shall include:

(I) A summary of:

(A) The procedures and requirements for amending the declaration that are set forth in the declaration;

(B) The proposed amendment to the declaration;

(C) The effect of and reason for the proposed amendment, including a statement of the circumstances that make the amendment necessary or advisable;

(D) The results of any vote taken with respect to the proposed amendment; and

(E) Any other matters that the association believes will be useful to the court in deciding whether to grant the petition; and

(II) As exhibits, copies of:

(A) The declaration as originally recorded and any recorded amendments to the declaration:

(B) The text of the proposed amendment;

(C) Copies of any notices sent pursuant to subparagraph (I) of paragraph (a) of this subsection (7); and

(D) Any other documents that the association believes will be useful to the court in deciding whether to grant the petition.

(c) Within three days of the filing of the petition, the district court shall set a date for hearing the petition. Unless the court finds that an emergency requires an immediate hearing, the hearing shall be held no earlier than forty-five days and no later than sixty days after the date the association filed the petition.

(d) No later than ten days after the date for hearing a petition is set pursuant to paragraph (c) of this subsection (7), the association shall:

(I) Send notice of the petition by any written means allowed pursuant to the provisions regarding notice to members in sections 7-121-402 and 7-127-104, C.R.S., of the "Colorado Revised Nonprofit Corporation Act:, articles 121 to 137 of title 7, C.R.S., to any unit owner, by first-class mail, postage prepaid or by hand delivery to any declarant, and by first-class mail, postage prepaid, to any lender that holds a security interest in one or more units and is entitled by the declaration or any underwriting guidelines or requirements of that lender or of the federal national mortgage association, the federal home loan mortgage corporation, the federal housing administration, the veterans administration, or the government national mortgage corporation to vote on the proposed amendment. The notice shall include:

(A) A copy of the petition which need not include the exhibits attached to the original petition filed with the district court:

(B) The date the district court will hear the petition ; and

(C) A statement that the court may grant the petition and order the proposed amendment to the declaration unless any declarant entitled by the declaration to vote on the proposed amendment, the federal housing administration, the veterans administration, more than thirty-three percent of the unit owners entitled by the declaration to vote on the proposed amendment, or more than thirty-three percent of the lenders that hold a security interest in one or more units and are entitled by the declaration to vote on the proposed amendment file written objections to the proposed amendment with the court prior to the hearing.

(II) File with the district court:

(A) A list of the names and mailing addresses of declarants, unit owners, and lenders that hold a security interest in one or more units and that are entitled by the declaration to vote on the proposed amendment; and

(B) A copy of the notice required by subparagraph (I) of this paragraph (d).

(e) The district court shall grant the petition after hearing if it finds that:

(I) The association has complied with all requirements of this subsection (7);

(II) No more than thirty-three percent of the unit owners entitled by the declaration to vote on the proposed amendment have filed written objections to the proposed amendment with the court prior to the hearing;

(III) Neither the federal housing administration for the veterans administration is entitled to approve the proposed amendment, or if so entitled has not filed written objections to the proposed amendment with the court prior to the hearing;

(IV) Either the proposed amendment does not eliminate any rights or privileges designated in the declaration as belonging to a declarant or no declarant has filed written objections to the proposed amendment with the court prior to the hearing;

(V) Either the proposed amendment does not eliminate any rights or privileges designated in the declaration as belonging to any lenders that hold security interests in one or more units and that are entitled by the declaration to vote on the proposed amendment or no more than thirty-three percent of such lenders have filed written objections to the proposed amendment with the court prior to the hearing; and

(VI) The proposed amendment would neither terminate the declaration nor change the allocated interests of the unit owners as specified in the declaration, except as allowed pursuant to section 38-33.3-315.

(f) Upon granting a petition, the court shall enter an order approving the proposed amendment and requiring the association to record the amendment in each county that includes all or any portion of the common interest community. Once recorded, the amendment shall have the same legal effect as if it were adopted pursuant to any requirements set forth in the declaration.

§ 38-33.3-218, C.R.S. Termination of common interest community.

(1) Except in the case of a taking of all the units by eminent domain, or in the case of foreclosure against an entire cooperative of a security interest that has priority over the declaration, a common interest community may be terminated only by agreement of unit owners of units to which at least sixty-seven percent of the votes in the association are allocated or any larger percentage the declaration specifies. The declaration may specify a smaller percentage only if all of the units in the common interest community are restricted exclusively to nonresidential uses.

(1.5) No planned community that is required to exist pursuant to a development or site plan shall be terminated by agreement of unit owners, unless a copy of the termination agreement is sent by certified mail or hand delivered to the governing body of every municipality in which a portion of the planned community is situated or, if the planned community is situated in an unincorporated area, to the board of county commissioners for every county in which a portion of the planned community is situated.

(2) An agreement of unit owners to terminate must be evidenced by their execution of a termination agreement or ratifications thereof in the same manner as a deed, by the requisite number of unit owners. The termination agreement must specify a date after which the agreement will be void unless it is recorded before that date. A termination agreement and all ratifications thereof must be recorded in every county in which a portion of the common interest community is situated and is effective only upon recordation.

(3) In the case of a condominium or planned community containing only units having horizontal boundaries described in the declaration, a termination agreement may provide that all of the common elements and units of the common interest community must be sold following termination. If, pursuant to the agreement, any real estate in the common interest community is to be sold following termination, the termination agreement must set forth the minimum terms of-the sale.

(4) In the case of a condominium or planned community containing any units not having horizontal boundaries described in the declaration, a termination agreement may provide for sale of the common elements, but it may not require that the units be sold following termination, unless the declaration as originally recorded provided otherwise or all the unit owners consent to the sale.

(5) Subject to the provisions of a termination agreement described in subsections (3) and (4) of this section, the association, on behalf of the unit owners, may contract for the sale of real estate in a common interest community following termination, but the contract is not binding on the unit owners until approved pursuant to subsections (1) and (2) of this section. If any real estate is to be sold following termination, title to that real estate, upon termination, vests in the association

as trustee for the holders of all interests in the units. Thereafter, the association has all the powers necessary and appropriate to effect the sale. Until the sale has been concluded and the proceeds thereof distributed, the association continues in existence with all the powers it had before termination. Proceeds of the sale must be distributed to unit owners and lienholders as their interests may appear, in accordance with subsections (8), (9), and (10) of this section taking into account the value of property owned or distributed that is not sold so as to preserve the proportionate interests of each unit owner with respect to all property cumulatively. Unless otherwise specified in the termination agreement, as long as the association holds title to the real estate, each unit owner and the unit owner's successors in interest have an exclusive right to occupancy of the portion of the real estate that formerly constituted the unit. During the period of that occupancy, each unit owner and the unit owner's successors in interest remain liable for all assessments and other obligations imposed on unit owners by this article or the declaration.

(6) (a) In a planned community, if all or a portion of the common elements are not to be sold following termination, title to the common elements not sold vests in the unit owners upon termination as tenants in common in fractional interests that maintain, after taking into account the fair market value of property owned and the proceeds of property sold, their respective interests as provided in subsection (10) of this section with respect to all property appraised under said subsection (10), and liens on the units shift accordingly.

(b) In a common interest community, containing units having horizontal boundaries described in the declaration, title to the units not to be sold following termination vests in the unit owners upon termination as tenants in common in fractional interests that maintain, after taking into account the fair market value of property owned and the proceeds of property sold, their respective interests as provided in subsection (10) of this section with respect to all property appraised under said subsection (10), and liens on the units shift accordingly. While the tenancy in common exists, each unit owner and the unit owner's successors in interest have an exclusive right to occupancy of the portion of the real estate that formerly constituted such unit.

(7) Following termination of the common interest community, the proceeds of any sale of real estate, together with the assets of the association, are held by the association as trustee for unit owners and holders of liens on the units as their interests may appear.

(8) Upon termination of a condominium or planned community, creditors of the association who obtain a lien and duly record it in every county in which any portion of the common interest community is located are to be treated as if they had perfected liens on the units immediately before termination or when the lien is obtained and recorded, whichever is later.

(9) In a cooperative, the declaration may provide that all creditors of the association have priority over any interests of unit owners and creditors of unit owners. In that event, upon termination, creditors of the association who obtain a lien and duly record it in every county in which any portion of the cooperative is located are to be treated as if they had perfected liens against the cooperative immediately before termination or when the lien is obtained and recorded, whichever is later. Unless the declaration provides that all creditors of the association have that priority:

(a) The lien of each creditor of the association which was perfected against the association before termination becomes, upon termination, a lien against each unit owner's interest in the unit as of the date the lien was perfected;

(b) Any other creditor of the association who obtains a lien and duly records it in every county in which any portion of the cooperative is located is to be treated upon termination as if the creditor had perfected a lien against each unit owner's interest immediately before termination or when the lien is obtained and recorded, whichever is later;

(c) The amount of the lien of an association's creditor described in paragraphs (a) and (b) of this subsection (9) against each unit owner's interest must dc proportionate to the ratio which each unit's common expense liability bears to the common expense liability of all of the units;

(d) The lien of each creditor of each unit owner which was perfected before termination continues as a lien against that unit owner's unit as 01 the date the lien was perfected; and

(e) The assets of the association must be distributed to all unit owners and all lienholders as their interests may appear in the order described above. Creditors of the association are not entitled to payment from any unit owner in excess of the amount of the creditor's lien against that unit owner's interest.

(10) The respective interests of unit owners referred to in subsections (5) to (9) of this section are as follows:

(a) Except as provided in paragraph (b) of this subsection (10), the respective interests of unit owners are the combined fair market values of their units, allocated interests, any limited common elements, and, in the case of a planned community, any tenant in common interest, immediately before the termination, as determined by one or more independent appraisers selected by the association. The decision of the independent appraisers shall be distributed to the unit owners and becomes final unless disapproved within thirty days after distribution by unit owners of units to which twenty-five percent of the votes in the association are allocated. The proportion of any unit owner's interest to that of all unit owners is determined by dividing the fair market value of that unit owner's unit and its allocated interests by the total fair market values of all the units and their allocated interests.

(b) If any unit or any limited common element is destroyed to the extent that an appraisal of the fair market value thereof prior to destruction cannot be made, the interests of all unit owners are:

(I) In a condominium, their respective common element interests immediately before the termination;

(II) In a cooperative, their respective ownership interests immediately before the termination; and

(III) In a planned community, their respective common expense liabilities immediately before the termination.

(11) In a condominium or planned community, except as provided in subsection (12) of this section, foreclosure or enforcement of a lien or encumbrance against the entire common interest community does not terminate, of itself, the common interest community. Foreclosure or enforcement of a lien or encumbrance against a portion of the common interest community other than withdrawable real estate does not withdraw that portion from the common interest community. Foreclosure or enforcement of a lien or encumbrance against withdrawable real estate does not withdraw, of itself, that real estate from the common interest community, but the person taking title thereto may require from the association, upon request, an amendment to the declaration excluding the real estate from the common interest community prepared, executed, and recorded by the association.

(12) In a condominium or planned community, if a lien or encumbrance against a portion of the real estate comprising the common interest community has priority over the declaration and the lien or encumbrance has not been partially released, the parties foreclosing the lien or encumbrance, upon foreclosure, may record an instrument excluding the real estate subject to that lien or encumbrance from the common interest community. The board of directors shall reallocate interests as if the foreclosed section were taken by eminent domain by an amendment to the declaration prepared, executed, and recorded by the association.

§ 38-33.3-219, C.R.S. Rights of secured lenders.

(1) The declaration may require that all or a specified number or percentage of the lenders who hold security interests encumbering me units approve specified actions of the unit owners or the association as a condition to the effectiveness of those actions, but no requirement for approval may operate to:

(a) Deny or delegate control over the general administrative affairs of the association by the unit owners or the executive board; or

(b) Prevent the association or the executive board from commencing, intervening in, or settling any solicitation or proceeding; or

(c) Prevent any insurance trustee or the association from receiving and distributing any insurance proceeds pursuant to section 38-33.3-313.

§ 38-33.3-220, C.R.S. Master associations.

(1) If the declaration provides that any of the powers of a unit owners' association described in section 38-33.3-302 are to be exercised by or maybe delegated to a master association, all provisions of this article applicable to unit owners' associations apply to any such master association except as modified by this section.

(2) Unless it is acting in the capacity of an association described in section 38-33.3-301, a master association may exercise the powers set forth in section 38-33.3-302 (1) (b) only to the extent such powers are expressly permitted to be exercise by a master association in the declarations of common interest communities which are part of the master association or expressly described in the delegations of power from those common interest communities to the master association.

(3) If the declaration of any common interest community provides that the executive board may delegate certain powers to a master association, the members of the executive board have no liability for the acts or omissions of the master association with respect to those powers following delegation.

(4) The rights and responsibilities of unit owners with respect to the unit owners' association set forth in sections 38-33.3-303, 38-33.3-308, 38-33.3-309, 38.33.3-310, and 38-33.3-312 apply in the conduct of the affairs of a master association only to persons who elect the board of a master association, whether or not those persons are otherwise unit owners within the meaning of this article.

(5) Even if a master association is also an association described in section 38-33.3-301, the articles of incorporation and the declaration of each common interest community, the powers of which are assigned by the declaration or delegated to the master association, must provide that the executive board of the master association be elected after the period of declarant control, if any, in one of the following ways:

(a) All unit owners of all common interest communities subject to the master association may elect all members of the master association's executive board.

(b) All members of the executive boards of all common interest communities subject to the master association may elect all members of the master association's executive board.

(c) All unit owners of each common interest community subject to the master association may elect specified members of the master association's executive board.

(d) All members of the executive board of each common interest community subject to the master association may elect specified members of the master association's executive board.

§ 38-33.3-221, C.R.S. Merger or consolidation of common interest communities.

(1) Any two or more common interest communities of the same form of ownership, by agreement of the unit owners as provided in subsection (2) of this section, may be merged or consolidated into a single common interest community. In the event of a merger or consolidation, unless the agreement otherwise provides, the resultant common interest community is the legal successor, for all purposes, of all of the preexisting common interest communities, and the operations and activities of all associations of the preexisting common interest communities are merged or consolidated into a single association that holds all powers, rights, obligations, assets, and liabilities of all preexisting associations.

(2) An agreement of two or more common interest communities to merge or consolidate pursuant to subsection (1) of this section must be evidenced by an agreement prepared, executed, recorded, and certified by the president of the association of each of the preexisting common interest communities following approval by owners of units to which are allocated the percentage of votes in each common interest community required to terminate that common interest community. The agreement must be recorded in every county in which a portion of the common interest community is located and is not effective until recorded.

(3) Every merger or consolidation agreement must provide for the reallocation of the allocated interests in the new association among the units of the resultant common interest community either by stating the reallocations or the formulas upon which they are based.

§ 38-33.3-221.5, C.R.S. Withdrawal from merged common interest community

(1) A common interest community that was merged or consolidated with another common interest community, or is party to an agreement to do so pursuant to section 38-33.3-221, may withdraw from the merged or consolidated common interest community or terminate the agreement to merge or consolidate, without the consent of the other common interest community or communities involved, if the common interest community wishing to withdraw meets all of the following criteria:

- (a) It is a separate, platted subdivision;
- (b) Its unit owners are required to pay into two common interest communities or separate unit owners' associations;
- (c) It is or has been a self-operating common interest community or association continuously for at least twenty-five years;
- (d) The total number of unit owners comprising it is fifteen percent or less of the total number of unit owners in the merged or consolidated common interest community or association;
- (e) Its unit owners have approved the withdrawal by a majority vote and the owners of units representing at least seventy-five percent of the allocated interests in the common interest community wishing to withdraw participated in the vote; and
- (f) Its withdrawal would not substantially impair the ability of the remainder of the merged common interest community or association to:
  - (I) Enforce existing covenants;
  - (II) Maintain existing facilities; or
  - (III) Continue to exist.

(2) If an association has met the requirements set forth in subsection (1) of this section, it shall be considered withdrawn as of the date of the election at which its unit owners voted to withdraw.

§ 38-33.3-222, C.R.S. Addition of unspecified real estate.

In a common interest community, if the right is originally reserved in the declaration, the declarant, in addition to any other development right, may amend the declaration at any time during as many years as are specified in the declaration to add additional real estate to the common interest community without describing the location of that real estate in the original declaration; but the area of real estate added to the common interest community pursuant to this section may not exceed ten percent of the total area of real estate described in section 38-33.3-205 (1) (c) and (1) (h), and the declarant may not in any event increase the number of units in the common interest community beyond the number stated in the original declaration pursuant to section 38-33.3-205 (1) (d), except as provided in section 38-33.3-217(4).

§ 38-33.3-223, C.R.S. Sale of unit – disclosure to buyer.

(Repealed, May 26, 2006)

XI. Management of the Common Interest Community

§ 38-33.3-301, C.R.S. Organization of unit owners' association.

A unit owners' association shall be organized no later than the date the first unit in the common interest community is conveyed to a purchaser. The membership of the association at all times shall consist exclusively of all unit owners or, following termination of the common interest community, of all former unit owners entitled to distributions of proceeds under section 38-33.3-218, or their heirs, personal representatives, successors, or assigns. The association shall be organized as a nonprofit, not-for-profit, or for-profit corporation or as a limited liability company in accordance with the laws of the state of Colorado; except that the failure of the association to incorporate or organize as a limited liability company will not adversely affect either the existence of the common interest community for purposes of this article or the rights of persons acting in reliance upon such existence, other than as specifically provided in section 38-33.3-316. Neither the choice of entity nor the organizational structure of the association shall be deemed to affect its substantive rights and obligations under this article.

§ 38-33.3-302, C.R.S. Powers of unit owners' association.

(1) Except as provided in subsections (2) and (3) of this section, and subject to the provisions of the declaration, the association, without specific authorization in the declaration, may:

- (a) Adopt and amend bylaws and rules and regulations;
- (b) Adopt and amend budgets for revenues, expenditures, and reserves and collect assessments for common expenses from unit owners;
- (c) Hire and terminate managing agents and other employees, agents, and independent contractors;
- (d) Institute, defend, or intervene in litigation or administrative proceedings in its own name on behalf of itself or two or more unit owners on matters affecting the common interest community;
- (e) Make contracts and incur liabilities;
- (f) Regulate the use, maintenance, repair, replacement, and modification of common elements;
- (g) Cause additional improvements to be made as a part of the common elements;
- (h) Acquire, hold, encumber, and convey in its own name any right, title, or interest to real or personal property, subject to the following exceptions:

(I) Common elements in a condominium or planned community may be conveyed or subjected to a security interest only pursuant to section 38-33.3-312; and

(II) Part of a cooperative may be conveyed, or all or part of a cooperative may be subjected to a security interest, only pursuant to section 38-33.3-312;

(i) Grant easements, leases, licenses, and concessions through or over the common elements;

(j) Impose and receive any payments, fees, or charges for the use, rental, or operation of the common elements other than limited common elements described in section 38-33.3-202 (1) (b) and (1) (d);

(k) Impose charges for late payment of assessments, recover reasonable attorney fees and other legal costs for collection of assessments and other actions to enforce the power of the association, regardless of whether or not suit was initiated, and, after notice and an opportunity to be heard, levy reasonable fines for violations of the declaration, bylaws, and rules and regulations of the association;

(l) Impose reasonable charges for the preparation and recordation of amendments to the declaration or statements of unpaid assessments;

(m) Provide for the indemnification of its officers and executive board and maintain directors' and officers' liability insurance;

(n) Assign its right to future income, including the right to receive common expense assessments, but only to the extent the declaration expressly so provides;

(o) Exercise any other powers conferred by the declaration or bylaws;

(p) Exercise all other powers that may be exercised in this state by legal entities of the same type as the association; and

(q) Exercise any other powers necessary and proper for the governance and operation of the association.

(2) The declaration may not impose limitations on the power of the association to deal with the declarant that are more restrictive than the limitations imposed on the power of the association to deal with other persons.

(3) (a) Any managing agent, employee, independent contractor, or other person acting on behalf of the association shall be subject to this article to the same extent as the association itself would be.

(b) Decisions concerning the approval or denial of a unit owner's application for architectural or landscaping changes shall be made in accordance with standards and procedures set forth in the declaration or in duly adopted rules and regulations or bylaws of the association, and shall not be made arbitrarily or capriciously.

(4) (a) The association's contract with a managing agent shall be terminable for cause without penalty to the association. Any such contract shall be subject to renegotiation.

(b) Notwithstanding section 38-33.3-117 (1.5) (g), this subsection (4) shall not apply to an association that includes time-share units, as defined in section 38-33-110 (7).

§ 38-33.3-303, C.R.S. Executive board members and officers.

(1) (a) Except as provided in the declaration, the bylaws, or subsection (3) of this section or any other provisions of this article, the executive board may act in all instances on behalf of the association.

(b) Notwithstanding any provision of the declaration or bylaws to the contrary, all members of the executive board shall have available to them all information related to the responsibilities and operation of the association obtained by any other member of the executive board. This information shall include, but is not necessarily limited to, reports of detailed monthly expenditures, contracts to which the association is a party, and copies of communications, reports, and opinions to and from any member of the executive board or any managing agent, attorney, or accountant employed or engaged by the executive board to whom the executive board delegates responsibilities under this article.

(2) Except as otherwise provided in subsection (2.5) of this section:

(a) If appointed by the declarant, in the performance of their duties, the officers and members of the executive board are required to exercise the care required of fiduciaries of the unit owners.

(b) If not appointed by the declarant, no member of the executive board and no officer shall be liable for actions taken or omissions made in the performance of such member's duties except for wanton and willful acts or omissions.

(2.5) With regard to the investment of reserve funds of the association, the officers and members of the executive board shall be subject to the standards set forth in section 7-128-401, C.R.S.; except that, as used in that section:

(a) "Corporation" or "nonprofit corporation" means the association.

(b) "Director" means a member of the association's executive board.

(c) "Officer" means any person designated as an officer of the association and any person to whom the executive board delegates responsibilities under this article, including, without limitation, a managing agent, attorney, or accountant employed by the executive board.

(3) (a) The executive board may not act on behalf of the association to amend the declaration, to terminate the common interest community, or to elect members of the executive board or determine the qualifications, powers and duties, or terms of office of executive board members, but the executive board may fill vacancies in its membership for the unexpired portion of any term.

(b) Committees of the association shall be appointed pursuant to the governing documents of the association or, if the governing documents contain no applicable provisions, pursuant to section 7-128-206, C.R.S. The person appointed after August 15, 2009, to preside over any such committee shall meet the same qualifications as are required by the governing documents of the association for election or appointment to the executive board of the association.

(4) (a) Within ninety days after adoption of any proposed budget for the common interest community, the executive board shall mail, by ordinary first-class mail, or otherwise deliver a summary of the budget to all the unit owners and shall set a date for a meeting of the unit owners to consider the budget. Such meeting shall occur within a reasonable time after mailing or other delivery of the summary, or as allowed for in the bylaws. The executive board shall give notice to the unit owners of the meeting as allowed for in the bylaws. Unless the declaration requires otherwise, the budget proposed by the executive board does not require approval from the unit owners and it will be deemed approved by the unit owners in the absence of a veto at the noticed meeting by a majority of all unit owners, or if permitted in the declaration, a majority of a class of unit owners, or any larger percentage specified in the declaration, whether or not a quorum is present. In the event that the proposed budget is vetoed, the periodic budget last proposed by the executive board and not vetoed by the unit owners must be continued until a subsequent budget proposed by the executive board is not vetoed by the unit owners.

(b) (I) At the discretion of the executive board or upon request pursuant to subparagraph (II) or (III) of this paragraph (b) as applicable, the books and records of the association shall be subject to an audit, using generally accepted auditing standards, or a review, using statements on standards for accounting and review services, by an independent and qualified person selected by the board. Such person need not be a certified public accountant except in the case of an audit. A person selected to conduct a review shall have at least a basic understanding of the principles of accounting as a result of prior business experience, education above the high school level, or bona fide home study. The audit or review report shall cover the association's financial statements, which shall be prepared using generally accepted accounting principles or the cash or tax basis of accounting.

(II) An audit shall be required under this paragraph (b) only when both of the following conditions are met:

(A) The association has annual revenues or expenditures of at least two hundred fifty thousand dollars; and

(B) An audit is requested by the owners of at least one-third of the units represented by the association.

(III) A review shall be required under this paragraph (b) only when requested by the owners of at least one-third of the units represented by the association.

(IV) Copies of an audit or review under this paragraph (b) shall be made available upon request to any unit owner beginning no later than thirty days after its completion.

(V) Notwithstanding section 38-33.3-117 (1.5) (h), this paragraph (b) shall not apply to an association that includes time-share units, as defined in section 38-33-110 (7).

(5) (a) Subject to subsection (6) of this section:

(I) The declaration, except a declaration for a large planned community, may provide for a period of declarant control of the association, during which period a declarant, or persons designated by such declarant, may appoint and remove the officers and members of the executive board. Regardless of the period of declarant control provided in the declaration, a period of declarant control terminates no later than the earlier of sixty days after conveyance of seventy-five percent of the units that may be created to unit owners other than a declarant, two years after the last conveyance of a unit by the declarant in the ordinary course of business, or two years after any right to add new units was last exercised.

(II) The declaration for a large planned community may provide for a period of declarant control of the association during which period a declarant, or persons designated by such declarant, may appoint and remove the officers and members of the executive board. Regardless of the period of declarant control provided in the declaration, a period of declarant control terminates in a large planned community no later than the earlier of sixty days after conveyance of seventy-five percent of the maximum number of units that may be created under zoning or other governmental development approvals in effect for the large planned community at any given time to unit owners other than a declarant, six years after the last conveyance of a unit by the declarant in the ordinary course of business, or twenty years after recordation of the declaration.

(b) A declarant may voluntarily surrender the right to appoint and remove officers and members of the executive board before termination of the period of declarant control, but, in that event, the declarant may require, for the duration of the period of declarant control, that specified actions of the association or executive board, as described in a recorded instrument executed by the declarant, be approved by the declarant before they become effective.

(c) If a period of declarant control is to terminate in a large planned community pursuant to subparagraph (II) of paragraph (a) of this subsection (5), the declarant, or persons designated by the declarant, shall no longer have the right to appoint and remove the officers and members of the executive board unless, prior to the termination date, the association approves an extension of the declarant's ability to appoint and remove no more than a majority of the executive board by vote of a majority of the votes entitled to be cast in person or by proxy, other than by the declarant, at a meeting duly convened as required by law. Any such approval by the association may contain conditions and limitations. Such extension of declarant's appointment and removal power, together with any conditions and limitations approved as provided in this paragraph (c), shall be included in an amendment to the declaration previously executed by declarant.

(6) Not later than sixty days after conveyance of twenty-five percent of the units that may be created to unit owners other than a declarant, at least one member and not less than twenty-five percent of the members of the executive board must be elected by unit owners other than the declarant. Not later than sixty days after conveyance of fifty percent of the units that may be created to unit owners other than a declarant, not less than thirty-three and one-third percent of the members of the executive board must be elected by unit owners other than the declarant.

(7) Except as otherwise provided in section 38-33.3-220 (5), not later than the termination of any period of declarant control, the unit owners shall elect an executive board of at least three members, at least a majority of whom must be unit owners other than the declarant or designated representatives of unit owners other than the declarant. The executive board shall elect the officers. The executive board members and officers shall take office upon election.

(8) Notwithstanding any provision of the declaration or bylaws to the contrary, the unit owners, by a sixty-seven percent vote of all persons present and entitled to vote at any meeting of the unit owners at which a quorum is present, may remove any member of the executive board with or without cause, other than a member appointed by the declarant or a member elected pursuant to a class vote under section 38-33.3-207 (4).

(9) Within sixty days after the unit owners other than the declarant elect a majority of the members of the executive board, the declarant shall deliver to the association all property of the unit owners and of the association held by or controlled by the declarant, including without limitation the following items:

(a) The original or a certified copy of the recorded declaration as amended, the association's articles of incorporation, if the association is incorporated, bylaws, minute books, other books and records, and any rules and regulations which may have been promulgated;

(b) An accounting for association funds and financial statements, from the date the association received funds and ending on the date the period of declarant control ends. The financial statements shall be audited by an independent certified public accountant and shall be accompanied by the accountant's letter, expressing either the opinion that the financial statements present fairly the financial position of the association in conformity with generally accepted accounting principles or a disclaimer of the accountant's ability to attest to the fairness of the presentation of the financial information in conformity with generally accepted accounting principles and the reasons therefore. The expense of the audit shall not be paid for or charged to the association.

(c) The association funds or control thereof;

(d) All of the declarant's tangible personal property that has been represented by the declarant to be the property of the association or all of the declarant's tangible personal property that is necessary for, and has been used exclusively in, the operation and enjoyment of the common elements, and inventories of these properties;

(e) A copy, for the nonexclusive use by the association, of any plans and specifications used in the construction of the improvements in the common interest community;

(f) All insurance policies then in force, in which the unit owners, the association, or its directors and officers are named as insured persons;

(g) Copies of any certificates of occupancy that may have been issued with respect to any improvements comprising the common interest community;

(h) Any other permits issued by governmental bodies applicable to the common interest community and which are currently in force or which were issued within one year prior to the date on which unit owners other than the declarant took control of the association;

(i) Written warranties of the contractor, subcontractors, suppliers, and manufacturers that are still effective;

(j) A roster of unit owners and mortgagees and their addresses and telephone numbers, if known, as shown on the declarant's records;

(k) Employment contracts in which the association is a contracting party;

(l) Any service contract in which the association is a contracting party or in which the association or the unit owners have any obligation to pay a fee to the persons performing the services; and

(m) For large planned communities, copies of all recorded deeds and all recorded and unrecorded leases evidencing ownership or leasehold rights of the large planned community unit owners' association in all common elements within the large planned community.

§ 38-33.3-304, C.R.S. Transfer of special declarant rights.

(1) A special declarant right created or reserved under this article may be transferred only by an instrument evidencing the transfer recorded in every county in which any portion of the common interest community is located. The instrument is not effective unless executed by the transferee.

(2) Upon transfer of any special declarant rights the liability of a transferor declarant is as follows:

(a) A transferor is not relieved of any obligation or liability arising before the transfer and remains liable for warranty obligations imposed upon such transferor by this article. Lack of privity does not deprive any unit owner of standing to bring an action to enforce any obligation of the transferor.

(b) If a successor to any special declarant right is an affiliate of a declarant, the transferor is jointly and severally liable with the successor for the liabilities and obligations of the successor which relate to the common interest community.

(c) If a transferor retains any special declarant rights but transfers other special declarant rights to a successor who is not an affiliate of the declarant, the transferor is liable for any obligations or liabilities imposed on a declarant by this article or by the declaration relating to the retained special declarant rights and arising after the transfer.

(d) A transferor has no liability for any act or omission or any breach of a contractual or warranty obligation arising from the exercise of a special declarant right by a successor declarant who is not an affiliate of the transferor.

(3) Unless otherwise provided in a mortgage instrument, deed of trust, or other agreement creating a security interest, in case of foreclosure of a security interest, sale by a trustee under an agreement creating a security interest, tax sale, judicial sale, or sale under bankruptcy or receivership proceedings of any units owned by a declarant or real estate in a common interest community subject to development rights, a person acquiring title to all the property being foreclosed or sold succeeds to only those special declarant rights related to that property held by that declarant which are specified in a written instrument prepared, executed, and recorded by such person at or about the same time as the judgment or instrument or by which such person obtained title to all of the property being foreclosed or sold.

(4) Upon foreclosure of a security interest, sale by a trustee under an agreement creating a security interest, tax sale, judicial sale, or sale under bankruptcy act or receivership proceedings of all interests in a common interest community owned by a declarant:

(a) The declarant ceases to have any special declarant rights; and

(b) The period of declarant control terminates unless the instrument which is required by subsection (3) of this section to be prepared, executed, and recorded at or about the same time as the judgment or instrument conveying title provides for transfer of all special declarant rights to a successor declarant.

(5) The liabilities and obligations of persons who succeed to special declarant rights are as follows:

(a) A successor to any special declarant right who is an affiliate of a declarant is subject to all obligations and liabilities imposed on any declarant by this article or by the declaration.

(b) A successor to any special declarant right, other than a successor described in paragraph (c) or (d) of this subsection (5) or a successor who is an affiliate of a declarant, is subject to all obligations and liabilities imposed by this article or the declaration:

(I) On a declarant which relate to the successor's exercise or non exercise of special declarant rights; or

(II) On the declarant's transferor, other than:

(A) Misrepresentations by any previous declarant;

(B) Warranty obligations on improvements made by any previous declarant or made before the common interest community was created;

(C) Breach of any fiduciary obligation by any previous declarant or such declarant's appointees to the executive board; or

(D) Any liability or obligation imposed on the transferor as a result of the transferor's acts or omissions after the transfer.

(c) A successor to only a right reserved in the declaration to maintain models, sales offices, and signs, if such successor is not an affiliate of a declarant, may not exercise any other special declarant right and is not subject to any liability or obligation as a declarant.

(d) A successor to all special declarant rights held by a transferor who succeeded to those rights pursuant to the instrument prepared, executed, and recorded by such person pursuant to the provisions of subsection (3) of this section may declare such successor's intention in such recorded instrument to hold those rights solely for transfer to another person. Thereafter, until transferring all special declarant rights to any person acquiring title to any unit or real estate subject to development rights owned by the successor or until recording an instrument permitting exercise of all those rights, that successor may not exercise any of those rights other than the right held by such successor's transferor to control the executive board in accordance with the provisions of section 38-33.3-303 (5) for the duration of any period of declarant control, and any attempted exercise of those rights is void. So long as a successor declarant may not exercise special declarant rights under this subsection (5), such successor declarant is not subject to any liability or obligation as a declarant, other than liability for the successor's acts and omissions under section 38-33.3-303 (4).

(6) Nothing in this section subjects any successor to a special declarant right to any claims against or other obligations of a transferor declarant, other than claims and obligations arising under this article or the declaration.

§ 38-33.3-305, C.R.S. Termination of contracts and leases of declarant.

(1) The following contracts and leases, if entered into before the executive board elected by the unit owners pursuant to section 38-33.3-303 (7) takes office, may be terminated without penalty by the association, at any time after the executive board elected by the unit owners pursuant to section 38-33.3-303 (7) takes office, upon not less than ninety days' notice to the other party:

(a) Any management contract, employment contract, or lease of recreational or parking areas or facilities;

(b) Any other contract or lease between the association and a declarant or an affiliate of a declarant; or

(c) Any contract or lease that is not bona fide or was unconscionable to the unit owners at the time entered into under the circumstances then prevailing.

(2) Subsection (1) of this section does not apply to any lease the termination of which would terminate the common interest community or reduce its size, unless the real estate subject to that lease was included in the common interest community for the purpose of avoiding the right of the association to terminate a lease under this section or a proprietary lease.

§ 38-33.3-306, C.R.S. Bylaws.

(1) In addition to complying with applicable sections, any, of the "Colorado Business Corporation Act", articles 101 to 117 of title 7, C.R.S., or the "Colorado Revised Nonprofit Corporation Act", articles 121 to 131 of title 7, C.R.S., if the common interest community is organized pursuant thereto, the bylaws of the association must provide:

(a) The number of members of the executive board and the titles of the officers of the association;

(b) Election by the executive board of a president, a treasurer, a secretary, and any other officers of the association the bylaws specify;

(c) The qualifications, powers and duties, and terms of office of, and manner of electing and removing, executive board members and officers and the manner of filling vacancies;

(d) Which, if any, of its powers the executive board or officers may delegate, to other persons or to a managing agent;

(e) Which of its officers may prepare, execute, certify, and record amendments to the declaration on behalf of the association; and

(f) A method for amending the bylaws.

(2) Subject to the provisions of the declaration, the bylaws may provide for any other matters the association deems necessary and appropriate.

(3) (a) If an association with thirty or more units delegates powers of the executive board or officers relating to collection, deposit, transfer, or disbursement of association funds to other persons or to a managing agent, the bylaws of the association shall require the following:

(I) That the other persons or managing agent maintain fidelity insurance coverage or a bond in an amount not less than fifty thousand dollars or such higher amount as the executive board may require;

(II) That the other persons or managing agent maintain all funds and accounts of the association separate from the funds and accounts of other associations managed by the other persons or managing agent and maintain all reserve accounts of each association so managed separate from operational accounts of the association;

(III) That an annual accounting for association funds and a financial statement be prepared and presented to the association by the managing agent, a public accountant, or a certified public accountant.

(b) Repealed, effective May 23,1996.

§ 38-33.3-307, C.R.S. Upkeep of the common interest community.

(1) Except to the extent provided by the declaration, subsection (2) of this section, or section 38-33.3-313 (9), the association is responsible for maintenance, repair, and replacement of the common elements, and each unit owner is responsible for maintenance, repair, and replacement of such owner's unit. Each unit owner shall afford to the association and the other unit owners,

and to their agents or employees, access through such owner's unit reasonably necessary for those purposes. If damage is inflicted, or a strong likelihood exists that it will be inflicted, on the common elements or any unit through which access is taken, the unit owner responsible for the damage, or expense to avoid damage, or the association if it is responsible, is liable for the cost of prompt repair.

(1.5) Maintenance, repair or replacement of any drainage structure or facilities, or other public improvements required by the local governmental entity as a condition of development of the common interest community or any part thereof shall be the responsibility of the association, unless such improvements have been dedicated to and accepted by the local governmental entity for the purpose of maintenance, repair, or replacement or unless such maintenance, repair, or replacement has been authorized by law to be performed by a special district or other municipal or quasi-municipal entity.

(2) In addition to the liability that a declarant as a unit owner has under this article, the declarant alone is liable for all expenses in connection with real estate within the common interest community subject to development rights. No other unit owner and no other portion of the common interest community is subject to a claim for payment of those expenses. Unless the declaration provides otherwise, any income or proceeds from real estate subject to development rights inures to the declarant. If the declarant fails to pay all expenses in connection with real estate within the common interest community subject to development rights, the association may pay such expenses, and such expenses shall be assessed as a common expense against the real estate subject to development rights, and the association may enforce the assessment pursuant to section 38-33.3-316 by treating such real estate as if it were a unit. If the association acquires title to the real estate subject to the development rights through foreclosure or otherwise, the development rights shall not be extinguished thereby, and thereafter, the association may succeed to any special declarant rights specified in a written instrument prepared, executed, and recorded by the association in accordance with the requirements of section 38-33.3-304(3).

(3) In a planned community, if all development rights have expired with respect to any real estate, the declarant remains liable for all expenses of that real estate unless, upon expiration, the declaration provides that the real estate becomes common elements or units.

§ 38-33.3-308, C.R.S. Meetings.

(1) Meetings of the unit owners, as the members of the association, shall be held at least once each year. Special meetings of the unit owners may be called by the president, by a majority of the executive board, or by unit owners having twenty percent, or any lower percentage specified in the bylaws, of the votes in the association. Not less than ten nor more than fifty days in advance of any meeting of the unit owners, the secretary or other officer specified in the bylaws shall cause notice to be hand delivered or sent prepaid by United States mail to the mailing address of each unit or to any other mailing address designated in writing by the unit owner. The notice of any meeting of the unit owners shall be physically posted in a conspicuous place, to the extent that such posting is feasible and practicable, in addition to any electronic posting or electronic mail notices that may be given pursuant to paragraph (b) of subsection (2) of this section. the notice shall state the time and place of the meeting and the items on the agenda, including the general nature of any proposed amendment to the declaration or bylaws, any budget changes, and any proposal to remove an officer or member of the executive board.

(2) (a) All regular and special meetings of the association's executive board, or any committee thereof, shall be open to attendance by all members of the association or their representatives. Agendas for meetings of the executive board shall be made reasonably available for examination by all members of the association or their representatives.

(b) (I) The association is encouraged to provide all notices and agendas required by this article in electronic form, by posting on a web site or otherwise, in addition to printed form. If such electronic means are available, the association shall provide notice of all regular and special meetings of unit owners by electronic mail to all unit owners who so request and who furnish the association with their electronic mail addresses. Electronic notice of a special meeting shall be given as soon as possible but at least twenty-four hours before the meeting.

(II) Notwithstanding section 38-33.3-117 (1.5) (i), this paragraph (b) shall not apply to an association that includes time-share units, as defined in section 38-33-110 (7), C.R.S.

(2.5) (a) Notwithstanding any provision in the declaration, bylaws, or other documents to the contrary, all meetings of the association and board of directors are open to every unit owner of the association, or to any person designated by a unit owner in writing as the unit owner's representative.

(b) At an appropriate time determined by the board, but before the board votes on an issue under discussion, unit owners or their designated representatives shall be permitted to speak regarding that issue. The board may place reasonable time restrictions on persons speaking during the meeting. If more than one person desires to address an issue and there are opposing views, the board shall provide for a reasonable number of persons to speak on each side of the issue.

(c) Notwithstanding section 38-33.3-117 (1.5) (i), this subsection (2.5) shall not apply to an association that includes time-share units, as defined in section 38-33-110 (7).

(3) The members of the executive board or any committee thereof may hold an executive or closed door session and may restrict attendance to executive board members and such other persons requested by the executive board during a regular or specially announced meeting or a part thereof. The matters to be discussed at such an executive session shall include only matters enumerated in paragraphs (a) to (e) of subsection (4) of this section.

(4) Matters for discussion by an executive or closed session are limited to:

(a) Matters pertaining to employees of the association or involving the employment, promotion, discipline, or dismissal of an officer, agent, or employee of the association;

(b) Consultation with legal counsel concerning disputes that are the subject of pending or imminent court proceedings or matters that are privileged or confidential between attorney and client;

(c) Investigative proceedings concerning possible or actual criminal misconduct;

(d) Matters subject to specific constitutional, statutory, or judicially imposed requirements protecting particular proceedings or matters from public disclosure;

(e) Any matter the disclosure of which would constitute an unwarranted invasion of individual privacy.

(f) Review of or discussion relating to any written or oral communication from legal counsel.

(4.5) Upon the final resolution of any matter for which the board received legal advice or that concerned pending or contemplated litigation, the board may elect to preserve the attorney-client privilege in any appropriate manner, or it may elect to disclose such information, as it deems appropriate, about such matter in an open meeting.

(5) Prior to the time the members of the executive board or any committee thereof convene in executive session, the chair of the body shall announce the general matter of discussion as enumerated in paragraphs (a) to (e) of Subsection (4) of this section.

(6) No rule or regulation of the board or any committee thereof shall be adopted during an executive session. A rule or regulation may be validly adopted only during a regular or special meeting or after the body goes back into regular session following an executive session.

(7) The minutes of all meetings at which an executive session was held shall indicate that an executive session was held, and the general subject matter of the executive session.

§ 38-33.3-309, C.R.S. Quorums.

(1) Unless the bylaws provide otherwise, a quorum is deemed present throughout any meeting of the association if persons entitled to cast twenty percent, or, in the case of an association with over one thousand unit owners, ten percent, of the votes which may be cast for election of the executive board are present, in person or by proxy at the beginning of the meeting.

(2) Unless the bylaws specify a larger percentage, a quorum is deemed present throughout any meeting of the executive board if persons entitled to cast fifty percent of the votes on that board are present at the beginning of the meeting or grant their proxy, as provided in section 7-128-205(4),C.R.S.

§ 38-33.3-310, C.R.S. Voting – proxies.

(1) (a) If only one of the multiple owners of a unit is present at a meeting of the association, such owner is entitled to cast all the votes allocated to that unit. If more than one of the multiple owners are present, the votes allocated to that unit may be cast only in accordance with the agreement of a majority in interest of the owners, unless the declaration expressly provides otherwise. There is majority agreement if any one of the multiple owners casts the votes allocated to that unit without protest being made promptly to the person presiding over the meeting by any of the other owners of the unit.

(b) (I) (A) Votes for contested positions on the executive board shall be taken by secret ballot. This sub-subparagraph (A) shall not apply to an association whose governing documents provide for election of positions on the executive board by delegates on behalf of the unit owners.

(B) At the discretion of the board or upon the request of twenty percent of the unit owners who are present at the meeting or represented by proxy, if a quorum has been achieved, a vote on any matter affecting the common interest community on which all unit owners are entitled to vote shall be by secret ballot.

(C) Ballots shall be counted by a neutral third party or by a committee of volunteers. Such volunteers shall be unit owners who are selected or appointed at an open meeting, in a fair manner, by the chair of the board or another person presiding during that portion of the meeting. The volunteers shall not be board members and, in the case of a contested election for a board position, shall not be candidates.

(D) The results of a vote taken by secret ballot shall be reported without reference to the names, addresses, or other identifying information of unit owners participating in such vote.

(II) Notwithstanding section 38-33.3-117 (1.5) (j), this paragraph (b) shall not apply to an association that includes time-share units, as defined in section 38-33-110 (7).

(2) (a) Votes allocated to a unit may be cast pursuant to a proxy duly executed by a unit owner. A proxy shall not be valid if obtained through fraud or misrepresentation. Unless otherwise provided in the declaration, bylaws, or rules of the association, appointment of proxies may be made substantially as provided in section 7-127-203, C.R.S.

(b) If a unit is owned by more than one person, each owner of the unit may vote or register protest to the casting of votes by the other owners of the unit through a duly executed proxy. A unit owner may not revoke a proxy given pursuant to this section except by actual notice of revocation to the person presiding over a meeting of the association. A proxy is void if it is not dated or purports to be revocable without notice. A proxy terminates eleven months after its date, unless it provides otherwise.

(c) The association is entitled to reject a vote, consent, written ballot, waiver, proxy appointment, or proxy appointment revocation if the secretary or other officer or agent authorized to tabulate votes, acting in good faith, has reasonable basis for doubt about the validity of the signature on it or about the signatory's authority to sign for the unit owner.

(d) The association and its officer or agent who accepts or rejects a vote, consent, written ballot, waiver, proxy appointment, or proxy appointment revocation in good faith and in accordance with the standards of this section are not liable in damages for the consequences of the acceptance or rejection.

(e) Any action of the association based on the acceptance or rejection of a vote, consent, written ballot, waiver, proxy appointment, or proxy appointment revocation under this section is valid unless a court of competent jurisdiction determines otherwise.

(3) (a) If the declaration requires that votes on specified matters affecting the common interest community be cast by lessees rather than unit owners of leased units:

(I) The provisions of subsections (1) and (2) of this section apply to lessees as if they were unit owners;

(II) Unit owners who have leased their units to other persons may not cast votes on those specified matters; and

(III) Lessees are entitled to notice of meetings, access to records, and other rights respecting those matters as if they were unit owners.

(b) Unit owners must also be given notice, in the manner provided in section 38-33.3-308, of all meetings at which lessees are entitled to vote.

(4) No votes allocated to a unit owned by the association may be cast.

§ 38-33.3-310.5, C.R.S. Executive board – conflicts of interest – definitions.

(1) Section 7-128-501, C.R.S., shall apply to members of the executive board; except that, as used in that section:

(a) "Corporation" or "nonprofit corporation" means the association.

(b) "Director" means a member of the association's executive board.

(c) "Officer" means any person designated as an officer of the association and any person to whom the board delegates responsibilities under this article, including, without limitation, a managing agent, attorney, or accountant employed by the board.

§ 38-33.3-311, C.R.S. Tort and contract liability.

(1) Neither the association nor any unit owner except the declarant is liable for any cause of action based upon that declarant's acts or omissions in connection with any part of the common interest community which that declarant has the responsibility to maintain. Otherwise, any action alleging an act or omission by the association must be brought against the association and not against any unit owner. If the act or omission occurred during any period of declarant control and the association gives the declarant reasonable notice of and an opportunity to defend against the action, the declarant who then controlled the association is liable to the association or to any unit owner for all tort losses not covered by insurance suffered by the association or that unit owner and all costs that the association would not have incurred but for

such act or omission. Whenever the declarant is liable to the association under this section, the declarant is also liable for all expenses of litigation, including reasonable attorney fees, incurred by the association. Any statute of limitation affecting the association's right of action under this section is tolled until the period of declarant control terminates. A unit owner is not precluded from maintaining an action contemplated by this section by being a unit owner or a member or officer of the association.

(2) The declarant is liable to the association for all funds of the association collected during the period of declarant control which were not properly expended.

§ 38-33.3-312, C.R.S. Conveyance or encumbrance of common elements.

(1) In a condominium or planned community, portions of the common elements may be conveyed or subjected to a security interest by the association if persons entitled to cast at least sixty-seven percent, of the votes in the association, including sixty seven percent of the votes allocated to units not owned by a declarant, or any larger percentage the declaration specifies, agree to that action; except that all owners of units to which any limited common element is allocated must agree in order to convey that limited common element or subject it to a security interest. The declaration may specify a smaller percentage only if all of the units are restricted exclusively to nonresidential uses. Proceeds of the sale are an asset of the association.

(2) Part of a cooperative may be conveyed and all or part of a cooperative may be subjected to a security interest by the association if persons entitled to cast at least sixty-seven percent of the votes in the association, including sixty-seven percent of the votes allocated to units not owned by a declarant, or any larger percentage the declaration specifies, agree to that action; except that, if fewer than all of the units or limited common elements are to be conveyed or subjected to a security interest, then all unit owners of those units, or the units to which those limited common elements are allocated, must agree in order to convey those units or limited common elements or subject them to a security interest. The declaration may specify a smaller percentage only if all of the units are restricted exclusively to nonresidential uses. Proceeds of the sale are an asset of the association. Any purported conveyance or other voluntary transfer of an entire cooperative, unless made in compliance with section 38-33.3-218, is void.

(3) An agreement to convey, or subject to a security interest, common elements in a condominium or planned community, or, in a cooperative, an agreement to convey, or subject to a security interest, any part of a cooperative, must be evidenced by the execution of an agreement, in the same manner as a deed, by the association. The agreement must specify a date after which the agreement will be void unless approved by the requisite percentage of owners. Any grant, conveyance, or deed executed by the association must be recorded in every county in which a portion of the common interest community is situated and is effective only upon recordation.

(4) The association, on behalf of the unit owners, may contract to convey an interest in a common interest community pursuant to subsection (1) of this section, but the contract is not enforceable against the association until approved pursuant to subsections (1) and (2) of this section and executed and ratified pursuant to subsection (3) of this section. Thereafter, the association has all powers necessary and appropriate to effect the conveyance or encumbrance, including the power to execute deeds or other instruments.

(5) Unless in compliance with this section, any purported conveyance, encumbrance, judicial sale, or other transfer of common elements or any other part of a cooperative is void.

(6) A conveyance or encumbrance of common elements pursuant to this section shall not deprive any unit of its rights of ingress and egress of the unit and support of the unit.

(7) Unless the declaration otherwise provides, a conveyance or encumbrance of common elements pursuant to this section does not affect the priority or validity of preexisting encumbrances.

(8) In a cooperative, the association may acquire, hold, encumber, or convey a proprietary lease without complying with this section.

§ 38-33.3-313, C.R.S. Insurance.

(1) Commencing not later than the time of the first conveyance of a unit to a person other than a declarant, the association shall maintain, to the extent reasonably available:

(a) Property insurance on the common elements and, in a planned community, also on property that must become common elements, for broad form covered causes of loss; except that the total amount of insurance must be not less than the full insurable replacement cost of the insured property less applicable deductibles at the time the insurance is purchased and at each renewal date, exclusive of land, excavations, foundations, and other items normally excluded from property policies; and

(b) Commercial general liability insurance against claims and liabilities arising in connection with the ownership, existence, use, or management of the common elements, and, in cooperatives, also of all units, in an amount, if any, specified by the common interest community instruments or otherwise deemed sufficient in the judgment of the executive board but not less than any amount specified in the association documents, insuring the executive board, the unit owners' association, the management agent, and their respective employees, agents, and all persons acting as agents. The declarant shall be included as an additional insured in such declarant's capacity as a unit owner and board member. The unit owners shall be included as additional insureds but only for claims and liabilities arising in connection with the ownership, existence, use, or management of the common elements and, in cooperatives, also of all units. The insurance shall cover claims of one or more insured parties against other insured parties.

(2) In the case of a building that is part of a cooperative or that contains units having horizontal boundaries described in the declaration, the insurance maintained under paragraph (a) of subsection (1) of this section must include the units but not the finished interior surfaces of the walls, floors, and ceilings of the units. The insurance need not include improvements and betterments installed by unit owners, but if they are covered, any increased charge shall be assessed by the association to those owners.

(3) If the insurance described in subsections (1) and (2) of this section is not reasonably available, or if any policy of such insurance is canceled or not renewed without a replacement policy therefore having been obtained, the association promptly shall cause notice of that fact to be hand delivered or sent prepaid by United States mail to all unit owners. The declaration may require the association to carry any other insurance, and the association in any event may carry any other insurance it considers appropriate, including insurance on units it is not obligated to insure, to protect the association or the unit owners.

(4) Insurance policies carried pursuant to subsections (1) and (2) of this section must provide that:

(a) Each unit owner is an insured person under the policy with respect to liability arising out 9f such unit owner's interest in the common elements or membership in the association;

(b) The insurer waives its rights to subrogation under the policy against any unit owner or member of his household;

(c) No act or omission by any unit owner, unless acting within the scope of such unit owner's authority on behalf of the association, will void the policy or be a condition to recovery under the policy; and

(d) If, at the time of a loss under the policy, there is other insurance in the name of a unit owner covering the same risk covered by the policy, the association's policy provides primary insurance.

(5) Any loss covered by the property insurance policy described in paragraph (a) of subsection (1) and subsection (2) of this section must be adjusted with the association, but the insurance proceeds for that loss shall be payable to any insurance trustee designated for that purpose, or otherwise to the association, and not to any holder of a security interest. The insurance trustee

or the association shall hold any insurance proceeds in trust for the association unit owners and lienholders as their interests may appear. Subject to the provisions of subsection (9) of this section, the proceeds must be disbursed first for the repair or restoration of the damaged property, and the association, unit owners, and lienholders are not entitled to receive payment of any portion of the proceeds unless there is a surplus of proceeds after the property has been completely repaired or restored or the common interest community is terminated.

(6) The association may adopt and establish written nondiscriminatory policies and procedures relating to the submittal of claims, responsibility for deductibles, and any other matters of claims adjustment. To the extent the association settles claims for damages to real property, it shall have the authority to assess negligent unit owners causing such loss or benefiting from such repair or restoration all deductibles paid by the association. In the event that more than one unit is damaged by a loss, the association in its reasonable discretion may assess each unit owner a pro rata share of any deductible paid by the association.

(7) An insurance policy issued to the association does not obviate the need for unit owners to obtain insurance for their own benefit.

(8) An insurer that has issued an insurance policy for the insurance described in subsections (1) and (2) of this section shall issue certificates or memoranda of insurance to the association and upon request, to any unit owner or holder of a security interest. Unless otherwise provided by statute, the insurer issuing the policy may not cancel or refuse to renew it until thirty days after notice of the proposed cancellation or nonrenewal has been mailed to the association, and each unit owner and holder of a security interest to whom a certificate or memorandum of insurance has been issued, at their respective last-known addresses.

(9) (a) Any portion of the common interest community for which insurance is required under this section which is damaged or destroyed must be repaired or replaced promptly by the association unless:

(I) The common interest community is terminated, in which case section 38-33.3-218 applies;

(II) Repair or replacement would be illegal under any state or local statute or ordinance governing health or safety;

(III) Sixty seven percent of the unit owners, including every owner of a unit or assigned limited common element that will not be rebuilt, vote not to rebuild; or

(IV) Prior to the conveyance of any unit to a person other than the declarant, the holder of a deed of trust or mortgage on the damaged portion of the common interest community rightfully demands all or a substantial part of the insurance proceeds.

(b) The cost of repair or replacement in excess of insurance proceeds and reserves is a common expense. If the entire common interest community is not repaired or replaced, the insurance proceeds attributable to the damaged common elements must be used to restore the damaged area to a condition compatible with the remainder of the common interest community, and, except to the extent that other persons will be distributees, the insurance proceeds attributable to units and limited common elements that are not rebuilt must be distributed to the owners of those units and the owners of the units to which those limited common elements were allocated, or to lienholders, as their interests may appear, and the remainder of the proceeds must be distributed to all the unit owners or lienholders, as their interests may appear, as follows:

(I) In a condominium, in proportion to the common element interests of all the units; and

(II) In a cooperative or planned community, in proportion to the common expense liabilities of all the units; except that, in a fixed or limited equity cooperative, the unit owner may not receive more of, the proceeds than would satisfy the unit owner's entitlements under the declaration if the unit owner leaves the cooperative. In such a cooperative, the proceeds that remain after satisfying the unit owner's obligations continue to be held in trust by the association for the benefit of the cooperative. If the unit owners vote not to rebuild any unit, that unit's allocated interests are automatically reallocated upon the vote as if the unit had been condemned under section 38-33.3-107, and the association promptly shall prepare, execute, and record an amendment to the declaration reflecting the reallocations.

(10) If any unit owner or employee of an association with thirty or more units controls or disburses funds of the common interest community, the association must obtain and maintain, to the extent reasonably available, fidelity insurance. Coverage shall not be less in aggregate than two months' current assessments plus reserves, as calculated from the current budget of the association.

(11) Any person employed as an independent contractor by an association with thirty or more units for the purposes of managing a common interest community must obtain and maintain fidelity insurance in an amount not less than the amount specified in subsection (10) of this section, unless the association names such person as an insured employee in a contract of fidelity insurance, pursuant to subsection (10) of this section.

(12) The association may carry fidelity insurance in amounts greater than required in subsection (10) of this section and may require any independent contractor employed for the purposes of managing a common interest community to carry more fidelity insurance coverage than required in subsection (10) of this section.

(13) Premiums for insurance that the association acquires and other expenses connected with acquiring such insurance are common expenses.

§ 38-33.3-314, C.R.S. Surplus funds.

Unless otherwise provided in the declaration, any surplus funds of the association remaining after payment of or provision for common expenses and any prepayment of or provision for reserves shall be paid to the unit owners in proportion to their common expense liabilities or credited to them to reduce their future common expense assessments.

§ 38-33.3-315, C.R.S. Assessments for common expenses.

(1) Until the association makes a common expense assessment, the declarant shall pay all common expenses. After any assessment has been made by the association, assessments shall be made no less frequently than annually and shall be based on a budget adopted no less frequently than annually by the association.

(2) Except for assessments under subsections (3) and (4) of this section and section 38-33.3- 207 (4) (a) (IV), all common expenses shall be assessed against all the units in accordance with the allocations set forth in the declaration pursuant to section 38-33.3-207 (1) and (2). Any past-due common expense assessment or installment thereof shall bear interest at the rate established by the association not exceeding twenty-one percent per year.

(3) To the extent required by the declaration:

(a) Any common expense associated with the maintenance, repair, or replacement of a limited common element shall be assessed against the units to which that limited common element is assigned, equally, or in any other proportion the declaration provides;

(b) Any common expense or portion thereof benefiting fewer than all of the units shall be assessed exclusively against the units benefited; and

(c) The costs of insurance shall be assessed in proportion to risk, and the costs of utilities shall be assessed in proportion to usage.

(4) If any common expense is caused by the misconduct of any unit owner, the association may assess that expense exclusively against such owner's unit.

(5) If common expense liabilities are reallocated, common expense assessments and any installment thereof not yet due shall be recalculated in accordance with the reallocated common expense liabilities.

(6) Each unit owner is liable for assessments made against such owner's unit during the period of ownership of such unit. No unit owner may be exempt from liability for payment of the assessments by waiver of the use or enjoyment of any of the common elements or by abandonment of the unit against which the assessments are made.

(7) Unless otherwise specifically provided in the declaration or bylaws, the association may enter into an escrow agreement with the holder of a unit owner's mortgage so that assessments may be combined with the unit owner's mortgage payments and paid at the same time and in the same manner; except that any such escrow agreement shall comply with any applicable rules of the federal housing administration, department of housing and urban development, veterans' administration, or other government agency.

§ 38-33.3-316, C.R.S. Lien for assessments.

(1) The association, if such association is incorporated or organized as a limited liability company, has a statutory lien on a unit for any assessment levied against that unit or fines imposed against its unit owner. Unless the declaration otherwise provides, fees, charges, late charges, attorney fees, fines, and interest charged pursuant to section 38-33.3-302 (1) (j), 1 (k), and (1) (1), section 38-33.3-313 (6), and section 38-33-315 (2) are enforceable as assessments under this article. The amount of the lien shall include all those items set forth in this section from the time such items become due. If an assessment is payable in installments, each installment is a lien from the time it becomes due, including the due date set by any valid association acceleration of installment obligations.

(2) (a) A lien under this section is prior to all other liens and encumbrances on a unit except:

(I) Liens and encumbrances recorded before the recordation of the declaration and, in a cooperative, liens and encumbrances which the association creates, assumes, or takes subject to;

(II) A security interest on the unit which has priority over all other security interests on the unit and which was recorded before the date on which the assessment sought to be enforced became delinquent, or, in a cooperative, a security interest encumbering only the unit owner's interest which has priority over all other security interests on the unit and which was perfected before the date on which the assessment sought to be enforced became delinquent; and

(III) Liens for real estate taxes and other governmental assessments or charges against the unit or cooperative.

(b) Subject to paragraph (d) of this subsection (2), a lien under this section is also prior to the security interests described in subparagraph (II) of paragraph (a) of this subsection (2) to the extent of:

(I) An amount equal to the common expense assessments based on a periodic budget adopted by the association under section 38-33.3-315 (J) which would have become due, in the absence of any acceleration, during the six months immediately preceding institution by either the association or any party holding a lien senior to any part of the association lien created under this section of an action or a nonjudicial foreclosure either to enforce or to extinguish the lien.

(II) Deleted by amendment effective 4-3 0-93

(c) This subsection (2) does not affect the priority of mechanics' or material men's liens or the priority of liens for other assessments made by the association. A lien under this section is not subject to the provisions of part 2 of article 41 of this title or to the provisions of section 15 -11-201, C.R.S.

(d) The association shall have the statutory lien described in subsection (1) of this section for any assessment levied or fine imposed after June 30, 1993. Such lien shall have the priority described in this subsection (2) if the other lien or encumbrance is created after June 30, 1992.

(3) Unless the declaration otherwise provides, if two or more associations have liens for assessments created at any time on the same property, those liens have equal priority.

(4) Recording of the declaration constitutes record notice and perfection of the lien. No further recordation of any claim of lien for assessments is required.

(5) A lien for unpaid assessments is extinguished unless proceedings to enforce the lien are instituted within six years after the full amount of assessments become due.

(6) This section does not prohibit actions or suits to recover sums for which subsection (1) of this section creates a lien or to prohibit an association from taking a deed in lieu of foreclosure.

(7) The association shall be entitled to costs and reasonable attorney fees incurred by the association in a judgment or decree in any action or suit brought by the association under this section.

(8) The association shall furnish to a unit owner or such unit owner's designee or to a holder of a security interest or its designee upon written request, delivered personally or by certified mail, first-class postage prepaid, return receipt, to the association's registered agent, a written statement setting forth the amount of unpaid assessments currently levied against such owner's unit. The statement shall be furnished within fourteen calendar days after receipt of the request and is binding on the association, the executive board, and every unit owner. If no statement is furnished to the unit owner or holder of a security interest or their designee, delivered personally or by certified mail, first-class postage prepaid, return receipt requested, to the inquiring party, then the association shall have no right to assert a lien upon the unit for unpaid assessments which were due as of the date of the request.

(9) In any action by an association to collect assessments or to foreclose a lien for unpaid assessments, the court may appoint a receiver of the unit owner to collect all sums alleged to be due from the unit owner prior to or during the pending of the action. The court may order the receiver to pay any sums held by the receiver to the association during the pending of the action to the extent of the association's common expense assessments.

(10) In a cooperative, upon nonpayment of an assessment on a unit, the unit owner may be evicted in the same manner as provided by law in the case of an unlawful holdover by a commercial tenant, and the lien may be foreclosed as provided by this section.

(11) The association's lien may be foreclosed by any of the following means:

(a) In a condominium or planned community, the association's lien may be foreclosed in like manner as a mortgage on real estate.

(b) In a cooperative whose unit owners' interests in the units are real estate as determined in accordance with the provisions of section 38-33.3-105, the association's lien must be foreclosed in like manner as a mortgage on real estate.

(c) In a cooperative whose unit owners' interests in the units are personal property, as determined in accordance with the provisions of section 38-33.3-105, the association's lien must be foreclosed as a security interest under the "Uniform Commercial Code", title 4, C.R.S.

§ 38-33.3-316.5, C.R.S. Time share estate – foreclosure – definitions.

(1) As used in this section, unless the context otherwise requires:

(a) "Junior lienor" has the same meaning as set forth in section 38-38-100.3 (12), C.R.S.

(b) "Obligor" means the person liable for the assessment levied against a time share estate pursuant to section 38 33.3-316 or the record owner of the time share estate.

(c) "Time share estate" has the same meaning as set forth in section 38-33-110 (5).

(2) A plaintiff may commence a single judicial foreclosure action pursuant to section 38-33.3-316 (11), joining as defendants multiple obligors with separate time share estates and the junior lienors thereto, if:

(a) The judicial foreclosure action involves a single common interest community;

(b) The declaration giving rise to the right of the association to collect assessments creates default and remedy obligations that are substantially the same for each obligor named as a defendant in the judicial foreclosure action;

(c) The action is limited to a claim for judicial foreclosure brought pursuant to section 38-33.3-316 (11); and

(d) The plaintiff does not allege, with respect to any obligor, that the association's lien is prior to any security interest described in section 38-33.3-316 (2) (a) (II), even if such a claim could be made pursuant to section 38-33.3-316 (2) (b) (I).

(3) In a judicial foreclosure action in which multiple obligors with separate time share estates and the junior lienors thereto have been joined as defendants in accordance with this section:

(a) In addition to any other circumstances where severance is proper under the Colorado rules of civil procedure, the court may sever for separate trial any disputed claim or claims;

(b) If service by publication of two or more defendants is permitted by law, the plaintiff may publish a single notice for all joined defendants for whom service by publication is permitted, so long as all information that would be required by law to be provided in the published notice as to each defendant individually is included in the combined published notice. Nothing in this paragraph (b) shall be interpreted to allow service by publication of any defendant if service by publication is not otherwise permitted by law with respect to that defendant.

(c) The action shall be deemed a single action, suit, or proceeding for purposes of payment of filing fees, notwithstanding any action by the court pursuant to paragraph (a) of this subsection (3), so long as the plaintiff complies with subsection (2) of this section.

(4) Notwithstanding that multiple obligors with separate time share estates may be joined in a single judicial foreclosure action, unless otherwise ordered by the court, each time share estate foreclosed pursuant to this section shall be subject to a separate foreclosure sale, and any cure or redemption rights with respect to such time share estate shall remain separate.

(5) The plaintiff in an action brought pursuant to this section is deemed to waive any claims against a defendant for a deficiency remaining after the foreclosure of the lien for assessment and for attorney fees related to the foreclosure action.

§ 38-33.3-317, C.R.S. Association records.

(1) (a) The association shall keep financial records sufficiently detailed to enable the association to comply with section 38-33.3-316 (8) concerning statements of unpaid assessments.

(b) The association shall keep as permanent records minutes of all meetings of unit owners and the executive board, a record of all actions taken by the unit owners or executive board by written ballot or written consent in lieu of a meeting, a record of all actions taken by a committee of the executive board in place of the executive board on behalf of the association, and a record of all waivers of notices of meetings of unit owners and of the executive board or any committee of the executive board.

(c) (I) The association or its agent shall maintain a record of unit owners in a form that permits preparation of a list of the names and addresses of all unit owners, showing the number of votes each unit owner is entitled to vote.

(II) Notwithstanding section 38-33.3-117 (1) (l), this paragraph (c) shall not apply to a unit, or the owner thereof, if the unit is a time-share unit, as defined in section 38-33-110 (7).

(d) The association shall maintain its records in written form or in another form capable of conversion into written form within a reasonable time.

(2) (a) Except as otherwise provided in paragraph (b) of this subsection (2), all financial and other records shall be made reasonably available for examination and copying by any unit owner and such owner's authorized agents.

(b) (I) Notwithstanding paragraph (a) of this subsection (2), a membership list or any part thereof may not be obtained or used by any person for any purpose unrelated to a unit owner's interest as a unit owner without consent of the executive board.

(II) Without limiting the generality of subparagraph (I) of this paragraph (b), without the consent of the executive board, a membership list or any part thereof may not be:

(A) Used to solicit money or property unless such money or property will be used solely to solicit the votes of the unit owners in an election to be held by the association;

(B) Used for any commercial purpose; or

(C) Sold to or purchased by any person.

(3) The association may charge a fee, which may be collected in advance but which shall not exceed the association's actual cost per page, for copies of association records.

(4) As used in this section, "reasonably available" means available during normal business hours, upon notice of five business days, or at the next regularly scheduled meeting if such meeting occurs within thirty days after the request, to the extent that:

(a) The request is made in good faith and for a proper purpose;

(b) The request describes with reasonable particularity the records sought and the purpose of the request; and

(c) The records are relevant to the purpose of the request.

(5) In addition to the records specified in subsection (1) of this section, the association shall keep a copy of each of the following records at its principal office:

(a) Its articles of incorporation, if it is a corporation, or the corresponding organizational documents if it is another form of entity;

(b) The declaration;

(c) The covenants;

(d) Its bylaws;

(e) Resolutions adopted by its executive board relating to the characteristics, qualifications, rights, limitations, and obligations of unit owners or any class or category of unit owners;

(f) The minutes of all unit owners' meetings, and records of all action taken by unit owners without a meeting, for the past three years;

(g) All written communications within the past three years to unit owners generally as unit owners;

(h) A list of the names and business or home addresses of its current directors and officers;

(i) Its most recent annual report, if any; and

(j) All financial audits or reviews conducted pursuant to section 38-33.3-303 (4) (b) during the immediately preceding three years.

(6) This section shall not be construed to affect:

(a) The right of a unit owner to inspect records:

(I) Under corporation statutes governing the inspection of lists of shareholders or members prior to an annual meeting; or

(II) If the unit owner is in litigation with the association, to the same extent as any other litigant; or

(b) The power of a court, independently of this article, to compel the production of association records for examination on proof by a unit owner of proper purpose.

(7) This section shall not be construed to invalidate any provision of the declaration, bylaws, the corporate law under which the association is organized, or other documents that more broadly defines records of the association that are subject to inspection and copying by unit owners, or that grants unit owners freer access to such records; except that the privacy protections contained in paragraph (b) of subsection (2) of this section shall supersede any such provision.

§ 38-33.3-318, C.R.S. Association as trustee.

With respect to a third person dealing with the association in the association's capacity as a trustee, the existence of trust powers and their proper exercise by the association may be assumed without inquiry. A third person is not bound to inquire whether the association has the power to act as trustee or is properly exercising trust powers. A third person, without actual knowledge that the association is exceeding or improperly exercising its powers, is fully protected in dealing with the association as if it possessed and properly exercised the powers it purports to exercise. A third person is not bound to assure the proper application of trust assets paid or delivered to the association in its capacity as trustee.

§ 38-33.3-319, C.R.S. Other applicable statutes.

To the extent that provisions of this article conflict with applicable provisions in the "Colorado Business Corporation Act", articles 101 to 117 of title 7, C.R.S., the "Colorado Revised Nonprofit Corporation Act", articles 121 to 137 of title 7, C.R.S., the "Uniform Partnership Law", article 60 of title 7, C.R.S., the "Colorado Uniform Partnership Act (1997)", article 64 of title 7, C.R.S., the "Colorado Uniform Limited Partnership Act of 1981", article 62 of title 7, C.R.S., article 1 of this title, article 55 of title 7, C.R.S., article 33.5 of this title, and section 39-1-103 (10), C.R.S., and any other laws of the state of Colorado which now exist or which are subsequently enacted, the provisions of this article shall control.

XIII. Cooperative Housing Corporations

* *§ 38-33.5-101, C.R.S. Method of formation – purpose*

Cooperative housing corporations may be formed by any three or more adult residents of this state associating themselves to form a cooperative or nonprofit corporation, pursuant to articles 55, 56, or 58 of title 7, C.R.S., or the "Colorado Revised Nonprofit Corporation Act", articles 121 to 137 of title 7, C.R.S. The specified purpose of the entity must be to provide each stockholder in or member of the entity with the right to occupy, for dwelling purposes, a house or an apartment in a building owned or leased by the entity.

§ 38-33.5-102, C.R.S. Requirements for articles of incorporation of cooperative housing corporations.

(1) In addition to any other requirements for articles of incorporation imposed by the "Colorado Revised Nonprofit Corporation Act", articles 121 to 137 of title 7, C.R.S. 1973, such articles of incorporation shall, in the case of cooperative housing corporations, include the following provisions:

(a) That the corporation shall have only one class of stock outstanding;

(b) That each stockholder is entitled, solely by reason of his ownership of stock in the corporation, to occupy, for dwelling purposes, a house or an apartment in a building owned or leased by the corporation;

(c) That the interest of each stockholder in the corporation shall be inseparable from and appurtenant to the right of occupancy, and shall be deemed an estate in real property for all purposes, and shall not be .deemed personal property;

(d) That no stockholder is entitled to receive any distribution not out of earnings and profits of the corporation except on a complete or partial liquidation of the corporation.

§ 38-33.5-103, C.R.S. Provisions relating to taxes, interest, and depreciation on corporate property.

(1) The bylaws of a cooperative housing corporation shall provide that no less than eighty percent of the gross income of the corporation in any taxable year shall be derived from payments from "tenant-stockholders". For the purposes of this article, "tenant-stockholder" means an individual who is a stockholder in the corporation and whose stock is fully paid when measured by his proportionate share of the value of the corporation's equity in the property.

(2) The bylaws shall further provide that each tenant-stockholder shall be credited with his proportionate payment of real estate taxes paid or incurred in any year on the buildings and other improvements owned or leased by the corporation in which the "tenant-stockholder's" living quarters are located, together with the land to which such improvements are appurtenant, and likewise with respect to interest paid or incurred by the corporation as well as depreciation on real and personal property which are proper deductions related to the said lands and improvements thereon for purposes of state and federal income taxation.

§ 38-33.5-104, C.R.S. Financing of cooperative housing – stock certificates held by tenant stockholders.

Stock certificates or membership certificates issued by cooperative housing corporations to tenant-stockholders shall be valid securities for investment by savings and loan associations, when the conditions imposed by sections 11-41-119 (13), C.R.S. are met.

§ 38-33.5-105, C.R.S. Provisions to be included in proprietary lease or right of tenancy issued by corporation.

(1) Every stockholder of a cooperative housing corporation shall be entitled to receive from the corporation a proprietary lease or right of tenancy document which shall include the following provisions:

(a) That no sublease in excess of one year, amendment, or modification to such propriety lease or right of tenancy in the property shall be permitted or created without the lender's prior written consent; and

(b) That the security for a loan against the tenant-stockholder's interest shall be in the nature of a real property security interest, and any default of such loan shall entitle the lender to treat such default in the same manner as a default of a loan secured by real property.

§ 38-33.5-106, C.R.S. Exemption from securities laws.

Any stock certificate or other evidence of membership issued by a cooperative housing corporation as an investment in its stock or capital to tenant-stockholders of such corporation is exempt from securities laws contained in article 51 of title 11, C.R.S.

Chapter 5:
Landmark Case Law and Opinions

An * in the left margin indicates a change in the statute, rule, or text since the last publication of the manual.

I. Supreme Court Decision on Practice of Law by Brokers

Colorado brokers are allowed to render services to their clients to a greater degree than are brokers in other states. The practicing real estate broker, of necessity, must work closely with practicing lawyers. Each practitioner zealously guards the legal field of his or her endeavor. In Colorado, a real estate broker renders service to his or her client beyond merely procuring a buyer. Colorado brokers should familiarize themselves with the Colorado Supreme Court's decisions in the cases of (1) *Conway-Bogue Realty Investment Co. v. Denver Bar Association*, (2) *Title Guaranty Co. v. Denver Bar Association*, and (3) *Record Abstract & Title Co. v. Denver Bar Association.*

In the case of *Conway-Bogue Realty Investment Co. v. Denver Bar Association*, 312 P.2d 998 (Colo. 1957), the Colorado Supreme Court addressed whether real estate brokers should be enjoined from preparing certain legal documents relating to and affecting real estate and the title thereto (such as receipts and options for purchase, contracts of sale, deeds, deeds of trust, and leases), and from giving advice to the parties regarding the legal effect of the documents.

In rendering its decision, the Colorado Supreme Court stated:

> The first question to be determined is:
>
> Does the preparation of receipts and options, deeds, promissory notes, deeds of trust, mortgages, releases of encumbrances, leases, notice terminating tenancies, demands to pay rent or vacate by completing standard and approved printed forms, coupled with the giving of explanation or advice as to the legal effect thereof, constitute the practice of law?
>
> This question we answer in the affirmative.
>
> . . .
>
> The remaining and most difficult question to be determined is:
>
> Should the defendants as licensed real estate brokers (none of whom are licensed attorneys) be enjoined from preparing in the regular course of their business the instruments enumerated above, at the requests of their customers and only in connection with transactions involving sales of real estate, loans on real estate or the leasing of real estate which transactions are being handled by them?
>
> This question we answer in the negative.
>
> . . .
>
> The testimony shows, and there is no effort to refute the same, that there are three counties in Colorado that have no lawyers, ten in each of which there

5. Case Law

is only one lawyer, seven in each of which there are only two lawyers; that many persons in various areas of the state reside at great distances from any lawyer's office. The testimony shows without contradiction that the practices sought to be enjoined are of at least 50 years uninterrupted duration; that a vast majority of the people of the state who buy, sell, encumber and lease real estate have chosen real estate brokers rather than lawyers to perform the acts herein complained of. Though not controlling, we must make note of the fact that the record is devoid of evidence of any instance in which the public or any member thereof, layman or lawyer has suffered injury by reason of the act of any of the defendants sought to be enjoined. Likewise, though not controlling, we take judicial notice of the fact that the legislature of the state, composed of 100 members from all walks of life and every section of the state, usually called upon by their constituents to adopt legislation designed to eliminate evils and protect the public against practices contrary to the public welfare, has never taken any steps to prevent continuation of the alleged evil which we are now asked to enjoin.

. . .

We feel that to grant the injunctive relief requested, thereby denying to the public the right to conduct real estate transactions in the manner in which they have been transacted for over half a century, with apparent satisfaction, and requiring all such transactions to be conducted through lawyers, would not be in the public interest. The advantages, if any, to be derived by such limitation are outweighed by the conveniences now enjoyed by the public in being permitted to choose whether their brokers or their lawyers shall do the acts or render the service which plaintiffs seeks to enjoin.

Summary of Decision on Practice of Law by Brokers

The following is an excellent summary of the case given by John E. Gorsuch, legal counsel for the Colorado Association of Realtors, quoted from the August 1957 issue of the Colorado Real Estate News:

It should be kept in mind that the Court states that the practices in question do amount to the practice of law. The Court says that it will not enjoin real estate brokers from doing these simple acts, however, under the circumstances indicated, because of the Court's express belief that the public's best interest will be served by continuing the present practice. The present practice, however, means the practice shown by the evidence. In other words, the broker's activity is limited to the following circumstances:

1. His office must be connected with the transaction as broker.
2. There must be no charge for preparing the documents other than the normal commission.
3. The documents must be prepared on commonly used printed, standard, and approved forms.

It is clear from the decision that the broker should not, under any circumstances:

1. Prepare any legal documents as a business, courtesy or favor, for any transaction with which he is not connected as broker, either with or without pay.
2. He should not prepare any documents which cannot be properly prepared on the standard and approved printed form.
3. He clearly should not draw wills, contracts, agreements and so forth, except the initial binder contract or other customary agreements of the type used to bind the transaction or sale.
4. In addition, it would appear in the best interests of the public and also in conformity with the Court's opinion for the broker to:
    a. Always recommend to the purchaser that the title be examined.
    b. Inform the parties that each has a right to have the papers prepared by an attorney of their own choosing.
    c. Advise the parties that each has a right to be represented at the closing by an attorney if they desire.
    d. In spite of the permission to prepare such documents, there will inevitably arise situations in which the legal complications are beyond the knowledge of the broker. In such instances an attorney's assistance should always be sought.

> In conclusion, it could be said that the Supreme Court will allow the brokers to prepare these legal documents on standard and approved printed forms by filling in the blanks therein, with information obtained from the usual sources, in transactions with which they are connected as brokers, when they receive no compensation for these acts other than their ordinary commission. It is to the interest of every broker that these limitations be properly recognized and followed so that the Supreme Court would not have a reason to change its opinion at a future date.

The final words of Mr. Gorsuch's summary bear repeating: "It is to the interest of every broker that these limitations be properly recognized and followed so that the Supreme Court would not have a reason to change its opinion at a future date."

With privilege granted, there must be no abuse. The same authority that granted it may take a privilege such as this away. A privilege respected may be retained. A careless regard is not sufficient. There must be a careful determination and application of what is authorized practice of law by a real estate broker.

The court in its decision referred to the use of "standard and approved" forms, but did not elaborate. Consequently, it was necessary to establish what is a STANDARD and what is an APPROVED form.

Any form purchased from a stationery store or a printer may or may not be a "standard and approved" form. The printer is under no obligation to determine what is standard or what is approved. However, a real estate broker may have such an obligation. Therefore, the brokers needed some guidance and support in their determination of what is a standard and approved form.

In the years following the *Conway-Bogue* decision, the business of real estate practice grew rapidly. There appeared to be less and less standardization of legal forms. Each association of brokers, each locality, and even individual brokers used their own forms, often times drafted with personal prejudice.

The real estate industry became concerned that its privilege to practice law, within the limited sphere, might be abrogated by the court. In 1970, the Colorado Association of Real Estate Boards passed a resolution requesting the Real Estate Commission to approve standard forms and to make their use compulsory. In response to this request, the Real Estate Commission held public hearings on the question. The consensus of opinion drawn from the hearings was almost unanimous: the industry wanted the Commission to use its authority to standardize forms throughout the state. As a result, the Commission in 1971 promulgated and adopted Rule F, which was submitted to the Attorney General. The Attorney General concluded that Rule F was a constitutional exercise of the Commission's rule-making authority.

Rule F covers forms for listing contracts, sales contracts, exchange contracts, disclosure forms, settlement sheets, extension agreements, and counterproposals. At the time of this writing, Rule F does not cover forms for business opportunity listing or sales contracts, management agreements, leases, warranty deeds, etc. In these areas, the broker must use his or her best judgment.

In 1993, the legislature gave the Commission statutory authority to promulgate standard forms for use by real estate licensees. (See § 12-61-803(4), C.R.S.)

In the area of listing and conveyancing covered by Rule F, it is to the advantage of the general public and of real estate licensees to use the Commission-approved forms. Much of the wording used in these approved forms has been interpreted by the Colorado Supreme Court and its meaning is known. Other portions have been rewritten to conform to Colorado Supreme Court opinion when older provisions have been found invalid. Economic conditions have also necessitated changes. Changes can also be expected in the Commission-approved forms, but reasonable notice will always be given to licensed brokers.

Companion Decision on Practice of Law

On the same day as *Conway-Bogue*, the Colorado Supreme Court decided the cases of *Title Guaranty Co. v. Denver Bar Association* and *Record Abstract & Title Co. v. Denver Bar Association*, which were taken as companion cases from which one decision was rendered (see 312 P.2d 1011 (Colo. 1957)).

In these two cases, the Denver Bar Association sought to enjoin the title company and the abstract company from preparing certain legal documents for others, giving advice as to their legal effect, and performing other acts that allegedly constituted the unauthorized practice of law.

The court reduced the issues to three:

1. Wherein one of the defendant corporations prepared papers incidental to the making of a loan from funds belonging to the corporation.

The court held that in such a case, the defendant may prepare the notes, deeds of trust, or mortgages incidental to making the loans. The defendant could not be restrained even if at the time of the closing the defendant had a firm commitment for the sale of the loan.

2. In situations where the parties involved in the transaction used an "escrow service" or "closing service" provided by the defendant corporations wherein they draft deeds, promissory notes, trust deeds, mortgages, and receipt and option contracts, and the defendants set a minimum fee and a sliding scale of charges for this service.

The court mentioned that the defendants actively solicited such business, although it was the same service that real estate brokers rendered as an incident of their business and without separate charge. The court held that the defendants were conducting a separate, distinct, and other business, much of which constituted the practice of law and could properly be restrained.

3. The third problem presented was where the defendant's "closing service" was used and the defendant also sold title insurance on the property involved.

The court held that the defendants could be enjoined and that the "escrow service" or "closing service" was not necessary or incidental to the issuance of title insurance. The court further held that the attorneys employed by them were representing the corporation and not the parties involved. The court said in part, "To hold otherwise would be to authorize corporations to practice law for compensation."

The court began its opinion by stating that it should be read and considered in connection with the opinion on the case between the real estate brokers and the lawyers.

II. Licensee Acting on Own Account—Commission Jurisdiction

The Commission staff is often asked whether it can investigate complaints against a licensee where the licensee is not involved as an agent in the transaction. The answer is yes. The Commission can investigate and take disciplinary action against a licensee acting on the licensee's own account where the licensee acts in a dishonest manner. Typical examples are where the licensee/owner does not disclose a known defect, fails to disclose the licensee's licensed status as a purchaser, or provides fraudulent information on a loan application.

Printed in relevant part below is the Colorado Court of Appeals case of *Seibel v. Colorado Real Estate Commission*, 530 P.2d 1290 (Colo. App. 1974) in which the issue of the Commission's jurisdiction over "non-agency" activities arose.

Ed. Note: The statutes cited in this opinion are now found in §§ 12-61-101 through -811, C.R.S.

> This appeal raises the question of jurisdiction of the Colorado Real Estate Commission over acts of a broker in negotiating the acquisition of an interest in real estate for his own use. The hearing officer and the Colorado Real Estate Commission, directly, and the district court, by implication, all concluded that the real estate brokers licensing act, C.R.S. 1963, 117-1-1, *et seq.*, and rules adopted by the commission pursuant to that statute do apply to the conduct of licensed brokers in real estate matters relating to actions taken for their own account. We affirm.
>
> Appellant (Seibel) is a licensed real estate broker. Intending to purchase a home owned by persons named Debord for his own use, he signed a receipt and option agreement, proceeding through the listing broker, Roberts. Seibel was not able to close on the agreed date, and accepted return of his deposit.

Several days later, one Arvidson signed a receipt and option agreement relating to the same property, again proceeding through Roberts. Seibel was not aware of this transaction. He personally contacted the Debords and attempted to have them sign a new contract for sale of the property to him. This proposed contract stated that Seibel and Roberts would divide the commission equally. All of the contacts by Seibel with the Debords regarding the second contract were made without the consent or approval of the listing broker.

After Seibel learned of the Arvidson contract, he recorded the original receipt and option agreement. The Debord-Arvidson sale was closed with $500 being placed in escrow to cover the cost of a possible quiet title suit to clear the records of the Seibel contract.

Pursuant to statute, proceedings were held before a hearing officer of the Colorado Real Estate Commission on alleged violations of both the real estate brokers licensing act and a commission rule. The hearing officer found that the commission had jurisdiction, that Seibel was guilty of improper and dishonest dealing in making direct contact with the sellers, that Seibel had violated both C.R.S. 1963, 117-1-12(1)(t), and Real Estate Commission Rule E-13, and therefore recommended that his license be suspended for a period of not less than thirty nor more than ninety days.

C.R.S. 1963, 117-l-12(1)(t), proscribes conduct "which constitutes dishonest dealing." Real Estate Commission Rule E-13 specifies that: "A real estate broker shall not negotiate a sale, exchange, lease or listing contract of real property directly with an owner for compensation from such owner if he knows that such owner has a written unexpired contract in connection with such property which grants an exclusive right to sell to another broker, or which grants an exclusive agency to another broker.

The Real Estate Commission approved and adopted the findings of the hearing officer, and suspended Seibel's license for a period of thirty days. The district court reversed the commission's finding that Seibel had violated the statute, but affirmed the finding that he had violated Rule E-13. The matter was remanded to the commission to impose whatever penalty the commission felt was warranted for the violation of the rule. The commission thereupon suspended plaintiff's license for ten days, and this appeal followed.

Seibel urges that 1965 Perm. Supp., C.R.S. 1963, 117-1-2(4), provides him a specific exemption from the authority of the commission in this case, since he was attempting to buy the home for his personal use and was not acting as a real estate broker. The pertinent paragraphs of this section state that:

"(a) The terms 'real estate broker' or 'real estate salesman,' as used in this article, shall not apply to any of the following:

. . . .

(e) Any owner of real estate acting personally, or a corporation acting through its officers, or regular salaried employees, in his or its own behalf with respect to property owned or leased by him or it, except as provided in subsection (2) of this section;

(f) Any person, firm, partnership, association acting personally, or a corporation acting through its officers or regular salaried employees, in his or its own behalf as principal in acquiring or in negotiating to acquire any interest in real estate . . . ."

. . .

Considering the statute in light of these principles, we conclude that the purpose of the exemption section of 1965 Perm. Supp., C.R.S. 1963, 117-1-2(4), is to permit an owner of property to sell it, or to permit one to purchase property for his own account without having to procure a real estate license. These paragraphs have no application to the matter of discipline of licensed real estate brokers and salesmen. To interpret the statute as Seibel urges, would be to adopt an illogical and unduly restrictive meaning of the regulatory provisions of the entire statute.

. . . .

Hence, we conclude that where a real estate broker is dealing in real estate for his own account, the Colorado Real Estate Commission has jurisdiction over his acts and can suspend or revoke his license for proven violations of the licensing statute or of the commission's rules. A broker can no more be allowed to violate the rules of the Real Estate Commission when purchasing property for his own account than he can when purchasing it for a client.

III. Attorney General's Opinion on Business Opportunities

Michael B. Gorham,
Deputy Director Division of Real Estate

Dear Mr. Gorham:

I am responding to your request of February 9, 1983, for an attorney general's opinion concerning the requirement of a real estate license to receive a commission in the sale of a business opportunity and possible exceptions to that requirement.

QUESTIONS PRESENTED AND CONCLUSIONS

Your questions ask

1. A person receives compensation for performing acts as basically set forth in C.R.S. 1973, 12-61-101(2)(i). Does the statute require such a person to obtain a real estate broker's license where the change in ownership or interest in real estate is an integral part of the business or business opportunity transaction, but is not negotiated or offered by the person? The answer to your first question is "yes", unless the person falls within one of the statutory exemptions contained in C.R.S. 1973, 12-61-101(4), as amended, or C.R.S. 1973, 12-61-101(2)(i).

2. If the answer to No. 1, is "yes" under what circumstances, if any, could a person involve himself in the transfer of a business or business opportunity for compensation without violating C.R.S. 1973, 12-61-101(2)(i).

The statute under consideration, C.R.S. 1973, 12-61-101(2)(i), grants an exception to the requirement of a real estate license to receive a commission for the sale of a business opportunity. Other circumstances where a license is not required are those situations within the ambit of C.R.S. 1973, 12-61-101(4), *et seq.*

ANALYSIS

C.R.S. 1973, 12-61-101(2)(i), as amended, sets forth a definition of a "real estate broker" in the sale of a business opportunity. The statute states:

(2) "Real estate broker" or "broker" means any person, firm, partnership, association, or corporation who, in consideration of compensation by fee, commissions, salary, or anything of value or with the intention of receiving or collecting such compensation, engages in or offers or attempts to engage in, either directly or indirectly, by a continuing course of conduct or by any single act or transaction, any of the following acts:

(I) Negotiating or attempting or offering to negotiate the listing, sale, purchase, exchange or lease of a business or business opportunity or the goodwill thereof or any interest therein when such act or transaction involves directly or indirectly any change in the ownership or interest in real estate, or in leasehold interest or estate, or in a business or business opportunity which owns an interest in real estate or in a leasehold unless such act is performed by any broker-dealer or insurer-dealer licensed under the provisions of article 51 of title 11, C.R.S. 1973, who is actually engaged generally in the business of offering, selling, purchasing or trading in securities or any officer, partner, salesman, employee or other authorized representative or agent thereof;

C.R.S. § 12-61-101(2)(i) was adopted in 1965 in response to the Colorado Supreme Court's decision in *Cary v. Borden Co.*, 153 Colo. 344, 386 P.2d 585 (1963). In that case, the supreme court, based on the old definition of a real estate broker found in C.R.S. § 117-1-2(1), adopted the minority New York rule and allowed recovery of a commission by an unlicensed person in the sale of a business opportunity where the interest in real estate was not the dominant feature of the whole transaction.

In *Broughall v. Black Forest Development Co.*, 196 Colo. 503, 593 P.2d 314 (1978), the Colorado Supreme Court found that the legislative intent of C.R.S. § 12-61-101(2)(i) in changing the definition of a real estate broker was to bring Colorado in line with the majority New Jersey rule. That rule defines a real estate broker to include anyone who negotiates any transaction that directly or indirectly involves a change in ownership in real estate or who negotiates a change in ownership of a business or business opportunity which includes an interest in real estate or in a leasehold. *Kenny v. Patterson Milk & Cream Co., Inc.*, 110 N.J.L. 141, 164 A. 274 (1932). This definition does not require that the change in the interest in real estate or in a leasehold be negotiated. Nor does the definition require that the change in ownership or interest in real estate be an integral part of the transaction. Furthermore, the transaction is not severable so that an unlicensed person may receive a commission on the portion of the sale not involving real estate, if the transfer as a whole involves the transfer of an interest in land or a leasehold. *Broughall v. Black Forest Development Co.*, supra.

C.R.S. 1973, 12-61-101(2)(i) does not require that the transfer of an interest in real estate or a leasehold be negotiated or offered to bring one within the definition of a real estate broker. It only requires that one negotiate a transfer of a business or business opportunity, and that the business or business opportunity include an interest in real estate or a leasehold.

Furthermore, the statute in question sets forth a very broad definition of "negotiating". "Negotiating" has been interpreted to mean the simple act of introducing the buyer and seller, thus bringing that act under the license laws and requiring a license before receiving a commission on the sale of a business opportunity. *Brakhage v. Georgetown Associates*, 33 Colo. App. 385, 523 P.2d 145 (1974).

Because the answer to question 1 is "yes" I will set forth the circumstances under which a person could receive compensation for the sale of a business opportunity, although not licensed as a real estate broker.

[The Opinion sets forth all of the exceptions to licensing requirements under 12-61-101(4). These are not repeated for the sake of brevity.]

Therefore, if a person falls within one of these exceptions, he does not need to obtain a real estate broker's license.

Summary

The change in the licensing law to bring Colorado under the majority New Jersey rule requires that a person must be licensed to receive compensation for the sale of a business or business opportunity where there is also a transfer of an interest in real estate or a leasehold, no matter whether the interest or leasehold is negotiated or if the interest is insignificant in comparison to the rest of the transaction. Also, the transaction must not be separable so that one can avoid the licensing requirement and collect compensation on the basis of the sale of the business or business opportunity only.

Circumstances under which persons may receive compensation without a license are set forth in the exception provided in § 12-61-101(2)(i), C.R.S. and the exception to the definitions of "real estate broker" found in § 12-61-101(4), C.R.S.

Ed. Note: The license law statutes cited in this opinion are now found in § 12-61-101(2), C.R.S.

Chapter 6: Interests in Land History

An * in the left margin indicates a change in the statute, rule, or text since the last publication of the manual.

I. Introduction

Modern real property law has evolved from the English feudal system of land ownership. The basic concept of the feudal system was that the king, as owner of all the land, would grant large tracts of land to faithful lords in return for allegiance and service. The lords then granted portions of their land to lesser nobles, and so on. These grants, called "**feuds**," continued on down to the "**villeins**" who lived on and cultivated the land. Except for the monarch and the villeins, each person occupied a dual position as both overlord to his tenant and tenant to his overlord.

The land itself was considered to owe services to the lord; the tenant performed those services. The service due was specified at the time the tenant received a land grant. Thus, a tenant might owe rent to the overlord and this overlord might owe "knight (or military) service" on the same land to a higher lord. In addition to the services, there were certain "**incidents**" due from all feuds, such as homage (a ceremonial pledge of personal loyalty) and relief (the payment of a sum by the heir of the tenant for the right to inherit—an ancient inheritance tax).

Land ownership is the basis of power and wealth. More than a system of land ownership, the feudal system was also a system of government, establishing an economic structure and a military organization. Because there was no centralized administration for the kingdom, discipline and order were effectively maintained through the series of lord-and-vassal relationships.

The relationship between the English Crown and the American colonies was essentially feudal. For example, according to the Maryland Charter, the feudal services due were the delivery of two Indian arrows on Tuesday of Easter week and one-fifth of all the gold and silver ore found within the boundaries of the land grant. After the revolution, the feudal position of the English Crown presumably passed to the states. In most states, the concept of feudal tenure was abolished by statute or judicial decision. In a few, the technical concept of feudal tenure may technically still exist. As a practical matter, all states now follow the "**allodial theory**" of land ownership, meaning an owner holds land in absolute independence, owing nothing to the state as overlord. Of course, the state always retains jurisdiction over land within its borders, including the four governmental rights discussed in this chapter.

II. Kinds of Interests in Land

A unique concept of Anglo-American land law is that of "**estates**." Estate types derived from the feudal system and are either "**freehold**" (ownership) estates or "**non-freehold**" (non-owned) estates. Freehold estates were normal holdings under the feudal system, and are: (1) fee simple absolute, (2) defeasible (or base or qualified) fee, (3) fee tail, and (4) life estate. Non-freehold estates appear to have begun primarily as a moneylender's device and did not have the dignity of feudal stature. Non-freehold estates are: (1) estate for years, (2) estate from period-to-period, (3) estate at will, and (4) estate at sufferance.

An estate is the type of ownership in land, and determines the duration of an individual's right of possession and right of use. For example, if a "fee simple" owner leases property to a tenant for ten years, both have interests in the property. The tenant's estate is called an "estate for years" and entitles the tenant to assert the right of exclusive possession against anyone, including the owner. The tenant must not abuse the property and has a limited right of use. The owner retains the right to possession at the end of the lease term—a present right to future possession. This interest of the owner is known as a "**reversion**."

The law concerning interests in land is extremely technical and complex. The following discussion is simplified and condensed.

A. Freehold Estates

Fee simple absolute

Often called a fee or a fee simple, this is the most comprehensive bundle of ownership rights known in law. This bundle of rights includes the rights to possess, use, enjoy, control, and dispose. A condominium is a fee simple estate created in air space.

Although fee simple is the highest degree of land ownership recognized by law, it is never absolute ownership (such as owning this book, for example). An owner's fee simple title is always subject to governmental and private limitations that apply equally to all types of estates in land.

The four major governmental limitations on land are:

1. **Police Power** – the right to impose reasonable limitations to protect and promote the health, safety, and general welfare of the public;
2. **Eminent Domain** – the right to take private property for public use in return for payment of just compensation;
3. **Taxation** – the right to impose taxes for governmental support and to proceed against the land for non-payment; and
4. **Escheat** – the right to acquire title to property owned by a person who dies without leaving a will (intestate) or heirs-at-law.

Private limitations upon the use of land are usually classified as:

1. **Deed Restrictions** – imposed by a grantor, such as requiring that all structures built upon the land must be of brick veneer, or that the property may only be used for a specific purpose;
2. **Mortgages** – a security claim of the mortgagee (lender) upon the property preventing use or change that would injure the property's value;
3. **Leases** – an agreement that suspends the fee holder's right to use and possess for some period of time; and
4. **Easements** – a right to cross over the property of the fee holder without interference.

Defeasible fee

A defeasible fee, also called a base or qualified fee, is a fee simple subject to a special limitation, a condition subsequent, or an executory limitation.

A fee simple subject to a "**special limitation**" automatically terminates the fee upon the happening of a specified event. Example: An owner in fee simple absolute conveys to another person and his or her heirs so long as the land is used for church purposes. This conveyance may last forever. But if the land ceases to be used for church purposes, ownership automatically reverts to the grantor, or to the grantor's successors-in-interest.

A fee simple subject to a "**condition subsequent**" gives the grantor, or the grantor's successors-in-interest, the power to terminate the grantee's estate upon the happening of a specified event. Example: If an owner in fee simple absolute conveys with a restriction against alcohol being sold on the premises, the owner shall have the right to re-enter for breach of this condition. Differing from a special limitation described above, this interest does not revert automatically upon the breach of the condition, but continues until the original owner exercises power of termination by re-entry.

Unlike the first two types of defeasible fees, a fee simple subject to an "**executory limitation**" does not return to the grantor but passes automatically to some third party upon the happening of a specified event. Example: An owner in fee simple absolute conveys with a limitation holding that if the grantee dies without surviving children, then the fee automatically passes to a third party named in the deed.

Fee tail

A fee tail estate historically created an estate along family lines. The first grantee could not re-convey the land, but was obligated to continue downward inheritance as long as there were lineal descendants. Upon failure of the chain, the land would automatically revert to the grantor or grantor's successors-in-interest. Fee tail estates are considered unsuited to American culture, and have been abolished or modified in all states. Some states provide that a conveyance, which under common law would have created a fee tail, now conveys a fee simple absolute. Other states, including Colorado, provide that the first grantee holds a life estate and the first heirs take a fee simple title. (See § 38-30-106, C.R.S.)

Life estate

A fee simple owner conveying to another for his or her lifespan creates an estate for life. Upon the grantee's death, the fee reverts to the grantor or grantor's successors-in-interest. Similar to a lease, the grantee may not make unreasonable use of the property or do anything that would decrease the value of the grantor's reversionary interest.

A life estate could also be created by a conveyance for as long as the grantee lives and then to a third party named in the deed. Alternatively, a life estate may also be based on the life of a third party instead of the grantee.

Although abolished in Colorado, there are two "legal" life estates automatically created by law and recognized in a few states today: dower and curtesy. (See § 15-11-112, C.R.S.)

Dower

Dower is a life interest of one-third of any real estate owned by a husband during the marriage given to his wife upon his death. The husband could not defeat the dower by conveying before death. If a wife had joined her husband in conveying the property, she was held to have waived her dower right.

Curtesy

Curtesy is a life estate in all of the real property owned by a wife during the marriage given to her husband upon her death, provided a child was born from their marriage. As in dower, a conveyance by the wife would not terminate the husband's curtesy right unless he joined in the conveyance.

B. Non-Freehold Estates

Non-freehold estates are "**leasehold**" interests. These are more fully discussed in Chapter 20, "Property Management and Leases."

Estate for years (tenancy for years)

An estate for years is one for a *fixed period of time*, whether for a day, one year, or 99 years. A conveyance from landlord to tenant for ten years creates an estate for years.

Estate from period-to-period (periodic tenancy)

Such an estate exists when there is *no definite agreed-upon duration* or termination date, but the rental period is fixed at a certain amount per week, month, or year. These estates are usually created by implication rather than express provision. Either party may terminate this estate by giving the statutory notice of termination at the expiration of any rental period.

Estate at will (tenancy at will)

Expressed or implied, an estate at will *may be terminated at the will of either party*. Upon the giving of proper notice, either the tenant or landlord may cancel the estate at any time.

Estate at sufferance (tenancy at sufferance)

This estate arises when the *tenant wrongfully holds over* after the expiration of the lease term.

III. Concurrent Interests

An estate in land may be owned by one person (in severalty), or by two or more persons concurrently. The two most important types of co-ownership are joint tenancy and tenancy in common.

A. Joint Tenancy

All co-owners are equally entitled to the use, enjoyment, control, and possession of the land or its equivalent in rents and profits. The best-known characteristic of joint tenancy is the "**right of survivorship**." Upon the death of one joint tenant, the decedent's rights pass immediately to the surviving tenant(s). Death of a joint tenant does not affect title, as the title is vested equally in all joint tenants rather than individually.

According to common law, joint tenancy must feature **"four unities**": time, title, interest, and possession. Joint tenants must acquire title at the same time, be named in the same deed, hold exactly equal interests, and be entitled to equal rights of possession. A conveyance from an owner in severalty to herself and her spouse could not have created a joint tenancy under common law because the unities of time and title were missing. However, under Colorado law such a deed would create a joint tenancy:

§ 38-31-101, C.R.S. Joint tenancy expressed in instrument – when.

(1) Except as otherwise provided in subsection (3) of this section and in section 38-31-201, no conveyance or devise of real property to two or more natural persons shall create an estate in joint tenancy in real property unless, in the instrument conveying the real property or in the will devising the real property, it is declared that the real property is conveyed or devised in joint tenancy or to such natural persons as joint tenants. The abbreviation "JTWROS" and the phrase "as joint tenants with right of survivorship" or "in joint tenancy with right of survivorship" shall have the same meaning as the phrases "in joint tenancy" and "as joint tenants". Any grantor in any such instrument of conveyance may also be one of the grantees therein.

(1.5) (a) The doctrine of the four unities of time, title, interest, and possession is continued as part of the law of this state subject to subsections (1), (3), (4), (5), (6), and (7) of this section and paragraph (b) of this subsection (1.5).

(b) Subsections (1), (3), (4), (5), (6), and (7) of this section are intended and shall be construed to clarify, supplement, and, limited to their express terms, modify the doctrine of the four unities.

(c) For purposes of this subsection (1.5), the "doctrine of the four unities of time, title, interest, and possession" means the common law doctrine that a joint tenancy is created by conveyance or devise of real property to two or more persons at the same time of the same title to the same interest with the same right of possession and includes the right of survivorship.

(2) (Deleted by amendment, L. 2006, p. 240, § 1, effective July 1, 2006.)

(3) A conveyance or devise to two or more personal representatives, trustees, or other fiduciaries shall be presumed to create an estate in joint tenancy in real property and not a tenancy in common.

(4) An estate in joint tenancy in real property shall only be created in natural persons; except that this limitation shall not apply to a conveyance or devise of real property to two or more personal representatives, trustees, or other fiduciaries. Any conveyance or devise of real property to two or more persons that does not create or is not presumed to create an estate in joint tenancy in the manner described in this section shall be a conveyance or devise in tenancy in common or to tenants in common.

(5) (a) Except as provided in sections 38-35-118 and 38-41-202 (4), a joint tenant may sever the joint tenancy between himself or herself and all remaining joint tenants by unilaterally executing and recording an instrument conveying his or her interest in real property to himself or herself as a tenant in common. The joint tenancy shall be severed upon recording such instrument. If there are two or more remaining joint tenants, they shall continue to be joint tenants as among themselves.

(b) Filing a petition in bankruptcy by a joint tenant shall not sever a joint tenancy.

(6) (a) The interests in a joint tenancy may be equal or unequal. The interests in a joint tenancy are presumed to be equal and such presumption is:

(I) Conclusive as to all persons who obtain an interest in property held in joint tenancy when such persons are without notice of unequal interests and have relied on an instrument recorded pursuant to section 38-35-109; and

(II) Rebuttable for all other persons.

(b) This subsection (6) does not bar claims for equitable relief as among joint tenants, including but not limited to partition and accounting.

(c) Upon the death of a joint tenant, the deceased joint tenant's interest is terminated. In the case of one surviving joint tenant, his or her interest in the property shall continue free of the deceased joint tenant's interest. In the case of two or more surviving joint tenants, their interests shall continue in proportion to their respective interests at the time the joint tenancy was created.

(d) For purposes of the "Colorado Medical Assistance Act", articles 4, 5, and 6 of title 25.5, C.R.S., a joint tenancy shall be deemed to be a joint tenancy with equal interests among the joint tenants regardless of the language in the deed or other instrument creating the joint tenancy.

(7) Nothing in this section shall be deemed to abrogate any existing case law to the extent that such case law establishes other means of severing a joint tenancy.

As one author put it, there is nothing sacred about joint tenancy. Any joint tenant can terminate the relationship by a conveyance or a contract to convey, or through involuntary transfer (*e.g.*, foreclosure or tax sale). When a joint tenancy is terminated, either voluntarily or involuntarily, the remaining co-owners then become tenants in common.

B. Tenancy in Common

Tenancy in common is an estate in land held by two or more persons with *only the unity of possession.* Unlike joint tenants, tenants in common may take title at different times and may receive their interests through different deeds. But each is entitled to the undivided possession of the property, according to their proportionate share and subject to the rights of possession of the other tenants. Upon the death of a tenant in common, there is no right of survivorship. The decedent's interest passes according to his or her will or the state law of descent and distribution.

IV. Concurrent Conveyances

Ownership of a home by a husband and wife is usually declared by the deed to be in "joint tenancy" or as "tenants in common." Each has advantages and disadvantages.

The automatic and immediate right of survivorship that accompanies joint tenancy eliminates some legal complications of probate in the event of the death of one of the parties. However, inheritance taxes are assessable and evidence of the death must be recorded. Joint tenancy ensures the survivor a fair share of the marital property and the property does pass free of the claims of unsecured creditors.

Disadvantages of joint tenancy may arise if marital difficulties occur or if one of the parties has obligations or responsibilities (*e.g.*, children) resulting from a previous marriage. The financial and tax situation of the parties may also favor tenancy in common.

Although it is helpful and proper to explain the meaning of "joint tenancy" or "tenancy in common," a broker must *never advise a client what type of conveyance is best.* To do so exceeds the role of broker and constitutes the unauthorized practice of law.

V. Homestead Exemption

Under § 38-41-201, C.R.S.,

> (1) Every homestead in the state of Colorado shall be exempt from execution and attachment arising from any debt, contract, or civil obligation not

> exceeding in actual cash value in excess of any liens or encumbrances on the homesteaded property in existence at the time of any levy of execution thereon:
>
> (a) The sum of sixty thousand dollars if the homestead is occupied as a home by an owner thereof or an owner's family; or
>
> (b) The sum of ninety thousand dollars if the homestead is occupied as a home by an elderly or disabled owner, an elderly or disabled spouse of an owner, or an elderly or disabled dependent of an owner.

The terms "householder" and "owner of the property" also include a person holding equity under a land contract or other agreement where such person possesses the property, but the sellers' or vendors' rights are always superior to any homestead.

If the debt, contract, or civil obligation that is the basis for the execution and attachment was entered into or incurred *after* July 1, 1975, the homestead exemption *will be created automatically* as long as the requirements outlined in §§ 38-41-203 and -205, C.R.S., are met. (See § 38-41-202, C.R.S.) Section 38-41-203, C.R.S., states that homesteaded property is only exempt while occupied as a home by the owner or owner's family. Section 38-41-205, C.R.S., states that "[t]he homestead . . . may consist of a house and lot or lots or of a farm consisting of any number of acres."

If, however, "the debt, contract, or civil obligation . . . was entered into or incurred prior to July 1, 1975," the owner or spouse must record in the office of the clerk and recorder of the county where the property is situated an instrument in writing (which should be acknowledged) describing the property, setting forth the nature and source of the owner's interest therein, and stating that the owner is homesteading the property.

A surviving joint tenant spouse will have the same homestead exemption as the deceased joint tenant. If there is no surviving spouse, the surviving minor children will hold the exemption. This survival occurs without the need for occupancy. Homestead exemptions do not pass to an unrelated joint tenant (*i.e.*, they pass only to spouse, parent, or minor child).

If the homestead was created automatically, the owner may convey or encumber the property without the signature of the owner's spouse. If the owner or owner's spouse recorded the homestead exemption as described above, then both spouses must execute any conveyance or encumbrance.

A homestead exemption may be released in writing signed by the party or parties who could convey the property. A statement contained in a mortgage, deed of trust, or other instrument creating a lien and waiving or releasing the homestead subordinates the homestead to that particular lien. The homestead exemption would stand against any other judgment creditor who had not secured such a waiver.

If a homestead property is sold, the person entitled to the homestead may keep the sale proceeds separate, and, if identified, the proceeds will be exempt from execution or attachment for one year. If the proceeds are used to buy a new home, there will be a homestead exemption on the new home. However, the homestead exemption does not defeat the rights of the holder of a purchase-money mortgage.

Before any creditor may proceed with execution and attachment of a homesteaded property, the creditor must file an affidavit with the clerk and recorder attesting that the equity in the property exceeds the amount of the exemption. This must be supported by the affidavit of an independent appraiser stating the fair market value of the property. If the amount offered at the sale does not exceed 70 percent of fair market value as shown in the affidavit, all proceedings to sell the property will terminate. If the sale succeeds, the creditor must pay the expenses of the sale, prior liens, and the homestead exemption before satisfying the creditor's own judgment. The balance, if any, would go to the homesteader.

VI. Easements

An easement is a limited right to enter and use another person's land.

An "**appurtenant easement**" attaches to and benefits the land owned by the easement holder. This is the "**dominant estate**." The land burdened by an easement is the "**servient estate**." Appurtenant easements pass with the title to the dominant estate and pass with the land, even if not mentioned in the deed. Easements for light and air are appurtenant, although they may limit the usage of the land subject to the easement.

An **"easement in gross"** belongs to and benefits the owner personally rather than the land itself. The right to run a utility line across another person's land is an example of an easement in gross. Easements in gross are assignable and permanent.

Easements are normally created by written contract or an express grant in a deed signed by the owner of the land over which the easement lies (the servient estate). Easements may also be created by prescription, *i.e.*, by long uninterrupted use without the consent of the owner. Abandonment would terminate a prescriptive easement.

Easements may also be created by implication of law. Such an easement may be so implied when an owner sells land that is inaccessible except through land belonging to the seller. Because the new owner must have access to owned land, an easement may be implied.

Ordinarily, easements are terminated by a written release or quitclaim deed given by the holder of the dominant estate to the owner of the servient estate. Easements may also be terminated by destruction of the servient estate or by a merger of the dominant and servient estates into one parcel.

VII. Adverse Possession

Adverse possession is the right of an occupant of land to acquire superior title against the owner of record without the owner's concurrence, provided the occupancy has been actual, notorious, hostile, visible, and continuous for a required statutory period. This right of adverse possession can be inherited, but there can be no intervening tenancy.

In Colorado the required adverse possession statutory periods are:

1. 18 years – without the consent of the owner of record, without color of title or payment of property taxes. (See § 38-41-101, C.R.S.)
2. 7 years – with color of title and/or with payment of seven years of property taxes. (See § 38-41-108, C.R.S.)

HB 08-1148, effective July 2008, made the first substantive statutory change in Colorado adverse possession law in over 100 years.

§ 38-41-101, C.R.S. Limitation of eighteen years.

(1) No person shall commence or maintain an action for the recovery of the title or possession or to enforce or establish any right or interest of or to real property or make an entry thereon unless commenced within eighteen years after the right to bring such action or make such entry has first accrued or within eighteen years after he or those from, by, or under whom he claims have been seized or possessed of the premises. Eighteen years' adverse possession of any land shall be conclusive evidence of absolute ownership.

(2) The limitation provided for in subsection (1) of this section shall not apply against the state, county, city and county, city, irrigation district, public, municipal, or quasi-municipal corporation, or any department or agency thereof. No possession by any person, firm, or corporation, no matter how long continued, of any land, water, water right, easement, or other property whatsoever dedicated to or owned by the state of Colorado, or any county, city and county, city, irrigation district, public, municipal, or quasi-municipal corporation, or any department or agency thereof shall ever ripen into any title, interest, or right against the state of Colorado, or such county, city and county, city, public, municipal, or quasi-municipal corporation, irrigation district, or any department or agency thereof.

(3) (a) In order to prevail on a claim asserting fee simple title to real property by adverse possession in any civil action filed on or after July 1, 2008, the person asserting the claim shall prove each element of the claim by clear and convincing evidence.

(b) In addition to any other requirements specified in this part 1, in any action for a claim for fee simple title to real property by adverse possession for which fee simple title vests on or after July 1, 2008, in favor of the adverse possessor and against the owner of record of the real property under subsection (1) of the section, a person may acquire fee simple title to real property by adverse possession only upon satisfaction of each of the following conditions:

(I) The person presents evidence to satisfy all of the elements of a claim for adverse possession required under common law in Colorado; and

(II) Either the person claiming by adverse possession or a predecessor in interest of such person had a good faith belief that the person in possession of the property of the owner of record was the actual owner of the property and the belief was reasonable under the particular circumstances.

(4) Notwithstanding any other provision of this section, the provisions of subsections (3) and (5) of this section shall be limited to claims of adverse possession for the purpose of establishing fee simple title to real property and shall not apply to the creation, establishment, proof, or judicial confirmation or delineation of easements by prescription, implication, prior use, estoppel, or otherwise, nor shall the provisions of subsections (3) or (5) of this section apply to claims or defenses for equitable relief under the common-law doctrine of relative hardships, or claims or defenses governed by any other statute of limitations specified in this article. Nothing in this section shall be construed to mean that any elements of a claim for adverse possession that are not otherwise applicable to the creation, establishment, proof, or judicial confirmation or delineation of easements by prescription, implication, prior use, estoppel, or otherwise are made applicable pursuant to the provisions of this section.

(5) (a) Where the person asserting a claim of fee simple title to real property by adverse possession prevails on such claim, and if the court determines in its discretion that an award of compensation is fair and equitable under the circumstances, the court may, after an evidentiary hearing separately conducted after entry of the order awarding title to the adverse possessor, award to the party losing title to the adverse possessor:

(I) Damages to compensate the party losing title to the adverse possessor for the loss of the property measured by the actual value of the property as determined by the county assessor as of the most recent valuation for property tax purposes. If the property lost has not been separately taxed or assessed from the remainder of the property of the party losing title to the adverse possessor, the court shall equitably apportion the actual value of the property to the portion of the owner's property lost by adverse possession including, as appropriate, taking into account the nature and character of the property lost and of the remainder.

(II) An amount to reimburse the party losing title to the adverse possessor for all or a part of the property taxes and other assessments levied against and paid by the party losing title to the adverse possessor for the period commencing eighteen years prior to the commencement of the adverse possession action and expiring on the date of the award or entry of final non appealable judgment, whichever is later. If the property lost has not been separately taxed or assessed from the remainder of the property of the party losing title to the adverse possessor, such reimbursement shall equitably apportion the amount of the reimbursement to the portion of the owner's property lost by adverse possession, including, as appropriate, taking into account the nature and character of the property lost and of the remainder. The amount of the award shall bear interest at the statutory rate from the dates on which the party losing title to the adverse possessor made payment of the reimburseable taxes and assessments.

(b) At any hearing conducted under this subsection (5), or in the event that adverse possession is claimed solely as a defense to an action for damages based upon a claim for trespass, forcible entry, forcible detainer, or similar affirmative claims by another against the adverse possessor, and not to seek an award of legal title against the claimant, the burden of proof shall be by a preponderance of the evidence. If the defendant is claiming adverse possession solely as a defense to an action and not to seek an award of legal title, the defendant shall so state in a pleading filed by the defendant within ninety days after filing an answer or within such longer period as granted by the court in the court's discretion, and any such statement shall bind the defendant in the action.

Effective date—applicability. This act shall take effect July 1, 2008. The provisions of section 38-41-101(3)(a), Colorado Revised Statutes, in section 1 of this act shall apply to civil actions filed on or after said date. All other provisions of this act shall apply to claims for title to real property for which fee simple title vests in favor of the adverse possessor and against the owner of record of the real property on or after said date.

VIII. Combined Types of Ownership

Section 38-32-101, C.R.S., provides that estates or interests above the surface of the ground may be validly created in persons or corporations other than the owners of the land below ground, and shall be deemed to be estates, rights, and interests in lands.

The Condominium Act effective prior to July 1, 1992 defined a condominium as an individual air space unit together with an interest in the common elements appurtenant to such unit. This definition means that an owner does not individually own the land underneath the structure. A condominium owner holds title to his or her unit within a defined air space, and the unit owners own the land, the hallways, and all the common elements as tenants in common.

Although a condominium complex may appear visually similar to an apartment complex, it is really a subdivision with many owners. Because each unit is truly an estate in land above the surface, a "declaration" must be filed with the county clerk and recorder so that each unit is properly and legally described, and may be taxed or mortgaged separately.

Pursuant to the Colorado Common Interest Ownership Act (CCIOA) effective July 1, 1992, **"common interest community"** means real estate described in a declaration that obligates each unit owner to pay for real estate taxes, insurance premiums, and maintenance or improvement of other real estate described in a declaration. Ownership of a unit does not include leasehold interests of less than 40 years, including renewal options measured from the date the initial term commences. (See § 38-33.3-103(8) C.R.S.)

Pursuant to CCIOA, **"condominium"** means a common-interest community in which portions of the real estate are designated for separate ownership and the separate owners commonly own the remainder. A common-interest community is not a condominium unless the undivided interests in the "**common elements**" are vested in the unit owners. (See § 38-33.3-103(9), C.R.S.) Prior to July 1, 1992, a condominium was defined only as an air space estate, but under CCIOA a condominium may include single-family lots.

CCIOA defines **"planned community"** as a common-interest community that is not a condominium or cooperative. A condominium or cooperative may be part of a planned community. (See § 38-33.3-103(22), C.R.S.) A planned community may have homeowners' association ownership of the common elements rather than undivided interests by the individual unit or lot owners as tenants in common. A planned community may also include a common-interest community with no common elements. However, the individual unit or lot owner is obligated to pay for such expenses as real estate taxes, insurance premiums, and maintenance or improvement of other real estate, such as private roads or a common greenbelt as described in a declaration.

A **"planned unit development"** (PUD) may also be a common-interest community and may consist of unit owners in duplexes, townhouses, condominiums, and single-family residences. Some or all of the owners may either hold common ownership in land or facilities such as a greenbelt, a playground, or a swimming pool, or are obligated for payment of expenses in addition to the individually owned land underneath each owner's residence. Commonly owned elements, expenses, conditions, or obligations must be in a recorded declaration.

A **"time-share** or **interval"** estate is a variation in conventional ownership. Time-shares are usually sold to vacation-seeking consumers in recreational areas. Time-sharing is based on the premise that most people do not require a year-round vacation home. Condominium units are time-shares when sold or leased for specific periods repeated each year (*e.g.*, four weeks out of each year). Several owners of one condominium unit each have a specified annual period of ownership or tenancy.

Time-share interests may be either fee simple deeded, or a non-deeded "right-to-use." Right-to-use is a contractual or membership interest granting exclusive occupancy to either a specified or any available unit for a set time period each year. Right-to-use interests usually run for a limited number of years and have the effect of a leasehold interest. Although right-to-use purchasers do not hold actual fee interest, bankruptcy laws extend equal protection to such owners in the event of a bankruptcy by the owner or developer.

Time-shares may be created by dividing a fee simple estate into several time-period fee simple estates or leases, or by dividing a lease into several subleases. Dividing owned or leased property into a number of right-to-use contracts for defined time periods may also create time-shares. Tenancy in common owners can, by contract, create time-shares for certain periods of the year. Membership agreements may also create time-shares.

Exchange companies facilitate the trading of owned or leased time-shares for the use of someone else's time-share in another recreational area for annual fees.

Time-share developers must register with the Commission as subdivision developers, and licensed real estate brokers must conduct all sales.

Ownership in a community apartment project may be accomplished by having all unit owners become tenants in common, with each owner being given the exclusive right to occupy a specific apartment.

A stock cooperative or "**cooperative housing corporation**" is formed as a non-profit corporation intended to provide each stockholder with the right to occupy a house or an apartment in a building owned or leased by the corporation. Each stockholder receives a proprietary lease or right-of-tenancy document.

Although sales of such interests in a cooperative housing corporation have elsewhere been regarded as a sale of securities, such sales in Colorado are deemed by statute to be real estate and are exempt from the Colorado Securities Act. The same statute also enables banks and associations to make first mortgage loans on a stockholder's interest. (See §§ 38-33.5-101, *et seq.*, and 11-41-110, C.R.S.).

Cooperative housing corporations, condominiums, and time-shares are treated as subdivisions.

The following portions of the Colorado Revised Statutes are also useful for real estate brokers:

- Title 38, Article 32 – Estates Above the Surface
- Title 38, Article 33 – Condominium Ownership Act
- Title 38, Article 33.3 – Colorado Common Interest Ownership Act
- Title 38, Article 33.5 – Cooperative Housing Corporations – Housing for Members
- Title 12, Article 61, Part 4 –Subdivisions, printed in Chapter 4.)

Chapter 7: Land Descriptions

An * in the left margin indicates a change in the statute, rule, or text since the last publication of the manual.

I. Introduction

While the location of land is commonly referred to by street number and city, it is necessary to use the legal description in the preparation of instruments relating to the title and use of real estate. Numerous methods of description have been developed for the purpose of achieving greater accuracy and precision in identifying the land. The more common methods of land description are:

1. United States Governmental Survey System (GSS), also known as the "rectangular survey system";
2. Metes and bounds;
3. Recorded subdivision plat; and
4. Colorado Coordinate System.

II. The United States Governmental Survey System

Soon after the Revolutionary War ended and new areas were added to the public domain, it became apparent to our government's leaders that a plan had to be worked out for selling and locating lands in the western territory. Thomas Jefferson authored a plan that was adopted by Congress in modified form on May 20, 1785. Under this law, the first surveys took place in the state of Ohio. Ohio was the testing ground for the rectangular survey system and some changes were made in the law as a result of experience gained there. The second survey started in Indiana around 1810. By this time the system was well established; it now extends westward to the Pacific Ocean. This system was not used within the area of the original colonies in America, where land locations were made in irregular form and without any orderly plan.

The object of the government survey was to create a checkerboard of identical squares covering a given area. The largest squares measure 24 miles on each side and are called **"quadrangles."** Each quadrangle is further divided into 16 squares called **"townships"** whose boundaries each measure six miles. Columns of townships are called ranges, and are numbered sequentially east or west of one of 36 **"principal meridians**." In most of Colorado, ranges are numbered west from the 6th principal meridian, which is located near Lincoln, Nebraska. The centerline of Colorado Boulevard in Denver is exactly 402 miles west of the 6th principal meridian. An east-west row of townships is a **"tier"** or township and is numbered sequentially north or south from its baseline. In most of Colorado, the main baseline lies approximately on the 40 degree parallel or line of latitude. This line is an extension of the Kansas-Nebraska border, and runs just north of the city of Brighton in Adams County.

Most of Colorado was surveyed in relation to the 6th principal meridian and 40 degrees latitude baseline. However, several counties in southwestern Colorado were surveyed using the New Mexico principal meridian and the New Mexico baseline as a starting point. Also, certain portions of Mesa and Delta Counties in western Colorado are measured from the Ute Meridian (located just east of Grand Junction) as the north-south survey line and an arbitrary baseline. These non-standard reference lines were implemented to expedite a survey in support of a plan to settle Ute Indians in and around what was later to become the city of Grand Junction. Because no surveys at that time had been extended west of the Continental Divide, a new meridian and a new baseline were established with no connection to the GSS.

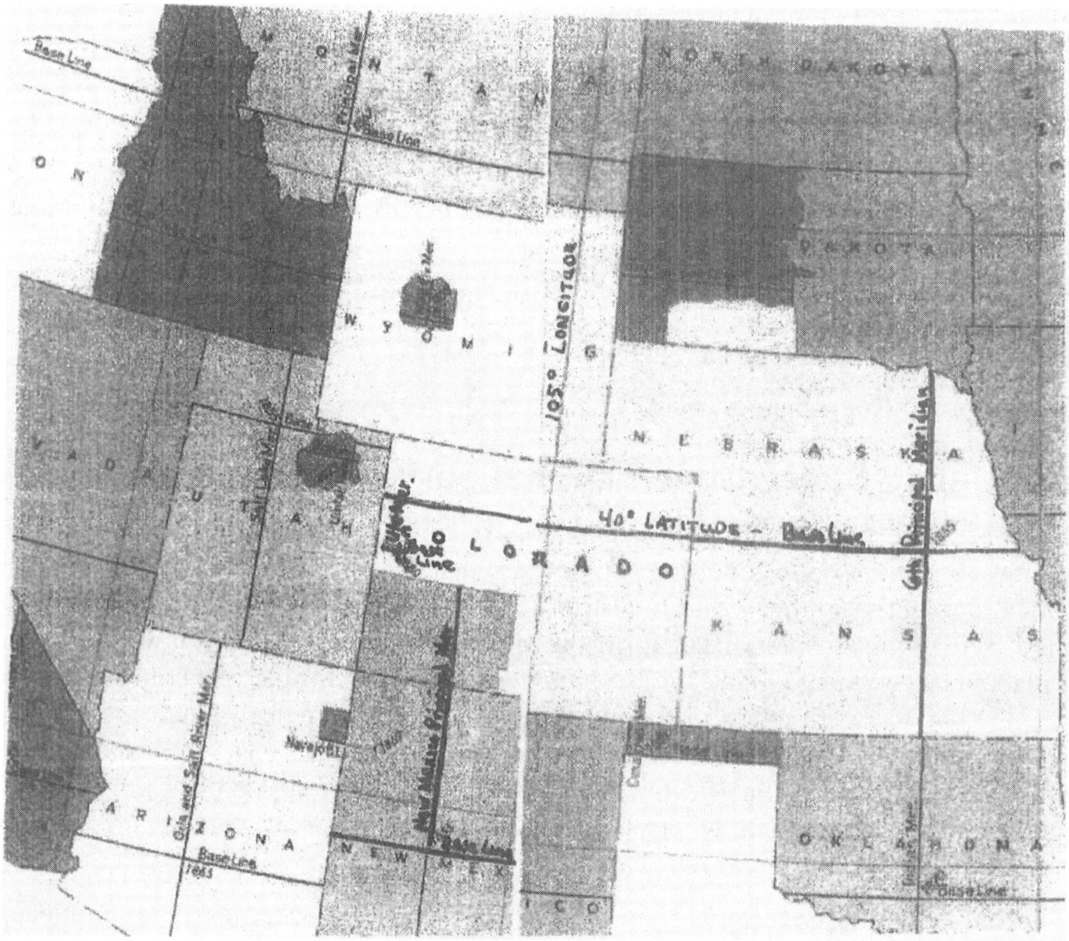

Because of the curvature of the earth, the meridians and north-south ranges converge as they extend toward the North Pole. To maintain a precise six-mile width, and to preserve the square shape of a township, range lines jog outward at each quadrangle (24 miles) so that they are again six miles apart.

The north and west tiers of sections of the township are closing sections. Discrepancies of closure between the interior section line and exterior boundary line surveys are adjusted. These sections usually contain more or less than the 640 acres in a normal section.

A township is six miles square (6 mi. x 6 mi. = 36 square miles). Each square mile is called a **"section,"** and contains 640 acres. Within each township, sections are numbered from 1 to 36 beginning in the northeast corner, counting west to Section 6, then down to Section 7 and back east to Section 12, following a back and forth course to Section 36 in the southeastern-most corner of each township. For purposes of legal description, sections are further divided into fractions, such as half-sections (320 acres), quarter-sections (160 acres), etc. Legal descriptions are then made in a building-block fashion from small to large, for example, referring to the southwest quarter of the northeast quarter of Section XX, Township XX North (of a particular base line), Range XX West (of a particular meridian).

A section is the smallest subdivision usually surveyed by government surveyors, marked at each section corner with a "survey monument."

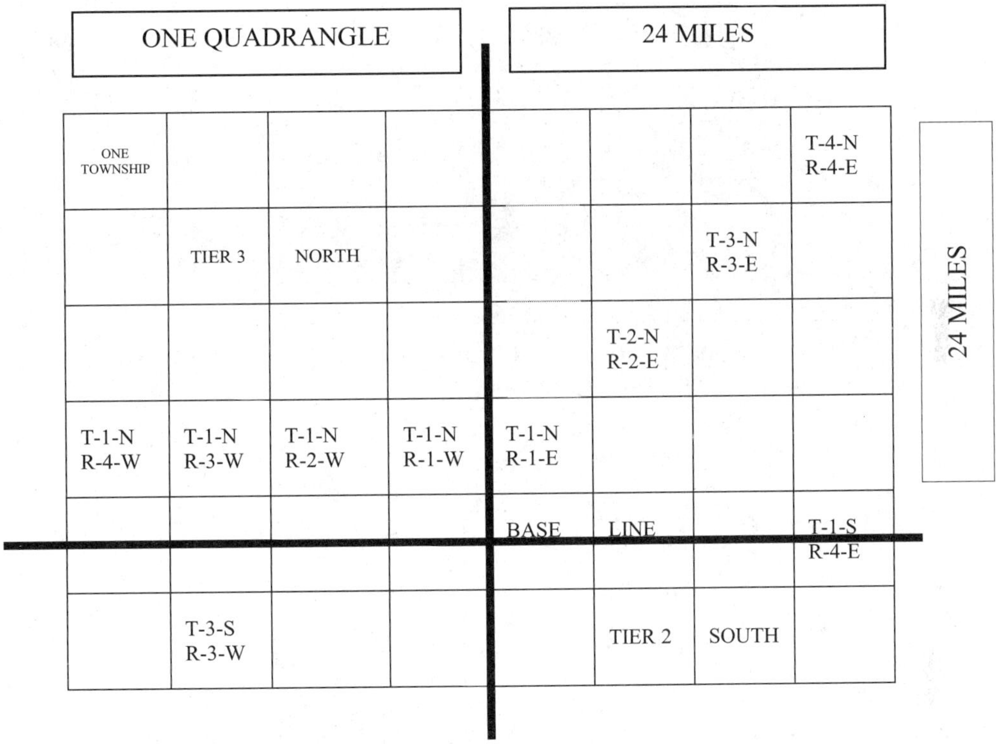

The above sketch shows ranges (numbered east and west of the 6th principal meridian) and townships (numbered north and south of a baseline). There are two quadrangles, one on either side of the 6th principal meridian above the base line. A portion of two additional quadrangles is shown below the base line. A tier is a horizontal row of ranges.

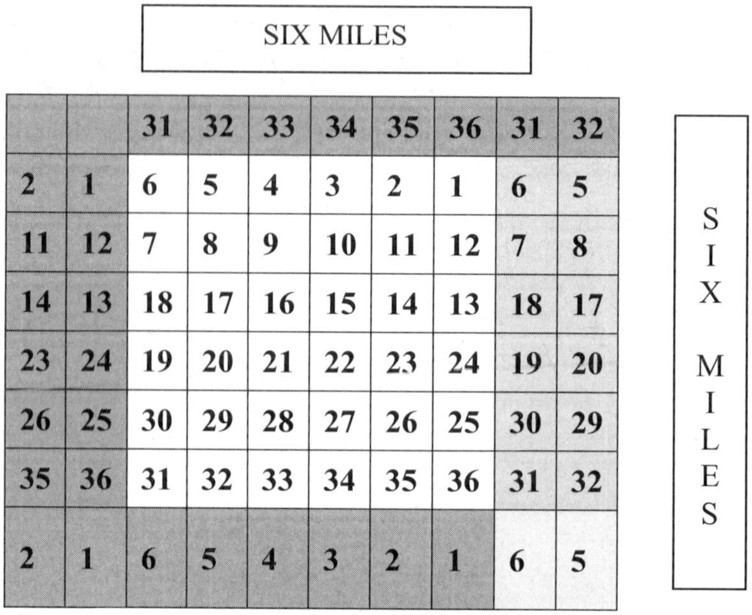

Township map showing 36 numbered sections as connected to sections of adjacent townships

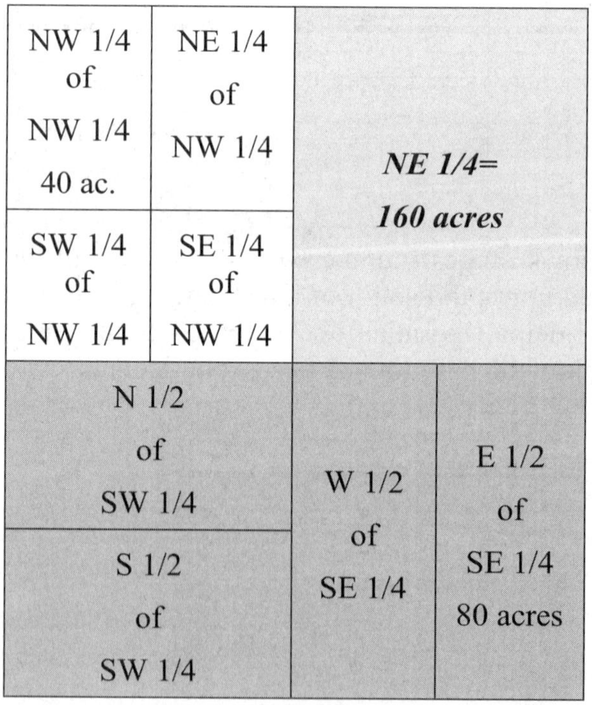

Example of a fractional breakdown of a section (640 acres) of land

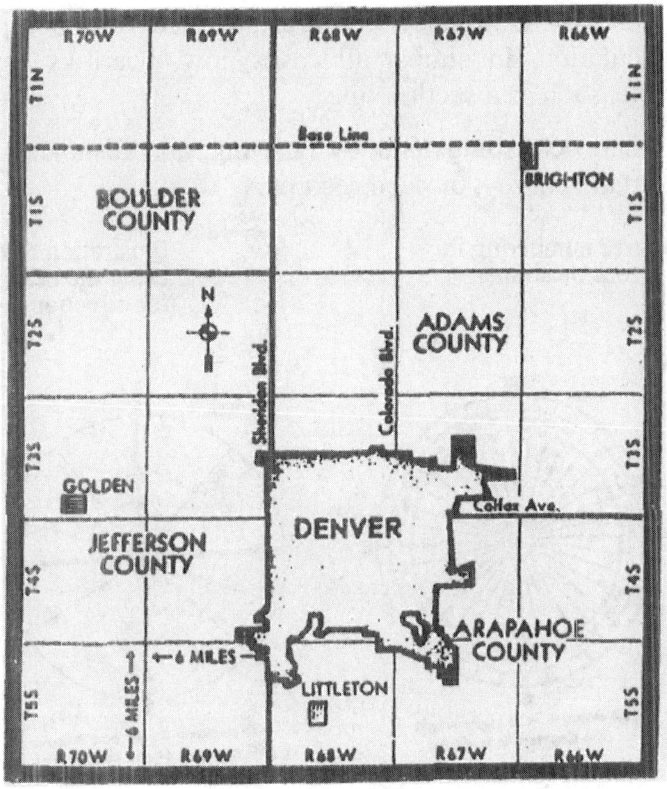

Map showing Denver and Vicinity in terms of the actual Townships, (tiers) and Ranges

III. Metes and Bounds Descriptions

When land cannot be identified by the governmental survey system, it is described by metes and bounds. Metes means measures of length and bounds means boundaries. The United States and Canada are the only countries in the world using the GSS. In the rest of the world, tracts of land are surveyed and described by metes and bounds—usually by identifying a point of beginning and the boundaries in relation to a recognized marker or monument or to natural features such as streams, bridges, piles of stones, or trees.

Metes and bounds are used in Colorado when it is necessary or desirable to describe a tract with irregular boundaries not conforming to the GSS. However, such a survey or description rarely relies on natural features for location. As used in this state, metes and bounds surveys and descriptions are irregular parts of a section or some subdivision of a section. They always tie to some established corner or line of the GSS or to a recognized point on a recorded subdivision plat. Professional land surveyors establish metes and bounds, and are the only persons qualified to sanction "official" surveys.

A. Bearing System

Metes and bounds are expressed in bearings and distances. The direction of a line—its "**bearing**"—is always stated in terms of its angle from north-south (expressed in degrees (°), minutes ('), and seconds (")), followed by its direction east or west of that north-south line, (*e.g.*, N 70 degrees, 19 minutes E., or S 24 degrees, 10' W). A cardinal direction of due north, south, east, or west is expressed as such.

In unsurveyed areas, meridians were established by compass or astronomical observations and calculation. In almost all cases now, bearings are determined from an already established line, such as a section line.

It is important when describing land by bearings and distances to state the source of information, such as grant, survey, or deed records.

Degree numbering in the four quadrants.

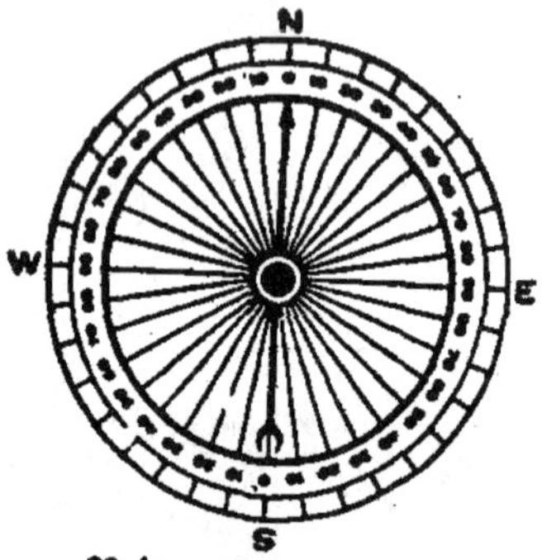

90 degrees in a right angle
360 degrees in a circle

Illustration of description using the bearing for directions.

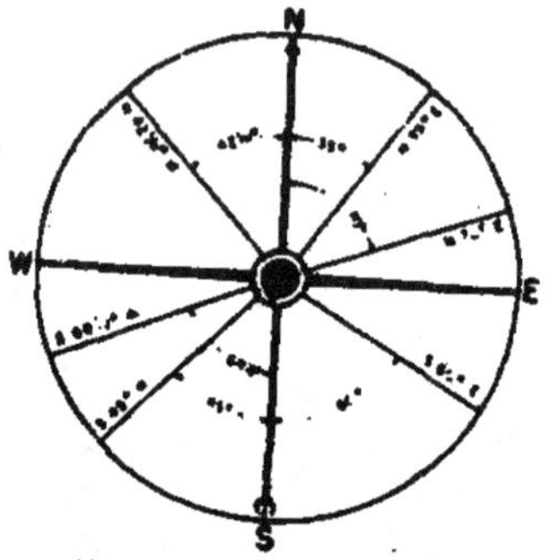

60 seconds equal one minute
60 minutes equal one degree

Example of Metes and Bounds Legal Description

A tract of land in the Northwest one-quarter of the Northwest one-quarter (N/W 1/4, NW 1/4) of Section 30, Township 1 South, Range 60 West of the 6th P.M., described as follows: Commencing from the Northwest corner of said Section 30; thence South 20 degrees 30 minutes East 140.60 feet to the point of beginning (POB); thence North 88 degrees 55 minutes East 200.00 feet; thence South 125.0 feet; thence South 88 degrees 55 minutes West 200.00 feet; thence North 125.00 feet to the POB, County of Adams, State of Colorado.

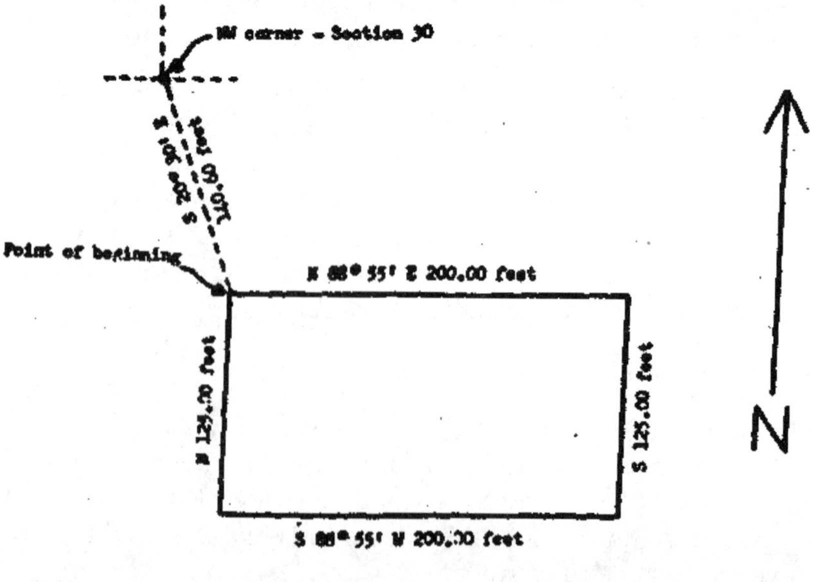

B. Azimuth System

The Azimuth system differs from bearings in that it expresses all directions in terms of the clockwise angle from North from zero (North) through 360 degrees (also North), instead of being broken into four quadrants. Thus, instead of N 70 degrees W, the Azimuth system would refer to that same boundary as "290 degrees," moving clockwise from due North as the starting point, through 180 degrees (due South), then 270 degrees (due West). Surveyors often use it in their work, but generally convert it to the usual bearing description. It is seldom used in legal descriptions.

IV. Recorded Subdivision Plat

A single large tract of land is typically developed into subdivisions. The small parcels of land within a subdivision are called lots and blocks. Subdivisions usually propose streets, alleys, public utility easements, and such other information that the owner and local government desire to include as part of the development plan. A survey is conducted and a map called a subdivision plat is made. Plats must then be recorded in the office of the county clerk and recorder. Recording enables permanent description of a parcel of land as a certain lot and block of the recorded subdivision map, instead of by metes and bounds. The plat map itself shows the boundaries and specific measurements of each lot.

In most cases it is unlawful for any subdivider or agent of a subdivider to transfer title or sell any subdivided land before a final subdivision plat of the subdivided land has been approved by the county board of commissioners and recorded or filed with the clerk and recorder. Violations carry a penalty for each parcel sold. (See § 30-28-110, C.R.S.)

Also, the boundaries of a subdivided block on which a lot is located must be visibly marked before a contract for sale is signed. Lot boundaries must be staked within one year from the effective date of the contract. The burden is on the seller of the subdivided lots to provide for this surveying, unless a block is sold as a unit, in which case the burden is on the subsequent seller. (See §§ 38-51-105(3)(a) and (5), C.R.S.)

The legal description of the shaded site in this illustration would be written as follows:

Lot five (5), Block two (2), Capitol Hill Subdivision, an addition to the City and County of Denver, State of Colorado, according to the recorded plat in the office of the County Clerk and Recorder of said county.

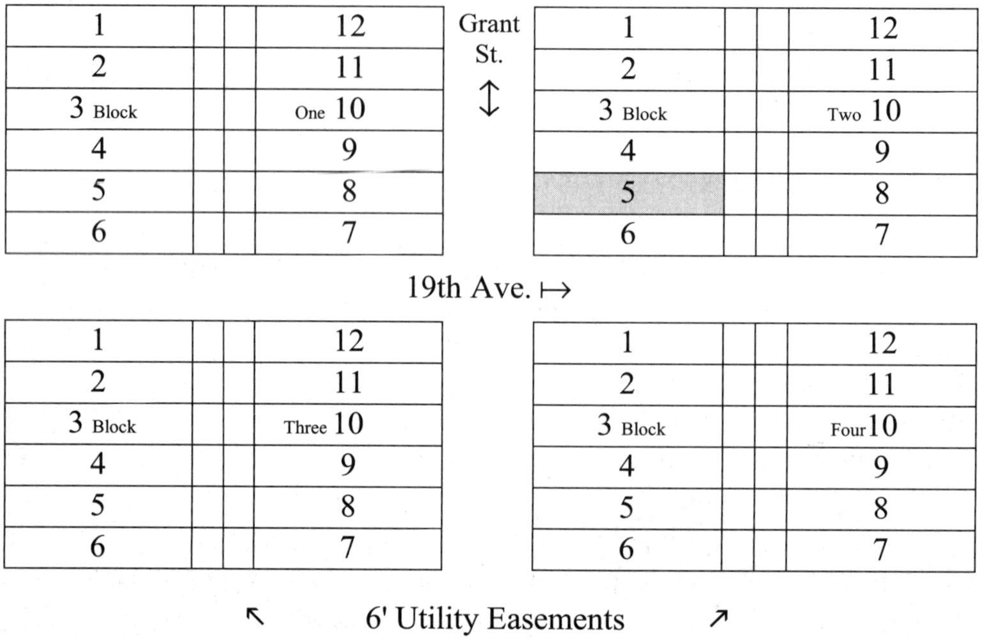

V. Surveys and Certificates

There are many methods and purposes for describing and identifying property that a real estate licensee will encounter and with which he or she should be familiar.

The "**land survey**" plat includes a scale drawing of the boundaries of a parcel of land, which is compiled by a series of exact and precise linear and angular measurements taken from a known point of origin developed by mathematical principles of surveying. The purpose of the land survey plat is to determine, locate, and/or restore real property boundaries. The land survey plat will also indicate any conflicting boundary evidence and any recorded and/or apparent rights-of-way or easements.

The "**improvement survey**" plat is comprised of the same precise information as is the land survey plat mentioned above, and also indicates the location of all structures (improvements) on the parcel of land. The improvement survey plat also shows visible encroachments and any fences, hedges, or walls on or within two feet of both sides of all boundaries. The improvement survey plat details all visible above-ground utilities and all underground utilities for which there is visible surface evidence.

An "**improvement location certificate (ILC)**" is another method of describing and approximately locating property, and is often required by lenders and insurance companies. It offers certain reasonable assurances regarding potential boundary or encroachment problems that may affect their interests. It also illustrates the location of improvements and conditions of the property. However, it is based on assumptions regarding boundary location and is *not a precise survey.* An ILC is typically used in single-family residential transactions for property located within a subdivision. It is a method of depicting property to which most real estate licensees will have the most exposure. A licensee should be familiar with the differences between land and improvement surveys and an ILC.

An ILC is:

1. A representation of boundaries and improvements based on a surveyor's general knowledge in a given area;
2. A depiction of the property boundaries showing the size and shape of a parcel that is based on the legal description provided in the warranty deed;
3. A document signed and sealed by a professional land surveyor who has certain professional responsibilities for its accuracy; and
4. A representation of the location of improvements, encroachments, and easements based on their relationship to a reasonable estimate of the location of property lines.

An ILC is not:

1. A survey;
2. Evidence of exact boundary location;
3. A precise property corner locator;
4. To be legally relied upon for locations of property lines or future improvements.

Sometimes an ILC will indicate a possible encroachment or other evidence of a boundary dispute. In this case, a true survey (*i.e.*, improvement survey plat or land survey plat) would be required to clarify or resolve any discrepancies. A real estate licensee should never represent that an ILC is a survey.

The following is a sample improvement location certificate:

LEGAL DESCRIPTION

Lots 15 and 15G,
Block D,
PLUM CREEK THREE,
County of Boulder,
State of Colorado.

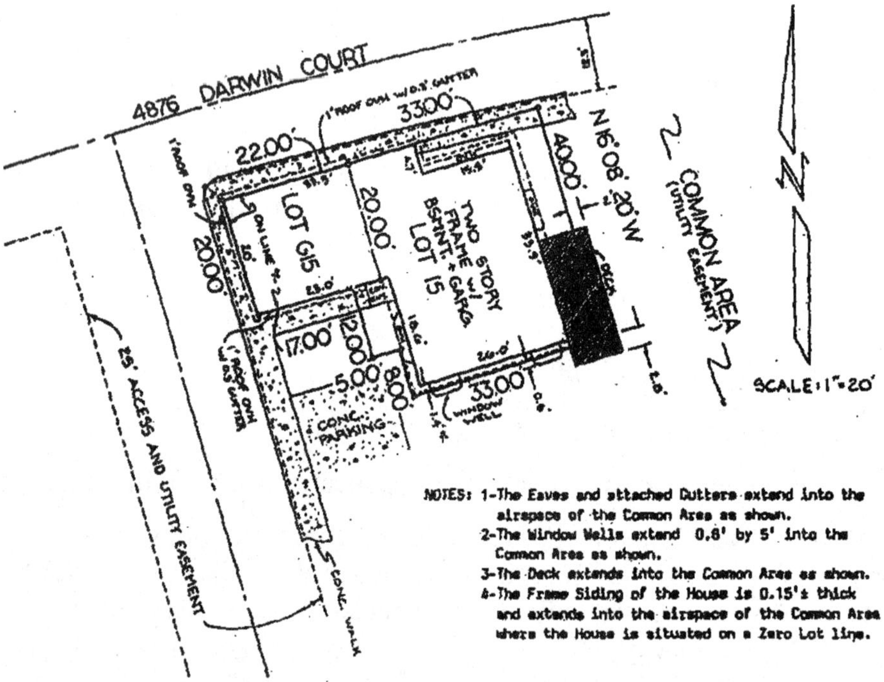

NOTES: 1-The Eaves and attached Gutters extend into the airspace of the Common Area as shown.
2-The Window Wells extend 0.8' by 5' into the Common Area as shown.
3-The Deck extends into the Common Area as shown.
4-The Frame Siding of the House is 0.15'± thick and extends into the airspace of the Common Area where the House is situated on a Zero Lot line.

FLOOD INFORMATION
The subject property is located in Zone C, the area of minimal flooding according to the FEMA Flood Insurance Rate Map; Community-Panel No. 080024-0120-D, dated August 4, 1988.

John B. Guyton, Colorado L.S. #16406

IMPROVEMENT LOCATION CERTIFICATE

TO____________________ AND TO ____________________

I hereby certify that the improvements on the described parcel, except utility connections, are entirely within the boundaries of said parcel, except as shown, that there are no encroachments upon the described premises by improvements on any adjoining premises, except as indicated, and that there is no apparent evidence or sign of any easement crossing or burdening any part of said parcel, except as noted. I further certify that this improvement location certificate is not a land survey plat or improvement survey plat, and that it is not to be relied upon for the establishment of fence, building or other future improvements lines.

VI. Colorado Coordinate System

The Colorado Coordinate System became effective July 1, 1967 under §§ 38-52-101, *et seq.*, C.R.S. This statute is permissive in nature and is not mandatory.

The system is based on defining a point by its distance from two perpendicular baselines (*i.e.*, one north-south axis and an intersecting east-west axis). The intersection of such defined lines in each Colorado coordinate zone then serves as the beginning point of a legal description.

The survey divides Colorado into roughly equal horizontal zones—North, Central, and South. Counties located in the northern one-third are designated "Colorado Coordinate System, North Zone," and the same applies to the Central and South zones. When a tract of land overlaps two zones, it may be described with reference to either zone, and names the zone from which its measurement originates in the legal description.

The coordinates used to express a point in any zone of this system are two distances, expressed in number of feet, measured to two decimal places. The east-west direction is known as the "X-coordinate" and a north-south direction is known as the "Y-coordinate." These coordinates conform to those on the "Colorado Coordinate System" of the National Geodetic Survey within the State of Colorado.

Whenever the "Colorado Coordinate System" is used to describe a tract of land in a document that also legally describes the same tract by reference to a subdivision, or to the GSS, the Colorado Coordinates are supplemental to the other description. In the event of a conflict between two descriptions, the GSS description prevails over the Colorado Coordinates unless such coordinates are upheld by adjudication.

For further information on the Colorado Coordinate System of land description, refer to the statute or consult a professional land surveyor.

Example of a Metes and Bounds Description Using the Colorado Coordinate System as Supplemental Information

Commencing at the corner of Section 20, 21, 28 and 29, T 4 S, R 75 W, 6th P.M. and bearing North 22 degrees, 15 minutes West 202.50 feet to the point of beginning which is marked by a 5/8" diameter iron rod set in concrete; thence bearing North 79 degrees 45 minutes West 155 feet to a brass marker set in a granite ledge and stamped “2928,” said brass marker having grid coordinates X = 1,916,572.14' and Y = 624,697.82' on the Colorado Coordinate System, Central Zone; thence South 22 degrees 45 minutes West 106.50 feet; thence South 70 degrees 15 minutes East 145 feet;, thence North 25 degrees 30 minutes E 133.50 feet to the Point of Beginning.

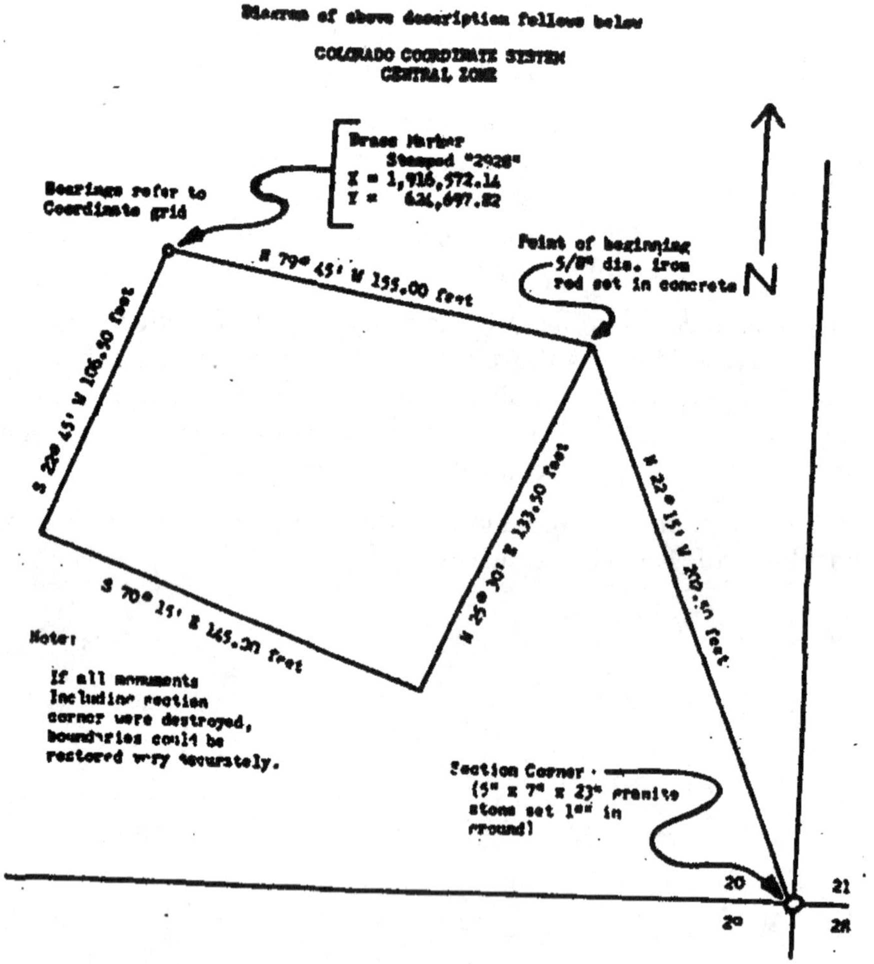

Any description is legal and valid if it unquestionably identifies the property. The phrase “legal description” refers to one of the types of land description explained in this chapter. These types of descriptions are more precise and accurate than informal descriptions such as street addresses.

Table of Land Measurement

LINEAR MEASURE	
7.92 inches	= 1 link
12 inches	= 1 foot
3 feet	= 1 yard
25 links	= 1 rod
100 links	= 1 chain
16 1/2 feet	= 1 rod
5 1/2 yards	= 1 rod
40 rods	= 1 furlong
8 furlongs	= 1 mile
66 feet	= 1 chain
80 chains	= 1 mile
320 rods	= 1 mile
8,000 links	= 1 mile
5,280 feet	= 1 mile
1,760 yards	= 1 mile

SQUARE MEASURE	
144 sq. in.	= 1 sq. foot
9 sq. feet	= 1 sq. yard
30 1/4 sq. yards	= 1 sq. rd.
16 sq. rods	= 1 sq. chain
1 sq. yard	= 272 1/4 sq. ft.
1 sq. chain	= 4356 sq. ft.
10 sq. chains	= 1 acre
160 sq. rods	= 1 acre
4,840 sq. yards	= 1 acre
43,560 sq. ft.	**= 1 acre**
640 acres	**= 1 sq. mile**
1 sq. mile	**= 1 section**
36 sq. miles	**= 1 township**
6 miles square	**= 1 township**
1 sq. mile	= 2.59 sq. kilometer

VII. Metric System

Most of the world does its measuring in metes. The metric system is called the International System (IS) of Units, and it is the measurement standard in nearly all countries of the world. The United States is slowly moving toward the metric system.

The metric system progresses logically in units of 10. Measurement prefixes have the same meanings whether measuring length, volume, or mass, the most common being micro- (one-millionth); milli- (one-thousandth); centi- (one-hundredth); deci- (one-tenth); mega- (1,000,000 x the base); kilo- (1,000 x the base); hecto- (100 x the base); and deka- (10 x the base).

The basic dimension of the metric system is the meter (approx. 3.28 feet). All dimensions of length may be expressed as variations of a meter—millimeter (mm), centimeter (cm), meter (m), or kilometer (km). To convert between the units, you need only move the decimal point to the right or left.

The basic metric unit of land measurement is the hectare (abbreviated as ha.), a square with each side 100 meters long, covering an area of 10,000 square meters. A hectare is equivalent to 2.471 acres.

U.S. TO METRIC		**METRIC TO U.S.**	
LENGTH			
1 inch	= 25.4 millimeters (mm)	1 millimeter (mm)	= 0.04 inch
1 foot	= 0.3 meter (m)	1 meter (m)	= 3.28 feet
1 yard	= 0.9 meter (m)	1 meter (m)	= 1.09 yards
1 mile	= 1.6 kilometer (km)	1 kilometer (km)	= 0.62 mile
AREA			
1 sq. inch	= 6.5 sq. centimeters (cm2)	1 sq. centimeter	= .16 sq. inch
1 sq. foot	= .09 sq. meter (m2)	1 square meter	= 10.76 sq. feet
1 sq. yard	= .84 sq. meter (m2)	1 square meter	= 1.2 sq. yards
1 acre	= .4 hectare (ha)	1 hectare	= 2.471 acres
1 sq. mile	= 2.6 sq. kilometers (km2)	1 sq. kilometer	= .39 sq. mile

Metric System			
Unit	Abbreviation	Number of Meters	Approx. U.S. Equivalent
Length			
Myriameter	mym	10,000	6.2 miles
Kilometer	km	1,000	.62 miles
Hectometer	hm	100	109.36 yards
Decameter	dkm	10	32.81 feet
Decimeter	dm	.1	3.94 inches
Centimeter	cm	.01	.3973 inches
Millimeter	mm	.001	.04 inches
Area			
Square Kilometer	sq. km or km	1,000,000	.3861 square miles
Hectare	ha	10,000	2.471 acres
Are	a	100	119.6 square yards
Centiare	ca	1	10.76 square feet
Square Centimeter	sq. cm or cm2	.0001	.155 square inches

Chapter 8:
Deeds and Transfer of Title

An * in the left margin indicates a change in the statute, rule, or text since the last publication of the manual.

I. Introduction

Before the modern-day concept of land ownership, title to real estate was evidenced primarily by possession of the land and the power to defend the land against others. The earliest method of transferring title to real property was simply surrender of possession by the claimant to another.

The use of deeds to convey real property has a long and colorful history. Personal property has always been transferred by giving possession of the thing itself. In feudal land transfers, the seller presented a clod of dirt from the land to the buyer in the presence of witnesses to symbolize delivery of title. Today, the delivery of the deed constitutes the actual transfer of title to the land.

Title to real property transfers from one person to another by one of four general means:

1. Descent;
2. Will;
3. Involuntary alienation; or
4. Voluntary alienation.

Title transfers "**by descent**" when a person dies without leaving a will (intestate). All states have statutes of descent and distribution providing for the orderly disposition of real property for those who die intestate. Such statutes typically distribute property to the nearest relatives, on the presumption that this would have been the desire of the deceased. According to the Colorado Probate Code, a portion of which is printed below, distribution of the largest share of the property of the decedent, and never less than half of the estate, descends to the surviving spouse.

§ 15-11-101, C.R.S. Intestate estate.

(1) Any part of a decedent's estate not effectively disposed of by will or otherwise passes by intestate succession to the decedent's heirs as prescribed in this code, except as modified by the decedent's will.

(2) A decedent by will may expressly exclude or limit the right of an individual or class to succeed to property of the decedent passing by intestate succession. If that individual or a member of that class survives the decedent, the share of the decedent's intestate estate to which that individual or class would have succeeded passes as if that individual or each member of that class had disclaimed his or her intestate share.

§ 15-11-102, C.R.S. Share of spouse.

The various possible circumstances describing the decedent, his or her surviving spouse, and their surviving descendants, if any, are set forth in this section to be utilized in determining the intestate share of the decedent's surviving spouse. If more than one circumstance is applicable, the circumstance that produces the largest share for the surviving spouse shall be applied. The intestate share of a decedent's surviving spouse is:

(1) The entire intestate estate if:

(a) No descendant or parent of the decedent survives the decedent; or

(b) All of the decedent's surviving descendants are also descendants of the surviving spouse and there is no other descendant of the surviving spouse who survives the decedent;

(2) The first three hundred thousand dollars, plus three-fourths of any balance of the intestate estate, if no descendant of the decedent survives the decedent, but a parent of the decedent survives the decedent;

(3) The first two hundred twenty-five thousand dollars, plus one-half of any balance of the intestate estate, if all of the decedent's surviving descendants are also descendants of the surviving spouse and the surviving spouse has one or more surviving descendants who are not descendants of the decedent;

(4) The first one hundred fifty thousand dollars, plus one-half of any balance of the intestate estate, if one or more of the decedent's surviving descendants are not descendants of the surviving spouse.

(5) (Deleted by amendment, L. 2009, (HB 09-1287), ch. 310, p. 1671, § 3, effective July 1, 2010.)

(6) The dollar amounts stated in this section shall be increased or decreased based on the cost of living adjustment as calculated and specified in section 15-10-112.

(Applies on or after July 1, 2010, to governing instruments executed by decedents who die on or after July 1, 2010)

Any part of the intestate estate not passing to the decedent's surviving spouse under § 15-11-102, C.R.S., or to the decedent's surviving designated beneficiary under § 15-11-102.5, C.R.S., passes to the nearest surviving relatives in accordance with § 15-11-103, C.R.S.

Title to property of a decedent more often transfers "**by will**." The laws of each state give a person a limited right to dispose of property after death. A person who dies leaving a last will and testament is said to have died "**testate**." In no state may a decedent completely exclude a spouse from distribution of his or her property. Under the Colorado Probate Code, a surviving spouse is entitled to a share of the estate even if there is a will to the contrary. (See § 15-11-201, C.R.S.)

"**Involuntary alienation**" (alienation as used here means "transfer") is a transfer without the owner's consent. Examples of such involuntary transfers are tax sales and sales to foreclose a mortgage or to enforce mechanics' or other liens. Involuntary alienation also occurs if title is lost through "**adverse possession**," a situation in which an owner is not making use of the property and an adverse claimant possesses the real estate openly and notoriously, hostile to, and to the exclusion of the owner for a period of time as required by law (18 years in Colorado).

"**Voluntary alienation**," by gift, loan, trade, or sale is the normal mode of real estate transfer, whereby either all or some of the owner's rights are voluntarily transferred to another. Examples of such transfers are: a buy-sell contract consummated by delivery of a deed, transfer of title by a deed of trust or mortgage as security for the payment of a note, or a lease.

The "**right of alienation**" is one of the "bundle of rights" of real estate ownership, allowing one to transfer ownership of real property to another. Living persons generally convey title by the execution and delivery of a deed. A "**deed**" is a legal instrument in writing, duly executed and delivered, whereby a grantor (owner) conveys to a grantee some right, title, or interest in or to the real estate.

Real estate may also be conveyed by deed to a person (*e.g.*, an individual, partnership, or corporation) as trustee for the benefit of a third party. The trustee then holds legal title and the third party holds the equitable title and receives the benefits.

A. Types of Deeds

There are four major classifications of deeds:

1. General warranty deed;
2. Special warranty deed;
3. Bargain and sale deed; and
4. Quitclaim deed.

The types of deeds differ solely in the degree of protection that the grantor promises or warrants to the grantee. No type of deed transfers any greater or lesser interest than another. For example, if a grantor conveys title in fee simple by a general warranty deed, the same fee simple ownership is transferred as if he or she had used a quitclaim deed. However, the general warranty deed grantor promises to defend against any loss incurred due to any title defect, whereas transfer by quitclaim deed contains no such warrant.

General Warranty Deed

A general warranty deed is one in which the grantor warrants or guarantees title against defects that existed before the grantor acquired title or that arose during the grantor's ownership. It does not warrant against encumbrances or defects arising from the grantee's own acts. The usual covenants or warranties contained in a general warranty deed are:

1. **Covenant of seisin.** Guarantees the grantor's ownership and that he or she has the right to convey it. The fact that the property is mortgaged or is subject to some restriction does not breach this covenant.

2. **Covenant against encumbrances.** Guarantees that there are no encumbrances or claims against the property except those specifically excluded in the deed.

3. **Covenant of quiet enjoyment.** Guarantees that the grantee will not be evicted or disturbed in possession of the property. Threats or claims by a third party do not breach this covenant. The grantee would have to actually be dispossessed before being entitled to seek recovery against the grantor under this covenant.

4. **Covenant of further assurance.** Guarantees that the grantor will procure and deliver any other instruments that are subsequently necessary to make the title good.

5. **Covenant of warrant forever.** Guarantees that the grantee shall have title to and possession of the property. Sometimes considered part of "quiet enjoyment."

The first two covenants relate to the past, and generally do not "run with the land"—meaning that only the current grantee may sue the grantor for a breach. The last three covenants protect against future defects and are said to run with the land—allowing any subsequent grantee to seek remedy for breach against any previous grantor. According to § 38-30-121, C.R.S., "covenants of seisin, peaceable possession, freedom from encumbrances, and warranty contained in any conveyance of real estate, or any interest therein, shall run with the premises and inure to the benefit of all subsequent purchasers and encumbrancers."

Special Warranty Deed

The grantor of a special warranty deed warrants the title only against defects arising after the grantor acquired the property and not against title defects arising before that time.

Bargain and Sale Deed

Technically, any deed that recites a consideration and purports to convey the real estate is a bargain and sale deed. Thus, many quitclaim and warranty deeds are also deeds of bargain and sale. Bargain and sale deeds often contain a covenant against the grantor's acts, whereby the grantor warrants only that the grantor has done nothing to harm the title. This covenant would not run with the land. Examples of bargain and sale deeds with a covenant against the grantor's acts are an executor's or personal representative's deed, a beneficiary's deed, an administrator's deed, and a conservator's or guardian's deed.

Quitclaim Deed

The grantor of a quitclaim deed warrants absolutely nothing. A quitclaim deed transfers the grantor's present interest in the land, if any. A quitclaim deed is frequently used to clear up a technical defect in the chain of title, to release lien claims against the property, to remove an owner in a multiple ownership situation, or when someone changes their name (*e.g.*, to a married name). Examples of such deeds are correction deeds and deeds of release.

B. Usual Elements of Deeds

In general, the usual elements of a deed are:

1. Written instrument;
2. Parties – grantor and grantee;
3. Recital of consideration;
4. Words of conveyance;
5. Description of the property;
6. Signature;
7. Delivery and acceptance;
8. Exceptions and restrictions;
9. Warranties and covenants;
10. Date;
11. Acknowledgment; and
12. Recording.

The first seven elements above are absolutely essential for a valid deed. The other five are recommended, but will not invalidate a deed if omitted:

1. **Written Instrument.** A deed must be in writing to be effective. The Colorado statute of frauds, § 38-10-106, C.R.S., requires: "No estate or interest in lands, other than leases for a term not exceeding one year, nor any trust or power over or concerning lands or in any manner relating thereto shall be created, granted, assigned, surrendered,

or declared, unless by act or operation of law, or by deed or conveyance in writing subscribed by the party creating, granting, assigning, surrendering, or declaring the same, or by his lawful agent thereunto authorized by writing." Note the two exceptions to the requirement of a written instrument are: (1) a lease for a term not exceeding one year, and (2) an interest or estate created by operation of law.

The courts may set aside a deed altered in any manner after delivery to the grantee. This means that all blanks on preprinted forms must be filled in according to the requirements of law and the intention of the parties.

2. **Parties: Grantor and Grantee.** A valid deed must clearly name or designate the grantor who is conveying interest in the property. The grantor's name must be identical to the name shown as the grantee in the conveyance by which the grantor received title. A minor discrepancy in name may not invalidate the deed, but could lead to legal challenge. A natural person grantor should be of sound mind. If a grantor is a minor and not of legal age, the conveyance may later be set aside and the grantor could recover the property.

   A deed is void if it fails to designate with reasonable certainty the grantee to whom title passes. Colorado deeds dated after January 1, 1977 must include the legal address of the grantee, including a road or street address. County clerks and recorders may reject a deed that does not comply. (See § 38-35-109(2), C.R.S.)

3. **Recital of Consideration.** A deed is valid without tangible consideration, but should contain at least a recital of consideration (*e.g.*, for $1.00, or for love and affection). Lack of consideration does not render a gift conveyance void, but may preclude a donee (receiver of the gift) from enforcing warranty deed covenants against the donor (grantor). A gift deed may also be set aside on grounds of fraud. For example, the grantor's creditors may set aside a deed gifting property to defraud creditors. If the deed recites consideration, the burden of proving lack of consideration is on the one who attacks the deed.

   Section 39-13-102, C.R.S., requires a "documentary fee" on real property conveyances where the consideration is more than $500. Each county clerk and recorder must collect one penny per one hundred dollars (sale price x .0001) of consideration whenever a deed is recorded. The documentary fee aids county tax assessors in determining property values. Section 39-14-102, C.R.S., requires the grantor and/or grantee to provide a "declaration" to the property tax administrator along with all conveyance documents subject to a documentary fee when presented for recording. It is a criminal offense to misstate actual consideration to the clerk and recorder. The assessor may impose a penalty of $25.00 or twenty-five one-thousandths of one percent of the sale price, whichever is greater, for failure of the grantee to submit the declaration. The deed itself is valid whether consideration shown on the face of the instrument is true and actual or nominal.

4. **Words of Conveyance or Quitclaim.** A deed must contain words that manifest intent to transfer title, or else it is ineffective. No specific words are required, but "sell and convey," "grant, bargain, sell, and convey," or "convey and warrant" are commonly used. The word "quitclaim" is substituted for "convey" in a quitclaim deed.

5. **Description of the Property.** A deed is not valid unless it legally describes the real estate conveyed or quitclaimed. Any description that clearly identifies the property is

sufficient, but using the same legal description used in previous deeds to the same parcel avoids discrepancies in the records and possible future title litigation. Courts may be liberal in holding rather ambiguous descriptions to be valid, but a court action is a high price to pay to correct technical errors that could have been avoided when drafting the legal description.

Any deed recorded after July 1, 1992, where the legal description has been newly created, must contain the name and address of the person who created the new legal description; however, failure to include this information will not affect the validity or the recordability of the deed. (See § 38-35-106.5, C.R.S.)

Section 38-35-122, C.R.S., provides that in addition to the legal description, the street address or identifying numbers on buildings, and the assessor's schedule or parcel number, must appear on the document of title. However, failure to include this additional information will not render the document ineffective or the title unmarketable.

A deed normally contains words following the description indicating that all the appurtenances go with the land. All improvements go with the land as appurtenances.

6. **Signature.** A deed not signed by the grantor is invalid. If there is more than one grantor (*e.g.*, joint tenants), each must sign the deed. A few states, primarily in the east, require a seal for a deed to be valid. Colorado and most states have abolished the requirement for a seal. Colorado does not require that the signature of the grantor be witnessed.

7. **Delivery and Acceptance.** To be effective, a deed must be both delivered by the grantor and accepted by the grantee. The intent of the grantor determines delivery. Presenting a deed to the grantee for examination does not constitute delivery. The grantor must deliver with intent to pass title to the grantee. Under § 38-35-101, C.R.S., an acknowledged and recorded deed presumes effective delivery.

   Effective delivery must occur while the grantor is alive. If a grantor executes a deed, retains it, and directs it to be delivered to the grantee at the grantor's death, the deed does not pass title. A grantor may deliver a deed to a third party to be held and delivered later to the grantee, but to be effective, the grantor must surrender all right to control or recover the deed.

8. **Exceptions and Restrictions.** A grantor is assumed to convey property free and clear of all encumbrances. Therefore, the deed usually provides that the grantor conveys the property "free and clear of all encumbrances except . . ."—followed by the exception, such as: "subject to a deed of trust (complete description)"; or "subject to an easement (complete description)"; or "subject to all encumbrances and restrictions of record."

   A grantor may restrict the grantee's right to use the real estate conveyed, as long as such restrictions are reasonable and not contrary to public policy. The use of such deed restrictions, or "**restrictive covenants**," is an old practice deriving from the bundle of property rights. An owner has the right of free alienation, that is, the right to dispose of his or her interest in any manner whatsoever. Once deed restrictions are established, they run with the land, limiting its use by all future grantees. Covenants are standard features in subdivisions and are intended to benefit all the landowners.

Typical restrictions deal with the minimum size of the house, type of building or roofing material, or exclusion of commercial establishments. Well-formulated deed restrictions have a stabilizing effect on property values. Homeowners are protected against forbidden uses, and may rest assured that a nuisance business will not be a neighbor or that a neighbor's house will meet certain minimum standards. Deed restrictions must be enforced through court action brought by any party for whose benefit the restrictions were imposed.

9. **Warranties and Covenants.** Warranties are not an essential requirement of a valid deed. A grantor may transfer interest by a quitclaim deed, giving no warranty of any kind, or by a general warranty deed, wherein the grantor makes numerous warrants to the grantee. Section 38-30-113, C.R.S., specifies a short-form warranty deed whereby every deed that is similar to the statutory form, and which includes the words "and warrant(s) the title," automatically implies the usual general warranty deed covenants.

   In 2005, § 38-30-113(1)(d), C.R.S., added that a properly executed deed conveys the grantor's interest, if any, in any vacated street, alley, or other right-of-way that adjoins the real property "unless the transfer of such interest is expressly excluded in the deed."

10. **Date.** A date is not essential for a valid deed, although it is a universal custom to date all deeds. A dated deed might obviously prevent future question or controversy concerning the time of delivery of the deed.

11. **Acknowledgment.** An acknowledgment is a declaration made by a person (grantor) to a notary public, or other authorized official, that the grantor executed the instrument and did so freely and voluntarily. The official fills out a certificate of acknowledgment customarily printed on the deed. Section 38-35-101, C.R.S., provides: "No officer . . . shall take or certify such acknowledgments unless the person making the same is personally known to such officer to be the identical person he represents himself to be . . . . It shall not be necessary to state such fact in his certificate of acknowledgment attached to any instrument affecting title to real property."

    In most states, including Colorado, a deed is valid and may be recorded without being notarized. Many states, however, require acknowledgment as a condition of recording.

    It is always sound practice to have a deed acknowledged before recording because of the presumption of proper delivery and acceptance (see number 7 above). An acknowledged deed may be evidence if a title controversy arises. An unacknowledged deed may only be used as evidence of the transaction if it has been recorded ten years or more and proven in court that the deed was properly executed. (See § 38-35-106, C.R.S.)

    The facts in a deed recorded for 20 years or more may be read in evidence and received as prima facie evidence of these facts. (See § 38-35-107, C.R.S.)

12. **Recording.** A deed is valid even if it is not recorded. The wording of the Colorado recording statute is permissive ("may be") rather than mandatory ("must be").

    Recording offers a two-fold benefit. It protects an innocent purchaser or encumbrancer from acting in ignorance of an unrecorded instrument, and it provides "**constructive notice**," a legally conclusive presumption that all persons have knowledge of recorded instruments. It is in the grantee's best interest to record the deed immediately.

Lack of acknowledgment does not invalidate constructive notice. A recorded deed that is not acknowledged still serves notice to subsequent purchasers. (See § 38-35-106, C.R.S.)

In addition to constructive notice, a purchaser or encumbrancer may have "**actual notice**" of another's right or claim. For instance, a purchaser is presumed to have actual notice of all rights and claims of parties in possession of the property, so that even if the right or claim is unrecorded, the purchaser cannot defeat it.

Chapter 9:
Evidence of Title

An * in the left margin indicates a change in the statute, rule, or text since the last publication of the manual.

I. Introduction

A prudent buyer of real estate will demand that the seller furnish proof of ownership. A deed naming the seller as grantee may not be adequate proof. This deed itself, or the previous owner's title, may be defective. The seller may own something less than fee simple title; title may be legally unmerchantable or may be heavily encumbered by liens or restrictions. The buyer needs to know the exact state of the seller's title. The lender also has a vested interest by virtue of accepting a mortgage as security for repayment of the loan.

"**Evidence of title**" is concerned with absolute proof of the nature of real estate ownership. The three major evidences of title are: (1) an abstract and opinion, (2) title insurance, and (3) a Torrens certificate of title.

II. Abstract and Opinion

All states provide for the public recording of every document by which any estate or interest in land is created, transferred or encumbered. In Colorado, the clerk and recorder of the county in which the real property is situated records the deed. (§§ 38-35-109(l) and (3), C.R.S.). This law also provides that any document affecting rights in real estate must be recorded in order to provide notice to persons other than those having actual knowledge of the document. In addition, the law provides:

> Any person who offers to have recorded . . . any document purporting to . . . affect the title to real property, knowing or having a reason to know that such document is forged or groundless, contains a material misstatement or false claim, or is otherwise invalid, shall be liable to the owner of such real property for the sum of not less than one thousand dollars or for actual damages caused thereby, whichever is greater, together with reasonable attorney fees.

Public records are a reliable history of the ownership of a tract of land. An "**abstract of title**" is a summary of the material parts of every recorded instrument affecting the title to a piece of real estate. Today abstractors typically photocopy the legal instrument history of a property rather than merely summarize it.

To the average purchaser, an abstract does not afford knowledge of the state of the title to the real estate. The purchaser still needs the "**opinion**" of an attorney to certify the legal nature of the seller's title and of any defects, liens, encumbrances, or other rights that may be disclosed in the abstract.

A. Liability

An abstractor does not guarantee title to the real estate. The law imposes only the duty to exercise due care in the preparation of the abstract. If an abstractor negligently omits or incorrectly summarizes a document, the abstractor can be held liable for any loss suffered by the purchaser. Likewise, an attorney can only be held liable for damages that are caused by the attorney's negligence in the examination of the abstract. As an example, the attorney is liable for any loss caused by failure to discover an existing, recorded lien contained in the abstract.

B. Risks

No evidence of title can completely and conclusively reveal the exact state of the title to real property. For instance, an abstract and opinion may indicate that the seller has clear title, but if the chain of title contains a forged deed, then title did not legally pass. There is no way of knowing from the abstract whether a deed is forged or not. Nor will an abstract reveal the rights of parties in possession, *i.e.*, a valid lease. The abstract may show title in one person but another may possibly have superior right through adverse possession. Fortunately, such things rarely happen. With an abstract and opinion together with a physical examination of the property, a buyer can be reasonably certain of obtaining good title.

III. Title Insurance

Title insurance is a contract that protects the insured against loss occurring through defects in title to real property. As in other insurance policies, the property owner transfers risk of loss to the insurer. A title company will not insure a bad title any more than a life insurance company will insure a dying person.

Basically, a title insurance policy provides that the company will indemnify the owner against any loss sustained because of a defect in title, provided that the defect is not specifically excluded in the policy. Further, the insurance company agrees to defend any lawsuit attacking the title based on a claimed defect that is covered by the insurance provisions. Examples of typical standard exclusions that the policy does not insure against are:

1. Rights or claims of parties in possession not shown of record, including unrecorded easements or leases;
2. Any facts that an accurate survey would show;
3. Mechanics liens, or any rights thereto, where such liens or rights are not recorded; and
4. Taxes and assessments not yet due or payable and special assessments not yet certified to the county treasurer's office.

Title policies also list exclusions of record pertaining to the specific property, such as mortgages, easements and covenants. Both standard and non-standard exclusions may sometimes be deleted or insured against if specifically requested.

The date of a title policy is very important. The title insurance company guarantees against loss occurring because of defects existing on or before the date of the policy. Defects that come into existence after the effective date of the title policy are not covered.

A. Owner's versus Mortgagee's Policies

Title insurance companies will issue a separate policy to the owner and to the mortgagee (lender). An owner's policy protects the owner's equitable interest in the property and is not transferable. Upon resale, the new purchaser must obtain a new or reissued title policy. A mortgagee's policy protects the mortgagee, and only to the extent of the mortgagee's interest (loan balance). A mortgagee's policy does normally transfer if the note and mortgage are sold together (an assumption).

Unlike other insurance, title insurance premiums are a one-time, up-front fee. Premiums are based upon the amount of insurance purchased. Premiums charged by title companies must be filed with the Colorado Division of Insurance and are available to the public. The owner's equity is only protected by an owner's policy.

B. Title Insurance Commitments

Shortly after receiving an order for title insurance, the company will issue a commitment showing what it is willing to insure and under what circumstances. Commitments are usually issued free of charge if there is a contract of sale on the property. If ordered prior to entering into a contract, or for a purchaser "to be determined" (TBD), the title company must make a charge for the commitment.

The use of title insurance may not relieve the purchaser of the need for legal advice on the title. A title insurance company may avoid liability through exclusions that may affect future marketability of title. It may be prudent for a purchaser's attorney to examine the title insurance commitment and its exclusions. Sufficient time should be allowed in the contract time line if the buyer elects an attorney examination.

Title insurance policies are the most popular evidence of title in urban areas. Abstracts are physically cumbersome, and when large blocks of mortgages or trust deeds are sold to banks or other financial institutions, the investors usually prefer a title policy.

C. Division of Insurance

The Colorado Division of Insurance regulates title insurance companies. The Real Estate Commission and Division of Insurance strive to create a homogenous regulatory environment for the two industries, particularly in the closing of real estate transactions. Toward this end, the Division of Insurance developed a set of questions and answers relating to statutory and regulatory requirements. The Real Estate Commission has endorsed the answers.

Question: Why can't I receive a free "TBD" commitment? Is there any alternative?

Answer: If a "TBD" commitment is used by a real estate licensee to obtain a listing or by a seller to ascertain the status of the title prior to entering into a contract, this is a legitimate expense of the licensee and/or the seller. A "TBD" commitment is in fact a commitment that is ordered prior to the time of a real estate sales contract or, in the case of a re-finance, prior to the time of loan approval. Pursuant to Section 6(D), Paragraph 5 of Regulation 3-5-1, title companies must properly charge for these commitments. However, should these commitments ultimately result in a policy of title insurance, any charge made may be credited against the final title policy charge.

As noted in Section 6(D), Paragraph 4 of Regulation 3-5-1, a title company is not required to charge for a commitment furnished in good faith in furtherance of a bona fide sale, purchase, or loan transaction which for good reason is not consummated.

Title companies give sufficient information in the form of an ownership and encumbrance report or "O&E" to allow a licensee who has a listing to perform most necessary functions. Although title companies also must charge for O&Es, the cost is often far less than that of a TBD commitment.

Question: Can title insurers continue to provide support, services or other items of value to individual real estate licensees, lenders or others?

Answer: In some cases, yes. Insurance Regulation 3-5-1 requires that any services provided to settlement producers (including real estate licensees, mortgage brokers, and lenders) be charged for at fair market value. Free services and other items of value are prohibited.

Question: Who pays for closing fees that are required by Regulation 3-5-1?

Answer: The division of insurance does not take a position on who should pay closing fees or, for that matter, the title insurance policy fees. These fees are a matter of negotiation between the parties. However, based upon local practice and custom, the division believes that these may be paid in the following manner:

A) The title insurance policy premium by the seller.

B) The closing and settlement services fee, exclusive of document preparation, by seller and/or buyer.

C) Document preparation/scrivener function by the broker/licensee.

Question: Regulation 3-5-1 requires title entities to provide closing and settlement services only with written closing instruction. Do we have such instruction?

Answer: Yes. Closing instruction forms are available through the real estate commission.

Question: How do I comply with the requirement for "good funds?"

Answer: There are three primary ways to comply with the "good funds" section:

A) Using funds that have been deposited and are available for immediate withdrawal, (*e.g.*, wire transfers, checks that have been deposited two to three days in advance of closing, or electronic fund transfer between two separate accounts in the same bank.

B) As a consequence of an agreement with the financial institution in which the funds are to be deposited and the financial institution upon which the funds are drawn. This would include so called "Good Funds" agreements (between mortgage broker, warehouse bank, and title company); the written guarantee of the bank upon which an earnest money deposit is drawn; or cashier's, certified, or teller's checks (under the theory that these instruments have the agreement for immediate withdrawal of the issuing institution).

C) Close the transaction, wait for the money to become available for withdrawal, and then disburse.

Question: How can I close and have money be disbursed at the table?

Answer:
A) The funds have been deposited in the title company's financial institution and they are available for immediate withdrawal. This includes wire transfers and checks deposited in advance.
B) Certified, cashier's, teller's checks and other instruments as defined by Federal Regulation CC, 12 CFR, Part 229.10(c), are considered "good funds" by the division of insurance and allow for immediate disbursement under the theory that these instruments have the agreement for immediate withdrawal of the issuing institution.
C) By virtue of a "Good Funds" agreement or any written agreement wherein the bank upon which the check is drawn agrees to guarantee to the title company that funds are available for immediate withdrawal.

Question: How do I make my earnest money deposits acceptable under the definition of "good funds?"

Answer: By depositing them with the title company two or three days in advance; converting them to cashier's, certified, or teller's checks; electronic or wire transfers; or by virtue of a written agreement with the bank upon which the funds are drawn.

D. Application of the Good Funds Laws

In July 2002, the Division of Real Estate and the Division of Insurance issued Bulletin No. 02-02, a Joint Position Statement Concerning the Application of the Good Funds Laws. While the specific bulletin was retired by the Division of Insurance, its text is still relevant for a discussion on the application of the laws as they relate to real estate closings.

The good funds statute (§ 38-35-125(2), C.R.S.) provides, in relevant part:

> *No person or entity that provides closing and settlement services for a real estate transaction shall disburse funds as a part of such services until those funds have been* ***received*** *and are either:* ***available for immediate withdrawal as a matter of right*** *from the financial institution in which the funds have been deposited; or available for immediate withdrawal as a consequence of an agreement of a financial institution in which the funds are to be deposited or a financial institution upon which the funds are to be drawn.*

The same statute defines funds "available for immediate withdrawal as a matter of right" to include any wire transfer or any certified check, cashier's check or teller's check. Thus, a cashier's check or wired funds (most typically used) that have been received by the entity providing closing and settlement services are considered "good funds".

Division of Insurance regulation 3-5-1(7)(I) parallels § 38-35-125, C.R.S. and provides that "All title insurance entities shall comply with the 'good funds law'." In addition, Division of Insurance regulation 3-5-1(6)(D)(2) specifies that failure to comply with the good funds laws constitutes an unlawful inducement for the referral of title insurance business proscribed by § 10-11-108, C.R.S.

The federal courts interpreted Colorado's good funds laws in *Guardian Title v. Matrix*, 141 F.Supp.2d 1277 (D.Colo. 2001). The court held that good funds laws govern title entities that engage in closing and settlement services. *See id.* at 1279. Failure to comply with the good funds statute is a deceptive trade practice and violates insurance regulation 3-5-1. *See id.* at 1280-81. The court stated: "The Good Funds law was developed as a solution to 'the need to insure that the title company or other party responsible for real estate closings has 'good funds' **in hand** before closing the transactions'". *Id.* at 1281.

Based on the above, it is the position of the Division of Real Estate and Division of Insurance that Colorado's good funds law and insurance regulation 3-5-1(7)(I) require that a title entity must have good funds "**in hand**" (*e.g.*, wired funds, certified check, cashier's check, tellers check) **before it disburses funds** as part of its settlement services.

Further, it is the position of the Division of Real Estate and Division of Insurance that a title company which withdraws funds from its account in the form of a cashier's check, but (1) maintains complete control and possession of the check; and (2) does not disburse (pay out) until **delivery** and receipt of "good funds" relating to the specific transaction, complies with the good funds laws.

By way of example, it is common in a real estate transaction for funds to come to the closing from at least two sources, the buyer and the lender. It is also common for a seller to ask for closing proceeds in the form of a cashier's check, drawn on the title entity's account. Applying the 'good funds' law and insurance regulation 3-5-1, the title company could cause a cashier's check to be issued from its account and have the check available for the seller at closing. The title entity could not disburse to the seller until "good funds" were received or "in hand" from the buyer and lender. "In hand" means that a cashier's check has been received by the title entity or, in the case of a wire transfer, has been wired into the title entity's account.

Once the transaction closes and the cashier's check is paid to the seller, the title entity is responsible for immediately depositing the buyer's "good funds" into its account. If the transaction does not close, the title entity is responsible for immediately re-depositing its cashier's check into its account. In that manner, no other customer of the title entity is harmed.

IV. Torrens Certificate of Title

Sir Robert Torrens, a British businessman, developed a system of real estate title registration in 1857 based on the system used to register ships. The registry of ships briefly and clearly showed the condition of a ship's title by listing the name of the ship's owner and all liens and encumbrances against it. A modern comparison would be an automobile title, which shows on one document the name of the owner and any existing liens or encumbrances. About a dozen states, including Colorado, have a Torrens Title Registration Act (see §§ 38-36-101, *et seq.*, C.R.S.).

A. Methods of Registration

To register title to land under the Torrens system, the owner files a written application with the appropriate court for the county in which the property is located. The court then holds proceedings to ascertain the state of the title. All persons known to have an interest or claim in the property are served personal notice of the registration proceedings. All other persons have constructive notice through newspaper publication. The proceedings equate in essence to a quiet-title lawsuit.

After the hearing, the court issues a decree of confirmation of title and registration. When the court's decree is filed with the registrar of titles (county clerk and recorder), an original certificate of title is issued setting forth the court's findings as to the owner, owner's interest, and all liens, claims, encumbrances and other rights, if any, against the property. The registrar then issues an "owner's duplicate certificate of ownership." Ninety days after the issuance of this decree, no person may maintain any action that challenges the findings set forth in the decree. The owner of the real estate is then conclusively presumed to have title as decreed.

B. Transfer of Torrens Title

Section 38-36-155, C.R.S., related to conveying registered land, reads as follows:

> An owner of registered land conveying the same, or any portion thereof, in fee, shall execute a deed of conveyance which the grantor shall file with the registrar of titles in the county where the land lies. The owner's duplicate certificate shall be surrendered at the same time, and shall be by the registrar marked "canceled". The original certificate of title shall also be marked "canceled". The registrar of titles shall thereupon enter in the register of titles a new certificate of title to the grantee, and shall prepare and deliver to such grantee an owner's duplicate certificate. All encumbrances, claims, or interests adverse to the title of the registered owner shall be stated upon the new certificate, except insofar as they may be simultaneously released or discharged. When only a part of the land described in a certificate is transferred, or some estate or interest in the land remains in the transferor, a new certificate shall be issued to him for the part, estate, or interest remaining to him.

The Torrens certificate is the rarest of the three evidences of title discussed above, but it is used in certain parts of eastern Colorado.

Chapter 10: Appraiser Regulation

An * in the left margin indicates a change in the statute, rule, or text since the last publication of the manual.

I. The Colorado Board of Real Estate Appraisers

The Colorado Board of Real Estate Appraisers ("Board") meets each month and consists of seven members who are appointed by the Governor. The overall objective of the Board is to protect the public. In order to do so, the Colorado legislature has granted the Board rule-making authority for matters related to the profession of real estate appraisers. Rules are made after notice and public hearings in which all interested parties may participate.

The Division of Real Estate ("Division") is part of the Department of Regulatory Agencies and is responsible for budgeting, purchasing, and related management functions. The director of the Division is an administrative officer who executes the directives of the Board and is given statutory authority in all matters delegated by the Board. The Board exercises its duties and authority through licensing, certification, and enforcement.

II. Appraiser Licensing and Certification

In 1990, legislature passed laws governing the practice of real estate appraisal in Colorado in response to the federal "Financial Institutions Reform, Recovery and Enforcement Act of 1989" ("FIRREA"). This enabling legislation has been amended several times since being adopted. The full text of the statutes, §§ 12-61-701 through 12-61-718, C.R.S., is reprinted in this chapter.

The Colorado Board of Real Estate Appraisers is composed of three appraisers, a county assessor, a commercial banker with mortgage lending experience, and two public members. The Board has a program manager and statutory authority for rule-making and appraiser discipline. The Board's rule-making implements Colorado law in a manner consistent with federal regulations.

Unless a specific exemption applies, any person acting as a real estate appraiser in this state must be licensed as provided by §§ 12-61-701, *et seq.* Among other things, any person who performs real estate appraisals for federally related loans in Colorado must be registered, licensed, or certified by the Division. Exceptions to the definition of "real estate appraiser" are found in § 12-61-702(5)(b), C.R.S., and include, among others, licensed real estate brokers who provide an opinion of value that is not represented as an appraisal and is not used for purposes of obtaining financing, *i.e.*, broker price opinions and comparable market analysis. Other exceptions are provided for corporations valuing property they own, may purchase, or may sell, and for appraisers of personal property (chattels), water rights, or mineral rights. State, county, and city right-of-way agents are exempt when they value properties worth $5,000 or less. However, staff appraisers employed in county tax assessment offices must be registered, licensed, or certified.

Colorado appraisal licensing and certification law, rules, and practices must be reviewed and approved by the Federal Appraisal Subcommittee, which is made up of representatives of the Federal Deposit Insurance Corporation, the Office of Thrift Supervision, the Comptroller of the Currency, the Federal Reserve System, the National Credit Union Administration, and the

Department of Housing and Urban Development. The Appraisal Foundation, a private non-profit appraisal organization, is charged with developing the qualifications for appraisers and standards for appraisals. It has no legislative power.

Federal financial regulatory agencies have developed rules as to what appraiser and appraisal related requirements must be met for valuation of properties in "federally related transactions." These rules vary slightly between agencies.

In general, the standards for the development and reporting of an appraisal are those of the Uniform Standards of Professional Appraisal Practice ("USPAP") as developed, interpreted, and amended by The Appraisal Standards Board ("ASB") of The Appraisal Foundation.

III. Levels of Appraiser Licensure

Colorado appraiser law and Board rules establish four levels of licensure: (1) Registered Appraiser, (2) Licensed Appraiser, (3) Certified Residential Appraiser, and (4) Certified General Appraiser. The level of licensure determines what properties an appraiser may appraise and are as follows:

Registered Appraiser: A Registered Appraiser is a person who has been issued a registration by the Board as a result of meeting the education and examination requirements for Registered Appraisers. No experience is required to become a Registered Appraiser. Registered Appraisers are trainees who must be supervised. The scope of practice for a Registered Appraiser is those properties the supervising appraiser is permitted and competent to appraise. A Registered Appraiser may also work as an appraiser employee of a county assessor and perform all real estate appraisals required to fulfill the official duties of such a position.

Licensed Appraiser: A Licensed Appraiser is a person who has been issued a license by the Board as a result of meeting the education, examination, and experience requirements for Licensed Appraisers. The Licensed Appraiser classification qualifies the appraiser to appraise, if competent for the assignment, non-complex 1-4 unit residential properties having a transaction value of less than $1 million and complex 1-4 unit residential properties having a transaction value of less than $250,000. The terms "Complex Residential Property" and "Transaction Value" are defined by Board Rule and the Real Property Appraiser Qualification Criteria of the Appraisal Qualifications Board. A Licensed Appraiser may also work as an appraiser employee of a county assessor and perform all real estate appraisals required to fulfill the official duties of such a position.

Certified Residential Appraiser: A Certified Residential Appraiser is a person who has been issued a certified credential by the Board as a result of meeting the education, examination, and experience requirements for Certified Residential Appraisers. The Certified Residential Appraiser classification qualifies the appraiser to appraise, if competent for the assignment, 1-4 unit residential properties without regard to transaction value or complexity. The classification includes the appraisal of vacant or unimproved land that is utilized for 1-4 family purposes or for which the highest and best use is for 1-4 family purposes, but does not include land for which a subdivision analysis is necessary. A Certified Residential Appraiser may also work as an appraiser employee of a county assessor and perform all real estate appraisals required to fulfill the official duties of such a position.

Certified General Appraiser: A Certified General Appraiser is a person who has been issued a certified credential by the Board as a result of meeting the education, examination, and experience requirements for Certified General Appraisers. The Certified General appraiser classification qualifies the appraiser to appraise, if competent for the assignment, all types of real property.

IV. Requirements for Appraiser Licensure

In general, there are three requirements that must be met for appraiser licensure: education, examination, and experience. The specific requirements in these areas are different for each level of licensure (Registered Appraiser, Licensed Appraiser, Certified Residential Appraiser, and Certified General Appraiser). The requirements are fully described in the Board rules. A general summary is as follows:

Registered Appraiser:

Education: An applicant submitting an application for licensure as a Colorado Registered Appraiser shall meet the following real estate appraisal education module requirements, or the substantial equivalent thereof, as set forth in the Required Core Curriculum and Guide Note 1 of the 2008 Real Property Appraiser Qualification Criteria adopted by the Appraiser Qualifications Board of the Appraisal Foundation on February 20, 2004, and amended through May 5, 2006, with an effective date of January 1, 2008 and incorporated by reference in Rule 1.32:

- Basic Appraisal Principles: 30 hours
- Basic Appraisal Procedures: 30 hours
- 15-hour National USPAP Course: 15 hours

Examination: Applicants must successfully complete the Registered Appraiser examination as provided in Chapter 4 of the Board Rules. A passing score on an examination is valid for two years from the examination date. Failure to file a complete application or registration within the two-year period will result in the examination grade being void.

Experience: No experience is required to apply for licensure as a Registered Appraiser.

Licensed Appraiser:

Education: An applicant submitting an application as a Colorado Licensed Appraiser shall meet the following real estate appraisal education module requirements, or the substantial equivalent thereof, as set forth in the Required Core Curriculum and Guide Note 1 of the 2008 Real Property Appraiser Qualification Criteria adopted by the Appraiser Qualifications Board of The Appraisal Foundation February 20, 2004, and amended through May 5, 2006, with an effective date of January 1, 2008, and incorporated by reference in Rule 1.32:

- Basic Appraisal Principles: 30 Hours
- Basic Appraisal Procedures: 30 Hours
- 15-Hour National USPAP Course: 15 Hours
- Residential Market Analysis and Highest and Best Use: 15 Hhours
- Residential Appraiser Site Valuation and Cost Approach: 15 Hours
- Residential Sales Comparison and Income Approaches: 30 Hours
- Residential Report Writing and Case Studies: 15 Hours.

Examination: Applicants must successfully complete the Licensed Appraiser examination as provided in Chapter 4 of the Board Rules. A passing score on an examination is valid for two years from the examination date. Failure to file a complete application for licensure within the two-year period will result in the examination grade being void.

Experience: An applicant submitting an application shall demonstrate to the satisfaction of the Board that the applicant completed at least 2,000 hours of appraisal experience in conformance with the provisions of Chapter 5 of these Rules and all of the applicant's experience was obtained after January 30, 1989 and in compliance with the Uniform Standards of Professional Appraisal Practice (USPAP). Pursuant to § 12-61-706(9), C.R.S., real estate appraisal experience shall have been gained across a period of not less than 12 months.

Certified Residential Appraiser:

Education: An applicant submitting an application for licensure as a Colorado Certified Residential Appraiser shall meet the education requirements set forth in Board Rule 2.3A4 and the following real estate appraisal education module requirements, or the substantial equivalent thereof, as set forth in the Core Curriculum and Guide Note 1 of the 2008 Real Property Appraiser Qualification Criteria adopted by the Appraiser Qualifications Board of The Appraisal Foundation on February 20, 2004, and amended through May 5, 2006, with an effective date of January 1, 2008, as incorporated by reference in Rule 1.32:

- Basic Appraisal Principles: 30 Hours
- Basic Appraisal Procedures: 30 Hours
- 15-Hour National USPAP Course: 15 Hours
- Residential Market Analysis and Highest and Best Use: 15 Hours
- Residential Appraiser Site Valuation and Cost Approach: 15 Hours
- Residential Sales Comparison and Income Approaches: 30 Hours
- Residential Report Writing and Case Studies: 15 Hours
- Statistics, Modeling and Finance: 15 Hours
- Advanced Residential Applications and Case Studies: 15 Hours
- Appraisal Subject Matter Electives: 20 Hours

In addition, applicants for the Certified Residential Appraiser credential must hold an Associate's degree or higher from an accredited college, junior college, community college, or university, or have successfully completed at least 21 semester credit hours or 31.5 quarter credit hours including all of the following topics: (1) English Composition; (2) Principles of Economics (Micro or Macro); (3) Finance; (4) Algebra, Geometry, or higher mathematics; (5) Statistics; (6) Computer Science; and (7) Business or Real Estate Law. Credits earned through the College Level Examination Program (CLEP) are acceptable to meet this requirement.

Examination: Applicants must successfully complete the Certified Residential Appraiser examination as provided in Chapter 4 of the Board Rules. A passing score on an examination is valid for two years from the examination date. Failure to file a complete application within the two-year period will result in the examination grade being void.

Experience: An applicant submitting an application for licensure as a Colorado Certified Residential Appraiser shall demonstrate to the satisfaction of the Board that the applicant completed at least 2,500 hours of appraisal experience in conformance with the provisions of Chapter 5 of these Rules and all of the applicant's experience was obtained after January 30, 1989 and in compliance with the Uniform Standards of Professional Appraisal Practice

(USPAP). Pursuant to § 12-61-706(9), C.R.S., real estate appraisal experience shall have been gained across a period of not less than 24 months.

Certified General Appraiser:

Education: An applicant submitting an application received in the offices of the Board on and after January 1, 2010 for licensure as a Colorado Certified General Appraiser shall meet the education requirements set forth in Board Rule 2.4A4 and the following real estate appraisal education module requirements, or the substantial equivalent thereof, as set forth in the Core Curriculum of the 2008 Real Property Appraiser Qualification Criteria adopted by the Appraiser Qualifications Board of The Appraisal Foundation on February 20, 2004, and amended through May 5, 2006, with an effective date of January 1, 2008, as incorporated by reference in Rule 1.32:

- Basic Appraisal Principles: 30 Hours
- Basic Appraisal Procedures: 30 Hours
- 15-Hour National USPAP Course: 15 Hours
- General Appraiser Market Analysis and Highest and Best Use: 30 Hours
- Statistics, Modeling and Finance: 15 Hours
- General Appraiser Sales Comparison Approach: 30 Hours
- General Appraiser Site Valuation and Cost Approach: 30 Hours
- General Appraiser Income Approach: 60 classroom Hours
- General Appraiser Report Writing and Case Studies: 30 Hours
- Appraisal Subject Matter Electives: 30 Hours

In addition, applicants for the Certified General Appraiser credential must hold a Bachelor's degree or higher from an accredited college or university, or have successfully completed at least 30 semester credit hours or 45 quarter credit hours in the following collegiate subject matter courses from an accredited college, junior college, community college, or university: (1) English Composition; (2) Macro Economics; (3) Micro Economics; (4) Finance; (5) Algebra, Geometry, or higher mathematics; (6) Statistics; (7) Computer Science; (8) Business or Real Estate Law; and (9) two elective courses in accounting, geography, agricultural economics, business management, or real estate.

Examination: Applicants must successfully complete the Certified General Appraiser examination as provided in Chapter 4 of the Board Rules. A passing score on an examination is valid for two years from the examination date. Failure to file a complete application within the two-year period will result in the examination grade being void.

Experience: An applicant submitting an application for licensure as a Colorado Certified General Appraiser shall demonstrate to the satisfaction of the Board that the applicant completed at least 3,000 hours of appraisal experience in conformance with the provisions of Chapter 5 of these Rules and all of the applicant's experience was obtained after January 30, 1989 and in compliance with the Uniform Standards of Professional Appraisal Practice (USPAP). Pursuant to § 12-61-706(9), C.R.S., real estate appraisal experience shall have been gained across a period of not less than 30 months and shall include at least 1,500 hours of appraisal of non-residential property, as defined in Chapter 1 of these Rules.

V. Continuing Education Requirements

An initial registration, license, or certification issued to an appraiser is valid through December 31 of the year of issue. Appraisers who obtain their initial registration, license, or certification before July 1 of any calendar year must complete at least 14 hours of approved appraiser continuing education before December 31. Appraisers who renew their registration, license, or certification will be issued a three-year credential and must complete at least 42 hours of approved appraiser continuing education during the three-year renewal cycle. During their three-year renewal cycle, appraisers must successfully complete the seven-hour National Uniform Standards of Professional Appraisal Practice (USPAP) Update Course. Each seven-hour USPAP Update Course may count toward the 42 hours of required continuing education.

Title 12, Article 61, Part 7, Colorado Revised Statutes – Real Estate Appraisers

§ 12-61-701, C.R.S. Legislative declaration

The general assembly finds, determines, and declares that this part 7 is enacted pursuant to the requirements of the federal "Real Estate Appraisal Reform Amendments", Title XI of the federal "Financial Institutions Reform, Recovery, and Enforcement Act of 1989". The general assembly further finds, determines, and declares that this part 7 is intended to implement the minimum requirements of federal law in the least burdensome manner to real estate appraisers.

§ 12-61-702, C.R.S. Definitions

As used in this part 7, unless the context otherwise requires:

(1) "Appraisal", "appraisal report", or "real estate appraisal" means a written analysis, opinion, or conclusion relating to the nature, quality, value, or utility of specified interests in, or aspects of, identified real estate. Such terms include a valuation, which is an opinion of the value of real estate, and an analysis, which is a general study of real estate not specifically performed only to determine value; except that such terms include any valuation completed by any appraiser employee of a county assessor as defined in section 39-1-102 (2), C.R.S. Such terms do not include an analysis, valuation, opinion, conclusion, notation, or compilation of data by an officer, director, or regular salaried employee of a financial institution or its affiliate, made for internal use only by the said financial institution or affiliate, concerning an interest in real estate that is owned or held as collateral by the said financial institution or affiliate which is not represented or deemed to be an appraisal except to the said financial institution, the agencies regulating the said financial institution, and any secondary markets that purchase real estate secured loans. Any such appraisal prepared by an officer, director, or regular salaried employee of said financial institution who is not registered, licensed, or certified under this part 7 shall contain a written notice that the preparer is not registered, licensed, or certified as an appraiser under this part 7.

(2) "Board" means the board of real estate appraisers created in section 12-61-703.

(2.3) "Commission" means the conservation easement oversight commission created in section 12-61-721 (1).

(2.5) "Consulting services" means services performed by an appraiser that do not fall within the definition of an "independent appraisal" in subsection 4.5 of this section. "Consulting services" includes, but is not limited to, marketing, financing and feasibility studies, valuations, analyses, and opinions and conclusions given in connection with real estate brokerage, mortgage banking, and counseling and advocacy in regard to property tax assessments and appeals thereof; except that, if in rendering such services, the appraiser acts as a disinterested third party, the work shall be deemed an independent appraisal and not a consulting service. Nothing in this subsection (2.5) shall be construed to preclude a person from acting as an expert witness in valuation appeals.

(3) "Division" means the division of real estate.

(4) "Director" means the director of the division of real estate.

(4.3) "Financial Institution" means any "bank" or "savings association" as such terms are defined in 12 U.S.C. Sec. 1813, Any state or industrial bank incorporated under Title XI, C.R.S., any state or federally chartered credit union, or any company which has direct or indirect control over any of such entities.

(4.5) "Independent appraisal" means an engagement for which an appraiser is employed or retained to act as a disinterested third party in rendering an unbiased analysis, opinion, or conclusion relating to the nature, quality, value or utility of specified interests in or aspects of identified real estate.

(5) (a) "Real estate appraiser" or "appraiser" means any person who provides for a fee or a salary an estimate of the nature, quality, value, or utility of an interest in, or aspect of, identified real

estate and includes one who estimates value and who possesses the necessary qualifications, ability, and experience to execute or direct the appraisal of real property.

(b) "Real estate appraiser" does not include:

(I) Any person who conducts appraisals strictly of personal property;

(II) Any person licensed as a broker pursuant to part 1 of this article who provides an opinion of value that is not represented as an appraisal and is not used for purposes of obtaining financing.

(III) Any person licensed as a certified public accountant pursuant to article 2 of title 12, C.R.S., and otherwise regulated, provided such opinions of value for real estate are not represented as an appraisal;

(IV) Any corporation, which is acting through its officers or regular salaried employees, when conducting a valuation of real estate property rights owned, to be purchased, or sold by the corporation;

(V) Any person who conducts appraisals strictly of water rights or of mineral rights;

(VI) Any right-of-way acquisition agent employed by a public entity who provides an opinion of value that is not represented as an appraisal when the property being valued is five thousand dollars or less;

(VII) Any officer, director, or regular salaried employee of a financial institution or its affiliate who makes, for internal use only by the said financial institution or affiliate, an analysis, evaluation, opinion, conclusion, notation, or compilation of data with respect to an appraisal so long as such person does not make a written adjustment of the appraisal's conclusion as to the value of the subject real property;

(VIII) Any officer, director, or regular salaried employee of a financial institution or its affiliate who makes such an internal analysis, valuation, opinion, conclusion, notation, or compilation of data concerning an interest in real estate that is owned or held as collateral by the financial institution or its affiliate.

(6) Repealed

12-61-703, C.R.S. Board of real estate appraisers – creation – compensation – immunity –subject to termination

(1) There is hereby created in the division a board of real estate appraisers consisting of seven members appointed by the governor with the consent of the senate. Of such members, three shall be licensed or certified appraisers, one of whom shall have expertise in eminent domain matters, one shall be a county assessor in office, one shall be an officer or employee of a commercial bank experienced in real estate lending, and two shall be members of the public at large not engaged in any of the businesses represented by the other members of the board. Of the members of the board appointed for terms beginning July 1, 1990, the commercial bank member, the county assessor member, and two of the appraiser members shall be appointed for terms of three years, and the public member and the remaining appraiser members shall be appointed for terms of one year. Members of the board appointed after July 1, 1990, shall hold office for a term of three years. The additional public member of the board of real estate appraisers authorized by this subsection (1) shall not be appointed before the earliest date on which one of the four appraiser members' terms expires after July 1, 1996. In the event of a vacancy by death, resignation, removal, or otherwise, the governor shall appoint a member to fill out the unexpired term. The governor shall have the authority to remove any member for misconduct, neglect of duty, or incompetence.

(2) The board shall exercise its powers and perform its duties and functions under the division as if transferred thereto by a type 1 transfer as such transfer is defined in the "Administrative Organization Act of 1968", article 1 of title 24, C.R.S.

(2.5) (a) The general assembly finds, determines, and declares that the organization of the board under the division as a type 1 agency will provide the autonomy necessary to avoid potential conflicts of interest between the responsibility of the board in the regulation of real estate appraisers and the responsibility of the division in the regulation of real estate brokers and salesmen. The general assembly further finds, determines, and declares that the placement of the board as a type 1 agency under the division is consistent with the organizational structure of state government.

(b) (I) Repealed

(II) Repealed

(III) Repealed

(c) Repealed

(3) Each member of the board shall receive the same compensation and reimbursement of expenses as those provided for members of board and commissions in the division of registrations pursuant to section 24-34-102 (13), C.R.S. Payment for all such per diem compensation and expenses shall be made out of annual appropriations from the division of real estate cash fund provided for in section 12-61-705.

(4) Members of the board, consultants, and expert witnesses shall be immune from suit in any civil action based upon any disciplinary proceedings or other official acts they performed in good faith pursuant to this part 7.

(5) A majority of the board shall constitute a quorum for the transaction of all business, and actions of the board shall require a vote of a majority of such members present in favor of the action taken.

(6) This part 7 is repealed, effective July 1, 2013. Prior to such repeal, the board of real estate appraisers shall be reviewed as provided in section 24-34-104, C.R.S.

§ 12-61-704, C.R.S. Powers and duties of the board

(1) In addition to all other powers and duties imposed upon it by law, the board has the following powers and duties:

(a) To promulgate and amend, as necessary, rules and regulations pursuant to article 4 of title 24, C.R.S., for the implementation and administration of this part 7 and as required to comply with the federal "Real Estate Appraisal Reform Amendments", Title XI of the federal "Financial Institutions Reform, Recovery, and Enforcement Act of 1989"; and with any requirements imposed by amendments to such federal law. The board shall not establish any requirements that are more stringent than the requirements of any applicable federal law.

(b) To charge application, examination, and registration license and certificate renewal fees established pursuant to section 12-61-111.5 from all applicants for registration, licensure, certification, examination, and renewal under this part 7. No fees received from applicants seeking registration, licensure, certification, examination, or renewal shall be refunded.

(c) (I) To keep all records of proceedings and activities of the board conducted under authority of this part 7, which records shall be open to public inspection at such time and in such manner as may be prescribed by rules and regulations formulated by the board.

(II) The board shall not be required to maintain or preserve licensing history records of any person licensed or certified under the provisions of this part 7 for any period of time longer than seven years.

(d) Through the department of regulatory agencies and subject to appropriations made to the department of regulatory agencies, to employ administrative law judges on a full-time or part-time basis to conduct any hearings required by this part 7. Such administrative law judges shall be appointed pursuant to part 10 of article 30 or title 24, C.R.S.

(e) To issue, deny, or refuse to renew a registration, license or certificate pursuant to this part 7;

(f) To take disciplinary actions in conformity with this part 7;

(g) To delegate to the director the administration and enforcement of this part 7 and the authority to act on behalf of the board on such occasions and in such circumstances as the board directs;

(h) (I) To develop, purchase or contract for any examination required for the administration of this part 7, to offer each such examination at least twice a year or, if demand warrants, at more frequent intervals, and to establish a passing score for each examination that reflects a minimum level or competency;

(II) If study materials are developed by a testing company or other entity, the board shall make such materials available to persons desiring to take examinations pursuant to this part 7. The board may charge fees for such materials to defray any costs associated with making such materials available.

(i) In compliance with the provisions of Article 4 of Title 24, C.R.S., to make investigations, subpoena persons and documents, which subpoenas may be enforced by a court of competent jurisdiction if not obeyed, hold hearings, and take evidence in all matters relating to the exercise of the board's power under this part 7.

(j) Pursuant to Section 1119 (b) of Title XI of the federal "Financial Reform, Recovery, and Enforcement Act of 1989", to apply, if necessary, for a federal waiver of the requirement relating to certification or licensing of a person to perform appraisals and to make the necessary written determinations specified in said section for purposes of making such application.

§ 12-61-705, C.R.S. Fees, penalties and fines collected under part 7

All fees, penalties, and fines collected pursuant to this part 7, not including fees retained by contractors pursuant to contracts entered into in accordance with section 12-61-103, 12-61-706, or 24-34-101, shall be transmitted to the state treasurer, who shall credit the same to the division of real estate cash fund, created in Section 12-61-111.5.

§ 12-61-706, C.R.S. Qualifications for appraiser's license and certification – continuing education

(1) (a) The board shall, by rule, prescribe requirements for the initial registration, licensing, or certification of persons under this part 7 to meet the requirements of the federal "Real Estate Appraisal Reform Amendments", Title XI of the federal "Financial Institutions Reform, Recovery, and Enforcement Act of 1989" and shall develop, purchase or contract for examinations to be passed by applicants. The board shall not establish any requirements for initial registration, licensing, or certification that are more stringent than the requirements of any applicable federal law; except that all applicants shall pass an examination offered by the board. If there is no applicable federal law, the board shall consider and may use as guidelines the most recent available criteria published by the appraiser qualifications board of the Appraisal Foundation or its successor organization.

(b) The four levels of appraiser licensure, pursuant to paragraph (a) of this subsection (1), shall be defined as follows:

(I) "Certified General Appraiser" means an appraiser meeting the requirements set by the board for general certification;

(II) "Certified Residential Appraiser" means an appraiser meeting the requirements set by the board for residential certification;

(III) "Licensed Appraiser" means an appraiser meeting the requirements set by the board for a license;

(IV) "Registered Appraiser" means an appraiser meeting the requirements set by the board for registration.

(2) The board shall, by rule, prescribe continuing education requirements for persons registered, licensed, or certified under this part 7 as needed to meet the requirements of the federal "Real Estate Appraisal Reform Amendments", Title XI of the federal "Financial Institutions Reform, Recovery, and Enforcement Act of 1989". The board shall not establish any continuing education requirements that are more stringent than the requirements of any applicable law; except that all persons registered, licensed, or certified under this part 7 shall be subject to continuing education requirements. If there is no applicable federal law, the board shall consider and may use as guidelines the most recent available criteria published by the appraiser qualifications board, of the Appraisal Foundation or its successor organization. The Board shall not grant continuing education credits for attendance at the Board's meetings.

(3) Any provision of this section to the contrary notwithstanding, the criteria established by the board for the registration, licensing, or certification of appraisers pursuant to this part 7 shall not include membership or lack of membership in any appraisal organization.

(4) Repealed (effective 7-1-96)

(5) (a) Subject to section 12-61-714 (2), all appraiser employees of county assessors shall be registered, licensed, or certified as provided in subsections (1) and (2), of this section. Obtaining and maintaining a registration, license or certificate under any one of said subsections (1) and (2), shall entitle an appraiser employee of a county assessor to perform all real estate appraisals required to fulfill such person's official duties.

(b) Appraiser employees of county assessors shall be subject to all provisions of this part 7; except that appraiser employees of county assessors who are employed to appraise real property shall not be subject to disciplinary actions by the board on the ground that they have performed appraisals beyond their level of competency when appraising real estate in fulfillment of their official duties. County assessors, if registered, licensed or certified as provided in subsections (1) and (2) of this section shall not be subject to disciplinary actions by the board on the ground that they have performed appraisals beyond their level of competency when appraising real estate in fulfillment of their official duties.

(c) All reasonable costs incurred by an appraiser employee of a county assessor to obtain and maintain a registration, license, or certificate pursuant to this section shall be paid by the county.

(6) Repealed

(7) Repealed

(8) Repealed

(9) The board shall not issue an appraiser's license as referenced in subparagraph (III) of paragraph (b) of subsection (1) of this section unless the applicant has at least twelve months appraisal experience.

§ 12-61-707, C.R.S. Expiration of licenses – renewal

(1) (a) All registrations, licenses or certificates shall expire pursuant to a schedule established by the director and shall be renewed or reinstated pursuant to this section. Upon compliance with this section and any applicable rules of the board regarding renewal, including the payment of a renewal fee plus a reinstatement fee established pursuant to paragraph (b) of this subsection (1) the expired registration, license or certificate shall be reinstated. No real estate appraiser's registration, license or certificate that has not been renewed for a period greater than two

years shall be reinstated, and such person shall be required to make new application for registration, license or certification.

(b) A person who fails to renew his or her registration, license, or certificate prior to the applicable renewal date may have it reinstated if the person does any one of the following:

(I) Makes proper application, within thirty-one days after the date of expiration, by payment of the regular three-year renewal fee;

(II) If proper application is made after thirty one days after the date of expiration, but within one year, after the date of expiration, by payment of the regular three year renewal fee and payment of a reinstatement fee equal to one-third of the regular three year renewal fee; or

(III) If proper application is made more than one year, but within two years, after the date of expiration, by payment of the regular three year renewal fee and payment of a reinstatement fee equal to two-thirds of the regular three year renewal fee.

(2) In the event the federal registry fee to be collected by the board and transmitted to the federal financial institutions examination council is adjusted during the period prior to expiration of a registration, license or certificate, the board shall collect the amount of the increase in such fee from the holder of the registration, license or certificate and shall forward such amount to the said council on an annual basis.

(3) (a) If the applicant has complied with this section and any applicable rules and regulations of the board regarding renewal, except for the continuing education requirements pursuant to section 12-61-706, the licensee may renew the license on inactive status. An inactive license may be activated if the licensee submits written certification of compliance with section 12-61-706 for the previous licensing period. The board may adopt rules establishing procedures to facilitate such a reactivation.

(b) The holder of an inactive license shall not perform a real estate appraisal in conjunction with a debt instrument that is federally guaranteed, in the federal secondary market, or regulated pursuant to Title 12, U.S.C.

(c) The holder of an inactive license shall not hold himself or herself out as having an active license pursuant to this Part 7.

§ 12-61-708, C.R.S. Licensure or certification by endorsement

(1) (a) The board may issue a license or certification to an appraiser by endorsement to engage in the occupation of real estate appraisal to any applicant who has a license, registration, or certification in good standing as a real estate appraiser under the laws of another jurisdiction if the applicant presents proof satisfactory to the board that, at the time of application for a Colorado registration, license or certificate by endorsement, the applicant possesses credentials and qualifications which are substantially equivalent to the requirements of this part 7; or

(b) The jurisdiction that issued the applicant a license or certificate to engage in the occupation of real estate appraisal has a law similar to this subsection (1) pursuant to which it licenses or certifies persons who are licensed real estate appraisers in this state.

(1.2) The board may specify by rules and regulation what shall constitute substantially equivalent credentials and qualifications and the manner in which credentials and qualifications of an applicant will be reviewed by the board.

(2) Pursuant to Section 1122 (a) of Title XI of the federal "Financial Institutions Reform, Recovery, and Enforcement Act of 1989", the board shall recognize, on a temporary basis, the license or certification of an appraiser issued by another state if:

(a) Repealed (effective 7-1-96)

(b) The appraiser's business is of a temporary nature; and

(c) The appraiser applies for and is granted a temporary practice permit by the board.

§ 12-61-709, C.R.S. Denial of license or certificate – renewal

(1) The board is empowered to determine whether an applicant for registration, licensure, or certification possesses the necessary qualifications for registration, licensure, or certification required by this part 7. The board may consider such qualities as the applicant's truthfulness and honesty and whether the applicant has been convicted of a crime involving moral turpitude.

(2) If the board determines that an applicant does not possess the applicable qualifications required by this part 7, or such applicant has violated any provision of this part 7 or the rules and regulations promulgated by the board or any board order, the board may deny the applicant a registration, license or certificate pursuant to section 12-61-707; and, in such instance, the board shall provide such applicant with a statement in writing setting forth the basis of the board's determination that the applicant does not possess the qualifications or professional competence required by this part 7. Such applicant may request a hearing on such determination as provided in section 24-4-104 (9), C.R.S.

§ 12-61-710, C.R.S. Prohibited activities – grounds for disciplinary actions – procedures

(1) A real estate appraiser is in violation of this part 7 if the appraiser:

(a) Has been convicted of a felony or has had accepted by a court a plea of guilty or nolo contendere to a felony if the felony is related to the ability to act as a real property appraiser. A certified copy of the judgment of court of competent jurisdiction of such conviction or plea shall be conclusive evidence of such conviction or plea. In considering the disciplinary action, the board shall be governed by the provisions of section 24-5-101, C.R.S.

(b) Has violated, or attempted to violate, directly or indirectly, or assisted in or abetted the violation of, or conspired to violate any provision or term of this part 7 or rule or regulation promulgated pursuant to this part 7 or any order of the board established pursuant to this part 7;

(c) Has accepted any fees, compensation, or other valuable consideration to influence the outcome of an appraisal;

(d) Has used advertising which is misleading, deceptive, or false;

(e) Has used fraud or misrepresentation in obtaining a license or certificate under this part 7;

(f) Has conducted an appraisal in a fraudulent manner or used misrepresentation in any such activity;

(g) Has acted or failed to act in a manner which does not meet the generally accepted standards of professional appraisal practice as adopted by the board by rule and regulation. A certified copy of a malpractice judgment of a court of competent jurisdiction shall be conclusive evidence of such act or omission, but evidence of such act or omission shall not be limited to a malpractice judgment;

(h) Has performed appraisal services beyond his level of competency;

(i) Has been subject to an adverse or disciplinary action in another state, territory, or country relating to a license, certification, registration, or other authorization to practice as an appraiser. A disciplinary action relating to a registration, license or certificate as an appraiser registered, licensed or certified under this part 7 or any related occupation in any other state, territory, or country for disciplinary reasons shall be deemed to be prima facie evidence of grounds for disciplinary action or denial of registration, licensure or certification by the board. This paragraph (i) shall apply only to violations based upon acts or omissions in such other state, territory, or country that are also violations of this part 7.

(2) If an applicant, a registrant, a licensee, or a certified person has violated any of the provisions of this section, the board may deny or refuse to renew any registration, license or certificate, or, as specified in subsections (2.5) and (5) of this section, revoke or suspend any registration, license or certificate, issue a letter of admonition to an applicant, a registrant, a licensee or a certified person, place a registrant, licensee or certified person on probation, or impose public censure.

(2.5) When a complaint or an investigation discloses an instance of misconduct by a registered, licensed, or certified appraiser that in the opinion of the board does not warrant formal action by the board but should not be dismissed as being without merit, the board may send a letter of admonition by certified mail to the appraiser against whom a complaint was made. The letter shall advise the appraiser of the right to make a written request, within twenty days after receipt of the letter of admonition, to the board to begin formal disciplinary proceedings as provided in this section to adjudicate the conduct or acts on which the letter was based.

(3) A proceeding for discipline of a registrant, licensee or certified person may be commenced when the board has reasonable grounds to believe that a registrant, licensee or a certified person has committed any act or failed to act pursuant to the grounds established in subsection (1) of this section or when a request for a hearing is timely made under subsection (2.5) of this section.

(4) Disciplinary proceedings shall be conducted in the manner prescribed by the "State Administrative Procedure Act", article 4 or title 24, C.R.S.

(5) As authorized in subsection (2) of this section, disciplinary actions by the board may consist of the following:

- (a) Revocation of a registration, license or certificate.
  - (I) Revocation of a registration, license or certificate by the board shall mean that the registered, licensed or certified person shall surrender his or her registration, license or certificate immediately to the board.
  - (II) Any person whose registration, license or certificate to practice is revoked is rendered ineligible to apply for any registration, license or certificate issued under this part 7 until more than two years have elapsed from the date of surrender of the registration, license or certificate. Any re-application after such two-year period shall be treated as a new application.
- (b) Suspension of a license. Suspension of a registration, license or certificate by the board shall be for a period to be determined by the board.
- (c) Probationary status. Probationary status may be imposed by the board. If the board places a registrant, licensee or certified person on probation, it may include such conditions for continued practice as the board deems appropriate to assure that the registrant, licensee or certified person is otherwise qualified to practice in accordance with generally accepted professional standards of professional appraisal practice as adopted by rule and regulation of the board, including any or all of the following:
  - (I) The taking by him of such courses of training or education as may be needed to correct deficiencies found in the hearing;
  - (II) Such review or supervision of his practice as may be necessary to determine the quality of his practice and to correct deficiencies therein; and
  - (III) The imposition of restrictions upon the nature of his appraisal practice to assure that he does not practice beyond the limits of his capabilities.
- (d) Repealed
- (e) Public censure. If after notice and hearing the director or the director's designee determines that the licensee has committed any of the acts specified in this section, the board may impose public censure.

(6) In addition to any other discipline imposed pursuant to this section, any person who violated the provisions of this part 7 or the rules and regulations of the board promulgated pursuant to this article may be penalized by the board upon a finding of a violation pursuant to article 4 or title 24, C.R.S., as follows:

(a) In the first administrative proceeding against any person, a fine of not less than three hundred dollars but not more than five hundred dollars per violation;

(b) In any subsequent administrative proceeding against any person for transactions occurring after a final agency action determining that a violation of this part 7 has occurred, a fine of not less than one thousand dollars but not more than two thousand dollars.

(7) Complaints of record in the office of the board and the results of staff investigations shall be closed to public inspection, during the investigatory period and until dismissed or until notice of hearing and charges are served on a licensee, except as provided by court order. Complaints of record that are dismissed by the Board and the results of investigation of such complaints shall be closed to public inspection, except as provided by court order. The Board's records shall be subject to sections 24-72-203 and 24-72-204, C.R.S., regarding public records and confidentiality.

(8) Any person participating in good faith in the making of complaint or report or participation in any investigative or administrative proceeding before the board pursuant to this article shall be immune from any liability, civil or criminal, that otherwise might result by reason of such action.

(9) Any board member having an immediate personal, private, or financial interest in any matter pending before the board shall disclose that fact to the board and shall not vote upon such matter.

(10) Any registrant, licensee or certified person having direct knowledge that any person has violated any of the provisions of this part 7 shall report such knowledge to the board.

(11) The board, on its own motion or upon application, at any time after the imposition of any discipline as provided in this section may reconsider its prior action and reinstate or restore such registration, license or certificate or terminate probation or reduce the severity of its prior disciplinary action. The taking of any such further action or the holding of a hearing with respect thereto shall rest in the sole discretion of the board.

§ 12-61-711, C.R.S. Judicial review of final board actions and orders

Final actions and orders of the board under sections 12-61-709 and 12-61-710 appropriate for judicial review shall be judicially reviewed in the court of appeals, in accordance with section 24-4-106 (11), C.R.S.

§ 12-61-712, C.R.S. Unlawful acts – real estate appraiser license required

(1) It is unlawful for any person to:

(a) Violate any provision of section 12-61-710(1)(c), (1)(e), or (1)(f), or to perform a real estate appraisal in conjunction with a debt instrument that is federally guaranteed or in the federal secondary market or regulated pursuant to title 12, U.S.C., without first having obtained a registration, license, or certificate from the board pursuant to this part 7.

(b) Accept a fee for an independent appraisal assignment that is contingent upon:

(I) The reporting of a predetermined analysis, opinion, or conclusion; or

(II) The analysis, opinion, or conclusion reached; or

(III) The consequences resulting from the analysis, opinion, or conclusion;

(c) Misrepresent a consulting service as an independent appraisal;

(d) Fail to disclose, in connection with a consulting service for which a contingent fee is or will be paid, the fact that a contingent fee is or will be paid.

(2) Any person who violates any provision of subsection (1) of this section commits a class 1 misdemeanor and shall be punished as provided in section 18-1.3-501, C.R.S. Any person who

subsequently violates any provision of subsection (1) of this section within five years after the date of a conviction for a violation of subsection (1) of this section commits a class 5 felony and shall be punished as provided in section 18-1.3-401, C.R.S.

(3) A person who represents property owners in tax or valuation protests and appeals pursuant to Title 39, C.R.S., shall be exempt from the licensing requirements of this part 7.

§ 12-61-713, C.R.S. Injunctive proceedings

(1) The board may, in the name of the people of the state of Colorado, through the attorney general of the state of Colorado, apply for an injunction in any court of competent jurisdiction to perpetually enjoin any person from committing any act prohibited by the provisions of this part 7.

(2) Such injunctive proceedings shall be in addition to and not in lieu of all penalties and other remedies provided in this part 7.

(3) When seeking an injunction under this section, the board shall not be required to allege or prove either that an adequate remedy at law does not exist or that substantial or irreparable damage would result from a continued violation.

§ 12-61-714, C.R.S. Requirement for appraisers to be licensed – special provisions for certain public employees

(1) Except as provided in subsection (2) of this section, unless a federal waiver is applied for and granted pursuant to section 12-61-704 (1) (j), on and after July 1, 1991, any person acting as a real estate appraiser in this state shall be licensed as provided in this part 7, and, on and after said date, no person shall practice without such a registration, license or certificate or hold himself out to the public as a real estate appraiser unless registered, licensed or certified pursuant to this part 7.

(2) Any appraiser employee of any county assessor who is employed to appraise real property shall be registered, licensed or certified as provided in the part 7, and shall have two years from the date of taking office or the beginning of employment to comply with the provisions of this part 7.

§ 12-61-715, C.R.S. Duties of board under federal law

(1) The board shall:

(a) Transmit to the appraisal subcommittee of the federal financial institutions examinations council, no less than annually, a roster listing individuals who have received a registration, certificate or license as provided in this part 7;

(b) Collect from individuals who have received a certificate or license as provided in this part 7 an annual registry fee of not more than twenty-five dollars, unless the appraisal subcommittee of the federal financial institutions examinations council adjusts the fee up to a maximum of fifty dollars, and transmit such fee to the federal financial institutions examinations council on an annual basis; and

(c) Conduct its business and promulgate rules and regulations in a manner not inconsistent with Title XI of the federal "Financial Institutions Reform, Recovery and Enforcement Act of 1989", as amended.

§ 12-61-716, C.R.S. Business entities

(1) A corporation, partnership, bank, savings and loan association, savings bank, credit union, or other business entity may provide appraisal services if such appraisal is prepared by individuals registered, certified or licensed in accordance with this part 7. An individual who is not a registered, certified or licensed appraiser may assist in the preparation of an appraisal if:

(a) The assistant is under the direct supervision of a registered, certified or licensed appraiser; and

(b) The final appraisal document is approved and signed by an individual who is a registered, certified or licensed appraiser.

§ 12-61-717, C.R.S. Provisions found not to comply with federal law null and void – severability

If any provision of this part 7 is found by a court of competent jurisdiction or by the appropriate federal agency not to comply with any provision of the federal "Financial Institutions Reform, Recovery, and Enforcement Act of 1989", such provision shall be null and void, but the remaining provisions of this part 7 shall be valid unless such remaining provisions alone are incomplete and are incapable of being executed in accordance with the legislative intent of this part 7.

§ 12-61-718, C.R.S. Scope of article – regulated financial institutions – de minimis exemption

(1) (a) This article shall not apply to an appraisal relating to any real estate-related transaction or loan made or to be made by a financial institution or its affiliate if such real estate-related transaction or loan is excepted from appraisal regulations established by the primary federal regulator of said financial institution and the appraisal is performed by:

(I) An officer, director, or regular salaried employee of the financial institution or its affiliate; or

(II) A real estate broker licensed under this article with whom said institution or affiliate has contracted for performance of the appraisal,

(b) Such appraisal shall not be represented or deemed to be an appraisal except to the said financial institution, the agencies regulating the said financial institution, and any secondary markets that purchase real estate secured loans. Such appraisal shall contain a written notice that the preparer is not registered, licensed, or certified as an appraiser under this part 7. Nothing in this subsection (1) shall be construed to exempt a person registered, licensed, or certified as an appraiser under this part 7 from regulation as provided in this part 7.

(2) Nothing in this article shall be construed to limit the ability of any federal or state regulator of a financial institution to require the financial institution to obtain appraisals as specified by the regulator.

(3) Repealed.

. Rule Making of the Board of Real Estate Appraisers

Pursuant to § 12-61-704(1)(a), C.R.S., the Colorado Board of Real Estate Appraisers engages in rule making to implement Colorado law in a manner consistent with the requirements of Title XI of the federal Financial Institutions Reform, Recovery and Enforcement Act of 1989.

The rule making process is set by § 24-4-103, C.R.S., and involves notice to the public, hearing(s), adoption of rules, and publication. General notice is accomplished through filing with the Secretary of State and publication in the Colorado Register. Specific notice is provided by mail to interested parties. To request mailing of rule-making notices, send a written request for placement on the rule-making notice list to: Rule Making Notice List, Colorado Board of Appraisers, 1560 Broadway, Suite 925, Denver, CO 80202.

While rule making may occur at any time, the Board prefers to adopt new and amended rules in the fall, with January 1 of the next year as the effective date. Rules are published in the Colorado Real Estate Manual.

DEPARTMENT OF REGULATORY AGENCIES
DIVISION OF REAL ESTATE
BOARD OF REAL ESTATE APPRAISERS
4 CCR 725-2

RULES OF THE COLORADO BOARD OF REAL ESTATE APPRAISERS

Ed. Note: For the most current information, please refer to the Division of Real Estate website: www.dora.state.co.us/real-estate

CHAPTER 1: DEFINITIONS

* 1.1 The Appraisal Foundation (TAF): TAF is the organization that is the source of appraisal standards, qualifications and ethical conduct in all valuation disciplines to assure public trust in the valuation profession.

* 1.2 Appraisal Qualifications Board (AQB) of The Appraisal Foundation: The AQB establishes the minimum education, experience and examination requirements for real property appraisers to obtain state certifications. In addition, the AQB performs a number of ancillary duties related to real property and personal property appraiser qualifications.

* 1.3 Appraiser Standards Board (ASB) of The Appraisal Foundation: The ASB develops, interprets and amends the Uniform Standards of Professional Appraisal Practice (USPAP).

1.4 Examination: The examination(s) developed or contracted for by the Board and issued or approved by the AQB.

1.5 FIRREA: The Financial Institutions Reform, Recovery and Enforcement Act of 1989.

* 1.6 Board: The Colorado Board of Real Estate Appraisers created and further defined pursuant to §12-61-703, C.R.S.

1.7 Applicant: Any person applying for a license or temporary practice permit, or applying for renewal of a license.

* 1.8 Initial License: The first license granted by the Board to an applicant pursuant to §12-61-706, C.R.S. An applicant may apply for an initial license at any credential level as long as all requirements for such credential level have been met pursuant to Chapter 3 of these Rules. An initial license is valid through December 31 of the year of issue.

1.9 Colorado Real Estate Appraiser Licensing Act: That portion of Colorado statutes known as Section 12-61-701, *et seq*., Colorado Revised Statutes, as amended.

* 1.10 Uniform Standards of Professional Appraisal Practice (USPAP): Those standards of professional practice promulgated by the Appraisal Standards Board of The Appraisal Foundation and adopted in Chapter 11 of these Rules through incorporation by reference.

1.11 Board Rules or Rules: Those rules adopted by the Colorado Board of Real Estate Appraisers pursuant to Section 12-61-704(1)(a), C.R.S., as amended.

* 1.12 Registered (Trainee) Appraiser: A Registered Appraiser is a trainee who has been granted a license pursuant to §12-61-706(1)(b)(IV), C.R.S. as a Registered Appraiser by the Board as a result of meeting the real estate appraisal education and examination requirements established by Board Rule 2.1, The AQB, or as a result of licensure through endorsement from another state as provided by Chapter 9 of these Rules. The scope of practice for the Registered or Trainee Appraiser shall be those properties that the supervising appraiser is permitted and competent to appraise, or as allowed by §12-61-706(5), C.R.S.

1.13 Licensed Appraiser: A person who has been granted a license pursuant to § 12-61-706(1)(b)(III), C.R.S. as a Licensed Appraiser by the Board as a result of meeting the real estate appraisal education, real estate appraisal experience and real estate appraisal examination requirements established by Board Rule 2.2, the AQB, or as a result of licensure through endorsement from another state as provided by Chapter 9 of these Rules, which license is in good standing. The usual scope of practice for the Licensed Appraiser shall be, if competent for the assignment, appraisal of non-complex one to four unit residential properties having a transaction value of less than $1,000,000 and complex one to four unit residential properties having a transaction value of less than $250,000, or as allowed by Section 12-61-706 (5), C.R.S.

* 1.14 Certified Residential Appraiser: A person who has been granted a license pursuant to § 12-61-706(1)(b)(II), C.R.S. as a Certified Residential Appraiser by the Board as a result of meeting the real estate appraisal education, real estate appraisal experience and real estate appraisal examination requirements established by Board Rule 2.3, the AQB, or as a result of licensure through endorsement from another state as provided by Chapter 9 of these Rules, which license is in good standing. The usual scope of practice for the Certified Residential Appraiser shall be, if competent for the assignment, appraisal of one to four unit residential properties without regard to transaction value or complexity, or as allowed by Section 12-61-706 (5), C.R.S. Such scope of practice includes vacant or unimproved land that is to be used for development for a one to four unit residential property, or vacant or unimproved land for which the highest and best use is a one to four unit residential property. The scope of practice for a Certified Residential Appraiser does not include vacant or unimproved land that has the potential for subdivision development for which the subdivision development analysis method of land valuation is necessary and applicable.

1.15 Certified General Appraiser: A person who has been granted a license pursuant to § 12-61-706(1)(b)(I), C.R.S. as a Certified General Appraiser by the Board as a result of meeting the real estate appraisal education, real estate appraisal experience and real estate appraisal examination requirements established by Board Rule 2.4, the AQB, or as a result of licensure through endorsement from another state as provided by Chapter 9 of these Rules, which license is in good standing. The scope of practice for the Certified General Appraiser shall be, if competent for the assignment, appraisal of all types of real property.

1.16 Residential Property: Properties comprising one to four residential units; also includes building sites suitable for development to one to four residential units. Residential property does not include land for which a subdivision analysis or appraisal is necessary.

1.17 Non-Residential Property: Properties other than those comprised of one to four residential units and building sites suitable for development to one to four residential units. Non-residential property includes, without limitation, properties comprised of five or more dwelling units, farm and ranch, retail, manufacturing, warehousing, and office properties, large vacant land parcels and other properties not within the definition of residential property.

1.18 Temporary Practice Permit: A permit issued pursuant to Section 12-61-708 (2), C.R.S., (as amended) and Chapter 10 of these rules allowing an appraiser licensed in another jurisdiction to appraise property in Colorado under certain conditions without obtaining Colorado licensure.

1.19 Title XI, FIRREA: That part of the Financial Institutions Reform, Recovery and Enforcement Act of 1989 known as the Appraisal Reform Amendments, and also known as 12 U.S.C. Section 3331 through 12 U.S.C. Section 3351.

* 1.20 Contingent Fee: Compensation paid to a person who is licensed as a registered, licensed or certified appraiser, as a result of reporting a predetermined value or direction of value that favors the cause of the client, the amount of value opinion, the attainment of a stipulated result, or the occurrence of a subsequent event directly related to the appraiser's opinion and specific to the assignment's purpose. A person licensed as a registered, licensed or certified appraiser employed by a business entity which is compensated by a contingent fee is considered to be compensated by a contingent fee.

1.21 Licensee: A collective term used to refer to a person who has been licensed by the Board as a Registered Appraiser, Licensed Appraiser, Certified Residential Appraiser or Certified General Appraiser.

* 1.22 Distance education: Educational methodologies and presentation techniques other than traditional classroom formats, including and without limitation, live teleconferencing, cd-rom or disk based computer presentations, written or electronic correspondence courses, internet on-line learning, video and audio tapes, and others.

1.23 Complex Residential Property: Properties comprising one to four residential dwelling units, or land suitable for development to one to four residential units exhibiting complex appraisal factors such as atypical form of ownership, atypical size, atypical design characteristics, atypical locational characteristics, atypical physical condition characteristics, landmark designation, non-conforming zoning, lack of appraisal data, and other similar factors. Complex residential property does not include land for which a subdivision analysis or appraisal is necessary.

1.24 Signature: As defined in the Uniform Standards of Professional Appraisal Practice incorporated by reference in Board Rule 11.1, and including all methods of indicating a signature, such as, without limitation, a handwritten mark, digitized image, coded authentication number, stamped impression, embossed or applied seal, or other means.

* 1.25 Supervisory Appraiser: Any active licensee who acts in a supervisory role in the development and reporting of appraisals, appraisal reports, and other appraisal work products. Includes, without limitation, any licensee who signs a report in a manner indicating they exert control over the action of any Trainee or Licensee, or who acts to guide or manage the work of any Trainee or Licensee. A supervisory appraiser is required to be in good standing with the Board, with no disciplinary actions taken against the supervising licensee's license during the three years preceding the period of supervision.

1.26 Qualifying education: real estate appraisal education courses completed for credit toward the licensing requirements set forth in Chapter 2 of these Board Rules and meeting the requirements of Chapter 3 of these Board Rules. Qualifying education courses must be at least 15 classroom hours in length and must include an examination. Qualifying education courses may be used to satisfy the continuing education requirements set forth in Chapter 7 of these Board Rules.

1.27 Continuing education: real estate and real estate appraisal related courses completed for credit toward meeting the continuing education requirements set forth in Chapter 7 of these Board Rules. Continuing education courses meeting the requirements of Chapter 3 of these Board Rules may be acceptable for credit toward meeting qualifying education requirements.

1.28 Transaction value: for purposes of these rules transaction value means:

A. For appraisal assignments carried out as part of a loan transaction, the amount of the loan; or

B. For appraisal assignments carried out for other than a loan transaction, the market value of the real property interest.

1.29 Appraisal process: the analysis of factors that bear upon value, including definition of the appraisal problem, gathering and analyzing data, applying appropriate valuation approaches and methods, arriving at an opinion of value and reporting the opinion of value.

1.30 Accredited college, junior college, community college or university: a higher education institution accredited by the Commission on Colleges, a regional or national accreditation association, or an accrediting agency that is recognized by the U. S. Secretary of Education.

* 1.31 Repealed.

1.32 2008 Real Property Appraiser Qualification Criteria: Pursuant to Section 12-61-706, (1) and (2), C.R.S. (as amended), the Board incorporates by reference in compliance with Section 24-4-103(12.5), C.R.S., the 2008 Real Property Appraiser Qualification Criteria adopted by the Appraiser Qualifications Board of The Appraisal Foundation on February 20, 2004, and as amended through May 5, 2006, including the Required Core Curricula, Guide Notes and

Interpretations thereof. Amendments to the 2008 Real Property Appraiser Qualification Criteria adopted subsequent to May 5, 2006 are not included in this rule. A certified copy of the 2008 Real Property Appraiser Qualification Criteria is on file and available for public inspection with the Program Administrator at the offices of the Board of Real Estate Appraisers at 1560 Broadway, Suite 925, Denver, Colorado. Copies of the 2008 Real Property Appraiser Qualification Criteria incorporated under this rule may be examined at any state publications depository library. The 2008 Real Property Appraiser Qualification Criteria may be examined at the Internet website of The Appraisal Foundation at www.appraisalfoundation.org, and copies may be ordered through that mechanism. The Appraisal Foundation may also be contacted at 1155 15th Street, NW, Suite 1111, Washington, DC 20005, or by telephone at (202) 347-7722 or by telefax at (202) 347-7727. The 2008 Real Property Appraiser Qualification Criteria shall go into effect on January 1, 2008.

* 1.33 Credential Upgrade: An existing licensee, who has been granted a license pursuant to 12-61-706, C.R.S., may submit an application to the Board requesting an upgrade of the licensee's credential if the licensee has completed the real estate appraisal education, experience, and examination requirements as defined in Chapter 2 of these Rules for the credential for which the licensee is applying. If the Board grants the requested credential, the upgraded license will expire on the same date of the licensee's current license cycle, prior to the upgrade.

1.34 Draft Appraisal: An appraisal that does not bear the appraiser's signature and is identified and labeled as a "draft". The purpose of issuing a draft appraisal cannot be to allow the client and/or the intended user(s) to influence the appraiser.

1.35 Amendment: A written modification of any appraisal, which is dated and signed by the appraiser, and delivered to the client. An amendment is a true and integral component of an appraisal. Amendments may also be referred to as correction pages.

* 1.36 Good Standing: Not having been subject to a stipulation and final agency order, or a final agency order for a period of five years, or had a license revoked or permanently surrendered for any of the violations enumerated under §§12-61-710 or 12-61-712, C.R.S. A license will be considered to be in good standing five years following the execution of the stipulation and final order, or the final agency order, and upon successful completion of all terms. If a licensee has an executed stipulation for diversion, the license will not be in good standing with the Board until all terms of the stipulated agreement have been successfully completed.

CHAPTER 2: REQUIREMENTS FOR LICENSURE AS A REAL ESTATE APPRAISER

* 2.1 An applicant for licensure as a Colorado Registered Appraiser shall successfully complete the following requirements or the substantial equivalent thereof, as set forth in the Required Core Curriculum and Guide Note 1 of the 2008 Real Property Appraiser Qualification Criteria adopted by the Appraiser Qualifications Board of the Appraisal Foundation on February 20, 2004 and amended through May 5, 2006, with an effective date of January 1, 2008, and incorporated by reference in Rule 1.32:

A. Real estate appraisal education:
   1. Basic Appraisal Principles: 30 hours;
   2. Basic Appraisal Procedures: 30 hours; and
   3. 15-Hour National USPAP Course: 15 hours.

B. Real estate appraisal examination: successful completion of the Registered Appraiser examination as provided in Chapter 4 of these Rules.

* 2.2 An applicant for licensure as a Colorado Licensed Appraiser shall successfully complete the following requirements or the substantial equivalent thereof, as set forth in the Required Core Curriculum and Guide Note 1 of the 2008 Real Property Appraiser Qualification Criteria adopted by the Appraiser Qualifications Board of the Appraisal Foundation on February 20, 2004, and amended through May 5, 2006, with an effective date of January 1, 2008, and incorporated by reference in Rule 1.32:

A. Real estate appraisal education:
   1. Basic Appraisal Principles: 30 hours;
   2. Basic Appraisal Procedures: 30 hours
   3. 15-Hour National USPAP Course: 15 hours;
   4. Residential Market Analysis and Highest and Best Use: 15 hours;
   5. Residential Appraiser Site Valuation and Cost Approach: 15 hours;
   6. Residential Sales Comparison and Income Approaches: 30 hours; and
   7. Residential Report Writing and Case Studies: 15 hours.

B. Real estate appraisal experience: An applicant shall demonstrate to the satisfaction of the Board that the applicant completed at least 2,000 hours of appraisal experience in conformance with the provisions of Chapter 5 of these Rules and all of the applicant's experience was obtained after January 30, 1989 and in compliance with the Uniform Standards of Professional Appraisal Practice (USPAP). Pursuant to §12-61-706(9), C.R.S., real estate appraisal experience shall be gained over a period of not less than 12 months.

C. Real estate appraisal examination: successful completion of the Licensed Appraiser examination as provided in Chapter 4 of these Rules.

* 2.3 An applicant for licensure as a Colorado Certified Residential Appraiser shall successfully complete the following requirements or the substantial equivalent thereof, as set forth in the Required Core Curriculum and Guide Note 1 of the 2008 Real Property Appraiser Qualification Criteria adopted by the Appraiser Qualifications Board of the Appraisal Foundation on February 20, 2004, and amended through May 5, 2006, with an effective date of January 1, 2008, and incorporated by reference in Rule 1.32:

A. Real estate appraisal education:
   1. Basic Appraisal Principles: 30 hours;
   2. Basic Appraisal Procedures: 30 hours;
   3. 15-hour National USPAP Course: 15 hours;
   4. Residential Market Analysis and Highest and Best Use: 15 hours;
   5. Residential Appraiser Site Valuation and Cost Approach: 15 hours;
   6. Residential Sales Comparison and Income Approaches: 30 hours;
   7. Residential Report Writing and Case Studies: 15 hours;
   8. Statistics, Modeling and Finance: 15 hours;
   9. Advanced Residential Applications and Case Studies: 15;
   10. Appraisal Subject Matter Electives: 20; and
   11. Hold an associate degree, or higher, from an accredited college, junior college, community college or university as defined in Board Rule 1.30; or
   12. Successfully complete at least 21 semester credit hours or 32 quarter credit hours in the following collegiate subject matter courses from an accredited college, junior college, community college or university as defined in Board Rule 1.30. Courses in all the listed topics shall be completed. No topics shall be omitted. Credits earned through the college level examination program ("CLEP") are acceptable to meet this requirement.
       A. English Composition;
       B. Principles of Economics;
       C. Finance;
       D. Algebra, Geometry or Higher Mathematics;
       E. Statistics;
       F. Computer Science; and
       G. Business or Real Estate Law.

B. Real estate appraisal experience:
An applicant for licensure as a Colorado Certified Residential Appraiser shall demonstrate to the satisfaction of the Board that the applicant completed at least 2,500 hours of appraisal experience in conformance with the provisions of Chapter 5 of these Rules and all of the applicant's experience was obtained after January 30, 1989 and in compliance with the

Uniform Standards of Professional Appraisal Practice (USPAP). Real estate appraisal experience shall have been gained across a period of not less than 24 months.

C. Real estate appraisal examination: Successful completion of the Certified Residential Appraiser examination as provided in Chapter 4 of these Rules.

* 2.4 An applicant for licensure as a Colorado Certified General Appraiser shall successfully complete the following requirements or the substantial equivalent thereof, as set forth in the Required Core Curriculum and Guide Note 1 of the 2008 Real Property Appraiser Qualification Criteria adopted by the Appraiser Qualifications Board of the Appraisal Foundation on February 20, 2004, and amended through May 5, 2006, with an effective date of January 1, 2008, as incorporated by reference in Rule 1.32:

A. Real estate appraisal education:

1. Basic Appraisal Principles: 30 hours;
2. Basic Appraisal Procedures: 30 hours;
3. 15-hour National USPAP Course: 15 hours;
4. General Appraiser Market Analysis and Highest and Best Use: 30 hours;
5. Statistics, Modeling and Finance: 15 hours;
6. General Appraiser Sales Comparison Approach: 30 hours;
7. General Appraiser Site Valuation and Cost Approach: 30 hours;
8. General Appraiser Income Approach: 60 hours;
9. General Appraiser Report Writing and Case Studies: 30 hours;
10. Appraisal Subject Matter Electives: 30 hours; and
11. Hold a bachelor's degree or higher from an accredited college or university as defined in Board Rule 1.30, or
12. Successfully complete not less than 30 semester credit hours or 45 quarter credit hours in the following collegiate subject matter courses from an accredited college, junior college, community college or university as defined in Board Rule 1.30. Courses in all of the listed topics shall be successfully completed. No topics shall be omitted. Credits earned through the college level examination program ("CLEP") are acceptable to meet this requirement.
    A. English Composition;
    B. Macro Economics;
    C. Micro Economics;
    D. Finance;
    E. Algebra, Geometry or Higher Mathematics;
    F. Statistics;
    G. Computer Science;
    H. Business or Real Estate Law; and
    I. Two elective courses in Accounting, Geography, Agricultural Economics, Business Management or Real Estate.

B. Real estate appraisal experience:
An applicant submitting an application received in the offices of the Board for licensure as a Colorado Certified General Appraiser shall demonstrate to the satisfaction of the Board that the applicant completed at least 3,000 hours of appraisal experience in conformance with the provisions of Chapter 5 of these Rules and all of the applicant's experience was obtained after January 30, 1989 and in compliance with the Uniform Standards of Professional Appraisal Practice (USPAP). Real estate appraisal experience shall have been gained across a period of not less than 30 months and shall include at least 1,500 hours of appraisal of non-residential property, as defined in Chapter 1 of these Rules.

C. Real estate appraisal examination: Successful completion of the Certified General Appraiser examination as provided in Chapter 4 of these Rules.

* 2.5 Repealed.

* 2.6 Repealed.

* 2.7 Repealed.

CHAPTER 3: STANDARDS FOR REAL ESTATE APPRAISAL QUALIFYING EDUCATION PROGRAMS

3.1 All qualifying education requirements may be completed at any time prior to filing of the application for registration, licensure or certification.

3.2 Appraisal education and training courses shall be taken from providers approved by the Board. In order to be approved, the course shall meet the following standards at the time it is offered:

A. The course was developed by persons qualified in the subject matter and instructional design;
B. The program content is current;
C. The instructor is qualified with respect to course content and teaching methods;
D. The number of participants and the physical facilities are consistent with the teaching method and;
E. The course includes an examination for measuring the information learned.

3.3 The following may be approved as providers of appraisal education and training provided the standards set forth in Rule 3.2 are maintained and provided they have complied with all other requirements of the State of Colorado:

A. Universities, colleges, junior colleges or community colleges accredited by a regional accrediting body accredited by the council on post secondary accreditation;
B. Professional appraisal and real estate related organizations;
C. State or federal government agencies;
D. Proprietary schools holding valid certificates of approval from the Colorado Division of Private Occupational Schools, Department of Higher Education;
E. As to courses completed in other jurisdictions, providers approved by such other jurisdiction, provided that the jurisdiction's appraiser regulation program has been determined to be in compliance with FIRREA;
F. As to courses approved under the course approval program of The Appraisal Foundation, the providers of such courses, and
G. Such other providers as the Board may approve upon petition of the course provider or the applicant in a form acceptable to the Board.

3.4 As to course work offered on or after January 1, 1991, in order to be approved by the Board, each course provider shall maintain, and provide to the Board upon request, information regarding the course offerings including, but not limited to the following:

A. Course outline or syllabus;
B. All texts, workbooks, hand outs or other course materials;
C. Instructors and their qualifications, including selection, training and evaluation criteria;
D. Course examinations;
E. Dates of course offerings; and
F. Location of course offerings;

3.5 The number of hours credited shall be equivalent to the actual number of contact hours of in-class instruction and testing. An hour of appraisal education and training is defined as at least 50 minutes of instruction out of each 60-minute segment. For distance education courses, the number of hours credited shall be that number of hours allowed by the Course Approval Program of The Appraisal Foundation.

3.6 In order to be approved as qualifying education and training, a course must be at least 15 hours in duration and must include an examination pertinent to the material covered. Courses may be comprised of segments of not less than one classroom hour.

3.7 Appraisal education and training courses must be successfully completed by the applicant. Except as otherwise provided in Rule 3.8, successful completion means the applicant has attended the class, participated in class activities and achieved a passing score on the course examination.

Teaching of approved appraisal education and training courses shall constitute successful completion.

3.8 Credit will be granted for classroom hours where the applicant obtained credit from the course provider by challenge examination without attending the course, provided that such credit was granted by the provider prior to July 1, 1990 and provided further that the Board is satisfied with the quality of the challenge examination administered.

3.9 The responsibility for establishing that a particular course or other program for which credit is claimed is acceptable rests upon the applicant.

3.10 Each applicant shall provide a signed statement, under penalty of perjury, attesting to the successful completion of the required hours of appraisal education and training on a form prescribed by the Board. The Board reserves the right to require an applicant or licensee to provide satisfactory documentary evidence of completion of appropriate course work.

3.11 Hours of appraisal education and training accepted in satisfaction of the education requirement of one level of registration, licensure or certification may be applied toward the requirement for another level and need not be repeated. Applicants are responsible for demonstrating coverage of the required topics.

3.12 The following factors shall be used to convert university, college, junior college and community college course credits into classroom hours:

A. Semester Credits x 15.00 = Classroom Hours

B. Quarter Credits x 10.00 = Classroom Hours

3.13 Applicants shall successfully complete a course or series of courses of appraisal education and training which build upon and augment previous courses. Courses which substantially repeat other course work in terms of content and level of instruction will not be accepted. The Board will give appropriate consideration to courses where substantive changes in content have occurred.

3.14 To be acceptable for qualifying real estate appraisal education, distance education offerings must incorporate methods and activities that promote active student engagement and participation in the learning process. Among those methods and activities acceptable are written exercises which are graded and returned to the student, required responses in cd-rom, disk and on-line computer based presentations, provision for students to submit questions during teleconferences, and examinations proctored by an independent third party. Simple reading, viewing or listening to materials is not sufficient engagement in the learning process to satisfy the requirements of this rule.

3.15 As to qualifying education courses completed in other jurisdictions with appraiser regulatory programs established in conformance with Title XI, FIRREA, the Board will accept the number of classroom hours of education accepted by that jurisdiction.

3.16 To be acceptable for qualifying real estate appraisal education, distance education courses shall meet the other requirements of this Chapter 3, and shall include a written, closed book final examination proctored by an independent third party, or other final examination testing procedure acceptable to the Board. Examples of acceptable examination proctors include public officials who do not supervise the student, secondary and higher education school officials, and public librarians. Failure to observe this requirement may result in rejection of the course and/or course provider by the Board for that applicant, and may result in the Board refusing or withdrawing approval of any courses offered by the provider.

* 3.17 All qualifying education courses in the Uniform Standards of Professional Appraisal Practice begun on and after January 1, 2003 shall be in the form of a course approved under the course approval program of the Appraiser Qualifications Board of The Appraisal Foundation, and taught by an instructor certified by the Appraiser Qualifications Board of The Appraisal Foundation and who is a state certified appraiser.

3.18 Course providers shall provide each student who successfully completes a qualifying real estate appraisal education course in the manner prescribed in Board Rule 3.7 a course completion certificate. The Board will not mandate the exact form of course certificates, however, the following information shall be included:

A. Name of course provider;

B. Course title, which shall describe topical content, or 2008 Real Property Appraiser Qualification Criteria Core Curriculum module title;

C. Course number, if any;

D. Course dates;

E. Number of classroom hours;

F. Statement that the required examination was successfully completed;

G. Course location, which for distance education modalities shall be the principal place of business of the course provider;

H. Name of student; and

I. For all Uniform Standards of Professional Appraisal Practice courses begun on and after January 1, 2003, the name(s) and Appraiser Qualifications Board Uniform Standards of Professional Appraisal Practice instructor certification number(s) of the instructor(s).

3.19 The provisions of Board Rule 3.3 notwithstanding, real estate appraisal qualifying education courses begun on and after January 1, 2004 and offered through distance education modalities must be approved through the Course Approval Program of The Appraisal Foundation. The Board will not accept distance education courses begun on and after January 1, 2004 that have not been approved through the Course Approval Program of The Appraisal Foundation.

3.20 All qualifying education courses in the Uniform Standards of Professional Appraisal Practice (USPAP) shall be presented using the most recent edition of the Uniform Standards of Professional Appraisal Practice and the most recent version of the National USPAP Course (real property) or equivalent as approved by the Course Approval Program of The Appraisal Foundation, with the exception that courses begun in the three months preceding the effective date of a new edition may be presented using the next succeeding USPAP edition and course version, if available from The Appraisal Foundation.

* 3.21 All qualifying education courses begun on or after January 1, 2008 must be approved through the Course Approval Program of the Appraiser Qualifications Board of the Appraisal Foundation, except as otherwise may be approved in advance and in writing by the Director of the Colorado Division of Real Estate (the "Director") on a limited case by case basis where the Director determines that the public would not be served if course approval were required through the Course Approval Program of the Appraiser Qualifications Board of the Appraisal Foundation for a particular course. Course providers seeking approval of qualifying education courses that have not been approved through the Course Approval Program of the Appraiser Qualifications Board of the Appraisal Foundation shall provide the Director with all requested information the Director deems necessary.

CHAPTER 4: STANDARDS FOR REAL ESTATE APPRAISAL LICENSING EXAMINATIONS

4.1 Any person wishing to apply for any appraiser's license shall register for and achieve a passing score on the appropriate level of examination with the testing service designated by the Board. No other examination results will be accepted. The appropriate levels of examination for the respective levels of licensure are as follows:

License Level	Examination
Registered Appraiser	Registered Appraiser
Licensed Appraiser	Licensed Real Property Appraiser
Certified Residential Appraiser	Certified Residential Appraiser
Certified General Appraiser	Certified General Appraiser

4.2 Examinees shall comply with the standards of test administration established by the Board and the testing service.

4.3 A passing score on an examination shall be valid for two years from the examination date. Failure to file a complete application within the two year period will result in the examination grade being void.

4.4 Examinations will be given only to duly qualified applicants for an appraiser's license; however, one instructor from each appraisal qualifying education course provider approved pursuant to Rule 3.3 may take the examination one time during any 12 month period in order to conduct research for course content.

4.5 Each examination for a license may, as determined by the Board, be a separate examination.

4.6 Examinations developed or contracted for by the Board for licensed and certified appraisers shall comply with Title XI, FIRREA.

4.7 Repealed.

4.8 Examinees may use financial calculators during the examination process. The memory functions of any such calculator shall be cleared by the testing service staff prior to the beginning and after the conclusion of the examination.

CHAPTER 5: STANDARDS FOR REAL ESTATE APPRAISAL EXPERIENCE

5.1 The following areas of appraisal activity shall constitute acceptable appraisal experience under this Chapter:

A. Fee and staff appraisal;
B. Ad valorem tax appraisal;
C. Review appraisal;
D. Appraisal analysis;
E. Real estate counseling;
F. Highest and best use analysis;
G. Feasibility analysis/study; and
H. Such other experience as the Board may accept upon petition by the applicant in a form acceptable to the Board.

5.2 An applicant must have made a substantial contribution to the appraisal process and arrived at a conclusion of value in any appraisal claimed as evidence of meeting experience requirements. Only those real property appraisals, appraisal reviews or appraisal consulting assignments culminating in a written or oral report and workfile compliant with the Uniform Standards of Professional Appraisal Practice shall be acceptable as evidence of meeting appraisal experience requirements.

5.3 Reports or file memoranda claimed as evidence of meeting experience requirements shall:

A. As to reports or file memoranda completed prior to July 1, 1991, such reports or file memoranda shall have been prepared in conformance with the generally accepted standards of professional appraisal practice for the type of real estate as of the time the work was completed; and
B. As to reports or file memoranda completed on or after January 1, 1991, such reports or file memoranda shall have been prepared in conformance with the Uniform Standards of Professional Appraisal Practice as promulgated by the Appraisal Standards Board of The Appraisal Foundation on January 30, 1989 and amended through the date of completion of the report or file memoranda.

5.4 Each applicant shall provide a statement signed under penalty of perjury, attesting to acceptable completion of the required appraisal experience on a form provided by the Board.

5.5 The Board reserves the right to verify an applicant's or licensee's evidence of appraisal experience by such means as it deems necessary, including, but not limited to requiring the following:

A. Submission of a detailed log of appraisal activity on the form or in the manner specified by the Board;
B. Submission of appraisal reports, workfiles or file memoranda;

C. Employer affidavits or interviews;
D. Client affidavits or interviews; and
E. Submission of appropriate business records.

5.6 Repealed.

5.7 On and after January 1, 2005, and prior to January 1, 2008, to be acceptable for licensing purposes, real estate appraisal experience gained by an unlicensed person or a person licensed at the Registered Appraiser level shall be gained under the following conditions:

A. The unlicensed person or Registered Appraiser shall be under the active, diligent and personal supervision of a supervising appraiser who has been a Licensed Appraiser as defined by Board Rule 1.13 for at least two years, or a Certified Residential Appraiser as defined by Board Rule 1.14, or a Certified General Appraiser as defined by Board Rule 1.15. The provisions of this Rule 5.7 a shall not apply to an unlicensed person or Registered Appraiser employed in the office of a Colorado county assessor when appraising real estate in fulfillment of their official duties;

B. The Licensed Appraiser, Certified Residential Appraiser or Certified General Appraiser acting as supervisor shall be in good standing with the Board. For purposes of this rule, good standing is defined as not having been subject to any disciplinary action under Section 12-61-710 (5)(a), (b), or (c), C.R.S., during the preceding two (2) years;

C. Real estate appraisal experience gained in conformance with Board Rule 5.7 prior to January 1, 2008 shall continue to be acceptable after January 1, 2008. Real estate appraisal experience gained on and after January 1, 2008 shall be gained in conformance with Board Rule 5.8.

5.8 On and after January 1, 2008, to be acceptable for licensing purposes, real estate appraisal experience gained by an unlicensed person or a person licensed at the Registered Appraiser level shall be gained under the following conditions:

A. The unlicensed person or Registered Appraiser shall be under the active, diligent and personal supervision of a Certified Residential Appraiser as defined by Board Rule 1.14, or a Certified General Appraiser as defined by Board Rule 1.15. The provisions of this Rule 5.8 a shall not apply to an unlicensed person or Registered Appraiser employed in the office of a Colorado county assessor when appraising real estate in fulfillment of their official duties;

B. The Certified Residential Appraiser or Certified General Appraiser acting as supervisor shall be in good standing with the Board. For purposes of this rule, good standing is defined as not having been subject to any disciplinary action under Section 12-61-710 (5)(a), (b), or (c), C.R.S., during the preceding two (2) years;

C. The Certified Residential Appraiser or Certified General Appraiser acting as supervisor shall not supervise more than three (3) unlicensed persons or Registered Appraisers at any one time; and

D. Real estate experience gained in conformance with Board Rule 5.7 prior to January 1, 2008 shall continue to be acceptable after January 1, 2008. Real estate appraisal experience gained on and after January 1, 2008 shall be gained in conformance with Board Rule 5.8.

5.9 Each application for licensure pursuant to Board Rules 2.2, 2.3, and 2.4 shall be accompanied by a log of real estate appraisal experience. The log of real estate appraisal experience claims submitted in support of an application for licensure shall be on the form or in the manner specified by the Board. Such log shall be subject to the following requirements:

A. The log shall include statements certifying to the accuracy and truthfulness of the information therein;

B. Signatures shall be individual handwritten marks. Photocopied, computer generated, stamped or other facsimile signatures are not acceptable. No one other than the applicant or supervisory appraiser shall sign the certifications.

5.10 Driving time in the market neighborhood of the subject property for inspection of the subject and comparable properties may qualify as part of appraisal experience.

5.11 An applicant for licensure as a Colorado Licensed Appraiser, a Colorado Certified Residential Appraiser or a Colorado Certified General Appraiser must demonstrate that the applicant is capable of performing appraisals that are compliant with the Uniform Standards of Professional Appraisal Practice. In accordance with Board Rule 5.5, the Board may verify an applicant's appraisal experience by such means as it deems necessary, including but not limited to requiring the applicant to submit a detailed log of appraisal experience and appraisal reports and work files. Staff within the Colorado Division of Real Estate or appraisers selected by the Colorado Division of Real Estate may review an applicant's appraisal reports and work files to determine whether the applicant is capable of performing appraisals that are compliant with USPAP. Such review shall not be considered an "Appraisal Review" as defined by USPAP. An appraiser performing a review of appraisal reports and work files in accordance with this rule shall not be required to perform a USPAP Standard 3 appraisal review.

CHAPTER 6: APPLICATION FOR INITIAL LICENSURE

6.1 An applicant for licensure as a registered, licensed or certified appraiser shall complete all requirements prior to filing the application, including education, experience (if required) and examination.

6.2 Each applicant shall submit original documentary evidence of a passing score on the appropriate examination with the application.

6.3 An application is deemed complete at the time all required supporting documents and fees are received at the Board offices.

6.4 Repealed.

6.5 Licenses shall be issued by the Board as soon as practicable after receipt of a complete application, required fees and all supporting documentation. The Board reserves the right to require additional information and documentation from an applicant, and to verify any information and documentation submitted.

6.6 Submission of an application does not guaranty issuance of a license, or issuance of a license within a specific period of time. Applicants shall observe the provisions of Section 12-61-714, C.R.S. and Board Rules Chapter 12. Applicants shall not represent themselves as being licensees of the Board until receipt of the Board issued license document.

6.7 Pursuant to Section 12-61-709(1), C.R.S., an applicant who has been convicted of, entered a plea of guilty to, or entered a plea of nolo contendere to any felony, or any crime involving moral turpitude, or any other like crime under Colorado law, federal law, or the laws of another state within the ten (10) years preceding application shall file with his or her application an addendum to the application in a form prescribed by the Board. Such addendum shall be supported and documented by, without limitation, the following:

A. Court documents, including original charges, disposition, pre-sentencing report and certification of completion of terms of sentence;
B. Police officer's report;
C. Probation or parole officer's report;
D. A written personal statement explaining the circumstances surrounding each violation, and including the statement "I have no other violations either past or pending";
E. Letters of recommendation; and
F. Employment history for the preceding five years.

6.8 Prior to application for licensure a person who has been convicted of, entered a plea of guilty to, or entered a plea of nolo contendere to any felony, or any crime involving moral turpitude, or any other like crime under Colorado law, federal law, or the laws of another state within the preceding ten (10) years may request the Board to issue a preliminary advisory opinion regarding the possible effect of such conduct on an application for licensure. A person requesting such an opinion is not an applicant for licensure. The Board may, at its sole discretion, issue such an opinion, which shall not be binding on the Board or limit the authority of the Board to investigate a later application for licensure. The issuance of such an opinion by the Board shall not act to prohibit a person from submitting an application for licensure. A person requesting such an opinion shall do so in a request form prescribed by the Board. Such request form shall be supported and documented by, without limitation, the following:

A. Court documents, including original charges, disposition, pre-sentencing report and certification of completion of terms of sentence;
B. Police officer's report(s);
C. Probation or parole officer's report(s);
D. A written personal statement explaining the circumstances surrounding each violation, and including the statement "I have no other violations either past or pending";
E. Letters of recommendation; and
F. Employment history for the preceding five years.

6.9 Repealed

CHAPTER 7: CONTINUING EDUCATION REQUIREMENTS

7.1 For initial licenses issued on or after July 1 of any year, there shall be no continuing education requirement as a condition of renewal of such initial license that expires December 31 of the year of issue as defined in Board Rule 1.8. For initial licenses issued before July 1 of any year, there shall be an obligation to complete 14 hours of continuing education as a condition of renewal before the initial license expires on December 31 of the year of issue as defined in Board Rule 1.8. Continuing education requirements established by this Chapter 7 shall apply to all other license renewals.

7.2 Except as provided under Board Rule 7.1, each applicant for renewal of a license shall complete at least 42 classroom hours of real estate appraisal continuing education during the three-year period preceding expiration of the license to be renewed. All licensees renewing a license at the end of a three-year licensing period shall complete the National Uniform Standards of Professional Appraisal Practice Update Courses set forth in Board Rule 7.19. All National Uniform Standards of Professional Appraisal Practice Update Courses begun on and after January 1, 2003 must comply with Board Rule 7.19. Continuing education requirements must be completed after the effective date of the license to be renewed and prior to the expiration of such license. Upon written request and receipt of the supporting documentation established by the Board, the Board may grant a deferral for continuing education compliance for licensees returning from active military duty. Credential holders returning from active military duty may be placed on active status for up to 90 days pending completion of all continuing education requirements established pursuant to chapter 7.

7.3 Continuing appraisal education programs and courses shall be taken from providers approved by the Board. In order to be approved by the Board, programs shall meet the following standards:

A. The program shall have been developed by persons qualified in the subject matter and instructional design;
B. The program shall be current;
C. The instructor shall be qualified with respect to course content and teaching methods;
D. The number of participants and the physical facilities are consistent with the teaching method(s).

7.4 The following may be approved as providers of continuing appraisal education and training provided the standards set forth in Rule 7.3 are maintained and provided they have complied with all other requirements of the State of Colorado:

A. Universities, colleges, junior colleges or community colleges accredited by a regional accrediting body accredited by the Council on Post Secondary Accreditation;
B. Professional appraisal and real estate related organizations;
C. State or federal government agencies;

D. Proprietary schools holding valid certificates of approval from the Colorado Division of Private Occupational Schools, Department of Higher Education
E. As to courses completed in other jurisdictions, providers approved by such other jurisdiction, provided that the jurisdiction's appraiser regulation program has been determined to be in compliance with Title XI, FIRREA;
F. As to courses approved under the course approval program of The Appraisal Foundation, the providers of such courses; and
G. Such other providers as the Board may approve upon petition of the course provider or the applicant in a form acceptable to the Board.

7.5 In order to be approved by the Board, each continuing education provider shall at its expense maintain, and provide to the Board on request, information regarding the program offerings including, but not limited to the following:
A. Course outline or syllabus;
B. All texts, workbooks, hand outs or other course materials;
C. Instructors and their qualifications, including selection, training and evaluation criteria;
D. Course examinations (if any);
E. Dates of course offerings;
F. Location of course offerings;
G. Record of participation;

* 7.6 In order to be approved as continuing appraisal education a program or course shall be at least 2 classroom hours in duration including examination time (if any). Continuing appraisal education programs and courses are intended to maintain and improve the appraiser's skill, knowledge and competency. Continuing appraisal education courses and programs may include, without limitation, these real estate and real estate appraisal related topics:
A. Ad valorem taxation;
B. Arbitration;
C. Business courses related to practice of real estate appraisal;
D. Construction cost estimating;
E. Ethics and standards of professional practice;
F. Land use planning, zoning and taxation;
G. Management, leasing, brokerage and timesharing;
H. Property development;
I. Real estate appraisal (valuation/evaluation);
J. Real estate law;
K. Real estate litigation;
L. Real estate financing and investment;
M. Real estate appraisal related computer applications;
N. Real estate securities and syndication;
O. Real property exchange; and
P. Such other topics as the Board may approve, upon its own motion or upon petition by the course provider or the licensee in a form acceptable to the Board.

7.8 The Board may consider alternatives to continuing appraisal education programs and courses such as teaching, authorship of textbooks or articles, educational programs development or similar activities for up to one-half of the required continuing education. Licensees desiring continuing appraisal education credit for alternative activities must petition the Board for approval in a form acceptable to the Board. Such petition for approval of alternatives to continuing appraisal education programs and courses shall be submitted to the Board in writing for review and possible approval prior to commencement of the alternative activity.

7.9 The act of applying for renewal or reinstatement shall constitute a statement under penalty of perjury in the second degree that the licensee had the present intent of affirmatively stating the licensee had complied with the continuing education requirements of Colorado statutes and Board

Rules. The Board reserves the right to require a renewal applicant or licensee to provide satisfactory documentary evidence of completion of continuing appraisal education requirements. The Board may at its option require such submission as part of the renewal process or subsequent to renewal.

7.10 With the exception of the 7-hour National Uniform Standards of Professional Appraisal Practice Update Course(s) required pursuant to Board Rule 7.19, applicants for renewal of a license may complete the required hours of continuing appraisal education at any time during the licensing period preceding expiration.

7.11 To complete continuing education requirements an appraiser may repeat courses or programs previously completed, subject to the limitation that no course or program may be repeated more frequently than once every two (2) years, except as authorized by the Board. Courses or programs in appraisal ethics and the Uniform Standards of Professional Appraisal Practice are not subject to this limitation.

7.12 In order to receive credit, continuing appraisal education courses and programs shall be successfully completed by the holder of the license to be renewed. Successful completion means attendance at the class or program and participation in class activities. Successful completion of courses undertaken through distance education requires compliance with the provisions of Board Rule 7.14. Teaching of continuing appraisal education courses and programs shall constitute successful completion, however, credit shall be given for only one presentation of a particular course or program during each renewal period.

7.13 The number of hours credited shall be equivalent to the actual number of contact hours of in class instruction and testing. An hour of appraisal education and training is defined as at least 50 minutes of instruction out of each 60-minute segment. For distance education courses, the number of hours credited shall be that number of hours allowed by the Course Approval Program of The Appraisal Foundation.

7.14 To be acceptable for real estate appraisal continuing education, distance education offerings shall include methods and activities which promote active student engagement and participation in the learning process. Among those methods and activities acceptable are written exercises which are graded and returned to the student, required responses in cd-rom, disk and on-line computer based presentations, provision for students to submit questions during teleconferences, and examinations proctored by an independent third party. Simple reading, viewing or listening to materials is not sufficient engagement in the learning process to satisfy the requirements of this rule.

7.15 As to continuing education courses and programs completed in other jurisdictions with appraiser regulatory programs established in conformance with Title XI, FIRREA, the Board shall accept the number of classroom hours of continuing education accepted by that jurisdiction.

7.16 Repealed.

7.17 Prior to enrolling in a continuing education course presenting topics other than those listed in Board Rule 7.6.A-O, a licensee shall request Board approval of such course or topic. Failure to request and receive approval of such course or topic prior to commencement of the course may result in Board refusal to accept the course for continuing education credit.

7.18 To be acceptable for continuing education credit, continuing education course content must have a clear application to real estate appraisal practice. The following topics or types of courses are not acceptable for satisfaction of the continuing education requirements established by these rules: motivational courses, personal growth or self-improvement courses, general business courses and general computing courses.

7.19 All licensees shall complete successfully a 7-hour National Uniform Standards of Professional Appraisal Practice Update Course, or its equivalent, every two calendar years. Such 7-hour National Uniform Standards of Professional Appraisal Practice Update Course shall be in the form of a course approved by the Appraiser Qualifications Board of The Appraisal Foundation, and taught by an instructor certified by the Appraiser Qualifications Board of The Appraisal Foundation and who is also a state certified appraiser. Equivalency shall be determined through the Appraiser Qualifications Board Course Approval Program or by an alternate method established by the Appraiser Qualifications Board.

7.20 A licensee who is a resident of a jurisdiction other than the State of Colorado may comply with the continuing education requirements of this Chapter 7 by documenting, at the request of the Board, compliance with the continuing education requirements of their jurisdiction of residence. In the event the jurisdiction of residence does not impose continuing education requirements consistent with the criteria promulgated by the Appraiser Qualifications Board of The Appraisal Foundation, the licensee shall comply with the continuing education requirements established by this Chapter 7.

7.21 A licensee who renews a license subject to a continuing education requirement shall retain documentary evidence of compliance with these continuing education requirements for a period of not less than five (5) years after the expiration of the license being renewed.

7.22 Course providers shall provide each student who successfully completes a continuing education course in the manner prescribed in Board Rule 7.12 a course completion certificate. The Board will not mandate the exact form of course certificates, however, the following information shall be included:

A. Name of course provider;
B. Course title, which shall describe topical content;
C. Course number, if any;
D. Course dates;
E. Number of classroom hours;
F. Statement that the required examination was successfully completed, if an examination is a regular part of the course;
G. Course location, which for distance education modalities shall be the principal place of business of the course provider;
H. Name of student; and
I. For Uniform Standards of Professional Appraisal Practice courses begun on and after January 1, 2003, the name and Appraiser Qualifications Board Uniform Standards of Professional Appraisal Practice instructor certification number of the instructor.

7.23 The provisions of Board Rule 7.4 notwithstanding, real estate appraisal continuing education courses begun on and after January 1, 2004 and offered through distance education modalities must be approved through the Course Approval Program of The Appraisal Foundation. The Board will not accept distance education courses begun on and after January 1, 2004 that have not been approved through the Course Approval Program of The Appraisal Foundation.

CHAPTER 8: RENEWAL, REINSTATEMENT, SURRENDER, REVOCATION OF LICENSURE

8.1 Prior to the expiration of any license the holder thereof shall make application for renewal of same in the form and manner provided by the Board, and pay the specified fees. The act of applying for renewal shall constitute a statement under penalty of perjury in the second degree that the licensee had the present intent of affirmatively stating the licensee had complied with the continuing education requirements of Colorado statutes and Board Rules.

8.2 After expiration of an unrenewed license but before the thirty-first day following the date of expiration, the holder of such license may reinstate same by applying for reinstatement in the form and manner provided by the Board, and paying the specified renewal fees. The act of applying for reinstatement shall constitute a statement under penalty of perjury in the second degree that the licensee had the present intent of affirmatively stating the licensee had complied with the continuing education requirements of Colorado statutes and Board Rules.

8.3 On and after the thirty-first day following the date of expiration, and before the end of the first year following the date of expiration, the holder of an expired license may reinstate same by applying in the form and manner provided by the Board, and paying the specified fees plus a reinstatement fee equal to one third of the base renewal fee. For purposes of this rule, the base renewal fee is defined as the total renewal fee less the National Appraiser Registry fee collected by the Board and remitted to the federal Appraisal Subcommittee. The act of applying for reinstatement shall constitute a statement under penalty of perjury in the second degree that the licensee had the present intent of affirmatively stating the licensee had complied with the continuing education requirements of Colorado statutes and Board Rules.

8.4 After the end of the first year following the date of expiration, and before the end of the second year following the date of expiration, the holder of an expired license may reinstate same by applying in the form and manner provided by the Board, and paying the specified fees plus a reinstatement fee equal to two thirds of the base renewal fee. For purposes of this rule, the base renewal fee is defined as the total renewal fee less the National Appraiser Registry fee collected by the Board and remitted to the federal Appraisal Subcommittee. The act of applying for reinstatement shall constitute a statement under penalty of perjury in the second degree that the licensee had the present intent of affirmatively stating the licensee had complied with the continuing education requirements of Colorado statutes and Board Rules.

8.5 No holder of an expired license which may be reinstated may apply for a new license of the same type. Such person shall reinstate the expired license as provided in these rules. Nothing in this Rule 8.5 shall act to prevent a person from applying for and receiving a license or certificate with higher qualification requirements than those of the expired license.

8.6 Each licensee shall provide the Board with the following information: (1) a current mailing address and phone number for the licensee; (2) a current email address for the licensee or a letter explaining why the licensee cannot provide an email address; and (3) such other contact information as may be required by the Board from time to time. Each licensee shall inform the Board within ten (10) calendar days of any change in such contact information on a form or in the manner prescribed by the Board. A mailing address for the licensee will be posted on the Division of Real Estate's public website, and it is the licensee's responsibility to inform the Division of Real Estate of any required changes to the mailing address shown for the licensee on the Division of Real Estate's public website. The address shown for the licensee on the Division of Real Estate's public website shall be considered the licensee's address of record.

8.7 Repealed.

8.8 The holder of a registration, license, certificate or temporary practice permit may surrender such to the Board. The Board may deem a surrendered registration, license, certificate or temporary practice permit as permanently relinquished. Such surrender shall not remove the holder from the jurisdiction of the Board for acts committed while holding a registration, license, certificate or temporary practice permit. A person who surrenders a registration, license, certificate or temporary practice permit may not reinstate same, but must reapply and meet the current requirements for initial licensure.

8.9 Upon revocation, suspension, surrender or expiration of a license or temporary practice permit the holder shall:

A. Immediately cease all activities requiring licensure or a temporary practice permit;

B. In the instance of revocation, suspension or surrender, immediately return the license document or temporary practice permit to the Board;

C. Immediately cease all actions which represent the holder to the public as being licensed or being the holder of a temporary practice permit, including, without limitation, the use of advertising materials, forms, letterheads, business cards, correspondence, internet website content, statements of qualifications and the like.

8.10 A licensee who has not completed continuing education requirements established pursuant to Chapter 7 of these rules may not renew or reinstate licensure on inactive status unless the Board determines that extenuating circumstances existed which caused the deficiency in the continuing education requirements. The Board may require a written request and supporting documentation to determine that an extenuating circumstance exists or existed. A licensee desiring to renew or reinstate licensure on inactive status must submit their renewal or reinstatement on an inactive status application directly to the Board at the designated office of the Board. Failure to submit the renewal or reinstatement on inactive status application directly to the Board at the designated office of the Board shall result in renewal or reinstatement on active status.

8.11 A licensee may, without limitation, renew or reinstate licensure on inactive status for subsequent renewal periods by complying with the requirements of Rule 8.10.

8.12 Renewal or reinstatement of licensure on inactive status may be elected at the time of application for renewal or reinstatement. A licensee may not renew or reinstate on active status and then change to inactive status, unless advance, written approval is given by the Board. A licensee who has renewed or reinstated on active status is subject to the continuing education requirements for renewal or reinstatement of licensure.

* 8.13 A licensee who has renewed or reinstated on inactive status may change to active status by submitting a written request to the Board. The act of requesting a change from inactive status to active status shall constitute a statement under penalty of perjury in the second degree that the licensee had the present intent of affirmatively stating the licensee had complied with the continuing education requirements of Colorado statutes and Board rules. The Board shall require any licensee requesting a change from inactive status to active status to document completion of continuing education before implementing the change.

8.14 No person whose license has expired may represent themselves in any manner which creates the impression of holding active licensure. A person whose license has expired may refer to the fact of previous licensure by the Board by stating the dates of active licensure in parentheses after the license title, or by placing the word "expired" in parentheses after the license title.

8.15 No person whose license is on inactive status may represent themselves in any manner which creates the impression of holding active licensure. A person whose license is on inactive status may refer to the fact of previous active licensure or current inactive licensure by stating the dates of active licensure in parentheses after the license title, or by placing the word "inactive" in parentheses after the license title.

8.16 No person whose license has expired may represent themselves in any manner which creates the impression of holding inactive licensure.

CHAPTER 9: LICENSURE AND CERTIFICATION BY ENDORSEMENT

9.1 Pursuant to Section 12-61-708(1), C.R.S. (as amended), licensure by endorsement shall be subject to the following restrictions and requirements:

A. The Board may issue licenses by endorsement only to those persons holding an active license from another jurisdiction which is substantially equivalent to those described in Board Rules 1.13, 1.14 or 1.15, with qualification requirements substantially equivalent to those in Board Rules 2.2, 2.3 or 2.4, respectively. Licensure by endorsement is not available to persons holding licensure in another jurisdiction at a trainee, apprentice, associate, intern or other entry level similar to that defined in Board Rule 1.12.

B. The applicant must be the holder of an active license in good standing under the laws of another jurisdiction;

C. The appraiser regulatory program of the jurisdiction where the applicant holds an active license in good standing must not have been disapproved by the appropriate authority under 12 U.S.C.A., Section 3347, FIRREA;

D. The applicant must apply for licensure by endorsement on a form provided by the Board, pay the specified fees and meet all other Board requirements;

E. The applicant must apply for and be issued by the Board a license by endorsement prior to undertaking appraisal activities in Colorado that would require licensure in Colorado; and

F. A license issued by endorsement shall be subject to the same renewal requirements as a license issued pursuant to Section 12-61-706, C.R.S. (as amended), and Board Rules Chapters 7 and 8.

CHAPTER 10: TEMPORARY PRACTICE IN COLORADO

10.1 Pursuant to Sections 12-61-701, 12-61-704(1)(a), 12-61-708(1), 12-61-715(1)(c), C.R.S. (as amended) and in conformance with 12 U.S.C.A. Section 3351(a), FIRREA, a Temporary Practice Permit may be issued to the holder of an active appraiser's license from another state. Such Temporary Practice Permit shall be subject to the following restrictions and requirements:

A. The applicant must apply for and be issued a Temporary Practice Permit prior to undertaking appraisal activities in Colorado that would require licensure in Colorado;

B. The applicant shall identify in writing the appraisal assignment(s) to be completed under the Temporary Practice Permit prior to being issued a Temporary Practice Permit;

C. The Temporary Practice Permit shall be valid only for the appraisal assignment(s) listed thereon;

D. The applicant must be the holder of an active license in good standing under the laws of another state;

E. The state in which the applicant holds an active license in good standing must impose licensure requirements that are in conformance with FIRREA;

F. The appraiser regulatory program of the state where the applicant holds a license in good standing must not have been disapproved by the appropriate authority under the provisions of 12 U.S.C.A. Section 3347, FIRREA;

G. The applicant must apply for a Temporary Practice Permit on a form provided by the Board, pay the specified fees, and meet all other Board requirements; and

H. Pursuant to Section 12-61-708 (1.2), C.R.S., Temporary Practice Permits are available only to persons holding active licensure in another jurisdiction at levels substantially equivalent to those defined in Board Rules 1.13, 1.14 and 1.15. Temporary Practice Permits are not available to persons holding licensure in another jurisdiction at a trainee, apprentice, associate, intern or other entry level similar to that defined in Board Rule 1.12.

10.2 No person may be issued more than two Temporary Practice Permits in any rolling twelve-month period.

10.3 A Temporary Practice Permit issued pursuant to this Chapter 10 shall be valid for the period of time necessary to complete the original assignment(s) listed thereon, including time for client conferences and expert witness testimony. A Temporary Practice Permit issued pursuant to this Chapter 10 shall not be valid for completion of additional or update assignments involving the same property or properties. Additional or update assignments involving the same property or properties are new assignments, requiring a new Temporary Practice Permit or licensure by endorsement as provided in Chapter 9 of these Rules.

CHAPTER 11: STANDARDS OF PROFESSIONAL APPRAISAL PRACTICE

11.1 Pursuant to Section 12-61-710(1)(g), C.R.S. (as amended), the Board adopts, and incorporates by reference in compliance with Section 24-4-103(12.5), C.R.S., as the generally accepted standards of professional appraisal practice the definitions, preamble, rules, standards and standards rules and statements of the Uniform Standards of Professional Appraisal Practice as promulgated by the Appraisal Standards Board of the Appraisal Foundation on January 30, 1989 and amended through April 3, 2009 and known as the 2010-2011 edition. Amendments to the Uniform Standards of Professional Appraisal Practice subsequent to April 3, 2009 are not included in this Rule. A certified copy of the Uniform Standards of Professional Appraisal Practice is on file and available for public inspection with the Program Manager at the offices of the Board of Real Estate Appraisers at 1560 Broadway, Suite 925, Denver, Colorado. Copies of the Uniform Standards of Professional Appraisal Practice adopted under this rule may be examined at any state publications depository library. The 2010-2011 edition of the Uniform Standards of Professional Appraisal Practice may be examined at the Internet website of The Appraisal Foundation at www.appraisalfoundation.org, and copies may be ordered through that mechanism. The Appraisal Foundation may also be contacted at 1155 15th Street, NW, Suite 1111, Washington, DC 20005, or by telephone at (202) 347-7722 or by telefax at (202) 347-7727. The 2008 edition of the Uniform Standards of Professional Appraisal Practice, incorporating the amendments made through June 8, 2007 shall remain in effect through December 31, 2009. Beginning January 1, 2010, the 2010-2011 edition of the Uniform Standards of Professional Appraisal Practice shall be in effect.

11.2 A licensee appraiser using the services of an unlicensed assistant under the provisions of Section 12-61-716, C.R.S. (as amended), or the services of another licensee in the preparation of appraisals or other work products shall, consistent with the Uniform Standards of Professional Appraisal Practice, supervise each such assistant or licensee in an active, diligent and personal manner, and describe the research, analysis and reporting contributions of each such assistant or other licensee in each such report or other work product.

11.3 When disclosing a contingent fee arrangement pursuant to Section 12-61-702(2.5), Section 12-61-710(1)(g), and Section 12-61-712(1)(b), (c) and (d), C.R.S. (as amended), Board Rule 1.20, and the ETHICS RULE and Standards 4 and 5 of the Uniform Standards of Professional Appraisal Practice, a licensee shall do so in a clear and unequivocal manner in any oral report, and in the letter of transmittal, summary of salient facts and conclusions, statement of limiting conditions, and certifications of any written report.

The Board has chosen not to require specific contingent fee disclosure language, believing that licensees will use language appropriate to each situation. However, the Board recommends the following model language as being a "safe harbor":

> "[name of firm or individual] has been retained to provide consulting services and is being compensated in whole or part on the basis of [state the basis of the contingency, such as achieving a property tax saving through a reduction in valuation for assessment, achieving a change in zoning, approval of a development plan, etc.]. This disclosure of a contingent fee is intended to comply with the requirements of Colorado law, Rules of the Colorado Board of Real Estate Appraisers and the Uniform Standards of Professional Appraisal Practice."

CHAPTER 12: LICENSE TITLES, LICENSE DOCUMENTS, AND SIGNATURES

12.1 The descriptive license titles defined in Board Rules 1.12, 1.13, 1.14, 1.15 and 1.18 shall only be used by persons who hold such Board issued license or permit in good standing.

12.2 The descriptive license titles defined in Board Rules 1.12, 1.13, 1.14, 1.15 and 1.18 may only be used to refer to the individual holder of a license or permit in good standing, and shall not be used in such manner as to create the impression that any other person or group of persons, including a corporation, partnership or other business entity, holds such a license or permit.

12.3 No person shall use any title, designation or abbreviation issued by a private professional appraisal organization in a manner that creates the impression of licensure by the Board.

12.4 In each appraisal report or other appraisal related work product the license held by the appraiser(s) shall be clearly identified by using the license titles defined in Board Rules 1.12, 1.13, 1.14 and 1.15 and including the license number. Such license titles and numbers shall be identified wherever the licensee signs, by any means or method, the report or other work product, including, but not limited to the:

A. Letter of transmittal;

B. Certification of the appraiser(s); and

C. Appraisal or other work product report form or document, including addenda thereto.

12.5 Repealed.

12.6 An appraiser practicing in Colorado under authority of a Temporary Practice Permit shall identify the state where they hold licensure, the type of license and the license number, and shall further state they hold a Temporary Practice Permit and state the permit number in all instances where license type and number are required under this Chapter 12.

12.7 The real estate appraiser's license or temporary practice permit document and identification card issued to an initial or renewal applicant shall remain the property of the Board. Such document and card shall be surrendered to the Board immediately upon demand. The reasons for such demand may include, but are not limited to, suspension, revocation, stipulated settlement or failure to pay required fees.

12.8 When complying with Rule 12.4 an appraiser shall use the full license or permit title in Rules 1.12, 1.13, 1.14, 1.15, and 1.18, or shall use the appropriate abbreviation as listed below, followed by the license or permit number. Use of initials only, such as RA, LA, CRA, CGA, or TP to identify the type of license or permit is prohibited except when necessary to comply with federally implemented data collection or reporting requirements (for example Fannie Mae or Freddie Mac implemented policies or guidelines).

Registered Appraiser:	Reg. App. or Reg. Appr.
Licensed Appraiser:	Lic. App. or Lic. Appr.
Certified Residential Appraiser:	Crt. Res. App. or Cert. Res. Appr.
Certified General Appraiser:	Crt. Gen. App. or Cert. Genl. Appr.
Temporary Practice Permit:	Temp. Prac. Pmt.

12.9 Repealed.

12.10 When stating the type of license or permit held, and the number thereof, an appraiser may make use of an impression, provided such impression is legible on each copy of the appraisal report or other work product.

12.11 Where appraisal report forms or other work product forms do not allow space for placing the information required by Rule 12.4 immediately following the name and signature of the appraiser the required information shall be placed in the closest reasonable available space on the same page.

12.12 The holder of a license or permit in good standing may copy the license or permit document for inclusion in an appraisal report or other appraisal work product. Such copy shall have the word "COPY" boldly marked across the face of the copy, in letters at least one inch in height, at least one half inch in width, and with a stroke width of at least one eighth inch. The word "COPY" marked on such copy shall be placed so as to substantially overlay the printed portions of the license or permit document.

12.13 The requirements of this chapter shall be complied with in any electronic copy or transmittal of an appraisal report or other appraisal related work product.

12.14 No holder of a license or temporary practice permit, or any other person, shall make or cause to be made or allow to be made, any alteration to a Board-issued license or permit document or copy thereof, other than as provided in Board Rule 12.12.

12.15 No licensee or other person may affix or cause to be affixed the name or signature of a licensee to an appraisal report or other appraisal related work product without the express permission of the licensee to do so for that assignment, report or other work product. No licensee shall give blanket permission for affixing their signature to appraisal reports or other work products.

12.16 No licensee shall permit, through action or inaction, their name or signature to be affixed to an appraisal report or other appraisal related work product without their first personally examining and approving the final version of such report or other work product.

CHAPTER 13: DISCIPLINARY PROCEDURES

13.1 Complaints alleging violation of Section 12-61-701, *et seq.* , C.R.S. or the Rules of the Board of Real Estate Appraisers shall be in writing on a form or in the manner prescribed by the Board.

Nothing in this rule shall act to prevent the Board from acting upon its own motion to open a complaint.

13.2 Pursuant to Section 12-61-704(1)(d), C.R.S., and Section 24-4-105(3), C.R.S., any disciplinary hearing conducted on behalf of the Board may, at the discretion of the Board, be conducted by an Administrative Law Judge from the Office of Administrative Courts of the Department of Personnel & Administration.

13.3 Pursuant to Section 12-61-710(7), C.R.S., complaints of record in the offices of the Board and the results of staff investigations shall be closed to public inspection, except as provided by court order, during the investigatory period and until notice of hearing and charges are served on the licensee. Pursuant to Section 12-61-710(7), C.R.S., Section 24-72-203, C.R.S., and Section 24-72-204, C.R.S., complaints of record that are dismissed by the Board and the results of investigation of such complaints shall be closed to public inspection, except as provided by court order.

13.4 When an appraiser licensed under the provisions of Section 12-61-701, *et seq.*, C.R.S., (as amended) has been sent written notification from the Board that a complaint has been filed against the appraiser, such appraiser shall submit to the Board a written answer. Such written answer shall address all of the issues raised in the complaint in a substantive manner. Mailing by first class mail to the last known address in the records of the Board shall constitute such written notification. Failure to submit a written answer within the time set by the Board in its notification shall be grounds for disciplinary action unless the Board has granted a written extension of time for the answer.

13.5 The holder of a Board-issued license or permit shall inform the Board in writing within ten (10) days of any disciplinary action taken by any other state, district, territorial, or provincial real estate appraiser or real estate brokerage licensing authority. For purposes of this rule, disciplinary action shall include, without limitation, actions such as fines, required education, probation, suspension, revocation, letters of censure, debarment, required supervision, and the like.

13.6 Pursuant to Section 24-34-106, C.R.S., when a licensee is required to complete real estate appraisal education as part of a disciplinary action, no portion of any such courses or programs completed to satisfy the terms of a disciplinary action shall be creditable toward continuing education or qualifying education requirements.

13.7 The holder of a Board-issued license or permit shall inform the Board in writing within ten days of conviction of, entering a plea of guilty to, or entering a plea of nolo contendere to any felony, or any crime involving moral turpitude, or any other like crime under Colorado law, federal law, or the laws of other states. A certified copy of the judgment of a court of competent jurisdiction of such conviction or other official record indicating that such plea was entered shall be conclusive evidence of such conviction or plea in any hearing under Section 12-61-701, *et seq.*, C.R.S., or these Rules.

13.8 An investigation performed by staff within the Colorado Division of Real Estate or an appraiser selected by the Colorado Division of Real Estate to perform an investigation is not considered an "Appraisal Review" as defined by USPAP. An appraiser performing an investigation in accordance with this rule shall not be required to perform a USPAP Standard 3 appraisal review.

13.9 A licensee shall respond in writing to any correspondence from the Board requiring a response. The written response shall be submitted within the time period provided by the Board. The Board shall send such correspondence to the licensee's address of record with the Board. Failure to submit a timely written response shall be grounds for disciplinary action.

13.10 Exceptions and Board Review of Initial Decisions:

A. Written form, service, and filing requirements

1. All designations of record, requests, exceptions, and responsive pleadings ("pleadings") must be in written form, mailed with a certificate of mailing to the board and the opposing party.

2. All pleadings must be filed with the board by 5:00 p.m. on the date the filing is due. These rules do not provide for any additional time for service by mail. Filing is the receipt of a pleading by the board.
3. Any pleadings must be served on the opposing party by mail or by hand delivery on the date on which the pleading is filed with the board.
4. All pleadings must be filed with the board and not the office of administrative courts. Any designations of record, requests, exceptions or responsive pleadings filed in error with the office of administrative courts will not be considered. The board's address is:
   Colorado Board of Real Estate Appraisers
   1560 Broadway, Suite 925
   Denver, CO 80202

B. Authority to Review
   1. The board hereby preserves the board's option to initiate a review of an initial decision on its own motion pursuant to § 24-4-105(14)(a)(ii) and (b)(iii), C.R.S. outside of the thirty day period after service of the initial decision upon the parties without requiring a vote for each case.
   2. This option to review shall apply regardless of whether a party files exceptions to the initial decision.

C. Designation of Record and Transcripts
   1. Any party seeking to reverse or modify the initial decision of the administrative law judge shall file with the board a designation of the relevant parts of the record for review ("designation of record"). Designations of record must be filed with the board within twenty days of the date on which the board mails the initial decision to the parties' address of record with the board.
   2. Even if no party files a designation of record, the record shall include the following:
      A. All pleadings;
      B. All applications presented or considered during the hearing;
      C. All documentary or other exhibits admitted into evidence;
      D. All documentary or other exhibits presented during the hearing;
      E. All matters officially noticed;
      F. Any findings of fact and conclusions of law proposed by any party; and
      G. Any written brief filed.
   3. Transcripts: transcripts will not be deemed part of a designation of record unless specifically identified and ordered. Should a party wish to designate a transcript or portion thereof, the following procedures apply:
      A. The designation of record must identify with specificity the transcript or portion thereof to be transcribed. For example, a party may designate the entire transcript, or may identify witness(es) whose testimony is to be transcribed, the legal ruling or argument to be transcribed, or other information necessary to identify a portion of the transcript.
      B. Any party who includes a transcript or a portion thereof as part of the designation of record must order the transcript or relevant portions by the date on which the designation of record must be filed (within twenty days of the date on which the board mails the initial decision to the parties).
      C. When ordering the transcript, the party shall request a court reporter or transcribing service to prepare the transcript within thirty days. The party shall timely pay the necessary fees to obtain and file with the board an original transcription and one copy within thirty days.
      D. The party ordering the transcript shall direct the court reporter or transcribing service to complete and file with the board the transcript and one copy of the transcript within thirty days.

E. If a party designates a portion of the transcript, the opposing party may also file a supplemental designation of record, in which the opposing party may designate additional portions of the transcript. This supplemental designation of record must be filed with the board and served on the other party within ten days after the date on which the original designation of record was due.

F. An opposing party filing a supplemental designation of record must order and pay for such transcripts and portions thereof within the deadlines set forth above. An opposing party must also cause the court reporter to complete and file with the board the transcript and one copy of the transcript within thirty days.

G. Transcripts that are ordered and not filed with the board in a timely manner by the reporter or transcription service due to non-payment, insufficient payment or failure to direct as set forth above will not be considered by the board.

D. Filing of Exceptions and Responsive Pleadings

1. Any party wishing to file exceptions shall adhere to the following timelines:

   A. If no transcripts are ordered, exceptions are due within thirty days from the date on which the board mails the initial decision to the parties. Both parties' exceptions are due on the same date.

   B. If transcripts are ordered by either party, the following procedure shall apply. Upon receipt of transcripts identified in all designations of record, the board shall mail notification to the parties stating that the transcripts have been received by the board. Exceptions are due within thirty days from the date on which such notification is mailed. Both parties' exceptions are due on the same date.

2. Either party may file a responsive pleading to the other party's exceptions. All responsive pleadings shall be filed within 10 days of the date on which the exceptions were filed with the board. No other pleadings will be considered except for good cause shown.

3. The board may in its sole discretion grant an extension of time to file exceptions or responsive pleadings, or may delegate the discretion to grant such an extension of time to the board's designee.

E. Request for Oral Argument

1. All requests for oral argument must be in writing and filed by the deadline for responsive pleadings. Requests filed after this time will not be considered.

2. It is within the sole discretion of the board to grant or deny a request for oral argument. If oral argument is granted, both parties shall have the opportunity to participate.

3. Each side shall be permitted ten minutes for oral argument unless such time is extended by the board or its designee.

CHAPTER 14: DECLARATORY ORDERS PURSUANT TO SECTION 24-4-105 (11), C.R.S.

14.1 Any person may petition the Board for a declaratory order to terminate controversies or to remove uncertainties as to the applicability to the petitioner of any statutory provisions or of any rule or order of the Board.

14.2 The Board will determine, in its discretion and without notice to petitioner, whether to rule upon any such petition. If the Board determines that it will not rule upon such a petition, the Board shall promptly notify the petitioner in writing of its action and state the reasons for such action.

14.3 In determining whether to rule upon a petition filed pursuant to this rule, the Board will consider the following matters, among others:

A. Whether a ruling on the petition will terminate a controversy or remove uncertainties as to the applicability to petitioner of any statutory provision or rule or order of the Board.

B. Whether the petition involves any subject, question or issue which is the subject of a formal or informal matter or investigation currently pending before the Board or a court involving one or more of the petitioners.

C. Whether the petition involves any subject, question or issue which is the subject of a formal or informal matter or investigation currently pending before the Board or a court but not involving any petitioner.

D. Whether the petition seeks a ruling on a moot or hypothetical question or will result in an advisory ruling or opinion.

E. Whether the petitioner has some other adequate legal remedy, other than an action for declaratory relief pursuant to Rule 57, C.R.C.P., which will terminate the controversy or remove any uncertainty as to the applicability to the petitioner of the statute, rule or order in question.

14.4 Any petition filed pursuant to this rule shall set forth the following:

A. The name and address of the petitioner and whether the petitioner holds a registration, license or certificate issued pursuant to Section 12-61-701 et. seq. C.R.S. (as amended).

B. The statute, rule or order to which the petition relates.

C. A concise statement of all of the facts necessary to show the nature of the controversy or uncertainty and the manner in which the statute, rule or order in question applies or potentially applies to the petitioner.

14.5 If the Board determines that it will rule on the petition, the following procedures shall apply:

A. The Board may rule upon the petition based solely upon the facts presented in the petition. In such a case:

1. Any ruling of the Board will apply only to the extent of the facts presented in the petition and any amendment to the petition.
2. The Board may order the petitioner to file a written brief, memorandum or statement of position.
3. The Board may set the petition, upon due notice to the petitioner, for a non-evidentiary hearing.
4. The Board may dispose of the petition on the sole basis of the matters set forth in the petition.
5. The Board may request the petitioner to submit additional facts, in writing. In such event, such additional facts will be considered as an amendment to the petition.
6. The Board may take administrative notice of facts pursuant to the Administrative Procedures Act, Section 24-4-105 (8), C.R.S., (as amended), and may utilize its experience, technical competence and specialized knowledge in the disposition of the petition.
7. If the Board rules upon the petition without a hearing, it shall promptly notify the petitioner of its decision.

B. The Board may, in its discretion, set the petition for hearing, upon due notice to petitioner, for the purpose of obtaining additional facts or information or to determine the truth of any facts set forth in the petition or to hear oral argument on the petition. The notice to the petitioner setting such hearing shall set forth, to the extent known, the factual or other matters into which the Board intends to inquire. For the purpose of such a hearing, to the extent necessary, the petitioner shall have the burden of proving all of the facts stated in the petition, all of the facts necessary to show the nature of the controversy or uncertainty and the manner in which the statute, rule or order in question applies or potentially applies to the petitioner and any other facts the petitioner desires the Board to consider.

14.6 The parties to any proceeding pursuant to this rule shall be the Board and the petitioner. Any other person may seek leave of the Board to intervene in such a proceeding, and leave to intervene will be granted at the sole discretion of the Board. A petition to intervene shall set forth the same matters as required by section 14.4 of this Rule. Any reference to a "petitioner" in this Rule also refers to any person who has been granted leave to intervene by the Board.

14.7 Any declaratory order or other order disposing of a petition pursuant to this Rule shall constitute agency action subject to judicial review pursuant to Section 24-4-106, C.R.S., (as amended).

CHAPTER 15: WRITTEN NOTICES – BANKING EXEMPTIONS

15.1 Pursuant to Section 12-61-702 (1), C.R.S., (as amended), any appraisal, analysis, valuation, opinion, conclusion, notation or compilation prepared by an officer, director or regular salaried employee of a financial institution as defined in Section 12-61-702 (6), C.R.S., (as amended) , who is not a registered, licensed or certified appraiser under the provisions of Section 12-61-701, *et seq*., C.R.S., (as amended), shall contain the following written notice:

> "NOTICE: The preparer of this appraisal is not licensed as a real estate appraiser under the laws of the State of Colorado."

15.2 Pursuant to Section 12-61-718 (1), C.R.S., (as amended), any appraisal prepared for a financial institution as defined in Section 12-61-702 (1), C.R.S. (as amended), where the real estate related transaction or loan made or to be made is excepted from appraisal regulations established by the primary federal regulator of the defined financial institution, by any person who is not a registered, licensed or certified appraiser under the provisions of Section 12-61-701, *et seq*., C.R.S. (as amended) shall contain the following written notice:

> "NOTICE: The preparer of this appraisal is not licensed as a real estate appraiser under the laws of the State of Colorado."

15.3 The notices required under Section 12-61-702 (1) and Section 12-61-718 (1), C.R.S. (as amended), and Board Rules 15.1 and 15.2 shall:

A. Be placed on the first or cover page of each such appraisal, analysis, valuation, opinion, conclusion, notation or compilation, and on any page containing a value conclusion, signature or certification of the preparer;

B. Be placed on each copy of each such appraisal, analysis, valuation, opinion, conclusion, notation or compilation;

C. Be clearly legible in any xerographic or other reproduction of each such appraisal, analysis, valuation, opinion, conclusion, notation or compilation; and

D. Be in a type size not smaller than the type size used in the body of any such appraisal, analysis, valuation, opinion, conclusion, notation or compilation.

15.4 The notices required under Section 12-61-702 (1) and Section 12-61-718 (1), C.R.S. (as amended) and Board Rules 15.1 and 15.2 may be provided through use of a rubber stamped impression, provided such impression meets the requirements of Board Rule 15.3.

15.5 The notice requirements established under Section 12-61-702 (1) and Section 12-61-718 (1), C.R.S. (as amended) and Board Rules 15.1 and 15.2 shall be complied with in any electronic copy or transmittal of any such appraisal, analysis, valuation, opinion, conclusion, notation or compilation.

CHAPTER 16: CONSERVATION EASEMENT APPRAISALS

16.1 Affidavit for Conservation Easement Appraisals

Pursuant to § 12-61-719 (1), C.R.S. any appraiser who conducts an appraisal for a conservation easement shall submit a copy of the completed appraisal to the Board within thirty days following signature and delivery of the appraisal to the client. The appraisal shall be accompanied by an affidavit from the appraiser. Pursuant to Section 12-61-719 (2), the affidavit submitted with a conservation easement appraisal shall be in a form approved by the Board. The form entitled, "Affidavit for Conservation Easement Appraisals" has been approved by the Board and must be submitted to the Division of Real Estate by an appraiser who conducts an appraisal for a conservation easement, together with a copy of the conservation easement appraisal. The affidavit for conservation easement appraisals is posted to the Division of Real Estate's website. Specimen forms are also available for review and inspection in the Colorado Real Estate manual and in the office of the Division of Real Estate. The Board will no longer post the form in the Code of

Colorado Regulations and hereby withdraws any forms previously posted in the Code of Colorado Regulations.

16.2 A draft appraisal, as defined by board rule 1.34, does not have to be submitted to the Division of Real Estate pursuant to §12-61-719(1), C.R.S.

16.3 Pursuant to §12-61-719(1), C.R.S, the following appraisals are required to be submitted to the Division of Real Estate with the prescribed fee:

A. Any and all appraisals that assess the value of a conservation easement;

B. Any and all amendments to appraisals that assess the value of a conservation easement; or

C. Any review of an appraisal that contains an opinion of value.

16.4 All licensees who prepare and sign an appraisal for a conservation easement pursuant to section 39-22-522, C.R.S., on or after July 1, 2011, shall have completed the "Conservation Easement Appraiser Update Course" once every other year. The "Conservation Easement Appraiser Update Course" shall be developed by the Division of Real Estate and presented by the Division of Real Estate or a provider approved by the Division of Real Estate.

VII. Appendix – Affidavit for Conservation Easement Appraisals

For Division Use:
Date Received

AFFIDAVIT FOR CONSERVATION EASEMENT APPRAISALS

If more than one appraiser signed the certification in the appraisal, each must complete and sign a separate affidavit.

This affidavit and the appraisal for which it was completed must be submitted to the Division of Real Estate within 30 days following delivery of the signed appraisal to the client. Failure to do so may result in disciplinary action pursuant to §12-61-719(6) C.R.S.

I ____

(Full Name) (Colorado Appraiser License Number)

Do hereby affirm:

1. a. My client ❑ ***is*** the Internal Revenue Service, which precludes me from completing the remainder of this affidavit and submitting the appraisal as required by Colorado law, if my client is the Internal Revenue Service, I have attached proof of this relationship to the affidavit and the prescribed fee. OR

   b. My client ❑ ***is not*** the Internal Revenue Service.

2. The following information is accurate:

   a. Full name of any <u>other</u> appraiser(s) who signed the appraisal:

   ____

   b. This affidavit is for a (check one that best applies):

   ❑ First appraisal submitted for the appraised conservation easement

   ❑ Second appraisal with a different scope of work or duplicated appraisal with the same scope of work (first appraisal DRE reference # ____________________)

   ❑ Appraisal review with a value opinion (reviewed appraisal DRE reference # ____________________)

   c. Conservation easement transaction type (check one that best applies):

   ❑ Donation Only

   ❑ Purchase Only (of the conservation easement interest, not for funding of transaction costs)

   ❑ Bargain Sale (partial sale of the conservation easement interest, not for funding of transaction costs)

   d. Effective date of the appraisal (Month/Day/Year): ____________________

   e. Appraised Fair Market Value of the conservation easement:____________________

   f. Conservation easement holder(s):____________________

   g. County(ies) where conservation easement is located:____________________

   h. Acres encumbered by the appraised conservation easement:____________________

   i. Total acres of the appraised property:____________________

   j. Grantor(s) full legal name(s):____________________

   k. The full legal name(s) of the signatory(ies) for the grantor:____________________

   ____

Revised on 10/28/2010 Page 1 of 4

3. The appraisal ❑ ***is*** ❑ ***is not*** for submission to the Division of Real Estate and/or the Department of Revenue as evidence of a charitable donation eligible for a state tax credit.

4. The appraisal ❑ ***is*** ❑ ***is not*** for a transaction involving a grant from the Great Outdoors Colorado Trust Fund.

5. If applicable, the increase in value of any other property owned by the donor or a related person, whether or not such property is contiguous is (i.e. "enhancement" [see Treasury Regulation §1.170A-14(h)(3)(i)]):

   $________________________________.

6. In estimating the value of the subject property after encumbrance by the conservation easement I ❑ ***have*** ❑ ***have not*** considered if an increase in the value of the subject property (contiguous property owned by a donor and the donors family [Treasury Regulations], larger parcel [UASFLA] or as defined in USPAP), caused by the granting of the easement has occurred.

7. If applicable, the grantor of the easement:

   a. and any family member, as defined in Section 267(c)4 of the Internal Revenue Code of 1986 as amended ❑ ***does; or*** ❑ ***does not*** own property contiguous to the property encumbered by the conservation easement;

   b. and/or a related person, as defined in Section 267(b) of the Internal Revenue Code of 1986 as amended ❑ ***does; or*** ❑ ***does not*** own any other property, whether contiguous or not to the appraised property whose value may be increased as a result of the grant of the appraised conservation easement.

   c. If I answered affirmative to part a. or b. of this question the family member(s) and/or related person(s) natural or juristic are (please provide full legal name):

   ____

8. This appraisal ❑ ***is*** ❑ ***is not*** for a conservation easement that is part of a multi-stage (increased land area or restrictions) or partial (land area) encumbrance conservation easement transaction (AKA phasing or phased conservation easement).

9. The appraised property ❑ ***has*** ❑ ***has not*** transferred ownership, been optioned or listed within three years of the effective date of the appraisal.

   a. If yes provide the following information (attached additional sheet as needed):

      i. Date of transfer, option or listing within the last three years (Month/Day/Year):________________

      ii. Consideration provided:____

      iii. Names of parties:____

   b. If yes, the most recent transfer, option, or listing ❑ ***was*** ❑ ***was not*** given significant weight in determining the value before the easement.

10. My opinion of the value of the property unencumbered and encumbered by the conservation easement or easements using the following approaches/techniques is (if an approach is not applicable indicate N/A).

	Value Before Easement	Value After Easement
Sales Comparison Approach	$	$
Cost Approach	$	$
Income Approach (other than the subdivision approach)	$	$
Subdivision Approach	$	$
Other (please specify)	$	$

11. In the appraisal I ❑ ***did*** ❑ ***did not*** derive and allocate separate values for sand and gravel, minerals, water, and/or improvements. If I did derive such separate values, they were allocated to each applicable item before and after the granting of the conservation easement, as follows (if no separate values were derived indicate N/A):

	Value Before Easement	Value After Easement
Sand and Gravel	$	$
Minerals	$	$
Water	$	$
Improvements	$	$

12. I signed and delivered the appraisal to my client on (Month/Day/Year) ______________________.

13. I last completed the *Conservation Easement Appraiser Update Course,* as required by Board Rule 16.4, on

(Month/Day/Year) ____.

14. I ❑ ***have*** ❑ ***have not*** relinquished an appraisal license issued by any state or territory of the United States.

Please list state or territory as applicable:______________________________________

15. I ❑ ***have*** ❑ ***have not*** had formal disciplinary action resulting from a final judgment (all applicable appeals have been exhausted, waived or not exercised) taken against me by any regulatory body in Colorado or any other State or jurisdiction. Details of any disciplinary actions resulting from a final judgment are set out below (including but not limited to complaint number, complaint date, type of action taken and details of penalization):

____

____

16. I have conducted _____ # previous conservation easement appraisals.

17. Initial_____ I have complied with the education requirements established by the Colorado Board of Real Estate Appraisers for conservation easement appraisals pursuant to 39-22-522 C.R.S. and 12-61-719(7) C.R.S.

18. Initial_____ If applicable, I have met the minimum education and experience requirements as set forth in applicable regulations prescribed by the Secretary of the Treasury and/or any other regulations prescribed by the federal government therefore I am a qualified appraiser as defined in Section 170(f)11 E(II) of the Internal Revenue Code of 1986, as amended, due to my having completed the required education, and having acquired relevant professional experience, in conservation easement appraisals.

19. Initial_____ If applicable, I have not been prohibited by the Secretary of the Treasury from practicing before the Internal Revenue Service under Section 330(c) of Title 31 of the United States Code at any time during a 3-year period ending on the date that this appraisal was signed.

20. Initial_____ If applicable, this appraisal is a qualified appraisal as defined in Section 170(f)11 E(i) of the Internal Revenue Code of 1986 as amended and has been conducted by me in accordance with generally accepted appraisal practice standards (USPAP) and any regulations prescribed by the Secretary of the Treasury.

21. Initial_____ I am competent and have the necessary experience, to complete the analysis presented in this conservation easement appraisal.

22. Initial_____ If applicable, my client may submit this affidavit to the Division of Real Estate as part of the Application for a Conservation Easement Tax Credit Certificate, in doing so I certify that the conservation easement value (#2e, above) and enhancement value (#5, above) reported in this affidavit are supported by a qualified appraisal as defined in Section 170(f)11 E(i) of the Internal Revenue Code of 1986 as amended and that the appraisal report conforms to the Uniform Standards of Professional Appraisal Practice. I will submit the appraisal and duplicate copy of the affidavit to the Division of Real Estate within 30 days of signing and delivering it to my client.

Under penalties of perjury, I declare that to the best of my knowledge and belief, this affidavit is true, correct and complete.

______________________	______________________	______________
Authorized Signature	Title	Date
______________________	______________________	
Printed Name of Signatory	Telephone Number	

The Division will refuse receipt of an incomplete or incorrectly completed Affidavit submitted in accordance with C.R.S. §12-16-719 or as part of an application for a tax credit certificate.

Appraisers:

You must submit a hard copy of this Affidavit along with the prescribed fee and a signed copy of the conservation easement appraisal (hard copy or PDF) to the:

Division of Real Estate
Conservation Easement Program
1560 Broadway, Suite 925
Denver, CO 80202

Revised on 10/28/2010

Page 4 of 4

Chapter 11:
Conservation Easements

An * in the left margin indicates a change in the statute, rule, or text since the last publication of the manual.

I. Introduction

In 2008, Colorado's appraiser statutes were amended by the passage of HB 1353, the Conservation Easement Bill, to prevent abuses of the state's popular land-preservation tax credit program.

This new legislation creates a nine-member Conservation Easement Oversight Commission ("commission"), appointed by the governor, that will meet at least quarterly to review applications for conservation easement holder certification and to review any other issues referred to the commission by any state agency.

Duties of the commission will be to:

- Advise the Division of Real Estate regarding minimum qualifications for certification of conservation easement holders by reviewing the applicant's process for approving a conservation easement, the applicant's stewardship practices, the applicant's financial records, and the applicant's system of governance and ethics.
- Advise the Division of Real Estate on unqualified conservation easement holders.
- Advise the Division of Real Estate and Department of Revenue regarding the efficacy of conservation easement transactions, valuations, and capabilities of conservation easement holders.

Under the new law, appraisers must submit all conservation easement appraisals to the Division of Real Estate. All organizations holding conservation easements must be certified by the Division of Real Estate. The Department of Revenue is now authorized to share information with the Division of Real Estate and the Conservation Easement Oversight Commission. The Department of Revenue must review conservation easements when the IRS is conducting an audit.

II. Limiting the Amount of State Tax Credit That May Be Claimed

In response to Colorado's budgetary shortfall in 2010, the total amount of tax credits allowed for conservation easement donations is limited to $26 million a year for 2011, 2012, and 2013. Based on HB 10-1197, this limit or "cap" will expire at the end of 2013 and will not restrict any 2014 claims or conservation easement donations involving a tax credit.

The Division of Real Estate will administer the cap by issuing tax credit certificates to taxpayers that submit a claim. Issuance of the certificate will be in the order in which the claims are received by the Division of Real Estate. The Division of Real Estate must issue the certificate upon receipt of a claim. The Division of Real Estate will track the amount the claims each year and notify the public when a $26 million cap for that tax year has been reached.

Once the $26 million cap is reached for a given tax year, any claim received by the Division of Real Estate will be placed on a wait list and will receive a tax credit certificate for a subsequent tax year that has not reached the $26 million cap limitation.

The Department of Revenue will not allow a tax credit claim unless a tax credit certificate is first issued by the Division of Real Estate for a conservation easement in 2011 through 2013.

III. Conservation Easement Statutes

§ 12-61-719, C.R.S. Conservation easement appraisals – fund created

(1) Any appraiser who conducts an appraisal for a conservation easement shall submit a copy of the completed appraisal to the division within thirty days following the completion of the appraisal. For purposes of this section, "completion of the appraisal" shall mean that the certification page, as defined in the uniform standards for professional appraisal practice, promulgated by the appraisal standards board, shall have been signed by the appraiser and the appraisal has been delivered to the client of the appraiser. The appraisal shall be accompanied by an affidavit from the appraiser that includes, but is not limited to, the following:

(a) A statement specifying the value of the unencumbered property and the total value of the conservation easement in gross along with details of what methods the appraiser used to determine these values;

(b) If the appraisal separately allocates the values of sand and gravel, minerals, water, or improvements, a statement of the separate value of the sand and gravel, minerals, water, or improvements before and after the conservation easement in gross is granted;

(c) An acknowledgment specifying whether a subdivision analysis was used to establish the conservation value in the appraisal;

(d) A statement clarifying whether or not the landowner or a family member as defined in section 267(c)(4) of the federal "Internal Revenue Code of 1986", as amended, owns other property contiguous to the property encumbered by the appraised conservation easement or owns other property, of which the value may be increased by the donation of the property encumbered by the appraised conservation easement, whether contiguous or not, owned by the landowner or related person as defined in section 267(b) of the federal "Internal Revenue Code of 1986", as amended;

(e) A statement specifying how the appraiser satisfies the qualified appraiser and licensing requirements set forth in section 39-22-522(3.3), C.R.S.;

(f) A statement verifying the date and method by which the appraiser has met any specified classroom education requirements established by the board for conservation easement appraisals pursuant to subsection (7) of this section; and

(g) A statement specifying the number of previous conservation easement appraisals conducted by the appraiser.

(2) An affidavit submitted in accordance with the provisions of this section shall be in a form approved by the board. The board shall have the authority to promulgate rules concerning the form and content of the affidavit. Such rules shall be promulgated in accordance with article 4 of title 24, C.R.S. A copy of the affidavit and the completed appraisal shall be provided to the landowner.

(3) The division shall review the information submitted in accordance with this section to ensure that it is complete and shall record and maintain the information submitted as part of the affidavit in an electronic database. The division shall have the authority to share the information with the department of revenue. Notwithstanding the provisions of part 2 of article

72 of title 24, C.R.S., the division's custodian of records shall deny the right of inspection of any appraisal, affidavit, or other record related to information submitted in accordance with the provision of this section unless and until such time as the division files a notice of charges related to the information.

(4) The board in its discretion may, or upon receiving a written complaint from any person shall, investigate the activities of any appraiser who submits any information in accordance with the provisions of this section. The investigation shall consider whether the appraiser complied with the uniform standards of professional appraisal practice and any other provision of law. In conducting the investigation, the division shall have the authority to consult with the commission.

(5) If the board determines that a material violation of the uniform standards of professional appraisal practice or a substantial misstatement of value has occurred in any appraisal submitted in accordance with this section, the board shall notify the department of revenue regarding the appraisal and provide the department with a copy of the appraisal and a summary of the division's findings.

(6) If an appraiser fails to file an appraisal, affidavit, or other information as required by this section, the board shall have the authority to take disciplinary action as provided in section 12-61-710.

(7) The board shall have the authority to establish classroom education and experience requirements for an appraiser who prepares an appraisal for a conservation easement pursuant to section 39-22-522, C.R.S. Such requirements shall be established to ensure that appraisers have a sufficient amount of training and expertise to accurately prepare appraisals that comply with the uniform standards of professional appraisal practice and any other provision of law related to the appraisal of conservation easements. A credit for a conservation easement shall not be allowed unless the appraiser who prepared the appraisal of the easement met all requirements established in accordance with this subsection (7) in effect at the time the appraisal was completed.

(8) Any appraiser who submits a copy of an appraisal to the division in accordance with the requirements of this section shall pay the division a fee as prescribed by the division. The fee shall cover the costs of the division in administering the requirements of this section. The division shall have the authority to accept and expend gifts, grants, and donations for the purposes of this section. The state treasurer shall credit fees, gifts, grants, and donations to the conservation easement appraisal review fund, which fund is hereby created in the state treasury. Moneys in the fund shall be annually appropriated to the division for the purposes of implementing and administering this section and shall not revert to the general fund at the end of any fiscal year. The fund shall be maintained in accordance with section 24-75-402, C.R.S. On or before January 1, 2009, and on or before each January 1 thereafter, the division shall certify to the general assembly the amount of the fee prescribed by the division pursuant to this subsection (8).

§ 12-61-720, C.R.S. Certification of conservation easement holders – fund created – rules – repeal

(1) The division shall, in consultation with the commission created in section 12-61-721, establish and administer a certification program for qualified organizations under section 170(h) of the federal "Internal Revenue Code of 1986", as amended, that hold conservation easements for which a tax credit is claimed pursuant to section 39-22-522, C.R.S. The purpose of the program shall be to:

(a) Establish minimum qualifications for certifying organizations that hold conservation easements to encourage professionalism and stability; and

(b) Identify fraudulent or unqualified applicants as defined by the rules of the division to prevent them from becoming certified by the program.

(2) The certification program shall be established and commence accepting applications for certification no later than January 1, 2009. The division shall conduct a review of each application and consider the recommendations of the commission before making a final determination to grant or deny certification. In reviewing an application and in granting certification, the division and the commission may consider:

(a) The applicant's process for reviewing, selecting, and approving a potential conservation easement;

(b) The applicant's stewardship practices and capacity, including the ability to maintain, monitor, and defend the purposes of the easement;

(c) An audit of the applicant's financial records;

(d) The applicant's system of governance and ethics regarding conflicts of interest and transactions with related parties as described in section 267(b) of the federal "Internal Revenue Code of 1986", as amended, donors, board members, and insiders. For purposes of this paragraph (d), "insiders" means board and staff members, substantial contributors, parties related to those above, those who have an ability to influence decisions of the organization, and those with access to information not available to the general public.

(e) Any other information deemed relevant by the division or the commission; and

(f) The unique circumstances of the different entities to which this certification applies as set forth in subsection (4) of this section.

(3) At the time of submission of an application, and each year the entity is certified pursuant to this section, the applicant shall pay the division a fee as prescribed by the division. The fee shall cover the costs of the division and the commission in administering the certification program for entities that hold conservation easements for which tax credits are claimed pursuant to section 39-22-522, C.R.S. The division shall have the authority to accept and expend gifts, grants, and donations for the purposes of this section. The state treasurer shall credit fees, gifts, grants, and donations collected pursuant to this subsection (3) to the conservation easement holder certification fund, which fund is hereby created in the state treasury. Moneys in the fund shall be annually appropriated to the division for the purposes of implementing and administering this section and shall not revert to the general fund at the end of any fiscal year. The fund shall be maintained in accordance with section 24-75-402, C.R.S. On or before January 1, 2009, and on or before each January 1 thereafter, the division shall certify to the general assembly the amount of the fee prescribed by the division pursuant to this subsection (3).

(4) The certification program shall apply to:

(a) Nonprofit entities holding easements on property with conservation values consisting of recreation or education, protection of environmental systems, or preservation of open space;

(b) Nonprofit entities holding easements on property for historic preservation; and

(c) The state and any municipality, county, city and county, special district, or other political subdivision of the state that holds an easement.

(5) The certification program may contain a provision allowing for the expedited or automatic certification of an entity that is currently accredited by national land conservation organizations that are broadly accepted by the conservation industry.

(6) The commission shall meet at least quarterly and make recommendations to the division regarding the certification program. The division shall have the authority to determine whether an applicant for certification possesses the necessary qualifications for certification required by the rules adopted by the division. If the division determines that an applicant does not possess the applicable qualifications for certification or that the applicant has violated any provision of

this part 7, the rules promulgated by the division, or any division order, the division may deny the applicant a certification or deny the renewal of a certification; and, in such instance, the division shall provide the applicant with a statement in writing setting forth the basis of the division's determination. The applicant may request a hearing on the determination as provided in section 24-4-104(9), C.R.S. The division shall notify successful applicants in writing. An applicant that is not certified may reapply for certification in accordance with procedures established by the division.

(7) The division shall implement the certification program in a manner that either commences accepting applications for certification:

(a) At the same time for all types of entities that hold conservation easements; or

(b) During the first year of the program for entities described in paragraph (a) of subsection (4) of this section and during the second year of the program for entities described in paragraphs (b) and (c) of subsection (4) of this section, and other entities.

(8) Beginning one year after the division commences accepting applications to certify the type of entity that holds a conservation easement in accordance with the provisions of subsection (7) of this section, a tax credit may be claimed for the easement pursuant to section 39-22-522, C.R.S., only if the entity has been certified in accordance with the provisions of this section at the time the donation of the easement is made. The division shall make information available to the public concerning the date that it commences accepting applications for entities that hold conservation easements and the requirements of this subsection (8).

(9) [Deleted]

(10) The division shall maintain and update an online list that can be accessed by the public of the organizations that have applied for certification and whether each has been certified, rejected for certification, or had its certification revoked or suspended in accordance with the provisions of this section.

(11) The division shall have the authority to investigate the activities of any entity that is required to be certified pursuant to this section and to impose discipline for noncompliance, including but not limited to the suspension or revocation of a certification or the imposition of fines. The division shall have the authority to promulgate rules for the certification program and discipline authorized by this section. Such rules shall be promulgated in accordance with article 4 of title 24, C.R.S.

(12) Nothing in this section shall be construed to:

(a) Affect any tax credit that was claimed pursuant to section 39-22-522, C.R.S., prior to the time certification was required by this section; or

(b) Require the certification of an entity that holds a conservation easement for which a tax credit is not claimed pursuant to section 39-22-522, C.R.S.

(13) This section is repealed, effective July 1, 2018.

§ 12-61-721, C.R.S. Conservation easement oversight commission – created – repeal

(1) There is hereby created in the division a conservation easement oversight commission consisting of nine members as follows:

(a) One member representing the great outdoors Colorado program shall be appointed by and serve at the pleasure of the state board of the great outdoors Colorado trust fund established in article XXVII of the state constitution;

(b) One member representing the department of natural resources shall be appointed by and serve at the pleasure of the executive director of the department;

(c) One member representing the department of agriculture shall be appointed by and serve at the pleasure of the executive director of the department;

(d) Six members appointed by the governor as follows with at least one member with the following qualifications or representing the following interests:

(I) A local land trust;

(II) A statewide or national land trust;

(III) A local government open space or land conservation agency;

(IV) An historic preservation organization with experience in easements on properties of historical significance;

(V) A certified general appraiser with experience in conservation easements who meets any classroom education and experience requirements established by the board in accordance with section 12-61-719; and

(VI) A landowner that has donated a conservation easement in Colorado.

(2) In making appointments to the commission, the governor shall consult with the three members of the commission appointed pursuant to paragraphs (a) to (c) of subsection (1) of this section and with appropriate organizations representing the particular interest or area of expertise that the appointee represents. Not more than three of the governor's appointees serving at the same time shall be from the same political party. In making the initial appointments, the governor shall appoint three members for terms of two years. All other appointments by the governor shall be for a term of three years. No member shall serve more than two consecutive terms. In the event of a vacancy by death, resignation, removal, or otherwise, the governor shall appoint a member to fill the unexpired term. The governor shall have the authority to remove any member for misconduct, neglect of duty, or incompetence.

* (3) The commission shall advise the division and the department of revenue regarding conservation easements for which a state income tax credit is claimed pursuant to section 39-22-522, C.R.S. At the request of the division or the department, the commission shall review conservation easement transactions, applications, and other documents and advise the division and the department regarding conservation values, consistent with section 170 (h) of the federal "Internal Revenue Code of 1986", as amended, the capacity of conservation easement holders, and the integrity and accuracy of conservation easement transactions related to the tax credits.

(4) The commission shall meet not less than once each quarter to review applications for conservation easement holder certification submitted in accordance with section 12-61-720 and to review any other issues referred to the commission by the division, the department of revenue, or any other state entity. The division shall convene the meetings of the commission and provide staff support as requested by the commission. A majority of the members of the commission shall constitute a quorum for the transaction of all business, and actions of the commission shall require a vote of a majority of such members present in favor of the action taken.

(5) On or before January 1, 2009, the commission shall establish a conflict of interest policy to ensure that any member of the commission shall be disqualified from performing any act that conflicts with a private pecuniary interest of the member or from participating in the deliberation or decision- making process for certification for an applicant represented by such member.

(6) Each member of the commission shall receive the same compensation and reimbursement of expenses as those provided for members of boards and commissions in the division of registrations pursuant to section 24-34-102(13), C.R.S. Payment for all such per diem compensation and expenses shall be made out of annual appropriations from the conservation easement holder certification fund created in section 12-61-720(3).

* (6.5) Commission members shall be immune from liability in accordance with the provisions of the "Colorado Governmental Immunity Act", article 10 of title 24, C.R.S.

(7) This section is repealed, effective July 1, 2018. Prior to such repeal, the commission shall be reviewed as provided in section 24-34-104, C.R.S.

§ 12-61-722, C.R.S. Conservation Easement tax credit certificates

(1) The division shall receive claims from and issue certificates to certified conservation easement holders for income tax credits for conservation easements donated during the 2011, 2012, and 2013 calendar years in accordance with the provisions of section 39-22-522(2.5), C.R.S. Nothing in this section shall be construed to restrict or limit the authority of the division to enforce the provisions of this part 7. The division may promulgate rules in accordance with article 4 of title 24, C.R.S., for the issuance of the certificates. In promulgating any such rules, the division may include but shall not be limited to provisions governing the following:

(a) The review of the tax credit certificate;

(b) The administration and financing of the certification process;

(c) The notification to the public regarding the aggregate amount of certificates that have been issued and that are on the wait list;

(d) The notification to the taxpayer, the entity to which the easement was granted, and the department of revenue regarding the certificates issued; and

(e) Any other matters related to administering the provisions of section 39-22-522(2.5), C.R.S.

§ 24-33-112, C.R.S. Conservation easement holders – submission of information

(1) Any organization that accepts a donation of a conservation easement in gross for which a state income tax credit is claimed in accordance with the provisions of section 39-22-522, C.R.S., shall submit the following information to the department of revenue and the division of real estate in the department of regulatory agencies:

(a) The number of conservation easements held by the organization in Colorado;

(b) The number of acres subject to each conservation easement held in Colorado, except properties for which the sole conservation purpose is historic preservation;

(c) The names of the board members if the organization is a private nonprofit organization or the names of the elected or appointed officials if the organization is a public entity;

(c.5) The date on which the organization received certification pursuant to section 12-61-720, C.R.S.; and

(d) A signed statement from the organization acknowledging that:

(I) The organization has a commitment to protect the conservation purpose of the donation and has the resources to enforce the restrictions; and

(II) The organization has adequate resources and policies in place to provide annual monitoring of each conservation easement held by the organization in Colorado, except for any conservation easement granted to a local government that did not involve a charitable donation.

(2) An organization that accepts a conservation easement in the calendar year commencing January 1, 2008, shall submit the information required by subsection (1) of this section prior to accepting the easement, but in no event later than April 15 of that calendar year. An organization shall not accept any donation of a conservation easement in gross for which a credit is claimed unless the organization has submitted the information required by this subsection (2) with the department of revenue, the department of agriculture, and the

department of natural resources. The department of natural resources and the department of agriculture shall make the information available to the public upon request.

(3) An organization that accepts a conservation easement in any calendar year commencing on or after January 1, 2009, shall submit the information required by subsection (1) of this section prior to accepting the easement, but in no event later than April 15 of that calendar year. An organization shall not accept any donation of a conservation easement in gross for which a credit is claimed unless the organization has submitted the information required by this subsection (3) with the department of revenue and the division of real estate. The department of revenue and the division of real estate shall make the information available to the public upon request.

(4) Federal agencies that accept conservation easements for which a state income tax credit is claimed are exempt from the submission of information required in subsection (1) of this section and, in any calendar year commencing on or after January 1, 2008, shall be exempt from the filing requirements of subsections (2) and (3) of this section. Conservation easements accepted by federal agencies may receive the state tax credit without the federal agency having filed the information required by this section.

§ 39-21-113, C.R.S. Reports and returns – repeal

(17) Notwithstanding any other provision of this section, the executive director may require that such detailed information regarding a claim for a credit for the donation of a conservation easement in gross pursuant to section 39-22-522 and any appraisal submitted in support of the credit claimed be given to the division of real estate in the department of regulatory agencies and the conservation easement oversight commission created pursuant to section 12-61-721(1), C.R.S., as the executive director determines is necessary in the performance of the department's functions relating to the credit. The executive director may provide copies of any appraisal and may file a complaint regarding any appraisal as authorized pursuant to section 39-22-522(3.3). Notwithstanding the provisions of part 2 of article 72 of title 24, C.R.S., in order to protect the confidential financial information of a taxpayer, the executive director shall deny the right to inspect any information or appraisal required in accordance with the provisions of this subsection (17).

* (17.5) (a) Notwithstanding the provisions of this section, the executive director may provide such detailed information pertinent to a claim for a credit for the donation of a conservation easement pursuant to section 39-22-522 to taxpayers, including donors and transferees, with cases involving common or related issues of fact or law. The executive director or the executive director's duly authorized agents may also provide such information to the parties to a consolidated administrative hearing pursuant to 39-22-522.5 (5) (a) as necessary and appropriate for the efficient and fair resolution of disputes.

(b) Persons who receive taxpayer information pursuant to paragraph (a) of this subsection (17.5) shall be subject to the provisions of this section, including the limitations in subsection (4) of this section and the penalties in subsection (6) of this section regarding disclosure of taxpayer information.

§ 39-22-522, C.R.S. Credit against tax – conservation easements

(1) For purposes of this section, "taxpayer" means a resident individual or a domestic or foreign corporation subject to the provisions of part 3 of this article, a partnership, S corporation, or other similar pass-through entity, estate, or trust that donates a conservation easement as an entity, and a partner, member, and subchapter S shareholder of such pass-through entity.

(2) For income tax years commencing on or after January 1, 2000, and, with regard to any credit over the amount of one hundred thousand dollars, for income tax years commencing on or after January 1, 2003, subject to the provisions of subsections (4) and (6) of this section, there shall

be allowed a credit with respect to the income taxes imposed by this article to each taxpayer who donates during the taxable year all or part of the value of a perpetual conservation easement in gross created pursuant to article 30.5 of title 38, C.R.S., upon real property the taxpayer owns to a governmental entity or a charitable organization described in section 38-30.5-104(2), C.R.S. The credit shall only be allowed for a donation that is eligible to qualify as a qualified conservation contribution pursuant to section 170(h) of the internal revenue code, as amended, and any federal regulations promulgated in connection with such section. The amount of the credit shall not include the value of any portion of an easement on real property located in another state.

* (2.5) Notwithstanding any other provision of this section, for income tax years commencing during the 2011, 2012, and 2013 calendar years, a taxpayer conveying a conservation easement in 2011, 2012, or 2013 and claiming a credit pursuant to this section shall, in addition to any other requirements of this section, submit a claim for the credit to the division of real estate in the department of regulatory agencies. The division shall issue a certificate for the claims received in the order submitted. After certificates have been issued for credits that exceed an aggregate of twenty-two million dollars for all taxpayers for income tax years commencing in each of the 2011 and 2012 calendar years and thirty-four million dollars for each income tax year commencing in the 2013 calendar year, any claims that exceed the amount allowed for a specified calendar year shall be placed on a wait list in the order submitted and a certificate shall be issued for use of the credit in 2012 or 2013. The division shall not issue credit certificates that exceed twenty-two million dollars for each income tax year commencing in the 2011 and 2012 calendar years and thirty-four million dollars for each income tax year commencing in the 2013 calendar year. No claim for a credit shall be allowed for any income tax year commencing during the 2011, 2012, or 2013 calendar years unless a certificate has been issued by the division. The right to claim the credit shall be vested in the taxpayer at the time a credit certificate is issued. The division may promulgate rules in accordance with article 4 of title 24, C.R.S., for the issuance of certificates in accordance with this subsection (2.5).

(3) In order for any taxpayer to qualify for the credit provided for in subsection (2) of this section, the taxpayer shall submit the following in a form approved by the executive director to the department of revenue at the same time as the taxpayer files a return for the taxable year in which the credit is claimed:

(a) A statement indicating whether a deduction was claimed on the taxpayer's federal income tax return for a conservation easement in gross;

(b) A statement that reflects the information included in the noncash charitable contributions form used to claim a deduction for a conservation easement in gross on a federal income tax return and whether the donation was made in order to get a permit or other approval from a local or other governing authority;

(c) A statement to be made available to the public by the department of revenue that includes a summary of the conservation purposes as defined in section 170(h) of the internal revenue code that are protected by the easement; the county, township, and range where the easement is located; the number of acres subject to the easement; the amount of the tax credit claimed; and the name of the organization holding the easement;

(d) A summary of a qualified appraisal that meets the requirements set forth in subsection (3.3) of this section; however, if requested by the department of revenue, the taxpayer shall submit the appraisal itself;

(e) A copy of the appraisal and accompanying affidavit from the appraiser submitted to the division of real estate in the department of regulatory agencies in accordance with the provisions of section 12-61-719, C.R.S.

(f) If the holder of the conservation easement is an organization to which the certification program in section 12-61-720, C.R.S., applies, a sworn affidavit from the holder of the conservation easement in gross that includes the following:

(I) An acknowledgment that the holder has filed the information with the department of revenue and the division of real estate in accordance with section 24-33-112, C.R.S.;

(II) An acknowledgment of whether the transaction is part of a series of transactions by the same donor; and

(III) An acknowledgment that the holder has reviewed the completed Colorado gross conservation easement credit schedule to be filed by the taxpayer and that the property is accurately described in the schedule.

(3.3) The appraisal for a conservation easement in gross for which a credit is claimed shall be a qualified appraisal from a qualified appraiser, as those terms are defined in section 170(f)(11) of the internal revenue code. The appraisal shall be in conformance with the uniform standards for professional appraisal practice promulgated by the appraisal standards board of the appraisal foundation and any other provision of law. The appraiser shall hold a valid license as a certified general appraiser in accordance with the provisions of part 7 of article 61 of title 12, C.R.S. The appraiser shall also meet any education and experience requirements established by the board of real estate appraisers in accordance with section 12-61-719(7), C.R.S. If there is a final determination, other than by settlement of the taxpayer, that an appraisal submitted in connection with a claim for a credit pursuant to this section is a substantial or gross valuation misstatement as such misstatements are defined in section 1219 of the federal "Pension Protection Act of 2006", Pub.L. 109-280, the department shall submit a complaint regarding the misstatement to the board of real estate appraisers for disciplinary action in accordance with the provisions of part 7 of article 61 of title 12, C.R.S.

(3.5) (a) The executive director shall have the authority, pursuant to subsection (8) of this section, to require additional information from the taxpayer or transferee regarding the appraisal value of the easement, the amount of the credit, and the validity of the credit. In resolving disputes regarding the validity or the amount of a credit allowed pursuant to subsection (2) of this section, including the value of the conservation easement for which the credit is granted, the executive director shall have the authority, for good cause shown and in consultation with the division of real estate and the conservation easement oversight commission created in section 12-61-721(1), C.R.S., to review and accept or reject, in whole or in part, the appraisal value of the easement, the amount of the credit, and the validity of the credit based upon the internal revenue code and federal regulations in effect at the time of the donation. If the executive director reasonably believes that the appraisal represents a gross valuation misstatement, receives notice of such a valuation misstatement from the division of real estate, or receives notice from the division of real estate that an enforcement action has been taken by the board of real estate appraisers against the appraiser, the executive director shall have the authority to require the taxpayer to provide a second appraisal at the expense of the taxpayer. The second appraisal shall be conducted by a certified general appraiser in good standing and not affiliated with the first appraiser that meets qualifications established by the division of real estate. In the event the executive director rejects, in whole or in part, the appraisal value of the easement, the amount of the credit, or the validity of the credit, the procedures described in sections 39-21-103, 39-21-104, 39-21-104.5, and 39-21-105 shall apply.

(b) In consultation with the division of real estate and the conservation easement oversight commission created in section 12-61-721(1), C.R.S., the executive director shall develop and implement a separate process for the review by the department of revenue of gross conservation easements. The review process shall be consistent with the statutory obligations of the division and the commission and shall address gross conservation easements for which the department of revenue has been informed that an audit is being performed by the internal revenue service. The executive director shall share information used in the review of gross conservation easements with the division. Notwithstanding part 2 of article 72 of title 24, C.R.S., in order to protect the confidential financial information of a taxpayer, the division and the commission shall deny the right to inspect any information provided by the executive director in accordance with this paragraph (b). On or before January 1, 2009, the executive director shall report to the general assembly on the status of the development and implementation of the process required by this paragraph (b).

(3.7) If the gain on the sale of a conservation easement in gross for which a credit is claimed pursuant to this section would not have been a long-term capital gain, as defined under the internal revenue code, if, at the time of the donation, the taxpayer had sold the conservation easement at its fair market value, then the value of the conservation easement in gross for the purpose of calculating the amount of the credit shall be reduced to the taxpayer's tax basis in the conservation easement in gross. The tax basis of a taxpayer in a conservation easement shall be determined and allocated pursuant to sections 170(e) and 170(h) of the internal revenue code, as amended, and any federal regulations promulgated in connection with such sections. This subsection (3.7) shall be applied in a manner that is consistent with the tax treatment of qualified conservation contributions under the internal revenue code and the federal regulations promulgated under the internal revenue code.

(4) (a) (I) For a conservation easement in gross created in accordance with article 30.5 of title 38, C.R.S., that is donated prior to January 1, 2007, to a governmental entity or a charitable organization described in section 38-30.5-104(2), C.R.S., the credit provided for in subsection (2) of this section shall be an amount equal to one hundred percent of the first one hundred thousand dollars of the fair market value of the donated portion of such conservation easement in gross when created, and forty percent of all amounts of the donation in excess of one hundred thousand dollars; except that in no case shall the credit exceed two hundred sixty thousand dollars per donation.

(II) For a conservation easement in gross created in accordance with article 30.5 of title 38, C.R.S., that is donated on or after January 1, 2007, to a governmental entity or a charitable organization described in section 38-30.5-104(2), C.R.S., the credit provided for in subsection (2) of this section shall be an amount equal to fifty percent of the fair market value of the donated portion of such conservation easement in gross when created; except that in no case shall the credit exceed three hundred seventy-five thousand dollars per donation.

(III) In no event shall a credit claimed by a taxpayer filing a joint federal return, or the sum of the credits claimed by taxpayers filing married separate federal returns, exceed the dollar limitations of this paragraph (a).

(b) For income tax years commencing on or after January 1, 2000, in the case of a joint tenancy, tenancy in common, partnership, S corporation, or other similar entity or ownership group that donates a conservation easement as an entity or group, the amount of the credit allowed pursuant to subsection (2) of this section shall be allocated to the entity's owners, partners, members, or shareholders in proportion to the owners', partners', members', or shareholders' distributive shares of income or ownership percentage from such entity or group. For income tax years commencing on or after January 1, 2000, but prior to January 1, 2003, the total aggregate amount of the credit allocated to such owners, partners, members, and shareholders shall not exceed one hundred thousand dollars, and, if any refund is claimed pursuant to subparagraph (I) of paragraph (b) of subsection (5) of this section, the aggregate amount of the refund and the credit claimed by such partners, members, and shareholders shall not exceed twenty thousand dollars for that income tax year. For income tax years commencing on or after January 1, 2003, but prior to January 1, 2007, the total aggregate amount of the credit allocated to such owners, partners, members, and shareholders shall not exceed two hundred sixty thousand dollars, and, if any refund is claimed pursuant to subparagraph (I) of paragraph (b) of subsection (5) of this section, the aggregate amount of the refund and the credit claimed by such owners, partners, members, and shareholders shall not exceed fifty thousand dollars for that income tax year. For income tax years commencing on or after January 1, 2007, the total aggregate amount of the credit allocated to such owners, partners, members, and shareholders shall not exceed three hundred seventy-five thousand dollars, and, if any refund is claimed pursuant to subparagraph (I) of paragraph (b) of subsection (5) of this section, the aggregate amount of the refund and the credit claimed by such owners, partners, members, and shareholders shall not exceed fifty thousand dollars for that income tax year.

(5) (a) If the tax credit provided in this section exceeds the amount of income tax due on the income of the taxpayer for the taxable year, the amount of the credit not used as an offset against income taxes in said income tax year and not refunded pursuant to paragraph (b) of this subsection (5) may be carried forward and applied against the income tax due in each of the twenty succeeding income tax years but shall be first applied against the income tax due for the earliest of the income tax years possible. Any amount of the credit that is not used after said period shall not be refundable.

(b) (I) Subject to the requirements specified in subparagraphs (II) and (III) of this paragraph (b), for income tax years commencing on or after January 1, 2000, if the amount of the tax credit allowed in or carried forward to any tax year pursuant to this section exceeds the amount of income tax due on the income of the taxpayer for the year, the taxpayer may elect to have the amount of the credit not used as an offset against income taxes in said income tax year refunded to the taxpayer.

(II) A taxpayer may elect to claim a refund pursuant to subparagraph (I) of this paragraph (b) only if, based on the financial report prepared by the controller in accordance with section 24-77-106.5, C.R.S., the controller certifies that the amount of state revenues for the state fiscal year ending in the income tax year for which the refund is claimed exceeds the limitation on state fiscal year spending imposed by section 20(7)(a) of article X of the state constitution and the voters statewide either have not authorized the state to retain and spend all of the excess state revenues or have authorized the state to retain and spend only a portion of the excess state revenues for that fiscal year.

(III) If any refund is claimed pursuant to subparagraph (I) of this paragraph (b), then the aggregate amount of the refund and amount of the credit used as an offset against income taxes for that income tax year shall not exceed fifty thousand dollars for that income tax year. In the case of a partnership, S corporation, or other similar pass-through entity that donates a conservation easement as an entity, if any refund is claimed pursuant to subparagraph (I) of this paragraph (b), the aggregate amount of the refund and the credit claimed by the partners, members, or shareholders of the entity shall not exceed the dollar limitation set forth in this subparagraph (III) for that income tax year. Nothing in this subparagraph (III) shall limit a taxpayer's ability to claim a credit against taxes due in excess of fifty thousand dollars in accordance with subsection (4) of this section.

(6) A taxpayer may claim only one tax credit under this section per income tax year; except that a transferee of a tax credit under subsection (7) of this section may claim an unlimited number of credits. A taxpayer who has carried forward or elected to receive a refund of part of the tax

credit in accordance with subsection (5) of this section shall not claim an additional tax credit under this section for any income tax year in which the taxpayer applies the amount carried forward against income tax due or receives a refund. A taxpayer who has transferred a credit to a transferee pursuant to subsection (7) of this section shall not claim an additional tax credit under this section for any income tax year in which the transferee uses such transferred credit.

(7) For income tax years commencing on or after January 1, 2000, a taxpayer may transfer all or a portion of a tax credit granted pursuant to subsection (2) of this section to another taxpayer for such other taxpayer, as transferee, to apply as a credit against the taxes imposed by this article subject to the following limitations:

(a) The taxpayer may only transfer such portion of the tax credit as the taxpayer has neither applied against the income taxes imposed by this article nor used to obtain a refund;

(b) The taxpayer may transfer a pro-rated portion of the tax credit to more than one transferee;

(c) A transferee may not elect to have any transferred credit refunded pursuant to paragraph (b) of subsection (5) of this section;

(d) For any tax year in which a tax credit is transferred pursuant to this subsection (7), both the taxpayer and the transferee shall file written statements with their income tax returns specifying the amount of the tax credit that has been transferred. A transferee may not claim a credit transferred pursuant to this subsection (7) unless the taxpayer's written statement verifies the amount of the tax credit claimed by the transferee.

(e) To the extent that a transferee paid value for the transfer of a conservation easement tax credit to such transferee, the transferee shall be deemed to have used the credit to pay, in whole or in part, the income tax obligation imposed on the transferee under this article, and to such extent the transferee's use of a tax credit from a transferor under this section to pay taxes owed shall not be deemed a reduction in the amount of income taxes imposed by this article on the transferee;

(f) The transferee shall submit to the department a form approved by the department. The transferee shall also file a copy of the form with the entity to whom the taxpayer donated the conservation easement.

(g) A transferee of a tax credit shall purchase the credit prior to the due date imposed by this article, not including any extensions, for filing the transferee's income tax return;

(h) A tax credit held by an individual either directly or as a result of a donation by a pass-through entity, but not a tax credit held by a transferee unless used by the transferee's estate for taxes owed by the estate, shall survive the death of the individual and may be claimed or transferred by the decedent's estate. This paragraph (h) shall apply to any tax credit from a donation of a conservation easement made on or after January 1, 2000.

(i) The donor of an easement for which a tax credit is claimed or the transferor of a tax credit transferred pursuant to this subsection (7) shall be the tax matters representative in all matters with respect to the credit. The tax matters representative shall be responsible for representing and binding the transferees with respect to all issues affecting the credit, including, but not limited to, the charitable contribution deduction, the appraisal, notifications and correspondence from and with the department of revenue, audit examinations, assessments or refunds, settlement agreements, and the statute of limitations. The transferee shall be subject to the same statute of limitations with respect to the credit as the transferor of the credit.

(j) Final resolution of disputes regarding the tax credit between the department of revenue and the tax matters representative, including final determinations, compromises, payment of additional taxes or refunds due, and administrative and judicial decisions, shall be binding on transferees.

(8) The executive director of the department of revenue may promulgate rules for the implementation of this section. Such rules shall be promulgated in accordance with article 4 of title 24, C.R.S.

(9) Any taxpayer who claims a credit for the donation of a conservation easement contrary to the provisions of this section shall be liable for such deficiencies, interest, and penalties as may be specified in this article or otherwise provided by law.

(10) On or before July 1, 2008, the department of revenue shall create a report, which shall be made available to the public, on the credits claimed in the previous year in accordance with this section. For each credit claimed for a conservation easement in gross, the report shall summarize by county where the easement is located, the acres under easement, the appraised value of the easement, the donated value of the easement, and the name of any holders of the easement; except that the department shall combine such information for multiple counties where necessary to ensure that the information for no fewer than three easements is summarized for any county or combination of counties in the report. The report shall be updated annually to reflect the same information for any additional credits that have been granted since the previous report.

(11) On or before December 31, 2007, the department of revenue shall create a report, which shall be made available to the public, with as much of the information specified in paragraph (c) of subsection (3) of this section as is available to the department, summarized by county, for each tax credit claimed for a conservation easement in gross for tax years commencing on or after January 1, 2000.

Chapter 12:
Mortgage Loan Originators

An * in the left margin indicates a change in the statute, rule, or text since the last publication of the manual.

I. Introduction

In 2003, the Department of Regulatory Agencies received a request to initiate a review of the mortgage loan origination industry to determine whether regulation was appropriate. Accordingly, pursuant to § 24-34-104.1(2), C.R.S., a sunrise review was conducted and completed October 14, 2005. In summary, the review addressed Colorado's current regulatory environment with respect to mortgage transactions and the possibility for public harm.

Colorado was one of two states (the other being Alaska) that had no regulatory oversight of mortgage loan originators. The sunrise review also concluded that there was significant risk to consumers, as mortgage financing often represented their largest financial transaction. The review highlighted an inherent conflict of interest between the consumer, who seeks the lowest possible interest rate, and the mortgage loan originator, who receives compensation from higher interest rates. Ultimately, the sunrise review identified a need for regulatory oversight to ensure consumer protection. As a result, the Mortgage Broker Registration Act, House Bill 06-1161, was passed by the Colorado General Assembly in 2006.

The Mortgage Broker Registration Act provided a minimal registration program for mortgage loan originators. Registration required a completed criminal background check, a $25,000 surety bond, a completed application, and payment of the $200 application fee. Due to the wave of foreclosures and the mortgage fraud epidemic, the Colorado General Assembly passed four new mortgage broker bills in the 2007 session. These included House Bill 07-1322, Senate Bill 07-085, Senate Bill 07-216, and Senate Bill 07-203. Governor Bill Ritter, Jr. signed all four bills into law on June 1, 2007. This legislation created a significant change in Colorado's regulatory environment. House Bill 07-1322 contained measures to prevent mortgage fraud and established comprehensive definitions of prohibited conduct for mortgage loan originators. Senate Bill 07-085 prohibited mortgage loan originators from coercing or intimidating appraisers for the purpose of influencing an appraiser's independent judgment. Senate Bill 07-216 established that mortgage loan originators have a duty of good faith and fair dealing in all communications and transactions with a borrower. Finally, Senate Bill 07-203 required the development of a licensure program and the establishment of grounds for disciplinary actions.

In July of 2008, Congress passed the Housing and Economic Recovery Act of 2008. A small portion of this Act is Title V – The S.A.F.E. Mortgage Licensing Act, which may also be cited as the Secure and Fair Enforcement for Mortgage Licensing Act of 2008. In summary, this bill sets minimum national licensing standards for mortgage loan originators and requires that all mortgage loan originators be registered on the Nationwide Mortgage Licensing System and Registry. Additionally, this law requires licensure for a few new groups of individuals and loan originators , including: loan originators working for non-profit organizations; loan originators working in chattel financing related to mobile and manufactured housing; loan originators working for affiliates of depositories; and independent contractor loan processors and underwriters. The S.A.F.E. Act was essentially a mandate for states to ensure that their laws are consistent with this federal mandate. Furthermore, the S.A.F.E. Act mandates the development of the Nationwide Mortgage Licensing System and Registry. This registry will benefit Colorado, because it will be possible to track individuals across state lines. In order to adopt provisions defined in the S.A.F.E. Act, the Colorado General Assembly passed House Bill 09-1085 in May of 2009 ; it became effective August 5, 2009.

In 2009, the Federal Housing and Finance Agency established a policy decision requiring Fannie Mae and Freddie Mac to only purchase mortgage loans if they contained a unique identifier for the individual mortgage loan originator and the mortgage company. Because Colorado, at that time, was one of two states (the other being Hawaii) that did not have any oversight regarding mortgage companies, the Colorado General Assembly acted and passed House Bill 10-1141. This law became effective on August 11, 2010 and requires mortgage companies to be registered on the Nationwide Mortgage Licensing System and Registry. Furthermore, this law established some standards of conduct for mortgage companies, including: document retention; advertising standards; and a prohibition on mortgage companies hiring unlicensed mortgage loan originators. Additionally, this law transforms the Mortgage Loan Originator Program from a director-model program to a board-model program. The defined board consists of five members, three of which are to be licensed mortgage loan originators and two that are representatives of the public at large. The transition to the new Board of Mortgage Loan Originators is an important change for Colorado's Mortgage Loan Originator regulatory program.

Since the inception of the mortgage regulatory program, there have been seven laws that have been passed. Additionally, there have been close to 40 rules that have been promulgated, many of which were adopted on an emergency basis. This regulatory program has seen a consistent change in licensing requirements, standards of conduct, and prohibitions. The mission of the Department of Regulatory Agencies is consumer protection. The Colorado Division of Real Estate now has the tools to protect Colorado consumers and ensure fair competition through aggressive enforcement and responsible implementation.

II. Mortgage Loan Originator Licensing and Mortgage Company Registration Act

Colorado Revised Statutes Title 12, Article 61, Part 9

§ 12-61-901, C.R.S. Short title

This part 9 shall be known and may be cited as the "Mortgage Loan Originator Licensing and Mortgage Company Registration Act".

§ 12-61-902, C.R.S. Definitions

As used in this part 9, unless the context otherwise requires:

(1) "Affiliate" means a person who, directly or indirectly, through intermediaries controls, is controlled by, or is under the common control of another person addressed by this part 9.

* (1.2) "Affordable housing dwelling unit" means an affordable housing dwelling unit as defined in section 29-26-102, C.R.S.

(1.3) "Board" means the board of mortgage loan originators created in section 12-61-902.5.

(1.5) "Borrower" means any person who consults with or retains a mortgage loan originator in an effort to obtain or seek advice or information on obtaining or applying to obtain a residential mortgage loan for himself, herself, or persons including himself or herself, regardless of whether the person actually obtains such a loan.

* (1.7) "Community development organization" means any community housing development organization or community land trust as defined by the federal "Cranston-Gonzalez National Affordable Housing Act of 1990" or a community-based development organization as defined by the federal "Housing and Community Development Act of 1974", that is also either a private or public nonprofit organization that is exempt from taxation under section 501 (a) of the federal "Internal Revenue Code of 1986" pursuant to section 501 (c) of the federal "Internal Revenue Code of 1986", 26 U.S.C. sec. 501 (a) and 501 (c), and that receives funding from the United States department of housing and urban development, Colorado division of housing, Colorado housing and finance authority, or United States department of agriculture rural development, or through a grantee of the United States department of housing and urban development, purely for the purpose of community housing development activities.

(2) "Depository institution" has the same meaning as set forth in the "Federal Deposit Insurance Act", 12 U.S.C. sec. 1813 (c), and includes a credit union.

(3) "Director" means the director of the division of real estate.

(4) "Division" means the division of real estate.

(4.3) "Dwelling" shall have the same meaning as set forth in the federal "Truth in Lending Act", 15 U.S.C. sec. 1602 (v).

(4.5) "Federal banking agency" means the board of governors of the federal reserve system, the comptroller of the currency, the director of the office of thrift supervision, the national credit union administration, or the federal deposit insurance corporation.

* (4.6) "HUD-approved housing counseling agency" means an agency that is either a private or public nonprofit organization that is exempt from taxation under section 501 (a) of the federal "Internal Revenue Code of 1986" pursuant to section 501 (c) of the federal "Internal Revenue Code of 1986", 26 U.S.C. sec. 501 (a) and 501 (c), and approved by the United States department of housing and urban development, in accordance with the housing counseling program handbook section 7610.1 and 24 CFR 214.

(4.7) "Individual" means a natural person.

(4.9) (a) "Loan processor or underwriter" means an individual who performs clerical or support duties at the direction of, and subject to supervision by, a state-licensed loan originator or a registered loan originator.

(b) As used in this subsection (4.9), "clerical or support duties" includes duties performed after receipt of an application for a residential mortgage loan, including:

(I) The receipt, collection, distribution, and analysis of information commonly used for the processing or underwriting of a residential mortgage loan; and

(II) Communicating with a borrower to obtain the information necessary to process or underwrite a loan, to the extent that the communication does not include offering or negotiating loan rates or terms or counseling consumers about residential mortgage loan rates or terms.

(5) "Mortgage company" means a person other than an individual who, through employees or other individuals, takes residential loan applications or offers or negotiates terms of a residential mortgage loan.

(5.5) "Mortgage lender" means a lender who is in the business of making residential mortgage loans if:

(a) The lender is the payee on the promissory note evidencing the loan; and

(b) The loan proceeds are obtained by the lender from its own funds or from a line of credit made available to the lender from a bank or other entity that regularly loans money to lenders for the purpose of funding mortgage loans.

(6) (a) "Mortgage loan originator" means an individual who:

(I) Takes a residential mortgage loan application; or

(II) Offers or negotiates terms of a residential mortgage loan.

(b) "Mortgage loan originator" does not include:

(I) An individual engaged solely as a loan processor or underwriter;

(II) A person that only performs real estate brokerage or sales activities and is licensed or registered pursuant to part 1 of this article, unless the person is compensated by a mortgage lender or a mortgage loan originator;

(III) A person solely involved in extensions of credit relating to time share plans, as defined in 11 U.S.C. sec. 101 (53D);

(IV) An individual who is servicing a mortgage loan; or

(V) A person that only performs the services and activities of a dealer, as defined in section 24-32-3302, C.R.S.

(6.3) "Nationwide mortgage licensing system and registry" means a mortgage licensing system developed pursuant to the federal "Secure and Fair Enforcement for Mortgage Licensing Act of 2008", 12 U.S.C. sec. 5101 *et seq.*, to track the licensing and registration of mortgage loan originators and that is established and maintained by:

(a) The conference of state bank supervisors and the American association of residential mortgage regulators, or their successor entities; or

(b) The secretary of the United States department of housing and urban development.

(6.5) "Nontraditional mortgage product" means a mortgage product other than a thirty-year, fixed-rate mortgage.

(7) "Originate a mortgage" means to act, directly or indirectly, as a mortgage loan originator.

(7.5) "Person" means a natural person, corporation, company, limited liability company, partnership, firm, association, or other legal entity.

* (7.6) "Quasi-government agency" means an agency that is either a private or public nonprofit organization that is exempt from taxation under section 501 (a) of the federal "Internal Revenue Code of 1986" pursuant to section 501 (c) of the federal "Internal Revenue Code of 1986", 26 U.S.C. sec. 501 (a) and 501 (c), and was created to operate in accordance with article 4 of title 29, C.R.S., as a public housing authority.

(7.7) "Real estate brokerage activity" means an activity that involves offering or providing real estate brokerage services to the public, including, without limitation:

(a) Acting as a real estate agent or real estate broker for a buyer, seller, lessor, or lessee of real property;

(b) Bringing together parties interested in the sale, purchase, lease, rental, or exchange of real property;

(c) Negotiating, on behalf of any party, any portion of a contract relating to the sale, purchase, lease, rental, or exchange of real property, other than matters related to financing for the transaction;

(d) Engaging in an activity for which a person engaged in the activity is required under applicable law to be registered or licensed as a real estate agent or real estate broker; or

(e) Offering to engage in any activity, or act in any capacity related to such activity, described in this subsection (7.7).

(8) "Residential mortgage loan" means a loan that is primarily for personal, family, or household use and that is secured by a mortgage, deed of trust, or other equivalent, consensual security interest on a dwelling or residential real estate upon which is constructed or intended to be constructed a single-family dwelling or multiple-family dwelling of four or fewer units.

(9) "Residential real estate" means any real property upon which a dwelling is or will be constructed.

* (9.5) "Self-help housing organization" means a private or public nonprofit organization that is exempt from taxation under section 501 (a) of the federal "Internal Revenue Code of 1986" pursuant to section 501 (c) of the federal "Internal Revenue Code of 1986", 26 U.S.C. sec. 501 (a) and 501 (c), and that purely originates residential mortgage loans with interest rates no greater than zero percent for borrowers who have provided part of the labor to construct the dwelling securing the loan or that receives funding from the United States department of agriculture rural development section 502 mutual self-help housing program for borrowers that have provided part of the labor to construct the dwelling securing the loan.

(10) "Servicing a mortgage loan" means collecting, receiving, or obtaining the right to collect or receive payments on behalf of a mortgage lender, including payments of principal, interest, escrow amounts, and other amounts due on obligations due and owing to the mortgage lender.

(11) "State-licensed loan originator" means an individual who is:

(a) A mortgage loan originator or engages in the activities of a mortgage loan originator;

(b) Not an employee of a depository institution or a subsidiary that is:

(I) Owned and controlled by a depository institution; and

(II) Regulated by a federal banking agency;

(c) Licensed or required to be licensed pursuant to this part 9; and

(d) Registered as a state-licensed loan originator with, and maintains a unique identifier through, the nationwide mortgage licensing system and registry.

(12) "Unique identifier" means a number or other identifier assigned to a mortgage loan originator pursuant to protocols established by the nationwide mortgage licensing system and registry.

§ 12-61-902.5, C.R.S. Board of mortgage loan originators – creation – compensation – enforcement of part after board creation – immunity

(1) There is hereby created in the division a board of mortgage loan originators, consisting of five members appointed by the governor with the consent of the senate. Of the members, three shall be licensed mortgage loan originators and two shall be members of the public at large not engaged in mortgage loan origination or mortgage lending. Of the members of the board appointed for terms beginning on and after August 11, 2010, two of the members appointed as mortgage loan originators and one of the members appointed as a member of the public at large shall be appointed for terms of two years, and one of the members appointed as a mortgage loan originator and one of the members appointed as a member of the public at large shall serve for terms of four years. Thereafter, members of the board shall hold office for a term of four years. In the event of a vacancy by death, resignation, removal, or otherwise, the governor shall appoint a member to fill the unexpired term. The governor shall have the authority to remove any member for misconduct, neglect of duty, or incompetence.

* (2) (a) The board shall exercise its powers and perform its duties and functions under the department of regulatory agencies as if transferred to the department by a **type 1** transfer, as such transfer is defined in the "Administrative Organization Act of 1968", article 1 of title 24, C.R.S.

(b) Notwithstanding any other provision of this part 9, on and after the creation of the board by this section, the board shall exercise all of the rule-making, enforcement, and administrative authority of the director set forth in this part 9. The board has the authority to delegate to the director any enforcement and administrative authority under this part 9 that the board deems necessary and appropriate. If the board delegates any enforcement or administrative authority under this part 9 to the director, the director shall only be entitled to exercise such authority as specifically delegated in writing to the director by the board.

(3) Each member of the board shall receive the same compensation and reimbursement of expenses as those provided for members of boards and commissions in the division of registrations pursuant to section 24-34-102 (13), C.R.S. Payment for all per diem compensation and expenses shall be made out of annual appropriations from the mortgage loan originator licensing cash fund created in section 12-61-908.

(4) Members of the board, consultants, and expert witnesses shall be immune from suit in any civil action based upon any disciplinary proceedings or other official acts they performed in good faith pursuant to this part 9.

(5) A majority of the board shall constitute a quorum for the transaction of all business, and actions of the board shall require a vote of a majority of the members present in favor of the action taken.

(6) (a) All rules promulgated by the director prior to August 11, 2010, shall remain in full force and effect until repealed or modified by the board. The board shall have the authority to enforce any previously promulgated rules of the director under this part 9 and any rules promulgated by the board.

(b) Nothing in this section shall affect any action taken by the director prior to August 11, 2010. No person who, on or before August 11, 2010, holds a license issued under this part 9 shall be required to secure an additional license under this part 9, but shall otherwise be subject to all the provisions of this part 9. A license previously issued shall, for all purposes, be considered a license issued by the board under this part 9.

§ 12-61-903, C.R.S. License required – rules

(1) (a) On or after August 5, 2009, unless licensed by the board, an individual shall not originate a mortgage, offer to originate a mortgage, act as a mortgage loan originator, or offer to act as a mortgage loan originator. On or after December 31, 2010, unless licensed by the board and registered with the nationwide mortgage licensing system and registry as a state-licensed loan originator, an individual shall not originate or offer to originate a mortgage or act or offer to act as a mortgage loan originator.

(b) On and after January 1, 2010, a licensed mortgage loan originator shall apply for license renewal in accordance with subsection (4) of this section every calendar year as determined by the board by rule.

(c) (Deleted by amendment, L. 2009, (HB 09-1085), ch. 303, p. 1615, § 1, effective August 5, 2009.)

(1.5) An independent contractor may not engage in residential mortgage loan origination activities as a loan processor or underwriter unless the independent contractor is a state-licensed loan originator.

(2) An applicant for initial licensing as a mortgage loan originator shall submit to the board the following:

(a) A criminal history record check in compliance with subsection (5) of this section;

(b) A disclosure of all administrative discipline taken against the applicant concerning the categories listed in section 12-61-905 (1) (c); and

(c) The application fee established by the board in accordance with section 12-61-908.

(3) (a) In addition to the requirements imposed by subsection (2) of this section, on or after August 5, 2009, each individual applicant for initial licensing as a mortgage loan originator shall have satisfactorily completed a mortgage lending fundamentals course approved by the board and consisting of at least nine hours of instruction in subjects related to mortgage lending. In addition, the applicant shall have satisfactorily completed a written examination approved by the board.

(b) The board may contract with one or more independent testing services to develop, administer, and grade the examinations required by paragraph (a) of this subsection (3) and to maintain and administer licensee records. The contract may allow the testing service to recover from applicants its costs incurred in connection with these functions. The board may contract separately for these functions and may allow the costs to be collected by a single contractor for distribution to other contractors.

(c) The board may publish reports summarizing statistical information prepared by the nationwide mortgage licensing system and registry relating to mortgage loan originator examinations.

(4) An applicant for license renewal shall submit to the board the following:

(a) A disclosure of all administrative discipline taken against the applicant concerning the categories listed in section 12-61-905 (1) (c); and

(b) The renewal fee established by the board in accordance with section 12-61-908.

(5) (a) Prior to submitting an application for a license, an applicant shall submit a set of fingerprints to the Colorado bureau of investigation. Upon receipt of the applicant's fingerprints, the Colorado bureau of investigation shall use the fingerprints to conduct a state and national criminal history record check using records of the Colorado bureau of investigation and the federal bureau of investigation. All costs arising from such criminal history record check shall be borne by the applicant and shall be paid when the set of fingerprints is submitted. Upon completion of the criminal history record check, the bureau shall forward the results to the board. The board may acquire a name-based criminal history record check for an applicant who has twice submitted to a fingerprint-based criminal history record check and whose fingerprints are unclassifiable.

(b) If the board determines that the criminal background check provided by the nationwide mortgage licensing system and registry is a sufficient method of screening license applicants to protect Colorado consumers, the board may, by rule, authorize the use of that criminal background check instead of the criminal history record check otherwise required by this subsection (5).

(5.5) (a) On and after January 1, 2010, in connection with an application for a license as a mortgage loan originator, the applicant shall furnish information concerning the applicant's identity to the nationwide mortgage licensing system and registry. The applicant shall furnish, at a minimum, the following:

(I) Fingerprints for submission to the federal bureau of investigation and any government agency or entity authorized to receive fingerprints for a state, national, or international criminal history record check; and

(II) Personal history and experience, in a form prescribed by the nationwide mortgage licensing system and registry, including submission of authorization for the nationwide mortgage licensing system and registry to obtain:

(A) An independent credit report from the consumer reporting agency described in the federal "Fair Credit Reporting Act", 15 U.S.C. sec. 1681a (p); and

(B) Information related to any administrative, civil, or criminal findings by a government jurisdiction.

(b) An applicant is responsible for paying all costs arising from a criminal history record check and shall pay such costs upon submission of fingerprints.

(c) The board may acquire a name-based criminal history record check for an applicant who has twice submitted to a fingerprint-based criminal history record check and whose fingerprints are unclassifiable.

(5.7) Any individual who obtains a license pursuant to this part 9 prior to January 1, 2010, shall furnish at least the following information concerning the individual's identity to the nationwide mortgage licensing system and registry:

(a) Fingerprints for submission to the federal bureau of investigation and any government agency or entity authorized to receive fingerprints for a state, national, or international criminal history record check; and

(b) Personal history and experience in a form prescribed by the nationwide mortgage licensing system and registry, including submission of authorization for the nationwide mortgage licensing system and registry to obtain:

(I) An independent credit report from the consumer reporting agency described in the federal "Fair Credit Reporting Act", 15 U.S.C. sec. 1681a (p); and

(II) Information related to any administrative, civil, or criminal findings by a government jurisdiction.

(6) Before granting a license to an applicant, the board shall require the applicant to post a bond as required by section 12-61-907.

(7) The board shall issue or deny a license within sixty days after:

(a) The applicant has submitted the requisite information to the board and the nationwide mortgage licensing system and registry, including, but not limited to, the completed application, the application fee, and proof that the applicant has posted a surety bond and obtained errors and omissions insurance; and

(b) The board receives the completed criminal history record check and all other relevant information or documents necessary to reasonably ascertain facts underlying the applicant's criminal history.

(8) (a) The board may require, as a condition of license renewal on or after January 1, 2009, continuing education of licensees for the purpose of enhancing the professional competence and professional responsibility of all licensees.

(b) Continuing professional education requirements shall be determined by the board by rule; except that licensees shall be required to complete at least eight credit hours of continuing education each year. The board may contract with one or more independent service providers to develop, review, or approve continuing education courses. The contract may allow the independent service provider to recover from licensees its costs incurred in connection with these functions. The board may contract separately for these functions and may allow the costs to be collected by a single contractor for distribution to other contractors.

(9) (a) The board may require contractors and prospective contractors for services under subsections (3) and (8) of this section to submit, for the board's review and approval, information regarding the contents and materials of proposed courses and other documentation reasonably necessary to further the purposes of this section.

(b) The board may set fees for the initial and continuing review of courses for which credit hours will be granted. The initial filing fee for review of materials shall not exceed five hundred dollars, and the fee for continued review shall not exceed two hundred fifty dollars per year per course offered.

(10) The board may adopt reasonable rules to implement this section. The board may adopt rules necessary to implement provisions required in the federal "Secure and Fair Enforcement for Mortgage Licensing Act of 2008", 12 U.S.C. sec. 5101 *et seq.*, and for participation in the nationwide mortgage licensing system and registry.

(11) In order to fulfill the purposes of this part 9, the board may establish relationships or contracts with the nationwide mortgage licensing system and registry or other entities designated by the nationwide mortgage licensing system and registry to collect and maintain records and process transaction fees or other fees related to licensees or other persons subject to this part 9.

(12) The board may use the nationwide mortgage licensing system and registry as a channeling agent for requesting information from or distributing information to the department of justice, a government agency, or any other source.

* ### *§ 12-61-903.1, C.R.S. Registration required – rules*

(1) On or after January 1, 2011, each mortgage company shall register with the nationwide mortgage licensing system and registry, unless exempted by rule by the board, and shall renew such registration each calendar year based on the following criteria:

(a) (I) The mortgage company is legally operating in the state of Colorado in accordance with standards determined and administered by the Colorado secretary of state; and

(II) The mortgage company is not legally barred from operating in Colorado.

(b) Sole proprietors, general partnerships, and other mortgage companies not otherwise required to register with the secretary of state shall register using a trade name.

§ 12-61-903.3, C.R.S. License or registration inactivation

(1) The board may inactivate a state license or a registration with the nationwide mortgage licensing system and registry when a licensee has failed to:

(a) Comply with the surety bond requirements of sections 12-61-903 (6) and 12-61-907;

(b) Comply with the errors and omissions insurance requirement in section 12-61-903.5 or any rule of the board that directly or indirectly addresses errors and omissions insurance requirements;

(c) Maintain current contact information, surety bond information, or errors and omissions insurance information as required by this part 9 or by any rule of the board that directly or indirectly addresses such requirements;

(d) Respond to an investigation or examination;

(e) Comply with any of the education or testing requirements set forth in this part 9 or in any rule of the board that directly or indirectly addresses education or testing requirements; or

(f) Register with and provide all required information to the nationwide mortgage licensing system and registry.

§ 12-61-903.5, C.R.S. Errors and omissions insurance – duties of the board – certificate of coverage – when required – group plan made available – effect

(1) (a) Every licensee under this part 9 shall maintain errors and omissions insurance to cover all activities contemplated under this part 9.

(b) The requirements of this subsection (1) shall not apply to:

(I) A mortgage loan originator with an inactive license or registration; or

(II) An attorney licensed as a loan originator who maintains a policy of professional malpractice insurance that provides coverage for errors and omissions for activities of the attorney licensee regulated by this part 9.

(2) The board shall determine the terms and conditions of coverage required under this section, including the minimum limits of coverage, the permissible deductible, and permissible exemptions. Each licensee subject to the requirements of this section shall maintain evidence of coverage, in a manner satisfactory to the board, demonstrating continuing compliance with the required terms.

§ 12-61-903.7, C.R.S. License renewal

(1) In order for a licensed mortgage loan originator to renew a license issued pursuant to this part 9, the mortgage loan originator shall:

(a) Continue to meet the minimum standards for issuance of a license pursuant to this part 9;

(b) Satisfy the annual continuing education requirements set forth in section 12-61-903 (8) and in rules adopted by the board; and

(c) Pay applicable license renewal fees.

(2) If a licensed mortgage loan originator fails to satisfy the requirements of subsection (1) of this section for license renewal, the mortgage loan originator's license shall expire. The board shall adopt rules to establish procedures for the reinstatement of an expired license consistent with the standards established by the nationwide mortgage licensing system and registry.

§ 12-61-904, C.R.S. Exemptions

* (1) Except as otherwise provided in section 12-61-911, this part 9 does not apply to the following, unless otherwise determined by the federal bureau of consumer financial protection or the United States department of housing and urban development:

(a) (Deleted by amendment, L. 2010, (HB 10-1141), ch. 280, p. 1289, § 10, effective August 11, 2010.)

* (b) With respect to a residential mortgage loan, a person, estate, or trust that provides mortgage financing for the sale of no more than three properties in any twelve-month period to purchasers of such properties, each of which is owned by such person, estate, or trust and serves as security for the loan;

(c) A bank and a savings association as these terms are defined in the "Federal Deposit Insurance Act", a subsidiary that is owned and controlled by a bank or savings association, employees of a bank or savings association, employees of a subsidiary that is owned and controlled by a bank or savings association, credit unions, and employees of credit unions;

(d) An attorney who renders services in the course of practice, who is licensed in Colorado, and who is not primarily engaged in the business of negotiating residential mortgage loans;

(e) (Deleted by amendment, L. 2007, p. 1716, § 2, effective June 1, 2007, and p. 1734, § 6, effective January 1, 2008.)

(f) A person who:

(I) Funds a residential mortgage loan that has been originated and processed by a licensed person or by an exempt person;

(II) Does not solicit borrowers in Colorado for the purpose of making residential mortgage loans; and

(III) Does not participate in the negotiation of residential mortgage loans with the borrower, except for setting the terms under which a person may buy or fund a residential mortgage loan originated by a licensed or exempt person.

(g) A loan processor or underwriter who is not an independent contractor and who does not represent to the public that the individual can or will perform any activities of a mortgage loan originator. As used in this paragraph (g), "represent to the public" means communicating, through advertising or other means of communicating or providing information, including the use of business cards, stationery, brochures, signs, rate lists, or other promotional items, that the individual is able to provide a particular service or activity for a consumer.

* (h) To the extent that it is providing programs benefitting affordable housing dwelling units, an agency of the federal government, the Colorado government, or any of Colorado's political subdivisions or employees of an agency of the federal government, of the Colorado government, or of any of Colorado's political subdivisions;

* (i) Quasi-government agencies, HUD-approved housing counseling agencies, or employees of quasi-government agencies or HUD-approved housing counseling agencies;

* (j) Community development organizations or employees of community development organizations;

* (k) Self-help housing organizations or employees of self-help housing organizations or volunteers acting as an agent of self-help housing organizations.

(2) The exemptions in subsection (1) of this section shall not apply to persons acting beyond the scope of such exemptions.

* (3) The board may adopt reasonable rules modifying the exemptions in this section in accordance with rules adopted by the federal bureau of consumer financial protection or the United States department of housing and urban development.

§ 12-61-904.5, C.R.S. Originator's relationship to borrower – rules

(1) A mortgage loan originator shall have a duty of good faith and fair dealing in all communications and transactions with a borrower. Such duty includes, but is not limited to:

(a) The duty to not recommend or induce the borrower to enter into a transaction that does not have a reasonable, tangible net benefit to the borrower, considering all of the circumstances, including the terms of a loan, the cost of a loan, and the borrower's circumstances;

(b) The duty to make a reasonable inquiry concerning the borrower's current and prospective income, existing debts and other obligations, and any other relevant information and, after making such inquiry, to make his or her best efforts to recommend, broker, or originate a residential mortgage loan that takes into consideration the information submitted by the borrower, but the mortgage loan originator shall not be deemed to violate this section if the borrower conceals or misrepresents relevant information; and

(c) The duty not to commit any acts, practices, or omissions in violation of section 38-40-105, C.R.S.

(2) For purposes of implementing subsection (1) of this section, the board may adopt rules defining what constitutes a reasonable, tangible net benefit to the borrower.

(3) A violation of this section constitutes a deceptive trade practice under the "Colorado Consumer Protection Act", article 1 of title 6, C.R.S.

§ 12-61-905, C.R.S. Powers and duties of the board

(1) The board may deny an application for a license, refuse to renew, or revoke the license of an applicant or licensee who has:

(a) Filed an application with the board containing material misstatements of fact or omitted any disclosure required by this part 9;

(b) Within the last five years, been convicted of or pled guilty or nolo contendere to a crime involving fraud, deceit, material misrepresentation, theft, or the breach of a fiduciary duty, except as otherwise set forth in this part 9;

(c) Except as otherwise set forth in this part 9, within the last five years, had a license, registration, or certification issued by Colorado or another state revoked or suspended for fraud, deceit, material misrepresentation, theft, or the breach of a fiduciary duty, and such discipline denied the person authorization to practice as:

(I) A mortgage broker or a mortgage loan originator;
(II) A real estate broker, as defined by section 12-61-101 (2);
(III) A real estate salesperson;
(IV) A real estate appraiser, as defined by section 12-61-702 (5);
(V) An insurance producer, as defined by section 10-2-103 (6), C.R.S.;
(VI) An attorney;
(VII) A securities broker-dealer, as defined by section 11-51-201 (2), C.R.S.;
(VIII) A securities sales representative, as defined by section 11-51-201 (14), C.R.S.;
(IX) An investment advisor, as defined by section 11-51-201 (9.5), C.R.S.; or
(X) An investment advisor representative, as defined by section 11-51-201 (9.6), C.R.S.;

(d) Been enjoined within the immediately preceding five years under the laws of this or any other state or of the United States from engaging in deceptive conduct relating to the brokering of or originating a mortgage loan;

(e) Been found to have violated the provisions of section 12-61-910.2;

(f) Been found to have violated the provisions of section 12-61-911;

(g) Had a mortgage loan originator license or similar license revoked in any jurisdiction; except that a revocation that was subsequently formally nullified shall not be deemed a revocation for purposes of this section;

(h) At any time preceding the date of application for a license or registration, been convicted of, or pled guilty or nolo contendere to, a felony in a domestic, foreign, or military court if the felony involved an act of fraud, dishonesty, breach of trust, or money laundering; except that, if the individual obtains a pardon of the conviction, the individual shall not be deemed convicted for purposes of this paragraph (h);

(i) Been convicted of, or pled guilty or nolo contendere to, a felony within the seven years immediately preceding the date of application for a license or registration;

(j) Not demonstrated financial responsibility, character, and general fitness to command the confidence of the community and to warrant a determination that the individual will operate honestly, fairly, and efficiently, consistent with the purposes of this part 9;

(k) Not completed the prelicense education requirements set forth in section 12-61-903 and any applicable rules of the board; or

(l) Not passed a written examination that meets the requirements set forth in section 12-61-903 and any applicable rules of the board.

(2) The board may investigate the activities of a licensee or other person that present grounds for disciplinary action under this part 9 or that violate section 12-61-910 (1).

(3) (a) If the board has reasonable grounds to believe that a mortgage loan originator is no longer qualified under subsection (1) of this section, the board may summarily suspend the mortgage loan originator's license pending a hearing to revoke the license. A summary suspension shall conform to article 4 of title 24, C.R.S.

(b) The board shall suspend the license of a mortgage loan originator who fails to maintain the bond required by section 12-61-907 until the licensee complies with such section.

(4) The board or an administrative law judge appointed pursuant to part 10 of article 30 of title 24, C.R.S., shall conduct disciplinary hearings concerning mortgage loan originators and mortgage companies. Such hearings shall conform to article 4 of title 24, C.R.S.

(5) (a) Except as provided in paragraph (b) of this subsection (5), an individual whose license has been revoked shall not be eligible for licensure for two years after the effective date of the revocation.

(b) If the board or an administrative law judge determines that an application contained a misstatement of fact or omitted a required disclosure due to an unintentional error, the board shall allow the applicant to correct the application. Upon receipt of the corrected and completed application, the board or administrative law judge shall not bar the applicant from being licensed on the basis of the unintentional misstatement or omission.

(6) (a) The board or an administrative law judge may administer oaths, take affirmations of witnesses, and issue subpoenas to compel the attendance of witnesses and the production of all relevant papers, books, records, documentary evidence, and materials in any hearing or investigation conducted by the board or an administrative law judge. The board may request any information relevant to the investigation, including, but not limited to, independent credit reports obtained from a consumer reporting agency described in the federal "Fair Credit Reporting Act", 15 U.S.C. sec. 1681a (p).

(b) Upon failure of a witness to comply with a subpoena or process, the district court of the county in which the subpoenaed witness resides or conducts business may issue an order requiring the witness to appear before the board or administrative law judge; produce the relevant papers, books, records, documentary evidence, testimony, or materials in question; or both. Failure to obey the order of the court may be punished as a contempt of court. The board or an administrative law judge may apply for such order.

(c) The licensee or individual who, after an investigation under this part 9, is found to be in violation of a provision of this part 9 shall be responsible for paying all reasonable and necessary costs of the division arising from subpoenas or requests issued pursuant to this subsection (6), including court costs for an action brought pursuant to paragraph (b) of this subsection (6).

(7) (a) If the board has reasonable cause to believe that an individual is violating this part 9, including but not limited to section 12-61-910 (1), the board may enter an order requiring the individual to cease and desist such violations.

(b) The board, upon its own motion, may, and, upon the complaint in writing of any person, shall, investigate the activities of any licensee or any individual who assumes to act in such capacity within the state. In addition to any other penalty that may be imposed pursuant to this part 9, any individual violating any provision of this part 9 or any rules promulgated pursuant to this article may be fined upon a finding of misconduct by the board as follows:

(I) In the first administrative proceeding, a fine not in excess of one thousand dollars per act or occurrence;

(II) In a second or subsequent administrative proceeding, a fine not less than one thousand dollars nor in excess of two thousand dollars per act or occurrence.

(c) All fines collected pursuant to this subsection (7) shall be transferred to the state treasurer, who shall credit such moneys to the mortgage company and loan originator licensing cash fund created in section 12-61-908.

(8) The board shall keep records of the individuals licensed as mortgage loan originators and of disciplinary proceedings. The records kept by the board shall be open to public inspection in a reasonable time and manner determined by the board.

(9) (a) The board shall maintain a system, which may include, without limitation, a hotline or web site, that gives consumers a reasonably easy method for making complaints about a mortgage loan originator.

(b) (Deleted by amendment, L. 2009, (HB 09-1085), ch. 303, p. 1621, § 1, effective August 5, 2009.)

(10) The board shall promulgate rules to allow licensed mortgage loan originators to hire unlicensed mortgage loan originators under temporary licenses. If an unlicensed mortgage loan originator has initiated the application process for a license, he or she shall be assigned a temporary license for a reasonable period until a license is approved or denied. The licensed mortgage loan originator who employs an unlicensed mortgage loan originator shall be held responsible under all applicable provisions of law, including without limitation this part 9 and section 38-40-105, C.R.S., for the actions of the unlicensed mortgage loan originator to whom a temporary license has been assigned under this subsection (10).

* ***§ 12-61-905.1, C.R.S. Powers and duties of the board over mortgage companies – fines – rules***

(1) With respect to mortgage companies, the board may deny an application for registration; refuse to renew, suspend, or revoke the registration; enter cease-and-desist orders; and impose fines as set forth in this section as follows:

(a) If the board has reasonable cause to believe a person is acting without a license or registration;

(b) If the mortgage company fails to maintain possession, for future use or inspection by an authorized representative of the board, for a period of four years, of the documents or records prescribed by the rules of the board or to produce such documents or records upon reasonable request by the board or by an authorized representative of the board;

(c) If the mortgage company employs or acts through individuals subject to its control who are unlicensed at the time of hire and not in the process of becoming licensed, who are required to be licensed pursuant to this part 9, or if the mortgage company, after notice, continues to employ or act through individuals subject to its control whose required licenses are not valid; or

(d) If the mortgage company directs, makes, or causes to be made, in any manner, a false or deceptive statement or representation with regard to the rates, points, or other financing terms or conditions for a residential mortgage loan, engages in bait and switch advertising as that term is used in section 6-1-105 (1) (n), C.R.S., or violates any rule of the board that directly or indirectly addresses advertising requirements.

(2) (a) The board upon its own motion or upon the complaint in writing of any person may investigate the activities of any registered mortgage company or any mortgage company that is acting in a capacity that requires registration pursuant to this part 9.

(b) The board may fine a mortgage company that has violated this section or any rules promulgated pursuant to this section as follows:

(I) In the first administrative proceeding, a fine not in excess of one thousand dollars per act or occurrence;

(II) In a second or subsequent administrative proceeding, a fine not in excess of two thousand dollars per act or occurrence.

(c) All fines collected pursuant to this section shall be transmitted to the state treasurer, who shall credit such moneys to the mortgage company and loan originator licensing cash fund created in section 12-61-908.

(3) The board may adopt reasonable rules for implementing this section.

(4) Nothing in this section automatically imputes a violation to the mortgage company if a licensed agent or employee, or an individual agent or employee who is required to be licensed, violates any other provision of this part 9.

§ 12-61-905.5, C.R.S. Disciplinary actions – grounds – procedures – rules

(1) The board, upon its own motion or upon the complaint in writing of any person, may investigate the activities of any mortgage loan originator. The board has the power to impose an administrative fine in accordance with section 12-61-905, deny a license, censure a licensee, place the licensee on probation and set the terms of probation, order restitution, order the payment of actual damages, or suspend or revoke a license when the board finds that the licensee or applicant has performed, is performing, or is attempting to perform any of the following acts:

(a) Knowingly making any misrepresentation or knowingly making use of any false or misleading advertising;

(b) Making any promise that influences, persuades, or induces another person to detrimentally rely on such promise when the licensee could not or did not intend to keep such promise;

(c) Knowingly misrepresenting or making false promises through agents, salespersons, advertising, or otherwise;

(d) Violating any provision of the "Colorado Consumer Protection Act", article 1 of title 6, C.R.S., and, if the licensee has been assessed a civil or criminal penalty or been subject to an injunction under said act, the board shall revoke the licensee's license;

(e) Acting for more than one party in a transaction without disclosing any actual or potential conflict of interest or without disclosing to all parties any fiduciary obligation or other legal obligation of the mortgage loan originator to any party;

(f) Representing or attempting to represent a mortgage loan originator other than the licensee's principal or employer without the express knowledge and consent of that principal or employer;

(g) In the case of a licensee in the employ of another mortgage loan originator, failing to place, as soon after receipt as is practicably possible, in the custody of that licensed mortgage loan originator-employer any deposit money or other money or fund entrusted to the employee by any person dealing with the employee as the representative of that licensed mortgage loan originator-employer;

(h) Failing to account for or to remit, within a reasonable time, any moneys coming into his or her possession that belong to others, whether acting as a mortgage loan originator, real estate broker, salesperson, or otherwise, and failing to keep records relative to said moneys, which records shall contain such information as may be prescribed by the rules of the board relative thereto and shall be subject to audit by the board;

(i) Converting funds of others, diverting funds of others without proper authorization, commingling funds of others with the licensee's own funds, or failing to keep such funds of others in an escrow or a trustee account with a bank or recognized depository in this state, which account may be any type of checking, demand, passbook, or statement account insured by an agency of the United States government, and to keep records relative to the deposit that contain such information as may be prescribed by the rules of the board relative thereto, which records shall be subject to audit by the board;

(j) Failing to provide the parties to a residential mortgage loan transaction with such information as may be prescribed by the rules of the board;

(k) Unless an employee of a duly registered mortgage company, failing to maintain possession, for future use or inspection by an authorized representative of the board, for a period of four years, of the documents or records prescribed by the rules of the board or to produce such documents or records upon reasonable request by the board or by an authorized representative of the board;

(l) Paying a commission or valuable consideration for performing any of the functions of a mortgage loan originator, as described in this part 9, to any person who is not licensed under this part 9 or is not registered in compliance with the federal "Secure and Fair Enforcement for Mortgage Licensing Act of 2008", 12 U.S.C. sec. 5101 *et seq*.;

(m) Disregarding or violating any provision of this part 9 or any rule adopted by the board pursuant to this part 9; violating any lawful orders of the board; or aiding and abetting a violation of any rule, order of the board, or provision of this part 9;

(n) Conviction of, entering a plea of guilty to, or entering a plea of nolo contendere to any crime in article 3 of title 18, C.R.S., in parts 1 to 4 of article 4 of title 18, C.R.S., in article 5 of title 18, C.R.S., in part 3 of article 8 of title 18, C.R.S., in article 15 of title 18, C.R.S., in article 17 of title 18, C.R.S., or any other like crime under Colorado law, federal law, or the laws of other states. A certified copy of the judgment of a court of competent jurisdiction of such conviction or other official record indicating that such plea was entered shall be conclusive evidence of such conviction or plea in any hearing under this part 9.

(o) Violating or aiding and abetting in the violation of the Colorado or federal fair housing laws;

(p) Failing to immediately notify the board in writing of a conviction, plea, or violation pursuant to paragraph (n) or (o) of this subsection (1);

(q) Having demonstrated unworthiness or incompetency to act as a mortgage loan originator by conducting business in such a manner as to endanger the interest of the public;

(r) (Deleted by amendment, L. 2009, (HB 09-1085), ch. 303, p. 1625, § 1, effective August 5, 2009.)

(s) Procuring, or attempting to procure, a mortgage loan originator's license or renewing, reinstating, or reactivating, or attempting to renew, reinstate, or reactivate, a mortgage loan originator's license by fraud, misrepresentation, or deceit or by making a material misstatement of fact in an application for such license;

(t) Claiming, arranging for, or taking any secret or undisclosed amount of compensation, commission, or profit or failing to reveal to the licensee's principal or employer the full amount of such licensee's compensation, commission, or profit in connection with any acts for which a license is required under this part 9;

(u) Exercising an option to purchase in any agreement authorizing or employing such licensee to sell, buy, or exchange real estate for compensation or commission except when such licensee, prior to or coincident with election to exercise such option to purchase, reveals in writing to the licensee's principal or employer the full amount of the licensee's profit and obtains the written consent of such principal or employer approving the amount of such profit;

(v) Fraud, misrepresentation, deceit, or conversion of trust funds that results in the payment of any claim pursuant to this part 9 or that results in the entry of a civil judgment for damages;

(w) Any other conduct, whether of the same or a different character than specified in this subsection (1), that evinces a lack of good faith and fair dealing;

(x) Having had a mortgage loan originator's license suspended or revoked in any jurisdiction or having had any disciplinary action taken against the mortgage loan originator in any other jurisdiction. A certified copy of the order of disciplinary action shall be prima facie evidence of such disciplinary action.

(2) (Deleted by amendment, L. 2009, (HB 09-1085), ch. 303, p. 1625, § 1, effective August 5, 2009.)

(3) Upon request of the board, when any mortgage loan originator is a party to any suit or proceeding, either civil or criminal, arising out of any transaction involving a residential mortgage loan and the mortgage loan originator participated in the transaction in his or her capacity as a licensed mortgage loan originator, the mortgage loan originator shall supply to the board a copy of the complaint, indictment, information, or other initiating pleading and the answer filed, if any, and advise the board of the disposition of the case and of the nature and amount of any judgment, verdict, finding, or sentence that may be made, entered, or imposed therein.

(4) This part 9 shall not be construed to relieve any person from civil liability or criminal prosecution under the laws of this state.

(5) Complaints of record in the office of the board and the results of staff investigations shall be closed to public inspection during the investigatory period and until dismissed or until notice of hearing and charges are served on a licensee, except as provided by court order. Complaints of record that are dismissed by the board and the results of investigation of such complaints shall be closed to public inspection, except as provided by court order. The board's records shall be subject to sections 24-72-203 and 24-72-204, C.R.S., regarding public records and confidentiality.

(6) When a complaint or an investigation discloses an instance of misconduct that, in the opinion of the board, does not warrant formal action by the board but that should not be dismissed as being without merit, the board may send a letter of admonition by certified mail, return receipt requested, to the licensee against whom a complaint was made and a copy of the letter of admonition to the person making the complaint, but the letter shall advise the licensee that the licensee has the right to request in writing, within twenty days after proven receipt, that formal disciplinary proceedings be initiated to adjudicate the propriety of the conduct upon which the letter of admonition is based. If such request is timely made, the letter of admonition shall be deemed vacated, and the matter shall be processed by means of formal disciplinary proceedings.

(7) All administrative fines collected pursuant to this section shall be transmitted to the state treasurer, who shall credit the same to the mortgage company and loan originator licensing cash fund created in section 12-61-908.

(8) (a) The board shall not consider an application for licensure from an individual whose license has been revoked until two years after the date of revocation.

(b) If an individual's license was suspended or revoked due to conduct that resulted in financial loss to another person, no new license shall be granted, nor shall a suspended license be reinstated, until full restitution has been made to the person suffering such financial loss. The amount of restitution shall include interest, reasonable attorney fees, and costs of any suit or other proceeding undertaken in an effort to recover the loss.

(9) When the board or the division becomes aware of facts or circumstances that fall within the jurisdiction of a criminal justice or other law enforcement authority upon investigation of the activities of a licensee, the board or division shall, in addition to the exercise of its authority under this part 9, refer and transmit such information, which may include originals or copies of documents and materials, to one or more criminal justice or other law enforcement authorities for investigation and prosecution as authorized by law.

§ 12-61-905.6, C.R.S. Hearing – administrative law judge – review – rules

(1) Except as otherwise provided in this section, all proceedings before the board with respect to disciplinary actions and denial of licensure under this part 9, at the discretion of the board, may be conducted by an authorized representative of the board or an administrative law judge pursuant to sections 24-4-104 and 24-4-105, C.R.S.

(2) Proceedings shall be held in the county where the board has its office or in such other place as the board may designate. If the licensee is employed by another licensed mortgage loan originator or by a real estate broker, the board shall also notify the licensee's employer by mailing, by first-class mail, a copy of the written notice required under section 24-4-104 (3), C.R.S., to the employer's last-known business address.

(3) The board, an authorized representative of the board, or an administrative law judge shall conduct all hearings for denying, suspending, or revoking a license or certificate on behalf of the board, subject to appropriations made to the department of personnel. Each administrative law judge shall be appointed pursuant to part 10 of article 30 of title 24, C.R.S. The administrative law judge shall conduct the hearing in accordance with sections 24-4-104 and 24-4-105, C.R.S. No license shall be denied, suspended, or revoked until the board has made its decision.

(4) The decision of the board in any disciplinary action or denial of licensure under this section is subject to judicial review by the court of appeals. In order to effectuate the purposes of this part 9, the board has the power to promulgate rules pursuant to article 4 of title 24, C.R.S.

(5) In a judicial review proceeding, the court may stay the execution or effect of any final order of the board; but a hearing shall be held affording the parties an opportunity to be heard for the purpose of determining whether the public health, safety, and welfare would be endangered by staying the board's order. If the court determines that the order should be stayed, it shall also determine at the hearing the amount of the bond and adequacy of the surety, which bond shall be conditioned upon the faithful performance by such petitioner of all obligations as a mortgage loan originator and upon the prompt payment of all damages arising from or caused by the delay in the taking effect of or enforcement of the order complained of and for all costs that may be assessed or required to be paid in connection with such proceedings.

(6) In any hearing conducted by the board or an authorized representative of the board in which there is a possibility of the denial, suspension, or revocation of a license because of the conviction of a felony or of a crime involving moral turpitude, the board or its authorized representative shall be governed by section 24-5-101, C.R.S.

§ 12-61-905.7, C.R.S. Subpoena – misdemeanor

(1) The board or the administrative law judge appointed for hearings may issue subpoenas, as described in section 12-61-905 (6), which shall be served in the same manner as subpoenas issued by district courts and shall be issued without discrimination between public or private parties requiring the attendance of witnesses or the production of documents at hearings.

(2) Any person who willfully fails or neglects to appear and testify or to produce books, papers, or records required by subpoena, duly served upon him or her in any matter conducted under this part 9, is guilty of a misdemeanor and, upon conviction thereof, shall be punished by a fine of one hundred dollars, or imprisonment in the county jail for not more than thirty days for each such offense, or by both such fine and imprisonment. Each day such person so refuses or neglects constitutes a separate offense.

§ 12-61-906, C.R.S. Immunity

A person participating in good faith in the filing of a complaint or report or participating in an investigation or hearing before the board or an administrative law judge pursuant to this part 9 shall be immune from any liability, civil or criminal, that otherwise might result by reason of such action.

§ 12-61-907, C.R.S. Bond required

(1) Before receiving a license, an applicant shall post with the board a surety bond in the amount of twenty-five thousand dollars or such other amount as may be prescribed by the board by rule. A licensed mortgage loan originator shall maintain the required bond at all times.

(2) The surety shall not be required to pay a person making a claim upon the bond until a final determination of fraud, forgery, criminal impersonation, or fraudulent representation has been made by a court with jurisdiction.

(3) The surety bond shall require the surety to provide notice to the board within thirty days if payment is made from the surety bond or if the bond is cancelled.

§ 12-61-908, C.R.S. Fees – cash fund – created

(1) The board may set the fees for issuance and renewal of licenses and registrations under this part 9. The fees shall be set in amounts that offset the direct and indirect costs of implementing this part 9 and section 38-40-105, C.R.S. The moneys collected pursuant to this section shall be transferred to the state treasurer, who shall credit them to the mortgage company and loan originator licensing cash fund.

(2) There is hereby created in the state treasury the mortgage company and loan originator licensing cash fund. Moneys in the fund shall be spent only to implement this part 9 and section 38-40-105, C.R.S., and shall not revert to the general fund at the end of the fiscal year. The fund shall be subject to annual appropriation by the general assembly.

(3) For the 2009-10 fiscal year, the division is authorized to expend up to one hundred twelve thousand dollars or such other amount as may be appropriated by the general assembly from the mortgage company and loan originator licensing cash fund for purposes of paying the development costs assessed by the conference of state bank supervisors, or its successor organization, for participating in the nationwide mortgage licensing system and registry. However, the board shall use its discretion in determining whether expenditure of these moneys is necessary for compliance with the federal "Secure and Fair Enforcement for Mortgage Licensing Act of 2008" or participation in the nationwide mortgage licensing system and registry.

§ 12-61-909, C.R.S. Attorney general – district attorney – jurisdiction

The attorney general shall have concurrent jurisdiction with the district attorneys of this state to investigate and prosecute allegations of criminal violations of this part 9.

§ 12-61-910, C.R.S. Violations – injunctions

(1) (a) Any individual violating this part 9 by acting as a mortgage loan originator in this state without having obtained a license or by acting as a mortgage loan originator after that individual's license has been revoked or during any period for which said license may have been suspended is guilty of a class 1 misdemeanor and shall be punished as provided in section 18-1.3-501, C.R.S.; except that, if the violator is not a natural person, the violator shall be punished by a fine of not more than five thousand dollars.

(b) Each residential mortgage loan negotiated or offered to be negotiated by an unlicensed person shall be a separate violation of this subsection (1).

(2) (Deleted by amendment, L. 2007, p. 1742, § 11, effective January 1, 2008.)

(3) The board may request that an action be brought in the name of the people of the state of Colorado by the attorney general or the district attorney of the district in which the violation is alleged to have occurred to enjoin a person from engaging in or continuing the violation or from doing any act that furthers the violation. In such an action, an order or judgment may be entered awarding such preliminary or final injunction as is deemed proper by the court. The notice, hearing, or duration of an injunction or restraining order shall be made in accordance with the Colorado rules of civil procedure.

(4) A violation of this part 9 shall not affect the validity or enforceability of any mortgage.

§ 12-61-910.2, C.R.S. Prohibited conduct – influencing a real estate appraisal

(1) A mortgage loan originator shall not, directly or indirectly, compensate, coerce, or intimidate an appraiser, or attempt, directly or indirectly, to compensate, coerce, or intimidate an appraiser, for the purpose of influencing the independent judgment of the appraiser with respect to the value of a dwelling offered as security for repayment of a residential mortgage loan. This prohibition shall not be construed as prohibiting a mortgage loan originator from requesting an appraiser to:

(a) Consider additional, appropriate property information;

(b) Provide further detail, substantiation, or explanation for the appraiser's value conclusion; or

(c) Correct errors in the appraisal report.

§ 12-61-910.3, C.R.S. Rule-making authority

The board has the authority to promulgate rules as necessary to enable the board to carry out the board's duties under this part 9.

§ 12-61-910.4, C.R.S. Nontraditional mortgage products – consumer protections – rules – incorporation of federal interagency guidance

The board shall adopt rules governing the marketing of nontraditional mortgage products by mortgage loan originators. In adopting such rules, the board shall incorporate appropriate provisions of the final "Interagency Guidance on Nontraditional Mortgage Product Risks" released on September 29, 2006, by the office of the comptroller of the currency and the office of thrift supervision in the federal department of the treasury, the board of governors of the federal reserve system, the federal deposit insurance corporation, and the national credit union administration, as such publication may be amended.

§ 12-61-911, C.R.S. Prohibited conduct – fraud – misrepresentation – conflict of interest – rules

(1) A mortgage loan originator, including a mortgage loan originator otherwise exempted from this part 9 by section 12-61-904 (1) (b), shall not:

(a) Directly or indirectly employ any scheme, device, or artifice to defraud or mislead borrowers or lenders or to defraud any person;

(b) Engage in any unfair or deceptive practice toward any person;

(c) Obtain property by fraud or misrepresentation;

(d) Solicit or enter into a contract with a borrower that provides in substance that the mortgage loan originator may earn a fee or commission through the mortgage loan originator's "best efforts" to obtain a loan even though no loan is actually obtained for the borrower;

(e) Solicit, advertise, or enter into a contract for specific interest rates, points, or other financing terms unless the terms are actually available at the time of soliciting, advertising, or contracting from a lender with whom the mortgage loan originator maintains a written correspondent or loan agreement under section 12-61-913;

(f) Fail to make a disclosure to a loan applicant or a noninstitutional investor as required by section 12-61-914 and any other applicable state or federal law;

(g) Make, in any manner, any false or deceptive statement or representation with regard to the rates, points, or other financing terms or conditions for a residential mortgage loan or engage in "bait and switch" advertising;

(h) Negligently make any false statement or knowingly and willfully make any omission of material fact in connection with any reports filed by a mortgage loan originator or in connection with any investigation conducted by the division;

(i) Advertise any rate of interest without conspicuously disclosing the annual percentage rate implied by such rate of interest;

* (j) Fail to comply with any requirement of the federal "Truth in Lending Act", 15 U.S.C. sec. 1601 and Regulation Z, 12 CFR 226; the "Real Estate Settlement Procedures Act of 1974", 12 U.S.C. sec. 2601 and Regulation X, 24 CFR 3500; the "Equal Credit Opportunity Act", 15 U.S.C. sec. 1691 and Regulation B, 12 CFR 202.9, 202.11, and 202.12; Title V, Subtitle A of the financial services modernization act of 1999 (known as the "Gramm-Leach-Bliley Act"), 12 U.S.C. secs. 6801 to 6809; the federal trade commission's privacy rules, 16 CFR 313-314, mandated by the "Gramm-Leach-Bliley Act"; the "Home Mortgage Disclosure Act of 1975", 12 U.S.C. sec. 2801 et seq. and Regulation C, home mortgage disclosure, 12 CFR 203; the "Federal Trade Commission Act", 15 U.S.C. sec. 45(a); the "Telemarketing and Consumer Fraud and Abuse Prevention Act", 15 U.S.C. secs. 6101 to 6108; and the federal trade commission telephone sales rule, 16 CFR 310, as amended, in any advertising of residential mortgage loans or any other applicable mortgage loan originator activities covered by the acts. The board may adopt rules requiring mortgage loan originators to comply with other applicable federal statutes and regulations.

(k) Fail to pay a third-party provider, no later than thirty days after the recording of the loan closing documents or ninety days after completion of the third-party service, whichever comes first, unless otherwise agreed or unless the third-party service provider has been notified in writing that a bona fide dispute exists regarding the performance or quality of the third-party service;

(l) Collect, charge, attempt to collect or charge, or use or propose any agreement purporting to collect or charge any fee prohibited by section 12-61-914 or 12-61-915; or

(m) Fail to comply with any provision of this part 9 or any rule adopted pursuant to this part 9.

§ 12-61-911.5, C.R.S. Acts of employee – mortgage loan originator's liability

An unlawful act or violation of this part 9 upon the part of an agent or employee of a licensed mortgage loan originator shall not be cause for disciplinary action against a mortgage loan originator unless it appears that the mortgage loan originator knew or should have known of the unlawful act or violation or had been negligent in the supervision of the agent or employee.

§ 12-61-912, C.R.S. Dual status as real estate broker – requirements

(1) Unless a mortgage loan originator complies with both subsections (2) and (3) of this section, he or she shall not act as a mortgage loan originator in any transaction in which:

(a) The mortgage loan originator acts or has acted as a real estate broker or salesperson; or

(b) Another person doing business under the same licensed real estate broker acts or has acted as a real estate broker or salesperson.

(2) Before providing mortgage-related services to the borrower, a mortgage loan originator shall make a full and fair disclosure to the borrower, in addition to any other disclosures required by this part 9 or other laws, of all material features of the loan product and all facts material to the transaction.

(3) (a) A real estate broker or salesperson licensed under part 1 of this article who also acts as a mortgage loan originator shall carry on such mortgage loan originator business activities

and shall maintain such person's mortgage loan originator business records separate and apart from the real estate broker or sales activities conducted pursuant to part 1 of this article. Such activities shall be deemed separate and apart even if they are conducted at an office location with a common entrance and mailing address if:

(I) Each business is clearly identified by a sign visible to the public;

(II) Each business is physically separated within the office facility; and

(III) No deception of the public as to the separate identities of the broker business firms results.

(b) This subsection (3) shall not require a real estate broker or salesperson licensed under part 1 of this article who also acts as a mortgage loan originator to maintain a physical separation within the office facility for the conduct of its real estate broker or sales and mortgage loan originator activities if the board determines that maintaining such physical separation would constitute an undue financial hardship upon the mortgage loan originator and is unnecessary for the protection of the public.

§ 12-61-913, C.R.S. Written contract required – effect

(1) Every contract between a mortgage loan originator and a borrower shall be in writing and shall contain the entire agreement of the parties.

(2) A mortgage loan originator shall have a written correspondent or loan agreement with a lender before any solicitation of, or contracting with, any member of the public.

§ 12-61-914, C.R.S. Written disclosure of fees and costs – contents – limits on fees – lock-in agreement terms – rules

(1) Within three business days after receipt of a loan application or any moneys from a borrower, a mortgage loan originator shall provide to each borrower a full written disclosure containing an itemization and explanation of all fees and costs that the borrower is required to pay in connection with obtaining a residential mortgage loan, specifying the fee or fees that inure to the benefit of the mortgage loan originator. A good-faith estimate of a fee or cost shall be provided if the exact amount of the fee or cost is not determinable. Except as required by paragraph (c) of subsection (2) of this section, this subsection (1) shall not be construed to require disclosure of the distribution or breakdown of loan fees, discounts, or points between the mortgage loan originator and any mortgage lender or investor.

(2) The written disclosure shall contain the following information:

(a) The annual percentage rate, finance charge, amount financed, total amount of all payments, number of payments, amount of each payment, amount of points or prepaid interest, and the conditions and terms under which any loan terms may change between the time of disclosure and closing of the loan. If the interest rate is variable, the written disclosure shall clearly describe the circumstances under which the rate may increase, any limitation on the increase, the effect of an increase, and an example of the payment terms resulting from an increase.

(b) The itemized costs of any credit report, appraisal, title report, title insurance policy, mortgage insurance, escrow fee, property tax, insurance, structural or pest inspection, and any other third-party provider's costs associated with the residential mortgage loan;

(c) If applicable, the amount of any commission or other compensation to be paid to the mortgage loan originator, including the manner in which the commission or other compensation is calculated and the relationship of the commission or other compensation to the cost of the loan received by the borrower;

(d) If applicable, the cost, terms, duration, and conditions of a lock-in agreement and whether a lock-in agreement has been entered, whether the lock-in agreement is guaranteed by the mortgage loan originator or lender, and, if a lock-in agreement has not been entered, disclosure in a form acceptable to the board that the disclosed interest rate and terms are subject to change;

(e) A statement that, if the borrower is unable to obtain a loan for any reason, the mortgage loan originator must, within five days after a written request by the borrower, give copies of each appraisal, title report, and credit report paid for by the borrower to the borrower and transmit the appraisal, title report, or credit report to any other mortgage loan originator or lender to whom the borrower directs the documents to be sent;

(f) Whether and under what conditions any lock-in fees are refundable to the borrower; and

(g) A statement providing that moneys paid by the borrower to the mortgage loan originator for third-party provider services are held in a trust account and any moneys remaining after payment to third-party providers will be refunded.

(3) If, after the written disclosure is provided under this section, a mortgage loan originator enters into a lock-in agreement with a borrower or represents to the borrower that the borrower has entered into a lock-in agreement, the mortgage loan originator shall deliver or send by first-class mail to the borrower a written confirmation of the terms of the lock-in agreement within three days, including Saturdays, after the agreement is entered or the representation is made. The written confirmation shall include a copy of the disclosure made under paragraph (d) of subsection (2) of this section.

(4) (a) Except as otherwise provided in paragraph (b) of this subsection (4), a mortgage loan originator shall not charge any fee that inures to the benefit of the mortgage loan originator and that exceeds the fee disclosed on the written disclosure pursuant to this section unless:

(I) The need to charge the fee was not reasonably foreseeable at the time the written disclosure was provided; and

(II) The mortgage loan originator has provided to the borrower, at least three business days prior to the signing of the loan closing documents, a clear written explanation of the fee and the reason for charging a fee exceeding that which was previously disclosed.

(b) If the borrower's closing costs on the final settlement statement, excluding prepaid escrowed costs of ownership as defined by the board by rule, do not exceed the total closing costs in the most recent good-faith estimate, excluding prepaid escrowed costs of ownership, no other disclosures shall be required by this subsection (4).

§ 12-61-915, C.R.S. Fee, commission, or compensation – when permitted – amount

(1) Except as otherwise permitted by subsection (2) or (3) of this section, a mortgage loan originator shall not receive a fee, commission, or compensation of any kind in connection with the preparation or negotiation of a residential mortgage loan unless a borrower actually obtains a loan from a lender on the terms and conditions agreed to by the borrower and mortgage loan originator.

(2) If the mortgage loan originator has obtained for the borrower a written commitment from a lender for a loan on the terms and conditions agreed to by the borrower and the mortgage loan originator, and the borrower fails to close on the loan through no fault of the mortgage loan originator, the mortgage loan originator may charge a fee, not to exceed three hundred dollars, for services rendered, preparation of documents, or transfer of documents in the borrower's file that were prepared or paid for by the borrower if the fee is not otherwise prohibited by the federal "Truth in Lending Act", 15 U.S.C. sec. 1601, and Regulation Z, 12 CFR 226, as amended.

(3) A mortgage loan originator may solicit or receive fees for third-party provider goods or services in advance. Fees for any goods or services not provided shall be refunded to the borrower, and

the mortgage loan originator may not charge more for the goods and services than the actual costs of the goods or services charged by the third-party provider.

* *§ 12-61-916, C.R.S. Confidentiality*

(1) Except as otherwise provided in the federal "Secure and Fair Enforcement for Mortgage Licensing Act of 2008", 12 U.S.C. sec. 5111, the requirements under any federal law or law of this state regarding privacy or confidentiality of any information or material provided to the nationwide mortgage licensing system and registry, and any privilege arising under federal or state law, including the rules of any federal or state court with respect to such information or material, shall apply to the information or material after it has been disclosed to the nationwide mortgage licensing system and registry. The information or material may be shared with all state and federal regulatory officials with mortgage industry oversight authority without the loss of privilege or confidentiality protections provided by federal or state law.

(2) The board may enter into agreements with other government agencies, the conference of state bank supervisors, the American association of residential mortgage regulators, or other associations representing government agencies as established by rule.

(3) Information or material that is subject to privilege or confidentiality pursuant to subsection (1) of this section shall not be subject to the following:

(a) Disclosure under a federal or state law governing the disclosure to the public of information held by an officer or agency of the federal government or the respective state; or

(b) Subpoena, discovery, or admission into evidence in any private civil action or administrative process, unless with respect to a privilege held by the nationwide mortgage licensing system and registry regarding the information or material, the person to whom the information or material pertains waives the privilege, in whole or in part.

* *§ 12-61-917, C.R.S. Mortgage call reports – reports of violations*

(1) The board may require each licensee or registrant to submit to the nationwide mortgage licensing system and registry mortgage call reports, which shall be in the form and contain the information required by the nationwide mortgage licensing system and registry.

(2) The board may report violations of this part 9, enforcement actions, and other relevant information to the nationwide mortgage licensing system and registry.

* *§ 12-61-918, C.R.S. Unique identifier – clearly displayed*

Each person required to be licensed or registered shall show his or her or the entity's unique identifier clearly on all residential mortgage loan application forms and any other documents as specified by the board by rule or order.

* *§ 12-61-919, C.R.S. Repeal of part*

(1) This part 9 is repealed, effective July 1, 2013.

(2) Prior to its repeal, the department of regulatory agencies shall review the licensing of mortgage loan originators and the registration of mortgage companies in accordance with section 24-34-104, C.R.S. The department shall include in its review of mortgage loan originators and mortgage companies an analysis of the number and types of complaints made about mortgage loan originators and mortgage companies and whether the licensing of mortgage loan originators and the registration of mortgage companies correlates with public protection from fraudulent activities in the residential mortgage loan industry.

III. Standards for Mortgage Lending and Servicing

§ 38-40-101, C.R.S. Mortgage broker fees – escrow accounts – unlawful act – penalty

(1) Any funds, other than advanced for actual costs and expenses to be incurred by the mortgage broker on behalf of the applicant for a loan, paid to a mortgage broker as a fee conditioned upon the consummation of a loan secured or to be secured by a mortgage or other transfer of or encumbrance on real estate shall be held in an escrow or a trustee account with a bank or recognized depository in this state. Such account may be any type of checking, demand, passbook, or statement account insured by an agency of the United States government.

(2) It is unlawful for a mortgage broker to misappropriate funds held in escrow or a trustee account pursuant to subsection (1) of this section.

(3) The withdrawal, transfer, or other use or conversion of any funds held in escrow or a trustee account pursuant to subsection (1) of this section prior to the time a loan secured or to be secured by mortgage or other transfer of or encumbrance on real estate is consummated shall be prima facie evidence of intent to violate subsection (2) of this section.

(4) Any mortgage broker violating any of the provisions of subsection (2) of this section commits theft as defined in section 18-4-401, C.R.S.

(5) Any mortgage broker violating any of the provisions of subsection (1) or (2) of this section shall be liable to the person from whom any funds were received for the sum of one thousand dollars plus actual damages caused thereby, together with costs and reasonable attorney fees. No lender shall be liable for any act or omission of a mortgage broker under this section.

(6) As used in this section, unless the context otherwise requires, "mortgage broker" means a person, firm, partnership, association, or corporation, other than a bank, trust company, savings and loan association, credit union, supervised lender as defined in section 5-1-301 (46), C.R.S., insurance company, federal housing administration approved mortgagee, land mortgagee, or farm loan association or duly appointed loan correspondents, acting through officers, partners, or regular salaried employees for any such entity, that engages in negotiating or offering or attempting to negotiate for a borrower, and for commission, money, or other thing of value, a loan to be consummated and funded by someone other than the one acting for the borrower.

§ 38-40-102, C.R.S. Disclosure of costs – statement of terms of indebtedness

(1) Any person regularly engaged in the making of loans secured by a mortgage or deed of trust on a one-to-four-family dwelling shall provide to any applicant for a loan to be secured by such a mortgage or deed of trust a good faith estimate, as a dollar amount or range, of each charge for a settlement service to be charged by the lender and paid by the applicant or a third party at the time of the making of the loan for which the application is made. Such disclosure shall be delivered to the applicant, and to any third party who will be liable on the loan and to the seller if the name and address of the third party and seller is known to the lender at the time of the application, in the same manner and at the same time as the good faith estimate required by the federal "Real Estate Settlement Procedures Act of 1974," 12 U.S.C. sec. 2601, *et seq.* If the lender conditionally guarantees any of the terms of the loan for which the application is made, there shall be delivered to the applicant a written statement of the conditions of such guaranty, including the period of time within which the consummation of the loan must occur in order for the guaranty to be honored.

(2) A person shall not state terms of an indebtedness to an applicant which are in conflict with the good faith estimate and which he knows to be false or unavailable at the time of the statement or at the time of closing of the agreement creating the indebtedness.

(3) As used in this section, unless the context otherwise requires, the terms "good faith estimate," "person," and "settlement service" shall have the same meanings as given to such terms in the federal "Real Estate Settlement Procedures Act of 1974," 12 U.S.C. sec. 2601, *et seq*., and in regulation X, 24 C.F.R. part 3500, issued by the United States secretary of housing and urban development pursuant to such act.

(4) The provisions of this section shall not apply to a loan to be made by a bank, trust company, savings and loan association, credit union, federal housing administration approved mortgagee, or supervised lender as defined in section 5-1-301 (46), C.R.S., that will be secured by a mortgage or deed of trust other than a first mortgage or deed of trust having priority as a lien on the real property over any other mortgage or deed of trust.

§ 38-40-103, C.R.S. Servicing of mortgages and deeds of trust – liability for interest or late fees for property taxes

(1) (a) (I) Any person who regularly engages in the collection of payments on mortgages and deeds of trust for owners of evidences of debt secured by mortgages or deeds of trust shall promptly credit all payments which are received and which are required to be accepted by such person or his agent and shall promptly perform all duties imposed by law and all duties imposed upon the servicer by such evidences of debt, mortgages, or deeds of trust creating or securing the indebtedness.

(II) No more than twenty days after the date of transfer of the servicing or collection rights and duties to another person, the transferor of such rights and duties shall mail a notice addressed to the debtor from whom it has been collecting payments at the address shown on its records, notifying such debtor of the transfer of the servicing of his or her debt and the name, address, and telephone number of the transferee of the servicing.

(b) The debtor may continue to make payments to the transferor of the servicing of his or her loan until a notice of the transfer is received from the transferee containing the name, address, and telephone number of the new servicer of the loan to whom future payments should be made. Such notice may be combined with the notice required in subparagraph (II) of paragraph (a) of this subsection (1). It shall be the responsibility of the transferor to forward to the transferee any payments received and due after the date of transfer of the loan.

(2) The servicer of a loan shall respond in writing within twenty days from the receipt of a written request from the debtor or from an agent of the debtor acting pursuant to written authority from the debtor for information concerning the debtor's loan, which is readily available to the servicer from its books and records and which would not constitute the rendering of legal advice. Any such response must include the telephone number of the servicer. The servicer shall not be liable for any damage or harm that might arise from the release of any information pursuant to this section.

(3) The servicer of a loan shall annually provide to the debtor a summary of activity related to the loan. Such a summary shall contain, but need not be limited to, the total amount of principal and interest paid on the loan in that calendar year.

(4) The servicer of a loan shall be liable for any interest or late fees charged by any taxing entity if funds for the full payment of taxes on the real estate have been held in an escrow account by such servicer and not remitted to the taxing entity when due.

§ 38-40-105, C.R.S. Prohibited acts by participants in certain mortgage loan transactions – unconscionable acts and practices – definitions

(1) The following acts by any mortgage broker, mortgage originator, mortgage lender, mortgage loan applicant, real estate appraiser, or closing agent, other than a person who provides closing

or settlement services subject to regulation by the division of insurance, with respect to any loan that is secured by a first or subordinate mortgage or deed or trust lien against a dwelling are prohibited:

(a) To knowingly advertise, display, distribute, broadcast, televise, or cause or permit to be advertised, displayed, distributed, broadcast, or televised, in any manner, any false, misleading, or deceptive statement with regard to rates, terms, or conditions for a mortgage loan;

(b) To make a false promise or misrepresentation or conceal an essential or material fact to entice either a borrower or a creditor to enter into a mortgage agreement when, under the terms and circumstances of the transaction, he or she knew or reasonably should have known of such falsity, misrepresentation, or concealment;

(c) To knowingly and with intent to defraud present, cause to be presented, or prepare with knowledge or belief that it will be presented to or by a lender or an agent thereof any written statement or information in support of an application for a mortgage loan that he or she knows to contain false information concerning any fact material thereto or if he or she knowingly and with intent to defraud or mislead conceals information concerning any fact material thereto;

(d) To facilitate the consummation of a mortgage loan agreement that is unconscionable given the terms and circumstances of the transaction;

(e) To knowingly facilitate the consummation of a mortgage loan transaction that violates, or that is connected with a violation of, section 12-61-911, C.R.S.

(f) (Deleted by amendment, L. 2009, (HB 09-1085), ch. 303, p. 1638, § 4, effective August 5, 2009.)

(1.5) (Deleted by amendment, L. 2009, (HB 09-1085), ch. 303, p. 1638, § 4, effective August 5, 2009.)

(1.7) (a) A mortgage broker or mortgage originator shall not commit, or assist or facilitate the commission of, the following acts or practices, which are hereby deemed unconscionable:

(I) Engaging in a pattern or practice of providing residential mortgage loans to consumers based predominantly on acquisition of the foreclosure or liquidation value of the consumer's collateral without regard to the consumer's ability to repay a loan in accordance with its terms; except that any reasonable method may be used to determine a borrower's ability to repay. This subparagraph (I) shall not apply to a reverse mortgage that complies with article 38 of title 11, C.R.S.

(II) Knowingly or intentionally flipping a residential mortgage loan. As used in this subparagraph (II), "flipping" means making a residential mortgage loan that refinances an existing residential mortgage loan when the new loan does not have reasonable, tangible net benefit to the consumer considering all of the circumstances, including the terms of both the new and refinanced loans, the cost of the new loan, and the consumer's circumstances. This subparagraph (II) applies regardless of whether the interest rate, points, fees, and charges paid or payable by the consumer in connection with the refinancing exceed any thresholds specified by law.

(III) Entering into a residential mortgage loan transaction knowing there was no reasonable probability of payment of the obligation by the consumer.

(b) Except as this subsection (1.7) may be enforced by the attorney general or a district attorney, only the original parties to a transaction shall have a right of action under this subsection (1.7), and no action or claim under this subsection (1.7) may be brought against a purchaser from, or assignee of, a party to the transaction.

(2) (a) Except as provided in subsection (5) of this section, if a court, as a matter of law, finds a mortgage contract or any clause of the contract to have been unconscionable at the time it was made, the court may refuse to enforce the contract, or it may enforce the remainder of the contract without the unconscionable clause, or it may so limit the application of any unconscionable clause as to avoid any unconscionable result.

(b) When it is claimed or appears to the court that the contract or any clause thereof may be unconscionable, the parties shall be afforded a reasonable opportunity to present evidence as to its commercial setting, purpose, and effect, to aid the court in making the determination.

(c) (I) In order to support a finding of unconscionability, there must be evidence of some bad faith overreaching on the part of the mortgage broker or mortgage originator such as that which results from an unreasonable inequality of bargaining power or under other circumstances in which there is an absence of meaningful choice on the part of one of the parties, together with contract terms that are, under standard industry practices, unreasonably favorable to the mortgage broker, mortgage originator, or lender.

(II) This paragraph (c) shall not apply to an unconscionable act or practice under subsection (1.7) of this section.

(3) A violation of this section shall be deemed a deceptive trade practice as provided in section 6-1-105 (1) (uu), C.R.S.

(4) The provisions of this section are in addition to and are not intended to supersede the deceptive trade practices actionable at common law or under other statutes of this state.

(5) No right or claim arising under this section may be raised or asserted in any proceeding against a bona fide purchaser of such mortgage contract or in any proceeding to obtain an order authorizing sale of property by a public trustee as required by section 38-38-105.

(6) The following acts by any real estate agent or real estate broker, as defined in section 12-61-101, C.R.S., in connection with any residential mortgage loan transaction, are prohibited:

(a) If directly engaged in negotiating, originating, or offering or attempting to negotiate or originate for a borrower a residential mortgage loan transaction, the real estate agent or real estate broker shall not make a false promise or misrepresentation or conceal an essential or material fact to entice either a borrower or lender to enter into a mortgage loan agreement when the real estate agent or real estate broker actually knew or, under the terms and circumstances of the transaction, reasonably should have known of such falsity, misrepresentation, or concealment.

(b) If not directly engaged in negotiating, originating, or offering or attempting to negotiate or originate for a borrower a residential mortgage loan transaction, the real estate agent or real estate broker shall not make a false promise or misrepresentation or conceal an essential or material fact to entice either a borrower or lender to enter into a mortgage loan agreement when the real estate agent or real estate broker had actual knowledge of such falsity, misrepresentation, or concealment.

(7) As used in this section, unless the context otherwise requires:

(a) "Consumer" has the meaning set forth in section 5-1-301, C.R.S.

(b) "Dwelling" has the meaning set forth in section 5-1-301, C.R.S.

(c) "Mortgage broker" has the same meaning as "mortgage loan originator" as set forth in section 12-61-902, C.R.S.

(d) "Mortgage lender" has the meaning set forth in section 12-61-902, C.R.S.

(e) "Mortgage originator" has the same meaning as "mortgage loan originator" as set forth in section 12-61-902, C.R.S.

(f) "Originate" has the same meaning as "originate a mortgage" as set forth in section 12-61-902, C.R.S.

(g) "Residential mortgage loan" has the meaning set forth in section 12-61-902, C.R.S.

IV. Loan Fraud

Legislative declaration

(1) The general assembly hereby determines that mortgage lending has a significant effect upon Colorado's economy; an estimated two trillion five hundred billion dollars in mortgage loans were made in the United States in 2005; an estimated eighty percent of reported mortgage fraud involves collusion by industry insiders; and Colorado's per capita incidents of mortgage fraud is one of the ten highest in the nation.

(2) The general assembly hereby declares that the high rates of mortgage fraud in Colorado are unacceptable and that residential mortgage fraud shall not be tolerated. The general assembly further declares that the goals of Colorado law are to deter residential mortgage fraud and to make the victim whole.

§ 18-4-401, C.R.S. Theft

(9) (a) If a person is convicted of or pleads guilty or nolo contendere to theft by deception and the underlying factual basis of the case involves the mortgage lending process, a minimum fine of the amount of pecuniary harm resulting from the theft shall be mandatory, in addition to any other penalty the court may impose.

(b) A court shall not accept a plea of guilty or nolo contendere to another offense from a person charged with a violation of this section that involves the mortgage lending process unless the plea agreement contains an order of restitution in accordance with part 6 of article 1.3 of this title that compensates the victim for any costs to the victim caused by the offense.

(c) The district attorneys and the attorney general have concurrent jurisdiction to investigate and prosecute a violation of this section that involves making false statements or filing or facilitating the use of a document known to contain a false statement or material omission relied upon by another person in the mortgage lending process.

(d) Documents involved in the mortgage lending process include, but are not limited to, uniform residential loan applications or other loan applications; appraisal reports; HUD-1 settlement statements; supporting personal documentation for loan applications such as W-2 forms, verifications of income and employment, bank statements, tax returns, and payroll stubs; and any required disclosures.

(e) For the purposes of this subsection (9):

(I) "Mortgage lending process" means the process through which a person seeks or obtains a residential mortgage loan, including, without limitation, solicitation, application, or origination; negotiation of terms; third-party provider services; underwriting; signing and closing; funding of the loan; and perfecting and releasing the mortgage.

(II) "Residential mortgage loan" means a loan or agreement to extend credit, made to a person and secured by a mortgage or lien on residential real property, including, but not limited to, the refinancing or renewal of a loan secured by residential real property.

(III) "Residential real property" means real property used as a residence and containing no more than four families housed separately.

§ 13-21-125, C.R.S. Civil actions for theft in the mortgage lending process

A person who suffers damages as a result of a violation of section 18-4-401, C.R.S., in the mortgage lending process, as defined by section 18-4-401 (9) (e) (I), C.R.S., shall have a private civil right of action against the perpetrator, regardless of whether the perpetrator was convicted of the crime. A claim arising under this section shall not be asserted against a bona fide purchaser of a mortgage contract.

§ 18-5-208, C.R.S. Dual contracts to induce loan

It is a class 3 misdemeanor for any person to knowingly make, issue, deliver, or receive dual contracts for the purchase or sale of real property. The term "dual contracts," either written or oral, means two separate contracts concerning the same parcel of real property, one of which states the true and actual purchase price and one of which states a purchase price in excess of the true and actual purchase price, and is used, or intended to be used, to induce persons to make a loan or a loan commitment on such real property in reliance upon the stated inflated value.

. . . .

Loan fraud has become one of the largest areas of white-collar crime and is a recurring subject of Commission disciplinary actions. Loan fraud includes falsified loan applications; fictitious income, employment, or deposit verifications; false occupancy claims; undisclosed buyer rebates or credits; and a host of other items, which can be considered dual contracting.

Loan fraud may also result in disbarment by HUD from all federal programs, large fines, and federal prosecution. Since virtually all loan programs are affiliated with the federal government in either the primary or secondary mortgage market, disbarment can mean the end of a career in real estate, appraisal, and lending or related fields.

* V. Mortgage Loan Originator Rules

DEPARTMENT OF REGULATORY AGENCIES
Division of Real Estate

RULES REGARDING MORTGAGE LOAN ORIGINATORS
4 CCR 725-3

* RULE 1-1-1 [Repealed Eff. 02/14/2011]

* RULE 1-1-2 MORTGAGE LOAN ORIGINATOR TEMPORARY LICENSE

* **Section 1. Authority**

The statutory basis for this rule entitled **1-1-2 Mortgage Loan Originator Temporary License**, is § 12-61-910.3, C.R.S.

The notice proposes to add rule 1-1-2. The rule establishes a temporary license for mortgage loan originators.

* **Section 2. Scope and Purpose**

Section 12-61-905(10), C.R.S., requires the Board of Mortgage Loan Originators to promulgate rules that allow licensed mortgage loan originators to hire unlicensed mortgage loan originators under temporary licenses. The purpose of this regulation is to define the parameters under which an individual may receive a temporary license.

* **Section 3. Applicability**

This rule applies to all individuals required to be licensed pursuant to sections 12-61-902 and 12-61-903, C.R.S.

* **Section 4. 1-1-2 Mortgage Loan Originator Temporary License**

* 1. Mortgage loan originators who demonstrate to the Board a good-faith effort to comply with the requirements pursuant to Colorado Revised Statutes 12-61-901, *et seq.*, may be issued a temporary license upon completion of the requirements set forth below:
* a. The individual has completed all requirements required by the Nationwide Mortgage Licensing System and Registry, including payment of requisite fees, and has been approved by the Board of Mortgage Loan Originators on the Nationwide Mortgage Licensing System and Registry;
b. Prior to submitting an application, a set of fingerprints for a criminal history record check must be submitted to the Colorado Bureau of Investigation (CBI);
c. Acquisition of a surety bond as required by § 12-61-907, C.R.S. and in accordance with any rule of the Director that directly or indirectly addresses surety bond requirements;
d. Acquisition of the errors and omissions insurance required by § 12-61-903.5, C.R.S. and in accordance with any rule of the Director that directly or indirectly addresses errors and omissions insurance requirements;
e. Completion of the mortgage loan originator application; and
f. Payment of the application fee established by the Director.

* 2. Only individuals who are licensed as state-licensed loan originators may hire and sponsor unlicensed mortgage loan originators under the temporary license provision.
* a. Licensed mortgage loan originators who employ and sponsor such a temporarily licensed mortgage loan originator shall be held responsible under all applicable provisions of law, including without limitation the Mortgage Loan Originator Licensing and Mortgage Company Registration Act and section 38-40-105, C.R.S., for the actions of the temporarily licensed mortgage loan originator to whom a temporary license has been assigned, and are personally subject to all applicable penalties under the law.
i. Licensed mortgage loan originators shall notify the Division of Real Estate, in a manner acceptable to the Director, of exact dates of hire and termination of employment for unlicensed mortgage loan originators. Sponsoring mortgage brokers or mortgage loan originators shall complete the Mortgage Broker Temporary License Update Form, found on the Division of Real Estate website at http://www.dora.state.co.us/real-estate/mortgage/MBForms.htm, and forward to the Division of Real Estate, in a manner acceptable to the Director, all other information required for the possible receipt of a temporary license.
ii. Licensed mortgage loan originators shall be held responsible for the activity of an unlicensed mortgage brokers or mortgage loan originators through and including the date of termination and required notification of such termination to the Division of Real Estate.

* 3. Temporary licenses shall expire 120 days after completion of the mortgage loan originator license application or when the temporary license is terminated by a licensed mortgage loan originator with whom the temporary licensee is operating under.

4. Individuals seeking temporary licenses shall be granted one temporary license. Additional or extended temporary licenses shall be prohibited.
5. Individuals seeking a temporary license shall complete the paper version of the mortgage broker or mortgage loan originator license application posted on the Division of Real Estate's website at http://www.dora.state.co.us/real-estate/mortgage/MBForms.htm.
6. Temporary licensees shall request on the application that the Director inactivate their temporary license upon determination by the Director that the requirements of the law have not been met. Applicants shall be notified via e- mail, fax or U.S. mail to the contact information provided to the Division of Real Estate in the applicant's mortgage loan originator license application.
7. Any temporary license issued by the Director shall have the same force and effect of the license required by § 12-61-901, *et seq.*, C.R.S. for the period of time it is in effect.
8. Once the applicant fully complies with the terms of the law as determined by the Director, the Director shall license the applicant in accordance with § 12-61-903, C.R.S.
9. Due to the changes defined in this rule, the names of temporary licensees will be posted to the Division of Real Estate website at http://www.dora.state.co.us/real-estate/mortgagebroker-registration.htm.''

* RULE 1-1-4 MORTGAGE LOAN ORIGINATOR LICENSE RENEWAL, REINSTATEMENT AND RE-APPLICATION

* **Section 1. Authority**

The statutory basis for this rule, entitled **1-1-4 Mortgage Loan Originator License Renewal, Reinstatement and Re-Application**, is § 12-61-910.3, C.R.S.

The notice proposes to add rule 1-1-4. The rule defines the license renewal process for mortgage loan originators.

* **Section 2. Scope and Purpose**

Due to the three year license cycle that has been in place, there has been no need to date to define the renewal process. As a result of the S.A.F.E. Act and subsequent passage of House Bill 09-1085, the license cycle has been changed from a three year cycle to an annual cycle. As a result, mortgage loan originators must renew their licenses annually. Additionally, licensees are now required to be registered with the Nationwide Mortgage Licensing System and Registry. The Director of the Division of Real Estate has determined that it is most appropriate to mimic timelines and processes associated with the Nationwide Mortgage Licensing System and Registry. Failing to do so would cause tremendous confusion on the part of the licensee pool.

The purpose of this rule is to clearly define the transition from a three year license cycle to an annual license cycle and to define the license renewal process.

* **Section 3. Applicability**

This rule applies to mortgage loan originators as that term is defined in § 12-61-902(6), C.R.S. and includes those persons who originate a mortgage, offer to originate a mortgage, act as a mortgage loan originator, or offer to act as a mortgage loan originator. This rule applies to all individuals required to be licensed pursuant to §§ 12-61-902 and 12-61-903, C.R.S.

* **Section 4. 1-1-4 Mortgage Loan Originator License Renewal, Reinstatement and Re-Application**

1. Transitioning from a three year license cycle to an annual license cycle.
   a. For licensees whose licenses are set to expire at any point in 2009, the Director will administratively change the expiration date to December 31, 2009.

   b. For licensees whose licenses are set to expire on or after January 1, 2010, the Director will administratively change the expiration date to December 31, 2010.

2. Renewal Process for active licensees.
   a. Currently, there are two existing databases that licensees shall independently renew their license through annually. The two independent databases include:
      i. The license database managed by the Division of Real Estate. This database may be located by visiting the Division of Real Estate website at http://www.dora.state.co.us/real-estate/index.htm.
      ii. The registration database managed by the Nationwide Mortgage Licensing System and Registry. This database is located at http://www.stateregulatoryregistry.org/NMLS/AM/Template.cfm?Section=Home3.
   b. Mortgage loan originators renewing, reinstating or re-applying for registration through the Nationwide Mortgage Licensing System and Registry shall do so in accordance with established timelines, policies and procedures set forth by the Nationwide Mortgage Licensing System and Registry. The Nationwide Mortgage Licensing System and Registry may collect fees for the purpose of registration applications, renewal applications, reinstatement applications, credit reports, criminal background checks and for other processes associated with registration through the nationwide database.
   c. The Director shall issue or deny a license renewal or reinstatement application within thirty days after the applicant has submitted all of the information necessary for license renewal or reinstatement and after the Director has received all information necessary to make a determination regarding the applicants' compliance.
   d. Regarding the license database managed by the Division of Real Estate, mortgage loan originators may renew or reinstate their license online or may do so by submitting a paper renewal or reinstatement application. Individuals who choose to submit a paper renewal or reinstatement application shall pay an administrative fee prescribed by the Director in addition to the renewal or reinstatement fee due to the administrative burden placed on the Division of Real Estate. The fee for reinstatement is one and one half times the amount of the current renewal fee.
   e. For both databases, the license renewal period begins November 1st of each calendar year and ends December 31st of each calendar year. Individuals who renew their license shall only do so if they are compliant with all provisions of the Mortgage Loan Originator Licensing Act and all Director rules.
   f. All licenses expire at 12 midnight on December 31st of each calendar year if the licensee has not properly renewed their license.
   g. If a license has expired, individuals may choose to reinstate their mortgage loan originator license. The reinstatement period for both databases begins January 1st of each calendar year and ends on the last day of February of each calendar year. Individuals who reinstate their license shall only do so if they are compliant with all provisions of the Mortgage Loan Originator Licensing Act and all Director rules.
   h. Individuals who fail to renew or reinstate their license shall re-apply with both in order for the Division of Real Estate to review their applications and determine whether the individual is compliant with the licensing requirements.
   i. All renewal, reinstatement or application fees shall be prescribed by the Director.

3. Renewal Process for inactive licensees.
   a. Individuals with inactive licenses shall renew their license annually. Individuals with inactive licensees are not required to maintain compliant errors and omissions insurance or a compliant surety bond, but they are required to stay current on all continuing education requirements in order to renew their license.
   b. Mortgage loan originators may renew or reinstate their inactive license online or may do so by submitting a paper renewal or reinstatement application. Individuals who choose to

submit a paper renewal or reinstatement application shall pay an administrative fee prescribed by the Director in addition to the renewal or reinstatement fee due to the administrative burden placed on the Division of Real Estate. The fee for reinstatement is one and one half times the amount of the current renewal fee.

c. Currently, there are two existing databases that inactive licensees shall independently renew their license through annually. The two independent databases include:
   i. The license database managed by the Division of Real Estate. This database may be located by visiting the Division of Real Estate website at http://www.dora.state.co.us/real-estate/index.htm.
   ii. The registration database managed by the Nationwide Mortgage Licensing System and Registry. This database is located at http://www.stateregulatoryregistry.org/NMLS/AM/Template.cfm?Section=Home3.

d. For both databases, the renewal period begins November 1 of each calendar year and ends December 31st of each calendar year. Individuals who renew their license shall only do so if they are compliant with all provisions of the Mortgage Loan Originator Licensing Act and all Director rules.

e. All inactive licenses expire at 12 midnight on December 31st of each calendar year if the license has not been properly renewed.

f. If a license has expired, individuals may choose to reinstate their inactive mortgage loan originator license. The reinstatement period for both databases begins January 1 of each calendar year and ends on the last day of February of each calendar year. Individuals who reinstate their license shall only do so if they are compliant with all provisions of the Mortgage Loan Originator Licensing Act and all Director rules.

g. Individuals who fail to renew or reinstate their inactive license shall re-apply in order for the Division of Real Estate to review their applications and determine whether the individual is compliant with the licensing requirements.

h. All renewal, reinstatement or application fees shall be prescribed by the Director.

i. The Director shall issue or deny a license renewal or reinstatement application within thirty days after the applicant has submitted all of the information necessary for license renewal or reinstatement and after the Director has received all information necessary to make a determination regarding the applicants' compliance.

4. Renewal, reinstatement or re-application fees.
   a. All fees collected for the purpose of applying for license renewal, reinstatement or re-application are non-refundable.

5. Re-application.
   a. Individuals who have taken the requisite courses and who have passed the test in accordance with Director rules within the immediately preceding three years of an application and who are compliant with the annual continuing education requirements will not need to duplicate the educational requirements upon re-application.

6. Individuals who do not have an active license are prohibited from practicing as a mortgage loan originator. Additionally, individuals who do not have an active license are prohibited from engaging in any mortgage related activities which require licensure pursuant to the Colorado Mortgage Loan Originator Licensing Act, Director rule or as prescribed by Director position statement.

* RULE 1-1-5 PRELIMINARY ADVISORY OPINIONS

* **Section 1. Authority**

The statutory basis for this rule, entitled **1-1-5 Preliminary Advisory Opinions**, is § 12-61-910.3, C.R.S.

The notice proposes to add rule 1-1-5. The rule establishes a preliminary advisory opinion process for individuals concerned about how existing license laws may apply to their circumstances.

* **Section 2. Scope and Purpose**

In 2006, Colorado was one of two states, the other being Alaska, that had no regulatory oversight regarding mortgage brokers. In 2006, the Colorado General Assembly acted and passed House Bill 06-1161. In 2007, due to the state of the real estate market and the foreclosure crisis, the Colorado General Assembly enacted and passed House Bill 07-1322, Senate Bill 07-216, Senate Bill 07-085, and Senate Bill 07-203. In 2008, Congress passed the Housing and Economic Recovery Act of 2008. The Housing and Economic Recovery Act of 2008 contained the S.A.F.E. Act, which established minimum national licensing standards for mortgage loan originators and mandated states to adopt such provisions. As a result, in 2009 the Colorado General Assembly acted and passed House Bill 09-1085 to ensure compliance with the S.A.F.E. Act.

While Colorado was one of the last states to establish regulatory oversight of mortgage brokers, the registration and licensing laws have seen significant changes. The investment of time, energy and resources have increased with each passing bill. As a result, the purpose of this rule is to define a preliminary advisory process where potential applicants may have their specific circumstances reviewed by the Board or an authorized representative of the Board and be provided an opinion regarding whether or not they are likely to receive a license approval or a license denial. In doing so, potential applicants will be able to receive guidance prior to acquiring and paying for the requisite errors and omissions insurance, surety bond, finger prints for submission, completion of required educational courses and passage of the appropriate test. The purpose of this preliminary advisory rule is to define a preliminary advisory opinion process for prospective licensees.

* **Section 3. Applicability**

This rule applies to mortgage loan originators as that term is defined in § 12-61-902(6), C.R.S. This rule applies to all individuals required to be licensed pursuant to §§ 12-61-902 and 12-61-903, C.R.S.

* **Section 4. 1-1-5 Preliminary Advisory Opinions**

1. Potential applicants for a state license or a registration through the Nationwide Mortgage Licensing System and Registry (the "NMLS&R") may submit information in order for the Board or an authorized representative of the Board to reasonably ascertain the likelihood of license or registration approval through a defined preliminary advisory opinion process.
2. Potential applicants may request a preliminary advisory opinion for any of the following reasons:
   a. If the individual has been convicted, plead guilty or nolo contendere to any crime under Colorado law, federal law, District of Columbia law, or under the laws of any other states or territories, Puerto Rico, Guam, American Samoa, the Trust Territory of the Pacific Islands, Virgin Islands and the Northern Mariana Islands;
   b. If the individual has been enjoined in the immediately preceding five (5) years under the laws of this or any other state, District of Columbia or any other territories, Puerto Rico, Guam, American Samoa, the Trust of the Pacific Islands, Virgin Islands and the Northern Mariana Islands from in engaging in deceptive conduct relating to the origination of a mortgage loan;
   c. If the individual has had other professional licenses, certifications or registrations issued by Colorado, the District of Columbia, any other states or territories, Puerto Rico, Guam, American Samoa, the Trust Territory of the Pacific Islands, Virgin Islands and the Northern Mariana Islands revoked or suspended for fraud, theft, deceit, material misrepresentations or the breach of a fiduciary duty and such suspension or revocation denied authorization to practices as: a mortgage loan originator or similar license; real estate broker; real estate appraiser; an insurance producer; an attorney; a securities

broker-dealer; a securities sales representative; an investment advisor; or an investment advisor representative; or

d. If the individual has been assessed a civil or criminal penalty for violating any provision of the Colorado Consumer Protection Act.

3. Individuals requesting a preliminary advisory opinion shall complete the Preliminary Advisory Worksheet posted on the Division of Real Estate website found at http://www.dora.state.co.us/real-estate/mortgage/MBForms.htm. Additionally, individuals requesting a preliminary advisory opinion shall pay a fee identical to the license application fee for applicants as prescribed by the Director. Such fee will be applied as the license application fee if the individual chooses to apply.

4. Individuals requesting a preliminary advisory opinion shall submit all corresponding, or relevant documents related to any conduct or actions described in Section 4, subsection 2 of this rule. Incomplete requests will not be processed. The Board or an authorized representative of the Board may, at any time, request additional information regarding the preliminary advisory opinion request. Such corresponding, relevant or related documents may include, but are not limited to:
   a. Police officer reports;
   b. Dispositions documents;
   c. Court documents;
   d. Original charges documents;
   e. Stipulated agreements; or
   f. Final Agency Orders.

5. Additionally, individuals requesting a preliminary advisory opinion shall submit a written and signed personal explanation and detailed account of the facts and circumstances.

6. Any preliminary advisory opinion shall not be binding on the Board or limit the Board's authority to investigate a future formal application for licensure.

7. An individual seeking a preliminary advisory opinion under this rule is not an applicant for licensure and the issuance of an unfavorable opinion shall not prevent such individual from making application for licensure pursuant to the Mortgage Loan Originator Licensing Act.

8. The Board or an authorized representative of the Board will provide a favorable or an unfavorable opinion.

* RULE 1-1-6 RESIDENTIAL MORTGAGE LOANS

* **Section 1. Authority**

The statutory basis for this rule, entitled Licensure for Individuals Engaged in Origination Activities on Investment Properties and other Similar Types of Lending for Properties of Four or Fewer Units, is § 12-61-910.3, C.R.S.

The notice proposes to add rule 1-1-6. The rule requires licensure for individuals that engage in loan origination activities on investment properties and other similar forms of lending.

* **Section 2. Scope and Purpose**

The purpose of this rule is to clarify the licensing requirement for individuals who originate residential mortgage loans on properties of four or fewer residential units.

A residential mortgage loan is defined in section 12-61-902(8), C.R.S., as:

> ". . . a loan that is primarily for personal, family, or household use and that is secured by a mortgage, deed of trust, or other equivalent, consensual security interest on a dwelling or residential real estate upon which is constructed or intended to be

constructed a single-family dwelling or multiple-family dwelling of four or fewer units."

The Board of Mortgage Loan Originators interprets this definition to include loans secured by a residential property of four or fewer units that is intended for development, rehabilitation, resale, or rental of such property.

* **Section 3. Applicability**

This rule applies to all individuals required to be licensed pursuant to §§ 12-61-902 and 12-61-903, C.R.S.

* **Section 4. 1-1-6 Residential Mortgage Loans**

1. A residential mortgage loan that is secured by a mortgage deed of trust, or other equivalent consensual security interest on a dwelling or residential real estate upon which is constructed or intended to be constructed a residential property of four or fewer units includes, but is not limited to:
    a. A loan whereupon the residential property is used, or intended for use as, a rental property.
    b. A loan whereupon the residential property is used, or intended for, development or rehabilitation purposes.
    c. A loan whereupon the residential real estate is used, or intended for, construction of a property of four or fewer residential units.
    d. A loan whereupon the residential property is purchased to be resold.
2. Individuals who take loan applications for, or who offer or negotiate terms of residential mortgage loans, as defined in section 4, subsection 1 of this rule, meet the definition of a mortgage loan originator pursuant to Colorado law and are required to be licensed as state-licensed loan originators, as this term is defined in section 12-61-902(11), C.R.S., pursuant to section 12-61-903, C.R.S. Additionally, all such persons are required to comply with all provisions defined in the Mortgage Loan Originator Licensing and Mortgage Company Registration Act and all rules promulgated by the Board of Mortgage Loan Originators.

* **Section 5. Enforcement**

1. Noncompliance with this rule, whether defined or reasonably implied in the rule, may result in the imposition of any of the sanctions allowable under Colorado law, including, but not limited to:
    a. Cease and desist order;
    b. Permanent injunction;
    c. Imposition of fines; and
    d. Restitution for any financial loss.

* RULE 1-1-7 LOAN MODIFIER LICENSURE AND THE REQUIRED USE OF A LOAN MODIFICATION CONTRACT

* **Section 1. Authority**

The statutory basis for this rule, entitled **1-1-7 Loan Modifier Licensure and the Required Use of a Loan Modification Contract**, is § 12-61-910.3, C.R.S.

This notice proposes to add rule 1-1-7. The rule requires licensure for individuals who directly or indirectly take residential loan modification applications or who negotiate, offer, or attempt to negotiate or offer loan modifications. Direct managers of such individuals also must be licensed. Finally, this rule requires that individuals who offer or negotiate loan modifications use the Colorado Loan Modification Services Contract prescribed by this rule.

* **Section 2. Scope and Purpose**

The Board of Mortgage Loan Originators finds that a rule regarding loan modifications is necessary in order to provide clarity to the industry. The Board has learned of individuals negotiating loan modification terms for borrowers and has received many inquiries regarding the applicability of current mortgage loan originator licensing law. Specifically, individuals are communicating directly with borrowers and borrowers' lenders in order to negotiate terms of a loan modification. In many instances, Colorado consumers are being charged high up front fees regardless of services rendered. The Board has also learned that consumers are being advised to cease making mortgage payments, even when they are already delinquent on payments. Additionally, there are existing loan modification services that are offered by U.S. Department of Housing and Urban Development (HUD) approved non-profit 501(c)(3) agencies which employ housing counselors around the State of Colorado. Such HUD-approved services are offered by housing counselors for free and are not associated with any compensation or other benefit from the borrower to the housing counselor. The purpose of this rule is to clearly notify loan modifiers (those who engage in the act of directly or indirectly negotiating a loan modification) of the applicability of Colorado mortgage loan originator laws and to require the use of a loan modification contract.

* **Section 3. Applicability**

This rule applies to all individuals required to be licensed pursuant to §§ 12-61-902 and 12-61-903, C.R.S.

* **Section 4. Definitions**

A. "HUD approved housing counseling agency" means an agency which is either a private or public nonprofit organization that is exempt from taxation under section 501(A) pursuant to section 501(C), of the internal revenue code of 1996, 26, U.S.C. 501(A) and 501(C), and approved by the U.S. Department of Housing and Urban Development, in accordance with Housing Counseling Program Handbook 7610.1 and Code of Federal Regulations Title 24, Part 214.

B. "Short sale" means the sale of a real property for less than the mortgage loan balance. In the settlement of the short sale transaction the existing mortgage is extinguished. Any deficiency created from the settlement of the transaction may be transformed into a promissory note, charged off, forgiven, or pursued as a judgment against the previous owner.

C. "Loan modification" means a temporary or permanent change in one or more of the terms of a mortgagor's existing loan, allows the loan to be reinstated, and often results in a more affordable mortgage payment. The borrower retains ownership of the real property and the mortgage note and the deed of trust remains intact.

D. "Loan modifier" means an individual who in the course of the person's business, vocation, or occupation offers to assist, provide, or negotiate on behalf of a borrower to facilitate the receipt of a loan modification from the borrower's current mortgage lender, generally for a fee or other thing of value.

* **Section 5. 1-1-7 Loan Modifier Licensure and the Required Use of a Loan Modification Contract**

1. Section 12-61-902(6)(a), C.R.S. defines a mortgage loan originator as an individual who takes a residential mortgage loan application or offers or negotiates terms of a residential mortgage loan. It is the Board's position that individuals offering or negotiating loan modifications meet the definition of a mortgage loan originator. Pursuant to section 12-61-903(1)(a), C.R.S, all persons who meet the definition of a mortgage loan originator are required to be licensed. As a result, individuals who directly or indirectly take residential loan modification applications or

who negotiate, offer, or attempt to negotiate or offer loan modifications are required to be licensed as Colorado mortgage loan originators.

2. Pursuant to section 12-61-902(7), C.R.S., individuals who directly supervise individuals who take residential loan modification applications or individuals who negotiate, offer, or attempt to negotiate or offer loan modifications are required to be licensed as mortgage loan originators and as state-licensed loan originators by July 31, 2010.
3. All individuals required to be licensed shall comply with all other provisions of the Colorado Mortgage Loan Originator Licensing Act and all Board rules.
4. Individuals taking loan modification applications or offering or negotiating loan modifications are required to use a loan modification contract which complies with the Mortgage Loan Originator Licensing Act and the Foreclosure Protection Act.
5. The Board has created the Colorado Loan Modification Services Contract to ensure compliance with the aforementioned laws. This contract may be found on the Division of Real Estate's website at http://www.dora.state.co.us/real-estate/mortgage/MBForms.htm. Loan modifiers shall use this form or an alternate form, if such alternate form clearly includes all information required on the suggested form, as determined by the Board.
6. The Colorado Loan Modification Services Contract prescribed by this regulation shall be completed when an application is taken.
7. This rule shall not be construed to include employees of HUD approved housing counseling agencies who are providing advice or general information on loan modifications in an ancillary manner relating to their general housing counseling services or duties.
8. The Board's position on this matter shall not be construed to include employees of mortgage loan servicing companies operating on behalf of the borrowers' mortgage lenders.
9. Licensed Real Estate Brokers engaged in licensed activities when performing services within the above defined short sale transactions do not need to maintain a license as a mortgage loan originator. If a real estate broker engages in the activities of providing loan modification services (those not included in the activities of short sales) as defined above, loan modification services are defined as outside the scope of licensed real estate broker activities and therefore, separate licensure as a mortgage loan originator is required. See MLO 1.5 Position Statement.
10. As set forth in section 12-61-904(1)(d), C.R.S., an attorney who renders services in the course of practice, who is licensed in Colorado, and who is not primarily engaged in the business of negotiating residential mortgage loans or loan modifications is not required to be licensed as a mortgage loan originator, but is required to comply with all non-licensing provisions of current mortgage loan originator law set forth in sections 12-61-901 through 12-61-915, C.R.S.

* **Section 6. Enforcement**

1. Noncompliance with this rule, whether defined or reasonably implied in the rule, may result in the imposition of any of the following sanctions allowable under Colorado law, including, but not limited to:
    a. Cease and desist orders;
    b. Permanent injunctions;
    c. Revocation;
    d. Refusal to renew a license;
    e. Refusal to issue a license;
    f. Imposition of fines; and
    g. Restitution for any financial loss.

* RULE 1-2-1 [Repealed 08/30/2009]

* RULE 1-2-2 SURETY BOND REQUIREMENTS FOR MORTGAGE LOAN ORIGINATORS

* **Section 1. Authority**

The Board of Mortgage Loan Originators updates the following permanent rule entitled, **1-2-2 Surety Bond Requirements for Mortgage Loan Originators**, according to the authority prescribed in §§ 12-61-907 and 910.3, C.R.S.

The notice proposes to update rule 1-2-2. The rule establishes surety bond requirements for mortgage loan originators.

* **Section 2. Scope and Purpose**

The purpose of this rule is to define the surety bond requirements for mortgage loan originators or any other individual required to be licensed pursuant to § 12-61-902 and § 12-61-903, C.R.S.

* **Section 3. Applicability**

This rule applies to all individuals required to be licensed pursuant to § 12-61-902 and § 12-61-903, C.R.S.

* **Section 4. 1-2-2 Surety Bond Requirements for Mortgage Loan Originators**

1. Mortgage loan originators are deemed compliant with the surety bond requirement if their surety bond meets the requirements defined in one of the following three options:
   a. Option 1 – Mortgage loan originators, at a minimum, may acquire and maintain an individual surety bond if:
      i. The surety bond is in the amount of $25,000.00;
      ii. The surety bond is in conformance with all relevant Colorado statutory requirements;
      iii. The surety bond is exclusive to covering acts contemplated under current Colorado mortgage loan originator licensing laws;
      iv. The surety bond is not applicable to any conduct or transactions outside the jurisdiction of the Board of Mortgage Loan Originators (the "Board"); and
      v. The surety bond is identical to the individual surety bond form developed and approved by the Board. Acceptable surety bond forms may be found on the Division of Real Estate website at http://www.dora.state.co.us/real-estate/applications/mortgagebroker/index.htm
   b. Option 2 – Mortgage loan originators who are employees or exclusive agents for companies with less than 20 individuals who are required to be licensed pursuant to current Colorado mortgage loan originator licensing laws and who do not work for more than one company, may, at a minimum, operate under their company's surety bond if the surety bond meets the following criteria:
      i. The surety bond is in the amount of $100,000.00;
      ii. The surety bond is in conformance with all relevant Colorado statutory requirements;
      iii. The surety bond is exclusive to covering acts of all of the company's W-2 employees or exclusive agents contemplated under current Colorado mortgage loan originator licensing laws; and
      iv. The surety bond is identical to the company surety bond form developed and approved by the Board. Acceptable surety bond forms may be found on the Division of Real Estate website at http://www.dora.state.co.us/real-estate/applications/mortgagebroker/index.htm
   c. Option 3 – Mortgage loan originators who are W-2 employees or exclusive agents for companies with 20 or more individuals who are required to be licensed pursuant to

current Colorado mortgage loan originator licensing laws and who do not work for more than one company, may, at a minimum, operate under a company's surety bond if the surety bond meets the following criteria:

i. The surety bond is in the amount of $200,000.00;

ii. The surety bond is in conformance with all relevant Colorado statutory requirements;

iii. The surety bond is exclusive to covering acts of all of the company's W-2 employees contemplated under current Colorado mortgage loan originator licensing laws; and

iv. The surety bond is identical to the company surety bond form developed and approved by the Board. Acceptable surety bond forms may be found on the Division of Real Estate website at http://www.dora.state.co.us/real-estate/applications/mortgagebroker/index.htm

2. Regarding company surety bonds, the company shall provide the Board or an authorized representative of the Board with any and all requested surety bonds relevant to this rule or current mortgage loan originator license laws and shall verify and provide adequate proof regarding the timeline of employment for each individual operating under such company policy. Failure on the part of the company to provide such information shall result in non-compliance regarding the surety bond requirement for individual licensees operating under such company bond.

3. Mortgage loan originators shall use the Mortgage Loan Originator Licensing Update Form to ensure surety bond information is clearly and concisely disclosed and that all information required by this rule is current. This form may be found on the Division of Real Estate's website at http://www.dora.state.co.us/real-estate/mortgage/MBForms.htm .

   a. Mortgage loan originators shall forward this form by mail or personal delivery to the following address:

      i. Division of Real Estate – Attn: Mortgage Loan Originator Licensing Department
      1560 Broadway, Suite 925
      Denver, CO. 80202

4. Additionally, mortgage loan originators may update all of the information required in this rule electronically. They may access their information through the following website: https://eservices.psiexams.com/index_login.jsp. After entering their password and username, mortgage loan originators may update all information without any fees or costs associated with such action.

5. Applicants for licensure, renewal, and reinstatement shall comply with this rule and §§ 12-61-903 and 907, C.R.S., in a manner prescribed by the Board. Any licensee who so fails to obtain and maintain a surety bond in accordance with this rule or fails to provide proof of continuous coverage shall be subject to disciplinary action.

* **Section 5. Enforcement**

1. Noncompliance with this rule, whether defined or reasonably implied in the rule, may result in the imposition of any of the sanctions allowable under Colorado law, including, but not limited to:

   a. Revocation;

   b. Refusal to renew a license;

   c. Imposition of fines; and

   d. Restitution for any financial loss.

RULE 1-3-1 ERRORS AND OMISSIONS INSURANCE FOR MORTGAGE LOAN ORIGINATORS

Section 1. Authority

The Director of the Division of Real Estate adopts the following permanent rule entitled **1-3-1 Errors and Omissions Insurance for Mortgage Loan Originators**, according to her authority as found in §§ 12-61-903.5 and 910.3, C.R.S.

The notice proposes to add rule 1-3-1. The rule establishes errors and omissions coverage for mortgage loan originators.

Section 2. Scope and Purpose

Section 12-61-903.5, C.R.S. requires the Director to determine the terms and conditions of coverage required, including the minimum limits of coverage, the permissible deductible and permissible exemptions. The purpose of this rule is to define the requisite errors and omissions coverage.

* **Section 3. Applicability**

This rule applies to all individuals required to be licensed pursuant to §§ 12-61-902 and 12-61-903, C.R.S.

* **Section 4. 1-3-1 Errors and Omissions Insurance for Mortgage Loan Originators**

1. Mortgage loan originators are deemed compliant with the errors and omissions insurance requirements if their errors and omissions insurance meets the requirements defined in one of the following three options:
    a. Option 1 – Mortgage loan originators, at a minimum, may acquire and maintain individual errors and omissions insurance in their own name with the following terms of coverage:
        i. The contract and policy are in conformance with all relevant Colorado statutory requirements;
        ii. Coverage includes all acts for which a mortgage loan originator license is required, except those illegal, fraudulent or other acts which are normally excluded from such coverage;
        iii. Coverage shall encompass all types of transactions conducted by the mortgage broker and shall be in the individual mortgage loan originators' name;
        iv. Coverage is for not less than $ 100,000.00 for each licensed individual per covered claim, with an annual aggregate limit of not less than $ 300,000.00 per licensed individual; and
        v. Coverage contains a deductible no greater than $ 1,000.00 or a deductible no greater than $ 20,000.00 for policies insuring primarily reverse mortgage transactions.
    b. Option 2 – Mortgage loan originators who are employees or exclusive agents for companies with less than 20 individuals who are required to be licensed pursuant to the Mortgage Loan Originator Licensing Act and who do not work for more than one company, at a minimum, may operate under the companies errors and omissions insurance policy if the policy meets the following terms of coverage:
        i. The contract and policy are in conformance with all relevant Colorado statutory requirements;
        ii. Coverage includes all acts for which a mortgage loan originator license is required, except those illegal, fraudulent or other acts which are normally excluded from such coverage;
        iii. Coverage shall include all activities contemplated under current Colorado mortgage loan originator licensing laws and states this in the policy;

iv. Coverage shall encompass all types of transactions conducted by all of the mortgage loan originators employed at the company or by all mortgage loan originators who are exclusive agents of the company;

v. Coverage is for not less than $ 1,000,000.00 per covered claim, with an annual aggregate limit of not less than $ 2,000,000.00 that is exclusive to Colorado consumers; and

vi. Coverage contains a deductible no greater than $ 50,000.00.

c. Option 3 – Mortgage loan originators who are W-2 employees or exclusive agents for companies with 20 or more employees and who do not work for more than one company, at a minimum, may operate under the companies errors and omissions insurance policy if the policy meets the following terms of coverage:

i. The contract and policy are in conformance with all relevant Colorado statutory requirements;

ii. Coverage includes all acts for which a mortgage loan originator license is required, except those illegal, fraudulent or other acts which are normally excluded from such coverage;

iii. Coverage shall include all activities contemplated under current Colorado mortgage loan originator licensing laws and states this in the policy;

iv. Coverage shall encompass all types of transactions conducted by all of the mortgage loan originators employed at the company or by all mortgage loan originators who are exclusive agents of the company;

v. Coverage shall encompass all types of transactions conducted by all of the mortgage loan originators employed at the company;

vi. Coverage is for not less than $ 1,000,000.00 per covered claim, with an annual aggregate limit of not less than $ 4,000,000.00 that is exclusive to Colorado consumers; and

vii. Coverage contains a deductible no greater than $ 100,000.00.

2. Regarding company errors and omissions insurance policies, the company shall provide the Director or an authorized representative of the Director with any and all requested errors and omissions insurance policies relevant to this rule or the Mortgage Loan Originator Licensing Act and shall verify and provide adequate proof regarding the timeline of employment for each individual operating under such company policy. Failure on the part of the company to provide such information shall result in non-compliance regarding the errors and omissions insurance requirement for individual licensees operating under such a company policy.

* 3. Mortgage Loan originators shall use the Mortgage Loan Originator Licensing Update Form to ensure their errors and omissions insurance information is current and clearly and concisely disclosed. This form may be found on the Division of Real Estate's website at http://www.dora.state.co.us/real-estate/mortgage/MBForms.htm .

a. Mortgage loan originators shall forward this form by mail or personal delivery to the following address:

i. Division of Real Estate – Attn: Mortgage Loan Originator Licensing Department
1560 Broadway, Suite 925
Denver, CO. 80202

4. Additionally, mortgage loan originators may update all of the information required in this rule electronically. They may access their information through the following website: https://eservices.psiexams.com/index_login.jsp. After entering their password and username, mortgage loan originators may update all information without any fees or costs associated with such action.

5. For information regarding errors and omissions insurance providers, visit the Division of Real Estate's website at http://www.dora.state.co.us/real-estate/index.htm.

6. Applicants for licensure, renewal and reinstatement shall comply with this rule and § 12-61-903.5, C.R.S. in a manner prescribed by the Director. Any licensee who so fails to obtain and maintain errors and omissions coverage in accordance with this regulation or fails to provide proof of continuous coverage shall be subject to disciplinary action.

Section 5. Enforcement

1. Noncompliance with this rule, whether defined or reasonably implied in the rule, may result in the imposition of any of the sanctions allowable under Colorado law, including, but not limited to:
   a. Revocation;
   b. Refusal to renew a license;
   c. Imposition of fines; and
   d. Restitution for any financial loss.

RULE 1-4-1 LICENSING EDUCATION, EXAMINATION AND CONTINUING EDUCATION REQUIREMENTS

* **Section 1. Authority**

The Board of Mortgage Loan Originators updates the following permanent rule entitled **1-4-1 Licensing Education, Examination and Continuing Education Requirements**, according to the authority prescribed in §§ 12-61-903(3), 12-61-903(8), 12-61-910.3, and 24-4-103, C.R.S.

* **Section 2. Scope and Purpose**

The purpose of this rule is to clarify the education requirements for mortgage loan originators to first obtain their state license and then maintain that license by completing continuing education requirements. It is vital to consumer protection and to a competent mortgage loan originator practice that mortgage loan originators understand applicable State and Federal laws. Please contact the Division of Real Estate if you have any questions.

Pursuant to § 12-61-903(3)(a), C.R.S. mortgage loan originators must complete at least nine (9) hours of fundamental mortgage lending coursework and satisfactorily complete a corresponding written examination.

Additionally, in July of 2008, the Housing and Economic Recovery Act of 2008 was signed into law. Title V of the Housing and Economic Recovery Act of 2008 is the S.A.F.E. Mortgage Licensing Act. The S.A.F.E. Mortgage Licensing Act defines minimum national licensing standards for mortgage loan originators and requires states to adopt such provisions. The S.A.F.E. Mortgage Licensing Act requires that pre-licensing education and testing be developed and administered by the Nationwide Mortgage Licensing System and Registry. As a result, Colorado's education and testing requirements were updated in order to conform to provisions defined in the S.A.F.E. Mortgage Licensing Act, House Bill 09-1085 and with standards established by the Nationwide Mortgage Licensing System and Registry. Consequently, this rule outlines how existing licensees may become compliant and how new applicants will be affected.

* **Section 3. Applicability**

This rule applies to all individuals required to be licensed pursuant to §§ 12-61-902 and 12-61-903, C.R.S.

* **Section 4. Licensing Education and Examination**

1. Applicant and Licensee Education Requirements
   (a) All mortgage loan originators who obtain a Colorado mortgage loan originator license prior to January 1, 2009 must complete the Director developed and approved 40 hours of licensing education and pass a two-part written licensing examination by January 1, 2009. Individuals who fail to comply with this requirement may file for an extension.

Extensions may be granted through and including March 31, 2009 and shall only be applied for beginning December 1, 2008 and ending January 30, 2009. Mortgage loan originators requesting an education extension shall:

* i. Complete the education extension form. This form may be found on the Division of Real Estate's website at http://www.dora.state.co.us/real-estate/mortgage/MBForms.htm;

ii. Pay a $100.00 extension fee by money order or a cashier check;

* iii. Request that the Director inactivate their mortgage loan originator license if they fail to pass the written examination in accordance with this rule by March 31, 2009. A licensee's inactive status will remain in effect until passage of the mortgage loan originator examination and subsequent request for activation;

* iv. Provide the Director with an original copy of the requisite surety bond, a power of attorney and proof of errors and omissions insurance.

(b) Individuals who fail to pass the requisite written examination by January 1, 2009 and who fail to comply with the extension process defined in this rule are subject to all forms of discipline authorized by the Mortgage Loan Originator Licensing Act. Additionally, the license renewal, reinstatement or reactivation fees for such individuals will automatically be increased by $ 500.00, due to the related increase in administrative burden.

(c) The Director has created the Mortgage Loan Originator Education Extension Form. This form may be found on the Division of Real Estate's website at http://www.dora.state.co.us/real-estate/mortgage/MBForms.htm.

(d) On or after January 1, 2009 and prior to January 1, 2010, each individual applicant for initial licensing as a mortgage loan originator must complete, within the three years immediately preceding the date of the application, 40 hours of licensing education and pass a two-part exam approved by the Director of the Division of Real Estate prior to applying for a mortgage loan originator license.

* (e) For individuals licensed prior to January 1, 2010, in addition to the requirements outlined in section 4(1)(d) of this rule, you must register on the Nationwide Mortgage Licensing System and Registry and as a state-licensed loan originator. In order to do so, you must apply to Colorado through the Nationwide Mortgage Licensing System and Registry by December 17, 2010, pay the certification invoice issued by the Nationwide Mortgage Licensing System and Registry by December 31, 2010, and pass the national portion of the two-part S.A.F.E. Mortgage Loan Originator exam developed and administered by the Nationwide Mortgage Licensing System and Registry or by a company contracted by the Nationwide Mortgage Licensing System and Registry to develop and administer the two part S.A.F.E. Mortgage Loan Originator exam.

(f) On or after January 1, 2010, each individual applicant shall complete, within the three years immediately preceding the date of the applications, the 20 hours of pre-licensing education requirements developed, administered and approved by the Nationwide Mortgage Licensing System and Registry or by a company contracted by the Nationwide Mortgage Licensing System and Registry to develop, administer and approve the 20 hours of pre-licensing education and pass the two-part S.A.F.E. Mortgage Loan Originator exam also developed and administered by the Nationwide Mortgage Licensing System and Registry or by a company contracted by the Nationwide Mortgage Licensing System and Registry to develop and administer the S.A.F.E. Mortgage Loan Originator exam prior to completing the applications for a state-licensed loan originator license.

2. Certificate of Completion

(a) Mortgage loan originator applicants and licensees must receive a certification of completion from their education provider evidencing the successful completion of the respective licensing education coursework before scheduling any of the requisite examinations.

(b) Prior to January 1, 2010, mortgage loan originator applicants and licensees must ensure that their education provider files a certificate of completion with the examination provider establishing the successful completion of the respective licensing education coursework before scheduling the exam. The education provider must file the certificate of completion with the approved examination provider electronically or in such manner as prescribed by the Director.

3. Licensing Education Passing Score

* (a) Prior to January 1, 2010, the mortgage loan originator written licensing examination consisted of two parts. The two parts consisted of the Federal, State and Consumer Protection Laws portion and the Mortgage Lending Basics and Ethics portion. On or after January 1, 2009 and prior to January 1, 2010, an individual shall not be considered to have passed the written test unless the individual achieves a test score of not less than seventy-five (75) percent correct answers on both the Federal and State Law portion of the exam and the Mortgage Lending Basics portion of the exam. If the applicant failed one of the two parts, the applicant could reschedule with the examination provider to retake only the portion of the exam that they failed. In no event is a passing score accepted beyond one year (365 days) from the date of the passing score.

* (b) On or after January 1, 2010, the S.A.F.E. Mortgage Loan Originator examination, developed and administered by the Nationwide Mortgage Licensing System and Registry or by a company contracted by the Nationwide Mortgage Licensing System and Registry to develop and administer the examination will consist of two parts. These two parts include a national component and a Colorado state specific component. On or after January 1, 2010, an individual shall pass the test in accordance with policies and procedures developed and administered by the Nationwide Mortgage Licensing System and Registry and in compliance with the S.A.F.E. Mortgage Licensing Act.

4. Qualifying Schools

(a) Prior to January 1, 2010, applicants and licensees must complete the requisite 40 hours of licensing education, approved by the Director, from any accredited degree-granting college or university or any private occupational school that has a certificate of approval from the Division of Private Occupational Schools in accordance with the provisions of article 59 of title 12, Colorado Revised Statutes.

(b) On or after January 1, 2010, applicants must complete the requisite 20 hours of licensing education from an educational provider approved by the Nationwide Mortgage Licensing System and Registry or by a company contracted by the Nationwide Mortgage Licensing System and Registry to approve educational providers.

5. Forty Hour Licensing Education Requirement

(a) Prior to January 1, 2010, mortgage loan originator applicants and licensees must successfully complete the required forty hours of licensing education through classroom instruction or an equivalent distance learning course offered in a manner as prescribed by the Director. For the purposes of this rule, distance learning shall not be construed to include home or correspondent education. Rather, equivalent distant or distance learning courses shall only include online courses that ensure through security features and functionality that an individual has spent the same amount of time on the online course as they would in a traditional classroom setting. Pursuant to the requirements in Part 1 of this rule, the following licensing education must be successfully completed prior to taking the examination and applying for a license:

i. A minimum of 19.5 hours in Federal and State Law;
ii. A minimum of 16 hours in Mortgage 101; and
iii. A minimum of 4.5 hours in Business and Trade Practices

6. Exemption Qualifications
   (a) Prior to January 1, 2010, as prescribed by the Director or person(s) authorized by the Director, qualifying mortgage loan originator applicants who meet the following criteria are exempt from having to complete the Mortgage Lending Basics and Ethics portion of the education coursework and respective examination. To qualify for the exemption, mortgage loan originators must meet all five requirements. They are as follows:
      i. Currently maintain a Colorado mortgage loan originator license.
      ii. Maintain a membership with a mortgage loan originator association approved for exemption by the Division of Real Estate.
      iii. Maintain a mortgage loan originator association designation that is current and in good standing.
      iv. Provide the association's letter of certification to the education course provider prior to completing coursework.
      v. Provide the association's letter of certification to an independent testing service contracted with by the Director, prior to taking the Federal and State Law exam.

   * (b) Prior to January 1, 2010, those who meet the criteria for exemption must complete the Federal and State Law portion of the licensing coursework and pass the Federal and State Law portion of the exam with a score of seventy-five (75) percent or higher.
7. Authority to Audit Education Provider
   * (a) The Board or the Board's designee may audit any mortgage loan originator courses offered and may request from each education provider or schools offering such courses, all related instructional materials, student attendance records and other information that may be necessary for an audit. The purpose of the audit is to ensure that education providers and schools adhere to the approved course of study, offer course material and instructions consistent with acceptable education standards and instruct in such a manner that the desired learning objectives are met. Failure to comply with this rule may result in the withdrawal of course approval.
8. Retesting
   (a) An individual may retake a test three (3) consecutive times with each consecutive taking occurring at least 30 days after the preceding test.
   (b) After failing three (3) consecutive tests, an individual shall wait at least six (6) months before taking the test again.
   (c) Individuals who fail to maintain a valid license for a period of five (5) years or longer shall retake the test prior to re-application, not taking into account any time during which such individual was licensed.

* **Section 5. Continuing Education**

1. The continuing education requirements for individuals licensed prior to January 1, 2009, shall begin after their first license renewal. Individuals licensed prior to January 1, 2009, shall complete at least 8 hours of continuing education courses reviewed and approved by the Nationwide Mortgage Licensing System and Registry or by a company contracted to review and approve continuing education courses and a two hour annual Colorado specific state update course reviewed and approved by the Division of Real Estate each calendar year and prior to subsequent license and registration renewals.
   a. Passage of the national portion of the S.A.F.E. Mortgage Loan Originator examination developed and administered by the Nationwide Mortgage Licensing System and Registry or by a company contracted by the Nationwide Mortgage Licensing System and Registry to develop and administer the national portion of the S.A.F.E. Mortgage Loan Originator examination shall satisfy one year of continuing education requirements if continuing education is required in the year in which the individual has passed the national portion

of the S.A.F.E. Mortgage Loan Originator exam as determined by the Nationwide Mortgage Licensing System and Registry.

2. The continuing education requirements for individuals licensed on or after January 1, 2009, shall begin after issuance of the initial license. Individuals licensed on or after January 1, 2009, shall complete at least 8 hours of continuing education courses reviewed and approved by the Nationwide Mortgage Licensing System and Registry or by a company contracted to review and approve continuing education courses and a two hour annual Colorado specific state update course reviewed and approved by the Division of Real Estate each calendar year and prior to license and registration renewals.
   a. Passage of the national portion of the S.A.F.E. Mortgage Loan Originator examination developed and administered by the Nationwide Mortgage Licensing System and Registry or by a company contracted by the Nationwide Mortgage Licensing System and Registry to develop and administer the national portion of the S.A.F.E. Mortgage Loan Originator examination shall satisfy one year of continuing education if continuing education is required in the year in which the individual has passed the national portion of the test as determined by the Nationwide Mortgage Licensing System and Registry.
3. For more information regarding the continuing education requirements, please review the Division of Real Estate website at http://www.dora.state.co.us/real-estate/mortgagebroker-registration.htm.

* 4. The Colorado Division of Real Estate will maintain a list of course providers approved to teach the Colorado two (2) hour annual update course on the Division website so interested parties may research and learn where the course is offered.

* 5. Licensee requirements:
   (a) All individuals required to be licensed as state-licensed mortgage loan originators and required to complete the Colorado two (2) hour annual update course shall maintain records of completion for a period of four (4) years.

* 6. Colorado two (2) hour annual update course provider requirements:
   (a) In order to provide and teach the Colorado two (2) hour annual update course, educators and trainers not exempt from the Colorado Division of Private Occupational Schools oversight, pursuant to 12-59-101, et seq., C.R.S., must be approved by the Colorado Division of Private Occupational Schools and approved by an authorized representative of the Board of Mortgage Loan Originators.
   (b) In order to provide and teach the Colorado two (2) hour annual update course, educators and trainers exempt from the Colorado Division of Private Occupational Schools oversight, pursuant to section 12-59-104, C.R.S., must be approved by an authorized representative of the Board of Mortgage Loan Originators.
   (c) If not approved by the Colorado Division of Private Occupational Schools, the trainer shall attend one train-the-trainer class, as developed and administered by the Colorado Division of Real Estate, prior to teaching the Colorado two (2) hour annual update course.
   (d) All education providers and trainers interested in teaching the Colorado two (2) hour annual update course shall apply each calendar year with the Colorado Division of Real Estate for approval in a manner prescribed by the Board of Mortgage Loan Originators; prior to teaching the course material. Educators and trainers that are exempt from the Division of Private Occupational Schools' oversight shall provide proof of such exemption.
   (e) All education providers and trainers interested in teaching the Colorado two (2) hour annual update course shall keep records of all individuals that have completed the Colorado two (2) hour annual update course and shall provide the Colorado Division of Real Estate with a quarterly list of such individuals by April 15 of each calendar year, July 15 of each calendar year, October 15 of each calendar year, January 15th of each

calendar year, and in a manner prescribed by the Board of Mortgage Loan Originators. Educators are required to keep records of course attendance for a period of four (4) years.

(f) All education providers shall provide the course material and applicable handouts to all students that have enrolled and completed the Colorado two (2) hour annual update course.

(g) All education providers and trainers shall provide a certificate of completion to all individuals that have completed the Colorado two (2) hour annual update course.

* RULE 1-5-1 MORTGAGE LOAN ORIGINATOR LICENSE AND REGISTRATION INACTIVATION AND REACTIVATION

* **Section 1. Authority**

The Board of Mortgage Loan Originators updates the following permanent rule entitled **1-5-1 Mortgage Loan Originator License and Registration Inactivation and Reactivation**, according to authority provided in section 12-61-910.3, C.R.S.

This notice proposes to update rule 1-5-1. The rule requires administrative fees to be collected when a mortgage loan originator seeks to reactivate their license after it has been inactivated for specific reasons.

* **Section 2. Scope and Purpose**

Section 12-61-903.3, C.R.S., allows the Board of Mortgage Loan Originators to inactivate licenses for specific reasons. The inactivation process creates an administrative burden on the Division of Real Estate, which includes ensuring the applicant is compliant with all licensing requirements. This task is similar in nature to review of a license application, but is often less intensive procedurally. Accordingly, the purpose of this rule is to establish an administrative fee collected upon reactivation for specific circumstances.

* **Section 3. Applicability**

This rule applies to all individuals required to be licensed pursuant to sections 12-61-902 and 12-61-903, C.R.S.

* **Section 4. 1-5-1 Mortgage Loan Originator License and Registration Inactivation and Reactivation**

1. If a mortgage loan originator license or registration is inactivated by the Board of Mortgage Loan Originators or an authorized representative of the Board for one or any combination of the following reasons, the mortgage loan originator shall pay an administrative fee determined by the Board, due to the related increase in administrative burden, in order to reactivate their license:
   a. The mortgage loan originator has failed or is failing to comply with the surety bond requirements of sections 12-61-903(6) and 12-61-907, C.R.S., or any rule of the Board that directly or indirectly addresses surety bond requirements;
   b. The mortgage loan originator has failed or is failing to comply with the errors and omissions insurance requirement in section 12-61-903.5, C.R.S., or any rule of the Board that directly or indirectly addresses errors and omissions insurance requirements;
   c. The mortgage loan originator has failed or is failing to maintain current contact information, surety bond information, or errors and omissions insurance information as required by the Mortgage Loan Originator Licensing and Mortgage Company Registration Act, or by any rule of the Board that directly or indirectly addresses such requirements;
   d. The mortgage loan originator has failed or is failing to respond to an investigation or examination;

e. The mortgage loan originator has failed or is failing to comply with any of the education or testing requirements set forth in the Mortgage Loan Originator Licensing and Mortgage Company Registration Act, or by any rule of the Board that directly or indirectly addresses education or testing requirements; or

f. The mortgage loan originator has failed to register with, and provide all required information to, the Nationwide Mortgage Licensing System and Registry.

2. Individuals who have an inactive license are prohibited from practicing as a mortgage loan originator. Additionally, individuals who have an inactive license are prohibited from engaging in any mortgage related activities which requires licensure pursuant to the Colorado Mortgage Loan Originator Licensing and Mortgage Company Registration Act, Board rule, or as prescribed by a Board position statement.

3. In order for an inactive mortgage loan originator license to be reactivated, the individual seeking reactivation shall provide the Division of Real Estate with proof of full compliance with current mortgage loan originator license law.

4. In order for an inactive mortgage loan originator license to be reactivated, the individual seeking reactivation must pay the requisite administrative fee. All administrative fees shall be collected in the form of a money order or a cashier's check.

5. The Board has created the Mortgage Loan Originator License Reactivation Form. This form may be found on the Division of Real Estate's website at http://www.dora.state.co.us/real-estate/mortgage/MBForms.htm.

* RULE 2-1-1 [Repealed 08/30/2009]

RULE 3-1-1 REASONABLE INQUIRY AND TANGIBLE NET BENEFIT

Section 1. Authority

The statutory basis for this rule entitled **3-1-1 Reasonable Inquiry and Tangible Net Benefit**, is § 12-61-910.3, C.R.S.

The notice proposes to add rule 3-1-1.

Section 2. Scope and Purpose

Section 12-61-904.5, C.R.S., states that mortgage loan originators shall have a duty of good faith and fair dealing in all communications and transactions with a borrower. Section 12-61-904.5(1)(b), C.R.S., requires mortgage loan originators to make a reasonable inquiry concerning the borrower's current and prospective income, existing debts and other obligations, and any other information known to the mortgage loan originator and, after making such inquiry, to make his or her best efforts to recommend, broker, or originate a residential mortgage loan that takes into consideration the information submitted by the borrowers. Additionally, section 12-61-904.5(1)(a), C.R.S., prohibits mortgage loan originators from recommending or inducing borrowers to enter into a transaction that does not have a reasonable, tangible net benefit to the borrower, considering all of the circumstances, including the terms of a loan, the cost of a loan, and the borrower's circumstances. After consulting with industry leaders, the Division has learned that there is uncertainty in the marketplace regarding the impact of these new provisions, specific to mortgage products and various documentation types. Documentation types include, but are not limited to: stated income; no income verification; no income disclosure; no asset verification; and no asset disclosure.

The mortgage lending community is uncertain if the aforementioned provisions prohibit non-traditional mortgage products and documentation types, since these provisions are new and have not been interpreted by the Division of Real Estate. This uncertainty could negatively impact the availability of mortgage credit to consumers. Due to the recent rise in foreclosures, the decline of the subprime market, and the closing of lenders on a national scale, the Division must adopt rules to clarify the new provisions in an effort to limit further reductions in mortgage credit. The purpose of this rule is to clarify uncertainties regarding reasonable inquiry and reasonable, tangible net benefit.''

Section 3. Definitions

A "Uniform Residential Loan Application" shall mean the Freddie Mac Form 65 or the Fannie Mae Form 1003 used in residential loan transactions on properties of four or fewer units. The Uniform Residential Loan Application forms defined in this rule are those editions of the forms that are current and effective on January 1, 2008 and do not include any later amendments or editions. The forms are available for inspection at the Division of Real Estate at 1560 Broadway, Suite 925, Denver, Colorado, 80202. These forms are posted on the Division of Real Estate's website at http://www.dora.state.co.us/real-estate/index.htm in the mortgage loan originator section under forms; the form(s) may be examined at any state publications depository library.

* **Section 4. Applicability**

This rule applies to all individuals required to be licensed pursuant to sections 12-61-902 and 12-61-903, C.R.S.

* **Section 5. 3-1-1 Reasonable Inquiry and Tangible Net Benefit**

1. Section 12-61-904.5(1)(b), C.R.S. does not prohibit specific mortgage products or documentation types. This provision requires the mortgage loan originator to recommend appropriate products.
   a. Mortgage loan originators shall only recommend appropriate products after reasonable inquiry has been made in order to understand borrower's current and prospective financial status.
   * b. Reasonable inquiry requires the mortgage loan originator to interview borrowers and discuss current and prospective income, including the income's source and likely continuance. Reasonable inquiry may not require the mortgage loan originator to verify such income.
   c. Mortgage loan originators have a duty to recommend mortgage products based on the information provided by the borrower.
2. Mortgage loan originators shall be deemed in compliance with Colorado law, § 12-61-904.5(1)(b), C.R.S., concerning reasonable inquiry, upon interviewing and discussing, with all applicable borrowers, all sections contained in the uniform residential loan application and upon completion of a Tangible Net Benefit Disclosure. The Tangible Net Benefit Disclosure is posted on the Division of Real Estate's website at http://www.dora.state.co.us/real-estate/mortgage/MBForms.htm.
3. A mortgage loan originator must first make a reasonable inquiry, in order to determine the reasonable, tangible net benefit for a borrower. The reasonable, tangible net benefit standard in § 12-61-904.5(1)(a), C.R.S., is inherently dependent upon the totality of facts and circumstances relating to a specific transaction. While the refinancing of certain home loans may clearly provide a reasonable, tangible net benefit, others may require closer scrutiny or consideration to determine whether a particular loan provides the requisite benefit to the borrower.
   a. When determining reasonable, tangible net benefit, there are many considerations mortgage loan originators shall take into account and discuss with prospective borrowers. If applicable, the required considerations for mortgage loan originators determining the requisite benefit shall include, but are not limited to:
      i. Lower payments;
      ii. Condensed amortization schedule;
      iii. Debt consolidation;

iv. Cash out;
v. Avoiding foreclosure;
vi. Negative amortization;
vii. Balloon payments;
viii. Variable rates;
ix. Interest only options;
x. Prepayment penalties; and
xi. Hybrid mortgage products.

4. The purpose or reason for a purchase or refinance transaction shall be identified by the borrower. A mortgage loan originator shall require that all borrowers describe, in writing, the reasons they are seeking a mortgage loan, a loan modification or to refinance an existing mortgage loan.
   a. It is the responsibility of the mortgage loan originator to ensure this information is acquired and accurately documented.
   b. Pursuant to § 12-61-904.5(1), C.R.S., a mortgage loan originator may not have demonstrated a duty of good faith and fair dealing in all communications and transactions with a borrower if it is determined that a mortgage loan originator completed the required purpose or reason for a purchase, loan modification or refinance transaction without consulting the borrower.

* 5. The Board developed a suggested disclosure form regarding reasonable, tangible net benefit. Alternate disclosures are acceptable if they include all information required on the suggested form, as determined by the Board.
   a. At the time of completing a loan application a mortgage loan originator shall complete a Tangible Net Benefit Disclosure with the borrower(s).
   b. The Tangible Net Benefit Disclosure shall also be completed with the borrower(s) prior to the borrower(s) signing loan closing documents if the reasonable, tangible net benefit has changed.
   c. Tangible Net Benefit disclosures shall be signed by both the mortgage loan originator and the borrowers.

* 6. Mortgage loan originators shall provide completed disclosure forms to all borrowers within three (3) business days of completion. Furthermore, mortgage loan originators must be able to provide proof to the Board or an authorized representative of the Board that the disclosure forms defined in this rule were in fact provided to the borrower within three (3) business days of completion.

7. Mortgage loan originators shall be presumed compliant with this rule when using the suggested form and when disclosures meet the timelines defined in this rule.

Section 6. Enforcement

1. Noncompliance with this rule, whether defined or reasonably implied in the rule, may result in the imposition of any of the sanctions allowable under Colorado law, including, but not limited to:
   a. Revocation;
   b. Refusal to renew a license;
   c. Imposition of fines; and
   d. Restitution for any financial loss.

* RULE 3-1-2 MORTGAGE LOAN ORIGINATOR AND MORTGAGE COMPANY DUTIES TO RESPOND AND PROVIDE REQUESTED DOCUMENTS FOR INVESTIGATIONS

* **Section 1. Authority**

The statutory basis for this rule entitled **3-1-2 Mortgage Loan Originator and Mortgage Company Duties to Respond and Provide Requested Documents for Investigations**, is section 12-61-910.3, C.R.S.

This notice proposes to update rule 3-1-2. The rule establishes that mortgage loan originators and mortgage companies have a duty to respond to and provide requested documentation for investigations conducted by the Board of Mortgage Loan Originators.

* **Section 2. Scope and Purpose**

Section 12-61-905(7)(b), C.R.S., states that the Board of Mortgage Loan Originators may, and, upon the complaint in writing of any person, shall, investigate the activities of any licensee or any individual who assumes to act in such capacity within the state. Section 12-61-905.5(1)(k), C.R.S., requires mortgage loan originators to maintain possession of the documents prescribed by the rules of the Board, for a period of four (4) years, for the future use or inspection by an authorized representative of the Board. Section 12-61-905.1(1)(b), C.R.S., requires mortgage companies to maintain possession of the documents or records prescribed by the rules of the Board, for a period of four (4) years, for the future use or inspection by an authorized representative of the Board. The purpose of this regulation is to define what documents should be retained for a period of four years and to require mortgage loan originators and mortgage companies to provide a written response and all requested documents to the Board or an authorized representative of the Board. Additionally, this regulation prescribes the time period in which all persons and entities shall respond to Board inquiries, including, but not limited to, document and information requests during investigations of complaints or any other investigation conducted for the purpose of determining compliance with the Mortgage Loan Originator Licensing and Mortgage Company Registration Act.

Section 3. Definitions

1. "Secure environment" means a system which implements the controlled storage and use of information.

* **Section 4. Applicability**

This rule applies to all persons required to be licensed or registered pursuant to sections 12-61-902 and 12-61-903, C.R.S.

* **Section 5. 3-1-2 Mortgage Loan Originator and Mortgage Company Duties to Respond and Provide Requested Documents for Investigations**

* 1. Persons required to be licensed or registered pursuant to sections 12-61-902 and 12-61-903, C.R.S., shall provide the Board or the Board's representative with all information required by this rule.
    a. Failure to provide all information requested by the Board or an authorized representative of the Board within a timeline established by the Board, or authorized representative of the Board, shall be grounds for disciplinary action and grounds for the imposition of fines unless the Board, or authorized representative of the Board, has granted an extension of time for the response.
        i. Mortgage loan originators and mortgage companies may ask for an extension of time to comply if:
            1. The request is done so in writing; and

2. The request is received by the Board or an authorized representative of the Board prior to the expiration date defined in the notification letter sent by the Board or an authorized representative of the Board.

ii. Any and all extensions granted are done so at the discretion of the Board or an authorized representative of the Board.

b. Failure to provide all requested information shall be grounds for disciplinary action and grounds for the imposition of fines regardless of whether the underlying complaint results in further investigation or subsequent action by the Board.

* 2. The response from the person shall contain the following:

a. If requested in the notification letter, the mortgage loan originator shall provide a complete and specific answer to the factual recitations, allegations or averments made in the complaint filed against the licensee, whether made by a member of the public, on the Board's own motion, or by an authorized representative of the Board;

b. The mortgage loan originator shall provide a complete and specific response to all questions, allegations, or averments presented in the notification letter; and

c. Any and all documents or records requested in the notification letter.

* 3. Mortgage companies shall maintain any and all documents collected, gathered, and provided for the purpose of negotiating and originating residential mortgage loans for a period of four (4) years. Additionally, mortgage companies shall maintain any and all documents used for the purpose of soliciting or marketing borrowers that were directed, made, or caused to be made by the mortgage company. These documents include but are not limited to:

a. All uniform residential loan applications (Form 1003);
b. All required state and federal disclosures;
c. Asset statements;
d. Income documentation;
e. Verification of employment;
f. Verification of deposit;
g. Lender submission forms;
h. Advertisements;
i. Flyers;
j. HUD-1 Settlement Statements;
k. Uniform Underwriting and Transmittal Summary (Form 1008); and
l. Credit report.

* 4. All mortgage loan originators shall maintain any and all documents used for the purpose of soliciting or marketing borrowers that were directed, made or caused to be made by the mortgage loan originator.

* 5. All documents required in this rule shall be kept in a secure environment. Electronic storage is acceptable as long as the information is accessible and kept in a secure environment.

Section 6. Enforcement

1. Noncompliance with this rule, whether defined or reasonably implied in the rule, may result in the imposition of any of the sanctions allowable under Colorado law, including, but not limited to:

a. Revocation;
b. Refusal to renew a license;
c. Imposition of fines; and
d. Restitution for any financial loss.

* RULE 3-1-3 MAINTAINING CURRENT CONTACT INFORMATION AND ALL INFORMATION REQUIRED FOR LICENSING

* **Section 1. Authority**

The statutory basis for this rule, entitled **Maintaining Current Contact Information and All Information Required for Licensing**, is section 12-61-910.3, C.R.S.

This notice proposes to update rule 3-1-3. The rule defines the requirement for mortgage loan originators and all other individuals required to be licensed to maintain contact information and all information required for licensing.

* **Section 2. Scope and Purpose**

In order to implement and enforce Colorado mortgage loan originator laws, the Board must have the ability to correspond or request documentation from licensees. Furthermore, licensees are responsible for maintaining specific requirements for licensing. These include, but are not limited to a surety bond and errors and omissions insurance. All licensees are responsible for maintaining such requirements.

The purpose of this rule is to ensure that licensees maintain current contact information and all information required for licensing to ensure the Board may adequately protect Colorado consumers.

Section 3. Definitions

1. "Address" means the street address, city, state and postal code.
2. "Physical Address" means the physical location of the property.
3. "Business Name" means the company for which individuals who originate a mortgage, offer to originate a mortgage, act as a mortgage loan originator, or offer to act as a mortgage loan originator are officers, partners, members, managers, owners, exclusive agents, contractors, independent contractors or employees.

* **Section 4. Applicability**

This rule applies to all individuals required to be licensed pursuant to sections 12-61-902 and 12-61-903, C.R.S.

* **Section 5. 3-1-3 Maintaining Current Contact Information and All Information Required for Licensing**

* 1. Individuals required to be licensed as state licensed loan originators shall maintain all current contact information and all information required for licensing, in a manner acceptable to the Board, including on the Division of Real Estate database and on the Nationwide Mortgage Licensing System and Registry. Failure to maintain the information identified in this rule shall be grounds for disciplinary action.
2. Contact information shall include, but is not limited to:
   a. E-mail address;
   b. Legal first, middle and last names;
   c. Physical home address;
   d. Home phone number;
   e. Business address;
   f. Business phone number; and
   g. Business name.
3. Information required for licensing includes, but is not limited to:
   a. Surety bond company;
   b. Surety bond number;
   c. Surety bond effective date;

d. Errors and omissions insurance provider;
e. Errors and omissions policy number;
f. Errors and omissions effective and expiration date; and
g. Convictions, pleas of guilt or nolo contendere for all crimes.

* 4. Individuals required to be licensed as a state licensed loan originator shall update the Board within thirty (30) days of any changes to the information defined in this rule on both the Division of Real Estate database and on the Nationwide Mortgage Licensing System and Registry.

5. The Director has created the Mortgage Loan Originator Licensing Update Form to ensure this information is clearly and concisely disclosed. This form may be found on the Division of Real Estate's website at http://www.dora.state.co.us/real-estate/mortgage/MBForms.htm. Mortgage loan originators shall use this form to ensure all information defined in this rule is current.
   a. Mortgage loan originators shall forward this form by mail or personal delivery to the following address:
      i. Division of Real Estate – Attn: Mortgage Broker Licensing Department
         1560 Broadway, Suite 925
         Denver, CO 80202

* 6. All individuals required to be licensed as state licensed loan originators shall maintain all information prescribed in this rule on the Nationwide Mortgage Licensing System and Registry and in conformance to procedures developed by the Nationwide Mortgage Licensing System and Registry.

* 7. Additionally, mortgage loan originators may update all of the information required in this rule electronically. They may access their information through the following website: https://eservices.psiexams.com/index_login.jsp. After entering their password and username, mortgage loan originators may update all information without any fees or costs associated with such action.

Section 6. Enforcement

1. Noncompliance with this rule, whether defined or reasonably implied in the rule, may result in the imposition of any of the sanctions allowable under Colorado law, including, but not limited to:
   a. Revocation;
   b. Refusal to renew a license;
   c. Imposition of fines; and
   d. Restitution for any financial loss.

RULE 3-1-4 PREPAYMENT PENALTIES

Section 1. Authority

The statutory basis for this rule, entitled **Prepayment Penalties**, is § 12-61-910.3, C.R.S.

The notice proposes to add rule 3-1-4. The rule addresses mortgage transactions that contain specific prepayment penalty terms.

* **Section 2. Scope and Purpose**

The Board has learned that some extended prepayment penalties lead to higher rates of foreclosure. Specifically, prepayment penalties which extend past the adjustment date of a mortgage loan often severely restrict the ability of the borrower to refinance or sell their property. Additionally, in higher rate environments, borrowers often have only two viable options: to absorb a much higher monthly payment or lose their home through foreclosure proceedings. The Board updates this rule in order to address the high rate of foreclosures in Colorado resulting from particular prepayment penalties.

Pursuant to § 12-61-904.5(1), C.R.S., mortgage loan originators have a duty of good faith and fair dealing in all communications and transactions with a borrower. This duty includes, but is not limited to, making a reasonable inquiry into a borrower's ability to repay a loan and recommending or inducing a borrower to enter into only those transactions that have a reasonable, tangible net benefit to the borrower.

The purpose of this rule is to establish a presumption that transactions which include a prepayment penalty that extends past the adjustment date of any teaser rate, payment rate, or interest rate included in the mortgage loan do not provide a reasonable, tangible net benefit to the borrower.

Section 3. Definitions

1. "Adjustable rate mortgage" means a mortgage in which the teaser rate, payment rate or the interest rate changes periodically and in some cases, may adjust according to corresponding fluctuations in an index.
2. "Adjustment date" means the date the teaser rate, payment rate or interest rate changes on an adjustable rate mortgage.
3. "Interest rate" means the rate used to calculate a borrower's monthly interest payment.
4. "Payment rate" means the rate used to determine a borrower's monthly payment.
5. "Teaser rate" means a temporary and often low introductory rate on an adjustable rate mortgage.
6. "Prepayment Penalty" means a fee assessed pursuant to the terms of the loan on a borrower who repays all or part of the principal of a loan before it is due. Prepayment penalties do not include interest payments of thirty (30) days or less that may be assessed pursuant to the terms of some FHA or VA loans. Prepayment penalties for the purpose of this rule do not include termination fees of $500.00 or less that are associated with home equity lines of credit.

* **Section 4. Applicability**

This rule applies to mortgage loan originators as that term is defined in § 12-61-902(6), C.R.S. This rule applies to all individuals required to be licensed pursuant to §§ 12-61-902 and 12-61-903, C.R.S.

* **Section 5. 3-1-4 Prepayment Penalties**

1. Mortgage loan originators who recommend or induce a borrower into a transaction that contains a prepayment penalty which extends past the adjustment date for any type of an adjustable rate mortgage shall be presumed to have violated their duty of good faith and fair dealing requirement pursuant to section 12-61-904.5, C.R.S. This includes, but is not limited to:
   a. Prepayment penalties that extend past the adjustment date of any teaser rate used to calculate a borrower's monthly mortgage payment;
   b. Prepayment penalties that extend past the adjustment date of any interest rate used to calculate a borrower's monthly mortgage payment;
   c. Prepayment penalties that extend past the adjustment date of any payment rate used to calculate a borrower's monthly mortgage payment; and
   d. Prepayment penalties that extend past the adjustment date of any like tool or instrument, similar to the teaser rate, payment rate or interest rate defined in this rule, used to calculate a borrower's monthly mortgage payment.

* 2. Information provided to consumers should clearly explain the ramifications of prepayment penalties. Borrowers should be informed of the existence of any prepayment penalty, how it will be calculated, and when it may be imposed. A prepayment penalty disclosure form may be prescribed by the Board, completion of which will constitute compliance with this section 5(2).

Section 6. Enforcement

1. Noncompliance with this rule, whether defined or reasonably implied in the rule, may result in the imposition of any of the sanctions allowable under Colorado law, including, but not limited to:
   a. Revocation;
   b. Refusal to renew a license;
   c. Imposition of fines; and
   d. Restitution for any financial loss.

* RULE 3-1-5 RESPONSIBILITY TO SUBMIT NMLS CALL REPORTS

* **Section 1. Authority**

The statutory authorities for this rule entitled 3-1-5 Responsibility **to Submit NMLS Call Reports**, are §§ 12-61-903 (10) and 12-61-910.3, C.R.S.

* **Section 2. Scope and Purpose**

Title V, section 1505(e), U.S.C. states that each mortgage loan originator licensee shall submit to the Nationwide Mortgage Licensing System and Registry (the "NMLS") reports of condition, which shall be in such form and shall contain such information as the NMLS may require.

* **Section 3. Applicability**

This rule applies to all state-licensed mortgage companies and all individuals required to be licensed pursuant to §§ 12-61-902 and 12-61-903, C.R.S.

* **Section 4. 3-1-5 Responsibility to Submit NMLS Call Reports**

1. Beginning January 1, 2012, all mortgage companies and mortgage loan originators must submit the NMLS Mortgage Call Report on a calendar quarterly basis in such form and shall contain such information as the NMLS may require.
2. A mortgage company must identify the applicable NMLS Mortgage Call Report. This includes, but is not limited to, the Standard Section and The Expanded Section of the NMLS Mortgage Call Report. The mortgage company must identify and complete the report on behalf of all employed mortgage loan originators or other mortgage loan originators that operate through their company.
3. If a mortgage company does not submit the NMLS Mortgage Call Report on behalf of their employed mortgage loan originators or other mortgage loan originators that operate through their company, an individualized NMLS Mortgage Call Report, as prescribed the NMLS, is required to be submitted by the individual mortgage loan originator.
4. The quarterly report is due within 45 days of the end of the quarter and the financial condition report of the Standard Section is due annually 90 days from the company's fiscal year end.
5. Mortgage companies and mortgage loan originators must comply with any rules, policies and procedures relating to the submission of a Mortgage Call Report that are prescribed by the NMLS.
6. Failure to properly submit a NMLS Mortgage Call Report in a timely manner prescribed by the NMLS shall prevent the mortgage company and/or the individual mortgage loan originator from renewing their NMLS registration and state license.

* **Section 5. Enforcement**

1. Noncompliance with this rule, whether defined or reasonably implied in the rule, may result in the imposition of any of the sanctions allowable under Colorado law, including, but not limited to:

a. Revocation;
b. Refusal to renew a license; and
c. Imposition of fines

* RULE 5-1-1 MORTGAGE LOAN ORIGINATOR CONTRACTS

Section 1. Authority

The statutory basis for this rule, entitled **Mortgage Loan Originator Contracts**, is § 12-61-910.3, C.R.S.

The notice proposes to update rule 5-1-1. The rule defines the requirement for mortgage loan originators to have contracts with borrowers and with mortgage lenders.

Section 2. Scope and Purpose

Section 12-61-913, C.R.S., requires contracts between a mortgage loan originator and a borrower to be in writing and to contain the entire agreement of the parties. This section also requires mortgage loan originators to have a written correspondent or loan originator agreement with a lender before any solicitation of, or contracting with, any member of the public. The purpose of this regulation is to define compliance with the contractual requirements.

Section 3. Applicability

This rule applies to mortgage loan originators as that term is defined in § 12-61-902(6), C.R.S. and includes those persons who originate a mortgage, offer to originate a mortgage, act as a mortgage loan originator, or offer to act as a mortgage loan originator. This rule applies to all individuals required to be licensed pursuant to §§ 12-61-902 and 12-61-903, C.R.S.

Section 4. 5-1-1 Mortgage Loan Originator Contracts

1. Section 12-61-913(1), C.R.S. states that every contract between a mortgage loan originator and a borrower shall be in writing and shall contain the entire agreement of the parties.
    a. Section 12-61-913(1), C.R.S. does not require a contract between a mortgage loan originator and a borrower. Rather, that if a contract does exist, such contract shall be in writing.
2. Section 12-61-913(2), C.R.S., states a mortgage loan originator shall have a written correspondent or loan originator agreement with a lender before any solicitation of, or contracting with, any member of the public.
    a. Mortgage loan originators are compliant with § 12-61-913(2), C.R.S. if they adhere to one of the following requirements:
        i. They individually have a written correspondent or loan originator agreement with a lender before any solicitation of, or contracting with, any member of the public;
        ii. They are an officer, partner, member, exclusive agent, or employee of a company that has a written correspondent or loan originator agreement with a lender before any solicitation of, or contracting with, any member of the public;
        iii. They are acting as an independent contractor and maintain a contractual agreement with a company that has a written correspondent or loan originator agreement with a lender before any solicitation of, or contracting with, any member of the public; or
        iv. They are an employee of a lender before any solicitation of, or contracting with, any member of the public.

Section 5. Enforcement

1. Noncompliance with this rule, whether defined or reasonably implied in the rule, may result in the imposition of any of the sanctions allowable under Colorado law, including, but not limited to:
   a. Revocation;
   b. Refusal to renew a license;
   c. Imposition of fines; and
   d. Restitution for any financial loss.

* RULE 5-1-2 MORTGAGE LOAN ORIGINATOR DISCLOSURES

* **Section 1. Authority**

The Board of Mortgage Loan Originators adopts the following permanent rule entitled **5-1-2 Mortgage Loan Originator Disclosures**, according to its statutory authority in section 12-61-910.3, C.R.S.

The notice proposes to update rule 5-1-2. The rule establishes required disclosures for mortgage loan originators.

* **Section 2. Scope and Purpose**

Section 12-61-914, C.R.S., requires mortgage loan originators, within three (3) business days after receipt of a loan application or any money from a borrower, to disclose specific details of a loan transaction to the borrower. These details include, but are not limited to: the annual percentage rate, finance charge, amount financed, total amount of all payments, third party costs, and terms of a lock-in agreement. The Board has learned that uncertainty exists in the mortgage industry regarding how and when to provide such disclosures.

The purpose of this rule is to ensure that disclosures, as set forth in section 12-61-914, C.R.S., are met and that borrowers are provided with accurate and clear disclosures regarding their mortgage loan transaction.

* **Section 3. Definitions**

A. "Truth-in-Lending Disclosure" means the disclosure form established by the Truth in Lending Act, specific to regulation Z, appendices H-2, H-3, H-4(a), (b), (c) and (d).

B. "Good Faith Estimate Disclosure" means the disclosure form established in the Real Estate Settlement Procedures Act, part 3500, appendix C.

C. "Rate" means the teaser rate, payment rate or interest rate used to determine a borrower's monthly payment or deferred interest specific to reverse mortgage transactions.

D. "Teaser rate" means a temporary and often low introductory rate on an adjustable rate mortgage.

E. "Payment rate" means the rate used to determine a borrower's monthly payment.

F. "Interest rate" means the rate used to calculate a borrower's monthly interest payment.

G. "Payment Type" means principal and interest, interest only or negative amortization.

H. "Fixed Term" means the length of time a teaser rate, payment rate or interest rate is fixed and will not adjust.

I. "Index" means the index for an adjustable rate mortgage.

J. "Initial Adjustment Cap" means the limit on how much the interest or payment rate can change at the first adjustment period.

K. "Life Cap" means the limit on how much the interest or payment rate can change over the life of the loan.

* **Section 4. Applicability**

This rule applies to mortgage loan originators as that term is defined in section 12-61-902(6), C.R.S., and includes those persons who originate a mortgage, offer to originate a mortgage, act as a mortgage loan originator, or offer to act as a mortgage loan originator.

* **Section 5. 5-1-2 Mortgage Loan Originator Disclosures**

1. Section 12-61-914 (1), C.R.S., requires that specific disclosures, set forth in § 12-61-914(2), C.R.S., be disclosed within three (3) business days after receipt of a loan application or any moneys from a borrower.
2. Section 12-61-914 (2)(a), C.R.S., states the written disclosures shall contain the annual percentage rate, finance charge, amount financed, total amount of all payments, number of payments, amount of each payment, amount of points or prepaid interest, and the conditions and terms under which any loan terms may change between the time of disclosure and closing of the loan. If the interest rate is variable, the written disclosure shall clearly describe the circumstances under which the rate may increase, any limitation on the increase, the effect of an increase, and an example of the payment terms resulting from such an increase.
   - * a. The Board has determined that the Truth in Lending Act Disclosure form is an acceptable manner in which to disclose the requirements set forth in section 12-61-914(2)(a), C.R.S.
   - b. Requirements defined in § 12-61-914(2)(a), C.R.S., shall be disclosed:
     - i. Within three (3) business days after receipt of a loan application or any moneys from a borrower;
     - ii. If, after the initial written disclosure is provided, a mortgage loan originator enters into a lock-in agreement, within three (3) business days thereafter, including Saturdays, and prior to the borrower signing loan closing documents; and
     - iii. If, after a mortgage loan originator enters into a lock-in agreement, the annual percentage rate increases from the annual percentage rate disclosed earlier by more than 1/8 of one (1) percentage point, within three (3) business days of such change and prior to the borrower signing loan closing documents.
3. Section 12-61-914(2)(b), C.R.S. states the disclosure shall contain the itemized costs of any credit report, appraisal, title report, title insurance policy, mortgage insurance, escrow fee, property tax, insurance, structural or pest inspection, and any other third-party provider's costs associated with the residential mortgage loan.
   - * a. Due to the 2010 changes to the HUD Good Faith Estimate Disclosure form, the Board has determined that this form no longer meets the requirements set forth in section 12-61-914(2)(b), C.R.S. As a result, the Board requires that all mortgage loan originators create and implement a form that itemizes the disclosure of all third-party fees and costs. The disclosure shall include mortgage loan originator and borrower signatures and dates in which the disclosure was completed and signed. A complete disclosure form shall be completed according to the following timelines outlined below.
     - i. Requirements defined in § 12-61-914(2)(b), C.R.S., shall be disclosed:
       1. Within three (3) business days after receipt of a loan application or any moneys from a borrower;
       2. If, after the initial written disclosure is provided, a mortgage loan originator enters into a lock-in agreement, within three (3) business days thereafter, including Saturdays, and prior to the borrower signing loan closing documents; and
       3. If, after a mortgage loan originator enters into a lock-in agreement, the annual percentage rate increases from the annual percentage rate disclosed earlier by more than 1/8 of one (1) percentage point, within three (3) business days of such change and prior to the borrower signing loan closing documents.

4. A mortgage loan originator shall not charge any fee that inures to the benefit of the mortgage loan originator and the mortgage company for which they are an officer, partner, member, exclusive agent, contractor, independent contractor or employee if such fee exceeds the fee disclosed on the previous written disclosure unless:
   a. The need to charge the fee was not reasonably foreseeable at the time the written disclosure was provided; and
   b. The mortgage loan originator has provided to the borrower, no less than three business days prior to the signing of the loan closing documents, a clear and written explanation of the fee and the reason for charging a fee exceeding that which was previously disclosed.

* 5. Section 12-61-914(2)(c), C.R.S. states that mortgage loan originators shall disclose the amount of any commission or other compensation to be paid to the mortgage loan originator, including the manner in which such commission or other compensation is calculated and the relationship of such commission or other compensation to the cost of the loan received by the borrower.

* a. Mortgage loan originators shall disclose compensation pursuant to provisions and timelines defined in the Real Estate Settlement Procedures Act, Real Estate Settlement Procedures Act Regulations, the Dodd-Frank Wall Street Reform and Consumer Protection Act, or according to any regulation adopted by the Consumer Financial Protection Bureau.

* b. To view any of the aforementioned laws, regulations or provisions, interested parties may visit the Division of Real Estate for access at: http://www.dora.state.co.us/real-estate/mortgage/mortgage_industry_links.htm.

6. Section 12-61-914(2)(d), C.R.S., states the written disclosure, if applicable, shall contain the cost, terms, duration, and conditions of a lock-in agreement and whether a lock-in agreement has been entered, whether the lock-in agreement is guaranteed by the mortgage broker or lender, and, if a lock-in agreement has not been entered, disclosure in a form acceptable to the Director that the disclosed interest rate and terms are subject to change. Section 12-61-914(2)(g), C.R.S. states the mortgage loan originator shall disclose whether and under what conditions any lock-in fees are refundable to the borrower.

* a. The Board has created the Colorado Lock-in Disclosure Form to ensure this information is clearly and concisely disclosed. This disclosure may be found on the Division of Real Estate's website at http://www.dora.state.co.us/real-estate/mortgage/MBForms.htm. Mortgage loan originators shall use this form or alternate form, if alternate form clearly includes all information required on the suggested form, as determined by the Board.

* b. This form or alternate form shall be used when disclosing lock-in agreements, or when the mortgage loan originator has not entered into a lock-in agreement, to borrowers on residential mortgage loan transactions.
   i. Mortgage loan originators shall disclose the amount of the teaser rate, payment rate or interest rate and also disclose the type of rate. Examples of the type of rate include, but are not limited to:
      1. Teaser rate;
      2. Payment rate; or
      3. Interest rate.
   ii. When disclosing the payment type, mortgage loan originators shall define if the payment type is a negative amortization payment, interest only payment or principal and interest payment.

* c. The lock-in agreement disclosure shall be completed and disclosed:
   i. Within three (3) business days after receipt of a loan application or any moneys from a borrower;
   ii. If, after the initial written disclosure is provided, a mortgage loan originator enters into a lock-in agreement, within three (3) business days thereafter, including

Saturdays and prior to the borrower signing loan closing documents, the mortgage broker shall deliver or send by first-class mail to the borrower, the written lock-in disclosure created by the Director; and

iii. If, after a mortgage loan originator enters into a lock-in agreement, the annual percentage rate increases from the annual percentage rate disclosed earlier by more than 1/8 of one (1) percentage point, within three (3) business days of such change and prior to the borrower signing loan closing documents.

* iv. If, after the mortgage loan originator enters into a lock-in agreement, there is a change to any of the information provided on the lock-in disclosure form, including but not limited to a lock-in extension.

* 7. Individuals who originate a mortgage or act as a mortgage loan originator are required to keep records of the disclosures required in this rule for a period of four (4) years, for the purposes of inspection by the Board or authorized representative of the Board.

a. All documents shall be kept in a secure environment. Electronic storage is acceptable as long as the information is accessible and kept in a secure environment.

* b. The company for whom the mortgage loan originator is an officer, partner, contractor, independent contractor, member, exclusive agent, or an employee may provide the requested documents to the Board. However, the mortgage loan originator is responsible for compliance with the Board's request and is subject to disciplinary action if the company fails or refuses to provide the requested documentation.

* 8. Mortgage loan originators shall provide completed disclosure forms to all borrowers within three (3) business days of completion. Furthermore, mortgage loan originators must be able to provide proof to the Board or an authorized representative of the Board that the disclosure forms defined in this rule were in fact provided to the borrower within three (3) business days of completion.

Section 6. Enforcement

1. Noncompliance with this rule, whether defined or reasonably implied in the rule, may result in the imposition of any of the sanctions allowable under Colorado law, including, but not limited to:
    a. Revocation;
    b. Refusal to renew a license;
    c. Imposition of fines; and
    d. Restitution for any financial loss.

* RULE 7-1-1 DUAL STATUS DISCLOSURE

* **Section 1. Authority**

The statutory basis for this rule entitled **7-1-1 Dual Status Disclosure**, is section 12-61-910.3, C.R.S.

This notice proposes to update rule 7-1-1. The rule requires mortgage loan originators to inform borrowers if they are also acting as the real estate broker on their transaction.

* **Section 2. Scope and Purpose**

Colorado statutes require mortgage loan originators, before providing mortgage services to the borrower, to disclose all material facts associated with the transaction. The Board has determined that individuals who operate with dual status licenses as real estate brokers and mortgage loan originators on the same transaction shall disclose this fact to the borrower. Additionally, this rule creates a new disclosure form that notifies borrowers of an individual's dual status and of the borrower's right to shop for alternate services.

The purpose of this rule is to clearly notify mortgage loan originators that their dual status as a real estate broker and a mortgage loan originator must be disclosed to the borrower. Furthermore, this rule establishes a disclosure form mortgage loan originators may use to disclose such relevant information.

* **Section 3. Applicability**

This rule applies to all individuals required to be licensed pursuant to sections 12-61-902 and 12-61-903, C.R.S.

* **Section 4. 7-1-1 Dual Status Disclosure**

1. Colorado law, specifically section 12-61-912, C.R.S., provides that a mortgage loan originator shall not act as a loan originator in any transaction in which (a) the mortgage loan originator acts or has acted as a real estate broker or salesperson; or (b) another person doing business under the same licensed real estate broker acts or has acted as a real estate broker or salesperson, unless the mortgage loan originator first makes a full and fair disclosure to the borrower of all material features of the loan product and all facts material to the transaction, in addition to any other disclosures required by law. Additionally, the mortgage loan originator must maintain his or her mortgage loan originator business activities and mortgage loan originator business records separate and apart from the real estate broker activities.
2. The Board prohibits individuals from acting as a mortgage loan originator and real estate broker, or real estate salesperson, on the same transaction unless they comply with this rule.
3. The Board has determined that dual status is a material fact to real estate transactions and shall be disclosed to the borrower(s).
4. The Board has created the Colorado Dual Status Disclosure Form to ensure this information is clearly and concisely disclosed. This disclosure may be found on the Division of Real Estate's website at http://www.dora.state.co.us/real-estate/mortgage/MBForms.htm. Mortgage loan originators shall use this form or an alternate form, if such alternate form clearly includes all information required on the suggested form, as determined by the Board.
5. The Colorado Dual Status Disclosure form shall be completed, disclosed, and provided to the borrower within three (3) business days after receipt of a loan application or any moneys from a borrower.
6. Persons who originate a mortgage, offer to originate a mortgage, act as a mortgage loan originator, or offer to act as a mortgage loan originator shall maintain the disclosure form defined by this rule for a period of four (4) years.
7. Furthermore, mortgage loan originators must be able to provide proof to the Board or an authorized representative of the Board that the disclosure forms defined in this rule were in fact provided to the borrower within three (3) business days of completion.

* **Section 5. Enforcement**

1. Noncompliance with this rule, whether defined or reasonably implied in the rule, may result in the imposition of any of the sanctions allowable under Colorado law, including, but not limited to:
   a. Revocation;
   b. Refusal to renew a license;
   c. Imposition of fines; and
   d. Restitution for any financial loss.

RULE 8-1-1 MORTGAGE LOAN ORIGINATOR ADVERTISING

* **Section 1. Authority**

The Board of Mortgage Loan Originators adopts the following rule entitled **8-1-1 Mortgage Loan Originator Advertising**, according to the authority found in § 12-61-910.3, C.R.S.

The notice proposes to update rule 8-1-1. The rule establishes advertising guidelines for mortgage loan originators and mortgage companies.

* **Section 2. Scope and Purpose**

Section 12-61-910.4, C.R.S., states the Board shall adopt rules regarding the marketing of nontraditional mortgages by mortgage loan originators. In adopting such rules, the Director is required to incorporate appropriate provisions of the final "Interagency Guidance on Nontraditional Mortgage Product Risks" released on September 29, 2006. While this rule incorporates provisions specific to nontraditional mortgage products, the requirements herein are applicable to all types of mortgage product advertisements.

Section 12-61-911(1)(j), C.R.S., in summary, prohibits mortgage loan originators from failing to comply with the Truth in Lending Act. The Truth in Lending Act defines specific requirements for advertising.

The purpose of this rule is to ensure that mortgage loan originators and mortgage companies are familiar with all current regulations that address advertising and to ensure the advertising of nontraditional mortgage products is addressed.

* **Section 3. Definitions**

1. "Interest Only Mortgage Loan" means a nontraditional mortgage on which, for a specified number of years the borrower is required to pay only the interest due on the loan, during which time, the rate may fluctuate or may be fixed. After the interest only period, the rate may be fixed or fluctuate, based on the prescribed index, and payments include both the principal and interest.
2. "Nontraditional Mortgage" means any mortgage product other than a 30-year fixed rate mortgage.
3. "Payment Option Arm" means a nontraditional adjustable rate mortgage that allows the borrower to choose from a number of different payment options. For example, each month, the borrower may choose a minimum payment option based on a "start" or introductory interest rate, an interest only payment option based on the fully indexed interest rate, or a fully amortizing principal and interest payment option based on a 15 year or 30 year loan term, plus any required escrow payments. The minimum payment option can be less than the interest accruing on the loan, resulting in negative amortization. After a specified number of years, or if the loan reaches a certain negative amortization cap, the required monthly payment amount is recast to require payments that will fully amortize the outstanding balance over the remaining loan term.
4. "Reduced Documentation" means a loan feature that is commonly referred to as "low doc/no doc," "no income/no asset," "stated income," or "stated assets." For mortgage loans with this feature, an institution sets reduced or minimal documentation standards to substantiate the borrower's income and assets.
5. "Simultaneous Second Lien Loan" means a lending arrangement where either a closed end second lien or a home equity line of credit is originated simultaneously with the first lien mortgage loan, typically in lieu of a higher down payment.

* 6. *Advertisement*: An "advertisement" is any *commercial message* that promotes consumer credit. "Advertisements" may appear:

   a. In newspapers, magazines, leaflets, flyers, catalogs, direct mail literature, or other printed material;
   b. On radio, television, or a public address system;
   c. On an inside or outside sign or display, or a window display;
   d. In point-of-sale literature, price tags, signs, and billboards; or
   e. Online, such as on the Internet.

7. "Annual Percentage Rate" means the charge for credit, stated as a percentage, and expressed as an annualized rate as defined by the Truth in Lending Act.
8. "Closed-end credit" includes all consumer credit that does not fit the definition of open-end credit. Closed-end credit consists of both sales credit and loans. In a typical closed-end credit transaction, credit is advanced for a specific timc period, and the "amount financed," "finance charge," and "schedule of payments" are agreed upon by the lender and the customer.
9. "Consumer credit" may be either closed-end or open-end credit. It is credit that is extended primarily for personal, family, or household purposes. It excludes business and agricultural loans, and loans exceeding $ 25,000 that are not secured by real property or a dwelling. It also must be extended by a "creditor".
10. "Credit Sale" is a transaction in which the seller is also the creditor, at least initially. Often, the seller-creditor will later assign the installment sales contract to another entity, such as a finance company or a bank.
11. "Creditor" is a person or organization (a) that regularly extends consumer credit for which a finance charge is required or that is repayable in more than four installments even without a finance charge, and (b) to whom the obligation is initially payable—for example, the finance company, bank, automobile dealer or other lender identified on the face of the credit agreement. A person or organization is considered to extend credit "regularly," if it has extended credit more than 25 times during the preceding year or more than 5 times for transactions secured by dwellings.
12. "Downpayment" is an amount paid to reduce the cash price of goods or services purchased in a credit sale transaction. The value of a trade-in is included in the downpayment. It can include a "pick-up" or deferred downpayment that is not subject to a finance charge and is due no later than the second regularly scheduled payment. The downpayment does not include any prepaid finance charges such as points.
13. "Finance Charge" is the dollar amount charged for credit. It includes interest and other costs, such as service charges, transaction charges, buyer's points, loan fees, and mortgage insurance. It also includes the premiums for credit life, accident, and health insurance, if required, and for property insurance, unless the buyer may select the insurer.
14. "Terms of Repayment" generally refers to the payment schedule, including the number, timing, and amount of the payments, including any final "balloon" payment, scheduled to repay the debt.

* **Section 4. Applicability**

This rule applies to mortgage loan originators as that term is defined in § 12-61-902(6), C.R.S. and mortgage companies as that term is defined in § 12-61-902(5), C.R.S.

* **Section 5. 8-1-1 Mortgage Loan Originator Advertising**

1. Mortgage loan originators shall comply with all advertising provisions, regulations and official staff commentary of the Truth in Lending Act (Regulation Z). Such provisions, regulations and official staff commentary include:
   a. Section 226.16; and
   b. Supplement I of Part 226 – Official Staff interpretations.

* 2. Mortgage loan originators and mortgage companies may review the Truth in Lending Act (Regulation Z) on the Division of Real Estate's website at http://www.dora.state.co.us/real-estate/index.htm. Additionally, mortgage loan originators and mortgage companies may also review the Truth in Lending Act (Regulation Z) at http://ecfr.gpoaccess.gov/cgi/t/text/text-idx?c=ecfr&sid=635f26c4af3e2fe4327fd25ef4cb5638&tpl=/ecfrbrowse/Title12/12cfr226_main_02.tpl.

* 3. Mortgage loan originators and mortgage companies may advertise only credit terms that are actually available to the consumer. "Bait and switch" credit or promotions are not allowed. For example, no advertisement may state that a specific installment payment or a specific downpayment can be arranged unless the creditor is prepared to make those arrangements. However, mortgage loan originators and mortgage companies may advertise terms that will be offered only for a limited time or terms that will become available at a known future date.

* 4. If a mortgage loan originator or a mortgage company advertises closed-end credit with a "triggering term," the mortgage loan originator and mortgage company also must disclose other major terms, including the annual percentage rate. This rule is intended to ensure that all important terms of a credit plan, not just the most attractive ones, appear in an ad. This includes all important terms that are advertised in ranges. The triggering terms for closed-end credit are:

   a. The amount of the downpayment expressed as either a percentage or dollar amount, in a "credit sale" transaction. Examples include, but are not limited to:
      i. "10% down"
      ii. "$10,000 down"
      iii. "90% financing"

   b. The amount of any payment expressed as either a percentage or dollar amount. Examples include, but are not limited to:
      i. "Monthly payments less than $ 650 on all our loan plans"
      ii. "Pay $ 300.00 per $ 100,000 amount borrowed"
      iii. "$ 650 per month"

   c. The number of payments or the period of repayment. Examples include, but are not limited to:
      i. "Up to thirty years to pay"
      ii. "180 months to pay"
      iii. "30-year mortgages available"

   d. The amount of any finance charge. Examples include, but are not limited to:
      i. "Financing costs less than $ 1,000 per year"
      ii. "Less than $ 1200 interest"

* e. Some statements about credit terms are too general to trigger additional disclosures. Examples of terms that do not trigger the required disclosures are:
      i. "No downpayment"
      ii. "Easy monthly payments"
      iii. "Low downpayment accepted"
      iv. "Pay weekly"
      v. "Terms to fit your budget"
      vi. "Financing available."

* f. General statements, such as "take years to pay" or "no closing costs," do not trigger further disclosures because they do not state or suggest the period of repayment or down payment cost. Advertisements that refer to a range of interest rates that may be provided are considered to advertise an interest rate and are considered a triggering term. The more specific the statement, the more likely it is to trigger additional disclosures.

* 5. If the ad for closed-end credit uses a triggering term, it also must include the following information:

a. The amount or percentage of the down-payment;
b. The terms of repayment; and
c. The "annual percentage rate," using that term or the abbreviation "APR." If the annual percentage rate may be increased after consummation of the credit transaction, that fact also must be stated.

* 6. If the ad shows the finance charge as a rate, that rate must be stated as an "annual percentage rate," using that term or the abbreviation "APR." The ad must state the annual percentage rate, even if it is the same as the simple interest rate. Disclosure of the annual percentage rate shall be disclosed as clearly and conspicuously as any interest rate in the advertisement. If the ad only shows a rate, and the APR is stated in the ad, no other credit information need be included: the "triggering term" requirement does not apply because the rate and APR are not triggering terms. Thus, an advertisement could simply state, "Assume 10% annual percentage rate" or "10% annual percentage rate mortgages available."

* a. All ads must state the annual percentage rate accurately. For example, some transactions include other components in the finance charge besides interest, such as "points" and mortgage insurance premiums paid by the buyer. As a result, the annual percentage rate may be higher than the simple interest rate, because the APR reflects the total cost of credit, including interest and other credit charges.

* b. As long as the ad includes the annual percentage rate, one also may state a simple annual rate or a periodic rate or both, applicable to an unpaid balance. However, the simple annual or periodic rate may not be more conspicuous in the advertisement than the annual percentage rate. For example, an advertisement may include the interest rate together with the annual percentage rate, as long as the interest rate is not more prominent than the APR.

7. Ads for variable-rate credit must state that the rate may increase or that it is subject to change, but need not explain how changes will be made.
   a. The following statement would satisfy this requirement.
      i. 8.5% annual percentage rate subject to increase or decrease.
   b. By contrast, an ad that promotes "9% APR graduated payment adjustable mortgages" (graduated payment mortgages plus an adjustable rate feature) would not comply with the law, because it does not state clearly that the rate may change.

8. The annual percentage rate in variable-rate financing ads must be accurate. To help calculate the APR, keep two principles in mind. First, remember there is only one APR per loan, regardless of how many interest rates may apply during the term of the loan. Second, assume that any "index" rates, such as the prime rate or the 6-month Treasury bill, used to determine future interest rate changes will remain constant during the life of the loan.

9. Special rules apply when you advertise a loan in which the seller or a third party "buys down" the interest rate during the early years of the loan.
   a. To comply with this requirement, you must determine the accurate annual percentage rate. First, ascertain whether the lower rates are stated as part of the credit contract between the consumer and the creditor. If so, you should take the buydown into account in calculating the annual percentage rate for the advertisement.
   b. If the lower rates are not part of the credit contract, the advertised annual percentage rate should not reflect the buydown. For example, suppose the seller agrees with the consumer to place funds in an escrow account. This escrow account will be drawn upon by the creditor to reduce the consumer's monthly payments during the term of the loan, but the consumer's credit obligation is not changed to reflect the lower effective rate and payments. In this situation, you should not consider the buydown in calculating the APR. Assuming the reduced rates are part of the credit contract between the consumer and lender, your ad might read as follows:

i. This buydown reduces your interest rate from 10½% to 8½% for the first year of your loan. APR 10½%.

c. If the interest rates in the buydown are not part of the credit agreement between the consumer and lender, because, for example, they are included in a separate contract between the consumer and the builder/seller, you still may show the reduced interest rates in the ad. But, if you do so, you must include all the rates, the limited terms to which they apply, and the annual percentage rate for the loan. The annual percentage rate that you disclose will not be based on the reduced interest rates, and therefore will be higher than those rates, as in the following example:

i. With this buydown, your interest rate for the first year of your loan is only 8½%. Rate for remainder of term is 10½%. 10¾% APR.

* d. If this information is advertised, the effect of a buydown on the monthly payments without triggering other disclosures may be disclosed. For example, an ad that states the above information also may say "with this buydown, your monthly payment for the first year of the mortgage will be only $615," or "save more than $100 per month the first year!" The use of these terms does not trigger disclosure of other information, other than the APR. But, if the ad shows the full term of the loan, such as "30-year financing", other required disclosures—namely, the downpayment, the terms of repayment, and the APR—must be shown, because the time period is a triggering term.

10. Adjustable rate mortgages (ARMs) often have a first-year "discount" or "teaser" feature in which the initial rate is substantially reduced. In these loans, the first year's rate is not computed in the same way as the rate for later years. Often, the "spread" or "margin" that is normally added to an "index," such as the one-year Treasury-note rate, to determine changes in the interest rate in the future is not included in the first year of a discounted ARM offered by a creditor.

a. Special rules, similar to those for buydowns, apply to advertising a discounted variable rate. An ad for this type of plan can show the simple interest rate during the discount period, as long as it also shows the annual percentage rate. However, in contrast to buydowns, the ad need not show the simple interest rate applicable after the discount period. For example, a plan with a low first year's interest rate (8%), but with a 10.25% rate in subsequent years, and additional credit costs, could be advertised as follows:

i. 8% first-year financing. APR 10.41%. APR subject to increase after closing.

b. As in buydowns, the annual percentage rate in discounted plans is a composite figure that must take into account the interest rates that are known at closing. In the above example, the disclosed APR must reflect the 8% rate for the first year, as well as, for example, the 10.25% rate applicable for the remainder of the term, plus any additional credit costs, such as buyer's points.

c. An ad for a discounted variable-rate loan, like an ad for a buydown, may show the effect of the discount on the payment schedule during the discount period without triggering other disclosures. An example of a disclosure that complies with Regulation Z is:

i. Interest rate only 8% first year. APR 10.50% subject to increase. With this discount, your monthly payments for the first year will be only $ 587.

11. In some transactions, particularly some graduated payment loans, the consumer's payments for the first few years of the loan may be based on an interest rate lower than the rate for which the consumer is liable. This situation is referred to as "negative amortization." As with buydowns, special rules apply when you advertise the "effective" or "payment" rates for these transactions.

a. Specifically, you may advertise these effective rates if you show the following information:

i. The "effective" or "payment" rate;

ii. The term of the reduced payments;

iii. The "note rate" at which interest is actually accruing; and
iv. The annual percentage rate.

b. The advertised annual percentage rate must take into account the interest for which the consumer is liable, even though it is not paid by the consumer during the period of reduced payments.

c. This type of financing could be advertised as:
   i. An effective first-year rate of only 1½ percent. Interest being charged at 10½ percent. 10¾% APR.

d. In contrast to an ad for a buydown or a discounted variable rate, an ad for an "effective" or "payment" rate may not show the monthly payments without triggering the other disclosures. You can, however, show the range of payments without showing all the intermediate payment amounts.

e. In addition to the information about the interest rate and APR, a complying ad for a "payment rate" plan also could state:
   i. Payments begin at $ 557.92 for the first year, ranging to $ 800.96 in years six through remainder of loan term.

12. The ad need not show all the different payments required during the life of the loan, if you advertise a mortgage in which the payments vary because:
   a. Payments include mortgage insurance premiums payable monthly or annually; or
   b. The loan has a "graduated payment" feature.
   c. These advertisements must state:
      i. the number and timing of payments,
      ii. the largest and smallest payments, and
      iii. the fact that the other payments will vary between those amounts.
   d. The following example, based upon a condominium with a $ 65,000 sale price, illustrates the terms of an advertisement for a loan with mortgage insurance.
      i. This example would comply with the disclosure requirements, assuming the information is printed clearly and conspicuously:
         1. Downpayment $ 15,000; 9.5% APR
         2. 360 monthly payments
         3. Payments 1-120 vary from $ 303.94 to $ 405.96
         4. Remaining 240 payments are $ 436.35.

13. When an advertisement promotes a variable-rate loan that is not a "discount" or a "buydown" and has no other special features, the advertisement contains triggering terms that require disclosure of the "terms of repayment," which include the payment amounts. In this ad, only one payment amount need be disclosed to comply with the law.
   a. To determine the proper payment disclosure, calculate the payment based on the interest rate that will be in effect initially during the loan, using the best information available at the time you run the ad. For example, suppose you want to determine the payments for a 30-year variable-rate mortgage in which rate changes will be based on the one-year Treasury bill index, and in which there is no discount and no additional "margin" added to the index.
   b. If that index is at 9.5% at the time you run the ad, you could disclose the payment amounts by developing an example, using 360 monthly payments based on the 9.5% rate.
   c. If you wish to offer a $ 100,000 condominium with a 20% downpayment , leaving an amount financed of $ 80,000, with no mortgage insurance and with all prepaid finance charges paid by the seller, the ad could state:
      i. Payments as low as $ 673 monthly. 30-year loan. 20% down. 9.5% APR subject to increase.

14. When an advertisement requiring disclosure of the payment schedule promotes a discounted variable-rate loan, rather than a variable rate plan with no special features, the advertised payment schedule must show all payment amounts that can be determined before consummation of the loan. For example, if the discounted rate is applicable for only one year, the advertisement should show a payment for the first year based on the reduced interest rate in effect for that year. If the interest rate is subject to annual increases thereafter, the advertisement must show a second payment amount based upon the interest rate that would have been in effect at consummation, except for the discount feature of the loan.
    a. Thus, for example, the payment schedule portion of an advertisement for a discounted variable-rate loan with a one-year discount might state:
        i. 1st year monthly payments are $ 585 and 2nd and subsequent years' monthly payments are $ 700.
    b. If the reduced rate plan has limits or "caps" on the amount that the interest rate or payments may increase in any year, the payment schedule must also show the effect of those caps. Suppose the plan has a cap that limits interest rate increases each year to 2%. Also suppose that interest rates for the loan are determined by the Treasury bill rate plus a 2% margin and that the Treasury bill rate at the time of your ad is 10%. The rate determined by this formula would be 12%, 10% plus the 2% margin. The creditor, however, has set the first-year rate at only 9% and the second-year rate can be no more than 11% because of the cap. In a 30-year loan for $ 100,000 with no other credit charges, your payment disclosures for this loan might read:
        i. 1st year's monthly payment are $ 804.62; 2nd year's monthly payments are $ 950.09; and 3rd year and subsequent year's monthly payments are $ 1024.34.

* 15. All advertisements shall have at least one (1) responsible person that is accountable. If the responsible party is an individual, their Colorado license number and their registration number approved on the Nationwide Mortgage Licensing System and Registry (the "NMLS") shall be clearly and conspicuously included in the advertisement. If the responsible party is a mortgage company, the company shall clearly and conspicuously include their NMLS approved registration number on all advertisements.

* 16. All advertisements shall clearly and conspicuously provide the following information:
    a. The mortgage company name; and
    b. The business phone number of the responsible party.

* 17. All advertisements shall clearly and conspicuously include the following statement:
    a. Regulated by the Division of Real Estate.

18. Advertisements containing an interest rate, payment rate, teaser rate or an annual percentage rate must be reasonably available on the day of the advertisement or the day the advertisement is received.

19. Advertisements containing an interest rate, payment rate, teaser rate or annual percentage rate must include all material terms and conditions specific to the rates advertised. Material terms and conditions include, but are not limited:
    a. Credit score;
    b. Debt to income ratios;
    c. Loan to value; and
    d. Occupancy type.

20. Advertisements promoting non-traditional mortgage products, as defined in this rule, must clearly demonstrate the type of product advertised.

Section 6. Enforcement

1. Noncompliance with this rule, whether defined or reasonably implied in the rule, may result in the imposition of any of the sanctions allowable under Colorado law, including, but not limited to:

a. Revocation;
b. Refusal to renew a license;
c. Imposition of fines; and
d. Restitution for any financial loss.

* VI. Position Statements

* Position Statement – MB 1.1 [Repealed]

* Position Statement – MB 1.2 [Repealed]

* Position Statement – MLO 1.3 – Licensing Required

Section 1. Scope and Purpose

The Director of the Division of Real Estate finds that a position statement regarding section 12-61-903(1)(c), C.R.S. is necessary to provide clarification to the mortgage industry. Section 12-61-903(1)(c), C.R.S. states that on or after January 1, 2008, unless licensed by the Director, aperson shall not originate a mortgage, offer to originate a mortgage, act as a mortgage loanoriginator, or offer to act as a mortgage loan originator. Section 12-61-902(6)(a), C.R.S. definesa mortgage loan originator as an individual who takes a residential mortgage loan application oroffers or negotiates terms of a residential mortgage loan. Section 12-61-902(7), C.R.S. definesoriginate a mortgage to act directly or indirectly as a mortgage loan originator. After consultingwith industry leaders, the Director has learned that uncertainty exists in the market placeregarding who is required to be licensed and who is not required to be licensed. The purpose ofthis position statement is to provide further clarification regarding this matter.

Section 2. Applicability

This position statement concerns individuals who originate a mortgage, offer to originate a mortgage, act as a mortgage loan originator, or offer to act as a mortgage loan originator.

* **Section 3. Position Statement – MLO 1.3 – License Required**

* 1. The Board's position regarding the above uncertainty is that persons who directly supervise individuals that take residential loan applications or offer or negotiate terms of a residential mortgage loan are required to be licensed.

* 2. Additionally, the Board's position is that individuals who perform purely administrative or clerical tasks do not fall within the definitions of originate a mortgage or mortgage loan originator. Administrative or clerical tasks include, but are not limited to:
   a. The receipt, collection, distribution and analysis of information common for the processing or underwriting of a residential mortgage loan; and
   b. Communicating with a consumer to obtain the information necessary for the processing or underwriting of a loan, to the extent that such communication does not include offering or negotiating loan rates or terms, or counseling consumers about residential mortgage loan rates or terms.

Section 4. Issuance Date

The Director of the Division of Real Estate issues this position statement January 7, 2008.

The Division of Real Estate revised this position statement and re-issued this position statement on Friday, September 11, 2009.

* The Board of Mortgage Loan Originators revised this position statement and re-issued this position statement on Wednesday, February 16, 2011.

* Position Statement – MLO 1.5 – Loan Modifications

* Section 1. Scope and Purpose

The Board of Mortgage Loan Originators ("Board") finds that a position statement regarding loan modifications is necessary in order to provide clarity to the industry. The Board has learned of individuals negotiating loan modification terms for borrowers and has received many inquiries regarding the applicability of current mortgage loan originator licensing law. Specifically, individuals are communicating directly with borrowers and borrowers' lenders in order to negotiate terms of a loan modification. In many instances, Colorado consumers are being charged high upfront fees regardless of services rendered. The Board has also learned that consumers are being advised to cease making mortgage payments, even when already delinquent on payments. Additionally, there are existing loan modification services that are offered by U.S. Department of Housing and Urban Development (HUD) approved non-profit 501(c)3 agencies which employ housing counselors around the State of Colorado. Such HUD-approved services are offered by housing counselors for free and are not associated with any compensation or other benefit from the borrower to the housing counselor. The purpose of this position statement is to clearly notify loan modifiers (those who engage in the act of directly or indirectly negotiating a loan modification) of the applicability of Colorado mortgage broker law.

* Section 2. Definitions

1. Short sale – A short sale is the sale of a real property for less than the mortgage loan balance. In the settlement of the short sale transaction the existing mortgage is extinguished. Any deficiency created from the settlement of the transaction may be transformed into a promissory note, charged off, forgiven, or pursued as a judgment against the previous owner.
2. Loan modification – A Loan Modification is a permanent change in one or more of the terms of a mortgagor's existing loan, allows the loan to be reinstated, and often results in a more affordable mortgage payment. The borrower retains ownership of the real property and the mortgage note and deed of trust remain intact.

* Section 3. Applicability

This position statement concerns individuals who originate a mortgage, offer to originate a mortgage, act as a mortgage loan originator, or offer to act as a mortgage loan originator.

* Section 4. Position Statement – MLO 1.5 – Loan Modifications

* 1. Section 12-61-902(7), C.R.S. defines originate a mortgage as to act directly or indirectly as a mortgage loan originator. It is the Board's position that individuals offering or negotiating loan modifications are, at a minimum, indirectly acting as mortgage loan originators. Pursuant to section 12-61-903(1)(a), Colorado Revised Statutes, all persons who meet the definition of originate a mortgage are required to be licensed. As a result, persons who directly or indirectly negotiate, originate, or offer or attempt to negotiate or originate loan modifications are currently required to be licensed as mortgage loan originators and are required to be licensed as state-licensed loan originators by July 31, 2010.

2. Additionally, persons who directly supervise individuals who negotiate, originate, or offer or attempt to negotiate or originate loan modifications for a commission or other thing of value are required to be licensed as mortgage loan originators.

* 3. 3.In addition to the licensing requirements, all individuals who directly or indirectly negotiate loan modifications for borrowers and their direct supervisors are required to comply with all

other provisions of Colorado mortgage loan originator licensing law and Board rules. This includes, but is not limited to:

a. A duty of good faith and fair dealing in all communications and transactions with borrowers;

b. A prohibition against making any promise that influences, persuades, or induces another person to detrimentally rely on such promise when the licensee could not or did not intend to keep such promise;

c. A prohibition against soliciting or entering into a contract with a borrower that provides in substance that the mortgage olan originator may earn a fee or commission through the mortgage broker's "best efforts" to obtain a loan even though no loan is actually obtained for the borrower; and

d. If the mortgage loan originator has obtained for the borrower a written commitment from a lender for a loan on the terms and conditions agreed to by the borrower and the mortgage loan originator, and the borrower fails to close on the loan through no fault of the mortgage loan originator, the mortgage loan originator may charge a fee, not to exceed three hundred dollars, for services rendered, preparation of documents, or transfer of documents in the borrower's file that were prepared or paid for by the borrower if the fee is not otherwise prohibited by the federal "Truth in Lending Act", 15 U.S.C. section 1601, and Regulation Z, 12 CFR 226, as amended.

* 4. The Board's position on this matter shall not be construed to include employees of non-profit HUD-approved housing counseling agencies as long as such individuals receive neither compensation nor anything of value for participation in loan modifications.

* 5. The Board's position on this matter shall not be construed to include employees of mortgage loan servicing companies operating on behalf of mortgage lenders.

6. Licensed Real Estate Brokers engaged in licensed activities when performing services within the above defined short sale transactions do not need to maintain a license as a mortgage loan originator. If a real estate broker engages in the activities of providing loan modification services (those not included in the activities of short sales) as defined above, loan modification services are defined as outside the scope of licensed real estate broker activities and as such separate licensure as a mortgage loan originator as defined in MLO 1.5 Position Statement.

7. As set forth in section 12-61-904(1)(d), C.R.S., an attorney who renders services in the course of practice, who is licensed in Colorado, and who is not primarily engaged in the business of negotiating residential mortgage loans or loan modifications is not required to be licensed as a mortgage loan originator, but is required to comply with all non-licensing provisions of current mortgage loan originator law set forth in sections 12-61-901 through 12-61-915, C.R.S.

8. Noncompliance may result in the imposition of any of the sanctions allowable under Colorado law, including, but not limited to:
   a. Imposition of fines;
   b. Restitution for any financial loss;
   c. Refusal to renew a license;
   d. Refusal to grant a license; and
   e. Revocation.

Section 5. Issuance Date

The Director of the Division of Real Estate issues this position statement November 19, 2008.

The Director of the Division of Real Estate revised this position statement December 11, 2008.

The Division of Real Estate revised this position statement and re-issued this position statement Friday, September 11, 2009.

* The Board or Mortgage Loan Originators revised this position statement on Wednesday, February 16, 2011.

* Position Statement – MLO 1.7 – Financial Responsibility Requirement

* Section 1. Scope and Purpose

In July of 2008, the Housing and Economic Recovery Act of 2008 was signed into law. Title V of the Economic Recovery Act of 2008 is the S.A.F.E. Mortgage Licensing Act. The S.A.F.E. Mortgage Licensing Act defines minimum national licensing standards for mortgage loan originators and requires states to adopt such provisions. The S.A.F.E. Mortgage Licensing Act requires that applicants for state-licensed loan originator licenses demonstrate financial responsibility, character and general fitness such as to command the confidence of the community and to warrant a determination that the mortgage loan originators will operate honestly, fairly and efficiently. Accordingly, the Colorado General Assembly passed House Bill 09-1085 in May of 2009. This bill was signed into law by Governor Bill Ritter Jr. on May 21, 2009. House Bill 09-1085 became effective on August 5, 2009. The Board of Mortgage Loan Originators ("Board") has received many inquiries from loan originators regarding the financial responsibility requirement. The purpose of this position statement is to create a presumption of compliance regarding the financial responsibility requirement for individuals licensed as state-licensed loan originators.

* Section 2. Applicability

This position statement concerns all individuals required to be licensed as state-licensed loan originators.

* Section 3. Position Statement – MB 1.7 – Financial Responsibility Requirement

The Board's position on this matter is there is a presumption of compliance with the financial responsibility requirement in section 12-61-905(1)(j), C.R.S. for individuals required to be licensed as state-licensed loan originators who have complied with the errors and omissions insurance requirements defined in section 12-61-903.5, C.R.S. and any Director rule that directly or indirectly addresses errors and omissions insurance requirements and who have complied with the surety bond requirements defined in sections 12-61-903(6) and 12-61-907, C.R.S. and any Board rule that directly or indirectly addresses surety bond requirements.

* Section 4. Issuance Date

The Director of the Division of Real Estate issues this position statement August 5, 2009.

* The Board of Mortgage Loan Originator revised this position statement on March 16, 2011.

* Position Statement – MLO 1.8 – Real Estate Brokerage Activity

* Section 1. Scope and Purpose

In July of 2008, the Housing and Economic Recovery Act of 2008 was signed into law. Title V of the Housing and Economic Recovery Act of 2008 is the S.A.F.E. Mortgage Licensing Act, which defines minimum national licensing standards for mortgage loan originators and requires states to adopt such provisions. Accordingly, the Colorado General Assembly passed House Bill 09-1085 in May of 2009. Governor Bill Ritter Jr. signed the bill into law on May 21, 2009 and it became effective on August 5, 2009. The Board of Mortgage Loan Originators ("Board") has received multiple inquiries regarding the potential requirement of licensure as a mortgage loan originator for those real estate brokers that discuss matters related to the financing for a transaction. The purpose of this position statement is to clarify real estate brokerage activities that involve transaction financing matters that are exempt from the Mortgage Loan Originator Licensing Act.

* **Section 2. Applicability**

This position statement concerns those licensed real estate brokers engaged in contract negotiations for the purchase, sale, lease, rental or exchange of real property when a residential mortgage loan is required to complete the transaction.

* **Section 3. Position Statement**

The Board is aware that pursuant to the real estate brokers licensing act, specifically § 12-61-801, C.R.S. *et seq.*, licensed Colorado real estate brokers are required to fulfill specific duties and obligations. Many of the duties prescribed by the act address financial matters involved in the contract for a real property transaction. Whether acting as a single agent or a transaction broker, a real estate broker must exercise reasonable skill and care, including but not limited to: 1) accounting for all money and property received in a timely manner; 2) keeping the parties fully informed of the transaction; 3) assisting the parties in complying with the terms and conditions of any contract including closing the transaction; and 4) making disclosures regarding adverse material facts pertaining to a principal's financial ability to perform the terms of the transaction and the buyer's intent to occupy the property as a principal residence. Without the informed consent of all parties, a transaction broker is prohibited from disclosing that a seller or buyer will agree to financing terms other than those offered. A single agent is prohibited from disclosing whether his or her client(s) will agree to financing terms other than those offered, unless the client consents. The Board is also cognizant that real estate brokers advise on fees relating to homeowner's associations, special assessments, appraisals, surveys, inspections, property insurance, and taxes.

Pursuant to § 12-61-902(7.7)(c), C.R.S., the aforementioned activities could be construed as requiring a mortgage loan originator's license since they involve "matters related to financing for the transaction" at the time of contract negotiation. However, the Board has determined these activities are exempt from the mortgage loan originator's licensing act. Specifically, § 12-61-902(6)(a), C.R.S. defines a mortgage loan originator as an individual who "takes a residential loan application" or "offers or negotiates terms of a residential mortgage loan." Real estate brokers engaging in these activities are required to be licensed as a mortgage loan originator.

* **Section 4. Issuance Date**

The Director of the Division of Real Estate issues this position statement November 10, 2009.

* The Board of Mortgage Loan Originators revised this position statement on March 16, 2011.

* VII. Colorado Specific Mortgage Loan Originator Forms

Dual Status Disclosure

The printed portions of this form, except differentiated additions, have been approved by the Colorado Real Estate Commission. (DSD 17-1-09) (Mandatory 8-09)

THIS DISCLOSURE IS MADE PURSUANT TO THE REQUIREMENTS OF THE COLORADO REAL ESTATE COMMISSION AND THE DIRECTOR OF THE COLORADO DIVISION OF REAL ESTATE.

DUAL STATUS DISCLOSURE
(REAL ESTATE BROKER AND MORTGAGE LOAN ORIGINATOR)

________________________, is a licensed real estate broker and a licensed mortgage loan originator in the State of Colorado.

THE BUYER/BORROWER IS NOT REQUIRED TO USE THE MORTGAGE LOAN ORIGINATOR'S SERVICES TO OBTAIN A MORTGAGE LOAN. THERE MAY BE OTHER MORTGAGE LOAN ORIGINATORS THAT PROVIDE SIMILAR SERVICES.

The Broker/Mortgage Loan Originator is acting in a dual capacity as a real estate broker and a mortgage loan originator in the transaction. The Broker/Mortgage Loan Originator ☐**Is** ☐ **Is Not** accepting a placement fee, commission or other valuable consideration for directly or indirectly placing a loan with a mortgage lender or its representative.

The Buyer/Borrower ____ ☐ **Does** ☐ **Does Not** consent to the Broker/Mortgage Loan Originator acting in a dual capacity as a licensed real estate broker and a licensed mortgage loan originator in the transaction. The Buyer/Borrower ☐ **Does** ☐ **Does Not** consent to the Broker/Mortgage Loan Originator receiving a placement fee, commission or other valuable consideration for placing a loan with a mortgage lender or its representative in the real estate transaction.

THIS IS NOT A CONTRACT AND IS NOT COMPREHENSIVE OF ALL DISCLOSURES REQUIRED BY §§ 12-61-101, C.R.S., et. seq., 12-61-801, C.R.S., et. seq., and 12-61-901, C.R.S., et. seq.

BUYER/BORROWER ACKNOWLEDGMENT:

The Buyer acknowledges receipt of this document on ______________.

______________________________ ______________________________

Buyer/Borrower Buyer/Borrower

BROKER/MORTGAGE LOAN ORIGINATOR ACKNOWLEDGMENT:

On __________________________, the Broker/Mortgage Loan Originator provided __________________________ (Buyer/Borrower) with a copy of this document via________________________ and retained a copy for the Broker's/Mortgage Loan Originator's records. Broker/Mortgage Loan Originator also acknowledges that Broker/Mortgage Loan Originator has made a full and fair disclosure to the Buyer/Borrower of all material features of the loan product and all facts material to the transaction.

____

Broker/Mortgage Loan Originator

Colorado Lock-in Disclosure Form

Colorado Lock-in Disclosure Form
Pursuant to sections 12-61-914(2)(d),(f) and (3), Colorado Revised Statutes

THIS FORM DESCRIBES HOW YOU MAY BE OFFERED A LOCK-IN. A LOCK-IN IS AN ARRANGEMENT IN WHICH AN INVESTOR/MORTGAGE LENDER RESERVES A TEASER RATE, PAYMENT RATE AND/OR INTEREST RATE DURING THE LOAN APPLICATION PROCESS FOR A SPECIFIC PERIOD OF TIME WHILE YOUR LOAN APPLICATION IS BEING REVIEWED AND UNDERWRITTEN. WHETHER YOUR LOAN WILL ACTUALLY BE APPROVED AND WILL CLOSE DURING THE TIME PERIOD DEPENDS ON A NUMBER OF CONDITIONS, SOME OF THEM BEYOND THE CONTROL OF YOUR MORTGAGE LOAN ORIGINATOR. TO LEARN MORE ABOUT LOCK-IN AGREEMENTS, PLEASE REVIEW THE FOLLOWING WEBSITE: http://www.federalreserve.gov/pubs/lockins/default.htm

__________________ Borrower First Name __________________ Borrower Last Name

__________________ Co-Borrower First Name __________________ Co-Borrower Last Name

__________________ Property Address __________________ City ______ State __________ Postal Zip Code

---

The following shall be completed, pursuant to § 12-61-914(2)(d), (f) and (3), C.R.S.

Interest Rate:

The interest rate your loan originator is offering you will be either an "Unlocked Rate" or a "Locked Rate". A locked rate is an interest rate that is guaranteed to you by the lender for a period of time and cannot change. The interest rate disclosed to you on this form should match the interest rate provided to you on the Good Faith Estimate (GFE), the Initial Loan Application (1003), and the Truth in Lending (TIL) forms.

The Interest Rate being offered to you is: ______________

Rate Lock Information:

The interest rate is either locked or not locked. If the interest rate is not locked, it can change up or down many times, even multiple times daily. If your interest rate is locked, it cannot raise or decline for a set period of time.

________ **Interest Rate** ______ **Locked** ______ **Not Locked** ____________ **Date Locked** ____________ **Date Locked Rate Expires**

There might be a Lock Fee associated with locking your interest rate.

________ **Lock In Fee (Yes or No)** __________________ **How much is the Lock In Fee In a Dollar Amount** ____________ **Is Lock In Fee Refundable? (Yes or No)**

Colorado Mortgage Loan Originator Lock-in Disclosure Form Revised February 24, 2011

Lock-in Extension:

Your interest rate lock guaranteeing a particular interest rate will expire at the end of the lock period indicated above under "Date Locked Rate Expires". If your loan has not closed prior to or on that date, you will need to extend that lock date for that interest rate prior to its expiration date to guarantee that rate for your loan. You should speak to your mortgage loan originator about this process. There may be a fee associated with this extension. Always ask your mortgage loan originator how much that fee is and who is responsible for paying that fee.

(The following fields are to be completed at time of any lock extension)

Date lock extended	Date new lock expires	Cost to extend (Dollar amount)	Who is responsible to pay extension fee

Loan Terms:

The loan term is how long that you will pay your guaranteed interest rate. That interest rate is "Fixed" for a set period. It could be fixed for the life of the loan or for a lesser period of time, often on what are called adjustable rate mortgages. If you have chosen or are being offered an Adjustable Rate Mortgage, also known as a Variable Rate Mortgage (ARM), your interest rate can go up or down after the "fixed period" of time. Refer to the Truth in Lending (TIL) disclosure provided to you by your mortgage loan originator to view possible **increases** in rate and payment after your initial fixed period in time and in order to view the **worst** case possible regarding the adjustment of your rate.

____

Loan term fixed for how many years

Type of Interest Rate:

The type of interest rate that you are being offered or have chosen may entail a payment that includes Principal and Interest **(PI).** This means that your loan balance will go down with each payment. A second option is for Interest Only **(IO)** loan terms. This means your loan amount will not decrease unless you pay extra money towards the balance of your loan. A final option includes a Negative Amortization **(NEG AM)** loan. This means that your loan balance will increase each month. Have your loan originator provide you with the maximum amount that your balance is allowed to increase before you will have to either refinance your loan or pay down the balance.

____

Type of Interest Rate
(Principal and interest (PI), interest only (IO) or negative Amortization (NA))

DO NOT SIGN THIS FORM UNLESS ALL BLOCKS ARE COMPLETED OR HAVE N/A. THIS FORM SHOULD HAVE BEEN COMPLETED, DATED AND SIGNED BY YOUR LOAN ORIGINATOR WITHIN 3 BUSINESS DAYS OF YOUR APPLICATION AND/OR OF YOUR LOCKED IN RATE AND/OR YOUR LOCK IN RATE EXTENSION AND/OR YOUR ANNUAL PERCENTAGE RATE (APR) CHANGING BY MORE THAN 1/8 PERCENT AS PROVIDED TO YOU ON YOUR TRUTH IN LENDING (TIL) DISCLOSURE.

Loan Originator Name	Colorado License Number	NMLS Registration Number

Loan Originator Signature	Date Prepared
Borrower Signature	Date Accepted
Co-Borrower Signature	Date Accepted

Colorado Mortgage Loan Originator Lock-in Disclosure Form   Revised February 24, 2011

Colorado Tangible Net Benefit Disclosure

Colorado Tangible Net Benefit Disclosure

Pursuant to section 12-61-904.5, 914(1)(e) and (g), Colorado Revised Statutes

Borrower Name: ______________________________
Co-Borrower Name: ______________________________
Property Address: ______________________
Mortgage Loan Originator: ______________________
Mortgage Loan Originator License #: ______________________
Date: ______________________

Section 12-61-904.5(a), C.R.S., states that a mortgage loan originator shall have a duty of good faith and fair dealing in all communications and transactions with a borrower. Such duty includes the duty to not recommend or induce the borrower to enter into a transaction that does not have a reasonable, tangible net benefit to the borrower, considering all of the circumstances, including the terms of a loan, the cost of a loan, and the borrower's circumstances. This disclosure is designed to assist borrowers and mortgage loan originators in determining if a proposed loan has a reasonable, tangible net benefit to the borrower.

If you, the borrower, are unable to obtain a loan for any reason, the mortgage loan originator must, within five days after a written request by the borrower, give copies of each appraisal, title report, and credit report paid for by the borrower to the borrower, and transmit the appraisal, title report, or credit report to any other mortgage loan originator or lender to whom the borrower directs the documents be sent.

All moneys paid by the borrower to the mortgage loan originator for third-party services are held in a trust account and any moneys remaining after payment to third-party providers will be refunded.

I/We understand:

The reasonable, tangible net benefit standard in § 12-61-904.5(1)(a), C.R.S., is inherently dependent upon the totality of facts and circumstances relating to a specific transaction. While the refinancing of certain home loans may clearly provide a reasonable, tangible net benefit, others may require closer scrutiny or consideration to determine whether a particular loan provides the requisite benefit to the borrower.

***Requires borrower and co-borrower initials when applicable. If not applicable, enter N/A.**

Purchase Transaction:

* _____ _____ The new loan will enable me to purchase a home or other residential real estate in Colorado.

Refinance Transaction:

* _____ _____ The new loan will have a lower interest rate or Annual Percentage Rate (APR) than my/our present loan.
* _____ _____ The new loan will have a lower monthly payment than my/our present loan.
* _____ _____ The new loan is a fixed rate loan.
* _____ _____ The new loan is refinancing a loan that permitted negative amortization (term) than my/our present loan.
* _____ _____ The new loan will have a shorter amortization schedule.
* _____ _____ The new loan will eliminate the need for private mortgage insurance.
* _____ _____ The new loan will consolidate other loans or current debt.
* _____ _____ The proceeds of the new loan will be used for purposes that are of such importance to me that I am willing to obtain a new loan, even if that loan has terms that may not be as favorable as my existing loan. Examples include, but are not limited to: medical expenses; home improvements; avoid foreclosure; or to pay educational expenses.

Regardless of the purpose of the new loan, we have considered the following:

* _____ _____ The new loan contains "negative amortization" features. This means that not all interest due is paid monthly and unpaid interest is added to the principal of the loan balance. Negative amortization reduces equity in a home.
* _____ _____ The new loan is an Adjustable Rate Loan. This means that the interest rate is the total of an index plus a margin and is subject to periodic adjustments both up and down depending on the movement of the index. I understand that if the index increases between adjustment dates, the payments may change.
* _____ _____ If the new loan is an ARM, I have considered how long the new monthly payment will be in effect before it adjusts.
* _____ _____ My income, as disclosed on the Uniform Residential Loan Application, Freddie Mac form 65 or Fannie Mae form 1003, attached hereto that will be used to repay the loan, after payment of other household expenses, is sufficient to make the mortgage payments. My disclosed income is stable and is unlikely to be discontinued or reduced.

Use the below space to describe any reasonable, tangible net benefit or additional considerations not contained in this form.

* _____ _____ ____
____

I/We certify that we have carefully read this disclosure. I/We understand there is no obligation to enter into any proposed loan. I/We agree that the proposed loan has a reasonable, tangible net benefit.

Borrower Signature	Date	Co-Borrower Signature	Date

Mortgage Loan Originator Printed Name	Mortgage Loan Originator Signature	Date

Revised Date 08/05/2009

Mortgage Loan Origination Agreement for a Loan Modification

MORTGAGE LOAN ORIGINATION AGREEMENT FOR A LOAN MODIFICATION

This agreement ("Agreement") is made this ________ day of ____________, 20____ between ____ [*include all home owners*] ("Borrower") and ________________________________ ("Mortgage Loan Originator").

1. Acknowledgement of Alternatives. Borrower acknowledges that Mortgage Loan Originator is being compensated for services that Borrower may be able to obtain at no charge from a not-for-profit HUD-approved housing counselor or the like or by contacting the Lender directly. BORROWER IS ADVISED TO CONTACT THE COLORADO FORECLOSURE PREVENTION HOTLINE OPERATED IN COOPERATION WITH THE COLORADO DIVISION OF HOUSING AT 1-877-601-4673 OR THE HUD HOUSING COUNSELING AND REFERRAL LINE AT 1-800-569-4287.

2. Scope of Work. Borrower wishes to employ Mortgage Loan Originator to negotiate with Borrower's current Lender who holds Subject Loan secured by a deed of trust on Subject Property to restructure Borrower's debt to achieve and maintain sustainable mortgage payments owing on the Subject Loan. The Borrower hereby grants to the Mortgage Loan Originator the right to apply for and negotiate a loan modification on behalf of the Borrower with respect to the existing Subject Loan(s) in the form of a first mortgage, second mortgage, or line of credit, liens, or any combination thereof on the Borrower's property ("Subject Property") located at:

____

Street Address City State Zip

The Borrower defines the right of the Mortgage Loan Originator to act on their behalf as:

[ ] Exclusive; or

[ ] Non-exclusive.

Subject Loan:
Lender/Lien Holder Name ("Lender"):
____
Loan/Account Number: ____
Loan: __________ (i.e. 1st Loan, 2nd Loan)
Loan Type: _____ (i.e. FHA, Conv. ARM)

1

Borrower Initials: ____ ____

Borrower's desired terms and/or goals for the refinance or loan modification are as follows: ____
____.

A completed Colorado Tangible Net Benefit Disclosure Form signed by all parties is attached and incorporated to this Agreement as **Exhibit A**. Mortgage Loan Originator will undertake commercially reasonable efforts to conclude a successful loan modification. Upon completion of Mortgage Loan Originator's analysis and research efforts, Mortgage Loan Originator shall present to Borrower the options which are, as a result of such research, available, including but not limited to practical ways to improve Borrower's present debt structure with Borrower's Lender(s). A non-exhaustive description of services to be provided by the Mortgage Loan Originator for the Borrower may include, as applicable and relevant to the Subject Loan on the Subject Property, are as follows:

a. Interview the Borrower, gather and review information about the Subject Loan and terms to include:

i. Subject Loan's principal balance, monthly payment amount, mortgage statements, loan documents, current interest rate, possible rate and/or payment adjustments, equity, loan payment history and correspondence from the Lender(s);

ii. Information about the Borrower's income and assets, including: pay stubs, W-2s, 1099s, benefit award letters, retirement and pension benefit statements, annuity statements, child support/alimony, tax returns, profit and loss statements, schedules of real estate owned, stock and mutual fund portfolio statements, bank statements, proof of any other income;

iii. Information about the Subject Property, including: property profile, comparable sales, active listings, and other applicable documents; and

iv. Information about the Borrower's ability to repay the Subject Loan, including: credit history, hardship circumstances, financial profile (assessment of income, assets, expenses and housing debt to income ratio);

b. Assist the Borrower in preparing a hardship summary/letter;

c. Prepare and submit loan modification request and package of supporting documents to Lender, including obtaining any necessary credit reports and verifications of employment;

d. Counsel the Borrower regarding the loan modification process and options;

e. Contact the Lender(s) to discuss/negotiate the loan modification request(s) and package of supporting documents;

2

Borrower Initials: ____ ____

f. Communicate regularly with the Lender(s) to attempt to negotiate new and more favorable loan terms on behalf of Borrower;

g. Communicate regularly with Borrower as to status updates, any additional requirements for updated documents or Lender requirements;

h. Assist Borrower in understanding and deciding about the modification terms offered by the Lender(s);

i. Attempt to negotiate and/or accomplish a loan modification for the Borrower. Successful loan modification performance by the Mortgage Loan Originator shall have occurred if the Borrower accepts one or more of the loan modifications set forth below:

i. Change adjustable interest rate to a fixed interest rate;
ii. Reduce fixed interest rate to a lower fixed interest rate;
iii. Reduce balance of the principal amount of the Subject Loan;
iv. Reduce adjustable interest rate / reduce caps of adjustable interest rate;
v. Stop upward adjustment of adjustable interest rate;
vi. Arrange for the delinquent payment amounts to be added to the end of Subject Loan;
vii. Arrange for the delinquent payment amounts to be added to a longer loan period;
viii. Arrange for the delinquent payment amounts to be accepted in an alternative payment plan;
ix. Eliminate or reduce the delinquent payment amounts; and/or
x. Arrange for the Lender to accept a trial repayment plan, discounted pay-off or forbearance agreement.

The Mortgage Loan Originator will complete the above services in subparagraphs a, b, and c, above, not later than thirty (30) calendar days from the date this agreement is made, as first above written. These services are focused on the Mortgage Loan Originator's efforts to vigorously and successfully seek through the Lender an offer to the Borrower (which offer shall be assessed by the Mortgage Loan Originator and clearly explained to the Borrower) of proactive loan modification solutions, which may provide the Borrower with the opportunity to remain in the Subject Property while making affordable loan payments.

2. Borrower's Obligations. Borrower will provide Mortgage Loan Originator with all information and documentation requested by Mortgage Loan Originator that is reasonably necessary for Mortgage Loan Originator to perform the services under this agreement. Failure by Borrower to provide Mortgage Loan Originator all the information requested within fourteen (14) days of the signing of this Agreement shall constitute a waiver by Borrower of Mortgage Loan Originator's obligation to perform the services under this Agreement. The Borrower

3

Borrower Initials: ____ ____

agrees to furnish the Mortgage Loan Originator with all applicable and relevant documents that will be required by the Mortgage Loan Originator and the Lender to assess the Borrower's financial status, including, without limitation, the following:

a. Mortgage statements-past three months;

b. Pay stubs - past two pay periods;

c. W-2 forms, 1099 forms, and/or tax returns-past 2 years;

d. Profit and loss statements-past 2 years (if self employed);

e. Bank statements-past 2 months;

f. Verification of any other income, benefit award letters, retirement statements, pension benefit statements;

g. Annuity statements, child support/alimony;

h. Schedules of real estate owned, stock and mutual fund portfolio statements;

i. Signed authorization for the Mortgage Loan Originator to contact Lender on Borrower's behalf; and

j. Signed authorization for the Mortgage Loan Originator to share confidential financial information with HFL (defined below).

The Borrower also agrees to provide additional updated information or documentation within five (5) days of the Mortgage Loan Originator's request. The Borrower further agrees to immediately notify the Mortgage Loan Originator of any change in the Borrower's address. Borrower represents and warrants to Mortgage Loan Originator that Borrower will at all times hereunder provide Mortgage Loan Originator with information that is accurate and true to the best of Borrower's knowledge and belief. Borrower agrees to hold Mortgage Loan Originator harmless from and against any liability arising from Borrower's breach in whole of in part of the representations and warranties contained in this Agreement.

3. No Guaranty. Borrower acknowledges that the Mortgage Loan Originator cannot guarantee that Lender will agree to a modification of the Subject Loan. Lender is not required to and is not obligated to modify the Subject Loan in any way and may not agree to any changes in the Subject Loan. Borrower has been advised that Mortgage Loan Originator does not promise or guarantee to stop any foreclosure or foreclosure proceedings or obtain any Public Trustee foreclosure sale date extensions, continuances, or withdrawals. Borrower understands and acknowledges that the services provided by Mortgage Loan Originator are not guaranteed, no particular result has been promised, and no prediction of a final result has been made. Nothing in this Agreement shall be construed as a promise or guarantee about the outcome of the matter.

4. Term. This authorization is effective immediately and for a period of ______ days thereafter unless otherwise canceled or extended by the parties. If a conforming refinance commitment or a loan modification offer is not obtained within such time, this Agreement shall be deemed canceled.

4

Borrower Initials: ____ ____

5. Commissions. In consideration of the services of Mortgage Loan Originator in securing and negotiating such refinance or loan modification, the Borrower agrees to pay Mortgage Loan Originator the total sum of $__________ ("Commission"), which shall be considered earned and immediately due and payable when a loan modification offer is received from Lender, conforming to the provisions specified above. In the event that a loan modification offer is not obtained for any reason, other than rejection by the Borrower, the Borrower shall have no obligation or liability to Mortgage Loan Originator for Mortgage Loan Origination commissions under this Agreement. A completed Colorado Mortgage Loan Originator Compensation Disclosure Form signed by all parties is attached and incorporated to this Agreement as **Exhibit B**.

6. Joint Representation. Borrower acknowledges that Mortgage Loan Originator intends to work with and pay ___________________________ a reasonable fee for actual services rendered in connection with securing, negotiating, and processing such refinance or loan modification, and Borrower consents to such an arrangement. It is expressly acknowledged that of the services described in paragraph 1, above, ___________________________ is expected to handle the processing of Borrower's file and communicating and negotiating with the Lender.

7. Rejection of Terms. The Borrower shall accept the loan modification if it conforms to the provisions described above. If the Mortgage Loan Originator has obtained for the borrower a written commitment from any lender for a refinance or loan modification on the terms and conditions set forth above and the Borrower fails to consummate the loan modification through no fault of the Mortgage Loan Originator, the Borrower shall pay a fee to the Mortgage Loan Originator of three hundred dollars ($300) for services rendered, preparation of documents, and/or transfer of documents in the Borrower's file.

8. Third-Party Fees. Borrower agrees to promptly pay all reasonable and necessary fees for third-party services such as credit reports, employment verification, appraisals, title work, or the like, necessary, desirable, or expedient to obtain or consummate a conforming refinance commitment or a loan modification. Mortgage Loan Originator may solicit or receive fees for third-party provider goods or services in advance. Fees for any goods or services not provided shall be refunded to the Borrower, and Mortgage Loan Originator may not charge more for the goods and services than the actual costs of the goods or services charged by the third-party provider. Borrower acknowledges that such fees may be non-refundable in the event that such services are actually rendered and a conforming refinance commitment or a loan modification offer is not obtained. In the event of cancellation of this Agreement, Borrower shall repay, within sixty (60) days after the date of cancellation, all funds paid or advanced in good faith prior to the receipt of notice of cancellation by the Mortgage Loan Originator under the terms of this Agreement, together with interest at the prime rate published by the federal reserve plus two percentage points, with the total interest rate not to exceed eight percent per year, from the date of expenditure until repaid by the Borrower.

5

Borrower Initials: ____ ____

9. Credit Report: Please note that a loan modification may negatively impact your credit score. To learn more about this, please contact a credit reporting agency for further information. Credit reporting agencies include: Equifax, Experian, and Transunion.

10. Other Compensation. Nothing contained herein shall preclude the Mortgage Loan Originator from receiving a fee or other remuneration from the Lender or other third party for services prior to or after the issuance of a written commitment from a lender for a refinance or loan modification to the extent allowed by applicable law, provided that the consideration is first fully disclosed in writing to the Borrower.

11. Waiver of Claims. Mortgage Loan Originator makes no warranty, expressed or implied, as to the fitness of any recommendation it may make to Borrower arising out of this Agreement. To the fullest extent allowed by applicable law, Borrower unconditionally waives any claim or right of action against Mortgage Loan Originator, its officers, directors, members, managers, employees, agents, loan originators, and assigns, arising out of this Agreement or for any damages that Borrower may incur by reasons of Borrower following any recommendation of Mortgage Loan Originator, Borrower's failure to follow any recommendation of Mortgage Loan Originator, or any other act or omission of Mortgage Loan Originator relating hereto.

12. Notice. Any cancellation or other notice required or permitted under this Agreement or under state law shall be deemed sufficiently given or served if sent by United States certified mail, return receipt requested, addressed as follows:

a. If to Mortgage Loan Originator:

____
____
____
____
E-mail: ____________________
Facsimile: __________________

b. If to Borrower:

____
____
____
____
E-mail: ____________________
Facsimile: __________________

The parties shall have the right from time to time to change the place notice is to be given under this paragraph by written notice thereof to the other party. A completed Notice of Cancellation is attached and incorporated as **Exhibit C**.

Borrower Initials: ____ ____

13. Miscellaneous Provisions.

a. The parties acknowledge and agree that each party is responsible for their respective tax obligations owed concerning the contemplated loan modification, Mortgage Loan Originator has made no representations concerning taxes, and Borrower has been encouraged to obtain advice from a competent tax advisor.

b. The parties acknowledge that they have had a full and fair opportunity to consult with legal counsel of their own choosing throughout all negotiations that preceded the execution of this Agreement, including in connection with their execution of this Agreement. No party shall be deemed the "drafting party" of this Agreement. Consequently, this Agreement shall be construed as a whole, according to its fair meaning and intent, and not strictly for or against any party hereto.

c. This Agreement shall be construed under the laws of the State of Colorado. Venue shall be in the county where the Subject Property is located.

d. Every provision of this Agreement is intended to be severable. If any provision of this Agreement or the application thereof shall, for any reason and to any extent, be invalid or unenforceable, neither the remainder of this Agreement nor the application of the provision to other persons, entities or circumstances shall be affected thereby, but instead shall be enforced to the maximum extent permitted by law.

e. This Agreement sets forth the entire agreement of the parties and fully supersedes any and all prior or contemporaneous negotiations, agreements or understandings between them pertaining to the subject matter hereof. The parties acknowledge that no party, nor agent, nor attorney of any arty has made any promise or representation whatsoever, express or implied, concerning the subject matter of this Agreement (or to induce the execution of this Agreement) which is not expressly set forth herein.

f. This Agreement may only be changed by an amendment executed in writing by all parties.

g. The parties represent they have read this Agreement, understand it, voluntarily agree to its terms and conditions, and sign it freely.

h. This Agreement shall be binding upon the parties' respective heirs, administrators, representatives, executors, successors and assigns.

7

Borrower Initials: ____ ____

i. This Agreement may be executed in counterparts, each of which shall be deemed an original, and all of which taken together shall constitute one and the same instrument. Facsimile or electronic signatures shall be effective as originals.

14. The parties acknowledge that this completed Agreement was provided to Borrowers for their review at least twenty-four hours prior to their signing on ________________________, 20___ at _____:____o'clock __.m.

IN WITNESS WHEREOF, the parties hereto executed this Agreement on the dates and times indicated below.

Borrower Initials: ____ ____

<u>Notice Required by Colorado Law</u>

_____________________ [*Mortgage Loan Originator*] **or (his/her/its) associate cannot ask you to sign or have you sign any document that transfers any interest in your home or property to (him/her/it) or (his/her/its) associate.**

____________________ [*Mortgage Loan Originator*] **or (his/her/its) associate cannot guarantee you that they will be able to refinance your home or arrange for you to keep your home.**

You may, at any time, cancel this contract, without penalty of any kind.

If you want to cancel this contract, mail or deliver a signed and dated copy of this notice of cancellation, or any other written notice, indicating your intent to cancel to ____ [*Mortgage Loan Originator*] **at** ____________________ [*address of Mortgage Loan Originator, including facsimile and electronic mail address*].

As part of any cancellation, you (the home owner) must repay any money actually spent on your behalf by ____________________ [*Mortgage Loan Originator*] **prior to receipt of this notice and as a result of this agreement, within sixty days, along with interest at the prime rate published by the federal reserve plus two percentage points, with the total interest rate not to exceed eight percent per year.**

This is an important legal contract and could result in the loss of your home. Contact an attorney or a housing counselor approved by the federal department of housing and urban development before signing.

[signatures appear on next page]

9

Borrower Initials: ____ ____

<table>
<tr><td>Borrower:

____
Print Name: ____________________________</td><td>Date: __________________
Time: __________________</td></tr>
<tr><td colspan="2">STATE OF COLORADO)
) ss.
_________ COUNTY OF ________________)

The foregoing instrument was acknowledged before me this _____ day of ___________, 20___.
Witness my hand and official seal.
My Commission Expires: ___________________

____
Notary Public
(Seal or Stamp)</td></tr>
<tr><td>Co-Borrower:

____
Print Name: ____________________________</td><td>Date: __________________
Time: __________________</td></tr>
<tr><td colspan="2">STATE OF COLORADO)
) ss.
_________ COUNTY OF ________________)

The foregoing instrument was acknowledged before me this _____ day of ___________, 20___.
Witness my hand and official seal.
My Commission Expires: ___________________

____
Notary Public
(Seal or Stamp)</td></tr>
</table>

10

Borrower Initials: ____ ____

<table>
<tr><td>Mortgage Loan Originator:

By: ______________________________
Print Name: ________________________
Title: ____________________________
Colo. License No. __________________</td><td>Date: _______________</td></tr>
<tr><td colspan="2">STATE OF COLORADO)
) ss.
_________ COUNTY OF ______________)

The foregoing instrument was acknowledged before me this _____ day of __________, 20___, by ____________________ [*name*] as __________________ [*title*] of _______________ ____________ [*company*]. Witness my hand and official seal.

My Commission Expires: _________________

____
Notary Public

(Seal or Stamp)</td></tr>
</table>

11

Borrower Initials: ____ ____

Exhibit C

Notice of Cancellation

Re: Mortgage Loan Origination Agreement for Refinance or Loan Modification dated ______________________, 20___.

To: __________________________ (*name of foreclosure consultant*)

____

____

____

____

(*Address of foreclosure consultant, including facsimile and electronic mail*)

I hereby cancel this contract.

_____________________ (*Date*)

_____________________ (*Home owner's signature*)

Borrower Initials: ____ ____

Chapter 13: Water Rights†

An * in the left margin indicates a change in the statute, rule, or text since the last publication of the manual.

I. Water Allocation Laws and Procedures

All water in natural surface streams and ground water in related aquifers (called "**tributary ground water**") in Colorado is owned by the public and is subject to the doctrine of prior appropriation. Ground water other than tributary ground water is allocated by different rules as described below. There is a rebuttable presumption under Colorado law that all surface water and ground water in Colorado is tributary to a natural surface stream.

A "**water right**" is the right to use a portion of the state's waters. A water right does not represent ownership of the water. It is a right to use a certain amount of water for a particular purpose under the restrictions stated in the court decree or well permit defining the water right.

The doctrine of "**prior appropriation**" is adopted and recognized in the Colorado Constitution in Article XVI, Sections 5 and 6. Prior appropriation means that the first user to divert water from a stream and put the water to beneficial use has a prior right to that source of water compared to later users. Under the prior appropriation system, water users do not share the burden of shortages. The prior user is entitled to divert the full amount of water to meet his or her entire water need before the next junior user is allowed to divert any water.

Water is appropriated, and a water right is created, by actions of the person who makes the appropriation. Physical diversion of water from a stream or a tributary aquifer, and application of that water to beneficial use, creates a water right. No further administrative or judicial action is necessary.

Under the prior appropriation system, the value and reliability of a water right is a function of its priority with respect to other water rights on the same stream system. In order to prioritize water rights, Colorado has adopted a statutory system of water right adjudication to determine the date of appropriation and priority of a water right with respect to other water rights. Adjudication means filing an application and proving to the court all of the aspects of a particular water right appropriation. The court then issues a decree that recites the relevant facts proved. The current adjudication statute is called the Water Right Determination and Administration Act of 1969, found at §§ 37-92-101, *et seq.*, C.R.S. Although a water right is created upon application of water to beneficial use, a water right owner is not entitled to have his or her water right administered within the priority system until he or she obtains a decree from a court confirming the water right priority.

Surface water includes all water in rivers, streams, lakes, wetlands and other natural waterways, and diffuse runoff. Ground water that is hydraulically connected to surface water—meaning that the ground water is replenished by surface water percolating into the ground or the ground water seeps into surface water bodies—is considered tributary ground

† The commentary portions of this chapter were written by Robert V. Trout. Mr. Trout is a partner at the law firm of Trout, Raley, Montaño, Witwer & Freeman, P.C., which is located in Denver.

water. Tributary ground water is subject to the doctrine of prior appropriation as a part of the surface water body to which it is hydraulically connected. Thus, wells withdrawing water from the South Platte alluvium (the shallow aquifer that is tributary to the South Platte River) are considered tributary to the South Platte River and are subject to senior "**surface water rights**" on that river. This means that wells withdrawing water from the South Platte River tributary aquifer may not be able to operate to withdraw water when they are not in priority with respect to senior surface water rights.

A surface water right or tributary ground water right is represented by a decree from a court that confirms the priority date and other important aspects of the water right, including the type of use (irrigation, domestic, commercial, industrial, or other uses), the amount, the time of use, the point of diversion, and the place of use. A water right decree does not usually determine the ownership of a water right. It only states thc identity of the claimant of the water right, who is usually—but not always—the owner. A water right is initially owned by the person or entity that actually diverted the water and applied it to beneficial use.

For administrative purposes, Colorado has been divided into seven water divisions, which are generally co-extensive with the seven major river basins that originate in the state. For instance, the South Platte River Basin is Water Division No. 1 and the Arkansas River Basin is Water Division No. 2. Each division has its own Water Court that has exclusive jurisdiction over all water matters in that division.

Water rights are administered, meaning that they are enforced, by the State Engineer's Office. Each water division has a division engineer's office that administers water rights in that division. Each division engineer supervises a number of water commissioners, who are the people who actually tell water users whether they can legally divert water under their water right at any given time. Water commissioners are the local police of the water administration system.

Ground water in Colorado is allocated under several different rules, depending upon its physical characteristics. As explained above, tributary ground water is subject to the doctrine of prior appropriation and is administered in conjunction with surface water rights in the river system to which it is tributary.

Another type of ground water classification, created by the legislature in the Ground Water Management Act of 1965, §§ 37-90-101, *et seq.*, C.R.S., is ground water within areas known as "**designated ground water basins**." Designated ground water basins are geographic areas containing ground water that: (1) in its natural course would not be available to and required for the fulfillment of decreed surface water rights, or (2) is in areas not adjacent to a continuously flowing natural stream in which ground water withdrawals have constituted the principal water usage for at least 15 years prior to designation of the basin. The basins are created by the Ground Water Commission through a formal hearing and order process. A modified doctrine of prior appropriation is applied in designated ground water basins, meaning that prior appropriation is applied but water levels in aquifers are allowed to decline over time even if this results in senior water rights losing their water supply. Rights to use designated ground water are represented by well permits issued by the Ground Water Commission. Colorado has eight designated ground water basins, which are generally located on the eastern plains.

Ground water may be so physically separated from surface water by impermeable layers or great distances so as to have little or no hydraulic connection with surface water. If such ground water is located outside of a designated ground water basin, and its withdrawal will not within 100 years deplete the flow of a natural stream at an annual rate greater than one-tenth of one percent of the annual rate of withdrawal, it is classified as "**non-tributary ground water**." By statute, § 37-90-137(4), C.R.S., the right to use non-tributary ground water is generally allocated based on the ownership of the overlying land, rather than the prior appropriation system. The owner of the overlying land may obtain a right to use non-tributary ground water by obtaining a well permit from the State Engineer's Office, or may seek to have the Water Court determine the non-tributary ground water rights before drilling a well. Ground water within the Dawson, Denver, Arapahoe, and Laramie-Fox Hills aquifers in the area known as the Denver Basin (a kidney-shaped area along the Front Range of Colorado between Greeley and Colorado Springs) is presumed to be non-tributary. Non-tributary ground water also occurs in other parts of the state.

The Colorado legislature has also defined a unique category of ground water located outside the boundaries of a designated ground water basin within the Dawson, Denver, Arapahoe, and Laramie-Fox Hills aquifers in the Denver Basin. Water within this classification is water that would otherwise not meet the definition of non-tributary ground water, and is known as "**not non-tributary ground water**." Not non-tributary ground water is also generally allocated on the basis of land ownership. Like non-tributary ground water, the owner of the overlying land may obtain a right to use not non-tributary ground water by obtaining a well permit from the State Engineer's Office or may seek to have the Water Court determine the not non-tributary ground water rights before drilling a well.

To avoid injury to senior surface water rights, the law now requires a judicially approved augmentation plan before junior tributary ground water rights and not non-tributary ground water rights can be pumped and used. An augmentation plan allows a water user to divert water out of priority so long as adequate replacement is made to the affected stream system and water rights in quantities and at times so as to prevent injury to the water rights of others.

Water rights can only be used for the purposes described in the applicable decree or permit and pursuant and subject to all of the other terms and conditions in the applicable decree or permit. For instance, an irrigation water right cannot be used for domestic or industrial purposes. The type, time and place of use, and other aspects of water rights can generally be changed if the change will not injure other water rights. Adjudicated water rights, including rights to non-tributary and not non-tributary ground water, must be changed in a proceeding filed in the applicable Water Court. Designated ground water rights must be changed in a proceeding filed with the Ground Water Commission. The change is usually evidenced by a change of water right decree issued by the Water Court or a changed well permit issued by the Ground Water Commission.

Surface and tributary ground water rights are subject to loss by abandonment. Abandonment occurs when there is a sustained period of non-use of the water right coupled with an intention to abandon. An intention to abandon can be inferred from an unreasonably long period of non-use. Abandonment of a water right can occur without any official court or administrative action or the execution of any document. Thus, when investigating the status of a water right, potential abandonment must always be considered.

II. Well Permits

A well is any structure or device used for the purpose or with the effect of obtaining ground water for beneficial use from an aquifer. A permit issued by the State Engineer's Office is required to construct a well, except in designated ground water basins where the well permit is issued by the Ground Water Commission. The State Engineer's Office maintains records of all well permits issued in the state.

A well permit for tributary ground water can only be issued by the State Engineer's Office if there is unappropriated water available for withdrawal by the proposed well and the vested rights of others will not be materially injured. Because most rivers in Colorado are already over-appropriated (meaning that there is often not enough water to satisfy existing water rights), this standard cannot be met in many areas of Colorado. To allow some low-density development in rural areas, there is a rebuttable presumption of no injury to other water users or existing wells if a proposed well will have a production capacity of less than 15 gallons per minute, and will be either: (1) the only well on a residential site located in a subdivision approved before June 1, 1972, and the well will be used solely for ordinary household purposes inside a single-family dwelling and will not be used for irrigation, or (2) the only well on a tract of land of 35 acres or more. These are commonly called "exempt" or "household use only" wells.

A well permit for non-tributary ground water and not non-tributary ground water is issued by the State Engineer's Office based on overlying land ownership. The well permit will only allow withdrawal of one percent of the amount of water calculated to exist in the aquifer underlying the land per year.

III. Conveying and Encumbering Water Rights

Water rights are represented by a number of different documents. Surface water rights, tributary ground water rights, non-tributary ground water rights, and not non-tributary ground water rights are usually represented by Water Court decrees. Rights to tributary ground water, non-tributary ground water, and not non-tributary ground water may also be represented by well permits. Designated ground water rights are usually represented by well permits. Water rights owned by mutual ditch or reservoir companies (commonly called ditch rights or reservoir rights) are usually represented by shares of stock in the mutual ditch or reservoir company, because the company itself usually owns the water rights.

Water rights in all of these forms are conveyed by a deed that should be recorded in the applicable county clerk and recorder's office in the same manner as a land deed. Well permits should also be conveyed by an assignment that is filed with the State Engineer's Office. Shares of stock in a mutual ditch or reservoir company are also conveyed by assignment and other procedures required by the company.

Water rights in all of these forms can also be encumbered by a deed of trust, except that a deed of trust usually may not encumber shares of stock in a mutual ditch or reservoir company. Security interests in shares of stock must be obtained and perfected under the terms of the Colorado Uniform Commercial Code.

Whether a particular deed to land conveys surface or tributary ground water rights depends upon the intention of the grantor, which is determined from the express terms of the deed. Thus, a deed may describe specific water rights that are conveyed. If a deed is silent as to surface or tributary ground water rights, the intentions of the grantor are to be determined by the circumstances, such as whether the water right is or is not incidental to and necessary to the beneficial enjoyment of the land. Where a deed is silent, no presumption arises as to the parties' intent regarding the transfer of surface or tributary ground water rights. The inclusion of a water right in a deed will not by itself prevent a later determination of abandonment.

The presumption is different with respect to non-tributary ground water. Rights to non-tributary ground water are presumed to pass with the land in a deed and are encumbered by a deed of trust encumbering the land, unless these rights are explicitly excepted from the deed. A party claiming that the non-tributary ground water was not transferred or encumbered with the land has the burden of proving that fact.

§ 38-30-102, C.R.S. Water rights conveyed as real estate – well permit transfers – legislative declaration – definitions

(1) The general assembly:

(a) Finds that the division of water resources in the department of natural resources needs timely and accurate data regarding well ownership in order to efficiently and accurately account for wells and to ensure that wells are properly constructed and maintained;

(b) Determines that current data concerning well ownership is inadequate and that a substantial number of residential real estate transactions that transfer ownership of a well are not reported to the division;

(c) Determines that current and accurate data is necessary for the state to notify well owners of any health, safety, water right, or stewardship issues pertaining to their ground water well; and

(d) Declares that this section is intended to provide the division with the information it needs to properly carry out its statutory duties.

(2) In the conveyance of water rights in all cases, except where the ownership of stock in ditch companies or other companies constitutes the ownership of a water right, the same formalities shall be observed and complied with as in the conveyance of real estate.

(3) (a) As used in this subsection (3):

(I) "Closing service" means closing and settlement services, as defined in section 10-11-102, C.R.S.

(II) "Division" means the division of water resources in the department of natural resources.

(III) "Person" means any individual, corporation, government or governmental subdivision or agency, business trust, estate, trust, limited liability company, partnership, association, or other legal entity.

(b) (I) On and after January 1, 2009, when a buyer of residential real estate enters into a transaction that results in the transfer of ownership of a small capacity well listed in section 37-90-105 (1) (a) or (1) (b), C.R.S., or a domestic exempt water well used for ordinary household purposes that is listed in section 37-92-602 (1) (b) or (1) (e), C.R.S., the buyer shall, prior to or at closing of the transaction, complete a change in ownership form for the well in compliance with section 37-90-143, C.R.S.; except that, if an existing well has not yet been registered with the division, the buyer shall complete a registration of existing well form for the well.

(II) The residential real estate contract approved by the real estate commission created in section 12-61-105, C.R.S., shall require the buyer to complete the appropriate form for the well and, if no person will be providing a closing service in connection with the transaction, to file the form with the division within sixty days after closing.

(c) (I) If a person provides a closing service in connection with a residential real estate transaction subject to this subsection (3), that person shall:

(A) Within sixty days after closing, submit the appropriate form to the division with as much information as is available, and the division shall be responsible for obtaining the necessary well registration information directly from the buyer; and

(B) Not be liable for delaying the closing of the transaction in order to ensure that the buyer completes the form required by subparagraph (I) of paragraph (b) of this subsection (3). If the closing is delayed pursuant to this sub-subparagraph (B), neither the buyer nor the seller shall have any claim under this section for relief against the buyer, the seller, the person who provided closing services, a title insurance company regulated pursuant to article 11 of title 10, C.R.S., or any person licensed pursuant to article 61 of title 12, C.R.S.

(II) If no person provides such closing service, the buyer shall submit the appropriate form within the deadline specified in sub-subparagraph (A) of subparagraph (I) of this paragraph (c) and pay the applicable fee.

IV. Disclosure of Potable Water Source

On and after January 1, 2008, Colorado law requires that a listing contract, contract of sale, or seller's property disclosure for residential land and residential improvements disclose in bold-faced type the source of potable water for the property, which can be one of the following:

1. Well (in which case a copy of the current well permit, if one is available, is to be provided);
2. Water provider (in which case the name and other information regarding the water provider is to be provided); or
3. Neither a well nor a water provider (in which case the source of the water is to be provided).

The disclosure statement is also required to state in bold-faced type that some water providers rely, to varying decrees, on nonrenewable water (which is generally considered to be non-tributary and not non-tributary ground water described above), and advise the prospective purchaser that he or she may wish to contact the water provider to determine the long-term sufficiency of that provider's water supplies.

Residential real estate located in incorporated cities and towns is almost always supplied potable water by a water provider (that is often part of the city or town government) such as the Denver Water Board in Denver and the Aurora Water Department in Aurora. Areas located near urban areas, such as areas adjacent to Fort Collins or Loveland, are sometimes supplied potable water by the adjacent municipality and are sometimes served by independent water districts. Some cities and towns are served by independent water districts that are not part of the city or town government.

Municipalities and water districts obtain their water from surface water sources and ground water. Denver, Aurora, and other large municipalities usually obtain all or most of their water from surface water rights. These surface water rights could divert water from streams large distances from the municipalities, such as the Colorado River basin in western Colorado for Denver, Aurora, and other municipalities. Municipalities and water districts also obtain water from tributary, non-tributary, not non-tributary, and designated ground water sources depending on their location.

Residential real estate in rural areas is most often supplied potable water from a well. The well can produce tributary ground water, non-tributary ground water, not non-tributary ground water, or designated ground water, depending upon the location. Such wells almost never produce water from more than one of these sources. In some cases, particularly in mountainous areas, residential real estate can obtain potable water from a small surface diversion or a spring.

§ 38-35.7-104, C.R.S. Disclosure of potable water source – rules

(1) (a) (I) By January 1, 2008, the real estate commission created in section 12-61-105, C.R.S., shall, by rule, require each listing contract, contract of sale, or seller's property disclosure for residential real property that is subject to the commission's jurisdiction pursuant to article 61 of title 12, C.R.S., to disclose the source of potable water for the property, which disclosure shall include substantially the following information:

THE SOURCE OF POTABLE WATER FOR THIS REAL ESTATE IS:
☐ **A WELL;**
☐ **A WATER PROVIDER, WHICH CAN BE CONTACTED AS FOLLOWS:**
NAME: ____________________
ADDRESS: ____________________
WEB SITE: ____________________
TELEPHONE: ____________________
☐ **NEITHER A WELL NOR A WATER PROVIDER. THE SOURCE IS [DESCRIBE]:** ____________________
SOME WATER PROVIDERS RELY, TO VARYING DEGREES, ON NONRENEWABLE GROUND WATER. YOU MAY WISH TO CONTACT YOUR PROVIDER TO DETERMINE THE LONG-TERM SUFFICIENCY OF THE PROVIDER'S WATER SUPPLIES.

(II) On and after January 1, 2008, each listing contract, contract of sale, or seller's property disclosure for residential real property that is not subject to the real estate commission's jurisdiction pursuant to article 61 of title 12, C.R.S., shall contain a disclosure statement in bold-faced type that is clearly legible in substantially the same form as is specified in subparagraph (I) of this paragraph (a).

(b) If the disclosure statement required by paragraph (a) of this subsection (1) indicates that the source of potable water is a well, the seller shall also provide with such disclosure a copy of the current well permit if one is available.

(2) The obligation to provide the disclosure set forth in subsection (1) of this section shall be upon the seller. If the seller complies with this section, the purchaser shall not have any claim under this section for relief against the seller or any person licensed pursuant to article 61 of title 12, C.R.S., for any damages to the purchaser resulting from an alleged inadequacy of the property's source of water. Nothing in this section shall affect any remedy that the purchaser may otherwise have against the seller.

(3) For purposes of this section, "residential real property" means residential land and residential improvements, as those terms are defined in section 39-1-102, C.R.S., but does not include hotels and motels, as those terms are defined in section 39-1-102, C.R.S; except that a mobile home and a manufactured home, as those terms are defined in section 39-1-102, C.R.S., shall be deemed to be residential real property only if the mobile home or manufactured home is permanently affixed to a foundation.

V. Special Considerations for Irrigated Land

Often the seller of an irrigated farm, raw land, or even a rural subdivision will need to be knowledgeable about associated water rights. Due to the intricacies of water systems and irrigated farms in Colorado, it is advisable for the seller of an irrigated farm to be prepared to inform the prospective purchaser of pertinent information on the water rights. Some suggestions as to the type of information that could be disclosed are as follows:

1. If the irrigation water is delivered by a ditch or canal, there are several things to be considered:

a. The number of shares of stock in the ditch or reservoir company that serves the farm that are proposed to be sold with the farm, and whether these are all of the shares that were historically used on the farm.

b. The average annual delivery of water under the canal and what months this delivery is normally received. Further, how often the water is historically available to land being sold. Not all canals run their water perpetually, with the usage to the shareholder being all the time that water is in the canal. Instead, some run their water in sections, with each section taking a turn for a specified period of continuous use, then moving on to the next section. Others use the call system—water, when available, being called by the user proportionate to his or her shares.

c. The prospective purchaser may also be interested in whether the bylaws of that canal company permit the sale of the water out of and separate from the land or the canal; also, whether the water can be transferred to another point of use within the canal system. The seller of such water rights should be familiar with the transfer procedures for the particular ditch or reservoir company, which may be by deed, of course, but may also involve the transfer of the ditch or reservoir company's stock certificate. The amount of any assessment on the shares of stock by the ditch or reservoir company would also be important.

2. If the farm is irrigated with wells, the following should be considered:

a. The prospective purchaser may be interested in whether the wells are tributary, and if so, whether the wells are covered by a court-adjudicated augmentation plan, whether the wells have been adjudicated in Water Court, and, if so, the date of adjudication, the priority date, and the amount allowed to be pumped. Of course, the prospective purchaser could also be interested in the physical condition of the wells and their current production capacity.

b. Irrigation wells may also be located in a designated ground water basin or may produce non-tributary or not non-tributary ground water. Here again, the prospective purchaser could be interested in the above information, plus information on aquifer levels in that particular basin, as aquifers in some basins have been depleted substantially in recent years. The energy supply for the water pumps and the cost of pumping the wells may also be important to a prospective buyer in these energy-conscious times.

VI. Water Conservation and Drought Mitigation

§ 37-60-126, C.R.S. Water conservation and drought mitigation planning – programs – relationship to state assistance for water facilities – guidelines

(*Ed. Note: The following is a portion (section (11) of Part 126 applicable to covenant controlled communities*)

(11) (a) Any section of a restrictive covenant that prohibits or limits xeriscape, prohibits or limits the installation or use of drought-tolerant vegetative landscapes, or requires cultivated vegetation to consist exclusively or primarily of turf grass is hereby declared contrary to public policy and, on that basis, that section of the covenant shall be unenforceable.

(b) As used in this subsection (11):

(I) "Executive board policy or practice" includes any additional procedural step or burden, financial or otherwise, placed on a unit owner who seeks approval for a landscaping change by the executive board of a unit owners' association, as defined in section 38-33.3-103, C.R.S., and not included in the existing declaration or bylaws of the association. An "executive board policy or practice" includes, without limitation, the requirement of:

(A) An architect's stamp;

(B) Pre-approval by an architect or landscape architect retained by the executive board;

(C) An analysis of water usage under the proposed new landscape plan or a history of water usage under the unit owner's existing landscape plan; and

(D) The adoption of a landscaping change fee.

(II) "Restrictive covenant" means any covenant, restriction, bylaw, executive board policy or practice, or condition applicable to real property for the purpose of controlling land use, but does not include any covenant, restriction, or condition imposed on such real property by any governmental entity.

(III) "Turf grass" means continuous plant coverage consisting of hybridized grasses that, when regularly mowed, form a dense growth of leaf blades and roots.

(IV) "Xeriscape" means the application of the principles of landscape planning and design, soil analysis and improvement, appropriate plant selection, limitation of turf area, use of mulches, irrigation efficiency, and appropriate maintenance that results in water use efficiency and water-saving practices.

(c) Nothing in this subsection (11) shall preclude the executive board of a common interest community from taking enforcement action against a unit owner who allows his or her existing landscaping to die; except that:

(I) Such enforcement action shall be suspended during a period of water use restrictions declared by the jurisdiction in which the common interest community is located, in which case the unit owner shall comply with any watering restrictions imposed by the water provider for the common interest community;

(II) Enforcement shall be consistent within the community and not arbitrary or capricious; and

(III) Once the drought emergency is lifted, the unit owner shall be allowed a reasonable and practical opportunity, as defined by the association's executive board, with consideration of applicable local growing seasons or practical limitations, to reseed and revive turf grass before being required to replace it with new sod.

§ 38-35.7-107, C.R.S. Water-smart homes option

(1) (a) Every person that builds a new single-family detached residence for which a buyer is under contract shall offer the buyer the opportunity to select one or more of the following water-smart home options for the residence:

(I) Installation of water-efficient toilets, lavatory faucets, and showerheads that meet or exceed the following water-efficient standards: toilets shall use no more than one and twenty-eight one-hundredths of a gallon per flush, lavatory faucets no more than one and one-half gallons per minute, and showerheads no more than two gallons per minute;

(II) If dishwashers or clothes washers are financed, installed, or sold as upgrades through the home builder, the builder shall offer a model that is qualified pursuant to the federal environmental protection agency's energy star program at the time of offering. Clothes washers shall have a water factor of less than or equal to six gallons of water per cycle per cubic foot of capacity.

* (III) If landscaping is financed, installed, or sold as upgrades through the home builder and will be maintained by the home owner, the home builder shall offer a landscape design that follows the landscape practices specified in this subparagraph (III) to ensure both the professional design and installation of such landscaping and

that water conservation will be accomplished. These best management practices are contained in the document titled: "Green Industry Best Management Practices (BMPs) for the Conservation and Protection of Water Resources in Colorado: Moving Toward Sustainability", 3rd release, and appendix, in May 2008, or this document's successors due to future inclusion of improved landscaping practices, water conservation advancements, and new irrigation technology. The best management practices specified in this subparagraph (III), through utilization of the proper landscape design, installation, and irrigation technology, accomplish substantial water savings compared to landscape designs, installation, and irrigation system utilization where these practices are not adhered to. The following best management practices and water budget calculator form the basis for the design and installation for the front yard landscaping option if selected by the homeowner as an upgrade:

(A) Xeriscape: To include the seven principles of xeriscape that provide a comprehensive approach for conserving water;

(B) Water budgeting: To include either a water allotment by the water utility for the property, if offered by the water utility, or a landscape water budget based on plant water requirements;

(C) Landscape design: To include a plan and design for the landscape to comprehensively conserve water and protect water quality;

(D) Landscape installation and erosion control: To minimize soil erosion and employ proper soil care and planting techniques during construction;

(E) Soil amendment and ground preparation: To include an evaluation of the soil and improve, if necessary, to address water retention, permeability, water infiltration, aeration, and structure;

(F) Tree placement and tree planting: To include proper soil and space for root growth and to include proper planting of trees, shrubs, and other woody plants to promote long-term health of these plants;

(G) Irrigation design and installation: To include design of the irrigation system for the efficient and uniform distribution of water to plant material and the development of an irrigation schedule;

(H) Irrigation technology and scheduling: To include water conserving devices that stop water application during rain, high wind, and other weather events and incorporate evapotranspiration conditions. Irrigation scheduling should address frequency and duration of water application in the most efficient manner; and

(I) Mulching: To include the use of organic mulches to reduce water loss through evaporation, reduce soil loss, and suppress weeds.

(IV) Installation of a pressure-reducing valve that limits static service pressure in the residence to a maximum of sixty pounds per square inch. Piping for home fire sprinkler systems shall comply with state and local codes and regulations but are otherwise excluded from this subparagraph (IV).

(b) The offer required by paragraph (a) of this subsection (1) shall be made in accordance with the builder's construction schedule for the residence. In the case of prefabricated or manufactured homes, "construction schedule" includes the schedule for completion of prefabricated walls or other subassemblies.

(2) Nothing in this section precludes a person that builds a new single-family detached residence from:

(a) Subjecting water-efficient fixture and appliance upgrades to the same terms and conditions as other upgrades, including charges related to upgrades, deposits required for upgrades, deadlines, and construction timelines;

(b) Selecting the contractors that will complete the installation of the selected options; or

(c) Stipulating in the purchase agreement or sales contract that water-efficient fixtures and appliances are based on technology available at the time of installation, such upgrades may not support all water-efficient fixtures or appliances installed at a future date, and the person that builds a new single-family detached residence is not liable for any additional upgrades, retrofits, or other alterations to the residence that may be necessary to accommodate water-efficient fixtures or appliances installed at a future date.

(3) This section does not apply to unoccupied homes serving as sales inventory or model homes.

(4) The upgrades described in paragraph (a) of subsection (1) of this section shall not contravene state or local codes, covenants, and requirements. All homes, landscapes, and irrigation systems shall meet all applicable national, state, and local regulations.

VII. Conclusion

From the foregoing, it should be evident that water law is a complicated subject, and the purpose of this section is to denote a few warning signals for the real estate professional. Real estate professionals should ensure proper conveyance of the right and the validity and value of court decrees and well permits, as well as other matters. The Real Estate Commission has developed an optional use form to assist brokers in gathering data for marketing property with water rights. The *Listing Firm's Well Checklist* was designed to help ensure that the seller and the listing broker cover all the bases in gathering data. It is not intended to become a part of a buy-sell contract, but obviously will drive the amount and type of information made available to a buyer. In many instances, it may be necessary to contact a competent water attorney, geologist, and/or water engineer concerning the status of water rights and their transfer.

VIII. Water Right Terminology

Absolute water right: A term often used to describe a water right under which water has been fully diverted and applied to beneficial use so that the water right is no longer a conditional water right, to distinguish it from a conditional water right.

Acre-foot: Volumetric measurement of water used for quantifying reservoir storage capacity and historic consumptive use and for other purposes. This is the amount of water that will cover an acre of land at a depth of one foot, or 325,851 gallons of water.

Adjudication: The judicial determination of the extent, nature, and limitations of a water right appropriation in a statutory court proceeding.

Appropriation: The application of a certain portion of the waters of the state of Colorado to a beneficial use.

Appropriation date: The date defining the priority of right to divert appropriated water in times of limited water supply.

Appropriator: A person who applies water to beneficial use so as to obtain a water right.

Aquifer: A subsurface water-bearing geological structure capable of storing and yielding water to streams, springs, or wells.

Augmentation: A detailed program to increase the supply of water available for beneficial use in a water basin or portion thereof by the development of new or alternate means or points of diversion, by a pooling of water resources, by water exchange projects, by providing substitute supplies of water, by the development of new sources of water, or by any other appropriate means.

Beneficial use: The use of that amount of water that is reasonable and appropriate under reasonably efficient practices to accomplish, without waste, the purpose for which the appropriation is lawfully made.

Conditional water right: A right to perfect a water right with a certain priority upon the completion, with reasonable diligence, of the appropriation upon which such water right is to be based.

Consumptive use: The amount of water that is consumed during its beneficial use so that it does not return to the waters of the state of Colorado.

Cubic foot per second (cfs): Measurement of flow rate of water in a running stream, a ditch or canal, or a pipeline. Water flowing at one cfs will deliver 448.8 gallons per minute or 648,000 gallons per day. One cfs flowing for 24 hours equals 1.983 acre-feet of water.

Direct flow water right: A water right that gives the owner thereof the right to divert water from a specified water source at a specified rate of flow for current use.

Historic use: The use to which a specified water right has previously or historically been put.

Junior appropriator: An appropriator whose right to use specified water is subject to a prior or senior right of another appropriator of the same water source.

Non-adjudicated or unadjudicated water right: A water right that has not been submitted to the appropriate court for adjudication. An unadjudicated water right is junior in priority to all water rights from the same source that have been adjudicated.

Point of diversion: The location at which water is removed from its natural course or location by means of a ditch, canal, flume, reservoir, bypass, pipeline, conduit, well, pump, or other structure or device.

Priority: The seniority, by date, as of which a water right is entitled to divert water and the relative seniority of a water right in relation to other water rights deriving their supply from a common source.

Senior appropriator: An appropriator whose water right has priority over another appropriator having a right to use water from a common water source.

Storage water right: A water right that gives the owner thereof the right to divert and store water from a specified water source in a specified volumetric amount for current or future use.

Water right: A real property right, either absolute or conditional, to use, in accordance with its priority, a certain portion of the waters of the state of Colorado by reason of the appropriation of such water, as confirmed by a Water Court decree or a Ground Water Commission well permit.

SOURCES OF INFORMATION

Rules, regulations, and statutes may be obtained from the Colorado Division of Water Resources, 1313 Sherman St., Room 821, Denver, CO 80203. Its website is www.water.state.co.us.

For further information, such as helpful publications, etc., the following agencies should be contacted: The Colorado Division of Water Resources; the Colorado Water Conservation

Board; Colorado State University, Civil Engineering Department; and the United States Geological Survey, Water Resources Branch, Denver Federal Center.

Chapter 14: Brokerage Relationships

An * in the left margin indicates a change in the statute, rule, or text since the last publication of the manual.

I. Introduction

A. Brokerage Relationships in Real Estate Act

Colorado is a national leader in the creation of real estate brokerage laws. For many years, the common law practice of agency guided relationships between the broker and the seller, landlord, buyer, or tenant. (For ease of reference, "seller, landlord, buyer, or tenant" when used together will be referred to as the "party" in this chapter.) Effective January 1, 1994, the "Brokerage Relationships in Real Estate Act" significantly changed Colorado license law by establishing two different types of working relationships between a broker and a party: single agency and transaction-brokerage. This legislation codified the duties and obligations of a real estate broker.

B. Establishing the Relationship

Parties now have two choices when engaging the services of a real estate broker. One choice is **transaction-brokerage**, where the broker *assists* one or more parties throughout the transaction without being an advocate for any party. Transaction brokerage is a non-agency relationship. The second relationship is **agency**, where the broker is an agent and *represents* only one party in the transaction. In addition to the "Uniform Duties" (described in Section V of this chapter) that both transaction-brokers and agents are obligated to perform under the Colorado real estate statutes, the broker acting as an agent is obligated to: (1) promote the interests of the party with the utmost good faith, loyalty, and fidelity, (2) seek a price or lease rate and terms that are acceptable to the party, and (3) counsel the party as to any material benefits or risks of a transaction.

C. Refining Agency Relationships

Before January 1, 2003, when a brokerage firm entered into an agency agreement with a party, all of the brokers in that firm would become agents of that party. Confidential information concerning the party and the transaction could be exchanged between brokers within the brokerage firm. The same broker or other brokers in the firm were permitted to work as the agent for the other party in the transaction—thus creating dual agency. The firm (and all the brokers in the firm) could represent both sides in the transaction. This brokerage arrangement created a potentially sensitive and difficult situation within the brokerage firm and resulted in problems and conflicts.

The second major change to Colorado's real estate brokerage relationships was the 2003 "Designated Brokerage Relationships in Real Estate Act." This statute created two types of brokers in a multiple-person brokerage firm—the "**employing broker**" and the "**employed broker**." The statute made each broker within the brokerage firm an independent, standalone broker for the purposes of establishing a brokerage relationship. In the past, the party entered into an agency or transaction-brokerage relationship with the brokerage firm. However, the new statute provided that the brokerage relationship is only between the individual broker and the party. The employing broker of the multiple-person brokerage firm was given the responsibility to designate either the employing broker or one or more employed brokers as the "**designated broker**" to work with a particular party in a specific real estate transaction. By making the relationship at the broker level rather than at the brokerage firm level and by prohibiting the imputation of information within the brokerage firm, the statute has simplified and improved the brokerage relationship between the broker and the party.

Colorado law provides brokerage relationship flexibility through the introduction and implementation of designated brokerage, agency, and transaction-brokerage. In Colorado, each brokerage relationship can be custom-designed for each specific personality, situation, and transaction. Written agreements, disclosures, , policies, and rules are in place to ensure that these brokerage relationships are properly presented and implemented for the benefit and protection of the public.

II. Real Estate Brokerage Basics

A. One-Person Firm

A brokerage employment contract is not a contract between the individual broker and the party. An employment contract is a contract between the *brokerage firm* and the party. If the employment contract is with a brokerage firm that consists of only one licensed natural person, then the brokerage firm and the individual broker are—for brokerage purposes—conceptually treated as one and the same. Hence, there is no reason to "designate" a broker to work with the party (as the broker could only designate himself or herself). With a one-person brokerage firm, there is no "designated broker."

B. Multiple-Person Firm

If the employment contract is with a brokerage firm that consists of more than one licensed natural person, the employing broker or an individual broker employed or engaged by that employing broker will be designated by the employing or supervising broker to work with the party as a designated broker. The employing or supervising broker may designate more than one of its individual brokers to work with a party as designated brokers.

A brokerage relationship exists only with the individual broker(s) so designated. The duties, obligations, and responsibilities of that relationship do not extend to the employing broker, brokerage firm, or to any other brokers employed or engaged by the brokerage firm.

C. Confidential Information

Preventing the imputation of knowledge and transmission of confidential information from the designated broker to the employing broker or an employed broker who has not been so designated is of paramount importance with designated brokerage. But at the same time, the employing broker and brokerage firm remain responsible for the supervision of the employed brokers of the brokerage firm and may have liability for the actions of the employed brokers. Under certain circumstances, these provisions could be contradictory, particularly if the employed designated broker was working, for example, with the seller and the employing broker was the designated broker for the buyer in the same transaction. Commission Rule E-45 addresses this potential conflict.

D. Supervision

Commission Rule E-45 states that a designated broker shall be permitted to reveal to a supervising broker, and a supervising broker shall be permitted to receive, confidential information as authorized by the informed consent of the party the designated broker is assisting or working with, without changing or extending the designated brokerage relationship beyond the designated broker. An employing broker is authorized by Commission Rule E-31 to delegate an experienced broker to perform some of the responsibilities of the employing broker to prevent a conflict of interest in a situation where the employing broker is actively representing one of the parties to a transaction.

All of the standard Commission-approved employment contracts contain a provision granting the party's consent to the designated broker's disclosure of confidential information to the employing broker or designee for the purpose of proper supervision, provided such employing broker or designee does not further disclose such information without consent of the party or use such information to the detriment of the party.

E. Intraoffice Relationships

As the result of the designated brokerage statute, a designated broker may work as a single agent for a seller or landlord and another designated broker in the same firm may work as a single agent for a buyer or tenant in the same transaction, and this designated brokerage arrangement does not create dual agency for either of the brokers, the employing broker, or the brokerage firm.

III. Agency

The agency relationship evolved from the master-servant relationship under English common law. The servant owed absolute loyalty to the master. This loyalty was superior to the servant's personal interests as well as the interests of others. Common law is established by court decisions. Under common law, the agent owes the principal five duties, including: (1) care: (2) obedience, (3) accounting, (4) loyalty (including confidentiality), and (5) disclosure. Statutory law is the law enacted by the legislature.

The "**agent**" is the individual who is authorized and consents to represent the interests of the principal. The "**principal**" is the individual hiring the agent and granting to the agent the authority to represent the principal. A "**fiduciary relationship**" exists between the agent and the principal, meaning the agent is held in a position of special trust and confidence by the principal.

There are three kinds of agents: (1) universal agents, (2) general agents, and (3) special agents. A "**universal agent**" has unlimited authority to perform any act on behalf of the principal. A "**general agent"** has far-reaching or wide authority to conduct a series of transactions of a continuous nature on behalf of the principal. For example, the vice-president of the western region of a company would be able to make all the decisions for the western region (but not so for the other regions). A "**special agent**" has only limited authority to conduct a single transaction for the principal. A real estate broker and an attorney are examples of special agents. In real estate, a "**single agent**" means a broker who is engaged by and represents only one party in a transaction.

An agent generally gains authority to act on behalf of a principal by entering into a contract. A contract is considered "**express authority**," where specific terms, duties, and responsibilities are established between the agent and the principal. A written listing agreement to sell a property is an example of an express authority. "**Implied authority**" is authority reasonably expected to permit the agent to be able to perform the scope of the agency. "**Apparent authority**" is when third parties reasonably believe an individual has authority to act and bind the principal based upon the principal's words or conduct. Although authority in an agency can be created expressly (written or oral), implied or by the imposition of apparent (ostensible) authority, Colorado real estate law specifically states that any agency relationship between a broker and a principal must be created by a written agreement signed by both parties.

Even when acting as an agent, the broker's right to bind a party is very restricted. A Commission-approved listing agreement does not give the broker the right to sign or initial legal documents for the party. Absent a power of attorney, the broker should not sign for a party on any document related to the real estate transaction.

For many years, Colorado real estate brokers worked with the public under the common law of agency. Brokers automatically became an agent of their party by entering into a listing for the sale or lease of the party's property. In 1993, the legislature decided that the duties and responsibilities associated with real estate brokerage relationships should be specifically defined in the statute. Section 12-61-804, C.R.S., defines the duties and obligations of a single agent engaged by a seller or landlord. Section 12-61-805, C.R.S., defines the duties and obligations of a single agent engaged by a buyer or tenant. All of these duties and obligations are summarized in the "Uniform Duties" section below.

IV. Transaction-Brokerage

Transaction-brokerage was created as a non-agency relationship. Under Colorado law, a broker is presumed to be a transaction-broker unless a single-agency relationship is created by a written agreement between the broker and the party. A "**transaction-broker**" assists one or more parties throughout a contemplated real estate transaction with communication, interposition, advisement, negotiation, contract terms, and the closing of such real estate transaction without being an agent or advocate for the interests of any party to such transaction. Section 12-61-807, C.R.S., defines the duties and obligations of a transaction-broker engaged by a party. All of these duties and obligations are summarized in the "Uniform Duties" section below.

V. Uniform Duties

In Colorado, a broker must be either an agent or a transaction-broker. If a broker is an agent, there must be a written agreement between the broker and the party. A broker may be a transaction-broker by either entering into a written agreement with the party or through disclosure only.

If a broker is acting either as an agent or as a transaction-broker in Colorado, there are 17 duties that the broker is responsible to perform. Since all of these duties are the same for agency and transaction-brokerage, they are called "**uniform duties**." If the broker and the party determine that the broker should be an agent, then the broker must agree to perform the three "**additional duties,**" described below.

As of January 1, 2006, the uniform duties and additional duties language outlined below appears in all Commission-approved employment contracts between the broker and a party.

By signing any of these agreements, the broker is agreeing to abide by and perform each of these duties. Therefore, it is imperative that the broker understand both the uniform and additional duties for agency.

A. Seller or Landlord Uniform Duties

Brokerage firm, acting through broker, shall provide brokerage services to the seller or landlord. The broker, acting as either a transaction-broker or a seller or landlord agent, shall perform the following *uniform duties* when working with seller or landlord:

1. Broker shall exercise reasonable skill and care for seller or landlord, including, but not limited to the following:
    a. Performing the terms of any written or oral agreement with seller or landlord;
    b. Presenting all offers to and from seller or landlord in a timely manner regardless of whether the property is subject to a contract for sale or a lease or letter of intent to lease;
    c. Disclosing to seller or landlord adverse material facts actually known by broker;
    d. Advising seller or landlord regarding the transaction and to obtain expert advice as to material matters about which broker knows but the specifics of which are beyond the expertise of broker;
    e. Accounting in a timely manner for all money and property received; and
    f. Keeping seller or landlord fully informed regarding the transaction.
2. Broker shall not disclose the following information without the informed consent of seller or landlord:
    a. That seller or landlord is willing to accept less than the asking price for the property or asking lease rate for the premises;
    b. What the motivating factors are for seller or landlord to sell the property or lease the premises;
    c. That seller or landlord will agree to financing or lease terms other than those offered;
    d. Any material information about seller or landlord unless disclosure is required by law or failure to disclose such information would constitute fraud or dishonest dealing; or
    e. Any facts or suspicions regarding circumstances that could psychologically impact or stigmatize the property or premises.
3. Seller or landlord consents to broker's disclosure of seller's or landlord's confidential information to the supervising broker or designee for the purpose of proper supervision, provided such supervising broker or designee shall not further disclose such information without consent of seller or landlord, or use such information to the detriment of seller or landlord.
4. Brokerage firm may have agreements with other sellers to market and sell their property. Broker may show alternative properties not owned by seller or landlord to other prospective buyers or tenants and list competing properties for sale or lease.

5. Broker shall not be obligated to seek additional offers to purchase or lease the property or premises while the property or premises is subject to a contract for sale or a lease or letter of intent to lease.

6. Broker has no duty to conduct an independent inspection of the property or premises for the benefit of a buyer or tenant and has no duty to independently verify the accuracy or completeness of statements made by seller or landlord or independent inspectors. Broker has no duty to conduct an independent investigation of a buyer's or tenant's financial condition or to verify the accuracy or completeness of any statement made by a buyer or tenant.

7. Seller or landlord shall not be liable for the acts of broker unless such acts are approved, directed, or ratified by the seller or landlord.

B. Seller or Landlord Agency – Additional Duties

If broker is a limited agent of seller or landlord (seller's or landlord's agent), broker has the following *additional duties*:

1. Promoting the interests of seller or landlord with the utmost good faith, loyalty, and fidelity.

2. Seeking a price and lease rates and terms that are acceptable to seller or landlord.

3. Counseling seller or landlord as to any material benefits or risks of a transaction that are actually known by broker.

C. Buyer or Tenant Uniform Duties

Brokerage firm, acting through broker, shall provide brokerage services to the buyer or tenant. Broker, acting as either a transaction-broker or a buyer or tenant agent, shall perform the following *uniform duties* when working with buyer or tenant:

1. Broker shall exercise reasonable skill and care for buyer or tenant, including, but not limited to the following:
   a. Performing the terms of any written or oral agreement with buyer or tenant;
   b. Presenting all offers to and from buyer or tenant in a timely manner regardless of whether buyer or tenant is already a party to a contract to purchase the property or a written agreement to lease the premises;
   c. Disclosing to buyer or tenant adverse material facts actually known by broker;
   d. Advising buyer or tenant regarding the transaction and to obtain expert advice as to material matters about which broker knows but the specifics of which are beyond the expertise of broker;
   e. Accounting in a timely manner for all money and property received; and
   f. Keeping buyer or tenant fully informed regarding the transaction.

2. Broker shall not disclose the following information without the informed consent of buyer or tenant:
   a. That buyer or tenant is willing to pay more than the purchase price offered for the property or lease rate offered for premises;
   b. What buyer's or tenant's motivating factors are;

c. That buyer or tenant will agree to financing or lease terms other than those offered;

d. Any material information about buyer or tenant unless disclosure is required by law or failure to disclose such information would constitute fraud or dishonest dealing; or

e. Any facts or suspicions regarding circumstances that could psychologically impact or stigmatize the property or premises.

3. Buyer or tenant consents to broker's disclosure of buyer's or tenant's confidential information to the supervising broker or designee for the purpose of proper supervision, provided such supervising broker or designee shall not further disclose such information without consent of buyer or tenant, or use such information to the detriment of buyer or tenant.

4. Broker may show properties in which the buyer or tenant is interested to other prospective buyers or tenants without breaching any duty or obligation to such buyer or tenant. Broker shall not be prohibited from showing competing buyers or tenants the same property and from assisting competing buyers or tenants in attempting to purchase or lease a particular property.

5. Broker shall not be obligated to seek other properties while buyer or tenant is already a party to a contract to purchase property or to a lease or letter of intent to lease.

6. Broker has no duty to conduct an independent inspection of the property for the benefit of buyer or tenant and has no duty to independently verify the accuracy or completeness of statements made by a seller or landlord or independent inspectors. Broker has no duty to conduct an independent investigation of buyer's or tenant's financial condition or to verify the accuracy or completeness of any statement made by buyer or tenant.

7. Broker shall disclose to any prospective seller or landlord all adverse material facts actually known by broker, including but not limited to adverse material facts concerning buyer's or tenant's financial ability to perform the terms of the transaction and whether buyer intends to occupy the property as a principal residence.

8. Buyer or tenant shall not be liable for the acts of broker unless such acts are approved, directed, or ratified by the buyer or tenant.

D. Buyer or Tenant Agency – Additional Duties

If broker is a limited agent of buyer or tenant (buyer's or tenant's agent), broker has the following *additional duties*:

1. Promoting the interests of buyer or tenant with the utmost good faith, loyalty, and fidelity.
2. Seeking a price or lease rate and terms that are acceptable to buyer or tenant.
3. Counseling buyer or tenant as to any material benefits or risks of a transaction that are actually known by broker.

VI. Entering into a Brokerage Relationship

A broker serving in a brokerage capacity may either be a single agent for one party or a transaction-broker with one or both parties. A broker shall be considered a transaction-broker unless a single-agency relationship is established through a written agreement between the broker and the party to be represented by such broker. If the transaction-broker undertakes any duties in addition to or different from those set forth in the statute, such additional duties shall be disclosed in writing and signed by the broker and the party.

A. Agency

Prior to engaging in any brokerage activities, a broker intending to establish a single-agency relationship with a party shall enter into a written agency agreement with the party to be represented. The agreement shall set forth the agent's duties as they appear in the agency sections of the statute and should set forth any other agreed-upon duties.

B. Transaction-Brokerage

Prior to engaging in any brokerage activities, a broker becomes a transaction-broker by doing one of the following: (1) entering into a written transaction-broker contract with the party, or (2) providing the party with a written transaction-brokerage disclosure with a signature block for the party to acknowledge receipt. If the disclosure is not signed, the broker shall note when the disclosure was presented.

C. Customer

The statute defines "customer" as a party to a real estate transaction with whom the broker has no brokerage relationship because such party has not engaged or employed a broker. A Brokerage Disclosure to Seller, explaining brokerage relationships, must be provided to a seller who does not have a working relationship with a real estate broker.

D. Permitted Relationships

Because there are different combinations of brokerage engagements, the statute defines which are permitted and not permitted.

Different Relationships with Same Party

A broker may work with a single party in separate transactions using different relationships including, but not limited to, selling one property as a seller agent and working with that seller in buying another property as a transaction-broker or buyer agent, provided the broker establishes separate relationships for each transaction.

Separate Transactions

A broker may work with a seller or landlord in one transaction and work with a buyer or tenant in another transaction.

No Double Agency Brokerage

A broker shall not enter into a brokerage relationship with one party as an agent and the other party as a transaction-broker in the same transaction. A broker who works with both the buyer and seller or landlord and tenant in the same real estate transaction may do so as: (1) a transaction-broker with both buyer and seller or landlord and tenant, (2) a single agent for the seller or landlord, treating the buyer or tenant as a customer, or (c) a single agent for the buyer or tenant, treating the seller or landlord as a customer. (See Rule E-40.)

In-House Transactions and Designated Brokerage

A brokerage firm may have one designated broker working as a single agent for the seller or landlord and another designated broker working as an agent for the buyer or tenant in the same real estate transaction without creating dual agency for the employing broker, brokerage firm, or any broker employed or engaged by that employing broker.

No Dual Agency

A broker shall not establish agency with the seller or landlord and the buyer or tenant in the same transaction.

Change of Status

A broker may switch or change from acting in one capacity to another. For example, a broker acting as a seller or landlord agent may change to a transaction-broker if agreed upon by the parties and the broker supplies a Change of Status – Transaction-Brokerage Disclosure (Form CS23).

VII. Mandatory Disclosures

A. Establishing the Brokerage Relationship

Colorado law provides a party with a number of ways to engage a real estate broker. Consequently, there are several brokerage relationship disclosures that may be presented by the broker to the party prior to the broker engaging in any activities that require a brokerage license.

Commission Rule E-35 states that "brokerage activities" occur when a broker elicits or accepts confidential information from a party concerning specific real estate needs, motivations, or financial qualifications. Activities such as an open house, preliminary conversations, or small talk concerning price range, location, property styles, or responding to general factual questions about properties that have been advertised for sale or lease do not qualify as triggering brokerage activities.

B. Mandatory Disclosures

All Commission-approved real estate brokerage employment contracts described above contain the following two mandatory disclosures to the party:

Counsel

"This is a binding contract. This form has important legal consequences and the parties should consult legal and tax or other counsel before signing."

Relationships

"Different brokerage relationships are available that include seller agency, landlord agency, buyer agency, tenant agency or transaction-brokerage."

C. Designated Brokerage Disclosure

When a party engages a broker from a multiple-person firm, that broker is a designated broker. Prior to engaging in any brokerage activities, the designated broker must advise the party in a written agreement that the brokerage relationship exists only with the designated broker and does not extend to the brokerage firm, the employing broker, or to any other brokers employed or engaged by the employing broker who are not so designated. The extent and limitations of the brokerage relationship with the designated broker must be disclosed to the party working with that designated broker.

D. Disclosure Forms

The Commission has approved brokerage relationship disclosure forms for presentation to potential parties prior to the broker engaging in any brokerage activities with those individuals. The forms should be presented to the appropriate individual upon initial contact or as soon as practical thereafter. The broker should fill in the appropriate form and attempt to secure a signature from the party to acknowledge receipt. If the disclosure is not signed, the broker must note when the disclosure was presented and retain a copy in the broker's files. These forms are disclosures only, and even if the party signs any of these forms, they are not considered contracts.

Definitions of Working Relationships (Form DD25)

This disclosure must be provided to any individual who requests definitions of these working relationships with brokers.

Brokerage Disclosure to Seller (For Sale by Owner) (Form SD16)

This disclosure is used when a broker comes in contact with a potential seller or landlord of a property and discusses the possible sale or leasing of that property. The property address must be included. Also, the broker must state whether: (1) the broker is an agent of a buyer or tenant and the seller or landlord is a customer, or (2) the broker is a transaction-broker.

Brokerage Duties Disclosure to Seller (REO and Non-CREC Approved Listing Agreements) (Form BDD56)

Brokerage Disclosure to Buyer/Tenant (Form BD24)

Brokerage Disclosure to Tenant (BDT20)

These disclosures are used when a broker comes in contact with a potential buyer or tenant and discusses the possible purchase or lease of property. The property address or requirements must be included. Also, the broker must state whether: (1) the broker is an agent of a seller or landlord and the buyer or tenant is a customer, or (2) the broker is a transaction-broker.

E. Other Disclosures

Notice to Parties

A broker who has already established a relationship with one party to a proposed transaction must advise, at the earliest reasonable opportunity, any other potential parties or their agents of such established relationship.

Transaction-Brokerage

Prior to engaging in any brokerage activity, a transaction-broker must disclose in writing to the party to be assisted that such broker is not acting as an agent for the other party and that the broker is acting as a transaction-broker.

Conflicts of Interest

Commission Rule E-25 states that when a broker is acting in a licensed capacity or when a broker sells, buys, or leases real property in which the broker has an ownership or financial interest, the broker has a continuing duty to disclose any known conflicts of interest. In addition, the broker must disclose in the real estate contract or in a separate document that the broker has an ownership interest in the property and is a licensed Colorado real estate broker.

Transaction Brokerage Versus Agency Commission position CP-31 states that before acting as a transaction-broker in transactions where neutrality is difficult, the broker should consider whether the transaction-brokerage arrangement is suitable, consult with the broker's supervising broker, and make any necessary disclosures. Some examples where transaction-brokerage may not be appropriate are negotiating the sale or purchase for for: (1) the broker's own account, (2) a spouse or family member of the broker, (3) a close personal friend or business associate of the broker, or (4) a repeat or regular party. Similarly, the broker may encounter certain agency situations or transactions where acting as an agent and advocate for a party could be difficult. In these circumstances, the broker should consider whether the agency arrangement is appropriate, consult with the broker's supervising broker, and act accordingly.

F. Change of Status

If a broker is acting as an agent for both a seller or landlord and a buyer or tenant and begins to assist those parties in the same real estate transaction, the broker is acting as a dual agent, which is not permitted under Colorado real estate law. The broker must immediately provide the written Change of Status – Transaction-Brokerage Disclosure (Form CS23) to the seller or landlord and buyer or tenant and begin working with both parties as a transaction-broker. The broker should attempt to secure the acknowledgements and signatures of the seller or landlord and buyer or tenant. However if that is not possible, the broker must complete the broker acknowledgement, sign the disclosure form, and retain a file copy. (See Rule E-41.)

VIII. Two Examples

A. One Broker for Both Sides of a Transaction

Broker Amy is working with Seller Sam who owns a home. Buyer Bob, who is not working with a broker, sees Broker Amy's open house sign, likes the home, and determines that he is interested in making an offer.

Agent/Customer

If Broker Amy is working as an agent for Seller Sam, then Broker Amy must treat Buyer Bob as a customer unless Broker Amy enters into a transaction brokerage relationship with Buyer Bob (if allowed by the listing agreement and confirmed by a Change of Status disclosure, Form CS-23). A "customer" is a party to a real estate transaction with whom the broker has no brokerage relationship because such party has not engaged or employed a broker. Broker Amy must present Commission-approved Form BD24, "Brokerage Disclosure to a Buyer," to Buyer Bob and check the box that states "Customer: The Broker is the Seller's agent and the Buyer is a customer."

Transaction-Broker

If Broker Amy is working as a transaction-broker with Seller Sam, then Broker Amy must also be a transaction-broker assisting Buyer Bob. A "transaction-broker" is a broker who assists one or more parties throughout a contemplated real estate transaction without being an agent or advocate for the interests of any party to such transaction. Broker Amy must present Commission-approved Form BD24, "Brokerage Disclosure to Buyer," to Buyer Bob and check the box that states "Transaction-Brokerage Only: The Broker is a transaction-broker assisting in the transaction."

B. Both Sides Represented

Broker Amy is working with Seller Sam who owns a home. Buyer Barbara is working with Broker Brad, and after they tour the home, Buyer Barbara decides she would like to make an offer. Depending upon the already-established brokerage relationships:

Agency

Broker Amy could be an agent for Seller Sam, and Broker Brad could be an agent for Buyer Barbara; or

Seller's Agent/Transaction-Broker

Broker Amy could be an agent for Seller Sam, and Broker Brad could be a transaction-broker assisting Buyer Barbara; or

Transaction- Broker/Buyer's Agent

Broker Amy could be a transaction-broker assisting Seller Sam and Broker Brad could be an agent for Buyer Barbara; or

Both Transaction-Brokers

Broker Amy could be a transaction-broker assisting Seller Sam and Broker Brad could be a transaction-broker for Buyer Barbara.

C. Prohibited Relationships

Dual Agency

Colorado statutes prohibit either broker from acting as an agent for both the seller and the buyer. Dual agency has been illegal since 2003.

Agency Limitation

A broker cannot be a transaction-broker assisting one party and be an agent for the other party in the same transaction.

IX. Duration of Relationships

Brokerage relationships between a broker and a party are in effect for certain specific periods of time. Colorado statutes define this time period and the duties and responsibilities after the relationship ends.

A. Term

The relationships commence at the time that the broker is engaged by a party and continue until performance or completion of the agreement by which the broker was engaged.

B. Termination

If the agreement by which the broker was engaged is not performed or completed for any reason, the relationship will end at the earlier of the following: (1) any date of expiration agreed upon by the broker and the party, or (2) by termination or relinquishment of the relationship.

C. No Duties after Termination

Except as otherwise agreed to in writing and except as set forth in the paragraph D below, a broker engaged as an agent or transaction-broker owes no further duty or obligation to the party after termination or expiration of the contract or completion of performance.

D. Responsibilities after Termination

A broker is responsible after termination or expiration of the contract or completion of performance for the following: (1) accounting for all moneys and property related to and received during the engagement, and (2) if the broker was acting as an agent, the broker must keep confidential all information received during the course of the engagement which was made confidential by request or instructions from the party, unless the party grants written consent to disclose such information, disclosure of such information is required by law, or the information is public or becomes public by the works or conduct of the party or from a source other than the broker.

X. Office Policies

Two Commission rules provide guidance for office policy relating to brokerage relationships. Commission Rule E-38 states that in a multiple-person firm, an employing broker or employed broker must be designated in writing by the employing broker to serve as a single agent or transaction-broker. In addition, Rule E-38 sets forth certain guidelines regarding individual and team brokerage employment contracts, substitute or additional brokers, and transaction-broker written disclosures. Rule E-39 states that a brokerage firm must adopt a written office policy that identifies and describes the relationships offered to the public by the brokers of that firm. A brokerage firm may elect to engage in agency only, transaction-brokerage only, or both.

XI. Compensation

The Colorado statutes set forth specific policies concerning the disclosure and payment of compensation to brokers.

A. Payment Does Not Establish Agency

Payment of compensation is not construed to establish an agency relationship between the broker and the party who paid the compensation. For example, one broker has an agency agreement with a seller and another broker has an agency agreement with a buyer in the same transaction. Even though the seller is the only party paying the commission and that payment is being shared by the seller's broker and buyer's broker, the seller's broker is working as a seller's agent only for the seller and the buyer's broker is working as a buyer's agent only for the buyer.

B. Multiple Payments

More than one party may compensate a broker for services in a transaction as long as all parties to the transaction have consented in writing to such multiple payments prior to entering into a contract to buy, sell, or lease.

C. Payer

The broker's compensation may be paid by the party, a third party, or by the sharing or splitting of a commission or compensation between brokers.

D. Approval to Share

A broker must obtain the written approval of the broker's party before the broker proposes to the other broker that the other broker be compensated by sharing compensation paid by such party.

E. Identity

Prior to entering into a brokerage employment contract, the identity of those parties, persons, or entities paying compensation or commissions to any broker must be disclosed to the parties to the transaction.

F. Out-of-State Brokers

Commission Rule E-23 states that a Colorado broker who cooperates with a broker who is licensed in another state or country may pay such out-of-state broker a finder's fee or share of the commission if: (1) such broker resides and maintains an office in the other state or county, (2) all advertising, negotiations, contracting, and conveyancing done in Colorado is performed in the name of the Colorado broker, and (3) all money collected prior to the closing is deposited in the name of the Colorado broker.

Chapter 15: Listings

An * in the left margin indicates a change in the statute, rule, or text since the last publication of the manual.

I. Introduction

A real estate broker has traditionally acted as a "**special agent**" authorized to conduct a single transaction for a buyer or seller. The broker's authority as a special agent for a seller is to find a purchaser who is ready, willing, and able to buy the single listed property, either on the terms set out by or acceptable to the seller. As a buyer's agent, the broker must locate a single property acceptable to the buyer. The broker, on occasion, may be a "**general agent**," such as when employed to manage a leased property over a long period, collect rent, hire custodial help, contract for repairs, etc.

As an alternative to acting as an agent for one of the parties, a Colorado broker may be engaged as a "**transaction-broker**." In fact, it is legally presumed that a real estate licensee in Colorado is acting as a transaction-broker unless there is a written agency agreement between the broker and the buyer or seller.

II. Right-to-Sell Agreements

The authority to act for a seller in a real estate transaction is given to the broker by means of a listing contract, which is simply an employment agreement between a property owner and the broker listing the property for sale. The listing may be either written or oral unless the broker is employed as an agent, in which case Colorado requires the agreement to be in writing. From a risk-reduction perspective, all listings should be in writing and signed by both the owner and the broker in order to avoid misunderstandings that may arise later on. Commission Rule E-11 requires that all written listing contracts provide a definite date for termination.

Absent a signed listing contract supporting a claim of employment, a broker is not entitled to compensation even if he or she procured the sale. The law will not assist "volunteers" in their claim of employment. Occasionally, a buyer and seller introduced by a broker may later consummate a private deal for which the broker tries to collect a commission. Unless the owner speaks or acts in a manner from which a listing contract could be implied, the broker will not collect. Proof of oral words or conduct or the intent or meaning thereof is difficult to establish in court. A prudent broker makes employment and its associated payment a certainty only by securing a signed listing contract.

Colorado listing agreements provide that property sold within a holdover period after the listing term, to any party with whom the listing broker negotiated and whose name the broker submitted to the owner in writing, entitles the broker to a commission, unless the property is subsequently listed with another broker.

III. Types of Seller Agreements

There are five general types of seller listing agreements: (1) net, (2) open, (3) exclusive agency, (4) exclusive right-to-sell, and (5) multiple listing. The five types relate to the degree of freedom the owner retains to either sell the property personally (without owing a commission) or to employ brokers to assist in the sale. The Real Estate Commission has approved both agency and transaction-broker listing forms for the most commonly used types of listings.

A. Net Listing

A net listing is a contract to find a buyer or lessee for the property at a certain "**net price to the owner**." For example: If an owner lists a property for $100,000 net, and the broker finds a buyer at $100,000 (or less), then the broker receives no commission. If the broker finds a buyer at $115,000, the broker retains $15,000 as earned commission. If the terms of a net listing agreement are challenged, courts may hold that the broker is not entitled to any amount exceeding the broker's usual commission. Additionally, a broker who abuses a net listing may be found in violation of § 12-61-113(l)(q), C.R.S., which deals with secret undisclosed profit. Because the Commission does not encourage net listings, there are no approved net-listing forms.

Net listings are generally out of favor in the sale of developed property. They are primarily used where the property is of a speculative nature. In addition to having no set price, an open net listing does not obligate the owner to restrict the listing to one broker. Thus, on an open net listing given to three different brokers, these brokers may offer the property for sale to the same prospect at three different prices. When several brokers quote different prices for the same property, there is a negative reflection on the honesty and integrity of the real estate industry.

B. Open Listing

Under an open listing, the owner lists the property with a broker at a specified price, agreeing to pay a commission on that price or any offer acceptable to the owner. However, the *owner retains the right to sell the property personally or to list the property with other brokers*. This type of listing my be more common in small communities, where the seller is likely to be acquainted with all or most of the brokers and does not wish to antagonize the others by listing with only one. *Only the broker who is the procuring cause of the sale is entitled to a commission.* If the owner sells directly to a buyer without broker involvement, the owner is not obligated to pay compensation to any broker holding an open listing.

C. Exclusive Agency Listing

Under an exclusive agency listing, the owner agrees that a commission will be payable only to the named broker, and that the property will not be listed with or sold by another broker. However, *if the owner sells to a buyer procured without broker's assistance, no commission is due.* An exclusive agency listing, as compared to the net or open listing, permits the broker to apply his or her best efforts, unhampered by possible interference from other brokers, but still subject to the uncertainty of an owner sale.

D. Exclusive Right-to-Sell Listing

This is similar to exclusive agency, except that the *broker is given the sole and exclusive right to sell the property during the listing period.* Even if the owner sells to a buyer procured by the owner, the broker is entitled to a commission. This type of listing is the most commonly used by brokers in Colorado. Brokers can apply their best efforts, secure in the knowledge that the right to a commission cannot be defeated by anyone during the listing period. The Commission-approved exclusive right-to-sell listing agreement is designed for use for both agency and transaction brokerage.

E. Multiple Listing

A multiple listing is not technically a separate kind of listing. It is, rather, a marketing arrangement. Broker-members of a local real estate association or multiple listing service (MLS) may combine to market their listings through the organization. Any member may then sell any property registered with the service and rely on a predetermined commission offered by the listing broker. The seller may choose whether to participate in MLS or an online property information exchange in the Commission-approved listing contracts. The seller also contracts in the listing as to which types of cooperating brokers will be offered how much compensation for bringing a buyer into the sale. Multiple listings are widely distributed and should never contain confidential seller information, such as the seller's motivation or willingness to accept a lower price or less favorable terms than those stated in the listing agreement.

Today, more and more listings are also being distributed statewide, nationally, and internationally over the Internet. Because many of these listing services do not require membership, it is wise for a cooperating broker to obtain a fee agreement prior to entering into negotiations.

IV. Right-to-Buy Agreements

The authority to act for a buyer in the purchase of real estate is secured by means of an employment agreement between the broker and buyer. The agreement engages the broker to locate a property for the buyer at an acceptable price and terms. The information above concerning seller listings also applies to buyer listings or right-to-buy agreements, including the requirement for a definite termination date and the inclusion of a holdover period. The Commission-approved exclusive right-to-buy contract is designed for use for both agency and transaction-brokerage.

Exclusive Right-to-Buy Contract

The broker agrees to assist (as a transaction-broker) or represent (as an agent) the purchaser or lessee by entering into a buyer listing agreement. The purchaser or lessee thus becomes the client/employer and compensates the broker for locating suitable property. With proper consent in the listing contract, the broker working with the buyer may seek compensation from the seller or the seller's broker. Brokers must make sure that clients fully understand the exclusive nature of this agreement. Clients who work with multiple brokers or directly with owners may create multiple contracts and commission obligations or precipitate litigation over breach of contract or procuring cause issues.

V. Change of Status

A broker may not represent one party as an agent and work as a transaction-broker with the other party in the same transaction. The principal to the agency agreement may agree to revert to transaction brokerage. To accommodate this change, the Commission listing forms contain a selection by the client at the time of the listing and a "Change of Status" form to notify the client at the time the "double ended" situation develops.

VI. Approved Forms

Commission Rule F-7 (see Chapter 2, "Commission Rules and Regulations") mandates the use of one of the standard Commission-approved seller or buyer listing contracts. If another listing contract is deemed necessary, an attorney representing one of the parties to the transaction must prepare it. Agency listings, whether for sellers or buyers, must be in writing. (See § 12-61-808(2)(b), C.R.S.)

VII. Broker Responsibility

Real estate brokers represent themselves to the public as possessing knowledge, ability, and skill in the field of real estate. The broker owes to the public the duty of exercising reasonable competence, judgment, and care in advising and rendering services. Real estate brokers fulfill these obligations by keeping abreast of social, economic, and legal developments affecting real property as well as changes to license law.

If a member of the public suffers a loss due to the actions or omissions of a broker, he or she may hold the broker liable in both civil action and in discipline before the real estate commission.

In addition to exercising reasonable skill and care, a broker acting as an agent for a buyer or seller must also advocate on behalf of the client to bring about a purchase or sale on the best possible terms. A transaction-broker, on the other hand, may not act as an advocate for one party's interests over those of the other party. All brokers, whether acting as an agent or transaction-broker, must observe all facets of the license law and exercise reasonable skill and care in performing the terms of the employment agreement. It is strongly recommended that every broker verify that the cooperating broker in a real estate transaction has an active license issued by the Colorado Real Estate Commission. This will ensure that both brokers are compliant and in observance of the license law.

A. Diligence in Pursuing the Objective of the Listing Agreement

A real estate broker has the duty to perform the terms of the employment agreement, including exerting reasonable effort to accomplish the sale or purchase of the property. If the broker does not perform, the owner is justified in voiding the contract. It is a violation of the listing agreement and license law for a broker to "sit" on a listing, that is, take a listing and make no attempt to sell or acquire the property. If a seller elects to set what the broker believes is an unreasonable list price, it is improper and unethical to take the listing and attempt to induce the seller to reduce the price. If the seller is not amenable to comparable properties and their market prices, the broker should refuse the listing.

Buyer brokers must actively fulfill their duty to identify the most appropriate property. A buyer broker must be reasonably available at the buyer's convenience to tour and show properties. It is never proper to suggest that buyers to view properties or attend open houses on their own. A buyer may never be considered an unlicensed personal assistant in the context of the Commission position statement on this subject.

B. Cancelled Listings

If a client unilaterally cancels an employment agreement during its original *unexpired* term, the listing broker may either accept the end of the employment or pursue a legal remedy. If the client attempts to re-list with another broker before the original listing expires, the second broker must emphatically caution the seller of potential liability for the payment of two commissions should the original broker bring civil action for breach of contract.

C. Conflicts of Interest

A broker must avoid even the appearance of conflict of interest with a client. Thus, a broker must clearly and fully disclose all aspects of a personal offer to purchase property listed with the broker or the broker's firm. The best action is to first abrogate the listing and then make the offer. A licensee should use a Commission-approved licensee buy-out addendum to the buy-sell contract in the purchase of a listed property. Similarly, of course, a buyer broker must not pursue the purchase of property shown to a client without clear assent from the client.

Colorado broker licenses may be suspended or revoked for acting for more than one party without the consent of all parties or for failing to disclose a conflict of interest. A seller wants to sell at the highest possible price; a buyer seeks to purchase at the lowest price. These interests are adversarial and irreconcilable. In attempting to serve two masters, a licensee may be in danger of sacrificing the interest of a buyer or seller to the broker's own interest.

D. Scope of Activity – Principal Consent

Within well-defined limits, a single broker may assist both parties to a transaction. This is allowed only with appropriate written consent of the parties to the transaction. By general custom, the broker is also permitted to represent both parties, with their knowledge and consent, and receive compensation from each in an exchange of properties. Again, the Commission-approved exchange agreement provides for such disclosure and consent.

A broker who, without the seller's express consent, informs a prospective buyer that his or her seller will accept an offer less than the asking price violates the license law. Likewise, a buyer broker, whether an agent or transaction-broker, is prohibited from informing the seller that the buyer will pay more than the offering price. A broker may never withhold an offer, either hiding the first one because of anticipating receipt of a second, higher offer, or hiding a subsequent higher offer fearing that it might kill the current deal. Brokers are required by statute to present all offers, including those received right up to closing.

E. Commission-Approved Forms

Real estate licensees are fortunate that Colorado is a leader in providing opportunities to participate in continuing education and conference programs, as well as providing approved forms for use by licensees. Approved listing forms address a wide range of current contractual issues in specific detail, particularly those of brokerage relationships. The Commission-approved seller's property disclosure forms deal with disclosure of the physical condition of residential or vacant land/farm and ranch property. Sellers are asked to certify that the disclosure is correct to the best of the seller's current, actual knowledge. Disclosure of property condition is optional. However, if a licensee chooses to use a disclosure form, it must be a Commission-approved version. If the seller declines to make such a disclosure, that provision should be stricken from the listing agreement, but not before advising the seller that buyers and buyer brokers often require completion of such a form.

A real estate broker has a statutory duty to account to members of the public for all funds received in the course of a transaction. The broker must keep accurate records and accounts and must keep any funds received on behalf of others in an identified trust account separate from funds belonging to the broker.

F. Closing Instructions

The Real Estate Commission, working in concert with the Division of Insurance, has developed a closing instructions form that must be used in conjunction with an approved listing contract. The closing instructions form provides for the appointment of a closing agent and outlines responsibility for payment of fees for closing services. The Commission's position is that this form be initiated, with the buyer or seller, at the time a listing is signed. The form can then be completed with the signatures of both parties at the time of acceptance of a sales contract, and delivered to the closing entity in advance.

It is impossible to anticipate all the varied situations that may raise questions concerning the broker's responsibilities. No safer guide for conduct exists than to treat others the way in which you would want to be treated.

G. Broker Compensation

In order to be entitled to compensation, a real estate broker must: (1) establish employment, (2) fulfill the terms of employment, and (3) get the transaction closed—unless defeated by the refusal of his or her client to consummate the sale as agreed upon.

Broker commissions have historically been paid by the seller out of the transaction proceeds with money the buyer brought into the transaction, typically computed as a percentage of the selling price. Listing brokers then often split this commission with a cooperating buyer broker. Brokers employed by buyers now often seek compensation directly from that buyer, a responsibility clearly delineated in the Commission-approved buyer listing agreements. More recently, brokers have turned to forms of compensation other than the traditional percentage, such as retainer or hourly fees, or combinations of either along with success fees.

Broker commissions are always freely and independently negotiable, established by agreement of the parties and not by law. To prevent controversy and clearly identify the intent of the parties, all compensation and terms of payment must be clearly stipulated in the employment contract. If the original fee or commission is changed, whether to facilitate a closing or to induce future business, this must be clearly spelled out in a written amendment to the contract. The Commission-approved listing contracts provide a section dealing with the splitting of fees with cooperating brokers.

Under Colorado law, a seller's broker is entitled to a commission if the seller refuses or neglects to correct a title defect, provided the contract would otherwise bind the purchaser to close the sale. If a buyer wrongfully refuses to complete the sale, a listing broker may receive compensation in the form of liquidated damages from the down payment forfeited by the purchaser. The broker's right in this instance is usually set forth in the contract to purchase or in the listing agreement or both.

If the purchaser makes an offer to buy conditional on some event, such as the ability to secure a loan, then he or she may rightfully cancel the contract if the condition does not occur. The buyer must have acted in good faith to secure the loan. In such event, the broker is not entitled to a commission.

If a buyer offers a different price or terms than agreed to in the original buyer agreement, or the seller accepts a different price or terms than contained in the original listing agreement, the broker(s) is entitled to a commission. Under these circumstances the parties have ratified, or given implied agreement to, variations in the terms of the original contract(s).

H. Sales Arrangements Between Brokers

An employment agreement (buyer or seller listing contract) is normally only between the broker and the principal. To help sell the property, it is common for the listing broker and seller to agree to offer compensation to other cooperating brokers, including buyer agents or transaction-brokers. Although unusual, buyer brokers may also offer compensation to cooperating brokers to help in locating a property for the buyer. The responsibility to pay a commission rests squarely with the listing broker.

Commission-approved seller listing contracts require the consent of the seller before a broker may offer commission splits to cooperating brokers.

If the broker's office policy offers various levels of compensation, such as one percentage to buyer agents and another to transaction-brokers, it must be clearly disclosed to the seller that such a policy could result in restricting market exposure or cooperation from other brokers.

Once determined, commission splits are usually communicated to other brokers through a multiple listing service. In the absence of a multiple listing service, commission letters or agreements between brokers are a common method of establishing agreement on the terms of sharing commissions. By whatever method, terms of cooperative commission sharing must be specifically agreed to in advance and clearly communicated to potential cooperating brokers.

Chapter 16: Contracts

An * in the left margin indicates a change in the statute, rule, or text since the last publication of the manual.

I. Introduction

Together with the laws of agency and brokerage relationships, an understanding of contract law is essential for real estate practitioners. A licensee constantly reviews contracts for purchases, lease agreements, and mortgages. In Colorado, real estate licensees are allowed to fill in blanks in standard contract forms. The competency and professionalism of the real estate licensee are always at stake when contracts are being written or explained.

Of all legal instruments, contracts are among the most important to our society and economic system. The stability and security of our business world are dependent upon the law of contracts. It ensures that parties perform their agreements by requiring that they either perform or pay for all loss or damage caused by non-performance. Furthermore, the specialized branches of business law, such as the sale of goods and services, negotiable instruments, partnerships and corporations, are all founded upon the law of contracts.

A contract may be defined as an agreement between two or more competent persons, having for its purpose a legal object, wherein the parties agree to act in a certain manner.

II. Essential Elements of a Contract

To be binding and enforceable at law, all contracts must have four essential elements: (1) mutual assent, (2) consideration, (3) competent parties, and (4) legal purpose.

1. **Mutual Assent.** Before a valid contract can exist, the parties must mutually consent to be bound by the terms of the agreement. Such mutual assent is evidenced or objectively set forth by the offer and acceptance. If the consent was obtained by fraud, misrepresentation, duress, undue influence, or mistake, then there is no real consent and, therefore, the element of mutual assent is absent. In certain cases, the law requires that the expression of the parties' mutual agreement be in writing to be enforceable.

   a. **Offer.** An offer is a promise by one party to act in a certain manner provided the other party will act in the manner requested. The one making the offer is called the offeror; the one to whom the offer is made is called the offeree.

      If a person says, "I'll give you $20 for that tire," that person is making an offer. They are saying, essentially, "I promise to pay you $20 if you will deliver to me the ownership and possession of the tire." Similarly, when a prospective buyer of real estate signs a contract to purchase property, they are making an offer to the seller to buy the property on stated terms and conditions. No contract exists until the seller agrees.

      To be effective, an offer first must be communicated to the offeree by a means selected by the offeror. Secondly, the offer must be intended as such. Whether it is intended as an offer depends, not on the offeror's subjective mental attitude, but on

16. Contracts

the reasonable interpretation given to the communication by the offeree. Expressions made in jest, anger, or excitement are generally not offers because the hearer should realize that the speaker is not, at the moment, seriously contemplating what is said. Thirdly, for an offer to be effective, it must be definite and certain as to its terms. If the offer is indefinite as to some of its terms, no mutual agreement can occur because reasonable persons could disagree as to the interpretation of the indefinite provisions. How long does an offer last? When does it cease? An offer can be terminated by a lapse of time, revocation, rejection, or operation of law.

(i) **Lapse of time.** The offer may specify the length of time it is to remain in effect. Upon expiration of that time, the offer ends. However, an expired offer may become effective if ratified. Ratification occurs if a person's acts or conduct validate an otherwise unenforceable act. For example, if a buyer gives a seller three days to accept the buyer's offer to purchase property and the seller accepts the offer on the fifth day, the offer would normally be considered dead because of lapse of time. However, if the buyer remained silent, allowed the contract to go to closing, and then backed out because the offer was accepted late, the buyer may be said to have ratified the contract through their conduct. If no time is specified, then the offer terminates upon the expiration of a reasonable length of time. Reasonable time is determined by all the surrounding circumstances; for instance, it is less in the case of an offer to sell perishable goods than for nonperishable goods.

(ii) **Revocation.** The offeror may revoke, cancel, or withdraw an offer at any time before acceptance, even if he or she had stated the offer would be held open for a certain period. Thus, a person may offer to sell or buy a vacant lot, telling the other party that they have ten days in which to accept. Two days later, if the other party has not accepted, the offeror may cancel without liability. But when an option exists, an offeror cannot withdraw their offer without liability. An option is a subsidiary contract to hold open an offer for a stated period of time. Many so-called options are not enforceable because consideration (something of legal value) has not been given in return for the option. In the above example, if the second party had paid or promised to pay $500 for the privilege of having ten days in which to decide, then there would be an option and the offeror could not withdraw the offer during that time.

(iii) **Rejection.** An offer is terminated by rejection or refusal of the offeree. If the offeree agrees to accept the offeror's proposal but on different terms, this is called a counteroffer and constitutes a rejection of the original offer.

(iv) **Operation of law.** Offers can be terminated automatically by operation of law. Generally, the death or insanity of either the offeror or offeree ends the offer. Destruction of the subject matter of the offer or a change of law making the object of the offer illegal will also terminate the offer.

b. **Acceptance.** The second step in achieving mutual assent is the acceptance, *i.e.*, the indication by the offeree that they are willing to be bound by the terms of the offer. In a real estate transaction, this is usually accomplished by the seller signing the offer to purchase made by the buyer.

To be effective, an acceptance must be made and communicated according to the manner, time, place, and terms specified in the offer. If not specified, then the acceptance must be made and communicated in a reasonable manner, according to the custom and usage of the trade in that locality.

c. **Reality of Consent.** For mutual assent to exist, consent must be given knowingly and voluntarily. If a party consents due to fraud, misrepresentation, undue influence, duress, or mistake, it would be unfair to hold them to the agreement. Therefore, when consent is obtained under these circumstances, the courts usually hold that there is no contract, or permit the innocent party to cancel the contract.

   When there is a mutual mistake as to material fact concerning the identity or existence of the subject matter, no contract results. But when the mistake concerns an unessential fact, relates to the value, or is made by only one party due to that party's carelessness, an enforceable contract will result. Thus, if the parties agree to buy and sell property at a certain address and there are two properties having the same address, and each party has in mind a different property, no contract results. But if one party has a mistaken belief as to the value of a piece of property, a good contract will result.

   Fraud and misrepresentation are self-explanatory and, when present, permit the innocent party to cancel the contract and, in appropriate cases, to recover damages suffered.

   Undue influence consists of the abuse of the control or influence that one person has over another because of their relationship. Duress consists of compelling a person, through fear, to do or to agree to do an act.

d. **Statute of Frauds.** To prevent fraud through perjury, the law requires that the parties' agreement evidencing their mutual assent be in writing in certain cases. As to real estate in Colorado, § 38-10-108, C.R.S., provides:

   > Every contract for the leasing for a longer period than one year or for the sale of any lands or any interest in lands is void unless the contract or some note or memorandum thereof expressing the consideration is in writing and subscribed by the party by whom the lease or sale is to be made.

   In Colorado, real estate contracts not signed by the seller are void, not voidable. Colorado differs from most other states that provide that "the party to be charged" (in a lawsuit by the other party) must have signed the contract.

   Other agreements that are declared void by law, unless in writing, are described in § 38-10-112, C.R.S.:

   > (a) Every agreement that by the terms is not to be performed within one year after the making thereof;
   >
   > (b) Every special promise to answer for the debt, default, or miscarriage of another person;
   >
   > (c) Every agreement, promise, or undertaking made upon consideration of marriage, except mutual promises to marry.

   Generally, the statute of frauds provides that no civil action can be brought to enforce a contract unless there is some writing signed by the party to be charged (in a civil action to enforce the contract). The writing does not have to be the "perfect" contract, but it does have to be sufficient to allow a court to determine that the parties intended to sell the property. Such things as: (1) the identity of the parties, (2) subject matter, (3) terms and conditions, (4) recital of consideration, and (5) signatures of the parties are necessary. Although Colorado's statute of frauds provides that only the seller must sign the real estate contract, the obvious best practice is for both parties to sign.

Some states have statute of frauds provisions in their real estate license laws. These laws provide that a real estate licensee will not be entitled to a commission unless there is a written employment agreement between the licensee and the buyer or seller. Although Colorado license law does not have such a statute of frauds provision, there is a statutory requirement that all agency listings and agency employment agreements be in writing.

e. **The Parol Evidence Rule.** The parol evidence rule is closely linked to the statute of frauds. It provides that an agreement in writing shows that the parties intend it as the final and complete expression of their agreement. Evidence of any earlier oral or written statements is not admissible to vary, add to, or contradict the terms of the writing. The word parol means "word" or "speech." Because the purpose of the statute of frauds is to prevent the possibility of nonexistent agreements being enforced by fraud or perjury, it makes sense to have a rule that requires the parties to live with what they have written. The parol evidence rule generally keeps parties from trying to introduce evidence in court that they really meant something other than what is stated in the written contract.

2. **Consideration.** Agreement alone does not make an enforceable contract. There must be consideration supporting the agreement. Many persons assume money is a requirement of consideration; but in the vast majority of cases the consideration for a promise is the return promise. The promise of the buyer to buy and the promise of the owner to sell constitute sufficient consideration to support their agreement—no deposit is necessary.

Consideration may be defined as a promise or an act of legal value bargained for and received in return for a promise. Both parties must receive consideration for their promises. Legal value is generally defined in terms of benefit or detriment. Thus, legal value is present if: (1) the one making the promise (or doing the act) thereby commits to something they were not previously obligated to do (detriment), and (2) the one receiving the promise (or act) thereby becomes entitled to something they would not previously have received (benefit). Both parties to an agreement usually receive some benefit and suffer some detriment.

When one party agrees to buy and another agrees to sell, each is agreeing to do something they were not obligated to do and each will receive something to which they were not entitled. But offering to pay a police officer $1,000 as a reward for recovering stolen property cannot be consideration for that offer. In promising to recover stolen property, a police officer is doing no more than he or she is already bound to do. A promise given without any return does not create a binding contract. Each party must in some way give legal value for what they receive.

Although the promise to pay for land, if written in the contract, is good consideration, the buyer customarily shows good faith by making a partial payment on the purchase price. This partial payment is called "earnest money" or "good faith money." It is a good indication that the buyer will perform as promised and pay for the land, because failing to do so will cause him or her to lose the money according to the contract's default provision.

3. **Competent Parties.** All parties are presumed to have the legal capacity to enter into contracts. But certain persons, for reasons of public policy or some disability, do not have full contractual capacity. Among these are minors, mental defectives, and intoxicated persons.

   In Colorado, a minor is an individual under 18 years of age. Minors have the right to cancel or disaffirm their contracts with no liability other than the return of any proceeds they received under such contract. Minors are given this right to protect them against their lack of experience, judgment, and ability. The burden is upon adults to ascertain that the person they deal with is of legal age. After reaching legal age, minors may ratify or approve previous contracts, which will then be binding on them.

   Insane persons are given the same protection as that given to minors, except that the contracts of a person judicially declared insane could never have had effect in the first place.

   The contract of an intoxicated person is usually binding, except where that person is so intoxicated as to be incapable of understanding the nature of the transaction. In that case, the intoxicated person may cancel or ratify the contract.

   A corporation's charter determines its contractual ability. Its capacity to contract may be related only to specific things or it may be related to broad areas of business transactions.

4. **Legal Purpose.** To be valid and enforceable, a contract must have a legal object for its purpose. The object cannot be to violate a valid statute. An agreement to commit a crime, a tort, or something contrary to public welfare is illegal. For example, an agreement to defraud someone, slander a person, or operate an unauthorized gambling operation is illegal. Dual contracting to induce a lender to make a loan on real estate without knowing the true terms of sale, such as the actual amount of down payment, is a criminal offense under § 18-5-208, C.R.S.

III. Matters to be Considered in Real Estate Contracts

The buy-sell contract is the most important document in a real estate transaction. This contract determines the kind of title to be conveyed, the type of deed, liens and encumbrances that the land will be sold subject to, and the manner of payment of the purchase price.

Numerous controversies involving real estate licensees arise out of contracts for the sale of property. Although dishonesty or wrongdoing on the part of the licensee is rare, disputes often stem from the licensee's lack of thoroughness or knowledge. Real estate brokers must continually strive to increase their own proficiency and that of their employed licensees in writing good contracts. It is an art to write a sound, workable contract that includes all important matters and is still reasonably clear and understandable. Although Colorado licensees are fortunate in having Commission-approved contract forms available, they must nevertheless pay close attention to completing these forms in a competent manner.

The following are the main items to be considered in drawing up real estate contracts. This list is not intended to be exhaustive; seldom are two real estate transactions alike. Only through careful study, experience, and guidance will the real estate licensee learn to recognize the essential items to be included in a given transaction.

A. Names and Signatures of the Parties

The seller and buyer must be named and properly designated as the seller (vendor) and buyer (vendee). If two or more persons own the property, all should be named and all should sign—unless, of course, only one is selling his or her interest. If two or more persons are buying the property, all should be named and all should sign, together with an election as to whether they are buying as joint tenants or tenants in common.

B. Sale Price and Payment Provisions

The contract is incomplete and unenforceable unless it contains the sales price. If there is no provision regarding the method of payment, the law presumes it is to be a cash sale. The contract should state, when applicable: (1) the amount of the deposit, (2) the amount to be paid at closing, (3) the method of payment, (4) the balance, either by assumption of the existing mortgage or by a new mortgage, and (5) any and all other pertinent financial provisions.

C. Description of the Property

The description of the real estate should be sufficiently definite to identify the land sold with reasonable certainty. Although the street address, with the city and state, is sometimes sufficient, it is better to use the legal description contained in the seller's deed. Even though the contract may not mention them, additional rights to the land such as easements, rights of way, and other appurtenances belonging to the land will automatically pass to the buyer in the transfer of ownership. For the sake of clarity and completeness, they should be mentioned in the contract. In addition, all items of personal property to be included in the sale should be listed.

D. Type of Deed

The contract should provide for the type of deed by which the property will be conveyed, whether by quitclaim, general warranty, or other kind of deed. In the event the type of deed is not stated, the courts will probably require that kind of deed that is customary to that particular type of transaction in that locality.

E. Condition of Title

Real estate sales contracts traditionally provide that title is to be merchantable, that is, free from defects and which a reasonably prudent buyer is willing to accept. Even without this provision, the law presumes that merchantable title is to be conveyed. Mortgages, tax liens, and other liens and encumbrances are considered defects. Therefore, if the property is to be conveyed subject to a mortgage or other encumbrance or restriction, the contract should clearly state so. Another customary provision states that the buyer will give written notice of defects of title, not excepted in the contract, and that the seller will clear up said defects by a given deadline. The seller has the duty of proving good title. A contract should require the owner to establish their title by furnishing evidence of ownership, such as an abstract of title or a title insurance commitment. In approved Colorado buy-sell contract forms, the seller does not specifically agree to provide merchantable title. However, the seller does agree to provide the buyer with a title insurance commitment, and, if the buyer objects to the merchantability of title, the seller must correct unsatisfactory title conditions or the contract will terminate.

F. Default Provisions

The rights of the parties should be stated in the event that one side fails to perform. The law, of course, gives the parties remedies for non-performance, but a lawsuit can be avoided if the parties mutually agree to a settlement beforehand. Therefore, provisions should be made as to the disposition of the buyer's deposit if the buyer defaults, and any other arrangements deemed appropriate. It is especially critical for brokers to counsel buyers on the meaning and effect of the loan commitment deadline in the Commission-approved buy-sell contract. A 100 percent commitment to fund a loan seldom exists, but buyers must have a sufficient level of understanding and comfort with their own and their lender's commitment as of that date, or face certain forfeiture of earnest money if the transaction does not close.

G. Contingency Provisions

A buyer may be willing to buy, but may first have to accomplish something, such as borrow additional money or sell a presently owned property. An offer to purchase must clearly state such conditions. It is possible that the seller may also wish to provide for some contingency. Poorly written contingencies are one of the major causes of disputes between the parties and complaints against real estate licensees. Any contingency clause must state not only the conditional situation or event, but also provide a definite method and deadline by which to accomplish the contingent requirement, remove the contingency, or terminate the contract, including disposition of earnest money.

H. Possession

If the time of closing the transaction is different from the time that possession of the premises is to be given to the buyer, the date and time of possession should be stated.

I. Apportionment or Adjustment

The contract should provide for the apportionment of all charges or assets concerning the property, such as taxes, assessments, water rents, interest on assumed encumbrances, mortgage insurance premiums, or rents.

J. Risk of Loss

If the property is damaged or destroyed by fire, flood, or storm after the contract is signed but before the deed is delivered, who suffers the loss—the seller or the buyer? The answer is not as simple as it seems.

In most jurisdictions, when a binding real estate contract exists, and where either party may enforce specific performance, the loss falls upon the buyer who is considered the owner of the property. The buyer holds what is known as "equitable title" even though legal title has not yet passed. The buyer can legally force the seller to convey the legal title. Also, the seller can force the buyer to accept the legal title and perform their part. This right is called specific performance; the parties lose this right only if they waive it in the contract.

Some courts interpret equitable title theory as unjustly putting the burden of loss on the buyer. Not being in possession, the buyer is unable to protect his or her interest. However, the majority of courts seem to hold that the loss falls on the buyer unless the contract provides otherwise. To avoid potential misunderstanding or controversy, it is important to clearly spell out risk in the contract. It is not unusual for the contract of sale to provide that the risk of loss remains with the seller.

IV. Colorado Buy-Sell Contract

Buy-sell contracts used by licensees are sometimes referred to as "preliminary," "earnest money," or "executory" contracts. They contain, among other provisions, a promise by the buyer to pay for the land and a promise by the seller to deliver a deed to the land. These contracts serve the purpose of establishing good faith until the time for payment and delivery of the deed. Buy-sell contracts are not recorded (except for a very good reason) because many such contracts fail and are never consummated. Recording would cloud the title to the property if delivery of a deed did not occur. However, an installment land contract, described later in this chapter, should always be recorded unless there is a specific agreement to the contrary.

The Real Estate Commission has an approved buy-sell contract for all types of properties: residential, residential income, commercial, and land. The default provisions shown in the contract below note the different remedies afforded.

> **TIME OF ESSENCE, DEFAULT AND REMEDIES.** Time is of the essence hereof. If any note or check received as Earnest Money hereunder or any other payment due hereunder is not paid, honored or tendered when due, or if any obligation hereunder is not performed or waived as herein provided, there shall be the following remedies:
>
> **21.1. If Buyer is in Default:**
>
> **21.1.1. Specific Performance.** Seller may elect to treat this Contract as canceled, in which case all Earnest Money (whether or not paid by Buyer) shall be paid to Seller and retained by Seller; and Seller may recover such damages as may be proper; or Seller may elect to treat this Contract as being in full force and effect and Seller shall have the right to specific performance or damages, or both.
>
> **21.1.2. Liquidated Damages, Applicable. This § 21.1.2 shall apply unless the box in § 21.1.1. is checked.** All Earnest Money (whether or not paid by Buyer) shall be paid to Seller, and retained by Seller. Both parties shall thereafter be released from all obligations hereunder. It is agreed that the Earnest Money specified in § 4.1 is LIQUIDATED DAMAGES, and not a penalty, which amount the parties agree is fair and reasonable and (except as provided in §§ 10.4, 22, 23 and 24), said payment of Earnest Money shall be SELLER'S SOLE AND ONLY REMEDY for Buyer's failure to perform the obligations of this Contract. Seller expressly waives the remedies of specific performance and additional damages.
>
> **21.2. If Seller is in Default:** Buyer may elect to treat this Contract as canceled, in which case all Earnest Money received hereunder shall be returned and Buyer may recover such damages as may be proper, or Buyer may elect to treat this Contract as being in full force and effect and Buyer shall have the right to specific performance or damages, or both.

The broker is in a position to strongly influence the choice of remedy. This position of influence should be used cautiously because there are circumstances when the use of a particular remedy may be injurious to one of the parties.

The liquidated damages provision is popular for various reasons. In the event of default by the buyer, the seller usually does not want to become involved in a lawsuit against the buyer in order to enforce the specific performance of the contract. The seller is usually more concerned about getting the property back on the market and making a successful sale. The broker has the same desire. The average buyer is not familiar with real estate transactions and is not aware of the possibility that he or she could be compelled to purchase the property. Usually, the buyer only understands that the earnest money is endangered.

The specific performance and damages remedy is appropriate, particularly if the buyer and seller are experienced in real estate dealings. It may be the fairest because it offers both parties an equal right to seek damages.

Earnest money deposits are another critical element of any contract. Earnest money should be adequate to demonstrate the buyer's serious intent to purchase and, in the event of the buyer's default, to compensate the seller for the act of taking the property off the market during the period prior to closing. Earnest money should apply only to partial payment of the purchase price. The form of earnest money, *e.g.*, check or promissory note, must be specified in the contract. If it is a note, it must have a definite due date. The Commission strongly recommends that notes not be taken with due dates of "at closing." Such notes create confusion as to the seller's forfeiture rights if closing does not occur and the buyer is at fault.

The Commission-approved buy-sell contract includes a mediation clause by which the parties agree to submit matters in dispute to mediation when the dispute cannot be otherwise resolved. Mediation is non-binding. If efforts at mediation do not resolve the dispute within 30 days of the written notice requesting mediation, the mediation terminates unless the parties mutually agree to continue.

If mediation fails to resolve an earnest money dispute the approved contract forms provide that the earnest money holder may await any proceeding or interplead the Earnest Money into a court of competent jurisdiction.. Under this provision, if the parties do not give mutual written instructions to the broker, the broker may "interplead" the money into court and let the court decide the matter. Although the broker may interplead without such a provision, the existence of the provision encourages the parties to reach a settlement. The provision also enables the court to relieve the broker from court costs and attorney fees. Nothing, of course, prohibits a broker from refunding an earnest money deposit to a buyer if, in the broker's judgment, that is what the contract calls for, but the broker may subsequently become liable to the seller if the disbursement is found to be wrongful. A broker may never unilaterally declare a forfeiture of the buyer's earnest money; only the seller has that right.

V. Competency in Preparing Contracts

The terms in any agreement to buy and sell real estate must be carefully drafted. Contingencies and promises must be completely defined. Consideration of the circumstances affecting the parties involved in the transaction must be carefully weighed before spelling out the terms.

A. Loan Contingency

The ordinary buyer can only buy if he or she is able to borrow sufficient funds on reasonable terms. Ethical procedure demands that the contract be made contingent upon the ability to secure such a loan. If a buyer is unable to buy unless the sale of his or her current home is consummated, any offer should reflect this contingency. Such a contingency is still needed even if there is a pending contract to sell the buyer's home, if the buyer requires the proceeds from the sale in order to purchase, because there is never complete certainty that a pending sale transaction will close.

B. Assumptions

When an existing mortgage will remain on the property after sale, the responsibility of the parties must be carefully set forth. The buyer may "assume and agree to pay" the existing mortgage or may buy the property "subject to" the existing mortgage. A seller will usually want the buyer to "assume and agree to pay" because it will make the buyer responsible on the original note along with the seller. In either case, both parties to the transaction should be informed of the resultant effect of the sale. Too often, unscrupulous buyers of equities have purchased "subject to" or even agreed to "assume and pay" an existing loan. They then collect rents from the property for as long as possible, while deliberately defaulting on the loan payments and letting the property go into foreclosure. A resulting deficiency judgment would be against the original owner and seller rather than the buyer. Such conduct, known as "equity skimming," is a criminal offense.

It is equally important for the broker to ensure that, if necessary, a buyer is properly qualified to assume a loan and that the assumption is properly processed through the lender. Licensees are subject to disciplinary action for failing to ensure that loan assumptions are finalized through the lending institution.

C. Buyer's Creditworthiness

The licensee's service to the seller (for which they are paid) is to procure a ready, willing, and able buyer. What is meant by "able"? Certainly it means more than the buyer's ability to execute the contract and make the initial payment. The licensee has a duty to the seller to make a reasonable effort to determine if the buyer is truly able to buy the property. If the buyer is assuming an existing loan, or if the seller is carrying back a purchase money mortgage or conveying by means of an installment land contract, the seller is in a high-risk position. There is no third-party lending institution to determine the buyer's qualifications. The typical residential seller is not a speculator, and does not wish to pursue foreclosure or to retake title to the sold property. The seller will likely depend upon the licensee for guidance. Although the licensee may have no legal obligations to investigate the buyer, the licensee at least has a duty to inform the seller of the inherent dangers in the transaction and to advise the seller to make some type of an investigation concerning the buyer's ability or willingness to pay.

A buyer may wish to use the seller's credit by having the seller secure a new loan or refinance the existing loan so that the buyer can purchase with less cash or no cash and without responsibility. The seller might also be induced to carry a second purchase money mortgage, which may even result in cash being given to the buyer at the time of closing. Thus, the buyer purchases without a down payment. This type of transaction may be perfectly proper if the seller knows the buyer or has faith in the buyer's creditworthiness.

However, this puts the seller in an extremely vulnerable position, and the broker should alert the seller to this fact.

D. Balloon Payments

If a buyer agrees to sign a second note and trust deed as part payment, the terms should be specifically set forth. If a note requires regular equal installments but will not be completely paid off at the time the note matures, a larger ("balloon") payment will be required at the maturity date. The buyer may be in danger of foreclosure if he or she is unable to raise the money for such a balloon payment. In such a case, the licensee should make the buyer and seller aware of this eventuality. At the time the balloon payment becomes due, the buyer may be dependent on the ability to refinance. Colorado law protects the borrower in this regard.

VI. Surveys

Many properties have not been properly surveyed. This is true particularly in areas that have not been formally subdivided into platted parcels. Some subdivided areas also contain irregular lot sizes, and the survey may be questionable. Both the frontage in running feet and the acreage, which determines square footage, are important and both should be verified before quoting figures to a buyer. In some cases, improvements, such as fences or garages, encroach on boundary lines and only a survey will reveal the problem. A broker may be liable in such situations because brokers are assumed to have greater knowledge than that of buyers and sellers. The broker should recommend to both the buyer and seller that a survey be made. (See Chapter 7, "Land Descriptions.")

VII. Dual Contracting and Loan Fraud

Another matter covered by law involves presenting a false contract with a larger purchase price to the lender than the price shown on the contract under which the parties intend to consummate the transaction. This is called dual contracting to induce a loan and is prohibited by the Colorado Criminal Code, § 18-5-208, C.R.S.

False or inflated down payments, failure to identify seller-assisted down payments or concessions, second trust deeds, "gift letters," or any other matter not fully and accurately reflected in a buy-sell contract and resulting settlement statement may result in severe disciplinary and sometimes even criminal action against a licensee.

VIII. Installment Contracts

* The installment land contract (ILC) is described in Chapter 17, "Trust Deeds and Liens," as a method of financing or a security device. It is also a method of effecting a sale. Commission Position 39 cautions:

* > "There is a significant potential for harm to the seller, buyer or assignee if the installment land contract is not properly drafted. Real estate brokers are prohibited from drafting a contract document that would reflect the terms of such a transaction as it would exceed their level of competency and is a matter requiring the expertise and advice of an attorney. Additionally, such behavior may be construed as the unauthorized practice of law by the real estate broker and subject to civil penalties. The contracts for these transactions should not

be prepared by a real estate broker; rather, the documents should be drafted by a licensed Colorado attorney-at-law engaged for each particular transaction."

* An ILC is a contract for delayed delivery of a deed, providing for periodic payments over a term of years, as does a promissory note. It is distinguished from the real estate buy-sell contract in that the buy-sell contract does not usually contain provisions for installment payments and is merely intended to hold the deal for a short period until the condition of title is accepted and deed is delivered to the buyer, normally at closing. An installment land contract must contain provisions required by statute and other customary provisions. There is no standard form of installment land contract approved by the Commission. The Commission revoked its approval of the installment land contract long ago.

A buy-sell contract may also be used to hold a deal until the execution of an installment land contract. In this case, the buy-sell agreement will of course not refer to delivery of a deed, but rather to the subsequent signing of an installment land contract.

If a buy-sell contract provides for specific performance as a remedy, it has the same effect as an ILC in that the seller is bound to convey the land to the buyer at some future time. At the signing of either type of contract, the buyer has an equitable interest in the real estate. In this situation, courts generally recognize that the "buyer becomes owner of the land in equity" and is called the "equitable owner."

Installment land contracts are more prevalent during periods of "tight" money or when a property is difficult to finance conventionally. Oftentimes a person with little or no cash for a down payment will be permitted to take possession of property under an installment land contract providing for monthly payments to the seller. The seller will still hold "legal" title, and the buyer will possess "equitable" title.

A preliminary contract for an ILC is not usually recorded unless a dispute arises and court action is imminent. It is always in the buyer's best interest to have the installment land contract recorded, and the Real Estate Commission requires that buyers of subdivisions registered with the Commission be so advised. Sellers of unimproved subdivided lands often have installment land contracts. If an ILC is not recorded, there is no notice to the world of the buyer's interest in the property, the buyer being completely at the mercy of the seller. The larger the buyer's down payment offer to the seller, the stronger the buyer's bargaining strength as to deed and trust deed arrangement.

Although the seller retains legal title under an installment land contract, he or she is not the actual owner of the real estate. The seller's interest in the contract is considered personalty, and would be treated as such in the distribution of the seller's estate in the event of his or her death. The seller would convey legal title interest in the property by formally assigning the contract. Any person buying a seller's legal title interest should make sure that the contract being assigned is of public record, and should receive the original signed ILC in the assignment. If a seller merely has a contract interest and is not the holder of legal title, the contract or assignment should so state.

The buyer's interest in an ILC is considered realty and generally is merchantable to a third person. If an ILC has a non-assignment clause, the seller's consent must be secured. Often, the contract will preclude the property from being mortgaged or leased. Of course the buyer under an ILC could not give a trust deed even if the contract permitted, because the buyer does not have a deed. A buyer's interest given as collateral for a loan would be secured by a mortgage. The wording of an assignment or new contract will determine whether the assignee is personally liable to make the remaining payments.

If there is an existing loan on the property, the ILC should state who is to make the payments. It is not enough to merely state that the property is subject to an existing loan. Such a statement would make the buyer responsible for both the contract price and for the seller's existing loan payments in order to protect equitable title interest. Usually it is the seller who continues to make the payments on the existing loan, and this should be stated in the contract. The contract should also provide that in the event the seller fails to make payments, the buyer is permitted to pay the lender directly and credit the amount paid against payments owed to the seller under the ILC.

An installment land contract usually provides that a deed to the property will be delivered when the full purchase price or a specified portion (*e.g.*, one-third or one-half) has been paid. This may create a problem if the seller is not able to execute and deliver the deed when it is due. A high level of trust is placed in the seller's ability to convey a future deed clear of all encumbrances. If the seller dies before the buyer fulfills the contract, other difficulties may arise; for example, the seller's interest may be tied up in estate proceedings. Therefore, if the seller is a natural person rather than a corporation, it is prudent to place the deed with an escrow agent at the time of sale, with proper instructions to deliver it when the buyer has complied with the contract. If a deed is being held in escrow and the seller assigns the contract, a new agreement with the original escrow agent is necessary to substantiate the chain of title to the property.

There is usually nothing to prevent the buyer from refinancing an installment land contract at any time and paying off the seller. As with any loan, however, terms or restrictions on prepayment should be clearly set out in the contract.

In the event of a default in payments under an ILC, the seller's remedies are limited by a forfeiture clause in the contract. The usual forfeiture clause gives the seller the choice of foreclosure or suing for payments when each comes due. Upon choosing one remedy, the other is lost. Thus, upon default, the seller usually keeps the money that has already been collected and forecloses to secure the return of the property.

A forfeiture clause usually demands that possession of the property be surrendered to the seller within 30 days or so after default. Even if in possession, however, the seller must still go to district court to foreclose. This would amount to strict foreclosure if the courts enforced the foreclosure clause. In mortgages or trust deeds, the courts will not enforce strict foreclosure, but in an installment land contract the courts may do so, if only partially, inasmuch as there is no public sale. A seller who chooses this remedy elects to rescind the contract and cannot get a deficiency judgment. The court, in its judgment, will often determine how long the buyer may keep possession, regardless of how many days are stated in the forfeiture provision. In one Colorado case, when the buyer had paid approximately one-third of the purchase price, the court required that the buyer be given six months to redeem.

Some sellers or their brokers attempt to avoid having to go to court to foreclose the contract. One popular but ineffective method of doing this is to have the buyer sign a quitclaim deed back to the seller up front, and escrow both the ILC and the quitclaim deed. The escrow agreement would provide for delivery of both the buyer's copy of the ILC and the quitclaim deed to the seller in the event of default. Adding the quitclaim deed to the escrow does not in any manner strengthen the position of the seller, as it would have been executed simultaneously with the ILC and does nothing to alter the underlying nature of the relationship between the parties. Foreclosure of an ILC is the only process by which the buyer may be dispossessed.

An installment land contract should be treated as a conveyance. Although it does not always happen, the buyer should demand evidence of title even though the title insurance or the abstract will not be delivered until the buyer complies with the contract terms. Commission Rule E-5 applies to an ILC and requires the broker to provide settlement sheets (showing the purchase price, the costs, the pro-rating, and how the purchase price is to be paid) to the parties.

The installment land contract is a complicated and flexible instrument. It is also salable, making for further complications. The seller, the buyer, or the assignee may all be hurt if the instrument is improperly drafted or used. Whether used as an instrument of conveyance or a security device, the Commission strongly recommends consultation with competent legal counsel when considering use of an installment land contract.

An ILC (contract for deed) must also provide for:

1. Designation of the public trustee of the county where the real property is located to act as escrow agent for the monthly payment by the purchaser of the monthly pro-rated property tax obligation on such property.
2. The payment to the public trustee of the seller's tax obligation at closing for the current year's property taxes.
3. The payment, by the purchaser, of the trustee's $75.00 fee once each year in April. (See § 38-35-126, C.R.S.)

These provisions must continue until the ILC is fulfilled and a deed to the property is delivered to the purchaser and recorded.

Section 38-35-126(1)(b), C.R.S., defines a contract for deed as

> a contract for the sale of real property which provides that the purchaser shall assume possession of the real property and the rights and responsibilities of ownership of the real property, but that the deed to such real property will not be delivered to the purchaser for at least one hundred and eighty days following the latest execution date on the contract for deed to real property and not until the purchaser has met certain conditions such as payment of the full contract price or a specified portion thereof.

Subsection (2) of the same statute requires the following:

> Within ninety days of executing and delivering a contract for deed to real property, the seller shall file with the county treasurer of the county wherein the real property is located a written notice of transfer by contract for deed to real property. Such notice shall not operate to convey title. Such notice shall include the name and legal address of the seller, the name and legal address of the purchaser, a legal description of the real property, the date upon which the contract for deed to real property was executed and delivered, and the date or conditions upon which the deed to the real property will be delivered to the purchaser, absent default. In addition, within ninety days of executing and

delivering the contract for deed to real property, the seller shall file a real estate transfer declaration with the county assessor of the county wherein the property is located, pursuant to the provisions of section 39-14-102, C.R.S.

The buyer has the option of voiding any contract for deed to real property that fails to designate the public trustee as escrow agent for deposit of property tax moneys or for which no written notice is filed with the county treasurer's office of the county assessor's office. Upon voidance of such contract, the buyer is entitled to the return of all payments made on the contract, with interest, and reasonable attorney fees and costs. This avoidance right expires seven years after the latest execution date on the contract for deed to real property, unless exercised prior to such date. (See § 38-35-126(3), C.R.S.)

According to § 38-35-126(4), C.R.S., the above sections do not apply if the:

1. Subject property is not divided into parcels less than one acre;
2. Developer (seller) pays the property tax or submits a bond or letter of credit within 30 days of the mailing of the notice of taxes due and prior to seeking reimbursement from the purchaser; or
3. Developer provides the notice of transfer mentioned in § 38-35-126(2), C.R.S.

IX. Manufactured, Modular, and Mobile Homes

The Division of Housing requires registration of persons who engage in the business of selling manufactured homes in Colorado under the Colorado Consumer Protection Act.

When engaging in the sale of mobile or manufactured homes, real estate brokers are subject to compliance with license law and the rules of the Real Estate Commission. A licensee may be disciplined for dishonest conduct or failure to account for money belonging to others. If the sale of a manufactured or mobile home is integrated with the sale or lease of land upon which the home is to be affixed or placed, a real estate license is required.

Manufactured and mobile homes may be conveyed by bill of sale if the sale is made prior to the home being affixed to the land. However, in the case of a manufactured home, a simple contract of sale would suffice because usually the manufactured home is immediately affixed to the land and would pass with a deed conveyance of the land.

Both mobile and modular homes are considered manufactured homes, and §§ 38-29-101, *et seq.*, C.R.S., govern title thereto.

A manufactured home seller must deliver a certificate of title to the buyer. Any person entitled to a certificate of title is required to make application to the director of revenue or the director's agent, who is the clerk and recorder of the county in which the manufactured home is located. Copies of all applications are forwarded to the county assessor for tax purposes. The certificate of title is mailed to the owner of the manufactured home, unless the home is mortgaged, in which case it is mailed to the mortgagee.

The notarized signature of the owner marks transfer of title. The buyer or transferee must present the transferred certificate, duly transferred, to the director of revenue or the director's agent within 30 days, along with an application for a new certificate of title. If a manufactured home is destroyed or dismantled, the certificate of title must be surrendered to the director or the director's authorized agent.

When a manufactured home is permanently affixed to the ground and no longer capable of being drawn over the public highways, the owner may surrender the certificate of title to the director's authorized agent with a request that the title be purged. With the consent of the mortgagee, the manufactured home will then become real property and the owner subject to all the rights and obligations of a real property owner.

Mobile homes and mobile home parks are subject to zoning requirements, and there is often a problem of finding suitable space. Collusion between the owner of a mobile home park and the seller of the mobile home is forbidden by statute. A mobile home seller may not pay or offer to pay cash or other consideration to the owner of a mobile home park to reserve space, and a mobile home park owner may not require that a mobile home be purchased from any particular seller as a condition of tenancy. Moreover, a mobile home park owner may not require selling or transfer fees from tenants or buyers. Colorado law also governs the amount of the security deposit and other matters. The **Mobile Home Park Act** (§§ 38-12-200.1, *et seq.*, C.R.S.) is printed in Chapter 25, "Related Real Estate Law.".

The construction of a manufactured or mobile home is subject to standards imposed by the Colorado Department of Local Affairs, Division of Housing, which are identical to those of the United States Department of Housing and Urban Development (HUD). Absent such federal regulations, manufactured housing must be reasonably consistent with the American National Standards Institute (ANSI) Standard A-119.1. Standards do not apply to sales made after the first purchase (see §§ 24-32-701, *et seq.*, C.R.S., as amended). The Colorado Department of Health establishes and enforces sanitary standards for mobile home parks (see §§ 25-1.5-201, *et seq.*, C.R.S.).

Prior to engaging in the sale of manufactured housing, a real estate licensee should become thoroughly familiar with the associated federal, state, and local requirements.

Ed. Note: See Chapter 25, "Related Real Estate Law," for legislation concerning the regulation of manufactured homes.

Chapter 17:
Trust Deeds and Liens

An * in the left margin indicates a change in the statute, rule, or text since the last publication of the manual.

I. Trust Deeds and Mortgages

A. Introduction and Background of Mortgages

The purchase of real estate usually involves a considerable sum of money. Rarely is full payment made in cash. In the great majority of real estate transactions, a purchaser makes a down payment in cash and arranges for a loan to cover the balance. Financing of this balance generally involves two legal instruments: a negotiable promissory note and a mortgage. A negotiable promissory note or bond is a writing signed by the maker containing an unconditional promise to pay a certain sum in money on demand or at some future time, and which is payable to the order of the payee or to the bearer of the instrument. A promissory note creates a debt for which the maker is personally liable. A mortgage is a legal document pledging or conveying a piece of real property as security for the indebtedness created by a promissory note.

In early English law, the mortgage was simply a deed conveying the property, from the mortgagor (borrower) to the mortgagee (lender). It contained a clause that defeated the conveyance when the mortgagor paid the debt on time. If the borrower defaulted, the mortgagee became the owner of the property. Foreclosure proceedings were not necessary and did not even exist.

Thereafter, a practice arose that permitted the borrower, in cases of extreme hardship, to repay the debt after default. The mortgagee was required to accept the delayed payment and convey the property back to the mortgagor. This right to pay and recover the property after default is known as the right (or equity) of redemption, and it soon became a matter of course in all cases of default. Mortgagees then attempted to insert a clause that required mortgagors to surrender their equity of redemption. However, common-law courts held this clause void, stating that because the needy borrowers were in no position to protect themselves, the courts would not let the lender take advantage of them. This left the lender in a somewhat difficult position of owning the land upon default but not being certain whether or not the mortgagor would redeem it.

A new practice emerged to remedy this situation. Upon mortgagee default and filing a petition with the court, a judge would decree that the mortgagor had only a certain amount of time, typically six months or a year, to redeem the property. After the lapse of the allotted time, the mortgagor's equity of redemption was barred and foreclosed, and the mortgagee became the absolute owner of the property. This procedure is called strict foreclosure and still may exist in some states.

Under strict foreclosure, the lender becomes the owner of property that may be worth many times the amount due, especially if the borrower had repaid most of the debt. If the value of the property was less than the mortgage balance, then the mortgagee lost the balance due, because under common law the lender had no personal right of recovery against the mortgagor. This injustice led to the next development—foreclosure through public sale.

Up to this point, the concept of a mortgage was based on ownership or "**title theory**," *i.e.*, that the mortgagor transferred the legal title of the property to the mortgagee.

Foreclosure through public sale gave rise to a new concept of the mortgage not as a conveyance of the land, but only as a lien upon the property. Thus, the lien would be enforced through a public sale rather than giving the lender title to the property. If the land sold for more than the debt, the mortgagee would be paid in full and the balance would be awarded to the borrower. It logically followed that if the property sold for less than the debt, then any other assets of the mortgagor would be available to the mortgagee through a deficiency judgment and by virtue of the borrower having signed a note or bond that was secured by the mortgage.

Under modern mortgage law in the United States, there are three theories as to the nature of mortgages: (1) lien, (2) title, and (3) intermediate theories. Most states, including Colorado (see § 38-35-117, C.R.S.), have adopted the lien theory in which a mortgage creates a lien and does not convey title. The mortgagor is entitled to possession until default and passage of the right of redemption. Foreclosure is through court action and a court-ordered public sale. The mortgagor is entitled to any excess funds over and above the amount of the debt and is liable personally for any deficiency. The security interest owned by the mortgagee is a personal property interest, and can be transferred only by assignment of the debt secured by the mortgage. When the debt is satisfied, the mortgage is automatically extinguished.

A few states have adopted a modified version of title theory in which the mortgagee is considered to have the legal title, subject only to the mortgagor's superior equitable ownership. Between default and foreclosure the mortgagee is entitled to possession, but must account for all rents and profits and apply them toward reduction of the mortgage debt. Foreclosure is generally by legal action and a court-ordered public sale. The mortgagor is entitled to any excess funds and is liable for any deficiency. Upon payment of the debt, the mortgagee's legal title is defeated. The mortgagee's interest is considered to be a real, rather than personal, property right. The difference today between lien and title theory is more technical than real. Some states have taken an intermediate position between title and lien theories, wherein legal title actually transfers to the mortgagee, but the enforcement of the mortgage upon default is in the nature of a lien.

II. The Foreclosure Process 2008

The following article was written by Jonathan A. Goodman, Esq. of the law firm Frascona, Joiner, Goodman and Greenstein, P.C., to describe the biggest changes in Colorado's new foreclosure law.

Foreclosure Revolution

http://www.frascona.com/resource/jag508foreclosurerev.htm

Question: What are the biggest changes in Colorado's new foreclosure law?

Summary

In Colorado, the foreclosure process historically gave borrowers two opportunities to pull their property out of foreclosure. Prior to the foreclosure sale, the borrower (and others) could "cure" monetary defaults. After the foreclosure sale, the owner could "redeem" the property. Under the new law, applicable to foreclosures filed after January 1, 2008, the time period which would otherwise have been available to an owner to redeem has been moved prior to the foreclosure sale date. Under the new law, the borrower has a longer time to cure and no redemption rights. The total duration of the foreclosure process remains essentially unchanged.

Longer Cure Period

Under the old and new laws, the foreclosure process is essentially commenced by the filing of a "Notice of Election and Demand" with the Public Trustee. The Public Trustee then has ten working days in which to record the Notice of Election and Demand at the Clerk & Recorder's office.

Under the old law, the Public Trustee was required to set up a public trustee's sale date in the 45-60 day window after the recording of the Notice of Election and Demand. The borrower had until noon on the day before the foreclosure sale date to cure the borrower's monetary defaults. In order to cure, the borrower had to tender all back payments, late fees, default interest, and other costs and expenses to restore the lender to the position the lender would have been in had the default not occurred. Because Public Trustee sale dates tended to be set closer to the end of the 45-60 day window, borrowers essentially had two months under the old law to cure. If the borrower, or someone else entitled to cure, did not cure, the property would be sold at a foreclosure sale.

Under the new law, the time otherwise given to an owner to redeem is now moved before the foreclosure sale date, giving the borrower a longer period of time to cure. The amount of time to cure now depends upon whether the property is considered agricultural or non-agricultural. Owners of non-agricultural property now have approximately four months to cure and owners of agricultural property have approximately seven months. (Determining whether a property is agricultural or non-agricultural is not intuitive, and explaining the detailed criteria for the distinction is beyond the scope of this article.)

No Owner's Right to Redeem

After the foreclosure sale, under the old law, the owner had the "owner's redemption period" to redeem the certificate of purchase from the highest bidder at the foreclosure sale. If the property was non-agricultural, the owner's redemption period lasted 75 days after the foreclosure sale. If the property was agricultural, then the owner had a six month redemption period.

If the owner did not redeem, then each junior lien holder had an opportunity to redeem. The junior lien holders would redeem in sequence, with the senior most lien junior to the lien being foreclosed having the first opportunity to redeem, and with each subsequent junior lien holder having the next opportunity to redeem out the prior redeeming lien holder. In order to redeem, junior lien holders (and the owner of the property) had to file notices of intent to redeem not later than fifteen days prior to the expiration of the owner's redemption period. The first redeeming lienor would have a ten-day window after the expiration of the owner's redemption period, and each subsequent lien holder would have the next five business day window to redeem.

Under the new foreclosure law, if the property is non-agricultural, the Public Trustee must set up the foreclosure sale in the 110-125 day window after the recording of the Notice of Election and Demand. If the property is agricultural, the foreclosure sale must be set up in the 215-230 day window after the recording of the Notice of Election and Demand. Under the new law the borrower still has until noon the day before the foreclosure sale to cure monetary defaults.

Under the new law, junior lien holders still have redemption rights. However, because there is no owner's redemption period, junior lien holders must now file their notices of intent to redeem within the 8 business day window after the foreclosure sale. The junior lien holders still have similar sequential redemption rights (the details of which are beyond the scope of this article).

Why Bother?

Different political constituencies had different reasons for changing the law. Generally, the new foreclosure process is simpler, should increase competitive bidding at foreclosure sales and makes homeowners less juicy as prey for unscrupulous foreclosure investors. Because borrowers are more likely to cure than to redeem, proponents of the change perceive that it is better to shift time to the more practical cure rights. Cures also tend to keep people in their homes more than redemptions. The few borrowers who actually redeemed tended to do so by selling the property. Some borrowers were under selling valuable redemption rights to clever (and sometimes worse than clever) foreclosure investors. The need to wait out an owner's redemption period discouraged third-party investors from bidding at the foreclosure sale. An increase in competitive bidding may cash out more foreclosing lenders, generate proceeds to apply against junior liens (reducing deficiency claims against owners), and generate funds to apply against the owner's equity (in the rare case where an owner with equity doesn't cure or sell the property prior to the foreclosure sale).

The two bills making the above changes total over one hundred pages. There are many nuances and changes to the law which are beyond the scope of this article. The purpose of this article has been merely to identify the most significant conceptual change for non-lawyers. Should any reader have a need to deal with a specific foreclosure or have an interest in the subtleties or multitude of other changes to Colorado foreclosures, he or she should consult an attorney.

III. Mortgages and Deeds of Trust

Although there are other mortgage devices, the mortgage and the deed of trust are the most prevalent. Both are found in Colorado, but the deed of trust to a public trustee is by far the most common.

A mortgage is a conditional conveyance of the real estate directly from the mortgagor (borrower) to the mortgagee (lender) to secure the indebtedness described therein. There are only two parties to a mortgage.

A deed of trust involves three parties. A trustor or grantor (borrower) conveys legal title via a trust deed to a public official (public trustee) of the county in which the property is situated. The public trustee holds title in trust for the lender (beneficiary) to secure payment of the indebtedness described in the deed of trust.

Upon compliance with the deed of trust provisions, the public trustee must release the deed of trust and reconvey the property back to the grantor. Upon default of the deed of trust's provisions, and after the trustor's right of redemption has expired, the public trustee is empowered to conduct a public sale, and to convey title to a new purchaser. A deed of trust to a public trustee may be foreclosed by public sale through the office of the public trustee or through the courts, at the option of the holder of the indebtedness.

In rare instances, a private trustee may hold a trust deed. According to Colorado law, such a trust deed is considered a mortgage and may be foreclosed only through the courts.

Upon payment of the indebtedness secured by a mortgage, a mortgage should be released by the mortgagee executing a release or satisfaction of mortgage, delivering the same to the mortgagor, who should record it in the office of the county clerk and recorder of the county in which property is situated. When the indebtedness secured by a deed of trust is paid, the procedure to procure a release thereof is to have the beneficiary execute a request for release of deed of trust and present it to the public trustee, together with the cancelled promissory note and deed of trust. The public trustee will then, upon receipt of the appropriate fee, execute the release of deed of trust. The release should be recorded in the clerk and recorder's office in the county in which the property is situated.

Because the deed of trust is the most commonly used real property encumbering instrument in Colorado, it is important to become acquainted with the more pertinent statutes dealing with it.

IV. Concerning Real Estate Foreclosures (Deeds of Trust)

House Bill 06-1387 was signed into law June 1, 2006, and is a comprehensive rewrite of the provisions pertaining to foreclosure processes. Brokers are cautioned to seek legal advice in matters pertaining to the public trustee and the foreclosure processes. Printed below for informational purposes are substantive portions of the law related to foreclosure process. *The following is not a complete listing of the law*; for a recitation of the entire law, access the Colorado General Assembly website at: www.leg.state.co.us.

§ 38-38-100.3, C.R.S. Definitions

As used in articles 37 to 39 of this title, unless the context otherwise requires:

(1) "Agricultural property" means property, none of which, on the date of recording of the deed of trust or other lien or at the time of the recording of the notice of election and demand or lis pendens, is:

- (a) Platted as a subdivision;
- (b) Located within an incorporated town, city, or city and county; or
- (c) Valued and assessed as other than agricultural property pursuant to sections 39-1-102 (1.6)(a) and 39-1-103(5), C.R.S., by the assessor of the county where the property is located.

(1.5) "Amended mailing list" means the amended mailing list in accordance with section 38-38-103 (2) containing the names and addresses in the mailing list as defined in section 38-38-100.3(14) and the names and addresses of the following persons:

- (a) The owner of the property, if different than the grantor of the deed of trust, as of the date and time of the recording of the notice of election and demand or lis pendens as shown in the records at the address indicated in such recorded instrument; and

(b) Each person, except the public trustee, who appears to have an interest in the property described in the combined notice by an instrument recorded prior to the date and time of the recording of the notice of election and demand or lis pendens with the clerk and recorder of the county where the property or any portion thereof is located at the address of the person indicated on the instrument, if the person's interest in the property may be extinguished by the foreclosure.

(2) "Attorney for the holder" means an attorney licensed and in good standing in the state of Colorado to practice law and retained by the holder of an evidence of debt to process a foreclosure under this article.

(3) "Certified copy" means, with respect to a recorded document, a copy of the document certified by the clerk and recorder of the county where the document was recorded.

(4) "Combined notice" means the combined notice of sale, right to cure, and right to redeem described in section 38-38-103(4)(a).

(5) "Confirmation deed" means the deed described in section 38-38-501 in the form specified in section 38-38-502 or 38-38-503.

(5.3) "Consensual lien" means a conveyance of an interest in real property, granted by the owner of the property after the recording of a notice of election and demand, that is not an absolute conveyance of fee title to the property. "Consensual lien" includes but is not limited to a deed of trust, mortgage or other assignment, encumbrance, option, lease, easement, contract, including an instrument specified in section 38-38-305, or conveyance as security for the performance of the grantor. "Consensual lien" does not include a lien described in section 38-38-306 or 38-33.3-316.

(5.7) "Corporate surety bond" means a bond issued by a person authorized to issue bonds in the state of Colorado with the public trustee as obligee, conditioned against the delivery of an original evidence of debt to the damage of the public trustee.

(6) "Cure statement" means the statement described in section 38-38-104(2)(a).

(7) "Deed of trust" means a security instrument containing a grant to a public trustee together with a power of sale.

(8) "Evidence of debt" means a writing that evidences a promise to pay or a right to the payment of a monetary obligation, such as a promissory note, bond, negotiable instrument, a loan, credit, or similar agreement, or a monetary judgment entered by a court of competent jurisdiction.

(9) "Fees and costs" means all fees, charges, expenses, and costs described in section 38-38-107.

(10) "Holder of an evidence of debt" means the person in actual possession of or person entitled to enforce an evidence of debt; except that "holder of an evidence of debt" does not include a person acting as a nominee solely for the purpose of holding the evidence of debt or deed of trust as an electronic registry without any authority to enforce the evidence of debt or deed of trust. For the purposes of articles 37 to 40 of this title, the following persons are presumed to be the holder of an evidence of debt:

(a) The person who is the obligee of and who is in possession of an original evidence of debt;

(b) The person in possession of an original evidence of debt together with the proper indorsement or assignment thereof to such person in accordance with section 38-38-101(6);

(c) The person in possession of a negotiable instrument evidencing a debt, which has been duly negotiated to such person or to bearer or indorsed in blank; or

(d) The person in possession of an evidence of debt with authority, which may be granted by the original evidence of debt or deed of trust, to enforce the evidence of debt as agent, nominee, or trustee or in a similar capacity for the obligee of the evidence of debt.

(11) "Junior lien" means a deed of trust or other lien or encumbrance upon the property for which the amount due and owing thereunder is subordinate to the deed of trust or other lien being foreclosed.

(12) "Junior lienor" means a person who is a beneficiary, holder, or grantee of a junior lien.

(12.5) "Lienor" includes without limitation the holder of a certificate of purchase or certificate of redemption for property, issued upon the foreclosure of a deed of trust or other lien on the property.

(13) "Lis pendens" means a lis pendens in accordance with section 38-35-110 that is recorded with the clerk and recorder of the county where the property or any portion thereof is located and that refers to a judicial action in which one of the claims is for foreclosure and sale of the property by an officer or in which a claim or interest in the property is asserted.

(14) "Mailing list" means the initial mailing list in accordance with section 38-38-101(1)(e) provided to the officer by the holder of the evidence of debt or the attorney for the holder containing the names and addresses of the following persons:

(a) The original grantor of the deed of trust or obligor under any other lien being foreclosed at the address shown in the recorded deed of trust or other lien being foreclosed and, if different, the last address, if any, shown in the records of the holder of the evidence of debt;

(b) Any person known or believed by the holder of the evidence of debt to be personally liable under the evidence of debt secured by the deed of trust or other lien being foreclosed at the last address, if any, shown in the records of the holder;

(c) The occupant of the property, addressed to "occupant" at the address of the property; and

(d) With respect to a public trustee sale, a lessee with an unrecorded possessory interest in the property at the address of the premises of the lessee and, if different, the address of the property, to the extent that the holder of the evidence of debt desires to terminate the possessory interest with the foreclosure.

(15) "Maintaining and repairing" means the act of caring for and preserving a property in its current condition or restoring a property to a sound or working condition after damage; except that "maintaining and repairing" shall not include, unless done pursuant to an order entered by a court of competent jurisdiction, any act of advancing a property to a better condition or any act that increases the quality of or adds to the improvements located on a property.

(16) "Notice of election and demand" means a notice of election and demand for sale related to a public trustee foreclosure under this article.

(17) "Officer" means the public trustee or sheriff conducting a foreclosure under this article.

(17.5) "Person" means any individual, corporation, government or governmental subdivision or agency, business trust, estate, trust, limited liability company, partnership, association, or other legal entity.

(18) "Property" means the portion of the property encumbered by a deed of trust or other lien that is being foreclosed under this article or the portion of the property being released from a deed of trust or other lien under article 39 of this title.

(19) "Publish", "publication", "republish", or "republication" means the placement by an officer of a legal notice that meets the requirements set forth in section 24-70-103, C.R.S., containing a combined notice that complies with the requirements of section 24-70-109, C.R.S., in a newspaper in the county or counties where the property to be sold is located. Unless otherwise specified by the attorney for the holder, the officer shall select the newspaper.

(20) "Qualified holder" means a holder of an evidence of debt, certificate of purchase, certificate of redemption, or confirmation deed that is also one of the following:

(a) A bank as defined in section 11-101-401(5), C.R.S.;

(b) An industrial bank as defined in section 11-108-101(1), C.R.S.;

(c) A federally chartered savings and loan association doing business in Colorado or a savings and loan association chartered under the "Savings and Loan Association Law," articles 40 to 46 of title 11, C.R.S.;

(d) A supervised lender as defined in section 5-1-301(46), C.R.S., that is licensed to make supervised loans pursuant to section 5-2-302, C.R.S., and that is either:

(I) A public entity, which is an entity that has issued voting securities that are listed on a national security exchange registered under the federal "Securities Exchange Act of 1934", as amended; or

(II) An entity in which all of the outstanding voting securities are held, directly or indirectly, by a public entity;

(e) An entity in which all of the outstanding voting securities are held, directly or indirectly, by a public entity that also owns, directly or indirectly, all of the voting securities of a supervised lender as defined in section 5-1-301(46), C.R.S., that is licensed to make supervised loans pursuant to section 5-2-302, C.R.S.;

(f) A federal housing administration approved mortgagee;

(g) A federally chartered credit union doing business in Colorado or a state-chartered credit union as described in section 11-30-101, C.R.S.;

(h) An agency or department of the federal government;

(i) An entity created or sponsored by the federal or state government that originates, insures, guarantees, or purchases loans or a person acting on behalf of such an entity to enforce an evidence of debt or the deed of trust securing an evidence of debt; or

(j) Any entity listed in paragraphs (a) to (i) of this subsection (20) acting in the capacity of agent, nominee except as otherwise specified in subsection (10) of this section, or trustee for another person.

(21) "Records" means the records of the county clerk and recorder of the county where the property is located.

(22) "Sale" means a foreclosure sale conducted by an officer under this article.

(23) "Secured indebtedness" means the amount owed pursuant to the evidence of debt without regard to the value of the collateral.

(24) "Statement of redemption" means the signed and acknowledged statement of the holder of the evidence of debt or the signed statement of the attorney for the holder as required by section 38-38-302(3) or the signed and acknowledged statement of the lienor or the signed statement of the attorney for the lienor as required by section 38-38-302(1)(f).

§ 38-38-101, C.R.S. Holder of evidence of debt may elect to foreclose

(1) **Documents required.** Whenever a holder of an evidence of debt declares a violation of a covenant of a deed of trust and elects to publish all or a portion of the property therein described for sale, the holder or the attorney for the holder shall file the following with the public trustee of the county where the property is located:

(a) A notice of election and demand signed and acknowledged by the holder of the evidence of debt or signed by the attorney for the holder;

(b) The original evidence of debt, including any modifications to the original evidence of debt, together with the original indorsement or assignment thereof, if any, to the holder of the evidence of debt or other proper indorsement or assignment in accordance with subsection (6) of this section or, in lieu of the original evidence of debt, one of the following:

(I) A corporate surety bond in the amount of one and one-half times the face amount of such original evidence of debt; or

(II) A copy of the evidence of debt and a certification signed and properly acknowledged by a holder of an evidence of debt acting for itself, or as agent, nominee, or trustee under subsection (2) of this section or a statement signed by the attorney for such holder, citing the paragraph of section 38-38-100.3(20) under which the holder claims to be a qualified holder and certifying or stating that the copy of the evidence of debt is true and correct and that the use of the copy is subject to the conditions described in paragraph (a) of subsection (2) of this section; or

(III) A certified copy of a monetary judgment entered by a court of competent jurisdiction.

(c) The original recorded deed of trust securing the evidence of debt and any original recorded modifications of the deed of trust or any recorded partial releases of the deed of trust, or in lieu thereof, one of the following:

(I) Certified copies of the recorded deed of trust and any recorded modifications of the deed of trust or recorded partial releases of the deed of trust; or

(II) Copies of the recorded deed of trust and any recorded modifications of the deed of trust or recorded partial releases of the deed of trust and a certification signed and properly acknowledged by a holder of an evidence of debt acting for itself or as an agent, nominee, or trustee under subsection (2) of this section or a signed statement by the attorney for such holder, citing the paragraph of section 38-38-100.3(20) under which the holder claims to be a qualified holder and certifying or stating that the copies of the recorded deed of trust and any recorded modifications of the deed of trust or recorded partial releases of the deed of trust are true and correct and that the use of the copies is subject to the conditions described in paragraph (a) of subsection (2) of this section;

(d) A combined notice pursuant to section 38-38-103 except that the combined notice may be omitted with the prior approval of the officer because the officer will supply the combined notice;

(e) A mailing list;

(f) Any affidavit recorded pursuant to section 38-35-109(5) affecting the deed of trust described in paragraph (c) of this subsection (1), which affidavit shall be accepted by the public trustee as modifying the deed of trust for all purposes under this article 38 only if the affidavit is filed with the public trustee at the same time as the other documents required under this subsection (1); and

(g) A statement executed by the holder of an evidence of debt, or the attorney for such holder, identifying, to the best knowledge of the person executing such statement, the name and address of the current owner of the property described in the notice of election and demand.

(h) A separate document notifying the public trustee that the property referred to in the notice of election and demand is property that requires posting under section 38-38-802. If the document required by this paragraph (h) is not filed at the time the documents required by paragraphs (a) to (e) of this subsection (1) are filed with the public trustee, and the holder determines at a later date that the property requires posting, the holder shall request that the public trustee rerecord the notice of election and demand. Thereafter, all deadlines for the foreclosure action shall be determined according to the date of the rerecording of the notice of election and demand as though the foreclosure was commenced on such date, and the public trustee shall collect a fee of seventy-five dollars from the holder. If the document required by this paragraph (h) is filed in error, the holder may withdraw it by filing with the public trustee an affidavit signed by the holder or the attorney for the holder affirming both that the document required by this paragraph (h) was filed in error and that the property has not been posted pursuant to section 38-38-802. In order to be effective, and thereby notify the public trustee that the property is not eligible for posting, such affidavit shall be filed with the public trustee no later than fifteen calendar days after the date of the determination of the public trustee that the filing is complete in accordance with section 38-38-102(1).

(2) **Foreclosure by qualified holder without original evidence of debt, original or certified copy of deed of trust, or proper indorsement.**

(a) A qualified holder, whether acting for itself or as agent, nominee, or trustee under section 38-38-100.3(20)(j), that elects to foreclose without the original evidence of debt pursuant to subparagraph (II) of paragraph (b) of subsection (1) of this section, or without the original recorded deed of trust or a certified copy thereof pursuant to subparagraph (II) of paragraph (c) of subsection (1) of this section, or without the proper indorsement or assignment of an evidence of debt under paragraph (b) of subsection (1) of this section shall, by operation of law, be deemed to have agreed to indemnify and defend any person liable for repayment of any portion of the original evidence of debt in the event that the original evidence of debt is presented for payment to the extent of any amount, other than the amount of a deficiency remaining under the evidence of debt after deducting the amount bid at sale, and any person who sustains a loss due to any title defect that results from reliance upon a sale at which the original evidence of debt was not presented. The indemnity granted by this subsection (2) shall be limited to actual economic loss suffered together with any court costs and reasonable attorney fees and costs incurred in defending a claim brought as a direct and proximate cause of the failure to produce the original evidence of debt, but such indemnity shall not include, and no claimant shall be entitled to, any special, incidental, consequential, reliance, expectation, or punitive damages of any kind. A qualified holder acting as agent, nominee, or trustee shall be liable for the indemnity pursuant to this subsection (2).

(b) In the event that a qualified holder or the attorney for the holder commences a foreclosure without production of the original evidence of debt, proper indorsement or assignment, or the original recorded deed of trust or a certified copy thereof, the qualified holder or the attorney for the holder may submit the original evidence of debt, proper indorsement or assignment, or the original recorded deed of trust or a certified copy thereof to the officer prior to the sale. In such event, the sale shall be conducted and administered as if the original evidence of debt, proper indorsement or assignment, or the original recorded deed of trust or a certified copy thereof had been submitted at the time of commencement of such proceeding, and any indemnities deemed to have been given by the qualified holder under paragraph (a) of this subsection (2) shall be null and void as to the instrument produced under this paragraph (b).

(c) In the event that a foreclosure is conducted where the original evidence of debt, proper indorsement or assignment, or original recorded deed of trust or certified copy thereof has not been produced, the only claims shall be against the indemnitor as provided in paragraph (a) of this subsection (2) and not against the foreclosed property or the attorney for the holder of the evidence of debt. Nothing in this section shall preclude a person liable for repayment of the evidence of debt from pursuing remedies allowed by law.

(3) **Foreclosure on a portion of property.** A holder of an evidence of debt may elect to foreclose a deed of trust under this article against a portion of the property encumbered by the deed of trust only if such portion is encumbered as a separate and distinct parcel or lot by the original or an amended deed of trust. Any foreclosure conducted by a public trustee against less than all of the property then encumbered by the deed of trust shall not affect the lien or the power of sale contained therein as to the remaining property. The amount bid at a sale of less than all of the

property shall be deemed to have satisfied the secured indebtedness to the extent of the amount of the bid.

(4) **Notice of election and demand.** A notice of election and demand filed with the public trustee pursuant to this section shall contain the following:

(a) The names of the original grantors of the deed of trust being foreclosed and the original beneficiaries or grantees thereof;

(b) The name of the holder of the evidence of debt;

(c) The date of the deed of trust being foreclosed;

(d) The recording date, county, book, and page or reception number of the recording of the deed of trust being foreclosed;

(e) The amount of the original principal balance of the secured indebtedness;

(f) The amount of the outstanding principal balance of the secured indebtedness as of the date of the notice of election and demand;

(g) A legal description of the property to be foreclosed as set forth in the documents to be provided to the public trustee pursuant to paragraph (c) of subsection (1) of this section;

(h) A statement of whether the property described in the notice of election and demand is all or only a portion of the property then encumbered by the deed of trust being foreclosed;

(i) A statement of the violation of the covenant of the evidence of debt or deed of trust being foreclosed upon which the foreclosure is based, which statement shall not constitute a waiver of any right accruing on account of any violation of any covenant of the evidence of debt or deed of trust other than the violation specified in the notice of election and demand; and

(j) The name, address, business telephone number, and bar registration number of the attorney for the holder of the evidence of debt, which may be indicated in the signature block of the notice of election and demand.

(k) A description of any changes to the deed of trust described in the notice of election and demand that are based on an affidavit filed with the public trustee under paragraph (f) of subsection (1) of this section, together with the recording date and reception number or book and page number of the recording of that affidavit in the records.

(5) **Error in notice.** In the event that the amount of the outstanding principal balance due and owing upon the secured indebtedness is erroneously set forth in the notice of election and demand or the combined notice, the error shall not affect the validity of the notice of election and demand, the combined notice, the publication, the sale, the certificate of purchase described in section 38-38-401, the certificate of redemption described in section 38-38-402, the confirmation deed as defined in section 38-38-100.3(5), or any other document executed in connection therewith.

(6) **Indorsement or assignment.**

(a) Proper indorsement or assignment of an evidence of debt shall include the original indorsement or assignment or a certified copy of an indorsement or assignment recorded in the county where the property being foreclosed is located.

(b) Notwithstanding the provisions of paragraph (a) of this subsection (6), the original evidence of debt or a copy thereof without proper indorsement or assignment shall be deemed to be properly indorsed or assigned if a qualified holder presents the original evidence of debt or a copy thereof to the officer together with a statement in the certification of the qualified holder or in the statement of the attorney for the qualified holder pursuant to subparagraph (II) of paragraph (b) of subsection (1) of this section that the party on whose behalf the foreclosure was commenced is the holder of the evidence of debt.

(7) **Multiple instruments.** If the evidence of debt consists of multiple instruments, such as notes or bonds, the holder of the evidence of debt may elect to foreclose with respect to fewer than all of such instruments or documents by identifying in the notice of election and demand and the combined notice only those to be satisfied in whole or in part, in which case the requirements of this section shall apply only as to those instruments or documents.

(8) **Assignment or transfer of debt during foreclosure.**

(a) The holder of the evidence of debt may assign or transfer the secured indebtedness at any time during the pendency of a foreclosure action without affecting the validity of the secured indebtedness. Upon receipt of written notice signed by the holder who commenced the foreclosure action or the attorney for the holder stating that the evidence of debt has been assigned and transferred and identifying the assignee or transferee, the public trustee shall complete the foreclosure as directed by the assignee or transferee or the attorney for the assignee or transferee. No holder of an evidence of debt, certificate of purchase, or certificate of redemption shall be liable to any third party for the acts or omissions of any assignee or transferee that occur after the date of the assignment or transfer.

(b) The assignment or transfer of the secured indebtedness during the pendency of a foreclosure shall be deemed made without recourse unless otherwise agreed in a written statement signed by the assignor or transferor. The holder of the evidence of debt, certificate of purchase, or certificate of redemption making the assignment or transfer and the attorney for the holder shall have no duty, obligation, or liability to the assignee or transferee or to any third party for any act or omission with respect to the foreclosure or the loan servicing of the secured indebtedness after the assignment or transfer. If an assignment or transfer is made by a qualified holder that commenced the foreclosure pursuant to subsection (2) of this section, the qualified holder's indemnity under said subsection (2) shall remain in effect with respect to all parties except to the assignee or transferee, unless otherwise agreed in a writing signed by the assignee or transferee if the assignee or transferee is a qualified holder.

(9) **Partial release from deed of trust.** At any time after the recording of the notice of election and demand but prior to the sale, a portion of the property may be released from the deed of trust being foreclosed pursuant to section 38-39-102 or as otherwise provided by order of a court of competent jurisdiction recorded in the county where the property being released is located. Upon recording of the release, the holder of the evidence of debt or the attorney for the holder shall pay the fee described in section 38-37-104(1)(b)(IX), amend the combined notice, and, in the case of a public trustee foreclosure, amend the notice of election and demand to describe the property that continues to be secured by the deed of trust or other lien being foreclosed as of the effective date of the release or court order. The public trustee shall record the amended notice of election and demand upon receipt. Upon receipt of the amended combined notice, the public trustee shall republish and mail the amended combined notice in the manner set forth in section 38-38-109(1)(b).

(10) **Deposit.** The public trustee may require a deposit of up to six hundred fifty dollars or the amount of the fee permitted pursuant to section 38-37-104(1)(b)(I), whichever is greater, at the time the notice of election and demand is filed, to be applied against the fees and costs of the public trustee. The public trustee may allow the attorney for the holder of the evidence of debt to establish one or more accounts with the public trustee, which the public trustee may use to pay the fees and costs of the public trustee in any foreclosure filed by the holder or the attorney for the holder, or through which the public trustee may transmit refunds or cures, excess proceeds, or redemption proceeds.

§ 38-38-102, C.R.S. Recording notice of election and demand – record of sale

(1) No later than ten business days following the receipt of the notice of election and demand, the public trustee shall cause the notice to be recorded in the office of the county clerk and recorder of the county where the property described in the notice is located.

(2) The public trustee shall retain in the public trustee's records a printed or electronic copy of the notice of election and demand and the combined notice, as published pursuant to section 38-38-103. Such records shall be available for inspection by the public at the public trustee's offices during the public trustee's normal business hours.

§ 38-38-103, C.R.S. Combined notice – publication – providing information

(1) (a) The public trustee shall mail a combined notice as described in subsection (4) of this section to the following persons as set forth in the initial mailing list as follows:

(I) No more than twenty calendar days after the recording of the notice of election and demand, to:

(A) The original grantor of the deed of trust or obligor under any other lien being foreclosed at the address shown in the recorded deed of trust or other lien being foreclosed and, if different, the last address, if any, shown in the records of the holder of the evidence of debt;

(B) Any person known or believed by the holder of the evidence of debt to be personally liable under the evidence of debt secured by the deed of trust or other lien being foreclosed at the last address, if any, shown in the records of the holder; and

(C) The occupant of the property, addressed to "occupant" at the address of the property;

(II) No more than sixty calendar days nor less than forty-five calendar days prior to the first scheduled date of sale, to the following persons as set forth in the supplemental or amended mailing list:

(A) The original grantor of the deed of trust or obligor under any other lien being foreclosed at the address shown in the recorded deed of trust or other lien being foreclosed and, if different, the last address, if any, shown in the records of the holder of the evidence of debt;

(B) The owner of the property as of the date and time of the recording of the notice of election and demand or lis pendens as shown in the records at the address indicated in such recorded instrument;

(C) Any person known or believed by the holder of the evidence of debt to be personally liable under the evidence of debt secured by the deed of trust or other lien being foreclosed, at the last address, if any, shown in the records of the holder;

(D) The occupant of the property, addressed to "occupant" at the address of the property; and

(E) Each person who appears to have an interest in the property described in the combined notice by an instrument recorded prior to the date and time of the recording of the notice of election and demand or lis pendens with the clerk and recorder of the county where the property or any portion thereof is located at the address of the person indicated on such instrument, if the person's interest in the property may be extinguished by the foreclosure.

(b) With respect to a public trustee sale, if a deed of trust being foreclosed has priority over a lessee who has an unrecorded possessory interest in the property and the holder of the evidence of debt desires to terminate the possessory interest with the foreclosure, the holder shall include on the mailing list the lessee together with the address of the premises of the lessee and, if different, the address of the property.

(c) If a recorded instrument does not specify the address of the party purporting to have an interest in the property under such recorded instrument, the party shall not be entitled to notice and any interest in the property under such instrument shall be extinguished upon the execution and delivery of a deed pursuant to section 38-38-501.

(2) (a) The holder of the evidence of debt or the attorney for the holder may deliver an amended mailing list to the officer from time to time, but no less than sixty-five calendar days prior to the actual date of sale. The officer shall send the notice pursuant to subsection (4) of this section to the persons on the amended mailing list no less than forty-five calendar days prior to the actual date of sale.

(b) Repealed (effective 1/8/08).

(3) The sheriff shall mail a combined notice as described in subsection (4) of this section to the persons named at the addresses indicated in a mailing list containing the names and addresses of the persons listed in subparagraph (II) of paragraph (a) of subsection (1) of this section no less than sixteen nor more than thirty calendar days after the holder of the evidence of debt or the attorney for the holder delivers to the sheriff the mailing list and the original or a copy of a decree of foreclosure or a writ of execution directing the sheriff to sell property.

(4) (a) The combined notices required to be mailed pursuant to subsections (1), (2), and (3) of this section shall contain the following:

(I) The information required by section 38-38-101(4);

(II) The statement: A notice of intent to cure filed pursuant to section 38-38-104 shall be filed with the officer at least fifteen calendar days prior to the first scheduled sale date or any date to which the sale is continued;

(III) The statement: A notice of intent to redeem filed pursuant to section 38-38-302 shall be filed with the officer no later than eight business days after the sale;

(IV) The name, address, and telephone number of each attorney, if any, representing the holder of the evidence of debt;

(V) The date of sale determined pursuant to section 38-38-108;

(VI) The place of sale determined pursuant to section 38-38-110; and

(VII) The statement as required by section 24-70-109, C.R.S.: The lien being foreclosed may not be a first lien.

(b) A legible copy of this section and sections 38-37-108, 38-38-104, 38-38-301, 38-38-304, 38-38-305, and 38-38-306 shall be sent with all notices pursuant to this section.

(5) (a) No more than sixty calendar days nor less than forty-five calendar days prior to the first scheduled date of sale, unless a longer period of publication is specified in the deed of trust or other lien being foreclosed, a deed of trust or other lien being foreclosed shall be deemed to require the officer to publish the combined notice, omitting the copies of the statutes under paragraph (b) of subsection (4) of this section and adding the first and last publication dates if not already specified in the combined notice, for four weeks, which means publication once each week for five consecutive weeks.

(b) The officer shall review all such publications of the combined notice for accuracy.

(c) The fees and costs to be allowed for publication of the combined notice shall be as provided by law for the publication of legal notices or advertising.

§ 38-38-104, C.R.S. Right to cure when default is nonpayment – right to cure for certain technical defaults

(1) Unless the order authorizing the sale described in section 38-38-105 contains a determination that there is a reasonable probability that a default in the terms of the evidence of debt, deed of trust, or other lien being foreclosed other than nonpayment of sums due thereunder has occurred, any of the following persons is entitled to cure the default if the person files with the officer, no later than fifteen calendar days prior to the date of sale, a written notice of intent to cure together with evidence of the person's right to cure to the satisfaction of the officer:

(a) (I) The owner of the property as of the date and time of the recording of the notice of election and demand or lis pendens as evidenced in the records;

(II) If the owner of the property is dead or incapacitated on or after the date and time of the recording of the notice of election and demand or lis pendens, the owner's heirs, personal representative, legal guardian, or conservator as of the time of filing of the notice of intent to cure, whether or not such person's interest is shown in the records, or any co-owner of the property if the co-owner's ownership interest is evidenced in the records as of the date and time of the recording of the notice of election and demand or lis pendens;

(III) A transferee of the property as evidenced in the records as of the time of filing of the notice of intent to cure if the transferee was the property owner's spouse as of the date and time of the recording of the notice of election and demand or lis pendens or if the transferee is wholly owned or controlled by the property owner, is wholly owned or controlled by the controlling owner of the property owner, or is the controlling owner of the property owner;

(IV) A transferee or owner of the property by virtue of merger or other similar event or by operation of law occurring after the date and time of the recording of the notice of election and demand or lis pendens; or

(V) The holder of an order or judgment entered by a court of competent jurisdiction as evidenced in the records after the date and time of the recording of the notice of election and demand or lis pendens ordering title to the property to be vested in a person other than the owner in connection with a divorce, property settlement, quiet title action, or similar proceeding;

(b) A person liable under the evidence of debt;

(c) A surety or guarantor of the evidence of debt; or

(d) A holder of an interest junior to the lien being foreclosed by virtue of being a lienor or lessee of, or a holder of an easement or license on, the property or a contract vendee of the property, if the instrument evidencing the interest was recorded in the records prior to the date and time of the recording of the notice of election and demand or lis pendens.

(2) (a) Promptly upon receipt of a notice of intent to cure by the officer, but no less than twelve calendar days prior to the date of sale, the officer shall transmit by mail, facsimile, or electronic means to the person executing the notice of election and demand a request for a statement of all sums necessary to cure the default. The statement shall be filed with the officer by the attorney for the holder or, if none, by the holder of the evidence of debt, and shall set forth the amounts necessary to cure as identified in paragraph (b) of this subsection (2), with the same detail as required for a bid pursuant to section 38-38-106.

(b) No later than 12 noon on the day before the sale, the person desiring to cure the default shall pay to the officer all sums that are due and owing under the evidence of debt and deed of trust or other lien being foreclosed and all fees and costs of the holder of the evidence of debt, including but not limited to all fees and costs of the attorney for the holder allowable under the evidence of debt, deed of trust, or other lien being foreclosed through the effective date set forth in the cure statement; except that any principal that would not have been due in the absence of acceleration shall not be included in such sums due.

(c) If a cure is made, interest for the period of any continuance pursuant to section 38-38-109 (1)(c) shall be allowed only at the regular rate and not at the default rate as may be specified in the evidence of debt, deed of trust, or other lien being foreclosed. If a cure is not made, interest at the default rate, if specified in the evidence of debt, deed of trust, or other lien being foreclosed, for the period of the continuance shall be allowed.

(d) Upon receipt of the cure amount and a withdrawal or dismissal of the foreclosure from the holder of the evidence of debt or the attorney for the holder, the officer shall deliver the cure amount, less the fees and costs of the officer, to the attorney for the holder or, if none, to the holder, the foreclosure shall be withdrawn or dismissed as provided by law, and the evidence of debt shall be returned uncancelled to the attorney for the holder of the evidence of debt or, if none, to the holder by the public trustee or to the court by the sheriff.

(3) Where the default in the terms of the evidence of debt, deed of trust, or other lien on which the holder of the evidence of debt claims the right to foreclose is the failure of a party to furnish balance sheets or tax returns, any person entitled to cure pursuant to paragraph (a) of subsection (2) of this section may cure such default in the manner prescribed in this section by providing to the holder or the attorney for the holder the required balance sheets, tax returns, or other adequate evidence of the party's financial condition so long as all sums currently due under the evidence of debt have been paid and all amounts due under paragraph (b) of subsection (2) of this section, where applicable, have been paid.

(4) Any person liable on the debt and the grantor of the deed of trust or other lien being foreclosed shall be deemed to have given the necessary consent to allow the holder of the evidence of debt or the attorney for the holder to provide the information specified in paragraph (a) of subsection (2) of this section to the officer and all other persons who may assert a right to cure pursuant to this section.

(5) A cure statement pursuant to paragraph (a) of subsection (2) of this section shall state the period for which it is effective. The cure statement shall be effective for at least ten calendar days after the date of the cure statement or until the last day to cure under paragraph (b) of subsection (2) of this section, whichever occurs first. The cure statement shall be effective for no more than thirty calendar days after the date of the cure statement or until the last day to cure under paragraph (b) of subsection (2) of this section, whichever occurs first. The use of good faith estimates in the cure statement with respect to interest and fees and costs is specifically authorized by this article, so long as the cure statement states that it is a good faith estimate effective through the last day to cure as indicated in the cure statement. The use of a good faith estimate shall not change or extend the period or effective date of a cure statement.

§ 38-38-105, C.R.S. Court order authorizing sale mandatory – notice of hearing for residential properties

(1) Repealed.

(2) On and after January 1, 2008, whenever a public trustee forecloses upon a deed of trust under this article, the holder of the evidence of debt or the attorney for the holder shall obtain an order authorizing sale from a court of competent jurisdiction to issue the same pursuant to rule 120 of the Colorado rules of civil procedure. The order shall recite the date the hearing was scheduled if no hearing was held, or the date the hearing was completed if a response was filed, which date in either case must be no later than the day prior to the last day on which an effective notice of intent to cure may be filed with the public trustee under section 38-38-104. The holder or the attorney for the holder shall cause a copy of the order to be provided to the public trustee

no later than 12 noon on the second business day prior to the date of sale. A sale held without an order authorizing sale shall be invalid.

(3) Not less than fifteen days before the date set for the hearing pursuant to rule 120 or other rule of the Colorado rules of civil procedure, the holder or the attorney for the holder seeking an order authorizing sale under this section for a residential property shall cause a notice of hearing as described in rule 120 (b) of the Colorado rules of civil procedure to be posted in a conspicuous place on the property that is the subject of the sale. If possible, the notice shall be posted on the front door of the residence, but if access to the door is not possible or is restricted, the notice shall be posted at an alternative conspicuous location, such as a gate or similar impediment.

§ 38-38-106, C.R.S. Bid required – form of bid

(1) The holder of the evidence of debt or the attorney for the holder shall submit a bid to the officer no later than 12 noon on the second business day prior to the date of sale as provided in this section. The holder or the attorney for the holder need not personally attend the sale. If the bid is not timely submitted, the officer shall continue the sale for one week and shall announce or post a notice of the continuance at the time and place designated for the sale.

(2) The holder of the evidence of debt shall submit a signed and acknowledged bid, or the attorney for the holder shall submit a signed bid, which shall specify the following amounts, itemized in substantially the following categories and in substantially the following form:

BID

To: ____

Public Trustee (or Sheriff) of the County (or City and County) of ____,
State of Colorado (hereinafter the "officer").

Date: ____________

____________, whose mailing address is ________________, bids the sum of
$____________ in your Sale No. _____ to be held on the ___ day of ______, 20___.

The following is an itemization of all amounts due the holder of the evidence of debt secured by the deed of trust or other lien being foreclosed.

Street address of property being foreclosed, if known: ________________

Regular ☐ / default ☐ rate of interest as of the date of sale: ____________

(Inapplicable items may be omitted):

Amounts due under the evidence of debt:

Principal	$ _______	
Interest	_______	
Late charges	_______	
Allowable prepayment penalties or premiums	_______	
Other amounts due under the evidence of debt (specify) ______________________	_______	
______________________	_______	
Category subtotal:		$ _______

Other fees and costs advanced by the holder of evidence of debt:

Property, general liability, and casualty insurance	_______
Property inspections	_______
Appraisals	_______
Taxes and assessments	_______
Utility charges owed or incurred	_______

Homeowner's association assessment paid	________	
Permitted amounts paid on prior liens	________	
Permitted lease payments	________	
Less impound/escrow account credit	________	
Plus impound/escrow account deficiency	________	
Other (describe) ________________________	________	
Category subtotal:		$ ________
Attorney fees and advances:		
Attorney fees	________	
Title commitments and insurances or abstractor charges	________	
Court docketing	________	
Statutory notice	________	
Postage	________	
Electronic transmissions	________	
Photocopies	________	
Telephone	________	
Other (describe) ________________________	________	
Category subtotal:		$ ________
Officer fees and costs:		
Officer statutory fee	________	
Publication charges	________	
Other (describe) ________________________	________	
Category subtotal:		$ ________
Total due holder of the evidence of debt		
Bid	$ ________	
Deficiency	$ ________	

I enclose herewith the following:

1. Order authorizing sale.
2. Check (if applicable) to your order in the sum of $________ covering the balance of your fees and costs.
3. Other: ______________________________.

Please send us the following:

1. Promissory note with the deficiency, if any, noted thereon
2. Refund for overpayment of officer's fees and costs, if any
3. Other: ______________________________.

Name of the holder of the evidence of debt
and the attorney for the holder:
Holder: ______________________________
Attorney: ______________________________
By: ______________________________
Attorney registration number: ____________
Attorney address: ______________________
Attorney business telephone: ____________

(3) Upon receipt of the initial bid from the holder of the evidence of debt or the attorney for the holder, the officer shall make such information available to the general public.

(4) The officer shall enter the bid by reading the bid amount set forth on the bid and the name of the person that submitted the bid or by posting or providing such bid information at the time and place designated for sale.

(5) Bids submitted pursuant to this section may be amended by the holder of the evidence of debt or the attorney for the holder in writing or electronically, as determined by the officer pursuant to section 38-38-112, no later than 12 noon the day prior to the sale, or orally at the time of sale if the person amending the bid is physically present at the sale. A bid submitted pursuant to this section may be modified orally at the time of sale if the person making the modification modifies and reexecutes the bid at the sale.

(6) The holder of the evidence of debt or the attorney for the holder shall bid at least the holder's good faith estimate of the fair market value of the property being sold, less the amount of unpaid real property taxes and all amounts secured by liens against the property being sold that are senior to the deed of trust or other lien being foreclosed and less the estimated reasonable costs and expenses of holding, marketing, and selling the property, net of income received; except that the holder or the attorney for the holder need not bid more than the total amount due to the holder as specified in the bid pursuant to subsection (2) of this section. The failure of the holder to bid the amount required by this subsection (6) shall not affect the validity of the sale but may be raised as a defense by any person sued on a deficiency.

(7) (a) Other than a bid by the holder of the evidence of debt not exceeding the total amount due shown on the bid pursuant to subsection (2) of this section, the payment of any bid amount at sale must be received by the officer no later than the date and time of the sale, or at an alternative time after the sale and on the day of the sale, as specified in writing by the officer. The payment shall be in the form specified in section 38-37-108. If the officer has not received full payment of the bid amount from the highest bidder at the sale pursuant to this subsection (7), the next highest bidder who has timely tendered the full amount of the bid under this subsection (7) shall be deemed the successful bidder at the sale.

(b) The officer may establish written policies relating to all aspects of the foreclosure sale that are consistent with the provisions of this article. The written policies shall be made available to the general public.

V. Master Form Mortgage or Deed of Trust

A. Master Form of Mortgage or Deed of Trust

Effective July 1, 2001, § 38-35-109(1.5), C.R.S., enables a master form of mortgage or deed of trust. The purpose of this law is to shorten the actual deed of trust, by recording the "master form" and then simply referring to the recorded provisions in the actual transaction instruments. Subsection (1.5) reads:

(a) Any person may record in the office of the county clerk and recorder of any county a master form mortgage or master form deed of trust. Such forms shall be entitled to recordation without any acknowledgement or signature; without identification of any specific real property; and without naming any specific mortgagor, mortgagee, trustor, beneficiary or trustee. Every instrument shall contain on the face of the document "master form recorded by (name of person causing instrument to be recorded)." The county clerk and recorder shall index such master forms in the grantee index under the name of the person causing it to be recorded.

(b) (I) Any of the provisions of such master form instrument may be incorporated by reference in any mortgage or deed of trust encumbering real estate situated within the state, if such reference in the mortgage or deed of trust states the following:

(A) That the master form instrument was recorded in the county in which the mortgage or deed of trust is offered for record;

(B) The date when recorded and the book or page or pages or reception or index number where such master form was recorded;

(C) That a copy of the provisions of the master form instrument was furnished to the person executing the mortgage or deed of trust; and

(D) If fewer than all of the provisions of the referenced master form are being adopted or incorporated, a statement identifying by paragraph, section, or other specification method that will clearly identify the incorporated provision or provisions, if in the absence of a specific designation, the entire referenced master form will be deemed to be incorporated.

(II) The recording of any mortgage or deed of trust, which has incorporated by reference any of the provisions of a master form as provided in this section, shall have the same effect as if such provisions of such master form had been set forth fully in the mortgage or deed of trust.

B. Acknowledged and Recorded for the Protection

Deeds of trust and mortgages, and all other instruments affecting real property, should be acknowledged and recorded for the protection of the holder of the interest. C.R.S. Section 38-35-109(1), C.R.S., states:

> All deeds, powers of attorney, agreements or other instruments in writing conveying, encumbering or affecting the title to real property, certificates and certified copies of orders, judgments and decrees of courts of record may be recorded in the office of the county clerk and recorder of the county where such real property is situated, except that all instruments conveying the title of real property to the state or a political subdivision shall be recorded pursuant to section 38-35-109.5. No such unrecorded instrument or document shall be valid against any person with any kind of rights in or to such real property who first records and those holding rights under such person, except between the parties thereto and against those having notice thereof prior to acquisition of such rights. This is a race-notice recording statute. In all cases where by law an instrument may be filed in the office of a county clerk and recorder, the filing thereof in such office shall be equivalent to the recording thereof, and the recording thereof in the office of such county clerk and recorder shall be equivalent to the filing thereof.

A subsequent innocent purchaser or encumbrancer with no actual knowledge of a prior unrecorded claim will be given a superior right. Unacknowledged recorded instruments constitute notice to subsequent purchasers or encumbrancers. But unless they have been of record for the required ten years, they may not be introduced as evidence until their validity is proven.

VI. Usual Elements of a Deed of Trust or Mortgage

The following list serves only as a reference to the usual elements of a deed of trust or mortgage. A competent attorney or other person with considerable experience in these matters should carefully check these instruments, because many varied and complex details must be adjusted to fit each particular case.

1. **Date.** Though not essential, inclusion of the date might prevent later controversy as to when the security interest was conveyed.

2. **Parties.** All parties to a mortgage or trust deed must be named and clearly designated. In a mortgage, they are the mortgagor (grantor) and mortgagee (grantee). In a deed of

trust, they are the trustor (grantor), public trustee and beneficiary. The name of the grantor must be exactly the same as on the deed by which the grantor acquired title.

3. **Consideration.** Consideration is the money loaned to the trustor or mortgagor, usually to assist in purchasing the property. The statement regarding the consideration should contain the following:
   a. Description of the indebtedness;
   b. Amount;
   c. Maturity date;
   d. Method of repayment of the principal amount;
   e. Interest rate and time of payment;
   f. Interest coupon notes, if any; and
   g. Conditions of default as to principal and interest.
4. **Words of Conveyance.** The words of conveyance should be "*does hereby convey to*" or something similar. This gives the trustee or mortgagee an interest in the property that will serve as security.
5. **Legal Description.** This is necessary to identify the real estate subject to the security interest. This description should read the same as that contained in the deed by which title is transferred.
6. **Conditions (trust deed) or Covenants (mortgage).** Usually contains requirements such as keeping the property insured, paying taxes and assessments, and maintaining improvements in good repair. See more conditions in the next section.
7. **Method of sale in case of default.** The beneficiary of a trust deed may foreclose by public sale through the office of the public trustee or through the courts. In Colorado, the mortgagee or beneficiary of a private trust deed may foreclose only through the courts.
8. **Exceptions as to prior liens, if any.**
9. **Signature of the trustor/mortgagor.**
10. **Acknowledgment.** Signing before a notary public is the simplest means of establishing the instrument's proper execution and validity.
11. **Recording.** Recording in the office of the county clerk and recorder of the county in which the property is situated is necessary to protect the interest of the beneficiary or mortgagee against the claim of persons who may thereafter acquire an interest in the property without actual notice of the mortgage or trust deed.

In addition to the above, the following elements may be contained in the mortgage or trust deed:

1. Provision for a higher rate of interest in all notes after maturity;
2. An acceleration clause, which provides that a default continuing more than a specified time gives the holder of the indebtedness the right to declare all indebtedness to be due and payable immediately without notice;
3. A waiver of homestead rights;

4. A reservation of the right to pay taxes if they remain unpaid when due, adding the amount so paid together with interest at a specified rate to the principal sum;
5. A requirement that the property be insured in companies acceptable to the holder of the indebtedness and the standard mortgage clause added to these policies. If the grantor fails to so insure, the grantee should be given the right to insure, adding the cost together with interest at a specified rate to the indebtedness;
6. Provision for the appointment of a receiver upon the occurrence of a default;
7. In case of a foreclosure or a trustee's sale, provision for:
   a. All the costs of such suits, advertising, sale, and conveyance, including attorneys, solicitors, stenographers, trustee's fees, outlays for documentary evidence, and costs of abstract and examination of title.
   b. All monies advanced by the holders of the indebtedness with interest thereupon from the time the advances were made.
   c. The accrued interest remaining unpaid on the indebtedness.
   d. All of the principal money remaining unpaid.
8. In the case of trust deeds, provision for a reconveyance of the property by the trustee to the grantor, upon the payment of the principal and interest and the performance of the covenants and agreements contained in the instrument; or
9. In a case where a private trustee is used, a provision for a successor in trust in case of the trustee's inability to act.

VII. Assumption of Indebtedness

A buyer and seller may wish to transfer title with the existing loan remaining as a lien upon the property. This is accomplished by a provision in the contract whereby the buyer assumes and agrees to pay the existing indebtedness.

However, assumption is subject to limitations that may be present in the mortgage or trust deed contract. Mortgages and trust deeds often contain a provision to the effect that if the subject property is conveyed, the entire balance of the loan becomes due (strict due-on-sale). This has the same effect as an acceleration clause in the event of default.

The above restriction may alternatively preclude conveyance without the lender's consent (due-on-sale). This enables the lender to adjust (usually upwards) the interest rate or other terms of the loan. If conveyance is made without the lender's consent, the lender may call the entire balance of the loan due.

VIII. Section 38-30-165, C.R.S., Limit on Interest Rate Increase

Section 38-30-165, C.R.S., limits interest rate increases on an assumption to one percent per annum above the existing interest rate on the indebtedness for trust deeds executed on or after July 1, 1975. On October 15, 1982, a new federal law preempted all state laws in this area. Lenders may now enforce a due-on-sale clause no matter when the mortgage or trust deed was executed.

Lenders need not necessarily have a due-on-sale provision in their trust deeds or mortgages. The Real Estate Commission has approved three types of trust deeds for mandatory use by licensees when preparing deeds of trust on behalf of their principals. One contains a strict due-on-sale clause. The second contains a modified due-on-sale clause, which makes the loan assumable if the purchaser is creditworthy. The third type of trust deed contains no due-on-sale clause, and the loan is fully assumable.

IX. The Promissory Note

In the real estate financing process, the principal promissory note or bond is the evidence of the debt for which the mortgage or deed of trust is the security. This note is an unconditional promise in writing, signed by the maker, agreeing to pay on demand or at some future time, a certain sum of money to the payee or bearer. A promissory note creates a personal liability on the part of the maker. In the event of a default, if the security is insufficient to cover the indebtedness, the holder of the note may obtain a deficiency judgment for the balance due and proceed against all other property and assets of the debtor.

The holder of a note secured by the mortgage or trust deed may sell or transfer the note to another. If the note is secured by a deed of trust, the holder simply endorses the note over to the successor holder. No separate transfer instrument is necessary. But if the note is secured by a mortgage, in addition to the endorsement of the note, the mortgage should also be separately assigned in writing to the new holder and the assignment should be recorded.

The reason for recording an assignment of a mortgage but not a deed of trust is to better preserve an unbroken chain of title. Unless default occurs in the payment of the note, a release or satisfaction of the security instrument will eventually be executed. In the instance of a deed of trust, the release is executed by the public trustee, who remains the same no matter how many times the note may have changed hands. In a mortgage, the current legal holder of the note, who would have changed each time the note was transferred, will execute the release instrument. A recorded assignment of a mortgage to each new note-holder gives constructive notice of the person who must execute the release thereof.

X. Second Mortgage or Trust Deed

An owner of real property encumbered by a deed of trust or mortgage may secure a second loan, secured by a second trust deed or mortgage. A second trust deed stands in a subordinate position to the first as to priority of lien claim in case of a foreclosure. The recording date of the first deed of trust before the recording of the second legally establishes the priorities of right. If the first trust deed was unrecorded but the holder of the second had actual knowledge of the existence of the first at the time of the second transaction, the first trust deed would still have priority.

When the first deed of trust is satisfied, subsequent encumbrances move upward in priority. The second trust deed would then become first in priority, the third becomes second, and so on. However, the priority of instruments may be controlled by their terms. For instance, the terms of a second deed of trust may allow its lien to continue to be subordinate to the existing first, or any substitution thereof, thus allowing the owner to replace the first deed of trust with another without disturbing the position of the lien holders below the first. This advantage is often very important to the grantor in matters pertaining to refinancing property.

XI. Installment Land Contract

* An installment land contract (ILC, or sometimes called a bond for title or a long-term escrow) is essentially another type of security instrument. A typical installment land contract provides for all the terms usually found in a buy-sell contract, but withholds a warranty deed transferring (legal) title until the full or some part of the purchase price has been paid. ILCs should be recorded. The buyer takes possession and assumes all the risks and responsibilities of ownership. The buyer covenants to insure, repair, pay taxes and assessments, etc., of the property for the benefit of the seller. The buyer is considered to have an equitable interest in the land in much the same way as a mortgagor. See the topic index in the back of this manual for more information on installment land contracts.

* A purchaser under an installment land contract has the right of entry and possession, but if there are no improvements on the land that can be physically occupied, there is no actual notice of the purchaser's interest given to the public. Some subdividers have sold vacant land by means of installment land contracts. Although it is advisable that all installment land contracts be recorded, it is especially important to record if the land is vacant.

* An ILC should contain an escrow provision whereby a copy of the contract and a warranty deed from the seller to the purchaser are delivered to an escrow agent. Upon performance of the covenants in the contract by the purchaser, the escrow agent would then deliver the warranty deed. This type of contract is but another security device that can be used in the financing of real estate. An installment land contract must also contain other provisions required by statute and other customary provisions. There is no standard form of installment land contract approved by the Commission. The Commission revoked its approval of the installment land contract long ago.

* Commission Position 39 cautions:

> "There is a significant potential for harm to the seller, buyer or assignee if the installment land contract is not properly drafted. Real estate brokers are prohibited from drafting a contract document that would reflect the terms of such a transaction as it would exceed their level of competency and is a matter requiring the expertise and advice of an attorney. Additionally, such behavior may be construed as the unauthorized practice of law by the real estate broker and subject to civil penalties. The contracts for these transactions should not be prepared by a real estate broker; rather, the documents should be drafted by a licensed Colorado attorney-at-law engaged for each particular transaction."

XII. Liens

A. Introduction

A lien is a right given by law to a creditor to have a debt or charge satisfied out of the property belonging to the debtor. For the purpose of convenience, liens may be classified as either specific or general. A "**specific lien**" attaches to and affects only a certain piece(s) of property, such as a mortgage, property tax, assessment, mechanics' lien, vendee's lien, vendor's lien, or an attachment. A "**general lien**" may attach to and affect all the property of the debtor, *e.g.*, a judgment lien, federal or state tax lien, or a lien for a decedent's debts.

B. Specific Liens

Mortgage

A mortgage secures or guarantees payment of the amount due to the lender or creditor by conditionally transferring an interest in the property to the lender. A mortgage is specific to one property. The lien becomes null and void upon the payment of the debt.

Taxes and assessments

Property taxes, special assessments, and water and sewer charges levied by law rather than usage become a specific lien on specific real property to which they pertain. The taxing body, usually the city or county, may take action resulting in the sale of the property if these charges are not paid.

Property subject to general ad valorem property tax is assessed on January 1 each year for the previous year, and a lien for the tax attaches on the same day. Property taxes are a perpetual lien upon the real estate until paid (including penalties, charges, and interest that may accrue). Property tax liens have priority over all other liens, regardless of filing date.

Real property taxes may be paid as follows: one-half on or before the last day of February, and the remaining one-half on or before June 15, or the entire tax may be paid on or before the last day of April. (See § 39-10-104.5, C.R.S.)

As soon as the first one-half installment becomes delinquent (*i.e.*, March 1), interest penalty accrues until the date of payment; except that, if the first installment is made after the last day of February, but not later than 30 days after the mailing by the treasurer of the tax statement pursuant to § 39-10-103(l)(a), C.R.S., no such delinquent interest shall accrue. For the single-payment option, interest accrues as of May 1. On June 16, all unpaid taxes of the preceding year become delinquent, and an interest penalty will be assessed in addition to any previous penalty that has accrued. (See § 39-10-104.5(3)(a), C.R.S.)

When an instrument of conveyance does not' specify who will pay the current year taxes, the grantee pays if the conveyance is made before July 1, and the grantor is responsible for paying if the conveyance is after June 30. (See § 39-1-108, C.R.S.) Proper real estate practice would have the instrument of conveyance contain a provision for apportionment of the taxes to the date of transfer.

The following various authorities determine the property tax:

a. The "**county assessor**," publicly elected in 62 counties (and appointed in the City and County of Denver), determines the assessed valuation of the property. The valuation for assessment of all taxable residential property is determined by statute and is 9.35 percent of its actual value and 29 percent for commercial and raw land. (See §§ 39-1-104 and -104.2(3)(h), C.R.S.)

b. An elected "**board of county commissioners**" (except in the City and County of Denver, where the authorized body is created by the city charter) determines the "**mill levy**," which is a fractional part of the assessed valuation. A "mill" is one-thousandth of a dollar. Eighty-five mills may be expressed as a fraction of a dollar ($.085), both of which equate to $85 of tax for each $1,000 of assessed valuation. This levy is made no later than November 15 each year.

c. A county "**board of equalization**," (except for the City and County of Denver) is composed of the above county commissioners, who become the board of equalization from the second Monday in July until the last working day of July each year. In this capacity, they review the assessor-prepared roll of all taxable property located in the county, and hear appeals from protests filed with the county assessor. If an owner is dissatisfied with the decision of the county board of equalization, the owner may within 30 days:

   (i) Appeal to the county commissioners for binding arbitration. An arbitrated decision will be final and not subject to review;

   (ii) Appeal to the (state) board of assessment appeals. When a decision of the board of assessment appeals is adverse to an owner, the owner has 30 days in which to appeal to the state court of appcals; or

   (iii) Appeal to the district court in which the property is located. When a court decision is adverse to an owner, the owner has 45 days in which to appeal to the state court of appeals.

d. The three-member quasi-judicial "**board of assessment appeals**" hears appeals concerning local property tax assessments, utilities assessments, and decisions of the property tax administrator. (See § 39-2-123, C.R.S.)

e. The division of property taxation reviews the methods used by the county assessors and the county boards of equalization, and examines where it is alleged in writing that property has not been properly appraised or valued. It also conducts an annual school for assessors.

f. The "**state board of equalization**" consists of the governor, speaker of the house of representatives (or designee), president of the senate (or designee), and two members appointed by the governor with the consent of the senate. The two appointed members must be qualified appraisers or former assessors, or have knowledge and experience in property taxation. The board meets each year on the second Monday in September to determine if each county has assessed at the percentage of actual value prescribed by law. The board can act only on classes and subclasses of property and not on individual assessments. The board may also meet at the governor's call.

Before the first day of September of each year, county treasurers notify delinquent taxpayers by mail of the amount of delinquency and penalty interest thereon and afford 15 days from the time of mailing the said notice to pay the tax. Treasurers then make a list of all the county lands with delinquent taxes, publish the list, and designate the date for public sale. If such a list is made later than September 1, a sale held under that list is still valid. (See § 39-11-101, C.R.S.)

Delinquent tax sales commence on or before the second Monday in December of each year and are held at the treasurer's office in each county. (See § 39-11-109, C.R.S.) Such property is "sold" to the person who pays the delinquent taxes, penalty interest, and costs due, and who further pays the highest bid over these amounts in cash.

The owner (or agent or assignee) may redeem real property sold for taxes at any time before the issuance of a treasurer's deed. The person redeeming must pay to the county treasurer the amount for which the property was sold together with interest from the date of sale. (See § 39-12-103, C.R.S.)

The county treasurer issues a certificate of purchase to the high bidder at the tax sale. A certificate of purchase is assignable, and if the property has not been redeemed, the certificate holder may request the treasurer to give notice of the sale to every person in actual possession or occupancy of the property, to the person in whose name the property was taxed, and to publish such notice. After notice and publication, the treasurer will issue a treasurer's deed to the holder of a certificate of purchase. (See §§ 39-11-117 and 39-12-105, C.R.S.)

After a treasurer's deed is issued, executed, delivered, and recorded, it is presumed to be validly acknowledged. After the deed has been recorded for five years, (nine years if the delinquent owner is legally disabled at the time the deed was issued), the delinquent taxpayer has no legal course by which to recover the land. A holder of a treasurer's deed may initiate a "**quiet title**" suit in order to acquire merchantable title before the expiration of the five- or nine-year period. (See §§ 39-12-101 and -104, C.R.S.)

Special improvements are assessed in proportion to the benefits to the real estate, as determined by the ordering authority. Such assessments are a perpetual lien against the land and have priority over all liens except property tax liens. Special assessments for local improvements are due and payable within 30 days after final publication of the assessing ordinance, although it is common for special assessments to permit an owner to pay by installments with interest. The number of installments, the period of payment, and the rate of interest are determined by the ordering authority and set forth in the assessing ordinance. In case of default in the payment of any installment, the county treasurer may sell the property in the same manner, and with the same effect as provided for in the sale of real estate in default of payment of the general property taxes. (See §§ 31-25-501, *et seq.*, C.R.S.)

Mechanics' lien

Mechanics, material suppliers, contractors, subcontractors, builders, and all other persons rendering professional or skilled service, performing labor upon, or furnishing materials used in the construction, alteration, or repair of any structure or improvement upon land are given a lien upon the property. Mechanics' liens are all effective as of the time the work first commenced and are superior to all subsequently filed or unrecorded liens or encumbrances of which the lienor had no actual knowledge. The order of priority among different mechanic lien claimants is:

1. First, liens of laborers or mechanics working by the day or piece;
2. Second, liens of all other subcontractors or suppliers whose claims are either entirely or principally for materials; and
3. Third, liens of all other principal contractors.

In order to preserve a lien for work performed or materials furnished, a lienor must serve the property owner (or agent) and principal contractor with notice of intent to file a lien at least 10 days before recording the lien statement. The lienor must serve this notice personally or by registered or certified mail. (See § 38-22-109(3), C.R.S.)

Lienors in the first class must file with the county clerk and recorder within two months after completion of the improvement. Lien statements of the second and third class must be filed within four months after completion of the work. (See §§ 38-22-109(4) and (5), C.R.S.)

No mechanics' lien shall hold a property longer than six months after the last work is performed or materials furnished, or completion of the improvement unless a lawsuit is brought within that time to enforce the lien and, unless a notice stating that such action has been commenced, shall have been recorded within that time in the county clerk and recorder's office. (See § 38-22-110, C.R.S.)

The purchaser of a single- or-double family dwelling is given some protection against hidden liens. No lien may encumber such property unless the purchaser had actual knowledge of unpaid lien claimants at the time of conveyance, or unless a lien statement or notice had been recorded within one month after completion of the work or prior to the conveyance, whichever is later. (See § 38-22-125, C.R.S.)

The "**disburser**" (usually the lender or owner) who distributes partial payments as mechanics' work progresses must record a notice stating the name and address of the owner, the principal contractor, if any, the disburser, and the legal description of the land. Lien claimants may give the disburser written notice that they are contracting on matters that may affect the property. Upon such notice being received, the disburser must pay the claimant before paying the claimant's contractor. If the disburser fails to do this and the claimant suffers loss, the disburser is personally liable. (See §§ 38-22-126(4), (5), (6), and (7), C.R.S.)

Funds disbursed to a contractor in accordance with a contract are declared to be in trust for the payment of subcontractors, material suppliers, and laborers. Except for good faith differences of opinion or the existence of performance bonds, wrongful expenditure of these funds constitutes the crime of theft. (See §§ 38-22-127(1) and (5), C.R.S.)

Vendee's lien

If a seller (vendor) defaults in performing the contract, a purchaser (vendee) has a lien against the property for return of all money paid under the terms of the sales agreement. This is an equitable lien and is enforceable by foreclosure.

Vendor's lien

If a seller does not receive the entire sum agreed upon from the buyer, the seller has a lien against the property for any unpaid balance. Like the vendee's lien, this is an equitable charge and is enforceable by foreclosure.

Attachment

An attachment is an encumbrance on property of a defendant in a pending lawsuit for money damages. Colorado and most states permit issuance of a writ of attachment only under special circumstances, such as when the defendant goes into hiding or is about to fraudulently convey or transfer the property. A plaintiff obtaining an attachment must file a bond to protect the defendant against any loss caused by the attachment in the event the plaintiff loses the case.

Lis Pendens

A "**lis pendens**" is not technically a lien upon property; it is constructive notice that a claim against the property exists, and persons could take title to the property only subject to the outcome of the lawsuit. By filing a lis pendens a few days before the expiration of one's lien, a mechanics' lien claimant can keep the lien alive beyond six months.

Fraudulent liens

In some cases, persons have filed liens for false or groundless claims. Although they have no legal effect, such liens can tie up a property being sold and cause legal expense before being declared invalid. Today, any person filing such a claim is civilly liable to the owner of the real property for not less than $1,000 or actual damages caused. In addition, the person commits a misdemeanor punishable by up to two years' imprisonment or a $5,000 fine, or both. (See Commission Position Statement CP-25 in Chapter 3 regarding recording contracts and real estate licensees' lien status.)

C. General Liens

Judgments

A judgment results from the determination of the rights of the parties through an action at law. Not all judgments involve monetary awards, but a monetary judgment awarded to a plaintiff may become a lien upon the defendant's real property. Some states provide that a judgment must be entered into the judgment docket and indexed before a lien is created. Other states require that a judgment must be recorded in the county recorder's office before the lien becomes effective. Colorado law provides that the judgment lien attaches when the transcript of the docket entry of the judgment, certified by the clerk of the court, is filed (for recording) in the office of the county clerk and recorder. The judgment then becomes a lien on all of the defendant's current or future real property located in that county. The judgment may be filed in any county in the state where the defendant owns property, and the lien thus created continues for six years from the entry of said judgment in the judgment docket. (See § 13-52-102(1), C.R.S.)

Federal tax liens

Federal tax liens may attach to real property because of violation of federal income tax laws, non-payment of gift taxes, or because of the transfer of the real estate through the owner's death.

When a taxpayer is delinquent in the payment of federal income tax, the government may issue a tax warrant that, when filed in the county wherein the taxpayer's real property is located, becomes a lien upon the real estate. Many people believe federal tax liens to have some high priority, but they are only prioritized among other liens or encumbrances by date filed.

Federal government liens for gift taxes are a lien against gift property and continue for ten years. This lien, too, is subordinate to all prior filed liens and encumbrances upon the property.

A federal inheritance or estate tax becomes a lien upon all personal and real property of the decedent. It continues for ten years and stands in priority by date filed.

State tax liens

Like the federal government, Colorado may also acquire liens against real property for the non-payment of state income taxes. A lien for delinquent state income tax becomes a lien upon the taxpayer's real property. This lien priority is established by date of filing and continues for six years unless paid.

Decedent's debts

A decedent's real property passes upon death to the devisees named in a will or if he or she dies intestate (*i.e.*, without a will) according to state laws of descent and distribution. The devisee or heir at law takes title to the property subject to existing liens or encumbrances, and to rights of creditors of the estate. Debts against the estate are paid first out of personal property not specifically bequeathed, then from that which is specifically bequeathed. If the personalty is insufficient to satisfy all debts, then the real property may be sold to pay the remaining debts. Thus, title to a decedent's real estate may be subject to a lien in favor of creditors of the estate.

Chapter 18:
Closing Statements

An * in the left margin indicates a change in the statute, rule, or text since the last publication of the manual.

I. Introduction

A real estate closing, or settlement, is the formal procedure by which title passes from seller to buyer and a final accounting is given for all funds received or paid. Closing procedures vary from state to state and even within state borders. In Colorado, title companies normally conduct closings. Real estate brokers, attorneys, or independent closing agents may also conduct closings.

The closing is created through the Contract to Buy and Sell, with the majority of the closing terms determined from the negotiations of the buyer and seller. The contract, along with title documents, a tax certificate, and lender loan documents make up the pieces the closer will use to create the "Closing Statement" for each party. This chapter will cover the rules and requirements for closings and then work through three different closing examples.

II. Rules and Requirements for Closings

A. Responsibility for Closing

The question of who conducts the closing is a contractual matter between the buyer, seller, and closing entity. Although real estate closers are not regulated, Colorado Division of Insurance Regulation 3-5-1 requires that title companies close real estate transactions only pursuant to written instructions. Further, the regulation requires title companies to execute closing instructions approved by the Real Estate Commission if the instructions are executed (signed) by all parties to the real estate transaction and delivered to the title company in advance of the closing and settlement. The Colorado Real Estate Commission-approved Closing Instructions form is required by Rule F-7 when it is appropriate for the broker to prepare instructions. The Contract to Buy and Sell § 4.2 states: "*If Earnest Money Holder is other than the Brokerage Firm identified in § 32 or § 33 below, Closing Instructions signed by Buyer, Seller and Earnest Money Holder must be obtained on or before delivery of Earnest Money to Earnest Money Holder.*" Listing brokers and brokerage firms using title companies to hold earnest money are required to have a completed Closing Instructions form signed by the buyer and seller prior to depositing the funds with the title company. Brokers using title companies to perform closings should have the completed Closing Instructions form, signed before title deadline, in the closed file regardless of who is holding the earnest money.

While the majority of closings are completed by a title company's closing section, this does not relieve the employed designated broker and that broker's employing broker of the responsibility from verifying that the closing statement is accurate. Real estate brokers are required by Rules E-4 and E-5 to provide copies of complete and accurate closing statements to buyers and sellers for any transaction in which the broker assists or acts in a real estate capacity. The designated listing broker and any designated buyer's broker must carefully review their respective closing statements for accuracy even if they will not conduct the closing. Failure to properly review closing documents could result in charges of incompetence or a breach of the broker's statutory or fiduciary duty.

> E-5. Pursuant to 12-61-113 (l)(h), at time of closing, the individual licensee who has established a brokerage relationship with the buyer or seller or who works with the buyer or seller as a customer, either personally or on behalf of an employing broker, shall be responsible for the proper closing of the transaction and shall provide, sign and be responsible for an accurate, complete and detailed closing statement as it applies to the party with whom the brokerage relationship has been established. If signed by an employed licensee, closing statements shall be delivered to the employing broker immediately following closing. Nothing in this rule shall relieve an employing broker of the responsibility for fulfilling supervisory responsibilities pursuant to 12-61-103 (6) (c), 12-61-113(l) (o), 12-61-118 C.R.S and Rules E-31 and E-32.

A designated broker who attends the closing must sign the Closing Statement and is primarily responsible for providing a proper Closing Statement to the party the broker assisted or represented. A broker associate must deliver a copy of the statement to the employing broker immediately after the closing.

If the designated broker is unable to attend a closing, the employing broker may designate another broker to attend, in which case both designated brokers assume joint responsibility for the accuracy of the closing statements. The employing broker is responsible for the supervision of both brokers, which gives all three brokers responsibility for an accurate closing. (See Rule E-5(e).)

B. Preparation of Legal Documents

Although buyers and sellers may be charged a fee for closing, no fee may be charged for preparation of legal documents, except by an attorney representing the buyer or seller. The *Conway-Bogue* decision granted real estate brokers the right to prepare certain legal documents, but prohibits licensees from charging a separate fee for such service. The companion *Title Guaranty* case specifically prohibits title companies from preparing legal documents. Today, title companies only fill in blanks on legal documents under explicit instructions from the broker responsible for the closing. The listing broker who is responsible for completing the deed, bill of sale, and any notes and deeds of trust called for in the contract uses the second section of the Closing Instructions form to hire the title company as scrivener to complete the legal forms. The listing broker will be responsible for paying for all legal documents and for their accuracy. (See CP-7, Commission Position on Closing Costs.)

C. Good Funds

In Colorado, on the settlement date all parties, including the broker, buyer, lender, and sometimes the seller, must furnish good funds for amounts due. No disbursements may be made until all funds are available for immediate withdrawal as "**good funds**" in accordance with § 38-35-125, C.R.S. Disbursements from closing may be made only after the closing entity has received good funds. Good funds are considered to be electronically transferred funds; certified, cashier's, or teller's checks; and other funds that are either received in sufficient time prior to closing to be eligible for immediate withdrawal or are guaranteed by the depository on which they are drawn. (Note: cash is not considered to be good funds under this statute.)

D. Closing Statements (SS 60-9-08) (Formerly called Settlement Statements)

The required Closing Statements (SS 60-9-08) provided to the seller and buyer reflects only that party's credits and debits. Dates of adjustments, names of payees of notes, etc., are shown on the final Closing Statement. Each Closing Statement must be prepared in conformance with Commission Rules E-4 and 5.

E. Signing the Closing Statement

The broker(s) attending the closing must sign and secure the signed approval and acceptance of the buyer and the seller on a copy of their respective closing statements for their own protection and for future inspection by the Real Estate Commission. Original signatures are not required on the copies retained in the office transaction file per § 24-71-101(1), C.R.S. Copies of signed statements satisfy the record retention requirement.

F. Broker Closing Records

The employing or independent broker must retain copies of the pertinent documents listed under "Transaction Files and the Retention of Records" in Chapter 19, "Escrow Records," for four years.

G. Escrow Tax Reserve Account Refunds

The tax reserve has no relationship to the proration of the current year's taxes; the reserve is the amount the lender is collecting from the buyer to pay the property taxes in the future when the bill comes due. This reserve is based on the lender's loan requirement and state law, § 39-1-119, C.R.S. This law provides that any amount held on May 20 in excess of 3/12 of the taxes paid that year must be refunded to the borrower on or before May 30. Payments to a reserve escrow account must be adjusted annually upon reasonable belief of substantial improvements to the property or upon official notification of an increase in the actual amount of taxes levied. Failure to make a refund is subject to interest and penalty.

H. Internal Revenue Service Reporting – Real Estate Sales

Generally, a transaction that consists in whole or in part of a *sale or exchange* for money, indebtedness, property, or services, or any present or future ownership interest must be reported to the IRS on Form 1099-S. This includes many real estate transactions.

However, there are several general exemptions from required 1099-S reporting. One of the most common is the sale or exchange of a "**principal residence**," including stock ownership in a cooperative housing corporation, for $250,000 or less ($500,000 or less for married persons), and the person responsible for closing the transaction receives an acceptable **"Written Assurance Certification"** in the form prescribed by Rev. Proc. 98-20, 1998-1 C.B. 549. Further information, instructions, and forms should be obtained from professional legal counsel. IRS materials may be obtained from www.irs.gov.

I. Certain Cash Transactions

In general, each person engaged in a trade or business who, in the course of that trade or business, receives more than $10,000 in "cash" in one transaction or two or more related transactions within 12 months, must file "**Form 8300**" and give a copy to each party named in the form. Voluntary filings may be made for suspicious transactions of similar or lesser amounts. The report must be retained for five years after the date filed, and fines and penalties apply for failing to file required information. This report is not required if the entity or party receiving the funds meets guidelines under the IRS rule. Further information, instructions, and forms should be obtained from professional legal counsel. IRS materials may be obtained from: www.irs.gov.

J. FIRPTA Withholding

Withholding of Tax on Dispositions of United States Real Property Interests

The disposition of a U.S. real property interest by a foreign person (the transferor) is subject to the Foreign Investment in Real Property Tax Act of 1980 (FIRPTA) income tax withholding. FIRPTA authorized the United States to tax foreign persons on dispositions of U.S. real property interests. A disposition means "disposition" for any purpose of the Internal Revenue Code. This includes, but is not limited to, a sale or exchange, liquidation, redemption, gift, and transfers. A U.S. real property interest includes sales of interests in parcels of real property as well as sales of shares in certain U.S. corporations that are considered U.S. real property holding corporations.

Persons purchasing U.S. real property interests (transferee) from foreign persons, certain purchasers' agents, and settlement officers are required to withhold 10 percent of the amount realized (special rules for foreign corporations). Withholding is intended to ensure U.S. taxation of gains realized on disposition of such interests. The transferee/buyer is the withholding agent. If you are the transferee/buyer, you must find out if the transferor is a foreign person. If the transferor is a foreign person and you fail to withhold, you may be held liable for the tax. For cases in which a U.S. business entity such as a corporation or partnership disposes of a U.S. real property interest, the business entity itself is the withholding agent. For more information, see: www.irs.gov/businesses/small/international/article/0,,id=105000,00.html.

K. Nonresident of Colorado Withholding

Colorado law calls for a possible withholding of potential income tax from the gain on the sale of a property sold by non-Colorado residents. The seller is subject to withholding tax if the seller lives or will live outside of Colorado and the sales price is greater than $100,000. There are several exemptions from this requirement, the primary being the sale of a principal residence that has no withholding . The amount of tax to be withheld is the lower of 2% of the sales price or the seller's entire net proceeds, the balance due the seller. It is the responsibility of the closing entity to collect and send the tax to the Colorado Department of Revenue. The closing entity can be a real estate broker, an attorney, or the closing company. The text of the law (§ 39-22-604.5, C.R.S.) is printed in Chapter 23, "Tax Factors Pertaining to Real Estate Practice," or by statute number at www.revenue.state.co.us/.

L. Real Estate Settlement Procedures Act (RESPA)

Federal law places certain requirements on lenders concerning to closing real estate transactions and related matters. The Real Estate Settlement Procedures Act (RESPA) is administered by the Department of Housing and Urban Development (HUD). Almost all lenders that make first-lien loans on one-to-four family units, including condominiums, cooperative units, and mobile homes, are subject to RESPA. Construction loans are not covered.

RESPA requires lenders to provide the applicant, at the time of the loan application or within three days following, a booklet explaining the costs involved and giving a "good faith estimate" (GFE), showing the loan terms and the settlement charges incurred if they go forward with the loan process and are approved for the loan. It explains which charges can change before settlement and which charges must remain the same. It also contains a shopping chart allowing the borrower to easily compare multiple mortgage loans and settlement costs, making it easier to shop for the best loan. The booklet must also disclose the lender's business relationship with any company that the borrower is required to use in legal services, title insurance, or searches.

In addition, under RESPA, no seller of property may require, directly or indirectly, as a condition of selling the property, that title insurance be purchased by the buyer from any particular title insurance company. The penalty for violation of this provision is a fine of up to three times all charges made for the title insurance.

In the usual Colorado transaction, the seller contracts to pay for the title insurance policy and may therefore select the title company without fear of penalty. The purchase of a mortgagee's title policy does not involve the seller, but rather, the lender imposes this requirement on the borrower. A buyer normally purchases a mortgagee's title policy from the same title company used by the seller because it costs less than buying it from another title company. This may create a problem if the listing broker orders an owner's title insurance policy for the seller and thus indirectly influences the buyer's purchase of the mortgagee's policy from the same company to save money. If the buyer is paying for extended coverage for the owner's policy, the buyer may then also determine the title company to provide the coverage. It may be advisable for brokers to have a buyer designate a title insurance company in the written contract.

The lender or lender's agent must also prepare a Uniform Settlement Sheet prescribed by HUD (HUD Form 1) and may not charge for its preparation. The HUD-1 must be mailed or delivered to the borrower and the seller on the date of settlement, or as soon thereafter as is practicable. The lender must retain a record copy for two years. The borrower has the right to inspect the HUD-1 completed to set forth those items that are known to the settlement agent at the time of inspection during the business day immediately preceding the day of closing. The lender may ask the broker for help in preparing the HUD-1, believing that the broker has easier access to some of the information that must be recorded.

The federal government has not pre-empted the states in the area of closing real estate transactions. Colorado law and Commission rule prevail for Colorado closings. The Commission has found that the lender's duties under RESPA regarding closings are not the equivalent of requirements placed on Colorado licensees. The Commission has presently taken the position that buyers and sellers are better protected under law and rule administered by the Commission concerning closing statements. Therefore, it may not be assumed that lender compliance with RESPA fulfills a broker's obligations concerning Colorado law.

M. Special Taxes

Special assessments, such as street paving, storm sewer improvements, etc., if they were installed at the time of sale, even though not yet assessed, are generally paid by the seller under the terms of the approved contract forms, and are never prorated. The amount of such taxes may be obtained from the county treasurer's office if the improvements are already assessed. The reason for debiting the seller is that the buyer has contracted for clear title other than named exceptions. Special taxes are often amortized and paid in installments with the ongoing ad valorem taxes, and therefore it is not unusual for the buyer to agree by contract to assume the balance of taxes due for special improvements. If special assessments are assumed, notation should be made of the amount assumed in the description column on this line, and no entry in either the debit or credit column. On a new loan, the lender may require that the seller pay special taxes at time of closing.

III. The Closing Process

While real estate brokers may complete all closing documents and hold closings in the broker's office, it is more typical for a title company to perform the task. Most often, the closing is done by the closing section of the title company that is supplying the owner's title policy. Even when using a closing company, the listing broker or brokerage will pay for the legal documents created by the closer. The listing broker and listing brokerage is responsible for the overall closing, with the designated brokers being responsible for the accuracy of the closing statement for the party they represent.

Using the Contract to Buy and Sell and other documents, the closer produces a closing statement for the seller and buyer. This statement will show all the debits and credits of the party and the final balance of money the party is to receive or needs to bring to close the transaction. Typically, the seller receives money from, and the buyer brings money to, the closing. A number of items in the closing are simply debits and credits between the seller and buyer, such as sales price, prorated property taxes, water, and HOA dues. Other items will be deducted from the party who agreed by contract or tradition to pay the bill; this amount will show as a credit to broker or closer to collect the funds to make the payment. It is helpful to think of the broker credit column as credit in equals a check out, as all broker credit items are bills that will need to be paid from the closing proceeds. Typically, it is not the broker but the closer who is paying these bills, but the broker is responsible to verify that all figures are correct. Similarly, the broker debit column can be thought of as debit in equals a deposit to the broker. This column is used to record funds the broker has or is receiving, *e.g.*, earnest money and net loan proceeds.

Credit items for the seller or buyer improve that party's bottom line; credits increase what the seller will receive and decrease what the buyer will bring. Debits are the opposite—a debit decreases what the seller will receive and increases what the buyer will bring. The sales price, for example, is always a seller credit and a buyer debit. If not specified in the contract, a charge will be debited to the party who receives the benefit, or according to government regulation or local custom.

Some items will be prorated, which means split between the parties. These items represent ongoing expenses or income such as taxes, water and sewer, HOA dues, rent, and interest on loans. The item is split between the parties based on the number of days each party owns the property during the billing period.

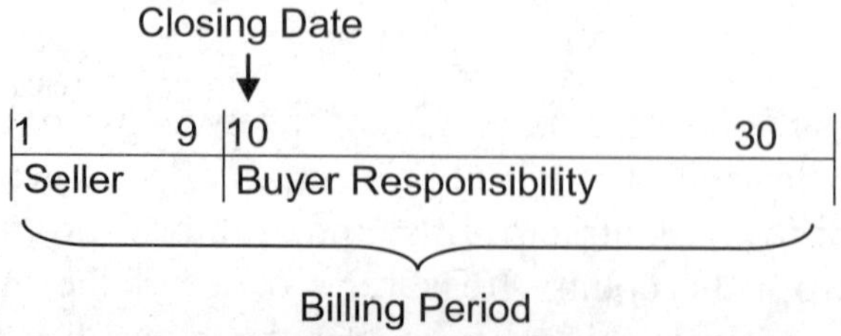

Which party owes the other depends on whether the bill was paid in advance by the seller, or will be paid after closing by the buyer. The illustrations below show how to determine which party will pay in a proration.

Bills Paid in Arrears

Seller owes Buyer: solve the <u>left side</u> of time line

- Paid in arrears by buyer after closing
- Includes items such as: real estate taxes, and interest on most real estate loans

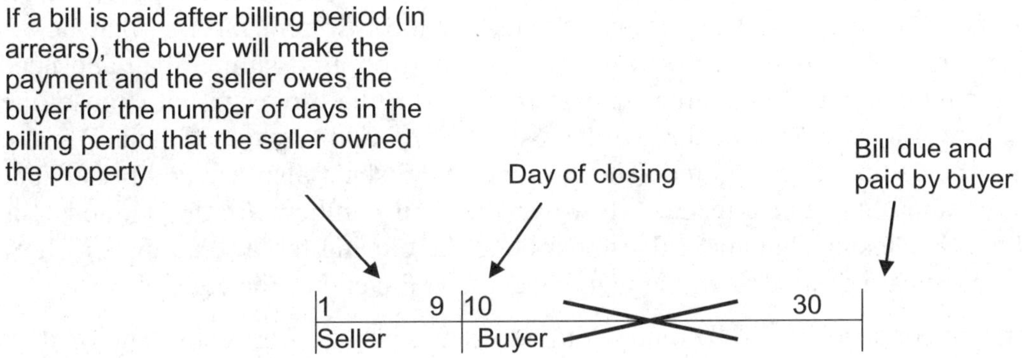

Bills Paid in Advance

Buyer owes Seller: solve the <u>right side</u> of time line

- Paid by seller in advance - before closing (*i.e.*, "prepaid," "paid," "was paid," "has already paid")
- Water and HOA fees are often paid in advance

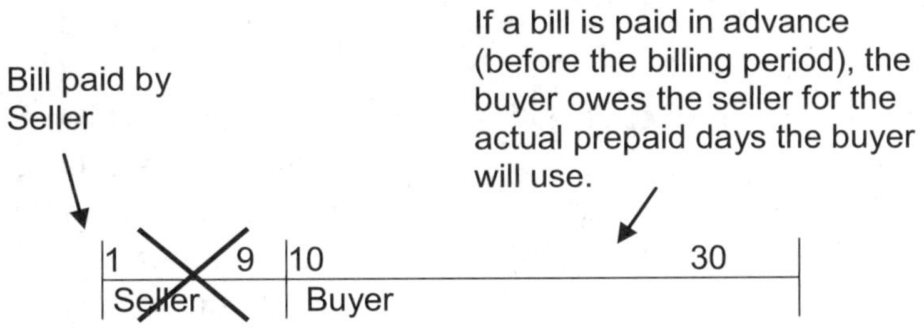

Calculating the Amount owed

The formula for determining the amount of the proration is always the same.

Bill amount ÷ Number of days in billing period * Number of days owed = Amount owed

In the Commission-approved Colorado contract forms, the buyer owns the property all day on the day of closing. On the Colorado portion of the broker licensing examination, all prorations (unless otherwise stated) are based on a 365-day year and/or the actual number of calendar days in the specific month.

IV. Closing Examples

The following examples illustrate preparation of several real estate closing worksheets. While not all encompassing, they illustrate good closing procedures and requirements. The illustrations assume selection of certain options available in the contract forms and are not intended to be all-inclusive. All fees charged and interest rates used in the following illustrations are examples and may only approximate actual market rates. The provisions of the contract govern who pays for certain items and how they are prorated in the settlement.

A broker who is closing in his or her office might use the worksheet (SS61-9-08) to determine what each party's debit and credits are. (Students also use the worksheet to learn how to allocate and balance a closing.) If the title on a line in the worksheet does not match what the broker needs, the broker simply crosses out the title and inserts what he or she needs. For example, if a broker is preparing for a closing on an assumed loan and needs to record the amount of interest the seller will owe the buyer, the broker might choose line 20, **Interest on New Loan,** cross out the words "New Loan," add "Assumed Loan," and enter the amount to be debited and credited. The approved worksheet also has additional space at the end to add other charges as needed. However the final numbers are determined, it is the seller and buyer's Closing Statement that must be at the closing table. Examples of how the Closing Statements are created from the worksheet are at the end of the chapter.

The general concepts of HUD and Colorado settlements, prorations, and real estate mathematics are discussed more fully in generally available real estate texts.

A. Final Settlement with a Seller Carry Loan

The first example is of a simple seller carry transaction. The closing company will be preparing the documents, including a note and deed of trust for the seller. The following paragraphs explain the computation of the charges and credits to each party for this basic transaction, and the worksheet follows. This transaction is then illustrated as a closing when the buyer assumes the seller's existing loan and then with the buyer receiving a new loan.

1. Facts

On April 22, the listing broker secures a written offer from Harold R. and A. Jean Blue with an earnest money deposit of $5,000. The buyers agree to purchase at the listed price of $250,000 if the sellers will accept a note and trust deed in the amount of $200,000. The sellers have requested that the buyer supply them with a mortgagee title policy and a credit report in order to approve the seller carry loan. The seller is also going to collect reserves for the property taxes of five months and hazard insurance of two months because the seller, acting as a lender, will be paying these bills when they come due in the future.

The sellers accepted the offer and authorized the broker to procure a title commitment. The title commitment was delivered to the sellers and buyers and their respective attorneys. The buyers' loan application was approved, by the sellers, in the amount of $200,000 at 7½ percent interest per year, amortized monthly over a period of 30 years. The first payment on the new loan is due on July 1, the first day of the first complete month after the loan closing date. By contract, the buyer is to obtain and pay for an appraisal.

Both the buyers and sellers complete "Closing Instructions" authorizing the closing company to collect all funds and to make all disbursements. The closing is held on May 10.

The following is an explanation of how each item is charged and adjusted on the worksheet. Each numbered item is identically numbered on the worksheet and Closing Statement. Worksheet items not pertinent to this transaction are omitted. Many of the items will carry through all three examples.

It is important to remember that the worksheet and Closing Statements show only money that is coming in and going out at the closing table. This means, most typically, that the buyers will have a credit for a loan they are using to buy the property. If the loan is a seller carry or being assumed from the seller, the seller will have a corresponding debit for the loan amount. The reason in either case is that the seller will not receive that money at the closing table. The seller, if giving the buyer a loan, will receive payments over the agreed period. In the case of an assumption, the loan amount is what the seller still owes and the buyer is taking over. In both cases, the loan amount represents money the seller will not receive at closing.

1. **Selling Price** – $250,000. Credit Seller and Debit Buyer.
2. **Deposit (Earnest Money) Paid** – $5,000. Credit Buyer and Debit Broker. Note that each debit to the Broker is money that the Broker has collected or will collect. A broker credit is money the Broker has paid or will pay out of the escrow account. Think of it as a broker debit is a deposit into the Broker's account, and a broker credit is a check that will be written out of the account.
3. **Principal amount of new Loan Payable to** Seller – $200,000. Credit Buyer (money the buyer does not have to bring to closing, but will be applied to the purchase price). Debit Seller, as this money the Seller will not receive at the closing table.
5. **1st Loan Payoff to**: the Acme Loan Co. – $30,000. Credit Broker/Closer, since the Broker will write the check to pay off the Seller's loan. (In most cases, it is the closing company that is writing the checks.) Debit Seller, because it is the Seller's obligation. In order to determine the amount of the payoff, the Broker/Closer requested a payoff statement from the Acme Loan Co. This statement shows the net balance after adjustments of interest, penalties, and credits the Seller may have in the way of tax or insurance reserves.
7. **Taxes for Preceding Year:** $2,051.30 was paid for the year preceding closing and noted in the left-hand column, but not entered in the debit/credit columns. If not paid, they would be Debit Seller, and in this case, the full amount would be a Credit to Broker, who would pay them because the unpaid taxes would be a lien on the property. On a new loan, the lender would deduct any unpaid prior taxes from the loan and pay them for the same reason.
8. **Taxes for Current Year:** $724.98. This is prorated based on last year's taxes ($2,051.30), per check box in the contract. Property taxes are paid in arrears in Colorado, so the prorated amount will always be a debit to the Seller and a credit to the Buyer. All Commission-approved sales contract forms state that taxes will be prorated to (but not including) the closing date. The Seller owned the property from January 1 through May 9, therefore, Debit Seller 129 days' taxes at $5.620000 per day, and Credit Buyer the same amount. This is an adjustment between the parties and not a broker credit (payment), as the Buyer will pay the current year's taxes when due next year. Prorating is based on the actual 365 (or 366) days in the year.

Line 8: Taxes for Current Year:
Taxes for the preceding year were $2,051.30, and this amount will be used to determine the current year's taxes.

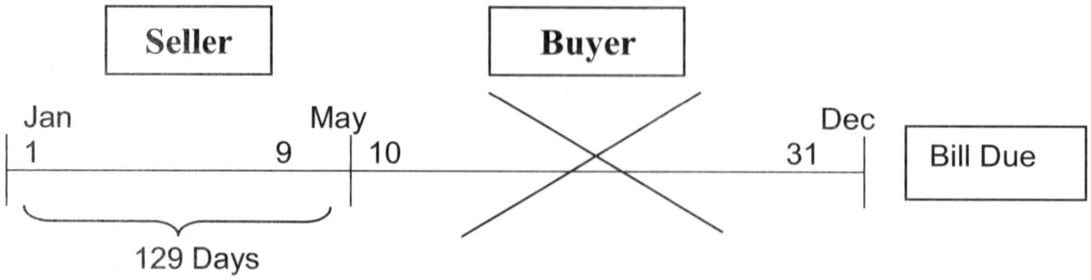

Months	Days (Seller owes)	
Jan.	31	
Feb.	28	$2051.30 ÷ 365 x 129 = $724.98
Mar.	31	
Apr.	30	
May	9	DEBIT Seller, CREDIT Buyer, who will pay in the future
	129	

13. **Appraisal Fee:** $350. The buyer has requested and agreed to pay for the appraisal. The cost of the appraisal, per the contract, can be paid for by either the Seller or Buyer, depending on which box is checked. The amount will be a Debit Buyer and Credit Broker, who will pay the bill.

20. **Interest on New Loan** – $904.11. Because the Buyer's first loan installment will be due July 1 (and will include interest in arrears for all of June but none of May), and the loan starts on May 10, the Buyer will owe the Seller for May 10 through May 31 (22 days), to be paid at closing. Debit Buyer, Credit Seller.

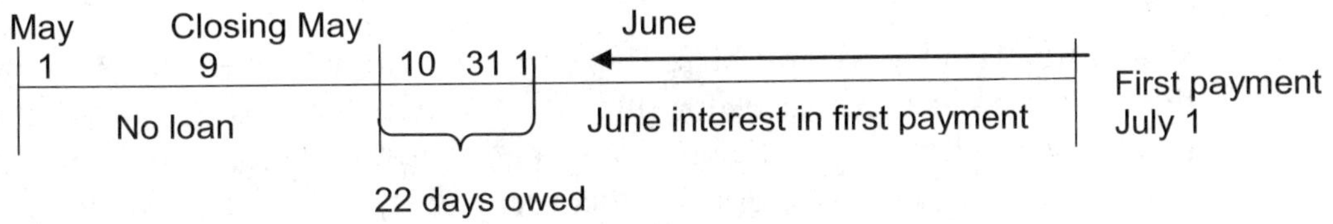

\$200,000 x 7.5% ÷ 365 DAYS = \$41.0959 per day

Interest on the new loan is \$41.0959 x 22 days = \$904.11

22. **Premium for New Hazard Insurance** – \$675.00. The Seller has required a one-year hazard insurance policy to be purchased, and requires the Buyer to pay in full at closing. Debit Buyer, Credit Broker, who will pay the bill.

23. **Reserves Deposited with Lender**

    23 a. **Hazard Insurance Reserve** – \$112.50. The Seller will collect the loan in monthly installments, along with one month's insurance to be held in reserve so that sufficient funds are on hand to pay the annual premium when due. The Seller will require a two-month reserve. Debit Buyer, Credit Seller to hold to pay the insurance bill when due.

    23 c. **Tax Reserve** – \$854.65. As with the insurance reserve, the Seller requires a five-month reserve be maintained in escrow, at \$170.93 per month with five months collected at closing to pay for the months that have already passed and are due. Debit Buyer and Credit Seller.

25. **Real Estate Closing Fee** – \$200.00. The closing instructions and sales contract specify the amount and who will be charged for allowable closing costs. In this case, the parties, by contract, agree to split the charge for the closing company to complete the closing. Debit Buyer and Seller each \$100.00, and Credit Broker the full \$200.

27. **Title Insurance Premium Owners Policy** – \$1,500.00. The Seller has agreed by contract to give evidence of merchantable title, therefore Debit Seller and Credit Broker, who will pay the bill.

28. **Owner's Extended Coverage-** \$100.00. The Seller, by contract, has agreed to pay the additional charge for coverage to delete the standard expectations listed in § 7.1, Evidence of Title. Debit Seller, Credit Broker.

29. **Title Insurance premium** – **Lender's Policy** (Mortgagee's) \$525. The Seller has requested that the Buyer supply the Seller title coverage in the Seller's role as lender. Debit Buyer, Credit Broker.

31. **Certificate of Taxes Due** – \$15.00. This certificate from the county treasurer's office is the Buyer's insurance that the county may not subsequently claim any taxes other than as stated on the certificate. Debit Buyer and Credit Broker. In this example, since there is no contract provision to the contrary, the Buyer (person who benefits) is debited. However, the Department of Housing and Urban Development (HUD) requires this to be a Seller charge on government-insured loans. The broker licensing examination will specify the party to be charged.

36. **Recording**

36 a. **Warranty Deed** – $10.00. The Buyer is the primary beneficiary of recording the warranty deed because it will make the transfer into the Buyer's name a matter of public record. Debit Buyer and Credit Broker, who will write the check to pay the county clerk and recorder's fees.

36 b. **Deeds of Trust** – 5 pages @ $10 for the first page, $5 for each additional page + $1 surcharge = $31.00 to record the deed of trust. This is the obligation of the Buyer. Debit Buyer, Credit Broker.

36 c. **Release of Existing Trust Deed** – $20.00. This releases the original Acme Loan Co. lien, which the Seller and title company want recorded to prove it was cleared. Debit Seller, Credit Broker.

38. **Documentary Fee** – $25.00. State law (§ 39-13-102, C.R.S.) requires the person recording an instrument of conveyance, such as a warranty deed, to pay a documentary fee to the clerk and recorder in the amount of one cent for each one hundred dollars (.01 per $100) of consideration, inclusive of any loan. ($250,000 x .0001 = $25.00). If the total consideration is $500 or less, there is no fee. Debit Buyer, Credit Broker.

45. **Water and/or Sewer Escrow** – $55.09. If the water or sewer is metered, then there is no proration. However, a final reading often needs to be made, and the closer will hold funds in escrow to pay the final bill, usually two to three times the average amount due. Once it is paid, the closer will send any balance to the Seller. In this example, the Seller paid a $96.40 water bill in advance on April 1 for three months (91 actual days), so this bill will need to be prorated. The Seller will have used 39 days of the 91-day period, leaving the Buyer to enjoy prepaid water for 52 days, therefore, Debit Buyer and Credit Seller $55.09 ($96.40 ÷ 91 days x 52 remaining days). Broker writes no check here; it is merely an adjustment between the parties.

$94.60 water and sewer. Paid – April 1 through June 30 (91 days).

May	22
June	30
	52

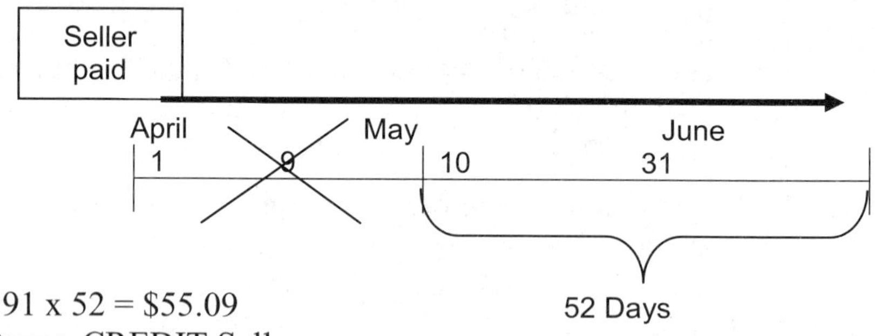

$94.60 ÷ 91 x 52 = $55.09
DEBIT Buyer, CREDIT Seller

53. **Broker's Fee** – $12,500.00. Debit Seller, Credit Broker.

54. **Other**

54 a. **Title Examination by the Buyer's attorney** – $100.00. Debit Buyer, Credit Broker.

54 b. **Title examination by the Seller's attorney** – $100.00. Debit Seller, Credit Broker.

54 c. **Credit Report** – $65.00. Debit Buyer, Credit Broker.

2. Sub-Totals

The totals of each column of debits and credits are made only for the convenience of the closing entity and for a better understanding by the parties in determining the balances or differences between the debits and credits of each party.

3. Balance Due to Seller

The balance due to Seller is $6,881.37. This amount is the difference between the total of the Seller's credits and debits, and is the amount the Seller will actually receive in cash for their home. Remember, most of the Seller's payment will come over time as the Buyer makes the loan payments. This amount is also recorded as a Broker credit since the Broker will disburse all money and write a check to the Seller for the amount owed.. If the Seller owed more than they were receiving, then both the Seller and Buyer would bring money to the closing and the amount would show under the Broker debit column.

4. Balance Due from Buyer

The balance due from the Buyer is $48,097.37. This is the difference between the total of the Buyer's credits and the Buyer's debits. The Buyer must bring this amount in good funds to accomplish the purchase at the time of final settlement. This amount is also entered as a Broker debit, since the Broker will collect and deposit this money.

5. Totals

After entering the amount due to or due from the Seller, the total Seller debits and credits must be equal, and the same is true for the Buyer and Broker totals. If the columns do not balance, then the sheet is incorrect. A Broker's column that does not balance is often from an issue in the Seller or Buyer columns.

6. Closing Statements

The worksheet on the next page will provide the itemized dollar amounts that will be transferred to the required closing statements for the Seller and Buyer. The Broker does not receive a Closing Statement (Form SS60-9-08).

7. Worksheet for Real Estate Settlement – Seller Carry Loan

See narrative on previous pages

SELLER: John R. and Mary L. Winter PURCHASER: Harold R. and A. Jean Blue

PROPERTY ADDRESS: 7373 West Flamingo Road

SETTLEMENT DATE: May 10, 20xx DATE OF PRORATION: May 9, 20xx

LEGAL DESCRIPTION: Lots 6 & 7, Block 14, Graham Heights, City of Lakewood, County of Jefferson, CO.

		SELLER		BUYER		BROKER	
	Description	DEBIT	CREDIT	DEBIT	CREDIT	DEBIT	CREDIT
1	Selling Price		$250,000.00	$250,000.00			
2	Deposit paid to: Mile High				$5,000.00	$5,000.00	
3	Principal amount of new 1st Loan	200,000.00			200,000.00		
5	1st Loan Payoff to: Acme	30,000.00					30,000.00
7	Taxes Prior Year: – Pd. $2,051.30						
8	Taxes Current Year	724.98			724.98		
	(129 days x $5.620000 per day)						
13	Appraisal Fee			350.00			350.00
20	Interest on New Loan						
11	(22 days x $41.0959 per day)		904.11	904.11			
22	Premium for New Hazard Ins.			675.00			675.00
23	Reserves Deposited with Lender						
	23 a. Hazard Ins. Reserve		112.50	112.50			
	23 c. County Prop. Tax Reserve		854.65	854.65			
25	Real Closing Fee (split)	100.00		100.00			200.00
27	Title Insurance Premium – Owner	1,500.00					1,500.00
28	Owner's Extended Coverage	100.00					100.00
29	Title Insurance Premium – Lender			525.00			525.00
31	Certificate of Taxes Due			15.00			15.00
36	Recording						
	36 a. Warranty Deed			10.00			10.00
	36 b. Deed of Trust			31.00			31.00
	36 c. Release Acme	20.00					20.00
38	Documentary Fee			25.00			25.00
45	Water and/or Sewer						
	(52 days x $1.059341 per day)		55.09	55.09			
53	Broker's Fee	12,500.00					12,500.00
54	Other						
	54. a. Buyer's Atty.			100.00			100.00
	54. b. Seller's Atty.	100.00					100.00
	54. c. Credit Report			65.00			65.00
	SUBTOTALS	$245,044.98	$251,926.35	$253, 822.35	$205,724.98	$5,000.00	$46,216.00
	DUE TO/[redacted]: SELLER	$6,881.37					$6,881.37
	DUE [redacted]/FROM: BUYER				$48,097.37	$48,097.37	
	TOTALS	$251,926.35	$251,926.35	$253, 822.35	$253, 822.35	$53,097.37	$53,097.37

Line numbers above correspond to numbering on Closing Statement SS60-9-08.

B. Final Settlement with an Assumed Loan

1. Introduction

The next closing statement will have the buyer assuming the seller's loan of $200,000. FHA and VA are two types of loans that allow qualifying buyers to assume the loan the seller originated. The advantage to the buyer is not having to pay loan costs such as appraisal, loan discount points, or origination fees.

2. Assumption Statement

In various circumstances, a purchaser, with consent of the seller and lender, may assume and pay an existing loan. The terms for assumption are part of the Contract to Buy and Sell.

The listing broker will request an assumption statement. This statement is prepared by the lending institution holding the existing deed of trust or mortgage and will contain all the requirements for assumption and the figures for closing. The following is an example of this type of information, which the closing company will use to prepare a closing statement. All of this information will be as of a certain date, in this case, a closing on May 10.

- The loan balance and term. The loan balance on May 1 is $200,000.00, due in 25 years. The loan balance will be a debit to the seller and credit to the buyer. Note: All loans are always a credit to the buyer.
- The rate of interest, amount paid, or the amount of interest earned but not yet due. The statement shows the interest rate is 7.5%, paid in arrears. The next payment is due on May 1; the seller will make the payment on May 1 and this payment will pay for April's interest. This means that when the buyer makes the June payment, it will pay interest for May. The seller will owe the buyer interest on the loan for the portion of May the seller was in the property, in this case nine days (shown below). The assumption statement would also show the amount of any delinquent payments.
- The tax reserve escrowed for the benefit of the mortgagor (the same as in the prior examples in this chapter).
- The insurance reserve escrowed for the benefit of the mortgagor (the same as in the prior examples in this chapter).
- The face amount, date, term, and premium of the existing homeowners insurance policy, and whether or not paid. For this example, the buyer obtains a new policy in the amount of $675.
- The loan transfer fee is $2,000. The statement also states what the lender requires before transferring the loan, *e.g.*, a copy of the contract or deed, or updating the title policy after the closing and conveyance.
- New owner's monthly payment, including principal, interest, taxes, and hazard insurance. This worksheet will use the same data from the prior examples in this chapter.

3. Other Charges and Adjustments for a Loan Assumption

No single real estate transaction will contain every type of charge or adjustment. All closings are similar, but each is unique. The following will explain some of the more common types of charges and adjustments for closing an assumed loan.

Although this entire chapter on closings ascribes obligations to the buyer or seller, any of these obligations may be reversed or changed by contract, unless prohibited by statute or government regulation.

The numbering below conforms to that found on Commission-approved Worksheets and Closing Statements.

20. **Interest on ~~New Loan~~ Assumed Loan.** There is no line for interest on an assumed loan, so when using the worksheet, the broker simply crosses out "New Loan" and notes this is an assumed loan. When a sale is made "subject to" an existing loan that will be assumed by the buyer, and when *interest is charged in arrears*, as in this example, then interest due on the loan from the due date of the last payment to date of settlement should be a *seller debit and buyer credit.* Interest for a monthly-amortized loan with a current unpaid principal balance of $200,000.00 at 7.5 percent interest paid in arrears, closing on May 10 is as follows:

    $200, 000 x 7.5% ÷ 12 months = $1,250.00 per month

    $1,250.00 ÷ 31 days (in May) = $40.3226 per day.

    $40.3226 x 9 days (May l-9) owned by seller = $362.90

    Debit seller/Credit buyer.

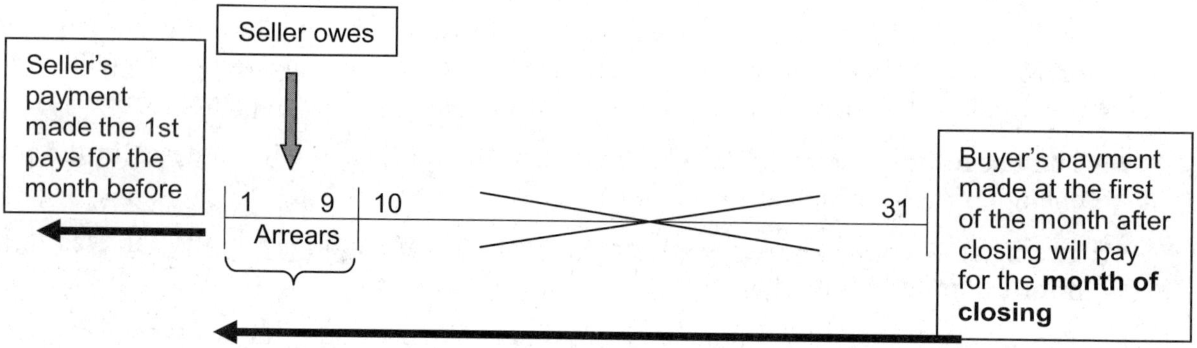

The buyer will then not be penalized when making the June 1 payment, including interest in arrears for the entire month of May, because the buyer will have been compensated at closing for the seller's nine days of interest responsibility.

The above daily rate is based on the 31 actual calendar *days in May* (or the actual closing month), based on the *outstanding principal balance* after the last payment.

This differs from the calculation for interest on a new loan, shown in the new loan, Item 20. Divide the annual interest by the actual number of days in the year to calculate the per diem figure for a new loan. In an assumed loan, because the payment has already been amortized, the interest for the month is determined by dividing by the 12 months in a year. In a new loan, for interest owed for the month of closing, 365 days are used to get the amount.

Loan Payment Due. Any loan payment due or delinquent should be charged to the seller and credited to the broker to pay. This could change the interest and reserve account picture if the buyer is assuming the loan. In this case, the buyer will pay this amount outside of closing.

23 a and c. **Hazard-Insurance and County Tax Reserve Accounts.** On home loans, most lending institutions today require that at least one month's taxes and insurance be paid with each monthly installment. This is to be placed in the mortgagor's trust account to be available for payment of taxes and insurance when due. In a transaction where an existing loan is being assumed and there is a tax or insurance trust account, this amount is *credited to the seller and debited to the buyer.* All similar escrow accounts are "sold" or charged to the purchaser at the closing, to return money to the seller who will not owe the future bill and set up the account to collect for what the buyer will owe.

39. **Transfer Fee.** This is a charge by the lender for changing the loan records from seller to buyer. Unless otherwise agreed between buyer and seller, this would be a Debit Buyer and Credit Broker.

4. Worksheet for Real Estate Settlement – Assumed Loan

(See narrative on previous pages)

SELLER: John R. and Mary L. Winter PURCHASER: Harold R. and A. Jean Blue

PROPERTY ADDRESS: 7373 West Flamingo Road

SETTLEMENT DATE: May 10, 20xx DATE OF PRORATION: May 9, 20xx

LEGAL DESCRIPTION: Lots 6 & 7, Block 14, Graham Heights, City of Lakewood, County of Jefferson, CO.

		SELLER		BUYER		BROKER	
	Description	DEBIT	CREDIT	DEBIT	CREDIT	DEBIT	CREDIT
1	Selling Price		$250,000.00	$250,000.00			
2	Deposit paid to: Mile High				$5,000.00	$5,000.00	
3	Principal amount of ~~new~~ Assumed Loan	200,000.00			200,000.00		
7	Taxes Prior Year: – Pd. $2,051.30						
8	Taxes Current Year (129 days x $5.620000 per day)	724.98			724.98		
20	Interest on ~~New~~ Assumed Loan						
11	$40.3226 x 9 days	362.90			362.90		
22	Premium for New Hazard Ins.			675.00			675.00
23	Reserves Deposited with Lender						
	23 a. Hazard Ins. Reserve		112.50	112.50			
	23 c. County Prop. Tax Reserve		854.65	854.65			
25	Real Closing Fee (split)	100.00		100.00			200.00
31	Certificate of Taxes Due			15.00			15.00
36	Recording						
	36 a. Warranty Deed			10.00			10.00
	36 b. Deed of Trust			31.00			31.00
38	Documentary Fee			25.00			25.00
39	Transfer Fee			2,000.00			2,000.00
45	Water and/or Sewer (52 days x $1.059341 per day)		55.09	55.09			
53	Broker's Fee	12,500.00					12,500.00
	SUBTOTALS	$213,687.88	$251,022.24	$253,878.24	$206,087.88	$5,000.00	$15,456.00
	DUE TO/[redacted]: SELLER	$37,334.36					$37,334.36
	DUE [redacted]D/FROM: BUYER				$47,790.36	$47,790.36	
	TOTALS	$251,022.24	$251,022.24	$253,878.24	$253,878.24	$52,790.36	$52,790.36

Line numbers above correspond to numbering on Closing Statement SS60-9-08.

C. Final Settlement with a New Loan

When the buyer is to receive a new loan, the lender's figures and requirements become part of the closing process and closing statement. Typically, the lender hires the closing company to collect and pay bills, similar to what the broker has been doing in previous examples. Any item that might affect the loan or title is now going to be paid for by the lender, not the broker. These loans are called single entry, as many items will appear on the worksheet and closing statement only as a debit to the party that is obligated to make the payment.

For example, the seller will be debited for the title insurance they have by contract agreed to purchase, but there will be no corresponding credit to the broker to pay the title company for this bill. An easy way to conceptualize what is happening to the money is to think of an new, invisible column, in which the lender is receiving the credit, just as the broker's column was used; the lender will write checks for items credited into their column. At the end of the worksheet the broker/closer will need to write a check to pay the seller's net proceed. To balance all of these costs, on a new loan there is always a debit (deposit) for net loan proceeds into the broker's account, the worksheet will now balance, and the broker will have the funds to complete the closing.

In the Lender Loan Statement, the lender states the full amount of the loan the buyer will receive or be credited, the total amount of expenses the lender is paying for, and the difference, which is the net /loan proceeds the broker will receive.

Example:	Total Loan	$200,000.00
	Loan costs paid for by lender	$ 36,822.26
	Net Loan Proceeds to broker	$163,177.74

1. New Loan Lender Statement

The various charges that a lending institution will make to protect their interest will vary from lender to lender. A loan statement from the lending institution using the data from the prior sample problem would probably appear similar to the example below. Note: the appraisal was paid for by the buyer when the appraisal was ordered, and it has been Paid Outside Closing (P.O.C.); however, the charge must be accounted for, and will still show on the Worksheet and Closing Statement with the notation "P.O.C."

Sample Lender's New Loan Statement

Face amount of loan to Buyer:	$200,000.00
Amounts charged by Lender to make the loan:	
Pay-off existing note	$ 30,000.00
Appraisal fee $350 P.O.C.	0
Owner's title policy with extended coverage	1,600.00
Mortgagee's Title Insurance	525.00
Recording Fees	
Warranty Deed	10.00
1st Trust Deed	31.00
Release – Acme Loan Co.	20.00

Documentary Fee	25.00
Tax Reserve	854.65
Loan Origination Fee (1%)	2,000.00
New Hazard Insurance Premium	675.00
Hazard Insurance Reserve	112.50
Interest on Loan May 10-31 (22 days)	904.11
Credit Report	65.00
Subtotal charges made by Lender:	$ 36,822.26
Net Loan Proceeds	$163,177.74

The loan statement above in no way relieves the designated brokers of the responsibility to prepare and provide a closing statement for their client or customer. The loan company has deducted these payouts from the amount of the loan, regardless of which party will be debited. Loan companies may also vary as to which of the costs they wish to collect and pay. Lender-paid items must be appropriately debited or credited by the closing entity as shown on the new loan worksheet below. Lenders are not concerned about which party pays a particular item unless the loan is governed by VA, FHA, or other regulations.

Rule E-5(g) requires a broker to reconcile the net loan proceeds shown on the loan statement, with the final payment due from the buyer and the final payment due to the seller. This reconciliation may be done by the broker or closing entity on a worksheet, a computer, or in any equivalent form. The broker must retain a copy of the reconciliation statement in the transaction file and make it available for audit by a representative of the Commission.

Broker Reconciliation Statement for New Loan

	Received	**Paid – Out**
Net Loan Proceeds (Closing Entity)	**$163,158.74**	
Earnest Money Deposit (Broker Escrow)	5,000.00	
Total Money Due from Buyer (Closing Entity)	**49,666.37**	
Other payouts made by broker (Closing Entity)		
Tax Certificate		15.00
Closing Fee		200.00
Broker's Fee		12,500.00
Total Amount Due Seller (Closing Entity)		205,110.11
Totals (See Broker/Closer Column on new loan Worksheet)	$217,825.11	$217,825.11

When the reconciliation above is made on the standard Worksheet for settlement (SS61-9-08), the theory is the same. All debits and credits in the "Broker" column are understood by contract and closing instructions to have been actually collected or disbursed by the lender or closing entity rather than the broker.

2. Worksheet for Real Estate Settlement – New Loan

(See narrative on previous pages)

SELLER: John R. and Mary L. Winter PURCHASER: Harold R. and A. Jean Blue

PROPERTY ADDRESS: 7373 West Flamingo Road

SETTLEMENT DATE: May 10, 20xx DATE OF PRORATION: May 9, 20xx

LEGAL DESCRIPTION: Lots 6 & 7, Block 14, Graham Heights, City of Lakewood, County of Jefferson, CO.

		SELLER		BUYER		BROKER	
	Description	DEBIT	CREDIT	DEBIT	CREDIT	DEBIT	CREDIT
1	Selling Price		$250,000.00	$250,000.00			
2	Deposit paid to: Mile High				$5,000.00	$5,000.00	
3	Principal amount of new 1st Loan				200,000.00		
5	1st Loan Payoff to: Acme	30,000.00					
7	Taxes Prior Year: – Pd. $2,051.30						
8	Taxes Current Year	724.98			724.98		
	(129 days x $5.620000 per day)						
13	Appraisal Fee P.O.C. $350						
20	Interest on New Loan						
	(22 days x $41.0959 per day)			904.11			
11	Loan Origination Fee			2,000.00			
22	Premium for New Hazard Ins.			675.00			
23	Reserves Deposited with Lender						
	23 a. Hazard Ins. Reserve			112.50			
	23 c. County Prop. Tax Reserve			854.65			
25	Real Closing Fee (split)	100.00		100.00			200.00
27	Title Insurance Premium – Owner			1,500.00			
28	Owner's Extended Coverage	100.00					
29	Title Insurance Premium – Lender			525.00			
31	Certificate of Taxes Due			15.00			15.00
36	Recording						
	36 a. Warranty Deed			10.00			
	36 b. Deed of Trust			31.00			
	36 c. Release Acme	20.00					
38	Documentary Fee			25.00			
45	Water and/or Sewer						
	(52 days x $1.059341 per day)		55.09	55.09			
53	Broker's Fee	12,500.00					12,500.00
54	Other						
	54. a. Credit Report			65.00			
	54. b. Credit Buyer Owner's	1,500.00			1,500.00		
	Net Loan Proceeds					163,177.74	
	SUBTOTALS	$44,944.98	$250,055.09	$256,872.35	$207,224.98	168,177.74	$12,715.00
	DUE TO/[redacted]: SELLER	$205,110.11					$205,110.11
	DUE [redacted]/FROM: BUYER				$49,647.37	$49,647.37	
	TOTALS	$250,055.09	$250,055.09	$256,872.35	$256,872.35	$217,825.11	$217,825.11

V. Closing Statement

From the Worksheet, the broker/closer creates individual Closing Statements for the seller and buyer. The Closing Statement shows only the figures for that party and does not reflect any payments made by the broker or lender. See following examples.

A. Seller's Closing Statement – New Loan

The printed portions of this form, except differentiated additions, have been approved by the Colorado Real Estate Commission. (SS60-9-08) (Mandatory 1-09)

☐ **ESTIMATE** ☒ **FINAL**

CLOSING STATEMENT

☒ **SELLER'S** ☐ **BUYER'S**

PROPERTY ADDRESS: 7373 West Flamingo Road Lakewood Co, 80237

SELLER: John R. and Mary L. Winter BUYER: Harold R. and A. Jean Blue

SETTLEMENT DATE: May 10, 20XX DATE OF PRORATION: May 10, 20XX

LEGAL DESCRIPTION: 6 & 7, Block 14, Graham Heights, City of Lakewood, County of Jefferson, CO

	DEBIT	CREDIT
Selling Price		$250,000.00
Deposit paid to: Mile High		
Principal amount of new 1st Loan		
1st Loan Payoff to: Acme	30,000.00	
Taxes Prior Year: – Pd. $2,051.30		
Taxes Current Year	724.98	
(129 days x $5.620000 per day)		
Real Closing Fee (split)	100.00	
Title Insurance Premium – Owner	1,500.00	
Owner's Extended Coverage	100.00	
Recording		
36 c. Release Acme	20.00	
Documentary Fee		
Water and/or Sewer		
(52 days x $1.059341 per day)		55.09
Broker's Commission	12,500.00	
SUBTOTALS	$44,944.98	$250,055.09
DUE TO[redacted]M: SELLER	$205,110.11	
DUE TO/FROM: BUYER		
TOTALS	$250,055.09	$250,055.09

APPROVED AND ACCEPTED

Buyer/Seller ______________________________

Buyer/Seller ______________________________

Brokerage Firm's Name: ______________________________

B. Buyer's Closing Statement – New Loan

The printed portions of this form, except differentiated additions, have been approved by the Colorado Real Estate Commission. (SS60-9-08) (Mandatory 1-09)

☐ **ESTIMATE** ☒ **FINAL**

CLOSING STATEMENT

☐ **SELLER'S** ☒ **BUYER'S**

PROPERTY ADDRESS: 7373 West Flamingo Road Lakewood Co, 80237

SELLER: John R. and Mary L. Winter BUYER: Harold R. and A. Jean Blue

SETTLEMENT DATE: May 10, 20XX DATE OF PRORATION: May 10, 20XX

LEGAL DESCRIPTION: 6 & 7, Block 14, Graham Heights, City of Lakewood, County of Jefferson, CO

	Description	DEBIT	CREDIT
1	Selling Price	$250,000.00	
2	Deposit paid to: Mile High		$5,000.00
3	Principal amount of new 1st Loan		200,000.00
	Buyer's Credit Owner's Policy		1,500.00
7	Taxes Prior Year: – Pd. $2,051.30		
8	Taxes Current Year		724.98
	(129 days x $5.620000 per day)		
11	Loan Origination Fee	2,000.00	
13	Appraisal Fee P.O.C. $350		
20	Interest on New Loan		
	(22 days x $41.0959 per day)	904.11	
22	Premium for New Hazard Ins.	675.00	
23	Reserves Deposited with Lender		
	23 a. Hazard Ins. Reserve	112.50	
	23 c County Prop. Tax Reserve	854.65	
25	Real Closing Fee (split)	100.00	
	Title Insurance Premium – Owner	1,500.00	
29	Title Insurance Premium – Lender	525.00	
31	Certificate of Taxes Due	15.00	
36	Recording		
	36 a. Warranty Deed	10.00	
	36 b. Deed of Trust	31.00	
38	Documentary Fee	25.00	
45	Water and/or Sewer		
	(52 days x $1.059341 per day)	55.09	
54	Other		
	54. a. Credit Report	65.00	
	SUBTOTALS	$256,872.35	$207,224.98
	DUE TO/FROM: SELLER		
	DUE [redacted]/FROM: BUYER		$49,647.37
	TOTALS	$256,872.35	$256,872.35

APPROVED AND ACCEPTED

Buyer/Seller ______________________________

Buyer/Seller ______________________________

Brokerage Firm's Name: ______________________

Broker ___________________________________

VII. Other Settlement Items

The items below, while not used in the example closings, appear with enough frequency that a broker should be familiar with them and understand how they affect the closing.

9. **Personal Property Taxes.** Personal property taxes will not be involved unless the property was used for business or income-producing purposes. If such personal property is included in the sale, these taxes are prorated as ad valorem property tax would be prorated. When title passes, the tax responsibility also passes from seller to buyer. Personal property tax situations are more frequently encountered in business opportunity transactions. Some counties demand advance payment of these taxes for the current year and they will be prorated to date of closing.

A. Loan Fees

Typically, these fees are paid by the buyer; however, money the buyer receives from the seller in the form of concessions is often used to cover all or part of these expenses. All are costs related to the buyer's new loan. Mortgage brokers in Colorado are required by law to give buyers a full disclosure and accounting of all loan fees being charged. This section is used to account for and separate these fees for the buyer at closing.

11. **Origination Charge.** The lender and mortgage broker's charges (including processing fees, underwriting fees, document preparation fees, etc.) and points(s) for origination the loan. An adjustment is made in the form of a credit or a charge for broker credits or points paid and the final number is the Adjust Origination Charge.

16. **Tax Service Fee.** If the lender uses a tax service to collect and pay the taxes, there may be a fee to set up this service.

17. **Flood Certification.** This is a fee charged to certify that the property is not in a flood zone. If the property is found to be in a flood zone, the lender will likely require the buyer to acquire flood insurance.

21. **Mortgage Insurance Premium/PMI.** Private mortgage insurance is usually required on loans with a loan-to-value ratio above 80%. Debit Buyer.

26. **Loan closing fee.** If there is a separate fee for the closing company to close the loan, in addition to the real estate, the fee is shown here.

30. **Endorsements.** These are additions added to the Mortgagee's title policy to further protect the lender.

B. HOA Fees

41. **HOA-CIC Document Procurement Fee.** If the Home Owner's Association (HOA) charges for copies of the Common Interest Community (CIC) documents the buyer has requested, the fee will show here. The contract calls for the seller to supply copies to the buyer. Debit Seller, Credit Broker.

42. **HOA Transfer/Status Letter Fee.** The seller has agreed in the contract to provide a status letter; if there is a charge for the letter, the amount will be posted here.

43. **HOA Dues.** The amount of any prorated dues, which are most often paid in advance, will be shown here. If paid in advance, Credit Seller and Debit Buyer the prorated share.

44. **HOA Working Capital.** A charge to buyer or seller by the HOA for capital is shown in this section.

C. Rentals

50. **Rents/Rent Proration.** Adjustment should be made for any rent collected by the seller from a tenant in advance, typically for a month. The prorated share for the rental period is always credited to the buyer, who will not receive possession after closing, and debited to the seller, who collected the rent for the entire period. Delinquent rents are not prorated.

51. **Security Deposits.** If the property is a rental and the seller is holding a tenant's security deposit, the full amount will be debited from the seller and credited to the buyer. By contract, the seller agrees to inform the tenant of the new owner's name and address.

D. Seller Concessions

52. **Seller's Concessions.** This total amount of money the seller has agreed to give the buyer to assist in paying costs of buying the property.

Closings are one of the highlights of a real estate broker's job. This is when all the broker's hard work pays off and the brokerage gets paid. Many complications can arise in the closing of a real estate transaction. Not all variations can be foreseen. When all parties are present at a closing, new contracts may evolve, there may be a necessity for escrow agreements, or rental agreements may be necessary if occupancy is not given at the time of transfer of title. The broker is responsible for ensuring that any contractual changes made at closing are reduced to writing. Brokers should continue their education on the subject of closings throughout their careers.

VIII. Statutes, Rules, and Position Statements Affecting Closings

A. Statutes

§ 38-35-125, C.R.S.	Good funds
§ 39-13-102, C.R.S.	Documentary fee
§ 39-1-119, C.R.S.	Lender reserve
§ 39-22-604.5, C.R.S.	2% withholding tax for nonresident sellers
§ 24-71-101(1), C.R.S.	Electronic signatures
§ 12-61-103(6)(c), C.R.S.	Employing broker supervision responsibility
§ 12-61-113(l)(o), C.R.S.	Employing broker supervision responsibility
§ 12-61-118, C.R.S.	Employing broker negligent supervision

B. Rules

E-3	Licensee must produce records; HOA records belong to HOA
E-4	Document preparation and duplicates
E-5	Closing responsibility; closing statement distribution
E-31	Reasonable supervision
E-32	High-level of supervision
F-7	Use of Commission Approved Forms; re: closing instructions

C. Commission Position Statements:

CP-7 Commission Position on Closing Costs

VIII. Useful Closing Web Sites

To view the most current approved forms:
http://www.dora.state.co.us/real-estate/contracts/contracts.htm

Questions regarding IRS reporting:
http://www.irs.gov.

FIRPTA Withholding:
http://www.irs.gov/businesses/small/international/article/0,,id=105000,00.html

Colorado Nonresident withholding:
http://www.revenue.state.co.us/

RESPA:
http://www.hud.gov/offices/hsg/ramh/res/respa_hm.cfm

Chapter 19:
Escrow Records

An * in the left margin indicates a change in the statute, rule, or text since the last publication of the manual.

I. Introduction

This chapter presents the general concepts and guidelines necessary to establish and maintain all escrow accounting records. Regulations governing these operations are found in §§ 12-61-102, -103(7) and (8), and -113(1), C.R.S.; Rules E-1 through E-5, E-21, and E-29 through E-32; and the subdivision references cited in Part IV of this chapter. Other laws related to real estate practice and property management are presented in Chapters 20, 24, and 25. Important information about industry developments, legislation, or changes in regulations is published quarterly in the *Colorado Real Estate News*. Licensing information, applications, portions of the manual, and past newsletters are published at: www.dora.state.co.us/real estate/. New brokers may obtain startup information from the Small Business Assistance Center, website at www.coloradosbdc.org.

A. Concepts and Responsibilities – A Chapter Summary

The **"Escrow Accounting Equation"** is the cornerstone for all related accounting processes. It states that at any given point in time, the reconciled escrow bank account ***cash balance*** must equal the corresponding escrow ***account liabilities*** per contract.

When the employing broker receives any money belonging to others, five obligations are generally undertaken: (1) the broker receives custody of the escrow cash asset as a "fiduciary" or "trustee," rather than as its legal owner; (2) the broker agrees to perform various duties for another, who is termed a "beneficiary" in the Commission regulations; (3) the custody, control, ownership, and use of each escrow asset is governed by the underlying contractual agreement, any applicable regulation, or other superseding law; (4) the broker is required to deposit and account for these assets in a prescribed manner; and (5) the broker remains responsible for the outcome of these acts when others perform them on his or her behalf.

Escrow bank accounts are unique "accounting entities," which are separate in purpose and function from the other accounts commonly used in a real estate business. "Escrow" and "trust" are synonymous descriptive terms for the broker's fiduciary account in all Commission regulations. This type of account excludes money handled for ongoing personal business income, expenses, commissions, and/or other non-licensed business transactions. Funds belonging to the same "common class" of beneficiaries are normally deposited into a "pooled" escrow bank account, unless otherwise prohibited by other law or agreement between the parties concerned. In other cases, the broker may choose to open a separate escrow bank account for funds held in each separate engagement. This structure is frequently found in the sale of luxury homes where large earnest money deposits are held in separate interest-bearing accounts, when the company manages broker-owned properties, or when the broker manages other significant accounting entities. The use of separate trust accounts for each significant entity provides greater protection against possible "illegal commingling of funds," described below. Diagrams showing the typical flow of funds and common company bank account structures for sales and management companies are included in this chapter.

The general concepts and responsibilities for maintaining escrow accounts apply to all types of real estate accounting activity. Common functional activities include establishing and maintaining bank accounts; collecting, evaluating, and recording accounting information; maintaining transaction files; reconciling accounts with related real estate business records and documents; reporting accounting activity to interested parties; training and supervising staff; and storing records for later use.

Each escrow bank account must have a corresponding set of office accounting records. These may be kept manually or by use of a computer. The terms for the required records are: a "journal," the individual "beneficiary ledgers," the "broker's ledger," the "monthly bank reconciliation worksheet," and the related "property transaction files." Sample accounting records and transactions are illustrated in Part II, Section D of this chapter; blank forms are found in the chapter appendix. These forms may be modified within the constraints of Rule E-1(p) to suit business needs.

The bank reconciliation process used for maintaining escrow accounts differs in a significant way from other methods used to reconcile personal or other business accounts. The goals of this process are to ensure that proper records have been established for actual events and to verify the information recorded in the office records agrees with the activity shown on the monthly bank statement. This requires examining certain financial provisions found in the pending sales contracts, leases, management agreements, and related business records and recording the financial data in the corresponding escrow account journal and ledgers. The total resulting "contractual liability" is then reconciled to the escrow bank account cash balance at a given point in time. The results are summarized on a form called the "bank reconciliation worksheet." Absent missing documents, unintentional errors, or internal fraud, this "worksheet" is a snapshot of the overall condition of the escrow accounting equation. If a properly prepared worksheet balances, it indicates that all escrow liabilities are fully funded and all financial obligations are properly reported in both the accounting and banking records. When the worksheet does not balance, the cause may be due to more serious conditions described next.

In order to avoid illegal commingling of funds, proper control over paying expenses must be maintained on a day-to-day basis; this means *never overspend or misuse* any beneficiary's available cash balance. Such misuse is described as "converting" (stealing) and/or "diverting" (borrowing or loaning) money without authorization. These practices endanger the public interest by removing the beneficiary's property from the account without settling the corresponding contractual liability as agreed; the resulting cash shortage will mean that in the event of any unexpected termination of business after the misuse, some liabilities cannot be paid from the available escrow account cash balance. Other practices often accompanying this condition are: (1) failing to deposit funds into an authorized account, (2) failing to account for the activity performed, (3) misrepresenting the status of financial information to others, and (4) other ongoing uncorrected accounting errors. The Commission may impose administrative discipline in these cases, and other civil or criminal statutes may also apply.

The general function of a journal is similar (but not necessarily equivalent) to a check register. The journal reports information about all events causing a change in the escrow bank balance over a given period of time. The function of each individual beneficiary ledger is to account for the information pertaining to all changes in the amount of cash held for a specific party during the same period of time.

Because of the possibility for internal theft, blind trust in the "equality" of the accounting equation will not guarantee that the intervening escrow accounting entries were properly made or represent corresponding real events. The employing broker and another officer or company owner, with assistance from an appointed and independent internal audit committee, should establish, review, and perform the following ***critical supervisory functions*** on an ongoing basis: (1) examine all company banking and accounting activity for proper operation, (2) review the quality of all services provided by all associates and any affiliated businesses entities, (3) maintain effective channels of communication, community feedback, and personal involvement in key operating processes, (4) enforce and promptly correct improper practices or violations of company policy, and (5) provide adequate compensation, necessary training, and adequate supervision to minimize the "controllable" means, motivation, and opportunity for financial harm to the public.

II. Sales Escrow Accounts

A. The Escrow Bank Account

General Operation

The Federal Deposit Insurance Corporation (FDIC) provides "dollar-for-dollar" insurance coverage for money held in all accounts maintained by a specific depositor-beneficiary at an insured bank up to a maximum amount of $100,000 per person. Supplemental private deposit insurance should be considered when this amount is exceeded.

The broker's use of a non-escrow business checking account for escrow money will result in commingled ownership of these funds. The identity of the individual depositors or their personal financial interest in the total bank account balance will not be determinable from the bank's own legal records. As a result, this type of account will only qualify for $100,000 of FDIC insurance coverage in total. In the event of a bank failure, each depositor would be reimbursed according to the percentage his or her balance constitutes to the total account balance. Any excess of funds deposited over the share of the coverage will be treated as "uninsured loss," which will be the broker's responsibility. To overcome this limitation, the bank's customer deposit agreement must identify the broker as a "fiduciary," and the records prescribed in Rule E-1(p) must be kept on a day-to-day basis. If those conditions are met, each beneficiary's coverage will be extended to the full $100,000 limit per individual depositor. The escrow account title format shown on the next page must be used to show the fiduciary nature of any real estate escrow account owned by the broker.

The employing broker, a licensed sole proprietor, the corporation, the partnership, or the LLC are the only "persons" authorized by statute to own and operate company escrow accounts. Employed brokers may not establish company escrow accounts in their own names. However, they may be designated as alternate signers on any escrow or company bank account, as long as the employing broker can independently operate all company-owned escrow accounts. In order for the broker to delegate the authority to perform accounting duties to another, the duties must be accepted in a dated and signed job description. The employed broker is then primarily accountable for the outcome of the acts and duties within their control, and the employing broker will have responsibility for supervision of the duty as well.

The following diagram illustrates common alternative flows of funds through an escrow account:

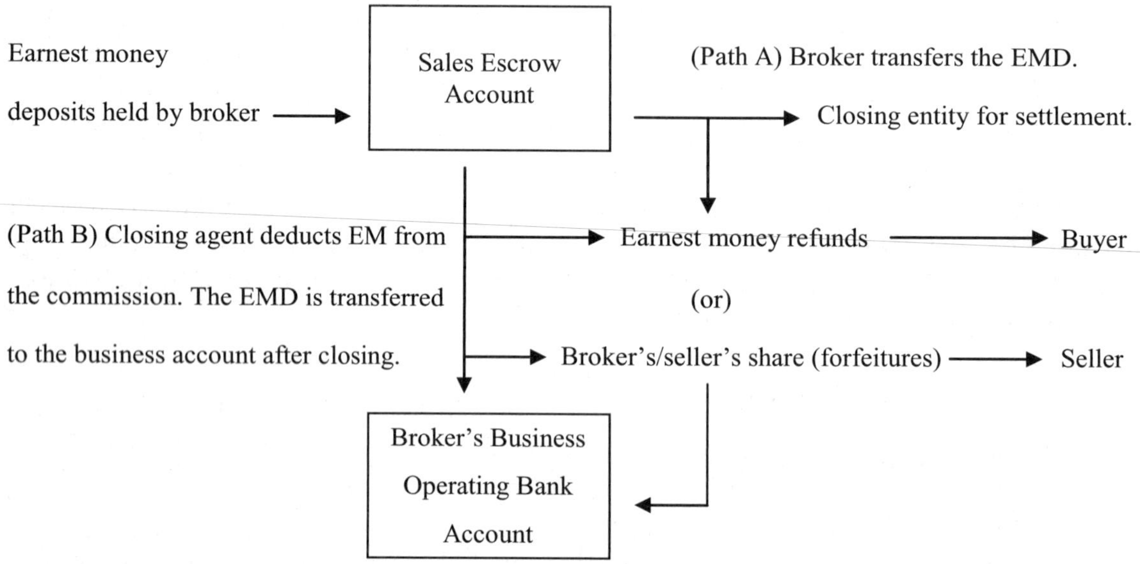

How to Open Escrow Bank Accounts

Public notice of the fiduciary nature of the escrow bank account must be given by the identification shown on the bank's customer deposit agreement described in Step 2:

1. Select a Colorado depository that offers FDIC insurance coverage or as authorized for the specific engagement. Information about the financial strength of various institutions may be obtained from the Weiss Research Group, 877-925-4833, www.weissgroupinc.com.
2. Include the following "**fiduciary elements**" in the account title. These must identify the true owner of the account, specify the type or purpose of account being established (sales, management, homeowner association, etc.), include one of the fiduciary words "escrow" or "trust," state the employing broker's personal name, and show his or her fiduciary capacity as "broker." The employing broker must be able to independently control and operate all escrow bank accounts, but others may be designated as signatories as well. These elements may be abbreviated to facilitate printing the broker's monthly bank statement heading, checks, and deposit stock. The general account title format follows:

   Licensed brokerage name and/or d.b.a. (brokerage TIN/SSN)

   Type of escrow, broker's name, broker

   Statement mailing address
3. Obtain copies of the customer deposit agreement and signature card(s) and retain them with office escrow records for later Commission inspection. Update these records whenever there is a change of authorized signatories or bank ownership.

4. Execute the "Notice of Escrow or Trust Account" (see Appendix, Exhibit A). This form may be typed on the broker's stationary. Retain for later inspection.
5. In order to reduce the risk of accounting error and internal theft, select (and/or design) company checking supplies that provide a clear record of individual accountability for all accounting and banking operations performed on the broker's behalf. Electronic imaging of banking records (and other office files) is permitted when reproductions and endorsements are easily readable and are retrievable upon reasonable request (see Rule E-6). The personal name of the employing broker acting for a corporation, partnership, or limited liability company is not required on deposit slips or check stock.
6. Please note: The first line of the account heading is reserved for the legal identification and TIN/SSN of the true account owner. Never use a third-party name or TIN/SSN identification number on a company-owned account, as this practice may enable the other owner(s) to independently transact business without the broker's consent. The fiduciary elements shown in Step 2 are not required if the account is owned by a third party, *e.g.*, a homeowner's association or a commercial property owner; is to be managed by the broker; and the broker is only added as another signor on the account. All independent account signors should understand the applicability and scope of any "setoff or seizure rights" stated in the bank deposit agreement.

Other Types of Escrow Accounts

The following guidelines apply to the use of interest-bearing accounts, stock market investments, Colorado Association of Realtors Housing Opportunity Fund (CARHOF) accounts for affordable housing programs, credit union accounts, and the transfer of earnest money deposits to a third party or closing entity.

Written disclosure and consent must be obtained for use of a passbook interest-bearing account or certificate of deposit. This requires a description of the account used, the risks involved, any applicable restrictions or penalties, and an agreement for the ownership of any subsequent income or loss. If there is no disclosure or consent from the beneficiary, any earnings belong to the beneficiary and any loss or penalty will be the broker's responsibility. The interest earned will normally appear on the monthly bank statement, and must be recorded in the broker's journal and/or allocated to the ledger of each beneficiary-owner. Any interest contractually retained by the broker must be entered on the "broker's ledger." An IRS Form 1099-INT must be sent to the beneficiary at year-end.

The city of Boulder currently requires the payment of a statutory rate of interest to tenants residing in that jurisdiction. Contact the city of Boulder or the Boulder County Apartment Association at (303) 494-9048 for further information on the current requirements. The simplest way of dealing with this matter is to use a non-interest-bearing account and fund the tenant interest payment by charging the statutory amount to the owner. Otherwise, the broker will have to account for and periodically allocate the differences in market and statutory rates to the owners concerned. The solution is a business policy decision that should be disclosed in the management agreement.

In general, a broker may not independently establish an escrow bank account outside Colorado, or deposit money belonging to others in a stock market or institutional "cash-asset management investment account," without the informed written consent and specific waiver of the applicable statutory requirements by those concerned. However, Commission policy permits the deposit of credit card receipts into an out-of-state bank clearing account (to secure lower processing rates) if the broker's records are able to track individual transactions in and out of the clearing account by name, date, purpose, and amount. In contrast, any investment made solely in the broker's name, where escrow funds are pledged as collateral for brokerage credit, capital loans, or as security for other institutional investments and/or debt, is prohibited. Similarly, an investment of escrow funds is prohibited when federal insurance coverage only applies to the sponsoring institution or its agents for unlawful events, but fails to insure the beneficiaries on a "dollar-for-dollar" basis.

Credit union escrow or trust accounts do not meet the escrow requirements of § 12-61-113(1)(g.5), C.R.S., and are therefore not suitable depositories for money belonging to others. See Rule E-1(b).

Participation in CARHOF or a similar non-profit qualified community affordable housing program is voluntary. The interest earned is transferred to the program as the interest beneficiary only (IBO), using the CARHOF program non-profit tax identification number. The term "CARHOF (IBO)" may appear on the left side of either the first or second line in the account format shown in Step 2, according to bank requirements. The term "CARHOF IBO" is not printed on company check stock or deposit slips. Other company programs that are established by the broker to benefit needy employees, a class of citizens, a favorite social service, a medical organization, or a charity are not eligible for treatment as a "qualified community housing program." The commissioners voted to limit such participation to non-profit real estate activities within their jurisdiction. This limitation does not prevent a written agreement between parties in a specific transaction to distribute interest earned to whomever they wish. Further information is available from the local board or Colorado Association of Realtors, (303) 790-7099.

When a contract is amended to allow the transfer of the earnest money to a third party or "closing entity," the broker will not need to maintain the normal escrow accounting records required by Rule E-1(p). Instead, Rule E-1(o) requires retention of the following items in the property transaction file: (1) a signed and dated receipt from the third party designated to hold the funds, (2) a copy of the earnest money check, and (3) a copy of any endorsement needed to make this transfer. The type of depository account used by the third party must be consistent with that provided in the approved contract form. The party (or parties) concerned must approve the terms and costs of any third party "custodial/escrow agreement" used in the transaction; however, such agreements will not "automatically nullify" the duties found in other Commission-approved forms.

Special Use of Accounts

The provisions of Rules E-1(i), E-16, and E-1(f)(5) affect how various bank accounts may be used.

Rule E-1(i) allows a broker to manage less than seven single-family residential units and maintain the rents collected in the sales escrow account. Any related security deposits may also be held in this account. The opposite case applies to earnest money deposits received by a property management broker; these may be placed in the security deposit account or held intact in the owner's management escrow account with the usual accounting records.

Rule E-16 allows the liability ("financial responsibility") for the timely return of a tenant's security deposit to be transferred from the broker to the property owner when there is a consistent agreement to this effect in the management agreement/addendum, and in an accompanying notice to the tenant in the lease/addendum or by first-class mail. The security deposit may then be paid directly to the property owner, held in the owner's management escrow account, or used as that owner's management operating capital. This option may not be advisable when poor business relationships exist among those concerned.

Rule E-1(f)(5) requires use of an additional "pooled escrow account," separate from other third-party client trust accounts, when the broker has an "ownership interest" in a partnership, joint venture, or syndication and receives compensation for selling or leasing such property. The broker may also choose to establish a separate escrow account for each "significant accounting entity" owned or otherwise managed and be in compliance with this and other rules. When a licensee personally receipts for security deposits in the management of his or her own property, that obligation is personal and the use of escrow accounts is not required. An employing broker's written company policy should address an associate's responsibility to clearly differentiate and separate "personal business" from other normal company activities. Under Commission case law, the licensee acting for his or her "own account" remains responsible to perform all promises made, to account for the funds received, and to disclose their licensed status to others (see Rule E-25).

B. The Cash Receipts and Disbursements Journal (The "Journal")

General Concepts

The "journal" is described in Rule E-1(p)(1) and is maintained when the broker receives or is designated as custodian for any money belonging to others, as defined in Rule E-1(g). A blank form is in the chapter appendix, Exhibit B.

The journal, the corresponding ledgers, the bank account, and the related contractual liabilities are always intended to be self-balancing and equal to each other. The journal is maintained on a "cash-basis" unless the beneficiaries agree to use accrual accounting. Cash-basis accounting means that receipts and payments are recorded when received for deposit or paid. The journal remains open until the corresponding bank account and open ledgers are closed.

Intentionally reporting expenses as "paid," or amounts as "received" in any escrow record or corresponding accounting or beneficiary report, without mailing the check or making a bank deposit, is a serious form of misrepresentation, failure to account, and possible fraud. Brokers can create similar conditions when they receipt for funds specified in the contract but do not take possession of the money and/or deposit it in a reasonable time.

Concerns may arise as to the validity of an acceptance of an offer when a faxed copy of the earnest money check is submitted to the listing broker or designated custodian. The absence of an actual earnest money check at the time of (or one day after) the acceptance does not invalidate the contract. Other provisions will normally provide the necessary "legal consideration" to make the acceptance binding. Some financial institutions are willing to accept a fax copy of a check as the maker's authorization for transfer of funds to a designated custodial account. Brokers are advised to have prior written agreement for use of this process, verify the receipt of "good funds" by the designated custodian, and communicate the results promptly to those concerned.

The "ending journal balance" includes all money held in escrow (pending closing or final disposition) for all beneficiaries, including any unearned funds belonging or ultimately due to the broker and/or the results of other bank adjustments and service charges. The escrow cash account balance is normally shown in the current asset section of the escrow account balance sheet, while the total for the corresponding total for all pending ledgers appears in the current liability section. Changes in these ending balance sheet amounts are explained by the transactional data recorded in the cash receipts and disbursements journal during the monthly accounting period. A negative escrow bank balance, an accounts receivable, or a debit balance in the escrow accounts payable or the escrow "equity" section may be the result of error or illegal commingling of funds.

A general policy of accepting cash (legal tender) in ongoing transactions is discouraged without corresponding fidelity insurance and effective internal controls. Most thefts are not detected until the loss reaches $20,000 to $35,000, and recovery depends on proving a person's specific responsibility for the disappearance. Certain cash sums totaling $10,000 or more require reporting on IRS Form 8300, per Publication 1544, which is available from www.irs.gov/.

Handling Earnest Money and Making Deposits

Rules E-1(m), (n), and (o) require the timely deposit of escrow funds and govern who is to receipt for and hold such money.

There are several accepted options for handling earnest money. These funds may be held: (1) in an account specifically identified in the sales agreement, (2) in an escrow account maintained by the buyer's agent, (3) in the listing agent's escrow account, or (4) in any other account acceptable to the buyer and seller.

The party designated to hold the deposit must be clearly identified in the sales contract. A check for the earnest money should accompany the offer until it is accepted. A buyer's agent holding the deposit may forward a copy of the earnest money check with the offer. If the offer is rejected, this broker may simply return the check to the prospect. Submitting an offer to a seller that specifies the receipt of earnest money without actual receipt and deposit of the money in a reasonably agreed-upon time is a serious misrepresentation and may violate federal law or HUD regulation.

Unless otherwise agreed, earnest money deposits held by the specified broker must be deposited not later than the *third* business day after notice of acceptance of the contract. The broker should keep a copy of the validated escrow deposit slip and earnest money check in the office transaction file for later inspection. The initial deposit slip and/or a subsequent wire transfer form to a third party or closing entity must show the buyer's name and the related property description, and must be recorded in the journal and the specific beneficiary's ledger. If a promissory note is initially received as the earnest money deposit, no entry of the deposit is made until the note is redeemed. The use of a promissory note must be authorized in the contract and must include a specific date for redemption. Timely collection of the note is essential, and notice of a failure to redeem the note on its due date must be communicated promptly to the seller. A failure to inform the seller of a default on the note may result in a complaint for misrepresenting the status of the contract.

Money received for property management and short-term rentals must be deposited within five business days after receipt unless the parties agree otherwise. All other types of money belonging to others must be deposited not later than the *third* business day after receipt or as provided in the agreement with those concerned.

Earnest Money Disputes and Unclaimed Property

The broker should retain correspondence that shows reasonable efforts were made to return refundable amounts to the proper beneficiary, or that such amounts were transferred to the appropriate state "escheat fund" for later distribution.

If the beneficiary cannot be contacted and the last known address is outside Colorado, the escheat laws of that state should be followed. If the state has no escheat law, then the property must be transferred to the Colorado State Treasurer's "Great Colorado Payback Fund," per § 38-13-103, C.R.S. This normally occurs no later than five years after abandonment.

When a party fails to cash a refund check six to twelve months after its issue, or if the broker has reason to presume the funds have been abandoned, a "stop payment" order may be issued to the bank and the amount will be added back to the journal balance. The funds are then entered on an "Unclaimed Property Ledger," and a note of this event is made on the original beneficiary's ledger to close it out and place it in the property transaction file. Any subsequent activity is reported on this continuing ledger, showing the status or disposition of such property through the appropriate escheat fund. If a party later claims this amount before transfer to the escheat fund, a new check is issued and recorded in the unclaimed property ledger and the escrow account journal. A copy of the new check should also be placed in the property transaction file. Unclaimed and undisputed items may be transferred to the Colorado Fund prior to the end of the five-year period.

If a dispute over ownership of a deposit develops, the guidelines found in the Commission position statement on earnest money deposits (CP-6) should be followed. If a court refuses to accept custody of funds tendered, the money must be held in escrow until there is a resolution of the dispute, a release is obtained from one party, the statutory record-keeping period under § 12-61-113(1)(i), C.R.S., has expired (four years), or there is good reason to believe the dispute has been abandoned. Subject to legal advice or further instructions from the parties concerned, the disputed but abandoned funds may be transferred to the escheat fund in the original depositor's name. When earnest money is held by a third-party closing entity, where return of the deposit to a buyer is not disputed and the buyer cannot be located but agreed to pay all or part of any third-party escrow agreement fee, then the broker may instruct the third-party closing entity to distribute the "net amount" to the appropriate escheat fund. The Commission has no guidance on making this business decision.

If the licensed real estate business is terminated before any notice of dispute is received, and the amount is abandoned, the money may be delivered to the appropriate escheat fund in the original depositor's name. Further information, other state search links, and software for reporting these items in Colorado can be obtained from Colorado Great Payback office by calling (800) 825-2111 or online at www.colorado.gov/treasury/gcp/.

C. The Beneficiary's Ledger Record (The "Ledger")

General Concepts

The "ledger record" is described in Rule E-1(p)(2). This record separates one person's transactional activity from all other data recorded in the journal and processed through the escrow bank account. Blank forms for the beneficiary and broker's ledgers are found in the chapter appendix, Exhibit C.

There are two types of ledgers used for normal escrow accounting functions: those for **external beneficiaries** assisted or represented during the engagement (the seller, buyer, a management property owner, the tenant, or unclaimed property described in the preceding subsection), and for the **internal beneficiary**, the employing broker, who maintains the account and/or provides any financing services to the external beneficiaries per Rules E-1(f)(4) and (p)(5). The "broker's ledger" record is described below. According to industry custom, the ledger maintained for each guest stay in short-term (hotel type) property management is called a "folio."

In a manual record-keeping system, all pending ledgers are usually maintained in a three-ring notebook and are alphabetized by client name or by address; different buyers may have deposits on the same ledger, and these should be identified as "backup offers." Closed ledgers are kept with copies of the deposit slip and earnest disbursement checks in the property transaction file. The journal pages are placed in front of the pending ledgers and broker's ledger in this notebook.

When a separate savings account is maintained for each beneficiary with proper disclosure and authorization for the use of interest-bearing accounts, the monthly bank statement will satisfy the record-keeping requirements for both the "journal" and a "ledger." However, the bank may charge a higher service fee for extensive use of these temporary accounts and may restrict the number of open accounts allowed to one broker at a time. This shortcut method is acceptable with maintenance of proper identification of individual parties in the deposit slips and check memo lines.

Choose a software program that has journal and ledger capabilities. Responsibility for ensuring compliance with Commission requirements rests with the broker and not the software developer. The broker may consult with the financial examination section to ensure that any proposed system will meet regulatory requirements. The cost and/or accounting skill required for proper use of software will vary according to the software program selected. The more complex software applications are generally designed for trained and/or experienced accounting personnel to use in high-volume business operations. A general real estate software resource for brokers is found at the end of this section.

Ledger Operation

A new beneficiary ledger/software sub-account record is opened or established when the broker receives, as the designated contractual custodian, any money as defined in Rule E-1(g), or when the broker places company funds in the escrow account to pay bank operating expenses. Each beneficiary ledger is "closed" when all funds pertaining to the transaction have been disbursed according to contract or operation of law, or when the escrow account is no longer used and any remaining funds have been distributed to the proper parties or a state escheat fund. Any interest earned on the account that appears on the monthly bank statement and that is owned by a beneficiary is recorded in the journal and the appropriate ledger(s).

Each beneficiary ledger must show the names of the parties to the specific transaction, the address or description of the property, transaction dates, check numbers, transaction amounts, a resulting balance, any appropriate deposit/receipt or transaction file reference numbers, and any other information of interest to the broker. The ending balance in an electronic accounting system may be determined when the accounts are reconciled, but care must be taken to never overspend or misuse the beneficiary's available cash balance.

Any rental income and expense and any security deposit held by the broker will generally be reported on separate owner and tenant ledgers. To simplify record keeping for small residential property management activities per Rule E-1(i), the tenant security deposit and rental revenues or expenses may be reported on that owner's ledger. When the broker is responsible for return of a deposit, care must be taken to never spend this money for the ongoing operation of the owner's property. Security deposits must be returned in a timely manner with proper accounting per § 38-12-103(1), C.R.S. The procedure for transfer of the responsibility for return of the security deposit to the owner is set forth in Rule E-16 and in the Commission position statement CP-5, Advance Rental and Tenant Security Deposits.

All ongoing owner expenses and net proceeds should be paid from the escrow account directly to the parties concerned. These amounts should not be transferred to the "company operating account" for payment, as that account is the personal property of the brokerage company and is subject to other setoff or seizure rights by other business creditors. All expenses paid to sell or manage any property must be fully funded by the available cash balance held on behalf of that beneficiary, unless the broker advances additional money to the owner, or other cash reserves are held in escrow pursuant to an agreement with that person. Borrowing funds from the amounts held for other beneficiaries constitutes *overspending the beneficiary's ledger*, creates a shortage in the bank account, and is an illegal commingling of funds. An owner of several properties may authorize the broker to offset the surplus funds of one property against the negative balance of another, so long as the net result is positive on a cash basis and the ownership of the properties is identical.

The Broker's Ledger

Many banks pay interest and charge monthly fees and other costs for maintaining an escrow account. The broker may keep money in escrow to pay these costs, conduct in-office closings, prevent possible overspending of ledger balances, and "offset" advances of money for unexpected client/customer repairs or "NSF" items (non-sufficient funds). This record normally constitutes an escrow account payable (liability) to the broker/company for the amount deposited. Amounts advanced from the broker's ledger must be collected as "good funds" in 45-90 days.

Rules E-1(f)(4) and (p)(5) require an accounting for any advance of money made to a beneficiary in both the journal and the beneficiary ledger affected. This practice places the broker in the role of financing the client's business activity. An alternative is to require the client to maintain a reserve balance for unforeseen emergencies and other contingencies. This is common in property management operations where there are absentee owners, variable operating expenses, or other monthly payments that require consistent collection of "good funds" from the tenants. If the broker makes an advance, it becomes that beneficiary's property and must be used accordingly. The expenditures and the subsequent repayment by the owner must be recorded on both the beneficiary's ledger and in the journal. The amount advanced must appear on the owner's accounting report, and any interest charged for the advance must be disclosed in the management agreement. When using a computerized accounting system, the advance is recorded by making a deposit (debit) to the escrow cash account and a credit (non-operating income) to the specific owner's (ledger) account. Expenses and repayments are paid from the cash account and charged to the specific owner balances affected. Accounting for management commissions earned and withdrawn from an escrow account is also illustrated in the broker's ledger in the section appendix, Exhibit C.

Using "estimated" amounts due the broker without subsequently reconciling and adjusting such amounts to actual earnings for the accounting month frequently results in illegal commingling of funds. See Rule E-1(f)(6). When real estate sales are closed in-house, any miscellaneous closing expenses and unexpected changes in service fees must be paid from the broker's own ledger and then should be collected according to the contract from the party concerned. Any uncollectible costs should not be written off against the general account balance; they are paid from funds held in the broker's ledger.

The following section will illustrate the general escrow accounting concepts, use of the escrow account journal and ledgers, and the bank reconciliation process. These processes apply to all other real estate escrow accounts.

D. Illustrated Escrow Accounting Transactions

Background Information

You are a new business and have two listings under contract. In addition, you will manage another single-family residential property for Carter Smith and hold the security deposit for the tenant, Rose Bloom. The sales escrow account was properly established as a CARHOF interest-bearing account. You use a manual accounting system. The following events are first recorded in the appropriate ledgers and then the journal using the transaction reference numbers indicated in (*parentheses*). The month of May 2010 has just ended and the bank statement was received on June 3, 2010. The May escrow bank reconciliation worksheet is shown later in this section.

Monthly Transactions:

(1) A deposit of $250.00 is made by the broker to open the account and purchase supplies on April 1, 2010. The bank charged $175.00 for business checks. CARHOF interest is assumed to be $1.00 for April and $10.00 for May. These amounts are withdrawn by the bank and are paid to CARHOF the next month. A "√" means the item had cleared the account and appeared on the bank statement (not shown).

(2) $5,000.00 was received on April 15, 2010 from Harold and Jean Blue for purchase of 7373 West Flamingo Road (This is to illustrate the use of escrow records for an in-house closing—see the first closing problem in Chapter 18, "Closing Statements," of the manual). The broker will close this transaction on May 10, 2010.

(3) The Blues obtained a loan for $190,750.00, which they deposit with the broker for closing. They also deposit the down payment of $4,188.43 per the broker's settlement worksheet on May 5. Broker makes all disbursements per the credit column on the settlement worksheet and pays the seller's proceeds on May 15 in "good funds."

(4) Rose Bloom rents Carter Smith's home on May 1, for $1,500.00 per month. Rent is due on the 5th and the tenant also pays the $1,500.00 security deposit due per the lease. The broker charges 10 percent of gross rent as the management fee and pays the owner's monthly mortgage of $800.00 no later than the 15th. The tenant pays all

utilities and trash directly to the city vendor. The management fee is scheduled to be withdrawn on the last day of the month. Proceeds are mailed to the owner by the 10th day of the next month.

(5) Carter Smith gives the broker a check for $175.00 to repair the furnace on May 29 at an estimated cost of $175.00. The bank returned this payment as "NSF" on May 30 after the broker mailed the monthly proceeds check. Smith repaid this amount in cash on June 1. (NOTE: The tenant deposit must be held intact as a refundable security deposit. If the furnace repair cost is actually $300.00 and is paid on May 30, this "theoretical" expense would be partially offset by the $85.00 balance on the broker's ledger and the $1,200.00 in the owner's ledger, however, and an **"unfunded amount"** of $215.00 would have been "borrowed" from the tenant's security deposit in violation of Rule E-1(q). This is an example of an event the broker must properly handle in property management.)

Ledger Entries by date:

BROKER'S LEDGER — Sales Escrow Account # 987654							Page 1
Ref	Date	Check	Description	√	Payment	Deposit	Balance
(1)	4-1-10		Broker Funds to Open Account	√		250.00	250.00
	4-1-10	101	Checking Supplies purchased	√	175.00		75.00
	4-30-10	Bnk Credit	Carhof interest earned April	√		1.00	76.00
	5-1-10	Bnk Debit	Sweep Carhof interest April	√	1.00		75.00
	5-30-10	Bnk Credit	Carhof interest for May	√		10.00	85.00

BUYER LEDGER: Harold & Jean Blue, 111 1st Ave, Salt Lake City, UT SELLER: John & Mary Gray LISTING 4-01-10 NEW ADDRESS: 7373 W. Flamingo Road, Lakewood, CO CLOSING DATE: May 10, 2010 CLOSED 5-10-10							
Ref	Date	Check	Description	√	Payment	Deposit	Balance
(2)	4-15-10		Earnest Money Deposit	√		5,000.00	5000.00
(3)	5-10-10		Lender Loan Proceeds	√		190,750.00	195,750.00
	5-10-10		Down payment for closing	√		4,188.43	199,938.43
	"	102	Acme Loan-Pay off of 1st	√	46,450.00		153,488.43
	"	103	Title Ins Mortgagee Premium	√	575.00		152,913.43
	"	104	Cnty Clerk recording/release fees	√	62.00		152,851.43
	"	105	Buyer 's Atty.-title exam	√	75.00		152,776.43
	"	106	Dept of Rev- State Doc fee & 2%	√	4095.38		148,681.05
	"	107	County-Tax Certificate	√	15.00		148,666.05
(3)	5-10-10	108	Lender Tax Reserve	√	854.65		147,811.40
	"	109	Hazard Ins. Premium & Reserve	√	787.50		147,023.90
	"	110	1% fee & interest on new loan	√	2,769.79		144,254.11
	"	111	Survey Cost	√	65.00		144,189.11
	"	112	Lender Credit Report Company	√	50.00		144,139.11
	"	113	Broker's Commission	√	11,400.00		132, 739.11
	"	114	New Lender 's Atty.- title exam	√	75.00		132,664.11
	"	115	Broker-document preparation	√	100.00		132,564.11
	"	116	Seller 's Net Proceeds Paid	√	132,564.11		0.00

MANAGEMENT LEDGER TENANT: Rose Bloom (303-550-0001) OWNER: Carter Smith (303-550-0000) RENTAL: 123 W. Flamingo Road OWNER ADDRESS: 10050 Grape Ct. Lakewood, CO. 89100 RENT PER MONTH: $500/mo due on 5th BANK: United Nat'l. Bank, Loan # xxxx-xxx – Due on 15th SEC DEPOSIT: $1,500.00 LEASE EXPIRES: 4-30-11 MANAGEMENT FEE: 10% of Gross Rents							
Ref	Date	Check	Description	√	Payment	Deposit	Balance
4	5-5-10		Rent and security deposit for Rose Bloom – 1 yr. Lease	√		3,000.00	3,000.00
	5-10-10	117	United National Bank loan	√	800.00		2,200.00
5	5-29-10		Owner funds to repair furnace	√		175.00	2,375.00
(4)	5-30-10	118	10% Management fee	√	150.00		2,225.00
	"	119	Owner Proceeds May 06	√	550.00		1,675.00
(5)	"	Actual Month end balance	Owner deposit was NSF	√	175.00		1,500.00
	"	Theoretical for illustration only*	Assumed but not actual repair of furnace to illustrate a shortage in the Sec Deposit. *		300.00*		1,200.00*

The total funds actually held in escrow for all pending ledgers at May 31, 2010 is **$1,585.00 ($85.00 + 1,500.00)**. This agrees with the month-end journal balance shown below. Note: the journal below is presented in very abbreviated form to save publishing space; this should not be done in actual practice:

SALES ESCROW JOURNAL May 2010							Page 1 of____
Ref	Date	Check	Description	√	Payment	Deposit	Balance
			Balance Forward from April 30, 2010	√			$5,076.00
(1)	5-1-10	Debit	Bank Interest Sweep	√	1.00		5,075.00
(2)	5-1-10		Rose Bloom Rent & Security Deposit – May	√		3,000.00	8,075.00
(3)	5-10-10		Blue Loan & Down payment	√		194,938.43	203,013.43
		102-116	Blue Closing, 7373 W. Flamingo	√	199,938.43		3,075.00
(5)	5-29-10		Bloom Repair Deposit-Smith	√		175.00	3,250.00
	5-30-10	Debit	Bloom Repair-Smith NSF	√	175.00		3,075.00
(4)	5-10 to 5-30-10	117-119	Bloom-Mortgage, rental expense Commission and proceeds	√	1,500.00		1,575.00
(6)	5-30-10	Credit	Record CARHOF Interest May 2010	√		10.00	$1,585.00

The Bank Reconciliation Process

The purpose of reconciliation is to verify that the records for the account are in balance per the escrow accounting equation. The bank reconciliation worksheet form is shown in the chapter appendix, Exhibit D.

Rule E-1(p)(3) requires the ending bank statement cash balance to be reconciled with the office journal and ledger account cards during any month when there has been escrow account activity. Each open ledger balance (*not just a lump-sum total*) is individually listed on the left side as shown below, or in additional attached sheets if necessary. The ending journal balance on the date of reconciliation is entered underneath the total for all pending ledgers. The bank balance is reconciled on the right side of the worksheet; it must balance with the cash shown in the journal and all ledgers. It is recommended that the "date of reconciliation" be the date of the latest bank statement, even though the actual date of performing this process is usually later.

Assuming that the bank statement balance on May 30, 2010 is $1,585.00, and that there are no outstanding items or errors on the statement, the reconciliation worksheet below would be prepared using the data above. In addition, the broker should carefully perform the verifying tests noted below.

<table>
<tr><td colspan="2">Mile High Realty Sales Escrow Account 000-0000-0
Bank reconciliation for month ending May 30, 2010
Prepared by: Linda Smith</td><td colspan="2">Date reconciled: June 5, 2010
Date of reconciliation: May 30, 2010
Reviewed by: John Smith, Broker</td></tr>
<tr><td>Escrow Liabilities per pending ledgers on 5-30-10
Description</td><td>Ledger Balance</td><td>Ending Bank Statement Bal 5-30-10:</td><td>$ 1,585.00</td></tr>
<tr><td>Broker (Company) Ledger</td><td>$ 85.00</td><td>Add: Outstanding Deposits mailed to bank on or before May 30, 2010</td><td>0 .00</td></tr>
<tr><td>123 W. Flamingo Sec Deposit</td><td>1,500.00</td><td>Subtotal:</td><td>$ 1,585.00</td></tr>
<tr><td></td><td></td><td>Subtract: Outstanding Checks</td><td>0.00</td></tr>
<tr><td></td><td></td><td>Reconciled Bank Balance: 5-30-10</td><td>√ $ 1,585.00</td></tr>
<tr><td>Total Pending Ledgers 5-30-10</td><td>√ $ 1,585.00</td><td colspan="2">√ This means all records agree with the actual escrow liabilities per the contracts and all banking activity is properly reported in the accounting records.</td></tr>
<tr><td>Ending Journal Balance 5-30-10</td><td>√ $ 1,585.00</td><td colspan="2"></td></tr>
</table>

For simplicity, the Commission recommends reconciling the bank balance to the ending checkbook and journal cash balance per the office records, but other accepted methods may be used, *e.g.*, reconciling the books to the cash in the bank, and/or using a "four column cash reconciliation," with a supplemental listing of all pending ledgers and outstanding items on attached sheets.

All contracts must be examined to confirm that the total amount of money that should have been received has been properly deposited. Investigate and correct any errors or omissions immediately. Any transfer of funds between related accounts must be made in a timely manner, *i.e.*, rent and security deposit payments combined on one check. If this is not done, a shortage will develop in the security deposit account, and refundable deposits may be erroneously paid to property owners as net proceeds. Collecting these amounts later may be difficult.

An authorized independent company custodian should have personal responsibility to account for retention, access, and use of banking records, receipt books, computer backups, and hard copy printouts of all accounting records. Someone independent of the accounting department should review monthly bank reconciliation and the items listed for errors or other irregularities. The reviewer should trace transfers and outstanding items to subsequent payments and deposits on later statements. Look for unrecorded statement items or those that are contrary to other company policy and practices.

E. Transaction Files and the Retention of Records

The records of licensed brokerage activity must be retained for *four* years per § 12-61-113(1)(i), C.R.S. Rules E-4 and E-5, as well as the Commission position statement on record-keeping (CP-9), control the contents of the broker's property transaction file. Rule E-3 requires any licensee to produce appropriate records concerning licensed activity and operation of the trust accounts upon the request of the Commission.

Except for times in which the documents are being reviewed or executed, the current transaction files should be kept at the broker's office in a secure, central location. The broker should review all pending sales transaction files and any leases and management agreements executed by associates for possible correction or follow-up attention. A copy of the earnest money check with a copy of the deposit slip should be placed in the transaction file. Associates may retain copies of contract documents (and pay for them) according to the broker's office policy or employment agreement.

Duplicate signatures are acceptable for all records maintained in the broker's transaction file per Rule E-4. "Duplicate" means photocopy, carbon copy, or facsimile, or electronic copies that contain a digital or electronic signature as defined in § 24-71-101(1), C.R.S.

A broker must maintain a duplicate of the original of any document (except deeds, promissory notes, and deeds of trust or mortgages prepared for the benefit of third-party lenders) that was prepared by or on behalf of the licensee and pertains to the consummation of the leasing, purchase, sale, or exchange of real property in which the broker participates as a broker. The payoff statement and new loan statement monetarily affect the settlement statement and should be retained by the broker concerned. Cooperating brokers, including brokers acting as agents for buyers in a specific real estate transaction, shall have the same requirements for retention of duplicate records as is stated above, except that a cooperating broker who is not a party to the listing contract need not retain a copy of the listing contract or the seller's settlement statement.

A broker is not required to retain copies of existing public records, title commitments, loan applications, lender-required disclosures, or related affirmations from independent third-party closing entities after the settlement date. The broker must retain documents bearing a duplicate signature for the disclosures required by Rule F-7. The broker engaged by a party must ensure that the final sales agreement, settlement statement, or amendment of the settlement, delivered at closing for that party's tax reporting or future use, bears duplicate signatures or as authorized by the parties concerned.

The following is a *checklist for common records* to retain in the both the listing and selling broker's property transaction file. Other ancillary documents and agreements executed between the parties and the closing entity or lender are not required.

SALES FILES

- Lead-based paint disclosures for residential property built before 1978;
- Exclusive right-to-buy/sell, or agency or open listing agreement and amendments (listing broker only);
- Disclosure of brokerage relationships;
- Disclosure of compensation for services and income from affiliated entities;
- Disclosure of the source of residential property square footage;
- Contract to buy/sell/exchange real estate, counterproposals, amendments, and attachments;
- Current marketing/MLS information used in the transaction;
- Inspection notice;
- Seller's property disclosure statement;
- Actual closing instructions, negotiated before the actual date of closing;

- Copy of any power of attorney (show recording data if closed in-house);
- Copy of earnest money check, validated escrow bank deposit slip (or receipt below);
- Signed and dated receipt for earnest money held by third-party closing entity;
- Copy of earnest money note;
- Buyer's financial information, if "owner-carry" financing;
- Rental/occupancy agreement before closing date (have separate security deposit);
- Estimated closing costs/estimated monthly expenses prepared by licensee;
- Settlement statement (or equivalent computer form) for the party represented or assisted;
- Side agreement/amendment to revise a settlement statement;
- Promissory note (unsigned, marked "COPY");**
- Closing entity commission check remittance less earnest money amount if applicable;
- Tax reports required by government agencies (Colorado withholding tax);**
- Escrow receipts or collection agreements continuing after closing;
- Accounting for use of advance retainer fees;
- Six-column worksheet for settlement (or equivalent computer form);**
- Deed (copy showing recording data if closed in-house);**
- Deed of trust (copy showing recording data if closed in-house);** and
- Other legal documents prepared by the broker.**

**Required only when the broker personally prepares the document, conducts the closing in-house without use of a title company, and/or is responsible for recording of any documents.

MANAGEMENT FILES

- Current/past management and/or short-term reservation management agreements;
- Current/past lease or rental occupancy agreements with tenants and guests;
- Lead-based paint disclosures for residential property built before 1978;
- Disclosure of brokerage relationships and/or listing contracts to lease;
- Disclosure of compensation, service income from affiliated entities;
- Brokerage accounting records, bank reconciliation, tax and owner reports;
- Ongoing contracts, bids, invoices, service provider billings, and correspondence with client;
- Legal notices, actions, and accounting reports affecting owner/occupant/tenant funds;
- Documentation for commissions earned versus taken or charged to others;
- Prompt assessment, timely (45-90 days) collection, restitution of all money due escrow; and
- Documentation verifying reported receipts, income, and all expenses paid for another.

F. Administrative Matters

Changing Employing Brokers

Each corporation, partnership, or limited liability company is recognized as a distinct, licensed entity. The designated natural person, *i.e.*, the "employing" or "acting" broker, is responsible for the ongoing maintenance of all records concerning licensed real estate activity and supervision of the escrow accounting process.

If the acting broker leaves employment with the licensed entity, the licensed entity retains the continuing responsibility for maintenance of all escrow records. The departing broker is personally responsible for delivering these records to the licensed entity, and must properly account for all trust funds transferred to the new broker. The acting broker serves only as a caretaker or trustee during the period of licensed tenure as the acting broker. A form for documenting a change in broker is found in the chapter appendix, Exhibit H.

An exception to this situation occurs when a licensed business entity is dissolved. The final acting broker then becomes personally responsible for making all final disbursements and accounting for all trust funds. That broker must maintain all records for a period of four years. Upon dissolution of an individual proprietorship, records maintenance remains the responsibility of the individual proprietor broker and his or her heirs. Closing the business and the pending transactions should be done according to the Commission position statement CP-8, Assignment of Contracts and Escrowed Funds. An attorney or another qualified unlicensed party may complete this process on behalf of the surviving heirs of the individual proprietorship. The forms for applying for a transfer or change in the broker's license status may be found at: www.dora.state.co.us/real-estate/. See Rule A-26 for the process of securing a temporary business entity broker license.

Good Funds

Rule E-36 requires that "good funds" be held and disbursed for closing. Such money is: (1) immediately available for withdrawal as a matter of right from the financial institution where deposited, or (2) is available for such withdrawal as the consequence of an agreement of an institution in which the funds are to be deposited or a financial institution upon which the funds are to be drawn. The agreement must be for the benefit of the licensee providing the closing service; all contingencies and conditions must be satisfied before any funds may be disbursed. Good funds are required for closing by the Colorado Consumer Protection Act, § 6-1-105(1)(v), C.R.S.

Examples of good funds are: cash, wire transfers, telephone transfers between accounts in the same bank, cashier's checks, certified checks, teller checks (issued by a savings and loan), tri-party agreements in which the financial institution unconditionally guarantees the lender's check, deposits of earnest money that clear the buyer's bank before closing, transfers of a buyer's earnest money to a closing agent (with prior consent of the parties) that clear the broker's bank before closing, offsets of earnest money deposits against earned commissions by the closing agent, and Federal Home Loan Bank checks.

Closing Instructions

Colorado Division of Insurance Regulation 3-5-1 requires that written closing instructions from all necessary parties be provided to the closing entity for any real estate transaction. Further, the regulation requires the title entity to execute closing instructions approved by the

Commission if the instructions were executed by all parties to the real estate transaction and delivered to the closing entity in advance of the closing and settlement. The Commission closing instructions form is found in Chapter 26, "Commission-Approved and Miscellaneous Forms," and is required by Rule F-7. The Commission's closing instructions and earnest money receipt or an equivalent form must be delivered to the closing agent in time to prepare the final settlement.

Signing Settlement Statements

Rule E-5(f) requires the licensee to sign and approve the settlement statement of the party they assist or represent. The settlement statement must also show the name of the employing broker where applicable. The Commission recommends that each licensee and supervising broker review the final contract and proposed settlement statement before closing. The licensee, or an alternate, who consents to attend a closing on behalf of the absent licensee, is responsible for furnishing a proper settlement statement at closing. The employing broker is responsible to see that the licensee is competent in such responsibilities. A copy of the signed settlement statement shall be delivered to the employing broker immediately after the closing. Original signatures are no longer required for the broker's transaction file.

If the closing involves a *new loan* made to the purchaser where the lending institution deducts costs before distributing the loan proceeds prior to final settlement, the loan proceeds must be reconciled with the amounts due to or from the seller and buyer. The new loan reconciliation is described and illustrated in Chapter 18, "Closing Statements." The broker's debit and credit columns of the "Worksheet For a Real Estate Settlement" or an equivalent closing entity form may be used for this purpose. The reconciliation must also be delivered to the employing broker after closing.

Closing Fees

Commission position statement CP-7, Closing Costs, and Rule E-37 state that there is no obligation for a broker to prepare any legal document as part of a real estate transaction or closing. However, as the result of the *Conway-Bogue* decision (see Chapter 5, "Landmark Case Law and Opinions"), brokers may prepare certain legal documents and complete standard and approved forms.

Certain fees are generally charged for preparation of real estate documents and closings: (1) a fee for closing and preparing *non-legal documents* such as the settlement statements, and (2) a fee for preparing *legal documents* executed by the parties, *i.e.*, contracts, deeds, notes, deeds of trust, mortgages, and other security instruments. Upon agreement of the parties, fees for preparing non-legal documents may be charged to anyone. However, in the absence of an attorney representing one of the parties to the transaction, the broker must pay any fees for preparing legal documents. The broker must ensure that the proper parties pay for the closing costs. Brokers may charge (with written authorization from the parties) for the transactions that they close "in-house," when such charges are not tied to preparation of legal documents. The broker may not designate his or her own attorney to prepare the documents, and then pass these charges to the parties, as if the attorney were representing them.

IRS/State Reports

IRS Form 8300, "Report of Cash Payment Over $10,000," received in a trade or business, must be filed when cash (currency) is received by the broker from the same person in any one year as the result of single, connected, or related transactions. The report and further instructions may be obtained at the IRS website at www.irs.gov/. Civil and criminal penalties may result from a failure to comply with reporting requirements.

Sellers must provide the closing agent with their complete name, address, and taxpayer identification number or Social Security number for reporting income from the sale or exchange of property. The person who actually provides the closing service makes this report on Form 1099-S. The Colorado Department of Revenue requires withholding 2 percent of the sales price *or* the net proceeds shown on the bottom of the settlement statement, whichever is less, from the sale of Colorado property in an amount of $100,000 or more by non-resident individuals, including foreign partnerships and corporations not registered with the Secretary of State, or having no Colorado business address immediately following the sale. The tax must be withheld and the forms prepared by the individual or entity actually providing the closing service. This is reported on Form DR-1083 and is remitted with payment on Colorado Form 1079. Further instructions, exemptions, and forms may be obtained by calling the Colorado Department of Revenue at (303) 238-3278. See basic text of this law in Chapter 23, "Tax Factors Pertaining to Real Estate Practice;" § 39-22-604.5, C.R.S.; or http://www.colorado.gov/revenue, select "Taxes", then "Tax Forms" to locate forms by form number or name.

Private Bank Account Insurance

Brokers may be able to purchase private insurance coverage for all escrow and operating checking accounts with deposits in excess of the FDIC coverage as added protection from a bank failure. Information on such coverage can be obtained from the broker's insurance agent.

Computer Forms

Personal computers may be used to generate standard and approved forms if the following requirements are met: (1) the Commission-approved language must be exactly reproduced, (2) the software must not allow alteration of the approved standard language in day-to-day operation, (3) the software must produce fill-in and allowable transaction-specific language in a font clearly differentiated from the standard, approved contract language, (4) contract print must be easily readable, (5) blank spaces shall not be filled in by the licensee, prior to negotiation with the parties. See Commission Rule F-1 in Chapter 26, "Commission-Approved and Miscellaneous Forms."

Software Resources

The Commission does not recommend or endorse any specific software, and provides the following information for further investigation and analysis by the licensee: (1) Texas A&M College Station (1-979-845-2031) publishes a synopsis of current software (400+) applications available for real estate firms, (2) Institute of Real Estate Management, 430 N. Michigan Ave., Chicago, IL 60610-9025, phone (800) 837-0706, fax (800) 338-4736. Colorado chapters may be contacted through C.A.R., (303) 790-7099.

Commission Audits

Statewide examinations are conducted in response to public complaints or on a routine cyclical basis. The examination is performed on-site to examine the handling of escrow funds and the maintenance of other required business records. The broker is selected from the licensing database of eligible brokers or registered developers. Audits of certain brokers and developers may be done by correspondence. Upon completion of an audit, the examiner will meet with the broker or registered developer's representatives to discuss any findings. The examiner will then mail a written report of the results to the broker for explanation and correction. All completed audit reports are filed electronically for future reference. It is important for brokers to ensure that prior corrections continue to be followed. Repeated findings are considered matters that warrant official Commission action.

III. Property Management Records

A. Management Accounting Requirements

General Concepts

The responsibilities and concepts described in Parts I and II become more critical in the supervision of property management activities.

The accounting cycles are more complex and intensified, as more transactions must be processed in a shorter time. The financial interest of each beneficiary must be maintained to prevent illegal commingling of funds. Ongoing operations must be effectively managed to maintain accurate and timely records, while administering customer and client services each month.

The management activity undertaken will affect the accounting system used, and care must be taken to choose the type of product best suited for the proposed business operation. If software is used, it must:

1. Classify and report current, year-to-date, and selected period financial information pertaining to the financial interests of the owner, tenant, and any related homeowner association by property and unit managed on the cash and accrual basis;
2. Control cash flows and ongoing expenditures;
3. Produce current or prior bank account reconciliations with the corresponding escrow liabilities in detail upon demand;
4. Account for the use of different escrow bank account structures;
5. Track managerial and administrative information for the property manager and owner, per Chapter 20, "Property Management and Leases;" and
6. Emphasize the "custodial/trustee responsibilities of the Colorado broker in accounting for the funds of others," as distinct from the "ownership/investor role" used in most commercial software design and operation.

Account Structures and the Flow of Funds

A typical full-service management company would generally have the following account structures for long- or short-term management operations involving associations and broker-owned properties. These activities were introduced in Part II.

LONG TERM MANAGEMENT

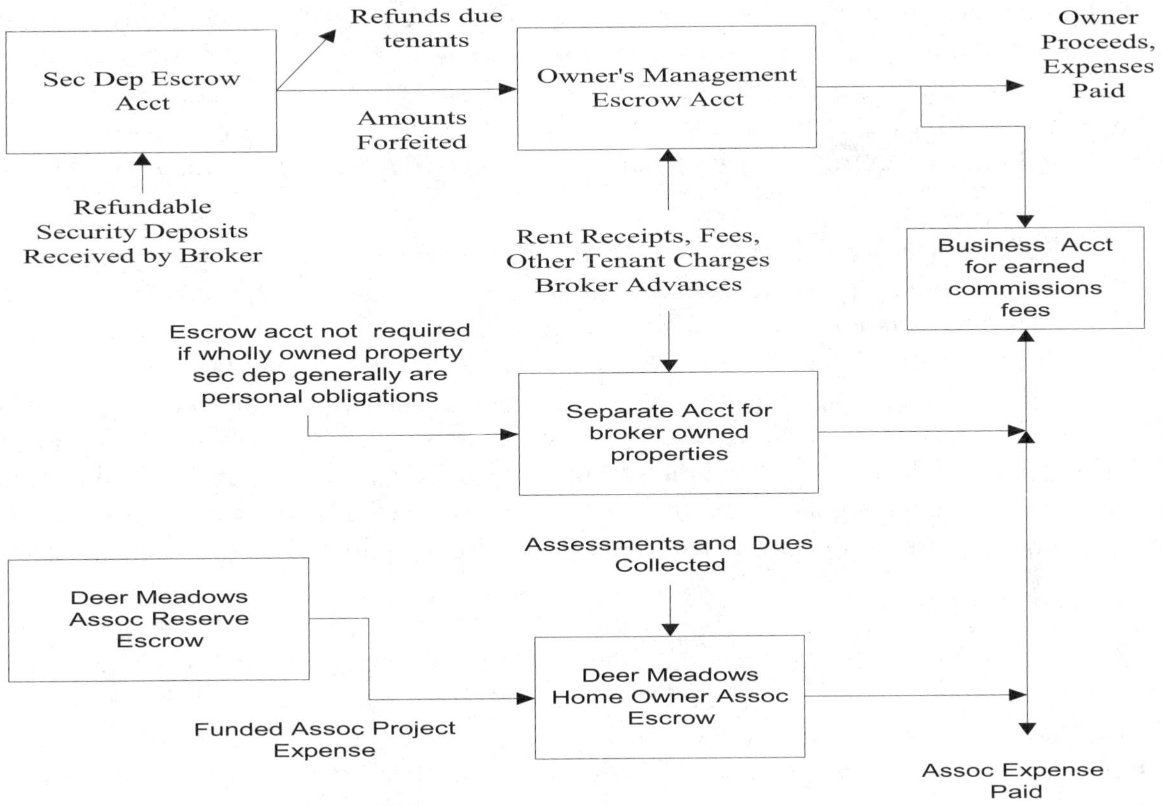

SHORT TERM FUNDS FLOW

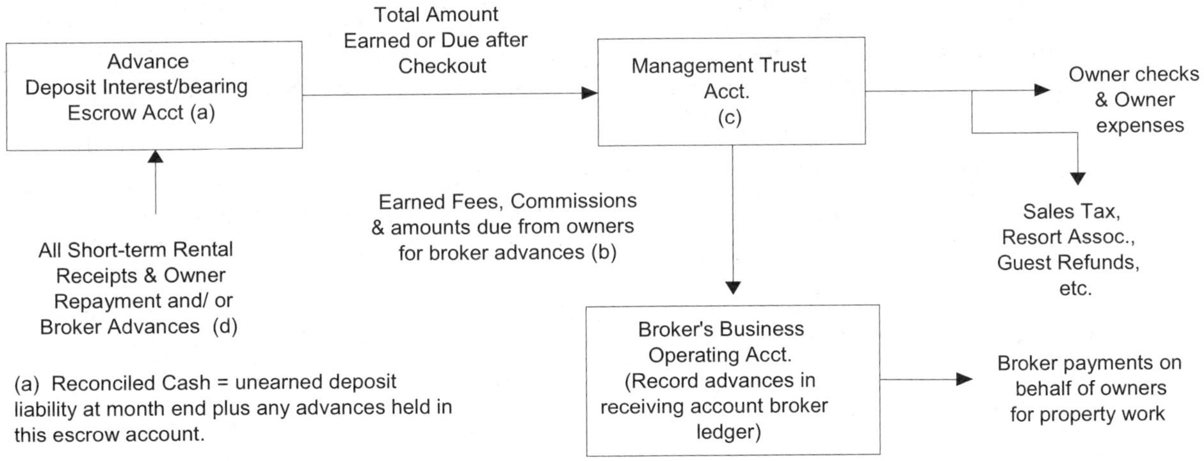

(a) Reconciled Cash = unearned deposit liability at month end plus any advances held in this escrow account.

(b) Use actual earned not estimated per Rule E-1(f)(6) and Ch. 18 exhibit J.

(c) Reconciled Cash = amounts held for owners + broker's ledger balance + other unpaid amounts held in this escrow account.

(d) Broker Advances/Owner Repayments can be directly deposited to the Advance Deposit Acct. and reported as a reimbursement when the expense is paid.

Account Operation

The accounts illustrated above may exist in addition to the sales escrow account. Information on how to establish and identify a required escrow account is found in Part II, Section A. Separate long- and short-term bank accounts are not required if the records differentiate and report each activity separately. However, management of associations of more than 30 units requires the use of separate accounts for each association and individual reserve fund. (See § 38-33.3-306(3)(a), C.R.S.)

Residential property management duties may range from simple upkeep and caring for an absentee owner's property to the management of large apartment or commercial or common interest owner associations, to managing short-term resort properties for many different owners. The basic accounting records for such activities are illustrated in simple form in Part II, Section D. Basically, the manager receives inflows of escrow cash from tenants/guests in the form of rent, homeowner association assessments, special fees, advance rent, security deposits, owner cash reserves, or reimbursement for broker advances, and pays this money out to various third parties as owner and tenant expenses, refunds, or owner rental proceeds. In addition, the broker may manage reserves for future expenditures or improvement funds.

Internal Controls

An effective and efficient "internal control structure" must be developed for business operations in order to establish personal accountability for performance of the critical steps of the company's accounting cycle. Professional advice is recommended as the size and complexity of the business increases. The structure must adequately separate and monitor three basic "incompatible" functions: (1) the transaction authorization and approval process, (2) the responsibilities for the physical control and custody of the escrow assets and/or the records creating or changing escrow liabilities, and (3) the accounting, record-keeping and external reporting functions. The employing broker must avoid delegating job duties in a manner that allows one person to independently perform and/or supervise all three functions from start to finish. Some guidelines concerning these functions based on audit findings are:

1. The responsibility for collection of company receipts and making the corresponding bank deposits should be separated, and be separate from the responsibility for maintaining the accounting records;
2. Avoid combining the responsibility for the custody for any escrow asset with the independent ability to control the related transactional information and/or to create or alter the corresponding contractual records of the liability;
3. The responsibility for authorizing write-offs and/or adjustments to amounts due the company should be based on independent collection efforts by a third party or the employing broker's own investigation of the facts reported;
4. The responsibility for conducting licensed activity on behalf of the employing broker should be separated from the responsibility for maintaining the primary accounting records and/or controlling the reporting processes associated with those efforts;
5. The broker should maintain full disclosure and reliable sources of ongoing, unfiltered communications with all parties affected by operating policies involving potential conflicts of interest; and

6. The broker must be alert for and monitor circumstances that may give rise to the means, motivation, or opportunity for misuse of funds, *e.g.*, accepting cash (legal tender), signing blank checks, using cash receipts as a petty cash fund, not verifying voided or outstanding checks and deposits in the bank reconciliation, etc.

A "self-authenticating" cash receipt and/or coversheet deposit form, with the detail information required in Rule E-1(p)(6), should be used to account for the physical custody and deposit of cash. The receipt must be signed and dated by a designated "cashier" *and* the person making the payment; the person paying must maintain the carbon receipt as proof of payment. The person collecting receipts must formally account for all receipts in his or her custody monthly, and for the receipts given to a designated "courier" for deposit; both the cashier and courier must count and *countersign a dated cover sheet* showing the receipt numbers and individual amounts included in each bank deposit. A ranking independent staff member should compare the monthly amounts due per the rent receivable roll, pending folios, and leases with the corresponding bank deposits and verify the receivables due are accounted for and were properly deposited. Any delinquent or missing receipt items should be confirmed with the party concerned and immediately reported to the employing/supervising broker. Each cash receipt form should be magnetically coded and numbered to simplify the reconciliation process by appearing on the monthly bank statement like returned checks. Some companies require the use of money orders from nearby banks as an alternative to handling cash receipts and then allow tenants to deduct the order cost from the rent due.

Authority to make telephone transfers or electronic withdrawals should be limited to the broker and a knowledgeable manager. The bank should receive written instructions to verify the identity of the caller and record this with the corresponding teller's name on each returned transfer/withdrawal form.

In short-term management, all guest receipts should be deposited directly into the advance rental/security deposit account to ensure: (1) there is only one authorized point of entry into the escrow accounting system, (2) any authorized brokerage income from the proper use of an interest-bearing account can be maximized, and (3) there is greater control over the transfer of earned income and miscellaneous receipts into the management escrow account. The management escrow account is the one account to be used to distribute all authorized payments to others. The use of manual checks prepared outside the normal accounting system may be avoided or closely monitored by the designated broker.

All used/unused company deposit slips, pre-numbered receipt books, sequentially numbered receipt forms, and blank check stock must be accounted for periodically and limited to controlled usage by authorized persons. Access to this inventory should be assigned to a specific person and/or the broker. Unused or new pre-numbered receipts, receipt books, check books, and unused stock should never be left unsupervised outside the control of an authorized custodian. Unnumbered bank items are difficult to control, costly to account for, and are always easy to misuse.

In long-term management, payments to vendors, owners, and tenants should generally be made from the account where the amount was first deposited. When the use of separate escrow bank accounts is required, some incentive may be given to encourage the separate payment of rent, security deposits, or other amounts requiring use of separate escrow accounts. Company policy should require tenants to use separate checks that can be deposited directly into the proper account. Every internal transfer duplicates the cost of accounting and increases the risk of error, misapplication, or theft. This policy should accommodate good business practice and occasional tenant hardships. It should require preparation of a corresponding escrow check to transfer the necessary amount to the proper account *at the same time* the customer's check is deposited. Failure to properly identify and transfer this money results in a corresponding shortage in the security deposit account. This error will not be easy to find if the identity of the tenant and the amounts paid are not shown individually on the deposit slip per Rule E-1(p)(6).

Unrecorded or uncorrected non-sufficient funds (NSF) items or bank errors will create a similar problem in the owner's management escrow account. NSF items may be offset by money maintained in the broker's ledger. The appropriate amount should be based on normal rates of occurrence.

Creation of an Unlicensed Company

Brokers who allow associates to manage property or perform real estate related services on the broker's behalf through the licensed brokerage entity are generally responsible for the results and must supervise those activities per Rules E-29 through E-32. A licensee may also sell and/or manage personally owned property as a private party with disclosure per Rule E-25. In this case, the licensee must avoid any impression that this activity is performed on behalf of his or her broker in a licensed capacity. See Commission position statement, CP-15, Sale of Items Related to Real Estate, in Chapter 3. A licensee who performs any exempt activity is still subject to the jurisdiction of the Commission. See *Seibel v. Colorado Real Estate Commission* in Chapter 5, "Landmark Case Law and Opinions," and § 12-61-113 (1)(g), C.R.S., in Chapter 1, "Real Estate Broker License Law." Even though the licensee has the general duty to act honestly and in good faith, to properly remit any funds received, and to perform all duties promised when performing exempt activity, the escrow accounts and records prescribed by Rule E-1 and E-1(p) are not required by license law for this activity.

Broker who acts as a "Conduit"

A "**conduit**" means that the broker only collects money on behalf of another and deposits the same to the owner's bank account without any additional signatory power or right of withdrawal. No trust account is required in this case. The broker should have a written agreement as to the duties required and keep a record showing the collection and proper deposit to the owner's account of funds received.

B. Required Management Records

The following ledger records are required to control and account for money belonging to others. These are in addition to the escrow bank accounts and the journal.

Tenant/guest Rental Ledger

This record shows each customer's payment history, any amount due, plus other fees or charges. For single-family management, the tenant's payment information may be kept on the owner's ledger card, but in multi-family (apartment) management, a separate record should be kept for each tenant renting a unit. The use of a "continuous tenant ledger by unit" (for each unit rented) lends itself to errors and internal misuse of funds because the amounts held or due for a specific tenant are difficult to isolate. See chapter appendix, Exhibits E and F.

A different ledger form is used for *short-term management* and is called the guest folio. It may be designed to suit company needs. The form must facilitate accounting for all unearned advance deposits in the monthly bank reconciliation; it also accounts to the guest for the amounts received and due on the check-in date, and contains the following general information:

Folio Number: ____________	Guest Name ____________
Dates of Stay ____________	Rental Address ____________
Reservation Confirmation No. ______	Reservation Date ____________
Guest Address and Telephone No. ____________	
Nights Rented _____ X Rate per/night $________ = Total Due $__________	
Less Travel Agent Fees & Discounts	(__________)
Add Security or Advance Deposit Due to the Company	__________
Special Packages Ordered by Guest	__________
Total Amount Due Company from Guest by Check-In Date:	$__________
Less Amount(s) Paid on ______ by ____________	(__________)
______ " ____________	(__________)
Balance Due at Check-In " ____________	$__________
Refund/Cancellation Paid Guest on ______ by Check ________	
(Company refund policies and other disclosures are printed and mailed to the guest upon receipt of a reservation).	

Owner's Ledger

All cash received or paid in managing the owner's property is itemized by individual transaction on this record. This ledger may be used to prepare a separate owner accounting report or may be mailed as the monthly statement with any net amount due to or from the owner. A sample form is found in the chapter appendix, Exhibit G.

Proper maintenance and scrutiny of the owner cash balance reported is the easiest way to prevent illegal commingling of funds between individual same-owner properties in a "pooled" escrow account. If the owner lacks the necessary capital in one property, the broker may transfer the funds needed from another identically owned property, assuming there is a surplus on the other property ledger and the transfer is authorized in the management agreement. If there are no additional owner funds on hand, then as a business decision consistent with the terms of the management agreement, the broker may advance the money needed from the broker's ledger, and reimburse this advance from the owner's future income. The various uses of the broker's ledger make it an absolute necessity in any escrow accounting or software system.

In short-term property management, the owner's share of advance rental deposit income and the expenses paid by the broker are reported on the owner's ledger after the checkout date. The amount earned is transferred into the owner's management escrow account. The owner's accounting report shows the disposition of any security deposit held, the rental fee earned during the month by guest name or folio number, any amounts refunded, the broker's fee, any advances due or repaid, plus any other operating expenses paid on behalf of the owner per the management agreement, and the current and year-to-date summaries of the net proceeds for each unit managed. The reported items must reference specific guest reservations, folios, and other appropriate business documents per Rule E-1(p)(4) by unit number and date, *e.g.*, receipt numbers, vendor billings, invoices, and paid check numbers.

Owner's Property File

This file contains all records of the broker's performance of duties and obligations required by the terms of the management agreement, lease, or short-term occupancy contract. It is similar to the "closing file" maintained by sales brokers and should contain the following records: (1) management agreements, amendments, and addenda; (2) leases, reservation policies, occupancy records, and agreements with guests; (3) legal notices affecting the tenants or occupants and disclosures required by the Commission; (4) ongoing vendor or service provider contracts, competitive bids and estimates, invoices, vendor billings, and owner authorizations for repairs or special maintenance work apart from that contained in the management agreement; (5) monthly accounting reports, tax reports, or other information required by federal agencies affecting the use or disposition of money belonging to others; (6) schedules or reports of commissions and fees earned; and (7) evidence showing assessment and timely collection (45-90 days) of all money due to the broker's escrow account.

Tax Reports

The accounting data maintained by the broker as the agent for the owner is reported on IRS Form 1099. Information on reporting duties and suppliers of forms are available from the IRS. State tax information may be obtained from the Colorado Department of Revenue. City and county tax reporting is required and should be discussed with the business tax representatives concerned.

Business Licenses

Brokers who rent short-term occupancies must first obtain business licenses and register such activity (when required) with local authorities. The broker must collect and remit state and local sales and use taxes and maintain the necessary accounting records for inspection by other agencies. State tax information is available from the State Sales Tax Division at the Colorado Department of Revenue. Contact the local city and county offices for additional information concerning possible professional licenses or registration of business activities required in your area.

Management Reports Provided to Owners

The broker is required to provide an accurate and timely accounting report to the owner for the stewardship of funds received or disbursed on behalf of the owner. In the absence of another agreement, Commission rules E-1(p)(4) and E-2 require an accounting report to be furnished to a property owner within 30 days of the end of any month in which such funds were received or disbursed. A sample form is shown in the chapter appendix, Exhibit H.

The accounting report may show totals for various classes of income and expenditures, provided other detail is maintained to identify the individual receipts and expenditures included in the totals. The most common forms for the reports to owners are: (1) the balance sheet and income statement, and (2) the owner's statement of account. The statement of account is usually a manual tabulation of the beginning management cash balance plus receipts less payments equals ending cash balance. The same formula may be used to report or analyze the changes in other trust accounts.

The owner's accounting report must be complete and accurate in reporting management operations. Escrow account transactions are generally reported on a cash basis. Care must be taken to report factual data, *e.g.*, expenditures charged to a owner on the report implies that checks have been mailed and are not being held in the broker's office, income reported has been fully collected, and cash balances for various trust accounts are accurate representations of the owner's corresponding rights and obligations with respect to these accounts.

Commissions Earned and Paid

Commissions and fees are a matter of contract between the broker and the parties concerned. The contract should be written to avoid confusion and disputes over the actual terms. Rule E-1(f)(6) states: "In the absence of a specific written agreement to the contrary, commissions, fees and other charges collected by a broker for performing any service on behalf of another are considered 'earned' and available for use by the broker only after all contracted services have been performed and there is no remaining right of recall by others for such money."

Two accounting practices are followed for the withdrawal of fees and commissions from the escrow account. The "accounting rule" provides that such fees are not earned and available to the broker until the service has been fully performed and the occupant leaves the premises. Under the "tax rule," such fees are earned when the broker has the right per contract to use the money received. Rule E-1(f)(6) applies the accounting rule, unless the parties agree otherwise. The management agreement and lease/reservation agreement must clearly and consistently disclose the nature of all fees and commissions charged to the parties concerned. Use of the "accounting rule" is a recommended approach. The delay between the date of check-in and the accounting cycle end date, when actual proceeds checks are cut, gives the broker additional time to make adjustments for late bills from vendors and/or account for changes in services billed to guests without borrowing from unearned advance deposits. The general industry "guest cancellation policy" below also illustrates the accounting rule. The time of a refundable cancellation may vary from 30 to 45 days before check-in, depending on the seasonal demand for the unit. The "tax rule" results in the deposit becoming non-refundable as early as upon receipt, but spending these amounts before the rental is used may create later hardships for the broker.

Rule E-1(f)(6) also requires an accounting for any commissions and fees or other charges withdrawn in a single and usually "estimated lump-sum disbursement" from a management escrow bank account. Such an accounting must be shown by corresponding entries in the journal <u>and</u> the individual ledgers of those affected. The rule was adopted to prevent continuous guessing as to what amount is earned and payable to the broker; this approach follows "a one-sided journal entry," where no corresponding amounts are recorded in the individual owner ledgers. In companies where different commissions are charged to owners of different units, control over the accounting for earned commissions will soon be lost. The broker must be able to provide a schedule, upon request, which breaks down all components of the amounts included in any lump-sum disbursement. The schedule can be made by a custom computer report or manually prepared. The ledger entries must report such disbursements in accordance with Rule E-1(p)(2) and include the date or time period for each individual transaction, rental, or occupancy. § 12-61-113(1)(g), C.R.S., requires the broker to account for any money belonging to others coming into the broker's possession; this includes money paid to the owner, tenant, guest, other vendors and service providers, and/or other governmental agencies, as well as the resulting commissions and fees paid. See the chapter appendix, Exhibit I.

Guest Cancellation Policy

These terms are generally found in the reservation agreement for rentals of short-term occupancies (30 days or less). The policy specifies when the prospective guest's advance deposit becomes non-refundable. By general industry practice, an advance deposit becomes non-refundable 30-45 days prior to the guest check-in date (depending on company policy and the season in which the unit is rented). At that time, the non-refundable deposit belongs to the owner and may only be withdrawn for any earned brokerage fees or commissions according to the management agreement. According to local custom, the broker may deduct a travel agent fee before paying the net amount of any earned brokerage fees or commission to the broker's company.

Management of short-term rentals does not currently require licensure as a real estate broker. But if the activity is conducted through a licensed brokerage, the licensee is not exempt from the jurisdiction of the Commission, must maintain the escrow and record-keeping requirements found in §§ 12-61-113(1)(g), (g.5), and (k), C.R.S., and Rule E-1, and the broker must account for commissions and fees earned according to Rule E-1(f)(6).

The following time line illustrates how to determine the unearned advance deposit liability on the date the account is reconciled based on the funds held "now" per the accounting equation:

Now — All folios with check-in dates 30 to 45 days from now

Non-Refundable Period | = Liability for future guest deposits = Cash in Escrow Now

Ownership of the Management Records and Business Termination

A broker who manages property and homeowner associations may receive requests from the owner or homeowner association for originals or copies of the escrow records. In such cases, the broker should follow the procedures below.

A licensed broker managing a common interest (homeowner) association is generally the temporary custodian and trustee for the association records. Such records generally pertain to any budgeting, financial, or ongoing administration of the association business and related operating policies, conducted by the broker pursuant to the management agreement. These records belong to the association, not the broker. Rule E-3 requires that all such records be promptly returned to the association upon termination of the broker's employment. A broker may retain file copies at the broker's own expense.

When there is a change in the managing entity employed by the property owner, the ownership of property management records and the cost of making requested copies might also become a point of conflict. The broker should anticipate and address this issue in the initial management agreement. There is no Commission requirement mandating that the broker absorb the costs of any record duplication. An alternative process, such as inspection or audit by the landlord or client during a "window period," might be more acceptable than billing a large sum for producing extensive duplicate copies. The broker may not use the requirement to keep escrow records as a reason to prevent furnishing adequate information or documentation concerning the performance of duties or representations made in the accounting reports upon request of the owner, new manager, or association. The broker as a "custodian" of the information maintains ongoing records, association-vendor contracts, assessment and collection records, legal actions, association bank accounts, and association accounting records. The records utilized for such management should be delivered to the owner upon termination of the employment.

It is recommended that the broker obtain an itemized receipt from any new manager or the association board, stating they have received all records and accounts that were previously in the broker's custody. This statement should acknowledge the statutory requirement applicable to the broker for retention of these records for four years and waive any claim against the broker for release of such records in the event of subsequent loss or destruction.

If the broker questions the certainty of obtaining records at a later time and no waiver is granted, the broker should copy the financial statements, independent audit reports, and/or any minutes of meetings concerning key contractual duties performed or unresolved issues, the supporting bank statements and monthly reconciliations prepared, along with related management agreements, sample leases and/or occupancy agreements, and sample disclosures required by the Commission. Verification of reported receipts or expense is important to the Commission, the property owner, and other governmental entities. The broker's records, whether originals or copies, must provide a clear paper trail from the depositor to the authorized payee and show "money belonging to others" was properly utilized for authorized purposes.

If the change of brokers is within a licensed entity, the departing broker should follow the guidelines found in this chapter under "Change of Employing Broker."

Required Disclosures

In addition to the lead-based paint and brokerage relationship disclosures required by Rules E-40 and F-7, Rule E-1(p)(8) requires written disclosure and consent for any compensation for services billed to clients and customers. The broker must disclose the use of any affiliated business entity (including those owned by related parties) to provide services to property owners.

A broker may sometimes add administrative overhead or other similar mark-up fees to a vendor's invoice as compensation for arranging or overseeing the service. This increased amount may then be erroneously reported in the owner's accounting statement as if it is the "true" cost of the job charged by the vendor. This may result in a valid complaint on dishonest dealing. Similarly, use of an affiliated or related business entity that does not have to compete for the job at "arm's length" may have the same result. Section 6-1-105, C.R.S., provides for damages to an injured party in any civil litigation for deceptive trade practices (see Chapter 25, "Related Real Estate Law").

To comply with Rule E-1(p)(8), first obtain prior written consent for payment of any additional compensation in the management agreement or a signed and dated addendum as the situation warrants. Next, disclose the fixed percentage of markup in these agreements and show the dollar amount added to the cost of the service rendered or provided in the owner's monthly or periodic accounting statement. This avoids any question about the client/customer's actual receipt of such disclosures by showing the added cost in the broker's own accounting report, rather than in a separate invoice attached to the report. If there are variable or unique rates and prices used, these should also be disclosed and pre-authorized in the management agreement or addendum. Additionally, disclose the use of any affiliated or controlled business entity providing such service, the billing rates used, and a general statement to the effect that the broker may or may not realize a profit in providing such services. Finally, maintain the internal accounting records, invoices, and reports showing compliance with the terms of the agreement(s). Brokers are advised to review and update any old or outdated agreements and should consult with resources available from IREM, NARPM, BOMA, CAR, and their own attorney in this matter.

C. Accounting for Security and Advance Rental Deposits

Rule E-16 applies to all licensed brokers

The following requirements should be followed in residential and/or commercial property management. Rule E-16 states:

> A broker receipting for security deposits shall not deliver such deposits to an owner without the tenant's written authorization in a lease or unless written notice has been given to the tenant by first class mail. Such notice must be given in a manner so that the tenant will know who is holding the security deposit and the specific requirements for the procedure in which the tenant may request return of the deposit. If a security deposit is delivered to an owner, the management agreement must place financial responsibility on the owner for its return, and in the event of a dispute over ownership of the deposit, must authorize disclosure by the broker to the tenant of the owner's true name and current mailing address. The broker shall not contract with the tenant to use the security deposit for the broker's own benefit.

Commission position statement CP-5, Advance Rental and Security Deposits, expounds on this rule. The goal is to have consistent terms for the responsibility to return any security deposit in both the lease and management agreement or addenda thereto. These requirements are not met when the lease provides that the owner holds the deposit and the management agreement is silent on the matter. Such inconsistency may create an unfunded and undisclosed financial liability for the property owner. The broker must account for the return, forfeiture, or transfer of the tenant deposit per the requirements of §§ (1), (2), and (4), C.R.S.; see Chapter 20, "Property Management and Leases."

Local Requirements

The City of Boulder currently requires payment of a stated rate of interest to tenants for any security deposits held for residential housing leased in that city. (See City Ordinances 4969 and 7158, Title 12). The broker should inform the property owner of this requirement and may have to assess the owner for any difference between the "statutory rate" and the lower "market rate" of interest when accounting for return of the deposit upon termination of the lease.

Advance Deposits

Under the property management agreement, a broker must transfer all escrowed money belonging to the owner of the property at reasonable and agreed upon times with the accounting required by Rules E-1(p) or E-2. If such money is subject to recall by the guest/occupant, it must be escrowed until rightfully earned per Rule E-1(f)(6), and then must be transferred or credited to the property owner. A broker has no right to use an unearned advance deposit that is subject to recall. Deposits that are not subject to recall by the guest/occupant may not be transferred to the broker's business operating account or used for the broker's benefit unless this is specifically authorized as an earned commission in the management agreement with the property owner.

Offsetting Refundable Deposits Against Broker Expenses

Questions arise over whether a broker may pay certain expenses from refundable deposit amounts held in trust. The answer depends on the ownership of these funds.

A broker has no ownership in earnest money held in a sales transaction. If the seller and broker terminate a listing agreement when the parties are unable to close a transaction, and the buyer is not in default, the broker may not use the deposit money to pay expenses that would have been due from the seller out of a later earned commission. The deposit must be returned to prospective buyer intact. If the buyer has forfeited the deposit, the broker is not entitled to any of the earnest money unless there is a previous written agreement with the seller to share the amount forfeited. The provisions of Commission position statement CP-6, Earnest Money Deposits, should be followed when ownership of the deposit is disputed.

Similarly, the broker has no ownership interest in management funds held as refundable security or advance deposits. Lease and management agreements often allow the broker to collect and retain late fees, non-sufficient funds charges, and other fees from tenants. Such fees are for the benefit of the broker, and Rule E-16 prohibits withholding such amounts from a refundable security deposit. Section 38-12-103(1), C.R.S., provides that the deposit may be withheld for non-payment of rent, repair work, or cleaning contracted for by the tenant for the benefit of the property owner, not the broker. Section 38-12-103(7), C.R.S., also states that any provision in the rental agreement whereby any provision of § 38-12-103(1) is waived shall be deemed to be against public policy and shall be "void" (*i.e.*, not legally binding).

A broker who holds a refundable deposit does so for the benefit of the owner and tenant. If the deposit is slowly liquidated to collect fees owed to the broker, the owner's security is jeopardized both by a loss of financial assurance against damage and by the tenant's loss of motivation to properly care for the property. Further, the owner could become fully liable for return of the full deposit (plus treble damages if paid late) even though the tenant might owe money for late fees and other charges to the broker.

If the broker has gained proper agreement for the collection of fees in both the management agreement and lease or occupancy agreement, then upon termination of the lease or occupancy, the order of deduction should be: first to the owner (for property damages, etc.) and then to the tenant less any late fees or other costs due the broker. If the balance is not adequate to pay the broker, the broker must seek collection directly from the tenant concerned. The concepts above also apply to brokers who receive advance short-term deposits. Care should be taken to ensure that all associates understand the proper handling of refundable deposits.

Office Policy Manuals

Commission Rules E-29 through E-32 require brokers to demonstrate reasonable supervision over all licensees and non-licensed employees, including but not limited to secretaries, bookkeepers, and personal assistants of licensed employees. To comply with these supervision Rules, brokers who employ others are required to establish an office policy manual. This is in addition to the requirements for a written brokerage relationship policy (Rule E-39), a policy to protect confidential information (Rule E-39), and designation brokerage relationships (Rule E-38), whether performing sales or management activities. The following topical guidelines (as applicable) are suggested for office policy manuals.

Sales Transactions

- Parties responsible for delegated duties/agreements;
- Preparation and review of contracts prior to closing;
- Handling earnest money deposits, disputes, and releases;
- Backup contracts;
- Closing documents and closing instructions for the broker's agent;
- Maintenance/custody of contract files;
- Escrow records and written procedures for handling business operations;
- Fair housing/affirmative action marketing;
- Staff training – dissemination of information, staff meetings;
- Use of personal assistants;
- Guaranteed buyouts;
- Investor purchases;
- Non-qualifying assumptions and owner financing;
- Licensee's purchase and sale of property;
- Listing procedures and release of listings;
- Rental occupancy before closing;
- Computer system – data control, backup, and physical security; and
- Internal audit and supervisory reviews of business operations.

Management Activity

- Operating policies and required disclosures;
- Use of unlicensed on-site managers;
- Administration of rentals and leasing activity;
- Items under "Sales" above, where applicable;
- Supervision of accounting services, records, and reporting to others;
- Cash handling, collection of delinquent rents and deposits;
- Ownership/management of rental properties by agents;
- Administration and policies for in-house services;
- Maintenance of records and business reports by any outside service;
- Advances of funds on behalf of clients/customers;

- Cancellation of agreements and termination of services;
- Related services performed by affiliated entities;
- Backup and disaster recovery plan for loss of business records;
- Eviction and legal action; and
- Return of security and advance deposits.

Accounting Problems to Avoid

The following list highlights some general but common audit problems found in management audits.

1. The software used reconciles to a "net" cash balance, where positive owner ledgers are offset against negative (overspent) balances with a resulting cash shortage. This may result from use of the accrual basis of accounting by "default" in the installation process, or by allowing payment of expenses in anticipation of future revenues. It is acceptable for the same owner of different properties to offset negative balance properties against other positive ones if the end result is positive.
2. Failing to print out the bank reconciliation in detail at the time the account is reconciled. Some software programs will not retroactively reproduce earlier reconciliations with the corresponding current liability detail. This weakens internal control and increases the difficulty of reconstructing prior records in the event of a system "crash." The reconciliation should be printed on the actual date of reconciliation, which is normally the same as the ending bank statement date. When Quicken, Quickbooks, or similar software programs are used, brokers may keep the escrow reports by month in yearly, tabulated notebooks. The first section is the monthly ending journal balance (the monthly check register), the second section is the listing of pending ledgers at month end, the third is the monthly detail bank reconciliation printout, and the fourth is a copy of the escrow bank statement.
3. Using fictitious deposits in transit and/or outstanding checks to "plug" the reconciled bank balance on the reconciliation worksheet. "Plug" means to balance the reconciliation by using arbitrary or nonexistent items to force the reconciled bank balance to agree with company records. While this condition may be a simple fix, it may mask an ongoing internal theft of funds in any bank account. Brokers should inspect the items shown on the reconciliation worksheet carefully, and review the corresponding bank statement, journal, and ledgers before accepting the report as valid. Outstanding amounts should clear quickly. Fictitious "voids" are common tools used to conceal unauthorized account withdrawals.
4. Making "John Doe" deposits and/or payments without recording or maintaining appropriate supporting information in the accounting deposit/check records. This may be due to over-extended job duties or poor record keeping, but may also conceal serious errors or thefts of trust assets. This condition may lead to complaints for failing to account for money belonging to others.
5. "We'll wait and fix that again in the next audit." Section 12-61-103, C.R.S., grants the broker's license on the basis of demonstrated competency to transact business in a manner that protects the public interest. A repeated failure to correct audit conditions is contrary to the requirements of Rule E-30(f). The audit representation letter affirms

the broker's agreement to maintain required corrections in place after the examination is completed.

IV. Subdivisions and Associations

A. General

This part describes the financial accounting requirements applicable to brokers and developers who list and/or market property registered with the Commission as a subdivision. All brokers actively marketing these subdivisions must ensure that the applicable provisions of Rule E-1 are followed. Developer sales contracts and disclosure forms are individually approved during the subdivision registration process and must be used for the sale of a registered subdivision property. The form used by the developer should be studied and understood by the real estate broker. Developers, if not required to use licensed brokers under the exemptions found in § 12-61-101(2)(b), C.R.S., may still be subject to other accounting and record-keeping requirements contained in any applicable sales or management agreement, declaration, and bylaws; the Subdivision Developers Act, §§ 12-61-405(1)(e) and (g), C.R.S.; Commission Rules S-23(n) and S-36; and/or the Colorado Common Interest Ownership Act, §§ 38-33.3-101, *et seq.*, C.R.S.

The goal of the regulatory process is to ensure that there is reasonable disclosure of all material matters at the time of the sale, and to ensure that the purchaser's ownership interest in the land is conveyed according to the terms of the contract, free and clear of any overriding or superior encumbrances. Commission accounting requirements for developers differ in significant ways from those applicable to brokers. Rule S contains significantly fewer requirements than Rule E.

Use of Licensed Brokers

Subdivision property registered in Colorado must be sold by actively licensed brokers, unless exempt under § 12-61-101(2)(b), C.R.S. In the absence of an agreement/contract to the contrary, brokers for these sales must escrow funds received in accordance with Rules E-1, E-1(k) and (1), and S-23(i) and (j). The broker must account for and remit such money according to the sales contract and/or the employment agreement with the developer and/or association and keep the applicable escrow records.

Subdivision Registration

Any agreement/contract for the sale or lease of property is voidable by the purchaser and unenforceable by the developer unless that developer was duly registered under the Subdivision Developers' Act at the time the contract was made.

Developers are required to register with the Commission if they market Colorado property to others, or if they sell out-of-state property in Colorado, which is:

1. Divided (cumulatively) into 20 or more interests intended solely for residential use;
2. A conversion (cumulatively) of an existing structure into a common interest community of 20 or more residential units;
3. A group of 20 or more time-shares intended for residential use; or
4. A group of 20 or more proprietary leases in a cooperative housing corporation.

Registration is not required for:

1. Selling memberships in campgrounds;
2. Bulk sales between developers;
3. Residential property not previously occupied that is to be constructed and where the consideration paid includes the cost of the residential building(s) or new home(s);
4. Lots, which at the time of closing or lease, are situated on a street improved to the standards of those maintained by the county where the lot resides, and which have a feasible plan for water and sewage disposal, and which have phone, electric, and utility services adequate to serve the lots under applicable city, county, state, or federal laws;
5. Any subdivision that is or has been required to be approved after September 1, 1972 by a regional, county, or municipal planning authority. Questions may be directed to the licensing section at (303) 894-2166 or (303) 894-2334.

The developer's registration expires on December 31 of each year, and a developer is not authorized to transact business after expiration. A registration that has expired may be reinstated within two years after such expiration upon payment of the renewal fee if the developer meets all other requirements of the developer's act.

Contract Provisions

All contracts used to market registered property must include the following (other disclosures are required by Rule S-23 in an attached disclosure document):

1. The names of the licensed real estate office and broker responsible for making the sale;
2. The purchaser's *five-day right of rescission* immediately above the purchaser's signature line;
3. A statement that a title commitment and/or title insurance policy will be delivered, unless otherwise agreed, Rule S-23(k), S-31 and S-32;
4. A statement concerning the time for delivery of deed after closing or payment of all installment amounts due, Rule S-30;
5. A statement of any taxes, special authority/district taxes, or assessments to which the purchaser may be subject, whether existing, proposed, or unpaid at the time of contracting, Rule S-23(f);
6. A statement of any taxes, special authority/district taxes, or assessments to which the purchaser may be subject, whether existing, proposed, or unpaid at the time of contracting; and
7. Seller and landlord disclosure of lead-based paint hazards for housing built before 1978, per Rule F-7. This HUD disclosure became effective September 6, 1996 for sales and rentals of more than four residential dwellings. There are severe penalties for non-disclosure. See the HUD pamphlet titled "Protect Your Family From Lead in Your Home."

B. Accounting Requirements for Registered Developers

Commission Requirements for Sales and Leasing

Commission requirements are found in Rule S-36 and § 12-61-406(2.5)(b), C.R.S. The developer must retain the following records for a period of seven years:

1. Rule S-36 (1) requires copies of the sales contract, lease agreement, financing agreement, settlement statements, title commitment/insurance policy, trust deed, escrow agreement, and other documents (disclosures) executed by the parties to effect the sale or transfer of any interest in the subdivision to purchasers be maintained at a Colorado place of business (or to reasonably produce such upon request). Brokers selling subdivision property must ensure that settlement statements are accurate and must show that any applicable association dues, transfer taxes, or other membership fees are properly prorated, or paid by the party as agreed in the contract, Rule S-23.
2. Rule S-36 (2) requires a record showing the receipt and disbursement of any money or assets received or paid on behalf of any purchaser or similar association managed or "controlled" (through actual voting rights held) by the developer.
3. Any Commission-approved escrow agreement with an independent third party and the related receipt and disbursement records showing the transfer of funds received from potential purchasers of reservations in an uncompleted project or pending subdivision registration under such escrow agreement, § 12-61-402, C.R.S., and Rule S-20. Brokers engaged in the sale of reservation agreements must also comply with escrow requirements as the designated trustee and independent third party. The developer may not directly or indirectly control the handling of funds by the escrow agent, control the process of maintaining records of the agent's account activities, or exercise any independent right of withdrawal over the funds held, apart from the Commission-approved escrow agreement.
4. Pursuant to § 38-33.3-315, C.R.S., the "declarant/developer" shall pay all common expenses until the association makes a common expense assessment and shall pay assessments on unsold units according to the allocations as set forth in the declaration; the declarant alone is liable for all expenses in connection with real estate in the common interest community that is subject to "development rights," § 38-33.3-307, C.R.S. The association shall keep financial records sufficient to enforce liens for unpaid assessments under § 38-33.3-316, C.R.S., and minutes of official meetings and association activity required by the recorded declaration.
5. In addition to the above, the following requirements must be met under the Colorado Common Interest Ownership Act (CCIOA), if applicable, when a developer transfers control to the association membership in accordance with §§ 38-33.3-303(5), (6), and (9), C.R.S.:
   (a) Original or certified copies of the recorded declaration, articles of incorporation, bylaws, minutes book, and any rules and regulations that may have been promulgated.
   (b) An accounting for all association funds, including audited financial statements with an accompanying opinion of an independent certified public accountant that the statements present fairly the financial position in accordance with generally

accepted accounting principles or a disclaimer of such attestation. The developer shall pay the cost for examination of the association financial statements.

(c) All association funds or control thereof.

(d) Inventories of personal property represented by the developer to be the property of the association or which has been exclusively used in the operation and enjoyment of the common elements.

(e) Copies of plans and specifications used in the construction of improvements in the common interest community.

(f) All insurance policies then in force in which the unit owners, the association, or its directors and officers are named as insured persons.

(g) Copies of any certificates of occupancy issued for improvements comprising the common interest community.

(h) Any other permits issued by governmental bodies applicable to the common interest community one year prior to transfer of control to the members of the community.

(i) Written warranties of contractors, suppliers, and manufacturers still in force.

(j) A roster of unit owners and mortgagees and their addresses and known telephone numbers.

(k) Employment contracts between the association and others.

(l) Any service contract between the association and its membership with others.

(m) For large, planned communities, copies of all recorded deeds and recorded or unrecorded leases evidencing rights in the community and its common elements.

C. Management of Common Interest Associations

The developer's record-keeping duty is found in Rule S-36 (2), § 12-61-405(1)(e), C.R.S., and, when applicable, §§ 38-33.3115, -117, and -118, C.R.S. The Commission has jurisdiction over the developer during the time the developer controls the financial operation of the association by controlling the actual voting membership on the association board of directors. After the developer has transferred control of the common interest association to the membership, the developer is governed by CCIOA.

Pooled bank accounts are not allowed for the management of any common interest owner (homeowner) association consisting of 30 or more units under the provisions of § 38-33.3-306(3), C.R.S. This law requires the use of separate accounts for each association and association reserve account, the presentation of an annual accounting for association activities, and a financial statement prepared by the manager, a public or certified public accountant, and the maintenance of not less than $50,000 in fidelity bond insurance (or more per bylaws) for the manager and others who perform management activities on behalf of the association. Brokers who manage associations in their licensed company accounts must use separate escrow accounts per Rule E-1.

Preexisting Subdivisions

Accounting for developer-controlled subdivisions created in Colorado before July 1, 1992 (which have not elected treatment under § 38-33.3-118, C.R.S.) is generally governed by the provisions of declaration and bylaws or the applicable sections of the Subdivision Act.

During the period of control of the association, beginning in January 1990, and for seven years thereafter, the developer must maintain annual records, which reasonably show that there was no diversion, conversion, or failure to account for any association funds. See Rules S-36 and S-23(n).

Sections 38-33.3-117(1) and (3), C.R.S., of CCIOA do not replace preexisting bylaws in regard to: (1) the process for transfer of control to the association members (§ 38-33.3-303), or (2) the requirement to keep separate association accounts for funds and reserves held by the developer as manager of 30 or more units (§ 38-33.3-306). The bylaws will frequently require more detailed records for interim inspections by association members and to prepare audited financial statements for the period of management while the developer controlled the association.

New Subdivisions

For subdivisions created after July 1, 1992, or those electing treatment under CCIOA, the record-keeping requirements of Rules S-23(n) and S-36 are supplemented by CCIOA, including § 38-33.3-306(3)(a). A developer who manages an association of 30 or more units must keep the records showing compliance with the following statutory requirements for a seven-year period. Such records must be reasonably available for inspection by members of the association or the Commission at the developer's and/or broker's Colorado business office and shall include:

1. The association bank accounts, monthly statements, and returned items according to § 38-33.3-306(3), C.R.S., for the operating funds and reserves belonging to each association. If the manager engaged is a licensed broker, then separate escrow accounts shall be used, unless there is another agreement or law to the contrary. It is recommended that the written agreement between the association and manager specifically identify the nature and requirements of the accounts and records to be used.
2. Property, general liability, and fidelity insurance or bond (for 30 or more units), and/or proper notice to the owners of any cancellation or the unavailability of such insurance, § 38-33.3-313, C.R.S.
3. The minutes for all association board meetings per the applicable bylaws, § 38-33.3-308, C.R.S.
4. Records necessary for transfer of control to the association. See detailed itemization found in §§ 38-33.3-303(9) and 38-33.3-314 through -317, C.R.S. These sections require accounting records for the proper dispossession of any surplus association funds, amounts of assessments collected and uncollected or delinquent, interest and penalties, liens filed, association minutes, and other related membership voting records.
5. Records for the payment of association dues assessed to the developer for all unsold units, intervals, or lots by the prescribed due date.
6. Records for any amount billed to the association for services provided to the association and any expense incurred in rendering such services. Such matters must be disclosed in the renewal of the developer's registration and in the disclosures required by Rule S-23(n).

V. Appendix – Sample Forms

A. Notice of Escrow or Trust Account

TO ____
(Name of Bank or Depository)

Pursuant to § 12-61-103(7), C.R.S., I, ___________________________ am the employing broker for ____
(Name of Licensed Real Estate Company)

Furthermore, pursuant to §§ 12-61-113(1)(g.5) and (k), C.R.S., Colorado Division of Real Estate Rule E-1, and Federal Deposit Insurance Corporation (FDIC) requirements, I am required to maintain a "escrow" or "trust" account with a bank or recognized depository in the State of Colorado for the purpose of holding money belonging to others. With regard to any account that is designated as an "escrow" or "trust" account, the said account(s) is/are maintained with you as a depository for money belonging to persons other than myself or my brokerage company in my fiduciary capacity as a licensed Colorado real estate broker under the provisions of § 12-61-103(7), C.R.S., and Rule E-1(g).

DATED this _________________ day of ___________________________, 20______.

____
(Signature of Employing Broker)

ACKNOWLEDGEMENT OF RECEIPT

I, a duly authorized representative of ____, the bank or depository identified above and acknowledge receipt of the above "NOTICE OF ESCROW OR TRUST ACCOUNT" on _______day of _____________, 20______.

____
(Representative's Signature and Title)

Rev 4/05

B. Escrow Account Journal

Escrow Account Journal **Page _______**

For ________________________ Account

Date Year	Check No.	Description of Transaction	Payments	Deposits	Journal Balance
			Balance Forward		

C. The Beneficiary and Broker Ledger Cards

FOR EACH BENEFICIARY (SALES/UNCLAIMED PROPERTY)

BUYER ______________________ **SELLER** ______________________
LISTING ADDRESS ____
CLOSING DATE ________________ **LISTING** ______________________

DATE	CHECK	DESCRIPTION	PAYMENT	DEPOSIT	BALANCE

FOR BROKER/COMPANY FUNDS IN ANY ACCOUNT

BROKER / COMPANY LEDGER **CARD NO** ________
FOR ______________________ **ESCROW ACCOUNT**

DATE	CHECK	DESCRIPTION	PAYMENT	DEPOSIT	BALANCE

D. The Bank Reconciliation Worksheet

ACCOUNT TITLE ________________ ACCOUNT NUMBER ________________

STATEMENT DATE ________________ DATE RECONCILED ________________

PREPARED BY ________________ REVIEWED BY ________________

ENTER LEDGER BALANCES ON STATEMENT DATE BY BUYER NAME OR PROPERTY ADDRESS BELOW:

BROKER'S LEDGER $____________

____________ ____________

____________ ____________

____________ ____________

____________ ____________

____________ ____________

____________ ____________

____________ ____________

____________ ____________

____________ ____________

____________ ____________

____________ ____________

____________ ____________

LEDGER BALANCES PER ATTACHED LIST $____________

TOTAL LEDGERS $____________

JOURNAL BALANCE ON STATEMENT DATE $____________

ENTER ENDING BANK STATEMENT BALANCE ON STATEMENT DATE $________

ADD: ALL UNCLEARED DEPOSITS:

DATE	AMOUNT	DATE	AMOUNT

TOTAL OUTSTANDING DEPOSITS $________

SUBTOTAL $________

SUBTRACT: OUTSTANDING CHECKS:

NUMBER	AMOUNT	NUMBER	AMOUNT

TOTAL CONTINUATION SHEET (S) $________

RECONCILIED BANK BALANCE $________

RECONCILED BANK BALANCE SHOULD = JOURNAL AND TOTAL LEDGER BALANCES ON LEFT SIDE

REV 5/06

E. Tenant Ledger

MULTI-FAMILY DWELLINGS

TENANT(S) ______________________________ UNIT ______________
______________________________ PHONE ______________
______________________________ ______________

OWNER NAME & ADDRESS ______________________________
____

LEASE DATE ________ EXPIRATION ________ RENT $ ________ UTIL $ ________

LATE FEES $ ________ OTHER $ ________ *SEC DEP $ ________ (OWNER HOLDS)

REMARKS ______________________________
____

* MAY BE OPERATING CAPTIAL WHEN OWNER HOLDS—OTHERWISE USE SEPARATE ACCT & LEDGER

DATE COLLECTED	RENT &SEC DEP DUE	UTILITIES DUE	OTHER CHARGES	AMOUNTS DEPOSITED	UNPAID BALANCE
BAL FWD $					

F. Tenant Security Deposit Ledger

FOR MULTI-FAMILY PROPERTIES

TENANT(S) ______________________________ **UNIT** ______________
______________________________ **PHONE** ______________
______________________________ ______________

WORK ADDRESS ______________________________
PRIOR ADDRESS ______________________________
LEASE DATE _____ **EXPIRATION** ______ **LEASING COMPANY** ______________

SEC DEP $ __________ **UTILITY $**__________ **PET $** __________ **OTHER $** ___________

SEC DEP HELD BY ___ **OWNER** _____ **BROKER PRIOR COMPANY** ______________
REMARKS ______________________________
____

DATE	CHECK	DESCRIPTION	PAYMENTS	DEPOSITS	BALANCE

G. Owner's Ledger

OWNER'S LEDGER

OWNER NAME ______________________ ACCT/CARD NO ____________
PROPERTY ADDRESS ______________________
OWNER'S ADDRESS ______________________
OWNER PHONE ____________ MGMT AGRMNT DATE ____________ EXPIRES ____________
MGT FEE % ____________ OTHER FEES ______________________
RENTAL AMT $ ____________ SEC DEP AMT $ ____________ HELD BY ____________
TENANT(S) ______________________ LEASE ________ EXPIRES ______
______________________ PHONE ____________
REMARKS ______________________
____

DATE	CHECK	DESCRIPTION	PAYMENTS	DEPOSITS	BALANCE
				BALANCE FORWARD $	

H. Change of Employing Broker Affidavit

CHANGE OF EMPLOYING BROKER AFFIDAVIT

I, ____, License No. _____________,
am the current employing broker for ____
____
____

I hereby affirm to the best of my current knowledge and belief that all escrow account and escrow account liabilities stated herein or incorporated by reference are a complete and accurate representation of all "money belonging to others," as defined in Commission Rule E-1(g), which is held or controlled by me in my fiduciary capacity as the company's employing broker on this ____________ day of ______________, 20____. The escrow bank accounts listed below or as incorporated by reference are fully funded for all corresponding escrow liabilities incurred on the above date. The funds held in the escrow account(s) listed below are hereby transferred to the new employing broker and/or the continuing company officer(s) and/or director(s), with all corresponding escrow records and transaction files required by §§ 12-61-113(1)(g),(g.5), and (k), C.R.S., and Rule E-1:

Bank	Account Number	Purpose	Reconciled Balance	(Date)

The foregoing records, accounts, and cash balances are accepted as complete and accurate in all material respects by the undersigned parties, who release the departing broker from further obligation for the maintenance, custody, and duty to account for new deposits, payments, and banking events after the said date above. The undersigned parties agree to maintain the records received for the time required under § 12-61-113(1)(i), C.R.S., at the licensed business location or company's storage facility.

Executed this _________ day of ________________________________, 20 ____
by: ______________________________________, License No ______________,
Departing Employing Broker
and:

____, License No ______________,
New Employing Broker,
and/or by:

____
____
____
Officers and Directors (of the continuing company) Rev 4/00

I. Schedule of Commissions Earned Versus Amounts Taken

YEAR TO DATE – NOVEMBER 30, 20XX

DATE 20XX	CHECK NUMBER	FILE REFERENCE OR PROPERTY	COMM %	GROSS REVENUE	EARNED COMM	FEES	TOTAL EARNED	TOTAL TAKEN	BROKER'S LEDGER
BAL FWD	$		N/A	425,000.00	55,129.00	6,077.50	61,206.50	58,766.99	2,439.51
11/1	1001	SmithB &B (45 day)	10	5,000.00	500.00	_	500.00	500.00	_
11/1	1002	Hill Top 44 (60 day)	10	5,000.00	500.00	45.73	545.73	545.73	_
11/10	1100	Folio 341 99	40	10,000.00	4,000.00	55.95	4,055.95	2,555.95	1,500.00
11/10	1100	Folio 200 11	40	9,000.00	3,600.00	"	3,600.00	3,600.00	_
11/10	1100	Folio 34889	40	15,000.00	6,000.00	_	6,000.00	6,000:00	_
11/10	1100	Folio 33521	40	2,000.00	800.00	_	800.00	800:00	_
11/28	1200	Folio 33521	40	5,500.00	2,200.00	300.00	2,500.00	2,200.00	300.00
11/30	Deposit	Folio 200 11	40	(9,000.00)	(3,600.00)	_	(3,600.00)	_	(3,600.001
ENDING BALANCE 11/31/20XX $			N/A	$467,500.00	$69,129.00	$6,479.18	$75,608.18	$74,968.67	$639.51

Chapter 20:
Property Management and Leases

An * in the left margin indicates a change in the statute, rule, or text since the last publication of the manual.

I. Introduction

Over the years, residential and commercial property management has developed into complex and profitable real estate specialties. Property managers are responsible for many trillions of dollars in real property market value on a long-term basis. Many firms are devoted exclusively to property management, and others have set up autonomous property management divisions to profit from the economic stability of management income during periods of slow sales activity. Some other firms simply do occasional property management as an accommodation to their sales listing clients.

Property managers offer a variety of extensive services and shoulder varying degrees of responsibility in the performance of their duties to the owners and tenants. Property managers are considered "**general agents**," performing multiple functions as compared to sales licensees who, as "**special agents**," are employed for a limited duration to market a specific property.

Whatever the scope of the management, if a broker or brokerage company is soliciting tenants, executing leases, collecting rents and security deposits, supervising repairs and improvements, and collecting a fee for such services, that person or company is performing property management and should become very familiar not only with this chapter, but also with Chapter 19, "Escrow Records," Chapter 24, "Colorado Fair Housing Act," and Chapter 4, "Subdivision Laws."

Occasionally, employed brokers are tempted to perform residential property management without their employing broker's knowledge or consent. An employed broker is prohibited from performing residential property management outside of the knowledge and supervision of his or her employing broker. Section 12-61-103(10), C.R.S., requires all business to be conducted only in the licensed name of the employing broker. Employing brokers must be aware of their employed brokers' activities, supervise all employed brokers' activities, and maintain proper accounting of any moneys obtained by the employed broker in accordance with Rule E-1 and § 12-61-113(1)(f), C.R.S. Further, the employing broker should have a clearly written policy as to the firm's offering of management services, and outline specifically how the firm and its employees will conduct such services.

The increasing use of computers and various software programs has improved the profitability and efficiency of property management as well as homeowner association management. However, software programs vary considerably, and property managers should thoroughly study any application prior to implementation. Some commercial software programs may lack the ability to customize formats for residential clients. Some managers have developed record-keeping systems using word processors or accounting systems. The suggested forms in Chapter 19, "Escrow Records," may be helpful whether using computerized, manual, or a combination of both types of record-keeping.

Property managers face challenges of age of construction, cash flow requirements, vacancy rates, heating and cooling concerns, and electrical and plumbing needs, as well as EPA guidelines for radon, asbestos, and lead-based paint, plus both federal and state fair housing and civil rights regulations and the state-mandated warranty of habitability, and carbon monoxide detector requirements. Additionally, sound management and accounting practices must be followed to avoid commingling of funds among the properties managed.

Professional property managers perform a variety of functions and must be able to advise on heating, cooling, painting, decorating, roofs, pests, insurance, the sales market, and household appliances, and must know when to refer to other professionals such as financial or tax advisors or attorneys. Property managers should be adept at problem resolution, negotiations, accounting, budgeting, and sales.

A working knowledge of landlord/tenant law, access to a competent attorney, effective communication skills, and the ability to organize and delegate effectively, as well as good time-management skills and stress-reduction techniques, are also necessary for efficient property management. While an average sales licensee may handle two or three transactions a month, a professional property manager with an inventory of 200 units may be executing five to six leases, as well as collecting and disbursing income from all 200 units, every month. The dollar value of each transaction may be smaller, but the manager is most often responsible for the entire value of the property and over an extensive period of time. The skills involved are equally important. A homeowner association manager may handle 1,000 units comprised of many small or several large communities.

At the outset, a property manager must clearly understand the owner's needs and desires for the property. Management plans must support the owner's objectives of short- or long-term ownership, long-term investment, or other income needs. As the management contract continues over time, the manager must excel at clear and prompt communications with the owner.

A property manager may decide to specialize in a particular type of property or to service many types. Property management specialties may include:

- Single family homes, attached or detached (condos, townhomes);
- Multi-unit buildings (residential or office);
- Government-assisted housing;
- Retail properties;
- Shopping centers;
- Office or industrial complexes;
- Resort or short-term rental properties;[†] and
- Homeowners associations.

([†] A Colorado real estate license is not required for the above specialty or for those exempt under the provisions of § 12-61-101, C.R.S., who lease or manage apartment buildings or condominiums, such as regularly salaried onsite managers employed by building owners or homeowners associations. However, many such specialists are Colorado real estate licensees, sometimes because they perform other activities that do require a license. Accordingly, brokers who perform services that may not require licensure must still follow the

Commission E-Rules applicable under their employment agreements. See Commission position statement CP-19, Short Term Occupancy Agreements.)

Several national organizations exist to assist property managers in the various management specialties. Each offers a wealth of information, networking opportunities, and referral services, as well as professional education courses and designations.

NARPM® National: The National Association of Residential Property Managers. 638 Independence Parkway, Suite 100, Chesapeake, VA 23320, Phone: (800) 782-3452, Fax: (866) 466-2776, E-mail: info@narpm.org, Website: www.narpm.org. Appealing to managers of smaller residential properties: single-family homes, individual condos or townhomes, and 2-12 unit apartment houses, **NARPM** is independent of the National Association of REALTORS® and does not require members to be REALTORS®. **NARPM** does require its members to hold a real estate license except in those states in which no license is required for property managers. There are chapters of **NARPM** in Denver, Colorado Springs, Grand Junction, and Northern Colorado, with members throughout the state. Several professional designations are available.

IREM: The Institute of Real Estate Management. 430 North Michigan Avenue, Chicago, IL 60611, Phone: (800) 837-0706, Fax: (800) 338-4736, E-mail: custserv@irem.org, Website: www.irem.org. This organization is an affiliate of the National Association of REALTORS® and requires its members to be REALTORS®. **IREM** awards the Certified Property Manager (CPM) designation to those members who successfully complete a rigorous series of courses. **IREM** tends to draw managers of commercial ventures or large apartment houses.

* **CAI: The Community Associations Institute.** 6402 Arlington Blvd., Suite 500, Falls Church, VA 22042, Phone: (888) 224-4321, Fax: (703) 684-1581, Website: www.caionline.org. This group is independent of the National Association of REALTORS® and specializes in the concerns of professional homeowners association managers. There are active chapters in both northern and southern Colorado. CAI awards several professional designations.

BOMA: The Building Owners and Managers Association.

NAA: The National Apartment Association. 4300 Wilson Blvd., Suite 400, Arlington, VA, 22203, Phone: (703) 518-6141, Fax: (703) 248-9440, Website: www.naahq.org. There are chapters of NAA in the Denver metro area, Weld County, Northern Colorado, and Southern Colorado.

The eight organizations listed in Part VII of this chapter offer literature, seminars, and other information to improve their members' professionalism.

II. Management Functions

A property manager's primary concern should be to obtain the highest possible income stream consistent with protecting the owner's capital investment and preserving a good owner-manager-tenant relationship.

The following list, although not all-inclusive, outlines what is usually expected of a property manager:

1. Establish the rental schedule.

2. Merchandise the space and collect the rents.
3. Supervise maintenance schedules and repairs.
4. Develop a tenant relations policy with tenant unions and tenants desiring a representative voice in the management of the project.
5. Develop employee policies and supervise employee performance. Have an employee manual of policies and instructions.
6. Maintain proper accounting records and make regularly scheduled reports to the owner.
7. Qualify and investigate tenant credit.
8. Prepare and execute leases.
9. Prepare decorating, renovation, or repair specifications and obtain estimates.
10. Hire, instruct, and maintain qualified and willing personnel to staff the building(s). Expect results.
11. Audit and pay bills, account for the return or forfeiture of tenant security deposits, bill tenants for utilities, and collect and disburse late fees.
12. Advertise and publicize vacancies through appropriate media.
13. Plan and supervise alterations and modernizing programs.
14. Inspect vacant space frequently and periodically.
15. Keep abreast of the times and stay posted on competitive market conditions.
16. Pay insurance premiums and taxes. Recommend adequate insurance coverage.
17. Keep abreast of health building code standards and the Americans with Disabilities Act, which require public buildings to meet all safety and access standards.
18. Provide for maximum-security provisions, understanding that the landlord is responsible for reasonable measures to safeguard tenants against intruders.
19. Develop an annual budget for the financial operations plan with the owner.
20. Manage affairs for homeowner associations. See Chapter 4, "Subdivision Laws."

The property manager's responsibilities do not end with the collection of rents and reporting income and expenses. The professional manager must be equipped to counsel the owner on a myriad of problems, including the following:

1. Analyses and recommendations regarding vacant land and proposed and existing buildings.
2. Economic analyses and supervision of planned remodeling and renovation.
3. Economic surveys and analyses of trade areas.
4. Analyses of rental rates and trends.
5. Budgeting for operating cash flows and unexpected costs or seasonal fluctuations in rental income.

6. Working with municipalities and aid organizations.
7. EPA and State regulations for renovations and construction.

Each property and category has its own character and its own set of problems. When taking on an unfamiliar assignment, an unwary broker may be overburdened with property management problems and may have to choose between neglecting the brokerage business and facing the wrath of an irate owner. A broker performing property management must recognize his or her staff's time and experience limitations.

Property management is a time-consuming process, and scheduling of labor prevalent problem. A shortage of qualified personnel is no defense for failure to fulfill fiduciary or contract duties to an owner. A competent manager should not assume additional accounts without adequate time or the technology to service them.

The business relationship between the property manager and owner is based on a current written management agreement. A manager should also have a current written agreement executed by the tenant(s) and landlord. If a lease is not required, all agreements concerning both parties' privileges and responsibilities should be in writing and signed by the parties concerned. It is wise to secure the owner's written consent for significant changes in such duties or other special services to be performed by the broker on behalf of the owner.

The management of short-term occupancies (30 days or less) under a broker's license requires diligence in complying with §§ 12-61-113(l)(g), (g.5), and (q), C.R.S. Complaints against licensees can generally be categorized into three areas: (1) a failure to plan for the seasonal cash flows inherent in vacation rental management, (2) a failure to supervise and properly maintain required records and accounts, and (3) a failure to disclose how management fees and commissions are earned in both the management agreement and reservation/cancellation policies. Please refer to "short-term occupancies" in the Index for further information.

Finally, the property manager must consider the rights and interests of the tenant in ongoing or temporary management during the listing period. The broker should consult the owner and tenant when scheduling showings of listed property. See Chapter 24, "Fair Housing," for federal and Colorado fair housing considerations.

* General information regarding tenant/landlord disputes is available from the Community Housing Service at (303) 831-1750 or the **Resident Relations Help Line** at (303) 320-1611.

III. Merchandising Rental Space

Rental space reacts to changes in supply and demand in the marketplace. A manager needs to estimate the strength of consumer pressure. Consumers normally shop the market and rent the space that best meets their financial and aesthetic needs.

As a rule of thumb, it takes five qualified prospects per unit to lease out a property under ideal market conditions. If more are required, then something may be wrong with the price, the manager's effort, or the attractiveness of the property. If the property rents on the basis of a rental for every qualified prospect, then the rental price asked may be too low. These ratios, of course, vary with the character of the particular building. Furnished apartments, for example, may rent with one renter to three prospects, whereas deluxe units may require six to nine prospects per rental.

It is imperative that a property manager counsel owners carefully prior to taking over an account and identify which problems may be curable and which may not. For example, a building that is not soundproof is not economically feasible to cure, and as a result, it limits the clientele to quiet people.

If a property suffers from cumulative maintenance problems, a disproportionate amount of time may be required of a property manager, thus causing management expenses to exceed potential fee income. Buildings that have been cheaply constructed and suffer from accelerated obsolescence are extremely vulnerable to rental competition from newer buildings, again contributing to higher turnover. One short-term owner savings is to forego a preventive maintenance program. However, preventive maintenance normally costs much less than paying to correct serious deferred maintenance problems later.

Many apartment buildings are over-encumbered as a result of improper initial projections or rent schedules barely sufficient to meet operating expenses and debt service even at 100 percent occupancy. This should be ascertained in advance in order to avoid negative cash flow. These cash shortages often lead to inadequate maintenance. The effect is cumulative and may seriously affect the manager's ability to maintain high occupancy. A manager must judge each property on its own merits before deciding whether or not to manage it. Brokers need to know and be able to advise their clients on changing rental markets.

Brokers who wish to engage in property management should carefully study Chapter 19, "Escrow Records." No area of real estate needs more diligent records maintenance than property management.

Rental location agents are mentioned in § 12-61-113(1.5), C.R.S. Brokers who receive advance fees from prospective tenants for furnishing information on available rentals must keep records of such funds according to § 12-61-113(g), C.R.S., and Rule E-l.

IV. General Accounting Concepts

A licensed property manager is a trustee primarily responsible for the supervision, accounting, and use of "money belonging to others." Any recallable trust account cash balance must always equal the corresponding trust account contractual liability at the same point in time. Trust accounts are generally maintained on a "cash basis." Funds belonging to one owner may never be "loaned" as unauthorized supplemental operating capital to finance expenditures of other owners (or the broker). (See §§ 12-61-113(l)(g), (g.5), and (n), C.R.S.; Rules E-l(f), (g), (p), and (q), E-29, and E-30.)

The following relationships govern operation of all double-entry management accounting systems:

BALANCE SHEET

ASSETS		=	LIABILITIES		+	CAPITAL & RESERVES	
Debit	Credit		Debit	Credit		Debit	Credit
Increase		=		Increase		Increase	
	Decrease	=	Decrease				Decrease

Assets: Cash balances for unpaid owner income, tenant security deposits, advance rental deposits, owner cash reserves, owner inventory and equipment on the property.

<u>Liabilities</u>: Mortgage principal, taxes, tenant or guest deposits.

<u>Capital</u>: Owner reserves, equipment replacement reserves, owner draws from net income earned, net income and retained earnings.

INCOME STATEMENT

NET INCOME			**REVENUE**			**EXPENSE**	
Debit	Credit		Debit	Credit		Debit	Credit
	Increase	=		Increase		Increase	
Decrease		=	Decrease				Decrease

<u>Revenue</u>: Rent receipts, late fees, forfeited tenant deposits, utility charges collected from tenants, other operating income payable after expenses to the owner. Owner payments to provide working capital (reserves) are not property income.

<u>Expense</u>: Payments or journal entries to record the cost of operating the property under the terms authorized in the management agreement or lease or addendum thereto.

In the context of rental management, cash receipts generally increase assets, net income, and capital. They are debited to cash and credited to the appropriate liability, revenue, or a capital account. Cash disbursements decrease (credit) a cash account and are debited to the appropriate liability, expense, or capital account.

The accounting system in a management operation should have the capability to integrate owner/tenant/property/service activity and non-financial marketing data with the accounting transactions. The system should provide the capability to reproduce reports, data, and bank reconciliations upon demand for any prior period. The accounting/management database should allow access to immediate information for:

- Tenant/guest amounts owed versus collected.
- Tenant by name/unit charges and receipts.
- Common area charges/special package prices.
- Tenant unit rental history/personal data.
- Deposits collected or held by current broker.
- Leases/agreements/amendments/coming expiration dates.
- Correspondence/evictions/addenda.
- Scheduled occupancy/vacancy dates.
- Accounting for security deposit refunds.
- Late fees and other tenant charges.
- Properties/units under management.
- Property/unit identification/marketing data.
- Owner/insurance/lender information.
- Management agreements/amendments/correspondence.
- Vendors and scheduled payments for mortgages, etc.
- Maintenance/remodeling/written authorizations.
- Accounting reports/multiple bank account capacity.

The foregoing information is critical, but the accounting system to produce such data need not be expensive. Good word-processing programs can maintain much of the management data required in transaction files. Several small-business accounting software programs comply with the requirements of Rule E-l. A broker must train assistants, establishing appropriate office policies, and understand and oversee operation of the accounting system and any software, or else problems or complaints will soon develop.

Managers must disclose brokerage relationships to property owners and prospective tenants using Commission-approved forms. For property owners, the broker, if performing leasing activities, is required to enter into the appropriate Exclusive Right-to-Lease Listing Agreement specific to the type of brokerage relationship offered (either Landlord Agency or Transaction-Broker, the current form is LC57-8-10). As an alternative to the listing agreement, the broker may use the Brokerage Duties Addendum to Property Management Agreement, current form BDA55-5-09, (if the management agreement includes leasing by the property manager/broker), executed by both the broker and property owner.

For prospective tenants, the broker must either enter into the appropriate Exclusive Tenant Contract specific to the type of brokerage relationship offered (Tenant Agency or Transaction-Broker, current form is ETC59-8-10), or the current Brokerage Disclosure to Buyer or Tenant (current forms are BDT24-5-09 and BDT20-5-09). Also, the broker should disclose in writing the specific duties pertaining to the brokerage relationship offered to prospective tenants pursuant to Rule E-35. If a property owner or prospective tenant requests information about types of brokerage relationships other than those offered by the broker, the broker could give the owner or tenant the current Definitions of Working Relationships (or use the Listing Agreement or Disclosure form given to owner or tenant noted in this paragraph).

Brokers must have written consent from the party assisted or represented to assess and receive any "**mark-ups**" and/or other compensation for services performed by any third party or affiliated business entity. (See Rule E-l(p)(8).) The purpose of this rule is to facilitate full disclosure of all forms of compensation under §§ 12-61-113(l)(c.5) and (q) and 6-1-105, C.R.S. This applies to management companies that mark-up the charges billed by independent maintenance companies, add a percentage to the cost billed by others for administrative overhead, or receive any transaction-specific income from an affiliated business entity. The broker must maintain office records that verify prior written consent for these amounts and account for the additional amounts or percentages charged to others.

V. Security Deposits

A. Introduction

Property managers may incur serious problems if they fail to properly handle security deposits. To avoid these problems, property managers should become thoroughly familiar with the requirements in the following provisions of Colorado law:

Title 38, Article 12, C.R.S. 1973 Security Deposits-Wrongful Withholding

§ 38-12-101, C.R.S. Legislative declaration

The provisions of this part 1 shall be liberally construed to implement the intent of the general assembly to insure the proper administration of security deposits and protect the interests of tenants and landlords.

§ 38-12-102, C.R.S. Definitions

As used in this part 1, unless the context otherwise requires:

(1) "Normal wear and tear" means that deterioration which occurs, based upon the use for which the rental unit is intended, without negligence, carelessness, accident, or abuse of the premises or equipment or chattels by the tenant or members of his household, or their invitees or guests.

(2) "Security deposit" means any advance or deposit of money, regardless of its denomination, the primary function of which is to secure the performance of a rental agreement for residential premises or any part thereof.

§ 38-12-103, C.R.S. Return of security deposit

(1) A landlord shall, within one month after the termination of a lease or surrender and acceptance of the premises, whichever occurs last, return to the tenant the full security deposit deposited with the landlord by the tenant, unless the lease agreement specifies a longer period of time, but not to exceed sixty days. No security deposit shall be retained to cover normal wear and tear. In the event that actual cause exists for retaining any portion of the security deposit, the landlord shall provide the tenant with a written statement listing the exact reasons for the retention of any portion of the security deposit. When the statement is delivered, it shall be accompanied by payment of the difference between any sum deposited and the amount retained. The landlord is deemed to have complied with this section by mailing said statement and any payment required to the last known address of the tenant. Nothing in this section shall preclude the landlord from retaining the security deposit for nonpayment of rent, abandonment of the premises, or nonpayment of utility charges, repair work, or cleaning contracted for by the tenant.

(2) The failure of a landlord to provide a written statement within the required time specified in subsection (1) of this section shall work a forfeiture of all his rights to withhold any portion of the security deposit under this section.

(3) (a) The willful retention of a security deposit in violation of this section shall render a landlord liable for treble the amount of that portion of the security deposit wrongfully withheld from the tenant, together with reasonable attorneys' fees and court costs; except that the tenant has the obligation to give notice to the landlord of his intention to file legal proceedings a minimum of seven days prior to filing said action.

(b) In any court action brought by a tenant under this section, the landlord shall bear the burden of proving that his withholding of the security deposit or any portion of it was not wrongful.

(4) Upon cessation of his interest in the dwelling unit, whether by sale, assignment, death, appointment of a receiver, or otherwise, the person in possession of the security deposit, including but not limited to the landlord, his agent, or his executor, shall, within a reasonable time:

(a) Transfer the funds, or any remainder after lawful deductions under subsection (1) of this section, to the landlord's successor in interest and notify the tenant by mail of such transfer and of the transferee's name and address; or

(b) Return the funds, or any remainder after lawful deductions under subsection (1) of this section, to the tenant.

(5) Upon compliance with subsection (4) of this section, the person in possession of the security deposit shall be relieved of further liability.

(6) Upon receipt of transferred funds under subsection (4)(a) of this section, the transferee, in relation to such funds, shall be deemed to have all of the rights and obligations of a landlord holding the funds as a security deposit.

(7) Any provision, whether oral or written, in or pertaining to a rental agreement whereby any provision of this section for the benefit of a tenant or members of his household is waived shall be deemed to be against public policy and shall be void.

§ 38-12-104, C.R.S. Return of security deposit – hazardous condition – gas appliance

(1) Anytime service personnel from any organization providing gas service to a residential building become aware of any hazardous condition of a gas appliance, piping, or other gas equipment, such personnel shall inform the customer of record at the affected address in writing of the hazardous condition and take any further action provided for by the policies of such personnel's employer. Such written notification shall state the potential nature of the hazard as a fire hazard or a hazard to life, health, property, or public welfare and shall explain the possible cause of the hazard.

(2) If the resident of the residential building is a tenant, such tenant shall immediately inform the landlord of the property or the landlord's agent in writing of the existence of the hazard.

(3) The landlord shall then have seventy-two hours excluding a Saturday, Sunday, or a legal holiday after the actual receipt of the written notice of the hazardous condition to have the hazardous condition repaired by a professional. "Professional" for the purposes of this section means a person authorized by the state of Colorado or by a county or municipal government through license or certificate where such government authorization is required. Where no person with such government authorization is available, and where there are no local requirements for government authorization, a person who is otherwise qualified and who possesses insurance with a minimum of one hundred thousand dollars public liability and property damage coverage shall be deemed a professional for purposes of this section. Proof of such repairs shall be forwarded to the landlord or the landlord's agent. Such proof may also be used as an affirmative defense in any action to recover the security deposit, as provided for in this section.

(4) If the landlord does not have the repairs made within seventy-two hours excluding a Saturday, Sunday, or a legal holiday, and the condition of the building remains hazardous, the tenant may opt to vacate the premises. After the tenant vacates the premises, the lease or other rental agreement between the landlord and tenant becomes null and void, all rights and future obligations between the landlord and tenant pursuant to the lease or other rental agreement terminate, and the tenant may demand the immediate return of all or any portion of the security deposit held by the landlord to which the tenant is entitled. The landlord shall have seventy-two hours following the tenant's vacation of the premises to deliver to the tenant all of, or the appropriate portion of, the security deposit plus any rent rebate owed to the tenant for rent paid by the tenant for the period of time after the tenant has vacated. If the seventy-second hour falls on a Saturday, Sunday, or legal holiday, the security deposit must be delivered by noon on the next day that is not a Saturday, Sunday, or legal holiday. The tenant shall provide the landlord with a correct forwarding address. No security deposit shall be retained to cover normal wear and tear. In the event that actual cause exists for retaining any portion of the security deposit, the landlord shall provide the tenant with a written statement listing the exact reasons for the retention of any portion of the security deposit. When the statement is delivered, it shall be

accompanied by payment of the difference between any sum deposited and the amount retained. The landlord is deemed to have complied with this section by mailing said statement and any payments required by this section to the forwarding address of the tenant. Nothing in this section shall preclude the landlord from withholding the security deposit for nonpayment of rent or for nonpayment of utility charges, repair work, or cleaning contracted for by the tenant. If the tenant does not receive the entire security deposit or a portion of the security deposit together with a written statement listing the exact reasons for the retention of any portion of the security deposit within the time period provided for in this section, the retention of the security deposit shall be deemed willful and wrongful and, not withstanding the provisions of section 38-12-103 (3), shall entitle the tenant to twice the amount of the security deposit and to reasonable attorney fees.

B. City Ordinances Concerning Security Deposits

The City of Boulder requires payment of a stated rate of interest to a tenant for any security deposit held under a residential lease. This excludes leasing of mobile home park space. The person in possession of the deposit must return and account for the amount and interest due within 30 days after the latter of termination or surrender and acceptance of the lease. (Ordinances 4969 and 7158, Title 12–Chapter 2, Landlord/Tenant Relations.) Brokers should check for similar requirements in other cities where leasing activity is conducted.

C. Guidelines for the Property Manager Regarding Security Deposits

A manager should inspect a property prior to occupancy and document the condition of the premises. When the tenant vacates and has caused no damage other than normal wear and tear, the deposit must be returned to the tenant.

Accounting for security deposits is extremely important and must be performed pursuant to Commission Rules E-l and E-16 and Commission position statement CP-5, Advance Rentals and Security Deposits (see Chapter 3). These deposits must generally be placed into a security deposit escrow account and returned as soon as possible to the tenant, when refundable. The practice of making refund checks jointly payable to a tenant and a new property manager or owner only delays the refund process and may result in public complaints. Some owners and management companies apply security deposits toward the last month's rent. This practice may result in owner liability because advance rental deposits may be subject to earning interest, whereas security deposits generally are not. The broker should review local or county ordinances for further information.

Both the management agreement and the lease or rental agreement should contain authority for the manager to control security deposits. If there is no written procedure pertaining to these deposits, each party to the agreement injecting his or her own ideas may result in confusion and resentment. Thus, it is best that both the lease and the management agreement spell out in writing the intent of all parties to the contract concerning the disposition of security deposit funds. A broker may transfer tenant security deposits to a property owner only pursuant to Commission position statement CP-5, Advance Rentals and Security Deposits. This position statement is summarized in Rule E-16; see also "Offsetting Broker Expenses Against Refundable Deposits" in Chapter 19, "Escrow Records."

A written agreement is also useful in the event of a change in ownership or management of a building. The new owner or manager may simply refer to the tenancy agreement to determine the amount of the deposit, and the tenant has a copy as proof.

The amount of a security deposit varies according to the rent paid, the size of the unit, whether the unit is furnished or not, and the type of equipment included (*e.g.*, washer, dryer, dishwasher, air conditioner). Policies vary, and competition plays a part in the amount of security deposit that may be obtained, but a good rule of thumb would be 50 percent to 100 percent of one month's rent.

Unclaimed security deposits and other forms of "money belonging to others" must be reported and remitted by the property manager to the Colorado State Treasurer under the provisions of the "Unclaimed Property Act," §§ 38-13-101, *et seq.*, C.R.S. Unclaimed property reports are filed by November 1 each year. Unclaimed property is generally that which has been held for five years or more. Forms and instructions may be obtained from The Great Colorado Payback Offices, 1580 Logan St., Suite 500, Denver, CO 80203, Phone: (800) 825-2111, Website: www.colorado.gov/treasury/gcp/.

VI. Leases

A. Introduction

A lease is both a contract and a conveyance. It sets forth the terms of the agreement between the parties (landlord and tenant; lessor and lessee) whereby the right to possess and use the property for a certain period of time is transferred from one to the other. The interest in the property transferred may be nominal, such as a lease for one month; or it may be a very substantial 99-year lease. A lease for one year or less may be oral. A lease for longer than one year is required to be in writing to be enforceable under the statute of frauds. A written lease is always preferable because it furnishes objective proof of the terms agreed to by the parties.

A lease is an agreement between a lessor and a lessee whereby the lessee takes possession and receives the use and profits of an estate in real property for a certain period of time in return for which the lessor receives the lessee's performance and payment according to the conditions of the agreement.

B. Leasehold Tenancies

Leasehold estates can be classified into four types: (1) tenancy for years, (2) periodic tenancy, (3) tenancy at will, and (4) tenancy at sufferance.

Tenancy for years

A tenancy for years is for a fixed period of time (*e.g.*, one day or 99 years). The termination date is set at the time the lease is executed. A tenancy for years ends on the last day of the lease term, with no need to give notice.

Periodic tenancy

A periodic tenancy exists when the rental period is indefinitely renewable for a series of same durations (*e.g.*, week-to-week or month-to-month). The most common example is a residential lease requiring a tenant to pay monthly rent, but with no definite termination date. Periodic tenancies are generally created by implication and not by an express provision. According to Colorado law, and that of most states, such tenancies require the giving of proper notice for their termination. Notice to terminate is discussed below under "Termination of leases."

Tenancy at will

A tenancy at will provides that either party may terminate the lease whenever he or she chooses to do so. A tenancy at will also exists when the agreement allows a tenant to occupy the premises until sold, or until the landlord is ready to construct a new building, or some other indefinite happening. Similar to a periodic tenancy, a tenancy at will requires the giving of proper notice for its termination.

Tenancy at sufferance

A tenancy at sufferance arises when a tenant remains in wrongful possession after a lease has ended. In this situation, the tenant is called a "**holdover tenant**." The landlord may treat the tenant as a trespasser and initiate eviction, or may elect to accept the tenant for a similar term and conditions as in the previous lease. The choice is the landlord's; the tenant has none. If a tenant holds over due to reasons beyond his or her control, such as illness, the tenant may be held liable only for the reasonable rental of the holdover period.

C. Types of Leases

Ground lease

A ground lease is a tenancy for years whereby a parcel of unimproved land is let for a typically extended period of time. This usually allows a building to be erected on the land by the tenant and provides for the disposition of the building at the end of the lease. The landowner may become entitled to the building upon the payment of all, part, or none of the value of the building, depending upon the agreement. In the absence of an agreement, the building legally becomes real property and belongs to the landowner, who is not required to reimburse the tenant.

A long-term ground lease can offer considerable advantage to a tenant. When land values run as high as $10,000 and more per front foot, considerable capital is required to invest in the land alone. Add the cost of a building to this, and the investment may exceed an investor's resources. But under a long-term ground lease, the land part of the financing problem is solved. Such a lease may be considered as borrowing of the capital value of the land for the term of the lease. The ground rent paid to the owner is, in this sense, interest on the value of the land. The land itself plus the improvements erected by the tenant become security for the "loan." A transaction with such ample security is indeed a good investment for the fee holder.

Big businesses and investors do not hesitate to deal with such long-term leases, provided the location involved is suitable to their purposes. In addition, long-term leases involve a tax advantage. If purchased, the price of land is a capital investment and is not deductible; in fact, the ground is not even depreciable. But rent paid by a tenant is a deductible business expense. The landowner benefits from a reduced income tax liability on the rent received over the years compared to an immediate and large capital gains tax if the property had been sold to the tenant.

A long-term ground lease holds another advantage for an owner of valuable land lacking sufficient finances to develop it. An owner may induce a tenant to make suitable improvements by means of rent concessions. With appropriate improvements, the fee holder's land will increase in value, with the increase benefiting the owner at the end of the lease. Such leases often provide for the increases in value to be matched by increased ground rent at suitable intervals. This is what is known as a "**step-up lease**" or "**graduated lease**." Two common ways to provide for these increases in rent are to: (1) provide for a fixed increase at stated intervals, or (2) provide for the increase to be based upon the appraised value of the property, determined by an arbitration committee. Although the first method has the advantage of being clear and definite, it may be too inflexible to meet changing economic conditions over a long period of years. The second method involves an arbitration committee, usually composed of one member selected by the tenant, one by the landlord, and the third selected by agreement of these two. This committee then applies a fixed capitalization rate to the appraised value of the property at regular intervals. This method establishes a currently reasonable rental, but may be difficult to implement if the committee members cannot agree. Some authorities on long-term leases claim that fixed rentals for the entire period give the greatest satisfaction to both parties, enabling stable, long-term business planning. Other authorities feel that such a fixed rental program works a hardship on the tenant in a recessionary period and a hardship upon the owner in an inflationary period.

Percentage lease

Percentage leases are used for commercial establishments, generally retail stores, and usually provide for a fixed minimum rent plus a percentage of the tenant's gross sales. Gross sales or gross income must be clearly defined and should provide for such things as returned merchandise, discounts for prompt payment made to customers, sales to employees, mail-order sales, services rendered at cost (such as clothing alterations), and income from vending machines. Detailed provisions should be made concerning the tenant's records and the landlord's right to examine or audit the tenant's books. Satisfactory use of percentage leases requires thorough knowledge and expert judgment.

Sky lease

A sky lease or lease of air space usually creates a tenancy for years, generally for a long period of time. In 1910, the Cleveland Athletic Club executed one of the first such leases, leasing the air space above a five-story building and erecting eight additional stories. The club paid rent for its space along with the improvement taxes, but not land taxes. The upper eight stories were to revert to the lessor at the end of the term upon the payment of its appraised value. This type of lease is based upon the common-law right of a fee holder to use his or her land from the center of the earth to the dome of the skies. Today, the governmental right to regulate air traffic has limited this property right.

One of the most interesting utilizations of air space involves the Merchandise Mart in Chicago. The building is constructed over the tracks of the Chicago and Northwestern Railroad, erected on piers 23 feet above the earth's surface, leaving space necessary for the operation of the railway.

Within the state of Colorado there exist a few such leases or sales of air space. In 1953, the Colorado legislature enacted a statute enabling the creation of estates, rights, and interests in areas above the surface of the ground and the transfer of such interests in the same manner as interests in land. (See §§ 38-32-101, *et seq.*, C.R.S.)

Net lease

A net lease requires the tenant to pay rent plus all or a substantial part of the cost of operations and maintenance. Various expressions are used in real estate to describe the many variations in net lease transactions. For instance, if a lease provides for the tenant to pay utilities, real estate taxes and assessments, etc., it might be referred to as "net" lease. If the lease additionally provides for the tenant to insure the premises, it might be referred to as "net-net." Both parties must be absolutely certain of their responsibilities in a net lease.

Gross lease

A gross lease is the opposite of a net lease. The rent typically includes all owner-paid operating costs associated with the premises.

Farm lease

Farm leases are based on the same principles as other leases. The farm tenant may pay rent based on a crop-sharing basis. The owner agrees to give possession to the land and improvements thereon, and perhaps to furnish the equipment, and the tenant agrees to furnish the labor and capital to farm the land in a sound, reasonable manner and to pay a specified share of the crops. Alternatively, the rental may be a fixed sum. Farm leases vary in terms and conditions by region and community.

Farm management has become one of the leading and most specialized branches of real estate. A farm manager must know soils, crops most suitable to the various types of soils, land conservation techniques, and the numerous other things necessary for successful modern farming.

D. Elements of a Lease

As stated earlier, a lease is both a contract and a conveyance. As a contract, it embodies the agreement of the parties. As a conveyance, it transfers an interest in land, the right to possess and use it for a certain time. The following are the more common lease elements.

1. **Date:** Although not essential, a date can prevent controversy as to questions of time and related problems, such as the portion of the rent due for a partial month or year.
2. **Parties:** Must have legal capacity to enter a contract, and be clearly named and designated. If there are multiple owners or tenants, all should be parties to the lease.
3. **Consideration:** A lease is not enforceable without consideration. The lessee's payment (or promise to pay) and the lessor's delivery of (or promise to deliver) possession are typical considerations supporting the lease.
4. **Description of the Property:** A lease must describe the premises with reasonable certainty. Tenancy of only part of an improvement, use of basement storage space, assignment of parking spaces, or other facilities should be clearly described.
5. **Words of Conveyance:** The lease should clearly state the extent and nature of the interest being conveyed, including the duration of the lease and the lessee's rights.
6. **Conditions and Exceptions:** All conditions imposed on a lessee's tenancy and exceptions to the rights that normally accrue to a tenant should be set forth.
7. **Lessor's and Lessee's Covenants:** Any and all covenants to be fulfilled by either party should be included in the lease.
8. **Signatures:** A lease for longer than one year must be in writing and signed by the parties. The best evidence of the parties' mutual assent is a signed instrument. If a

lessee takes possession without signing, only the lessor need sign to create a valid lease. The lessee's taking possession is evidence of his or her assent to the lease.

9. **Seal:** A seal is not generally required, except in the case of corporations and governmental agencies.
10. **Delivery:** Like a deed, a lease must be delivered to be effective.
11. **Recording:** A lease need not be recorded to be valid. However, a long-term lease may be extremely valuable and should be recorded. As a rule, a landlord does not furnish a tenant with title evidence, but in the case of a long-term lease, a tenant might require the owner to prove clear title.
12. **Acknowledgment:** A lease need not be acknowledged. Again, in the case of a valuable lease that will be recorded, acknowledgment of the signatures should be made.
13. **Lead-Based Paint Disclosure.**
14. **Any City or County Regulations on Occupancy.**

Some other lease clauses that may apply include: cost-of-living adjustment; handling of the security deposits; use of premises; acceptance of the premises by lessee; surrender of premises at end of term; maintenance, repair, and alterations of premises during term; responsibility for payment of utilities; personal and real property taxes; entry and inspection by lessor's agents; assignment and subletting; agent hold-harmless clause; repossession due to unpaid rent; abandonment of premises by the tenant; holding over; future sale of premises; cessation of lease by condemnation or destruction of premises; right of the lessor to mortgage or subordinate; sign regulation; renewal options; termination notice; and disposition of deposits/records upon change of property managers.

E. Termination of Leases

Leases may be terminated in four major ways: (1) expiration of the term, (2) surrender and acceptance, (3) breach of conditions of the lease, and (4) eviction of the tenant.

Expiration of the term of the lease

A **tenancy for years** ends on the last day of the term, with no notice-to-quit required. Section 13-40-107(4), C.R.S., states: "No notice to quit shall be necessary from or to a tenant whose term is, by agreement, to end at a time certain." If a lease is oral, the lessor should give the periodic statutory notice-to-quit in writing in order to avoid potential conflict over the term of the oral agreement.

To terminate a **periodic tenancy** or a **tenancy-at-will**, the party (lessor or lessee) desiring to end the lease must serve a written notice to quit. The notice must describe the premises, state the time the tenancy will terminate, be signed by the party (or agent) giving such notice, and be served not less than a statutorily specified time before the end of the tenancy period. Required notice periods under § 13-40-107, C.R.S., are:

- Year-to-year tenancy or longer: three months prior or earlier.
- Six months or more but less than a year: one month prior or earlier.
- Month-to-month or up to but less than six months: at least 10 days' prior notice.
- Tenancy at will: minimum three-day notice.

Notice must be delivered to the tenant or other person occupying the premises, or by leaving a copy with some person, a member of the tenant's family above the age of 15, residing on or in charge of the premises; or if no one is on the premises at the time service is attempted, by posting a copy in some conspicuous place on the premises.

Section 13-40-107.5(1), C.R.S., provides for a three-day expedited eviction of certain undesirable and dangerous persons who demonstrate that they (or their guests) are "unfit to coexist with their neighbors and co-tenants" by committing infractions known in the law as "substantial violations." These include various violent or drug-related felonies as well as endangerment of persons and property. These acts are considered severe enough to give the landlord a remedy of expedited eviction. However, the statute specifically states that victims of domestic abuse, and persons who could not have reasonably known of or prevented the substantial violations but did immediately notify law enforcement, are exempt from any expedited eviction action.

A holdover tenant is not entitled to notice to quit. If a lease is for a definite term and the tenant does not surrender possession of the property at the end of the term, the landlord may elect to hold the tenant for an additional like term. Such election must be accompanied by some act on the part of the landlord that signifies an intention to accept the tenant, such as receiving the next rent payment. Unless the landlord in some way indicates intent to retain the tenant, the tenant remains a tenant at sufferance.

The tenant does not have any right of election in such a case; only the landlord. It is a common practice—and potential pitfall—to include in the lease an automatic renewal clause, which provides that unless an agreed-upon notice of a certain number of days (*e.g.*, 30 or 60) is given by either party, the lease will be continued automatically from the end of the term for a like period.

Surrender and acceptance

A mutual agreement to terminate a lease without obligation on the part of either the landlord or tenant is a termination by surrender of the lease and an acceptance thereof.

Breach of conditions

Failure by either the lessor or lessee to perform agreed-upon conditions or covenants constitute a breach of the lease and may permit the injured party to cancel the lease.

Eviction of the tenant

An eviction may be either actual or constructive. Actual eviction occurs when a tenant is ousted from the premises, completely or partially, either by an act of the landlord or by someone with superior title. Constructive eviction occurs when the leased premises deteriorate to such physical condition, owing to some act or omission of the landlord, that the tenant is unable to use the premises for the purpose intended. Failure to furnish heat or other facilities contemplated by the lease or any other deprivation of use by the lessor is also a constructive eviction.

Termination under other conditions

If leased property is taken for public use by condemnation, any lease is terminated. The tenant is entitled to compensation for the value of the unexpired portion of the lease, and the tenant's claim is superior to that of the landlord.

The foreclosure of a mortgage or other lien may terminate the lease. If the mortgage or other lien was prior in time to the lease, and the tenant had either actual notice or constructive notice of the lien, then foreclosure will terminate the lease.

F. Duties and Liabilities of the Parties

A carefully drafted lease will clearly set forth all the duties and responsibilities of the parties, and avoid ambiguities that might lead to controversy. Absent a complete written lease setting forth all terms, the law presumes certain agreements on the part of the parties. For instance, unless there is an agreement to pay rent in advance, the law presumes that rent is not due until the end of a rental period.

A tenant may use the premises in any lawful, appropriate way not expressly restricted in the lease. If the premises are unsuitable for the specified purpose of the lease, the landlord, unless having agreed to do so, need not remodel the property but the tenant may do so. A commercial landlord may compete or lease to a competing business within the same building unless the lease so prohibits.

A lease of business property automatically gives a tenant the right to maintain signs on the leased property advertising the business, in compliance with state, county, and city regulations. Unless expressly granted, no such right to advertise exists for leased residential property, such as when a doctor, real estate broker, or other professional maintains an office in a leased residence.

In multiple-unit commercial or residential property, the landlord has a duty to keep the premises warm and habitable, unless each unit has its own facilities. Provisions as to the furnishing of gas, electricity, heat, hot water, and other services should be incorporated in the lease.

Unless a lease provides otherwise, a landlord is generally not required to keep the premises in repair. Neither is the tenant required to make repairs. Provision for repair and for the scope of the duties of the party obligated to keep the premises in repair should be clearly delineated in the lease. An agreement to repair does not impose the duty to rebuild if the premises are accidentally destroyed. A landlord is not required to repair and make habitable property that is uninhabitable at the time of making the lease. The tenant is presumed to have full knowledge of the condition of the property and should specify any desired repairs.

A lessor has no right to enter the leased premises. A landlord's right to enter upon the premises to inspect the property or to show it to prospective purchasers or lessees is limited to what is spelled out in the agreement.

As a general rule, a person occupying the property is liable to others for injury caused by the condition of the property. An occupant is also liable to others for any nuisance resulting from the occupant's use that interferes with others' use and enjoyment of their property.

A landlord is not generally liable for injury to a tenant or a tenant's family caused by the property's condition, unless such condition is latent (*i.e.*, hidden) and the landlord had knowledge of such latent, dangerous condition. A landlord may be held liable to persons using the sidewalks or highway abutting the property for injury caused by dangerous conditions on the property. In such a case, a landlord's liability continues only until a reasonable time after the tenant takes possession and has the opportunity to correct the dangerous condition, whereupon the tenant becomes responsible. It is advisable that the parties agree as to responsibility for injury to other persons, and for the responsible party to secure protection by means of liability insurance.

A landlord usually retains control over entrances, hallways, elevators, stairways, and other portions of multi-unit property. In such cases, the landlord is liable for injury to the tenants, their guests, or business visitors caused by dangerous conditions in these areas resulting from landlord negligence. As a general rule, partial or total destruction of the premises by fire or other accident does not relieve a tenant from the obligation to pay rent. Some states feel this common-law rule is too harsh and have enacted statutes stating that destruction or damage making the property unfit for occupancy terminates the lease and relieves a tenant from paying rent. It is strongly recommended that lease provisions cover such emergencies.

Unless the provisions of the lease prohibit, a tenant may assign or sublet the premises. The lessee would remain liable to the lessor for the performance of all the original lease conditions. Most leases prohibit subletting or assignment without the lessor's prior consent.

A landlord who re-enters leased premises effectively evicts the tenant and relieves the tenant from all liability for future rent, unless the lease specifies otherwise. If the lease authorizes a landlord to re-enter and re-let the premises without terminating the lease in the event a tenant vacates the premises, a court may hold the tenant liable for rent the tenant agreed to pay, less any amount the landlord received from the new tenant. Many lease agreements provide that upon tenant default a landlord may: (1) declare the term of the lease ended, re-enter the premises, expel the tenant, and take possession of the premises, or (2) re-let the premises and apply the rent from the new tenant's lease to the lease of the old tenant, with the old tenant being responsible for any balance due.

The above discussion should indicate the extreme desirability of having a carefully drafted lease, which clearly sets forth all the conditions and covenants of the tenancy and all the duties and responsibilities of each party.

G. 2008 Warranty of Habitability Act (Residential Properties)

§ 38-12-501, C.R.S. Legislative declaration – matter of statewide concern – purposes and policies

(1) The general assembly hereby finds and declares that the provisions of this part 5 are a matter of statewide concern. Any local government ordinance, resolution, or other regulation that is in conflict with this part 5 shall be unenforceable.

(2) The underlying purposes and policies of this part 5 are to:

- (a) Simplify, clarify, modernize, and revise the law governing the rental of dwelling units and the rights and obligations of landlords and tenants;
- (b) Encourage landlords and tenants to maintain and improve the quality of housing; and
- (c) Make uniform the law with respect to the subject of this part 5 throughout Colorado.

§ 38-12-502, C.R.S. Definitions

As used in this part 5, unless the context otherwise requires:

(1) "Common areas" means the facilities and appurtenances to a residential premises, including the grounds, areas, and facilities held out for the use of tenants generally or whose use is promised to a tenant.

(2) "Dwelling unit" means a structure or the part of a structure that is used as a home, residence, or sleeping place by a tenant.

(3) "Landlord" means the owner, manager, lessor, or sublessor of a residential premises.

(4) "Rental agreement" means the agreement, written or oral, embodying the terms and conditions concerning the use and occupancy of a residential premises.

(5) "Residential premises" means a dwelling unit, the structure of which the unit is a part, and the common areas.

(6) "Tenant" means a person entitled under a rental agreement to occupy a dwelling unit to the exclusion of others.

§ 38-12-503, C.R.S. Warranty of habitability

(1) In every rental agreement, the landlord is deemed to warrant that the residential premises is fit for human habitation.

(2) A landlord breaches the warranty of habitability set forth in subsection (1) of this section if:

(a) A residential premises is uninhabitable as described in section 38-12-505 or otherwise unfit for human habitation; and

(b) The residential premises is in a condition that is materially dangerous or hazardous to the tenant's life, health, or safety; and

(c) The landlord has received written notice of the condition described in paragraphs (a) and (b) of this subsection (2) and failed to cure the problem within a reasonable time.

(3) When any condition described in subsection (2) of this section is caused by the misconduct of the tenant, a member of the tenant's household, a guest or invitee of the tenant, or a person under the tenant's direction or control, the condition shall not constitute a breach of the warranty of habitability. It shall not be misconduct by a victim of domestic violence or domestic abuse under this subsection (3) if the condition is the result of domestic violence or domestic abuse and the landlord has been given written notice and evidence of domestic violence or domestic abuse as described in section 38-12-402(2)(a).

(4) In response to the notice sent pursuant to paragraph (c) of subsection (2) of this section, a landlord may, in the landlord's discretion, move a tenant to a comparable unit after paying the reasonable costs, actually incurred, incident to the move.

(5) Except as set forth in this part 5, any agreement waiving or modifying the warranty of habitability shall be void as contrary to public policy.

(6) Nothing in this part 5 shall:

(a) Prevent a landlord from terminating a rental agreement as a result of a casualty or catastrophe to the dwelling unit without further liability to the landlord or tenant; or

(b) Preclude a landlord from initiating an action for nonpayment of rent, breach of the rental agreement, violation of section 38-12-504, or as provided for under article 40 of title 13, C.R.S.

§ 38-12-504, C.R.S. Tenant's maintenance of premises

(1) In addition to any duties imposed upon a tenant by a rental agreement, every tenant of a residential premises has a duty to use that portion of the premises within the tenant's control in a reasonably clean and safe manner. A tenant fails to maintain the premises in a reasonably clean and safe manner when the tenant substantially fails to:

(a) Comply with obligations imposed upon tenants by applicable provisions of building, health, and housing codes materially affecting health and safety;

(b) Keep the dwelling unit reasonably clean, safe, and sanitary as permitted by the conditions of the unit;

(c) Dispose of ashes, garbage, rubbish, and other waste from the dwelling unit in a clean, safe, sanitary, and legally compliant manner;

(d) Use in a reasonable manner all electrical, plumbing, sanitary, heating, ventilating, air-conditioning, elevators, and other facilities and appliances in the dwelling unit;

(e) Conduct himself or herself and require other persons in the residential premises within the tenant's control to conduct themselves in a manner that does not disturb their neighbors' peaceful enjoyment of the neighbors' dwelling unit; or

(f) Promptly notify the landlord if the residential premises is uninhabitable as defined in section 38-12-505 or if there is a condition that could result in the premises becoming uninhabitable if not remedied.

(2) In addition to the duties set forth in subsection (1) of this section, a tenant shall not knowingly, intentionally, deliberately, or negligently destroy, deface, damage, impair, or remove any part of the residential premises or knowingly permit any person within his or her control to do so.

(3) Nothing in this section shall be construed to authorize a modification of a landlord's obligations under the warranty of habitability.

§ 38-12-505, C.R.S. Uninhabitable residential premises

(1) A residential premises is deemed uninhabitable if it substantially lacks any of the following characteristics:

(a) Waterproofing and weather protection of roof and exterior walls maintained in good working order, including unbroken windows and doors;

(b) Plumbing or gas facilities that conformed to applicable law in effect at the time of installation and that are maintained in good working order;

(c) Running water and reasonable amounts of hot water at all times furnished to appropriate fixtures and connected to a sewage disposal system approved under applicable law;

(d) Functioning heating facilities that conformed to applicable law at the time of installation and that are maintained in good working order;

(e) Electrical lighting, with wiring and electrical equipment that conformed to applicable law at the time of installation, maintained in good working order;

(f) Common areas and areas under the control of the landlord that are kept reasonably clean, sanitary, and free from all accumulations of debris, filth, rubbish, and garbage and that have appropriate extermination in response to the infestation of rodents or vermin;

(g) Appropriate extermination in response to the infestation of rodents or vermin throughout a residential premises;

(h) An adequate number of appropriate exterior receptacles for garbage and rubbish, in good repair;

(i) Floors, stairways, and railings maintained in good repair;

(j) Locks on all exterior doors and locks or security devices on windows designed to be opened that are maintained in good working order; or

(k) Compliance with all applicable building, housing, and health codes, which, if violated, would constitute a condition that is dangerous or hazardous to a tenant's life, health, or safety.

(2) No deficiency in the common area shall render a residential premises uninhabitable as set forth in subsection (1) of this section, unless it materially and substantially limits the tenant's use of his or her dwelling unit.

(3) Unless otherwise stated in section 38-12-506, prior to being leased to a tenant, a residential premises must comply with the requirements set forth in section 38-12-503(1), (2)(a), and (2)(b).

§ 38-12-506, C.R.S. Opt-out

(1) If a dwelling unit is contained within a mobile home park, as defined in section 38-12-201.5(3), or if there are four or fewer dwelling units sharing common walls or located on the same parcel, as defined in section 30-28-302(5), C.R.S., all of which have the same owner, or if the dwelling unit is a single-family residential premises:

(a) A good faith rental agreement may require a tenant to assume the obligation for one or more of the characteristics contained in section 38-12-505(1)(f), (1)(g), and (1)(h), as long as the requirement is not inconsistent with any obligations imposed upon a landlord by a governmental entity for the receipt of a subsidy for the residential premises; and

(b) For any dwelling unit for which a landlord does not receive a subsidy from any governmental source, a landlord and tenant may agree in writing that the tenant is to perform specific repairs, maintenance tasks, alterations, and remodeling, but only if:

(I) The agreement of the parties is entered into in good faith and is set forth in a separate writing signed by the parties and supported by adequate consideration;

(II) The work is not necessary to cure a failure to comply with section 38-12-505(3); and

(III) Such agreement does not affect the obligation of the landlord to other tenants' residential premises.

(2) For a single-family residential premises for which a landlord does not receive a subsidy from any governmental source, a landlord and tenant may agree in writing that the tenant is to perform specific repairs, maintenance tasks, alterations, and remodeling necessary to cure a failure to comply with section 38-12-505(3), but only if:

(a) The agreement of the landlord and tenant is entered into in good faith and is set forth in a writing that is separate from the rental agreement, signed by the parties, and supported by adequate consideration; and

(b) The tenant has the requisite skills to perform the work required to cure a failure to comply with section 38-12-505(3).

(3) To the extent that performance by a tenant relates to a characteristic set forth in section 38-12-505(1), the tenant shall assume the obligation for such characteristic.

(4) If consistent with this section a tenant assumes an obligation for a characteristic set forth in section 38-12-505(1), the lack of such characteristic shall not make a residential premises uninhabitable.

§ 38-12-507, C.R.S. Breach of warranty of habitability – tenant's remedies

(1) If there is a breach of the warranty of habitability as set forth in section 38-12-503(2), the following provisions shall apply:

(a) Upon no less than ten and no more than thirty days written notice to the landlord specifying the condition alleged to breach of the warranty of habitability and giving the landlord five business days from the receipt of the written notice to remedy the breach, a tenant may terminate the rental agreement by surrendering possession of the dwelling unit. If the breach is remediable by repairs, the payment of damages, or otherwise and the landlord adequately remedies the breach within five business days of receipt of the notice, the rental agreement shall not terminate by reason of the breach.

(b) A tenant may obtain injunctive relief for breach of the warranty of habitability in any court of competent jurisdiction. In any proceeding for injunctive relief, the court shall determine actual damages for a breach of the warranty at the time the court orders the injunctive relief. A landlord shall not be subject to any court order for injunctive relief if the landlord tenders the actual damages to the court within two business days of the order. Upon application by the tenant, the court shall immediately release to the tenant the damages paid by the landlord. If the tenant vacates the leased premises, the landlord shall not be permitted to rent the premises again until such time as the unit would be in compliance with the warranty of habitability set forth in section 38-12-503(1).

(c) In an action for possession based upon nonpayment of rent in which the tenant asserts a defense to possession based upon the landlord's alleged breach of the warranty of habitability, upon the filing of the tenant's answer the court shall order the tenant to pay into the registry of the court all or part of the rent accrued after due consideration of expenses already incurred by the tenant based upon the landlord's breach of the warranty of habitability.

(d) Whether asserted as a claim or counterclaim, a tenant may recover damages directly arising from a breach of the warranty of habitability, which may include, but are not limited to, any reduction in the fair rental value of the dwelling unit, in any court of competent jurisdiction.

(2) If a rental agreement contains a provision for either party in an action related to the rental agreement to obtain attorney fees and costs, then the prevailing party in any action brought under this part 5 shall be entitled to recover reasonable attorney fees and costs.

§ 38-12-508, C.R.S. Landlord's defenses to a claim of breach of warranty – limitations on claiming a breach

(1) It shall be a defense to a tenant's claim of breach of the warranty of habitability that the tenant's actions or inactions prevented the landlord from curing the condition underlying the breach of the warranty of habitability.

(2) Only parties to the rental agreement or other adult residents listed on the rental agreement who are also lawfully residing in the dwelling unit may assert a claim for a breach of the warranty of habitability.

(3) A tenant may not assert a claim for injunctive relief based upon the landlord's breach of the warranty of habitability of a residential premises unless the tenant has given notice to a local government within the boundaries of which the residential premises is located of the condition underlying the breach that is materially dangerous or hazardous to the tenant's life, health, or safety.

(4) A tenant may not assert a breach of the warranty of habitability as a defense to a landlord's action for possession based upon a nonmonetary violation of the rental agreement or for an action for possession based upon a notice to quit or vacate.

(5) If the condition alleged to breach the warranty of habitability is the result of the action or inaction of a tenant in another dwelling unit or another third party not under the direction and control of the landlord and the landlord has taken reasonable, necessary, and timely steps to abate the condition, but is unable to abate the condition due to circumstances beyond the landlord's reasonable control, the tenant's only remedy shall be termination of the rental agreement consistent with section 38-12-507(1)(a).

(6) For public housing authorities and other housing providers receiving federal financial assistance directly from the federal government, no provision of this part 5 in direct conflict with any federal law or regulation shall be enforceable against such housing provider.

§ 38-12-509, C.R.S. Prohibition on retaliation

(1) A landlord shall not retaliate against a tenant for alleging a breach of the warranty of habitability by discriminatorily increasing rent or decreasing services or by bringing or threatening to bring an action for possession in response to the tenant having made a good faith complaint to the landlord or to a governmental agency alleging a breach of the warranty of habitability.

(2) A landlord shall not be liable for retaliation under this section, unless a tenant proves that a landlord breached the warranty of habitability.

(3) Regardless of when an action for possession of the premises where the landlord is seeking to terminate the tenancy for violation of the terms of the rental agreement is brought, there shall be a rebuttable presumption in favor of the landlord that his or her decision to terminate is not retaliatory. The presumption created by this subsection (3) cannot be rebutted by evidence of the timing alone of the landlord's initiation of the action.

(4) If the landlord has a right to increase rent, to decrease service, or to terminate the tenant's tenancy at the end of any term of the rental agreement and the landlord exercises any of these rights, there shall be a rebuttable presumption that the landlord's exercise of any of these rights was not retaliatory. The presumption of this subsection (4) cannot be rebutted by evidence of the timing alone of the landlord's exercise of any of these rights.

§ 38-12-510, C.R.S. Unlawful removal or exclusion

It shall be unlawful for a landlord to remove or exclude a tenant from a dwelling unit without resorting to court process, unless the removal or exclusion is consistent with the provisions of article 18.5 of title 25, C.R.S., and the rules promulgated by the state board of health for the cleanup of an illegal drug laboratory or is with the mutual consent of the landlord and tenant or unless the dwelling unit has been abandoned by the tenant as evidenced by the return of keys, the substantial removal of the tenant's personal property, notice by the tenant, or the extended absence of the tenant while rent remains unpaid, any of which would cause a reasonable person to believe the tenant had permanently surrendered possession of the dwelling unit. Such unlawful removal or exclusion includes the willful termination of utilities or the willful removal of doors, windows, or locks to the premises other than as required for repair or maintenance. If the landlord willfully and unlawfully removes the tenant from the premises or willfully and unlawfully causes the termination of heat, running water, hot water, electric, gas, or other essential services, the tenant may seek any remedy available under the law, including this part 5.

§ 38-12-511, C.R.S. Application

(1) Unless created to avoid its application, this part 5 shall not apply to any of the following arrangements:

   (a) Residence at a public or private institution, if such residence is incidental to detention or the provision of medical, geriatric, education, counseling, religious, or similar service;

   (b) Occupancy under a contract of sale of a dwelling unit or the property of which it is a part, if the occupant is the purchaser, seller, or a person who succeeds to his or her interest;

   (c) Occupancy by a member of a fraternal or social organization in the portion of a structure operated for the benefit of the organization;

   (d) Transient occupancy in a hotel or motel that lasts less than thirty days;

   (e) Occupancy by an employee or independent contractor whose right to occupancy is conditional upon performance of services for an employer or contractor;

   (f) Occupancy by an owner of a condominium unit or a holder of a proprietary lease in a cooperative;

(g) Occupancy in a structure that is located within an unincorporated area of a county, does not receive water, heat, and sewer services from a public entity, and is rented for recreational purposes, such as a hunting cabin, yurt, hut, or other similar structure;

(h) Occupancy under rental agreement covering a residential premises used by the occupant primarily for agricultural purposes; or

(i) Any relationship between the owner of a mobile home park and the owner of a mobile home situated in the park.

(2) Nothing in this section shall be construed to limit remedies available elsewhere in law for a tenant to seek to maintain safe and sanitary housing.

H. Carbon Monoxide Alarms

§ 38-45-101, C.R.S. Definitions

(1) "Carbon monoxide alarm" means a device that detects carbon monoxide and that:

(a) Produces a distinct, audible alarm;

(b) Is listed by a nationally recognized, independent product-safety testing and certification laboratory to conform to the standards for carbon monoxide alarms issued by such laboratory or any successor standards;

(c) Is battery powered, plugs into a dwelling's electrical outlet and has a battery backup, is wired into a dwelling's electrical system and has a battery backup, or is connected to an electrical system via an electrical panel; and

(d) May be combined with a smoke detecting device if the combined device complies with applicable law regarding both smoke detecting devices and carbon monoxide alarms and that the combined unit produces an alarm, or an alarm and voice signal, in a manner that clearly differentiates between the two hazards.

(2) "Dwelling unit" means a single unit providing complete independent living facilities for one or more persons, including permanent provisions for living, sleeping, eating, cooking, and sanitation.

(3) "Fuel" means coal, kerosene, oil, fuel gases, or other petroleum products or hydrocarbon products such as wood that emit carbon monoxide as a by-product of combustion.

(4) "Installed" means that a carbon monoxide alarm is installed in a dwelling unit in one of the following ways:

(a) Wired directly into the dwelling's electrical system;

(b) Directly plugged into an electrical outlet without a switch other than a circuit breaker; or

(c) If the alarm is battery-powered, attached to the wall or ceiling of the dwelling unit in accordance with the national fire protection association's standard 720, or any successor standard, for the operation and installation of carbon monoxide detection and warning equipment in dwelling units.

(5) "Multi-family dwelling" means any improved real property used or intended to be used as a residence and that contains more than one dwelling unit. Multi-family dwelling includes a condominium or cooperative.

(6) "Operational" means working and in service in accordance with manufacturer instructions.

(7) "Single-family dwelling" means any improved real property used or intended to be used as a residence and that contains one dwelling unit.

§ 38-45-102, C.R.S. Carbon monoxide alarms in single-family dwellings – rules

(1) (a) Notwithstanding any other provision of law, the seller of each existing single-family dwelling offered for sale or transfer on or after July 1, 2009, that has a fuel-fired heater or

appliance, a fireplace, or an attached garage shall assure that an operational carbon monoxide alarm is installed within fifteen feet of the entrance to each room lawfully used for sleeping purposes or in a location as specified in any building code adopted by the state or any local government entity.

(b) By July 1, 2009, the real estate commission created in section 12-61-105, C.R.S., shall by rule require each listing contract for residential real property that is subject to the commission's jurisdiction pursuant to article 61 of title 12, C.R.S., to disclose the requirements specified in paragraph (a) of this subsection (1).

(2) Notwithstanding any other provision of law, every single-family dwelling that includes either fuel-fired appliances or an attached garage where, on or after July 1, 2009, interior alterations, repairs, fuel-fired appliance replacements, or additions, any of which require a building permit, occurs or where one or more rooms lawfully used for sleeping purposes are added shall have an operational carbon monoxide alarm installed within fifteen feet of the entrance to each room lawfully used for sleeping purposes or in a location as specified in any building code adopted by the state or any local government entity.

(3) No person shall remove batteries from, or in any way render inoperable, a carbon monoxide alarm, except as part of a process to inspect, maintain, repair, or replace the alarm or replace the batteries in the alarm.

§ 38-45-103, C.R.S. Carbon monoxide alarms in multi-family dwellings – rules

(1) (a) Notwithstanding any other provision of law, the seller of every dwelling unit of an existing multi-family dwelling offered for sale or transfer on or after July 1, 2009, that has a fuel-fired heater or appliance, a fireplace, or an attached garage shall assure that an operational carbon monoxide alarm is installed within fifteen feet of the entrance to each room lawfully used for sleeping purposes or in a location as specified in any building code adopted by the state or any local government entity.

(b) By July 1, 2009, the real estate commission created in section 12-61-105, C.R.S., shall by rule require each listing contract for residential real property that is subject to the commission's jurisdiction pursuant to article 61 of title 12, C.R.S., to disclose the requirements specified in paragraph (a) of this subsection (1).

(2) Notwithstanding any other provision of law, every dwelling unit of a multi-family dwelling that includes fuel-fired appliances or an attached garage where, on or after July 1, 2009, interior alterations, repairs, fuel-fired appliance replacements, or additions, any of which require a building permit, occurs or where one or more rooms lawfully used for sleeping purposes are added shall have an operational carbon monoxide alarm installed within fifteen feet of the entrance to each room lawfully used for sleeping purposes or in a location as specified in any building code adopted by the state or any local government entity.

(3) No person shall remove batteries from, or in any way render inoperable, a carbon monoxide alarm, except as part of a process to inspect, maintain, repair, or replace the alarm or replace the batteries in the alarm.

§ 38-45-104, C.R.S. Carbon monoxide alarms in rental properties

(1) Except as provided in subsection (5) of this section, any single-family dwelling or dwelling unit in a multi-family dwelling used for rental purposes and that includes fuel-fired appliances or an attached garage where, on or after July 1, 2009, interior alterations, repairs, fuel-fired appliance replacements, or additions, any of which requires a building permit, occurs or where one or more rooms lawfully used for sleeping purposes are added shall be subject to the requirements specified in sections 38-45-102 and 38-45-103.

(2) Except as provided in subsection (5) of this section, each existing single-family dwelling or existing dwelling unit in a multi-family dwelling that is used for rental purposes that has a

change in tenant occupancy on or after July 1, 2009, shall be subject to the requirements specified in sections 38-45-102 and 38-45-103.

(3) (a) Notwithstanding any other provision of law, the owner of any rental property specified in subsections (1) and (2) of this section shall:

(I) Prior to the commencement of a new tenant occupancy, replace any carbon monoxide alarm that was stolen, removed, found missing, or found not operational after the previous occupancy;

(II) Ensure that any batteries necessary to make the carbon monoxide alarm operational are provided to the tenant at the time the tenant takes residence in the dwelling unit;

(III) Replace any carbon monoxide alarm if notified by a tenant as specified in paragraph (c) of subsection (4) of this section that any carbon monoxide alarm was stolen, removed, found missing, or found not operational during the tenant's occupancy; and

(IV) Fix any deficiency in a carbon monoxide alarm if notified by a tenant as specified in paragraph (d) of subsection (4) of this section.

(b) Except as provided in paragraph (a) of this subsection (3), the owner of a single-family dwelling or dwelling unit in a multi-family dwelling that is used for rental purposes is not responsible for the maintenance, repair, or replacement of a carbon monoxide alarm or the care and replacement of batteries for such an alarm.

(4) Notwithstanding any other provision of law, the tenant of any rental property specified in subsections (1) and (2) of this section shall:

(a) Keep, test, and maintain all carbon monoxide alarms in good repair;

(b) Notify, in writing, the owner of the single-family dwelling or dwelling unit of a multi-family dwelling, or the owner's authorized agent, if the batteries of any carbon monoxide alarm need to be replaced;

(c) Notify, in writing, the owner of the single-family dwelling or dwelling unit of a multi-family dwelling, or the owner's authorized agent, if any carbon monoxide alarm is stolen, removed, found missing, or found not operational during the tenant's occupancy of the single-family dwelling or dwelling unit in the multi-family dwelling; and

(d) Notify, in writing, the owner of the single-family dwelling or dwelling unit of a multi-family dwelling, or the owner's authorized agent, of any deficiency in any carbon monoxide alarm that the tenant cannot correct.

(5) Notwithstanding the requirements of section 38-45-103 (1) and (2), so long as there is a centralized alarm system or other mechanism for a responsible person to hear the alarm at all times in a multi-family dwelling used for rental purposes, such multi-family dwelling may have an operational carbon monoxide alarm installed within twenty-five feet of any fuel-fired heater or appliance, fireplace, or garage or in a location as specified in any building code adopted by the state or any local government entity.

(6) No person shall remove batteries from, or in any way render inoperable, a carbon monoxide alarm, except as part of a process to inspect, maintain, repair, or replace the alarm or replace the batteries in the alarm.

§ 38-45-105, C.R.S. Municipal or county ordinances regarding carbon monoxide alarms

Nothing in this article shall be construed to limit a municipality, city, home rule city, city and county, county, or other local government entity from adopting or enforcing any requirements for the installation and maintenance of carbon monoxide alarms that are more stringent than the requirements set forth in this article.

§ 38-45-106, C.R.S. Limitation of liability

(1) No person shall have a claim for relief against a property owner, an authorized agent of a property owner, a person in possession of real property, or an installer for any damages resulting from the operation, maintenance, or effectiveness of a carbon monoxide alarm if the property owner, authorized agent, person in possession of real property, or installer installs a carbon monoxide alarm in accordance with the manufacturer's published instructions and the provisions of this article.

(2) A purchaser shall have no claim for relief against any person licensed pursuant to article 61 of title 12, C.R.S., for any damages resulting from the operation, maintenance, or effectiveness of a carbon monoxide alarm if such licensed person complies with rules promulgated pursuant to sections 38-45-102 (1) (b) and 38-45-103 (1) (b). Nothing in this subsection (2) shall affect any remedy that a purchaser may otherwise have against a seller.

VII. Sources of Information and Training

- The National Center for Housing Management under the sponsorship of the Department of Housing and Urban Development of the U.S. government.
- The National Association of Homebuilders.
- The National Apartment Association.
- The Institute of Real Estate Management associated with the National Association of Realtors.
- Building Owners and Managers Association.
- Educational Institute for the American Hotel & Motel Association.
- National Association of Realtors.
- National Association of Residential Property Managers.

These national associations usually have local chapters affiliated with them. The national organizations collect income and operating expense data from their members. The expense ratios are useful guides that managers use to check their individual properties' operating expense against the average expense shown for that city. Several associations offer educational courses and information useful in all forms of property management.

VIII. Mobile Home Park Tenancies

Colorado law specifically provides for the method of termination of a lease in a mobile home park. Management must give written notice to remove an owner's unit from the premises within not less 60 days from the date notice is served. The manager must provide the homeowner with a statement of reasons for termination. Management may increase rent only after 60 days' written notice to the homeowners.

The law also covers regulations of tenancy, amount of security deposits, fees or fines, collection of utility charges, etc. (see §§ 38-12-201, *et seq.*, C.R.S.) The Mobile Home Park Act is printed in Chapter 25, "Related Real Estate Law."

Chapter 21: Farm and Ranch Brokerage

An * in the left margin indicates a change in the statute, rule, or text since the last publication of the manual.

I. Introduction

A large segment of the Colorado economy is devoted to agriculture. A wide variety of products are produced on property ranging from rangeland to irrigated land to mountain hay meadows to fruit farms. It is a complex area of real property that provides both an opportunity and a challenge for real estate licensees. There is opportunity because tremendous wealth is involved; no other group in Colorado values the ownership of land more than ranchers and farmers. It is a challenge because farmers and ranchers demand service for the commissions they pay—and service in this field involves much effort and knowledge. Rural real estate involves many problems that are not found in urban property transactions. The successful person in this type of brokerage must have solutions to the problems and understand all the factors involved in determining rural real property values.

The sale of a farm or ranch is also the sale of a business. This has become more obvious as the traditional family farm or ranch increasingly has been replaced by sophisticated corporate entities. Although a property may include land, personal property, and water rights, the marginal value of a farm or ranch is largely determined by the income it produces. A real estate licensee dealing in farms or ranches therefore must have a strong knowledge of agricultural finance and economics in addition to an appreciation of the physical assets to be conveyed. Such knowledge can include areas as diverse as the price of winter wheat, changing developmental and demographic patterns, and new developments in fertilizers and pest control.

Successful farm and ranch brokers exercise a great deal of care in listing properties for sale. Many problems can be avoided by planning carefully in this phase of a real estate operation. Showing a farm or ranch involves much more than showing a house in an urban setting. Consequently, when a licensee accepts a listing of rural property, the real estate licensee must have a sound knowledge of the property and surrounding area.

In developing a list of farms and ranches for sale, a licensee should consider specializing either in certain types of properties or in a given area. By restricting the area of operation, a licensee can gradually become an expert in that field. For example, if a real estate licensee becomes familiar with every farm and every farmer in the south half of a county, he or she will be recognized as an authority and will obtain good listings there. If a licensee learns about dairy farms and becomes acquainted with owners of this kind of property, the licensee's services will be in demand by those wishing to sell dairy farms. As a licensee becomes more experienced, he or she can expand their area of geographic expertise or may branch out into different specialties (*e.g.*, orchards or wheat farms).

Before an owner signs an exclusive listing, a complete statement of all the important information concerning the property should be developed. Sample listing sheets appear in this chapter. The licensee should go further and develop a brochure or brief that gives a complete description of the property, along with pictures and charts. Some brokers even use aerial photographs to better present the qualities of the land to prospective buyers. The extent of the listing information will depend on the complexity of the transaction.

The following maps are useful in the analysis of a farm or ranch:

1. Map showing all improvements (location and description);
2. Map showing all water, streams, springs, wells, lakes, water holes, etc.;
3. Map showing vegetation cover from the Bureau of Land Management;
4. Map of mineral ownership;
5. Plot of the ranch on a road map showing accessibility to roads, railroads, air fields, etc.

The listing broker must also obtain full financial data concerning operation of the property. In the past, financial records were often incomplete due to resistance from owners or inconsistent record keeping. Today, this situation has changed to the point where a licensee often deals not only with an owner, but also with accountants, lenders, and attorneys. Financial information must be maintained in strict confidentiality. Potential purchasers should be provided such information only after being fully qualified and with the owner's consent.

Water rights should be carefully studied and described not only as to the date of decree and amounts of water decreed, but also as to actual delivery of water year after year in both wet and dry years. Additional information on water rights is available in Chapter 13, "Water Rights". A list of Commission-approved contract forms is located in Chapter 26 and the Commission-approved well checklist form is located at the end of this chapter.

Precipitation and temperature figures should be developed for the past few years, because they are important in determining winter conditions, winter feed needs, etc. Hay and grain production on the ranch for several years back should be determined. These figures tie into the wintering analysis that the broker is making.

All minerals should be checked, as they might be the greatest asset of the property. Also, in the sale of the property, the minerals can be sold separately to the purchaser of the land or to someone else.

Inquiries should also be made of the owner concerning the existence of possible hazardous waste sites. These could include abandoned fuel storage tanks or chemical dumps and could result in serious problems if not disclosed to potential purchasers.

A very important factor in the sale of a ranch is the carrying capacity. How many animal units will the ranch support? Sometimes this is a historical fact based on the number of cattle that have been run on the ranch over a period of years. If the ranch has Bureau of Land Management (BLM) lands within its boundaries, the BLM may have the A.U. (animal unit) figures for the ranch. Check to see if the carrying capacity has been increased by range seeding and by water hole development.

Farm and ranch experts look for buyers in basically the same areas where they search for listings. The licensee keeps in contact with as many people as possible that are related to the industry, such as machinery companies and farm organizations. Probate judges and trust officers often provide leads on prospective buyers. Real estate professionals watch newspaper stories about farm sales and condemnations, and become acquainted with investors who make a practice of buying rural property. Government agencies buy land, as do factories and land developers. A successful broker knows who buys land, and catalogs and analyzes their needs. Foreclosures should also be monitored.

Many buyers want farm or ranch land for special uses such as grass sod farms or horse-breeding farms. Some farm or ranch lands may be suitable for recreational or subdivision development. Other buyers may be interested in securing income tax benefits.

Buyer qualification is critical in the sale of a farm or ranch. This is particularly true if the seller is going to finance all or part of the sale by carrying back a mortgage or trust deed. Qualification should include not only a buyer's ability to complete the purchase, but also evidence that the buyer can successfully operate the farm or ranch after the sale. Licensees should encourage sellers to seek professional assistance in evaluating buyer qualifications.

Sources of funding for agricultural properties are more varied than for urban residential properties. These include not only banks and mortgage companies, but also insurance companies, pension plans, and real estate investment trusts (REITs). A farm and ranch broker should have a complete list of all the sources of money available for financing. Most sales will hinge on the ability of the broker to bring the moneylender and buyer together on satisfactory terms. The licensee should also be familiar with the sources of funds made available by the federal government. These include the Federal Land Bank, the Farmers Home Administration, the Federal Land Bank Association, and the Federal Intermediate Credit Banks. These institutions are designed to meet unusual demands on the part of farmers and ranchers. Real estate brokers can contact these agencies to get more information about the services they provide. Appraisers may also be a valuable source of information concerning financing.

Selling to and for syndicates is a device employed by many farm and ranch professionals. This takes specialized knowledge on the part of the licensee and should be explored carefully. A knowledge of securities law is vital to such transactions, which may also require the involvement of a licensed securities dealer.

A farm and ranch broker should recognize the influence that income tax has on the purchase and sale of real estate and should know where to get expert advice in this area.

Finally, in relation to selling farms and ranches, the manager is someone who can help directly or indirectly in the sale. The knowledge needed in managing a farm is very similar to the knowledge required to properly present the farm to a prospective buyer. Furthermore, the sale of a farm or ranch may depend on the ability of the broker to furnish a manager for the property after the sale. Consequently, many successful offices incorporate a management department in their business operation.

This chapter is merely an introduction for real estate licensees to the highly specialized field of farm and ranch brokerage. Experience is the great teacher in this field. Also review Chapter 7, Land Descriptions and Chapter 13, Water Rights when working on a farm or ranch sale.

The listing contract forms used for farms and ranches are similar to those used for the listing of other types of real estate. However, the information necessary for the sale of a farm or a ranch is much more detailed. Following is a short glossary of terms and basic farm and ranch information sheets.

II. Farm and Ranch Glossary

National Forest: A forest or watershed reservation administered by the Forest Service, United States Department of Agriculture.

Grazing Preference on National Forest: An established preference to graze certain numbers and classes of livestock upon a National Forest for a specified time and subject to rules and regulations adopted by the Forest Service.

Grazing District – Taylor Grazing Act: An administrative subdivision of range lands under the jurisdiction of the Bureau of Land Management, established pursuant to Section 3 of the Taylor Grazing Act to facilitate management of BLM forage resources. Grazing on the public lands within such districts was formerly regulated by the Grazing Service.

Grazing Licenses: A grant of grazing rights for a specified number and class of livestock on a designated area of grazing-district lands for a specified period, usually not more than one year.

Grazing Permit: An authorization to graze a set number and class of livestock on a designated area of grazing-district lands during specified seasons each year for a period of usually 10 years.

Section 15 Grazing Lease: A lease which authorizes the use of public lands outside of grazing districts (Taylor Grazing Act) for the grazing of livestock for a specified period.

State Lease: A lease in which the state of Colorado, as landlord, grants grazing, agricultural, and other rights to land under the jurisdiction of the state board of land commissioners.

EXAMPLE
FARM INFORMATION

Date ____________________ Farm Listing ____________________
State ____________________ Irrigated ____________________
County ____________________ Dry Land ____________________
Co. Seat ____________________

Name of Farm ____________________ Nearest Town ____________________
Total Acres __________ Direction from Town __________ Distance __________
Roads __________ Distance School __________ High School __________ Bus ________
Domestic Water __________ Stock Water __________ Soil __________
Acres Cultivated ________ Irrigated ________ Non-Irrigated ________ Sub-Irrigated ________
Acres Alfalfa ________ Native ________ Total Tons ________ Pasture ________
Crops Now Growing ____
____
Following crops are/are not included in sale price ____________________
____
Irrigation Wells ________ Depth ________ Power ________ Name of Pump ________
Capacity of Lakes ________ or Well ________ Reservoirs ________ Fences ________

Main House Construction __________ No. of Rooms ______ Roof ______ Foundation ______
Basement ____________ Gas _____________ Electricity _____________ Bath ______________
Water System _____________ Heat __________________ Condition Improv. _____________
____

Other Living Quarters ____
Barns and Out Buildings ____
____
____

Name of Tenant _________________________ Address ___________________________________
Term of Lease __________________________ Crop or Share Rent ________________________
Water Rights ____
Water Assessments ____
What Mineral Rights Go? _________________________________ Taxes ___________________
Comments (General impression of farm) (Advantages and disadvantages) _______________
____
____
____
____
____

Owner ____ Phone _________________________
Address ____ Possession Date ________________
Price __________________________________ Terms ____________________________________
Loan Information: Original Amount $______________________ Interest Rate _____________
Payments Due ___________________________ How Payable ______________________________
Present Balance $_______________________ Can it be paid off? _______________________
Mortgagee ______________________________ Address __________________________________
Can new loan be secured? ___________ Amount ____________________ Interest __________
Legal Description ____
____

RANGE ______

TOWNSHIP ______

6	5	4	3	2	1
7	8	9	10	11	12
18	17	16	15	14	13
19	20	21	22	23	24
30	29	28	27	26	25
31	32	33	34	35	36

North

Date ______________________

The foregoing statements are substantially correct.

(Owner) ____

(Owner) ____
Address ____
____

EXAMPLE
RANCH INFORMATION

Date ______________________________ Ranch Listing
State______________________________ Cattle ___________ Sheep ___________
County ____________________________ Mountain ________ Plains ___________

Co. Seat ___________________________ Carrying Capacity
Altitude at Ranch ___________________ No. of Cows _____ Hd Mo's __________
No. of Steers _____ Hd Mo's __________
No. of Sheep _____ Hd Mo's __________

Total Acres ________ Direction from Town ___________ Distance ______________
Name of Ranch ____________________________ Nearest Town _______________
Acres Deeded ______ State Lease ___ Acres at $________ Per Year - Exp. Date ______
Private Lease ______ Acres at $_________ Per ______________________________
Year-(Written-Verbal) Exp. Date ____
BLM Lease ________ Acres at $___ Per Year-Term Exp. Date ______________
BLM Permit _______ Head at $______ Per ____________________________
Head-Season of ____________________________ to ___________________________
Forest Permit ______ Head at $_________ Per ______________________________
Head-Season of ______________________ to _________________________________
Name of Forest____________ Likelihood of cut (Yes-No) _______ What Percent ______
Name of Ranger or Supervisor and Address ____________________________________
Acres in Hay _______ Kind _______ Average Tonnage ________ Quality ___________
Acres Farmed ______ What Crops ______________ Average Yields _______________
Acres in Pasture _____ Acres Sub-Irr. Pasture ___________ Acres Dry Pasture ________
Acres Waste Land ____
Predominant Range Grasses _______ Condition of Range _________________________
Water Rights _______ Name of Stream ____ No. of Cu. Ft. ______ Date of Priority _____
Stream or Lake s _______________________ Miles of Stream ____________________
Stock Water Creek ________ Springs ___________Ponds ______ Windmills ________
Distance to Grade School _______________________ Bus (Yes-No) ________________
Distance to High School ________________________ Bus (Yes-No) ________________
Kind of Road in to Ranch _________ Miles to Main Road _______ No. or Type _______
Is there good winter shelter? _______ Kind _____________ Annual Precipitation ______
Describe Climate _________________ Winters ____________ Summers _____________
Condition of fences ________ Kind ______________ No. of Pastures _______________

Improvements

Describe fully - type - condition - water supply - bath - elec. (Yes-No) source ___________
____
Are buildings neat and attractive? (Yes-No) Lawn (Yes-No) Shade trees (Yes-No) ________
Explain carrying capacity and best type of operation___________________________
____
Livestock or Ranch (Included - Not included) in sale price, No. of Cattle __ No. of Sheep __
When purchased by present owner? _______ Why is ranch for sale? _______________
Will hay crop be included in sale? (Yes-No) If not, at what price per ton? $___________

Real estate Taxes $_______________ Personal Taxes $_______________

Any Poisonous Weeds? ___________ What Mineral Rights Go? _______________

Comments (general impression of ranch, any hunting, fishing, or recreation facilities?)

____

Owner _______________________________ Ranch Phone ___________

Address_______________________________ Bus. Phone ___________

Name of (Foreman-Tenant) _______________ Remuneration___________

Price of Ranch $_______________ Terms _______________

Possession will be given _______________________

Price of livestock if not included with ranch $_______________

Following described equipment (is-is not) included in sale price ___________

Legal Description (if too long attach rider) _______________

____

Loan Information ___________ Township: ___________ Range: ___________

Is there a loan? (Yes-No)

Original Amt. $________

Int. Rate _____% Due____

When Made __________

How Payable __________

Present Balance $_______

Can it be paid off? ______

Mortgagee __________

Address __________

____

____

Other Indebtedness _____

Lender __________

6	5	4	3	2	1
7	8	9	10	11	12
18	17	16	15	14	13
19	20	21	22	23	24
30	29	28	27	26	25
31	32	33	34	35	36

LEGEND

Buildings ■

Fences

Railroads

Streams

Wells o

Windmills oX

Reservoir

Ponds

Timber

Deeded (Red)

State Lease (Yellow)

BLM (Blue)

Private Lease (Green)

Date_______________

The foregoing statements are substantially correct.

(Owner) _______________________

(Owner) _______________________

Address _______________________

____

EXAMPLE
LISTING FIRM'S WELL CHECKLIST

[THIS CHECKLIST IS FOR SELLER AND LISTING FIRM'S INTERNAL USE ONLY.]

Date: ______________________

Seller: ____

Property: ____

Copy of Well Permit attached ☐ Yes ☐ No

I. Domestic (Exempt) Wells: ☐ Household use only

A. Confirm with State or Division Engineer as to:
1) Permit or Registration No: ______________________
2) Statement of Beneficial Use filed ☐ Yes ☐ No
3) Location: ______________________
4) Permitted uses: ______________________
5) Restrictions: ______________________
6) Decreed: ☐ Yes ☐ No
a. Water Court Docket No: ______________________
7) Other, copy of report, etc. ______________________
8) Augmentation Plan ☐ Yes ☐ No
9) Well placed on Inactive Status ☐ Yes ☐ No

B. Pump Test ☐ Yes Date ________ ☐ No
GPM ______________________

C. Potability test ☐ Yes Date ________ ☐ No
Results: ______________________

D. Cistern ☐ Yes ☐ No

E. Pump
Type ______________________
Age ______________________

F. Shared use ☐ Yes ☐ No
Shared with ______________________

II. Other (Fee) Wells:

A. Confirm with State or Division Engineer or Ground Water Commission as to:
1) Permit or Registration No: ______________________
2) Statement of Beneficial Use filed ☐ Yes ☐ No
3) Place of use/location: ______________________
4) Pumping rate, volumetic limit: ______________________
5) Metered ☐ Yes ☐ No
a. Subject to Metering Order ☐ Yes ☐ No
6) Permitted uses and restrictions:
a. Irrigation: ______________________
b. Industrial: ______________________
c. Commercial: ______________________
d. Municipal: ______________________

7) Decreed: ☐ Yes ☐ No
   a. Water Court Docket No: ______________________
8) Source: ______________________
   a. Tributary to: ______________________
      (1) Augmentation by: ______________________
         (a) Decree, Docket No: ______________________
         (b) Administrative approval ☐ Yes ☐ No
            (i) Cost of augmentation: $______________
            (ii) Membership fee: $______________
            (iii) Cost of water: $______________
   b. Designated Ground Water (Ground Water Commission): __________
      (1) Designated Basin: ______________________
      (2) Management District: ______________________
         (a) Contact information: ______________________
   c. Non-Tributary/Not-Nontributary: ☐ Yes ☐ No
      (1) Name of formation (aquifer) ______________________
      (2) Permit conditions: ______________________
      (3) Decree provisions: ______________________

> **Caution: Water rights can be very technical and complex.** Counsel of appropriate experts, such as attorneys or brokers who specialize in water rights, water engineers and well drillers, should be sought. Valuable general and specific information can also be obtained from the Office of the State Engineer, Division of Water Resources, Colorado Department of Natural Resources, at 303-866-3581 (general), 303-866-3587 (groundwater information), and the Water Division Office for the county in which a property is located. The State Engineer's Office also has a useful Guide to Colorado Water Rights, Well Permits, and Administration available at www.water.state.co.us.

Chapter 22: Business Opportunities

An * in the left margin indicates a change in the statute, rule, or text since the last publication of the manual.

I. Introduction

The sale of business opportunities requires a real estate broker's license when the transaction involves a change of ownership or leasehold in real estate (see § 12-61-101(2)(a)(I), C.R.S.). The Colorado Attorney General has interpreted this statute to hold that conveyance of a business opportunity is not severable from an interest in land. Furthermore, an unlicensed person may not receive a commission on the portion of the conveyance not involving real estate (*i.e.*, a business opportunity), if the transfer as a whole involves an ownership or leasehold interest in land.

The sale of a business opportunity may be less or more complicated than the sale of real estate. There are usually more representations to be made. A portion of the sale is intangible, and therefore values are difficult to determine. A broker should recommend attorney representation to each party to the transaction.

II. Matters to be Considered

The following information is essential to successfully brokering a business opportunity.

1. **Name of business.**
2. **Location of business.**
3. **Name of owner, address, and phone number.**
4. **Price.** Be sure that the price quoted in the listing contract includes the broker's fee.
5. **Terms.** The amount of cash the seller demands and how large a note and purchase money chattel mortgage the seller will carry. Lending institutions may not finance business opportunity transactions; therefore, the broker should nail down financing arrangements with the seller at the time of securing the listing contract.
6. **License, Franchise, or Distributorship.** If a business involves a license, franchise, or distributorship, arrangements must be made to ensure that rights are transferred and perhaps become a condition of the contract.

   If the business involves the sale of liquor, both the appropriate municipal agency and the Colorado Department of Revenue must issue licenses. The requirements are stringent and the investigation of the applicant is quite thorough. Requirements include a copy of the purchase agreement; evidence of the transfer if corporate stock is sold; a copy of the lease, lease assignment, or deed; trade name affidavit; health and hospital inspection certificate; bill of sale; receipt for personal property taxes paid; the source of financing; and fingerprinting.

   If a distributorship is involved, the manufacturer must consent and may demand certain financial standards before consenting to the transfer.

Other businesses also may require licenses of various kinds before the buyer may operate the business.

7. **Lease.** A licensee should inspect the lease to determine any special conditions and the remaining term. The monthly rental is always important because of its relationship to the business income. Determine if the lease is assignable. Since most leases prohibit assignment without the lessor's consent, such consent must be obtained. If the lessor charges for consent, the seller will be obligated for this expense and should be told so. It is better for the seller if the buyer obtains a new lease, because the seller will remain liable to the lessor on a lease assignment if the buyer later defaults on any terms. A licensee might also propose a sale to the lessor.
8. **Fixtures.** When the sale includes fixtures, check to make sure that they belong to the seller. For example, under some lease provisions, fixtures belong to the lessor on termination of the lease and therefore cannot be included in the sale.
9. **Equipment.** It is advisable to prepare a list of the equipment and determine if it is marketable and if the price is fair.
10. **Stock or Inventory.** Without an actual inventory, the broker should establish the value of the stock as closely as possible based on wholesale cost. Find out if there is any unsalable stock. Of course, at the time of closing, there must be an accurate and detailed inventory.
11. **Number of Employees.** It is important to establish the dollar amount of the payroll, and especially the status of payroll taxes.
12. **Income, Gross and Net.** The broker should review CPA reports or a copy of income tax returns (or both) for previous years. This is a risky situation for the licensee insofar as representations to the buyer. Agency laws on representation and disclosure apply with particular force in a business sale because there are so many different facts that may be material to the purchase. The seller's attorney may want to include a clause in the contract stating that the seller has made no representations regarding the business and that the buyer has made their own inspection of the business and takes all goods, fixtures, and other property "as is," without any warranties. Such a clause gives only limited protection and will not safeguard the seller against a clear showing of fraudulent misrepresentation. The broker should choose records that can be verified when he or she uses them for purposes of making a sale. It may be advisable to provide an income or profit-and-loss statement for the seller to complete.
13. **Accounts Receivable.** Sometimes a business sale includes all the outstanding customer accounts receivable, that is, the right to collect all outstanding bills owed to the seller by previous customers. In such a case, the seller "assigns" these accounts to the buyer. Such an assignment should be in the contract. But even with the assignment made, it is up to the buyer to effect the transfer. The buyer should notify each account of the change in ownership and the assignment of the account, and provide instructions on how and where to make future payments. Otherwise, the customer may continue to make payments to the original owner and the buyer would have no recourse. Sometimes the agreement of sale may provide for a notice or letter to go out to all customers over the signatures of both seller and buyer, announcing the change in management and reassuring the customer that they will get the same good service from the new owner. Such a letter could also include notice of assignment of the accounts. In assigning accounts, the seller should

affirmatively make no representations or warranties regarding the ability to collect such accounts. Only in rare cases would a seller be willing to guarantee full or a percentage of collection on accounts receivable.

14. **Number of Years Business Operated.** To establish the stability of the business.
15. **Reason for Selling.** The buyer will want to know this.
16. **Covenant Not to Compete.** The buyer of a business that is a going concern may seek assurance that the seller will not go back into business on a competitive basis at some other location. Thus, if buying a restaurant from a seller who expresses an intent to retire, the buyer should obtain a specific contractual promise that the seller will neither operate nor buy another restaurant in the same locality for a specified period of time (*e.g.*, five years). Otherwise, if the seller finds that retirement is not as expected, he or she might decide to go back into business and draw from previous loyal customers. This kind of clause is called a "restrictive covenant" or "covenant not to compete" and is enforceable. It should be limited as to time and territory to the extent necessary to protect the goodwill for which the buyer is paying. If the agreement does not include such a covenant, there is no protection for the buyer, and the seller may compete immediately after the sale. The buyer can, of course, show by oral evidence that the seller represented that he or she would not compete (constituting grounds for rescission for fraud) or that there was a promise made orally that the seller would not compete (which may be difficult to prove absent a carefully written contract embodying the entire agreement).

III. The Uniform Commercial Code

The Uniform Commercial Code (UCC) repealed past laws on chattel mortgages. Under the current code, there must be a security agreement of some type between the parties. A chattel mortgage may still be the security agreement, although other forms of security agreements are superseding the chattel mortgage form. The UCC further provides, with a few exceptions, that a financing statement must be filed in order to perfect the security interest. When the financing statement covers timber, minerals, or other fixtures that are or will become attached to real estate, it must be filed with the county clerk and recorder in the county where the real property exists. In other instances, the financing statement is filed with the Secretary of State. (See § 4-9-301, C.R.S.)

In 1994 and 1995, a board was created within the Colorado Department of State charged with implementing a central indexing system for simplifying the filing and retrieval of all security interests. The system does not replace the need to record documents affecting real estate with the county clerk and recorder pursuant to § 38-35-109, C.R.S.

A security agreement is sufficient for filing if it contains the same information that is required by law to be included in the financing statement. The necessary information consists of the names and addresses of the debtor and secured party, the Social Security number and tax identification number of the debtor, and a statement indicating the types and description of the collateral. (See the examples in this chapter.)

A maturity date extending five years or less is effective until the maturity date plus 60 days. With longer maturity dates, the statement is effective for five years from the date of filing. A continuation statement may be filed within certain time limitations (see § 4-9-515, C.R.S.). Failure to file a continuation statement within the required period does not affect the validity of the security agreement. The filing is merely for giving constructive notice that the debt exists.

The complete Uniform Commercial Code, effective July 1, 1966, covers many facets of personal property sales; therefore, business opportunity transactions may be affected by the law on sales, commercial paper, bank deposits and collections, letters of credit, warehouse receipts, bills of lading, investment securities, and other documents of title.

IV. The Colorado Use Tax

The Colorado Use Tax (§§ 39-26-201, *et seq.*, C.R.S.) is a form of sales tax, payable on the transfer of furniture, equipment, etc. The *buyer* is obligated to pay this tax by statute. The broker has the duty to inform the buyer of this obligation.

Occasionally, but perhaps more often than in other real estate transactions, the broker may wish to receive an advance fee for services in the sale because of the expense involved in the promotion of a business opportunity. In such a case, the broker must comply with Commission Rule E-2.

A. Forms and Settlement

The sample forms shown in this chapter are typical of a business opportunity transaction, but are not necessarily all-inclusive. If the real estate is to be conveyed with the business, the broker would use a Commission-approved exclusive right-to-sell listing contract for real estate, amend it to describe the business, and also provide a bill of sale.

The closing statement forms for a real estate transaction may be used for business opportunity transactions with very little alteration. The worksheet in this chapter indicates the sale of a business, including goodwill, lease, and fixtures, for a price of $14,500. The cost of the inventory is listed separately and is $7,850. The seller in this transaction is taking a note in the amount of $17,000, secured by a purchase money chattel mortgage. The same principles apply in the debiting and crediting of the parties. The sample transaction shown on the worksheet in this chapter should be self-explanatory. Of course, the broker will sign and provide the seller and buyer each with a statement of their respective debits and credits, and the broker will retain a signed copy from both parties. Compliance with Commission Rule E-5 is also necessary.

It is not enough to say that the sale of business opportunities is a specialized field. The field itself is further divided into specialties. There are brokers who deal only in motels; others are experts in liquor outlets or restaurants. Some brokers concentrate on the negotiation of corporate sales, where stock transfers are necessary.

Business Opportunity Worksheet

Seller:			Buyer:			
Property Address:						
Settlement Date: January 15, 2XXX			Proration Date: January 15, 2XXX			
Legal Description:						
	Seller		Buyer		Broker	
	Debit	Credit	Debit	Credit	Debit	Credit
Price: (Business, lease, fixtures)		*14,500.00*	*14,500.00*			
Inventory: (On closing date)		*7,850.00*	*7,850.00*			
Deposit:				*1,500.00*	*1,500.00*	
Security agreement payable to:	*17,000.00*			*17,000.00*		
Security agreement assigned:						
Interest on loan assumed						
Recording: financing statement			*2.00*			*2.00*
trade name affidavit			*1.50*			*1.50*
Bulk Transfer Notice:	*7.50*					*7.50*
Lease security deposit:		*600.00*	*600.00*			
Lease transfer fee:						
Personal property taxes: $240.00						
Seller 1/2 mo. Buyer 11 1/2 mo.	*10.00*		*230.00*			*240.00*
Water rent:						
Rental income: $340.00/mo (Pd.)		*170.00*	*170.00*			
Special Taxes:						
Insurance: (ZYX Co.)		*172.50*	*172.50*			
Term: 1 yr Exp.: Dec. 31 Prem.:						
New insurance:						
Attorney's fee:						
Seller:	*100.00*					*100.00*
Buyer:			*100.00*			*100.00*
Other:						
Commission on sale:	*1,450.00*					*1,450.00*
Subtotals	*$18,567.50*	*$23,292.50*	*$23,626.00*	*$18,500.00*	*$1,500.00*	*$1,901.00*
Balance due to/from seller	*$4,725.00*					*$4,725.00*
Balance due to/from buyer				*$5,126.00*	*$5,126.00*	
TOTALS	*$23,292.50*	*$23,292.50*	*$23,626.00*	*$23,626.00*	*$6,626.00*	*$6,626.00*

Income Statement

COMPANY NAME: ______________________________
LOCATION: ______________________________
INCOME STATEMENT (Profit and Loss) for periods indicated.
Current Period is for __________ months End Date__________

UNAUDITED	Period	Period	Period
GROSS SALES AND REVENUES			
MERCHANDISE COSTS (Adjustment inv.)			
GROSS PROFIT			
OVERHEAD COSTS AND OUT OF POCKET			
Utilities and phone (exclusive income)			
Insurance			
Advertising and other selling			
Repairs and maintenance			
Supplies and miscellaneous			
Legal and accounting			
Rent			
Business (auto-transportation)			
Other:			
TOTAL			
WAGES, SALARIES, PAYROLL TAXES			
Wages			
Salaries			
Taxes			
Owner-Partner draw			
Total compensation costs			
MARGIN FOR OVERHEAD AND PROFIT			
BUSINESS PROFIT before depreciation & int.			

Source of information: _________ Owner __________ CPA __________ Bookkeeper

B. Colorado UCC Financing Statements

Brokers are advised to contact the Colorado Secretary of State office for information on approved financing statement forms: www.sos.state.co.us.

§ 4-9-502, C.R.S. Contents of financing statement – record of mortgage as financing statement – time of filing financing statement

(a) Subject to subsection (b) of this section, a financing statement is sufficient only if it:

(1) Provides the name of the debtor;

(2) Provides the name of the secured party or a representative of the secured party; and

(3) Indicates the collateral covered by the financing statement.

(b) Except as otherwise provided in section 4-9-501 (b), to be sufficient, a financing statement that covers as-extracted collateral or timber to be cut, or which is filed as a fixture filing and covers goods that are or are to become fixtures, must satisfy subsection (a) of this section and also:

(1) Indicate that it covers this type of collateral;

(2) Indicate that it is to be filed for record in the real property records;

(3) Provide a description of the real property to which the collateral is related sufficient to give constructive notice of a mortgage under the law of this state if the description were contained in a record of the mortgage of the real property; and

(4) If the debtor does not have an interest of record in the real property, provide the name of a record owner.

(c) A record of a mortgage is effective, from the date of recording, as a financing statement filed as a fixture filing or as a financing statement covering as-extracted collateral or timber to be cut only if:

(1) The record indicates the goods or accounts that it covers;

(2) The goods are or are to become fixtures related to the real property described in the record or the collateral is related to the real property described in the record and is as-extracted collateral or timber to be cut;

(3) The record satisfies the requirements for a financing statement in this section other than an indication that it is to be filed in the real property records; and

(4) The record is duly recorded.

(d) A financing statement may be filed before a security agreement is made or a security interest otherwise attaches.

§ 4-9-521, C.R.S. Uniform form of written financing statement and amendment

(a) A filing office that accepts written records may not refuse to accept a written initial financing statement in the form and format adopted from time to time by the secretary of state, except for a reason set forth in section 4-9-516 (b).

(b) A filing office that accepts written records may not refuse to accept a written record in the form and format adopted from time to time by the secretary of state, except for a reason set forth in section 4-9-516 (b).

Chapter 23:
Tax Factors Pertaining to Real Estate Practice

An * in the left margin indicates a change in the statute, rule, or text since the last publication of the manual.

I. Introduction

This chapter presents a general overview of the rules for individual taxpayers that pertain to the acquisition, ownership, and sale of residential real estate. Professional assistance is required to determine the tax consequences or reporting requirements that may pertain to a specific real estate transaction. One should permanently retain all original contracts, settlement statements, and related banking records for such ownership for subsequent tax reporting.

The use of a property generally drives the tax consequences and reporting of its ownership. Property is commonly held for purposes such as personal use, business operations, or investment purposes, and these purposes may change and intermingle during the life cycle of ownership. The method of tax accounting used by the taxpayer also determines deductibility and reporting rules. In "**cash basis**" accounting, benefits (income and expenses) are considered reportable or deductible when "constructively received" in cash or an equivalent form, or actually paid. Under the "**accrual basis**," one reports income when earned, that is, when the right to receive the income has occurred. Expenses are likewise deductible when incurred, that is, when all events have occurred that fix the amount of the expense and create a tax liability for the individual. The purpose of accrual accounting is to better match reporting of income with the associated expenses of generating it. IRS accounting requirements are found in Publication 538.

Some resources for tax information are the *U.S. Master Tax Guide*, published annually by Commerce Clearing House, www.cch.com, and various IRS *Publications and Forms* that may be viewed and downloaded at www.irs.gov. These documents and forms may be read online, but the user will need the latest version of Adobe Acrobat or similar software to print most documents on a home computer. The discussion of tax rules in the following sections is based on material contained in these references in effect for 2010. Tax law changes are found in IRS Publication 553.

II. Ownership of a Personal Residence

Federal tax law provides extensive tax benefits for purchase and ownership of a home. These benefits deal with buying expenses, new provisions for financing purchases, qualified deductible residential interest, property taxes, non-business theft and casualty losses, moving expenses, and business or rental use of a home. They are described in IRS Publications 17 (Your Federal Income Tax), 523 (Selling Your Home), 527 (Residential Rental Property), 530 (Tax Information for Homeowners), 547 (Casualties, Disasters, and Thefts), 551 (Basis of Assets), 587 (Business Use of Your Home), 936 (Home Mortgage Interest Deduction) and Form 8396 (Mortgage Interest Credit), 590 (Individual Retirement Arrangements (IRAs)), and 225 (Farmer's Tax Guide).

A. Buying Expenses

A buyer may find certain settlement and closing costs deductible, capitalized (added to the cost or "basis" of the property), or of no tax benefit. The deductibles generally include discount points and loan origination fees for the purchase or construction of a principal residence. Points paid to finance the purchase of a second home or to refinance an existing mortgage must be deducted over the life of the loan, not in the year in which they are paid. Prorated mortgage interest is also tax-deductible in the year of purchase or sale. Non-deductible items generally include other settlement costs such as appraisal fees, notary fees, VA funding fees, points not separately paid for by the borrower at closing for property improvements (these are generally deducted over the life of the loan), title insurance, survey costs, legal fees, and other similar costs. Non-deductible items are added to the basis of the property and will ultimately reduce the gain or increase the taxpayer's loss in a subsequent sale. See Publication 530 for more information.

B. IRA Withdrawal Used to Fund Purchase

Current legislation allows first-time homebuyers to use IRA distributions to fund up to $10,000 of the cost of their new home without incurring the 10 percent early distribution penalty even if they are under age 59½ (Publication 590). A first-time homebuyer can be the individual, a spouse, or a child, grandchild, or parent of the individual or spouse. To qualify, a buyer must have had no present ownership interest in a principal residence during the two-year period ending on the date of acquisition of the new residence. Special rules apply to armed forces members or owners of property outside the U.S. The date of acquisition is the date a binding contract to purchase the property is executed, or the date when construction of the principal residence begins. IRA disbursements can be used to pay the costs of acquiring, constructing, or reconstructing a residence, and include any reasonable and common cost of settlement, financing, or closing the transaction. However, any amount withdrawn must be used to pay qualified acquisition costs within 120 days of the date of withdrawal.

C. Qualified Residential Mortgage Interest

Qualified residence interest is interest that is paid or accrued during the tax year on acquisition or home equity indebtedness with respect to any qualified residence. A "qualified residence" for this deduction is defined as a house, condominium, mobile home, houseboat, house trailer, or any other facility (excluding unimproved vacant land) that has sleeping quarters, a toilet, and cooking facilities. A qualified second home is one that is used by the owner at least 14 days or 10 percent of the total number of days that it is rented to others, whichever is greater. If a second home is not rented to others, it may be a qualified home regardless of whether a taxpayer uses it during the year or not. A taxpayer who rents out a second residence may deduct mortgage interest only if the property meets the test of a "qualified residence." If a taxpayer does not satisfy these tests, then the residence is considered rental property rather than a qualified second home, and may be subject to the passive activity rules. These are very complex areas of tax law, and expert professional assistance is recommended. See Publication 925 (Passive Activity and At-Risk Rules) for more information.

A residence under construction can be treated as a qualified residence for up to 24 months, only if it actually becomes a qualified residence when ready for occupancy. The land upon which the construction is undertaken does not become a qualified residence until construction actually begins.

Residential interest generally includes mortgage interest on home acquisition debt of up to $1 million ($500,000 for married filing separately), plus up to $100,000 ($50,000 for a married person filing separately) on a qualifying home equity loan. Certain items can be included as home mortgage interest. These items include late payment charges on mortgage payment, redeemable ground rents, interest on stock purchased in a cooperative housing residence, certain "points" or loan origination fees paid by a purchaser or by a seller for the purchaser, and mortgage prepayment penalties. Acquisition indebtedness proceeds must generally be "traceable" to expenditures to acquire, construct, or substantially improve a qualified residence. Acquisition indebtedness includes debt used to refinance earlier indebtedness (meeting the definition for acquisition indebtedness) to the extent of the original indebtedness. IRS Publication 936 provides a special 90-day rule exception to the literal application of the tracing rules for expenditures on a qualified residence. This exception provides that debt incurred within 90 days after the completion of the construction or improvements is treated as incurred to construct or improve the residence to the extent those expenditures occur not more than 24 months before project completion, and after completion, up to the time the debt is incurred. A purchaser claiming an interest deduction for private seller-carry financing must include the name of the seller, the seller's address, and the seller's taxpayer identification number (TIN) on the purchaser's income tax return Schedule A. Failure to furnish this information is subject to a fine.

Note that "grandfathered debt" (pre-October 14, 1987 debt still of record on the property) is not subject to the $1 million acquisition debt ceiling, but any pre-October 14, 1987 debt reduces the ceiling for any new post-October 13, 1987 debt used to improve or refinance the property. Pre-October 14, 1987 debt does not have to be "traceable" as indicated above, but must be still secured by the residence at all times thereafter. Debt used to refinance the "grandfathered debt" qualifies for this same treatment to the extent of pre-October 14, 1987 debt principal. Home equity loans are limited to the lesser of $100,000 ($50,000 for a married person filing separately) or the fair market value of the residence less accession indebtedness including pre-October 14, 1987 grandfathered indebtedness.

D. Mortgage Interest Credit

* This credit may be available for first-time homebuyers whose income is below the median income in the area where they live. This credit is intended to help lower-income individuals afford home ownership. To be eligible for this credit, the buyer must obtain a "mortgage credit certificate" from a participating state or local agency before making any offer to buy a home or seek a loan. The Mortgage Credit Certificate program does not expire as long as the home remains a taxpayer's principal residence and mortgage payments are being made. According to the State Division of Housing, 1-866-327-8877, and Colorado Housing and Finance Authority (CHFA), (303) 297-2432, this program is also available for the qualified refinance of an adjustable rate mortgage loan originated after December 31, 2001 and before January 1, 2008. More information can be obtained from CHFA's website at www.chfainfo.com. The program allows a dollar-to-dollar reduction of income tax liability on 20 percent of mortgage interest, reducing the amount of federal taxes owed. The CHFA Mortgage Credit Certificate program is available statewide; however, certain targeted areas have different income and purchase price limits and no first time homebuyer requirements.

Any tax credit obtained is reported to the IRS on Form 8396. The borrower may have to recapture (repay) all or part of the benefit received from that program when the home is sold or otherwise disposed of. See Publication 523 for further federal information.

E. Mortgage Insurance Premiums

Amounts paid for qualified mortgage insurance can be treated as home mortgage interest. The insurance must be in connection with home acquisition debt, and the insurance contract must have been issued after 2006 and before December 31, 2010 (scheduled to expire then). Qualified mortgage insurance is defined as mortgage insurance provided by the Department of Veterans Affairs, the Federal Housing Administration, or the Rural Housing Service, and private mortgage insurance.

F. Property Taxes

Real property tax includes local, state, and foreign taxes levied on the value of real property. It does not include special assessments for local benefits or improvements that increase the value of the property, such as sidewalks, streets, and water or sewer systems.

Property taxes are generally deductible by the person(s) on whom they are levied in the year they are accrued or paid. In the year of acquisition or sale, both the buyer and seller must apportion among themselves any real property taxes levied for applicable "real property tax year." The date of sale and the statutory date the taxes become due govern how to determine the prorated amount that each party may deduct, according to the number of days each party held ownership of the property. Computation of the prorated property tax amount is illustrated in Chapter 18, "Closing Statements."

In Colorado, the current year's property taxes come due the following January 1. Cash basis taxpayers generally cannot take any property tax deduction for taxes placed in escrow through monthly payments until the escrow holder pays the tax. Lenders will report the deductible amount to the borrower annually for preparation of the return.

When the seller pays prorated taxes at closing on the date of sale, the seller will deduct that amount on Schedule A. Delinquent taxes due from the seller that were included in the contract price are not deductible. The buyer adds this amount to the cost (basis) of the property purchased.

Transfer taxes charged by some local tax authorities on the sale of a personal residence are not deductible. The person paying this tax may adjust the basis of the property by such amount.

G. Personal Property Taxes

To qualify for this itemized deduction, the tax must meet three tests: (1) it must be charged on personal property, (2) it must be based only on the value of the property, and (3) it must be charged on a yearly basis, even if collected more or less than once a year. If the tax is partly based on value and partly based on other criteria, it may partially qualify to be deductible.

H. Non-business Casualty and Theft Losses

A casualty or theft loss results from the damage, destruction, or loss of property from an event that is direct, identifiable, sudden, unexpected, or unusual (see IRS Publication 547).

The amount of the loss is generally the lesser of: (1) the loss in fair market value before and after the event, and (2) the adjusted basis of the property before and after the event. A business casualty loss is fully deductible, while a personal loss is only a loss over $500 (a $100 floor in 2010 and thereafter), and is further limited to the net loss (above the floor) in excess of 10 percent of the taxpayer's adjusted gross income. The $500/$100 rule is applied to the loss from each event of casualty or theft only once, even if many pieces of property are affected. The 10 percent limitation also applies to the adjusted gross income of any estate and trust claiming a personal casualty or theft loss. Special rules are used for federally designated disaster areas. IRS Publication 584 (Casualty, Disaster, and Theft Loss Workbook (Personal-Use Property)) should be used to document and compute these losses.

Losses from progressive deterioration due to neglect or steadily operating environmental conditions, disease, drought, insects, accidental breakage, pets, and arson are not deductible. Landlords and tenants may claim theft and casualty losses on rental property. Special rules apply to situations where both casualty gains and losses occur. Incidental expenses may not be deducted, and the loss reported may not exceed the adjusted basis in the property destroyed or stolen. The taxpayer must itemize to deduct this loss.

I. Moving Expenses

Taxpayers may deduct (subject to certain limits) unreimbursed moving expenses related to taking a new job or changing jobs, including self-employment, if certain distance and subsequent time of employment tests are met. A taxpayer may also deduct these expenses if the taxpayer expects to meet these tests in the following consecutive year. Only reasonable expenses for the circumstances surrounding the move can be deducted, such as certain storage costs, cost of moving household goods, and traveling to a new location, including lodging. Certain expenses, such as expenses of buying and selling a home, expenses of entering or breaking a lease, pre-move house-hunting expenses, and the cost of meals while traveling to a new residence are non-deductible. The new job location must be at least 50 miles farther from the old residence than the old job location was. In addition, an employee must work full-time in the general vicinity of the new job location for at least 39 weeks during the 12 months following the move. The 39-weeks period does not have to be consecutive or with the same employer, as long as the jobs are in the same general location and are classified as full-time work. Special rules apply to members of the armed forces; they are not required to meet the distance and time tests for a permanent change of duty station. See IRS Publications 17 and 521 for further information.

J. Business Use of Home (Home Offices)

According to Publication 587 (Business Use of Your Home), self-employed individuals who operate a home business and employees may be able to deduct certain expenses for the part of the home used for business.

There are two essential requirements that must be met in order to qualify for the deduction: (1) part of the home must be used for business purposes *regularly and exclusively*, and (2) the business part of the home must be either a principal place of business or the location where meetings with clients or customers are held in the normal course of conducting business. For a detached garage or other separate structures, the requirement is only that the building is used in connections with a trade or business. Deductions can also be claimed for the use of an area of the home for storage of inventory or product samples. There is an additional requirement for employees who telecommute from home: their business use of the home must be for the *employer's* convenience, *and* they cannot be renting any part of their home to the employer and then use the rented portion to perform services for the employer.

Deductible expenses for business use of a home include, but are not limited to, the business portion of real estate taxes, deductible mortgage interest, rent, casualty losses, utilities, insurance, depreciation, maintenance, and repairs. When calculating the amount that can be deducted for the business use of the home, the entire amount of expenses attributable solely to the portion of the home used in the business can be used. Deduction for expenses attributable to the whole house depends on the percentage of the home used for business. Any reasonable method can be used to calculate the business percentage, such as dividing the area used for business by the total area of the house, or dividing the number of rooms used for business by the total number of rooms in the house if all rooms are about the same size. The business portion of expenses is calculated by applying the business percentage to the total of each expense.

For qualified day-care providers who do not use any area exclusively for day care, the business portion is further limited by the ratio of the number of hours the area is used exclusively for business to the total number of hours the portion is available for any use.

If gross income from the business use of the home is less than the total business expenses, the deduction for certain expenses for the business use of the home, other than mortgage interest, taxes, and casualty losses, is limited. However, those business expenses that are disallowed on the current tax return can be carried forward to the next year and will be subject to the deduction limitations for that year. For additional information on business use of a home, see Publication 587.

III. Sale of a Personal Residence

When a taxpayer sells a principal residence, any loss is not deductible unless part of the residence was used in the taxpayer's business. IRS Publication 523 describes the reporting requirements for this type of transaction; Publication 544 describes the sale of rental property, second homes, or vacation property. A trade of homes is treated as a sale and purchase.

Any taxable gain that cannot be excluded is reported on Schedule D as a capital gain. A loss on the sale of the main home (excluding business use) is personal and is not deductible, but may need to be reported. The basis must be adjusted for any depreciation taken for any part of the home used in a trade or business. Points not deducted or amortized may be deductible in the year of sale. See "points" in Publication 936, Part I.

Gain or loss is the selling price of the home less expenses of the sale and less the adjusted basis in the home. Adjusted basis is generally the original cost plus certain closing costs, capital improvements and additions. Any depreciation allowed or allowable and discharge of qualified principal residence indebtedness that was excluded from income further decrease the basis.

The seller may be able to exclude up to $250,000 ($500,000 if married filing jointly) of any realized gain on the sale or exchange of a personal residence. Any gain properly excluded is not reported on the return.

Current tax rules allow reuse of the exclusion amount for any subsequent transaction meeting all of the following tests where a taxpayer: (1) has "ownership of the property for two of the five years before the current sale or exchange, (2) "used" by occupying it for periods totaling two years within the last five years, ending on the date of the sale or exchange, and (3) meets the "one-sale-in-two-years" criteria, where the $250,000/$500,000 exclusion was not used for the prior sale of any residence for the two-year period ending on the date of the current sale or exchange. If a seller does not satisfy these tests, he or she may qualify for a reduced maximum exclusion if the primary reason for the sale is a change in employment, health, or unforeseen circumstances. See Publication 523 for rules applicable to reduced exclusions, foreclosures, or other special situations, and instructions for worksheets to compute the gain or loss. Divorce property settlement rules are described in Publication 504, and Publication 544 deals with condemned property.

Additional rules apply to the replacement period for homes outside the U.S. and for members of the armed services.

If the property was used partly as a home and partly for business or as a rental property, the treatment of any gain on the sale depends on whether the business or rental part of the property is part of the home or separate from it. If the part of the property used for business or as a rental property is within the home, there is no need to allocate gain on the sale of the property between the business part and part used as a home. In addition, sale of the business or rental property does not have to be separately reported on Form 4797. However, the part of any gain equal to any depreciation allowed or allowable after May 6, 1997 cannot be excluded. If the business or rental part of the property is separate from the home, the gain cannot be excluded unless the taxpayer owned and lived in that part of the property for at least two years during the five-year period ending on the date of sale. If the test is not met, allocation of the gain is required and Form 4797 must be filed.

A. Installment Sales

A homeowner who carries back part of the sale price in the form of a note may defer payment of gains until received as installment payments. This allows a seller to spread payment of taxes over the life of the loan. The seller must charge a fair interest rate, and some restrictions apply to dealers and sellers of time-shares and residential lots. Form 6252 must be filed to report installment sale income. Additional information on this type of sale is contained in the chapters on contracts, deeds, and Publication 537. The broker should be familiar with the risks to both buyers and sellers, and advise the parties to seek legal counsel in such transactions.

B. Foreclosure

Upon default, abandonment, or conveyance in lieu of foreclosure, a gain in the form of discharge of debt may result to the mortgagor, or such gain may be used to reduce the basis of certain depreciable business property. In a foreclosure sale, the mortgagor generally recognizes a gain (or loss) in that the amount received exceeds (or is less than) the adjusted basis of the property sold. Transfers of property and abandonments are considered "sales" for tax purposes. The discharge of debt through cancellation in bankruptcy is generally not taxable income to the discharged debtor. Cancelled debt is also excluded from income to the extent that the taxpayer was insolvent immediately before the cancellation of debt (*i.e.*, total liabilities were greater than the fair market value of all assets).

Cancelled debt that is qualified principal residence indebtedness may be excluded from taxable income. Qualified principal residence indebtedness is any mortgage originated to buy, build, or substantially improve the taxpayer's principal residence, and must be secured by the principal residence. This exclusion does not apply to a cancellation of debt in a Chapter 11 bankruptcy case. The maximum amount that can be treated as qualified principal residence indebtedness is $2 million ($1 million if married filing separately). For additional information on qualified principal residence exclusion, insolvency determination, worksheets, and examples, see Publication 4681.

C. Colorado Withholding Tax on Certain Transfers of Real Estate

Closing entities are generally required to withhold the lesser of (1) two percent of the sales price, or (2) the entire net proceeds, as a tax on the sale of Colorado property when the seller has moved or will move out of state. The law is at the end of this chapter, and settlement procedures are shown in Chapter 18, "Closing Statements."

IV. Property Used in a Trade or Business

This section describes general rules for certain residential rental activities found in IRS Publication 527 (Residential Rental Property (Including Rental of Vacation Homes)) and other related references. Readers should review Publication 553 or other tax periodicals for additional information on specific transactions.

A. Rental Property Operations

When taxpayers rent out a home (including an apartment, condominium, mobile home, boat, or similar property), tax treatment of rental activities may be different depending on how much they use the property for personal use. If the taxpayer has no personal use, the property is treated as rental and all income is reported and expenses are deducted on Schedule E. When property is used for both personal and rental purposes, the property is considered personal use property or personal/rental residence. If the residence is rented for less than 15 days per year, it is treated as personal residence. The rental income is not included in income and mortgage interest and real estate taxes are allowed as itemized deductions. If the residence is rented out for 15 or more days, and it is used for personal purposes for the greater of: (1) more than 14 days, or (2) more than 10 percent of the rental days, it is treated as a personal/rental residence and expenses must be prorated between personal and rental use.

With some exceptions, property owners are required to report all rental amounts received in cash or services at fair market value on their return. Rental income includes any payment received for the use or occupation of the property. Advance rents (amounts received before the periods that they cover) are included in rental income in the year received, regardless of the period covered and accounting method used. Refundable security deposits that will be returned to the occupant are not income, except to the extent retained by the owner in excess of related expense. Property or services received as rent are included in rental income at the fair market value. Generally, the expenses of renting the property can be deducted from rental income. Most common rental expenses include, but are not limited to, advertising, cleaning and maintenance, insurance, utilities, depreciation, and repairs. Deductible expenses may exceed gross rental income, but a taxpayer must generally offset any "passive" rental loss from other "passive" income to deduct the loss. Any excess deductible loss is carried forward to the next tax year. See Publication 925 (Passive Activity and At-Risk Rules) for more information.

There is an exception for a "qualified person," where losses from real estate activities in which the person materially participates are not limited by the passive activity rules. The person may be able to deduct up to $25,000 of loss ($12,500 if married filing separately) from ordinary income. This deduction is phased out as adjusted gross income exceeds $100,000 and is eliminated at $150,000. A qualified person must own 10 percent of the value of all interests in the activity at all times and must "actively" participate in the operation of the property, both in the year of loss and in the year when any claim against income or certain credits is sought under the loss carryover provisions. IRS Publication 925 disallows this loss to owners of short-term and time-share rental activity, who fall into the classification of "passive" rental activity, due to a lack of material participation in operations, or who have averaged rentals of seven days or less. Stringent tests define "material participation," and professional advice is essential before taking this deduction.

There is also an exception for real estate professionals. If the taxpayer is deemed to have active participation in the activity, the rental activity is not considered to be passive and the taxpayer can fully deduct rental activity losses against ordinary income. However, the following conditions must be met: (1) more than 50 percent of the taxpayer's personal services during the tax year are performed in real estate business, and (2) the taxpayer performs more than 750 hours of services in real estate business during the year.

B. Depreciation

(Ed. Note: All references to "Section" numbers in the remainder of this chapter are to the Internal Revenue Code.)

Depreciation is an annual income tax deduction that allows the taxpayer to recover the cost or other basis of certain property over the time the taxpayer uses the property. Generally, real property (excluding the land and landscaping costs) and personal property used in a trade or business with a useful life of more than one year is depreciable.. Accounting and record keeping for depreciable items and costs is very important. The total amount of depreciation cannot exceed the basis of the depreciated property. The main factors in determining depreciation expense amount are: (1) the applicable tax law, (2) the basis in the property, (3) the recovery period, and (4) the depreciation method used. See Publication 946 (How to Depreciate Property).

A taxpayer must claim the correct amount of depreciation each year. This amount will be used to reduce the basis of the property, even if it was incorrectly reported or not taken on the return. The taxpayer must file an amended return to recover any unclaimed depreciation within three years from the filing date of the original return, or within two years from the date the tax was paid, whichever is later.

Generally, taxpayers must use the Modified Accelerated Cost Recovery System (MACRS) to depreciate residential rental property or tangible property placed in service after 1986. If rental property was placed in service before 1980 but before 1987, the Accelerated Cost Recovery System (ACRS) is used, and straight line or declining balance method over the useful life of the property is used if placed in service before 1981. The last two systems are described in Publication 534.

MACRS determines depreciation in one of two methods. Most rental property (buildings, structures, and structural components) is subject to the General Depreciation System (GDS). The taxpayer may elect to use the Alternative Depreciation System (ADS). The main difference in these methods is that the cost-recovery time period under GDS may be shorter than under ADS. The taxpayer should use IRS Publication 946 to determine the applicable recovery period and class of the property to be depreciated under these methods.

Taxpayers may elect to "expense" and deduct from taxable income, rather than to "capitalize" and depreciate over the useful life, certain qualifying Section 1245 assets (machinery and equipment), in the year of acquisition. Items expensed in this manner are known as "Section 179 Property." This election is made on Form 4562. The maximum deductible amount is reduced dollar-for-dollar for the cost of property placed in service in the amount over $800,000. The deduction taken cannot exceed the total taxable income generated from active conduct of any trade or business during the tax year. Any disallowed amount is carried forward for an indefinite number of years, subject to the ceiling for that particular tax year. However, only certain rental activities are eligible to take the Section 179 deduction. For additional information, see Publication 17.

Using an accelerated depreciation method may require filing Form 6251 to compute Alternative Minimum Tax. Accelerated depreciation includes MACRS, ACRS, and any other system resulting in a deduction greater than that computed by the Straight Line Depreciation Method. Straight line depreciation is the number "1" divided by the number of years of useful life, adjusted by any applicable tax "convention" for the specific class of property being depreciated, times the asset cost. The more common conventions are half-year or mid-quarter. In general, a half-year convention applies to personal property, under which such property placed in service or disposed of during a taxable year is treated as having been placed in service or disposed of at the midpoint of the year. If more than 40 percent of depreciable property is placed in service in the last quarter of the year, the mid-quarter convention must be used.

When personal use property is converted to rental use, the taxpayer must determine the basis of the property for purposes of depreciation. This is generally the lesser of the fair market value or the adjusted basis on the date it is placed into rental use. The determination of basis is described in IRS Publication 551 (Basis of Assets).

C. Certain Business Gains and Losses

In addition to taxable business expense deductions (see IRS Publication 535 (Business Expenses)), certain types of business property also produce special tax benefits through more favorable tax rates or deductions from ordinary income. These assets commonly are designated as Section 1231, 1245, and 1250 assets used in a taxpayer's trade or business and are treated under the rules for "capital gains or losses." Tax rules for these business items are found in IRS Publication 544 (Sales and Other Dispositions of Assets).

"Capital assets" include most everything owned and used for personal or investment purposes. Some examples are: stocks, bonds, personal residence, household furnishings, a personal automobile, jewelry, art collections, and similar items. Taxable gains or losses from the sale or exchange of capital assets are either classified as ordinary income or loss or as capital gain or loss. For individuals, net capital gain is taxed at a lower rate than ordinary income, and any capital losses are generally limited. The tax treatment of capital gains and losses depends on how long an asset is owned or held before sale. A sale or exchange of capital assets between related persons is generally taxed as ordinary income, and any loss is not deductible, except when corporate property is distributed in a complete liquidation.

In contrast, business real estate and depreciable business property is excluded from the definition of capital assets. Non-capital assets are defined as property held for resale to others (inventory), business or trade, accounts and notes receivable, depreciable property used in a trade or business, real property (including certain Section 197 intangibles) used in a trade or business, copyrights, literary, musical, or artistic compositions, and certain acquisitions of publications from a governmental agency. However, if non-capital assets qualify as Section 1231, 1245, or 1250 property, gains or losses from these transactions may receive "capital gains or loss" treatment.

In general, the sale or exchange of depreciable business property is treated under the rules for Section 1231 property. Other depreciable property under Sections 1245 and 1250 requires recapture of the depreciation allowed or allowable as ordinary income, and any gain in excess of that amount is treated as a Section 1231 capital gain. Section 1250 property requires recapture of any "additional depreciation" (in excess of straight line or other specific methods) as ordinary income.

Section 1231 assets are depreciable real and personal property held for more than one year and used in a trade or business. Some examples are: rental homes, rental dwelling units, business machinery, equipment, leaseholds, livestock, crops and timber, and any of these items that have been involuntarily converted. Their tax treatment, as ordinary or capital items, depends on whether there is a net 1231 gain or loss from all 1231 transactions. A net 1231 loss is an ordinary loss, and if a net 1231 gain, it is ordinary income up to the amount of any non-recaptured 1231 losses not offset against prior 1231 gains in the last five years. The remainder is long-term capital gain.

Section 1245 assets are tangible and intangible personal assets that have been subject to depreciation. Some examples are tangible personal property, such as furniture, bulk storage units, livestock, and office equipment (except for buildings and their structural components), used as an integral part of the business production process. The amount of gain treated as ordinary income from the sale, exchange, or involuntary conversion of Section 1245 property (including a sale and leaseback) is the lesser of: the depreciation or amortization allowed or allowable on the property, or the gain realized on the disposition (amount realized less adjusted basis). Certain limits apply to like-kind exchanges.

Section 1250 property is any real property that is depreciable but is not subject to recapture under Section 1245, that has never been used as Section 1245 property. Some examples are intangible property, such as leases of land, buildings, and major structural components. The amount of ordinary income is computed according IRS instructions in Publication 544, and any remaining gain follows the treatment for Section 1231 gain.

All of the gains or losses from Section 1231, 1245, and 1250 property are reported on Form 4797. All Section 1231 gains or losses are reported in Part 1 of this form, and any net gain from these transactions is carried to Schedule D as a long-term capital gain. Any net 1231 loss is carried to Part II of this form as an ordinary loss. Part IE handles the Section 1245 and 1250 items. If property held for use in a trade or business or for investment is exchanged solely for property of a like kind to be held either for use in trade or business or for investment, the gain or loss may be deferred, that is, not recognized in the current year.

However, the exchange must still be reported on Form 8824. Any gain or loss realized, but not recognized, adjusts the basis of like-kind property received in exchange.

The maximum capital gain rates on the net capital gain depend on the tax year and in what type of property the gain originates. "Net capital gain" is the excess of net long-term capital gain over net short-term capital loss for the year and is determined for individual taxpayers on Schedule D.

D. Tax Credits Applicable to Business Property

Tax credits applicable to business property include the general business credit, disabled access credit, low-income housing credit, and rehabilitation credit.

1. **Home Energy Tax Credits**

   Homeowners may qualify for a federal tax credit for making improvements or installing equipment designed to boost the energy-efficiency of a home.

   Qualifying energy-efficient property purchased and installed in a taxpayer's main home in the years 2006, 2007, 2009, or 2010 may be eligible for a tax credit. Examples of home improvements that could qualify as tax credits include, but are not limited to, exterior doors and windows, storm windows, skylights, metal roofs, insulation, central air conditioning and heating, geothermal heat pumps, and hot water boilers. Tax credits are available at 30 percent of the cost, up to $1,500 in 2010. A complete list of qualifying home improvement equipment can be found on EnergyStar website at www.energystar.gov. Certain types of solar panels, fuel cell power plants, small wind energy systems, and other similar equipment are eligible for a 30 percent tax credit with no maximum tax credit amount and are available through December 31, 2016.

   The tax credit for non-business energy property is restricted to improvements to and equipment installed at a primary residence. Improvements made on rental homes, second homes, or vacation properties are not eligible for this tax credit. For additional information, see Publication 17.

2. **General Business Credit** (combines credits and some described below)

   The investment credit (including the rehabilitation, energy, and reforestation credits), empowerment zone employment credit, welfare-to-work credit, Indian employment credit, employer Social Security credit, alcohol fuels credit, orphan drug credit, enhanced oil recovery credit, renewable electricity production credit, disabled access credit, and low-income housing credit are all combined into the General Business Credit (GBC). Taxpayers may qualify to deduct part or all of this and other specific unused credits listed above at the end of any carry-forward period.

   The GBC is claimed for multiple credits on Form 3800 (General Business Credit). This form is not used if the taxpayer claims only one credit. Instead, where there are no carry backs or carryovers of the amounts claimed, use the specific tax form for the credit claimed.

   The GBC is limited to the taxpayer's net income tax over: the greater of the taxpayer's "tentative minimum tax," or 25 percent of the taxpayer's net regular tax liability in excess of $25,000.

The Taxpayer Relief Act of 1997 changed the time period for carry back or carry forward of unused general business credits. For credits earned in years beginning after 1997, the carry back period is reduced to one year, and the carry forward period is 20 years. For credits earned on or before December 31, 1997, the unused credits are carried back three years and forward 15. Certain components of the GBC may be subject to recapture if a property is disposed of within five years after being placed in service, or if the property is owned by a "pass-through" entity, and when the credit was taken in a year that was subject to at-risk rules or to non-recourse financing limitations. Any recapture increases the property basis.

3. **Disabled Access Credit**

This component of the general business credit discussed above is subject to the same general limitations and carry back or carry forward provisions. It applies to expenditures made after November 5, 1990 to comply with the Americans with Disabilities Act to remove architectural, communication, transportation, or physical barriers to access or use of facilities by disabled persons. Deductions must meet standards set by the Architectural and Transportation Barriers Compliance Board as found in IRS regulations. The credit is available for qualifying small businesses. A "small business" is one that, for the preceding year, had 30 or fewer full-time employees, or had $1 million or less in gross receipts. Neither a deduction nor increase in basis is allowed for this credit.

4. **Rehabilitation Credit**

This credit is available for certain rehabilitations of qualified buildings first placed in service before 1936 and certified historic structures placed in service anytime. Qualified expenditures mean any amount charged to capital equipment in the reconstruction or rehabilitation of a nonresidential real property, a residential rental property, or real property with a class life of more than 12.5 years. Architectural and engineering fees, site survey fees, legal expenses, insurance premiums, development fees, cleanup, fire damage repair, and other related construction costs qualify if they are capitalized. The credit requires a basis reduction in an equal amount and a corresponding reduction in the basis of a partner's interest in a partnership or S corporation. Tax-exempt use of property does not qualify for this credit.

5. **Low-Income Housing Credit**

This is available for statutory low-income residential housing. It is claimed annually over a 10-year period on Form 8586 (Low-Income Housing Credit). The credit percentages are set so that the 10-year amounts will equal a present value of 70 percent of the basis of a comparable new building that is not federally subsidized and 30 percent of an existing building or federally subsidized new building. A higher credit is allowed for certain high-cost areas. Rehabilitation expenditures also qualify if they exceed $3,000 per unit.

A building generally qualifies if either: (1) 20 percent of the units are both rent-restricted and occupied by individuals with incomes of 50 percent or less of area median income, or (2) if at least 40 percent of the units are both rent-restricted and occupied by individuals with income of 60 percent or less of the area median income. Mixed income multifamily property may qualify despite one resident's high income, if the next low-income unit is rented to an individual on a rent-restricted basis. These tests must be satisfied over a 15-year commitment period, and the penalty for noncompliance is recapture of the credit taken.

The IRS issued proposed regulations (Reg-114664-97) on January 8, 1999 requiring state and local housing agencies and owners to monitor compliance with the rules. Monitoring activity requires annual reports to the IRS, inspections of the projects once every three years, and a review of local government building code violations. Owners must certify annually that a project is suitable for occupancy, submit reports of code violations, and obtain a CPA's opinion on the financial determination and certifications owners submit to the building inspection agency. The opinion includes the basis for the tax credit claimed. Please refer to Internal Revenue Code § 42 for further information.

6. **Colorado Vacant Commercial Building Rehabilitation Credit**

Under current Colorado legislation, the owner or tenant of a building in an enterprise zone that is at least 20 years old and that has been completely vacant for at least two years can claim a tax credit of 25 percent of the cost of rehabilitating such building for commercial use. The credit limit is $50,000 per building. See FYI 24 for additional information.

V. Federal Estate and Gift Taxation

A. Real Property

The estate tax is imposed on all testamentary transfers regardless of probate. A special estate tax lien attaches to all property in the decedent's gross estate upon death, whether or not it is assessed and filed by the taxing authority. Foreclosure against purchasers of such property without knowledge of this attachment has been upheld in court. An executor for the estate may elect to apply a special lien against specific property of sufficient value to pay all tax and interest due from the decedent.

* Under current legislation, the estate tax is repealed in 2010, but is completely reinstated in 2011 for estates valued at $5 million or more. In general, a return of the estate or trust must be filed by the fiduciary on Form 1041 when: the trust had gross income of $600 or more for the tax year, any beneficiary is a non-resident alien, or the bankruptcy estate has gross income equal to the sum of unified credit exemption plus the standard deduction for married persons filing separately. The filing amount is known as the "unified credit" because it is deducted from any tax due on the decedent's estate in excess of that amount. See Publications 950 and 553 for further information.

Determination of estate tax depends upon the value of the decedent's "gross estate," either at the date of death or by election at an alternative valuation date if elected six months later. Property held by the deceased, property transferred within three years before death, and property transferred with a retained power of alteration, amendment, or revocation is included. Certain deductions are subtracted from the gross estate, and credits may reduce taxes due.

Principal deductions are for funeral and estate administration, claims against the estate, mortgages, marital property settlements, charitable contributions, losses, and bequests to a surviving spouse. The unified credit is deductible from any tax remaining. The credit changes each year. In addition, credit may be taken for state death taxes, federal gift taxes, taxes paid on prior transfers, and foreign death taxes. The executor may elect to deduct the adjusted value of a qualified family-owned business interest up to a given amount from the gross estate, per instructions for Schedule T, Form 706.

B. Federal Gift Taxes

* Any transfer of money or property, whether real or personal, tangible or intangible, for less than an adequate consideration is a gift. A living donor's gift is subject to gift tax, although a taxpayer may transfer up to $13,000 (in 2011) each year ($26,000 if married and gift splitting is elected) without being subject to any tax or reporting requirement. This annual exclusion is not available for a gift of a future interest or incomplete gifts. In addition to the annual $13,000 exclusion, certain payments qualify for an unlimited exclusion: (1) amounts paid on behalf of a donee for tuition paid directly to an educational institution, (2) fees paid directly to a medical institution, (3) charitable gifts, and (4) the marital deduction (transfers between spouses).

> Ed. Note: See Publication 709 for further information about gift taxes.

VI. Tax Treatment of Various Legal Entities

A. Corporations

A corporation is taxed as a separate legal entity on reported income. Dividends paid are also taxable to the individual receiving them. Associations, joint stock companies, and insurance companies are taxed as corporations. Subchapter S corporations are not taxed on income, but serve as conduits for passing income, losses, and deductions to their stockholders.

B. Partnerships

A partnership is not a taxable entity. All income, loss, credits, and deductions pass through to the individual partners who share these items according to agreed-upon amounts in the partnership agreement. A partnership must file an informational tax return showing distributions to all partners.

C. S Corporations

The domestic small, closely held corporation may elect to be taxed as a pass-through entity. The requirements for election are to: have 100 or fewer consenting shareholders, file a timely election, and issue only one class of stock. The election can be revoked by certain actions of the shareholders. There are several restrictions on eligible shareholders, such as eligible shareholder must be an individual, estate, or certain type of trust, and an individual shareholder may not be a nonresident alien. For more details, see I.R.C. § 1361.

D. Limited Liability Companies (LLC)

A limited liability company (LLC) features many of the personal protections of a corporation, while preserving the tax benefits of a partnership and without an S corporation's restrictions on eligible members. An LLC with only one member can be treated as a disregarded entity and report its income and expenses on Schedule C or Schedule E. An LLC with more than one member may be treated as a partnership. Or, an LLC with one or more members may elect to be treated as a corporation for tax purposes.

E. Trusts

A trust takes title to property on behalf of someone else. Trusts are subject to taxation and are allowed deductions for income distributed to the beneficiaries, who must report the distribution. Real estate investment trusts are subject to strict tax requirements concerning forms of organization, sources of income, and allowable assets.

F. Homeowner Associations

If qualified, a homeowner association is taxed at 30 percent of its taxable income. "Exempt function income" derived from assessments on owner-members is generally not taxed. Taxable income includes amounts received as interest on sinking funds, amounts received for services provided to private property not owned by the association, and amounts received from members for special services provided. An association must annually elect to exclude exempt function income.

G. Real Estate Mortgage Investment Conduit (REMIC)

A REMIC is an entity formed to hold a fixed pool of mortgages. Tax provisions follow the class of ownership the taxpayer has in the REMIC. "Regular interest holders" are treated as debt holders of the REMIC. "Residual interest owners" are taxed on the prorated share of the REMIC net income, whether or not it is distributed. Both are taxed as ordinary income.

H. Tax Shelters

These are generally classified into two groups: "Projected Income Investments" and "Abusive Tax Shelters." An investor should seek tax and legal counsel to determine how the IRS classifies a shelter before making an investment.

A projected income investment is one not expected to substantially reduce the cumulative tax liability of any investor during the first five years the investment is offered for sale. Tax shelters previously qualified as projected income investments may lose such status. Such loss requires registration with the IRS and record keeping of sales between subsequent investors. Severe penalties may apply to any failure to keep records.

Internal Revenue Bulletins discuss abusive tax shelters. Such rulings bind the agency in enforcement of tax matters. The disallowance of tax deductions in such shelters may be accompanied by other severe tax penalties.

VII. Employed Real Estate Licensees

Commission Rule E-29 and the related Commission position statement CP-18, Payments to a Wholly Owned Employee Corporation (see Chapter 3), recognize independent contractor agreements with the employing broker. The payment of earned commissions by the employing broker to a wholly owned employee corporation is not considered payment to an unlicensed entity, pursuant to §§ 12-61-113(1) or -117, C.R.S.

This recognition does not relieve the employing broker of the statutory responsibility to train and supervise licensed associates pursuant to Rules E-29 through E-32. Wholly owned corporations for this purpose are not licensed with the Commission and may never transact licensed business or hold money belonging to others in its own name.

VIII. Withholding of State Income Tax on Proceeds from Transfers by Nonresidents of Real Property Located in Colorado

§ 39-22-604.5, C.R.S. Withholding tax – transfers of Colorado real property – nonresident transferors

(1) Except as otherwise provided in this section, in the case of any conveyance of a Colorado real property interest, the title insurance company or its authorized agent or any attorney, bank, savings and loan association, savings bank, corporation, partnership, association, joint stock company, trust, or unincorporated organization or any combination thereof, acting separately or in concert, that provides closing and settlement services as defined herein shall be required to withhold an amount equal to two percent of the sales price of the Colorado real property interest conveyed or the net proceeds resulting from such conveyance, whichever is less, when:

(a) The transferor is a person and either the return required to be filed with the secretary of the treasury pursuant to section 6045 (e) of the internal revenue code indicates or the authorization for the disbursement of the funds resulting from such transaction instructs that such funds be disbursed to a transferor with a last-known street address outside the boundaries of this state at the time of the transfer of the title to such Colorado real property interest or to the escrow agent of such transferor; or

(b) (I) The transferor is a corporation which immediately after the transfer of the title to the Colorado real estate interest has no permanent place of business in Colorado.

(II) For purposes of this section, a corporation has no permanent place of business in Colorado if all of the following apply:

(A) Such corporation is a foreign corporation;

(B) Such corporation does not qualify pursuant to law to transact business in Colorado; and

(C) Such corporation does not maintain and staff a permanent office in Colorado.

(2) No title insurance company or its authorized agent or any attorney, bank, savings and loan association, savings bank, corporation, partnership, association, joint stock company, trust, or unincorporated organization or any combination thereof, acting separately or in concert, that provides closing and settlement services as defined herein shall be required to withhold any amount pursuant to this section:

(a) If the sales price of the Colorado real property conveyed does not exceed one hundred thousand dollars;

(b) When the transferee is a bank or corporate beneficiary under a mortgage or beneficiary under a deed of trust and the Colorado real property interest is acquired in judicial or nonjudicial foreclosure or by deed in lieu of foreclosure;

(c) If the title insurance company or its authorized agent or any attorney, bank, savings and loan association, savings bank, corporation, partnership, association, joint stock company, trust, or unincorporated organization or any combination thereof, acting separately or in concert, that provides closing and settlement services as defined herein in good faith relies upon a written affirmation executed by the transferor, certifying under penalty of perjury one of the following:

(I) That the transferor, if a person, is a resident of Colorado;

(II) That the transferor, if a corporation, has a permanent place of business in Colorado;

(III) That the Colorado real property being conveyed is the principal residence of the transferor within the meaning of section 1034 of the internal revenue code; or

(IV) That the transferor will not owe tax reasonably estimated to be due pursuant to this article from the inclusion of the actual gain required to be recognized on the transaction in the gross income of the transferor.

(3) Any title insurance company or its authorized agent which is required to withhold any amount pursuant to this section and fails to do so shall be liable for the greater of the following amounts for such failure to withhold:

(a) Five hundred dollars;

(b) Ten percent of the amount required to be withheld pursuant to this section, not to exceed two thousand five hundred dollars.

(4) (a) Amounts withheld and payments made in accordance with this section shall be reported and remitted to the department of revenue in such form and at such time as specified by rule and regulation of the executive director. Written affirmations executed pursuant to paragraph (c) of subsection (2) of this section shall be submitted to the department of revenue pursuant to procedures specified by rule and regulation of the executive director.

(b) All of the other provisions of this article shall apply to and be effective as to the provisions of this section to the extent to which they are not inconsistent with this section, and all of the remedies available to the department of revenue for the administration, assessment, enforcement, and collection of tax under other sections of this article and article 21 of this title shall be available to the department of revenue and shall apply to the amounts required to be deducted and withheld pursuant to the provisions of this section, and all of the penalties, both civil and criminal, shall apply to this section.

(5) Whenever a title insurance company or its authorized agent provides escrow services as directed by the parties in compliance with the withholding requirements of this section, such title insurance company or its authorized agent shall charge the parties pursuant to the rates in effect at the time and filed with the division of insurance of the department of regulatory agencies as required by law.

(6) For purposes of this section, unless the context otherwise requires:

(a) "Authorized agent" means a title insurance agent, as defined in section 10-11-102 (9), C.R.S., who is responsible for closing and settlement services in the transaction.

(b) "Closing and settlement services" means closing and settlement services as defined in section 10-11-102 (3.5), C.R.S., and section 38-35-125, C.R.S.

(c) "Colorado real property interest" means an interest in real property located in Colorado and defined in section 897 (c) (1) (A) (i) of the internal revenue code.

(d) "Escrow agent" means an agent for the purpose of receiving and transferring funds to a principal.

(e) "Person" means any individual, estate, or trust who may be subject to taxation pursuant to part 1 of this article.

(f) "Sales price" means the sum of all of the following:

(I) The cash paid or to be paid, but shall not include stated or unstated interest or original issue discount as determined pursuant to sections 1271 to 1275 of the internal revenue code;

(II) The fair market value of other property transferred or to be transferred;

(III) The outstanding amount of any liability assumed by the transferee to which the Colorado real property interest is subject immediately before and after the transfer.

(g) "Title insurance company" means the title insurance company, as defined in section 10-11-102 (10), C.R.S., responsible for closing and settlement services in the transaction.

Ed. Note: See Chapter 11, "Conservation Easements," for tax factors pertaining to conservation easement holders.

Chapter 24:
Fair Housing

An * in the left margin indicates a change in the statute, rule, or text since the last publication of the manual.

I. Introduction

The following information is excerpted from the Federal Civil Rights Acts of 1866, 1870, and 1968 and the Fair Housing Amendments Act of 1988 as they apply to equal housing opportunity. The information is intended to be a broad overview of the fair housing provisions within the Federal Civil Rights Acts. A comprehensive listing of rules and interpretations of the 1968 and 1988 Acts can be obtained by contacting the Department of Housing and Urban Development (HUD), Office of Fair Housing and Equal Opportunity.

II. Federal Civil Rights Acts

A. Civil Rights Acts of 1866 and 1870 (42 U.S.C. §§ 1981 and 1982)

The Civil Rights Acts of 1866 and 1870, passed shortly after the passage of the Thirteenth Amendment to the Constitution (which eliminated slavery), are brief enough to be quoted in their entirety.

42 U.S.C. § 1981 – Equal rights under the law. "All persons within the jurisdiction of the United States shall have the same right in every State and Territory to make and enforce contracts, to sue, be parties, give evidence, and to the full and equal benefit of all laws and proceedings for the security of persons and property as is enjoyed by white citizens, and shall be subject to like punishment, pains, penalties, taxes, licenses, and exactions of every kind, and to no other." (May 1870)

42 U.S.C. § 1982 – Property rights of citizens. "All citizens of the United States shall have the same right, in every State and Territory, as is enjoyed by white citizens thereof to inherit, purchase, lease, sell, hold, and convey real and personal property." (April 1866)

Until 1987, it was assumed that the above two laws applied only to discrimination on the basis of race. The U.S. Supreme Court ruled then that they applied also to discrimination on the basis of ancestry or ethnicity (on its rationale that some ethnic or religious groups were considered different "races" when the law was enacted). However, neither can be used to make discrimination claims on other bases, such as sex, handicap, or familial status, found in the Fair Housing Act (Title VIII), and discussed below.

The above two laws apply to both real and personal property, and to both commercial and residential property, unlike the 1968 Fair Housing Act, which applies only to housing and land intended for housing. Therefore, licensees must ensure that the conduct of their business affords equal opportunity in commercial as well as residential transactions.

B. Fair Housing Act 1968, Amended 1988 (42 U.S.C. §§ 3601 to 3619)

Bases of Discrimination

Under the acts of 1866 and 1870, and the 1968 Fair Housing Act, real estate licensees must ensure that their residential real estate activities do not discriminate on the basis of **race, color, religion, sex,** and **national origin**.

The **Fair Housing Amendments Act of 1988** expanded the prohibition against unlawful discrimination to include two additional protected classes: **handicap** (both mental and physical) and **familial status**.

Handicap is defined as: "(1) a physical or mental impairment which substantially limits one or more of such person's major life activities, (2) a record of having such an impairment, or (3) being regarded as having such an impairment." The definition includes: alcoholism, HIV or the AIDS virus, certain physiological disorders, and specified types of anatomical losses. Mental illness, retardation, and psychological disorders are also considered handicaps. Further discussion of discrimination on the basis of handicap is contained in the sections entitled "Handicap," "Steering," and "Exclusionary Land Use," below.

Familial status is defined as children under age 18 living with parents or others with legal custody, or with a designee of the parent with written permission, a person who is pregnant, or a person who is seeking custody of a person under 18. The 1988 amendments made it illegal not only to refuse to rent or sell to families with children, but also made it illegal to designate a residential building, mobile home park, or even a section of a building as "adults only." There can be no rules, covenants, deed restrictions, bylaws, or agreements that discriminate against families with children, although in limited circumstances a residential community may be able to adopt rules about families with children if they are based on *safety* considerations (not the convenience of adults).

Charging per-person rental fees can also be considered discrimination on the basis of familial status, because such fees can be shown to have a discriminatory effect on families with children. One of the most difficult issues in familial status discrimination is the question of how many children may be allowed in a particular unit. HUD guidance has established that two persons per bedroom will be considered generally reasonable, but this is not absolute. If a charge is filed, consideration will be given to the overall size of the dwelling, size of the bedrooms, what other rooms might be used for sleeping areas, and any local zoning or occupancy codes.

There are specific exemptions from the protection of familial status for retirement communities or housing for the elderly. See a further explanation of the exemption for senior communities under "Exemptions," below.

Exemptions to Property Covered

1. A single-family home sold or rented† *by the owner*, if the owner: (1) does not own over three single-family homes, (2) does not use the services or facilities of a licensee or anyone in the business of selling or renting buildings, and (3) does not make, print, or publish any discriminatory advertising or statement;

   (†Note: The home itself is not exempt. The transaction *by the owner* is exempt. Actions by non-owners, such as homeowners associations, real estate brokers, cities, lenders, neighbors, etc. are not exempt. This is why an owner may be able to sell or rent a single-family home without coming under the federal Fair Housing Act, but a real estate broker may not.)

2. Rooms or units in dwellings occupied or intended to be occupied by no more than four families, if the owner lives in one of the units;

   (Note: Exemptions #1 and #2 are not found in Colorado law, except for familial status. See later explanation of the Colorado law.)

3. Religious organizations or societies that own and operate dwelling units for a non-commercial purpose may give preference or limit occupancy to persons of the same religion, unless membership in the religion is restricted on the basis of race, color, or national origin;

4. Private clubs that own or operate lodging for non-commercial purposes may limit occupancy or give preference to members; and

5. Housing for seniors may be exempt only from familial status protections if it meets one of the following three requirements:
   (a) Housing provided under a state or federal program that the secretary of HUD determines is designed and operated for elderly persons;
   (b) Housing in which 100 percent of the residents are 62 years of age or older; or
   (c) Housing in which 80 percent of the occupied units have at least one person 55 years of age or older and the housing publishes and adheres to policies demonstrating the intent to house persons over 55.

After May 3, 2000, the only way a community can convert to "over-55" housing is if it has been "wholly unoccupied for at least 90 days" for the purpose of renovation or rehabilitation. The Fair Housing Amendments Act of 1988 originally required that over-55 housing also provide "significant facilities and services" for persons over 55. This requirement was repealed on April 2, 1999, and gave until May 3, 2000 to transition to over-55 housing. HUD strongly suggests advertising as "Senior Housing," "55 and older community," or "retirement community," and warns that using the words "adult community" or "adult living" puts the community in danger of complaint, investigation, or litigation. The housing community must verify ages and update its age surveys at least every two years.

WARNING: If a fair housing complaint is filed alleging that housing was refused to families with children without meeting one of the three exemptions described above, any licensees who listed the property or participated in the sale or rental as an exempt senior property have a "good faith" exemption from money damages *only* if the community's "authorized representatives" have certified "in writing and under oath" that it complies with the exemption.

III. Illegal Practices Under Federal Law

- To refuse to show, rent, lease, sell, or transfer housing.
- To represent that property is not available for sale or rental, when in fact it is.
- To refuse to receive or transmit any bona fide offer to buy, sell, or lease housing.
- To discriminate in the terms, conditions, or privileges of housing.
- To discriminate in the provision of services or facilities of housing.

- To discriminate in making loans available, or in their terms, conditions, or privileges, for the purchase, construction, or maintenance of housing, or for loans secured by housing.
- To advertise any discriminatory preferences or limitations.

  Licensees must be aware that an advertisement need not explicitly mention race, religion, or other protected classes to be unlawful, and should avoid making or using any statement that could reasonably be interpreted as conveying a prohibited preference or limitation. For example, using a term such as "restricted" in an advertisement may violate the act unless it is clearly indicated that the restriction is not an unlawfully discriminatory one. Using models not in keeping with community race demographics has also been found to be discriminatory. Licensees are urged to consult the "Advertising Guidelines for Fair Housing" issued by the Secretary of HUD, which catalogue a number of phrases that are considered discriminatory. HUD regulations also prescribe the use of the equal housing logo and/or slogan in advertisements and require the posting of a HUD Equal Housing poster. Licensees are strongly encouraged to use the "Equal Housing Opportunity" logo or statement in anything that could possibly be considered an "advertisement," such as brochures, calling cards, and signs.
- To deny any person access to membership or to impose unequal terms in any multiple listing service or real estate broker's organization.
- To interfere with, coerce, or intimidate persons exercising fair housing rights, or persons aiding or encouraging others to exercise fair housing rights.
- To discriminate or retaliate against someone for opposing unfair housing practices or for testifying, assisting, or participating in an investigation, proceeding, or hearing.
- To discriminate in fire/title/homeowners insurance or in real estate appraisals.
- **Blockbusting:** Blockbusting is the practice of inducing or attempting to induce a person to sell or rent a dwelling by representing that persons of a certain race, disability, etc., are or may be moving into a neighborhood. Courts have ruled that this covers not only explicit representations about race, but also statements by real estate agents such as "changing neighborhood," "falling property values," "bad schools," or "undesirable elements," if used to solicit listings and sales. In racially transitional neighborhoods, where residents tend to be aware of racial change even without its being mentioned, a racial representation may reasonably be inferred from unusually heavy solicitation of listings, even if no explicit statements are made relative to new residents of a particular race or national origin.
- To "otherwise make unavailable" housing. This phrase includes:
  - **Steering:** Steering is any action or difference in service or information provided that might influence persons to select their own ethnic-identity neighborhoods or discourage living in certain areas. In a landmark case, *Gladstone Realtors v. Village of Bellwood*, 441 U.S. 91 (1979), the U.S. Supreme Court declared that the "otherwise make unavailable" prohibition in the Fair Housing Act prohibited steering, which it defined as "directing prospective home buyers interested in equivalent properties to different areas according to their race." *Id.* at 94. HUD

regulations issued after the passage of the 1988 Fair Housing Amendments Act define steering as discouraging anyone from inspecting, purchasing, or renting a dwelling, exaggerating drawbacks, or failing to inform persons of the desirable features of a community, communicating that someone would not be welcome in a community, or assigning any person to a particular building or floor based on a protected class. Steering includes such practices as renting or selling units only on the first floor to persons in wheelchairs, or renting or selling units to families with children only on certain floors, in designated buildings, or areas of rental, town-home, and condominium communities.

- **Exclusionary Land Use:** Courts have also ruled that the term "otherwise make unavailable" includes zoning regulations and decisions of local government, or covenants or actions of homeowners associations, which have the effect of preventing housing choices for minorities, women, or persons with disabilities. Until the addition of the handicapped protected class to Title VIII in 1988, most exclusionary land use resulted from denial of low-income housing or other actions by local government which had the effect of restricting minorities from living in certain areas. Since 1989, the major exclusionary land use litigation has been over placement in the community of group homes or other residential facilities for persons with mental or physical disabilities. Litigation on this issue is often also filed under the "refusal to make reasonable accommodations" section of the statute, discussed further under "Handicap," below. When licensees encounter opposition to selling or listing a home intended for the use of a group home for persons with disabilities, they should contact HUD or the Colorado Civil Rights Division (CCRD) for advice on how to proceed. Also, because the disabled are a protected class, licensees do not have to disclose that there is a group home for persons with disabilities in the neighborhood. In fact, they should not make a voluntary disclosure of this fact, in the same way that they would not volunteer to a customer the information that there are minorities in the neighborhood.
- **Redlining:** Redlining is a lender practice of refusing to grant loans or an insurance company refusing to issue policies in certain neighborhoods, usually characterized by a large number of persons in protected classes. It may also be considered redlining when loans or policies are not refused outright, but contain discriminatory terms or higher costs. Prior to the 1988 amendments, such practices or lack of services could be addressed only under the "otherwise make unavailable" section of the law, but discrimination in lending and other "real estate-related" services are now specifically listed as prohibitions in the Fair Housing Act. Nevertheless, such discriminatory treatment does exist, and licensees who suspect that their protected class customers are not being treated equally should consult with either HUD or the CCRD about possible charges.
- **Handicap:** The 1988 Fair Housing Amendments Act extended protections afforded to other classes to persons with mental or physical handicaps. Persons may not be refused housing or subjected to unequal terms or conditions because of their handicap. The statute excepts persons convicted of manufacturing or selling drugs and persons currently addicted to or using illegal drugs, as well as persons "whose tenancy would constitute a direct threat to the health or safety of other residents or whose tenancy would result in substantial physical damage to

the property of others." Although alcoholism, for example, is considered an impairment and is given protected status, this does not mean that the behavior or rental history of an alcoholic must be ignored in determining whether an applicant for housing is qualified. While an alcoholic or mentally impaired person may not be rejected based solely on his or her impairment, a landlord may consider "behavioral manifestations" of the condition. In determining qualifications, a housing provider may consider past rental history, violation of rules and laws, or a history of disruptive, abusive, or dangerous behavior. Housing providers may not presume, however, that applicants with certain disabilities are less likely to be qualified or are more likely to be dangerous, in the absence of specific proof. In the few cases that have been decided under the "direct threat" provisions, including one in the United States District Court for the District of Colorado, *Roe v. Housing Authority of the City of Boulder*, 909 F. Supp. 814 (D. Colo. 1995), courts have ruled that housing providers must first make a reasonable effort and accommodation to lessen or mitigate any possible threat before they may deny housing.

The Fair Housing Amendments Act of 1988 also added three definitions of discrimination that apply *only to persons with disabilities*:

- **Refusal to permit reasonable modifications**, at the expense of a handicapped person, to existing premises to give that person full enjoyment. Under this section, landlords, owners, and condominium associations must allow tenants or owners to make reasonable modifications to either the unit or to common areas, if necessary for the person's access or equal enjoyment of the housing. Further, landlords and homeowners associations may not increase the security deposit of a disabled tenant in anticipation of a request for future modifications. However, licensees should be cautious about suggesting that buyers or tenants make accessibility modifications at their own expense until determining whether the requested modification should have been designed into multifamily buildings constructed since March 13, 1991. (See the paragraph below on "a failure to design and construct multifamily housing" for further details.) Under a different federal law, the 1973 Rehabilitation Act, the landlord may be responsible for the cost of modifications if housing was partially or fully funded with federal funds. Another situation where the owner or homeowners association, not the occupant, might be responsible for the cost of modification is when the modification requested is a part of housing considered a "public accommodation" under the Americans with Disabilities Act (the ADA), such as sales/rental offices and common areas like pools and clubhouses rented out to the public. (See the subsequent section on the ADA.)

  In limited situations, such as when the modifications might not be usable by a subsequent non-disabled occupant, a landlord may require that a disabled tenant deposit a reasonable amount of money into an escrow account to cover the costs of restoration of the *interior* of the unit. Landlords or homeowners associations may not require restoration of modifications to the *exterior* of the unit, since exterior accessibility modifications may benefit other persons with disabilities.

- **Refusal to make reasonable accommodations** in rules, policies, practices, or services to accommodate the handicapped. Under this provision, housing providers, including homeowners associations, must waive or amend rules to accommodate persons with handicaps, such as providing assigned parking when parking is usually "first-come, first-served" or allowing guide, service, and companion animals in buildings that usually prohibit animals. Courts have also ruled that the word "rules" includes zoning regulations and covenants that preclude or put undue restrictions on group homes for persons with handicaps in residential neighborhoods. This means that cities and counties with zoning regulations limiting the number of unrelated people who may share a housing unit may have to make an exception to allow the establishment of a group home for persons with handicaps. As another example of the wide-ranging interpretation of this provision of the law, one court has required covenants not allowing businesses to be waived so that a handicapped person could operate a business from home.

- **Failure to design and construct handicap-accessible multifamily housing** containing four or more units, put into first occupancy after March 13, 1991. Any housing with four or more units in a single structure must comply with seven specific accessibility requirements: (1) an accessible entrance on an accessible route, (2) accessible and usable common use areas, (3) usable doors, (4) an accessible route into and through the unit, (5) light switches, electrical outlets, thermostats, and other environmental controls in accessible locations, (6) reinforced walls for grab bars, and (7) usable kitchens and bathrooms. Buildings with elevators must make all units accessible; buildings without elevators must make ground-floor units accessible.

  There is only one exception to the "four-or-more" requirement. It is HUD's interpretation of the law that two-story townhomes in a building without an elevator are not required to be accessible, because there is no "ground floor unit." Other than this, all other buildings with four or more units have accessibility requirements. Single-story units are considered "ground floor units" and must be accessible, as are single-story units with an unfinished basement or single-story units with an open loft. If the building has an elevator, then all units, even if they are two-story townhome style, must comply with accessibility requirements.

  Anyone involved in the design or construction of multifamily housing subject to the act may be held liable. This includes owners, developers, architects, site and electrical engineers, and construction companies. HUD considers that the usual one-year statute of limitations does not apply until the units have been brought into compliance, and so far, there has been no case ruling to the contrary. That means that there are thousands of non-compliant units in Colorado whose designers and builders may be subject to a complaint filed anytime in the future (see *Garcia v. Brockway*, 526 F.3d 456 (9th Cir. 2008).

Licensees who list or sell residential property defined as "multifamily housing" need to be very familiar with accessibility requirements and when they apply. Property, including individual units or whole multifamily buildings, changes hands without new purchasers being aware of whether the property is or is not in compliance. Although commercial brokers seem to be generally aware of the coverage of the ADA, there is less understanding of the Fair Housing Act accessibility mandates. The Colorado Civil Rights Division has investigated charges of "failure to design and construct" to fair housing standards and notes that sometimes contracts for the sale of apartment buildings refer to the ADA, even though this generally is the wrong law, except for rental offices in apartment buildings or common areas rented out to the public. Although licensees should not themselves certify whether multifamily buildings are in compliance, they are well advised to warn potential buyers to hire an architectural firm to make this assessment. (See the ADA section for further discussion of when the ADA applies versus when the Fair Housing Act applies.)

Enforcement: The amended fair housing act of 1988 provides that persons who believe they have been subjected to a discriminatory housing practice may file a complaint with either HUD's Office of Fair Housing and Equal Opportunity, or with the CCRD. HUD is mandated to refer housing discrimination complaints to any state or local public agency, if that agency has been certified as "substantially equivalent." Agencies receive this certification if the following are substantially equivalent to federal law: (1) substantive rights protected, (2) procedures followed by the agency, (3) remedies available to that agency, and (4) availability of judicial review of such agency's action.

The Colorado Civil Rights Division has had a memorandum of understanding (MOU) with HUD for joint processing of charges since 1981. Under this MOU, the Division accepts and investigates most state and federal charges at the same time, except for the following: (1) complaints that do not fall under both laws because of differences in the laws, (2) complaints against an agency of the federal government, and (3) complaints where the property is federally subsidized and there is also a complaint under Title VI, § 504 of the 1973 Rehabilitation Act or the Americans with Disabilities Act. HUD may also elect to investigate some cases it considers "systemic," such as those against companies with holdings both in and out of Colorado, issues of zoning laws and other local land use practices, or cases that raise a question of public importance.

Complaints must be filed *within one year* of the discriminatory action or termination of that discriminatory action. Complainants may bypass both HUD and the Colorado Civil Rights Division and file directly in federal or state district court within two years of the alleged discrimination. Complainants may also decide, at any stage of the conciliation and investigation process, to pull the complaint from HUD or the Colorado Civil Rights Division and file directly in court, unless a conciliation agreement has been reached with the consent of the complainant or unless a hearing before an administrative law judge (ALJ) has commenced. The HUD secretary, the attorney general of Colorado, and the Colorado Civil Rights Commission may also file a complaint upon their own initiative.

During the period beginning with the filing of a complaint and ending with a formal charge or dismissal, HUD or the CCRD will attempt to conciliate the complaint in order to achieve an agreement satisfactory to all parties and in keeping with public policy and the purposes of the fair housing acts. The CCRD calls this attempt to settle the case its "alternative dispute resolution," and uses the term "conciliation" only after the director has found "probable cause" that discrimination has occurred and a second attempt has been made to come to an agreement between the parties. The purpose of conciliation is to obtain assurances that the violation will be remedied and to protect the interest of the aggrieved person and other persons similarly situated.

If an agreement cannot be reached between the parties, then, after a full investigation, the agency carrying out the investigation issues a formal finding of "probable cause" or "no probable cause" (Colorado law) or "reasonable cause" or "no reasonable cause" (federal law), that discrimination has or has not occurred. "No cause" cases are dismissed unless appealed by the complainant. In "cause" cases, either the state or HUD will issue a formal complaint to be heard by an ALJ, unless either party requests, within 20 days of service of the complaint, that the matter be moved to a federal or state district court. Further efforts at an agreement will continue until the matter is heard before the ALJ or court. Courts or an ALJ can issue a final decision and award actual damages, injunctive or other equitable relief, and civil penalties. A court can also award punitive damages. There is no statutory limit on the amount of punitive damages that a judge or jury may award.

Violation of fair housing laws may affect a broker's Colorado real estate license. If a respondent licensee is found to have committed a discriminatory housing practice, then HUD or the CCRD will notify the Colorado Division of Real Estate. This notification will contain copies of the findings of fact, conclusions of law, and the final decision against the licensee with recommendations of revocation or other disciplinary action. Pursuant to Colorado license law, § 12-61-113(1)(m.5), C.R.S., any violation by a real estate agent or the aiding and abetting in the violation of the Colorado or federal fair housing laws is cause for the revocation of a real estate license and a maximum fine of $2,500.

Fair housing acts do not prohibit only clear, obvious, and intentional discrimination, but also make unlawful subtle forms of discriminatory treatment, as well as conduct that has discriminatory results, regardless of the motivation. Moreover, employing brokers may be liable for discriminatory acts by employed licensees. This is true even for a broker who has not personally violated the act, who has given perfunctory instructions to subagents to obey the law, and who was not aware of the licensee's violations. The duty to comply with the law cannot be delegated, and even a "silent partner" can be found in violation of the act when employees discriminate. On the good side, licensees are also protected by court rulings that anyone who has been harmed by a discriminatory housing act has standing to file a housing discrimination complaint. A broker who has lost a commission because of a discriminatory practice may file a charge and claim damages.

IV. Equal Credit Opportunity Act (ECOA) (15 U.S.C. §§ 1691, *et seq.*)

The Equal Credit Opportunity Act (ECOA) makes it unlawful to discriminate in the granting of credit on the basis of race, color, religion, national origin, sex, marital status, age, or because income comes from a public assistance program. Notice two classes here that are not found in the fair housing acts: "age" and "income from a public assistance program."

V. Americans with Disabilities Act

Real estate professionals need to be aware how the Americans with Disabilities Act (the ADA) will affect their practices. Title III of the ADA, "Nondiscrimination on the Basis of Disability by Public Accommodations and in Commercial Facilities," went into effect on January 26, 1992. The ADA does not generally apply to residential real estate except for on-site offices or common areas rented to the public. However, this section of the ADA may affect brokerage offices, licensees working with multifamily or commercial real estate, brokers who offer brokerage services, and employ others, and/or persons who teach real estate, in four ways, described below.

A. Licensee ADA Responsibilities in Conducting Real Estate Practices

Real estate brokerages and licensees have four basic responsibilities in the conduct of their real estate practices; to:

1. Not discriminate against persons with disabilities;

2. Make reasonable modifications in their procedures and policies so as to make their services available to persons with disabilities;
3. Take steps to ensure that persons with disabilities are not excluded or treated differently because of the absence of auxiliary aids or services; and
4. Remove architectural barriers.

Architectural barriers in existing facilities must be removed if removal is "readily achievable," *i.e.*, able to be carried out without much difficulty or expense. Barrier removal includes such things as installing ramps, widening doors, removing high-pile carpeting, rearranging furniture, and installing raised markings on elevator controls. If these cannot be done all at once, Department of Justice regulations specify an order of priority: first, accomplish access to the facility, next, access to the places where services or goods are available, then restroom access, then anything else necessary. ADA regulations also contain complex provisions that take effect when alterations are made to a place of public accommodation. Alterations can, in some cases, trigger requirements for additional remodeling to achieve accessibility. Building owners should not proceed with plans for office upgrade before review of ADA regulations on "alterations," "alterations: plan of travel," and "alterations: elevator exemption."

"Auxiliary aids" include such things as deaf interpreters, large print materials, and modification of equipment. Public accommodations should provide these unless doing so would fundamentally alter the nature of their services or result in an "undue burden," *i.e.*, significant difficulty or expense.

The ADA specifies factors that will be considered in evaluating "readily achievable" and "undue burden." These include the cost of the provision of auxiliary aids or removal of barriers, in relation to the financial resources of the site or, in some cases, the parent corporation.

The ADA places these responsibilities on the "public accommodation," as distinguished from a "place of public accommodation." Since the definition of "public accommodation" is "a private entity that owns, leases (or leases to), or operates a place of public accommodation," both the owner and the lessee are subject to the act's requirements. After considerable controversy over whether the lessor or lessee would be responsible for the removal of barriers and provision of auxiliary aids, final ADA regulations specify that "allocation of responsibility for the obligations of this part may be determined by lease or other contract." Unfortunately, this means that persons who rent from or to other parties must negotiate the details of ADA compliance in their leases. Although freely negotiable, the most common lease arrangements tend to hold the owner responsible for the common areas, and the lessee is made responsible within the leased portion.

B. Licensee ADA Responsibilities in Listing, Selling, Leasing, or Managing Property

Although licensees are not responsible for ensuring that the buildings they sell, lease, or manage are fully ADA accessible, they should be familiar with accessibility requirements in order to serve their clients. This would include a basic understanding of the requirements for buildings built both before and after the effective date of the ADA, and the lessor and lessee responsibilities briefly discussed above. Licensees would be unwise to claim that any building being leased or managed complies with the ADA, but instead should recommend that the parties hire a licensed architect or engineer to analyze compliance and/or estimate the cost to bring a building up to ADA standards.

Licensees involved in the sale, lease, or management of commercial or multifamily property must understand the differences between the accessibility requirements of the ADA and the Fair Housing Act. (See also the section above entitled "Failure to Design.") Parts of housing that are also "public accommodations" are subject to the ADA retrofit obligations discussed above, whereas housing built before the 1991 effective date of fair housing act accessibility mandates has no retrofit requirements.

A licensee who lists or sells apartment complexes should be aware that in ADA enforcement, the U.S. Department of Justice considers a rental or sales office in any housing facility to be a "public accommodation" subject to ADA requirements. Similarly, common areas, such as pools and clubhouses, are also "public accommodations" if they are rented out to the public, while common areas used only by residents and their guests are not. Some types of housing can be considered both "housing" under the Fair Housing Act and a "public accommodation" under the ADA. These include nursing homes, dormitories, some kinds of assisted living facilities, and time shares. Apartment, townhome, or condominium communities that are rented out on a short-term basis, like a hotel, may also be considered "public accommodations" with ADA responsibilities. Under ADA Title II, "Nondiscrimination on the Basis of Disability in State and Local Governments," housing built by, on behalf of, or for the use of state or local government is subject to the ADA.

Licensees who manage commercial buildings and public accommodations act as the owner's representative and are responsible for the same level of non-discrimination and accommodation as in the management of their own real estate practices (described), as well as the differences and overlap between the ADA and the Fair Housing Act.

C. ADA Responsibilities in Real Estate Instruction

The ADA provides that any private entity that offers examinations or courses related to licensing for professional or trade purposes must do so in a place and manner accessible to persons with disabilities, or offer alternative accessible arrangements. Real estate schools have to provide auxiliary aids and services for persons with disabilities (such as Braille or large-print texts and deaf interpreters), unless they can prove that this fundamentally alters the course or results in an undue burden. Exams for persons with disabilities must be offered as often as other examinations and in equally convenient locations, and the kind of exam must accommodate an individual's disability and accurately reflect that individual's aptitude.

D. ADA Responsibilities as Employers

One of the main provisions of the ADA is the section on the employment and treatment of persons with disabilities. Title I of the ADA, "Equal Employment Opportunity for Individuals with Disabilities," makes it illegal to discriminate against persons with physical or mental disabilities. It also places an affirmative duty on employers to provide reasonable accommodations for persons with disabilities, including such things as removing physical barriers, possibly restructuring jobs or schedules, modifying equipment, and providing auxiliary aids. Although Title I applies only to firms with 15 or more employees, and thus may not affect some real estate firms, a separate Colorado statute applies to firms with even one employee.

From this brief description of the ADA, it is apparent that all licensees need to be aware of its provisions as they affect their facilities and practices. In addition, those selling or leasing commercial real estate of others need to make themselves aware of the requirements for new buildings or alterations, and about owner and lessee responsibilities in complying with the ADA. The above discussion is only a brief summary of pertinent portions of the ADA. Copies of the regulations may be obtained from the Department of Justice by calling (202) 514-0301 or the ADA InfoCenter at (719) 444-0252 or (800)949-4232.

VI. Colorado Fair Housing Act

A. Title 24, Article 34, C.R.S.

Colorado enacted prohibitions against housing discrimination in 1959, becoming the first state in the nation to pass anti-discrimination laws pertaining to private property. The Colorado act even preceded the federal Fair Housing Act and prohibited discrimination based on **race, creed, color, national origin, or ancestry** in the renting or purchasing of housing.

In 1969, **sex** was added as a protected class, and in 1973, **marital status**† and **religion** were included. Eleven years before Congress added handicap to the federal fair housing act, Colorado included **physical handicap** in 1977 as a class to be protected from discrimination. After the federal Fair Housing Amendments Act in 1988 added handicap and familial status, the Colorado act was amended to add **familial status** and to expand the definition of handicap to include both physical and mental. Subsequently, all Colorado statutes were amended to replace the word "handicap" with "disability." Sexual orientation was added as a basis in 2008.

(†Note: Discrimination is permitted on the basis of marital status if complying with local zoning ordinance.)

All the actions listed in Part III as "Illegal Practices Under Federal Law" are likewise illegal under the Colorado fair housing statute. In addition, Colorado law has additional prohibitions that, although probably illegal under federal law, are more clearly spelled out in the Colorado fair housing law. These include:

1. To honor, or attempt to honor, any discriminatory covenant;
2. To segregate or separate in housing;
3. To make any inquiry, reference, or record that is discriminatory;
4. To discharge, demote, or discriminate in matters of compensation against an agent or employee for obeying the law; and
5. To require any person accompanied by an assistance dog to pay a charge for that dog. (See § 24-34-803, C.R.S.)

B. Major Differences Between the Federal and Colorado Fair Housing Acts

1. Colorado law covers commercial and residential property, Title VIII covers residential only.
2. Colorado law prohibits marital status discrimination, Title VIII does not.
3. Colorado law protects both ancestry and national origin, whereas federal law lists national origin only. Colorado law makes it illegal to discriminate on the basis of both creed and religion, whereas the federal law lists religion only.

4. Colorado exemptions to property covered are different from the federal law. *Except for familial status*, Colorado law does not exempt single-family homes or owner-occupied dwellings of up to four units from coverage. Colorado law does exempt senior housing from the prohibition against discriminating on the basis of familial status. (See also "Exemptions," above.) Colorado law exempts rooms for rent in a single-family home occupied by the owner or lessee and, like federal law, non-commercial housing operated by private clubs or religious organizations.

5. Under both Title VIII and Colorado law, ALJs can levy fines and award actual damages, and courts may award both actual and punitive damages. However, there is a difference between federal and state courts on the power to levy fines. Federal courts can levy fines only for pattern and practice cases and violations of conciliation agreements. Colorado courts may levy fines for any violation of the law.

6. Colorado law specifically states that it is not illegal to restrict the sale, rental, or development of housing designed or intended for persons with disabilities.

   (Note: Although age is not a protected class under either federal or Colorado law, it is illegal to discriminate on the basis of age in Aspen, Crested Butte, Denver, and Telluride.)

The rest of this chapter presents Colorado housing discrimination law, as well as the law on "Discrimination in Places of Public Accommodation," "Discriminatory Advertising," and "Persons with Disabilities-Civil Rights," all of which affect the practice of real estate.

VII. Colorado Civil Rights Division—Commission—Procedures

§ 24-34-301, C.R.S. Definitions

As used in parts 3 to 7 of this article, unless the context otherwise requires:

(1.5) "Commission" means the Colorado civil rights commission created by section 24-34-303.

(1.6) "Commissioner" means a member of the Colorado civil rights commission.

(2) "Director" means the director of the Colorado civil rights division, which office is created by section 24-34-302.

(2.5) (a) "Disability" means a physical impairment which substantially limits one or more of a person's major life activities and includes a record of such an impairment and being regarded as having such an impairment.

(b) (I) On and after July 1, 1990, as to part 5 of this article, disability shall also include such a person who has a mental impairment, but such term does not include any person currently involved in the illegal use of or addiction to a controlled substance.

(II) On and after July 1, 1992, as to parts 4, 6, and 7 of this article, disability shall also include such a person who has a mental impairment.

(III) The term "mental impairment" as used in subparagraphs (I) and (U) of this paragraph (b) shall mean any mental or psychological disorder such as developmental disability, organic brain syndrome, mental illness, or specific learning disabilities.

(3) "Division" means the Colorado civil rights division, created by section 24-34-302.

(4) Deleted by amendment effective July 1, 1993.

(5) "Person" means one or more individuals, limited liability companies, partnerships, associations, corporations, legal representatives, trustees, receivers, or the state of Colorado, and all political subdivisions and agencies thereof.

(6) "Respondent" means any person, agency, organization, or other entity against whom a charge is filed pursuant to any of the provisions of parts 3 to 7 of this article.

(7) "Sexual orientation" means a person's orientation toward heterosexuality, homosexuality, bisexuality, or transgender status or another person's perception thereof.

VIII. Housing Practices

§ 24-34-501, C.R.S. Definitions

(1) "Aggrieved person" means any person who claims to have been injured by a discriminatory housing practice or believes that he will be injured by a discriminatory housing practice that is about to occur.

(1.5) "Discriminate" includes both segregate and separate.

(1.6) "Familial status" means one or more individuals, who have not attained eighteen years of age, being domiciled with a parent or another person having legal custody of or parental responsibilities for such individual or individuals or the designee of such parent or other persons having such custody or parental responsibilities with the written permission of such parent or other person. Familial status shall apply to any person who is pregnant or is in the process of securing legal custody of any individual who has not attained eighteen years of age.

(2) "Housing" means any building, structure, vacant land, or part thereof offered for sale, lease, rent, or transfer of ownership; except that "housing" does not include any room offered for rent or lease in a single-family dwelling maintained and occupied in part by the owner or lessee of said dwelling as his household.

(3) "Person" has the meaning ascribed to such term in section 24-34-301 (5) and includes any owner, lessee, proprietor, manager, employee, or any agent of a person; but, for purposes of this part 5, "person" does not include any private club not open to the public, which as an incident to its primary purpose or purposes provides lodgings that it owns or operates for other than a commercial purpose unless such club has the purpose of promoting discrimination in the matter of housing against any person because of disability, race, creed, color, religion, sex, sexual orientation, marital status, familial status, national origin, or ancestry.

(4) "Restrictive covenant" means any specification limiting the transfer, rental, or lease of any housing because of disability, race, creed, color, religion, sex, sexual orientation, marital status, familial status, national origin, or ancestry.

(5) "Transfer", as used in this part 5, shall not apply to transfer of property by will or by gift.

(6) "Unfair housing practices" means those practices specified in section 24-34-502.

§ 24-34-502, C.R.S. Unfair housing practices prohibited

(1) It shall be an unfair housing practice and unlawful and hereby prohibited:

(a) For any person to refuse to show, sell, transfer, rent, or lease, or to refuse to receive and transmit any bona fide offer to buy, sell, rent, or lease, or otherwise make unavailable or deny or withhold from any person such housing because of disability, race, creed, color, sex, sexual orientation, marital status, familial status, religion, national origin, or ancestry; to discriminate against any person because of disability, race, creed, color, sex, sexual orientation, marital status, familial status, religion, national origin, or ancestry in the terms, conditions, or privileges pertaining to any housing or the transfer, sale, rental, or lease thereof or in the furnishing of facilities or services in connection therewith; or to cause to be made any written or oral inquiry or record concerning the disability, race, creed, color, sex, sexual orientation, marital status, familial status, religion, national origin, or ancestry of a person seeking to purchase, rent, or lease any housing; however, nothing in this paragraph (a) shall be construed to require a dwelling to be made available to an individual whose tenancy would constitute a direct threat to the health or safety of other individuals or whose tenancy would result in substantial physical damage to the property of others;

(b) For any person to whom application is made for financial assistance for the acquisition, construction, rehabilitation, repair, or maintenance of any housing to make or cause to be made any written or oral inquiry concerning the disability, race, creed, color, sex, sexual orientation, marital status, familial status, religion, national origin, or ancestry of a person seeking such financial assistance or concerning the disability, race, creed, color, sex, sexual orientation, marital status, familial status, religion, national origin, or ancestry of prospective occupants or tenants of such housing, or to discriminate against any person because of the disability, race, creed, color, sex, sexual orientation, marital status, familial status, religion, national origin, or ancestry of such person or prospective occupants or tenants in the terms, conditions, or privileges relating to the obtaining or use of any such financial assistance;

(c) (I) For any person to include in any transfer, sale, rental, or lease of housing any restrictive covenants, but shall not include any person who, in good faith and in the usual course of business, delivers any document or copy of a document regarding the transfer, sale, rental, or lease of housing which includes any restrictive covenants which are based upon race or religion, or reference thereto; or

(II) For any person to honor or exercise or attempt to honor or exercise any restrictive covenant pertaining to housing;

(d) For any person to make, print, or publish or cause to be made, printed, or published any notice or advertisement relating to the sale, transfer, rental, or lease of any housing that indicates any preference, limitation, specification, or discrimination based on disability, race, creed, color, religion, sex, sexual orientation, marital status, familial status, national origin, or ancestry;

(e) For any person: To aid, abet, incite, compel, or coerce the doing of any act defined in this section as an unfair housing practice; to obstruct or prevent any person from complying with the provisions of this part 5 or any order issued with respect thereto; to attempt either directly or indirectly to commit any act defined in this section to be an unfair housing practice; or to discriminate against any person because such person has opposed any practice made an unfair housing practice by this part 5, because he has filed a charge with the commission, or because he has testified, assisted, or participated in any manner in an investigation, proceeding, or hearing conducted pursuant to parts 3 and 5 of this article; or to coerce, intimidate, threaten, or interfere with any person in the exercise or enjoyment of, or on account of his having exercised or enjoyed, or on account of his having aided or encouraged, any other person in the exercise of any right granted or protected by parts 3 and 5 of this article;

(f) For any person to discharge, demote, or discriminate in matters of compensation against any employee or agent because of said employee's or agent's obedience to the provisions of this part 5;

(g) For any person whose business includes residential real estate-related transactions, which transactions involve the making or purchasing of loans secured by residential real estate or the provisions of other financial assistance for purchasing, constructing, improving, repairing, or maintaining a dwelling or the selling, brokering, or appraising of residential real property, to discriminate against any person in making available such a transaction or in fixing the terms or conditions of such a transaction because of race, creed, color, religion, sex, sexual orientation, marital status, disability, familial status, or national origin or ancestry;

(h) For any person to deny another person access to or membership or participation in any multiple-listing service, real estate brokers' organization or other service, organization, or facility related to the business of selling or renting dwellings or to discriminate against such person in the terms or conditions of such access, membership, or participation on account of race, creed, color, religion, sex, sexual orientation, disability, marital status, familial status, or national origin or ancestry;

(i) For any person, for profit, to induce or attempt to induce any person to sell or rent any dwelling by representations regarding the entry or prospective entry into the neighborhood of a person or persons of a particular race, color, religion, sex, sexual orientation, disability, familial status, creed, national origin, or ancestry;

(j) For any person to represent to any other person that any dwelling is not available for inspection, sale, or rental, when such dwelling is in fact available, for the purpose of discriminating against another person on the basis of race, color, religion, sex, sexual orientation, disability, familial status, creed, national origin, or ancestry.

(2) The provisions of this section shall not apply to or prohibit compliance with local zoning ordinance provisions concerning residential restrictions on marital status.

(3) Nothing contained in this part 5 shall be construed to bar any religious or denominational institution or organization which is operated or supervised or controlled by or is operated in connection with a religious or denominational organization from limiting the sale, rental, or occupancy of dwellings which it owns or operates for other than a commercial purpose to persons of the same religion, or from giving preference to such persons, unless membership in such religion is restricted on account of race, color, or national origin, nor shall anything in this part 5 prohibit a private club not in fact open to the public which, as an incident to its primary purpose or purposes provided lodgings which it owns or operates for other than a commercial purpose, from limiting the rental or occupancy of such lodgings to its members or from giving preference to its members.

(4) Deleted

(5) Nothing in this section shall be construed to prevent or restrict the sale, lease, rental, transfer, or development of housing designed or intended for the use of persons with disabilities.

(6) Nothing in this part 5 shall prohibit a person engaged in the business of furnishing appraisals of real property from taking into consideration factors other than race, creed, color, religion, sex, sexual orientation, marital status, familial status, disability, religion, national origin, or ancestry.

(7) (a) Nothing in this section shall limit the applicability of any reasonable local, state, or federal restrictions regarding the maximum number of occupants permitted to occupy a dwelling. Nor shall any provision in this section regarding familial status apply with respect to housing for older persons.

(b) As used in this subsection (7), "housing for older persons" means housing provided under any state or federal program that the division determines is specifically designed and operated to assist older persons, or is intended for, and solely occupied by, persons sixty-two years of age or older, or is intended and operated for occupancy by at least one person fifty-five years of age or older per unit. In determining whether housing intended and operated for occupancy by one person fifty-five years of age or older per unit qualifies as housing for older persons under this subsection (7), the division shall require the following:

(I) That the housing facility or community publish and adhere to policies and procedures that demonstrate the intent required under this paragraph (b);

(II) That at least eighty percent of the units be occupied by at least one person fifty-five years of age or older; and

(III) That the housing facility or community comply with rules promulgated by the commission for verification of occupancy. Such rules shall:

(A) Provide for verification by reliable surveys and affidavits; and

(B) Include examples of the types of policies and procedures relevant to a determination of such compliance with the requirements of subparagraph (H) of this paragraph (b). Such surveys and affidavits shall be admissible in administrative and judicial proceedings for the purposes of verification of occupancy in accordance with this section.

(c) Housing shall not fail to meet the requirements for housing for older persons by reason of persons residing in such housing as of March 12, 1989, who do not meet the age requirements of paragraph (b) of this subsection (7), provided that the new occupants of such housing meet the age requirements of paragraph (b) of this subsection (7) or by reason of unoccupied units, provided that such units are reserved for occupancy by persons who meet the age requirements of paragraph (b) of this subsection (7).

(d) (I) A person shall not be held personally liable for monetary damages for a violation of this part 5 if such person reasonably relied, in good faith, on the application of the exemption available under this part 5 relating to housing for older persons.

(II) For purposes of this paragraph (d), a person may only show good faith reliance on the application of an exemption by showing that:

(A) Such person has no actual knowledge that the facility or community is not or will not be eligible for the exemption claimed; and

(B) The owner, operator, or other official representative of the facility or community has stated, formally, in writing, that the facility or community complies with the requirements of the exemption claimed.

(8) (a) With respect to "familial status", nothing in this part 5 shall apply to the following:

(I) Any single-family house sold or rented by an owner if such private individual owner does not own more than three such single-family houses at any one time. In the case of the sale of any such single-family house by a private individual owner not residing in such house at the time of such sale or who was not the most recent resident of such house prior to such sale, the exemption granted by this subsection (8) shall apply only with respect to one such sale within any twenty-four month period. Such bona fide private individual owner shall not own any interest in, nor shall there be owned or reserved on his behalf, under any express or voluntary agreement, title to or any right to all or a portion of the proceeds from the sale or rental of more than three such single-family houses at any one time. The sale or rental of any such single-family house shall be excepted from the application of this subsection (8) only if such house is sold or rented:

(A) Without the use in any manner of the sales or rental facilities or the sales or rental services of any real estate broker, agent, or salesman, or of such facilities or services of any person in the business of selling or renting dwellings, or of any employee or agent of any such broker, agent, salesman, or person; and

(B) Without the publication, posting, or mailing, after notice, of any advertisement or written notice in violation of this section; but nothing in this section shall prohibit the use of attorneys, escrow agents, abstractors, title companies, and other such professional assistance as necessary to perfect or transfer the title.

(II) Rooms or units in dwellings containing living quarters occupied or intended to be occupied by no more than four families living independently of each other, if the owner actually maintains and occupies one of such living quarters as his residence.

(b) For the purposes of paragraph (a) of this subsection (8), a person shall be deemed to be in the business of selling or renting dwellings if:

(I) He has, within the preceding twelve months, participated as principal in three or more transactions involving the sale or rental of any dwelling or any interest therein;

(II) He has, within the preceding twelve months, participated as agent, other than in the sale of his own personal residence in providing sales or rental facilities or sales or rental services in two or more transactions involving the sale or rental of any dwelling or any interest therein; or

(III) He is the owner of any dwelling designed or intended for occupancy by, or occupied by, five or more families.

(9) Repealed.

§ 24-34-502.2, C.R.S. Unfair or discriminatory housing practices against persons with disabilities prohibited

(1) It shall be an unfair or discriminatory housing practice and unlawful and hereby prohibited:

(a) For any person to discriminate in the sale or rental of, or to otherwise make unavailable or deny, a dwelling to any buyer or renter because of a disability of the buyer or renter, or of any person who will reside in the dwelling after it is sold, rented, or made available, or of any person associated with such buyer or renter.

(b) For any person to discriminate against another person in the terms, conditions, or privileges of sale or rental of a dwelling or in the provision of services or facilities in connection with such dwelling because of a disability of that person, of any person residing in or intending to reside in that dwelling after it is so sold, rented, or made available, or of any person associated with that person.

(2) For purposes of this section, "discrimination" includes, but is not limited to:

(a) A refusal to permit, at the expense of the person with a disability, reasonable modifications of existing premises occupied or to be occupied by such person if such modifications are necessary to afford such person full enjoyment of the premises; except that, in the case of a rental, the landlord may, where it is reasonable to do so, condition permission for a modification on the renter agreeing to restore the interior of the premises to the condition that existed before the modification, reasonable wear and tear excepted;

(b) A refusal to make reasonable accommodations in rules, policies, practices, or services when such accommodations may be necessary to afford such person equal opportunity to use and enjoy a dwelling; and

(c) In connection with the design and construction of covered multifamily dwellings for first occupancy after the date that is thirty months after the date of enactment of the federal "Fair Housing Amendments Act of 1988", a failure to design and construct those dwellings in such a manner that the public use and common use portions of such dwellings are readily accessible to and usable by persons with disabilities. At least one building entrance shall be on an accessible route unless it is impractical to do so because of the terrain or the unusual characteristics of the site. All doors designed to allow passage into and within all premises within such dwellings shall be sufficiently wide to allow passage by persons with disabilities in wheelchairs, and all premises within such dwellings shall contain the following features of adaptive design:

(I) Accessible routes into and through the dwellings;

(II) Light switches, electrical outlets, thermostats, and other environmental controls in accessible locations;

(III) Reinforcements in bathroom walls to allow later installation of grab bars; and

(IV) Usable kitchens and bathrooms such that an individual in a wheelchair can maneuver about the space.

(3) Compliance with the appropriate requirements of the American national standard for buildings and facilities providing accessibility and usability for persons with physical disabilities (commonly cited as ANSI All7.1) suffices to satisfy the requirements of paragraph (c) of subsection (2) of this section.

(4) As used in this section, "covered multifamily dwellings" means:

(a) Buildings consisting of four or more units if such buildings have one or more elevators; and

(b) Ground floor units in other buildings consisting of four or more units.

§ 24-34-503, C.R.S. Refusal to show housing

If the charge alleging an unfair housing practice relates to the refusal to show the housing involved, the commission, after proper investigations as set forth in section 24-34-306, may issue its order that the housing involved be shown to the person filing such charge, and, if the respondent refuses without good reason to comply therewith within three days, then the commission or any commissioner may file a petition pursuant to section 24-34-509. The district court shall hear such matters at the earliest possible time, and the court may waive the requirement of security for a petition filed under this section. If the district court finds that the denial to show is based upon an unfair housing practice, it shall order the respondent to immediately show said housing involved and also to make full disclosure concerning the sale, lease, or rental price and any other information being then given to the public.

§ 24-34-504, C.R.S. Time limits on filing of charges

(1) Any charge alleging a violation of this part 5 shall be filed with the commission pursuant to section 24-34-306 within one year after the alleged unfair housing practice occurred, or it shall be barred.

(2) A civil action filed by the attorney general under this section shall be commenced not later than eighteen months after the date of the occurrence or the termination of the alleged discriminatory housing practice.

(3) The director, not later than ten days after filing or identifying additional respondents, shall serve on the respondent a notice identifying the alleged discriminatory housing practice and advising such respondent of the procedural rights and obligations of respondents under this part 5, together with a copy of the original charge.

(4) The director shall commence an investigation of any charge filed pursuant to subsection (1) of this section within thirty days of such filing. Within one hundred days after the filing of the charge, the director shall determine, based on the facts, whether probable cause exists to believe that a discriminatory housing practice has occurred or is about to occur, unless it is impracticable to do so or the director has approved a conciliation agreement with respect to the charge. If the director is unable to complete the investigation within one hundred days after the filing of the charge, the director shall notify the parties of the reasons for not doing so.

(4.1) After a determination by the director that probable cause exists to believe that a discriminatory housing practice has occurred or is about to occur, the commission shall issue a notice and complaint as provided in section 24-34-306(4). After such notice and complaint is issued by the commission, the complainant, respondent, or any aggrieved person on whose behalf the charge was filed may elect to have the claims asserted in the charge decided in a civil action in lieu of an administrative hearing. Such election shall be made in writing within twenty days after receipt of the notice and complaint issued by the Commission. The Commission shall provide notice of the election to all other parties to whom the notice and complaint relates.

(4.2) If all parties agree to have the charges decided in an administrative hearing, the Commission shall hold a hearing as provided in section 24-34-306. If any party elects a civil action, the Commission shall authorize the attorney general to commence and maintain a civil action in the appropriate state district court to obtain relief with respect to the discriminatory housing practice or practices alleged in the notice and complaint.

(4.3) Final administrative disposition of a charge filed pursuant to this section shall be made within one year of the date the charge was filed, unless it is impractical to do so. If the Commission is unable to do so, the Commission shall notify the complainant and the respondent, in writing, of the reasons that such disposition is impractical.

(5) Repealed.

§ 24-34-505, C.R.S. Charges by other persons

Any person whose employees, agents, employers, or principals, or some of them, refuse or threaten to refuse to comply with the provisions of this part 5 may make, sign, and file with the commission a verified written charge in duplicate asking the commission for assistance to obtain their compliance by conciliation or other remedial action.

§ 24-34-505.5, C.R.S. Enforcement by the attorney general

(1) Upon timely application, the attorney general may intervene in any civil action filed as provided in section 24-34-505.6 if the attorney general certifies that the case is of general public importance. Upon such intervention, the attorney general may obtain such relief as would be available to the director under section 24-34-306 in a civil action to which such section applies.

(2) Whenever the attorney general has probable cause to believe that any person or group of persons is engaged in a pattern or practice of resistance to the full enjoyment of any of the rights granted by this title or that any group of persons has been denied any of the rights granted by this title and such denial raises an issue of general public importance, the attorney general may commence a civil action in any appropriate district court.

(3) The attorney general may commence a civil action in any appropriate district court for appropriate relief with respect to:

 (a) A discriminatory housing practice referred to the attorney general by the commission under section 24-34-306; or

 (b) Breach of a conciliation agreement referred to the attorney general by the director under section 23-34-506.5.

(4) The attorney general, on behalf of the commission, division, or other party at whose request a subpoena is issued under this section, may enforce such subpoena in appropriate proceedings in the district court for the district in which the person to whom the subpoena was addressed resides, was served, or transacts business.

(5) Repealed.

§ 24-34-505.6, C.R.S. Enforcement by private persons

(1) Notwithstanding any provision of this article to the contrary, an aggrieved person may commence a civil action in an appropriate United States district court or state district court not later than two years after the occurrence or the termination of an alleged discriminatory housing practice or the breach of a conciliation agreement entered into under this title, whichever occurs last, to obtain appropriate relief with respect to such discriminatory housing practice or breach.

(2) The computation of such two-year period shall not include any time during which an administrative proceeding under this title was pending with respect to a complaint or charge under this title based upon such discriminatory housing practice. This subsection (2) does not apply to actions arising from a breach of a conciliation agreement.

(3) Notwithstanding any provision of this article to the contrary, an aggrieved person may commence a civil action under this section whether or not a charge has been filed under section 24-34-306 and without regard to the status of any such charge, but if the director or local agency has obtained a conciliation agreement with the consent of an aggrieved person, no action may be filed under this section by such aggrieved person with respect to the alleged discriminatory housing practice which forms the basis for such charge except for the purpose of enforcing the terms of such an agreement.

(4) An aggrieved person may not commence a civil action under this section with respect to an alleged discriminatory housing practice which forms the basis of a complaint issued by the Commission if an administrative law judge has commenced a hearing on the record under this title with respect to such complaint.

(5) At the request of the aggrieved person, the court may appoint an attorney in accordance with section 23-34-307 (9.5).

(6) In addition to the relief which may be granted in accordance with section 24-34-508, the following relief is available:

   (a) If the court finds that a discriminatory housing practice has occurred or is about to occur, the court may award to the plaintiff actual and punitive damages or may grant as relief, as the court deems appropriate, any permanent or temporary injunction, temporary restraining order, or other order, including an order enjoining the defendant from engaging in such practice or ordering such affirmative action as may be appropriate.

   (b) The court, in its discretion, may allow the prevailing party reasonable attorney fees and costs.

   (c) Relief granted under this section shall not affect any contract, sale, encumbrance, or lease consummated before the granting of such relief and involving a bona fide purchaser, encumbrancer, or tenant, without actual notice of the filing of a charge with the commission or a civil action under this section.

(7) Repealed.

§ 24-34-506, C.R.S. Probable cause

In making his determination on probable cause under the provisions of section 24-34-306 (2), the director shall find that probable cause exists if upon all the facts and circumstances a person of reasonable prudence and caution would be warranted in a belief that an unfair housing practice has been committed.

§ 24-34-506.5, C.R.S. Conciliation agreements

(1) A conciliation agreement arising out of a conciliation shall be an agreement between the respondent and the charging party, and shall be subject to approval by the director.

(2) A conciliation agreement may provide for binding arbitration of the dispute arising from the charge. Any such arbitration that results from a conciliation agreement may award appropriate relief, including monetary relief.

(3) Each conciliation agreement shall be made public unless the charging party and respondent otherwise agree and the director determines that disclosure is not required to further the purposes of this section.

(4) Whenever the director has reasonable cause to believe that a respondent has breached a conciliation agreement, the director shall refer the matter to the attorney general with a

recommendation that a civil action be filed under section 24-34-505.5 for the enforcement of such agreement.

(5) Repealed.

§ 24-34-507, C.R.S. Injunctive relief

(1) After the filing of a charge pursuant to section 24-34-306 (1), the commission or a commissioner designated by the commission for that purpose may file in the name of the people of the state of Colorado through the attorney general of the state a petition in the district court of the county in which the alleged unfair housing practice occurred, or of any county in which a respondent resides, seeking appropriate injunctive relief against such respondent, including orders or decrees restraining and enjoining him from selling, renting, or otherwise making unavailable to the complainant any housing with respect to which the complaint is made, pending the final determination of proceedings before the commission under this part 5.

(2) Any injunctive relief granted pursuant to this section shall expire by its terms within such time after entry, not to exceed sixty days, as the court fixes, unless within the time so fixed the order, for good cause shown, is extended for a like period or unless the party against whom the order is directed consents that it may be extended for a longer period. An affidavit of notice of hearing shall forthwith be filed in the office of the clerk of the district court wherein said petition is filed. The procedure for seeking and granting said injunctive relief, including temporary restraining orders and preliminary injunctions, shall be the procedure provided in the rules of civil procedure for courts of record in Colorado pertaining to injunctions, and the district court has power to grant such temporary relief or restraining orders as it deems just and proper.

(3) The district court shall hear matters on the request for an injunction at the earliest possible time.

(4) If, upon all the evidence at a hearing, the commission finds that a respondent has not engaged in any such unfair housing practice, the district court which has granted temporary relief or restraining orders pursuant to the petition filed by the commission or commissioner shall dismiss such temporary relief or restraining orders. Any person filing a charge alleging an unfair housing practice with the commission, a commissioner, or the attorney general may not thereafter apply, by himself or by his attorney-at-law, directly to the district court for any further relief under this part 5, except as provided in sections 24-34-307.

§ 24-34-508, C.R.S. Relief authorized

(1) In addition to the relief authorized by section 24-34-306 (9), the commission may order a respondent who has been found to have engaged in an unfair housing practice:

(a) To rehire, reinstate, and provide back pay to any employee or agent discriminated against because of his obedience to this part 5;

(b) To take affirmative action regarding the granting of financial assistance as provided in section 24-34-502 (1) (b) or the showing, sale, transfer, rental, or lease of housing;

(c) To make reports as to the manner of compliance with the order of the commission;

(d) To reimburse any person who was discriminated against for any fee charged in violation of this part 5 and for any actual expenses incurred in obtaining comparable alternate housing, as well as any storage or moving charges associated with obtaining such housing.

(e) To award actual damages suffered by the aggrieved person and injunctive or other equitable relief;

(f) To assess a civil penalty against the respondent in the following amounts:

(I) Not to exceed ten thousand dollars if the respondent has not been adjudged to have committed any prior discriminatory housing practice;

(II) Not to exceed twenty-five thousand dollars if the respondent has been adjudged to have committed any other discriminatory housing practice during the five-year period ending on the date of the filing of the charge;

(III) Not to exceed fifty thousand dollars if the respondent has been adjudged to have committed two or more discriminatory housing practices during the seven-year period ending on the date of the filing of the charge.

§ 24-34-509, C.R.S. Enforcement sought by commission

Upon refusal by a person to comply with any order, order pursuant to section 24-34-503, or regulation of the commission, the commission has authority to immediately seek an order in the district court enforcing the order or regulation of the commission. Such proceedings shall be brought in the district court in the county in which the respondent resides or transacts business.

§ 24-34-510, C.R.S. Repealed

IX. Discrimination in Places of Public Accommodation

§ 24-34-601, C.R.S. Discrimination in places of public accommodation

(1) As used in this part 6, "place of public accommodation" means any place of business engaged in any sales to the public and any place offering services, facilities, privileges, advantages, or accommodations to the public, including but not limited to any business offering wholesale or retail sales to the public; any place to eat, drink, sleep, or rest, or any combination thereof; any sporting or recreational area and facility; any public transportation facility; a barber shop, bathhouse, swimming pool, bath, steam or massage parlor, gymnasium, or other establishment conducted to serve the health, appearance, or physical condition of a person; a campsite or trailer camp; a dispensary, clinic, hospital, convalescent home, or other institution for the sick, ailing, aged, or infirm; a mortuary, undertaking parlor, or cemetery; an educational institution; or any public building, park, arena, theater, hall, auditorium, museum, library, exhibit, or public facility of any kind whether indoor or outdoor. "Place of public accommodation" shall not include a church, synagogue, mosque, or other place that is principally used for religious purposes.

(2) It is a discriminatory practice and unlawful for a person, directly or indirectly, to refuse, withhold from, or deny to an individual or a group, because of disability, race, creed, color, sex, sexual orientation, marital status, national origin, or ancestry, the full and equal enjoyment of the goods, services, facilities, privileges, advantages, or accommodations of a place of public accommodation or, directly or indirectly, to publish, circulate, issue, display, post, or mail any written, electronic, or printed communication, notice, or advertisement that indicates that the full and equal enjoyment of the goods, services, facilities, privileges, advantages, or accommodations of a place of public accommodation will be refused, withheld from, or denied an individual or that an individual's patronage or presence at a place of public accommodation is unwelcome, objectionable, unacceptable, or undesirable because of disability, race, creed, color, sex, sexual orientation, marital status, national origin, or ancestry.

(2.5) It is a discriminatory practice and unlawful for any person to discriminate against any individual or group because such person or group has opposed any practice made a discriminatory practice by this part 6 or because such person or group has made a charge, testified, assisted, or participated in any manner in an investigation, proceeding, or hearing conducted pursuant to this part 6.

(3) Notwithstanding any other provisions of this section, it is not a discriminatory practice for a person to restrict admission to a place of public accommodation to individuals of one sex if

such restriction has a bona fide relationship to the goods, services, facilities, privileges, advantages, or accommodations of such place of public accommodation.

§ 24-34-602, C.R.S. Penalty and civil liability

(1) Any person who violates section 24-34-601 shall be fined not less than fifty dollars nor more than five hundred dollars for each violation. A person aggrieved by the violation of section 24-34-601 shall bring an action in any court of competent jurisdiction in the county where the violation occurred. Upon finding a violation, the court shall order the defendant to pay the fine to the aggrieved party.

(2) For each violation of section 24-34-601, the person is guilty of a misdemeanor and, upon conviction thereof, shall be punished by a fine of not less than ten dollars nor more than three hundred dollars, or by imprisonment in the county jail for not more than one year, or by both such fine and imprisonment.

(3) A judgment in favor of the party aggrieved or punishment upon an indictment or information shall be a bar to either prosecution, respectively; but the relief provided by this section shall be an alternative to that authorized by section 24-34-306 (9), and a person who seeks redress under this section shall not be permitted to seek relief from the commission.

§ 24-34-603, C.R.S. Jurisdiction of county court – trial

The county court in the county where the offense is committed shall have jurisdiction in all civil actions brought under this part 6 to recover damages to the extent of the jurisdiction of the county court to recover a money demand in other actions. Either party shall have the right to have the cause tried by jury and to appeal from the judgment of the court in the same manner as in other civil suits.

§ 24-34-604, C.R.S. Time limits on filing of charges

Any charge filed with the commission alleging a violation of this part 6 shall be filed pursuant to section 24-34-306 within sixty days after the alleged discriminatory act occurred, and if not so filed, it shall be barred.

§ 24-34-605, C.R.S. Relief authorized

In addition to the relief authorized by section 24-34-306 (9), the commission may order a respondent who has been found to have engaged in a discriminatory practice as defined in this part 6 to rehire, reinstate, and provide back pay to any employee or agent discriminated against because of his obedience to this part 6; to make reports as to the manner of compliance with the order of the commission; and to take affirmative action, including the posting of notices setting forth the substantive rights of the public under this part 6.

X. Discriminatory Advertising

§ 24-34-701, C.R.S. Publishing of discriminative matter forbidden

No person, being the owner, lessee, proprietor, manager, superintendent, agent, or employee of any place of public accommodation, resort, or amusement, directly or indirectly, by himself or herself or through another person shall publish, issue, circulate, send, distribute, give away, or display in any way, manner, or shape or by any means or method, except as provided in this section, any communication, paper, poster, folder, manuscript, book, pamphlet, writing, print, letter, notice, or advertisement of any kind, nature, or description that is intended or calculated to discriminate or actually discriminates against any disability, race, creed, color, sex, sexual orientation, marital status, national origin, or ancestry or against any of the members thereof in the matter of furnishing or neglecting or refusing to furnish to them or any one of them any lodging, housing, schooling, or tuition or any accommodation, right, privilege, advantage, or convenience offered to or enjoyed by the general public or which states that any of the accommodations, rights, privileges, advantages, or conveniences of any such place of public accommodation, resort, or amusement shall or will be refused, withheld from, or denied to any person or class of persons on account of disability, race, creed, color, sex, sexual orientation, marital status, national origin, or ancestry or that the patronage, custom, presence, frequenting, dwelling, staying, or lodging at such place by any person or class of persons belonging to or purporting to be of any particular disability, race, creed, color, sex, sexual orientation, marital status, national origin, or ancestry is unwelcome or objectionable or not acceptable, desired, or solicited.

§ 24-34-702, C.R.S. Presumptive evidence

The production of any such communication, paper, poster, folder, manuscript, book, pamphlet, writing, print, letter, notice, or advertisement, purporting to relate to any such place and to be made by any person being the owner, lessee, proprietor, agent, superintendent, manager, or employee thereof, shall be presumptive evidence in any civil or criminal action or prosecution that the same was authorized by such person.

§ 24-34-703, C.R.S. Places of public accommodation, resort, or amusement

A place of public accommodation, resort, or amusement, within the meaning of this part 7, shall be deemed to include any inn, tavern, or hotel, whether conducted for the entertainment, housing, or lodging of transient guest or for the benefit, use, or accommodation of those seeking health, recreation, or rest, and any restaurant, eating house, public conveyance on land or water, bathhouse, barber shop, theater, and music hall.

§ 24-34-704, C.R.S. Exceptions

Nothing in this part 7 shall be construed to prohibit the mailing of a private communication in writing sent in response to specific written inquiry.

§ 24-34-705, C.R.S. Penalty

Any person who violates any of the provisions of this part 7 or who aids in, incites, causes, or brings about in whole or in part the violation of any such provisions, for each and every violation thereof, is guilty of a misdemeanor and, upon conviction thereof, shall be punished by a fine of not less than one hundred dollars nor more than five hundred dollars, or by imprisonment in the county jail for not less than thirty days nor more than ninety days, or by both such fine and imprisonment. The penalty provided by this section shall be an alternative to the relief authorized by section 24-34-306(9), and a person who seeks redress under this section shall not be permitted to seek relief from the commission.

§ 24-34-706, C.R.S. Time limits on filing of charges

Any charge filed with the commission alleging a violation of this part 7 shall be filed pursuant to section 24-34-306 within sixty days after the alleged discriminatory act occurred, and, if not so filed, it shall be barred.

§ 24-34-707, C.R.S. Relief authorized

In addition to the relief authorization by section 24-34-306(9), the commission may order a respondent who has been found to have violated any of the provisions of this part 7 to rehire, reinstate, and provide back pay to any employee or agent discriminated against because of his obedience to this part 7; to make reports as to the manner of compliance with the order of the commission; and to take affirmative action, including the posting of notices setting forth the substantive rights of the public under this part 7.

XI. Persons with Disabilities – Civil Rights

§ 24-34-801, C.R.S. Legislative declaration

(1) The general assembly hereby declares that it is the policy of the state:

(a) To encourage and enable the blind, the visually impaired, the deaf, the partially deaf, and the otherwise physically disabled to participate fully in the social and economic life of the state and to engage in remunerative employment;

(b) That the blind, the visually impaired, the deaf, the partially deaf, and the otherwise physically disabled shall be employed in the state service, the service of the political subdivisions of the state, the public schools, and in all other employment supported in whole or in part by public funds on the same terms and conditions as the able-bodied unless it is shown that the particular disability prevents the performance of the work involved;

(c) That the blind, the visually impaired, the deaf, the partially deaf, and the otherwise physically disabled have the same rights as the able-bodied to the full and free use of the streets, highways, sidewalks, walkways, public buildings, public facilities, and other public places;

(d) That the blind, the visually impaired, the deaf, the partially deaf, and the otherwise physically disabled are entitled to full and equal housing and full and equal accommodations, advantages, facilities, and privileges of all common carriers, airplanes, motor vehicles, railroad trains, motor buses, streetcars, boats, or any other public conveyances or modes of transportation, hotels, motels, lodging places, places of public accommodation, amusement, or resort, and other places to which the general public is invited, including restaurants and grocery stores; and that the blind, the visually impaired, the deaf, the partially deaf, or the otherwise physically disabled person assume the liability for any injury that he or she might sustain which is attributable solely to causes originating with the nature of the particular disability involved and otherwise subject only to the conditions and limitations established by law and applicable alike to all persons.

(e) Repealed

(f) Repealed

(2) Repealed

§ 24-34-802, C.R.S. Violation – penalty

Any person, firm, or corporation or the agent of any person, firm, or corporation that denies or interferes with the rights and the admittance to or enjoyment of the public facilities enumerated in section 24-34-801 (1) (b) to (1) (d) is guilty of a misdemeanor and, upon conviction thereof, shall be punished by a fine of not more than one hundred dollars, or by imprisonment in the county jail for not more than sixty days, or by both such fine and imprisonment.

§ 24-34-803, C.R.S. Rights of persons with assistance dogs

(1) A person with a disability, including but not limited to a blind, visually impaired, deaf, hard of hearing, or otherwise physically disabled person, has the right to be accompanied by an assistance dog specially trained for that person without being required to pay an extra charge for the assistance dog in or on the following places and subject to the conditions and limitations established by law and applicable alike to all persons:

(a) Public streets, highways, walkways, public buildings, public facilities and services, and other public places;

(b) Any place of public accommodation or on public transportation services; and

(c) Any housing accommodation offered for rent, lease, or other compensation in the state.

(2) A trainer of an assistance dog has the right to be accompanied by an assistance dog that the trainer is in the process of training without being required to pay an extra charge for the assistance dog in or on the following places:

(a) Public streets, highways, walkways, public buildings, public facilities and services, and other public places; and

(b) Any place of public accommodation or on public transportation services.

(3) (a) An employer shall not refuse to permit an employee with a disability who is accompanied by an assistance dog to keep the employee's assistance dog with the employee at all times in the place of employment. An employer shall not fail or refuse to hire or discharge any person with a disability, or otherwise discriminate against any person with a disability, with respect to compensation, terms, conditions, or privileges of employment because that person with a disability is accompanied by an assistance dog specially trained for that person.

(b) An employer shall make reasonable accommodation to make the workplace accessible for an otherwise qualified person with a disability who is an applicant or employee and who is accompanied by an assistance dog specially trained for that person unless the employer can show that the accommodation would impose an undue hardship on the employer's business. For purposes of this paragraph (b), "undue hardship" means an action requiring significant difficulty or expense.

(4) The owner or the person having control or custody of an assistance dog or an assistance dog in training is liable for any damage to persons, premises, or facilities, including places of housing accommodation and places of employment, caused by that person's assistance dog or assistance dog in training. The person having control or custody of an assistance dog or an assistance dog in training shall be subject to the provisions of section 18-9-204.5, C.R.S.

(5) A person with a disability is exempt from any state or local licensing fees or charges that might otherwise apply in connection with owning an assistance dog.

(6) The mere presence of an assistance dog in a place of public accommodation shall not be grounds for any violation of a sanitary standard, rule, or regulation promulgated pursuant to section 25-4-1604, C.R.S.

(7) As used in this section, unless the context otherwise requires:

(a) "Assistance dog" means a dog that has been or is being trained as a guide dog, hearing dog, or service dog. Such terms are further defined as follows:

(I) "Guide dog" means a dog that has been or is being specially trained to aid a particular blind or visually impaired person.

(II) "Hearing dog" means a dog that has been or is being specially trained to aid a particular deaf or hearing-impaired person.

(III) "Service dog" means a dog that has been or is being specially trained to aid a particular physically disabled person with a physical disability other than sight or hearing impairment.

(b) "Disability" has the same meaning as set forth in the federal "Americans with Disabilities Act of 1990", 42 U.S.C. sec. 12102 (2), as amended.

(c) "Employer" has the same meaning as set forth in the federal "Americans with Disabilities Act of 1990", 42 U.S.C. sec. 12111 (5), as amended.

(d) "Housing accommodations" means any real property or portion thereof that is used or occupied, or intended, arranged, or designed to be used or occupied, as the home, residence, or sleeping place of one or more persons but does not include any single family residence, the occupants of which rent, lease, or furnish for compensation not more than one room in that residence.

(e) "Places of public accommodation" means the following categories of private entities:

(I) Inns, hotels, motels, or other places of lodging, except establishments located within buildings actually occupied by the proprietor as the proprietor's residence containing five or fewer rooms for rent or hire;

(II) Restaurants, bars, cafeterias, lunchrooms, lunch counters, soda fountains, casinos, or other establishments serving food or drink, including any such facility located on the premises of any retail establishment;

(III) Gasoline stations or garages;

(IV) Motion picture theaters, theaters, billiard or pool halls, concert halls, stadiums, sports arenas, amusement or recreation parks, or other places of exhibition or entertainment;

(V) Auditoriums, convention centers, lecture halls, or other places of public gathering;

(VI) Bakeries, grocery stores, clothing stores, hardware stores, shopping centers, or other sales or retail establishments;

(VII) Laundromats, dry cleaners, banks, barber shops, beauty shops, travel services, shoe repair services, funeral parlors, offices of accountants or attorneys-at-law, pharmacies, insurance offices, professional offices of health care providers, hospitals, or other service establishments;

(VIII) Terminals, depots, or other stations used for specified purposes;

(IX) Museums, libraries, galleries, or other places of public display or collection;

(X) Parks, zoos, or other places of recreation;

(XI) Nursery, elementary, secondary, undergraduate, or graduate schools or other places of education;

(XII) Day care centers, senior citizen centers, homeless shelters, food banks, adoption agencies, or other social service center establishments;

(XIII) Gymnasiums, health spas, bowling alleys, golf courses, or other places of exercise or recreation;

(XIV) Any other establishment or place to which the public is invited; or

(XV) Any establishment physically containing or contained within any of the establishments described in this paragraph (e) that holds itself out as serving patrons of the described establishment.

(f) "Public transportation services" means common carriers of passengers or any other means of public conveyance or modes of transportation, including but not limited to airplanes, motor vehicles, railroad trains, motorbuses, streetcars, boats, or taxis.

(g) "Trainer of an assistance dog" means a person who is qualified to train dogs to serve as assistance dogs.

§ 24-34-804, C.R.S. Violations – penalties

(1) It is unlawful for any person, firm, corporation, or agent of any person, firm, or corporation to:

(a) Withhold, deny, deprive, or attempt to withhold, deny, or deprive any person with a disability or trainer of any of the rights or privileges secured in section 24-34-803;

(b) Threaten to interfere with any of the rights of persons with disabilities or trainers secured in section 24-34-803;

(c) Punish or attempt to punish any person with a disability or trainer for exercising or attempting to exercise any right or privilege secured by section 24-34-803; or

(d) Interfere with, injure, or harm, or cause another dog to interfere with, injure, or harm, an assistance dog.

(2) Any person who violates any provision of subsection (1) of this section commits a class 3 misdemeanor and shall be punished as provided in section 18-1-106, C.R.S.

(3) (a) Any person who violates any provision of subsection (1) of this section shall be liable to the person with a disability or trainer whose rights were affected for actual damages for economic loss, to be recovered in a civil action in a court in the county where the infringement of rights occurred or where the defendant resides.

(b) In any action commenced pursuant to this subsection (3), a court may award costs and reasonable attorney fees.

(4) Nothing in this section is intended to interfere with remedies or relief that any person might be entitled to pursuant to parts 3 to 7 of this article.

Chapter 25:
Related Real Estate Law

An * in the left margin indicates a change in the statute, rule, or text since the last publication of the manual.

I. Real Estate Settlement Procedures Act (RESPA)

12 U.S.C. § 2607. Prohibition against kickbacks and unearned fees

(a) **Business referrals.**

No person shall give and no person shall accept any fee, kickback, or thing of value pursuant to any agreement or understanding, oral or otherwise, that business incident to or a part of a real estate settlement service involving a federally related mortgage loan shall be referred to any person.

(b) **Splitting charges.**

No person shall give and no person shall accept any portion, split, or percentage of any charge made or received for the rendering of a real estate settlement service in connection with a transaction involving a federally related mortgage loan other than for services actually performed.

(c) **Fees, salaries, compensation, or other payments.**

Nothing in this section shall be construed as prohibiting (1) the payment of a fee (A) to attorneys at law for services actually rendered or (B) by a title company to its duly appointed agent for services actually performed in the issuance of a policy of title insurance or (C) by a lender to its duly appointed agent for services actually performed in the making of a loan, (2) the payment to any person of a bona fide salary or compensation or other payment for goods or facilities actually furnished or for services actually performed, (3) payments pursuant to cooperative brokerage and referral arrangements or agreements between real estate agents and brokers, (4) affiliated business arrangements so long as (A) a disclosure is made of the existence of such an arrangement to the person being referred and, in connection with such referral, such person is provided a written estimate of the charge or range of charges generally made by the provider to which the person is referred (i) in the case of a face-to-face referral or a referral made in writing or by electronic media, at or before the time of the referral (and compliance with this requirement in such case may be evidenced by a notation in a written, electronic, or similar system of records maintained in the regular course of business); (ii) in the case of a referral made by telephone, within 3 business days after the referral by telephone, (and in such case an abbreviated verbal disclosure of the existence of the arrangement and the fact that a written disclosure will be provided within 3 business days shall be made to the person being referred during the telephone referral); or (iii) in the case of a referral by a lender (including a referral by a lender to an affiliated lender), at the time the estimates required under 5(c) [12 USCS 2604(c)] are provided (notwithstanding clause (i) or (ii)); and any required written receipt of such disclosure (without regard to the manner of the disclosure under clause (i), (ii), or (iii)) may be obtained at the closing or settlement (except that a person making a face-to-face referral who provides the written disclosure at or before the time of the referral shall attempt to obtain any required written receipt of such disclosure at such time and if the person being referred chooses not to acknowledge the receipt of the disclosure at that time, that fact shall be noted in the written, electronic, or similar system of records maintained in the regular course of business by the person making the referral), (B) such person is not required to use any particular provider of settlement services, and (C) the only thing of value that is received from the arrangement, other than the payments permitted under this subsection, is a return on the ownership interest or franchise relationship, or (5) such other payments or classes of payments or other transfers as are specified in regulations prescribed by the Secretary, after consultation with the Attorney General, the Secretary of Veterans Affairs, the Federal Home Loan Bank Board, the Federal Deposit Insurance Corporation, the Board of Governors of the Federal Reserve System, and the Secretary of Agriculture. For purposes of the preceding sentence, the following shall not be considered a violation of clause (4)(B): (i) any arrangement that requires a buyer, borrower, or seller to pay for the services of an attorney, credit reporting agency, or real estate appraiser chosen by the lender to represent the lender's interest in a real estate transaction, or (ii) any arrangement where an attorney or law firm represents a client in a real estate transaction and issues or arranges for the issuance of a policy of title insurance in the transaction directly as agent or through a separate corporate title insurance agency that may be established by that attorney or law firm and operated as an adjunct to his or its law practice.

(d) Penalties for violations; joint and several liability; treble damages; actions for injunction by Secretary and by State officials; costs and attorney fees; construction of State laws.

(1) Any person or persons who violate the provisions of this section shall be fined not more than $10,000 or imprisoned for not more than one year, or both.

(2) Any person or persons who violate the prohibitions or limitations of this section shall be jointly and severally liable to the person or persons charged for the settlement service involved in the violation in an amount equal to three times the amount of any charge paid for such settlement service.

(3) No person or persons shall be liable for a violation of the provisions of subsection (c)(4)(A) of this section if such person or persons proves by a preponderance of the evidence that such violation was not intentional and resulted from a bona fide error notwithstanding maintenance of procedures that are reasonably adapted to avoid such error.

(4) The Secretary, the Attorney General of any State, or the insurance commissioner of any State may bring an action to enjoin violations of this section.

(5) In any private action brought pursuant to this subsection, the court may award to the prevailing party the court costs of the action together with reasonable attorneys fees.

(6) No provision of State law or regulation that imposes more stringent limitations on affiliated business arrangements shall be construed as being inconsistent with this section.

II. Manufactured Homes

§ 24-32-3311, C.R.S. Certification of factory-built residential and nonresidential structures

(1) (a) Factory-built structures manufactured, substantially altered or repaired, sold, or offered for sale within this state after the effective date of the rules promulgated pursuant to this part 33 shall bear an insignia of approval issued by the division and affixed by the division or an authorized quality assurance representative.

(b) Rented or leased factory-built structures that are occupied on or after March 1, 2009, shall bear an insignia of approval issued by the division and affixed by the division or an authorized quality assurance representative.

(2) Factory-built residential structures manufactured prior to March 31, 1971, shall be subject to any existing state or local government rules relating to the manufacture of the structures.

(3) Factory-built nonresidential structures manufactured prior to June 31, 1991, shall be subject to any existing state or local government rules relating to the manufacture of the structures.

(4) A factory-built structure bearing an insignia of approval issued by the division and affixed by the division or an authorized quality assurance representative pursuant to this part 33 shall be deemed to be designed and constructed in compliance with the requirements of all ordinances or rules, including those for electrical and plumbing, enacted or adopted by the state or by any local government that are applicable to the manufacture of factory-built structures to the extent that the design and construction relates to work performed in a factory or work that is completed at a site using components shipped with the factory-built structure as reflected in the approved plans for the factory-built structure. The determination by the board of the scope of such approval is final.

(5) No factory-built structures bearing an insignia of approval issued by the division and affixed by the division or an authorized quality assurance representative pursuant to this part 33 shall be in any way modified contrary to the rules promulgated pursuant to section 24-32-3305 prior to or during installation unless approval is first obtained from the division.

(6) All work at a site that is unrelated to the installation of a factory-built structure or components shipped with the factory-built structure, including additions, modifications, and repairs to a factory-built structure, shall be subject to applicable local government rules.

§ 24-32-3323, C.R.S.. Sellers of manufactured homes – registration

(1) Any person whose business involves the sale of manufactured homes shall be required to register with the division before engaging in the business of selling manufactured homes in Colorado. Any person who wishes to engage in the business of selling manufactured homes in Colorado through advertising or sales activities but who does not operate a retail location in Colorado shall obtain a single registration. Any person who wishes to engage in the business of selling manufactured homes from one or more retail locations in Colorado shall obtain a separate registration for each location. The registration requirements of this section shall not apply to any individual who, for a salary, commission, or compensation of any kind, is employed directly or indirectly by any registered manufactured home seller to sell or negotiate for the sale of manufactured homes.

(2) An application for a registration or renewal required by this section shall be submitted on a form provided by the division and shall be verified by a declaration signed, under penalty of perjury, by a principal of the manufactured home seller. The application shall contain, in addition to such other information regarding the conduct of the manufactured home seller's business as the division may reasonably require, the name, address, and position of each principal of the manufactured home seller and each person who exercises management responsibilities as part of the manufactured home seller's business activities. The application shall also contain the address and telephone number of each retail location operated by the applicant as well as the location and account number of the separate fiduciary account required by section 24-32-3324 (1). The declaration shall specify the date and location of the signing, and the division shall preserve the application and declaration and make them available for public inspection.

(3) A registration issued pursuant to subsection (2) of this section shall be valid for one year after the date of issuance. The amount of the registration fee shall be no more than two hundred dollars. If, after issuance of a registration, any of the required information submitted with the application for the registration pursuant to subsection (2) of this section becomes inaccurate, a principal of the manufactured home seller shall notify the division in writing of the inaccuracy within thirty days and provide the division with accurate updated information.

(4) For purposes of this section, a person is not engaged in the business of selling manufactured homes if the person:

(a) Is a natural person acting personally in selling a manufactured home owned or leased by the person;

(b) Sells a manufactured home in the course of engaging in activities that are subject to the provisions of article 61 of title 12, C.R.S., or activities that would be subject to the provisions but for a specific exemption set forth in article 61 of title 12, C.R.S.;

(c) Sells a manufactured home for salvage or nonresidential use; or

(d) Directly or indirectly sells, in any calendar year, three or fewer previously occupied manufactured homes that are owned by a manufactured home park owner and are located within one or more manufactured home parks in Colorado.

§ 24-32-3325, C.R.S. Contract for sale of manufactured home – requirements

(1) A seller who is required to register with the division pursuant to section 24-32-3323 shall make the following disclosures in any contract for the sale of a manufactured home:

(a) That the buyer may have no legal right to rescind the contract absent delinquent delivery of the manufactured home or the existence of a specific right of recission set forth in the contract;

(b) That the seller has a separate fiduciary account for the escrow of home sale down payments pending delivery of the manufactured home and a letter of credit, certificate of deposit, or surety bond filed with the division for the repayment of home sale down payments pending delivery of manufactured homes;

(c) That an aggrieved person may file a complaint for a refund of a down payment held in escrow by a seller of manufactured homes against the seller with the attorney general or with the district attorney for the district in which the sale occurs; and

(d) That an aggrieved person may bring a civil action pursuant to the provisions of the "Colorado Consumer Protection Act", article 1 of title 6, C.R.S., to remedy violations of manufactured home seller requirements in this part 33.

(2) A contract for the sale of a manufactured home by a person who is required to register with the division pursuant to section 24-32-3323 shall contain the following provisions:

(a) A date certain for the delivery of the manufactured home or a listing of specified delivery preconditions that must occur before a date certain for delivery can be determined; and

(b) A statement that if delivery of the manufactured home is delayed by more than sixty days after the delivery date specified in the contract of sale or by more than sixty days after the delivery preconditions set forth in the contract of sale have been met if no date certain for delivery has been set, the seller will either refund the manufactured home sale down payment or provide a reasonable per diem living expense to the buyer for the days between the delivery date specified in the contract or the sixty-first day after the delivery preconditions set forth in the contract have been met, whichever is applicable, and the actual date of delivery, unless the delay in delivery is unavoidable or caused by the buyer.

§ 24-32-3326, C.R.S. Unlawful manufactured home sale practices

(1) Any person who is required to register with the division pursuant to section 24-32-3323 engages in an unlawful manufactured home sale practice when the person:

(a) Fails to comply with the registration requirements of section 24-32-3323;

(b) Fails to comply with the escrow and bonding requirements of section 24-32-3324;

(c) Fails to include in any contract for the sale of a manufactured home any of the disclosures or contract provisions required by section 24-32-3325; or

(d) Fails to refund a manufactured home down payment or provide a reasonable per diem living expense in violation of the contractual provisions required by section 24-32-3325 (2) (b).

III. Mobile Home Park Act

§ 38-12-200.1. C.R.S. Short Title

This part 2 shall be known and may be cited as the "Mobile Home Park Act".

§ 38-12-200.2, C.R.S. Legislative declaration

The general assembly hereby declares that the purpose of this part 2 is to establish the relationship between the owner of a mobile home park and the owner of a mobile home situated in such park.

§ 38-12-201, C.R.S. Application of part 2

(1) This part 2 shall apply only to manufactured homes as defined in section 42-1-102 (106) (b), C.R.S.

(2) Repealed.

§ 38-12-201.3, C.R.S. Legislative declaration – increased availability of mobile home parks

The general assembly hereby finds and declares that mobile homes, manufactured housing, and factory-built housing are important and effective ways to meet Colorado's affordable housing needs. The general assembly further finds and declares that, because of the unique aspects of mobile homes and mobile home park ownership, there is a need to protect mobile home owners from eviction with short notice so as to prevent mobile home owners from losing their shelter as well as any equity in their mobile homes. The general assembly encourages local governments to allow and protect mobile home parks in their jurisdictions and to enact plans to increase the number of mobile home parks in their jurisdictions. The general assembly further encourages local governments to provide incentives to mobile home park owners to attract additional mobile home parks and to increase the viability of current parks.

§ 38-12-201.5, C.R.S. Definitions

As used in this part 2, unless the context otherwise requires:

(1) "Home owner" means any person or family of such person owning a mobile home that is subject to a tenancy in a mobile home park under a rental agreement.

(1.5) "Management" or "landlord" means the owner or person responsible for operating and managing a mobile home park or an agent, employee, or representative authorized to act on said management's behalf in connection with matters relating to tenancy in the park.

(2) "Mobile home" means a single-family dwelling built on a permanent chassis designed for long-term residential occupancy and containing complete electrical, plumbing, and sanitary facilities and designed to be installed in a permanent or semipermanent manner with or without a permanent foundation, which is capable of being drawn over public highways as a unit, or in sections by special permit, or a manufactured home as defined in section 38-29-102 (6) if the manufactured home is situated in a mobile home park.

(3) "Mobile home park" or "park" means a parcel of land used for the continuous accommodation of five or more occupied mobile homes and operated for the pecuniary benefit of the owner of the parcel of land, his agents, lessees, or assignees. Mobile home park does not include mobile home subdivisions or property zoned for manufactured home subdivisions.

(4) "Mobile home space", "space", "mobile home lot" or "lot" means a parcel of land within a mobile home park designated by the management to accommodate one mobile home and its accessory buildings and to which the required sewer and utility connections are provided by the mobile home park.

(5) "Premises" means a mobile home park and existing facilities and appurtenances therein, including furniture and utilities where applicable, and grounds, areas, and existing facilities held out for the use of home owners generally or the use of which is promised to the home owner.

(6) "Rent" means any money or other consideration to be paid to the management for the right of use, possession, and occupation of the premises.

(7) "Rental agreement" means an agreement, written or implied by law, between the management and the home owner establishing the terms and conditions of a tenancy, including reasonable rules and regulations promulgated by the park management. A lease is a rental agreement.

(8) Repealed.

(9) "Tenancy" means the rights of a home owner to use a space or lot within a park on which to locate, maintain, and occupy a mobile home, lot improvements, and accessory structures for human habitation, including the use of services and facilities of the park.

§ 38-12-202, C.R.S. Tenancy – notice to quit

(1) (a) No tenancy or other lease or rental occupancy of space in a mobile home park shall commence without a written lease or rental agreement, and no tenancy in a mobile home park shall be terminated until a notice to quit has been served. Said notice to quit shall be in writing and in the form specified in section 13-40-107(2), C.R.S. The property description required in section 13-40-107(2), C.R.S., shall be deemed legally sufficient if it states:

(I) The name of the landlord or the mobile home park;

(II) The mailing address of the property;

(III) The location or space number upon which the mobile home is situate; and

(IV) The county in which the mobile home is situate.

(b) Service of the notice to quit shall be as specified in section 13-40-108, C.R.S. Service by posting shall be deemed legally sufficient within the meaning of section 13-40-108, C.R.S., if the notice is affixed to the main entrance of the mobile home.

(c) (I) Except as otherwise provided in subparagraph (II) of this paragraph (c), the home owner shall be given a period of not less than sixty days to remove any mobile home from the premises from the date the notice is served or posted. In those situations where a mobile home is being leased to, or occupied by, persons other than its owner and in a manner contrary to the rules and regulations of the landlord, then in that event, the tenancy may be terminated by the landlord upon giving a thirty-day notice rather than said sixty-day notice.

(II) If the tenancy is terminated on grounds specified in section 38-12-203 (1) (f), the home owner shall be given a period of not less than ten days to remove any mobile home from the premises from the date the notice is served or posted.

(2) No lease shall contain any provision by which the home owner waives his or her rights under this part 2, and any such waiver shall be deemed contrary to public policy and shall be unenforceable and void. In those situations where a mobile home is being leased to, or occupied by, persons other than its owner and in a manner contrary to the rules and regulations of the landlord, then, in that event, the tenancy may be terminated by the landlord upon giving a thirty-day notice rather than said sixty-day notice.

(3) The landlord or management of a mobile home park shall specify, in the notice required by this section, the reason for the termination, as described in section 38-12-203, of any tenancy in such mobile home park. If the tenancy is being terminated based on the mobile home or mobile home lot being out of compliance with the rules and regulations adopted pursuant to section 38-12-203 (l)(c), the notice required by this section shall include a statement advising the home

owner that the home owner has a right to cure the noncompliance within thirty days of the date of service or posting of the notice to quit. The thirty-day period to cure any noncompliance set forth in this subsection (3) run concurrently with the sixty -day period to remove a mobile home from the premises as set forth in paragraphs (c) of subsection (1) and subsection (2) of this section. Acceptance of rent by the landlord or management of a mobile home park during the thirty-day right to cure period set forth in section 38-12-203 (1) (c) shall not constitute a waiver of the landlord's right to terminate the tenancy for any noncompliance set forth in section 38-12-203 (1) (c).

§ 38-12-202.5, C.R.S. Action for termination

(1) The action for termination shall be commenced in the manner described in section 13-40-110, C.R.S. The property description shall be deemed legally sufficient and within the meaning of section 13-40-110, C.R.S., if it states:

 (a) The name of the landlord or the mobile home park;

 (b) The mailing address of the property;

 (c) The location or space number upon which the mobile home is situate; and

 (d) The county in which the mobile home is situate.

(2) Service of summons shall be as specified in section 13-40-112, C.R.S. Service by posting shall be deemed legally sufficient within the meaning of section 13-40-112, C.R.S., if the summons is affixed to the main entrance of the mobile home.

(3) Jurisdiction of courts in cases of forcible entry, forcible detainer, or unlawful detainer shall be as specified in section 13-40-109, C.R.S.. Trial on the issue of possession shall be timely as specified in section 13-40-114, C.R.S., with no delay allowed for the determination of other issues or claims which may be severed at the discretion of the trial court.

(4) After commencement of the action and before judgment, any person not already a party to the action who is discovered to have a property interest in the mobile home shall be allowed to enter into a stipulation with the landlord and be bound thereby.

§ 38-12-203, C.R.S. Reasons for terminations

(1) A tenancy shall be terminated pursuant to this part 2 only for one or more of the following reasons:

 (a) Failure of the home owner to comply with local ordinances and state laws and regulations relating to mobile homes and mobile home lots;

 (b) Conduct of the home owner, on the mobile home park premises, which constitutes an annoyance to other home owners or interference with park management;

 (c) Failure of the home owner to comply with written rules and regulations of the mobile home park either established by the management in the rental agreement at the inception of the tenancy, amended subsequently thereto with the consent of the home owner, or amended subsequently thereto without the consent of the home owner on sixty days' written notice if the amended rules and regulations are reasonable; except that the home owner shall have thirty days from the date of service or posting of the notice to quit set forth in section 38-12-202 (3) to cure any noncompliance on the mobile home or mobile home lot before an action for termination may be commenced, except if local ordinances, state laws and regulations, park rules and regulations, or emergency, health, or safety situations require immediate compliance. If a home owner was in violation or noncompliance pursuant to this paragraph (c) and was given notice and a right to cure such noncompliance and within a twelve-month period from the date of service of the notice is in noncompliance of the same rule or regulation and is given notice of the second noncompliance, there shall be no right to cure the second noncompliance.

Regulations applicable to recreational facilities may be amended at the reasonable discretion of the management. For purposes of this paragraph (c), when the mobile home is owned by a person other than the owner of the mobile home park, the mobile home is a separate unit of ownership, and regulations that are adopted subsequent to the unit location in the park without the consent of the home owner and that place restrictions or requirements on that separate unit are prima facie unreasonable. Nothing in this paragraph (c) shall prohibit a mobile home park owner from requiring compliance with current park unit regulations at the time of sale or transfer of the mobile home to a new owner. Transfer under this paragraph (c) shall not include transfer to a co-owner pursuant to death or divorce or to a new co-owner pursuant to marriage.

(d) (I) Condemnation or change of use of the mobile home park. When the owner of a mobile home park is formally notified by a notice of intent to acquire pursuant to section 38-1-121 (1) or other similar provision of law, or a complaint in a condemnation action from an appropriate governmental agency that the mobile home park, or any portion thereof, is to be acquired by the governmental agency or may be the subject of a condemnation proceeding, the landlord shall, within seventeen days, notify the home owners in writing of the terms of the notice of intent to acquire or complaint received by the landlord.

(II) In those cases where the landlord desires to change the use of the mobile home park and where such change of use would result in eviction of inhabited mobile homes, the landlord shall first give the owner of each mobile home subject to such eviction a written notice of the landlord's intent to evict not less than six months prior to such change of use of the land, notice to be mailed to each home owner.

(e) The making or causing to be made, with knowledge, of false or misleading statements on an application for tenancy;

(f) Conduct of the home owner or any lessee of the home owner or any guest, agent, invitee, or associate of the home owner or lessee of the home owner, that:

(I) Occurs on the mobile home park premises and unreasonably endangers the life of the landlord, any home owner or lessee of the mobile home park, any person living in the park, or any guest, agent, invitee, or associate of the home owner or lessee of the home owner;

(II) Occurs on the mobile home park premises and constitutes willful, wanton, or malicious damage to or destruction of property of the landlord, any home owner or lessee of the mobile home park, any person living in the park, or any guest, agent, invitee, or associate of the home owner or lessee of the home owner;

(III) Occurs on the mobile home park premises and constitutes a felony prohibited under article 3, 4, 6, 7, 9,10,12, or 18 of title 18, C.R.S.; or

(IV) Is the basis for a pending action to declare the mobile home or any of its contents a class 1 public nuisance under section 16-13-303, C.R.S.

(2) In an action pursuant to this part 2, the landlord shall have the burden of proving that the landlord complied with the relevant notice requirements and that the landlord provided the home owner with a statement of reasons for the termination. In addition to any other defenses a home owner may have, it shall be a defense that the landlord's allegations are false or that the reasons for termination are invalid.

§ 38-12-204, C.R.S. Non-payment of rent – notice required for rent increase

(1) Any tenancy or other estate at will or lease in a mobile home park may be terminated upon the landlord's written notice to the home owner requiring, in the alternative, payment of rent or the

removal of the home owner's unit from the premises, within a period of not less than five days after the date notice is served or posted, for failure to pay rent when due.

(2) Rent shall not be increased without sixty days' written notice to the homeowner. In addition to the amount and the effective date of the rent increase, such written notice shall include the name, address, and telephone number of the mobile home park management, if such management is a principal owner, or owner of the mobile home park and, if the owner is other than a natural person, the name, address, and telephone number of the owner's chief executive officer or managing partner; except that such ownership information need not be given if it was disclosed in the rental agreement made pursuant to section 38-12-213.

§ 38-12-204.3, C.R.S. Notice required for termination

(1) Where the tenancy of a mobile home owner is being terminated under section 38-12-202 or section 38-12-204, the landlord or mobile home park owner shall provide such mobile home owner with written notice as provided for in subsection (2) of this section. Service of such notice shall occur at the same time and in the same manner as service of:

(a) The notice to quit as provided in section 38-12-202(1); or

(b) The notice of nonpayment of rent as provided in section 38-12-204(1).

(2) The notice required under this section shall be in at least ten-point type and shall read as follows:

IMPORTANT NOTICE TO THE HOME OWNER:

This notice and the accompanying notice to quit/notice of nonpayment of rent are the first steps in the eviction process. Any dispute you may have regarding the grounds for eviction should be addressed with your landlord or the management of the mobile home park or in the courts if an eviction action is filed. Please be advised that the "Mobile Home Park Act", part 2 of article 12 of title 38, Colorado Revised Statutes, may provide you with legal protection:

NOTICE TO QUIT: The landlord or management of a mobile home park must serve to a home owner a notice to quit in order to terminate a home owner's tenancy. The notice must be in writing and must contain certain information, including:

- The grounds for the termination of the tenancy;
- Whether or not the home owner has a right to cure under the "Mobile Home Park Act"; and
- That the home owner has a right to mediation pursuant to section 38-12-216, Colorado Revised Statutes, of the "Mobile Home Park Act"

NOTICE OF NONPAYMENT OF RENT: The landlord or management of a mobile home park must serve to a home owner a notice of nonpayment of rent in order to terminate a home owner's tenancy. The notice must be in writing and must require that the home owner either make payment of rent and any applicable fees due and owing or remove the owner's unit from the premises, within a period of not less than five days after the date the notice is served or posted, for failure to pay rent when due.

CURE PERIODS: If the home owner has a right to cure under the "Mobile Home Park Act", the landlord or management of a mobile home park cannot terminate a home owner's tenancy without first providing the home owner with a time period to cure the noncompliance. "Cure" refers to a home owner remedying, fixing, or otherwise correcting the situation or problem that caused the tenancy to be terminated pursuant to sections 38-12-202, 38-12-203, or 38-12-204, Colorado Revised Statutes.

COMMENCEMENT OF LEGAL ACTION TO TERMINATE THE TENANCY: After the last day of the notice period, a legal action may be commenced to take possession of the space leased by the home owner. In order to evict a home owner, the landlord or management of the mobile home park must prove:

- The landlord or management complied with the notice requirements of the "Mobile Home Park Act";
- The landlord or management provided the home owner with a statement of reasons for termination of the tenancy; and
- The reasons for termination of the tenancy are true and valid under the "Mobile Home Park Act".

A home owner must appear in court to defend against an eviction action. If the court rules in favor of the landlord or management of the mobile home park, the home owner will have not less than 48 hours from the time of the ruling to remove the mobile home and to vacate the premises. If a tenancy is being terminated pursuant to section 38-12-203 (1) (f), Colorado Revised Statutes, the home owner shall have not less than 48 hours from the time of the ruling to remove the home and vacate the premises. In all other circumstances, if the home owner wishes to extend such period beyond 48 hours but not more than thirty days from the date of the ruling, the home owner shall prepay to the landlord an amount equal to any total amount declared by the court to be due to the landlord, as well as a pro rata share of rent for each day following the court's ruling that the mobile home owner will remain on the premises. All prepayments shall be paid by certified check, by cashier's check, or by wire transfer and shall be paid no later than 48 hours after the court ruling.

§ 38-12-205, C.R.S. Termination prohibited

A tenancy or other estate at will or lease in a mobile home park may not be terminated solely for the purpose of making the home owner's space in the park available for another mobile home or trailer coach.

§ 38-12-206, C.R.S. Home owner meetings – assembly in common areas

Home owners shall have the right to meet and establish a homeowners' association. Meetings of home owners or the homeowners' association relating to mobile home living and affairs in their park common area, community hall, or recreation hall, if such a facility or similar facility exists, shall not be subject to prohibition by the park management if the common area or hall is reserved according to the park rules and such meetings are held at reasonable hours and when the facility is not otherwise in use; except that no such meetings shall be held in the streets or thoroughfares of the mobile home park.

§ 38-12-207, C.R.S. Security deposits – legal process

(1) The owner of a mobile home park or his agents may charge a security deposit not greater than the amount of one month's rent or two month's rent for multiwide units.

(2) Legal process, other than eviction, shall be used for the collection of utility charges and incidental service charges other than those provided by the rental agreement.

§ 38-12-208, C.R.S. Remedies

(1) (a) Upon granting judgment for possession by the landlord in a forcible entry and detainer action, the court shall immediately issue a writ of restitution which the landlord shall take to the sheriff. In addition, if a money judgment has been requested in the complaint and if service was accomplished by personal service, the court shall determine and enter

judgment for any amounts due to the landlord and shall calculate a pro rata daily rent amount that must be paid for the home to remain in the park. The court may rely upon information provided by the landlord or the landlord's attorney when determining the pro rata daily rent amount to be paid by the home owner. Upon receipt of the writ of restitution, the sheriff shall serve notice in accordance with the requirements of section 13-40-108, C.R.S., to the home owner of the court's decision and entry of judgment.

(b) The notice of judgment shall state that, at a specified time not less than forty-eight hours from the entry of judgment if a tenancy is being terminated pursuant to section 38-12-203 (1) (f) and, in all other instances, not less than forty-eight hours from the entry of judgment, which may be extended to not more than thirty days after the entry of judgment if the home owner has prepaid by certified check, by cashier's check, or by wire transfer no later than forty-eight hours after the court ruling to the landlord an amount equal to any total amount declared by the court to be due to the landlord, as well as a pro rata share of rent for each day following the court's ruling that the mobile home owner will remain on the premises, the sheriff will return to serve a writ of restitution and superintend the peaceful and orderly removal of the mobile home under that order of court. The notice of judgment shall also advise the home owner to prepare the mobile home for removal from the premises by removing the skirting, disconnecting utilities, attaching tires, and otherwise making the mobile home safe and ready for highway travel.

(c) Should the home owner fail to have the mobile home safe and ready for physical removal from the premises or should inclement weather or other unforeseen problems occur at the time specified in the notice of judgment, the landlord and the sheriff may, by written agreement, extend the time for the execution of the writ of restitution to allow time for the landlord to arrange to have the necessary work done or to permit the sheriff's execution of the writ of restitution at a time when weather or other conditions will make removal less hazardous to the mobile home.

(d) If the mobile home is not removed from the landlord's land on behalf of the mobile home owner within the time permitted by the writ of restitution, then the landlord and the sheriff shall have the right to take possession of the mobile home for the purposes of removal and storage. The liability of the landlord and the sheriff in such event shall be limited to gross negligence or willful and wanton disregard of the property rights of the home owner. The responsibility to prevent freezing and to prevent wind and weather damage to the mobile home lies exclusively with those persons who have a property interest in the mobile home; except that the landlord may take appropriate action to prevent freezing, to prevent wind and weather damage, and to prevent damage caused by vandals.

(e) (e) Reasonable removal and storage charges and the costs associated with preventing damage caused by wind, weather, or vandals can be paid by any party in interest. Those charges will run with the mobile home and whoever ultimately claims the mobile home will owe that sum to the person who paid it.

(2) (a) Prior to the issuance of said writ of restitution, the court shall make a finding of fact based upon evidence or statements of counsel that there is or is not a security agreement on the mobile home being subjected to the writ of restitution. A written statement on the mobile home owner's application for tenancy with the landlord that there is no security agreement on the mobile home shall be prima facie evidence of the nonexistence of such security agreement.

(b) In those cases where the court finds there is a security agreement on the mobile home subject to the writ of restitution and where that holder of the security agreement can be identified with reasonable certainty, then, upon receipt of the writ of restitution, the plaintiff shall promptly inform the holder of such security agreement as to the location of the mobile home, the name of the landlord who obtained the writ of restitution, and the time when the mobile home will be subject to removal by the sheriff and the landlord.

(3) The remedies provided in part 1 of this article and article 40 of title 13, C.R.S., except as inconsistent with this part 2, shall be applicable to this part 2.

§ 38-12-209, C.R.S. Entry fees prohibited – entry fee defined – security deposit – court costs

(1) The owner of a mobile home park, or the agent of such owner, shall neither pay to nor receive from an owner or a seller of a mobile home an entry fee of any type as a condition of tenancy in a mobile home park.

(2) As used in this section, "entry fee" means any fee paid to or received from an owner of a mobile home park or his agent except for:

(a) Rent;

(b) A security deposit against actual damages to the premises or to secure rental payments, which deposit shall not be greater than the amount allowed under this part 2. Subsequent to July 1, 1979, security deposits will remain the property of the home owner, and they shall be deposited into a separate trust account by the landlord to be administered by the landlord as a private trustee. For the purpose of preserving the corpus, the landlord will not commingle the trust funds with other money, but he is permitted to keep the interest and profits thereon as his compensation for administering the trust account.

(c) Fees charged by any state, county, town, or city governmental agency;

(d) Utilities;

(e) Incidental reasonable charges for services actually performed by the mobile home park owner or his agent and agreed to in writing by the home owner.

(3) The trial judge may award court costs and attorney fees in any court action brought pursuant to any provision of this part 2 to the prevailing party upon finding that the prevailing party undertook the court action and legal representation for a legally sufficient reason and not for a dilatory or unfounded cause.

(4) The management or the resident may bring a civil action for violation of the rental agreement or any provision of this part 2 in the appropriate court of the county in which the park is located. Either party may recover actual damages or, the court may in its discretion award such equitable relief as it deems necessary, including the enjoining of either party from further violations.

§ 38-12-210, C.R.S. Closed parks prohibited

(1) The owner of a mobile home park or his agent shall not require as a condition of tenancy in a mobile home park that the prospective home owner has purchased a mobile home from any particular seller or from any one of a particular group of sellers.

(2) Such owner or agent shall not give any special preference in renting to a prospective home owner who has purchased a mobile home from a particular seller.

(3) A seller of mobile homes shall not require as a condition of sale that a purchaser locate in a particular mobile home park or in any one of a particular group of mobile home parks.

(4) The owner or operator of a mobile home park shall treat all persons equally in renting or leasing available space. Notwithstanding the foregoing, nothing in this subsection (4) shall be construed to preclude owners and operators of mobile home parks from providing housing for older persons as defined in section 24-34-502 (7) (b), C.R.S.

§ 38-12-211, C.R.S. Selling fees prohibited

The owner of a mobile home park or his agent shall not require payment of any type of selling fee or transfer fee by either a home owner in the park wishing to sell his mobile home to another party or by any party wishing to buy a mobile home from a home owner in the park as a condition of tenancy in a mobile home park for the prospective buyer. This section shall in no way prevent the owner of a mobile home park or his agent from applying the normal park standards to prospective buyers before granting or denying tenancy or from charging a reasonable selling fee or transfer fee for service actually performed and agreed to in writing by the home owner. Nothing in this section shall be construed to affect the rent charged. The owner of a mobile home shall have the right to place a "for sale" sign on or in his mobile home. The size, placement, and character of such signs shall be subject to reasonable rules and regulations of the mobile home park.

§ 38-12-212, C.R.S. Certain types of landlord-seller agreements prohibited

A seller of mobile homes shall not pay or offer cash or other consideration to the owner of a mobile home park or his agent for the purpose of reserving spaces or otherwise inducing acceptance of one or more mobile homes in a mobile home park.

§ 38-12-212.3, C.R.S. Responsibilities of landlord – acts prohibited

(1) (a) Except as otherwise provided in this section, a landlord shall be responsible for and pay the cost of the maintenance and repair of:

(I) Any sewer lines, water lines, utility service lines, or related connections owned and provided by the landlord to the utility pedestal or pad space for a mobile home sited in the park; and

(II) Any accessory buildings or structures, including, but not limited to, sheds and carports, owned by the landlord and provided for the use of the residents; and.

(III) The premises as defined in section 38-12-201.5 (5).

(b) Any landlord who fails to maintain or repair the items delineated in paragraph (a) of this subsection (1) shall be responsible for and pay the cost of repairing any damage to a mobile home which results from such failure. The landlord shall ensure that all plumbing lines and connections owned and provided by the landlord to the utility pedestal or pad space for each mobile home in the mobile home park have plumbing that conformed to applicable law in effect at the time the plumbing was installed and that is maintained in good working order and running water and reasonable amounts of water at all times furnished to the utility pedestal or pad space and shall ensure that each pad space is connected to a sewage disposal system approved under applicable law; except that these conditions need not be met if:

(I) A mobile home is individually metered and the tenant occupying the mobile home fails to pay for water services;

(II) The local government in which the mobile home park is situated shuts off water service to a mobile home for any reason;

(III) Weather conditions present a likelihood that water pipes will freeze, water pipes to a mobile home are wrapped in heated pipe tape, and the utility company has shut off electrical service to a mobile home for any reason or the heat tape malfunctions for any reason; or

(IV) Running water is not available for any other reason outside the landlord's control.

(c) The landlord shall give a minimum of two days' notice to a mobile home owner if the water service will be disrupted for planned maintenance. The landlord shall attempt to give a reasonable amount of notice to home owners if water service is to be disrupted for any other reasons unless conditions are such that providing the notice would result in property damage, health, or safety concerns or when conditions otherwise require emergency repair.

(2) No landlord shall require a resident to assume the responsibilities outlined in subsection (1) of this section as a condition of tenancy in the mobile home park.

(3) Nothing in this section shall be construed as:

(a) Limiting the liability of a resident for the cost of repairing any damage caused by such resident to the landlord's property or other property located in the park; or

(b) Restricting a landlord or his agent or property manager from requiring a resident to comply with reasonable rules and regulations or terms of the rental agreement and any covenants binding upon the landlord or resident, including covenants running with the land which pertain to the clcanliness of such resident's lot and routine lawn and yard maintenance, exclusive of major landscaping projects.

§ 38-12-212.7, C.R.S.Landlord utilities account

(1) Whenever a landlord contracts with a utility for service to be provided to a resident, the usage of which is to be measured by a master meter or other composite measurement device, such landlord shall remit to the utility all moneys collected from each resident as payment for the resident's share of the charges for such utility service within forty-five days of the landlord's receipt of payment.

(2) If a landlord fails to timely remit utility moneys collected from residents as required by subsection (1) of this section, such utility may, after written demand therefor is served upon the landlord, require the landlord to deposit an amount equal to the average daily charge for the usage of such utility service for the preceding twelve months multiplied by the sum of ninety.

(3) Any utility which prevails in an action brought to enforce the provisions of this section shall be entitled to an award of its reasonable attorney fees and court costs.

§ 38-12-213, C.R.S. Rental agreement – disclosure of terms in writing

(1) The terms and conditions of a tenancy must be adequately disclosed in writing in a rental agreement by the management to any prospective home owner prior to the rental or occupancy of a mobile home space or lot. Said disclosures shall include:

(a) The term of the tenancy and the amount of rent therefor, subject to the requirements of subsection (4) of this section;

(b) The day rental payment is due and payable;

(c) The day when unpaid rent shall be considered in default;

(d) The rules and regulations of the park then in effect;

(e) The name and mailing address where a manager's decision can be appealed;

(f) All charges to the home owner other than rent.

(2) Said rental agreement shall be signed by both the management and the home owner, and each party shall receive a copy thereof.

(3) The management and the home owner may include in a rental agreement terms and conditions not prohibited by this part 2.

(4) The terms of tenancy shall be specified in a written rental agreement subject to the following conditions:

(a) The standard rental agreement shall be for a month-to-month tenancy.

(b) Upon written request by the home owner to the landlord, the landlord shall allow a rental agreement for a fixed tenancy of not less than one year if the home owner is current on all rent payments and is not in violation of the terms of the then-current rental agreement;

except that an initial rental agreement for a fixed tenancy may be for less than one year in order to ensure conformity with a standard anniversary date. A landlord shall not evict or otherwise penalize a home owner for requesting a rental agreement for a fixed period.

(c) A landlord may, in the landlord's discretion, allow a lease for a fixed period of longer than one year. In such circumstances, the requirements of paragraphs (a) and (b) of this subsection (4) shall not apply.

§ 38-12-214, C.R.S. Rules and regulations

(1) The management shall adopt written rules and regulations concerning all home owners' use and occupancy of the premises. Such rules and regulations are enforceable against a home owner only if:

(a) Their purpose is to promote the convenience, safety or welfare of the home owners, protect and preserve the premises from abusive use, or make a fair distribution of services and facilities held out for the home owners generally.

(b) They are reasonably related to the purpose for which they are adopted;

(c) They are not retaliatory or discriminatory in nature;

(d) They are sufficiently explicit in prohibition, direction, or limitation of the home owner's conduct to fairly inform him of what he must or must not do to comply.

§ 38-12-215, C.R.S. New developments and parks – rental of sites to dealers authorized

(1) The management of a new mobile home park or manufactured housing community development may require as a condition of leasing a mobile home site or manufactured home site for the first time such site is offered for lease that the prospective lessee has purchased a mobile home or manufactured home from a particular seller or from any one of a particular group of sellers.

(2) A licensed mobile home dealer or a manufactured home dealer may, by contract with the management of a new mobile home park or manufactured housing community development, be granted the exclusive right to first-time rental of one or more mobile home sites or manufactured home sites.

§ 38-12-216, C.R.S. Mediation, when permitted – court actions

(1) In any controversy between the management and a home owner of a mobile home park arising out of the provisions of this part 2, except for the non-payment of rent or in cases in which the health or safety of other home owners is in imminent danger, such controversy may be submitted to mediation by either party prior to the filing of a forcible entry and detainer lawsuit upon agreement of the parties.

(2) The agreement, if one is reached, shall be presented to the court as a stipulation. Either party to the mediation may terminate the mediation process at any time without prejudice.

(3) If either party subsequently violates the stipulation, the other party may apply immediately to the court for relief.

§ 38-12-217, C.R.S. Notice of sale of mobile home park – notice of change in use

(1) (a) The mobile home park owner shall notify the owners of all mobile homes in the park and the municipality in which the park is situated or, if none, the county in which the park is situated of his or her intent to change the use of the land comprising the park or to sell the park pursuant to paragraph (b) or (c) of this subsection (1), as applicable.

(b) If the mobile home park owner intends to sell the park, the notification shall be made only once for any particular contract to sell or trade and shall be by written notice mailed to each mobile home owner at the address shown on the rental agreement with the mobile home park owner at least ten days prior to the first scheduled closing for the sale or trade.

(c) If the mobile home park owner intends to change the use of the land comprising the mobile home park, the mobile home park owner shall give written notice to each mobile home owner at least one hundred eighty days before the change in use will occur. The mobile home park owner shall mail the written notice to each mobile home owner at the address shown on the rental agreement with the mobile home park owner.

(2) The provisions of paragraph (b) of subsection (1) of this section shall not apply to the sale of a mobile home park when such sale occurs between members of an immediate family, related business entities, members and managers of a limited liability company, shareholders, officers, and directors in a corporation, trustees and beneficiaries of a trust, or partners and limited liability partners in a partnership or limited liability partnership; except that such purchasers shall not change the use of the land comprising the mobile home park without complying with the notice provisions of this section. For purposes of this section, "immediate family" means persons related by blood or adoption.

§ 38-12-218, C.R.S. Mobile home owners – right to form a cooperative

One or more members of a homeowners' association may, at any time, form a cooperative for the purposes of offering to purchase or finance a mobile home park. A home owner shall be a member of the homeowners' association in order to participate in the cooperative, and participation in the cooperative shall be voluntary.

§ 38-12-219, C.R.S. Home owners' and landlords' rights

(1) Every home owner and landlord shall have the right to the following:

(a) Protection from abuse or disregard of state or local law by the landlord and home owners;

(b) Peaceful enjoyment of the home owner's mobile home space, free from unreasonable, arbitrary, or capricious rules and enforcement thereof; and

(c) Tenancy free from harassment or frivolous lawsuits by the landlord and homeowners.

§ 38-12-220, C.R.S. Private civil right of action

Any home owner who owns a home in a mobile home park where the landlord has violated any provision of this article shall have a private civil right of action against the landlord. In any such action, the home owner shall be entitled to actual economic damages and reasonable attorney fees and costs if the home owner is successful in the action.

§ 38-12-221, C.R.S. Access by counties and municipalities

Notwithstanding any other provision of law, upon a finding that the utilities in a park create a significant health or safety danger to park residents, the landlord of a mobile home park shall grant county or municipal officers or employees access to the mobile home park for the purposes of investigating or conducting a study related to such danger.

IV. Title to Manufactured Homes Act

§ 38-29-101, C.R.S. Short title

This part 1 shall be known and may be cited as the "Titles to Manufactured Homes Act".

§ 38-29-102, C.R.S. Definitions

As used in this article, unless the context otherwise requires:

(1) "Authorized agent" means the county clerk and recorder in each of the counties of the state, except in the city and county of Denver, and therein the manager of revenue, or such other official of the city and county of Denver as may be appointed by the mayor to perform functions related to the registration of manufactured homes, is the authorized agent.

(1.5) "Clerk and recorder" means the clerk and recorder of any county or city and county in the state of Colorado.

(2) "Dealer" means any person, firm, partnership, corporation, or association licensed under the laws of this state to engage in the business of buying, selling, exchanging, or otherwise trading in manufactured homes.

(3) "Department" means the department of revenue.

(4) "Director" means the executive director of the department of revenue.

(5) "Home" means any manufactured home as defined in subsection (6) of this section.

(6) "Manufactured home" means a preconstructed building unit or combination of preconstructed building units that is constructed in compliance with the federal manufactured home construction safety standard, as defined in section 24-32-3302(13), C.R.S. "Manufactured home" shall also include a mobile home, as defined in section 24-32-3302(24), C.R.S.

(7) "Manufacturer" means a person, firm, partnership, corporation, or association engaged in the manufacture of new manufactured homes.

(8) Repealed.

(9) "Mortgages" or "mortgage" or "chattel mortgage" means chattel mortgages, conditional sales contracts, or any other like instrument intended to operate as a mortgage or to create a lien on a manufactured home as security for an undertaking of the owner thereof or some other person; except that, as used in part 2 of this article, "mortgage" also includes mortgages, deeds of trust, and other liens on real property.

(10) "Owner" means any person, association of persons, firm, or corporation in whose name the title to a manufactured home is registered.

(11) "Person" means a natural person, association of persons, firm, partnership, or corporation.

(12) "State" includes the territories and the federal districts of the United States.

(13) "Verification of application form" means the form generated by an authorized agent upon receipt of a properly completed application for title submitted in accordance with section 38-29-107.

§ 38-29-103, C.R.S. Application

The provisions of this article shall apply to manufactured homes as defined in section 38-29-102(6).

§ 38-29-104, C.R.S. Administration

The director is charged with the duty of administering this part 1. For that purpose he or she is vested with the power to make such reasonable rules, prepare, prescribe, and require the use of such forms, and provide such procedures as may be reasonably necessary or essential to the efficient administration of this part 1.

§ 38-29-105, C.R.S. Authorized agents

The county clerk and recorder in each of the counties of the state, except in the city and county of Denver the manager of revenue or such other official of the city and county of Denver as may be appointed by the mayor to perform functions related to the registration of manufactured homes, is designated to be the authorized agent of the director and, under the direction of the director, is charged with the administration of the terms and provisions of this article and the rules that may from time to time be adopted for the administration thereof in the county in which such authorized agent holds office.

§ 38-29-106, C.R.S. Sale or transfer of manufactured home

Except as provided in section 38-29-114, no person shall sell or otherwise transfer a manufactured home to a purchaser or transferee thereof without delivering to such purchaser or transferee the certificate of title to such home, duly transferred in the manner prescribed in section 38-29-112, and no purchaser or transferee shall acquire any right, title, or interest in and to a manufactured home purchased by him unless and until he obtains from the transferor the certificate of title thereto, duly transferred to him in accordance with the provisions of this article.

§ 38-29-107, C.R.S. Applications for certificates of title

(1) In any case under the provisions of this article wherein a person who is entitled to a certificate of title to a manufactured home is required to make formal application to the director therefor, such applicant shall make application upon a form provided by the director in which appears a description of the manufactured home, including the manufacturer and model thereof, the manufacturer's number, the date on which said manufactured home was first sold by the dealer or manufacturer thereof to the initial user thereof, and a description of any other distinguishing mark, number, or symbol placed on said home by the manufacturer thereof for identification purposes, as may by rule be required by the director. Such application shall also show the applicant's source of title and the new or resale price of said manufactured home, whichever is applicable, paid by such applicant and shall include a description of all known mortgages and liens upon said manufactured home, each including the name of the legal holder thereof, the amount originally secured, the amount outstanding on the obligation secured at the time such application is made, the name of the county or city and county and state in which such mortgage or lien instrument is recorded or filed, and proof of the fact that no property taxes for previous years are due on such manufactured home. Such proof shall be a certificate of taxes, or an authentication of paid ad valorem taxes, issued by the county treasurer of the county in which the manufactured home is located. Such application shall be affirmed by a statement signed by the applicant and shall contain or be accompanied by a written declaration that it is made under the penalties of perjury in the second degree, as defined in section 18-8-503, C.R.S.

(2) In any case in which the manufactured home was affixed to the ground prior to July 1, 2008, and a certificate of permanent location was not filed and recorded, a person who is entitled to a certificate of title to a manufactured home shall make formal application to the director upon a form provided by the director. As part of the application, in addition to any information required pursuant to subsection (1) of this section, the applicant shall provide an affidavit of real property, a statement that the identification number has been verified pursuant to section 38-29-122 (3) (a), a certificate of removal, and a copy of all deeds recorded since the home was affixed to the ground. The director shall accept these documents as sufficient evidence of the applicant's proof of ownership of the manufactured home.

(3) (a) In any case in which the manufactured home was affixed to the ground after July 1, 2008, and a certificate of permanent location was filed and recorded, a person who is entitled to a certificate of title to a manufactured home shall make formal application to the director upon a form provided by the director. As part of the application, in addition to any information required pursuant to subsection (1) of this section, the applicant shall provide a copy of the recorded certificate of permanent location, a certificate of removal, a statement that the identification number has been verified pursuant to section 38-29-122 (3) (a), and a copy of all deeds recorded since the home was affixed to the ground. The director shall accept these documents as sufficient evidence of the applicant's proof of ownership of the manufactured home.

(b) In any case in which a manufactured home occupies real property subject to a long-term lease that has an express term of at least ten years, the manufactured home was affixed to the ground after July 1, 2008, and a certificate of permanent location was filed and recorded, a person who is entitled to a certificate of title to a manufactured home shall make formal application to the director upon a form provided by the director. As part of the application, in addition to any information required pursuant to subsection (1) of this section, the applicant shall provide a copy of the recorded certificate of permanent location, a statement that the identification number has been verified pursuant to section 38-29-122 (3) (a), and a copy of the recorded long-term lease. The director shall accept these documents as sufficient evidence of the applicant's proof of ownership of the manufactured home.

§ 38-29-108, C.R.S. Where application for certificates of title made – procedure

(1) An application for a certificate of title upon the sale, transfer, or movement into the state of any manufactured home that does not become real property pursuant to section 38-29-114(2) or section 38-29-117(6) shall be directed to the director and filed with the authorized agent of the county or city or city and county in which such manufactured home is to be located. Upon sale or transfer, an application for a certificate of title on a manufactured home shall be made within forty-five days of the receipt of a manufacturer's certificate or statement of origin or its equivalent. The authorized agents shall forward copies of all such applications to the county assessor. Any person, other than an individual selling a manufactured home used as his residence, who receives a commission or other valuable consideration for the transfer or sale of a manufactured home shall fulfill the application and notice requirements of this subsection (1).

(2) Repealed.

§ 38-29-109, C.R.S. Director may refuse certificate, when

The director shall use reasonable diligence in ascertaining whether the facts stated in any application and facts contained in other documents submitted to him with said application are true and, in appropriate cases, may require the applicant to furnish other and additional information regarding his ownership of the manufactured home and his right to have issued to him a certificate of title therefor. He may refuse to issue a certificate of title to such home if from his investigation he determines that the applicant is not entitled thereto.

§ 38-29-110, C.R.S. Certificates of title – contents

(1) All certificates of title to manufactured homes issued under the provisions of this article shall be subscribed by the director, or by some duly authorized officer or employee in the department in the name, place, and stead of the director, to which shall be affixed the seal of the department. Such certificate shall be mailed to the applicant, except as provided in section 38-29-111, and information of the facts therein appearing and concerning the issuance thereof shall be retained by the director and appropriately indexed and filed in his office. The certificate shall be in such form as the director may prescribe and shall contain, in addition to other information which he may by rule from time to time require, the manufacturer and model of the manufactured home for which said certificate is issued, the date on which said home therein described was first sold by the manufacturer or dealer to the initial user thereof, where such information is available, together with the serial number thereof, if any, and a description of such other marks or symbols as may be placed upon the home by the manufacturer thereof for identification purposes.

(2) Beginning January 1, 1983, there shall be issued a distinctive certificate of title identifying the home as a manufactured home. Any person in whose name a certificate of title to a mobile home, as defined in section 38-29-102(8), was issued prior to January 1, 1983, and which title is free and clear of all encumbrances, may apply to the director or one of his authorized agents

for a distinctive manufactured home certificate of title, accompanied by the fee required in section 38-29-138 to be paid for the issuance of a duplicate certificate of title; whereupon, a distinctive certificate of title shall be issued and disposition thereof made as required in this article.

§ 38-29-111, C.R.S. Disposition of certificates of title

(1) All certificates of title issued by the director shall be disposed of by him in the following manner:

(a) If it appears from the records in the director's office and from an examination of the certificate of title that the manufactured home therein described is not subject to a mortgage filed subsequent to August 1, 1949, or if such home is encumbered by a mortgage filed in any county of a state other than the state of Colorado, the certificate of title shall be delivered to the person who therein appears to be the owner of the home described, or such certificate shall be mailed to the owner thereof at his address as the same may appear in the application, the certificate of title, or other records in the director's office.

(b) If it appears from the records in the office of the director and from the certificate of title that the manufactured home therein described is subject to one or more mortgages filed subsequent to August 1, 1949, the director shall deliver the certificate of title issued by him to the mortgagee named therein or the holder thereof whose mortgage was first filed in the office of an authorized agent or shall mail the same to such mortgagee or holder at his address as the same appears in the certificate of title to said manufactured home.

§ 38-29-112, C.R.S. Certificate of title – transfer

(1) Upon the sale or transfer of a manufactured home for which a certificate of title has been issued, the person in whose name said certificate of title is registered, if he is other than a dealer, shall, in his own person or by his duly authorized agent or attorney, execute a formal transfer of the home described in the certificate, which transfer shall be affirmed by a statement signed by the person in whose name said certificate of title is registered or by his duly authorized agent or attorney and shall contain or be accompanied by a written declaration that it is made under the penalties of perjury in the second degree, as defined in section 18-8-503, C.R.S. The purchaser or transferee, within thirty days thereafter, shall present such certificate, duly transferred, together with his application for a new certificate of title to the director or one of his authorized agents, accompanied by the fee required in section 38-29-138 to be paid for the issuance of a new certificate of title; whereupon, a new certificate of title shall be issued and disposition thereof made as required in this article.

(1.3) Prior to the sale or transfer of a manufactured home for which a certificate of title has been issued, a holder of a mortgage that is the legal holder of certificate of title shall provide a copy of the certificate of title to any title insurance agent, title insurance company, or financial institution requesting information related to the payoff of the mortgage within fourteen days of the request.

(1.5) The purchaser or transferee of a manufactured home that becomes permanently affixed at an existing site or is transported to a site and is permanently affixed to the ground so that it is no longer capable of being drawn over the public highways shall present a certificate of transfer as required in subsection (1) of this section, together with his or her application for purging a manufactured home title and a certificate of permanent location, to the authorized agent of the county or city or city and county in which such manufactured home is located. The manufactured home shall become real property upon the filing and recording of the certificate of permanent location in accordance with section 38-29-202. The provisions of articles 30 to 44 of this title and of any other law of this state shall be applicable to manufactured homes that have become real property pursuant to this subsection (1.5) and to instruments creating, disposing of, or otherwise affecting such real property wherever such provisions would be applicable to estates, rights, and interests in land or to instruments creating, disposing of, or otherwise affecting estates, rights, and interest in land. The manufactured home for which a Colorado certificate of title has been issued shall continue to be valued and taxed separately from the land on which it sits until such time that the manufactured home becomes real property pursuant to this subsection (1.5).

(1.7) (a) If the conditions set forth in paragraph (b) of this subsection (1.7) are met, the legal holder of the certificate of title, within forty-five days, shall deliver to the title insurance agent who is the settlement agent related to the sale of the manufactured home the certificate of title or evidence that the holder has lost the certificate of title and requested a duplicate from the department. The holder shall mail or otherwise deliver the duplicate certificate of title to the title insurance agent within five business days of receipt from the department. Upon receipt from the holder, the title insurance agent shall present the certificate of title to the person in whose name the certificate of title is issued or his or her authorized agent or attorney to allow such person to execute a formal transfer as required by subsection (1) of this section.

(b) The provisions of paragraph (a) of this subsection (1.7) shall apply if:

(I) A title insurance agent acts as a settlement agent related to the sale of a manufactured home;

(II) The manufactured home that is sold is the subject of one or more mortgages that have been filed pursuant to section 38-29-128; and

(III) All holders of a mortgage on the manufactured home that have been filed pursuant to section 38-29-128 have been paid in full from the proceeds of the sale.

(2) Any person who violates any of the provisions of subsection (1) of this section is guilty of a misdemeanor and, upon conviction thereof, shall be punished by a fine of not less than two hundred fifty dollars nor more than one thousand dollars, or by imprisonment in the county jail for not less than ten days nor more than six months, or by both such fine and imprisonment.

(3) Any person who violates the provisions of subsection (1.3) or (1.7) of this section shall be liable to an injured person for any actual economic damages caused by the violation, to be recovered in a civil action in a court of competent jurisdiction.

§ 38-29-113, C.R.S. Lost certificates of title

(1) Upon the loss in the mails of any certificate of title to a manufactured home and accompanying papers which may be sent by an authorized agent to the director and upon an appropriate application of the owner or other person entitled to such certificate of title directed to the authorized agent therefor, such certificate of title may be reissued bearing such notations respecting existing mortgages on the home therein described as the records of the authorized agent and of the director may indicate are unreleased and constitute an encumbrance upon the home, which certificate of title shall be issued without charge.

(2) If the holder of any certificate of title loses, misplaces, or accidentally destroys any certificate of title to a manufactured home which he holds whether as the holder of a mortgage or as the owner of the home therein described, upon application therefor to the director, the director may issue a duplicate certificate of title as in other cases.

(3) Upon the issuance of any duplicate certificate of title as provided in this section, the director shall note thereon every mortgage shown to be unreleased and the lien of which is in force and effect as may be disclosed by the records in his office and shall dispose of such certificate as in other cases.

§ 38-29-114, C.R.S. New manufactured homes – bill of sale – certificate of title

(1) Upon the sale or transfer by a dealer of a new manufactured home, such dealer shall, upon the delivery thereof, make, execute, and deliver to the purchaser or transferee a good and sufficient bill of sale therefor, together with the manufacturer's certificate or statement of origin or the filing of a mortgage by the holder of such mortgage pursuant to section 38-29-128. Said bill of sale shall be affirmed by a statement signed by such dealer and shall contain or be accompanied by a written declaration that it is made under the penalties of perjury in the second degree, as defined in section 18-8-503, C.R.S., and the manufacturer's certificate or statement of origin shall be notarized. Both the bill of sale and the manufacturer's certificate or statement of origin shall be in such form as the director may prescribe, and shall contain, in addition to other information which he may by rule from time to time requirc, the manufacturer and model of the manufactured home so sold or transferred, the identification number placed upon the home by the manufacturer for identification purposes, the manufacturer's suggested retail price or the retail delivered price, and the date of the sale or transfer thereof, together with a description of any mortgage thereon given to secure the purchase price or any part thereof. Upon presentation of such a bill of sale to the director or one of his authorized agents, a new certificate of title for the home therein described shall be issued and disposition thereof made as in other cases. The transfer of a manufactured home which has been used by a dealer for the purpose of demonstration to prospective customers shall be made in accordance with the provisions of this section.

(2) Any purchaser of a new manufactured home that is transported to a site and permanently affixed to the ground so that it is no longer capable of being drawn over the public highways shall not be required to procure a certificate of title thereto as is otherwise required by this article. The purchaser shall file a certificate of permanent location along with the manufacturer's certificate or statement of origin or its equivalent with the clerk and recorder for the county or city and county in which the new manufactured home is permanently affixed to the ground. The manufactured home shall become real property upon the filing and recording of such documents in accordance with section 38-29-202. The provisions of articles 30 to 44 of this title and of any other law of this state shall be applicable to manufactured homes that have become real property pursuant to this subsection (2) and to instruments creating, disposing of, or otherwise affecting such real property wherever such provisions would be applicable to estates, rights, and interests in land or to instruments creating, disposing of, or otherwise affecting estates, rights, and interests in land.

§ 38-29-115, C.R.S. Sale to dealers – certificate need not issue

Upon the sale or transfer to a dealer of a manufactured home for which a Colorado certificate of title has been issued, formal transfer and delivery of the certificate of title thereto shall be made as in other cases; except that, so long as the home so sold or transferred remains in the dealer's inventory for sale and for no other purpose, such dealer shall not be required to procure the issuance of a new certificate of title thereto as is otherwise required in this article.

§ 38-29-116, C.R.S. Transfers by bequest, descent, law

Upon the transfer of ownership of a manufactured home by a bequest contained in the will of the person in whose name the certificate of title is registered, or upon the descent and distribution upon the death intestate of the owner of such home, or upon the transfer by operation of law, as in proceedings in bankruptcy, insolvency, replevin, attachment, execution, or other judicial sale, or whenever such manufactured home is sold to satisfy storage or repair charges or repossession is had upon default in the performance of the terms of any mortgage, the director or an authorized agent, upon the surrender of the certificate of title, if the same is available, or upon presentation of such proof of ownership of such home as the director may reasonably require and upon presentation of an application for a certificate of title, as required in section 38-29-107, a new certificate of title may thereupon issue to the person shown by such evidence to be entitled thereto, and disposition shall be made as in other cases.

§ 38-29-117, C.R.S. Certificates for manufactured homes registered in other states

(1) Whenever any resident of the state acquires the ownership of a manufactured home, located or to be located in the state of Colorado, by purchase, gift, or otherwise, for which a certificate of title has been issued under the laws of a state other than the state of Colorado, the person so acquiring such home upon acquiring the same shall make application to the director or his authorized agent for a certificate of title as in other cases.

(2) If any dealer acquires the ownership by any lawful means whatsoever of a manufactured home, the title to which is registered under the laws of and in a state other than the state of Colorado, such dealer shall not be required to procure a Colorado certificate of title therefor so long as such home remains in the dealer's inventory for sale and for no other purpose.

(3) Upon the sale by a dealer of a manufactured home, the certificate of title to which was issued in a state other than Colorado, the dealer shall immediately deliver to the purchaser or transferee such certificate of title from a state other than Colorado duly and properly endorsed or assigned to the purchaser or transferee, together with the dealer's statement, which shall contain or be accompanied by a written declaration that it is made under the penalties of perjury in the second degree, as defined in section 18-8-503, C.R.S., and which shall set forth the following:

 (a) That such dealer has warranted and, by the execution of such affidavit, does warrant to the purchaser or transferee and all persons claiming or who shall claim under, by, or through the named purchaser or transferee that, at the time of the sale, transfer, and delivery thereof by the dealer, the manufactured home therein described was free and clear of all liens and mortgages, except those which might otherwise appear therein;

 (b) That the home therein described is not stolen; and

 (c) That such dealer had good, sure, and adequate title thereto and full right and authority to sell and transfer the same.

(4) If the purchaser or transferee of the said manufactured home accompanies his application for a Colorado certificate of title to such home with the affidavit required by subsection (3) of this section and the duly endorsed or assigned certificate of title from a state other than Colorado, a Colorado certificate of title therefor may issue in the same manner as upon the sale or transfer of a manufactured home for which a Colorado certificate of title has been issued. Upon the issuance by the director of such certificate of title, he shall dispose of the same as provided in section 38-29-111.

(5) Each dealer, on or before the fifteenth day of each month, on a form to be provided therefor, shall prepare, subscribe, and send to the auto theft division of the Colorado state patrol a complete description of each manufactured home held by such dealer during the preceding calendar month, or any part thereof, the certificate of title to which was issued by a state other than the state of Colorado or which home was registered under the laws of a state other than the state of Colorado and for which no application for a Colorado certificate of title has been made as provided in this section.

(6) If any person acquires the ownership in a manufactured home for which a certificate of title has been issued under the laws of a state other than the state of Colorado and such home is transported to a site where it is permanently affixed to the ground so that it is no longer capable of being drawn over the public highways, such person shall not be required to procure a new certificate of title as is otherwise required by this article. The owner shall file a certificate of permanent location along with the certificate of title or the manufacturer's certificate or statement of origin or its equivalent with the clerk and recorder for the county or city and county in which the manufactured home is permanently affixed to the ground. The manufactured home shall become real property upon the filing and recording of such

documents in accordance with section 38-29-202. The provisions of articles 30 to 44 of this title and of any other law of this state shall be applicable to manufactured homes that have become real property pursuant to this subsection (6) and to instruments creating, disposing of, or otherwise affecting such real property wherever such provisions would be applicable to estates, rights, and interests in land or to instruments creating, disposing of, or otherwise affecting estates, rights, and interests in land.

§ 38-29-118, C.R.S. Surrender and cancellation of certificate – purge of certificate – penalty for violation

(1) The owner of any manufactured home for which a Colorado certificate of title has been issued, upon the destruction or dismantling of said manufactured home or upon its being sold or otherwise disposed of as salvage, shall surrender his or her certificate of title thereto to the director with the request that such certificate of title be cancelled and shall submit a certificate of destruction as set forth in section 38-29-204, and such certificate of title may there upon be cancelled. Any person who violates any of the provisions of this subsection (1) commits a class 1 petty offense and, upon conviction thereof, shall be punished as provided in section 18-1.3-503, C.R.S.

(2) The owner of any manufactured home for which a Colorado certificate of title has been issued, upon its being permanently affixed to the ground so that it is no longer capable of being drawn over the public highways, shall surrender his or her certificate of title thereto and file with the authorized agent of the county or city and county in which such manufactured home is located a request for purging of the manufactured home title and a certificate of permanent location. The manufactured home shall become real property upon the filing and recording of the certificate of permanent location in accordance with section 38-29-202. The provisions of articles 30 to 44 of this title and of any other law of this state shall be applicable to manufactured homes that have become real property pursuant to this subsection (2) and to instruments creating, disposing of, or otherwise affecting such real property wherever such provisions would be applicable to estates, rights, and interests in land or to instruments creating, disposing of, or otherwise affecting estates, rights, and interests in land. The manufactured home for which a Colorado certificate of title has been issued shall continue to be valued and taxed separately from the land on which it sits until such time that the manufactured home becomes real property pursuant to this subsection (2).

§ 38-29-119, C.R.S. Furnishing bond for certificates

(1) In cases where the applicant for a certificate of title to a manufactured home is unable to provide the director or the director's authorized agent with a certificate of title thereto, duly transferred to such applicant, a bill of sale therefor, or other evidence of the ownership thereof that satisfies the director of the right of the applicant to have a certificate of title issued to him or her, as provided in section 38-29-110, a certificate of title for such home may, nevertheless, be issued by the director upon the applicant therefor furnishing the director with his or her statement, in such form as the director may prescribe. There shall appear a recital of the facts and circumstances by which the applicant acquired the ownership and possession of such home, the source of the title thereto, and such other information as the director may require to enable him or her to determine what liens and encumbrances are outstanding against such manufactured home, if any, the date thereof, the amount secured thereby, where said liens or encumbrances are of public record, if they are of public record, and the right of the applicant to have a certificate of title issued to him or her. In situations involving an abandoned manufactured home located on an applicant's real property, a copy of an order or judgment for possession obtained through a civil eviction proceeding, along with proof of efforts to notify, via certified mail, regular mail, and posting as otherwise required by law, the prior owner of the potential removal or transfer of title of the home, as well as proof of ownership of the real

property on which the home is located, shall constitute sufficient evidence of the applicant's right to a certificate of title for the home. The statement shall contain or be accompanied by a written declaration that it is made under the penalties of perjury in the second degree, as defined in section 18-8-503, C.R.S., and shall accompany the formal application for the certificate as required in section 38-29-107.

(2) (a) If, from the affidavit of the applicant and such other evidence as may be submitted to him or her, the director finds that the applicant is the same person to whom a certificate of title for said home has previously been issued or that a certificate of title should be issued to the applicant, such certificate may be issued, in which event disposition thereof shall be made as in other cases. Except as provided by paragraph (b) of this subsection (2), no certificate of title shall be issued as provided in this section unless and until the applicant furnishes evidence of a savings account, deposit, or certificate of deposit meeting the requirements of section 11-35-101, C.R.S., or a good and sufficient bond with a corporate surety, to the people of the state of Colorado, in an amount equal to twice the actual value of the manufactured home according to the assessor's records, as of the time application for the certificate is made, conditioned that the applicant and his or her surety shall hold harmless any person who suffers any loss or damage by reason of the issuance thereof.

(b) An applicant shall not be required to furnish surety pursuant to this subsection (2) for a manufactured home that is twenty-five years old or older, if the applicant:

(I) Provides proof that no property taxes for previous years are due for the manufactured home;

(II) Has had a manufactured home identification inspection performed on the manufactured home; and

(III) Presents the information required in subsection (1) of this section with a title application, accompanied by the written declaration set forth therein.

(c) If any person suffers any loss or damage by reason of the issuance of the certificate of title as provided in this section, such person shall have a right of action against the applicant and, if applicable, the surety on his or her bond. The person who has suffered a loss or damage may proceed against the applicant, the surety, or against both the applicant and the surety.

§ 38-29-120, C.R.S. Where to apply for certificate of title

Except as may be otherwise provided by rule of the director, it is unlawful for any person who is a resident of the state to procure a certificate of title to a manufactured home in any county of this state other than the county in which such home is to be used as a residence. Any person who violates any of the provisions of this section or any rule of the director relating thereto, made pursuant to the authority conferred upon him in this article, is guilty of a misdemeanor and, upon conviction thereof, shall be punished by a fine of not less than fifty dollars nor more than one hundred dollars, or by imprisonment in the county jail for not less than ten days nor more than six months, or by both such fine and imprisonment.

§ 38-29-121, C.R.S. Altering or using altered certificate

Any person who alters or forges or causes to be altered or forged any certificate of title issued by the director pursuant to the provisions of this article, or any written transfer thereof, or any other notation placed thereon by the director or under his or her authority respecting the mortgaging of the manufactured home therein described or who uses or attempts to use any such certificate for the transfer thereof, knowing the same to have been altered or forged, commits a class 6 felony and shall be punished as provided in section 18-1.3-401, C.R.S.

§ 38-29-122, C.R.S. Substitute manufactured home identification numbers – inspection

(1) Any person required to make an application for a certificate of title to a manufactured home shall use the identification number placed upon the home by the manufacturer thereof or an identification number assigned to the home by the department. The certificate of title issued by the department shall use the identification number assigned to the manufactured home.

(2) On and after February 25, 1954, the identification number provided for in this section shall be accepted in lieu of any serial number provided for by law prior to said date.

(3) (a) The department may designate a manufactured home identification inspector to physically inspect a manufactured home in order to verify the following information: The identification number, the make of the manufactured home, the year of manufacture of the manufactured home, and such other information as may be required by the department. A manufactured home identification inspector may charge a fee for the inspection; except that such fee shall not exceed the reasonable costs related to the inspection. A manufactured home identification inspector shall notify the owner of the amount of the fee before commencing any verification activities. If the manufactured home identification inspector determines that the manufactured home identification number has been removed, changed, altered, or obliterated, the owner shall request that the department assign a distinguishing number to the manufactured home pursuant to section 38-29-123.

(b) The department may designate one or more of the following persons to be a manufactured home identification inspector charged with the functions set forth in paragraph (a) of this subsection (3):

(I) An authorized agent as defined in section 38-29-102 (1) or a person designated by such agent;

(II) A Colorado law enforcement officer;

(III) A person registered to sell manufactured homes pursuant to section 24-32-3323, C.R.S.; or

(IV) A county assessor.

§ 38-29-123, C.R.S. Assignment of a special manufactured home identification number by the department of revenue

The department is authorized to assign a distinguishing number to any manufactured home whenever there is no identifying number thereon or such number has been destroyed, obliterated, or mutilated. In such cases, the department shall provide a form on which the distinguishing number has been assigned to the manufactured home. The distinguishing number shall be affixed to the manufactured home in the door frame or fuse box or as determined by the department. The distinguishing number shall then be the manufactured home identification number. Such manufactured home shall be titled under such distinguishing number in lieu of the former number or absence thereof, or in the event that the manufactured home is affixed to the ground so that it is no longer capable of being drawn over the public highways, the owner shall file the form provided by the department on which the distinguishing number has been assigned with the clerk and recorder for the county or city and county in which the manufactured home is located. The clerk and recorder shall file and record such form in his or her office.

§ 38-29-124, C.R.S. Amended certificate to issue, when

If the owner of any manufactured home for which a Colorado certificate of title has been issued replaces any part of said home on which appears the identification number or symbol described in the certificate of title and by which said home is known and identified, by reason whereof such identification number or symbol no longer appears thereon, or incorporates the part containing the identification number or symbol into a manufactured home other than the one for which the original certificate of title was issued, immediately thereafter, such owner shall make application to the director or one of his authorized agents for an assigned identification number and an amended certificate of title to such manufactured home.

§ 38-29-125, C.R.S. Security interests upon manufactured homes

(1) Except as provided in this section, the provisions of the "Uniform Commercial Code", title 4, C.R.S., relating to the filing, recording, releasing, renewal, and extension of mortgages, as the term is defined in section 38-29-102(9), shall not be applicable to manufactured homes. Any mortgage intended by the parties thereto to encumber or create a lien on a manufactured home, to be effective as a valid lien against the rights of third persons, purchasers for value without notice, mortgagees, or creditors of the owner, shall be filed for public record and the fact thereof noted on the owner's certificate of title or bill of sale substantially in the manner provided in section 38-29-128; and the filing of such mortgage with the authorized agent and the notation by him of that fact on the certificate of title or bill of sale substantially in the manner provided in section 38-29-128 shall constitute notice to the world of each and every right of the person secured by such mortgage.

(2) The provisions of this section and section 38-29-128 shall not apply to any mortgage or security interest upon any manufactured home held for sale or lease which constitutes inventory as defined in section 4-9-102, C.R.S. As to such mortgages or security interests, the provisions of article 9 of title 4, C.R.S., shall apply, and perfection of such mortgages or security interests shall be made pursuant thereto, and the rights of the parties shall be governed and determined thereby.

§ 38-29-126, C.R.S. Existing mortgages not affected

Nothing in this article shall be construed to impair the rights of the holder of any lien on a manufactured home created by mortgage or otherwise prior to August 1, 1949, which remains unreleased and the undertaking which the lien thereof secures remains undischarged. Nothing in this article shall be construed to relieve the holders of such liens of the duty to file such instruments respecting the undertakings secured thereby as may be required by law to preserve the liens of such mortgages unimpaired.

§ 38-29-127, C.R.S. Foreign mortgages

No mortgage on a manufactured home, filed for record in any state other than the state of Colorado, shall be valid and enforceable against the rights of subsequent purchasers for value, creditors, or mortgagees having no actual notice of the existence thereof. If the certificate of title for such home, whether issued under the laws of this state or any other state, bears thereon any notation adequate to apprise a purchaser, creditor, or mortgagee of the existence of such mortgage at the time any third party acquires a right in the manufactured home covered thereby, such mortgage and the rights of the holder thereof shall be enforceable in this state the same and with like effect as though such mortgage were filed in the state of Colorado and noted on the certificate of title in the manner prescribed in section 38-29-128.

§ 38-29-128, C.R.S. Filing of mortgage

The holder of any mortgage on a manufactured home desiring to secure to himself the rights provided for in this article and to have the existence of the mortgage and the fact of the filing thereof for public record noted on the certificate of title to the manufactured home thereby encumbered shall present said mortgage or a duly executed copy or certified copy thereof and the certificate of title to the manufactured home encumbered to the authorized agent of the director in the county or city and county in which the manufactured home is located. Upon the receipt of said mortgage or executed copy or certified copy thereof and certificate of title, the authorized agent, if he is satisfied that the manufactured home described in the mortgage is the same as that described in the certificate of title, shall make and subscribe a certificate to be attached or stamped on the mortgage and on the certificate of title, in which shall appear the day and hour on which said mortgage was received for filing, the name and address of the mortgagee therein named and the name and address of the holder of such mortgage, if such person is other than the mortgagee named, the amount secured thereby, the date thereof, the day and year on which said mortgage was filed for public record, and such other information regarding the filing thereof in the office of the authorized agent as may be required by the director by rule, to which certificate the authorized agent shall affix his signature and the seal of his office.

§ 38-29-129, C.R.S. Disposition of mortgages by agent

(1) The authorized agent upon receipt of the mortgage shall file the same in his office separately and apart from records affecting real property and personal property, other than manufactured homes, which he may by law be required to keep. Such mortgage shall be appropriately indexed and cross-indexed:

(a) Under one or more of the following headings in accordance with such rules and regulations relating thereto as may be adopted by the director:

(I) Manufacturer, manufacturer's number, or serial number of manufactured homes mortgaged;

(II) The numbers of the certificates of title for manufactured homes mortgaged;

(b) Under the name of the mortgagee, the holder of such mortgage, or the owner of such mortgaged home; or

(c) Under such other system as the director may devise and determine to be necessary for the efficient administration of this article.

(2) All records of mortgages affecting manufactured homes shall be public and may be inspected and copies thereof made, as is provided by law respecting public records affecting real property.

§ 38-29-130, C.R.S. Disposition after mortgaging

Within forty-eight hours after a mortgage on a manufactured home has been filed in his office, the authorized agent shall mail to the director the certificate of title or bill of sale on which he has affixed his certificate respecting the filing of such mortgage. Upon the receipt thereof, the director shall note, on records to be kept and maintained by him in his office, the fact of the existence of the mortgage on such manufactured home and other information respecting the date thereof, the date of filing, the amount secured by the lien thereof, the name and address of the mortgagee and of the holder of the mortgage, if such person is other than the mortgagee, and such other information relating thereto as appears in the certificate of the authorized agent affixed to the certificate of title or bill of sale. The director shall thereupon issue a new certificate of title containing, in addition to the other matters and things required to be set forth in certificates of title, a description of the mortgage and all information respecting said mortgage and the filing thereof as may appear in the certificate of the authorized agent, and he shall thereafter dispose of said new certificate of title containing said notation as provided in section 38-29-111.

§ 38-29-131, C.R.S. Release of mortgages

(1) Upon the payment or discharge of the undertaking secured by any mortgage on a manufactured home that has been filed for record and noted on the certificate of title in the manner prescribed in section 38-29-128, the legal holder of the certificate of title, in a place to be provided therefor, shall make and execute such notation of the discharge of the obligation and release of the mortgage securing the same and set forth therein such facts concerning the right of the holder to so release said mortgage as the director may require by appropriate rule, which

satisfaction and release shall be affirmed by a statement signed by the legal holder of the certificate of title and shall contain or be accompanied by a written declaration that it is made under the penalties of perjury in the second degree, as defined in section 18-8-503, C.R.S. Thereupon, except as otherwise provided in section 38-29-112(1.7), the holder of the mortgage so released shall dispose of the certificate of title as follows:

(a) If it appears from an examination of the certificate of title that the manufactured home therein described is subject to an outstanding junior mortgage or mortgages filed for record subsequent to August 1, 1949, the holder shall deliver the certificate of title to the person so shown to be the holder of the mortgage which was filed earliest in point of time after the filing of the mortgage released or to the person or agent of the person shown to be the assignee or other legal holder of the undertaking secured thereby or shall mail the same to such mortgagee or holder thereof at his address as the same thereon appears. If such certificate is returned unclaimed, it shall thereupon be mailed to the director.

(b) If it appears from an examination of the certificate of title that there are no other outstanding mortgages against the manufactured home therein described, filed for record subsequent to August 1, 1949, upon the release of such mortgage as provided in this section, the holder thereof shall deliver the certificate of title to the owner of the home therein described or shall mail the same to him at his address as the same may therein appear. If for any reason said certificate of title is not delivered to the owner of the home therein described or is returned unclaimed upon the mailing thereof, it shall thereupon be mailed to the director.

§ 38-29-132, C.R.S. New certificate upon release of mortgage

Upon the release of any mortgage on a manufactured home, filed for record in the manner prescribed in section 38-29-128, the owner of the home encumbered by such mortgage, the purchaser from or transferee of the owner thereof as appears on the certificate of title, or the holder of any mortgage the lien of which was junior to the lien of the mortgage released, whichever the case may be, upon the receipt of the certificate of title, as provided in section 38-29-131, shall deliver the same to the authorized agent who shall transmit the same to the director as in other cases. Upon the receipt by the director of the certificate of title bearing thereon the release and satisfaction of mortgage referred to in section 38-29-131, he shall make such notation on the records in his office as shall show the release of the lien of such mortgage, shall issue a new certificate of title to the manufactured home therein described, omitting therefrom all reference to the mortgage so released, and shall dispose of the new certificate of title in the manner prescribed in other cases.

§ 38-29-133, C.R.S. Duration of lien of mortgage – extensions

(1) The duration of the lien of any mortgage on a manufactured home shall be for the full term of the mortgage, but the lien of the mortgage may be extended beyond the original term thereof for successive three-year periods during the term of the mortgage or any extension thereof upon the holder thereof presenting the certificate of title, on which the existence of the mortgage has been noted, to the authorized agent of the county wherein said mortgage is filed, together with a notarized written request for an extension of the mortgage or a written request that is made under the penalties of perjury in the second degree, as defined in section 18-8-503, C.R.S., , in which shall appear a description of the undertaking secured, to what extent it has been discharged or remains unperformed, and such other and further information respecting the same as may be required by appropriate rule of the director to enable him or her to properly record such extension upon the director's records.

(2) Upon receipt of a mortgage extension, the authorized agent shall make and complete a record of the extension and shall issue a new certificate of title on which the extension of the mortgage is noted. Thereafter the newly issued certificate of title shall be returned to the person shown thereon to be entitled thereto, the same as in other cases. If a mortgage noted on the certificate

of title has not been released or extended after its maturity date, the owner of the manufactured home described in the certificate of title may request that any references to the mortgages shown on the records of the authorized agent be removed, and upon the request, the authorized agent shall remove such references.

§ 38-29-134, C.R.S. Priority of mortgages

The liens of mortgages filed for record and noted on a certificate of title to a manufactured home, as provided in sections 38-29-128 and 38-29-135, shall take priority in the same order that the mortgages creating such liens were filed in the office of the authorized agent.

§ 38-29-135, C.R.S. Second or other junior mortgages

(1) On and after July 1, 1977, any person who takes a second or other junior mortgage on a manufactured home for which a Colorado certificate of title has been issued may file said mortgage for public record and have the existence thereof noted on the certificate of title with like effect as in other cases, in the manner prescribed in this section.

(2) Such second or junior mortgagee or the holder thereof shall file said mortgage with the authorized agent of the county wherein the manufactured home is located and shall accompany said mortgage with a written request to have the existence thereof noted on the certificate of title to the manufactured home covered thereby, subscribed by such mortgagee or holder, in which shall appear the names and addresses of the holders of all outstanding mortgages against the home described in said second or junior mortgage and the name and address of the person in possession of the certificate of title thereto. Upon the filing of such mortgage, the authorized agent shall note thereon the day and hour on which such mortgage was received by him and shall make and deliver a receipt therefor to the person filing the same.

(3) The authorized agent, by registered mail, return receipt requested, shall make a written demand on the holder of the certificate of title, addressed to such person at his address as the same may appear in said written request, that such certificate be delivered to the authorized agent for the purpose of having noted thereon such second or junior mortgage. Within fifteen days after the receipt of such demand, the person holding such certificate shall either mail or deliver the same to such authorized agent or, if he no longer has possession thereof, shall so notify the agent and, if he knows, shall likewise inform him where and from whom such certificate may be procured. Upon the receipt of such certificate, the authorized agent shall complete his application for a new title and record the number thereof on the mortgage, as in the case of a first mortgage, and shall thereafter transmit the current certificate of title and application for a new certificate of title to the director. Upon the receipt thereof, the director, as in the case of a first mortgage, shall thereupon issue a new certificate of title on which the existence of all mortgages on the manufactured home, including such second or junior mortgage, have been noted, which certificate he shall dispose of as in other cases.

(4) If any person lawfully in possession of a certificate of title to any manufactured home upon whom demand is made for the delivery thereof to the authorized agent omits, for any reason whatsoever, to deliver or mail the same to the authorized agent, such person shall be liable to the holder of such second or junior mortgage for all damage sustained by reason of such omission.

§ 38-29-136, C.R.S. Validity of mortgage between parties

Nothing in this article shall be construed to impair the validity of a mortgage on a manufactured home between the parties thereto as long as no purchaser for value, mortgagee, or creditor without actual notice of the existence thereof has acquired an interest in the manufactured home described therein, notwithstanding that the parties to said mortgage have failed to comply with the provisions of this article.

§ 38-29-137, C.R.S. Mechanics', warehouse, and other liens

Nothing in this article shall be construed to impair the rights of lien claimants arising under any mechanics' lien law in force and effect in this state or the lien of any warehouseman or any other person claimed for repairs on or storage of any manufactured home, when a mechanic's lien or storage lien has originated prior to the time any mortgage on said manufactured home has been filed for record, as provided in section 38-29-125, and such manufactured home has remained continuously in the possession of the person claiming such mechanic's lien or lien for storage, notwithstanding that no notation of such lien is made upon the certificate of title to the home in respect of which it is claimed.

§ 38-29-138, C.R.S. Fees

(1) (a) Upon filing with the authorized agent any application for a certificate of title, the applicant shall pay to the agent a fee of seven dollars and twenty cents, which shall be disposed pursuant to section 42-6-138, C.R.S.

(b) Repealed.

(2) Upon the receipt by the authorized agent of any mortgage for filing under the provisions of section 38-29-128, the agent shall be paid such fees as are prescribed by law for the filing of like instruments in the office of the county clerk and recorder in the county or city and county in which such mortgage is filed and shall receive, in addition, a fee of seven dollars and twenty cents for the issuance or recording of the certificate of title and the notation of the existence of said mortgage.

(3) Upon application to the authorized agent to have noted on a certificate of title the extension of any mortgage therein described and noted thereon, such authorized agent shall receive a fee of one dollar and fifty cents.

(4) Upon the release and satisfaction of any mortgage and upon application to the authorized agent for the notation thereof on the certificate of title in the manner prescribed in section 38-29-131, such authorized agent shall be paid a fee of seven dollars and twenty cents, which shall be disposed pursuant to section 42-6-138, C.R.S.

(5) For the issuance of any duplicate certificate of title, except as may be otherwise provided in this article, the agent shall be paid a fee of eight dollars and twenty cents, and, in all cases in which the department assigns a new identifying number to any manufactured home, the fee charged for such assignment shall be three dollars and fifty cents.

(6) The fees provided for in subsections (1) and (2) of this section shall not apply to the issuance of a certificate of title for a tax-deferred mobile home pursuant to the provisions of section 39-3.5-105(1)(b)(II), C.R.S.

§ 38-29-139, C.R.S. Disposition of fees

(1) All fees received by the authorized agent under the provisions of section 38-29-138(1) and (2), upon application being made for a certificate of title, shall be disposed of pursuant to section 42-6-138(1), C.R.S.

(2) All fees collected by the authorized agent under the provisions of section 38-29-138(5) shall be disposed of pursuant to section 42-6-138(2), C.R.S.

(3) All fees paid to the authorized agent under section 38-29-138(3) for the filing or extension of any mortgage on a manufactured home filed in his or her office shall be kept and retained by said agent to defray the cost thereof and shall be disposed of by him or her as provided by law; except that fees for this service that may be paid to the authorized agent in the city and county of Denver shall, by such agent, be disposed of in the same manner as fees retained by him or her that were paid upon application being made for a certificate of title.

§ 38-29-140, C.R.S. Director's records to be public

All records in the director's office pertaining to the title to any manufactured home shall be public records and shall be subject to the provisions of section 42-1-206, C.R.S. This shall include any records regarding ownership of and mortgages on any manufactured home for which a Colorado certificate of title has been issued.

§ 38-29-141, C.R.S. Penalties

(1) No person may:

- (a) Sell, transfer, or in any manner dispose of a manufactured home in this state without complying with the requirements of this article.
- (b) Deleted by amendment, L. 89, p. 1573, § 8, effective January 1, 1990.)

(2) Any person who violates any of the provisions of subsection (1) of this section for which no other penalty is expressly provided is guilty of a misdemeanor and, upon conviction thereof, shall be punished by a fine of not less than one hundred dollars nor more than five hundred dollars, or by imprisonment in the county jail for not less than ten days nor more than six months, or by both such fine and imprisonment.

§ 38-29-141.5, C.R.S. False oath

Any person who makes any application for a certificate of title, written transfer thereof, satisfaction and release, oath, affirmation, affidavit, statement, report, or deposition required to be made or taken under any of the provisions of this article and who, upon such application, transfer, satisfaction and release, oath, affirmation, affidavit, statement, report, or deposition, swears or affirms willfully and falsely in a matter material to any issue, point, or subject matter in question, in addition to any other penalties provided in this article, is guilty of perjury in the second degree, as defined in section 18-8-503, C.R.S.

§ 38-29-142, C.R.S. Repossession of manufactured home – owner must notify law enforcement agency – penalty

(1) If any mortgagee or his assignee or the agent of either repossesses a manufactured home because of default in the terms of a mortgage, the mortgagee or his assignee shall notify, either verbally or in writing, a law enforcement agency, as provided in this section, of the fact of such repossession, the name of the owner, and the name of the mortgagee or assignee. Such notification shall be made not later than twelve hours after the repossession occurs. If such repossession takes place in an incorporated city or town, the notification shall be made to the police department, town marshal, or other local law enforcement agency of such city or town, and, if such repossession takes place in the unincorporated area of a county, the notification shall be made to the county sheriff.

(2) Any mortgagee of a manufactured home or his assignee who violates the provisions of this section is guilty of a misdemeanor and, upon conviction thereof, shall be punished by a fine of not less than fifty dollars nor more than one hundred dollars.

§ 38-29-143, C.R.S. Change of location – penalty

(1) The owner shall file notice of any change of location within the county with the county assessor and the county treasurer or change of location from one county to another county with the county assessor and the county treasurer of each county within twenty days after such change of location occurs. For the purposes of this subsection (1), "owner" shall mean the owner at the time of the change of location.

(2) Any person who fails to file notice of any change of location as required by subsection (1) of this section is guilty of a misdemeanor traffic offense and, upon conviction thereof, shall be

punished by a fine of not less than one hundred dollars nor more than one thousand dollars. This shall be a strict liability offense.

§ 38-29-201, C.R.S. Verification of application form – supporting materials

(1) In all instances under part 1 of this article in which an application for a certificate of title is filed with an authorized agent pursuant to section 38-29-107, the authorized agent, in his or her capacity as the clerk and recorder, shall file and record the documents set forth in subsection (2) of this section in his or her office.

(2) (a) For an application for a certificate of title for a new manufactured home, the following documents shall be filed and recorded:

(I) The manufacturer's certificate or statement of origin or its equivalent; and

(II) (Deleted by amendment, L. 2009, (S.B. 09-040), ch. 9, p. 67, § 8, effective July 1, 2009.)

(III) The verification of application form.

(b) For an application for a certificate of title for which a bond is furnished pursuant to section 38-29-119(2), the following documents shall be filed and recorded:

(I) A copy of the written declaration required pursuant to section 38-29-119(1);

(II) A copy of the bond that was furnished; and

(III) The verification of application form.

(c) For all other applications for a certificate of title, the following documents shall be filed and recorded:

(I) A copy of the certificate of title presented to the authorized agent, if any; and

(II) The verification of application form.

(3) A verification of application form shall comply with the federal "Driver's Privacy Protection Act of 1994", 18 U.S.C. sec. 2721, *et seq.*

§ 38-29-202, C.R.S. Certificate of permanent location

(1) (a) If a manufactured home is permanently affixed to the ground so that it is no longer capable of being drawn over the public highways on or after July 1, 2008, the owner of the manufactured home shall file a certificate of permanent location.

(b) If the certificate of permanent location accompanies an application for purging a manufactured home title pursuant to section 38-29-112(1.5) or 38-29-118(2), the certificate shall be filed with the authorized agent for the county or city and county in which the manufactured home is located. For a manufactured home that occupies real property subject to a long-term lease that has an express term of at least ten years, a copy of the lease shall be filed along with the certificate. The authorized agent, in his or her capacity as the clerk and recorder, shall file and record the certificate of permanent location and, if applicable, the copy of the long-term lease in his or her office.

(c) If the certificate of permanent location is received in accordance with section 38-29-114(2) or 38-29-117(6), the certificate shall be filed with the clerk and recorder for the county or city and county in which the manufactured home is located. For a manufactured home that occupies real property subject to a long-term lease that has an express term of at least ten years, a copy of the lease shall be filed along with the certificate. The clerk and recorder shall file and record the certificate of permanent location, a copy of the bill of sale, a copy of the manufacturer's certificate or statement of origin or its equivalent, and, if applicable, the copy of the long-term lease in his or her office and destroy the original manufacturer's certificate or statement of origin or its equivalent.

(d) At least one of the owners of the manufactured home, as reflected on the certificate of title, the bill of sale, or the manufacturer's certificate or statement of origin or its equivalent, must be an owner of record of the real property to which the manufactured home is to be affixed or permanently located; except that this paragraph (d) shall not apply to any manufactured home that occupies real property subject to a long-term lease that has an express term of at least ten years.

(2) The property tax administrator shall establish the form of the certificate of permanent location. In addition to any other information that the administrator may require, the certificate shall include the following:

(a) The name and mailing address of the owner of the manufactured home;

(b) The name and mailing address of any holder of a mortgage on the manufactured home or on the real property to which the home has been affixed;

(c) The identification number of the manufactured home and the certificate of title number, if applicable;

(d) The manufacturer or make and year of the manufactured home;

(e) Attached to the certificate of permanent location, a certificate of taxes due, or an authentication of paid ad valorem taxes, issued by the county treasurer of the county in which the manufactured home is located;

(f) The legal description of the real property to which the manufactured home has been permanently affixed;

(g) The name of the legal owner or owners of the land upon which the home is affixed;

(h) The county or city and county in which the certificate of permanent location is filed;

(i) Verification that the manufactured home is permanently affixed to the ground so that it is no longer capable of being drawn over the public highways in accordance with any applicable county or city and county codes or requirements;

(j) Consent to the permanent location of the manufactured home by all holders of a security interest in the manufactured home;

(k) An affirmative statement of relinquishment and release of all rights in the manufactured home by all holders of a security interest in the manufactured home;

(l) An affirmative statement of relinquishment of all rights in the manufactured home by any owner on the certificate of title of the manufactured home who is not also an owner of the real property to which the manufactured home is to be affixed or permanently located. The provisions of this paragraph (l) shall not apply to any manufactured home that occupies real property subject to a long-term lease that has an express term of at least ten years.

(l.5) For any manufactured home that occupies real property subject to a long-term lease that has an express term of at least ten years, an affirmative statement that all owners of the real property and the manufactured home consent to the affixation of the manufactured home to the real property and an acknowledgment that, upon such affixation and upon the filing and recording of the certificate of permanent location, the manufactured home will become a part of the real property, subject to the reversion of the manufactured home to the owners of the home upon termination of the long-term lease; and

(m) An affirmative statement that all owners of the real property and the manufactured home consent to the affixation of the manufactured home to the real property and an acknowledgment that upon such affixation and upon the filing and recording of the certificate of permanent location the manufactured home will become a part of the real property and ownership shall be vested only in the title owners of the real property. Ownership in the manufactured home shall vest in the same parties and be subject to the same tenancies, encumbrances, liens, limitations, restrictions, and estates as the real property to which the manufactured home is affixed or permanently located. The provisions of this paragraph (m) shall not apply to any manufactured home that occupies real property subject to a long-term lease that has an express term of at least ten years.

(3) The certificate of permanent location shall be acknowledged and shall contain or be accompanied by a written declaration that the statements made therein are made under the penalties of perjury in the second degree, as defined in section 18-8-503, C.R.S.

§ 38-29-203, C.R.S. Certificate of removal

(1) (a) On or after July 1, 2008, a manufactured home shall not be removed from its permanent location unless the owner of the manufactured home files a certificate of removal. If a certificate of permanent location has not been previously filed and recorded for the manufactured home, the owner shall also file an affidavit of real property, described in section 38-29-208, along with the certificate of removal.

(b) The certificate of removal and the affidavit of real property, if any, along with the application for a new certificate of title required in part 1 of this article, shall be filed with the authorized agent for the county or city and county in which the manufactured home is located. The authorized agent, in his or her capacity as the clerk and recorder, shall file and record the certificate of removal and the affidavit of real property in his or her office.

(2) The property tax administrator shall establish the form of the certificate of removal. In addition to any other information that the administrator may require, the certificate shall include the following:

(a) The name and mailing address of the owner of the manufactured home;

(b) The name and mailing address of any holder of a mortgage on or lien against the real property on which the manufactured home was affixed or permanently located;

(c) The identification number of the manufactured home;

(d) The manufacturer or make and year of the manufactured home;

(e) Attached to the certificate of removal, a certificate of taxes due, or an authentication of paid ad valorem taxes, issued by the county treasurer of the county in which the manufactured home is located;

(f) The legal description of the real property from which the manufactured home was removed; and

(g) Consent of all lienholders and a release by all holders of a mortgage, only to the extent that the mortgage or lien applies to the manufactured home, to allow the removal of the manufactured home from its permanent location.

(2.5) (a) The provisions of this section shall apply to a manufactured home that occupies real property subject to a long-term lease that has an express term of at least ten years, except as set forth in paragraph (b) of this subsection (2.5).

(b) A landlord evicting a tenant who owns a manufactured home that occupies real property subject to a long-term lease that has an express term of at least ten years may cause the home to be removed from its permanent location without the owner first filing a certificate of removal if, within twenty days after such removal, the landlord files a certificate of removal accompanied by a copy of the notice of judgment or order for possession allowing the eviction of the home and the address of the location to which the home has been moved. Such certificate of removal shall comply with subsection (5) of this section and include the information required in subsection (2) of this section; except that paragraphs (e) and (g) of said subsection (2) shall not apply. The landlord shall file the certificate of removal and the additional information with the authorized agent for the county or city and county from which the manufactured home was removed.

(3) The consent of a mortgage or other lien holder on the certificate of removal shall serve as a full release of any interest against the manufactured home once the manufactured home is removed from the real property. The consent on the certificate of removal shall not release any interest of the mortgage or lien holder against the remaining real property.

(4) If consent of any mortgagee or lien holder is not given, the owner may file a corporate surety bond or any other undertaking with the clerk of the district court of the county in which the real property to which the manufactured home was affixed is situated. The bond or undertaking shall be in an amount equal to one and one-half times the amount of the mortgage or lien and shall be approved by a judge of the district court with which the bond or undertaking is filed. The bond or undertaking shall be conditioned that, if the mortgagee or lien holder shall be finally adjudged to be entitled to recover upon the mortgage or lien, the principal or his sureties shall pay to the mortgagee or lien holder the amount of the indebtedness together with any interest, costs, and other sums which the mortgagee or lien holder would be entitled to recover upon foreclosure of the mortgage or lien. Upon the filing of a bond or undertaking, the mortgage or lien against the property shall be forthwith discharged and released in full, and the real property described in the bond or undertaking shall be released from the mortgage or lien and from any action brought to foreclose the mortgage or lien, and the bond or undertaking shall be substituted. The clerk of the district court with which the bond or undertaking has been filed shall issue a certificate of release that shall be recorded in the office of the clerk and recorder of the county in which the real property to which the manufactured home was affixed is situated, and the certificate of release shall show that the property has been released from the mortgage or lien and from any action brought to foreclose the mortgage or lien.

(5) The certificate of removal shall be acknowledged and shall contain or be accompanied by a written declaration that the statements made therein are made under the penalties of perjury in the second degree, as defined in section 18-8-503, C.R.S.

§ 38-29-204, C.R.S. Certificate of destruction

* (1) (a) If a manufactured home is destroyed, dismantled, or sold or otherwise disposed of as salvage on or after July 1, 2008, the owner of the manufactured home or the person on whose property the manufactured home is situated shall file a certificate of destruction.

(b) If the certificate of destruction accompanies an application to cancel a certificate of title pursuant to section 38-29-118(1), the certificate shall be filed with the authorized agent for the county or city and county in which the manufactured home is or was located. The authorized agent, in his or her capacity as the clerk and recorder, shall file and record the certificate of destruction in his or her office.

(c) If an application to cancel a certificate of title is not required pursuant to section 38-29-118(1) because no certificate of title was ever issued or because the title has been purged, the certificate of destruction shall be filed with the county clerk and recorder for the county or city and county in which the manufactured home is or was located. The clerk and recorder shall file and record the certificate of destruction in his or her office.

* (d) (I) Notwithstanding any other provision of the law, if a manufactured home has been deemed materially dangerous or materially hazardous, pursuant to local building or health codes by a governmental entity, the person on whose real property the manufactured home is situated may file and record a certificate of destruction without attaching a certificated of taxes due or an authentication of paid ad valorem taxes and without surrendering a certificate of title or filing an application to cancel a certificate of title. Any certificate of destruction filed and recorded pursuant to this paragraph (d) shall be accompanied by the evidence of violation.

* (II) The certificate of destruction and the evidence of violation shall be filed and recorded with the clerk and recorder for the county or city and county I which the manufactured home is or was located. The clerk and recorder shall file and record the certificate of destruction with the evidence of violation in his or her office.

* (III) For purposes of this paragraph (d):

(A) "Evidence of violation" means a notice and order form a governmental entity that a manufactured home has been deemed materially dangerous or materially hazardous pursuant to local building or health codes and that all applicable cure periods have expired.

(B) "Governmental entity" means any federal agency, the state, or any county, town, city, or city and county.

(2) The property tax administrator shall establish the form of the certificate of destruction. In addition to any other information that the administrator may require, the certificate shall include the following:

(a) The name and mailing address of the owner of the manufactured home;

(b) The name and mailing address of each holder of a security interest in the manufactured home and all holders of a lien against the real property on which the manufactured home was affixed or permanently located;

(c) The identification number of the manufactured home;

(d) The manufacturer or make and year of the manufactured home;

(e) Attached to the certificate of destruction, a certificate of taxes due, or an authentication of paid ad valorem taxes, issued by the county treasurer of the county in which the manufactured home is located;

(f) The legal description of the real property on which the manufactured home was affixed or permanently located prior to destruction;

(g) A book and page or reception number reference for a certificate of permanent location that was previously filed related to the manufactured home, if any;

* (h) Consent of all lienholders to the destruction of the manufactured home, or proof that a request for such consent was sent by certified mail to such lienholders, along with proof that a copy of the request for such consent was mailed to the owner if the certificate of destruction is filed by the person on whose real property the manufactured home is situated, at their last-known address and a notarized declaration, signed under penalty of perjury, that no response was received within thirty days of the date of the mailing of the notice;

(i) Release of all holders of a mortgage to the extent that the mortgage applies to the manufactured home, or proof that a request for such consent was sent by certified mail to such mortgage holders at their last-known address and a notarized declaration, signed under penalty of perjury, that no response was received within thirty days of the date of the mailing of the notice; and

(j) Verification that the manufactured home has been destroyed, dismantled, or sold or otherwise disposed of as salvage.

(3) The certificate of destruction shall be acknowledged and shall contain or be accompanied by a written declaration that the statements made therein are made under the penalties of perjury in the second degree, as defined in section 18-8-503, C.R.S.

* (4) Any owner or person on whose real property the manufactured home is situated who fails to file a properly completed certificate of destruction when required pursuant to this section shall be responsible for all actual damages sustained by any affected party related to the manufactured home being destroyed, dismantled, or sold or otherwise disposed of as salvage.

§ 38-29-205, C.R.S. Authorized agent – forward to the clerk and recorder

If an authorized agent who receives a document for filing and recording pursuant to this part 2 is not the clerk and recorder for the county or city and county, the authorized agent shall forward such document to the clerk and recorder, for the clerk and recorder to file and record the document in his or her office.

§ 38-29-206, C.R.S. Recorded documents – index

Any document filed and recorded by a clerk and recorder pursuant to this part 2 shall be indexed in both the grantor and grantee indexes under the name of the owner or owners of the manufactured home and the owners of the land to which the manufactured home was affixed or permanently located at the time the document is required to be filed and recorded.

§ 38-29-207, C.R.S. Copy of certificates to assessor

The clerk and recorder shall forward a copy of a certificate of permanent location, certificate of removal, and certificate of destruction to the assessor for the county or city and county.

§ 38-29-208, C.R.S. Affidavit of real property

(1) Any person can prove that a manufactured home and the land upon which it has been permanently affixed is real property by filing an affidavit of real property with the clerk and recorder for the county or city and county in which the manufactured home is located. The clerk and recorder shall file and record the affidavit of real property in his or her office. Except as otherwise set forth in subsection (2) of this section, the affidavit of real property shall include the following:

   (a) An acknowledged statement by all owners that the manufactured home and real property to which the manufactured home is permanently affixed became real property pursuant to this article;

   (b) A statement from the county assessor that the manufactured home has been valued together with the land upon which it is affixed;

   (c) A statement from the county treasurer that taxes have been paid on the manufactured home and the land upon which it is affixed in the same manner as other real property, as that term is defined in section 39-1-102(14), C.R.S.;

   (d) Proof that a search of the director's records pursuant to section 42-1-206, C.R.S., was conducted and that no certificate of title was found for the manufactured home; and

   (e) Verification that the manufactured home is permanently affixed to the ground in accordance with any applicable county or city and county codes or requirements so that it is no longer capable of being drawn over the public highways.

(2) If a manufactured home occupies real property subject to a long-term lease that has an express term of at least ten years, then the affidavit of real property shall include the following:

   (a) A copy of the applicable long-term lease;

   (b) A statement from the county treasurer that taxes have been paid separately on the manufactured home and the land upon which it is affixed; and

   (c) The items set forth in paragraphs (a), (d), and (e) of subsection (1) of this section.

§ 38-29-209, C.R.S. Fees – disposition

(1) In all instances in which a document is to be filed and recorded pursuant to this part 2, the authorized agent or clerk and recorder, as the case may be, shall be paid such fees for each document so filed and recorded as are prescribed by law for the filing of like instruments in the office of the county clerk and recorder.

(2) The recording fees authorized by this section are in addition to any fees that are required pursuant to section 38-29-138.

(3) All fees paid pursuant to this section shall be kept and retained by the authorized agent or the clerk and recorder to defray the cost thereof and shall be disposed of by him or her as provided by law.

V. Nondisclosure of Information Psychologically Impacting Real Property

§ 38-35.5-101, C.R.S. Circumstances psychologically impacting real property – no duty for broker or salesperson to disclose

(1) Facts or suspicions regarding circumstances occurring on a parcel of property which could psychologically impact or stigmatize such property are not material facts subject to a disclosure requirement in a real estate transaction. Such facts or suspicions include, but are not limited to, the following:

  (a) That an occupant of real property is, or was at any time suspected to be, infected or has been infected with human immunodeficiency virus (HIV) or diagnosed with acquired immune deficiency syndrome (AIDS), or any other disease which has been determined by medical evidence to be highly unlikely to be transmitted through the occupancy of a dwelling place; or

  (b) That the property was the site of a homicide or other felony or of a suicide.

(2) No cause of action shall arise against a real estate broker or salesperson for failing to disclose such circumstance occurring on the property which might psychologically impact or stigmatize such property.

VI. Soil and Hazard Analyses of Residential Construction

§ 6-6.5-101, C.R.S. Disclosure to purchaser – penalty

(1) At least fourteen days prior to closing the sale of any new residence for human habitation, every developer or builder or their representatives shall provide the purchaser with a copy of a summary report of the analysis and the site recommendations. For sites in which significant potential for expansive soils is recognized, the builder or his representative shall supply each buyer with a copy of a publication detailing the problems associated with such soils, the building methods to address these problems during construction, and suggestions for care and maintenance to address such problems.

(2) In addition to any other liability or penalty, any builder or developer failing to provide the report or publication required by subsection (1) of this section shall be subject to a civil penalty of five hundred dollars payable to the purchaser.

(3) The requirements of this section shall not apply to any individual constructing a residential structure for his own residence.

VII. Uniform Power of Attorney Act

§ 15-14-702, C.R.S. Definitions

* Except as otherwise provided, under this part 7, and except as the context may otherwise require, in this part 7:

(1) "Agent" means a person granted authority to act for a principal under a power of attorney, whether denominated an agent, attorney-in-fact, or otherwise. The term includes an original agent, coagent, successor agent, and a person to which an agent's authority is delegated.

(2) "Durable", with respect to a power of attorney, means not terminated by the principal's incapacity.

(3) "Electronic" means relating to technology having electrical, digital, magnetic, wireless, optical, electromagnetic, or similar capabilities.

(4) "Good faith" means honesty in fact.

(5) "Incapacity" means inability of an individual to manage property or business affairs because the individual:

(a) Has an impairment in the ability to receive and evaluate information or make or communicate decisions even with the use of technological assistance; or

(b) Is:

(I) Missing;

(II) Detained, including incarcerated in a penal system; or

(III) Outside the United States and unable to return.

(6) "Person" means an individual, corporation, business trust, estate, trust, partnership, limited liability company, association, joint venture, public corporation, government or governmental subdivision, agency, or instrumentality, or any other legal or commercial entity.

(7) "Power of attorney" means a writing or other record that grants authority to an agent to act in the place of the principal, whether or not the term power of attorney is used.

(8) "Presently exercisable general power of appointment", with respect to property or a property interest subject to a power of appointment, means power exercisable at the time in question to vest absolute ownership in the principal individually, the principal's estate, the principal's creditors, or the creditors of the principal's estate. The term includes a power of appointment not exercisable until the occurrence of a specified event, the satisfaction of an ascertainable standard, or the passage of a specified period only after the occurrence of the specified event, the satisfaction of the ascertainable standard, or the passage of the specified period. The term does not include a power exercisable in a fiduciary capacity or only by will.

(9) "Principal" means an individual who grants authority to an agent in a power of attorney.

(10) "Property" means anything that may be the subject of ownership, whether real or personal, or legal or equitable, or any interest or right therein.

(11) "Record" means information that is inscribed on a tangible medium or that is stored in an electronic or other medium and is retrievable in perceivable form.

(12) "Sign" means, with present intent to authenticate or adopt a record:

(a) To execute or adopt a tangible symbol; or

(b) To attach to or logically associate with the record an electronic sound, symbol, or process.

(13) "State" means a state of the United States, the District of Columbia, Puerto Rico, the United States Virgin Islands, or any territory or insular possession subject to the jurisdiction of the United States.

(14) "Stocks and bonds" means stocks, bonds, mutual funds, and all other types of securities and financial instruments, whether held directly, indirectly, or in any other manner. The term does not include commodity futures contracts and call or put options on stocks or stock indexes.

§ 15-14-714, C.R.S. Agent's duties

(1) Notwithstanding provisions in the power of attorney, an agent that has accepted appointment shall:

(a) Act in accordance with the principal's reasonable expectations to the extent actually known by the agent and, otherwise, in the principal's best interest;

(b) Act in good faith; and

(c) Act only within the scope of authority granted in the power of attorney.

(2) Except as otherwise provided in the power of attorney, an agent that has accepted appointment shall:

(a) Act loyally for the principal's benefit;

(b) Act so as not to create a conflict of interest that impairs the agent's ability to act impartially in the principal's best interest;

(c) Act with the care, competence, and diligence ordinarily exercised by agents in similar circumstances;

(d) Keep a record of all receipts, disbursements, and transactions made on behalf of the principal;

(e) Cooperate with a person that has authority to make health care decisions for the principal to carry out the principal's reasonable expectations to the extent actually known by the agent and, otherwise, act in the principal's best interest; and

(f) Attempt to preserve the principal's estate plan, to the extent actually known by the agent, if preserving the plan is consistent with the principal's best interest based on all relevant factors, including:

(I) The value and nature of the principal's property;

(II) The principal's foreseeable obligations and need for maintenance;

(III) Minimization of taxes, including income, estate, inheritance, generation-skipping transfer, and gift taxes; and

(IV) Eligibility for a benefit, a program, or assistance under a statute or regulation.

(3) An agent that acts in good faith is not liable to any beneficiary of the principal's estate plan for failure to preserve the plan.

(4) An agent that acts with care, competence, and diligence for the best interest of the principal is not liable solely because the agent also benefits from the act or has an individual or conflicting interest in relation to the property or affairs of the principal.

(5) If an agent is selected by the principal because of special skills or expertise possessed by the agent or in reliance on the agent's representation that the agent has special skills or expertise, the special skills or expertise must be considered in determining whether the agent has acted with care, competence, and diligence under the circumstances.

(6) Absent a breach of duty to the principal, an agent is not liable if the value of the principal's property declines.

(7) An agent that exercises authority provided in the power of attorney to delegate to another person the authority granted by the principal or that engages another person on behalf of the principal is not liable for an act, error of judgment, or default of that person if the agent exercises care, competence, and diligence in selecting and monitoring the person.

(8) Except as otherwise provided in the power of attorney, an agent is not required to disclose receipts, disbursements, or transactions conducted on behalf of the principal unless ordered by a court or requested by the principal, a guardian, a conservator, another fiduciary acting for the principal, a governmental agency having authority to protect the welfare of the principal, or, upon the death of the principal, by the personal representative or successor in interest of the principal's estate. If so requested, within thirty days the agent shall comply with the request or provide a writing or other record substantiating why additional time is needed and shall comply with the request within an additional thirty days.

§ 15-14-726, C.R.S. Construction of authority generally

(1) Except as otherwise provided in the power of attorney, by executing a power of attorney that incorporates by reference a subject described in sections 15-14-727 to 15-14-740 or that grants to an agent authority to do all acts that a principal could do pursuant to section 15-14-724 (3), a principal authorizes the agent, with respect to that subject, to:

(a) Demand, receive, and obtain by litigation or otherwise money or another thing of value to which the principal is, may become, or claims to be entitled and conserve, invest, disburse, or use anything so received or obtained for the purposes intended;

(b) Contract in any manner with any person, on terms agreeable to the agent, to accomplish a purpose of a transaction and perform, rescind, cancel, terminate, reform, restate, release, or modify the contract or another contract made by or on behalf of the principal;

(c) Execute, acknowledge, seal, deliver, file, or record any instrument or communication the agent considers desirable to accomplish a purpose of a transaction, including creating at any time a schedule listing some or all of the principal's property and attaching it to the power of attorney;

(d) Initiate, participate in, submit to alternative dispute resolution, settle, oppose, or propose or accept a compromise with respect to a claim existing in favor of or against the principal or intervene in litigation relating to the claim;

(e) Seek on the principal's behalf the assistance of a court or other governmental agency to carry out an act authorized in the power of attorney;

(f) Engage, compensate, and discharge an attorney, accountant, discretionary investment manager, expert witness, or other advisor;

(g) Prepare, execute, and file a record, report, or other document to safeguard or promote the principal's interest under a statute or regulation;

(h) Communicate with any representative or employee of a government or governmental subdivision, agency, or instrumentality on behalf of the principal;

(i) Access communications intended for and communicate on behalf of the principal, whether by mail, electronic transmission, telephone, or other means; and

(j) Do any lawful act with respect to the subject and all property related to the subject.

§ 15-14-727, C.R.S. Real property

(1) Unless the power of attorney otherwise provides, language in a power of attorney granting general authority with respect to real property authorizes the agent to:

(a) Demand, buy, lease, receive, accept as a gift or as security for an extension of credit, or otherwise acquire or reject an interest in real property or a right incident to real property;

(b) Sell; exchange; convey with or without covenants, representations, or warranties; quitclaim; release; surrender; retain title for security; encumber; partition; consent to partitioning; subject to an easement or covenant; subdivide; apply for zoning or other governmental permits; plat or consent to platting; develop; grant an option concerning; lease; sublease; contribute to an entity in exchange for an interest in that entity; or otherwise grant or dispose of an interest in real property or a right incident to real property;

(c) Pledge or mortgage an interest in real property or right incident to real property as security to borrow money or pay, renew, or extend the time of payment of a debt of the principal or a debt guaranteed by the principal;

(d) Release, assign, satisfy, or enforce by litigation or otherwise a mortgage, deed of trust, conditional sale contract, encumbrance, lien, or other claim to real property that exists or is asserted;

(e) Manage or conserve an interest in real property or a right incident to real property owned or claimed to be owned by the principal, including:
 (I) Insuring against liability or casualty or other loss;
 (II) Obtaining or regaining possession of or protecting the interest or right by litigation or otherwise;
 (III) Paying, assessing, compromising, or contesting taxes or assessments or applying for and receiving refunds in connection with them; and
 (IV) Purchasing supplies, hiring assistance or labor, and making repairs or alterations to the real property;

(f) Use, develop, alter, replace, remove, erect, or install structures or other improvements upon real property in or incident to which the principal has, or claims to have, an interest or right;

(g) Participate in a reorganization with respect to real property or an entity that owns an interest in or right incident to real property and receive, and hold, and act with respect to stocks and bonds or other property received in a plan of reorganization, including:
 (I) Selling or otherwise disposing of them;
 (II) Exercising or selling an option, right of conversion, or similar right with respect to them; and
 (III) Exercising any voting rights in person or by proxy;

(h) Change the form of title of an interest in or right incident to real property; and

(i) Dedicate to public use, with or without consideration, easements or other real property in which the principal has or claims to have an interest.

VIII. Relief of Residential Taxpayers from Lien of Special District Taxes for General Obligation Indebtedness

Certification and Notice of Special District Taxes for General Obligation Indebtedness

§ 32-1-1601, C.R.S. Legislative declaration

The general assembly hereby finds and declares that special districts are political subdivisions and instrumentalities of the state of Colorado and local governments thereof. The general assembly further finds that defaults in payment of general obligation debts and the possibility of further defaults by some special districts have resulted in a general loss of confidence by investors in bonds and undertakings of all types issued or to be issued by local governments of the state and have imposed severe hardship on investors in general obligation bonds of special districts and upon owners of residential real property within such districts. The general assembly further finds that this Part 16 is necessary to protect the credit reputation of local governments of this state, to restore confidence of investors in local government obligations, and to protect owners of residential real property within special districts.

§ 32-1-1602, C.R.S. Definitions

As used in this part 16, unless the context otherwise requires:

(1) "General obligation debt" means an obligation of a special district created by a resolution of the special district authorizing the issuance of bonds or a contract, the obligations of which are backed by a pledge of the full faith and credit of the special district and a covenant to impose mill levies without limit to retire the bonds or fund the contractual obligation.

(2) "Special district" shall have the same meaning as provided in section 32-1-103 (20).

§ 32-1-1603, C.R.S. Separate mill levies – certification to county commissioners

After July 1, 1992, special districts which levy taxes for payment of general obligation debt shall certify separate mill levies to the board of county commissioners, one each for funding requirements of each such debt in accordance with the relevant contracts or bond resolutions which identifies each bond issue by series, date, coupon rate, and maturity and each contract by title, date, principal amount, and maturity and one for the remainder of the budget of said district.

§ 32-1-1604, C.R.S. Recording

Whenever a special district authorizes or incurs a general obligation debt, a notice of such action and a description of such debt in a form prescribed by the director of the division of local government in the department of local affairs shall be recorded by the special district with the county clerk and recorder in each county in which the district is located. The recording shall be done within thirty days after authorizing or incurring the debt.

§ 32-1-1605, C.R.S. Limitations on actions – prior law

Any claim for relief under section 32-1-1504, as it existed prior to July 1, 1992, shall be commenced on or before January 1,1993, and not thereafter.

§ 10-11-122, C.R.S. Title commitments

(1) Every title insurance agent or title insurance company shall provide, along with each title commitment issued for the sale of residential real property as defined in Section 39-1-102 (14.5), C.R.S., a statement disclosing the following information:

- (a) That the subject real property may be located in a special taxing district;
- (b) That a certificate of taxes due listing each taxing jurisdiction shall be obtained from the county treasurer or the county treasurer's authorized agent;
- (c) That information regarding special districts and the boundaries of such districts may be obtained from the board of county commissioners, the county clerk and recorder, or the county assessor.

(2) Failure of a title insurance agent or a title insurance company to provide the statement required by subsection (1) of this section shall subject such agent or company to the penalty provisions of section 10-3-111 but shall not affect or invalidate any provisions of the commitment for title insurance.

(3) Before issuing any title insurance policy, unless the proposed insured provides written instructions to the contrary, a title insurance agent or title insurance company shall obtain a certificate of taxes due or other equivalent documentation from the county treasurer or the county treasurer's authorized agent.

§ 38-35.7-101, C.R.S. Disclosure – special taxing districts – general obligation indebtedness

(1) Every contract for the purchase and sale of residential real property shall contain a disclosure statement in bold-faced type which is clearly legible and in substantially the following form:

> **SPECIAL TAXING DISTRICTS MAY BE SUBJECT TO GENERAL OBLIGATION INDEBTEDNESS THAT IS PAID BY REVENUES PRODUCED FROM ANNUAL TAX LEVIES ON THE TAXABLE PROPERTY WITHIN SUCH DISTRICTS. PROPERTY OWNERS IN SUCH DISTRICTS MAY BE PLACED AT RISK FOR INCREASED MILL LEVIES AND TAX TO SUPPORT THE SERVICING OF SUCH DEBT**

WHERE CIRCUMSTANCES ARISE RESULTING IN THE INABILITY OF SUCH A DISTRICT TO DISCHARGE SUCH INDEBTEDNESS WITHOUT SUCH AN INCREASE IN MILL LEVIES. BUYERS SHOULD INVESTIGATE THE SPECIAL TAXING DISTRICTS IN WHICH THE PROPERTY IS LOCATED BY CONTACTING THE COUNTY TREASURER, BY REVIEWING THE CERTIFICATE OF TAXES DUE FOR THE PROPERTY, AND BY OBTAINING FURTHER INFORMATION FROM THE BOARD OF COUNTY COMMISSIONERS, THE COUNTY CLERK AND RECORDER, OR THE COUNTY ASSESSOR.

[Ed. Note: The above disclosure is printed in all versions of the Real Estate Commission-approved "Contract to Buy and Sell Real Estate."]

(2) The obligation to provide the disclosure set forth in subsection (1) of this section shall be upon the seller, and, in the event of the failure by the seller to provide the written disclosure described in subsection (1) of this section, the purchaser shall have a claim for relief against the seller for all damages to the purchaser resulting from such failure plus court costs.

IX. Colorado Consumer Protection Act

Section 12-61-113(1)(c.5), C.R.S., which is printed in Chapter 1, lists as a cause for disciplinary action and possible revocation of a real estate license, the conviction of a violation of § 6-1-105(1), C.R.S., known as The Colorado Consumer Protection Act. The civil penalties for conviction include a payment of up to $100,000 to the state general fund and three times the amount of actual damages to the injured party in a private civil action.

Printed below are the portions of the law pertinent to the real estate industry.

§ 6-1-104, C.R.S. Cooperative reporting

The district attorneys may cooperate in a statewide reporting system by receiving, on forms provided by the attorney general, complaints from persons concerning deceptive trade practices listed in sections 6-1-105 and part 7 of this article and transmitting such complaints to the attorney general.

§ 6-1-105, C.R.S. Deceptive trade practices

(1) A person engages in a deceptive trade practice when, in the course of such person's business, vocation, or occupation, such person:

- (a) Knowingly passes off goods, services, or property as those of another;
- (b) Knowingly makes a false representation as to the source, sponsorship, approval, or certification of goods, services, or property;
- (c) Knowingly makes a false representation as to affiliation, connection, or association with or certification by another;
- (d) Uses deceptive representations or designations of geographic origin in connection with goods or services;
- (e) Knowingly makes a false representation as to the characteristics, ingredients, uses, benefits, alterations, or quantities of goods, food, services, or property or a false representation as to the sponsorship, approval, status, affiliation, or connection of a person therewith;
- (f) Represents that goods are original or new if he knows or should know that they are deteriorated, altered, reconditioned, reclaimed, used, or secondhand;

(g) Represents that goods, food, services, or property are of a particular standard, quality, or grade, or that goods are of a particular style or model, if he knows or should know that they are of another;

(h) Disparages the goods, services, property, or business of another by false or misleading representation of fact;

(i) Advertises goods, services, or property with intent not to sell them as advertised;

(j) Advertises goods or services with intent not to supply reasonably expectable public demand, unless the advertisement discloses a limitation of quantity;

(k) Advertises under the guise of obtaining sales personnel when in fact the purpose is to first sell a product or service to the sales personnel applicant;

(l) Makes false or misleading statements of fact concerning the price of goods, services, or property or the reasons for, existence of, or amounts of price reductions;

(m) Fails to deliver to the customer at the time of an installment sale of goods or services a written order, contract, or receipt setting forth the name and address of the seller, the name and address of the organization which he represents, and all of the terms and conditions of the sale, including a description of the goods or services, stated in readable, clear, and unambiguous language;

(n) Employs "bait and switch" advertising, which is advertising accompanied by an effort to sell goods, services, or property other than those advertised or on terms other than those advertised and which is also accompanied by one or more of the following practices:

(I) Refusal to show the goods or property advertised or to offer the services advertised;

(II) Disparagement in any respect of the advertised goods, property, or services or the terms of sale;

(III) Requiring tie-in sales or other undisclosed conditions to be met prior to selling the advertised goods, property, or services;

(IV) Refusal to take orders for the goods, property, or services advertised for delivery within a reasonable time;

(V) Showing or demonstrating defective goods, property, or services which are unusable or impractical for the purposes set forth in the advertisement;

(VI) Accepting a deposit for the goods, property, or services and subsequently switching the purchase order to higher-priced goods, property, or services; or

(VII) Failure to make deliveries of the goods, property, or services within a reasonable time or to make a refund therefor;

(o) Knowingly fails to identify flood-damaged or water-damaged goods as to such damages;

(p) Solicits door-to-door as a seller, unless the seller, within thirty seconds after beginning the conversation, identifies himself or herself, whom he or she represents, and the purpose of the call;

(p.3) to (p.7) Repealed.

(q) Contrives, prepares, sets up, operates, publicizes by means of advertisements, or promotes any pyramid promotional scheme;

(r) Advertises or otherwise represents that goods or services are guaranteed without clearly and conspicuously disclosing the nature and extent of the guarantee, any material conditions or limitations in the guarantee which are imposed by the guarantor, the manner in which the guarantor will perform, and the identity of such guarantor. Any representation that goods or services are "guaranteed for life" or have a "lifetime guarantee" shall contain, in addition to the other requirements of this paragraph (r), a conspicuous disclosure of the meaning of "life" or "lifetime" as used in such representation (whether that of the purchaser, the goods or services, or otherwise). Guarantees shall not be used which under normal conditions could not be practically fulfilled or which are for such a period of time or are otherwise of such a nature as to have the capacity and tendency of misleading purchasers or prospective purchasers into believing that the goods or services so guaranteed have a greater degree of serviceability, durability, or performance capability in actual use than is true in fact. The provisions of this paragraph (r) apply not only to guarantees but also to warranties, to disclaimer of warranties, to purported guarantees and warranties, and to any promise or representation in the nature of a guarantee or warranty; however, such provisions do not apply to any reference to a guarantee in a slogan or advertisement so long as there is no guarantee or warranty of specific merchandise or other property.

(s) and (t) Repealed.

(u) Fails to disclose material information concerning goods, services, or property which information was known at the time of an advertisement or sale if such failure to disclose such information was intended to induce the consumer to enter into a transaction;

(v) Disburses funds in connection with a real estate transaction in violation of section 38-35-125 (2), C.R.S.;

(w) Repealed.

(x) Violates the provisions of sections 6-1-203 to 6-1-205 or of part 7 of this article;

(y) Fails, in connection with any solicitation, oral or written, to clearly and prominently disclose immediately adjacent to or after the description of any item or prize to be received by any person the actual retail value of each item or prize to be awarded. For the purposes of this paragraph (y), the actual retail value is the price at which substantial sales of the item were made in the person's trade area or in the trade area in which the item or prize is to be received within the last ninety days or, if no substantial sales were made, the actual cost of the item or prize to the person on whose behalf any contest or promotion is conducted; except that, whenever the actual cost of the item to the provider is less than fifteen dollars per item, a disclosure that "actual cost to the provider is less than fifteen dollars" may be made in lieu of disclosure of actual cost. The provisions of this paragraph (y) shall not apply to a promotion which is soliciting the sale of a newspaper, magazine, or periodical of general circulation, or to a promotion soliciting the sale of books, records, audio tapes, compact discs, or videos when the promoter allows the purchaser to review the merchandise without obligation for at least seven days and provides a full refund within thirty days after the receipt of the returned merchandise or when a membership club operation is in conformity with rules and regulations of the federal trade commission contained in 16 CFR 425.

(z) Refuses or fails to obtain all governmental licenses or permits required to perform the services or to sell the goods, food, services, or property as agreed to or contracted for with a consumer;

(aa) Fails, in connection with the issuing, making, providing, selling, or offering to sell of a motor vehicle service contract, to comply with the provisions of article 11 of title 42, C.R.S.;

(bb) Repealed.

(cc) Engages in any commercial telephone solicitation which constitutes an unlawful telemarketing practice as defined in section 6-1-304;

(dd) Repealed.

(ee) Intentionally violates any provision of article 10 of title 5, C.R.S.;

(ee.5) to (ff) Repealed.

(gg) Fails to disclose or misrepresents to another person, a secured creditor, or an assignee by whom such person is retained to repossess personal property whether such person is bonded in accordance with section 4-9-629, C.R.S., or fails to file such bond with the attorney general;

(hh) Violates any provision of article 16 of this title;

(ii) Repealed.

(jj) Represents to any person that such person has won or is eligible to win any award, prize, or thing of value as the result of a contest, promotion, sweepstakes, or drawing, or that such person will receive or is eligible to receive free goods, services, or property, unless, at the time of the representation, the person has the present ability to supply such award, prize, or thing of value;

(kk) Violates any provision of article 6 of this title;

(ll) Knowingly makes a false representation as to the results of a radon test or the need for radon mitigation;

(mm) Violates section 35-27-113 (3) (e), (3) (f), or (3) (i), C.R.S.;

(nn) Repealed.

(oo) Fails to comply with the provisions of section 35-80-108 (1) (a), (1) (b), or (2) (f), C.R.S.;

(pp) Violates article 9 of title 42, C.R.S.;

(qq) Repealed.

(rr) Violates the provisions of part 8 of this article;

(ss) Violates any provision of part 33 of article 32 of title 24, C.R.S., that applies to the installation of manufactured homes;

(tt) Violates any provision of part 9 of this article;

(uu) Violates section 38-40-105, C.R.S.;

(vv) Violates section 12-55-110.3, C.R.S.;

(ww) Violates any provision of section 6-1-702;

(xx) Violates any provision of part 11 of this article;

(yy) Violates any provision of part 3 of article 5.5 of title 12, C.R.S.;

(zz) Violates any provision of section 6-1-717;

(aaa) Violates any provision of section 12-61-904.5, C.R.S.;

(bbb) Violates any provision of section 12-61-911, C.R.S.

(ccc) Violates the provisions of section 6-1-722.

(2) Evidence that a person has engaged in a deceptive trade practice shall be prima facie evidence of intent to injure competitors and to destroy or substantially lessen competition.

(3) The deceptive trade practices listed in this section are in addition to and do not limit the types of unfair trade practices actionable at common law or under other statutes of this state.

§ 6-1-113, C.R.S. Damages

(1) The provisions of this article shall be available in a civil action for any claim against any person who has engaged in or caused another to engage in any deceptive trade practice listed in this article. An action under this section shall be available to any person who:

(a) Is an actual or potential consumer of the defendant's goods, services, or property and is injured as a result of such deceptive trade practice, or is a residential subscriber, as defined in section 6-1-903(9), who receives unlawful telephone solicitation, as defined in section 6-1-903(10); or

(b) Is any successor in interest to an actual consumer who purchased the defendant's goods, services, or property; or

(c) In the course of the person's business or occupation, is injured as a result of such deceptive trade practice.

(2) Except in a class action or a case brought for a violation of section 6-1-709, any person who, in a private civil action, is found to have engaged in or caused another to engage in any deceptive trade practice listed in this article shall be liable in an amount equal to the sum of:

(a) The greater of:

(I) The amount of actual damages sustained; or

(II) Five hundred dollars; or

(III) Three times the amount of actual damages sustained, if it is established by clear and convincing evidence that such person engaged in bad faith conduct; plus

(b) In the case of any successful action to enforce said liability, the costs of the action together with reasonable attorney fees as determined by the court.

(2.3) As used in subsection (2) of this section, "bad faith conduct" means fraudulent, willful, knowing, or intentional conduct that causes injury.

(2.5) Notwithstanding the provisions of subsection (2) of this section, in the case of any violation of section 6-1-709, in addition to interest, costs of the action, and reasonable attorney fees as determined by the court, the prevailing party shall be entitled only to damages in an amount sufficient to refund moneys actually paid for a manufactured home not delivered in accordance with the provisions of section 6-1-709.

(2.7) Notwithstanding the provisions of subsection (2) of this section, in case of any violation of section 6-1-105 (1) (ss), the court may award reasonable costs of the action and attorney fees and interest, and in addition, the prevailing party shall be entitled only to damages in an amount sufficient to refund moneys actually paid for the installation of a manufactured home not installed in accordance with the provisions of part 33 of article 32 of title 24, C.R.S., that apply to the installation of manufactured homes.

(3) Any person who brings an action under this article that is found by the court to be groundless and in bad faith or for the purpose of harassment shall be liable to the defendant for the costs of the action together with reasonable attorney fees as determined by the court.

(4) Costs and attorney fees shall be awarded to the attorney general or a district attorney in all actions where the attorney general or the district attorney successfully enforces this article.

§ 6-1-703, C.R.S. Time shares – deceptive trade practices

(1) A person engages in a deceptive trade practice when, in the course of such person's business, vocation, or occupation, such person engages in one or more of the following activities in connection with the advertisement or sale of a time share:

(a) Misrepresents the investment, resale, or rental value of any time share; the conditions under which a purchaser may exchange the right to use accommodations or facilities in one location for the right to use accommodations or facilities in another location; or the period of time during which the accommodations or facilities contracted for will be available to the purchaser;

(b) Fails to allow any purchaser of a time share a right to rescind the sale within five calendar days after the sale;

(c) Fails to provide conspicuous notice on the contract of the right of a purchaser of a time share to rescind the sale either by telegram, mail, or hand delivery. For purposes of this section, notice of rescission is considered given, if by mail when postmarked, if by telegram when filed for telegraphic transmission, or if by hand delivery when delivered to the seller's place of business.

(d) Fails to refund any down payment or deposit made pursuant to a time share contract within seven days after the seller receives the purchaser's written notice of rescission.

§ 6-1-709, C.R.S. Sales of manufactured homes – deceptive trade practices

A person engages in a deceptive trade practice when, in the course of such person's business, vocation, or occupation, such personengages in conduct that constitutes an unlawful manufactured home sale practice as described in section 24-32-3326, C.R.S.

X. Disclosure – Methamphetamine Laboratory

CONCERNING MANDATORY DISCLOSURE IN CONNECTION WITH THE PURCHASE OF RESIDENTIAL REAL PROPERTY OF WHETHER THE PROPERTY HAS BEEN USED AS A METHAMPHETAMINE LABORATORY. (EFFECTIVE JANUARY 1, 2007)

§ 38-35.7-103, C.R.S. Disclosure – methamphetamine laboratory

(1) A buyer of residential real property has the right to test the property for the purpose of determining whether the property has ever been used as a methamphetamine laboratory.

(2) (a) Tests conducted pursuant to this section shall be performed by a certified industrial hygienist or industrial hygienist, as those terms are defined in section 24-30-1402, C.R.S., and in accordance with the procedures and standards established by rules of the state board of health promulgated pursuant to section 25-18.5-102, C.R.S. If the buyer's test results indicate that the property has been contaminated with methamphetamine or other contaminants for which standards have been established pursuant to section 25-18.5-102, C.R.S., and has not been remediated to meet the standards established by rules of the state board of health promulgated pursuant to section 25-18.5-102, C.R.S., the buyer shall promptly give written notice to the seller of the results of the test, and the buyer may terminate the contract. The contract shall not limit the rights to test the property or to cancel the contract based upon the result of the tests.

(b) The seller shall have thirty days after receipt of the notice to conduct a second independent test. If the seller's test results indicate that the property has been used as a methamphetamine laboratory but has not been remediated to meet the standards established by rules of the state board of health promulgated pursuant to section 25-18.5-102, C.R.S., then the second independent hygienist shall so notify the seller.

(c) If the seller receives the notice referred to in paragraph (b) of this subsection (2) or if the seller receives the notice referred to in paragraph (a) of this subsection (2) and does not elect to have the property retested pursuant to paragraph (b) of this subsection (2), then an illegal drug laboratory used to manufacture methamphetamine shall be deemed to have been discovered and the owner shall be deemed to have received notice pursuant to section 25-18.5-103 (1) (a), C.R.S. Nothing in this section shall prohibit a buyer from purchasing the property and assuming liability pursuant to section 25-18.5-103, C.R.S., if, on the date of closing, the buyer provides notice to the department of public health and environment of the purchase and assumption of liability and if the remediation required by section 25-18.5-103, C.R.S., is completed within ninety days after the date of closing.

(3) (a) Except as specified in subsection (4) of this section, the seller shall disclose in writing to the buyer whether the seller knows that the property was previously used as a methamphetamine laboratory.

(b) A seller who fails to make a disclosure required by this section at or before the time of sale and who knew of methamphetamine production on the property is liable to the buyer for:

(I) Costs relating to remediation of the property according to the standards established by rules of the state board of health promulgated pursuant to section 25-18.5-102, C.R.S.;

(II) Costs relating to health-related injuries occurring after the sale to residents of the property caused by methamphetamine production on the property; and

(III) Reasonable attorney fees for collection of costs from the seller.

(c) A buyer shall commence an action under this subsection (3) within three years after the date on which the buyer closed the purchase of the property where the methamphetamine production occurred.

(4) If the seller became aware that the property was once used for the production of methamphetamine and the property was remediated in accordance with the standards established pursuant to section 25-18.5-102, C.R.S., and evidence of such remediation was received by the applicable governing body in compliance with the documentation requirements established pursuant to section 25-18.5-102, C.R.S., then the seller shall not be required to disclose that the property was used as a methamphetamine laboratory to a buyer, and the property shall be removed from any government-sponsored informational service listing properties that have been used for the production of methamphetamine.

(5) For purposes of this section, "residential real property" includes a: Manufactured home; mobile home; condominium; townhome; home sold by the owner, a financial institution, or the federal department of housing and urban development; rental property, including an apartment; and short-term residence such as a motel or hotel.

Illegal Drug Laboratories

§ 25-18.5-101, C.R.S. Definitions

As used in this article, unless the context otherwise requires:

(1) "Board" means the state board of health in the department of public health and environment.

(2) (Deleted by amendment, L. 2009, (SB 09-060), ch. 140, p. 600, § 1, effective April 20, 2009.)

(2.5) "Governing body" means the agency or office designated by the city council or board of county commissioners where the property in question is located. If there is no such designation, the governing body shall be the county, district, or municipal public health agency, building department, and law enforcement agency with jurisdiction over the property in question.

(2.7) "Illegal drug laboratory" means the areas where controlled substances, as defined by section 18-18-102, C.R.S., have been manufactured, processed, cooked, disposed of, used, or stored and all proximate areas that are likely to be contaminated as a result of such manufacturing, processing, cooking, disposal, use, or storing.

(3) "Property" means anything that may be the subject of ownership, including, but not limited to, land, buildings, structures, and vehicles.

(4) "Property owner", for the purposes of real property, means the person holding record fee title to real property. "Property owner" also means the person holding the title to a manufactured home.

§ 25-18.5-102, C.R.S. Illegal drug laboratories – rules

The board shall promulgate health-protective rules that establish procedures for testing and evaluation of contamination and the acceptable standards for the cleanup of illegal drug laboratories involving methamphetamine.

§ 25-18.5-103, C.R.S. Discovery of illegal drug laboratory – property owner – cleanup – liability

(1) (a) Upon notification from a peace officer that chemicals, equipment, or supplies indicative of an illegal drug laboratory are located on a property, or when an illegal drug laboratory used to manufacture methamphetamine is otherwise discovered and the property owner has received notice, the owner of any contaminated property shall meet the clean-up standards for property established by the board in section 25-18.5-102; except that a property owner may, at his or her option and subject to paragraph (b) of this subsection (1), elect instead to demolish the contaminated property. If the owner elects to demolish the contaminated property, the governing body or, if none has been designated, the county, district, or municipal public health agency, building department, or law enforcement agency with jurisdiction over the area where the property is located may require the owner to fence off the property or otherwise make it inaccessible to persons for occupancy or intrusion.

(b) An owner of any personal property within a structure or vehicle contaminated by illegal drug laboratory activity shall have ten days after the date of discovery of the laboratory or contamination to remove or clean his or her personal property according to board rules. If the personal property owner fails to remove the personal property within ten days, the owner of the structure or vehicle may dispose of the personal property during the clean-up process without liability to the owner of the personal property for such disposition.

(2) Once a property owner has met the clean-up standards and documentation requirements established by the board, as evidenced by a copy of the results provided to the governing body, or has demolished the property, compliance with subsection (1) of this section shall establish immunity for the property owner from a suit for alleged health-based civil actions brought by any future owner, renter, or other person who occupies such property, or a neighbor of such property, in which the alleged cause of the injury or loss is the existence of the illegal drug laboratory used to manufacture methamphetamine; except that immunity from a civil suit is not established for the person convicted for the production of methamphetamine.

(3) A person who removes personal property or debris from a drug laboratory shall secure the property and debris to prevent theft or exposing another person to any toxic or hazardous chemicals until the property and debris is appropriately disposed of or cleaned according to board rules.

§ 25-18.5-104, C.R.S. Entry into illegal drug laboratories

If a structure or vehicle has been determined to be contaminated or if a governing body or law enforcement agency issues a notice of probable contamination, the owner of the structure or vehicle shall not permit any person to have access to the structure or vehicle unless the person is trained or certified to handle contaminated property pursuant to board rules or federal law.

§ 25-18.5-105, C.R.S. Drug laboratories – governing body – authority

(1) An illegal drug laboratory that has not met the clean-up standards set by the board in section 25-18.5-102 shall be deemed a public health nuisance.

(2) Governing bodies may enact ordinances or resolutions to enforce this article, including, but not limited to, preventing unauthorized entry into contaminated property; requiring contaminated property to meet clean-up standards before it is occupied; notifying the public of contaminated property; coordinating services and sharing information between law enforcement, building, public health, and social services agencies and officials; and charging reasonable inspection and testing fees.

XI. Common Interest Community Disclosure

§ 38-35.7-102, C.R.S. Disclosure – common interest community – obligation to pay assessments – requirement for architectural approval

(1) On and after January 1, 2007, every contract for the purchase and sale of residential real property in a common interest community shall contain a disclosure statement in bold-faced type that is clearly legible and in substantially the following form:

THE PROPERTY IS LOCATED WITHIN A COMMON INTEREST COMMUNITY AND IS SUBJECT TO THE DECLARATION FOR SUCH COMMUNITY. THE OWNER OF THE PROPERTY WILL BE REQUIRED TO BE A MEMBER OF THE OWNER'S ASSOCIATION FOR THE COMMUNITY AND WILL BE SUBJECT TO THE BYLAWS AND RULES AND REGULATIONS OF THE ASSOCIATION. THE DECLARATION, BYLAWS, AND RULES AND REGULATIONS WILL IMPOSE FINANCIAL OBLIGATIONS UPON THE OWNER OF THE PROPERTY, INCLUDING AN OBLIGATION TO PAY ASSESSMENTS OF THE ASSOCIATION. IF THE OWNER DOES NOT PAY THESE ASSESSMENTS, **THE ASSOCIATION COULD PLACE A LIEN ON THE PROPERTY AND POSSIBLY SELL IT TO PAY THE DEBT. THE DECLARATION, BYLAWS, AND RULES AND REGULATIONS OF THE COMMUNITY MAY PROHIBIT THE OWNER FROM MAKING CHANGES TO THE PROPERTY WITHOUT AN ARCHITECTURAL REVIEW BY THE ASSOCIATION (OR A COMMITTEE OF THE ASSOCIATION) AND THE APPROVAL OF THE ASSOCIATION. PURCHASERS OF PROPERTY WITHIN THE COMMON INTEREST COMMUNITY SHOULD INVESTIGATE THE FINANCIAL OBLIGATIONS OF MEMBERS OF THE ASSOCIATION. PURCHASERS SHOULD CAREFULLY READ THE DECLARATION FOR THE COMMUNITY AND THE BYLAWS AND RULES AND REGULATIONS OF THE ASSOCIATION.**

(2) (a) The obligation to provide the disclosure set forth in subsection (1) of this section shall be upon the seller, and, in the event of the failure by the seller to provide the written disclosure described in subsection (1) of this section, the purchaser shall have a claim for relief against the seller for actual damages directly and proximately caused by such failure plus court costs. It shall be an affirmative defense to any claim for damages brought under this section that the purchaser had actual or constructive knowledge of the facts and information required to be disclosed.

(b) Upon request, the seller shall either provide to the buyer or authorize the unit owners' association to provide to the buyer, upon payment of the association's usual fee pursuant to section 38-33.3-317 (3), all of the common interest community's governing documents and financial documents, as listed in the most recent available version of the contract to buy and sell real estate promulgated by the real estate commission as of the date of the contract.

(3) This section shall not apply to the sale of a unit that is a time share unit, as defined in section 38 33 110 (7).

XII. Equity Skimming

§ 18-5-802, C.R.S. Equity skimming of real property

(1) A person commits the crime of equity skimming of real property if the person knowingly:

(a) Acquires an interest in real property that is encumbered by a loan secured by a mortgage or deed of trust and the loan is in arrears at the time the person acquires the interest or is placed in default within eighteen months after the person acquires the interest ; and

(b) Either:

(I) Fails to apply all rent derived from the person's interest in the real property first toward the satisfaction of all outstanding payments due on the loan and second toward any fees due to any association of real property owners that charges such fees for the upkeep of the housing facility, or common area including buildings and grounds thereof, of which the real property is a part before appropriating the remainder of such rent or any part thereof for any other purpose except for the purpose of repairs necessary to prevent waste of the real property; or

(II) After a foreclosure in which title has vested pursuant to section 38-38-501, C.R.S., collects rent on behalf of any person other than the owner of the real property.

(2) Repealed.

(3) Equity skimming of real property is a class 5 felony.

(4) It shall be an affirmative defense to this section:

(a) That all deficiencies in all underlying encumbrances at the time of acquisition have been fully satisfied and brought current and that, in addition, any regular payments on the underlying encumbrances during the succeeding nine months after the date of acquisition have been timely paid in full; except that this shall not be an affirmative defense to a crime that includes the element set forth in subparagraph (II) of paragraph (b) of subsection (1) of this section;

(b) That any fees due to an association of real property owners for the upkeep of the housing facility, or common area including buildings and grounds thereof, of which the real property is a part have been paid in full.

(5) The provisions of this section shall not apply to any bona fide lender who accepts a deed in lieu of foreclosure or who forecloses upon the real property.

(6) The provisions of this section shall not apply to any bona fide purchaser who acquires fee title in any real property without agreeing to pay all underlying encumbrances and takes fee title subject to all underlying encumbrances, if the following written, verbatim warning was provided to the seller in capital letters of no less than ten-point, bold-faced type and acknowledged by the seller's signature:

WARNING: PURCHASER, ________,WILL NOT ASSUME OR PAY ANY PRESENT MORTGAGE, DEEDS OF TRUST, OR OTHER LIENS OR ENCUMBRANCES AGAINST THE PROPERTY. THE SELLER, ________, UNDERSTANDS HE/SHE WILL REMAIN RESPONSIBLE FOR ALL PAYMENTS DUE ON SUCH MORTGAGES, DEEDS OF TRUST, OR OTHER LIENS OR ENCUMBRANCES AND FOR ANY DEFICIENCY JUDGMENT UPON FORECLOSURE.

I HAVE HAD THE FOREGOING READ TO ME AND UNDERSTAND THE PURCHASER, ________, WILL NOT ASSUME ANY PRESENT MORTGAGES, DEEDS OF TRUST, OR OTHER LIENS OR ENCUMBRANCES AGAINST THE PROPERTY DESCRIBED AS: __________.

DATE SELLER _________.

XIII. Colorado Foreclosure Protection Act

§ 6-1-1101, C.R.S. Short title

This part 11 shall be known and may be cited as the "Colorado Foreclosure Protection Act".

§ 6-1-1102, C.R.S. Legislative declaration

The general assembly hereby finds, determines, and declares that home ownership and the accumulation of equity in one's home provide significant social and economic benefits to the state and its citizens. Unfortunately, too many home owners in financial distress, especially the poor, elderly, and financially unsophisticated, are vulnerable to a variety of deceptive or unconscionable business practices designed to dispossess them or otherwise strip the equity from their homes. There is a compelling need to curtail and to prevent the most deceptive and unconscionable of these business practices, to provide each home owner with information necessary to make an informed and intelligent decision regarding transactions with certain foreclosure consultants and equity purchasers, to provide certain minimum requirements for contracts between such parties, including statutory rights to cancel such contracts, and to ensure and foster fair dealing in the sale and purchase of homes in foreclosure. Therefore, it is the intent of the general assembly that all violations of this part 11 have a significant public impact and that the terms of this part 11 be liberally construed to achieve these purposes.

§ 6-1-1103, C.R.S. Definitions.

As used in this part 11, unless the context otherwise requires:

(1) "Associate" means a partner, subsidiary, affiliate, agent, or any other person working in association with a foreclosure consultant or an equity purchaser. "Associate" does not include a person who is excluded from the definition of an "equity purchaser" or a "foreclosure consultant".

(2) "Equity purchaser" means a person, other than a person who acquires a property for the purpose of using such property as his or her personal residence, who acquires title to a residence in foreclosure; except that the term does not include a person who acquires such title:

- (a) (Deleted by amendment, L. 2010, (HB 10-1133), ch. 350, p. 1615, § 1, effective January 1, 2011.)
- (b) By a deed in lieu of foreclosure to the holder of an evidence of debt, or an associate of the holder of an evidence of debt, of a consensual lien or encumbrance of record if such consensual lien or encumbrance is recorded in the real property records of the clerk and recorder of the county where the residence in foreclosure is located prior to the recording of the notice of election and demand for sale required under section 38-38-101, C.R.S.;
- (c) By a deed from the public trustee or a county sheriff as a result of a foreclosure sale conducted pursuant to article 38 of title 38, C.R.S.;
- (d) At a sale of property authorized by statute;
- (e) By order or judgment of any court;
- (f) From the person's spouse, relative, or relative of a spouse, by the half or whole blood or by adoption, or from a guardian, conservator, or personal representative of a person identified in this paragraph (f);
- (g) While performing services as a part of a person's normal business activities under any law of this state or the United States that regulates banks, trust companies, savings and loan associations, credit unions, insurance companies, title insurers, insurance producers, or escrow companies authorized to conduct business in the state, an affiliate or subsidiary of such person, or an employee or agent acting on behalf of such person; or

(h) As a result of a short sale transaction in which a short sale addendum form, as promulgated by the Colorado real estate commission, is part of the contract used to acquire a residence in foreclosure and such transaction complies with section 6-1-1121.

(3) "Evidence of debt" means a writing that evidences a promise to pay or a right to the payment of a monetary obligation, such as a promissory note, bond, negotiable instrument, a loan, credit, or similar agreement, or a monetary judgment entered by a court of competent jurisdiction.

(4) (a) "Foreclosure consultant" means a person who does not, directly or through an associate, take or acquire any interest in or title to a homeowner's property and who, in the course of such person's business, vocation, or occupation, makes a solicitation, representation, or offer to a home owner to perform, in exchange for compensation from the home owner or from the proceeds of any loan or advance of funds, a service that the person represents will do any of the following:

(I) Stop or postpone a foreclosure sale;

(II) Obtain a forbearance from a beneficiary under a deed of trust, mortgage, or other lien;

(III) Assist the home owner in exercising a right to cure a default as provided in article 38 of title 38, C.R.S.;

(IV) Obtain an extension of the period within which the home owner may cure a default as provided in article 38 of title 38, C.R.S.;

(V) Obtain a waiver of an acceleration clause contained in an evidence of debt secured by a deed of trust, mortgage, or other lien on a residence in foreclosure or contained in such deed of trust, mortgage, or other lien;

(VI) Assist the home owner to obtain a loan or advance of funds;

(VII) Avoid or reduce the impairment of the home owner's credit resulting from the recording of a notice of election and demand for sale, commencement of a judicial foreclosure action, or due to any foreclosure sale or the granting of a deed in lieu of foreclosure or resulting from any late payment or other failure to pay or perform under the evidence of debt, the deed of trust, or other lien securing such evidence of debt;

(VIII) In any way delay, hinder, or prevent the foreclosure upon the home owner's residence; or

(IX) Assist the home owner in obtaining from the beneficiary, mortgagee, or grantee of the lien in foreclosure, or from counsel for such beneficiary, mortgagee, or grantee, the remaining or excess proceeds from the foreclosure sale of the residence in foreclosure.

(b) The term "foreclosure consultant" does not include:

(I) A person licensed to practice law in this state, while performing any activity related to the person's attorney-client relationship with a home owner or any activity related to the person's attorney-client relationship with the beneficiary, mortgagee, grantee, or holder of any lien being enforced by way of foreclosure;

(II) A holder or servicer of an evidence of debt or the attorney for the holder or servicer of an evidence of debt secured by a deed of trust or other lien on any residence in foreclosure while the person performs services in connection with the evidence of debt, lien, deed of trust, or other lien securing such debt;

(III) A person doing business under any law of this state or the United States, which law regulates banks, trust companies, savings and loan associations, credit unions, insurance companies, title insurers, insurance producers, or escrow companies authorized to conduct business in the state, while the person performs services as part of the person's normal business activities, an affiliate or subsidiary of any of the foregoing, or an employee or agent acting on behalf of any of the foregoing;

(IV) A person originating or closing a loan in a person's normal course of business if, as to that loan:

(A) The loan is subject to the requirements of the federal "Real Estate Settlement Procedures Act of 1974", as amended, 12 U.S.C. sec. 2601 to 2617; or

(B) With respect to any second mortgage or home equity line of credit, the loan is subordinate to and closed simultaneously with a qualified first mortgage loan under sub-subparagraph (A) of this subparagraph (IV) or is initially payable on the face of the note or contract to an entity included in subparagraph (III) of this paragraph (b);

(V) A judgment creditor of the home owner, if the judgment is recorded in the real property records of the clerk and recorder of the county where the residence in foreclosure is located and the legal action giving rise to the judgment was commenced before the notice of election and demand for sale required under section 38-38-101, C.R.S.;

(VI) A title insurance company or title insurance agent authorized to conduct business in this state, while performing title insurance and settlement services;

(VII) A person licensed as a real estate broker under article 61 of title 12, C.R.S., while the person engages in any activity for which the person is licensed; or

(VIII) A nonprofit organization that solely offers counseling or advice to home owners in foreclosure or loan default, unless the organization is an associate of the foreclosure consultant.

(5) "Foreclosure consulting contract" means any agreement between a foreclosure consultant and a home owner.

(6) "Holder of evidence of debt" means the person in actual possession of or otherwise entitled to enforce an evidence of debt; except that "holder of evidence of debt" does not include a person acting as a nominee solely for the purpose of holding the evidence of debt or deed of trust as an electronic registry without any authority to enforce the evidence of debt or deed of trust. The following persons are presumed to be the holder of evidence of debt:

(a) The person who is the obligee of and who is in possession of an original evidence of debt;

(b) The person in possession of an original evidence of debt together with the proper indorsement or assignment thereof to such person in accordance with section 38-38-101 (6), C.R.S.;

(c) The person in possession of a negotiable instrument evidencing a debt, which has been duly negotiated to such person or to bearer or indorsed in blank; or

(d) The person in possession of an evidence of debt with authority, which may be granted by the original evidence of debt or deed of trust, to enforce the evidence of debt as agent, nominee, or trustee or in a similar capacity for the obligee of the evidence of debt.

(7) "Home owner" means the owner of a dwelling who occupies it as his or her principal place of residence, including a vendee under a contract for deed to real property, as that term is defined in section 38-35-126 (1) (b), C.R.S.

(8) (a) Except as otherwise provided in paragraph (b) of this subsection (8), "residence in foreclosure" means a residence or dwelling, as defined in sections 5-1-201 and 5-1-301, C.R.S., that is occupied as the home owner's principal place of residence and that is encumbered by a residential mortgage loan that is at least thirty days delinquent or in default.

(b) With respect to subpart 3 of this part 11, "residence in foreclosure" means a residence or dwelling, as defined in sections 5-1-201 and 5-1-301, C.R.S., that is occupied as the home owner's principal place of residence, is encumbered by a residential mortgage loan, and against which a foreclosure action has been commenced or as to which an equity purchaser otherwise has actual or constructive knowledge that the loan is at least thirty days delinquent or in default.

(9) "Short sale" or "short sale transaction" means a transaction in which the residence in foreclosure is sold when:

(a) A holder of evidence of debt agrees to release its lien for an amount that is less than the outstanding amount due and owing under such evidence of debt; and

(b) The lien described in paragraph (a) of this subsection (9) is recorded in the real property records of the county where the residence in foreclosure is located.

XIV. Foreclosure Consultants

§ 6-1-1104, C.R.S. Foreclosure consulting contract

(1) A foreclosure consulting contract shall be in writing and provided to and retained by the home owner, without changes, alterations, or modifications, for review at least twenty-four hours before it is signed by the home owner.

(2) A foreclosure consulting contract shall be printed in at least twelve-point type and shall include the name and address of the foreclosure consultant to which a notice of cancellation can be mailed and the date the home owner signed the contract.

(3) A foreclosure consulting contract shall fully disclose the exact nature of the foreclosure consulting services to be provided and the total amount and terms of any compensation to be received by the foreclosure consultant or associate.

(4) A foreclosure consulting contract shall be dated and personally signed, with each page being initialed, by each home owner and the foreclosure consultant and shall be acknowledged by a notary public in the presence of the home owner at the time the contract is signed by the home owner.

(5) A foreclosure consulting contract shall contain the following notice, which shall be printed in at least fourteen-point bold-faced type, completed with the name of the foreclosure consultant, and located in immediate proximity to the space reserved for the home owner's signature:

Notice Required by Colorado Law

_________ (Name) or (his/her/its) associate cannot ask you to sign or have you sign any document that transfers any interest in your home or property to (him/her/it) or (his/her/its) associate.

_________ (Name) or (his/her/its) associate cannot guarantee you that they will be able to refinance your home or arrange for you to keep your home.

You may, at any time, cancel this contract, without penalty of any kind.

If you want to cancel this contract, mail or deliver a signed and dated copy of this notice of cancellation, or any other

written notice, indicating your intent to cancel to _________ (name and address of foreclosure consultant) at _________ (address of foreclosure consultant, including facsimile and electronic mail address).

As part of any cancellation, you (the home owner) must repay any money actually spent on your behalf by _________ (name of foreclosure consultant) prior to receipt of this notice and as a result of this agreement, within sixty days, along with interest at the prime rate published by the federal reserve plus two percentage points, with the total interest rate not to exceed eight percent per year.

This is an important legal contract and could result in the loss of your home. Contact an attorney or a housing counselor approved by the federal department of housing and urban development before signing.

(6) A completed form in duplicate, captioned "Notice of Cancellation" shall accompany the foreclosure consulting contract. The notice of cancellation shall:

(a) Be on a separate sheet of paper attached to the contract;

(b) Be easily detachable; and

(c) Contain the following statement, printed in at least fourteen-point type:

Notice of Cancellation

(Date of contract)

To: (name of foreclosure consultant)

(Address of foreclosure consultant, including facsimile and electronic mail)

I hereby cancel this contract.

__________ (Date)

__________ (Home owner's signature)

(7) The foreclosure consultant shall provide to the home owner a signed, dated, and acknowledged copy of the foreclosure consulting contract and the attached notice of cancellation immediately upon execution of the contract.

(8) The time during which the home owner may cancel the foreclosure consulting contract does not begin to run until the foreclosure consultant has complied with this section.

§ 6-1-1105, C.R.S. Right of cancellation

(1) In addition to any right of rescission available under state or federal law, the home owner has the right to cancel a foreclosure consulting contract at any time.

(2) Cancellation occurs when the home owner gives written notice of cancellation of the foreclosure consulting contract to the foreclosure consultant at the address specified in the contract or through any facsimile or electronic mail address identified in the contract or other materials provided to the home owner by the foreclosure consultant.

(3) Notice of cancellation, if given by mail, is effective when deposited in the United States mail, properly addressed, with postage prepaid.

(4) Notice of cancellation need not be in the form provided with the contract and is effective, however expressed, if it indicates the intention of the home owner to cancel the foreclosure consulting contract.

(5) As part of the cancellation of a foreclosure consulting contract, the home owner shall repay, within sixty days after the date of cancellation, all funds paid or advanced in good faith prior to the receipt of notice of cancellation by the foreclosure consultant or associate under the terms of the foreclosure consulting contract, together with interest at the prime rate published by the federal reserve plus two percentage points, with the total interest rate not to exceed eight percent per year, from the date of expenditure until repaid by the home owner.

(6) The right to cancel may not be conditioned on the repayment of any funds.

§ 6-1-1106, C.R.S. Waiver of rights – void

(1) A provision in a foreclosure consulting contract is void as against public policy if the provision attempts or purports to:

(a) Waive any of the rights specified in this subpart 2 or the right to a jury trial;

(b) Consent to jurisdiction for litigation or choice of law in a state other than Colorado;

(c) Consent to venue in a county other than the county in which the property is located; or

(d) Impose any costs or fees greater than the actual costs and fees.

§ 6-1-1107, C.R.S. Prohibited acts

(1) A foreclosure consultant may not:

(a) Claim, demand, charge, collect, or receive any compensation until after the foreclosure consultant has fully performed each and every service the foreclosure consultant contracted to perform or represented that the foreclosure consultant would perform;

(b) Claim, demand, charge, collect, or receive any interest or any other compensation for a loan that the foreclosure consultant makes to the home owner that exceeds the prime rate published by the federal reserve at the time of any loan plus two percentage points, with the total interest rate not to exceed eight percent per year;

(c) Take a wage assignment, lien of any type on real or personal property, or other security to secure the payment of compensation;

(d) Receive any consideration from a third party in connection with foreclosure consulting services provided to a home owner unless the consideration is first fully disclosed in writing to the home owner;

(e) Acquire an interest, directly, indirectly, or through an associate, in the real or personal property of a home owner with whom the foreclosure consultant has contracted;

(f) Obtain a power of attorney from a home owner for any purpose other than to inspect documents as provided by law; or

(g) Induce or attempt to induce a home owner to enter into a foreclosure consulting contract that does not comply in all respects with this subpart 2.

§ 6-1-1108, C.R.S. Criminal penalties

A person who violates section 6-1-1107 is guilty of a misdemeanor, as defined in section 18-1.3-504, C.R.S., and shall be subject to imprisonment in county jail for up to one year, a fine of up to twenty-five thousand dollars, or both.

§ 6-1-1109, C.R.S. Unconscionability

(1) A foreclosure consultant or associate may not facilitate or engage in any transaction that is unconscionable given the terms and circumstances of the transaction.

(2) (a) If a court, as a matter of law, finds a foreclosure consultant contract or any clause of such contract to have been unconscionable at the time it was made, the court may refuse to enforce the contract, enforce the remainder of the contract without the unconscionable clause, or so limit the application of any unconscionable clause as to avoid an unconscionable result.

(b) When it is claimed or appears to the court that a foreclosure consultant contract or any clause of such contract may be unconscionable, the parties shall be afforded a reasonable opportunity to present evidence as to its commercial setting, purpose, and effect, to aid the court in making the determination.

(c) In order to support a finding of unconscionability, there must be evidence of some bad faith overreaching on the part of the foreclosure consultant or associate such as that which results from an unreasonable inequality of bargaining power or other circumstances in which there is an absence of meaningful choice for one of the parties, together with contract terms that are, under standard industry practices, unreasonably favorable to the foreclosure consultant or associate.

§ 6-1-1110, C.R.S. Language

A foreclosure consulting contract, and all notices of cancellation provided for therein, shall be written in English and shall be accompanied by a written translation from English into any other language principally spoken by the home owner, certified by the person making the translation as a true and correct translation of the English version. The translated version shall be presumed to have equal status and credibility as the English version.

XV. Equity Purchasers

§ 6-1-1111, C.R.S. Written contract required

Every contract shall be written in at least nine-point, legible type and fully completed, signed, and dated by the home owner and equity purchaser prior to the execution of any instrument quit-claiming, assigning, transferring, conveying, or encumbering an interest in the residence in foreclosure.

§ 6-1-1112, C.R.S. Written contract – contents – notice

(1) Every contract shall contain the entire agreement of the parties and shall include the following terms:

(a) The name, business address, and telephone number of the equity purchaser;

(b) The street address and full legal description of the residence in foreclosure;

(c) Clear and conspicuous disclosure of any financial or legal obligations of the home owner that will be assumed by the equity purchaser. If the equity purchaser will not be assuming any financial or legal obligations of the home owner, the equity purchaser shall provide to the home owner a separate written disclosure that substantially complies with section 18-5-802 (6), C.R.S.

(d) The total consideration to be paid by the equity purchaser in connection with or incident to the acquisition by the equity purchaser of the residence in foreclosure;

(e) The terms of payment or other consideration, including, but not limited to, any services of any nature that the equity purchaser represents will be performed for the home owner before or after the sale;

(f) The date and time when possession of the residence in foreclosure is to be transferred to the equity purchaser;

(g) The terms of any rental agreement or lease;

(h) The specifications of any option or right to repurchase the residence in foreclosure, including the specific amounts of any escrow deposit, down payment, purchase price, closing costs, commissions, or other fees or costs;

(i) A notice of cancellation as provided in section 6-1-1114; and

(j) The following notice, in at least nine-point bold-faced type, and completed with the name of the equity purchaser, immediately above the statement required by section 6-1-1114:

NOTICE REQUIRED BY COLORADO LAW

Until your right to cancel this contract has ended, (Name) or anyone working for __________ (Name) CANNOT ask you to sign or have you sign any deed or any other document.

(2) The contract required by this section survives delivery of any instrument of conveyance of the residence in foreclosure, but does not have any effect on persons other than the parties to the contract or affect title to the residence in foreclosure.

§ 6-1-1113, C.R.S. Cancellation

(1) In addition to any right of rescission available under state or federal law, the home owner has the right to cancel a contract with an equity purchaser until 12 midnight of the third business day following the day on which the home owner signs a contract that complies with this part 11 or until 12 noon on the day before the foreclosure sale of the residence in foreclosure, whichever occurs first.

(2) Cancellation occurs when the home owner personally delivers written notice of cancellation to the address specified in the contract or upon deposit of such notice in the United States mail, properly addressed, with postage prepaid.

(3) A notice of cancellation given by the home owner need not take the particular form as provided with the contract and, however expressed, is effective if it indicates the intention of the home owner not to be bound by the contract.

(4) In the absence of any written notice of cancellation from the home owner, the execution by the home owner of a deed or other instrument of conveyance of an interest in the residence in foreclosure to the equity purchaser after the expiration of the rescission period creates a rebuttable presumption that the home owner did not cancel the contract with the equity purchaser.

§ 6-1-1114, C.R.S. Notice of cancellation

(1) (a) The contract shall contain, as the last provision before the space reserved for the home owner's signature, a conspicuous statement in at least twelve-point bold-faced type, as follows:

You may cancel this contract for the sale of your house without any penalty or obligation at any time before _________ (Date and time of day). See the attached notice of cancellation form for an explanation of this right.

(b) The equity purchaser shall accurately specify the date and time of day on which the cancellation right ends.

(2) The contract shall be accompanied by duplicate completed forms, captioned "notice of cancellation" in at least nine-point bold-faced type if the contract is printed or in capital letters if the contract is typed, followed by a space in which the equity purchaser shall enter the date on which the home owner executed the contract. Such form shall:

(a) Be attached to the contract;

(b) Be easily detachable; and

(c) Contain the following statement, in at least nine-point type if the contract is printed or in capital letters if the contract is typed:

NOTICE OF CANCELLATION

________ (Enter date contract signed). You may cancel this contract for the sale of your house, without any penalty or obligation, at any time before ________ (Enter date and time of day). To cancel this transaction, personally deliver a signed and dated copy of this Notice of Cancellation in the United States mail, postage prepaid, to ________, (Name of purchaser) at ________ (Street address of purchaser's place of business) NOT LATER

THAN ________ (Enter date and time of day). I hereby cancel this transaction ________ (Date)

__________ (Seller's signature)

(3) The equity purchaser shall provide the home owner with a copy of the contract and the attached notice of cancellation.

(4) Until the equity purchaser has complied with this section, the home owner may cancel the contract.

§ 6-1-1115, C.R.S. Options through reconveyances

(1) A transaction in which a home owner purports to grant a residence in foreclosure to an equity purchaser by an instrument that appears to be an absolute conveyance and reserves to the home owner or is given by the equity purchaser an option to repurchase shall be permitted only where all of the following conditions have been met:

(a) The reconveyance contract complies in all respects with section 6-1-1112;

(b) The reconveyance contract provides the home owner with a nonwaivable thirty-day right to cure any default of said reconveyance contract and specifies that the home owner may exercise this right to cure on at least three separate occasions during such reconveyance contract;

(c) The equity purchaser fully assumes or discharges the lien in foreclosure as well as any prior liens that will not be extinguished by such foreclosure, which assumption or discharge shall be accomplished without violation of the terms and conditions of the liens being assumed or discharged;

(d) The equity purchaser verifies and can demonstrate that the home owner has or will have a reasonable ability to make the lease payments and to repurchase the residence in foreclosure within the term of the option to repurchase under the reconveyance contract. For purposes of this section, there is a rebuttable presumption that the home owner has a reasonable ability to make lease payments and to repurchase the residence in foreclosure if the home owner's payments for primary housing expenses and regular principal and interest payments on other personal debt do not exceed sixty percent of the home owner's monthly gross income; and

(e) The price the home owner must pay to exercise the option to repurchase the residence in foreclosure is not unconscionable. Without limitation on available claims under section 6-1-1119, a repurchase price exceeding twenty-five percent of the price at which the equity purchaser acquired the residence in foreclosure creates a rebuttable presumption that the reconveyance contract is unconscionable. The acquisition price paid by the equity purchaser may include any actual costs incurred by the equity purchaser in acquiring the residence in foreclosure.

§ 6-1-1116, C.R.S. Waiver of rights – void

(1) A provision in a contract between an equity purchaser and home owner is void as against public policy if it attempts or purports to:

(a) Waive any of the rights specified in this subpart 3 or the right to a jury trial;

(b) Consent to jurisdiction for litigation or choice of law in a state other than Colorado;

(c) Consent to venue in a county other than the county in which the property is located; or

(d) Impose any costs or fees greater than the actual costs and fees.

§ 6-1-1117, C.R.S. Prohibited conduct

(1) The contract provisions required by sections 6-1-1111 to 6-1-1114 shall be provided and completed in conformity with such sections by the equity purchaser.

(2) Until the time within which the home owner may cancel the transaction has fully elapsed, the equity purchaser shall not do any of the following:

(a) Accept from a home owner an execution of, or induce a home owner to execute, an instrument of conveyance of any interest in the residence in foreclosure;

(b) Record with the county recorder any document, including, but not limited to, the contract or any lease, lien, or instrument of conveyance, that has been signed by the home owner;

(c) Transfer or encumber or purport to transfer or encumber an interest in the residence in foreclosure to a third party; or

(d) Pay the home owner any consideration.

(3) Within ten days following receipt of a notice of cancellation given in accordance with sections 6-1-1113 and 6-1-1114, the equity purchaser shall return without condition the original contract and any other documents signed by the home owner.

(4) An equity purchaser shall make no untrue or misleading statements of material fact regarding the value of the residence in foreclosure, the amount of proceeds the home owner will receive after a foreclosure sale, any contract term, the home owner's rights or obligations incident to or arising out of the sale transaction, the nature of any document that the equity purchaser induces the home owner to sign, or any other untrue or misleading statement concerning the sale of the residence in foreclosure to the equity purchaser.

§ 6-1-1118, C.R.S. Criminal penalties

A person who violates section 6-1-1117 (2) or (3) or who intentionally violates section 6-1-1117 (4) is guilty of a misdemeanor, as defined in section 18-1.3-504, C.R.S., and shall be subject to imprisonment in county jail for up to one year, a fine of up to twenty-five thousand dollars, or both.

§ 6-1-1119, C.R.S. Unconscionability

(1) An equity purchaser or associate may not facilitate or engage in any transaction that is unconscionable given the terms and circumstances of the transaction.

(2) (a) If a court, as a matter of law, finds an equity purchaser contract or any clause of such contract to have been unconscionable at the time it was made, the court may refuse to enforce the contract, enforce the remainder of the contract without the unconscionable clause, or so limit the application of any unconscionable clause as to avoid an unconscionable result.

(b) When it is claimed or appears to the court that the contract or any clause thereof may be unconscionable, the parties shall be afforded a reasonable opportunity to present evidence as to its commercial setting, purpose, and effect, to aid the court in making the determination.

(c) In order to support a finding of unconscionability, there must be evidence of some bad faith overreaching on the part of the equity purchaser or associate such as that which results from an unreasonable inequality of bargaining power or under other circumstances in which there is an absence of meaningful choice for one of the parties, together with contract terms that are, under standard industry practices, unreasonably favorable to the equity purchaser or associate.

§ 6-1-1120, C.R.S. Language

(1) Any contract, rental agreement, lease, option or right to repurchase, and any notice, conveyance, lien, encumbrance, consent, or other document or instrument signed by a home owner, shall be written in English; except that, if the equity purchaser has actual or constructive knowledge that the home owner's principal language is other than English, the home owner shall be provided with a notice, written in the home owner's principal language, substantially as follows:

This transaction involves important and complex legal consequences, including your right to cancel this transaction within three business days following the date you sign this contract. You should consult with an attorney or seek assistance from a housing counselor by calling the Colorado foreclosure hotline at current, correct telephone number .

(2) If a notice in the home owner's principal language is required to be provided under subsection (1) of this section, the notice shall be given to the home owner as a separate document accompanying the written contract required by section 6-1-1111.

§ 6-1-105, C.R.S. Deceptive trade practices

(1) A person engages in a deceptive trade practice when, in the course of such person's business, vocation, or occupation, such person:

(xx) Violates any provision of part 11 of this article.

XVI. Notaries Public Act

§ 12-55-101, C.R.S. Short title

This part 1 shall be known and may be cited as the "Notaries Public Act".

§ 12-55-102, C.R.S. Definitions

As used in this part 1, unless the context otherwise requires:

(1) "Attested" means subscribed, signed, acknowledged, sworn to, affirmed, certified, verified, or attested to and includes other words and phrases that have a substantially similar meaning.

(1.1) "Electronic" means relating to technology having electrical, digital, magnetic, wireless, optical, electromagnetic, or similar capabilities.

(1.2) "Electronic record" means a record containing information that is created, generated, sent, communicated, received, or stored by electronic means.

(1.3) "Electronic signature" means an electronic sound, symbol, or process attached to or logically associated with an electronic record and executed or adopted by a person with the intent to sign the electronic record.

(1.4) "Misdemeanor involving dishonesty" means a violation of, or a conspiracy to violate, a civil or criminal law involving fraud, dishonesty, bribery, perjury, larceny, theft, robbery, extortion, forgery, counterfeiting, embezzlement, misappropriation of property, or any other offense adversely affecting such person's fitness to serve as a notary public.

(1.5) "Notarial acts" means those acts that a notary public is empowered to perform pursuant to section 12-55-110(1).

(2) "Notarization" means the performance of a notarial act.

(3) "Notary" or "notary public" means any individual appointed and commissioned to perform notarial acts.

§ 12-55-102.5, C.R.S. Disposition of fees

(1) All fees collected by the office of the secretary of state pursuant to this article shall be collected in the manner required by section 24-21- 104(3), C.R.S., and transmitted to the state treasurer, who shall credit the same to the notary administration cash fund, which fund is hereby created in the state treasury.

(2) The general assembly shall make annual appropriations from the notary administration cash fund for expenditures of the secretary of state incurred in the performance of the secretary of state's duties under this article.

(3) Pursuant to section 24-36-114, C.R.S., all interest derived from the deposit and investment of moneys in the notary administration cash fund shall be credited to the general fund.

(4) Notwithstanding any provision of this section to the contrary, on April 20, 2009, the state treasurer shall deduct five hundred seventy-five thousand dollars from the notary administration cash fund and transfer such sum to the general fund.

§ 12-55-103, C.R.S. Appointment – terms

Upon application pursuant to this part 1, the secretary of state may appoint and commission individuals as notaries public for a term of four years, unless said commission is revoked as provided in section 12-55-107. An applicant who has been denied appointment and commission may appeal such decision pursuant to article 4 of title 24, C.R.S. The secretary of state shall promptly notify the applicant in writing of such denial.

§ 12-55-103.5, C.R.S. Training

(1) The office of the secretary of state may enter into a contract with a private contractor or contractors to conduct notary training programs. The contractor or contractors may charge a fee for any such training program.

(2) The office of the secretary of state may promulgate rules to require notaries public to complete a training program.

§ 12-55-104, C.R.S. Application

(1) Every applicant for appointment and commission as a notary public shall complete an application form furnished by the secretary of state to be filed with the secretary of state, stating:

(a) That the applicant is a resident of Colorado who is at least eighteen years of age;

(b) That the applicant is able to read and write the English language;

(c) The addresses and telephone numbers of the applicant's business and residence in this state;

(d) That the applicant's commission as a notary public has never been revoked;

(e) That the applicant has not been convicted of a felony or, in the prior five years, a misdemeanor that disqualifies him or her from being a notary public pursuant to section 12-55-107(1)(b).

(2) The application shall include a handwritten sample of the applicant's official signature, the applicant's typed legal name, and the affirmation as provided in section 12-55-105. The application may also contain the applicant's electronic signature if the applicant is issued a journal.

(3) Subject to subsection (2) of this section, the secretary of state shall ensure, at the earliest practicable time, that an application pursuant to this article may be delivered electronically. All such applications shall be stored by the secretary of state in a medium that is retrievable by the secretary of state in perceivable form.

(4) On and after July 1, 2009, the secretary of state shall verify the lawful presence in the United States of each applicant through the verification process outlined in section 24-76.5-103 (4), C.R.S.

§ 12-55-105, C.R.S. Applicant's affirmation

Every applicant for appointment and commission as a notary public shall take the following affirmation in the presence of a person qualified to administer an affirmation in this state:

> "I, (name of applicant) solemnly affirm, under the penalty of perjury in the second degree, as defined in section 18-8-503, Colorado Revised Statutes, that I have carefully read the notary law of this state, and, if appointed and commissioned as a notary public, I will faithfully perform, to the best of my ability, all notarial acts in conformance with the law.
>
> (signature of applicant)
>
> ______________________
>
> Subscribed and affirmed before me this ______ day of ____________, 20___.
> (official signature and seal of person qualified to administer affirmation)."

§ 12-55-106, C.R.S. Repealed

§ 12-55-106.5, C.R.S. Notary's electronic signature – secretary of state

(1) In every instance, the electronic signature of a notary public shall contain or be accompanied by the following elements, all of which shall be immediately perceptible and reproducible in the electronic record to which the notary's electronic signature is attached: The notary's name; the words "NOTARY PUBLIC" and "STATE OF COLORADO"; a document authentication number issued by the secretary of state; and the words "my commission expires" followed by the expiration date of the notary's commission. A notary's electronic signature shall conform to any standards promulgated by the secretary of state.

(2) The secretary of state shall promulgate rules necessary to establish standards, procedures, practices, forms, and records relating to a notary's electronic signature.

(3) To the extent the provisions of this part 1 differ from the requirements of the federal "Electronic Signatures in Global and National Commerce Act", 15 U.S.C. sec. 7001, *et seq.*, the provisions of this part 1 are intended to modify, limit, or supercede the requirements of such act, as provided for in section 7002(a) of such act.

§ 12-55-106.7, C.R.S. Repealed

§ 12-55-107, C.R.S. Revocation of commission

(1) The secretary of state or the secretary of state's designee may deny the application of any person for appointment or reappointment, issue a letter of admonition, suspend a commission, or revoke the commission of any notary public during such notary's term of appointment, if the notary public:

- (a) Submits an application for commission and appointment that contains substantial and material misstatement or omission of fact;
- (b) Is convicted of official misconduct under this part 1 or any felony or, in the prior five years, a misdemeanor involving dishonesty;
- (c) Fails to exercise the powers or perform the duties of a notary public in accordance with this part 1;
- (d) Knowingly uses false or misleading advertising in which such notary represents that such notary has powers, duties, rights, or privileges that such notary does not possess by law;
- (e) Is found by a court of this state to have engaged in the unauthorized practice of law;
- (f) Ceases to fulfill the requirements applicable to such notary's most recent appointment;
- (g) Notarizes any blank document;
- (h) Knowingly uses false or misleading advertising to represent a level of authority not permitted to a notary public by law.

(1.5) Whenever the secretary of state or the secretary of state's designee believes that a violation of this article has occurred, the secretary of state or the secretary of state's designee may investigate any such violation. The secretary of state or the secretary of state's designee may also investigate possible violations of this article upon a signed complaint from any person.

(2) The secretary of state or the secretary of state's designee may revoke a notary's commission under the provisions of this part 1 only if action is taken pursuant to article 4 of title 24, C.R.S.

(3) After a notary public receives notice from the secretary of state or the secretary of state's designee that such notary's commission has been revoked, and unless such revocation has been enjoined, such notary shall immediately send or have delivered to the secretary of state such notary's journal of notarial acts, all other papers and copies relating to such notary's notarial acts, and such notary's official seal.

(4) A person whose notary commission has been revoked pursuant to this part 1 may not apply for or receive a commission and appointment as a notary.

§ 12-55-108, C.R.S. Reappointment – failure to be reappointed

Every notary public, before or at the expiration of such notary's commission, may submit an application for reappointment by submitting the same information and documents as required by sections 12-55-104 and 12-55-105 for the initial application. The secretary of state shall then determine whether the person shall be reappointed as a notary public. If the secretary of state determines such notary shall not be reappointed, the applicant may appeal such determination pursuant to article 4 of title 24, C.R.S.

§ 12-55-109, C.R.S. Certificate of appointment – recording

(1) The secretary of state is authorized to issue a certificate of authority qualifying said person as a notary public. The certificate shall also state the date of expiration of the commission and any other fact concerning such notary public which is required by the laws of this state.

(2) A notary public may record his certificate of authority in any county of this state and, after such recording, the county clerk and recorder of such county may issue a certificate that such person is a notary public, the date of expiration of his commission, and any other fact concerning such notary public which is required by the laws of this state.

(3) A notary public may exhibit to the judge or clerk of any court of record his certificate of authority, and the said judge or clerk may thereupon issue a certificate that such person is a notary public, the date of expiration of his commission, and any other fact concerning such notary which is required by the laws of this state.

§ 12-55-110, C.R.S. Powers and limitations

(1) Every notary public is empowered to:

(a) Take acknowledgments and other unsworn statements, proof of execution, and attest documents and electronic records;

(b) Administer oaths and affirmations;

(c) Give certificates or other statements as to a notarial act performed by such notary. Such acts shall include, but are not limited to, the giving of certificates as to, or certified copies of, any record or other document relating to a notarial act performed by such notary and certifying that a copy of a document is a true copy of another document or that a facsimile is a true facsimile of another document in accordance with section 12-55-120.

(d) Take depositions, affidavits, verifications, and other sworn testimony or statements;

(d.5) Perform any other act that is recognized or otherwise given effect under the law, rules, or regulations of another jurisdiction, including the United States, provided such other law, rule, or regulation authorizes a notary in this state to perform such act. However, no notary is empowered to perform an act under this paragraph (d.5) if such performance is prohibited by the law, rules, or regulations of this state.

(e) Perform any other act authorized by law, rules, or regulations;

(f) Present and give notice of dishonor and protest notes and other negotiable instruments as provided in part 5 of article 3 of title 4, C.R.S., or the corresponding laws of another jurisdiction.

(2) A notary public who has a disqualifying interest in a transaction may not legally perform any notarial act in connection with such transaction. For the purposes of this section, a notary public has a disqualifying interest in a transaction in connection with which notarial services are requested if he:

(a) May receive directly, and as a proximate result of the notarization, any advantage, right, title, interest, cash, or property exceeding in value the sum of any fee properly received in accordance with this part 1; or

(b) Is named, individually, as a party to the transaction.

(3) In no case shall a notary public notarize any blank document.

(4) No notary shall sign a certificate or other statements as to a notarial act to the effect that a document or any part thereof was attested by an individual, unless:

(a) Such individual has attested such document or part thereof while in the physical presence of such notary; and

(b) Such individual is personally known to such notary as the person named in the certificate, statement, document, or part thereof, or such notary receives satisfactory evidence that such individual is the person so named. For purposes of this paragraph (b), "satisfactory evidence" includes but is not limited to the sworn statement of a credible witness who personally knows such notary and the individual so named, or a current identification card or document issued by a federal or state governmental entity containing a photograph and signature of the individual who is so named.

§ 12-55-110.3, C.R.S. Advertisements for services – unauthorized practice of law – prohibited conduct – penalties

(1) (a) A notary public who is not a licensed attorney in the state of Colorado and who advertises, including by signage, his or her services in a language other than English shall include in the advertisement the following notice, both in English and in the language of the advertisement:

"I AM NOT AN ATTORNEY LICENSED TO PRACTICE LAW IN THE STATE OF COLORADO AND I MAY NOT GIVE LEGAL ADVICE OR ACCEPT FEES FOR LEGAL ADVICE."

(b) All written advertisements shall include the language exactly as written in paragraph (a) of this subsection (1). Such language shall be clearly visible. Oral advertisements or solicitations, including those on radio or television, shall contain the same message but shall not be required to use the exact language.

(2) A notary public who advertises in a language other than English shall post a list of fees permitted by law for notarial services. Such list shall be written in English and in the language of the advertisement and shall be posted in a highly visible location at the notary's place of business. Such list shall include the notice included in paragraph (a) of subsection (1) of this section.

(3) (a) A notary public who is not a licensed attorney in the state of Colorado shall not represent or advertise himself or herself as an immigration consultant or an expert on immigration matters.

(b) A notary public who is not an attorney licensed to practice law in Colorado is prohibited from:

(I) Providing any service that constitutes the unauthorized practice of law;

(II) Stating or implying that he or she is an attorney licensed to practice law in this state;

(III) Soliciting or accepting compensation to prepare documents for or otherwise represent the interest of another in a judicial or administrative proceeding, including a proceeding relating to immigration to the United States, United States citizenship, or related matters;

(IV) Soliciting or accepting compensation to obtain relief of any kind on behalf of another from any officer, agency, or employee of the state of Colorado or of the United States; or

(V) Using the phrase "notario" or "notario publico" to advertise the services of a notary public, whether by sign, pamphlet, stationery, or other written communication or by radio, television, or other nonwritten communication.

(4) Knowing and willful violation of the provisions of this section shall constitute a deceptive trade practice pursuant to section 6-1-105, C.R.S., and shall also constitute official misconduct pursuant to section 12-55-116.

§ 12-55-110.5, C.R.S. Accommodation of physical limitations

(1) A notary public may certify as to the subscription or signature of an individual when it appears that such individual has a physical limitation that restricts such individual's ability to sign by writing or making a mark, pursuant to the following:

(a) The name of an individual may be signed, or attached electronically in the case of an electronic record, by another individual other than the notary public at the direction and in the presence of the individual whose name is to be signed and in the presence of the notary public.

(b) The words "Signature written by" or "Signature attached by" in the case of an electronic record, "(name of individual directed to sign or directed to attach) at the direction and in the presence of (name as signed) on whose behalf the signature was written" or "attached electronically" in the case of an electronic record, or words of substantially similar effect shall appear under or near the signature.

(2) A notary public may use signals or electronic or mechanical means to take an acknowledgment from, administer an oath or affirmation to, or otherwise communicate with any individual in the presence of such notary public when it appears that such individual is unable to communicate verbally or in writing.

§ 12-55-111, C.R.S. Journal

(1) Every notary public shall keep a journal of every notarial act of the notary and, if required, give a certified copy of or a certificate as to any such journal or any of the notary's acts, upon payment of the notary's fee.

(2) For each notarial act, a notary's journal may contain the following information:

(a) The type and date of the notarial act;

(b) The title or type of document or proceeding that was notarized and the date of such document or proceeding, if different than the date of the notarization;

(c) The name of each person whose oath, affirmation, acknowledgment, affidavit, declaration, deposition, protest, verification, or other statement is taken;

(d) The signature and address of each person whose oath, affirmation, acknowledgment, affidavit, declaration, deposition, protest, verification, or other statement is taken;

(e) The signature, printed name, and address of each witness to the notarization;

(e.5) Deleted by Laws 2004, Ch. 337, § 5, eff. May 28, 2004.

(f) Any other information the notary considers appropriate to record that concerns the notarial act.

(3) (a) Subsection (1) of this section shall not apply to any document or electronic record where the original or a copy of such document or electronic record contains the information otherwise required to be entered in the notary's journal and such original or copy or electronic record is retained by the notary's firm or employer in the regular course of business.

(b) Notwithstanding any provision of this subsection (3) to the contrary, no firm, employer, or professionally licensed person shall prohibit an employee who is a notary from maintaining a journal of his or her notarial acts in the regular course of business of such firm, employer, or professionally licensed person.

(c) For purposes of this subsection (3), "firm" includes but is not limited to an office where the business of a real estate broker, lawyer, title insurance company, title insurance agent, or other licensed professional is regularly carried on and the records of such business are regularly maintained.

(4) Except as otherwise exempted by paragraph (a) of subsection (3) of this section or by another law of this state, for each electronic record or document signed by the notary public, the notary public shall record the document authentication number issued by the secretary of state for each document authenticated in the journal pursuant to this section.

§ 12-55-112, C.R.S. Official signature – rubber stamp seal – seal embosser notary's electronic signature

(1) At the time of notarization, a notary public shall sign such notary's official signature on every notary certificate or in the case of an electronic record, a notary public shall affix his or her electronic signature.

(2) Under or near such notary's official signature on every notary certificate, a notary public shall rubber stamp or emboss clearly and legibly such notary's official seal. The official notary seal shall contain only the outline of the seal, the name of the notary, exactly as such notary writes his or her official signature, the words "STATE OF COLORADO", and the words "NOTARY PUBLIC".

(3) Under or near such notary's official signature on every notary certificate, a notary public shall write or stamp "my commission expires (commission expiration date)".

(4) Every notary public may provide, keep, and use a seal embosser engraved to show such notary's name and the words "NOTARY PUBLIC" and "STATE OF COLORADO". The indentations made by the seal embosser shall not be applied on the document where the notary certificate appears in a manner that will render illegible or incapable of photographic reproduction any of the printed marks or writing.

(4.5) In the case of notarization of an electronic record, the application of a notary's electronic signature in lieu of a handwritten signature and rubber stamp seal or seal embosser is sufficient. A notary shall not use an electronic signature unless:

(a) The notary uses a journal if maintaining such journal is required by section 12-55-111; and

(b) The notary attaches to the document a document authentication number issued by the secretary of state.

(5) The illegibility of any of the information required by this section does not affect the validity of a document or transaction.

(6) For purposes of this section, "notary certificate" means a certificate or other statement of a notary relating to a notarial act performed by such notary.

§ 12-55-113, C.R.S. Lost journal or official seal

Every notary public shall send or have delivered notice to the secretary of state within thirty days after the notary loses or misplaces such notary's journal of notarial acts, or official seal, or the notary becomes aware that any other person has electronic control of his or her electronic signature. The fee payable to the secretary of state for recording notice of a lost journal, or seal, or that another person has electronic control of a notary's electronic signature shall be determined and collected pursuant to section 24-21-104(3), C.R.S.

§ 12-55-114, C.R.S. Change of name or address

(1) Every notary public shall send or have delivered notice to the secretary of state within thirty days after such notary changes the address of such notary's business or residence in this state. The fee payable to the secretary of state for recording notice of change of address shall be determined and collected pursuant to section 24-21-104(3), C.R.S.

(2) Every notary public shall send or have delivered notice to the secretary of state within thirty days after such notary changes such notary's name, including with the notification a sample of

such notary's handwritten official signature that contains such notary's surname and at least the initial of such notary's first name. The fee payable to the secretary of state for recording notice of change of notary's name shall be determined and collected pursuant to section 24-21-104(3), C.R.S.

§ 12-55-115, C.R.S. Death – resignation – removal from state

(1) If a notary public dies during the term of the notary's appointment, the notary's heirs or personal representative, as soon as reasonably possible after the notary's death, shall send or have delivered to the secretary of state the deceased notary's journal of notarial acts and the notary's seal, if available.

(2) If a notary public no longer desires to be a notary public or has ceased to have a business or residence address in this state, the notary shall send or have delivered to the secretary of state a letter of resignation, the notary's journal of notarial acts, and all other papers and copies relating to the notary's notarial acts, including the notary's seal. The notary's commission shall thereafter cease to be in effect.

§ 12-55-116, C.R.S. Official misconduct by a notary public – liability of notary or surety

(1) A notary public who knowingly and willfully violates the duties imposed by this part 1 commits official misconduct and is guilty of a class 2 misdemeanor.

(2) A notary public and the surety or sureties on his bond are liable to the persons involved for all damages proximately caused by the notary's official misconduct.

(3) Nothing in this article shall be construed to deny a notary public the right to obtain a surety bond or insurance on a voluntary basis to provide coverage for liability.

§ 12-55-117, C.R.S. Willful impersonation

Any person who acts as, or otherwise willfully impersonates, a notary public while not lawfully appointed and commissioned to perform notarial acts is guilty of a class 2 misdemeanor.

§ 12-55-118, C.R.S. Wrongful possession of journal or seal

Any person who unlawfully possesses and uses a notary's journal, an official seal, a notary's electronic signature, or any papers, copies, or electronic records relating to notarial acts is guilty of a class 3 misdemeanor.

§ 12-55-119, C.R.S. Affirmation procedures – form

(1) If an affirmation is to be administered by the notary public in writing, the person taking the affirmation shall sign his name thereto, and the notary public shall write or print under the text of the affirmation the fact that the document has been subscribed and affirmed, or sworn to before me in the county of ________, state of Colorado, this ______ day of ________, 20___.
(official signature, seal, and commission expiration date of notary).

(2) If an affirmation is to be administered by the notary public in an electronic record, the person taking the affirmation shall attach his or her electronic signature thereto. Within the affirmation, the notary shall add the fact that the document has been subscribed and affirmed, or sworn to before me in the county of ________, state of Colorado, this ______ day of ________, 20___.
(notary's electronic signature).

§ 12-55-120, C.R.S. Certified facsimiles of documents – procedure and form

(1) A notary public may certify a facsimile of a document if the original of the document is exhibited to him, together with a signed written request stating that:

(a) A certified copy or facsimile of the document cannot be obtained from the office of any clerk and recorder of public documents or custodian of documents in this state; and

(b) The production of a facsimile, preparation of a copy, or certification of a copy of the document does not violate any state or federal law.

(2) The certification of a facsimile shall be substantially in the following form:

"State of ____________, County (or City) of ____________, I, (name of notary) , a Notary Public in and for said state, do certify that on (date) , I carefully compared with the original the attached facsimile of (type of document) and the facsimile I now hold in my possession. They are complete, full, true, and exact facsimiles of the document they purport to reproduce.

(official signature, official seal, and commission expiration date of notary)."

§ 12-55-121, C.R.S. Fees

(1) The fees of notaries public may be, but shall not exceed, five dollars for each document attested by a person before a notary, except as otherwise provided by law. The fee for each such document shall include the following incidental services of such notary:

(a) Receiving evidence of such person's identity as enumerated in section 12-55-110(4);

(b) Administering an oath or affirmation to such person; and

(c) Signing and sealing a certificate or statement of such notary that is included in or attached to such document and evidences that the document was attested before such notary.

(2) In lieu of the fee authorized in subsection (1) of this section, a notary public may charge a fee, not to exceed ten dollars, for the notary's electronic signature.

§ 12-55-122, C.R.S. Applicability

This part 1 shall apply to all applications, both new and for reappointment, submitted to the office of secretary of state on or after July 1, 1981. Nothing in this part 1 shall be construed to revoke any notary public commission existing on July 1, 1981.

§ 12-55-123, C.R.S. Repeal of article

This article is repealed, effective July 1, 2018. Prior to such repeal, the appointment function of the secretary of state shall be reviewed as provided for in section 24-34-104, C.R.S.

XVII. Uniform Recognition of Acknowledgments Act

§ 12-55-201, C.R.S. Short title

This part 2 shall be known and may be cited as the "Uniform Recognition of Acknowledgments Act".

§ 12-55-202, C.R.S. Definitions

As used in this part 2, unless the context otherwise requires:

(1) "Notarial acts" means acts which the laws and regulations of this state authorize notaries public of this state to perform, including, but not limited to, the administering of oaths and affirmations, taking proof of execution and acknowledgments of instruments, and attesting documents.

§ 12-55-203, C.R.S. Recognition of notarial acts performed outside this state

(1) Notarial acts may be performed outside this state for use in this state with the same effect as if performed by a notary public of this state by the following persons authorized pursuant to the

laws and regulations of other governments, in addition to any other person authorized by the laws and regulations of this state:

(a) A notary public authorized to perform notarial acts in the place in which the act is performed;

(b) A judge, clerk, or deputy clerk of any court of record in the place in which the notarial act is performed;

(c) An officer of the foreign service of the United States, a consular agent, or any other person authorized by regulation of the United States department of state to perform notarial acts in the place in which the act is performed;

(d) A commissioned officer in active service with the armed forces of the United States and any other person authorized by regulation of the armed forces to perform notarial acts if the notarial act is performed for one of the following or his dependents: A merchant seaman of the United States, a member of the armed forces of the United States, or any other person serving with or accompanying the armed forces of the United States; or

(e) Any other person authorized to perform notarial acts in the place in which the act is performed.

§ 12-55-204, C.R.S. Authentication of authority of officer

(1) If the notarial act is performed by any of the persons described in section 12-55-203(1)(a) to (1)(d), other than a person authorized to perform notarial acts by the laws or regulations of a foreign country, the signature, rank, or title and serial number, if any, of the person are sufficient proof of the authority of a holder of that rank or title to perform the act. Further proof of his authority is not required.

(2) If the notarial act is performed by a person authorized by the laws or regulations of a foreign country to perform the act, there is sufficient proof of the authority of that person to act if:

(a) Either a foreign service officer of the United States resident in the country in which the act is performed or a diplomatic or consular officer of the foreign country resident in the United States certifies that a person holding that office is authorized to perform the act;

(b) Either the official seal of the person performing the notarial act is affixed to the document, or, in the case of an electronic record, such information that is required in lieu of a notary seal by the laws of the place granting notarial authority to the person performing the notarial act is attached to or logically associated with the document; or

(c) The title and indication of authority to perform notarial acts of the person appears either in a digest of foreign law or in a list customarily used as a source of such information.

(3) If the notarial act is performed by a person other than one described in subsections (1) and (2) of this section, there is sufficient proof of the authority of that person to act if the clerk of a court of record in the place in which the notarial act is performed certifies to the official character of that person and to his authority to perform the notarial act.

(4) The signature and title of the person performing the act are prima facie evidence that he is a person with the designated title and that the signature is genuine.

§ 12-55-205, C.R.S. Certificate of person taking acknowledgment

(1) The person taking an acknowledgment shall certify that:

(a) The person acknowledging appeared before him and acknowledged he executed the instrument; and

(b) The person acknowledging was known to the person taking the acknowledgment or that the person taking the acknowledgment had satisfactory evidence that the person acknowledging was the person described in and who executed the instrument.

§ 12-55-206, C.R.S. Recognition of certificate of acknowledgment

(1) The form of a certificate of acknowledgment used by a person whose authority is recognized under section 12-55-203 shall be accepted in this state if:

(a) The certificate is in a form prescribed by the laws or regulations of this state; or

(b) The certificate is in a form prescribed by the laws or regulations applicable in the place in which the acknowledgment is taken; or

(c) The certificate contains the words "acknowledged before me", or their substantial equivalent.

§ 12-55-207, C.R.S. Certificate of acknowledgment

(1) "Acknowledged before me" means:

(a) That the person acknowledging appeared before the person taking the acknowledgment; and

(b) That he acknowledged he executed the instrument; and

(c) That, in the case of:

(I) A natural person, he executed the instrument for the purposes therein stated;

(II) A corporation, the officer or agent acknowledged he held the position or title set forth in the instrument and certificate, he signed the instrument on behalf of the corporation by proper authority, and the instrument was the act of the corporation for the purpose therein stated;

(III) A partnership, the partner or agent acknowledged he signed the instrument on behalf of the partnership by proper authority and he executed the instrument as the act of the partnership for the purposes therein stated;

(IV) A person acknowledging as principal by an attorney in fact, he executed the instrument by proper authority as the act of the principal for the purposes therein stated;

(V) A person acknowledging as a public officer, trustee, administrator, guardian, or other representative, he signed the instrument by proper authority and he executed the instrument in the capacity and for the purposes therein stated; and

(d) That the person taking the acknowledgment either knew or had satisfactory evidence that the person acknowledging was the person named in the instrument or certificate.

§ 12-55-208, C.R.S. Short forms of acknowledgment

(1) The forms of acknowledgment set forth in this section may be used and are sufficient for their respective purposes under any law of this state. The forms shall be known as "Statutory Short Forms of Acknowledgment" and may be referred to by that name. The authorization of the following forms does not preclude the use of other forms:

(a) For an individual acting in his own right:

"State of ....

County of ....

The foregoing instrument was acknowledged before me this (date) by (name of person acknowledged).

(signature of person taking acknowledgment)

(title or rank)

(serial number, if any)";

(b) For a corporation:

"State of ....

County of ....

The foregoing instrument was acknowledged before me this (date) by (name of officer or agent, title of officer or agent) of (name of corporation acknowledging) a (state or place of incorporation, corporation, on behalf of the corporation.

(signature of person taking acknowledgment)

(title or rank)

(serial number, if any)";

(c) For a partnership:

"State of ....

County of ....

The foregoing instrument was acknowledged before me this (date) by (name of acknowledging partner or agent), partner (or agent) on behalf of (name of partnership), a partnership.

(signature of person taking acknowledgment)

(title or rank)

(serial number, if any)";

(d) For an individual acting as principal by an attorney in fact:

"State of ....

County of ....

The foregoing instrument was acknowledged before me this (date) by (name of attorney-in-fact) as attorney in fact on behalf of (name of principal).

(signature of person taking acknowledgment)

(title or rank)

(serial number, if any)";

(e) By any public officer, trustee, or personal representative:

"State of ....

County of ....

The foregoing instrument was acknowledged before me this (date) by (name and title of position).

(signature of person taking acknowledgment)

(title or rank)

(serial number, if any)".

§ 12-55-209, C.R.S. Acknowledgments not affected by this part 2

A notarial act performed prior to July 1, 1969, is not affected by this part 2. This part 2 provides an additional method of proving notarial acts. Nothing in this part 2 diminishes or invalidates the recognition accorded to notarial acts by other laws or regulations of this state.

§ 12-55-210, C.R.S. Uniformity of interpretation

This part 2 shall be so interpreted as to make uniform the laws of those states which enact it.

§ 12-55-211, C.R.S. Seals

Whenever any law, rule, or regulation requires the use of a seal, it shall be sufficient that a rubber stamp with a facsimile affixed thereon of the seal required to be used is placed or stamped upon the document requiring the seal with indelible ink or, in the case of an electronic record, attachment of such information that is required in lieu of a notary seal by the laws of the place granting notarial authority to the person performing the notarial act shall be sufficient in lieu of any other form of notary seal.

Chapter 26: Commission-Approved and Miscellaneous Forms

An * in the left margin indicates a change in the statute, rule, or text since the last publication of the manual.

I. Commission-Approved Forms

Through the adoption and promulgation of Commission Rule F, it became compulsory for all real estate brokers licensed by the State of Colorado to use Commission-approved forms in most of their contracting. Section 12-61-803(4), C.R.S., grants the Colorado Real Estate Commission statutory authority to promulgate standard forms for use by licensees.

One of the major purposes of the rule is to help to ensure broker compliance with the Colorado Supreme Court Conway-Bogue decision. (See the case summary in Chapter 5, "Landmark Case Law and Opinions.") A second purpose is to help promote uniformity in contracting to better protect the public. The privileges granted should not be abused by the real estate broker.

Rule F – Use of Commission-Approved Forms

F-1. Permitted and Prohibited Form Modifications

(a) No modifications shall be made to a Commission-approved form by a broker except as provided in rules promulgated by the Commission and as set forth in this Rule F-1 through F-7. For purposes of Rule F-1 through F-7, the term "Commission-approved form" means any form promulgated by the Commission; the term "broker" shall also include brokerage firm.

(b) A broker may add its firm name, address, telephone, e-mail, trademark or other identifying information on a Commission-approved form.

(c) A broker may add initial lines at the bottom of a page of any Commission-approved form.

(d) Any deletion to the printed body of a Commission-approved form, or any "Additional Provision" or "Addenda" which by its terms serves to amend or delete portions of the approved language, must result from negotiations or the instruction(s) of a party to the transaction and must be made directly on the printed body of the form by striking through the amended or deleted portion in a legible manner that does not obscure the deletion that has been made.

(e) Blank spaces on a Commission-approved form may be lengthened or shortened to accommodate the applicable data or information.

(f) Provisions that are inserted into blank spaces must be printed in a style or type that clearly differentiates such insertions from the style or type used for the Commission-approved form language.

(g) A broker may omit part or all of the following provisions of a Commission-approved "Contract to Buy and Sell Real Estate" (even if the provision is identified by a different Section number), or corresponding provisions in other Commission-approved forms, if such provisions do not apply to the transaction. In the event any provision is omitted, the provision's caption or heading must remain unaltered on the form followed by the words "OMITTED".

* 1. Section 2.5 Inclusions in its entirety or any of its subsections

* 2. Section 2.6 Exclusions

3. Section 4.4 Seller Concessions
4. Section 4.5 New Loan in its entirety or any of its subsections
5. Section 4.6 Assumption
6. Section 4.7 Seller or Private Financing
7. Section 5 Financing Conditions and Obligations in its entirety or any of its sections
8. Section 6 Appraisal Provisions in its entirety or any of its subsections
9. * Section 7.3 Homeowners' Association Documents in its entirety or any of its subsections
10. Section 8.4 Special Taxing Districts
11. * Section 8.5 Right of First Refusal or Contract Approval
12. * Section 10.6 Due Diligence Documents
13. * Section 10.7 Due Diligence Documents Conditions in its entirety or any of its subsections
14. * Section 10.8 Due Diligence—Environmental, ADA (CBS2, CBS3, CBS4)
15. * Section 10.7.3 Source of Potable Water (CBS4)
16. * Section 10.9 Existing Leases; Modification of Existing Leases; New Leases (CBS3, CBS4)
17. * [Deleted]
18. * [Deleted]
19. * [Deleted]
20. * Section 10.15 Existing Leases; Modification of Existing Leases; New Leases (CBS2)
21. * Section 11 Tenant Estoppel Statements in its entirety or any of its subsections (CBS2, CBS3, CBS4)
22. Section 15.3 Status and Transfer Letter Fees
23. Section 15.4 Local Transfer Tax
24. * Section 15.6 Sales and Use Tax
25. Section 16.2 Rents
26. Section 16.3 Association Assessments

(h) A broker may add an additional page to the "Contract to Buy and Sell Real Estate", "Counterproposal" and the "Agreement to Amend/Extend Contract", following such document, that contains the dates and deadlines information set forth in § 3, arranged in chronological date sequence.

(i) A broker may omit part or all of the following provisions of the "Counterproposal" and the "Agreement to Amend/Extend Contract" if such provisions do not apply to the transaction. In the event any provision is omitted, the provision's caption or heading must remain unaltered on the form followed by the words "OMITTED".

1. Section 3 Dates and Deadlines table
2. Section 4 Purchase Price and Terms [in the Counterproposal only]

(j) A broker may substitute the term "Landlord" for the term "Seller" and the term "Tenant" for the term "Buyer" in the Brokerage Disclosure to Buyer form, in the Brokerage Disclosure to Seller and Definitions of Working Relationships form when making disclosures in a lease transaction (or use the separate Broker Disclosure to Tenant form).

(k) A broker may add signature lines and identifying labels for the parties signature on a Commission-approved form.

(*l*) A broker may modify, strike or delete such language on a Commission-approved form as the Commission may from time to time authorize to be modified, stricken or deleted.

F-2. Additional Provisions

(a) The "Additional Provisions" section of a Commission-approved form must contain only those transaction-specific terms or acknowledgments that result from negotiations or the instruction(s) of the party(ies) to the transaction.

(b) A broker who is not a principal party to the contract may not insert personal provisions, personal disclaimers or exculpatory language in favor of the broker in the "Additional Provisions" section of a Commission-approved form.

F-3. Addenda

(a) If a broker originates or initiates the use of a preprinted or prepared addendum that modifies or adds to the terms of a Commission-approved contract form which does not result from the negotiations of the parties, such addendum must be prepared by:

 (1) an attorney representing the broker or brokerage firm; or

 (2) a principal party to the transaction; or

 (3) an attorney representing a principal party.

(b) An addendum permitted by this Rule F-3 (a), shall not be included within the body of, or in the "Additional Provisions" section of, a Commission-approved form.

(c) A broker who is not a principal party to the contract may not insert personal provisions, personal disclaimers or exculpatory language in favor of the broker in an addendum.

(d) If an addendum is prepared by a broker's attorney, the following disclosure must appear on the first page of the addendum in the same sized type as the size of type used in the addendum: "This addendum has not been approved by the Colorado Real Estate Commission. It was prepared by (insert licensed name of broker or brokerage firm's) legal counsel." Broker must retain the document prepared by broker's attorney for 4 years from the date such addendum was last used by the Broker and provide said document and the name of the attorney or law firm that prepared the addendum to the Commission upon request.

(e) If an addendum to a listing, tenant or right to buy contract, is prepared by a broker or brokerage firm, the following disclosure must appear on the first page of the addendum in the same sized type as the size of type used in the addendum: "This addendum has not been approved by the Colorado Real Estate Commission. It was prepared by (insert licensed name of broker or brokerage firm)."

F-4. Prohibited Provisions

No contract provision, including modifications permitted by Rules F-1 through F-3, shall relieve a broker from compliance with the real estate license law, section 12-61-101, et. seq., or the Rules of the Commission.

Pursuant to Rule E-12, when a written agreement contains a provision entitling the broker to a commission on a sale or purchase made after the expiration of the agreement, such provision must refer only to those persons or properties with whom or on which the broker negotiated during the term of the agreement, and whose names or addresses, were submitted in writing to the seller or buyer during the term of the agreement, including any extension thereof.

F-5. Explanation of Permitted Modifications

The broker shall explain all permitted modifications, deletions, omissions, insertions, additional provisions and addenda to the principal party and must recommend that the parties obtain expert advice as to the material matters that are beyond the expertise of the broker.

F-6. Commission-Approved Form Reproduction:

(a) Commission-approved forms used by a broker, including permitted modification made by a broker, shall be legible.

(b) Brokers generating Commission-approved forms through the use of a computer shall ensure that a security software program is utilized that prevents inadvertent change or prohibited modification of Commission-approved forms by the broker or other computer user.

* ### *F-7. Commission Approved Forms*

> Ed. Note: The most current version of approved forms can be found on the Division of Real Estate website at: **www.dora.state.co.us/real-estate/contracts/contracts.htm.**

Real estate brokers are required to use Commission-approved forms as appropriate to a transaction or circumstance to which a relevant form is applicable. Commission-approved forms are posted on the Division of Real Estate's website. Effective June 2009, the Commission will no longer post forms in the Code of Colorado Regulations. The Commission hereby withdraws all forms from the Code of Colorado Regulations. In instances when the Commission has not developed an approved form within the purview of this rule, and other forms are used, they are not governed by Rule F. Other forms used by a broker shall not be prepared by a broker, unless otherwise permitted by law.

* To obtain the forms promulgated by the real estate commission that are within the purview of Rule F, visit the Division of Real Estate website at: http://www.dora.state.co.us/real-estate/broker licensing.htm or the Division of Real Estate's offices at 1560 Broadway, Suite 925, Denver, Colorado 80202.

II. Appendix – Commission-Approved Forms

Editor's Note: Current versions of approved forms can be found on the Colorado Division of Real Estate website at http://www.dora.state.co.us/real-estate.

A. Exclusive Right-to-Sell Listing Contract (All Types of Properties) LC50-8-10

The printed portions of this form, except differentiated additions, have been approved by the Colorado Real Estate Commission. (LC50-8-10) (Mandatory 1-11)

THIS IS A BINDING CONTRACT. THIS FORM HAS IMPORTANT LEGAL CONSEQUENCES AND THE PARTIES SHOULD CONSULT LEGAL AND TAX OR OTHER COUNSEL BEFORE SIGNING.

Compensation charged by brokerage firms is not set by law. Such charges are established by each real estate brokerage firm.

DIFFERENT BROKERAGE RELATIONSHIPS ARE AVAILABLE WHICH INCLUDE BUYER AGENCY, SELLER AGENCY, OR TRANSACTION-BROKERAGE.

EXCLUSIVE RIGHT-TO-SELL LISTING CONTRACT

☐ **SELLER AGENCY** ☐ **TRANSACTION-BROKERAGE**

Date: ______________________________

1. AGREEMENT. Seller and Brokerage Firm enter into this exclusive, irrevocable contract (Seller Listing Contract) as of the date set forth above.

2. BROKER AND BROKERAGE FIRM.

☐ **2.1. Multiple-Person Firm.** If this box is checked, the individual designated by Brokerage Firm to serve as the broker of Seller and to perform the services for Seller required by this Seller Listing Contract is called Broker. If more than one individual is so designated, then references in this Seller Listing Contract to Broker shall include all persons so designated, including substitute or additional brokers. The brokerage relationship exists only with Broker and does not extend to the employing broker, Brokerage Firm or to any other brokers employed or engaged by Brokerage Firm who are not so designated.

☐ **2.2. One-Person Firm.** If this box is checked, Broker is a real estate brokerage firm with only one licensed natural person. References in this Seller Listing Contract to Broker or Brokerage Firm mean both the licensed natural person and brokerage firm who shall serve as the broker of Seller and perform the services for Seller required by this Seller Listing Contract.

3. DEFINED TERMS.

3.1. Seller: ____

3.2. Brokerage Firm: ____

3.3. Broker: ____

3.4. Property. The Property is the following legally described real estate in the County of _______________, Colorado:

known as No. ____,

Street Address City State Zip

together with the interests, easements, rights, benefits, improvements and attached fixtures appurtenant thereto, and all interest of Seller in vacated streets and alleys adjacent thereto, except as herein excluded.

3.5. Sale.

3.5.1. A Sale is the voluntary transfer or exchange of any interest in the Property or the voluntary creation of the obligation to convey any interest in the Property, including a contract or lease. It also includes an agreement to transfer any ownership interest in an entity which owns the Property.

☐ **3.5.2.** If this box is checked, Seller authorizes Broker to negotiate leasing the Property. Lease of the Property or Lease means any lease of an interest in the Property.

3.6. Listing Period. The Listing Period of this Seller Listing Contract shall begin on __________________________, and shall continue through the earlier of (1) completion of the Sale of the Property or (2) __________________________. Broker shall continue to assist in the completion of any sale or lease for which compensation is payable to Brokerage Firm under § 7 of this Seller Listing Contract.

3.7. Applicability of Terms. A check or similar mark in a box means that such provision is applicable. The abbreviation "N/A" or the word "Deleted" means not applicable. The abbreviation "MEC" (mutual execution of this contract) means the date upon which both parties have signed this Seller Listing Contract.

3.8. Day; Computation of Period of Days, Deadline.

3.8.1. Day. As used in this Seller Listing Contract, the term "day" shall mean the entire day ending at 11:59 p.m., United States Mountain Time (Standard or Daylight Savings as applicable).

3.8.2. Computation of Period of Days, Deadline. In computing a period of days, when the ending date is not specified, the first day is excluded and the last day is included, e.g., three days after MEC. If any deadline falls on a Saturday, Sunday or federal or Colorado state holiday (Holiday), such deadline ☐ **Shall** ☐ **Shall Not** be extended to the next day that is not a Saturday, Sunday or Holiday. Should neither box be checked, the deadline shall not be extended.

4. BROKERAGE RELATIONSHIP.

4.1. If the Seller Agency box at the top of page 1 is checked, Broker shall represent Seller as a Seller's limited agent (Seller's Agent). If the Transaction-Brokerage box at the top of page 1 is checked, Broker shall act as a Transaction-Broker.

4.2. In-Company Transaction – Different Brokers. When Seller and buyer in a transaction are working with different brokers, those brokers continue to conduct themselves consistent with the brokerage relationships they have established. Seller acknowledges that Brokerage Firm is allowed to offer and pay compensation to brokers within Brokerage Firm working with a buyer.

4.3. In-Company Transaction – One Broker. If Seller and buyer are both working with the same broker, Broker shall function as:

4.3.1. Seller's Agent. If the Seller Agency box at the top of page 1 is checked, the parties agree the following applies:

4.3.1.1. Seller Agency Only. Unless the box in § 4.3.1.2 (**Seller Agency Unless Brokerage Relationship with Both**) is checked, Broker shall represent Seller as Seller's Agent and shall treat the buyer as a customer. A customer is a party to a transaction with whom Broker has no brokerage relationship. Broker shall disclose to such customer Broker's relationship with Seller.

☐ **4.3.1.2. Seller Agency Unless Brokerage Relationship with Both.** If this box is checked, Broker shall represent Seller as Seller's Agent and shall treat the buyer as a customer, unless Broker currently has or enters into an agency or Transaction-Brokerage relationship with the buyer, in which case Broker shall act as a Transaction-Broker.

4.3.2. Transaction-Broker. If the Transaction-Brokerage box at the top of page 1 is checked, or in the event neither box is checked, Broker shall work with Seller as a Transaction-Broker. A Transaction-Broker shall perform the duties described in § 5 and facilitate sales transactions without being an advocate or agent for either party. If Seller and buyer are working with the same broker, Broker shall continue to function as a Transaction-Broker.

5. BROKERAGE DUTIES. Brokerage Firm, acting through Broker, as either a Transaction-Broker or a Seller's Agent, shall perform the following **Uniform Duties** when working with Seller:

5.1. Broker shall exercise reasonable skill and care for Seller, including, but not limited to the following:

5.1.1. Performing the terms of any written or oral agreement with Seller;

5.1.2. Presenting all offers to and from Seller in a timely manner regardless of whether the Property is subject to a contract for Sale;

5.1.3. Disclosing to Seller adverse material facts actually known by Broker;

5.1.4. Advising Seller regarding the transaction and advising Seller to obtain expert advice as to material matters about which Broker knows but the specifics of which are beyond the expertise of Broker;

5.1.5. Accounting in a timely manner for all money and property received; and

5.1.6. Keeping Seller fully informed regarding the transaction.

5.2. Broker shall not disclose the following information without the informed consent of Seller:

5.2.1. That Seller is willing to accept less than the asking price for the Property;

5.2.2. What the motivating factors are for Seller to sell the Property;

5.2.3. That Seller will agree to financing terms other than those offered;

5.2.4. Any material information about Seller unless disclosure is required by law or failure to disclose such information would constitute fraud or dishonest dealing; or

5.2.5. Any facts or suspicions regarding circumstances that could psychologically impact or stigmatize the Property.

5.3. Seller consents to Broker's disclosure of Seller's confidential information to the supervising broker or designee for the purpose of proper supervision, provided such supervising broker or designee shall not further disclose such information without consent of Seller, or use such information to the detriment of Seller.

5.4. Brokerage Firm may have agreements with other sellers to market and sell their property. Broker may show alternative properties not owned by Seller to other prospective buyers and list competing properties for sale.

5.5. Broker shall not be obligated to seek additional offers to purchase the Property while the Property is subject to a contract for Sale.

5.6. Broker has no duty to conduct an independent inspection of the Property for the benefit of a buyer and has no duty to independently verify the accuracy or completeness of statements made by Seller or independent inspectors. Broker has no duty to conduct an independent investigation of a buyer's financial condition or to verify the accuracy or completeness of any statement made by a buyer.

5.7. Seller understands that Seller shall not be liable for Broker's acts or omissions that have not been approved, directed, or ratified by Seller.

5.8. When asked, Broker ☐ **Shall** ☐ **Shall Not** disclose to prospective buyers and cooperating brokers the existence of offers on the Property and whether the offers were obtained by Broker, a broker within Brokerage Firm or by another broker.

6. ADDITIONAL DUTIES OF SELLER'S AGENT. If the Seller Agency box at the top of page 1 is checked, Broker is Seller's Agent, with the following additional duties:

6.1. Promoting the interests of Seller with the utmost good faith, loyalty and fidelity;

6.2. Seeking a price and terms that are set forth in this Seller Listing Contract; and

6.3. Counseling Seller as to any material benefits or risks of a transaction that are actually known by Broker.

7. COMPENSATION TO BROKERAGE FIRM; COMPENSATION TO COOPERATIVE BROKER. Seller agrees that any Brokerage Firm compensation that is conditioned upon the Sale of the Property shall be earned by Brokerage Firm as set forth herein without any discount or allowance for any efforts made by Seller or by any other person in connection with the Sale of the Property.

7.1. Amount. In consideration of the services to be performed by Broker, Seller agrees to pay Brokerage Firm as follows:

7.1.1. Sale Commission. (1) _______% of the gross purchase price or (2) ________________________________, in U.S. dollars.

7.1.2. Lease Commission. If the box in § 3.5.2 is checked, Brokerage Firm shall be paid a fee equal to (1) ______% of the gross rent under the lease, or (2) ____, in U.S. dollars, payable as follows: ____.

7.2. When Earned. Such commission shall be earned upon the occurrence of any of the following:

7.2.1. Any Sale of the Property within the Listing Period by Seller, by Broker or by any other person;

7.2.2. Broker finding a buyer who is ready, willing and able to complete the sale or lease as specified in this Seller Listing Contract; or

7.2.3. Any Sale (or Lease if § 3.5.2 is checked) of the Property within _______ calendar days subsequent to the expiration of the Listing Period (Holdover Period) (1) to anyone with whom Broker negotiated and (2) whose name was submitted, in writing, to Seller by Broker during the Listing Period, including any extensions thereof, (Submitted Prospect). Provided, however, Seller ☐ **Shall** ☐ **Shall Not** owe the commission to Brokerage Firm under this § 7.2.3 if a commission is earned by another licensed real estate brokerage firm acting pursuant to an exclusive agreement entered into during the Holdover Period and a Sale or Lease to a Submitted Prospect is consummated. If no box is checked above in this § 7.2.3, then Seller shall not owe the commission to Brokerage Firm.

7.3. When Applicable and Payable. The commission obligation shall apply to a Sale made during the Listing Period or any extension of such original or extended term. The commission described in § 7.1.1 shall be payable at the time of the closing of the Sale, or, if there is no closing (due to the refusal or neglect of Seller) then on the contracted date of closing, as contemplated by § 7.2.1 or § 7.2.3, or upon fulfillment of § 7.2.2 where the offer made by such buyer is not accepted by Seller.

7.4. Other Compensation. ____

7.5. Cooperative Broker Compensation. Broker shall seek assistance from, and Brokerage Firm offers compensation to, outside brokerage firms, whose brokers are acting as:

☐ **Buyer Agents:** _______% of the gross sales price or ______________________________, in U.S. dollars.

☐ **Transaction-Brokers:** _______% of the gross sales price or ______________________________, in U.S. dollars.

8. LIMITATION ON THIRD-PARTY COMPENSATION. Neither Broker nor the Brokerage Firm, except as set forth in § 7, shall accept compensation from any other person or entity in connection with the Property without the written consent of Seller. Additionally, neither Broker nor Brokerage Firm shall assess or receive mark-ups or other compensation for services performed by any third party or affiliated business entity unless Seller signs a separate written consent.

9. OTHER BROKERS' ASSISTANCE, MULTIPLE LISTING SERVICES AND MARKETING. Seller has been advised by Broker of the advantages and disadvantages of various marketing methods, including advertising and the use of multiple listing services (MLS) and various methods of making the Property accessible by other brokerage firms (e.g., using lock boxes, by-appointment-only showings, etc.), and whether some methods may limit the ability of another broker to show the Property. After having been so advised, Seller has chosen the following (check all that apply):

9.1. MLS/Information Exchange.

9.1.1. The Property ☐ **Shall** ☐ **Shall Not** be submitted to one or more MLS and ☐ **Shall** ☐ **Shall Not** be submitted to one or more property information exchanges. If submitted, Seller authorizes Broker to provide timely notice of any status change to such MLS and information exchanges. Upon transfer of deed from Seller to buyer, Seller authorizes Broker to provide sales information to such MLS and information exchanges.

9.1.2. Seller authorizes the use of electronic and all other marketing methods except: ______________________.

9.1.3. Seller further authorizes use of the data by MLS and property information exchanges, if any.

9.1.4. The Property Address ☐ **Shall** ☐ **Shall Not** be displayed on the Internet.

9.1.5. The Property Listing ☐ **Shall** ☐ **Shall Not** be displayed on the Internet.

9.2. Property Access. Access to the Property may be by:

☐ Lock Box

☐ ____

Other instructions: ____

9.3. Broker Marketing. The following specific marketing tasks shall be performed by Broker:

9.4. Brokerage Services. The Broker shall provide brokerage services to Seller.

10. SELLER'S OBLIGATIONS TO BROKER; DISCLOSURES AND CONSENT.

10.1. Negotiations and Communication. Seller agrees to conduct all negotiations for the Sale of the Property only through Broker, and to refer to Broker all communications received in any form from real estate brokers, prospective buyers, tenants or any other source during the Listing Period of this Seller Listing Contract.

10.2. Advertising. Seller agrees that any advertising of the Property by Seller (e.g., Internet, print and signage) shall first be approved by Broker.

10.3. No Existing Listing Agreement. Seller represents that Seller ☐ **Is** ☐ **Is Not** currently a party to any listing agreement with any other broker to sell the Property.

10.4. Ownership of Materials and Consent. Seller represents that all materials (including all photographs, renderings, images or other creative items) supplied to Broker by or on behalf of Seller are owned by Seller, except as Seller has disclosed in writing to Broker. Seller is authorized to and grants to Broker, Brokerage Firm and any MLS (that Broker submits the Property to) a nonexclusive irrevocable, royalty-free license to use such material for marketing of the Property, reporting as required and the publishing, display and reproduction of such material, compilation and data. This license shall survive the termination of this Seller Listing Contract.

10.5. Colorado Foreclosure Protection Act. The Colorado Foreclosure Protection Act (Act) generally applies if (1) the Property is residential (2) Seller resides in the Property as Seller's principal residence (3) Buyer's purpose in purchase of the Property is not to use the Property as Buyer's personal residence and (4) the Property is in foreclosure or Buyer has notice that any loan secured by the Property is at least thirty days delinquent or in default. If all requirements 1, 2, 3 and 4 are met and the Act otherwise applies, then a contract, between Buyer and Seller for the sale of the Property, that complies with the provisions of the Act is required. If the transaction is a Short Sale transaction and a Short Sale Addendum is part of the Contract between Seller and Buyer, the Act does not apply. It is recommended that Seller consult with an attorney.

11. PRICE AND TERMS. The following Price and Terms are acceptable to Seller:

11.1. Price. U.S. $________________

11.2. Terms. ☐ **Cash** ☐ **Conventional** ☐ **FHA** ☐ **VA** ☐ **Other:** ____________________

11.3. Loan Discount Points. ____

11.4. Buyer's Closing Costs (FHA/VA). Seller shall pay closing costs and fees, not to exceed $____________, that Buyer is not allowed by law to pay, for tax service and ____.

11.5. Earnest Money. Minimum amount of earnest money deposit U.S. $____________ in the form of ____________

11.6. Seller Proceeds. Seller will receive net proceeds of closing as indicated: ☐ **Cashier's Check** at Seller's expense; ☐ **Funds Electronically Transferred (Wire Transfer)** to an account specified by Seller, at Seller's expense; or ☐ **Closing Company's Trust Account Check**.

11.7. Advisory: Tax Withholding. The Internal Revenue Service and the Colorado Department of Revenue may require closing company to withhold a substantial portion of the proceeds of this Sale when Seller either (1) is a foreign person or (2) will not be a Colorado resident after closing. Seller should inquire of Seller's tax advisor to determine if withholding applies or if an exemption exists.

12. DEPOSITS. Brokerage Firm is authorized to accept earnest money deposits received by Broker pursuant to a proposed Sale contract. Brokerage Firm is authorized to deliver the earnest money deposit to the closing agent, if any, at or before the closing of the Sale contract.

13. INCLUSIONS AND EXCLUSIONS.

13.1. Inclusions. The Purchase Price includes the following items (Inclusions):

13.1.1. Fixtures. If attached to the Property on the date of this Seller Listing Contract, lighting, heating, plumbing, ventilating, and air conditioning fixtures, TV antennas, inside telephone, network and coaxial (cable) wiring and connecting blocks/jacks, plants, mirrors, floor coverings, intercom systems, built-in kitchen appliances, sprinkler systems and controls, built-in vacuum systems (including accessories), garage door openers including _______ remote controls; and

LC50-8-10. EXCLUSIVE RIGHT-TO-SELL LISTING CONTRACT **Page 4 of 7**

13.1.2. Personal Property. If on the Property whether attached or not on the date of this Seller Listing Contract: storm windows, storm doors, window and porch shades, awnings, blinds, screens, window coverings, curtain rods, drapery rods, fireplace inserts, fireplace screens, fireplace grates, heating stoves, storage sheds, and all keys. If checked, the following are included: ☐ **Water Softeners** ☐ **Smoke/Fire Detectors** ☐ **Security Systems** ☐ **Satellite Systems** (including satellite dishes); and

The Personal Property to be conveyed at closing shall be conveyed by Seller free and clear of all taxes (except personal property taxes for the year of closing), liens and encumbrances, except ________________________________. Conveyance shall be by bill of sale or other applicable legal instrument.

13.1.3. Trade Fixtures. The following trade fixtures: ________________________________

The Trade Fixtures to be conveyed at closing shall be conveyed by Seller, free and clear of all taxes (except personal property taxes for the year of closing), liens and encumbrances, except ________________________________. Conveyance shall be by bill of sale or other applicable legal instrument.

13.1.4. Parking and Storage Facilities. ☐ **Use Only** ☐ **Ownership** of the following parking facilities: ________ ____________________; and ☐ **Use Only** ☐ **Ownership** of the following storage facilities: ________________.

13.1.5. Water Rights. The following legally described water rights:

Any water rights shall be conveyed by ________________________ deed or other applicable legal instrument. The Well Permit # is ________________.

13.1.6. Growing Crops. The following growing crops:

13.2. Exclusions. The following are excluded (Exclusions): ________________________________

14. TITLE AND ENCUMBRANCES. Seller represents to Broker that title to the Property is solely in Seller's name. Seller shall deliver to Broker true copies of all relevant title materials, leases, improvement location certificates and surveys in Seller's possession and shall disclose to Broker all easements, liens and other encumbrances, if any, on the Property, of which Seller has knowledge. Seller authorizes the holder of any obligation secured by an encumbrance on the Property to disclose to Broker the amount owing on said encumbrance and the terms thereof. In case of Sale, Seller agrees to convey, by a ________________ deed, only that title Seller has in the Property. Property shall be conveyed free and clear of all taxes, except the general taxes for the year of closing.

All monetary encumbrances (such as mortgages, deeds of trust, liens, financing statements) shall be paid by Seller and released except as Seller and buyer may otherwise agree. Existing monetary encumbrances are as follows: ________________.

The Property is subject to the following leases and tenancies: ________________________________.

If the Property has been or will be subject to any governmental liens for special improvements installed at the time of signing a Sale contract, Seller shall be responsible for payment of same, unless otherwise agreed. Brokerage Firm may terminate this Seller Listing Contract upon written notice to Seller that title is not satisfactory to Brokerage Firm.

15. EVIDENCE OF TITLE. Seller agrees to furnish buyer, at Seller's expense, a current commitment and an owner's title insurance policy in an amount equal to the Purchase Price in the form specified in the Sale contract, or if this box is checked, ☐ **An Abstract of Title** certified to a current date.

16. ASSOCIATION ASSESSMENTS. Seller represents that the amount of the regular owners' association assessment is currently payable at $____________ per ____________ and that there are no unpaid regular or special assessments against the Property except the current regular assessments and except ________________________. Seller agrees to promptly request the owners' association to deliver to buyer before date of closing a current statement of assessments against the Property.

17. POSSESSION. Possession of the Property shall be delivered to buyer as follows: ________________________, subject to leases and tenancies as described in § 14.

18. MATERIAL DEFECTS, DISCLOSURES AND INSPECTION.

18.1. Broker's Obligations. Colorado law requires a broker to disclose to any prospective buyer all adverse material facts actually known by such broker including but not limited to adverse material facts pertaining to the title to the Property and the physical condition of the Property, any material defects in the Property, and any environmental hazards affecting the Property which are required by law to be disclosed. These types of disclosures may include such matters as structural defects, soil conditions, violations of health, zoning or building laws, and nonconforming uses and zoning variances. Seller agrees that any buyer may have the Property and Inclusions inspected and authorizes Broker to disclose any facts actually known by Broker about the Property.

18.2. Seller's Obligations.

18.2.1. Seller's Property Disclosure Form. A seller is not required by law to provide a written disclosure of adverse matters regarding the Property. However, disclosure of known material latent (not obvious) defects is required by law. Seller ☐ **Agrees** ☐ **Does Not Agree** to provide a Seller's Property Disclosure form completed to Seller's current, actual knowledge.

18.2.2. Lead-Based Paint. Unless exempt, if the improvements on the Property include one or more residential dwellings for which a building permit was issued prior to January 1, 1978, a completed Lead-Based Paint Disclosure (Sales) form must be signed by Seller and the real estate licensees, and given to any potential buyer in a timely manner.

18.2.3. Carbon Monoxide Alarms. Note: If the improvements on the Property have a fuel-fired heater or appliance, a fireplace, or an attached garage and one or more rooms lawfully used for sleeping purposes (Bedroom), Seller understands that Colorado law requires that Seller assure the Property has an operational carbon monoxide alarm installed within fifteen feet of the entrance to each Bedroom or in a location as required by the applicable building code, prior to offering the Property for sale or lease.

18.3. Right of Broker to Terminate. Although Broker has no obligation to investigate or inspect the Property, and no duty to verify statements made, Broker shall have the right to terminate this Seller Listing Contract if the physical condition of the Property, Inclusions, any proposed or existing transportation project, road, street or highway, or any other activity, odor or noise (whether on or off the Property) and its effect or expected effect on the Property or its occupants, or if any facts or suspicions regarding circumstances that could psychologically impact or stigmatize the Property are unsatisfactory to Broker.

19. FORFEITURE OF PAYMENTS. In the event of a forfeiture of payments made by a buyer, the sums received shall be divided between Brokerage Firm and Seller, one-half thereof to Brokerage Firm but not to exceed the Brokerage Firm compensation agreed upon herein, and the balance to Seller. Any forfeiture of payment under this section shall not reduce any Brokerage Firm compensation owed, earned and payable under § 7.

20. COST OF SERVICES AND REIMBURSEMENT. Unless otherwise agreed upon in writing, Brokerage Firm shall bear all expenses incurred by Brokerage Firm, if any, to market the Property and to compensate cooperating brokerage firms, if any. Neither Broker nor Brokerage Firm shall obtain or order any other products or services unless Seller agrees in writing to pay for them promptly when due (examples: surveys, radon tests, soil tests, title reports, engineering studies). Unless otherwise agreed, neither Broker nor Brokerage Firm shall be obligated to advance funds for the benefit of Seller in order to complete a closing. Seller shall reimburse Brokerage Firm for payments made by Brokerage Firm for such products or services authorized by Seller.

21. DISCLOSURE OF SETTLEMENT COSTS. Seller acknowledges that costs, quality, and extent of service vary between different settlement service providers (e.g., attorneys, lenders, inspectors and title companies).

22. MAINTENANCE OF THE PROPERTY. Neither Broker nor Brokerage Firm shall be responsible for maintenance of the Property nor shall they be liable for damage of any kind occurring to the Property, unless such damage shall be caused by their negligence or intentional misconduct.

23. NONDISCRIMINATION. The parties agree not to discriminate unlawfully against any prospective buyer because of the race, creed, color, sex, sexual orientation, marital status, familial status, physical or mental disability, handicap, religion, national origin or ancestry of such person.

24. RECOMMENDATION OF LEGAL AND TAX COUNSEL. By signing this document, Seller acknowledges that Broker has advised that this document has important legal consequences and has recommended consultation with legal and tax or other counsel before signing this Seller Listing Contract.

25. MEDIATION. If a dispute arises relating to this Seller Listing Contract, prior to or after closing, and is not resolved, the parties shall first proceed in good faith to submit the matter to mediation. Mediation is a process in which the parties meet with an impartial person who helps to resolve the dispute informally and confidentially. Mediators cannot impose binding decisions. The parties to the dispute must agree, in writing, before any settlement is binding. The parties will jointly appoint an acceptable mediator and will share equally in the cost of such mediation. The mediation, unless otherwise agreed, shall terminate in the event the entire dispute is not resolved within 30 calendar days of the date written notice requesting mediation is delivered by one party to the other at the party's last known address.

26. ATTORNEY FEES. In the event of any arbitration or litigation relating to this Seller Listing Contract, the arbitrator or court shall award to the prevailing party all reasonable costs and expenses, including attorney and legal fees.

27. ADDITIONAL PROVISIONS. (The following additional provisions have not been approved by the Colorado Real Estate Commission.)

28. ATTACHMENTS. The following are a part of this Seller Listing Contract:

29. NO OTHER PARTY OR INTENDED BENEFICIARIES. Nothing in this Seller Listing Contract shall be deemed to inure to the benefit of any person other than Seller, Broker and Brokerage Firm.

30. NOTICE, DELIVERY AND CHOICE OF LAW.

30.1. Physical Delivery. All notices must be in writing, except as provided in § 30.2. Any document, including a signed document or notice, delivered to the other party to this Seller Listing Contract, is effective upon physical receipt. Delivery to Seller shall be effective when physically received by Seller, any signator on behalf of Seller, any named individual of Seller or representative of Seller.

30.2. Electronic Delivery. As an alternative to physical delivery, any document, including any signed document or written notice may be delivered in electronic form only by the following indicated methods: ☐ **Facsimile** ☐ **Email** ☐ **Internet** ☐ **No Electronic Delivery**. Documents with original signatures shall be provided upon request of any party.

30.3. Choice of Law. This Seller Listing Contract and all disputes arising hereunder shall be governed by and construed in accordance with the laws of the State of Colorado that would be applicable to Colorado residents who sign a contract in this state for property located in Colorado.

31. MODIFICATION OF THIS SELLER LISTING CONTRACT. No subsequent modification of any of the terms of this Seller Listing Contract shall be valid, binding upon the parties, or enforceable unless made in writing and signed by the parties.

32. COUNTERPARTS. If more than one person is named as a Seller herein, this Seller Listing Contract may be executed by each Seller, separately, and when so executed, such copies taken together with one executed by Broker on behalf of Brokerage Firm shall be deemed to be a full and complete contract between the parties.

33. ENTIRE AGREEMENT. This agreement constitutes the entire contract between the parties, and any prior agreements, whether oral or written, have been merged and integrated into this Seller Listing Contract.

34. COPY OF CONTRACT. Seller acknowledges receipt of a copy of this Seller Listing Contract signed by Broker, including all attachments.

Brokerage Firm authorizes Broker to execute this Seller Listing Contract on behalf of Brokerage Firm.

Seller's Name: ______________________________

____
Seller's Signature Date

Address: ______________________________
____

Phone No.: ______________________________
Fax No: ______________________________
Electronic Address: ______________________________

Broker's Name: ______________________________

____
Broker's Signature Date

Address: ______________________________
____

Phone No.: ______________________________
Fax No: ______________________________
Electronic Address: ______________________________

Brokerage Firm's Name: ______________________________
Address: ______________________________
____

Phone No.: ______________________________
Fax No.: ______________________________
Electronic Address: ______________________________

B. Contract to Buy and Sell Real Estate (Residential) CBS1-10-11

The printed portions of this form, except differentiated additions, have been approved by the Colorado Real Estate Commission. (CBS1-10-11) (Mandatory 1-12)

THIS FORM HAS IMPORTANT LEGAL CONSEQUENCES AND THE PARTIES SHOULD CONSULT LEGAL AND TAX OR OTHER COUNSEL BEFORE SIGNING.

CONTRACT TO BUY AND SELL REAL ESTATE (RESIDENTIAL)

Date: ____________________________

AGREEMENT

1. AGREEMENT. Buyer, identified in § 2.1, agrees to buy, and Seller, identified in § 2.3, agrees to sell, the Property described below on the terms and conditions set forth in this contract (Contract).

2. PARTIES AND PROPERTY.

2.1. Buyer. Buyer, ____, will take title to the Property described below as ☐ **Joint Tenants** ☐ **Tenants In Common** ☐ **Other** ______________________________.

2.2. Assignability and Inurement. This Contract ☐ **Shall** ☐ **Shall Not** be assignable by Buyer without Seller's prior written consent. Except as so restricted, this Contract shall inure to the benefit of and be binding upon the heirs, personal representatives, successors and assigns of the parties.

2.3. Seller. Seller, ____, is the current owner of the Property described below.

2.4. Property. The Property is the following legally described real estate in the County of ______________, Colorado:

known as No. ____,

Street Address City State Zip

together with the interests, easements, rights, benefits, improvements and attached fixtures appurtenant thereto, and all interest of Seller in vacated streets and alleys adjacent thereto, except as herein excluded (Property).

2.5. Inclusions. The Purchase Price includes the following items (Inclusions):

2.5.1. Fixtures. If attached to the Property on the date of this Contract: lighting, heating, plumbing, ventilating and air conditioning fixtures, TV antennas, inside telephone, network and coaxial (cable) wiring and connecting blocks/jacks, plants, mirrors, floor coverings, intercom systems, built-in kitchen appliances, sprinkler systems and controls, built-in vacuum systems (including accessories), garage door openers including _______ remote controls.

Other Fixtures:

If any fixtures are attached to the Property after the date of this Contract, such additional fixtures are also included in the Purchase Price.

2.5.2. Personal Property. If on the Property whether attached or not on the date of this Contract: storm windows, storm doors, window and porch shades, awnings, blinds, screens, window coverings, curtain rods, drapery rods, fireplace inserts, fireplace screens, fireplace grates, heating stoves, storage sheds, and all keys. If checked, the following are included: ☐ **Water Softeners** ☐ **Smoke/Fire Detectors** ☐ **Security Systems** ☐ **Satellite Systems** (including satellite dishes).

Other Personal Property:

The Personal Property to be conveyed at Closing shall be conveyed by Seller free and clear of all taxes (except personal property taxes for the year of Closing), liens and encumbrances, except ______________________________. Conveyance shall be by bill of sale or other applicable legal instrument.

2.5.3. Parking and Storage Facilities. ☐ **Use Only** ☐ **Ownership** of the following parking facilities: ______________________; and ☐ **Use Only** ☐ **Ownership** of the following storage facilities: __________________.

2.5.4. Water Rights, Water and Sewer Taps.

2.5.4.1. Deeded Water Rights. The following legally described water rights:

Any water rights shall be conveyed by ☐ ______________________ **Deed** ☐ **Other** applicable legal instrument.

☐ **2.5.4.2. Well Rights.** If any water well is to be transferred to Buyer, Seller agrees to supply required information about such well to Buyer. Buyer understands that if the well to be transferred is a Small Capacity Well or a Domestic Exempt Water Well used for ordinary household purposes, Buyer shall, prior to or at Closing, complete a Change in Ownership form for the well. If an existing well has not been registered with the Colorado Division of Water Resources in the Department of Natural Resources (Division), Buyer shall complete a registration of existing well form for the well and pay the cost of registration. If no person will be providing a closing service in connection with the transaction, Buyer shall file the form with the Division within sixty days after Closing. The Well Permit # is ______________.

2.5.4.3. ☐ **Water Stock Certificates:**

2.5.4.4. ☐ **Water Tap** ☐ **Sewer Tap**

Note: Buyer is advised to obtain, from the provider, written confirmation of the amount remaining to be paid, if any, time and other restrictions for transfer and use of the tap.

2.5.4.5. Other Rights:

2.6. Exclusions. The following items are excluded (Exclusions):

3. DATES AND DEADLINES.

Item No.	Reference	Event	Date or Deadline
1	§ 4.2	Alternative Earnest Money Deadline	
		Title and Association	
2	§ 7.1	Record Title Deadline	
3	§ 7.2	Exceptions Request Deadline	
4	§ 8.1	Record Title Objection Deadline	
5	§ 8.2	Off-Record Title Deadline	
6	§ 8.2	Off-Record Title Objection Deadline	
7	§ 8.3	Title Resolution Deadline	
8	§ 7.3	Association Documents Deadline	
9	§ 7.3	Association Documents Objection Deadline	
10	§ 8.5	Right of First Refusal Deadline	
		Seller's Property Disclosure	
11	§ 10.1	Seller's Property Disclosure Deadline	
		Loan and Credit	
12	§ 5.1	Loan Application Deadline	
13	§ 5.2	Loan Conditions Deadline	
14	§ 5.3	Buyer's Credit Information Deadline	
15	§ 5.3	Disapproval of Buyer's Credit Information Deadline	
16	§ 5.4	Existing Loan Documents Deadline	
17	§ 5.4	Existing Loan Documents Objection Deadline	
18	§ 5.4	Loan Transfer Approval Deadline	
		Appraisal	
19	§ 6.2	Appraisal Deadline	
20	§ 6.2	Appraisal Objection Deadline	
		Survey	
21	§ 9.1	Current Survey Deadline	
22	§ 9.2	Current Survey Objection Deadline	
		Inspection and Due Diligence	
23	§ 10.2	Inspection Objection Deadline	
24	§ 10.3	Inspection Resolution Deadline	

25	§ 10.5	Property Insurance Objection Deadline	
26	§ 10.6	Due Diligence Documents Delivery Deadline	
27	§ 10.7	Due Diligence Documents Objection Deadline	
		Closing and Possession	
28	§ 12.3	**Closing Date**	
29	§ 17	Possession Date	
30	§ 17	Possession Time	
31	§ 28	**Acceptance Deadline Date**	
32	§ 28	**Acceptance Deadline Time**	

Note: Applicability of Terms.
Any box, blank or line in this Contract left blank or completed with the abbreviation "N/A", or the word "Deleted" means such provision in **Dates and Deadlines** (§ 3), including any deadline, is not applicable and the corresponding provision of this Contract to which reference is made is deleted.

The abbreviation "MEC" (mutual execution of this Contract) means the date upon which both parties have signed this Contract.

Note: If **FHA** or **VA** loan boxes are checked in § 4.5.3 (Loan Limitations), the **Appraisal Deadline** (§ 3) does **<u>Not</u>** apply to **FHA** insured or **VA** guaranteed loans.

4. PURCHASE PRICE AND TERMS.

4.1. Price and Terms. The Purchase Price set forth below shall be payable in U.S. Dollars by Buyer as follows:

Item No.	Reference	Item	Amount	Amount
1	§ 4.1	Purchase Price	$	
2	§ 4.2	Earnest Money		$
3	§ 4.5	New Loan		
4	§ 4.6	Assumption Balance		
5	§ 4.7	Seller or Private Financing		
6				
7				
8	§ 4.3	Cash at Closing		
9		**TOTAL**	$	$

4.2. Earnest Money. The Earnest Money set forth in this section, in the form of ____________________, shall be payable to and held by ____ (Earnest Money Holder), in its trust account, on behalf of both Seller and Buyer. The Earnest Money deposit shall be tendered with this Contract unless the parties mutually agree to an **Alternative Earnest Money Deadline** (§ 3) for its payment. If Earnest Money Holder is other than the Brokerage Firm identified in § 33 or § 34, Closing Instructions signed by Buyer, Seller and Earnest Money Holder must be obtained on or before delivery of Earnest Money to Earnest Money Holder. The parties authorize delivery of the Earnest Money deposit to the company conducting the Closing (Closing Company), if any, at or before Closing. In the event Earnest Money Holder has agreed to have interest on Earnest Money deposits transferred to a fund established for the purpose of providing affordable housing to Colorado residents, Seller and Buyer acknowledge and agree that any interest accruing on the Earnest Money deposited with the Earnest Money Holder in this transaction shall be transferred to such fund.

4.2.1. Alternative Earnest Money Deadline. The deadline for delivering the Earnest Money, if other than at the time of tender of this Contract is as set forth as the **Alternative Earnest Money Deadline** (§ 3).

4.2.2. Return of Earnest Money. If Buyer has a Right to Terminate and timely terminates, Buyer shall be entitled to the return of Earnest Money as provided in this Contract. If this Contract is terminated as set forth in § 25 and, except as provided in § 24, if the Earnest Money has not already been returned following receipt of a Notice to Terminate, Seller agrees to execute and return to Buyer or Broker working with Buyer, written mutual instructions, i.e., Earnest Money Release form, within three days of Seller's receipt of such form.

4.3. Form of Funds; Time of Payment; Funds Available.

4.3.1. Good Funds. All amounts payable by the parties at Closing, including any loan proceeds, Cash at Closing and closing costs, shall be in funds that comply with all applicable Colorado laws, including electronic transfer funds, certified check, savings and loan teller's check and cashier's check (Good Funds).

4.3.2. Available Funds. All funds required to be paid at Closing or as otherwise agreed in writing between the parties shall be timely paid to allow disbursement by Closing Company at Closing **OR SUCH PARTY SHALL BE IN DEFAULT**.

Buyer represents that Buyer, as of the date of this Contract, ☐ **Does** ☐ **Does Not** have funds that are immediately verifiable and available in an amount not less than the amount stated as Cash at Closing in § 4.1.

4.4. Seller Concession. Seller, at Closing, shall credit, as directed by Buyer, an amount of $______________ to assist with Buyer's closing costs, loan discount points, loan origination fees, prepaid items (including any amounts that Seller agrees to pay because Buyer is not allowed to pay due to FHA, CHFA, VA, etc.), and any other fee, cost, charge, expense or expenditure related to Buyer's New Loan or other allowable Seller concession (collectively, Seller Concession). Seller Concession is in addition to any sum Seller has agreed to pay or credit Buyer elsewhere in this Contract. Seller Concession shall be reduced to the extent it exceeds the amount allowed by Buyer's lender as set forth in the Closing Statement or HUD-1, at Closing.

4.5. New Loan.

4.5.1. Buyer to Pay Loan Costs. Buyer, except as provided in § 4.4, if applicable, shall timely pay Buyer's loan costs, loan discount points, prepaid items and loan origination fees, as required by lender.

4.5.2. Buyer May Select Financing. Buyer may pay in cash or select financing appropriate and acceptable to Buyer, including a different loan than initially sought, except as restricted in § 4.5.3 or § 30 (Additional Provisions).

4.5.3. Loan Limitations. Buyer may purchase the Property using any of the following types of loan: ☐ **Conventional** ☐ **FHA** ☐ **VA** ☐ **Bond** ☐ **Other** ____.

4.5.4. Good Faith Estimate – Monthly Payment and Loan Costs. Buyer is advised to review the terms, conditions and costs of Buyer's New Loan carefully. If Buyer is applying for a residential loan, the lender generally must provide Buyer with a good faith estimate of Buyer's closing costs within three days after Buyer completes a loan application. Buyer should also obtain an estimate of the amount of Buyer's monthly mortgage payment. If the New Loan is unsatisfactory to Buyer, Buyer shall have the Right to Terminate under § 25.1, on or before **Loan Conditions Deadline** (§ 3).

4.6. Assumption. Buyer agrees to assume and pay an existing loan in the approximate amount of the Assumption Balance set forth in § 4.1, presently payable at $______________ per ______________ including principal and interest presently at the rate of ________% per annum, and also including escrow for the following as indicated: ☐ **Real Estate Taxes** ☐ **Property Insurance Premium** ☐ **Mortgage Insurance Premium** and ☐ ____.

Buyer agrees to pay a loan transfer fee not to exceed $______________. At the time of assumption, the new interest rate shall not exceed ________% per annum and the new payment shall not exceed $______________ per ______________ principal and interest, plus escrow, if any. If the actual principal balance of the existing loan at Closing is less than the Assumption Balance, which causes the amount of cash required from Buyer at Closing to be increased by more than $______________, then Buyer shall have the Right to Terminate under § 25.1, on or before **Closing Date** (§ 3), based on the reduced amount of the actual principal balance.

Seller ☐ **Shall** ☐ **Shall Not** be released from liability on said loan. If applicable, compliance with the requirements for release from liability shall be evidenced by delivery ☐ **on or before Loan Transfer Approval Deadline** (§ 3) ☐ **at Closing** of an appropriate letter of commitment from lender. Any cost payable for release of liability shall be paid by __________________ in an amount not to exceed $______________.

4.7. Seller or Private Financing. Buyer agrees to execute a promissory note payable to ______________________, as ☐ **Joint Tenants** ☐ **Tenants In Common** ☐ **Other** ______________________________________, on the note form as indicated: ☐ **(Default Rate)** NTD81-10-06 ☐ **Other** ____ secured by a ____________ (1st, 2nd, etc.) deed of trust encumbering the Property, using the form as indicated: ☐ **Due on Transfer – Strict** (TD72-8-10) ☐ **Due on Transfer – Creditworthy** (TD73-8-10) ☐ **Assumable – Not Due on Transfer** (TD74-8-10) ☐ **Other** ____.

The promissory note shall be amortized on the basis of ____________ ☐ **Years** ☐ **Months**, payable at $______________ per ______________ including principal and interest at the rate of ________% per annum. Payments shall commence ______________________ and shall be due on the __________ day of each succeeding ______________. If not sooner paid, the balance of principal and accrued interest shall be due and payable ______________________________ after Closing. Payments ☐ **Shall** ☐ **Shall Not** be increased by ____________ of estimated annual real estate taxes, and ☐ **Shall** ☐ **Shall Not** be increased by ____________ of estimated annual property insurance premium. The loan shall also contain the following terms: (1) if any payment is not received within __________ days after its due date, a late charge of ________% of such payment shall be due; (2) interest on lender disbursements under the deed of trust shall be ________% per annum; (3) default interest rate shall be ________% per annum; (4) Buyer may prepay without a penalty except ______________________________________; and (5) Buyer ☐ **Shall** ☐ **Shall Not** execute and deliver, at Closing, a Security Agreement and UCC-1 Financing Statement granting the holder of the promissory note a ____________ (1st, 2nd, etc.) lien on the personal property included in this sale.

Buyer ☐ **Shall** ☐ **Shall Not** provide a mortgagee's title insurance policy, at Buyer's expense.

TRANSACTION PROVISIONS

5. FINANCING CONDITIONS AND OBLIGATIONS.

5.1. Loan Application. If Buyer is to pay all or part of the Purchase Price by obtaining one or more new loans (New Loan), or if an existing loan is not to be released at Closing, Buyer, if required by such lender, shall make an application verifiable by such lender, on or before **Loan Application Deadline** (§ 3) and exercise reasonable efforts to obtain such loan or approval.

5.2. Loan Conditions. If Buyer is to pay all or part of the Purchase Price with a New Loan, this Contract is conditional upon Buyer determining, in Buyer's sole subjective discretion, whether the New Loan is satisfactory to Buyer, including its availability, payments, interest rate, terms, conditions, and cost of such New Loan. This condition is for the benefit of Buyer. Buyer shall have the Right to Terminate under § 25.1, on or before **Loan Conditions Deadline** (§ 3), if the New Loan is not satisfactory to Buyer, in Buyer's sole subjective discretion. **IF SELLER DOES NOT TIMELY RECEIVE WRITTEN NOTICE TO TERMINATE, BUYER'S EARNEST MONEY SHALL BE NONREFUNDABLE,** except as otherwise provided in this Contract (e.g., Appraisal, Title, Survey).

5.3. Credit Information and Buyer's New Senior Loan. If Buyer is to pay all or part of the Purchase Price by executing a promissory note in favor of Seller, or if an existing loan is not to be released at Closing, this Contract is conditional (for the benefit of Seller) upon Seller's approval of Buyer's financial ability and creditworthiness, which approval shall be at Seller's sole subjective discretion. In such case: (1) Buyer shall supply to Seller by **Buyer's Credit Information Deadline** (§ 3), at Buyer's expense, information and documents (including a current credit report) concerning Buyer's financial, employment and credit condition and Buyer's New Senior Loan, defined below, if any; (2) Buyer consents that Seller may verify Buyer's financial ability and creditworthiness; (3) any such information and documents received by Seller shall be held by Seller in confidence, and not released to others except to protect Seller's interest in this transaction; and (4) in the event Buyer is to execute a promissory note secured by a deed of trust in favor of Seller, this Contract is conditional (for the benefit of Seller) upon Seller's approval of the terms and conditions of any New Loan to be obtained by Buyer if the deed of trust to Seller is to be subordinate to Buyer's New Loan (Buyer's New Senior Loan). If the Cash at Closing is less than as set forth in § 4.1 of this Contract or Buyer's New Senior Loan changes from that approved by Seller, Seller shall have the Right to Terminate under § 25.1, at or before Closing. If Seller disapproves of Buyer's financial ability, creditworthiness or Buyer's New Senior Loan, in Seller's sole subjective discretion, Seller shall have the Right to Terminate under § 25.1, on or before **Disapproval of Buyer's Credit Information Deadline** (§ 3).

5.4. Existing Loan Review. If an existing loan is not to be released at Closing, Seller shall deliver copies of the loan documents (including note, deed of trust, and any modifications) to Buyer by **Existing Loan Documents Deadline** (§ 3). For the benefit of Buyer, this Contract is conditional upon Buyer's review and approval of the provisions of such loan documents. Buyer shall have the Right to Terminate under § 25.1, on or before **Existing Loan Documents Objection Deadline** (§ 3), based on any unsatisfactory provision of such loan documents, in Buyer's sole subjective discretion. If the lender's approval of a transfer of the Property is required, this Contract is conditional upon Buyer's obtaining such approval without change in the terms of such loan, except as set forth in § 4.6. If lender's approval is not obtained by **Loan Transfer Approval Deadline** (§ 3), this Contract shall terminate on such deadline. Seller shall have the Right to Terminate under § 25.1, on or before Closing, in Seller's sole subjective discretion, if Seller is to be released from liability under such existing loan and Buyer does not obtain such compliance as set forth in § 4.6.

6. APPRAISAL PROVISIONS.

6.1. Lender Property Requirements. If the lender imposes any requirements or repairs (Requirements) to be made to the Property (e.g., roof repair, repainting), beyond those matters already agreed to by Seller in this Contract, Seller shall have the Right to Terminate under § 25.1, (notwithstanding § 10 of this Contract), on or before three days following Seller's receipt of the Requirements, based on any unsatisfactory Requirements, in Seller's sole subjective discretion. Seller's Right to Terminate in this § 6.1 shall not apply if, on or before any termination by Seller pursuant to this § 6.1: (1) the parties enter into a written agreement regarding the Requirements; or (2) the Requirements have been completed; or (3) the satisfaction of the Requirements is waived in writing by Buyer.

6.2. Appraisal Condition. The applicable Appraisal provision set forth below shall apply to the respective loan type set forth in § 4.5.3, or if a cash transaction, i.e. no financing, § 6.2.1 shall apply.

6.2.1. Conventional/Other. Buyer shall have the sole option and election to terminate this Contract if the Property's valuation is less than the Purchase Price determined by an appraiser engaged on behalf of ______________________. The appraisal shall be received by Buyer or Buyer's lender on or before **Appraisal Deadline** (§ 3). Buyer shall have the Right to Terminate under § 25.1, on or before **Appraisal Objection Deadline** (§ 3), if the Property's valuation is less than the Purchase Price and Seller's receipt of either a copy of such appraisal or written notice from lender that confirms the Property's valuation is less than the Purchase Price.

6.2.2. FHA. It is expressly agreed that, notwithstanding any other provisions of this Contract, the Purchaser (Buyer) shall not be obligated to complete the purchase of the Property described herein or to incur any penalty by forfeiture of Earnest Money deposits or otherwise unless the Purchaser (Buyer) has been given in accordance with HUD/FHA or VA requirements a written statement issued by the Federal Housing Commissioner, Department of Veterans Affairs, or a Direct

Endorsement lender, setting forth the appraised value of the Property of not less than $______________. The Purchaser (Buyer) shall have the privilege and option of proceeding with the consummation of this Contract without regard to the amount of the appraised valuation. The appraised valuation is arrived at to determine the maximum mortgage the Department of Housing and Urban Development will insure. HUD does not warrant the value nor the condition of the Property. The Purchaser (Buyer) should satisfy himself/herself that the price and condition of the Property are acceptable.

6.2.3. VA. It is expressly agreed that, notwithstanding any other provisions of this Contract, the purchaser (Buyer) shall not incur any penalty by forfeiture of Earnest Money or otherwise or be obligated to complete the purchase of the Property described herein, if the Contract Purchase Price or cost exceeds the reasonable value of the Property established by the Department of Veterans Affairs. The purchaser (Buyer) shall, however, have the privilege and option of proceeding with the consummation of this Contract without regard to the amount of the reasonable value established by the Department of Veterans Affairs.

6.3. Cost of Appraisal. Cost of any appraisal to be obtained after the date of this Contract shall be timely paid by ☐ **Buyer** ☐ **Seller**.

7. EVIDENCE OF TITLE AND ASSOCIATION DOCUMENTS.

7.1. Evidence of Title. On or before **Record Title Deadline** (§ 3), Seller shall cause to be furnished to Buyer, at Seller's expense, a current commitment for owner's title insurance policy (Title Commitment) in an amount equal to the Purchase Price, or if this box is checked, ☐ **An Abstract** of title certified to a current date. If title insurance is furnished, Seller shall also deliver to Buyer copies of any abstracts of title covering all or any portion of the Property (Abstract) in Seller's possession. At Seller's expense, Seller shall cause the title insurance policy to be issued and delivered to Buyer as soon as practicable at or after Closing. The title insurance commitment ☐ **Shall** ☐ **Shall Not** commit to delete or insure over the standard exceptions which relate to: (1) parties in possession, (2) unrecorded easements, (3) survey matters, (4) unrecorded mechanics' liens, (5) gap period (effective date of commitment to date deed is recorded), and (6) unpaid taxes, assessments and unredeemed tax sales prior to the year of Closing. Any additional premium expense to obtain this additional coverage shall be paid by ☐ **Buyer** ☐ **Seller**.

Note: The title insurance company may not agree to delete or insure over any or all of the standard exceptions. Buyer shall have the right to review the Title Commitment, its provisions and Title Documents (defined in § 7.2), and if not satisfactory to Buyer, Buyer may exercise Buyer's rights pursuant to § 8.1.

7.2. Copies of Exceptions. On or before **Record Title Deadline** (§ 3), Seller, at Seller's expense, shall furnish to Buyer and ______________________________, (1) copies of any plats, declarations, covenants, conditions and restrictions burdening the Property, and (2) if a Title Commitment is required to be furnished, and if this box is checked ☐ **Copies of any Other Documents** (or, if illegible, summaries of such documents) listed in the schedule of exceptions (Exceptions). Even if the box is not checked, Seller shall have the obligation to furnish these documents pursuant to this section if requested by Buyer any time on or before **Exceptions Request Deadline** (§ 3). This requirement shall pertain only to documents as shown of record in the office of the clerk and recorder in the county where the Property is located. The Abstract or Title Commitment, together with any copies or summaries of such documents furnished pursuant to this section, constitute the title documents (collectively, Title Documents).

7.3. Homeowners' Association Documents. The term Association Documents consists of all owners' associations (Association) declarations, bylaws, operating agreements, rules and regulations, party wall agreements, minutes of most recent annual owners' meeting and minutes of any directors' or managers' meetings during the six-month period immediately preceding the date of this Contract, if any (Governing Documents), most recent financial documents consisting of (1) annual balance sheet, (2) annual income and expenditures statement, and (3) annual budget (Financial Documents), if any (collectively, Association Documents).

7.3.1. Common Interest Community Disclosure. THE PROPERTY IS LOCATED WITHIN A COMMON INTEREST COMMUNITY AND IS SUBJECT TO THE DECLARATION FOR SUCH COMMUNITY. THE OWNER OF THE PROPERTY WILL BE REQUIRED TO BE A MEMBER OF THE OWNER'S ASSOCIATION FOR THE COMMUNITY AND WILL BE SUBJECT TO THE BYLAWS AND RULES AND REGULATIONS OF THE ASSOCIATION. THE DECLARATION, BYLAWS, AND RULES AND REGULATIONS WILL IMPOSE FINANCIAL OBLIGATIONS UPON THE OWNER OF THE PROPERTY, INCLUDING AN OBLIGATION TO PAY ASSESSMENTS OF THE ASSOCIATION. IF THE OWNER DOES NOT PAY THESE ASSESSMENTS, THE ASSOCIATION COULD PLACE A LIEN ON THE PROPERTY AND POSSIBLY SELL IT TO PAY THE DEBT. THE DECLARATION, BYLAWS, AND RULES AND REGULATIONS OF THE COMMUNITY MAY PROHIBIT THE OWNER FROM MAKING CHANGES TO THE PROPERTY WITHOUT AN ARCHITECTURAL REVIEW BY THE ASSOCIATION (OR A COMMITTEE OF THE ASSOCIATION) AND THE APPROVAL OF THE ASSOCIATION. PURCHASERS OF PROPERTY WITHIN THE COMMON INTEREST COMMUNITY SHOULD INVESTIGATE THE FINANCIAL OBLIGATIONS OF MEMBERS OF THE ASSOCIATION. PURCHASERS SHOULD CAREFULLY READ THE DECLARATION FOR THE COMMUNITY AND THE BYLAWS AND RULES AND REGULATIONS OF THE ASSOCIATION.

7.3.2. Association Documents to Buyer.

☐ **7.3.2.1. Seller to Provide Association Documents.** Seller shall cause the Association Documents to be provided to Buyer, at Seller's expense, on or before **Association Documents Deadline** (§ 3).

☐ **7.3.2.2. Seller Authorizes Association.** Seller authorizes the Association to provide the Association Documents to Buyer, at Seller's expense.

7.3.2.3. Seller's Obligation. Seller's obligation to provide the Association Documents shall be fulfilled upon Buyer's receipt of the Association Documents, regardless of who provides such documents.

Note: If neither box in this § 7.3.2 is checked, the provisions of § 7.3.2.1 shall apply.

7.3.3. Conditional on Buyer's Review. If the box in either § 7.3.2.1 or § 7.3.2.2 is checked, the provisions of this § 7.3.3 shall apply. Buyer shall have the Right to Terminate under § 25.1, on or before **Association Documents Objection Deadline** (§ 3), based on any unsatisfactory provision in any of the Association Documents, in Buyer's sole subjective discretion. Should Buyer receive the Association Documents after **Association Documents Deadline** (§ 3), Buyer, at Buyer's option, shall have the Right to Terminate under § 25.1 by Buyer's Notice to Terminate received by Seller on or before ten days after Buyer's receipt of the Association Documents. If Buyer does not receive the Association Documents, or if Buyer's Notice to Terminate would otherwise be required to be received by Seller after **Closing Date** (§ 3), Buyer's Notice to Terminate shall be received by Seller on or before three days prior to **Closing Date** (§ 3). If Seller does not receive Buyer's Notice to Terminate within such time, Buyer accepts the provisions of the Association Documents as satisfactory, and Buyer waives any Right to Terminate under this provision, notwithstanding the provisions of § 8.5.

8. RECORD TITLE AND OFF-RECORD TITLE MATTERS.

8.1. Record Title Matters. Buyer has the right to review and object to any of the Title Documents (Right to Object, Resolution) as set forth in § 8.3. Buyer's objection may be based on any unsatisfactory form or content of Title Commitment, notwithstanding § 13, or any other unsatisfactory title condition, in Buyer's sole subjective discretion. If Buyer objects to any of the Title Documents, Buyer shall cause Seller to receive Buyer's Notice to Terminate or Notice of Title Objection on or before **Record Title Objection Deadline** (§ 3). If Title Documents are not received by Buyer, on or before the **Record Title Deadline** (§ 3), or if there is an endorsement to the Title Commitment that adds a new Exception to title, a copy of the new Exception to title and the modified Title Commitment shall be delivered to Buyer. Buyer shall cause Seller to receive Buyer's Notice to Terminate or Notice of Title Objection on or before ten days after receipt by Buyer of the following documents: (1) any required Title Document not timely received by Buyer, (2) any change to the Title Documents, or (3) endorsement to the Title Commitment. If Seller receives Buyer's Notice to Terminate or Notice of Title Objection, pursuant to this § 8.1 (Record Title Matters), any title objection by Buyer and this Contract shall be governed by the provisions set forth in § 8.3 (Right to Object, Resolution). If Seller does not receive Buyer's Notice to Terminate or Notice of Title Objection by the applicable deadline specified above, Buyer accepts the condition of title as disclosed by the Title Documents as satisfactory.

8.2. Off-Record Title Matters. Seller shall deliver to Buyer, on or before **Off-Record Title Deadline** (§ 3), true copies of all existing surveys in Seller's possession pertaining to the Property and shall disclose to Buyer all easements, liens (including, without limitation, governmental improvements approved, but not yet installed) or other title matters (including, without limitation, rights of first refusal and options) not shown by public records, of which Seller has actual knowledge. Buyer shall have the right to inspect the Property to investigate if any third party has any right in the Property not shown by public records (such as an unrecorded easement, unrecorded lease, boundary line discrepancy or water rights). Buyer's Notice to Terminate or Notice of Title Objection of any unsatisfactory condition (whether disclosed by Seller or revealed by such inspection, notwithstanding § 13), in Buyer's sole subjective discretion, shall be received by Seller on or before **Off-Record Title Objection Deadline** (§ 3). If Seller receives Buyer's Notice to Terminate or Notice of Title Objection pursuant to this § 8.2 (Off-Record Title Matters), any title objection by Buyer and this Contract shall be governed by the provisions set forth in § 8.3 (Right to Object, Resolution). If Seller does not receive Buyer's Notice to Terminate or Notice of Title Objection, on or before **Off-Record Title Objection Deadline** (§ 3), Buyer accepts title subject to such rights, if any, of third parties of which Buyer has actual knowledge.

8.3. Right to Object, Resolution. Buyer's right to object to any title matters shall include, but not be limited to those matters set forth in §§ 8.1 (Record Title Matters), 8.2 (Off-Record Title Matters) and 13 (Transfer of Title), in Buyer's sole subjective discretion (collectively, Notice of Title Objection). If Buyer objects to any title matter, on or before the applicable deadline, Buyer shall have the choice to either (1) object to the condition of title, or (2) terminate this Contract.

8.3.1. Title Resolution. If Seller receives Buyer's Notice of Title Objection, as provided in § 8.1 (Record Title Matters) or § 8.2 (Off-Record Title Matters), on or before the applicable deadline, and if Buyer and Seller have not agreed to a written settlement thereof on or before **Title Resolution Deadline** (§ 3), this Contract shall terminate on the expiration of **Title Resolution Deadline** (§ 3), unless Seller receives Buyer's written withdrawal of Buyer's Notice of Title Objection (i.e., Buyer's written notice to waive objection to such items and waives the Right to Terminate for that reason), on or before expiration of **Title Resolution Deadline** (§ 3).

8.3.2. Right to Terminate – Title Objection. Buyer shall have the Right to Terminate under § 25.1, on or before the applicable deadline, based on any unsatisfactory title matter, in Buyer's sole subjective discretion.

8.4. Special Taxing Districts. SPECIAL TAXING DISTRICTS MAY BE SUBJECT TO GENERAL OBLIGATION INDEBTEDNESS THAT IS PAID BY REVENUES PRODUCED FROM ANNUAL TAX LEVIES ON THE TAXABLE PROPERTY WITHIN SUCH DISTRICTS. PROPERTY OWNERS IN SUCH DISTRICTS MAY BE PLACED AT RISK FOR INCREASED MILL LEVIES AND TAX TO SUPPORT THE SERVICING OF SUCH DEBT WHERE CIRCUMSTANCES ARISE RESULTING IN THE INABILITY OF SUCH A DISTRICT TO DISCHARGE SUCH

INDEBTEDNESS WITHOUT SUCH AN INCREASE IN MILL LEVIES. BUYERS SHOULD INVESTIGATE THE SPECIAL TAXING DISTRICTS IN WHICH THE PROPERTY IS LOCATED BY CONTACTING THE COUNTY TREASURER, BY REVIEWING THE CERTIFICATE OF TAXES DUE FOR THE PROPERTY, AND BY OBTAINING FURTHER INFORMATION FROM THE BOARD OF COUNTY COMMISSIONERS, THE COUNTY CLERK AND RECORDER, OR THE COUNTY ASSESSOR.

Buyer shall have the Right to Terminate under § 25.1, on or before **Off-Record Title Objection Deadline** (§ 3), based on any unsatisfactory effect of the Property being located within a special taxing district, in Buyer's sole subjective discretion.

8.5. Right of First Refusal or Contract Approval. If there is a right of first refusal on the Property, or a right to approve this Contract, Seller shall promptly submit this Contract according to the terms and conditions of such right. If the holder of the right of first refusal exercises such right or the holder of a right to approve disapproves this Contract, this Contract shall terminate. If the right of first refusal is waived explicitly or expires, or the Contract is approved, this Contract shall remain in full force and effect. Seller shall promptly notify Buyer in writing of the foregoing. If expiration or waiver of the right of first refusal or Contract approval has not occurred on or before **Right of First Refusal Deadline** (§ 3), this Contract shall then terminate.

8.6. Title Advisory. The Title Documents affect the title, ownership and use of the Property and should be reviewed carefully. Additionally, other matters not reflected in the Title Documents may affect the title, ownership and use of the Property, including, without limitation, boundary lines and encroachments, area, zoning, unrecorded easements and claims of easements, leases and other unrecorded agreements, and various laws and governmental regulations concerning land use, development and environmental matters. **The surface estate may be owned separately from the underlying mineral estate, and transfer of the surface estate does not necessarily include transfer of the mineral rights or water rights. Third parties may hold interests in oil, gas, other minerals, geothermal energy or water on or under the Property, which interests may give them rights to enter and use the Property.** Such matters may be excluded from or not covered by the title insurance policy. Buyer is advised to timely consult legal counsel with respect to all such matters as there are strict time limits provided in this Contract [e.g., **Record Title Objection Deadline** (§ 3) and **Off-Record Title Objection Deadline** (§ 3)].

9. CURRENT SURVEY REVIEW.

9.1. Current Survey Conditions. If the box in § 9.1.1 or § 9.1.2 is checked, Buyer, the issuer of the Title Commitment or the provider of the opinion of title if an abstract, and ____________________ shall receive a Current Survey, i.e., Improvement Location Certificate, Improvement Survey Plat or other form of survey set forth in § 9.1.2 (collectively, Current Survey), on or before **Current Survey Deadline** (§ 3). The Current Survey shall be certified by the surveyor to all those who are to receive the Current Survey.

☐ **9.1.1. Improvement Location Certificate.** If the box in this § 9.1.1 is checked, ☐ **Seller** ☐ **Buyer** shall order or provide, and pay, on or before Closing, the cost of an **Improvement Location Certificate.**

☐ **9.1.2. Other Survey.** If the box in this § 9.1.2 is checked, a Current Survey, other than an Improvement Location Certificate, shall be an ☐ **Improvement Survey Plat** ☐ ____________________. The parties agree that payment of the cost of the Current Survey and obligation to order or provide the Current Survey shall be as follows:

9.2. Survey Objection. Buyer shall have the right to review and object to the Current Survey. Buyer shall have the Right to Terminate under § 25.1, on or before the **Current Survey Objection Deadline** (§ 3), if the Current Survey is not timely received by Buyer or based on any unsatisfactory matter with the Current Survey, notwithstanding § 8.2 or § 13.

DISCLOSURE, INSPECTION AND DUE DILIGENCE

10. PROPERTY DISCLOSURE, INSPECTION, INDEMNITY, INSURABILITY, DUE DILIGENCE, BUYER DISCLOSURE AND SOURCE OF WATER.

10.1. Seller's Property Disclosure Deadline. On or before **Seller's Property Disclosure Deadline** (§ 3), Seller agrees to deliver to Buyer the most current version of the applicable Colorado Real Estate Commission's Seller's Property Disclosure form completed by Seller to Seller's actual knowledge, current as of the date of this Contract.

10.2. Inspection Objection Deadline. Unless otherwise provided in this Contract, Buyer acknowledges that Seller is conveying the Property to Buyer in an "as is" condition, "where is" and "with all faults". Seller shall disclose to Buyer, in writing, any latent defects actually known by Seller. Buyer, acting in good faith, shall have the right to have inspections (by one or more third parties, personally or both) of the Property and Inclusions (Inspection), at Buyer's expense. If (1) the physical condition of the Property, including, but not limited to, the roof, walls, structural integrity of the Property, the electrical, plumbing, HVAC and other mechanical systems of the Property, (2) the physical condition of the Inclusions, (3) service to the Property (including utilities and communication services), systems and components of the Property, e.g. heating and plumbing, (4) any proposed or existing transportation project, road, street or highway, or (5) any other activity, odor or noise (whether on or off the Property) and its effect or expected effect on the Property or its occupants is unsatisfactory, in Buyer's sole subjective discretion, Buyer shall, on or before **Inspection Objection Deadline** (§ 3):

10.2.1. Notice to Terminate. Notify Seller in writing that this Contract is terminated; or

10.2.2. Inspection Objection. Deliver to Seller a written description of any unsatisfactory physical condition that Buyer requires Seller to correct.

Buyer shall have the Right to Terminate under § 25.1, on or before **Inspection Objection Deadline** (§ 3), based on any unsatisfactory physical condition of the Property or Inclusions, in Buyer's sole subjective discretion.

10.3. Inspection Resolution Deadline. If an Inspection Objection is received by Seller, on or before **Inspection Objection Deadline** (§ 3), and if Buyer and Seller have not agreed in writing to a settlement thereof on or before **Inspection Resolution Deadline** (§ 3), this Contract shall terminate on **Inspection Resolution Deadline** (§ 3), unless Seller receives Buyer's written withdrawal of the Inspection Objection before such termination, i.e., on or before expiration of **Inspection Resolution Deadline** (§ 3).

10.4. Damage, Liens and Indemnity. Buyer, except as otherwise provided in this Contract or other written agreement between the parties, is responsible for payment for all inspections, tests, surveys, engineering reports, or any other work performed at Buyer's request (Work) and shall pay for any damage that occurs to the Property and Inclusions as a result of such Work. Buyer shall not permit claims or liens of any kind against the Property for Work performed on the Property at Buyer's request. Buyer agrees to indemnify, protect and hold Seller harmless from and against any liability, damage, cost or expense incurred by Seller and caused by any such Work, claim, or lien. This indemnity includes Seller's right to recover all costs and expenses incurred by Seller to defend against any such liability, damage, cost or expense, or to enforce this section, including Seller's reasonable attorney fees, legal fees and expenses. The provisions of this section shall survive the termination of this Contract.

10.5. Insurability. Buyer shall have the right to review and object to the availability, terms and conditions of and premium for property insurance (Property Insurance). Buyer shall have the Right to Terminate under § 25.1, on or before **Property Insurance Objection Deadline** (§ 3), based on any unsatisfactory provision of the Property Insurance, in Buyer's sole subjective discretion.

10.6. Due Diligence Documents. Seller agrees to deliver copies of the following documents and information pertaining to the Property (Due Diligence Documents) to Buyer on or before **Due Diligence Documents Delivery Deadline** (§ 3) to the extent such Due Diligence Documents exist and are in Seller's possession:

10.6.1. All current leases, including any amendments or other occupancy agreements, pertaining to the Property (Leases).

10.6.2. Other documents and information:

10.7. Due Diligence Documents Conditions. Buyer shall have the right to review and object to Due Diligence Documents, in Buyer's sole subjective discretion, or Seller's failure to deliver to Buyer all Due Diligence Documents. Buyer shall also have the unilateral right to waive any condition herein.

10.7.1. Due Diligence Documents Objection. Buyer shall have the Right to Terminate under § 25.1, on or before **Due Diligence Documents Objection Deadline** (§ 3), based on any unsatisfactory matter with the Due Diligence Documents, in Buyer's sole subjective discretion. If, however, Due Diligence Documents are not timely delivered under § 10.6, or if Seller fails to deliver all Due Diligence Documents to Buyer, then Buyer shall have the Right to Terminate under § 25.1 on or before the earlier of ten days after **Due Diligence Documents Objection Deadline** (§ 3) or Closing.

10.8. Buyer Disclosure. Buyer represents that Buyer ☐ **Does** ☐ **Does Not** need to sell and close a property to complete this transaction.

Note: Any property sale contingency should appear in **Additional Provisions** (§ 30).

10.9. Source of Potable Water (Residential Land and Residential Improvements Only). Buyer ☐ **Does** ☐ **Does Not** acknowledge receipt of a copy of Seller's Property Disclosure or Source of Water Addendum disclosing the source of potable water for the Property. Buyer ☐ **Does** ☐ **Does Not** acknowledge receipt of a copy of the current well permit. ☐ There is **No Well.**

Note to Buyer: SOME WATER PROVIDERS RELY, TO VARYING DEGREES, ON NONRENEWABLE GROUND WATER. YOU MAY WISH TO CONTACT YOUR PROVIDER (OR INVESTIGATE THE DESCRIBED SOURCE) TO DETERMINE THE LONG-TERM SUFFICIENCY OF THE PROVIDER'S WATER SUPPLIES.

10.10. Carbon Monoxide Alarms. Note: If the improvements on the Property have a fuel-fired heater or appliance, a fireplace, or an attached garage and include one or more rooms lawfully used for sleeping purposes (Bedroom), the parties acknowledge that Colorado law requires that Seller assure the Property has an operational carbon monoxide alarm installed within fifteen feet of the entrance to each Bedroom or in a location as required by the applicable building code.

10.11. Lead-Based Paint. Unless exempt, if the improvements on the Property include one or more residential dwellings for which a building permit was issued prior to January 1, 1978, this Contract shall be void unless (1) a completed Lead-Based Paint Disclosure (Sales) form is signed by Seller, the required real estate licensees and Buyer, and (2) Seller receives the completed and fully executed form prior to the time when this Contract is signed by all parties. Buyer acknowledges timely receipt of a completed Lead-Based Paint Disclosure (Sales) form signed by Seller and the real estate licensees.

10.12. Methamphetamine Disclosure. If Seller knows that methamphetamine was ever manufactured, processed, cooked, disposed of, used or stored at the Property, Seller is required to disclose such fact. No disclosure is required if the Property was remediated in accordance with state standards and other requirements are fulfilled pursuant to § 25-18.5-102, C.R.S. Buyer further acknowledges that Buyer has the right to engage a certified hygienist or industrial hygienist to test whether the Property has ever been used as a methamphetamine laboratory. Buyer shall have the Right to Terminate under § 25.1, upon Seller's receipt of Buyer's written notice to terminate, notwithstanding any other provision of this Contract, based on Buyer's test results that indicate the Property has been contaminated with methamphetamine, but has not been remediated to meet the standards established by rules of the State Board of Health promulgated pursuant to § 25-18.5-102, C.R.S. Buyer shall promptly give written notice to Seller of the results of the test.

11. COLORADO FORECLOSURE PROTECTION ACT. The Colorado Foreclosure Protection Act (Act) generally applies if: (1) the Property is residential, (2) Seller resides in the Property as Seller's principal residence, (3) Buyer's purpose in purchase of the Property is not to use the Property as Buyer's personal residence, and (4) the Property is in foreclosure or Buyer has notice that any loan secured by the Property is at least thirty days delinquent or in default. If the transaction is a Short Sale transaction and a Short Sale Addendum is part of this Contract, the Act does not apply. Each party is further advised to consult an attorney.

CLOSING PROVISIONS

12. CLOSING DOCUMENTS, INSTRUCTIONS AND CLOSING.

12.1. Closing Documents and Closing Information. Seller and Buyer shall cooperate with the Closing Company to enable the Closing Company to prepare and deliver documents required for Closing to Buyer and Seller and their designees. If Buyer is obtaining a new loan to purchase the Property, Buyer acknowledges Buyer's lender shall be required to provide the Closing Company in a timely manner all required loan documents and financial information concerning Buyer's new loan. Buyer and Seller will furnish any additional information and documents required by Closing Company that will be necessary to complete this transaction. Buyer and Seller shall sign and complete all customary or reasonably required documents at or before Closing.

12.2. Closing Instructions. Buyer and Seller agree to execute the Colorado Real Estate Commission's Closing Instructions. Such Closing Instructions ☐ **Are** ☐ **Are Not** executed with this Contract. Upon mutual execution, ☐ **Seller** ☐ **Buyer** shall deliver such Closing Instructions to the Closing Company.

12.3. Closing. Delivery of deed from Seller to Buyer shall be at closing (Closing). Closing shall be on the date specified as the **Closing Date** (§ 3) or by mutual agreement at an earlier date. The hour and place of Closing shall be as designated by______________________________________.

12.4. Disclosure of Settlement Costs. Buyer and Seller acknowledge that costs, quality, and extent of service vary between different settlement service providers (e.g., attorneys, lenders, inspectors and title companies).

13. TRANSFER OF TITLE. Subject to tender of payment at Closing as required herein and compliance by Buyer with the other terms and provisions hereof, Seller shall execute and deliver a good and sufficient ______________________________ deed to Buyer, at Closing, conveying the Property free and clear of all taxes except the general taxes for the year of Closing. Except as provided herein, title shall be conveyed free and clear of all liens, including any governmental liens for special improvements installed as of the date of Buyer's signature hereon, whether assessed or not. Title shall be conveyed subject to:

13.1. Those specific Exceptions described by reference to recorded documents as reflected in the Title Documents accepted by Buyer in accordance with **Record Title Matters** (§ 8.1),

13.2. Distribution utility easements (including cable TV),

13.3. Those specifically described rights of third parties not shown by the public records of which Buyer has actual knowledge and which were accepted by Buyer in accordance with **Off-Record Title Matters** (§ 8.2) and **Current Survey Review** (§ 9),

13.4. Inclusion of the Property within any special taxing district, and

13.5. Other______________________________________.

14. PAYMENT OF ENCUMBRANCES. Any encumbrance required to be paid shall be paid at or before Closing from the proceeds of this transaction or from any other source.

15. CLOSING COSTS, CLOSING FEE, ASSOCIATION FEES AND TAXES.

15.1. Closing Costs. Buyer and Seller shall pay, in Good Funds, their respective closing costs and all other items required to be paid at Closing, except as otherwise provided herein.

15.2. Closing Services Fee. The fee for real estate closing services shall be paid at Closing by ☐ **Buyer** ☐ **Seller** ☐ **One-Half by Buyer and One-Half by Seller** ☐ **Other**______________________________________.

15.3. Status Letter and Transfer Fees. Any fees incident to the issuance of Association's statement of assessments (Status Letter) shall be paid by ☐ **Buyer** ☐ **Seller** ☐ **One-Half by Buyer and One-Half by Seller** ☐ **None.** Any transfer fees assessed by the Association including, but not limited to, any record change fee, regardless of name or title of such fee (Association's Transfer Fee) shall be paid by ☐ **Buyer** ☐ **Seller** ☐ **One-Half by Buyer and One-Half by Seller** ☐ **None.**

15.4. Local Transfer Tax. ☐ **The Local Transfer Tax** of ________% of the Purchase Price shall be paid at Closing by ☐ **Buyer** ☐ **Seller** ☐ **One-Half by Buyer and One-Half by Seller** ☐ **None.**

15.5. Private Transfer Fee. Private transfer fees and other fees due to a transfer of the Property, payable at Closing, such as community association fees, developer fees and foundation fees, shall be paid at Closing by ☐ **Buyer** ☐ **Seller** ☐ **One-Half by Buyer and One-Half by Seller** ☐ **None.**

15.6. Sales and Use Tax. Any sales and use tax that may accrue because of this transaction shall be paid when due by ☐ **Buyer** ☐ **Seller** ☐ **One-Half by Buyer and One-Half by Seller** ☐ **None.**

16. PRORATIONS. The following shall be prorated to **Closing Date** (§ 3), except as otherwise provided:

16.1. Taxes. Personal property taxes, if any, special taxing district assessments, if any, and general real estate taxes for the year of Closing, based on ☐ **Taxes for the Calendar Year Immediately Preceding Closing** ☐ **Most Recent Mill Levy and Most Recent Assessed Valuation**, adjusted by any applicable qualifying seniors property tax exemption, or ☐ **Other** _________.

16.2. Rents. Rents based on ☐ **Rents Actually Received** ☐ **Accrued.** At Closing, Seller shall transfer or credit to Buyer the security deposits for all Leases assigned, or any remainder after lawful deductions, and notify all tenants in writing of such transfer and of the transferee's name and address. Seller shall assign to Buyer all Leases in effect at Closing and Buyer shall assume Seller's obligations under such Leases.

16.3. Association Assessments. Current regular Association assessments and dues (Association Assessments) paid in advance shall be credited to Seller at Closing. Cash reserves held out of the regular Association Assessments for deferred maintenance by the Association shall not be credited to Seller except as may be otherwise provided by the Governing Documents. Buyer acknowledges that Buyer may be obligated to pay the Association, at Closing, an amount for reserves or working capital. Any special assessment assessed prior to **Closing Date** (§ 3) by the Association shall be the obligation of ☐ **Buyer** ☐ **Seller.** Except however, any special assessment by the Association for improvements that have been installed as of the date of Buyer's signature hereon, whether assessed prior to or after Closing, shall be the obligation of Seller. Seller represents that the Association Assessments are currently payable at $______________ per ______________ and that there are no unpaid regular or special assessments against the Property except the current regular assessments and ______________________________. Such assessments are subject to change as provided in the Governing Documents. Seller agrees to promptly request the Association to deliver to Buyer before **Closing Date** (§ 3) a current Status Letter.

16.4. Other Prorations. Water and sewer charges, interest on continuing loan, and ______________________________.

16.5. Final Settlement. Unless otherwise agreed in writing, these prorations shall be final.

17. POSSESSION. Possession of the Property shall be delivered to Buyer on **Possession Date** (§ 3) at **Possession Time** (§ 3), subject to the following Leases or tenancies:

If Seller, after Closing, fails to deliver possession as specified, Seller shall be subject to eviction and shall be additionally liable to Buyer for payment of $______________ per day (or any part of a day notwithstanding § 18.1) from **Possession Date** (§ 3) and **Possession Time** (§ 3) until possession is delivered.

Buyer ☐ **Does** ☐ **Does Not** represent that Buyer will occupy the Property as Buyer's principal residence.

GENERAL PROVISIONS

18. DAY; COMPUTATION OF PERIOD OF DAYS, DEADLINE.

18.1. Day. As used in this Contract, the term "day" shall mean the entire day ending at 11:59 p.m., United States Mountain Time (Standard or Daylight Savings as applicable).

18.2. Computation of Period of Days, Deadline. In computing a period of days, when the ending date is not specified, the first day is excluded and the last day is included, e.g., three days after MEC. If any deadline falls on a Saturday, Sunday or federal or Colorado state holiday (Holiday), such deadline ☐ **Shall** ☐ **Shall Not** be extended to the next day that is not a Saturday, Sunday or Holiday. Should neither box be checked, the deadline shall not be extended.

19. CAUSES OF LOSS, INSURANCE; CONDITION OF, DAMAGE TO PROPERTY AND INCLUSIONS AND WALK-THROUGH. Except as otherwise provided in this Contract, the Property, Inclusions or both shall be delivered in the condition existing as of the date of this Contract, ordinary wear and tear excepted.

19.1. Causes of Loss, Insurance. In the event the Property or Inclusions are damaged by fire, other perils or causes of loss prior to Closing in an amount of not more than ten percent of the total Purchase Price (Property Damage), Seller shall be obligated to repair the same before **Closing Date** (§ 3). In the event such damage is not repaired within said time or if the damage exceeds such sum, this Contract may be terminated at the option of Buyer. Buyer shall have the Right to Terminate under § 25.1, on or before **Closing Date** (§ 3), based on any Property Damage not repaired before **Closing Date** (§ 3). Should Buyer elect to carry out this Contract despite such Property Damage, Buyer shall be entitled to a credit at Closing for all insurance proceeds that were received by Seller (but not the Association, if any) resulting from such damage to the Property and Inclusions, plus the amount of any deductible provided for in such insurance policy. Such credit shall not exceed the Purchase Price. In the event Seller has not received such insurance proceeds prior to Closing, the parties may agree to extend the **Closing Date** (§ 3) or, at the option of Buyer, Seller shall assign such proceeds at Closing, plus credit Buyer the amount of any deductible provided for in such insurance policy, but not to exceed the total Purchase Price.

19.2. Damage, Inclusions and Services. Should any Inclusion or service (including utilities and communication services), systems and components of the Property, e.g., heating or plumbing, fail or be damaged between the date of this Contract and Closing or possession, whichever shall be earlier, then Seller shall be liable for the repair or replacement of such Inclusion, service, system, component or fixture of the Property with a unit of similar size, age and quality, or an equivalent credit, but only to the extent that the maintenance or replacement of such Inclusion, service, system, component or fixture is not the responsibility of the Association, if any, less any insurance proceeds received by Buyer covering such repair or replacement. Seller and Buyer are aware of the existence of pre-owned home warranty programs that may be purchased and may cover the repair or replacement of such Inclusions.

19.3. Condemnation. In the event Seller receives actual notice prior to Closing that a pending condemnation action may result in a taking of all or part of the Property or Inclusions, Seller shall promptly notify Buyer, in writing, of such condemnation action. Buyer shall have the Right to Terminate under § 25.1, on or before **Closing Date** (§ 3), based on such condemnation action, in Buyer's sole subjective discretion. Should Buyer elect to consummate this Contract despite such diminution of value to the Property and Inclusions, Buyer shall be entitled to a credit at Closing for all condemnation proceeds awarded to Seller for the diminution in the value of the Property or Inclusions but such credit shall not include relocation benefits or expenses, or exceed the Purchase Price.

19.4. Walk-Through and Verification of Condition. Buyer, upon reasonable notice, shall have the right to walk through the Property prior to Closing to verify that the physical condition of the Property and Inclusions complies with this Contract.

20. RECOMMENDATION OF LEGAL AND TAX COUNSEL. By signing this document, Buyer and Seller acknowledge that the respective broker has advised that this document has important legal consequences and has recommended the examination of title and consultation with legal and tax or other counsel before signing this Contract.

21. TIME OF ESSENCE, DEFAULT AND REMEDIES. Time is of the essence hereof. If any note or check received as Earnest Money hereunder or any other payment due hereunder is not paid, honored or tendered when due, or if any obligation hereunder is not performed or waived as herein provided, there shall be the following remedies:

21.1. If Buyer is in Default:

☐ **21.1.1. Specific Performance.** Seller may elect to treat this Contract as canceled, in which case all Earnest Money (whether or not paid by Buyer) shall be paid to Seller and retained by Seller; and Seller may recover such damages as may be proper; or Seller may elect to treat this Contract as being in full force and effect and Seller shall have the right to specific performance or damages, or both.

21.1.2. Liquidated Damages, Applicable. This § 21.1.2 shall apply <u>unless the box in § 21.1.1. is checked</u>. All Earnest Money (whether or not paid by Buyer) shall be paid to Seller, and retained by Seller. Both parties shall thereafter be released from all obligations hereunder. It is agreed that the Earnest Money specified in § 4.1 is LIQUIDATED DAMAGES, and not a penalty, which amount the parties agree is fair and reasonable and (except as provided in §§ 10.4, 22, 23 and 24), said payment of Earnest Money shall be SELLER'S SOLE AND ONLY REMEDY for Buyer's failure to perform the obligations of this Contract. Seller expressly waives the remedies of specific performance and additional damages.

21.2. If Seller is in Default: Buyer may elect to treat this Contract as canceled, in which case all Earnest Money received hereunder shall be returned and Buyer may recover such damages as may be proper, or Buyer may elect to treat this Contract as being in full force and effect and Buyer shall have the right to specific performance or damages, or both.

22. LEGAL FEES, COST AND EXPENSES. Anything to the contrary herein notwithstanding, in the event of any arbitration or litigation relating to this Contract, prior to or after **Closing Date** (§ 3), the arbitrator or court shall award to the prevailing party all reasonable costs and expenses, including attorney fees, legal fees and expenses.

23. MEDIATION. If a dispute arises relating to this Contract, prior to or after Closing, and is not resolved, the parties shall first proceed in good faith to submit the matter to mediation. Mediation is a process in which the parties meet with an impartial person who helps to resolve the dispute informally and confidentially. Mediators cannot impose binding decisions. The parties to the dispute must agree, in writing, before any settlement is binding. The parties will jointly appoint an acceptable mediator and will share equally in the cost of such mediation. The mediation, unless otherwise agreed, shall terminate in the event the entire dispute is not resolved within thirty days of the date written notice requesting mediation is delivered by one party to the other at the party's last known address. This section shall not alter any date in this Contract, unless otherwise agreed.

24. EARNEST MONEY DISPUTE. Except as otherwise provided herein, Earnest Money Holder shall release the Earnest Money as directed by written mutual instructions, signed by both Buyer and Seller. In the event of any controversy regarding the Earnest Money (notwithstanding any termination of this Contract), Earnest Money Holder shall not be required to take any action. Earnest Money Holder, at its option and sole subjective discretion, may (1) await any proceeding, (2) interplead all parties and deposit Earnest Money into a court of competent jurisdiction and shall recover court costs and reasonable attorney and legal fees, or (3) provide notice to Buyer and Seller that unless Earnest Money Holder receives a copy of the Summons and Complaint or Claim (between Buyer and Seller) containing the case number of the lawsuit (Lawsuit) within one hundred twenty days of Earnest Money Holder's notice to the parties, Earnest Money Holder shall be authorized to return the Earnest Money to Buyer. In the event Earnest Money Holder does receive a copy of the Lawsuit, and has not interpled the monies at the time of any Order, Earnest Money Holder shall disburse the Earnest Money pursuant to the Order of the Court. The parties reaffirm the obligation of **Mediation** (§ 23). The provisions of this § 24 apply only if the Earnest Money Holder is one of the Brokerage Firms named in § 33 or § 34.

25. TERMINATION.

25.1. Right to Terminate. If a party has a right to terminate, as provided in this Contract (Right to Terminate), the termination shall be effective upon the other party's receipt of a written notice to terminate (Notice to Terminate), provided such written notice was received on or before the applicable deadline specified in this Contract. If the Notice to Terminate is not received on or before the specified deadline, the party with the Right to Terminate shall have accepted the specified matter, document or condition as satisfactory and waived the Right to Terminate under such provision.

25.2. Effect of Termination. In the event this Contract is terminated, all Earnest Money received hereunder shall be returned and the parties shall be relieved of all obligations hereunder, subject to §§ 10.4, 22, 23 and 24.

26. ENTIRE AGREEMENT, MODIFICATION, SURVIVAL. This Contract, its exhibits and specified addenda, constitute the entire agreement between the parties relating to the subject hereof, and any prior agreements pertaining thereto, whether oral or written, have been merged and integrated into this Contract. No subsequent modification of any of the terms of this Contract shall be valid, binding upon the parties, or enforceable unless made in writing and signed by the parties. Any obligation in this Contract that, by its terms, is intended to be performed after termination or Closing shall survive the same.

27. NOTICE, DELIVERY, AND CHOICE OF LAW.

27.1. Physical Delivery. All notices must be in writing, except as provided in § 27.2. Any document, including a signed document or notice, from or on behalf of Seller, and delivered to Buyer shall be effective when physically received by Buyer, any signatory on behalf of Buyer, any named individual of Buyer, any representative of Buyer, or Brokerage Firm of Broker working with Buyer (except for delivery, after Closing, of the notice requesting mediation described in § 23) and except as provided in § 27.2. Any document, including a signed document or notice, from or on behalf of Buyer, and delivered to Seller shall be effective when physically received by Seller, any signatory on behalf of Seller, any named individual of Seller, any representative of Seller, or Brokerage Firm of Broker working with Seller (except for delivery, after Closing, of the notice requesting mediation described in § 23) and except as provided in § 27.2.

27.2. Electronic Delivery. As an alternative to physical delivery, any document, including any signed document or written notice, may be delivered in electronic form only by the following indicated methods: ☐ **Facsimile** ☐ **Email** ☐ **Internet** ☐ **No Electronic Delivery**. If the box "No Electronic Delivery" is checked, this § 27.2 shall not be applicable and § 27.1 shall govern notice and delivery. Documents with original signatures shall be provided upon request of any party.

27.3. Choice of Law. This Contract and all disputes arising hereunder shall be governed by and construed in accordance with the laws of the State of Colorado that would be applicable to Colorado residents who sign a contract in Colorado for property located in Colorado.

28. NOTICE OF ACCEPTANCE, COUNTERPARTS. This proposal shall expire unless accepted in writing, by Buyer and Seller, as evidenced by their signatures below, and the offering party receives notice of such acceptance pursuant to § 27 on or before **Acceptance Deadline Date** (§ 3) and **Acceptance Deadline Time** (§ 3). If accepted, this document shall become a contract between Seller and Buyer. A copy of this document may be executed by each party, separately, and when each party has executed a copy thereof, such copies taken together shall be deemed to be a full and complete contract between the parties.

29. GOOD FAITH. Buyer and Seller acknowledge that each party has an obligation to act in good faith including, but not limited to, exercising the rights and obligations set forth in the provisions of **Financing Conditions and Obligations** (§ 5), **Record Title and Off-Record Title Matters** (§ 8), **Current Survey Review** (§ 9) and **Property Disclosure, Inspection, Indemnity, Insurability, Due Diligence, Buyer Disclosure and Source of Water** (§ 10).

ADDITIONAL PROVISIONS AND ATTACHMENTS

30. ADDITIONAL PROVISIONS. (The following additional provisions have not been approved by the Colorado Real Estate Commission.)

31. ATTACHMENTS. The following are a part of this Contract:

Note: The following disclosure forms **are attached** but are **not** a part of this Contract:

SIGNATURES

Buyer's Name: ________________	Buyer's Name: ________________
________________ Buyer's Signature Date	________________ Buyer's Signature Date
Address: ________________ ________________	Address: ________________ ________________
Phone No.: ________________	Phone No.: ________________
Fax No.: ________________	Fax No.: ________________
Electronic Address: ________________	Electronic Address: ________________

[NOTE: If this offer is being countered or rejected, do not sign this document. Refer to § 32]

Seller's Name: ________________	Seller's Name: ________________
________________ Seller's Signature Date	________________ Seller's Signature Date
Address: ________________ ________________	Address: ________________ ________________
Phone No.: ________________	Phone No.: ________________
Fax No.: ________________	Fax No.: ________________
Electronic Address: ________________	Electronic Address: ________________

32. COUNTER; REJECTION. This offer is ☐ **Countered** ☐ **Rejected.**
Initials only of party (Buyer or Seller) who countered or rejected offer ________________

END OF CONTRACT TO BUY AND SELL REAL ESTATE

33. BROKER'S ACKNOWLEDGMENTS AND COMPENSATION DISCLOSURE.
(To be completed by Broker working with Buyer)

Broker ☐ **Does** ☐ **Does Not** acknowledge receipt of Earnest Money deposit and, while not a party to the Contract, agrees to cooperate upon request with any mediation concluded under § 23. Broker agrees that if Brokerage Firm is the Earnest Money Holder and, except as provided in § 24, if the Earnest Money has not already been returned following receipt of a Notice to Terminate or other written notice of termination, Earnest Money Holder shall release the Earnest Money as directed by the written mutual instructions. Such release of Earnest Money shall be made within five days of Earnest Money Holder's receipt of the executed written mutual instructions, provided the Earnest Money check has cleared. Broker agrees that if Earnest Money Holder is other than the Brokerage Firm identified in § 33 or § 34, Closing Instructions signed by Buyer, Seller, and Earnest Money Holder must be obtained on or before delivery of Earnest Money to Earnest Money Holder.

Broker is working with Buyer as a ☐ **Buyer's Agent** ☐ **Seller's Agent** ☐ **Transaction-Broker** in this transaction.
☐ This is a **Change of Status.**

Brokerage Firm's compensation or commission is to be paid by ☐ **Listing Brokerage Firm** ☐ **Buyer** ☐ **Other** ____________.

Brokerage Firm's Name: ______________________
Broker's Name: ______________________

____
Broker's Signature   Date

Address: ______________________
____

Phone No.: ______________________
Fax No.: ______________________
Electronic Address: ______________________

34. BROKER'S ACKNOWLEDGMENTS AND COMPENSATION DISCLOSURE.
(To be completed by Broker working with Seller)

Broker ☐ **Does** ☐ **Does Not** acknowledge receipt of Earnest Money deposit and, while not a party to the Contract, agrees to cooperate upon request with any mediation concluded under § 23. Broker agrees that if Brokerage Firm is the Earnest Money Holder and, except as provided in § 24, if the Earnest Money has not already been returned following receipt of a Notice to Terminate or other written notice of termination, Earnest Money Holder shall release the Earnest Money as directed by the written mutual instructions. Such release of Earnest Money shall be made within five days of Earnest Money Holder's receipt of the executed written mutual instructions, provided the Earnest Money check has cleared. Broker agrees that if Earnest Money Holder is other than the Brokerage Firm identified in § 33 or § 34, Closing Instructions signed by Buyer, Seller, and Earnest Money Holder must be obtained on or before delivery of Earnest Money to Earnest Money Holder.

Broker is working with Seller as a ☐ **Seller's Agent** ☐ **Buyer's Agent** ☐ **Transaction-Broker** in this transaction.
☐ This is a **Change of Status.**

Brokerage Firm's compensation or commission is to be paid by ☐ **Seller** ☐ **Buyer** ☐ **Other** ____________________.

Brokerage Firm's Name: ______________________
Broker's Name: ______________________

____
Broker's Signature   Date

Address: ______________________
____

Phone No.: ______________________
Fax No.: ______________________
Electronic Address: ______________________

679

C. Lead-Based Paint Disclosures (Sales) LP45-5-04

The printed portions of this form except differentiated additions, have been approved by the Colorado Real Estate Commission. (LP45-5-04

Lead-Based Paint Disclosure (Sales)

Attachment to Contract to Buy and Sell Real Estate for the Property known as:

Street Address City State Zip

WARNING! LEAD FROM PAINT, DUST, AND SOIL CAN BE DANGEROUS IF NOT MANAGED PROPERLY

Penalties for failure to comply with Federal Lead-Based Paint Disclosure Laws include treble (3 times) damages, attorney fees, costs, and a penalty up to $10,000 (plus adjustment for inflation) for each violation.

Disclosure of Information on Lead-Based Paint and/or Lead-Based Paint Hazards

Lead Warning Statement

Every purchaser of any interest in residential real property on which a residential dwelling was built prior to 1978 is notified that such property may present exposure to lead from lead-based paint that may place young children at risk of developing lead poisoning. Lead poisoning in young children may produce permanent neurological damage, including learning disabilities, reduced intelligence quotient, behavioral problems, and impaired memory. Lead poisoning also poses a particular risk to pregnant women. The Seller of any interest in residential real property is required to provide the buyer with any information on lead-based paint hazards from risk assessments or inspections in the Seller's possession and notify the buyer of any known lead-based paint hazards. A risk assessment or inspection for possible lead-based paint hazards is recommended prior to purchase.

Seller's Disclosure to Buyer and Real Estate Licensee(s) and Acknowledgment

(a) Seller acknowledges that Seller has been informed of Seller's obligations. Seller is aware that Seller must retain a copy of this disclosure for not less than three years from the completion date of the sale.

(b) Presence of lead-based paint and/or lead-based paint hazards (check one box below):

❑ Seller has no knowledge of any lead-based paint and/or lead-based paint hazards present in the housing.

❑ Seller has knowledge of lead-based paint and/or lead-based paint hazards present in the housing (explain):

(c) Records and reports available to Seller (check one box below):

❑ Seller has no reports or records pertaining to lead-based paint and/or lead-based paint hazards in the housing.

❑ Seller has provided Buyer with all available records and reports pertaining to lead-based paint and/or lead-based paint hazards in the housing (list documents below):

Buyer's Acknowledgment

(d) Buyer has read the Lead Warning Statement above and understands its contents.

(e) Buyer has received copies of all information, including any records and reports listed by Seller above.

(f) Buyer has received the pamphlet "Protect Your Family From Lead in Your Home".

(g) Buyer acknowledges federal law requires that before a buyer is obligated under any contract to buy and sell real estate, Seller shall permit Buyer a 10-day period (unless the parties mutually agree, in writing, upon a different period of time) to conduct a risk assessment or inspection for the presence of lead-based paint and/or lead-based paint hazards.

(h) Buyer, after having reviewed the contents of this form, and any records and reports listed by Seller, has elected to (check one box below):

❑ Obtain a risk assessment or an inspection of the Property for the presence of lead-based paint and/or lead-based paint hazards, within the time limit and under the terms of Section 10 of the Contract to Buy and Sell Real Estate; or

❑ Waive the opportunity to conduct a risk assessment or inspection for the presence of lead-based paint and/or lead-based paint hazards.

Real Estate Licensee's Acknowledgment

Each real estate licensee signing below acknowledges receipt of the above Seller's Disclosure, has informed Seller of Seller's obligations and is aware of licensee's responsibility to ensure compliance.

Certification of Accuracy

I certify that the statements I have made are accurate to the best of my knowledge.

Date: ______________________________ Date: ______________________________

______________________________ ______________________________

Seller Seller

Date: ______________________________ Date: ______________________________

______________________________ ______________________________

Buyer Buyer

Date: ______________________________ Date: ______________________________

______________________________ ______________________________

Real Estate Licensee (Listing) Real Estate Licensee (Selling)

D. Seller's Property Disclosure (All Types of Properties) SPD19-10-11

The printed portions of this form, except differentiated additions, have been approved by the Colorado Real Estate Commission. (SPD19-10-11) (Mandatory 1-12)

THIS FORM HAS IMPORTANT LEGAL CONSEQUENCES AND THE PARTIES SHOULD CONSULT LEGAL AND TAX OR OTHER COUNSEL BEFORE SIGNING.

SELLER'S PROPERTY DISCLOSURE (ALL TYPES OF PROPERTIES)

THIS DISCLOSURE SHOULD BE COMPLETED BY SELLER, NOT BY BROKER.

Seller states that the information contained in this Disclosure is correct to Seller's CURRENT ACTUAL KNOWLEDGE as of this Date. **Any changes will be disclosed by Seller to Buyer promptly after discovery.** Seller hereby receipts for a copy of this Disclosure. **If the Property is part of a Common Interest Community, this Disclosure is limited to the Property or Unit itself, except as stated in Section L.** Broker may deliver a copy of this Disclosure to prospective buyers.

Note: **If an item is not present at the Property or if an item is not to be included in the sale, mark the "N/A" column. The Contract to Buy and Sell Real Estate, not this Disclosure form, determines whether an item is included or excluded; if there is an inconsistency between this form and the Contract, the Contract controls.**

Date: ______________________________

Property Address: ______________________________

Seller: ______________________________

I. IMPROVEMENTS

☐ **If this box is checked, there are no structures or improvements on the Property; do not complete Sections A-G.**

A.	**STRUCTURAL CONDITIONS** Do any of the following conditions **now exist or have they ever existed**:	Yes	No	Do Not Know	N/A	Comments
1	Structural problems					
2	Moisture and/or water problems					
3	Damage due to termites, other insects, birds, animals or rodents					
4	Damage due to hail, wind, fire or flood					
5	Cracks, heaving or settling problems					
6	Exterior wall or window problems					
7	Exterior Artificial Stucco (EIFS)					
8	Any additions or alterations made					
9	Building code, city or county violations					

B.	**ROOF** Do any of the following conditions **now exist**:	Yes	No	Do Not Know	N/A	Comments
1	Roof problems					
2	Roof material: ____________ Age ______ Roof material: ____________ Age ______					
3	Roof leak: Past					
4	Roof leak: Present					
5	Damage to roof: Past					
6	Damage to roof: Present					
7	Roof under warranty until ____________. Transferable ________					
8	Roof work done while under current roof warranty					
9	Skylight problems					
10	Gutter or downspout problems					

C.	APPLIANCES Are the following **now** in working condition:	IN WORKING CONDITION Yes	No	Do Not Know	Age If Known	N/A	Comments
1	Built-in vacuum system & accessories						
2	Clothes dryer						
3	Clothes washer						
4	Dishwasher						
5	Disposal						
6	Freezer						
7	Gas grill						
8	Hood						
9	Microwave oven						
10	Oven						
11	Range						
12	Refrigerator						
13	T.V. antenna: ☐ Owned ☐ Leased						
14	Satellite system or DSS dish: ☐ Owned ☐ Leased						
15	Trash compactor						

D.	ELECTRICAL & TELECOMMUNICATIONS Are the following **now** in working condition:	IN WORKING CONDITION Yes	No	Do Not Know	Age If Known	N/A	Comments
1	Security system: ☐ Owned ☐ Leased						
2	Smoke/fire detectors: ☐ Battery ☐ Hardwire						
3	Carbon Monoxide Alarm: ☐ Battery ☐ Hardwire						
4	Light fixtures						
5	Switches & outlets						
6	Aluminum wiring (110)						
7	Electrical: Phase _________ Voltage _________ Amps ________						
8	Telecommunications (T1, fiber, cable, satellite)						
9	Inside telephone wiring & blocks/jacks						
10	Abandoned communication cables: ☐ Yes ☐ No						
11	Ceiling fans						
12	Garage door opener						
13	Garage door control(s) #___________						
14	Intercom/doorbell						
15	In-wall speakers						
16	220 volt service						
17	Landscape lighting						

E.	MECHANICAL Are the following **now** in working condition:	IN WORKING CONDITION Yes	No	Do Not Know	Age If Known	N/A	Comments
1	Air conditioning:						
	Evaporative cooler						
	Window units						
	Central						
	Computer room						
2	Attic/whole house fan						
3	Vent fans						
4	Humidifier						

5	Air purifier						
6	Sauna						
7	Hot tub or spa						
8	Steam room/shower						
9	Pool						
10	Heating system: Type ______ Fuel ______ Type ______ Fuel ______						
11	Water heater: Number of ______ Fuel type ______ Capacity ______						
12	Fireplace: Type ______ Fuel ______						
13	Fireplace insert						
14	Stove: Type ______ Fuel ______						
15	When was fireplace/wood stove, chimney/flue last cleaned: Date: ______ ☐ Do not know						
16	Fuel tanks: ☐ Owned ☐ Leased						
17	Radiant heating system: ☐ Interior ☐ Exterior Hose Type ______						
18	Overhead door						
19	Entry gate system						
20	Elevator/escalators						
21	Lift/hoist/crane						

		IN WORKING CONDITION					
F.	**WATER, SEWER & OTHER UTILITIES** Are the following **now** in working condition:	**Yes**	**No**	**Do Not Know**	**Age If Known**	**N/A**	**Comments**
1	Water filter system: ☐ Owned ☐ Leased						
2	Water softener: ☐ Owned ☐ Leased						
3	Sewage problems: ☐ Yes ☐ No ☐ Do not know						
4	Lift station (sewage ejector pump)						
5	Drainage, storm sewers, retention ponds						
6	Grey water storage/use						
7	Plumbing problems: ☐ Yes ☐ No ☐ Do not know						
8	Sump pump						
9	Underground sprinkler system						
10	Fire sprinkler system						
11	Polybutylene pipe: ☐ Yes ☐ No ☐ Do not know						
12	Galvanized pipe: ☐ Yes ☐ No ☐ Do not know						
13	Backflow prevention device: ☐ Domestic ☐ Irrigation ☐ Fire ☐ Sewage						
14	Irrigation pump						
15	Well pump						

		IN WORKING CONDITION					
G.	**OTHER DISCLOSURES – IMPROVEMENTS**	**Yes**	**No**	**Do Not Know**	**Age If Known**	**N/A**	**Comments**
1	Included fixtures and equipment **now** in working condition						

II. GENERAL

H.	USE, ZONING & LEGAL ISSUES Do any of the following conditions **now exist**:	Yes	No	Do Not Know	N/A	Comments
1	Current use of the Property					
2	Zoning violation, variance, conditional use, violation of an enforceable PUD or non-conforming use					
3	Notice or threat of condemnation proceedings					
4	Notice of any adverse conditions from any governmental or quasi-governmental agency that have not been resolved					
5	Violation of restrictive covenants or owners' association rules or regulations					
6	Any building or improvements constructed within the past one year from this Date without approval by the Association or the designated approving body					
7	Notice of zoning action related to the Property					
8	Notice of ADA complaint or report					
9	Other legal action					

I.	ACCESS, PARKING, DRAINAGE & SIGNAGE Do any of the following conditions **now exist**:	Yes	No	Do Not Know	N/A	Comments
1	Any access problems					
2	Roads, driveways, trails or paths through the Property used by others					
3	Public highway or county road bordering the Property					
4	Any proposed or existing transportation project that affects or is expected to affect the Property					
5	Encroachments, boundary disputes or unrecorded easements					
6	Shared or common areas with adjoining properties					
7	Cross-parking agreement, covenants, easements					
8	Requirements for curb, gravel/paving, landscaping					
9	Flooding or drainage problems: Past					
10	Flooding or drainage problems: Present					
11	Signs: ☐ Owned ☐ Leased					
12	Signs: Government or private restriction problems					

J.	WATER & SEWER SUPPLY Do any of the following conditions **now exist**:	Yes	No	Do Not Know	N/A	Comments
1	Water Rights: Type ____________					
2	Water tap fees paid in full					
3	Sewer tap fees paid in full					
4	Subject to augmentation plan					
5	Well required to be metered					
6	Type of water supply: ☐ Public ☐ Community ☐ Well ☐ Shared Well ☐ Cistern ☐ None If the Property is served by a Well, a copy of the Well Permit ☐ **Is** ☐ **Is Not attached**. Well Permit #: ____________ ☐ Drilling Records ☐ Are ☐ Are not attached. Shared Well Agreement ☐ **Yes** ☐ **No**. The **Water Provider** for the Property can be contacted at: Name: ____________ Address: ____________ Web Site: ____________ Phone No.: ____________ ☐ There is neither a Well nor a Water Provider for the Property. The source of potable water for the Property is [describe source]: **SOME WATER PROVIDERS RELY, TO VARYING DEGREES, ON NONRENEWABLE GROUND WATER. YOU MAY WISH TO CONTACT YOUR PROVIDER (OR INVESTIGATE THE DESCRIBED SOURCE) TO DETERMINE THE LONG-TERM SUFFICIENCY OF THE PROVIDER'S WATER SUPPLIES.**					
7	Type of sanitary sewer service: ☐ Public ☐ Community ☐ Septic System ☐ None ☐ Other ____________ If the Property is served by an on-site septic system, supply to buyer a copy of the permit. Type of septic system: ☐ Tank ☐ Leach ☐ Lagoon					

K.	**ENVIRONMENTAL CONDITIONS** Do any of the following conditions **now exist or have they ever existed**:	**Yes**	**No**	**Do Not Know**	**N/A**	**Comments**
1	Hazardous materials on the Property, such as radioactive, toxic, or biohazardous materials, asbestos, pesticides, herbicides, wastewater sludge, radon, methane, mill tailings, solvents or petroleum products					
2	Underground storage tanks					
3	Aboveground storage tanks					
4	Underground transmission lines					
5	Animals kept in the residence					
6	Property used as, situated on, or adjoining a dump, land fill or municipal solid waste land fill					
7	Monitoring wells or test equipment					
8	Sliding, settling, upheaval, movement or instability of earth or expansive soils on the Property					
9	Mine shafts, tunnels or abandoned wells on the Property					
10	Within governmentally designated geological hazard or sensitive area					
11	Within governmentally designated flood plain or wetland area					
12	Governmentally designated noxious weeds (within last 3 years only) If yes, see Section O.					
13	Dead, diseased or infested trees or shrubs					
14	Environmental assessments, studies or reports done involving the physical condition of the Property					
15	Property used for any mining, graveling, or other natural resource extraction operations such as oil and gas wells					
16	Endangered species on the Property					
17	Archeological features, fossils, or artifacts on the Property					
18	Interior of improvements of Property tobacco smoke-free					
19	Other environmental problems					

L.	**COMMON INTEREST COMMUNITY – ASSOCIATION PROPERTY** Do any of the following conditions **now exist**:	**Yes**	**No**	**Do Not Know**	**N/A**	**Comments**
1	Property is part of an owners' association					
2	Special assessments or increases in regular assessments approved by owners' association but not yet implemented					
3	Has the Association made demand or commenced a lawsuit against a builder or contractor alleging defective construction of improvements of the Association Property (common area or property owned or controlled by the Association but outside the Seller's Property or Unit).					

M.	**OTHER DISCLOSURES – GENERAL** Do any of the following conditions **now exist**:	**Yes**	**No**	**Do Not Know**	**N/A**	**Comments**
1	Any part of the Property leased to others (written or oral)					
2	Written reports of any building, site, roofing, soils or engineering investigations or studies of the Property					
3	Any property insurance claim submitted (whether paid or not)					
4	Structural, architectural and engineering plans and/or specifications for any existing improvements					
5	Property was previously used as a methamphetamine laboratory and not remediated to state standards					
6	Government special improvements approved, but not yet installed, that may become a lien against the Property					

SPD19-10-11. SELLER'S PROPERTY DISCLOSURE (ALL TYPES OF PROPERTIES) **Page 5 of 7**

III. LAND

N.	CROPS, LIVESTOCK & LEASES Do any of the following conditions **now exist**:	Yes	No	Do Not Know	N/A	Comments
1	Crops being grown on the Property					
2	Seller owns all crops					
3	Livestock on the Property					
4	Any land leased from others: ☐ State ☐ BLM ☐ Federal ☐ Private ☐ Other ________					

O.	NOXIOUS WEEDS Do any of the following conditions **now exist**:					
	The Colorado Noxious Weed Management Act (35-5.5-101-119 C.R.S) enables County and City governments to implement noxious weeds management programs to reclaim infested acres and protect weed-free land. For a directory of county weed supervisors call 303-239-4173 or see: www.colorado.gov/ag/weeds.					
	Have any of the following occurred to the Property:	**Yes**	**No**	**Do Not Know**	**N/A**	**Comments**
1	Have any noxious weeds on the Property been identified?					
2	Have there been any weed enforcement actions on the Property?					
3	Has a noxious weed management plan for the Property been entered into?					
4	Have noxious weed management actions been implemented?					
5	Have herbicides been applied?					

P.	OTHER DISCLOSURES – LAND Do any of the following conditions **now exist**:	Yes	No	Do Not Know	N/A	Comments
1	Any part of the Property enrolled in any governmental programs such as Conservation Reserve Program (CRP), Wetlands Reserve Program (WRP), etc.					
2	Conservation easement					

Seller and Buyer understand that the real estate brokers do not warrant or guarantee the above information on the Property. Property inspection services may be purchased and are advisable. This form is **not** intended as a substitute for an inspection of the Property.

ADVISORY TO SELLER:

Failure to disclose a known material defect may result in legal liability.

The information contained in this Disclosure has been furnished by Seller, who certifies to the truth thereof based on Seller's CURRENT ACTUAL KNOWLEDGE.

_______________________________________ _______________________________________

Seller Date Seller Date

ADVISORY TO BUYER:

1. Even though Seller has answered the above questions to Seller's current actual knowledge, Buyer should thoroughly inspect the Property and obtain expert assistance to accurately and fully evaluate the Property to confirm the status of the following matters:
   a. the physical condition of the Property;
   b. the presence of mold or other biological hazards;
   c. the presence of rodents, insects and vermin including termites;
   d. the legal use of the Property and legal access to the Property;
   e. the availability and source of water, sewer, and utilities;

f. the environmental and geological condition of the Property;
g. the presence of noxious weeds; and
h. any other matters that may affect Buyer's use and ownership of the Property that are important to Buyer as Buyer decides whether to purchase the Property.

2. Seller states that the information is correct to "Seller's current actual knowledge" as of the date of this form. The term "current actual knowledge" is intended to limit Seller's disclosure only to facts actually known by the Seller and does not include "constructive knowledge" or "common knowledge" or what Seller "should have known" about the Property. The Seller has no duty to inspect the Property when this Disclosure is filled in and signed.

3. Valuable information may be obtained from various local/state/federal agencies, and other experts may assist Buyer by performing more specific evaluations and inspections of the Property.

4. Boundaries, location and ownership of fences, driveways, hedges, and similar features of the Property may become the subjects of a dispute between a property owner and a neighbor. A survey may be used to determine the likelihood of such problems.

5. Whether any item is included or excluded is determined by the contract between Buyer and Seller and not this Seller's Property Disclosure.

6. Buyer acknowledges that Seller does not warrant that the Property is fit for Buyer's intended purposes or use of the Property. Buyer acknowledges that Seller's indication that an item is "working" is not to be construed as a warranty of its continued operability or as a representation or warranty that such item is fit for Buyer's intended purposes.

7. Buyer hereby receipts for a copy of this Disclosure.

____
Buyer Date

____
Buyer Date

E. Inspection Notice NTC43-10-11

The printed portions of this form, except differentiated additions, have been approved by the Colorado Real Estate Commission. (NTC43-10-11) (Mandatory 1-12)

THIS FORM HAS IMPORTANT LEGAL CONSEQUENCES AND THE PARTIES SHOULD CONSULT LEGAL AND TAX OR OTHER COUNSEL BEFORE SIGNING.

INSPECTION OBJECTION

Date: ______________________

This document affects the contract dated ______________________, between ______________________ ______________________, (Seller) and ______________________ (Buyer) relating to the sale and purchase of the Property known as: ______________________ ______________________ (Contract). Terms used herein shall have the same meaning as in the Contract.

1. BUYER'S NOTIFICATION OF UNSATISFACTORY PHYSICAL CONDITION.

1.1. Pursuant to § 10.2.2 of the Contract, Buyer notifies Seller that Buyer requires Seller, on or before ______________, to correct or resolve the following unsatisfactory physical conditions of the Property or Inclusions:

____

____

____

If more space is required, attached are ________ additional pages.

1.2. A copy of the inspection report ☐ **Is** ☐ **Is Not** provided in conjunction with this Notice.

Pursuant to § 10.4 of the Contract, items set forth in § 1.1, or otherwise in this document, shall be paid by Seller.

Pursuant to § 10.3 of the Contract, if Buyer and Seller have not agreed in writing to a settlement of the above matters on or before the Inspection Resolution Deadline, the Contract will terminate unless Seller receives written notice from Buyer withdrawing this Inspection Objection no later than before expiration of the Inspection Resolution Deadline.

______________________________ ______________________________
Buyer Date Buyer Date

______________________________ ______________________________
Seller Date Seller Date

Seller: ☐ **Seller's Alternative Resolution in Part 2 of this document.**

☐ **Rejects** to correct all items in § 1.1 ____________________
Initials of Seller

2. SELLER'S ALTERNATIVE RESOLUTION:

____

____

____

Seller	Date	Seller	Date
Buyer	Date	Buyer	Date

Buyer: ☐ **Rejects** Seller's Alternative Resolution ____________________
Initials of Buyer

3. SURVIVAL. If any agreed upon correction requires action after Closing, the obligations agreed upon shall survive Closing.

4. BUYER'S WITHDRAWAL OF INSPECTION OBJECTION.

Buyer withdraws the Inspection Objection and elects to proceed with the Contract.

Buyer	Date	Buyer	Date

F. Counterproposal CP40-10-11

The printed portions of this form, except differentiated additions, have been approved by the Colorado Real Estate Commission. (CP40-10-11) (Mandatory 1-12)

THIS FORM HAS IMPORTANT LEGAL CONSEQUENCES AND THE PARTIES SHOULD CONSULT LEGAL AND TAX OR OTHER COUNSEL BEFORE SIGNING.

COUNTERPROPOSAL

Date: ______________________________

1. This Counterproposal shall supersede and replace any previous counterproposal. This Counterproposal amends the proposed contract dated ____________________ (Contract), between ____ (Seller), and ____ (Buyer), relating to the sale and purchase of the following legally described real estate in the County of ____________________, Colorado:

known as No. ____ (Property).
Street Address City State Zip

NOTE: If the table is omitted, or if any item is left blank or is marked in the "No Change" column, it means no change to the corresponding provision of the Contract. If any item is marked in the "Deleted" column, it means that the corresponding provision of the Contract to which reference is made is deleted.

2. § 3. DATES AND DEADLINES. [**Note:** This table may be omitted if inapplicable.]

Item No.	Reference	Event	Date or Deadline	No Change	Deleted
1	§ 4.2	Alternative Earnest Money Deadline			
		Title and Association			
2	§ 7.1	Record Title Deadline			
3	§ 7.2	Exceptions Request Deadline			
4	§ 8.1	Record Title Objection Deadline			
5	§ 8.2	Off-Record Title Deadline			
6	§ 8.2	Off-Record Title Objection Deadline			
7	§ 8.3	Title Resolution Deadline			
8	§ 7.3	Association Documents Deadline			
9	§ 7.3	Association Documents Objection Deadline			
10	§ 8.5	Right of First Refusal Deadline			
		Seller's Property Disclosure			
11	§ 10.1	Seller's Property Disclosure Deadline			
		Loan and Credit			
12	§ 5.1	Loan Application Deadline			
13	§ 5.2	Loan Conditions Deadline			
14	§ 5.3	Buyer's Credit Information Deadline			
15	§ 5.3	Disapproval of Buyer's Credit Information Deadline			
16	§ 5.4	Existing Loan Documents Deadline			
17	§ 5.4	Existing Loan Documents Objection Deadline			
18	§ 5.4	Loan Transfer Approval Deadline			
		Appraisal			
19	§ 6.2	Appraisal Deadline			
20	§ 6.2	Appraisal Objection Deadline			
		Survey			
21	§ 9.1	Current Survey Deadline			
22	§ 9.2	Current Survey Objection Deadline			

		Inspection and Due Diligence			
23	§ 10.2	Inspection Objection Deadline			
24	§ 10.3	Inspection Resolution Deadline			
25	§ 10.5	Property Insurance Objection Deadline			
26	§ 10.6	Due Diligence Documents Delivery Deadline			
27	§ 10.7	Due Diligence Documents Objection Deadline			
28	§ 10.8	Environmental Inspection Objection Deadline CBS2, 3, 4			
29	§ 10.8	ADA Evaluation Objection Deadline CBS2, 3, 4			
30	§ 11.2	Tenant Estoppel Statements Deadline CBS2, 3, 4			
31	§ 11.2	Tenant Estoppel Statements Objection Deadline CBS2, 3, 4			
		Closing and Possession			
32	§ 12.3	**Closing Date**			
33	§ 17	Possession Date			
34	§ 17	Possession Time			

3. § 4. PURCHASE PRICE AND TERMS. [**Note:** This table may be omitted if inapplicable.]

The Purchase Price set forth below shall be payable in U. S. Dollars by Buyer as follows:

Item No.	Reference	Item	Amount	Amount
1	§ 4.1	Purchase Price	$	
2	§ 4.2	Earnest Money		$
3	§ 4.5	New Loan		
4	§ 4.6	Assumption Balance		
5	§ 4.7	Seller or Private Financing		
6				
7				
8	§ 4.3	Cash at Closing		
9		**TOTAL**	$	$

4. ATTACHMENTS. The following are a part of this Counterproposal:

Note: The following disclosure forms **are attached** but are **not** a part of this Counterproposal:

5. OTHER CHANGES.

6. ACCEPTANCE DEADLINE. This Counterproposal shall expire unless accepted in writing by Seller and Buyer as evidenced by their signatures below and the offering party to this document receives notice of such acceptance on or before

______________________.
Date Time

If accepted, the Contract, as amended by this Counterproposal, shall become a contract between Seller and Buyer. All other terms and conditions of the Contract shall remain the same.

Buyer's Name: ______________________ Buyer's Name: ______________________

______________________ ______________________
Buyer's Signature Date Buyer's Signature Date

Address: ______________________
____
Phone No.: ______________________
Fax No.: ______________________
Electronic Address: ______________________

Address: ______________________
____
Phone No.: ______________________
Fax No.: ______________________
Electronic Address: ______________________

Seller's Name: ______________________

____
Seller's Signature Date

Address: ______________________
____
Phone No.: ______________________
Fax No.: ______________________
Electronic Address: ______________________

Seller's Name: ______________________

____
Seller's Signature Date

Address: ______________________
____
Phone No.: ______________________
Fax No.: ______________________
Electronic Address: ______________________

Note: When this Counterproposal form is used, the Contract is **not** to be signed by the party initiating this Counterproposal. Brokers must complete and sign the Broker's Acknowledgments and Compensation Disclosure portion of the Contract.

G. Agreement to Amend/Extend Contract AE41-10-11

The printed portions of this form, except differentiated additions, have been approved by the Colorado Real Estate Commission. (AE41-10-11) (Mandatory 1-12)

THIS FORM HAS IMPORTANT LEGAL CONSEQUENCES AND THE PARTIES SHOULD CONSULT LEGAL AND TAX OR OTHER COUNSEL BEFORE SIGNING.

AGREEMENT TO AMEND/EXTEND CONTRACT

Date: ______________________________

1. This agreement amends the contract dated ______________________ (Contract), between ______________________ ______________________ (Seller), and ______________________ (Buyer), relating to the sale and purchase of the following legally described real estate in the County of ______________, Colorado:

known as No. ____ (Property).
Street Address City State Zip

NOTE: If the table is omitted, or if any item is left blank or is marked in the "No Change" column, it means no change to the corresponding provision of the Contract. If any item is marked in the "Deleted" column, it means that the corresponding provision of the Contract to which reference is made is deleted.

2. § 3. DATES AND DEADLINES. [**Note:** This table may be omitted if inapplicable.]

Item No.	Reference	Event	Date or Deadline	No Change	Deleted
1	§ 4.2	Alternative Earnest Money Deadline			
		Title and Association			
2	§ 7.1	Record Title Deadline			
3	§ 7.2	Exceptions Request Deadline			
4	§ 8.1	Record Title Objection Deadline			
5	§ 8.2	Off-Record Title Deadline			
6	§ 8.2	Off-Record Title Objection Deadline			
7	§ 8.3	Title Resolution Deadline			
8	§ 7.3	Association Documents Deadline			
9	§ 7.3	Association Documents Objection Deadline			
10	§ 8.5	Right of First Refusal Deadline			
		Seller's Property Disclosure			
11	§ 10.1	Seller's Property Disclosure Deadline			
		Loan and Credit			
12	§ 5.1	Loan Application Deadline			
13	§ 5.2	Loan Conditions Deadline			
14	§ 5.3	Buyer's Credit Information Deadline			
15	§ 5.3	Disapproval of Buyer's Credit Information Deadline			
16	§ 5.4	Existing Loan Documents Deadline			
17	§ 5.4	Existing Loan Documents Objection Deadline			
18	§ 5.4	Loan Transfer Approval Deadline			
		Appraisal			
19	§ 6.2	Appraisal Deadline			
20	§ 6.2	Appraisal Objection Deadline			
		Survey			
21	§ 9.1	Current Survey Deadline			
22	§ 9.2	Current Survey Objection Deadline			

		Inspection and Due Diligence			
23	§ 10.2	Inspection Objection Deadline			
24	§ 10.3	Inspection Resolution Deadline			
25	§ 10.5	Property Insurance Objection Deadline			
26	§ 10.6	Due Diligence Documents Delivery Deadline			
27	§ 10.7	Due Diligence Documents Objection Deadline			
28	§ 10.8	Environmental Inspection Objection Deadline CBS2, 3, 4			
29	§ 10.8	ADA Evaluation Objection Deadline CBS2, 3, 4			
30	§ 11.1	Tenant Estoppel Statements Deadline CBS2, 3, 4			
31	§ 11.2	Tenant Estoppel Statements Objection Deadline CBS2, 3, 4			
		Closing and Possession			
32	§ 12.3	**Closing Date**			
33	§ 17	Possession Date			
34	§ 17	Possession Time			

3. Other dates or deadlines set forth in the Contract shall be changed as follows:

4. Additional amendments:

All other terms and conditions of the Contract shall remain the same.

This proposal shall expire unless accepted in writing by Seller and Buyer as evidenced by their signatures below and the offering party to this document receives notice of such acceptance on or before ______________________________.
Date Time

Buyer's Name: ______________________________ Buyer's Name: ______________________________

______________________________ ______________________________
Buyer's Signature Date Buyer's Signature Date

Seller's Name: ______________________________ Seller's Name: ______________________________

______________________________ ______________________________
Seller's Signature Date Seller's Signature Date

H. Closing Instructions CL8-8-10

The printed portions of this form, except differentiated additions, have been approved by the Colorado Real Estate Commission. (CL8-8-10) (Mandatory 1-11)

THIS FORM HAS IMPORTANT LEGAL CONSEQUENCES AND THE PARTIES SHOULD CONSULT LEGAL AND TAX OR OTHER COUNSEL BEFORE SIGNING.

CLOSING INSTRUCTIONS

Date: ______________________________

1. PARTIES, PROPERTY. ____, Seller, and ____, Buyer, engage ____, Closing Company, who agrees to provide closing and settlement services in connection with the Closing of the transaction for the sale and purchase of the Property known as No. ____,

Street Address City State Zip

and more fully described in the Contract to Buy and Sell Real Estate, dated ________________________, including any counterproposals and amendments (Contract).

2. INFORMATION, PREPARATION. Closing Company is authorized to obtain any information necessary for the Closing. Closing Company agrees to prepare, deliver and record those documents (excluding legal documents), and disburse all funds pursuant to the Contract that are necessary to carry out the terms and conditions of the Contract.

3. CLOSING FEE. Closing Company will receive a fee not to exceed $______________ for providing these closing and settlement services.

4. RELEASE, DISBURSEMENT. Closing Company is not authorized to release any signed documents or things of value prior to receipt and disbursement of Good Funds, except as provided in §§ 8, 9 and 10.

5. DISBURSER. Closing Company shall disburse all funds, including real estate commissions, except those funds as may be separately disclosed in writing to Buyer and Seller by Closing Company or Buyer's lender on or before Closing. All parties agree that no one other than the disburser can assure that payoff of loans and other disbursements will actually be made.

6. SELLER'S NET PROCEEDS. Seller will receive the net proceeds of Closing as indicated: ☐ **Cashier's Check**, at Seller's expense ☐ **Funds Electronically Transferred** (wire transfer) to an account specified by Seller, at Seller's expense ☐ **Closing Company's** trust account check.

7. CLOSING STATEMENT. Closing Company will prepare and deliver an accurate, complete and detailed closing statement to Buyer and Seller at time of Closing.

8. FAILURE OF CLOSING. If Closing or disbursement does not occur on or before Closing Date set forth in the Contract, Closing Company, except as provided herein, is authorized and agrees to return all documents, monies, and things of value to the depositing party, upon which Closing Company will be relieved from any further duty, responsibility or liability in connection with these Closing Instructions. In addition, any promissory note, deed of trust or other evidence of indebtedness signed by Buyer shall be voided by Closing Company, with the originals returned to Buyer and a copy to Buyer's lender.

9. RETURN OF EARNEST MONEY. Except as otherwise provided in § 10, Earnest Money Dispute, if the Earnest Money has not already been returned following receipt of a Notice to Terminate or other written notice of termination, Earnest Money Holder shall release the Earnest Money as directed by the written mutual instructions. Such release of Earnest Money shall be made within five days of Earnest Money Holder's receipt of the written mutual instructions signed by both Buyer and Seller, provided the Earnest Money check has cleared.

10. EARNEST MONEY DISPUTE. In the event of any controversy regarding the Earnest Money (notwithstanding any termination of the Contract), Earnest Money Holder shall not be required to take any action. Earnest Money Holder, at its option and sole subjective discretion, may (1) await any proceeding, (2) interplead all parties and deposit Earnest Money into a court of competent jurisdiction and shall recover court costs and reasonable attorney and legal fees, or (3) provide notice to Buyer and Seller that unless Earnest Money Holder receives a copy of the Summons and Complaint or Claim (between Buyer and Seller) containing the case number of the lawsuit (Lawsuit) within one hundred twenty days of Earnest Money Holder's notice to the parties, Earnest Money Holder shall be authorized to return the Earnest Money to Buyer. In the event Earnest Money Holder does receive a copy of the Lawsuit, and has not interpled the monies at the time of any Order, Earnest Money Holder shall disburse the Earnest Money pursuant to the Order of the Court.

11. SUBSEQUENT AMENDMENTS. Any amendments to, or termination of, these Closing Instructions must be in writing and signed by Buyer, Seller and Closing Company.

12. CHANGE IN OWNERSHIP OF WATER WELL. Within sixty days after Closing, Closing Company shall submit any required Change in Ownership form or registration of existing well form to the Division of Water Resources in the Department of Natural Resources (Division), with as much information as is available, and the Division shall be responsible for obtaining the necessary well registration information directly from Buyer. Closing Company shall not be liable for delaying Closing to ensure Buyer completes any required form.

13. WITHHOLDING. The Internal Revenue Service and the Colorado Department of Revenue may require Closing Company to withhold a substantial portion of the proceeds of this sale when Seller either (a) is a foreign person or (b) will not be a Colorado resident after Closing. Seller should inquire of Seller's tax advisor to determine if withholding applies or if an exemption exists.

14. ADDITIONAL PROVISIONS. (The following additional provisions have not been approved by the Colorado Real Estate Commission.)

15. COUNTERPARTS. This document may be executed by each party, separately, and when each party has executed a copy, such copies taken together shall be deemed to be a full and complete contract between the parties.

16. BROKER'S COPIES. Closing Company shall provide, to each broker in this transaction, copies of all signed documents that such brokers are required to maintain pursuant to the rules of the Colorado Real Estate Commission.

17. NOTICE, DELIVERY AND CHOICE OF LAW.

17.1. Physical Delivery. Except as provided in § 17.2, all notices must be in writing. Any notice or document to Buyer shall be effective when physically received by Buyer, any individual buyer, any representative of Buyer, or Brokerage Firm of Broker working with Buyer. Any notice or document to Seller shall be effective when physically received by Seller, any individual seller, any representative of Seller, or Brokerage Firm of Broker working with Seller. Any notice or document to Closing Company shall be effective when physically received by Closing Company, any individual of Closing Company, or any representative of Closing Company.

17.2. Electronic Delivery. As an alternative to physical delivery, any signed documents and written notice may be delivered in electronic form by the following indicated methods only: ☐ **Facsimile** ☐ **Email** ☐ **Internet** ☐ **No Electronic Delivery**. Documents with original signatures shall be provided upon request of any party.

17.3. Choice of Law. This contract and all disputes arising hereunder shall be governed by and construed in accordance with the laws of the State of Colorado that would be applicable to Colorado residents who sign a contract in this state for property located in Colorado.

Buyer's Name: ____________________	Buyer's Name: ____________________
____________________	____________________
Buyer's Signature Date	Buyer's Signature Date
Address: ____________________	Address: ____________________
Phone No.: ____________________	Phone No.: ____________________
Fax No.: ____________________	Fax No.: ____________________
Electronic Address: ____________________	Electronic Address: ____________________
Seller's Name: ____________________	Seller's Name: ____________________
____________________	____________________
Seller's Signature Date	Seller's Signature Date

Address: ______________________ Address: ______________________

Phone No.: ______________________ Phone No.: ______________________
Fax No.: ______________________ Fax No.: ______________________
Electronic Address: ______________________ Electronic Address: ______________________

Closing Company's Name: ______________________

Authorized Signature Title Date

Address: ______________________

Phone No.: ______________________
Fax No.: ______________________
Electronic Address: ______________________

(TO BE COMPLETED ONLY BY BROKER AND CLOSING COMPANY)

______________________ (Broker) ☐ **Working with Seller** ☐ **Working with Buyer** engages Closing Company as Broker's scrivener to complete, for a fee not to exceed $______________ at the sole expense of Broker, the following legal documents: ☐ **Deed** ☐ **Bill of Sale** ☐ **Colorado Real Estate Commission approved Promissory Note** ☐ **Colorado Real Estate Commission approved Deed of Trust**. Closing Company agrees to prepare, on behalf of Broker, the indicated legal documents pursuant to the terms and conditions of the Contract.

The documents stated above shall be subject to Broker's review and approval and Broker acknowledges that Broker is responsible for the accuracy of the above documents.

Brokerage Firm's Name: ______________________
Broker's Name: ______________________

Broker's Signature Date

Closing Company's Name: ______________________

Authorized Signature Title Date

Glossary

abstract of title. a summary or condensation of the essential parts of all recorded instruments which affect a particular piece of real estate, arranged in the order in which they were recorded.

acceleration clause. a clause in a contract by which the time for payment of a debt is advanced, usually making the obligation immediately due and payable, because of the breach of some condition, such as failure to pay an installment when due.

acceptance. an indication by an offeree of willingness to be bound by the terms of the offer.

acknowledgment. a declaration made by a person to a notary public, or other public official authorized to take acknowledgments, that the instrument was executed by the person and that it is a free and voluntary act.

acre foot. a term used in measuring the volume of water, equal to the quantity of water required to cover one acre one foot deep, or 43,560 cu. ft.

administrator. A person appointed by the court to administer the estate of a deceased person who died intestate (without leaving a will).

ad valorem. Latin meaning "according to value"; normally used to describe a tax based on the assessed value of real property.

adverse possession. the right of an occupant of land to acquire a superior title to the real estate against the record owner, where such possession has been actual, notorious, hostile, visible and continuous for the required statutory period (18 years in Colorado). Adverse possession promotes the productive use of land by giving title to the one putting the land to use.

affidavit. a written statement or declaration, sworn to or affirmed before some officer who has authority to administer an oath or affirmation.

agency. a legal relationship resulting from an agreement or contract, either expressed or implied, written or oral, whereby one person, the agent, is employed by another, called the principal, to do certain acts in dealing with a third party.

agent. any person, partnership, association, or corporation authorized or employed by another, called the principal, to act for, on behalf of, and subject to the control of the principal.

alienation. transfer of real property by one person to another.

amenities. in real estate, amenities are features such as location, outlook, or access to a park, lake, highway, view or the like which enhance the desirability of real estate and which contribute to the pleasure and enjoyment of the occupants.

amortization. liquidation or gradual retirement of a financial obligation by periodic installments.

appraisal. in real estate, an estimate of the quality or value of property; also refers to the report setting forth the estimate of value together with the basis for such conclusions.

appropriation. the act(s) involved in the taking and reducing to personal possession of water occurring in a stream or other body of water, and of applying such water to beneficial use.

appropriator. one who diverts and puts to beneficial use the water of a stream or other body of water, under a water right obtained through appropriation.

appurtenance. that which belongs to something else; something adapted to the use of the real property to which it is connected or belongs intended to be a permanent addition to the land. Appurtenances pass with the title to the land, e.g. a house, barn, garage, right-of-way, etc.

assessed valuation. an estimate of value by a unit of government for taxation purposes.

assessment. in real estate, the valuation of property in order to apportion a tax upon it.

assignee. the party to whom a legal right has been assigned or transferred.

assignment. transfer to another of a legal right.

assignor. the party who assigns or transfers a legal right.

attachment. a type of encumbrance, permitted only under special circumstances, which is placed against the real estate of a defendant in a pending law suit for money damages.

attorney's opinion. in real estate, the written opinion of an attorney-at-law regarding the marketability of title to real property based upon an examination of the abstract of title or the records in the county clerk and recorder's office.

animal unit (A.U.). the grazing capacity of land to properly sustain one animal and any offspring for one year.

balance sheet. a statement showing a company's financial position at the end of an accounting period by listing assets, liabilities and owner's equity.

balloon payment. a final lump-sum payment of an installment debt, much larger than all previous installments, and which pays the debt in full prior to its full amortization.

bargain and sale deed. any deed that recites consideration and purports to convey the real estate. A bargain and sale deed with a covenant against the grantor's acts warrants only that he or she has done nothing to harm or cloud the title.

beneficiary. the person who benefits from certain acts, e.g. a will; one receiving benefits, profits or advantage; one for whose benefit a trust is created.

bill of sale. a written instrument by which a person transfers right, title or interest in personal property to another.

blanket mortgage. a mortgage that covers more than one piece of property.

broker. a duly licensed person, firm, partnership, limited liability company, association, or corporation who, in consideration of compensation or with the intent of receiving such compensation, facilitates a real property transaction for another party. (See 12-61-101 C.R.S. for Colorado statutory definition – chapter 1 of this manual.)

building code. local government regulations specifying structural requirements of buildings.

buyer agent. a broker engaged by and representing the buyer in a real estate transaction.

capitalization rate. a percentage rate of change applied in the income approach to value.

cash basis accounting. recognizing revenue and expense when cash is received or disbursed rather than when earned or incurred. A service business not dealing in inventory has the option of using the cash or accrual basis of accounting. Individual taxpayers must use the accrual basis.

cash flow. cash receipts minus cash disbursements from an operation or asset. An annual cash flow statement shows total return after taxes.

caveat emptor. Latin phrase meaning "let the buyer beware.", formerly imposing a duty on the buyer to examine the products or property accepting them "as is".

certificate of reasonable value (CRV). Veterans Administration's certified appraisal of value of real property.

certificate of taxes. a written guaranty of the condition of the taxes on a certain property made by the county treasurer wherein the property is located. Any loss resulting from an error in a tax certificate shall be paid by the county that such treasurer represents.

chapter 7. provision of the 1978 Bankruptcy Reform Act that covers liquidations under a court appointed trustee.

chapter 11. provision of the 1978 Bankruptcy Reform Act that covers reorganizations where the debtor remains in control of the business and its operations.

chattel. property other than real estate, i.e. personal property; an item of movable property.

check. synonym for quadrangle, a 24 mile square tract of land in the Governmental Survey System.

cloud on title. an outstanding claim or encumbrance that affects or impairs title to the property.

cognovit note. one containing a confession of judgment (waiver of due process) by the borrower.

collateral security. some security additional to the personal obligation of the borrower, as a chattel mortgage or trust deed.

Colorado Association of REALTORS® – (C.A.R). the state organization of real estate licensees whose goal is the professional advancement of the real estate industry and whose membership is comprised of local real estate associations or boards.

Colorado Coordinate System. a method of land description based on measurements from the intersection of statutorily defined north-south and east-west axes; applied only in Delta and Ute Counties.

commingling. mixing money belonging to others with personal or business funds. Illegal commingling is using the money of one beneficiary for the benefit of another or failing to maintain such money in identified escrow accounts.

common interest community. real estate described in a declaration which obligates an individual unit owner to pay property tax, insurance premiums, maintenance or improvement on some declared real property owned in common. Ownership does not include a leasehold interest of less than forty years, measured from the date the initial term commences, including renewal options.

common-law. law evolving from usage, custom and judicial interpretation rather than legislated by statute. Common law originated in old English courts.

community property. property acquired by a husband and wife, or either, during marriage, by their industry and not by gift, belonging equally to husband and wife. Community property laws exist in only nine states: AZ, CA, ID, LA, NV, NM, OK, TX and WA.

condemnation. in real property law, the process by which property of a private owner is taken for public use, with compensation to the owner, under the governmental right of eminent domain.

condominium. a common interest community in which portions of the real estate are designated for separate ownership and the remainder of which is distributed for common ownership solely among separate owners. A common interest community is not a condominium unless the undivided interests in the common elements are vested in the unit owners.

consideration. a promise or an act of legal value bargained for and received in return for a promise; one of the essential elements of a contract.

construction mortgage. a short-term loan used to finance the building of a structure.

constructive (or legal) notice. the conclusive presumption that all persons have knowledge of the contents of a recorded instrument.

contract. an agreement, enforceable at law, between two or more competent persons, having a legal purpose, wherein the parties agree to act in a certain manner.

controller. the chief accounting executive of an organization responsible for (1) financial reporting, (2) tax administration, (3) management audits, (4) planning controls and (5) developing accounting systems and procedures.

conventional mortgage. a mortgage securing a loan made by private investors without governmental participation, i.e. not F.H.A.-insured or V.A.-guaranteed.

conversion. unauthorized appropriation of ownership rights over goods or property belonging to another; also altering one form of property to another such as changing a leasehold apartment building to freehold condominium ownership.

conveyance. an instrument in writing by which a person transfers some estate, interest, or title in real estate to another, such as a deed or lease.

covenant. a promise or agreement, usually in writing, to do or not do certain acts; also stipulations in a real estate conveyance document governing use of the property.

cubage. the product of multiplying width x height x depth (or length) of an object.

cubic foot per second. a unit of discharge for measurement of flowing liquid, equal to a flow of one cubic foot per second past a given section. Also called "second-foot".

cul-de-sac. a street which dead-ends in a semi-circle.

curtesy. a common-law life-estate in all of a wife's real property given to the husband upon her death, provided a child was born from their marriage; abolished in Colorado.

customer. a party to a real estate transaction with whom the broker has no brokerage relationship because such party has not engaged or employed a broker.

debenture. bonds issued without specific security and are secured only by the overall equity of the issuer.

declaration. a recorded instrument that defines boundaries and common elements of a condominium and establishes the basic rights and obligations of the owners. It also provides for the creation of an owners' association including a board of directors with authority to collect common expenses and otherwise act for the benefit of all owners.

dedication. transfer of land from private to public use, as streets in a platted subdivision.

deed. a legal instrument in writing, duly executed and delivered, whereby the owner (grantor) conveys to another (grantee) some right, title or interest in or to real estate.

deed restriction. a provision in a deed controlling or limiting the use of the land.

default. omission or failure to perform a legal duty; failure to meet an obligation when due.

defeasible fee (base- or qualified fee). a fee interest in land that is capable of being defeated or terminated upon the happening of a specified event.

deficiency judgment. a lien against borrower's remaining assets in an amount equal to the shortage between a foreclosure sale price less than the indebtedness owed.

depreciation. loss in value due to deterioration from ordinary wear and tear, action of the elements, functional or economic obsolescence.

designated broker. an employing or employed broker designated in writing by an employing broker to serve as a single agent or transaction-broker for a seller, landlord, buyer or tenant in a real estate transaction; does not include a real estate brokerage firm that consists of only one licensed natural person.

devise. a gift of real property by the last will and testament of a donor.

diversion. illegal or unauthorized use of entrusted funds.

documentary fee. a statutory Colorado tax of one cent per one hundred dollars (sale price x .0001) of consideration paid by a person recording an instrument of conveyance with a county clerk and recorder.

donee. receiver of a gift.

donor. giver of a gift.

dower. a common-law estate consisting of a one-third interest in a husband's real property given to his wife upon his death. abolished in Colorado.

due-on-sale clause. a provision in a mortgage or trust deed which allows the lender to call a promissory note due and payable in full immediately upon the sale or transfer of a secured property; allows a lender to raise the interest rate or force other changes in terms upon assumption of the loan.

duress. forcing action or inaction against a person's will.

earnest money. down payment made by a purchaser of real estate as evidence of good faith.

easement. a right or interest in the real property of another; the right to use another's land for a specific purpose, such as a right-of-way.

economic life. the period of time over which improved property may be profitably used.

eminent domain. a governmental right to take private property for public use through the process of condemnation, and with payment of just compensation.

employing broker. a license level qualifying a broker to employ other licensees, requiring two years of active licensed experience, a 24-hour "brokerage administration" course if licensed after December 31, 1996 and passage of the Colorado part of the broker licensing exam if upgrade to broker associate from salesperson was by means of the broker transition course.

encroachment. illegal intrusion of an improvement or other real property onto another's property.

encumbrance. a claim, lien, charge, or liability attached to and binding upon real property, such as a judgment, mortgage, mechanic's lien, lien for unpaid taxes, or right-of-way.

endorsement. signing one's name on a negotiable instrument with intent to transfer ownership; also an addition altering or clarifying coverage of an (title) insurance policy.

equity. the amount of an owner's interest in real estate exceeding its encumbrances.

equity of redemption. see redemption.

escheat. reversion of property to the state when an owner dies without leaving a will or legal heirs to whom the property may pass by lawful descent.

escrow. the state or condition of money or a deed held conditionally by a third party, called the escrow agent, pending the performance or fulfillment of some act or condition.

escrow account. any checking, demand, passbook or statement account insured by an agency of the United States government maintained in a Colorado depository for money that belongs to others.

escrow agreement. a written agreement whereby a grantor, promissor or obligor delivers certain instruments or property to an escrow agent, to be held until the happening of a contingency or performance of a condition, and then to be delivered to the grantee, promisee or obligee.

estate. the degree, quantity, nature and extent of a person's interest in real property; such as a fee simple absolute estate, or an estate for years.

estate (tenancy) at sufferance. an estate in land arising when the tenant wrongfully holds over after the expiration of the tenant's term; the landlord has the choice of evicting the tenant as a trespasser or accepting such tenant for a similar term and under the conditions of the tenant's previous holding.

estate (tenancy) at will. an interest in land terminable at the will of either the tenant or landlord.

estate (tenancy) for years. an interest in land for a fixed period of time, e.g. one day or 99 years.

estate from period-to-period (periodic tenancy). An interest in land with no contract date of termination. The rental period (week, month or year, etc.) renews by payment of the contract rent.

et al. Latin abbreviation for "et allus", meaning "and others".

et ux. Latin abbreviation for "et uxor", meaning "and wife".

eviction. dispossession by process of law; the act of depriving a person of the possession of land pursuant to a court judgment.

exclusive agency listing. a listing whereby the owner engages a real estate brokerage as sole broker for a specified period of time, while retaining the right to sell the property to a buyer that the owner finds without paying the broker a commission.

exclusive right-to-sell listing. a listing whereby the owner engages one real estate brokerage as sole broker for a specified period of time, entitling the broker to a commission regardless of who sells the property, including the owner.

execution. a writ issued by a court to the sheriff directing seizure and sale of a property to satisfy a debt; the act of signing a contract; completion of the terms of a contract.

executor. the person named in a will to carry out its provisions.

"fannie mae". The pronunciation of "FNMA" (Federal National Mortgage Association). provides a market for government secured mortgages held by primary lenders and provides them with a ready market so as to permit a greater turnover of money for loans.

fee simple absolute (fee or fee simple). the most comprehensive ownership of real property under law; the largest bundle of ownership rights possible.

fee tail. an estate in land which cannot be conveyed but which must descend to the heirs of the holder; abolished in Colorado.

F.H.A.-insured mortgage. a mortgage under which the Federal Housing Administration insures approved lenders against loan default.

fiduciary. a person in a position of trust relative to another party; confidential, as in a fiduciary relationship between an agent and the principal.

fixture. an article of personal property installed in or attached to land or an improvement in a permanent manner, so that it is considered a part of the real estate.

foreclosure. termination of property rights due to some default by the borrower; a judicial or public trustee process whereby secured property is sold to satisfy a debt.

grantee. a person to whom real estate is conveyed; the buyer.

grantor. a person who conveys real estate; the seller.

grazing district. an administrative subdivision of the range lands under the jurisdiction of the Bureau of Land Management, established pursuant to section 3 of the Taylor Grazing Act to facilitate management of BLM forage resources.

grazing lease section 15. a lease authorizing the use of public lands outside of grazing districts (Taylor Grazing Act) for the grazing of livestock for a specified period of time.

grazing licenses. a permit for the grazing of a set number and class of livestock on a designated area of grazing district lands for a specified time, usually less than one year.

grazing permit. a permit to graze a certain number and class of livestock on a designated area of grazing district lands during specified seasons each year for a period of usually 10 years.

grazing preference. a request to graze certain numbers and classes of livestock upon a national forest for a specified time and subject to rules and regulations adopted by the Forest Service.

gross income multiplier. a number used in the income approach to value used to compare potential desirability of income properties, and calculated by dividing sales price by gross annual income.

ground water. a pervious formation with sides and bottom of relatively impervious material, in which ground water is held or retained; also called subsurface water basin.

holdover tenant. one who fails to vacate leased property after the lease has expired.

homeowners association. an association or unit owners association formed as part of a common interest community.

homestead exemption. a/k/a "homestead" or "homestead right"; a fixed, statutory sum exempt from execution by creditors, and intended to protect a family home from foreclosure or sale for debts.

indemnify. to insure; to secure against loss.

independent broker. a license level qualifying a broker to work without the supervision of an employing broker, requiring two years of active licensed experience, and if upgrade to broker associate was by means of the broker transition course, passage of the Colorado part of the broker licensing exam.

installment land contract (ILC), also land contract, or installment contract; an agreement for the purchase of real estate on an installment basis, whereby the deed is withheld until all or a specified portion of the purchase price is paid.

inter alia. Latin meaning "among other things".

intestate. Dying without leaving a valid will.

joint tenancy. a type of co-ownership of real property featuring a right of survivorship and four unities (time, title, interest and possession).

judgment. final declaration of the rights of the parties by a court.

land. real property; all below the surface, the surface and the airspace above it, and that which is affixed to it permanently; synonymous with "real property", "realty", and "real estate"; often used to mean only the unimproved surface of the earth.

land economics. the production, distribution and consumption of wealth deriving from land classification and use.

landlord. an owner who has leased an estate-in-land to a tenant.

landlord agent. a broker engaged by and representing a landlord as an agent in a leasing transaction.

lease. an agreement under which a tenant receives possession and use of real property for a certain period of time and the landlord receives the payment of rent and/or the performance of other conditions.

leasehold. an estate or right in real property held under a lease.

legal description. a description recognized by law that is sufficient to locate and identify a property without oral testimony.

lessee. party who possesses an estate in realty under a lease; commonly referred to as tenant.

lessor. party who conveys a right or estate in realty to a lessee under a lease; commonly referred to as landlord.

lien. a right given by law to a creditor to have a debt or charge satisfied out of the value of real or personal property belonging to the debtor.

life estate. an estate or interest in real property held for the duration of the life of some certain person.

limited agent. an agent whose duties and obligations to a principal are only those set forth in C.R.S. 12-61-804 or 12-61-805, with any additional duties and obligations agreed to pursuant to section 12-61-803 (5).

lis pendens. a filing against specific property, giving public notice that an action at law is pending that may affect the title to the land.

listing. an agreement or contract of employment, either oral or written, whereby the owner authorizes the real estate broker to sell, exchange or lease real estate.

marketable (merchantable) title. a title free from reasonable doubt of defect; which can be readily sold or mortgaged to a reasonably prudent person; a title free from material defects or grave doubts and reasonably free from potential litigation.

market value. the price which a ready and able buyer, not forced to buy, would pay and which a ready and willing seller, not forced to sell, would accept, assuming that both parties are fully informed, act reasonably, and have sufficient time to consider the transaction with due care.

mechanics' lien. a lien created by statute which exists against real property in favor of persons who have performed work or furnished materials for the improvement of the real estate.

metes and bounds. a method of describing or locating real property; metes are measures of length and bounds are boundaries. This method starts from a well-marked point of beginning and follows the boundaries of the land until it returns once more to the point of beginning.

mill. one-tenth of a cent; a tax rate of one mill on the dollar or one-tenth of one percent of the assessed value of a property. (assessed value x .001)

mortgage. a conditional conveyance of property as security for the payment of a debt or the fulfillment of some obligation. Upon payment of the debt or performance of the obligation, a mortgage automatically becomes void.

mortgagee. the party (lender) to whom property is conveyed under a mortgage as security for the repayment of a loan or fulfillment of some obligation.

mortgagor. the party who gives a mortgage (borrower) conveying interest in the property to the lender as security for the obligation to repay a loan or fulfill some obligation.

multiple listing service (MLS). a marketing arrangement among real estate brokers whereby a seller authorizes the listing broker to share information and a pre-determined portion of a commission to any broker cooperating in the sale of the property.

mutual assent (meeting of the minds). agreement of the parties to the contract, mutually consenting to be bound by its exact terms; an essential contract element.

National Association of REALTORS©, (N.A.R.). a national association of real estate personnel whose goal is the professional advancement of the real estate industry and whose membership is comprised of state and local real estate associations or boards.

national forest. a forest or watershed reservation administered by the Forest Service, United States Department of Agriculture.

negotiable instrument. a written instrument containing a promise of payment, which can be endorsed from one person to another.

net listing. a listing contract whereby the owner is to receive a certain net price, with the broker receiving any excess over and above the net price as commission.

note. a written instrument acknowledging a debt and promising payment.

obsolescence. impairment of desirability and usefulness of the property resulting from economic, functional, physical, fashion, or other changes.

offer. to present for sale; or a proposal presented for acceptance or rejection which, if accepted, will form a binding contract.

offeree. one to whom an offer is made.

offeror. one who makes an offer.

open listing. a non-exclusive employment agreement in which an owner retains the right to list the property with other brokers.

option. a temporary right for a specified time, and for which a consideration is paid, during which an optionee may purchase or lease property at a set price.

optionee. one who requests, receives or stands to benefit from an option.

optionor. one who grants an option to another, usually the land owner.

party wall. a wall erected on a line between adjoining properties for the use of both properties.

patent. an instrument of conveyance of government-owned land to an individual.

percentage lease. A commercial lease of property in which the rent is based upon a percentage of the sales volume derived from the leased premises.

percolation (perc) test. determines if soil will take sufficient water seepage for use of a septic tank.

periodic tenancy. see estate from period-to-period.

personal property. all that is not real property; items of a temporary or movable nature.

personalty. synonym for personal property.

plat. a parcel or plot of land; also a method of land description referring to a recorded map (plat) of a subdivision or town which lays out boundaries, streets, easements etc.

police power. governmental right to enact legislation deemed necessary to protect and promote the health, safety and general welfare of the public. (License law is supported by this legal theory.)

power of attorney. a legal instrument authorizing another person to act in place of the person drawing the instrument.

principal. a person, partnership, association or corporation who authorizes or employs another, called the agent, to do certain acts on behalf of the principal.

principal note. a promissory note secured by the mortgage or trust deed.

property. anything which may be owned and its bundle of ownership rights; the right to use, possess, enjoy, and dispose of a thing in every legal way and to exclude everyone else from interfering with these rights; generally classified into two groups; personal and real.

public trustee. a county official to whom borrowers convey title to real property by trust deed for the benefit of the beneficiary (lender).

purchase money mortgage. a mortgage given by the purchaser to secure a loan for part or all of the purchase price. Such a mortgage becomes a lien on the property simultaneously with the passing of title, and if immediately recorded becomes prior to any lien against the purchaser.

quadrangle, (check). a square tract of land in the U.S. Governmental Survey System measuring 24 miles on each side.

quiet-title suit. an action in court to remove a defect, cloud or suspicion regarding the owner's legal rights to a parcel of real estate.

quitclaim deed. a deed in which the grantor warrants nothing, conveying only the grantor's present interest in the real estate, if any.

range. a six-mile wide strip of land that runs in a north-south direction. Ranges are determined by government survey and are numbered in numerical order east or west of a principal meridian.

real estate. real property, realty, land.

real property. land; the surface of the earth and whatever is erected, growing upon, or affixed to the land; including that which is below it and the airspace above it. synonymous with "land", "realty", and "real estate".

REALTOR®. a registered trade name exclusive to members of the National Association of REALTORS®.

realty. real property, land, real estate.

receiver. a court-appointed custodian who holds property pending final disposition of the matter before the court.

recording. entering an instrument in a book of public record in the office of the county clerk and recorder. recording constitutes "constructive" notice to all persons of the rights or claims contained in the instrument.

Rectangular Survey System. see U.S. Government Survey System.

redemption. the right of an owner to redeem or reclaim real estate by paying the debt or charge (such as mortgage or tax lien) after default, together with interest and costs. Specifically, **equity of redemption** is the right to redeem the property after default but before foreclosure. **Statutory right-of-redemption** refers to the right to redeem the property <u>after</u> foreclosure, or other enforcement action, within a certain time specified by statute. In Colorado, a mortgagor has a statutory right to redeem property any time within 75 days (residential) or six months (agricultural)) after foreclosure or three years after a tax sale.

release. the relinquishment or surrender of a right, claim, or interest.

release of lien. the discharge or release of specific property from the charge or lien of a judgment, mortgage or other claim.

restrictive covenant. a clause in a deed limiting the use of a property.

right of survivorship. a characteristic of joint-tenancy whereupon the death of one tenant triggers an automatic and immediate transfer of the decedent's property rights equally among the surviving tenant(s).

right-of-way. an easement or right to pass over another's land; also the strip of land used as roadbed by a railroad or used for a public purpose by other public utilities.

salesperson. an inactive license status in Colorado; in other jurisdictions, a license level authorized to perform real estate activity on behalf of a licensed real estate broker.

seisin. actual possession of real estate by a freehold estate owner; a typical warranty deed covenant.

seller agent. a broker engaged by and representing the seller in a real estate transaction.

single agent. a broker engaged by and representing only one party, i.e. buyer, seller, tenant or landlord in a real estate transaction.

special assessment. a tax against real property made by a unit of government to cover the proportionate cost of an improvement, such as a street or sewer.

special warranty deed. a deed in which the grantor warrants title only against defects arising during the grantor's ownership.

specific performance. a remedy compelling a party to perform or carry out the terms of a valid, existing contract.

state lease. an agreement between the state of Colorado and other parties for the use of lands under the jurisdiction of the State Board of Land Commissioners for grazing, agriculture and other lawful purposes.

statutory right of redemption. see redemption.

subordination clause. a clause in a mortgage or lease stating that the rights of the holder shall be secondary to a subsequent encumbrance or right of another person.

surrender. in leases, the cancellation of a lease by mutual consent of lessor and lessee.

survey. the measurement of a parcel of land and its characteristics.

Taylor Grazing Act. see grazing district.

tenancy at sufferance. see estate at sufferance.

tenancy at will. see estate at will.

tenancy-in-common. a type of co-ownership of an estate in land entitling each tenant to full possession of the property (unity of possession) regardless of proportionate share owned; tenancy-in-common contains no right of survivorship.

tenant agent. a broker engaged by and representing the tenant in a leasing transaction.

testate. a condition of death characterized by the decedent having left a valid will.

time-share. an interval interest in real estate which limits ownership or occupancy rights to specified time periods. Ownership may be either fee simple (deeded) or "right-to-use" (contractual or membership). In Colorado, time-share sales are subject to license law.

title. in real property, the right, or evidence of the right, to ownership.

title insurance. indemnification of a policyholder from loss due to a title defect, provided the loss does not result from a defect excluded by the policy provisions.

Torrens system. a system by which the registrar of Torrens (i.e. clerk and recorder) keeps and maintains title records pertaining to real property located in the county.

tort. a negligent or intentional wrong done to another for which the law will grant money damages in a civil action.

transaction-broker. a broker who assists one or more parties throughout a contemplated real estate transaction with communication, interposition, advisement, negotiation, contract terms, and the closing without being an agent or advocate for the interests of any party.

treasurer. a county official responsible for property tax administration; a chief executive in a firm responsible for (1) obtaining operating capital, (2) investor relations, (3) short-term financing, (4) banking policies, (5) asset custody, (6) credit and collections, (7) investment analysis, and (8) risk management.

treasurer's deed. a deed for property sold at public sale by the county for non-payment of taxes by the owner.

trust deed. a loan security instrument by which a borrower conveys title to a (usually public) trustee, to be held for the protection of a lender as security for the repayment of the debt. Upon payment of the debt a trust deed must be specifically released by the trustee.

United States Government (or Rectangular) Survey System (GSS). a land description method based on reference to governmental surveys.

usury. charging more than the legal rate of interest for the use of money.

V.A.-guaranteed mortgage. a mortgage backed by a Veterans Administration guarantee to the lender for a percentage of the loan amount.

vendee. buyer.

vendor. seller.

vicarious liability. a principal's liability for an agent's acts performed within the scope of the agency; specifically excluded by Colorado statute from a principal's liability unless the act or omission was approved, directed or ratified.

waiver. abandonment of some claim or right.

warranty deed, (general warranty deed). a deed in which the grantor warrants or guarantees the title to real property against defects during the grantor's ownership and as far back as a chain-of-title can be established.

writ of execution. a court order directing an officer of the court, usually the sheriff, to carry out the judgment or decree of the court.

Topical Index

Topical Index

Colorado Forms Committee Process

Colorado Forms Committee Established

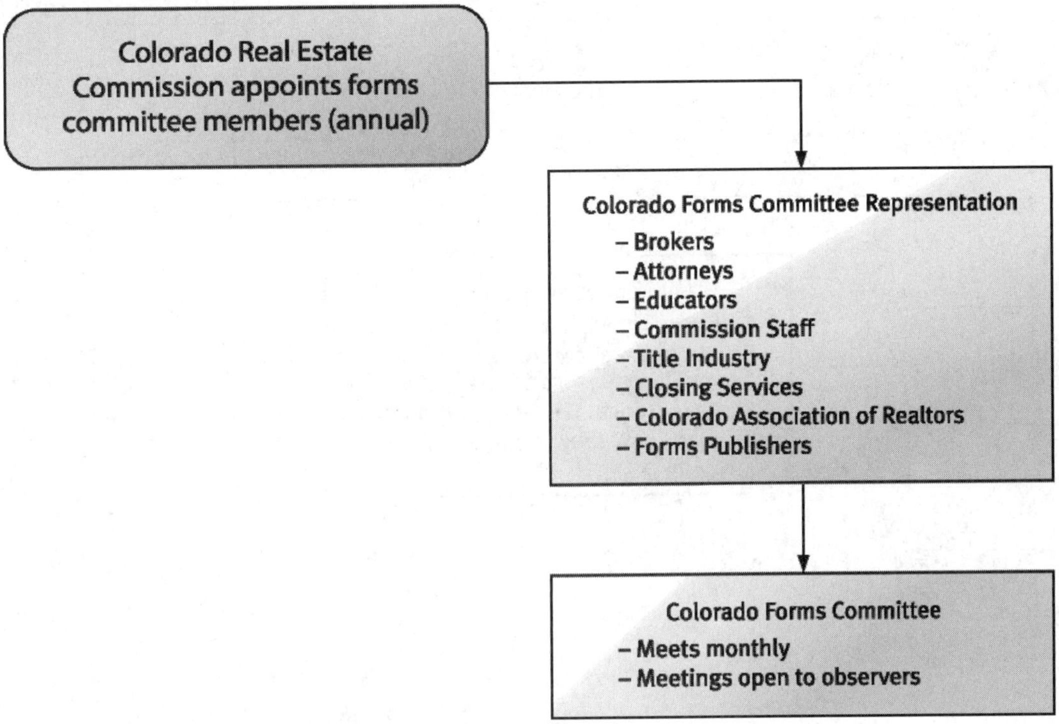

Colorado Forms Committee Monthly Activity

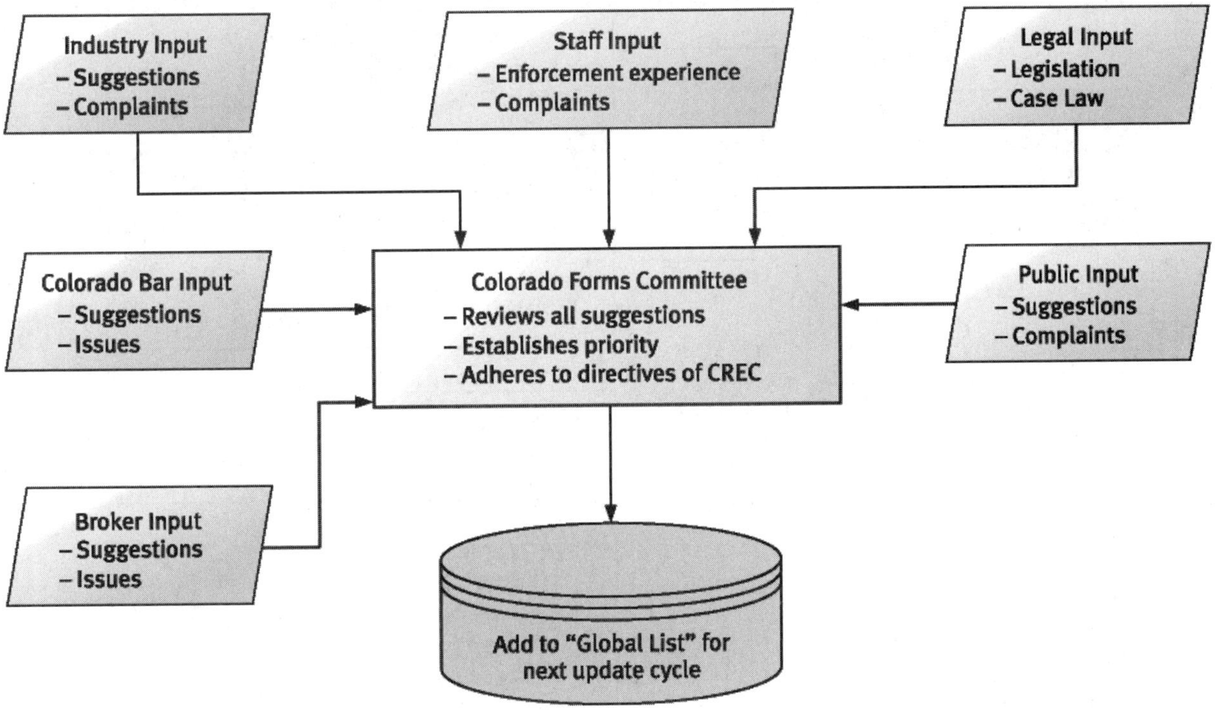

Chart provided by Garrett Quackenbush

Colorado Forms Committee Process

Colorado Forms Committee Update Cycle

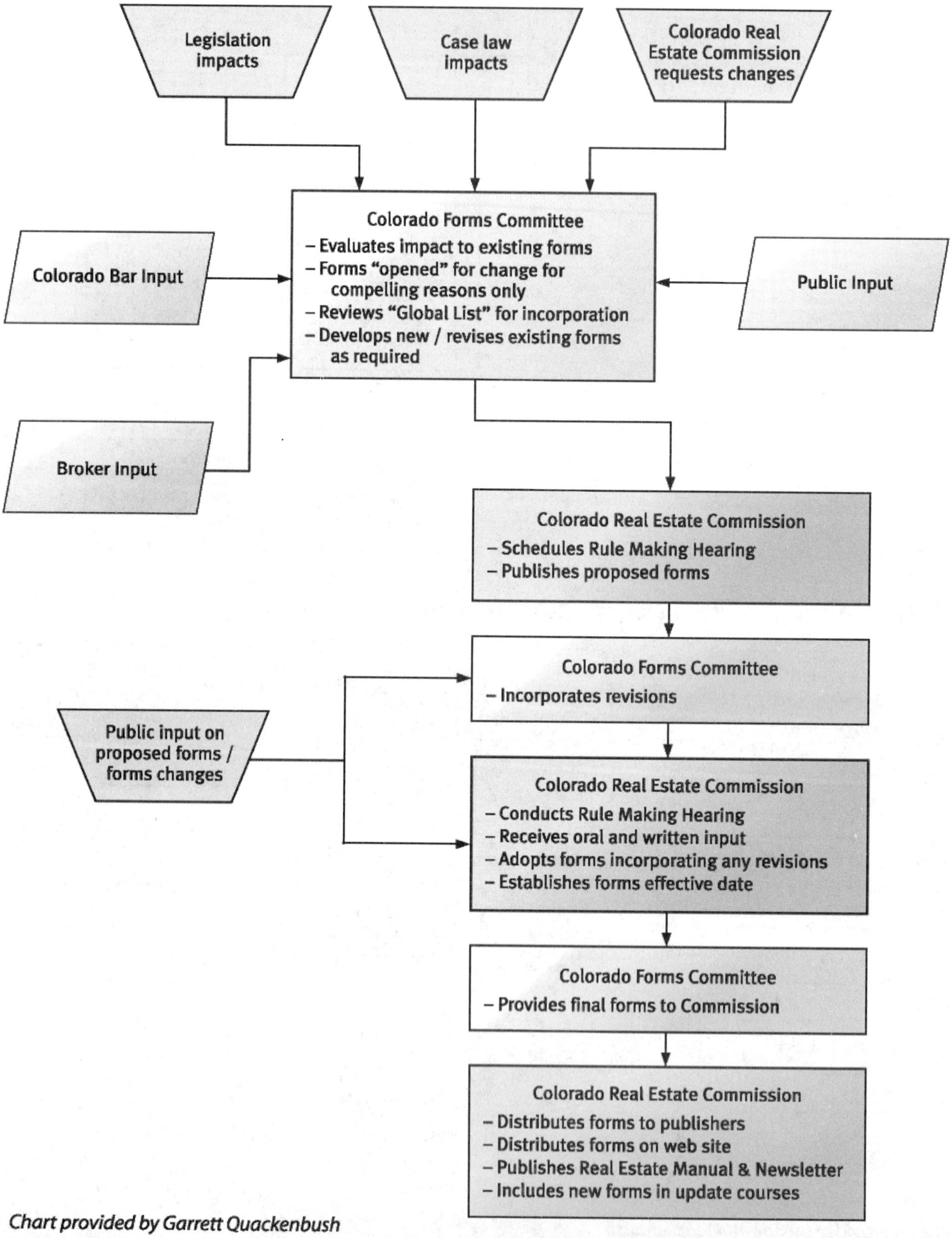

Chart provided by Garrett Quackenbush